CHARLIE
C

D0708220

Oxford Mini School GERMAN DICTIONARY

Editorial Manager: Valerie Grundy
New Edition: Nicholas Rollin
with the assistance of Marie-Louise Wasmeier

OXFORD
UNIVERSITY PRESS

OXFORD
UNIVERSITY PRESS

Great Clarendon Street, Oxford OX2 6DP

Oxford University Press is a department of the University of Oxford.
It furthers the University's objective of excellence in research,
scholarship, and education by publishing worldwide in

Oxford   New York

Auckland   Cape Town   Dar es Salaam   Hong Kong   Karachi
Kuala Lumpur   Madrid   Melbourne   Mexico City   Nairobi
New Delhi   Shanghai   Taipei   Toronto

With offices in

Argentina   Austria   Brazil   Chile   Czech Republic   France   Greece
Guatemala   Hungary   Italy   Japan   Poland   Portugal   Singapore
South Korea   Switzerland   Thailand   Turkey   Ukraine   Vietnam

Oxford is a registered trade mark of Oxford University Press
in the UK and in certain other countries

© Oxford University Press 2012

Database right Oxford University Press (maker)

First published 1998
Revised first edition 2002
Second edition 2004
Third edition 2007
This edition 2012

British Library Cataloguing in Publication Data
Data available

ISBN: 978 0 19 275710 4

10 9 8 7 6

Printed in China

Paper used in the production of this book is a natural, recyclable product
made from wood grown in sustainable forests. The manufacturing process
conforms to the environmental regulations of the country of origin.

In the case of more common words the dictionary also gives you a selection of phrases you will often want to use. In the entry for **hair** below you can find out how to use the translation **Haare** in different expressions:

hair *noun* **1** Haare (*plural*); **to comb your hair** sich (DAT) die Haare kämmen; **to wash your hair** sich (DAT) die Haare waschen; **to have your hair cut** sich (DAT) die Haare schneiden lassen; **she's had her hair cut** sie hat sich die Haare schneiden lassen; **2 a hair** ein Haar.

Note on the German Spelling Reform

The German spelling reform was adopted by German-speaking countries in July 1996. You will find all the new spellings in this dictionary. However, since you may come across old spellings if you are reading pre-reform German material, we have also given all the most frequent old spellings as headwords to help you locate the entry. These are cross-referred to the new spellings. Thus **As** is cross-referred to **Ass** but the old spelling of **Ausschuss** (**Ausschuß**) is not shown.

INTRODUCTION

This dictionary has been specially written for students who are in their first years of learning German all the way through to preparing for exams. We have paid particular attention to making the dictionary user-friendly. With the help of bold headwords, alphabet tabs, easy-to-follow signposts and examples, the right translation can quickly be found. The things students need to know about words in German are clearly shown. These include main parts of irregular verbs, noun plurals, and the case taken by prepositions.

Throughout the writing of this dictionary we have worked in close consultation with students, teachers, and examining boards. We gratefully acknowledge the examining boards AQA (formerly NEAB and SEG), OCR, and EDEXCEL, who have read and commented on the dictionary text.

Since the first edition of this dictionary there have been many changes in German life. Not least has been the introduction of the euro. This new edition of the dictionary takes full account of these changes and many new words and examples have been included in order to provide the best possible learner's dictionary of German at this level.

HOW A BILINGUAL DICTIONARY WORKS

A bilingual dictionary contains two languages. When you look up a word in one of the languages, it gives the translation for that word in the other language. This dictionary is divided into two halves which are separated by a section of dark-edged pages. In the first half you look up German words, which are in alphabetical order, to find out what they mean in English and in the second half you look up English words, also in alphabetical order, to find out how to say them in German.

At the entry, you will find not only **translations** but also other information that will help you get the right word and use it correctly. Here is a guide to the different things you will find in an entry:

headword	a word you look up in the dictionary
translation	translations are the only things that are in 'ordinary' type in the dictionary. They are always typed like this, and something which is typed in a different way can never be a translation
noun	word class (part of speech): tells you whether the word you are looking up is a noun, a verb, an adjective, or some other part of speech. A headword can be more than one part of speech. For instance, book can be a noun (she was reading a book) or a verb (I've booked the seats)
(*signpost*)	helpful information: to guide you to the right translation, to show you how to use the translation, or to give you extra information about either the headword or the translation
example	a phrase or sentence using the word you have looked up. You should read through them carefully to see if they are close to what you want to understand or say
der/die/das	gender: after a German noun to tell you whether it is masculine (der), feminine (die), or neuter (das)
(PL *die........*)	shows the plural form of a German noun
●	indicates a phrasal verb such as to carry on
★	shows an idiomatic expression such as over the moon
[27]	verb number – tells you which verb pattern to look at in the dark-edged of the dictionary
✧	indicates an irregular German verb
SEP	indicates that a German verb is separable such as ablenken (PERF lenkt ab)

USING THE DICTIONARY

To find out what a German word means

Suppose you want to find out what the German word **Tor** means. You need to use the first half of the dictionary to find the German word that you are looking for. To help you do this, the guide words at the top of each page show the alphabetical range of words on the pages you have open. You will know that all German nouns start with a capital letter. Notice that this makes no difference to the alphabetical order, nor do accented letters like **ü**.

When you find the entry for **Tor** you will find the translation but you will also see what the gender of **Tor** is. Nouns in German are either masculine, feminine, or neuter. These are shown in the dictionary as *der, die,* or *das*. You can see that **Tor** says *das* so it is neuter.

However, it often happens that a German word has more than one translation in English so you will see that the translation for **Tor** is divided into sections numbered **1** and **2**.

Tor *das* (Pl. die **Tore**) **1** gate; **2** goal;
  mit 3 zu 2 Toren gewinnen to win
  by 3 goals to 2.

The first translation is **gate** and the second is **goal**. You will need to look at both translations and see which fits best in the German sentence you are trying to understand, so:

Uli hat das Tor geöffnet means Uli opened the gate

BUT

Uli steht im Tor means Uli's in goal

In English, the plural of most nouns is formed by adding -s. In German there are quite a lot of ways of forming the plural and these are not always easy to recognize. To help you with this, we show the plural form after every noun headword. For instance, if you are trying to find out what the German word **Häuser** means, you can see immediately that it is the plural of **Haus** and so it means **houses**.

Haus *das* (Pl. die **Häuser**) **1** house;
  2 nach Hause home; zu Hause at
home.

German like English has certain words that you would use when chatting with friends but not in more formal situations. German words like this are marked (*informal*) like **flitzen** here:

flitzen *verb* (*informal*) (PERF **ist**
geflitzt) **1** to dash; **2** to whizz.

vi

You can think of a dictionary entry as being made out of different sorts of building bricks. In the entries below you can see how they fit together to help you find what you need. The more you use your dictionary the more confident you will feel about finding your way around it.

GERMAN-ENGLISH

headword in bold for easy look-up

aberglaübisch *adjective* superstitious.

word class (part of speech)

abfahren ◇*verb* (PRES **fährt ab**, IMPERF **fuhr ab**, PERF **ist abgefahren**) to leave; **Peter fährt morgen ganz früh ab** Peter is leaving very early tomorrow morning; **wann fährt der Zug nach Berlin ab?** when does the Berlin train leave?

main forms of irregular verbs

gender

Abfahrt *die* (PL die **Abfahrten**) **1** departure; **2** run (*on a ski slope*); **3** exit (*on a motorway*).

noun plurals in bold for easy look-up

Abfall *der* (PL die **Abfälle**) rubbish.

Abfalleimer *der* (PL die **Abfalleimer**) rubbish bin.

typical examples to show German in context

abfliegen ◇*verb* (IMPERF **flog ab**, PERF **ist abgeflogen**) **1** to take off; **die Maschine ist mit zehn Minuten Verspätung abgeflogen** the plane took off ten minutes late; **2** to leave (*by plane*); **ich fliege um elf Uhr ab** my plane leaves at 11 o'clock.

Abflug *der* (PL die **Abflüge**) departure.

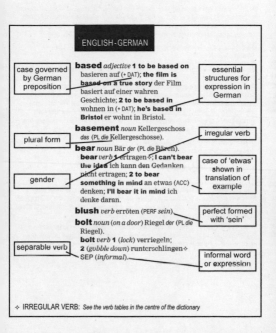

ENGLISH-GERMAN

case governed by German preposition

based *adjective* **1 to be based on** basieren auf (+ DAT); **the film is based on a true story** der Film basiert auf einer wahren Geschichte; **2 to be based in** wohnen in (+ DAT); **he's based in Bristol** er wohnt in Bristol.

essential structures for expression in German

basement *noun* Kellergeschoss das (PL die Kellergeschosse).

plural form

irregular verb

bear *noun* Bär der (PL die Bären). **bear** *verb* **1** ertragen◇; **I can't bear the idea** ich kann den Gedanken nicht ertragen; **2 to bear something in mind** an etwas (ACC) denken; **I'll bear it in mind** ich denke daran.

gender

case of 'etwas' shown in translation of example

blush *verb* erröten (PERF *sein*).

perfect formed with 'sein'

bolt *noun* (*on a door*) Riegel der (PL die Riegel).
bolt *verb* **1** (*lock*) verriegeln; **2** (*gobble down*) runterschlingen◇ SEP (*informal*).

separable verb

informal word or expression

◇ IRREGULAR VERB: *See the verb tables in the centre of the dictionary*

Finding an English word and how to say it in German

You can see that it is quite easy once you know how the dictionary works to look up a German word and find out what it means. Students usually find it harder to use the dictionary to find out how to say something in German. This dictionary is written specially to help you do this and to make it easy to find the right way of saying things in German.

Suppose you want to know how to say **garden** in German. Look up the word in the second part of the dictionary. If you follow the same method of going through the alphabetical order of the headwords as you did when you were looking up a German word, you will find **garden** on page 429.

garden *noun* Garten *der* (PL die Gärten).

Now you can see that the German word for **garden** is **Garten**. But if you want to make a sentence using a noun like **Garten** you need to know its gender. The dictionary shows you that it is *der* **Garten** so in the garden will be **im Garten**. It is not always as easy as this to know which German word you need. Sometimes there will be more than one German word for the English word you are looking up. When the dictionary gives you more than just one translation, it is very important to take the time to read through the whole entry. If you look up plug the entry looks like this:

plug *noun* **1** (*electrical*) Stecker *der* (PL die Stecker); **2** (*in a bath or sink*) Stöpsel *der* (PL die Stöpsel); **to pull out the plug** den Stöpsel herausziehen.

You can see that **1** tells you that the German word for an electrical plug is **Stecker** and **2** tells you that the word for a **plug** in a bath or a sink is **Stöpsel**. Remember that information which is either in brackets or italics or both is there to help you, but it will never be the translation itself.

Wherever there is more than one translation, depending on what meaning of the English word you are looking for, the dictionary will always help you to choose the right one. Often it is not enough to find the translation of one word.

Aa

Aal der (PL die **Aale**) eel.

ab preposition (+ DAT) from; **ab Montag** from Monday; **Kinder ab sechs Jahren** children from the age of six.

ab adverb **1** off; **der Henkel ist ab** the handle has come off; **ab ins Bett!** (informal) off (you go) to bed!; **2 ab und zu** now and again.

abbiegen ◇verb (IMPERF **bog ab**, PERF **ist abgebogen**) **1** to turn off; **nach rechts abbiegen** to turn off to the right; **2 biegen Sie an der Ampel (nach) links ab** turn left at the lights.

Abbildung die (PL die **Abbildungen**) illustration.

abbrechen ◇verb (PRES **bricht ab**, IMPERF **brach ab**, PERF **hat abgebrochen**) **1** to break off (a branch, negotiations); **Ruth brach ein paar Zweige ab** Ruth broke off a few branches; **2** to pull down (a building); **3** to cut short; **leider mussten wir unsere Ferien vorzeitig abbrechen** unfortunately we had to cut short our holidays; **er hat sein Studium aus finanziellen Gründen abgebrochen** he left university for financial reasons; **4** (PERF **ist abgebrochen**) **der Ast ist abgebrochen** the branch has broken off.

Abend der (PL die **Abende**) evening; **am Abend** in the evening; **heute Abend** this evening, tonight; **gestern Abend** yesterday evening,

last night; **wann esst ihr zu Abend?** when do you have dinner?

Abendbrot das evening meal.

Abendessen das (PL die **Abendessen**) supper, dinner (in the evening); **was gibt es zum Abendessen?** what are we having for supper?

Abendkurs der (PL die **Abendkurse**) evening course.

abends adverb in the evening.

Abenteurfilm der (PL die **Abenteuerfilme**) adventure film.

Abenteuer das (PL die **Abenteuer**) adventure.

aber conjunction but; **es ist zwar nützlich, aber zu teuer** it's useful, but too expensive.

aber adverb really; **das ist aber sehr nett von dir** that's really nice of you; **du bist aber groß!** aren't you tall!; **aber ja!** but of course!; **jetzt ist es aber Schluss!** that's it now!

abergläubisch adjective superstitious.

abfahren ◇verb (PRES **fährt ab**, IMPERF **fuhr ab**, PERF **ist abgefahren**) to leave; **Peter fährt morgen ganz früh ab** Peter is leaving very early tomorrow morning; **wann fährt der Zug nach Berlin ab?** when does the Berlin train leave?

Abfahrt die (PL die **Abfahrten**) **1** departure; **2** run (on a ski slope); **3** exit (on a motorway).

Abfall der (PL die **Abfälle**) rubbish.

Abfalleimer der (PL die **Abfalleimer**) rubbish bin.

abfliegen ✧*verb* (IMPERF **flog ab**, PERF **ist abgeflogen**) **1** to take off; **die Maschine ist mit zehn Minuten Verspätung abgeflogen** the plane took off ten minutes late; **2** to leave (*by plane*); **ich fliege um elf Uhr ab** my plane leaves at 11 o'clock.

Abflug der (PL die **Abflüge**) departure.

Abflussrohr das (PL die **Abflussrohre**) outlet, drain.

abfragen *verb* (PERF **hat abgefragt**) **1** to test; **sie fragt ihn Vokabeln ab** she's testing him on his vocabulary; **2** to call up (*on a computer*); **Adressen am Computer abfragen** to call up addresses on the computer.

Abgase (*plural noun*) exhaust fumes.

abgeben ✧*verb* (PRES **gibt ab**, IMPERF **gab ab**, PERF **hat abgegeben**) **1** to hand in (*homework, an application, lost property*); **2** to pass (*in football*); **den Ball abgeben** to pass the ball; **3 sich mit etwas abgeben** to spend time on something; **mit solchen Typen würde ich mich nicht abgeben** I wouldn't associate with blokes like that; **4 jemandem etwas abgeben** to give someone something; **gib mir ein Stück von deiner Schokolade ab** give me a piece of your chocolate; **5 er wird einen guten Lehrer abgeben** he'll make a good teacher.

abgelegen *adjective* remote.

abgemacht *adjective* agreed.

Abgeordnete der/die (PL die **Abgeordneten**) member of parliament.

abgießen *verb* (IMPERF **goss ab**, PERF **hat abgegossen**) **1** to pour away; **2** to drain (*vegetables*).

Abhang der (PL die **Abhänge**) slope.

abhängen¹ ✧*verb* (IMPERF **hing ab**, PERF **hat abgehangen**) **von jemandem abhängen** to depend on somebody; **von etwas abhängen** to depend on something; **es hängt vom Wetter ab, ob wir am Wochenende nach Wales fahren** whether or not we are going to Wales at the weekend depends on the weather.

abhängen² *verb* (PERF **hat abgehängt**) **1** to unhitch (*a trailer*); **2** to uncouple (*a train carriage*); **3** (*informal*) to shake off; **die Einbrecher hängten die Polizei schnell ab** the burglars soon shook off the police.

abhängig *adjective* dependent.

abheben ✧*verb* (IMPERF **hob ab**, PERF **hat abgehoben**) **1** to lift off; **2** to withdraw (*money*); **3** to answer the phone; **ich habe schon zweimal angerufen, aber niemand hat abgehoben** I've rung twice before, but nobody answered.

abholen *verb* (PERF **hat abgeholt**) **1** to collect; **2** to pick up; **ich hole dich am Bahnhof ab** I'll pick you up at the station.

Abitur das (PL die **Abiture**) A levels (*German students usually take Abitur at 19, sitting exams in four subjects, which they have to pass to* go on to university); **sein Abitur machen** to do your A levels.

Abiturient der (PL die Abiturienten) A-level student.

Abiturientin die (PL die Abiturientinnen) A-level student.

Abkommen das (PL die Abkommen) agreement.

abkürzen verb (PERF hat abgekürzt) 1 to abbreviate; **wie kürzt man das Wort ab?** how do you abbreviate that word?; 2 **den Weg abkürzen** to take a short cut.

Abkürzung die (PL die Abkürzungen) 1 abbreviation; **die Abkürzung für Europäische Union is EU** the abbreviation for European Union is EU; 2 short cut.

abladen ◇verb (PRES lädt ab, IMPERF lud ab, PERF hat abgeladen) to unload.

ablaufen ◇verb (PRES läuft ab, IMPERF lief ab, PERF ist abgelaufen) 1 to expire (passport, contract); 2 to drain off; **das Badewasser ablaufen lassen** to let the bathwater out; 3 to go off; **wie ist die Besprechung abgelaufen?** how did the meeting go?

Ablaufdatum der (PL die Ablaufdaten) expiry date.

ablegen verb (PERF hat abgelegt) 1 to take off; 2 **abgelegte Kleidung** cast-offs.

ablehnen verb (PERF hat abgelehnt) 1 to turn down (a position, money, an invitation); 2 to reject (an applicant, a suggestion).

ablenken verb (PERF hat abgelenkt) 1 to distract; **jemanden von seiner Arbeit ablenken** to distract somebody from their work; 2 **jemanden von seinen Sorgen ablenken** to take somebody's mind off their worries; 3 to divert (attention, suspicion); **vom Thema ablenken** to change the subject.

abliefern verb (PERF hat abgeliefert) 1 to deliver; 2 to hand in (an essay, a form, lost property); 3 to drop off; **die Kinder abliefern** to drop the children off.

abmachen verb (PERF hat abgemacht) 1 to take off; **kannst du den Deckel abmachen?** can you take off the lid?; 2 to agree; **wir müssen noch einen Termin für unser nächstes Treffen abmachen** we still have to agree on a date for our next meeting; **abgemacht!** agreed!; 3 to sort out; **das müsst ihr untereinander abmachen** you'll have to sort that out amongst yourselves.

Abmachung die (PL die Abmachungen) agreement.

abnehmen ◇verb (PRES nimmt ab, IMPERF nahm ab, PERF hat abgenommen) 1 to take off (remove); 2 **kann ich dir etwas abnehmen?** (carry) can I take something (for you)?; (help) can I do anything for you?; 3 **jemandem etwas abnehmen** to take something off somebody; **sie nehmen einem schnell zwanzig Euro ab** they'll soon take 20 euros off you; 4 to buy; 5 to decrease (in

a b c d e f g h i j k l m n o p q r s t u v w x y z

number); **6** to diminish; **7** to lose weight; **er hat schon vier Kilo abgenommen** he's already lost four kilos; **8** to answer the phone; **9 das nehme ich dir nicht ab** (*informal*) I don't buy that.

Abonnement *das* (PL die **Abonnements**) subscription.

abonnieren *verb* (PERF hat **abonniert**) to subscribe to.

abraten ⬦*verb* (PRES **rät ab**, IMPERF **riet ab**, PERF **hat abgeraten**) **jemandem von etwas abraten** to advise somebody against something.

abräumen *verb* (PERF hat **abgeräumt**) to clear away; **den Tisch abräumen** to clear the table.

abreagieren *verb* (PERF hat **abreagiert**) **1 seine Wut an jemandem abreagieren** to take your anger out on somebody; **2 sich abreagieren** to calm down.

Abreise *die* departure.

abreisen *verb* (PERF **ist abgereist**) to leave.

abreißen ⬦*verb* (IMPERF **riss ab**, PERF **hat abgerissen**) **1** to tear down (*a poster, notice*); **2** to demolish (*a building*); **3** (PERF **ist abgerissen**) to come off (*a button, for example*).

Absage *die* (PL die **Absagen**) refusal.

absagen *verb* (PERF hat **abgesagt**) **1** to cancel; **2 eine Einladung absagen** to turn down an invitation.

Absatz *der* (PL die **Absätze**) **1** heel (*of a shoe*); **2** paragraph.

abschaffen *verb* (PERF hat **abgeschafft**) **1** to abolish (*a regulation, capital punishment*); **2** to get rid of; **wir haben unseren Hund abgeschafft** we got rid of our dog.

abscheulich *adjective* horrible.

abschicken *verb* (PERF hat **abgeschickt**) to send off.

Abschied *der* (PL die **Abschiede**) **1** parting; **2** farewell; **3 Abschied nehmen** to say goodbye.

Abschleppdienst *der* breakdown service.

abschleppen *verb* (PERF hat **abgeschleppt**) **1** to tow away; **2 sich mit den Koffern abschleppen** (*informal*) to struggle along with the suitcases; **3 jemanden abschleppen** (*informal*) to pick somebody up.

Abschleppwagen *der* (PL die **Abschleppwagen**) breakdown truck.

abschließen ⬦*verb* (IMPERF **schloss ab**, PERF **hat abgeschlossen**) to lock.

Abschlussprüfung *die* (PL die **Abschlussprüfungen**) final exam.

abschneiden ⬦*verb* (IMPERF **schnitt ab**, PERF **hat abgeschnitten**) **1** to cut off; **ich schneide dir eine Scheibe Brot ab** I'll cut you a slice of bread; **2 gut/ schlecht abschneiden** to do well/ badly.

abschrecken *verb* (PERF hat abgeschreckt) to deter.

abschreiben ◇*verb* (IMPERF schrieb ab, PERF hat abgeschrieben) to copy.

Abseilen *das* abseiling.

abseits *adverb* **1** far away; **etwas abseits** a little way away; **2** offside (*in soccer*).

Absender *der* (PL die **Absender**) sender.

absetzen *verb* (PERF hat abgesetzt) **1** to take off (*your hat, glasses*); **2** to put down (*a bag, suitcase*); **3** to drop off; **ich setze euch am Bahnhof ab** I'll drop you off at the station; **4 die Pille absetzen** to stop taking the pill.

Absicht *die* (PL die **Absichten**) intention.

absichtlich *adverb* intentionally.

absolut *adjective* absolute.

absolut *adverb* absolutely; **das ist absolut unmöglich** that's absolutely impossible.

abspülen *verb* (PERF hat abgespült) **1** to rinse, to rinse off; **2** to do the washing up.

Abstand *der* (PL die **Abstände**) **1** distance; **in zwanzig Meter Abstand** at a distance of 20 metres; **Abstand halten** to keep your distance; **2** interval.

abstauben *verb* (PERF hat abgestaubt) to dust.

abstellen *verb* (PERF hat abgestellt) **1** to turn off (*the radio, a tap*); **2** to put down (*a suitcase, the shopping*); **3** to park (*the car*).

Abstimmung *die* (PL die **Abstimmungen**) vote.

abstreiten ◇*verb* (IMPERF stritt ab, PERF hat abgestritten) to deny.

abstürzen *verb* (PERF ist abgestürzt) **1** to fall; **2** to crash (*a plane*).

Abszess *der* (PL die **Abszesse**) abscess.

abtauen *verb* (PERF hat abgetaut) to defrost (*the fridge*).

Abteil *das* (PL die **Abteile**) compartment.

abteilen *verb* (PERF hat abgeteilt) **1** to divide up; **2** to divide off.

Abteilung *die* (PL die **Abteilungen**) department.

Abtreibung *die* (PL die **Abtreibungen**) abortion.

abtrocknen *verb* (PERF hat abgetrocknet) **1** to dry up; **2 sich abtrocknen** to dry yourself.

abwägen *verb* (IMPERF wog ab, PERF hat abgewogen) to weigh up.

abwärts *adverb* down.

Abwasch *der* washing-up.

abwaschen ◇*verb* (PRES wäscht ab, IMPERF wusch ab, PERF hat abgewaschen) **1** to wash up (*the dishes*); **2** to wash off (*dirt, marks*).

Abwasser *das* (PL die **Abwässer**) sewage.

Abwechslung *die* (PL die **Abwechslungen**) change; **zur Abwechslung** for a change.

abwerten *verb* (PERF hat abgewertet) to devalue.

abwertend *adjective* pejorative.

abwesend *adjective* absent.

Abwesenheit *die* absence.

abwischen *verb* (PERF **hat abgewischt**) to wipe.

abzählen *verb* (PERF **hat abgezählt**) to count.

Abzeichen *das* (PL **die Abzeichen**) badge.

abziehen ✧*verb* (IMPERF **zog ab**, PERF **hat abgezogen**) **1** to take off (*a sheet, backing*); **die Betten abziehen** to strip the beds; **2** to take out (*a key*); **3** to deduct, to take away; **4** to withdraw (*troops*); **5** (PERF **ist abgezogen**) to escape (*steam or smoke, for example*); **6** (PERF **ist abgezogen**) **sie sind gleich nach dem Essen abgezogen** (*informal*) they pushed off straight after the meal.

abzielen *verb* (PERF **hat abgezielt**) **etwas zielt auf etwas ab** something is aimed at something.

Abzweigung *die* (PL **die Abzweigungen**) turning.

ach *exclamation* oh!

Achsel *die* (PL **die Achseln**) shoulder.

Acht[1] *die* (PL **die Achten**) eight; **eine Acht schreiben** to write an eight.

Acht[2] *die* **1 Acht geben** to pay attention; **er sollte in der Schule besser Acht geben** he should pay more attention at school; **2 auf etwas/jemanden Acht geben** to look after something/somebody; **3 gib Acht!** watch out!; **4 sich in Acht nehmen** to be careful;

5 etwas außer Acht lassen to disregard something.

acht *number* eight; **um acht (Uhr)** at eight (o'clock); **um halb acht** at half past seven.

Achtel *das* (PL **die Achtel**) eighth.

achten *verb* (PERF **hat geachtet**) **1** to respect (*a person, an opinion*); **2 auf etwas achten** to pay attention to something; **3 auf jemanden achten** to look after somebody; **4 achte nicht darauf!** don't take any notice of it!

achter, achte, achtes *adjective* eighth; **jede achte Kiste** every eighth crate; **mein achter Geburtstag** my eighth birthday; **sie ging als Achte durchs Ziel** she finished eighth.

Achterbahn *die* (PL **die Achterbahnen**) roller coaster.

achtgeben SEE Acht[2].

achthundert *number* eight hundred.

achtmal *adverb* eight times.

Achtung *die* **1** respect; **Achtung vor jemandem haben** to have respect for somebody; **2 Achtung!** look out!; **Achtung, fertig, los!** on your marks, get set, go!; **'Achtung Stufe'** 'mind the step'.

achtzehn *number* eighteen.

achtzig *number* eighty.

Acker *der* (PL **die Äcker**) field.

addieren *verb* (PERF **hat addiert**) to add.

Ader *die* (PL **die Adern**) vein.

Adjektiv das (PL die **Adjektive**) adjective.

Adler der (PL die **Adler**) eagle.

adoptieren verb (PERF hat **adoptiert**) to adopt.

Adoption die (PL die **Adoptionen**) adoption.

Adoptiveltern plural noun adoptive parents.

Adoptivkind das (PL die **Adoptivkinder**) adopted child.

Adresse die (PL die **Adressen**) address.

adressieren verb (PERF hat **adressiert**) to address; **an wen soll ich den Brief adressieren?** who shall I address the letter to?

Advent der Advent.

Adventskalender der (PL die **Adventskalender**) Advent calendar.

Adventskranz der (PL die **Adventskränze**) Advent wreath.

Adverb das (PL die **Adverbien**) adverb.

Aerobic das aerobics.

Affe der (PL die **Affen**) 1 monkey; 2 ape.

Afrika das Africa; **aus Afrika** from Africa; **nach Afrika** to Africa.

Afrikaner der (PL die **Afrikaner**) African.

Afrikanerin die (PL die **Afrikanerinnen**) African.

afrikanisch adjective African.

AG[1] die (PL die **AGs**) (Aktiengesellschaft) Plc (Public limited company).

AG[2] die (PL die **AGs**) 1 work group; 2 school club.

Agentur die (PL die **Agenturen**) agency.

aggressiv adjective aggressive.

ähneln verb (PERF hat **geähnelt**) 1 to resemble; **er ähnelt seinem Vater sehr** he's very like his father; 2 **sich ähneln** to be alike.

ahnen verb (PERF hat **geahnt**) 1 to know; **das konnte ich wirklich nicht ahnen** I had no way of knowing that; **wer soll denn ahnen, dass ...?** who would know that ...?; 2 to suspect; **so etwas habe ich doch schon geahnt** I did suspect something like that.

ähnlich adjective 1 similar; 2 **jemandem ähnlich sein** to be like somebody; **jemandem ähnlich sehen** to look like somebody; 3 **ähnlich wie**; 4 **das sieht dir ähnlich!** (informal) that's just like you!

Ähnlichkeit die (PL die **Ähnlichkeiten**) similarity.

Ahnung die 1 idea; **hast du eine Ahnung, wie er heißt?** have you got any idea what he's called?; 2 **keine Ahnung!** no idea!; **er hat von Mode absolut keine Ahnung** he doesn't know a thing about fashion; 3 premonition.

ahnungslos adjective unsuspecting.

Ahorn der (PL die **Ahorne**) maple.

Aids das Aids.

Akademiker der (PL die **Akademiker**) university graduate.

a
b
c
d
e
f
g
h
i
j
k
l
m
n
o
p
q
r
s
t
u
v
w
x
y
z

a **Akademikerin** *die* (PL *die* **Akademikerinnen**) university graduate.

b

c **akademisch** *adjective* academic.

d **Akkusativ** *der* (PL *die* **Akkusative**) accusative.

e **Akne** *die* acne.

f **Akte** *die* (PL *die* **Akten**) file.

g **Aktentasche** *die* (PL *die* **Aktentaschen**) briefcase.

h **Aktion** *die* (PL *die* **Aktionen**)
i   **1** action; **in Aktion treten** to go into action; **2** campaign.

j **Aktiv** *das* active.

k **aktiv** *adjective* active.

l **Aktualisierung** *die* (PL *die* **Aktualisierungen**) **1** up-date;
m   **2** updating.

n **aktuell** *adjective* **1** topical; **ein aktuelles Thema** a topical issue; **2 nicht mehr aktuell** no longer relevant; **3** current; **eine aktuelle Sendung** a current-affairs programme.

o **Akzent** *der* (PL *die* **Akzente**)
p   **1** accent; **mit starkem Akzent sprechen** to speak with a strong accent; **2** accent (*on a letter*);
q   **3** stress; **den Akzent auf etwas legen** to stress something.

r **albern** *adjective* silly.

s **albern** *adverb* in a silly way.

t **Albtraum** *der* (PL *die* **Albträume**) nightmare.

u **Album** *das* (PL *die* **Alben**) album.

v **Algebra** *die* algebra.

w **Alkohol** *der* alcohol.

x

y

z

alkoholfrei *adjective* non-alcoholic.

Alkoholiker *der* (PL *die* **Alkoholiker**) alcoholic.

Alkoholikerin *die* (PL *die* **Alkoholikerinnen**) alcoholic.

alkoholisch *adjective* alcoholic.

All *das* space; **einen Satelliten ins All schicken** to send a satellite into space.

alle SEE **aller**.

Allee *die* (PL *die* **Alleen**) avenue.

allein *adjective, adverb* alone **1 sie waren allein im Zimmer** they were alone in the room; **jemanden allein lassen** to leave somebody alone; **2** on your own; **sie hat das ganz allein gezeichnet** she drew it all on her own; **3 von allein** by yourself, by itself (*automatically*); **4 allein stehend** single; **5 eine allein erziehende Mutter** a single mother; **der/die allein Erziehende** single parent; **6 nicht allein** not only; **7 allein der Gedanke** the mere thought.

alleinerziehend, alleinstehend SEE **allein**.

aller, alle, alles *pronoun* **1** all; **alle meine Freunde** all my friends; **alles Geld** all the money; **alle miteinander** all together; **2 alle Jungen in der Schule** all the boys in the school; **alle Bewohner der Stadt sind dagegen** all the people of the town are against it; **alles Gute!** all the best!; **Getränke aller Art** all kinds of drinks; **3 alle** (*plural*) all; **alle waren da** they were all there; **wir alle** all of us; **wir**

haben alle gesehen we saw all of them; **4 ohne allen Grund** without any reason; **5 alle beide** both of them; **6** every; **alle Tage** every day; **alle fünf Minuten** every five minutes; **7 alles** everything, everybody (*people*).

alle *adjective* **alle sein** (*informal*) to be all gone.

allerbester, allerbeste, allerbestes *adjective* **1** very best; **2 am allerbesten** best of all.

allerdings *adverb* **1** though; **das Essen ist gut, allerdings ziemlich teuer** the food's good, though rather expensive; **2** certainly (*yes*); **'tut das weh?' – 'allerdings!'** 'does it hurt?' – 'it certainly does!'.

Allergie *die* (PL **die Allergien**) allergy.

allergisch *adjective* allergic.

Allerheiligen *das* All Saints' Day.

allerlei *adjective* all sorts of; **allerlei Ausreden** all sorts of excuses.

allerletzter, allerletzte, allerletztes *adjective* very last.

alles SEE **aller.**

allgemein *adjective* **1** general; **2 im Allgemeinen** in general.

allgemein *adverb* **1** generally; **2 es ist allgemein bekannt, dass** ... it is common knowledge that ....

allmählich *adjective* gradual.

allmählich *adverb* gradually; **wir sollten allmählich gehen** it's time we got going.

Alltag *der* **1** daily routine; **2** weekday.

alltäglich *adjective* everyday (*event, sight*).

alltags *adverb* on weekdays.

Alpen *plural noun* **die Alpen** the Alps.

Alphabet *das* (PL **die Alphabete**) alphabet.

alphabetisch *adjective* alphabetical.

als *conjunction* **1** when; **als meine Freundin hier war** when my friend was here; **erst als** only when; **2** than (*as a comparison*); **er ist jünger als sie** he's younger than her; **3 lieber ... als ... rather ... than ...; ich würde lieber ins Kino gehen, als zum Essen** I'd rather go to the cinema than for a meal; **4** as; **als Frau kann ich das verstehen** as a woman, I can sympathize; **gerade als ich gehen wollte** just as I was about to leave; **5 als ob** as if; **als ob ich das nicht wüsste** as if I didn't know that!

also *adverb, conjunction* **1** so; **ich konnte ihn telefonisch nicht erreichen, also habe ich ihm ein Fax geschickt** I couldn't get through to him on the phone, so I sent him a fax; **2** then; **also kommst du mit?** you're coming too, then?; **also gut** all right then; **3** well; **also, wie gesagt** well, as I said before; **4 na also!** there you are!

alt *adjective* **1** old; **wie alt bist du?** how old are you?; **alt werden** to grow old; **2 alles beim Alten lassen** to leave everything as it was.

Altar der (PL die Altäre) altar.

Alter das (PL die Alter) 1 age; **in deinem Alter** at your age; **im Alter von zwanzig** at the age of twenty; 2 old age; **im Alter** in old age.

älter adjective 1 older; **mein Rad ist älter als deins** my bike is older than yours; 2 elder; **mein älterer Bruder** my elder brother; 3 elderly.

altern verb (PERF **ist gealtert**) to age.

Alternative die (PL die Alternativen) alternative.

Altersgenosse der (PL die Altersgenossen) person of one's own age.

Altersgenossin der (PL die Altersgenossinnen) person of one's own age.

Altersgrenze die (PL die Altersgrenzen) age limit.

Altersheim das (PL die Altersheime) old people's home.

ältester, älteste, ältestes adjective 1 oldest; 2 eldest; **der älteste Sohn** the eldest son.

Altglas das used glass.

Altglascontainer der (PL die Altglascontainer) bottle bank.

altmodisch adjective old-fashioned.

Altpapier das waste paper.

Altstadt die (PL die Altstädte) old town.

Alufolie die tin foil.

Aluminium das aluminium.

am = **an dem**; 1 **am Freitag** on Friday; 2 **am besten** the best; 3 **am teuersten** (the) most expensive; 4 **am höchsten** the highest; 5 **am Abend** in the evening.

Ameise die (PL die Ameisen) ant.

Amerika das America.

Amerikaner der (PL die Amerikaner) American.

Amerikanerin die (PL die Amerikanerinnen) American.

amerikanisch adjective American.

Ampel die (PL die Ampeln) traffic lights.

Amsel die (PL die Amseln) blackbird.

Amt das (PL die Ämter) 1 office; 2 exchange (telephone).

amtlich adjective official.

amüsant adjective amusing.

amüsieren verb (PERF **hat amüsiert**) 1 to amuse; 2 **sich amüsieren** to enjoy oneself; **amüsier dich gut!** enjoy yourself!; 3 **sich über etwas amüsieren** to find something funny.

an preposition (+ DAT or + ACC) (the dative is used when talking about position; the accusative shows movement or a change of place) 1 at; **an der Spitze** at the top; **sich an den Tisch setzen** to sit down at the table; **er arbeitet an der Schule** he works at the school; 2 on (attached to, when talking about time); **das Bild hängt an der Wand** the picture is on the wall; **an dem Tag** on that day; **ich habe am fünften März Geburtstag** my birthday is on the fifth of March;

3 to; **einen Brief an jemanden schicken** to send a letter to somebody; **4 an einer Krankheit sterben** to die of a disease; **5 an jemanden denken** to think of somebody; **6 sich an etwas erinnern** to remember something; **7 an (und für) sich** actually; **an sich ist das kein Problem** actually, it's no problem; **8 es liegt an dir, jetzt etwas zu unternehmen** it's up to you to do something now.

an *adverb* **1** on; **das Licht ist an** the light's on; **2 ohne etwas an** with nothing on; **3 an die dreißig Euro** about thirty euros; **4 von heute an** from today.

analysieren *verb* (PERF hat analysiert) to analyse.

Ananas die (PL die Ananas) pineapple.

Anästhetikum das (PL die Anästhetika) anaesthetic.

anbieten ◇*verb* (IMPERF bot an, PERF hat angeboten) to offer; **Anna bot mir an, mich nach Hause zu bringen** Anna offered to take me home.

Anblick der (PL die Anblicke) sight.

anbrennen ◇*verb* (IMPERF brannte an, PERF ist angebrannt) to burn; **das Essen ist angebrannt** the food's burnt.

Andenken das (PL die Andenken) **1** souvenir; **2 zum Andenken an unsere Ferien** to remind us of our holiday.

anderer, andere, anderes *adjective* **1** other; **ich nehme das andere T-Shirt** I'll have the other

T-shirt; **2** different; **3 ein anderer/ eine andere/ ein anderes** another; **ein anderes Mal** another time.

andere *pronoun* **1** der/die/das andere the other one; **nicht dieses Buch, sondern das andere** not that book, but the other one; **die anderen** the others; **die anderen kommen später** the others are coming later; **2 andere** other ones (*things, toys, etc.*); **3 ein anderer/ eine andere/ ein anderes** a different one (*thing*), someone else (*person*); **4 kein anderer** no one else; **5 unter anderem** among other things; **6 etwas anderes** something else; **7 alles andere** everything else.

andererseits *adverb* on the other hand.

andermal *adverb* **ein andermal** another time.

ändern *verb* (PERF hat geändert) **1** to change; **2** to alter (*a garment*); **3 sich ändern** to change; **sie hat sich sehr geändert** she's changed a lot.

anders *adverb* **1** differently; **2 anders aussehen** to look different; **3 niemand anders** nobody else; **jemand anders** somebody else; **4 anders als** different from; **du bist ganz anders als ich** you're quite different from me; **5 irgendwo anders** somewhere else.

anderthalb *number* one and a half.

Anerkennung die **1** appreciation; **2** recognition (*of a king, state*).

Anfall der (PL die **Anfälle**) fit.

Anfang der (PL die **Anfänge**)
1 beginning, start; **am Anfang** at
the beginning; **von Anfang an** from
the start; **zu Anfang** at first.

anfangen ◇verb (PRES **fängt an**,
IMPERF **fing an**, PERF **hat
angefangen**) 1 to begin, to start;
die Schule fängt um acht an
school starts at eight; **mit etwas
anfangen** to start (on) something;
2 bei einer Firma anfangen to
start working for a firm; **3 was soll
ich damit anfangen?** what am I
supposed to do with that? **4 damit
kann ich nichts anfangen** that's no
good to me (*it's no use*), it doesn't
mean anything to me (*I don't
understand it*).

Anfänger der (PL die **Anfänger**)
beginner.

Anfängerin die (PL die
Anfängerinnen) beginner.

anfassen verb (PERF **hat
angefasst**) 1 to touch; 2 to tackle
(*a problem, a task*); 3 to treat (*a
person*); **4 mit anfassen** to lend a
hand; **5 sich anfassen** to feel; **es
fasst sich weich an** it feels soft;
6 jemanden anfassen to take
somebody's hand; **sie hat ihrer
Mutter angefasst** she took her
mother's hand; **fasst euch an!** hold
hands!

anfragen verb (PERF **hat
angefragt**) to enquire, to ask.

anfreunden verb (PERF **hat sich
angefreundet**) 1 **sich anfreunden**
to make friends; **sie freundet sich
mit allen möglichen Leuten an** she

makes friends with all sorts of
people; **2 sich anfreunden** to
become friends; **wir haben uns
angefreundet** we've become
friends.

Anführungszeichen plural
noun inverted commas.

Angabe die (PL die **Angaben**)
1 piece of information; **2** serve (*in
tennis*); **3** showing off; **das ist nur
Angabe** he is/she is/they are only
showing off.

angeben ◇verb (PRES **gibt an**,
IMPERF **gab an**, PERF **hat
angegeben**) 1 to give (*your name, a
reason*); 2 to show off; 3 to indicate
(*on a map*); 4 to serve (*in tennis*).

Angeber der (PL die **Angeber**)
show-off.

Angeberin die (PL die
Angeberinnen) show-off.

Angebot das (PL die **Angebote**)
offer.

angehen ◇verb (IMPERF **ging an**,
PERF **ist angegangen**) 1 to come on
(*a radio, heating, a light*); 2 to
concern; **das geht auch dich
etwas an** it concerns you too; **das
geht dich nichts an** it's none of
your business; 3 (PERF **hat
angegangen**) to tackle (*problems,
difficulty, work*).

Angehörige der/die (PL die
Angehörigen) relative.

Angel die (PL die **Angeln**) fishing
rod.

Angelegenheit die (PL die
Angelegenheiten) 1 matter;

2 business; **das ist meine Angelegenheit** that's my business.

angeln verb (PERF **hat geangelt**)
1 to fish; **angeln gehen** to go fishing; **2** to catch (a fish).

Angelrute die (PL die **Angelruten**) fishing rod.

angemessen adjective adequate.

angenehm adjective pleasant.

angenehm exclamation pleased to meet you! (when introduced to somebody).

Angestellte der/die (PL die **Angestellten**) employee.

angewiesen adjective dependent; **auf etwas angewiesen sein** to be dependent on something; **auf jemanden angewiesen sein** to be dependent on somebody.

angewöhnen verb (PERF **hat angewöhnt**) **1** jemandem etwas **angewöhnen** to get somebody used to something; **2** sich etwas **angewöhnen** to get into the habit of doing something; **ich habe es mir angewöhnt, früh aufzustehen** I've got into the habit of getting up early.

Angewohnheit die (PL die **Angewohnheiten**) habit.

angreifen ◊verb (IMPERF **griff an**, PERF **hat angegriffen**) **1** to attack; **2** to affect (your health, voice).

Angriff der (PL die **Angriffe**) attack.

Angst die (PL die **Ängste**) **1** fear; **2 Angst haben** to be afraid; **vor jemandem Angst haben** to be afraid of somebody; **mir ist Angst** I'm afraid; **3** jemandem Angst **machen** to frighten somebody; **4 Angst vor einer Prüfung haben** to be worried about an exam; **Angst um jemanden haben** to be worried about somebody.

ängstlich adjective **1** nervous; **2** frightened; **3** anxious.

anhaben ◊verb (informal) (PRES **hat an**, IMPERF **hatte an**, PERF **hat angehabt**) to have on; **sie hat heute das neue Kleid an** she's got her new dress on today.

anhalten ◊verb (PRES **hält an**, IMPERF **hielt an**, PERF **hat angehalten**) **1** to stop; **2 den Atem anhalten** to hold your breath; **3** to last; **das schöne Wetter wird nicht lange anhalten** the nice weather won't last long; **4** jemanden zur **Arbeit anhalten** to urge somebody to work.

Anhalter der (PL die **Anhalter**) hitchhiker; **per Anhalter fahren** to hitchhike.

Anhalterin die (PL die **Anhalterinnen**) hitchhiker.

Anhang der (PL die **Anhänge**) appendix.

Anhänger der (PL die **Anhänger**) **1** supporter; **2** trailer; **3** label (on a suitcase); **4** pendant; **5** loop (for hanging up).

Anhängerin die (PL die **Anhängerinnen**) supporter.

anhören verb (PERF **hat angehört**) **1** to listen to (music, a CD); **sich etwas anhören** to listen to something; **ich kann ihn mir nicht länger anhören** I can't listen to

a b c d e f g h i j k l m n o p q r s t u v w x y z

him any longer; **2 sich anhören** to sound; **sich gut anhören** to sound good; **3 jemandem etwas anhören** to hear something in somebody's voice; **man hörte ihr die Verzweiflung an** you could hear the despair in her voice.

anklagen *verb* (PERF **hat angeklagt**) to accuse.

Ankleidekabine die (PL die **Ankleidekabinen**) changing cubicle.

anklicken *verb* (PERF **hat angeklickt**) etwas anklicken to click on something; **das Icon anklicken** to click on the icon.

ankommen ⋄*verb* (IMPERF **kam an**, PERF **ist angekommen**) **1** to arrive; **gut ankommen** to arrive safely; **2 (bei jemandem) gut ankommen** (*informal*) to go down well (with somebody); **3 ankommen auf** to depend on; **es kommt ganz darauf an** it all depends; **4 es drauf ankommen lassen** (*informal*) to take a chance; **5 auf ein paar Minuten kommt es nicht an** a few minutes don't matter.

ankündigen *verb* (PERF **hat angekündigt**) to announce.

Ankunft die (PL die **Ankünfte**) arrival.

Ankunftstafel die (PL die **Ankunftstafeln**) arrivals board.

Ankunftszeit die (PL die **Ankunftszeiten**) time of arrival.

Anlage die (PL die **Anlagen**) **1** gardens; **2** investment; **das Haus**

ist eine gute Anlage the house is a good investment; **3** plant (*industrial, for recycling, for example*); **4** enclosure; **als Anlage eingelegt** enclosed; **5** system (*music, loudspeakers, etc.*); **6** installation (*military*).

Anlass der (PL die **Anlässe**) **1** cause; **der Anlass ihres Streits** the cause of their row; **Anlass zu etwas geben** to give cause for something; **2** occasion; **ein festlicher Anlass** a festive occasion; **aus Anlass ihres Geburtstags** on the occasion of her birthday.

Anleitung die (PL die **Anleitungen**) instructions.

anmachen *verb* (PERF **hat angemacht**) **1** to turn on (*the light, radio, TV*); **2** to light (*a fire*); **3** to dress (*salad*); **4** (*informal*) to chat up (*a person*).

Anmeldeformular das (PL die **Anmeldeformulare**) registration form.

anmelden *verb* (PERF **hat angemeldet**) **1** to register (*a car, change of address*); **2 jemanden anmelden** to enrol somebody; **3 jemanden anmelden** to make an appointment for somebody; **sind Sie angemeldet?** do you have an appointment?; **4 ein Gespräch anmelden** to book a call (*on the phone*); **5 sich anmelden** to say that you're coming; **6 sich anmelden** to register your new address (*in Germany a change of address has to be registered at the 'Einwohnermeldeamt'*); **sich**

polizeilich anmelden to register with the police; **7 sich anmelden** to make an appointment; **sich beim Arzt anmelden** to make an appointment with the doctor; **8 sich anmelden** to check in (*at a hotel*); **9 sich anmelden** to enrol; **sich zu einem Abendkurs anmelden** to enrol for an evening course.

Anmeldung *die* (PL *die* **Anmeldungen**) **1** registration; **2** appointment.

annehmbar *adjective* acceptable.

annehmen ◇*verb* (PRES **nimmt an**, IMPERF **nahm an**, PERF **hat angenommen**) **1** to accept (*an invitation, help, a verdict*); **2** to take (*a call, name*); **3** to adopt (*a child, habit*); **4** to assume; **angenommen, dass** ... assuming that ...; **5** to suppose.

Annonce *die* (PL *die* **Annoncen**) (small) ad.

Anorak *der* (PL *die* **Anoraks**) **1** anorak; **2** cagoule.

anordnen *verb* (PERF **hat angeordnet**) **1** to arrange; **2** to order.

anpassen *verb* (PERF **hat sich angepasst**) **sich anpassen** to adapt.

anpassungsfähig *adjective* adaptable.

anprobieren *verb* (PERF **hat anprobiert**) to try on.

Anruf *der* (PL *die* **Anrufe**) (phone) call.

Anrufbeantworter *der* (PL *die* **Anrufbeantworter**) answering machine.

anrufen ◇*verb* (IMPERF **rief an**, PERF **hat angerufen**) **1** to ring, to phone; **ich rufe schnell mal meine Mutter an** I'll just quickly ring my mother; **2** to call to (*a passer-by*).

ans = **an das**; **ans Telefon gehen** to answer the phone.

Ansage *die* (PL *die* **Ansagen**) announcement.

Ansager *der* (PL *die* **Ansager**) announcer.

Ansagerin *die* (PL *die* **Ansagerinnen**) announcer.

anschalten *verb* (PERF **hat angeschaltet**) to switch on.

anschauen *verb* (PERF **hat angeschaut**) **1** to look at; **2 sich etwas anschauen** to look at something, to watch something (*on TV*); **sie schauten sich den neuen Film an** they saw the new film.

anscheinend *adverb* apparently.

Anschlag *der* (PL *die* **Anschläge**) **1** notice; **2** attack; **ein Anschlag auf den Präsidenten** an attack on the president.

Anschlagbrett *das* (PL *die* **Anschlagbretter**) notice board.

anschlagen ◇*verb* (PRES **schlägt an**, IMPERF **schlug an**, PERF **hat angeschlagen**) **1** to put up (*a notice, an announcement*); **2** to chip.

anschließen ◇*verb* (IMPERF **schloss an**, PERF **hat angeschlossen**) **1** to connect;

b
c
d
e
f
g
h
i
j
k
l
m
n
o
p
q
r
s
t
u
v
w
x
y
z

2 sich an etwas anschließen to follow something; **an den Vortrag schließt sich eine Diskussion an** the talk will be followed by a discussion; **3 sich jemandem anschließen** to join somebody; **sich einer Gruppe anschließen** to join a group.

anschließend *adverb*
1 afterwards; **2 anschließend an das Essen** after the meal.

Anschluss *der* (PL die **Anschlüsse**)
1 connection; **2 Anschluss finden** to make friends; **3 den Anschluss verlieren** to lose contact; **4 im Anschluss an** after.

anschnallen *verb* (PERF **hat sich angeschnallt**) **sich anschnallen** to fasten your seat belt.

Anschrift *die* (PL die **Anschriften**) address.

Anschuldigung *die* (PL die **Anschuldigungen**) accusation.

ansehen ✧*verb* (PRES **sieht an**, IMPERF **sah an**, PERF **hat angesehen**)
1 to look at; **sie sah mich nicht an** she didn't look at me; **2 sich etwas ansehen** to look at something (*on TV*) to watch something; **sich einen Film ansehen** to see a film; **3 sich eine Stadt ansehen** to look round a town; **4** to regard; **ich sehe ihn als meinen Freund an** I regard him as a friend.

Ansehen *das* **1** respect; **2** reputation.

Ansicht *die* (PL die **Ansichten**) view; **meiner Ansicht nach** in my view.

Ansichtskarte *die* (PL die **Ansichtskarten**) picture postcard.

ansprechen ✧*verb* (PRES **spricht an**, IMPERF **sprach an**, PERF **hat angesprochen**) **1** to speak to; **2** to appeal to; **die Musik spricht mich an** the music appeals to me; **3** to mention; **er hat den Skandal, in den sie verwickelt war, angesprochen** he mentioned the scandal she was involved in; **4 auf etwas ansprechen** to respond to something (*a treatment, for example*).

Anspruch *der* (PL die **Ansprüche**) **1** demand; **keine Ansprüche stellen** to make no demands; **2** claim (*for compensation*); **3 Anspruch auf etwas haben** to be entitled to something; **4 viel Zeit in Anspruch nehmen** to take up a lot of time; **5 etwas in Anspruch nehmen** to take advantage of something (*an offer, for example*).

anständig *adjective* **1** decent; **2** respectable.

anstarren *verb* (PERF **hat angestarrt**) to stare at.

anstatt *preposition* (+ GEN) instead of.

anstatt *conjunction* **anstatt zu arbeiten** instead of working.

ansteckend *adjective* infectious.

anstelle *preposition* (+ GEN) instead of.

anstellen *verb* (PERF **hat angestellt**) **1** to employ; **2** to turn on (*the TV, radio*); **3** (*informal*) to do; **was stellt ihr heute Abend noch an?** what are you doing tonight?; **wie kann ich es nur anstellen, dass ...?** what can I do to ...?; **4 sich anstellen** to queue; **5 sich anstellen** to make a fuss; **stell dich nicht so an!** don't make such a fuss!

Anstieg der (PL die **Anstiege**) **1** increase; **2** way up, ascent.

anstreichen ✧verb (IMPERF **strich an**, PERF **hat angestrichen**) to paint.

anstrengen verb (PERF **hat angestrengt**) **1** to tire; **ihr Besuch hat mich sehr angestrengt** their visit tired me out; **2 sich anstrengen** to make an effort.

anstrengend adjective tiring.

Anstrengung die (PL die **Anstrengungen**) effort.

Antarktis die die **Antarktis** the Antarctic.

Anteil der (PL die **Anteile**) **1** share; **mein Anteil an dem Gewinn** my share of the profit; **2 Anteil nehmen** to sympathize; **3 Anteil nehmen an** to take an interest in.

Antenne die (PL die **Antennen**) aerial.

Antibiotikum das (PL die **Antibiotika**) antibiotic.

antik adjective antique.

Antiquitäten plural noun antiques.

Antiseptikum das (PL die **Antiseptika**) antiseptic.

Antivirenprogramm das (PL die **Antivirenprogramme**) anti-virus software.

Antrag der (PL die **Anträge**) application; **einen Antrag stellen** to make an application.

Antragsformular das (PL die **Antragsformulare**) application form.

Antwort die (PL die **Antworten**) answer, reply; **jemandem eine Antwort geben** to give somebody an answer.

antworten verb (PERF **hat geantwortet**) to answer, to reply; **auf etwas antworten** to answer something; **jemandem antworten** to reply to somebody.

Anwalt der (PL die **Anwälte**) lawyer.

Anwältin die (PL die **Anwältinnen**) lawyer.

Anweisung die (PL die **Anweisungen**) instruction.

anwenden verb (PERF **hat angewendet**) **1** to use (a method, process, medicine); **2** to apply (a rule, law).

anwesend adjective present.

Anwesenheit die presence; **er gab es in meiner Anwesenheit zu** he admitted it in my presence.

Anzahl die number.

anzahlen verb (PERF **hat angezahlt**) to pay a deposit; **hundert Euro anzahlen** to pay a deposit of a hundred euros; **ein Auto anzahlen** to pay a deposit on a car.

Anzahlung die (PL die **Anzahlungen**) deposit.

Anzeichen das (PL die **Anzeichen**) sign.

a b c d e f g h i j k l m n o p q r s t u v w x y z

Anzeige die (PL die **Anzeigen**)
1 advertisement; **2** report (to the police); **(eine) Anzeige gegen jemanden erstatten** to report somebody to the police.

anzeigen verb (PERF **hat angezeigt**) **1** to report; **jemanden anzeigen** to report somebody to the police; **2** to show (the time, a date).

anziehen ◇verb (IMPERF **zog an**, PERF **hat angezogen**) **1** to attract; **2** to put on (clothes, the brakes); **3** to dress (a child or doll); **gut angezogen** well dressed; **4** to tighten (a knot, a screw); **5** sich anziehen to get dressed; **6** was soll ich anziehen? what shall I wear?

Anzug der (PL die **Anzüge**) suit.

anzünden verb (PERF **hat angezündet**) to light.

Apfel der (PL die **Äpfel**) apple.

Apfelsaft der (PL die **Apfelsäfte**) apple juice.

Apfelsine die (PL die **Apfelsinen**) orange.

Apotheke die (PL die **Apotheken**) chemist's, pharmacy.

Apotheker der (PL die **Apotheker**) chemist, pharmacist.

Apothekerin die (PL die **Apothekerinnen**) chemist, pharmacist.

Apparat der (PL die **Apparate**) **1** set (TV, radio); **2** camera; **3** phone; **am Apparat!** speaking!; **4** gadget.

Appartement das (PL die **Appartements**) flat.

Appetit der appetite; **guten Appetit!** enjoy your meal!

Aprikose die (PL die **Aprikosen**) apricot.

April der April; **am ersten April** on the first of April; **April, April!** April fool!; **jemanden in den April schicken** to play an April fool trick on somebody.

Aquarium das (PL die **Aquarien**) **1** aquarium; **2** tank (for fish).

Äquator der equator.

Araber der (PL die **Araber**) Arab.

Araberin die (PL die **Araberinnen**) Arab.

arabisch adjective **1** Arab; **die arabischen Länder** the Arab countries; **2** Arabian; **3** Arabic (number); **die arabische Sprache** Arabic.

Arbeit die (PL die **Arbeiten**) **1** work; **viel Arbeit haben** to have a lot of work; **von der Arbeit kommen** to come from work; **2** job; **3** test (at school); **4** sich viel Arbeit machen to go to a lot of trouble.

arbeiten verb (PERF **hat gearbeitet**) to work.

Arbeiter der (PL die **Arbeiter**) worker.

Arbeiterin die (PL die **Arbeiterinnen**) worker.

Arbeitgeber der (PL die **Arbeitgeber**) employer.

Arbeitnehmer der (PL die **Arbeitnehmer**) employee.

Arbeitsamt das (PL die **Arbeitsämter**) job centre.

arbeitslos adjective unemployed.

Arbeitslose der/die (PL die **Arbeitslosen**) unemployed person; **die Arbeitslosen** the unemployed.

Arbeitslosigkeit die unemployment.

Arbeitsplatz der (PL die **Arbeitsplätze**) 1 job; 2 desk.

Arbeitspraktikum das (PL die **Arbeitspraktika**) work experience.

Arbeitsstunde die (PL die **Arbeitsstunden**) working hour.

Arbeitszimmer das (PL die **Arbeitszimmer**) study.

Architekt der (PL die **Architekten**) architect.

Architektin die (PL die **Architektinnen**) architect.

Architektur die architecture.

Ärger der 1 annoyance; 2 trouble; **Ärger mit dem Auto haben** to have trouble with the car.

ärgerlich adjective 1 annoying; 2 annoyed; **er war darüber sehr ärgerlich** he was very annoyed about it.

ärgern verb (PERF hat geärgert) 1 to annoy; 2 sich ärgern to be annoyed, to get annoyed; **ich habe mich darüber geärgert** I was annoyed about it; **sich über jemanden ärgern** to get annoyed with somebody.

Arktis die die Arktis the Arctic; **in der Arktis** in the Arctic.

Arm der (PL die **Arme**) arm; **jemanden auf den Arm nehmen** (informal) to pull somebody's leg.

arm adjective poor.

Armband das (PL die **Armbänder**) bracelet.

Armbanduhr die (PL die **Armbanduhren**) wrist-watch.

Armee die (PL die **Armeen**) army.

Ärmel der (PL die **Ärmel**) sleeve.

Ärmelkanal der (English) Channel.

Armut die poverty.

arrangieren verb (PERF hat arrangiert) 1 to arrange; 2 sich arrangieren to come to an arrangement.

Art die (PL die **Arten**) 1 way; **auf diese Art** in this way; **auf seine Art** in his own way; 2 kind; **diese Art (von) Buch** this kind of book; **Bücher aller Art** books of all kinds; 3 species; **eine gefährdete Art** an endangered species; 4 nature; **es ist nicht seine Art, das zu tun** it's not (in) his nature to do that.

Arterie die (PL die **Arterien**) artery.

artig adjective well-behaved.

Artikel der (PL die **Artikel**) article; **der bestimmte/unbestimmte Artikel** the definite/indefinite article.

Arznei die (PL die **Arzneien**) medicine.

Arzneimittel das (PL die **Arzneimittel**) drug.

Arzt der (PL die **Ärzte**) doctor.

Ärztin die (PL die **Ärztinnen**) doctor.

ärztlich adjective medical.

ärztlich adverb **sich ärztlich behandeln lassen** to have medical treatment.

As SEE **Ass.**

Asche die (PL die **Aschen**) ash.

Aschenbecher der (PL die **Aschenbecher**) ashtray.

Aschermittwoch der Ash Wednesday.

Asiat der (PL die **Asiaten**) Asian.

Asiatin die (PL die **Asiatinnen**) Asian.

asiatisch adjective Asian.

Asien das Asia; **nach Asien** to Asia.

Ass das (PL die **Asse**) ace.

aß SEE **essen.**

Assistent der (PL die **Assistenten**) assistant.

Assistentin die (PL die **Assistentinnen**) assistant.

Ast der (PL die **Äste**) branch.

Asthma das asthma.

Astrologie die astrology.

Astronaut der (PL die **Astronauten**) astronaut.

Astronomie die astronomy.

Asyl das 1 asylum; **um politisches Asyl bitten** to apply for political asylum; 2 hostel (for the homeless).

Asylant der (PL die **Asylanten**) asylum-seeker.

Atelier das (PL die **Ateliers**) (artist's) studio.

Atem der breath; **außer Atem sein** to be out of breath.

atemlos adjective breathless.

Atemlosigkeit die breathlessness.

Athlet der (PL die **Athleten**) athlete.

Athletin die (PL die **Athletinnen**) athlete.

Atlantik der der Atlantik the Atlantic (Ocean); **im Atlantik** in the Atlantic.

Atlas der (PL die **Atlanten**) atlas.

atmen verb (PERF **hat geatmet**) to breathe.

Atmosphäre die (PL die **Atmosphären**) atmosphere.

Atom das (PL die **Atome**) atom.

atomar adjective atomic.

Atombombe die (PL die **Atombomben**) atomic bomb.

Atomwaffen plural noun nuclear weapons.

atomwaffenfrei adjective nuclear-free.

attraktiv adjective attractive.

ätzend adjective 1 corrosive; 2 caustic (wit, remark).

au exclamation 1 ouch!; 2 oh! (when surprised or enthusiastic); **au ja!** oh yes!

auch adverb 1 also, too; **Sophie war auch dabei** Sophie was also there, Sophie was there too; **ich auch** me too; **nicht nur ... sondern auch ...** not only ... but also ...; 2 **'ich gehe jetzt'** – **'ich auch'** I'm going now' – 'so am I'; **'er schläft'** – **'sie auch'** 'he's asleep' – 'so is she'; 3 **'ich bin nicht müde'** – **'ich auch nicht'** 'I'm not tired'-'neither am I'; **das weiß ich auch nicht** I don't know either; 4 **auch wenn** even if; 5 **wann auch** whenever; **was auch** whatever; **wo auch** wherever; **wer auch** whoever; 6 **wie dem auch sei**

however that may be; **7 lügst du auch nicht?** you're not lying, are you?

auf *preposition* (+ DAT *or* + ACC) *(the dative is used when talking about position; the accusative shows movement or a change of place)* **1** on; **das Buch liegt auf dem Tisch** the book's on the table; **er hat das Buch auf den Tisch gelegt** he put the book on the table; **2 ich war auf der Party** I was at the party; **ich gehe auf eine Party** I'm going to a party; **ich war auf der Post** I was at the post office; **er ist auf die Post gegangen** he went to the post office; **3 auf der Straße** in the street; **4 auf diese Art** in this way; **auf Deutsch** in German; **5** for *(indicating time or distance)*; **er ist auf ein paar Tage verreist** he's gone away for a few days; **6 auf seinen Rat hin** on his advice; **7 auf Wiedersehen!** goodbye!

auf *adverb* **1** open; **die Tür ist auf** the door is open; **Mund auf!** open your mouth!; **2** up *(out of bed)*, **auf sein** to be up; **er ist schon auf** he's already up; **3 auf einmal** suddenly; **4 auf einmal** at once *(at the same time)*; **5 auf und ab** up and down; **6 sich auf und davon machen** to make off.

aufbekommen ◇*verb* (IMPERF **bekam auf**, PERF **hat aufbekommen**) **1** to get open; **2 Hausaufgaben aufbekommen** to be given homework.

aufbewahren *verb* (PERF **hat aufbewahrt**) to keep.

aufblasen ◇*verb* (PRES **bläst auf**, IMPERF **blies auf**, PERF **hat aufgeblasen**) to blow up.

aufbleiben ◇*verb* (IMPERF **blieb auf**, PERF **ist aufgeblieben**) **1** to stay open; **wie lange bleiben die Geschäfte auf?** how long do the shops stay open?; **2** to stay up *(not go to bed)*.

aufbringen ◇*verb* (IMPERF **brachte auf**, PERF **hat aufgebracht**) **1** to raise *(money)*; **2** to find *(patience, strength)*; **3** to open; **ich bringe die Tür nicht auf** I can't open the door; **4 jemanden aufbringen** to make somebody angry; **5 Verständnis für etwas aufbringen** to be able to understand something.

aufeinander *adverb* **1** one on top of the other; **die Bretter aufeinander legen** to put the planks one on top of the other; **2 aufeinander liegen** to lie on top of each other; **3 aufeinander folgen** to follow one another; **4 aufeinander warten** to wait for each other; **5 aufeinander schießen** to shoot at each other; **6 aufeinander fahren** to collide with each other.

Aufenthalt *der* (PL **die Aufenthalte**) **1** stay; **2** stop *(pause in a journey)*; **zehn Minuten Aufenthalt haben** to stop for ten minutes.

Aufenthaltsraum *der* (PL **die Aufenthaltsräume**) **1** lounge; **2** recreation room.

Auffahrt *die* (PL **die Auffahrten**) **1** drive; **2** slip road.

auffallend *adjective* striking.

auffangen ⋄verb (PRES **fängt auf**, IMPERF **fing auf**, PERF **hat aufgefangen**) to catch.

aufführen verb (PERF **hat aufgeführt**) 1 to perform (a play); 2 to list (words, items); 3 sich **aufführen** to behave.

Aufführung die (PL die **Aufführungen**) performance.

auffüllen verb (PERF **hat aufgefüllt**) 1 to fill up; 2 to stock up.

Aufgabe die (PL die **Aufgaben**) 1 task; 2 exercise (at school); 3 question (in a test or an exam); 4 **Aufgaben** homework.

aufgeben ⋄verb (PRES **gibt auf**, IMPERF **gab auf**, PERF **hat aufgegeben**) 1 to give up; **ich gebe auf!** I give up!; 2 to post; 3 to check in (luggage); 4 to place (an advertisement, order); 5 **Hausaufgaben aufgeben** to set homework.

aufgehen ⋄verb (IMPERF **ging auf**, PERF **ist aufgegangen**) 1 to open (of a door or flower, for example); 2 to come undone (of a knot or zip, for example); 3 to rise (of the sun, moon); 4 to realize; **es ist mir aufgegangen, dass ...** I've realized that ...; 5 to work out (in maths); **zehn durch drei geht nicht auf** three into ten won't go.

aufgeregt adjective excited.

aufgeschlossen adjective open-minded.

aufgrund preposition (+ GEN) 1 because of; 2 on the strength of.

aufhaben ⋄verb (PRES **hat auf**, IMPERF **hatte auf**, PERF **hat aufgehabt**) 1 to have on (a hat); 2 **den Mund aufhaben** to have your mouth open; 3 **etwas aufhaben** to have homework to do; **viel aufhaben** to have a lot of homework; 4 to be open; **der Laden hat abends auf** the shop is open in the evening.

aufhalten ⋄verb (PRES **hält auf**, IMPERF **hielt auf**, PERF **hat aufgehalten**) 1 to hold open (a door); 2 to hold up, to keep (somebody from doing something); 3 **die Hand aufhalten** to hold out your hand; 4 **die Augen aufhalten** to keep your eyes open; 5 to check (inflation, an advance, unemployment); 6 **sich aufhalten** to stay; 7 **sich mit etwas aufhalten** to spend your time on something.

aufhängen verb (PERF **hat aufgehängt**) 1 to hang up (washing); 2 **sich aufhängen** to hang yourself.

aufheben ⋄verb (IMPERF **hob auf**, PERF **hat aufgehoben**) 1 to pick up (from the ground); 2 to keep; 3 to abolish (a law); 4 **gut aufgehoben sein** to be well looked after.

aufheitern verb (PERF **hat aufgeheitert**) 1 to cheer up; 2 **sich aufheitern** to brighten up (of the weather).

aufhören verb (PERF **hat aufgehört**) to stop; **aufhören zu arbeiten** to stop working.

aufklären verb (PERF **hat aufgeklärt**) 1 to solve (a crime);

2 to explain (*an event, incident*);
3 ein Kind aufklären to tell a child
the facts of life; **4 sich aufklären** to
be solved (*a misunderstanding or
mystery*); **5 sich aufklären** to clear
up; **das Wetter klärt sich auf** the
weather is clearing up.

Aufkleber *der* (PL *die* **Aufkleber**)
sticker.

auflegen *verb* (PERF **hat
aufgelegt**) **1** to put on; **2** to hang up
(*when phoning*); **3** to lay; **noch ein
Gedeck auflegen** to lay another
place (*at table*); **4** to publish; **ein
Buch neu auflegen** to reprint a
book.

auflösen *verb* (PERF **hat aufgelöst**)
1 to dissolve; **2** to close (*an
account*); **3 sich auflösen** to
dissolve; **4 sich auflösen** to break
up (*of a crowd, demonstration*);
5 der Nebel ist aufgelöst the
fog has lifted; **6 in Tränen
aufgelöst sein** to be in floods of
tears.

aufmachen *verb* (PERF **hat
aufgemacht**) **1** to open;
2 jemandem aufmachen to open
the door to somebody; **3** to undo (*a
zip, knot*); **4 sich aufmachen** to set
out.

aufmerksam *adjective*
1 attentive; **2 auf etwas
aufmerksam werden** to notice
something; **3 jemanden auf etwas
aufmerksam machen** to draw
somebody's attention to
something.

aufmuntern *verb* (PERF **hat
aufgemuntert**) to cheer up.

Aufnahme *die* (PL *die* **Aufnahmen**)
1 photograph; **2** recording;
3 admission (*to hospital, to a club*);
4 welcome.

Aufnahmeprüfung *die* (PL *die*
Aufnahmeprüfungen) entrance
exam.

Aufnahmetaste *die* (PL *die*
Aufnahmetasten) record button.

aufnehmen *◇verb* (PRES **nimmt
auf**, IMPERF **nahm auf**, PERF **hat
aufgenommen**) **1** to receive
(*guests*); **2** to take up (*an idea,
activity, a theme*); **3** to admit (*to
hospital, to a club*); **4** to
photograph; **5** to film; **6** to record
(*a song, a programme, a film*); **7 es
mit jemandem aufnehmen
können** to be a match for
somebody; **8** to take (*food, news*);
etwas gelassen aufnehmen to
take something calmly.

aufpassen *verb* (PERF **hat
aufgepasst**) **1** to pay attention;
2 to watch out; **3 auf jemanden
aufpassen** to look after somebody;
4 auf etwas aufpassen to keep an
eye on something; **pass auf meine
Tasche auf** keep an eye on my bag.

aufräumen *verb* (PERF **hat
aufgeräumt**) to tidy up.

aufrecht *adjective* upright.

aufregen *verb* (PERF **hat
aufgeregt**) **1** to excite; **2** to annoy;
3 sich aufregen to get worked up.

aufregend *adjective* exciting.

aufs = **auf das**.

Aufsatz *der* (PL *die* **Aufsätze**) essay.

a b c d e f g h i j k l m n o p q r s t u v w x y z

a

b

c

d

e

f

g

h

i

j

k

l

m

n

o

p

q

r

s

t

u

v

w

x

y

z

aufschieben ◇verb (IMPERF **schob auf**, PERF **hat aufgeschoben**) **1** to put off (an arrangement); **2** to slide open.

aufschlagen verb (PRES **schlägt auf**, IMPERF **schlug auf**, PERF **hat aufgeschlagen**) to open.

aufschließen ◇verb (IMPERF **schloss auf**, PERF **hat aufgeschlossen**) to unlock.

Aufschnitt der sliced cold meat and cheese.

aufschreiben ◇verb (IMPERF **schrieb auf**, PERF **hat aufgeschrieben**) to write down.

aufsehen ◇verb (PRES **sieht auf**, IMPERF **sah auf**, PERF **hat aufgesehen**) to look up.

Aufsehen das sensation, stir; **Aufsehen erregen** to cause a stir.

Aufseher der (PL die **Aufseher**) **1** supervisor; **2** warder (in a prison); **3** attendant (in a museum).

Aufseherin die (PL die **Aufseherinnen**) **1** supervisor; **2** warder (in a prison); **3** attendant (in a museum).

aufsetzen verb (PERF **hat aufgesetzt**) **1** to put on; **2** to draft; **3 sich aufsetzen** to sit up.

Aufsicht die **1** supervision; **2** supervisor.

Aufstand der (PL die **Aufstände**) rebellion.

aufstehen ◇verb (IMPERF **stand auf**, PERF **ist aufgestanden**) **1** to get up; **2** (PERF **hat aufgestanden**) to be open.

aufstellen verb (PERF **hat aufgestellt**) **1** to put up; **2** to set up (skittles, chess pieces); **3 eine Mannschaft aufstellen** to pick a team; **4 eine Liste aufstellen** to draw up a list; **5 sich aufstellen** to line up.

auftauen verb (PERF **ist aufgetaut**) **1** to thaw; **2** to defrost; **die Erdbeeren sind aufgetaut** the strawberries have defrosted; **3** (PERF **hat aufgetaut**) to defrost; **ich habe die Erbeeren aufgetaut** I've defrosted the strawberries.

aufteilen verb (PERF **hat aufgeteilt**) to divide up.

Auftrag der (PL die **Aufträge**) **1** job; **2** order (in business); **etwas in Auftrag geben** to order something; **3** instructions; **einen Auftrag ausführen** to carry out an instruction; **4 im Auftrag von** on behalf of.

auftreten ◇verb (PRES **tritt auf**, IMPERF **trat auf**, PERF **ist aufgetreten**) **1** to appear (on stage); **2** to arise (a problem, difficulty); **3** to behave; **4** to tread.

aufwachen verb (PERF **ist aufgewacht**) to wake up.

aufwachsen ◇verb (PRES **wächst auf**, IMPERF **wuchs auf**, PERF **ist aufgewachsen**) to grow up.

aufwecken verb (PERF **hat aufgeweckt**) to wake up.

aufziehen ◇verb (IMPERF **zog auf**, PERF **hat aufgezogen**) **1** to wind up (a clock or toy); **2** to draw (curtains); **3 jemanden aufziehen** (informal) to tease somebody; **4** to bring up (*a child*).

Aufzug der (PL die **Aufzüge**) lift; **ich fahre mit dem Aufzug runter** I'm going down in the lift.

Auge das (PL die **Augen**) **1** eye; **2 unter vier Augen** in private.

Augenarzt der (PL die **Augenärzte**) ophthalmologist.

Augenärztin die (PL die **Augenärztinnen**) ophthalmologist.

Augenblick der (PL die **Augenblicke**) moment; **im Augenblick** at the moment.

Augenbraue die (PL die **Augenbrauen**) eyebrow.

August der August.

aus *preposition* (+ DAT) **1** out of; **er hat es aus dem Fenster geworfen** he threw it out of the window; **2** from; **aus Spanien** from Spain; **aus Erfahrung** from experience; **3** made of; **aus Holz** made of wood; **4 aus Spaß** for fun; **5 aus der Mode** out of fashion; **6 aus Versehen** by mistake; **7 aus welchem Grund?** for what reason?; **8 aus ihr ist eine gute Rechtsanwältin geworden** she made a good lawyer; **aus ihm ist nichts geworden** he never made anything of his life.

aus *adverb* **1** off (*of a TV, radio*); **das Licht ist aus** the light is off; **Licht aus!** lights out!; **2** finished; **wenn das Spiel aus ist** when the game has finished; **3 von mir aus** as far as I'm concerned; **4 von sich aus** of your own accord.

ausbauen *verb* (PERF **hat ausgebaut**) **1** to extend (*a building*); **2** to build up.

ausbeuten *verb* (PERF **hat ausgebeutet**) to exploit.

ausbilden *verb* (PERF **hat ausgebildet**) to train.

Ausbildung die **1** training; **2** education.

ausbreiten *verb* (PERF **hat ausgebreitet**) **1** to unfold; **2** to spread; **3** to stretch (*one's arms etc*).

ausbuhen *verb* (PERF **hat ausgebuht**) to boo; **die Menge buhte den Schiedsrichter aus** the crowd booed the referee.

ausdehnen *verb* (PERF **hat ausgedehnt**) **1** to extend, to prolong; **2** to expand.

Ausdruck[1] der (PL die **Ausdrücke**) expression; **etwas zum Ausdruck bringen** to express something.

Ausdruck[2] der (PL die **Ausdrucke**) print-out.

ausdrucken *verb* (PERF **hat ausgedruckt**) to print out.

ausdrücken *verb* (PERF **hat ausgedrückt**) **1** to squeeze (*oranges, lemons*); **2** to express; **3 sich ausdrücken** to express oneself.

auseinander *adverb* **1** apart; **etwas auseinander nehmen** to take something apart; **auseinander halten** to tell apart; **2 auseinander gehen** to part; **3 auseinander schreiben** to write as separate words; **4 sich mit einem Problem auseinander setzen** to come to

a b c d e f g h i j k l m n o p q r s t u v w x y z

grips with a problem; **5 sich mit jemandem auseinander setzen** to have it out with somebody.

Ausfahrt die (PL die **Ausfahrten**)
1 exit; **2 'Ausfahrt freihalten'** 'keep clear'.

Ausfall der (PL die **Ausfälle**)
1 result; **2** failure, breakdown; **3** loss (of hair, teeth); **4** cancellation.

ausfallen ◇verb (PRES **fällt aus**, IMPERF **fiel aus**, PERF **ist ausgefallen**) **1** to be cancelled; **etwas ausfallen lassen** to cancel something; **2** to fall out (hair); **3** to fail (an engine, brakes, a signal); **4** to break down (a machine, a car, heating); **5** to turn out; **gut ausfallen** to turn out well.

Ausflug der (PL die **Ausflüge**)
outing, trip; **einen Ausflug machen** to go on an outing.

Ausfuhr die export.

ausführen verb (PERF **hat ausgeführt**) **1** to carry out (a plan); **2** to export (goods); **3** to take out; **er hat seine Freundin zum Essen ausgeführt** he took his girlfriend out for a meal; **4 den Hund ausführen** to take the dog for a walk.

ausführlich adjective detailed.

ausführlich adverb in detail.

ausfüllen verb (PERF **hat ausgefüllt**) **1** to fill in; **ein Formular ausfüllen** to fill in a form; **2 ihr Beruf als Lehrerin füllt sie ganz aus** teaching gives her great satisfaction.

Ausgabe die (PL die **Ausgaben**)
1 edition; **2** issue; **3 Ausgaben** expenditure.

Ausgang der (PL die **Ausgänge**)
1 exit; **'kein Ausgang'** 'no exit'; **2** end, ending; **3** result (of a game, discussion).

ausgeben ◇verb (PRES **gibt aus**, IMPERF **gab aus**, PERF **hat ausgegeben**) **1** to spend; **2** to hand out; **3 Fahrkarten ausgeben** to issue tickets; **4** to serve (food); **5 sich ausgeben als** to pretend to be; **6 einen ausgeben** (informal) to treat everybody (to a round of drinks for example).

ausgebucht adjective fully booked.

ausgehen ◇verb (PRES **geht aus**, IMPERF **ging aus**, PERF **ist ausgegangen**) **1** to go out; **mit Freunden ausgehen** to go out with friends; **2** to run out (of supplies); **3** to end; **schlecht ausgehen** to end badly; **4 davon ausgehen, dass ...** to assume that ...

ausgerechnet adverb
1 ausgerechnet heute today of all days; **2 ausgerechnet sie** she of all people.

ausgeschlossen adjective out of the question.

ausgestorben adjective **1** dead; **2** extinct.

ausgewogen adjective balanced.

ausgezeichnet adjective excellent.

ausgleichen verb (IMPERF **glich aus**, PERF **hat ausgeglichen**) to equalize; **sie haben in der letzten Minute ausgeglichen** they equalized in the last minute.

aushalten ◊*verb* (PRES **hält aus**, IMPERF **hielt aus**, PERF **hat ausgehalten**) **1** to stand; **2 es ist nicht zum Aushalten** it's unbearable.

Aushilfe die (PL die **Aushilfen**) temporary assistant, temp.

aushöhlen *verb* (PERF **hat ausgehöhlt**) to hollow out.

auskennen ◊*verb* (IMPERF **kannte sich aus**, PERF **hat sich ausgekannt**) **1 sich auskennen** to know your way around; **2 sich gut mit etwas auskennen** to know a lot about something.

auskommen ◊*verb* (IMPERF **kam aus**, PERF **ist ausgekommen**) **1** to manage; **mit fünfzig Euro auskommen** to manage on fifty euros; **2 mit jemandem gut auskommen** to get on well with somebody.

Auskunft die (PL die **Auskünfte**) **1** information; **2** information desk; **3** enquiries (*when phoning*).

auslachen *verb* (PERF **hat ausgelacht**) to laugh at.

ausladen ◊*verb* (PRES **lädt aus**, IMPERF **lud aus**, PERF **hat ausgeladen**) **1** to unload; **2 jemanden ausladen** (*informal*) to put somebody off.

Ausland das **im Ausland** abroad; **ins Ausland reisen** to travel abroad.

Ausländer der (PL die **Ausländer**) foreigner.

Ausländerin die (PL die **Ausländerinnen**) foreigner.

ausländisch *adjective* foreign.

Auslandsgespräch das (PL die **Auslandsgespräche**) international call.

ausleeren *verb* (PERF **hat ausgeleert**) to empty.

ausleihen ◊*verb* (IMPERF **lieh aus**, PERF **hat ausgeliehen**) **1** to lend; **2 sich etwas ausleihen** to borrow something.

ausmachen *verb* (PERF **hat ausgemacht**) **1** to turn off; **2** to put out; **3** to arrange; **wir haben ausgemacht, dass wir uns heute Abend treffen** we've arranged to meet up this evening; **4 das macht mir nichts aus** I don't mind; **macht es Ihnen etwas aus, wenn ...?** would you mind if ...?; **5 viel ausmachen** to make a great difference.

Ausnahme die (PL die **Ausnahmen**) exception.

ausnutzen *verb* (PERF **hat ausgenutzt**) **1** to use; **2** to take advantage of; **3** to exploit.

auspacken *verb* (PERF **hat ausgepackt**) to unpack.

Auspuff der (PL die **Auspuffe**) exhaust.

ausrechnen *verb* (PERF **hat ausgerechnet**) to work out.

Ausrede die (PL die **Ausreden**) excuse.

a

ausreichend *adjective*
1 sufficient; 2 fair, pass (*as a mark at school*).

b

Ausreise die (PL die **Ausreisen**) departure (*from a country*).

c

d

ausrichten *verb* (PERF **hat ausgerichtet**) jemandem etwas ausrichten to tell somebody something.

e

f

g

ausrufen *verb* (IMPERF **rief aus**, PERF **hat ausgerufen**) 1 to call out; 2 to call, to declare; allgemeine Wahlen ausrufen to call a general election.

h

i

j

Ausrufezeichen das (PL die **Ausrufezeichen**) exclamation mark.

k

l

ausruhen *verb* (PERF **hat sich ausgeruht**) sich ausruhen to have a rest.

m

n

ausrüsten *verb* (PERF **hat ausgerüstet**) to equip.

o

Ausrüstung die equipment.

p

ausschalten *verb* (PERF **hat ausgeschaltet**) 1 to switch off; 2 to eliminate.

q

r

ausschneiden ✧*verb* (IMPERF **schnitt aus**, PERF **hat ausgeschnitten**) to cut out.

s

t

Ausschuss der (PL die **Ausschüsse**) committee.

u

v

aussehen ✧*verb* (PRES **sieht aus**, IMPERF **sah aus**, PERF **hat ausgesehen**) to look.

w

x

Aussehen das appearance.

y

außen *adverb* 1 (on the) outside; von außen from the outside; 2 nach außen outwards.

z

Außenminister der (PL die **Außenminister**) Foreign Secretary, Foreign Minister.

außer *preposition* (+ DAT) 1 apart from, except (for); alle außer ihm everyone except (for) him; 2 out of; außer Sicht out of sight; außer Betrieb out of order; 3 außer Haus out; 4 außer sich sein to be beside yourself.

außer *conjunction* 1 except; außer sonntags except Sundays; 2 außer wenn unless.

außerdem *adverb* 1 as well; 2 besides.

äußerer, äußere, äußeres *adjective* 1 external (*injury, circumstances*); 2 outer (*layer, circle*); 3 outward (*appearance, effect*).

außergewöhnlich *adjective* unusual.

außerhalb *preposition* (+ GEN) outside.

außerhalb *adverb* außerhalb wohnen to live out of town.

Außerirdische der/die (PL die **Außerirdischen**) alien (*from outer space*).

äußerlich *adjective* 1 external; 2 outward (*appearance*).

außerordentlich *adjective* extraordinary.

äußerst *adverb* extremely.

Äußerung die (PL die **Äußerungen**) remark.

Aussicht die (PL die **Aussichten**) 1 prospect; etwas in Aussicht haben to have the prospect of something; **keine Aussichten auf Erfolg haben** to have no chance of success; **2** view; **ein Zimmer mit Aussicht aufs Meer** a room with a view of the sea.

Aussprache die (PL die Aussprachen) **1** pronunciation; **2** talk.

aussprechen ◇verb (PRES **spricht aus**, IMPERF **sprach aus**, PERF **hat ausgesprochen**) **1** to pronounce; **2** to express; **3** **lassen Sie ihn aussprechen** let him finish (speaking); **4** **sich aussprechen** to talk; **sich mit jemandem aussprechen** to have a talk with somebody; **5** **sich gegen etwas aussprechen** to come out against something; **sich für etwas aussprechen** to come out in favour of something; **6** **sich lobend über jemanden aussprechen** to speak highly of somebody.

aussteigen ◇verb (IMPERF **stieg aus**, PERF **ist ausgestiegen**) **1** to get out; **2** to get off.

ausstellen verb (PERF **hat ausgestellt**) **1** to display (in a shop); **2** to exhibit; **3** to make out (a certificate, bill); **4** to issue (a passport); **5** to switch off.

Ausstellung die (PL die Ausstellungen) exhibition.

ausstreichen ◇verb (IMPERF **strich aus**, PERF **hat ausgestrichen**) to cross out.

aussuchen verb (PERF **hat ausgesucht**) **1** to choose; **2** **sich etwas aussuchen** to choose something.

Austausch der exchange.

austauschen verb (PERF **hat ausgetauscht**) **1** to exchange; **2** to replace; **3** to substitute (a player).

Auster die (PL die Austern) oyster.

austragen ◇verb (PRES **trägt aus**, IMPERF **trug aus**, PERF **hat ausgetragen**) **1** to deliver (post, newspapers); **2** to hold (a race).

Australien das Australia; **aus Australien** from Australia.

Australier der (PL die Australier) Australian.

Australierin die (PL die Australierinnen) Australian.

australisch adjective Australian.

austreten ◇verb (PRES **tritt aus**, IMPERF **trat aus**, PERF **hat ausgetreten**) **1** to stamp out (a cigarette or fire); **2** to wear out (shoes); **3** (PERF **ist ausgetreten**) **aus einem Klub austreten** to leave a club; **ich trete aus** I'm leaving; **4** (informal) (PERF **ist ausgetreten**) to go to the loo.

austrinken ◇verb (IMPERF **trank aus**, PERF **hat ausgetrunken**) to drink up.

Ausverkauf der (PL die Ausverkäufe) sale.

ausverkauft adjective **1** sold out; **2** **ein ausverkauftes Haus** a full house (at the cinema or theatre).

Auswahl die (PL die Auswahlen) choice, selection; **wenig Auswahl haben** to have a limited selection.

Auswanderer der (PL die Auswanderer) emigrant.

a
b
c
d
e
f
g
h
i
j
k
l
m
n
o
p
q
r
s
t
u
v
w
x
y
z

Auswanderin die (PL die Auswanderinnen) emigrant.

auswandern verb (PERF ist ausgewandert) to emigrate; **nach Amerika auswandern** to emigrate to America.

Auswanderung die emigration.

auswärts adverb **1** away (in sport); **auswärts spielen** to play away; **2 auswärts essen** to eat out; **3 sie arbeitet auswärts** she doesn't work locally.

Auswärtsspiel das (PL die Auswärtsspiele) away game.

Ausweg der (PL die Auswege) way out.

Ausweis der (PL die Ausweise) **1** identity card; **2** card (for students or members); **3** pass.

auswendig adverb by heart.

auswirken verb (PERF hat sich ausgewirkt) **sich auf etwas auswirken** to have an effect on something.

ausziehen ◇verb (IMPERF zog aus, PERF hat ausgezogen) **1** to take off (clothes); **2** to undress; **3 sich ausziehen** to get undressed; **4** (PERF ist ausgezogen) to move out (move house); **wir ziehen nächste Woche aus** we're moving out next week.

Auszubildende der/die (PL die Auszubildenden) trainee.

Auto das (PL die Autos) car; **Auto fahren** to drive; **das Auto waschen** to wash the car.

Autobahn die (PL die Autobahnen) motorway.

Autobahnraststätte die (PL die Autobahnraststätten) motorway service area.

Autofahrer der (PL die Autofahrer) motorist.

Autogramm das (PL die Autogramme) autograph.

Automat der (PL die Automaten) machine.

automatisch adjective automatic.

Autor der (PL die Autoren) author.

Autorin die (PL die Autorinnen) authoress.

Autorität die authority.

Autoskooter der (PL die Autoskooter) bumper car, dodgem car.

Autostopp der per Autostopp **fahren** to hitchhike.

Autotelefon das (PL die Autotelefone) car phone.

Autounfall der (PL die Autounfälle) car accident.

Autoverleih der (PL die Autoverleihe) car hire (firm).

Axt die (PL die Äxte) axe.

Bb

Baby das (PL die Babys) baby.

Babysitting das babysitting; **Babysitting machen** to babysit.

Bach der (PL die Bäche) stream.

Backe die (PL die Backen) cheek.

backen ◇*verb* (PRES **bäckt**, IMPERF **backte**, PERF **hat gebacken**) to bake.

Bäcker *der* (PL die **Bäcker**) **1** baker; **2 beim Bäcker** at the baker's.

Bäckerei *die* (PL die **Bäckereien**) baker's.

Backofen *der* (PL die **Backöfen**) oven.

Backpflaume *die* (PL die **Backpflaumen**) prune.

Bad *das* (PL die **Bäder**) **1** bath; **2** bathroom; **3** pool (*for swimming*).

Badeanzug *der* (PL die **Badeanzüge**) swimsuit.

Badehose *die* (PL die **Badehosen**) swimming trunks.

Bademeister *der* (PL die **Bademeister**) swimming-pool attendant.

Bademeisterin *die* (PL die **Bademeisterinnen**) swimming-pool attendant.

Bademütze *die* (PL die **Bademützen**) bathing cap.

baden *verb* (PERF **hat gebadet**) **1** to have a bath; **2** to bathe (*in the sea*); **3** to bath (*wash somebody*).

Badetuch *das* (PL die **Badetücher**) bath towel.

Badewanne *die* (PL die **Badewannen**) bath (*tub*).

Badezimmer *das* (PL die **Badezimmer**) bathroom.

Bahn *die* (PL die **Bahnen**) **1** railway; **2** train; **mit der Bahn fahren** to go by train; **3** tram; **4** track (*in sport*); **5** lane (*on a track*); **6** path; **auf die schiefe Bahn geraten** to go off the rails.

Bahnhof *der* (PL die **Bahnhöfe**) (railway) station.

Bahnsteig *der* (PL die **Bahnsteige**) platform.

Bahnübergang *der* (PL die **Bahnübergänge**) level crossing.

bald *adverb* **1** soon; **bis bald!** see you soon!; **2 wird's bald!** (*informal*) get a move on!; **3** almost; **ich hätte bald vergessen, ihn anzurufen** I almost forgot to ring him.

baldig *adjective* speedy.

Balken *der* (PL die **Balken**) beam.

Balkon *der* (PL die **Balkons**) balcony.

Ball *der* (PL die **Bälle**) **1** ball; **Ball spielen** to play ball; **2** ball; **auf dem Ball** at the ball.

Ballett *das* (PL die **Ballette**) ballet.

Balletttänzer *der* (PL die **Balletttänzer**) ballet dancer.

Balletttänzerin *die* (PL die **Balletttänzerinnen**) ballet dancer.

Ballon *der* (PL die **Ballons**) balloon.

Banane *die* (PL die **Bananen**) banana.

Band[1] *das* (PL die **Bänder**) **1** ribbon; **2** tape (*for recording*); **etwas auf Band aufnehmen** to tape something; **3** production line; **am Band arbeiten** to work on the production line; **4 am laufenden Band** (*informal*) nonstop.

Band[2] *der* (PL die **Bände**) volume.

Band[3] *die* (PL die **Bands**) band.

band SEE **binden**.

Bank[1] die (PL die **Bänke**) bench.

Bank[2] die (PL die **Banken**) bank; **ich muss erst zur Bank gehen** I have to go to the bank first.

Bankkauffrau die (PL die **Bankkauffrauen**) bank clerk.

Bankkaufmann der (PL die **Bankkaufleute**) bank clerk.

Bankkonto das (PL die **Bankkonten**) bank account.

Banknote die (PL die **Banknoten**) banknote.

bankrott adjective bankrupt; **bankrott gehen/machen** to go bankrupt.

Bär der (PL die **Bären**) bear.

Bar die (PL die **Bars**) bar.

bar adjective (in) cash.

Bardame die (PL die **Bardamen**) barmaid.

barfuß adjective barefoot.

Bargeld das cash.

Barkeeper der (PL die **Barkeeper**) barman.

Barren der (PL die **Barren**) 1 bar; 2 parallel bars.

Bart der (PL die **Bärte**) beard.

bärtig adjective bearded.

Basel das Basle.

Basis die (PL die **Basen**) basis.

Bass der (PL die **Bässe**) bass.

basta exclamation and that's that!

basteln verb (PERF hat gebastelt) 1 to make (things); 2 sie bastelt gern she likes making things.

bat SEE bitten.

Batterie die (PL die **Batterien**) battery.

Bau der (PL die **Bauten**) 1 construction; **im Bau sein** to be under construction; 2 building; 3 building site; **auf dem Bau arbeiten** to work on a building site.

Bauarbeiten plural noun building work.

Bauarbeiter der (PL die **Bauarbeiter**) builder.

Bauarbeiterin die (PL die **Bauarbeiterinnen**) builder.

Bauch der (PL die **Bäuche**) stomach, belly.

Bauchschmerzen plural noun stomachache.

bauen verb (PERF hat gebaut) 1 to build; 2 einen Unfall bauen (informal) to have an accident.

Bauer der (PL die **Bauern**) 1 farmer; 2 pawn (in chess).

Bäuerin die (PL die **Bäuerinnen**) 1 farmer; 2 farmer's wife.

Bauernhof der (PL die **Bauernhöfe**) farm.

Baum der (PL die **Bäume**) tree.

Baumwolle die cotton.

Bausparkasse die (PL die **Bausparkassen**) building society.

Baustelle die (PL die **Baustellen**) building site.

Bayer der (PL die **Bayern**) Bavarian.

Bayerin die (PL die **Bayerinnen**) Bavarian.

Bayern das Bavaria; **aus Bayern** from Bavaria.

bay(e)risch adjective Bavarian.

beabsichtigen verb (PERF **hat beabsichtigt**) to intend.

beachten verb (PERF **hat beachtet**) 1 to take notice of; **beachte ihn einfach nicht** just don't take any notice of him; 2 to observe; 3 to follow (a rule, advice); 4 to obey; **die Verkehrsregeln beachten** to obey traffic regulations.

Beamte der (PL die **Beamten**) 1 civil servant (in Germany all public employees, such as teachers and policemen, are 'Beamte'); 2 official.

Beamtin die (PL die **Beamtinnen**) 1 civil servant; 2 official.

beanspruchen verb (PERF **hat beansprucht**) 1 to claim (benefit); 2 to take up (time, space); **jemanden beanspruchen** to take up somebody's time; 3 to demand (energy, attention); **die Arbeit beansprucht sie sehr** her work is very demanding; 4 to take advantage of (hospitality, services, help); **ich möchte Ihre Geduld nicht zu sehr beanspruchen** I don't want to try your patience.

Beanstandung die (PL die **Beanstandungen**) complaint.

beantragen verb (PERF **hat beantragt**) to apply for.

beantworten verb (PERF **hat beantwortet**) to answer.

bearbeiten verb (PERF **hat bearbeitet**) 1 to deal with; **einen Antrag bearbeiten** to deal with an application; 2 to adapt (a play); 3 to treat (wood, for example); **er hat die**

Oberfläche mit Wachs bearbeitet he's treated the surface with wax; 4 **jemanden bearbeiten, dass er etwas macht** (informal) to work on somebody so that he does something (persuade).

beaufsichtigen verb (PERF **hat beaufsichtigt**) to supervise.

Becher der (PL die **Becher**) 1 beaker, mug; 2 pot, carton (of yoghurt, cream).

Becherglas das (PL die **Bechergläser**) tumbler.

Becken das (PL die **Becken**) 1 basin; 2 pool (for swimming); 3 pelvis.

bedanken verb (PERF **hat sich bedankt**) **sich bedanken** to say thank you; **vergiss nicht, dich zu bedanken** don't forget to say thank you; **ich habe mich bei ihm bedankt** I thanked him.

Bedarf der 1 need; 2 **bei Bedarf** if required; 3 demand; **je nach Bedarf** according to demand.

bedauerlicherweise adverb unfortunately.

bedauern verb (PERF **hat bedauert**) 1 to regret; **ich bedaure kein Wort** I don't regret a single word; 2 **ich bedaure sehr, dass du nicht kommen kannst** I'm very sorry that you can't come; **bedaure!** sorry!; 3 **jemanden bedauern** to feel sorry for somebody.

bedecken verb (PERF **hat bedeckt**) to cover.

a
b
c
d
e
f
g
h
i
j
k
l
m
n
o
p
q
r
s
t
u
v
w
x
y
z

bedeckt *adjective* **1** covered; **2** overcast (*weather*); **gestern war es den ganzen Tag bedeckt** it was overcast all day yesterday.

bedenken ◇*verb* (IMPERF **bedachte**, PERF **hat bedacht**) to consider.

Bedenken *plural noun* **1** doubts; **Bedenken haben** to have doubts; **2 ohne Bedenken** without hesitation.

bedenklich *adjective* **1** worrying; **die Situation ist sehr bedenklich** the situation is very worrying; **2** dubious; **er hat bedenkliche Mittel angewendet, um sein Ziel zu erreichen** he's used dubious methods to achieve his aims; **3** serious.

bedeuten *verb* (PERF **hat bedeutet**) to mean.

bedeutend *adjective* **1** important; **2** considerable.

Bedeutung *die* (PL die **Bedeutungen**) **1** meaning; **2** importance.

bedienen *verb* (PERF **hat bedient**) **1** to serve; **hier wird man sehr schnell bedient** you get served very quickly here; **2** to operate; **3 sich bedienen** to help oneself.

Bedienstete *der/die* (PL die **Bediensteten**) servant.

Bedienung *die* (PL die **Bedienungen**) **1** service; **Bedienung inbegriffen** service included; **2** waiter, waitress; **3** shop assistant; **4** operation (*of a machine*).

Bedingung *die* (PL die **Bedingungen**) condition; **nur unter der Bedingung, dass du mitkommst** only on condition that you're coming with us.

bedrohen *verb* (PERF **hat bedroht**) to threaten.

bedroht *adjective* endangered.

Bedrohung *die* (PL die **Bedrohungen**) threat.

beeilen *verb* (PERF **hat sich beeilt**) **sich beeilen** to hurry (up); **beeilt euch!** hurry up!

beeindrucken *verb* (PERF **hat beeindruckt**) to impress.

beeinflussen *verb* (PERF **hat beeinflusst**) to influence.

beenden *verb* (PERF **hat beendet**) to end.

Beerdigung *die* (PL die **Beerdigungen**) funeral.

Beere *die* (PL die **Beeren**) berry.

Beet *das* (PL die **Beete**) **1** bed (*of flowers*); **2** patch (*of vegetables*).

befahl SEE **befehlen**.

Befehl *der* (PL die **Befehle**) **1** order; **2** command; **den Befehl über etwas haben** to be in command of something.

befehlen ◇*verb* (PRES **befiehlt**, IMPERF **befahl**, PERF **hat befohlen**) **1 jemandem befehlen, etwas zu tun** to order somebody to do something; **2** to give orders.

befestigen *verb* (PERF **hat befestigt**) **1** to fix; **etwas an der Wand befestigen** to fix something to the wall; **2** to fasten.

befinden ◇verb (IMPERF **befand sich**, PERF **hat sich befunden**) **sich befinden** to be; **sie befindet sich zur Zeit in Deutschland** she's in Germany at the moment.

befolgen verb (PERF **hat befolgt**) to follow.

befördern verb (PERF **hat befördert**) **1** to carry (people by bus or train); **2** to transport (goods by train or lorry); **3** to promote; **er ist zum Kommissar befördert worden** he's been promoted to superintendent.

befragen verb (PERF **hat befragt**) to question.

befreien verb (PERF **hat befreit**) **1** to free; **2** to exempt; **jemanden vom Wehrdienst befreien** to exempt somebody from military service; **3** **sich befreien** to free oneself.

Befreiung die liberation.

befreunden verb (PERF **hat sich befreundet**) **sich befreunden** to make friends.

befreundet adjective **mit jemandem befreundet sein** to be friends with somebody; **wir sind schon lange gut befreundet** we've been close friends for a long time.

befriedigen verb (PERF **hat befriedigt**) to satisfy.

befriedigend adjective satisfactory.

Befugnis die (PL die **Befugnisse**) authority.

begabt adjective gifted, talented.

Begabung die gift, talent.

begann SEE **beginnen**.

begegnen verb (PERF **ist begegnet**) **1 jemandem begegnen** to meet somebody; **etwas begegnen** to meet something; **2 sich begegnen** to meet (each other).

Begegnung die (PL die **Begegnungen**) meeting.

begehen ◇verb (IMPERF **beging**, PERF **hat begangen**) to commit.

begeistern verb (PERF **hat begeistert**) **1 jemanden für etwas begeistern** to fill somebody with enthusiasm for something; **2 sich begeistern** to get enthusiastic.

begeistert adjective enthusiastic.

Begeisterung die enthusiasm.

Beginn der beginning; **zu Beginn** at the beginning.

beginnen ◇verb (IMPERF **begann**, PERF **hat begonnen**) to begin, to start.

begleiten verb (PERF **hat begleitet**) to accompany; **jemanden begleiten** to accompany somebody; **er hat mich nach Hause begleitet** he took me home.

beglückwünschen verb (PERF **hat beglückwünscht**) to congratulate.

begonnen SEE **beginnen**.

begraben ◇verb (PRES **begräbt**, IMPERF **begrub**, PERF **hat begraben**) to bury.

begreifen ◇verb (IMPERF **begriff**, PERF **hat begriffen**) to understand.

a
b
c
d
e
f
g
h
i
j
k
l
m
n
o
p
q
r
s
t
u
v
w
x
y
z

begrenzen verb (PERF hat begrenzt) to limit.

Begriff der (PL die Begriffe) 1 concept; davon kann ich mir keinen Begriff machen I can't imagine that; 2 term; ein Begriff aus der Malerei a painting term; 3 im Begriff sein, etwas zu tun to be about to do something; 4 für meine Begriffe to my mind; 5 schwer von Begriff (informal) slow on the uptake.

Begründung die (PL die Begründungen) reason.

begrüßen verb (PERF hat begrüßt) 1 to greet; 2 to welcome.

Begrüßung die welcome.

begünstigen verb (PERF hat begünstigt) to favour.

behaart adjective hairy.

behaglich adjective cosy.

behalten ◇verb (PRES behält, IMPERF behielt, PERF hat behalten) 1 to keep; du kannst die CD behalten you can keep the CD; 2 to remember (a name).

Behälter der (PL die Behälter) container.

behandeln verb (PERF hat behandelt) 1 to treat; er ist sehr schlecht behandelt worden he's been treated very badly; einen Patienten behandeln to treat a patient; 2 to deal with (a subject, question).

Behandlung die (PL die Behandlungen) treatment.

behaupten verb (PERF hat behauptet) 1 to claim; 2 sich behaupten to assert oneself.

Behauptung die (PL die Behauptungen) claim.

beherrschen verb (PERF hat beherrscht) 1 to rule over (a country, people); 2 to control; 3 to know; 4 sich beherrschen to control oneself.

behilflich adjective jemandem behilflich sein to help somebody.

behindert adjective disabled, handicapped; ist er behindert? does he have a disability?

Behinderte der/die (PL die Behinderten) disabled person, handicapped person.

Behindertenheim das (PL die Behindertenheime) home for handicapped people.

Behinderung die 1 obstruction; 2 handicap, disability.

Behörde die (PL die Behörden) authority, authorities.

behüten verb (PERF hat behütet) to protect.

bei preposition (+ DAT) 1 near; die Diskothek beim Bahnhof the disco near the station; 2 at (indicating a place or time); bei mir at my place; beim Arzt at the doctor's; bei Beginn at the beginning; 3 bei seinen Eltern wohnen to live with your parents; 4 bei uns in der Firma in our firm; bei guter Gesundheit in good health; 5 bei einem Verlag arbeiten to work for a publisher; 6 bei Regen if it rains;

bei Nebel in fog; **bei Tag** by day; **7 etwas bei sich haben** to have something on you; **8 bei Morris** c/o Morris; **9 sich bei jemandem entschuldigen** to apologize to somebody; **10 bei der hohen Miete** with the high rent; **11 beim Fahren** while driving; **beim Lesen sein** to be reading; **beim Frühstück** at breakfast; **12 bei der Ankunft** on arrival.

beibringen ✧*verb* (PRES **bringt bei**, IMPERF **brachte bei**, PERF **hat beigebracht**) **jemandem etwas beibringen** to teach somebody something.

Beichte *die* (PL *die* **Beichten**) confession.

beichten *verb* (PERF **hat gebeichtet**) to confess.

beide *adjective, pronoun* **1** both; **ihr beide** both of you; **er hat seine beiden Eltern verloren** he has lost both his parents; **2 die ersten beiden** the first two; **eins von beiden** one of the two; **3 keiner von beiden** neither (of them); **4 beides** both; **er kann beides** - Klavier und Gitarre spielen he can do both - play the piano and the guitar; **5 dreißig beide** thirty all (*in tennis*).

beieinander *adverb* together.

Beifahrer *der* (PL *die* **Beifahrer**) passenger.

Beifahrerin *die* (PL *die* **Beifahrerinnen**) passenger.

Beifall *der* applause.

Beil *das* (PL *die* **Beile**) axe.

Beilage *die* (PL *die* **Beilagen**) **1** supplement (*to a paper*); **2** side-dish; **als Beilage Reis und Spinat** served with rice and spinach.

beiläufig *adjective* casual.

beilegen *verb* (PERF **hat beigelegt**) to enclose.

Beileid *das* condolences; **jemandem sein Beileid aussprechen** to offer your condolences to somebody.

beiliegen ✧*verb* (PRES **liegt bei**, IMPERF **lag bei**, PERF **hat beigelegen**) to be enclosed; **ein Scheck liegt bei** please find enclosed a cheque.

beiliegend *adjective* enclosed.

beim = bei dem.

Bein *das* (PL *die* **Beine**) leg.

beinahe *adverb* almost.

Beinbruch *der* (PL *die* **Beinbrüche**) broken leg; **das ist doch kein Beinbruch** (*informal*) it's not the end of the world.

beisammen *adverb* together.

beiseite *adverb* **1** aside; **etwas beiseite schieben** to push something aside; **2 etwas beiseite legen** to put something by; **3 das Geld beiseite schaffen** to hide the money away.

Beispiel *das* (PL *die* **Beispiele**) example; **zum Beispiel** for example; **mit gutem Beispiel vorangehen** to set a good example.

beispielsweise *adverb* for example.

beißen ✧*verb* (IMPERF **biss**, PERF **hat gebissen**) **1** to bite; **2** to sting (*of*

a
b
c
d
e
f
g
h
i
j
k
l
m
n
o
p
q
r
s
t
u
v
w
x
y
z

a
b
c
d
e
f
g
h
i
j
k
l
m
n
o
p
q
r
s
t
u
v
w
x
y
z

smoke, for example); **3 sich beißen to clash; die Farben beißen sich** the colours clash.

Beitrag der (PL die **Beiträge**) **1** contribution; **2** subscription; **3** premium (insurance fee); **4** article (in a newspaper).

beitragen ◇verb (PRES **trägt bei**, IMPERF **trug bei**, PERF **hat beigetragen**) **zu etwas beitragen** to contribute to something.

beitreten ◇verb (PRES **tritt bei**, IMPERF **trat bei**, PERF **ist beigetreten**) to join; **ich trete dem Fußballverein bei** I'm joining the football club.

bekam SEE **bekommen**.

bekämpfen verb (PERF **hat bekämpft**) **1** to fight; **2 sich bekämpfen** to fight.

bekannt adjective **1** well known; **2** familiar; **das kommt mir bekannt vor** that seems familiar; **3 mit jemandem bekannt sein** to know somebody; **4 für etwas bekannt sein** to be (well) known for something; **5 jemanden bekannt machen** to introduce somebody; **6 das ist mir bekannt** I know that; **7 etwas bekannt geben/machen** to announce something; **sie gab ihre Verlobung bekannt** she announced her engagement; **8 bekannt werden** to become known.

Bekannte der/die (PL die **Bekannten**) **1** acquaintance; **2** friend.

bekannt geben verb (PRES **gibt bekannt**, IMPERF **gab bekannt**, PERF

hat bekannt gegeben) to announce SEE **bekannt**.

bekanntlich adverb **Rauchen ist bekanntlich schädlich** as you know, smoking is bad for you.

beklagen verb (PERF **hat sich beklagt**) **sich beklagen** to complain.

Bekleidung die clothes, clothing.

bekommen ◇verb (IMPERF **bekam**, PERF **hat bekommen**) **1** to get; **Angst bekommen** to get frightened; **2** to catch (a cold, the train); **3 ein Kind bekommen** to have a baby; **4 was bekommen Sie?** (in a shop) can I help you? (in a restaurant) what would you like?; **5 was bekommen Sie dafür?** how much is it?; **6** (PERF **ist bekommen**) **fettes Essen bekommt mir nicht** fatty food doesn't agree with me; **7** (PERF **ist bekommen**) **die Ferien sind mir gut bekommen** the holiday did me good.

Belag der (PL die **Beläge**) **1** covering; **2** coating; **3** topping (on bread); **4** lining (of brakes).

belasten verb (PERF **hat belastet**) **1** to burden; **2** to put weight on (foot); **3** to pollute (the atmosphere); **4** to debit (an account); **5** to incriminate.

belästigen verb (PERF **hat belästigt**) **1** to bother; **2** to harass.

Belastung die **1** strain; **2** load; **3** burden; **4** pollution.

belaufen ◇verb (PRES **beläuft**, IMPERF **belief**, PERF **belaufen**) **sich auf etwas belaufen** to amount to something; **die Rechnung beläuft sich auf fünfhundert Euro** the bill amounts to five hundred euros.

belegen verb (PERF **hat belegt**) 1 to cover; 2 **eine Scheibe Brot mit Käse belegen** to put some cheese on a slice of bread; 3 to enrol for (a course); 4 to reserve (a seat); 5 **den ersten Platz belegen** to come first; 6 to prove (facts).

belegt adjective 1 occupied; 2 **der Platz ist belegt** this seat is taken; 3 **ein belegtes Brot** an open sandwich; 4 **die Nummer ist belegt** (when phoning) the number's engaged.

beleidigen verb (PERF **hat beleidigt**) to insult.

Beleidigung die (PL die **Beleidigungen**) insult.

Beleuchtung die lighting.

Belgien das Belgium.

Belgier der (PL die **Belgier**) Belgian.

Belgierin die (PL die **Belgierinnen**) Belgian.

belgisch adjective Belgian.

Belichtung die exposure.

beliebig adjective any; **eine beliebige Zahl** any number you like.

beliebig adverb **beliebig lange** as long as you like; **beliebig viele** as many as you like.

beliebt adjective popular.

Beliebtheit die popularity.

bellen verb (PERF **hat gebellt**) to bark.

belohnen verb (PERF **hat belohnt**) to reward.

Belohnung die (PL die **Belohnungen**) reward.

belügen verb (IMPERF **belog**, PERF **hat belogen**) to lie to.

bemerkbar adjective **sich bemerkbar machen** to attract attention, to become noticeable.

bemerken verb (PERF **hat bemerkt**) 1 to notice; 2 to remark; 3 **nebenbei bemerkt** by the way.

Bemerkung die (PL die **Bemerkungen**) remark.

bemitleiden verb (PERF **hat bemitleidet**) to pity.

bemühen verb (PERF **hat sich bemüht**) 1 **sich bemühen** to try; **sich sehr bemühen** to try hard; **er bemüht sich um eine Stelle** he's trying to get a job; 2 **sich um jemanden bemühen** to try to help somebody; 3 **bitte, bemühen Sie sich nicht** please don't trouble yourself.

Bemühung die (PL die **Bemühungen**) effort.

benachrichtigen verb (PERF **hat benachrichtigt**) 1 to inform; 2 to notify (officially).

benachteiligt adjective disadvantaged.

benehmen ◇verb (PRES **benimmt sich**, IMPERF **benahm sich**, PERF **hat sich benommen**) **sich benehmen** to behave; **benimm dich!** behave yourself!

Benehmen das behaviour.

a
b
c
d
e
f
g
h
i
j
k
l
m
n
o
p
q
r
s
t
u
v
w
x
y
z

beneiden *verb* (PERF **hat beneidet**) to envy; **jemanden um etwas beneiden** to envy somebody something.

benoten *verb* (PERF **hat benotet**) to mark.

benutzen *verb* (PERF **hat benutzt**) to use.

Benutzer *der* (PL *die* **Benutzer**) user.

Benutzerin *die* (PL *die* **Benutzerinnen**) user.

Benutzung *die* use.

Benzin *das* petrol.

beobachten *verb* (PERF **hat beobachtet**) to observe, to watch; **Vögel beobachten** to watch birds.

bequem *adjective* **1** comfortable; **2 machen Sie es sich bequem** make yourself at home; **3** lazy; **4** easy; **eine bequeme Lösung finden** to find an easy way out.

beraten ⬥*verb* (PRES **berät**, IMPERF **beriet**, PERF **hat beraten**) **1** to advise; **2 jemanden gut/schlecht beraten** to give somebody good/ bad advice; **3 sich beraten lassen** to get advice; **4 gut beraten sein** to be well advised; **5** to discuss (*a plan, matter*); **6 sich über etwas beraten** to discuss something.

Berater *der* (PL *die* **Berater**) adviser.

Beratung *die* (PL *die* **Beratungen**) **1** advice; **2** discussion; **3** consultation (*with a doctor*).

berauben *verb* (PERF **hat beraubt**) to rob.

berechnen *verb* (PERF **hat berechnet**) **1** to charge; **jemandem zehn Euro für etwas berechnen** to charge somebody ten euros for something; **2 jemandem zu viel berechnen** to overcharge somebody; **3** to calculate.

berechtigen *verb* (PERF **hat berechtigt**) **jemanden berechtigen, etwas zu tun** to give someone the right to do something.

berechtigt *adjective* justified.

Bereich *der* (PL *die* **Bereiche**) **1** area; **2** field (*in a profession*); **im Bereich Tourismus** in the field of tourism.

bereit *adjective* ready.

bereiten *verb* (PERF **hat bereitet**) **1** to make (*coffee, tea*); **2** to cause (*trouble, difficulty*); **leider hat es uns Schwierigkeiten bereitet** unfortunately it caused us some trouble; **3** to give (*a surprise, pleasure*).

bereits *adverb* already.

bereuen *verb* (PERF **hat bereut**) to regret.

Berg *der* (PL *die* **Berge**) **1** mountain; **2** hill.

bergab *adverb* downhill.

Bergarbeiter *der* (PL *die* **Bergarbeiter**) miner.

bergauf *adverb* uphill.

bergen ⬥*verb* (PRES **birgt**, IMPERF **barg**, PERF **hat geborgen**) to rescue.

Bergsteigen *das* mountaineering.

Bergsteiger der (PL die Bergsteiger) mountaineer, climber.

Bergsteigerin die (PL die Bergsteigerinnen) mountaineer, climber.

Bergwacht die mountain rescue.

Bergwerk das (PL die Bergwerke) mine.

Bericht der (PL die Berichte) report.

berichten verb (PERF hat berichtet) 1 to report; **die Zeitungen haben nichts davon berichtet** the newspapers didn't report anything about it; 2 **jemandem über etwas berichten** to tell somebody about something; **er hat mir über seine Ferien in Amerika berichtet** he told me about his holiday in America.

berücksichtigen verb (PERF hat berücksichtigt) to take into account.

Beruf der (PL die Berufe) 1 occupation; 2 profession; **ich bin Lehrerin von Beruf** I'm a teacher by profession; 3 trade; 4 **was sind Sie von Beruf?** what do you do for a living?

beruflich adjective 1 professional; 2 vocational (training).

beruflich adverb 1 **beruflich erfolgreich sein** to be successful in your career; 2 **viel beruflich unterwegs sein** to be away a lot on business.

Berufsberatung die careers advice.

Berufsschule die (PL die Berufsschulen) technical college.

berufstätig adjective working.

Berufsverkehr der rush-hour traffic.

beruhigen verb (PERF hat beruhigt) 1 to calm down; 2 to reassure; 3 **sich beruhigen** to calm down.

Beruhigungsmittel das (PL die Beruhigungsmittel) sedative, tranquillizer.

berühmt adjective famous.

berühren verb (PERF hat berührt) 1 to touch; 2 to touch on (a topic, an issue); 3 to affect; **ihre Geschichte berührte ihn seltsam** he was strangely affected by her story; 4 **sich berühren** to touch.

besaß SEE besitzen.

beschädigen verb (PERF hat beschädigt) to damage.

Beschädigung die (PL die Beschädigungen) damage; **der Sturm verursachte zahlreiche Beschädigungen** the storm caused considerable damage.

beschaffen¹ verb (PERF hat beschafft) to get; **kannst du mir nicht einen Job beschaffen?** can't you get me a job?

beschaffen² adjective so beschaffen sein, dass ... to be such that ...

beschäftigen verb (PERF hat beschäftigt) 1 to occupy (keep busy); 2 to employ (people); 3 **sich beschäftigen** to occupy yourself; 4 **ich beschäftige mich mit den**

a b c d e f g h i j k l m n o p q r s t u v w x y z

a
b
c
d
e
f
g
h
i
j
k
l
m
n
o
p
q
r
s
t
u
v
w
x
y
z

Kindern I'm busy with the children; **5 sich mit einem Fall beschäftigen** to deal with a case; **sein Aufsatz beschäftigt sich mit der Umweltverschmutzung** his essay deals with environmental pollution.

beschäftigt *adjective* **1** busy; **2** employed.

Beschäftigung *die* (PL die **Beschäftigungen**) **1** occupation; **2** activity.

Bescheid *der* (PL die **Bescheide**) **1** information; **2 jemandem Bescheid sagen** to let somebody know; **3 über etwas Bescheid wissen** to know about something.

bescheiden *adjective* modest.

Bescheinigung *die* (PL die **Bescheinigungen**) **1** certificate; **eine Bescheinigung des Arztes** a doctor's certificate; **2** (written) confirmation.

beschimpfen *verb* (PERF hat **beschimpft**) to abuse.

beschlagnahmen *verb* (PERF hat **beschlagnahmt**) to confiscate.

beschleunigen *verb* (PERF hat **beschleunigt**) **1** to speed up; **2** to accelerate; **der Lastwagen hinter uns hat plötzlich beschleunigt** the lorry behind us suddenly accelerated.

beschließen *◇verb* (IMPERF **beschloss**, PERF hat **beschlossen**) to decide.

Beschluss *der* (PL die **Beschlüsse**) decision.

beschränken *verb* (PERF hat **beschränkt**) to limit.

beschränkt *adjective* **1** narrow-minded; **2** dim; **sie ist ein bisschen beschränkt** she's a bit dim.

beschreiben *◇verb* (IMPERF **beschrieb**, PERF hat **beschrieben**) to describe.

Beschreibung *die* (PL die **Beschreibungen**) description.

beschuldigen *verb* (PERF hat **beschuldigt**) to accuse.

Beschuldigung *die* (PL die **Beschuldigungen**) accusation.

beschützen *verb* (PERF hat **beschützt**) to protect.

Beschwerde *die* (PL die **Beschwerden**) complaint.

beschweren *verb* (PERF hat sich **beschwert**) **sich beschweren** to complain; **ich habe mich bei den Nachbarn über ihn beschwert** I've complained to the neighbours about him.

beschwipst *adjective* tipsy.

beseitigen *verb* (PERF hat **beseitigt**) to remove.

Besen *der* (PL die **Besen**) broom.

besetzen *verb* (PERF hat **besetzt**) **1** to occupy; **2** to fill (*a post, role*); **3** to trim, to edge (*with lace or fur*).

besetzt *adjective* **1** occupied; **2 besetzt sein** to be engaged (*a phone, toilet*); **3** taken (*a table, seat*); **der Platz ist besetzt** this seat is taken; **4** full (*of a train, bus*); **der Zug ist voll besetzt** the train is full up.

Besetztzeichen das (PL die Besetztzeichen) engaged tone.

Besetzung die (PL die Besetzungen) 1 cast; 2 team; 3 occupation.

besichtigen verb (PERF hat besichtigt) 1 to look round (a town, museum); 2 to see (sights, a house).

Besichtigung die (PL die Besichtigungen) visit.

besinnungslos adjective unconscious.

Besitz der 1 property; 2 im Besitz einer Sache sein to be in possession of something.

besitzen ◇verb (IMPERF besaß, PERF hat besessen) 1 to own; sie besitzen ein Haus in Italien they own a house in Italy; 2 to have (talent, a quality).

Besitzer der (PL die Besitzer) owner.

Besitzerin die (PL die Besitzerinnen) owner.

besonderer, besondere, besonderes adjective 1 special; unter besonderen Umständen in special circumstances; 2 particular; ohne besondere Begeisterung without any particular enthusiasm; 3 keine besonderen Kennzeichen no distinguishing features.

Besonderheit die (PL die Besonderheiten) 1 special feature; 2 peculiarity.

besonders adverb particularly.

besorgen verb (PERF hat besorgt) to get; ich kann dir Karten besorgen I can get you tickets.

besorgt adjective worried.

besprechen ◇verb (PRES bespricht, IMPERF besprach, PERF hat besprochen) 1 to discuss; ich muss es erst mit meinen Eltern besprechen I'll have to discuss it with my parents first; 2 to review (a book, film).

Besprechung die (PL die Besprechungen) 1 meeting (at work); 2 discussion; 3 review (of a film, play).

besser adjective, adverb better; alles besser wissen to know better.

Besserung die 1 improvement; 2 gute Besserung! get well soon!

beständig adjective 1 constant; 2 settled (weather).

Bestandteil der (PL die Bestandteile) component.

bestätigen verb (PERF hat bestätigt) 1 to confirm; 2 to acknowledge (receipt); 3 sich bestätigen to be confirmed, to prove to be true.

beste SEE **besser.**

bestechen ◇verb (PRES besticht, IMPERF bestach, PERF hat bestochen) 1 to bribe; 2 to win over.

Bestechung die (PL die Bestechungen) bribery.

Besteck das (PL die Bestecke) cutlery.

a
b
c
d
e
f
g
h
i
j
k
l
m
n
o
p
q
r
s
t
u
v
w
x
y
z

bestehen ⟡*verb* (IMPERF **bestand**, PERF **hat bestanden**) **1** to exist; **2 es besteht die Gefahr, dass** ... there is a danger that ...; **noch besteht die Hoffnung, dass** ... there is still hope that ...; **3** to pass; **eine Prüfung bestehen** to pass an exam; **4 auf etwas bestehen** to insist on something; **5 aus etwas bestehen** to consist of something; **6 aus etwas bestehen** to be made of something.

bestellen *verb* (PERF **hat bestellt**) **1** to order (*goods*); **2** to reserve (*tickets*); **3** to tell; **jemandem etwas bestellen** to tell somebody something; **4 bestell ihm schöne Grüße** give him my regards; **5 kann ich etwas bestellen?** can I take a message?; **6** to send for; **jemanden zu sich bestellen** to send for somebody.

Bestellung *die* (PL *die* **Bestellungen**) **1** order (*for goods*); **2** reservation (*for tickets*).

bestens *adverb* very well; **das hat ja bestens geklappt** that worked out very well.

bester, beste, bestes *adjective* **1** best; **sein bestes Buch** his best book; **2 ich halte es für das Beste, wenn** ... I think it would be best if ...; **sein Bestes tun** to do your best; **3 einen Witz zum Besten geben** to tell a joke; **4 jemanden zum Besten halten** to pull somebody's leg.

am besten *adverb* best; **du bleibst am besten zu Hause** you'd best stay at home; **es ist am besten, wenn wir gleich anfangen** it's best if we get started straight away.

bestimmen *verb* (PERF **hat bestimmt**) **1** to fix (*a time, price*); **2** to decide (on); **etwas allein bestimmen** to decide (on) something on your own; **er bestimmt immer, was wir machen** he always decides what we're going to do; **3** to be in charge; **4 für jemanden bestimmt sein** to be meant for somebody; **5 für etwas bestimmt sein** to be intended for something (*a donation for a good cause, for example*).

bestimmt *adjective* **1** certain; **zu einer bestimmten Zeit** at a certain time; **2** particular; **suchen Sie etwas Bestimmtes?** are you looking for anything in particular?; **3** definite.

bestimmt *adverb* **1** certainly, definitely; **ich komme ganz bestimmt** I'm definitely coming; **2 er hat es bestimmt vergessen** he's bound to have forgotten; **3 du weißt es doch bestimmt** surely you must remember it.

Bestimmung *die* (PL *die* **Bestimmungen**) regulation.

bestrafen *verb* (PERF **hat bestraft**) to punish.

bestreiten ⟡*verb* (IMPERF **bestritt**, PERF **hat bestritten**) **1** to deny; **2** to dispute; **das möchte ich nicht bestreiten** I'm not disputing it; **3** to pay for.

bestürzt *adjective* upset.

Besuch der (PL die Besuche)
1 visit; **2** attendance (*at school*);
3 Besuch haben to have visitors/a
visitor; **4 bei Freunden zu Besuch
sein** to be staying with friends; **zu
Besuch kommen** to be visiting.

besuchen verb (PERF hat besucht)
1 to visit; **2** to go to (*an exhibition,
the theatre*); **die Schule besuchen**
to go to school; **3** to attend (*a
lecture*).

Besucher der (PL die Besucher)
visitor.

Besucherin die (PL die
Besucherinnen) visitor.

betätigen verb (PERF hat betätigt)
1 to operate; **2 die Bremse
betätigen** to apply the brakes;
3 sich politisch betätigen to be
involved in politics; **4 sich
künstlerisch betätigen** to do art;
5 sich als Reporter betätigen to
work as a reporter.

Betäubungsmittel das (PL die
Betäubungsmittel) anaesthetic.

Bete die Rote Bete beetroot.

beteiligen verb (PERF hat
beteiligt) **1** to give a share to;
**jemanden mit zehn Prozent an
einem Geschäft beteiligen** to give
somebody a ten percent share of a
business; **2 sich an etwas
beteiligen** to take part in
something; **3 kann ich mich an
eurem Spiel beteiligen?** can I join
in your game?

beten verb (PERF hat gebetet) to
pray.

Beton der concrete.

betonen verb (PERF hat betont) to
stress.

Betonung die (PL die Betonungen)
stress.

Betrag der (PL die Beträge)
amount.

betragen ◊verb (PRES beträgt,
IMPERF betrug, PERF hat betragen)
1 to amount to, to come to; **2 sich
betragen** to behave; **haben sich die
Kinder gut betragen?** did the
children behave well?

Betragen das behaviour.

betreffen ◊verb (PRES betrifft,
IMPERF betraf, PERF betroffen) to
concern; **was mich betrifft** as far as
I'm concerned.

betreten ◊verb (PRES betritt,
IMPERF betrat, PERF hat betreten)
1 to enter; **2 'Betreten verboten'**
'keep out', 'keep off' (*the grass, for
example*).

Betrieb der (PL die Betriebe)
1 business, firm; **2** activity; **es war
viel Betrieb** it was very busy; **3 in
Betrieb sein** to be working (*of a
machine*); **4 außer Betrieb** to
be out of order; **5 eine Maschine in
Betrieb setzen** to start up a
machine.

Betriebsferien plural noun
firm's holiday; **'Betriebsferien'**
'closed for the holidays'.

Betriebspraktikum das (PL die
Betriebspraktika) training course.

betrinken ◊verb (IMPERF betrank
sich, PERF hat sich betrunken) **sich
betrinken** to get drunk.

betrog SEE betrügen.

a
b
c
d
e
f
g
h
i
j
k
l
m
n
o
p
q
r
s
t
u
v
w
x
y
z

Betrug der **1** deception; **2** fraud; **was für ein Betrug** what a swindle!

betrügen ◇verb (IMPERF **betrog**, PERF **hat betrogen**) **1** to cheat; **jemanden um tausend Euro betrügen** to cheat somebody out of a thousand euros; **2** to be unfaithful to, to cheat on; **sie hat ihren Mann betrogen** she's been unfaithful to her husband.

betrunken adjective drunk.

Bett das (PL die **Betten**) bed; **ins Bett gehen** to go to bed; **das Bett machen** to make the bed.

Bettbezug der (PL die **Bettbezüge**) duvet cover.

betteln verb (PERF **hat gebettelt**) to beg.

Bettlaken das (PL die **Bettlaken**) sheet.

Bettler der (PL die **Bettler**) beggar.

Bettlerin die (PL die **Bettlerinnen**) beggar.

Bettwäsche die bed linen.

Bettzeug das bedding.

beugen verb (PERF **hat gebeugt**) **1** to bend; **2** to decline, to conjugate (in grammar); **3 sich nach vorn beugen** to bend forwards; **sich über etwas beugen** to bend over something; **4 sich aus dem Fenster beugen** to lean out of the window; **5 sich beugen** to submit.

Beule die (PL die **Beulen**) **1** bump; **2** lump; **3** dent.

beurteilen verb (PERF **hat beurteilt**) to judge.

Beutel der (PL die **Beutel**) bag.

Bevölkerung die (PL die **Bevölkerungen**) population.

bevor conjunction **1** before; **2 bevor nicht** until; **bevor er nicht unterschrieben hat** until he has signed.

bevorzugen verb (PERF **hat bevorzugt**) to prefer.

bewachen verb (PERF **hat bewacht**) to guard.

bewaffnen verb (PERF **hat bewaffnet**) to arm.

bewahren verb (PERF **hat bewahrt**) **jemanden vor etwas bewahren** to protect someone from something.

bewaffnet adjective armed.

bewährt adjective **1** reliable; **2** proven (method, design); **3 ein bewährtes Rezept** a well-tried recipe.

bewegen[1] verb (PERF **hat bewegt**) **1** to move; **2 sich bewegen** to take exercise; **3 sich bewegen** to move.

bewegen[2] ◇verb (IMPERF **bewog**, PERF **hat bewogen**) **jemanden dazu bewegen, etwas zu tun** to persuade somebody to do something.

bewegt adjective eventful.

Bewegung die (PL die **Bewegungen**) **1** movement; **2** exercise; **3 eine Maschine in Bewegung setzen** to start (up) a machine; **4 sich in Bewegung setzen** to start to move.

Beweis der (PL die **Beweise**) **1** proof; **2** belastende Beweise incriminating evidence; **3** token, sign.

beweisen ◇*verb* (IMPERF **bewies**, PERF **hat bewiesen**) **1** to prove; **2** to show.

bewerben ◇*verb* (PRES **bewirbt sich**, IMPERF **bewarb sich**, PERF **hat sich beworben**) **sich bewerben** to apply; **sich um eine Stelle bewerben** to apply for a job.

Bewerber *der* (PL **die Bewerber**) applicant.

Bewerberin *die* (PL **die Bewerberinnen**) applicant.

Bewerbung *die* (PL **die Bewerbungen**) application.

bewohnen *verb* (PERF **hat bewohnt**) to live in.

Bewohner *der* (PL **die Bewohner**) **1** resident; **2** inhabitant (*of a region*).

Bewohnerin *die* (PL **die Bewohnerinnen**) **1** resident; **2** inhabitant (*of a region*).

bewölkt *adjective* cloudy.

Bewölkung *die* clouds.

bewundern *verb* (PERF **hat bewundert**) to admire.

Bewunderung *die* admiration.

bewusst *adjective* **1** conscious; **2** deliberate; **3 sich etwas bewusst sein** to be aware of something; **ich war mir der Folgen bewusst** I was aware of the consequences.

bewusstlos *adjective* unconscious.

Bewusstsein *das* **1** consciousness; **2 bei vollem**

Bewusstsein sein to be fully conscious; **3 mir kam zu(m) Bewusstsein, dass** ... I realized that ....

bezahlbar *adjective* affordable.

bezahlen *verb* (PERF **hat bezahlt**) **1** to pay; **für etwas 10 Euro bezahlen** to pay 10 euros for something; **2** to pay for (*goods, food*); **er hat das Essen bezahlt** he paid for the meal.

Bezahlung *die* payment.

bezeichnend *adjective* typical.

beziehen ◇*verb* (IMPERF **bezog**, PERF **hat bezogen**) **1** to cover; **2 das Bett frisch beziehen** to put clean sheets on the bed; **3** to move into; **wann kannst du die neue Wohnung beziehen?** when will you be able to move into the new flat?; **4** to get (*goods, a pension*); **5** to take (*a newspaper*); **6 sich auf etwas/jemanden beziehen** to refer to something/somebody; **7 es bezieht sich** it's clouding over.

Beziehung *die* (PL **die Beziehungen**) **1** connection; **2** relationship; **3 Beziehungen** contacts; **Anna hat gute Beziehungen** Anna has good contacts; **4 diplomatische Beziehungen** diplomatic relations; **5 in dieser Beziehung** in this respect; **6 eine Beziehung zu etwas haben** to be able to relate to something (*to art, pop music, for example*).

beziehungsweise *conjunction* **1** or rather; **2** respectively.

Bezirk *der* (PL **die Bezirke**) district.

a b c d e f g h i j k l m n o p q r s t u v w x y z

Bezug der (PL die **Bezüge**) **1** cover (of a cushion, duvet, etc.); **2** connection; **keinen Bezug zu etwas haben** to be unable to relate to something; **3 auf etwas Bezug nehmen** to refer to something; **4 in Bezug auf** regarding; **5 mit Bezug auf Ihr Angebot** with reference to your offer.

bezweifeln verb (PERF **hat bezweifelt**) to doubt.

BH der (PL die **BHs**) bra.

Bibel die (PL die **Bibeln**) bible; **die Bibel** the Bible.

Bibliothek die (PL die **Bibliotheken**) library.

Bibliothekar der (PL die **Bibliothekare**) librarian.

Bibliothekarin die (PL die **Bibliothekarinnen**) librarian.

biegen ◇verb (IMPERF **bog**, PERF **hat gebogen**) **1** to bend; **2 sich biegen** to bend; **3** (PERF **ist gebogen**) to turn; **um die Ecke biegen** to turn the corner.

Biene die (PL die **Bienen**) bee.

Bier das (PL die **Biere**) beer.

Bierdeckel der (PL die **Bierdeckel**) beer mat.

bieten ◇verb (IMPERF **bot**, PERF **hat geboten**) **1** to offer; **2** to bid (at an auction); **3 es bietet sich die Möglichkeit** there is a possibility; **4** to present (a sight); **5 das lasse ich mir nicht bieten!** I won't put up with it!

Bikini der (PL die **Bikinis**) bikini.

Bild das (PL die **Bilder**) **1** picture; **jemanden ins Bild setzen** to put somebody in the picture; **2** scene.

bilden verb (PERF **hat gebildet**) **1** to form; **2 sich bilden** to form; **3 sich bilden** to educate yourself.

Bildschirm der (PL die **Bildschirme**) screen.

bildschön adjective (very) beautiful.

Bildung die **1** formation; **2** education.

billig adjective cheap.

Billion die (PL die **Billionen**) billion (a million million); **drei Billionen Euro** three Billion euros.

bin SEE **sein**.

Binde die (PL die **Binden**) **1** bandage; **2** sanitary towel.

binden ◇verb (IMPERF **band**, PERF **hat gebunden**) **1** to tie; **2** to bind (a book); **3** to make up (a bouquet); **4** to thicken (a sauce); **5 sich binden** to commit oneself.

Bindestrich der (PL die **Bindestriche**) hyphen.

Bindfaden der (PL die **Bindfäden**) (piece of) string.

Bindung die (PL die **Bindungen**) **1** tie; **2** relationship; **3** binding (on a ski).

Biokost die health food.

Biologie die biology.

biologisch adjective biological.

Birke die (PL die **Birken**) birch tree.

Birne die (PL die **Birnen**) **1** pear; **2** bulb.

bis *preposition* (+ ACC) **1** as far as; **dieser Zug fährt nur bis Passau** this train only goes as far as Passau; **2** up to; **Kinder bis zehn zahlen die Hälfte** children up to ten pay half; **bis jetzt** up to now; **bis zu** up to; **3** until, till (*with time*); **4** by; **bis dahin** by then; **5** bis auf except for; **alle sind durchgefallen bis auf die zwei Mädchen** everyone failed except for the two girls; **6 bis bald!** see you soon!; **7 von München bis Salzburg** from Munich to Salzburg; **von Montag bis Freitag** from Monday to Friday; **zwei bis drei Euro** two to three euros.

bis *conjunction* until, till; **sie bleibt, bis es dunkel wird** she's staying until it gets dark.

Bischof *der* (PL die Bischöfe) bishop.

bisher *adverb* so far.

bisherig *adjective* previous.

Riss *der* (PL die Bisse) bite.

biss SEE **beißen.**

bisschen *pronoun* **1** ein bisschen a bit; ; **ein bisschen Brot** a bit of bread; **2 kein bisschen** not a bit.

bissig *adjective* **1** vicious; **'Vorsicht bissiger Hund!'** 'beware of the dog!'; **2** cutting (*remark, tone*).

bist SEE **sein.**

Bitte *die* (PL die Bitten) request.

bitte *adverb* **1** please; **'möchten Sie Kuchen?' – 'ja bitte'** 'would you like some cake?' – 'yes please'; **2** you're welcome (*in reply to* thanks); **3** come in (*after a knock on the door*); **4** (*in a shop*) **bitte?** yes, please?; **5 wie bitte?** sorry?

bitten ◇*verb* (IMPERF bat, PERF hat gebeten) to ask; **jemanden um etwas bitten** to ask somebody for something.

bitter *adjective* bitter.

blamieren *verb* (PERF hat blamiert) **1** to disgrace; **2 jemanden blamieren** to embarrass somebody; **3 sich blamieren** to make a fool of yourself.

Blase *die* (PL die Blasen) **1** bubble; **2** blister; **3** bladder.

blasen ◇*verb* (PRES bläst, IMPERF blies, PERF hat geblasen) to blow.

Blasinstrument *das* (PL die Blasinstrumente) wind instrument.

Blaskapelle *die* (PL die Blaskapellen) brass band.

blass *adjective* pale.

Blatt *das* (PL die Blätter) **1** leaf; **2** sheet; **ein Blatt Papier** a sheet of paper; **3** page; **4** newspaper.

blau *adjective* **1** blue; **ein blau gestreiftes Kleid** a dress with blue stripes; **2 ein blaues Auge haben** to have a black eye; **3 ein blauer Fleck** a bruise; **4 blau sein** (*informal*) to be tight; **5 eine Fahrt ins Blaue** a mystery tour.

Blech *das* (PL die Bleche) **1** sheet metal; **2** tin; **3** baking tray; **4** brass (*in music*).

Blei *das* lead.

bleiben ❖*verb* (IMPERF **blieb**, PERF **ist geblieben**) **1** to stay, to remain; **2** to be left; **3** **bleiben Sie am Apparat** hold the line; **4** **bei etwas bleiben** to stick to something; **5** **ruhig bleiben** to keep calm; **6** **wo bleibt er so lange?** where has he got to?; **7** **etwas bleiben lassen** to not do something; **wenn du nicht mitkommen willst, dann lass es eben bleiben** if you don't want to come, then don't.

bleich *adjective* pale.

Bleichmittel *das* (PL **die Bleichmittel**) bleach.

bleifrei *adjective* unleaded.

Bleistift *der* (PL **die Bleistifte**) pencil.

Bleistiftspitzer *der* (PL **die Bleistiftspitzer**) pencil sharpener.

blenden *verb* (PERF **hat geblendet**) **1** to dazzle; **2** to blind.

blendend *adjective* **1** marvellous; **2** **es geht mir blendend** I feel great; **wir haben uns blendend amüsiert** we had a great time.

Blick *der* (PL **die Blicke**) **1** look; **2** glance; **3** **auf den ersten Blick** at first sight; **4** view; **ein Zimmer mit Blick aufs Meer** a room with a sea view.

blicken *verb* (PERF **hat geblickt**) **1** to look; **2** **sich blicken lassen** to show your face.

blieb SEE **bleiben**.

blies SEE **blasen**.

blind *adjective* blind.

Blinddarm *der* (PL **die Blinddärme**) appendix.

Blinddarmentzündung *die* (PL **die Blinddarmentzündungen**) appendicitis.

Blinde *der/die* (PL **die Blinden**) blind person, blind man/woman.

blinken *verb* (PERF **hat geblinkt**) **1** to flash; **2** to indicate (*of a car*).

Blinker *der* (PL **die Blinker**) indicator.

blinzeln *verb* (PERF **hat geblinzelt**) to blink.

Blitz *der* (PL **die Blitze**) **1** (flash of) lightning; **2** flash.

blitzen *verb* (PERF **hat geblitzt**) **1** to flash; **2** to sparkle; **3** **es hat geblitzt** there was a flash of lightning.

Block *der* (PL **die Blöcke**) **1** pad (*for writing on*); **2** (PL **die Blocks**) block (*of flats*).

Blockflöte *die* (PL **die Blockflöten**) recorder.

blöd *adjective* stupid.

Blödsinn *der* nonsense.

blond *adjective* blonde, fair-haired.

bloß *adverb* **1** only; **es kostet bloß fünf Euro** it's only five euros; **2** **warum hat er das bloß gemacht?** why on earth did he do it?; **3** **was mache ich bloß?** whatever shall I do?; **2** **fass das bloß nicht an!** don't touch it!

bloß *adjective* **1** bare (*feet*); **mit bloßem Auge** with the naked eye; **2** mere (*words, suspicion*); **der bloße Gedanke daran** the mere thought of it.

Blume *die* (PL **die Blumen**) flower.

Blumenkohl *der* cauliflower.

Bluse die (PL die **Blusen**) blouse.

Blut das blood.

Blutdruck der blood pressure.

Blüte die (PL die **Blüten**) blossom.

bluten verb (PERF hat geblutet) to bleed.

Blutgefäß das (PL die **Blutgefäße**) bloodvessel.

Blutprobe die (PL die **Blutproben**) blood test.

Blutwurst die (PL die **Blutwürste**) black pudding.

Bock der (PL die **Böcke**) **1** buck; **2** billy-goat; **3** ram; **4 Bock auf etwas haben** (informal) to fancy something; **5 einen Bock schießen** (informal) to make a blunder.

Bockwurst die (PL die **Bockwürste**) frankfurter.

Boden der (PL die **Böden**) **1** ground; **2** floor; **3** bottom (of a container); **4** loft, attic.

Bodensee der Lake Constance.

bog SEE **biegen**.

Bogen der (PL die **Bögen**) **1** curve; **2** arch; **3** turn (in skiing).

Bohne die (PL die **Bohnen**) bean.

bohren verb (PERF hat gebohrt) to drill.

Bohrer der (PL die **Bohrer**) drill.

Bohrinsel die (PL die **Bohrinseln**) oil rig.

Bohrmaschine die (PL die **Bohrmaschinen**) electric drill.

Bombe die (PL die **Bomben**) bomb.

Bonbon der (PL die **Bonbons**) sweet.

Boot das (PL die **Boote**) boat.

Bord[1] das (PL die **Borde**) shelf.

Bord[2] der **an Bord** on board; **über Bord** overboard.

Bordkarte die (PL die **Bordkarten**) boarding card.

borgen verb (PERF hat geborgt) **1** to borrow; **2 sich etwas borgen** to borrow something; **ich habe es mir von ihr geborgt** I borrowed it from her; **3 jemandem etwas borgen** to lend somebody something; **Evi hat mir ihr Buch geborgt** Evi lent me her book.

Börse die (PL die **Börsen**) stock exchange.

Börsenmakler der (PL die **Börsenmakler**) stock broker.

Borste die (PL die **Borsten**) bristle.

böse adjective **1** bad; **2** wicked; **3** naughty (child); **4** angry; **böse werden** to get angry; **ich bin ihm böse** I'm angry with him; **5 auf jemanden böse sein** to be cross with somebody.

boshaft adjective malicious.

bot SEE **bieten**.

Bote der (PL die **Boten**) messenger.

Botin die (PL die **Botinnen**) messenger.

Botschaft die (PL die **Botschaften**) **1** message; **2** embassy; **die britische Botschaft** the British Embassy.

Botschafter der (PL die **Botschafter**) ambassador.

Botschafterin die (PL die **Botschafterinnen**) ambassador.

a b c d e f g h i j k l m n o p q r s t u v w x y z

Bowle die (PL die **Bowlen**) punch (for drinking).

boxen verb (PERF **hat geboxt**) 1 to box; 2 to punch.

Boxer der (PL die **Boxer**) boxer.

brach SEE **brechen**.

brachte SEE **bringen**.

Branche die (PL die **Branchen**) (line of) business.

Branchenverzeichnis das (PL die **Branchenverzeichnisse**) classified directory.

Brand der (PL die **Brände**) fire.

Brandung die surf.

brannte SEE **brennen**.

Brasilianer der (PL die **Brasilianer**) Brazilian.

Brasilianerin die (PL die **Brasilianerinnen**) Brazilian.

braten ◇ verb (PRES **brät**, IMPERF **briet**, PERF **hat gebraten**) 1 to fry; 2 to roast.

Braten der (PL die **Braten**) 1 roast; 2 joint.

Brathähnchen das (PL die **Brathähnchen**) roast chicken.

Bratkartoffeln plural noun fried potatoes.

Bratpfanne die (PL die **Bratpfannen**) frying pan.

Bratwurst die (PL die **Bratwürste**) fried sausage.

Brauch der (PL die **Bräuche**) custom.

brauchbar adjective 1 usable; 2 useful.

brauchen verb (PERF **hat gebraucht**) 1 need; **ich brauche eine neue Birne für meine Lampe** I need a new bulb for my light; **du brauchst nur auf den Knopf zu drücken** all you need to do is press the button; **du brauchst nicht zu gehen** you needn't go; 2 **sie braucht es nur zu sagen** she only has to say (time); 3 to take (time); **wie lange brauchst du mit dem Auto?** how long does it take you by car?; 4 **ich könnte es gut brauchen** I could do with it.

brauen verb (PERF **hat gebraut**) to brew.

Brauerei die (PL die **Brauereien**) brewery.

braun adjective 1 brown; 2 **braun werden** to get a tan; **braun (gebrannt) sein** to be tanned.

Bräune die tan.

Brause die (PL die **Brausen**) fizzy drink.

Braut die (PL die **Bräute**) bride.

Bräutigam der (PL die **Bräutigame**) bridegroom.

Brautjungfer die (PL die **Brautjungfern**) bridesmaid.

Brautpaar das (PL die **Brautpaare**) bride and groom.

brav adjective good.

BRD die (Bundesrepublik Deutschland) FRG (Federal Republic of Germany).

brechen ◇ verb (PRES **bricht**, IMPERF **brach**, PERF **hat gebrochen**) 1 to break (an agreement, a record); 2 **sich den Arm brechen** to break your arm; **3** to vomit; **4** (PERF **ist gebrochen**) to break; **der Ast ist gebrochen** the branch broke.

breit *adjective* **1** wide; **2** broad; **3 die breite Masse** the general public.

Breite die (PL die **Breiten**) width.

Bremse die (PL die **Bremsen**) **1** brake; **2** horsefly.

bremsen *verb* (PERF **hat gebremst**) **1** to brake; **2** to slow down (*development, production*); **3 jemanden bremsen** (*informal*) to stop somebody; **er ist nicht mehr zu bremsen** there's no stopping him.

Bremslicht das (PL die **Bremslichter**) brake light.

Bromspedal das (PL die **Bremspedale**) brake pedal.

brennen ◇*verb* (IMPERF **brannte**, PERF **hat gebrannt**) **1** to burn; **2** to be on (*of a light*); **das Licht brennen lassen** to leave the light on; **3** to sting (*of a wound or sore*); **4 das Haus brennt** the house is on fire; **es brennt!** fire!; **5 darauf brennen, etwas zu tun** to be dying to do something

Brennnessel die (PL die **Brennnesseln**) stinging nettle.

Brennpunkt der (PL die **Brennpunkte**) focus.

Brett das (PL die **Bretter**) **1** board; **2** plank; **3** shelf.

Brezel die (PL die **Brezeln**) pretzel.

bricht SEE **brechen**.

Brief der (PL die **Briefe**) letter.

Brieffreund der (PL die **Brieffreunde**) pen friend.

Brieffreundin die (PL die **Brieffreundinnen**) pen friend.

Briefkasten der (PL die **Briefkästen**) **1** letterbox; **2** postbox.

Briefmarke die (PL die **Briefmarken**) stamp.

Brieftasche die (PL die **Brieftaschen**) wallet.

Briefträger der (PL die **Briefträger**) postman.

Briefträgerin die (PL die **Briefträgerinnen**) postwoman.

Briefumschlag der (PL die **Briefumschläge**) envelope.

Briefwechsel der correspondence.

briet SEE **braten**.

Brillant der (PL die **Brillanten**) diamond.

Brille die (PL die **Brillen**) glasses, spectacles.

bringen ◇*verb* (IMPERF **brachte**, PERF **hat gebracht**) **1** to bring; **2** to take; **Peter bringt dich nach Hause** Peter will take you home; **3 die Kinder ins Bett bringen** to put the children to bed; **4 einen Film im Fernsehen bringen** to show a film on television; **5** to publish (*an article*); **6** to yield (*interest, a profit*); **7 jemanden dazu bringen, etwas zu tun** to get somebody to do something; **8 mit sich bringen** to entail; **9 etwas hinter sich bringen** to get something over and done with; **10 es weit bringen** to go far;

11 jemanden auf eine Idee bringen to give somebody an idea; **12 es zu nichts bringen** to get nowhere; **13 das bringt's nicht!** (*informal*) that's no use!

Brise die (PL die **Brisen**) breeze.

Brite der (PL die **Briten**) Briton; **die Briten** the British.

Britin die (PL die **Britinnen**) Briton.

britisch *adjective* British.

Brokkoli der broccoli.

Brombeere die (PL die **Brombeeren**) blackberry.

Brosche die (PL die **Broschen**) brooch.

Broschüre die (PL die **Broschüren**) brochure.

Brot das (PL die **Brote**) **1** bread; **ein Brot** a loaf of bread; **2 ein Brot** a slice of bread.

Brötchen das (PL die **Brötchen**) roll.

Bruch der (PL die **Brüche**) **1** break; **2** fracture; **3** hernia; **4** fraction.

Bruchteil der (PL die **Bruchteile**) fraction.

Brücke die (PL die **Brücken**) bridge.

Bruder der (PL die **Brüder**) brother.

Brühe die (PL die **Brühen**) **1** broth; **2** stock (*for cooking*).

Brühwürfel der (PL die **Brühwürfel**) stock cube.

brüllen *verb* (PERF **hat gebrüllt**) to roar.

brummen *verb* (PERF **hat gebrummt**) **1** to buzz; **2** to growl (*of a bear*); **3** to hum (*of an engine*).

Brunnen der (PL die **Brunnen**) **1** well; **2** fountain.

Brüssel das Brussels.

Brust die (PL die **Brüste**) **1** chest; **2** breast.

Brustschwimmen das breaststroke.

brutto *adverb* gross.

BSE das (*bovine spongiforme Enzephalopathie*) BSE.

Bub der (PL die **Buben**) boy.

Buch das (PL die **Bücher**) book.

Buche die (PL die **Buchen**) beech.

buchen *verb* (PERF **hat gebucht**) to book.

Bücherei die (PL die **Büchereien**) library.

Bücherregal das (PL die **Bücherregale**) bookcase.

Buchhalter der (PL die **Buchhalter**) accountant, bookkeeper.

Buchhalterin die (PL die **Buchhalterinnen**) accountant, bookkeeper.

Buchhandlung die (PL die **Buchhandlungen**) bookshop.

Büchse die (PL die **Büchsen**) tin, can.

Büchsenöffner der (PL die **Büchsenöffner**) tin opener.

Buchstabe der (PL die **Buchstaben**) letter (*of the alphabet*); **ein großer Buchstabe** a capital letter; **ein kleiner Buchstabe** a small letter.

buchstabieren *verb* (PERF **hat buchstabiert**) to spell.

Bucht die (PL die **Buchten**) bay.

Buchung die (PL die **Buchungen**) booking, reservation.

bücken (PERF hat sich gebückt) **sich bücken** to bend down.

Buddhismus der Buddhism.

Bude die (PL die **Buden**) **1** hut; **2** stall; **3 meine Bude** (informal) my room, my pad.

Büfett das (PL die **Büfetts**) buffet.

Bügel der (PL die **Bügel**) hanger.

Bügeleisen das (PL die **Bügeleisen**) iron.

bügeln verb (PERF hat gebügelt) to iron.

Bühne die (PL die **Bühnen**) stage.

Bulle der (PL die **Bullen**) **1** bull; **2** (informal) cop.

Bummel der (PL die **Bummel**) stroll (around town).

bummeln verb (PERF ist gebummelt) **1** to stroll; **wir sind durch die Stadt gebummelt** we strolled around town; **2** (PERF hat gebummelt) to dawdle.

Bund[1] der (PL die **Bünde**) **1** association; **2** waistband.

Bund[2] das (PL die **Bunde**) bunch.

Bundesbürger der (PL die **Bundesbürger**) German citizen.

Bundeskanzler der (PL die **Bundeskanzler**) Federal Chancellor.

Bundesland das (PL die **Bundesländer**) (federal) state.

Bundesliga die (German) national football league.

Bundesrat der Upper House (of the German Parliament).

Bundesrepublik die Federal Republic.

Bundesstraße die (PL die **Bundesstraßen**) A road, major road.

Bundestag der Lower House (of the German Parliament).

Bundeswehr die (German) Army.

Bungalow der (PL die **Bungalows**) bungalow.

bunt adjective colourful.

Buntstift der (PL die **Buntstifte**) coloured pencil.

Burg die (PL die **Burgen**) castle.

Bürger der (PL die **Bürger**) citizen.

Bürgerin die (PL die **Bürgerinnen**) citizen.

Bürgermeister der (PL die **Bürgermeister**) mayor.

Bürgersteig der (PL die **Bürgersteige**) pavement.

Büro das (PL die **Büros**) office.

Büroklammer die (PL die **Büroklammern**) paper clip.

Bürste die (PL die **Bürsten**) brush.

bürsten verb (PERF hat gebürstet) to brush.

Bus der (PL die **Busse**) bus; **ich fahre mit dem Bus** I'm going by bus.

Busbahnhof der (PL die **Busbahnhöfe**) bus station.

Busch der (PL die **Büsche**) bush.

Busen der (PL die **Busen**) bosom.

Busfahrer der (PL die **Busfahrer**) bus driver.

a b c d e f g h i j k l m n o p q r s t u v w x y z

Busfahrerin die (PL die Busfahrerinnen) bus driver.

Busfahrkarte die (PL die Busfahrkarten) bus ticket.

Bushaltestelle die (PL die Bushaltestellen) bus stop.

Buslinie die (PL die Buslinien) bus route.

Bussard der (PL die Bussarde) buzzard.

Bußgeld das (PL die Bußgelder) fine.

Büstenhalter der (PL die Büstenhalter) bra.

Busverbindung die (PL die Busverbindungen) **1** bus connection; **2** bus line.

Butter die butter.

Butterbrot das (PL die Butterbrote) sandwich, bread and butter.

bzw. SEE beziehungsweise.

Cc

Café das (PL die Cafés) cafe.

Cafeteria die (PL die Cafeterias) cafeteria.

campen verb (PERF hat gecampt) to camp.

Camper der (PL die Camper) camper.

Camperin die (PL die Camperinnen) camper.

Camping das camping.

Campingbus der (PL die Campingbusse) camper (vehicle).

Campingkocher der (PL die Campingkocher) camping stove.

Campingplatz der (PL die Campingplätze) campsite.

CD die (PL die CDs) CD.

CD-Spieler der (PL die CD-Spieler) CD player.

Cello das (PL die Cellos) cello.

Cent der (PL die Cents) cent (in euro and dollar systems); **25 Cent** 25 cents.

Champignon der (PL die Champignons) mushroom.

Chance die (PL die Chancen) chance.

Chaos das chaos.

chaotisch adjective chaotic.

Charakter der (PL die Charaktere) character.

charmant adjective charming.

Charterflug der (PL die Charterflüge) charter flight.

Chatroom der (PL die Chatrooms) chatroom.

Chauvinist der (PL die Chauvinisten) chauvinist.

Chef der (PL die Chefs) **1** head (of a firm); **2** boss.

Chefin die (PL die Chefinnen) **1** head (of a firm); **2** boss.

Chemie die chemistry.

Chemikalie die (PL die Chemikalien) chemical.

Chemiker der (PL die Chemiker) chemist.

Chemikerin die (PL die **Chemikerinnen**) chemist.

chemisch *adjective* **1** chemical; **2 chemische Reinigung** dry-cleaning, dry-cleaner's.

Chicorée der chicory.

China das China.

Chinese der (PL die **Chinesen**) Chinese; **die Chinesen** the Chinese.

Chinesin die (PL die **Chinesinnen**) Chinese.

chinesisch *adjective* Chinese.

Chipkarte die (PL die **Chipkarten**) smart card.

Chips *plural noun* crisps.

Chirurg der (PL die **Chirurgen**) surgeon.

Chirurgin die (PL die **Chirurginnen**) surgeon.

Chlor das chlorine.

Chor der (PL die **Chöre**) choir.

Christ der (PL die **Christen**) Christian.

Christentum das Christianity.

Christin die (PL die **Christinnen**) Christian.

christlich *adjective* Christian.

Christus der Christ.

circa *adverb* approximately.

Clown der (PL die **Clowns**) clown.

Cola™ die (PL die **Colas**) Coke™.

Comic der (PL die **Comics**) cartoon.

Comicheft das (PL die **Comichefte**) comic.

Computer der (PL die **Computer**) computer; **ich spiele am** Computer I'm playing on the computer.

Computerprogramm das (PL die **Computerprogramme**) computer program.

Computerspiel das (PL die **Computerspiele**) computer game.

Container der (PL die **Container**) **1** container; **2** skip.

Cordsamt der corduroy.

Couch die (PL die **Couchs**) sofa.

Couchtisch der (PL die **Couchtische**) coffee table.

Cousin der (PL die **Cousins**) cousin.

Cousine die (PL die **Cousinen**) cousin SEE **Kusine**.

Creme die (PL die **Cremes**) **1** cream; **2** cream dessert.

Curry das **1** curry; **2** curry powder.

Currywurst die (PL die **Currywürste**) curried sausage.

Cursor der (PL die **Cursors**) cursor.

Dd

da *adverb* **1** there; **da draußen** out there; **da drüben** over there; **da sein** to be there; **man muss pünktlich da sein** you have to be there on time; **2 ist noch Brot da?** is there any bread left?; **3** here; **sind alle da?** is everyone here?; **da sind deine Handschuhe** here are your gloves; **4 ist Sabine da?** is Sabine about?; **5 von da an** from then on; **6 ich bin wieder da** I'm back; **7** so (*therefore*); **der Bus war**

a b c d e f g h i j k l m n o p q r s t u v w x y z

a
b
c
d
e
f
g
h
i
j
k
l
m
n
o
p
q
r
s
t
u
v
w
x
y
z

weg, da bin ich gelaufen the bus had gone, so I walked; **8 da kann man nichts machen** there's nothing you can do about it; **9 da, wo die Straße nach Stuttgart abzweigt** at the turning for Stuttgart.

da conjunction as, since; **da es gerade regnet** as it's raining.

dabei adverb **1** (included or next to) with it/him/her/them; **sie hatten die Kinder dabei** they had the children with them; **2 dicht dabei** close by; **3** (referring to something already mentioned) about it; **das Wichtigste dabei** the most important thing about it; **4** at the same time; **er malte ein Bild und sang dabei** he painted a picture and sang at the same time; **5** during this; **6 jemandem dabei helfen, etwas zu tun** to help somebody do something; **7 was hast du dir denn dabei gedacht?** what were you thinking of?; **8 dabei sein** to be there; **er ist dabei gewesen** he was there; **9 was ist denn dabei?** so what?; **10 dabei sein, etwas zu tun** to be just doing something; **ich war gerade dabei zu gehen** I was just about to leave; **11 dabei bleiben** to stick with it (an opinion, for example); **12** and yet, even though.

dabeibleiben ⬦verb (IMPERF blieb dabei, PERF ist dabeigeblieben) **1** to stay on (at an organisation); **2 er hat mit dem Training begonnen, ist aber nicht dabeigeblieben** he started training, but didn't keep it up.

dabeisein SEE **dabei**.

Dach das (PL die **Dächer**) roof.

Dachboden der (PL die **Dachböden**) loft, attic.

Dachgeschoss das (PL die **Dachgeschosse**) attic.

Dachrinne die (PL die **Dachrinnen**) gutter (on roof edge).

dachte SEE **denken**.

Dackel der (PL die **Dackel**) dachshund.

dadurch adverb **1** through it/ them; **das Wasser muss dadurch gelaufen sein** the water must have run through it; **2** as a result; **3** in this way; **ich nehme die U-Bahn, dadurch bin ich eine halbe Stunde eher da** I'll take the tube, that way I'll be there half an hour earlier.

dadurch conjunction **dadurch, dass** because.

dafür adverb **1** for it/them; **dafür kriegt man nicht viel** you won't get much for it/them; **2** instead; **wenn er schon nicht auf die Party gehen will, kann er dich dafür zum Essen einladen** if he doesn't want to go to the party he can take you for a meal instead; **3** but then (on the other hand); **4 dafür, dass** considering that; **5 ich kann nichts dafür** it's not my fault.

dagegen adverb **1** against it/ them; **ich bin dagegen** I'm against it; **2** for it/them (when swapping); **3** into it; **das Auto ist dagegen gefahren** the car drove into it; **4** by comparison; **5 hast du was**

dagegen? do you mind?; **6** however.

daheim *adverb* at home.

daher *adverb* **1** from there; **2** that's why.

dahin *adverb* **1** there; **2** bis dahin (*in the past*) until then, (*in the future*) by then; **3** jemanden dahin bringen, dass er etwas tut to get somebody to do something.

dahinten *adverb* over there.

dahinter *adverb* **1** behind it/them; **2** dahinter kommen to get to the bottom of it; ich bin endlich dahinter gekommen I finally got to the bottom of it.

dalassen ◇*verb* (PRES lässt da, IMPERF ließ da, PERF hat dagelassen) to leave there.

damals *adverb* at that time, then; wir wohnten damals in Berlin we were then living in Berlin.

Dame *die* (PL die Damen) **1** lady; **2** queen (*in chess or cards*); **3** draughts.

Damenbinde *die* (PL die Damenbinden) sanitary towel.

damit *adverb* **1** with it/them; ich will damit spielen I want to play with it; hör auf damit! stop it!; **2** by it; was meinst du damit? what do you mean by that?; **3** damit hat es noch Zeit there's no hurry (about that); **4** therefore, because of that; sie hat den zweiten Satz verloren und damit das Spiel she lost the second set and because of it the match.

damit *conjunction* so that; ich habe es aufgeschrieben, damit du es nicht vergisst I wrote it down so that you won't forget.

Damm *der* (PL die Dämme) **1** dam; **2** embankment.

dämmern *verb* (PERF hat gedämmert) es dämmert it is getting light, it is getting dark.

Dämmerung *die* **1** dawn; **2** dusk.

Dampf *der* (PL die Dämpfe) steam.

dämpfen *verb* (PERF hat gedämpft) **1** to steam (*in cooking*); **2** to muffle (*a sound*); **3** to dampen (*somebody's enthusiasm*).

dampfen *verb* (PERF hat gedampft) to steam.

Dampfer *der* (PL die Dampfer) steamer.

danach *adverb* **1** after it/them; **2** afterwards; kurz danach shortly afterwards; **3** danach suchen to look for it/them; **4** danach riechen to smell of it; **5** accordingly; **6** es sieht danach aus it looks like it.

Däne *der* (PL die Dänen) Dane.

daneben *adverb* **1** next to it/them; **2** by comparison.

Dänemark *das* Denmark.

Dänin *die* (PL die Däninnen) Dane.

dänisch *adjective* Danish.

Dank *der* **1** thanks; mit Dank zurück thanks for the loan; **2** vielen Dank thank you very much.

dank *preposition* (+ GEN *or* + DAT) thanks to.

a b c d e f g h i j k l m n o p q r s t u v w x y z

dankbar *adjective* **1** grateful; **2** rewarding.

danke *exclamation* thank you, thanks; **danke schön** thank you very much; **(nein) danke** no thank you, no thanks.

danken *verb* (PERF **hat gedankt**) **1** to thank; **2 nichts zu danken** don't mention it.

dann *adverb* then.

daran *adverb* **1** on it/them; **2 daran denken** to think of it/them; **3 dicht daran** close to it/them; **4 nahe daran sein, etwas zu tun** to be on the point of doing something; **5** about it/them; **daran ist nichts zu machen** there is nothing you can do about it; **6 es liegt daran, dass** ... it is because ...; **7 er ist daran gestorben** he died of it.

darauf *adverb* **1** on it/them; **2 darauf warten** to wait for it; **3 darauf antworten** to reply to it; **4** after that; **kurz darauf** shortly after that; **5 am Tag darauf** the day after; **6 am darauf folgenden Tag** the following day; **7 es kommt darauf an, ob** ... it depends whether ....

daraufhin *adverb* as a result.

daraus *adverb* **1** out of it/them, from it/them; **2 was ist daraus geworden?** what has become of it/them? **3 mach dir nichts daraus** don't worry about it.

darf, darfst SEE **dürfen**.

darin *adverb* **1** in it/them; **2** in that respect; **der Unterschied liegt**

darin, dass ... the difference is that ...

Darm *der* (PL *die* **Därme**) intestine(s).

darstellen *verb* (PERF **hat dargestellt**) **1** to represent; **2** to portray; **dieses Gemälde stellt Szenen aus dem Bürgerkrieg dar** this painting portrays scenes from the civil war; **3** to describe; **er stellt es so dar, als sei es meine Schuld** the way he describes it, it's all my fault; **4** to play (*in the theatre*).

Darsteller *der* (PL *die* **Darsteller**) actor.

Darstellerin *die* (PL *die* **Darstellerinnen**) actress.

darüber *adverb* **1** over it/them; **2** about it; **darüber sprechen** to talk about it; **3** more; **dreißig Euro oder darüber** thirty euros or more.

darum *adverb* **1** round it/them; **2 darum bitten** to ask for it; **3** that's why; **darum komme ich nicht** that's why I'm not coming; **4 ich sorge mich darum** I worry about it; **5 es geht darum, zu gewinnen** the main thing is to win; **6 darum geht es nicht** that's not the point; **7** because of that; **darum, weil** because.

darunter *adverb* **1** under it/them; **2 im Stock darunter** on the floor below; **3** among them; **mehrere Schüler, darunter zwei Zehnjährige** a number of pupils, among them two ten year olds; **4** less; **dreißig Euro oder darunter** thirty euros or less; **5 was**

a
b
c
d
e
f
g
h
i
j
k
l
m
n
o
p
q
r
s
t
u
v
w
x
y
z

verstehen Sie darunter? what do you understand by that?

das *article (neuter)* **1** the; **das Haus** the house; **2** that; **das Mädchen war es** it was that girl; **das da** that one.

das *pronoun* **1** which, that; **das Kleid, das ich im Schaufenster gesehen habe** the dress which I saw in the window; **2 das mit der Spitze** the one with the lace; **3** who; **das Mädchen, das gegenüber wohnt** the girl who lives opposite; **4** that; **das wusste ich nicht** I didn't know that; **das geht** that's all right.

Dasein *das* existence.

dasein SEE **da.**

dass *conjunction* **1** that; **ich freue mich, dass …** I'm very pleased that …; **2 ich verstehe nicht, dass Karin ihn mag** I don't understand why Karin likes him.

dasselbe *pronoun* the same, the same one.

Daten *plural noun* data.

Datenbank *die* (PL *die* **Datenbanken**) database.

Datenverarbeitung *die* data processing.

datieren *verb* (PERF **hat datiert**) to date.

Dativ *der* (PL *die* **Dative**) dative.

Datum *das* (PL *die* **Daten**) date.

Dauer *die* **1** duration; **2** length; **3 für die Dauer von fünf Jahren** for (a period of) five years; **4 von Dauer sein** to last; **5 auf die Dauer** in the long run; **auf Dauer** permanently.

Dauerkarte *die* (PL *die* **Dauerkarten**) season ticket.

dauern *verb* (PERF **hat gedauert**) **1** to last; **2 lange dauern** to take a long time; **es hat vier Wochen gedauert, bis der Brief hier ankam** it took four weeks for the letter to arrive.

dauernd *adjective* constant.

dauernd *adverb* constantly.

Dauerwelle *die* (PL *die* **Dauerwellen**) perm.

Daumen *der* (PL *die* **Daumen**) thumb.

Daunendecke *die* (PL *die* **Daunendecken**) duvet.

davon *adverb* **1** from it/them; **2** about it; **ich weiß nichts davon** I don't know anything about it; **3** of it/them; **die Hälfte davon** half of it/them; **4 das kommt davon** (*informal*) it serves you right; **5 was habe ich davon?** what's the point?; **6 abgesehen davon** apart from that.

davor *adverb* **1** in front of it/them; **2** beforehand; **3 Angst davor haben** to be frightened of it/them; **4 kurz davor sein, etwas zu tun** to be on the point of doing something.

dazu *adverb* **1** to it/them; **2** in addition; **noch dazu** in addition (to it); **3** with it, **was isst du dazu?** what are you having with it?; **4 ich habe keine Lust dazu** I don't feel like it; **5 jemanden dazu bringen, etwas zu tun** to get somebody to do something; **6 ich bin nicht dazu gekommen** I didn't get round to it; **7 er ist nicht dazu bereit** he's not prepared to do it.

dazugeben ✧*verb* (PRES **gibt dazu**, IMPERF **gab dazu**, PERF **hat dazugegeben**) to add.

dazugehören *verb* (PERF **hat dazugehört**) **1** to belong to it/them; **2** to go with it/them (*of accessories*); **alles, was dazugehört** everything that goes with it.

dazukommen ✧*verb* (IMPERF **kam dazu**, PERF **ist dazugekommen**) **1** to arrive; **2** to be added; **3 kommt noch etwas dazu?** would you like anything else?

dazwischen *adverb* **1** in between; **2** between them; **der Unterschied dazwischen** the difference between them.

dazwischenkommen ✧*verb* (PRES **kommt dazwischen**, IMPERF **kam dazwischen**, PERF **ist dazwischengekommen**) to crop up.

DB *die* (*Deutsche Bundesbahn*) German railways.

DDR *die* (*Deutsche Demokratische Republik*) GDR, East Germany; **in der ehemaligen DDR** in the former East Germany.

Debatte *die* (PL **die Debatten**) debate.

Decke *die* (PL **die Decken**) **1** blanket, cover; **2** (table)cloth; **ich habe eine neue Decke aufgelegt** I've put on a new tablecloth; **3** ceiling.

Deckel *der* (PL **die Deckel**) **1** lid; **2** top.

decken *verb* (PERF **hat gedeckt**) **1** to cover; **2 ein Tuch über etwas decken** to spread a cloth over something; **3 den Tisch decken** to lay the table; **4 jemanden decken** to cover up for somebody; **5 einen Spieler decken** to mark a player (*in sport*).

definieren *verb* (PERF **hat definiert**) to define.

Definition *die* (PL **die Definitionen**) definition.

dehnbar *adjective* elastic.

dehnen *verb* (PERF **hat gedehnt**) to stretch.

dein *adjective* your.

deiner, deine, deins *pronoun* yours; **meine Uhr ist kaputt, kann ich deine haben?** my watch is broken, can I take yours?

deinetwegen *adverb* **1** because of you; **2** for your sake.

deins SEE **deiner.**

deklinieren *verb* (PERF **hat dekliniert**) to decline.

Delfin *der* (PL **die Delfine**) dolphin.

Delle *die* (PL **die Dellen**) dent.

Delphin *der* (PL **die Delphine**) dolphin.

dem *article* (*dative*) **1** (to) the; **2 es liegt auf dem Tisch** it's on the table.

dem *pronoun* **1** to him; **gib es dem** give it to him; **2** to it, to that one;

3 to whom; **der Mann, dem ich das Geld gegeben habe** the man I gave the money to; **4** which; **das Messer, mit dem ich Zwiebeln schneide** the knife that I cut onions with.

demnächst *adverb* shortly.

Demokratie *die* (PL *die* **Demokratien**) democracy.

demokratisch *adjective* democratic.

Demonstrant *der* (PL *die* **Demonstranten**) demonstrator.

Demonstrantin *die* (PL *die* **Demonstrantinnen**) demonstrator.

Demonstration *die* (PL *die* **Demonstrationen**) demonstration.

demonstrieren *verb* (PERF **hat demonstriert**) to demonstrate.

den *article* (accusative) **1** the; **2 ich habe mir den Arm gebrochen** I've broken my arm.

den *pronoun* **1** him; **kennst du den?** do you know him?; **2** it, that one; **don kannst du gerne haben** you're welcome to it; **ich nehme den** I'll take that one; **3** who(m); **4** which; **der Mantel, den ich mir gekauft habe** the coat I bought.

denen *pronoun* (dative plural) **1** (to) them; **2** that, (to) whom; **die Menschen, denen sie geholfen hat** the people she helped.

denkbar *adjective* conceivable.

denken ◇*verb* (IMPERF **dachte**, PERF **hat gedacht**) **1** to think; **ich denke oft an dich** I often think of you;

2 das kann ich mir denken I can imagine.

Denkmal *das* (PL *die* **Denkmäler**) monument.

denn *conjunction* **1** because, for; **2 mehr denn je** more than ever.

denn *adverb* **1 wo denn?** where?; **2 was ist denn los?** so what's the matter?; **3 warum denn nicht?** why ever not?; **4 es sei denn** unless.

dennoch *conjunction* nevertheless.

deprimierend *adjective* depressing.

deprimiert *adjective* depressed.

der *article* **1** (masculine) the; **der Mann** the man; **2** (feminine and plural genitive) of the; **die Katze der Frau** the woman's cat; **der Ball der Kinder** the children's ball; **3** (dative) (to) the; of the; **ich gab es der Frau** I gave it to the woman.

der *pronoun* **1** who; **der Mann, der hier wohnt** the man who lives here; **2** which; **der Regenschirm, der mir gehört** the umbrella which is mine; **3** der da that one; **4** him, he.

deren *pronoun* **1** their; **die Kinder und deren Hund** the children and their dog; **2** whose; **3** of which.

derselbe *pronoun* the same, the same one.

des *article* **1** (masculine and neuter genitive singular) of the; **das Klingeln des Telefons** the ringing of the phone; **2 der Ball des Jungen** the boy's ball.

a b c **d** e f g h i j k l m n o p q r s t u v w x y z

a

b

c

d

e

f

g

h

i

j

k

l

m

n

o

p

q

r

s

t

u

v

w

x

y

z

deshalb *adverb* **1** therefore; **2** that's why.

Desinfektionsmittel *das* (PL die **Desinfektionsmittel**) disinfectant.

desinfizieren *verb* (PERF **hat desinfiziert**) to disinfect.

dessen *pronoun* **1** his; **2** its; **3** whose; **der Junge, dessen Mutter weint** the boy whose mother is crying; **4** of which.

desto *adverb* the; **je mehr, desto besser** the more the better.

deswegen *conjunction* **1** therefore; **2** that's why.

Detektiv *der* (PL die **Detektive**) detective.

deutlich *adjective* clear.

deutlich *adverb* **ich konnte ihn deutlich sehen** I could clearly see him.

Deutsch *das* German; **auf Deutsch** in German; **fließend Deutsch sprechen** to speak fluent German.

deutsch *adjective* German.

Deutsche *der/die* (PL die **Deutschen**) German; **er ist Deutscher** he's German.

Deutschland *das* Germany; **nach Deutschland** to Germany.

Devisen *plural noun* foreign currency.

Dezember *der* December; **am ersten Dezember** on the first of December; **im Dezember** in December.

Dezimalzahl *die* (PL die **Dezimalzahlen**) decimal (number).

d. h. (*das heißt*) i.e.

Dia *das* (PL die **Dias**) slide.

Diagnose *die* (PL die **Diagnosen**) diagnosis.

diagonal *adjective* diagonal.

Diagramm *das* (PL die **Diagramme**) diagram.

Dialekt *der* (PL die **Dialekte**) dialect.

Dialog *der* (PL die **Dialoge**) dialogue.

Diamant *der* (PL die **Diamanten**) diamond.

Diät *die* (PL die **Diäten**) diet; **jemanden auf Diät setzen** to put somebody on a diet.

dich *pronoun* **1** you; **2** yourself.

dicht *adjective* **1** thick (*fog*); **2** dense; **3** watertight; **4** airtight; **5** er ist nicht ganz dicht (*informal*) he's off his head.

dicht *adverb* **1** densely; **2** tightly; **3** close; **geh nicht so dicht an den Käfig** don't go so close to the cage; **dicht bei** close to.

Dichter *der* (PL die **Dichter**) poet.

Dichterin *die* (PL die **Dichterinnen**) poet.

Dichtung *die* (PL die **Dichtungen**) **1** poetry; **2** seal, washer.

dick *adjective* **1** thick; **2** swollen (*ankle, tonsils*); **3** fat (*person*).

Dickkopf *der* (PL die **Dickköpfe**) **1** stubborn person; **2** einen **Dickkopf haben** to be stubborn.

die *article* (*feminine and plural*) the; **die Frau** the woman; **die Bücher** the books.

die *pronoun* (*feminine and plural*) **1** who; **die Frau, die hier wohnt**

the woman who lives here; **die Frau, die ich kenne** the woman I know; **die Kinder, die ich gefragt habe** the children I asked; **2** which; **die Tasche, die ich gekauft habe** the bag I bought; **3** she, her; **4** them; **ich meine die** I mean them; **5 die da** that one, (*plural*) those.

Dieb der (PL die Diebe) thief.

Diebin die (PL die Diebinnen) thief.

Diebstahl der (PL die Diebstähle) theft.

Diele die (PL die Dielen) **1** hall; **2** floorboard.

dienen verb (PERF hat gedient) to serve.

Dienst der (PL die Dienste) service; **Dienst haben** to work, to be on duty (*of a soldier or doctor*).

Dienstag der (PL die Dienstage) Tuesday; **am Dienstag** on Tuesday.

dienstags adverb on Tuesdays.

dienstfrei adjective **1 ein dienstfreier Tag** a day off; **2 dienstfrei haben** to have time off, to be off duty.

dienstlich adverb on business.

Dienstreise die (PL die Dienstreisen) business trip.

diese SEE dieser.

Diesel der diesel.

dieselbe pronoun the same, the same one.

dieser, diese, dieses adjective **1** this; **2** these; **diese Äpfel** these apples.

dieses pronoun **1** this one; **mir gefällt dieses am besten** I like this one best; **2** these ones.

diesmal adverb this time.

Digitaluhr die (PL die Digitaluhren) **1** digital watch; **2** digital clock.

Diktat das (PL die Diktate) dictation.

Ding das (PL die Dinge) thing; **vor allen Dingen** above all; **das war ein Ding** (*informal*) that was quite something.

Dings der/die/das thingummy.

Dinosaurier der (PL die Dinosaurier) dinosaur.

Diplom das (PL die Diplome) diploma.

dir pronoun **1** you, to you; **sie hat es dir gegeben** she gave it to you; **ich verspreche dir, dass** ... I promise you that ...; **2 Freunde von dir** friends of yours; **3** yourself.

direkt adjective direct.

direkt adverb b direct; **der Bus fährt direkt zum Flughafen** the bus goes direct to the airport.

Direktor der (PL die Direktoren) **1** director; **2** headmaster, principal; **3** manager (*of a bank, theatre*).

Direktorin die (PL die Direktorinnen) **1** director; **2** headmistress, principal; **3** manager (*of a bank, theatre*).

Direktübertragung die (PL die Direktübertragungen) live transmission.

Dirigent der (PL die Dirigenten) conductor.

a
b
c
d
e
f
g
h
i
j
k
l
m
n
o
p
q
r
s
t
u
v
w
x
y
z

dirigieren verb (PERF **hat dirigiert**) to conduct.

Diskette die (PL die **Disketten**) floppy disk.

Diskettenlaufwerk das (PL die **Diskettenlaufwerke**) disk drive.

Disko die (PL die **Diskos**) disco.

Diskothek die (PL die **Diskotheken**) disco, discotheque.

Diskriminierung die discrimination; **die Diskriminierung von Frauen** discrimination against women.

Diskussion die (PL die **Diskussionen**) discussion; **zur Diskussion stehen** to be under discussion.

diskutieren verb (PERF **hat diskutiert**) to discuss.

Disziplin die (PL die **Disziplinen**) discipline.

DJH die (Deutsche Jugendherberge) German youth hostel (association).

DM die (Deutsche Mark) DM, Deutschmark SEE **Mark**.

D-Mark die (PL die **D-Mark**) Deutschmark, German mark SEE **Mark**.

doch adverb **1** yes (when you are contradicting somebody); '**hast du keinen Hunger?**' – '**doch!**' 'aren't you hungry?' – 'yes, I am!'; **2** after all; **sie hat ihn doch eingeladen** she invited him after all; **sie ist doch nicht gekommen** she hasn't come after all; **3** er hat doch meinen Brief bekommen? he did get my letter, didn't he?; **sie kommt doch?** she's coming, isn't she?; **4** anyway; **du hörst ja doch nicht auf mich** you won't listen to me anyway; **5 pass doch auf!** do be careful!.

doch conjunction but.

Doktor der (PL die **Doktoren**) doctor; **den Doktor machen** to do a doctorate.

Dokument das (PL die **Dokumente**) document.

Dokumentarfilm der (PL die **Dokumentarfilme**) documentary.

Dokumentarsendung die (PL die **Dokumentarsendungen**) documentary (programme).

dolmetschen verb (PERF **hat gedolmetscht**) to interpret.

Dolmetscher der (PL die **Dolmetscher**) interpreter.

Dolmetscherin die (PL die **Dolmetscherinnen**) interpreter.

Dom der (PL die **Dome**) cathedral.

Donau die Danube.

Donner der thunder.

donnern verb (PERF **hat gedonnert**) to thunder.

Donnerstag der (PL die **Donnerstage**) Thursday; **am Donnerstag** on Thursday.

donnerstags adverb on Thursdays.

doof adjective (informal) stupid.

Doppel das (PL die **Doppel**) **1** duplicate; **2** doubles (in sport).

Doppelbett das (PL die **Doppelbetten**) double bed.

Doppelfenster das (PL die **Doppelfenster**) double-glazed window; **wir haben Doppelfenster** we've got double glazing.

Doppelhaus das (PL die **Doppelhäuser**) semi-detached house.

Doppelklick der (PL die **Doppelklicks**) double-click (*with mouse*).

Doppelpunkt der (PL die **Doppelpunkte**) colon.

doppelt *adjective* 1 double; 2 in **doppelter Ausführung** in duplicate; 3 **die doppelte Menge** twice the amount.

doppelt *adverb* 1 doubly; 2 twice; **doppelt so viel** twice as much; **sich doppelt anstrengen** to try twice as hard.

Doppelzimmer das (PL die **Doppelzimmer**) double room.

Dorf das (PL die **Dörfer**) village.

Dorn der (PL die **Dornen**) thorn.

dort *adverb* there; **dort drüben** over there.

dorther *adverb* from there.

dorthin *adverb* there; **geht ihr jetzt dorthin?** are you going there now?

Dose die (PL die **Dosen**) tin, can.

dösen *verb* (PERF **hat gedöst**) to doze.

Dosenöffner der (PL die **Dosenöffner**) tin opener.

Dosierung die (PL die **Dosierungen**) dose.

Dosis die (PL die **Dosen**) dose.

Dotter der (PL die **Dotter**) yolk.

Dozent der (PL die **Dozenten**) lecturer.

Dozentin die (PL die **Dozentinnen**) lecturer.

Drache der (PL die **Drachen**) dragon.

Drachen der (PL die **Drachen**) kite.

Drachenfliegen das hang-gliding; **Drachenfliegen gehen** to go hang-gliding.

Draht der (PL die **Drähte**) 1 wire; 2 **er ist auf Draht** (*informal*) he's on the ball.

Drama das (PL die **Dramen**) drama.

Dramatik die drama.

dran *adverb* SEE **daran** 1 **ich bin dran** it's my turn; **wer ist dran?** whose turn is it?; 2 **gut dran sein** to be well off; 3 **arm dran sein** to be in a bad way; 4 **spät dran sein** to be late.

drängen *verb* (PERF **hat gedrängt**) 1 to push; 2 to press, to urge (*somebody*); 3 **sich drängen** to crowd; **die Leute drängten sich vor der Kasse** people crowded around the box-office.

drankommen ◇*verb* (IMPERF **kam dran**, PERF **ist drangekommen**) to have your turn; **wer kommt dran?** whose turn is it?

drauf *adverb* SEE **darauf** 1 **drauf und dran sein, etwas zu tun** to be on the point of doing something; 2 **gut drauf sein** (*informal*) to be in a good mood.

draußen *adverb* outside.

Dreck der dirt.

dreckig *adjective* dirty, filthy.

Drehbuch *das* (PL die **Drehbücher**)
1 screenplay; 2 script.

drehen *verb* (PERF **hat gedreht**)
1 to turn; **an etwas drehen** to turn
something; 2 to shoot (*a film*);
3 **sich drehen** to turn; 4 **sich im
Kreis drehen** to rotate; 5 **es dreht
sich um ihr Taschengeld** it's about
her pocket money.

Drei *die* (PL die **Dreien**) three.

drei *number* three.

Dreieck *das* (PL die **Dreiecke**)
triangle.

dreieckig *adjective* triangular.

dreifach *adjective* triple.

dreihundert *number* three
hundred.

dreimal *adverb* three times.

Dreirad *das* (PL die **Dreiräder**)
tricycle.

dreißig *number* thirty.

drei viertel *number* three-
quarters.

Dreiviertelstunde *die* (PL die
Dreiviertelstunden) three-
quarters of an hour.

dreizehn *number* thirteen.

drin *adverb* SEE **darin**; **drin sein** to
be inside.

dringend *adjective* urgent.

drinnen *adverb* 1 inside;
2 indoors.

dritt *adverb* **sie sind zu dritt** there
are three of them.

dritte SEE **dritter**.

Drittel *das* (PL die **Drittel**) third.

drittens *adverb* thirdly.

dritter, dritte, drittes *adjective*
third; **zum dritten Mal** for the third
time; **ein Dritter** a third person;
jeder Dritte, der mitwollte every
third person who wanted to come;
die Dritte Welt the Third World.

Droge *die* (PL die **Drogen**) drug.

drogenabhängig *adjective*
addicted to drugs.

Drogenabhängige *der/die* (PL die
Drogenabhängigen) drug addict.

Drogenabhängigkeit *die* drug
addiction.

drogensüchtig *adjective*
addicted to drugs.

Drogensüchtige *der/die* (PL die
Drogensüchtigen) drug addict.

Drogerie *die* (PL die **Drogerien**)
chemist's.

Drogist *der* (PL die **Drogisten**)
chemist.

Drogistin *die* (PL die **Drogistinnen**)
chemist.

drohen *verb* (PERF **hat gedroht**) to
threaten; **jemandem drohen** to
threaten somebody.

Drohung *die* (PL die **Drohungen**)
threat.

Drossel *die* (PL die **Drosseln**)
1 thrush (*bird*); 2 throttle.

drüben *adverb* over there.

Druck *der* 1 pressure; **jemanden
unter Druck setzen** to put
pressure on somebody; 2 printing;
3 (PL die **Drucke**) print.

drücken *verb* (PERF **hat gedrückt**)
1 to press; 2 **an der Tür drücken** to

push the door; **'bitte drücken'** 'push'; **3** to hug; **4** to pinch (*of shoes*); **5 die Preise drücken** to force down prices; **6 sich vor etwas drücken** (*informal*) to get out of something; **du hast dich mal wieder vor dem Aufräumen gedrückt** you've got out of tidying up again.

drucken *verb* (PERF **hat gedruckt**) to print.

Drucker *der* (PL die **Drucker**) printer.

Druckknopf *der* (PL die **Druckknöpfe**) press stud.

Druckluftmesser *der* (PL die **Druckluftmesser**) pressure gauge.

Drucksache *die* (PL die **Drucksachen**) printed matter.

Druckschrift *die* (PL die **Druckschriften**) **1** block letters; **2** type; **3** pamphlet.

Drüse *die* (PL die **Drüsen**) gland.

Dschungel *der* (PL die **Dschungel**) jungle.

du *pronoun* **1** you; **2** du sagen to say 'du' (to each other); **per du sein** to be on familiar terms ('*du*' *is used when talking to family members, close friends, or people of your own age; otherwise 'Sie' is used*).

Dudelsack *der* (PL die **Dudelsäcke**) bagpipes.

Duft *der* (PL die **Düfte**) fragrance, scent.

duften *verb* (PERF **hat geduftet**) to smell; **nach Lavendel duften** to smell of lavender.

dumm *adjective* **1** stupid; **2 das wird mir jetzt zu dumm** (*informal*) I've had enough of it; **3 so etwas Dummes!** how annoying!; **4 der Dumme sein** to draw the short straw.

dummerweise *adverb* stupidly.

Dummheit *die* (PL die **Dummheiten**) **1** stupidity; **2** stupid thing; **mach keine Dummheiten** don't do anything stupid.

Dummkopf *der* (PL die **Dummköpfe**) fool.

Dünger *der* (PL die **Dünger**) fertilizer.

dunkel *adjective* **1** dark; **ein dunkler Anzug** a dark suit; **2 im Dunkeln** in the dark; **3** vague (*idea*); **4** shady (*business*); **5** deep (*voice*).

Dunkelheit *die* darkness, dark; **bei Einbruch der Dunkelheit** at dusk.

dünn *adjective* **1** thin; **2** weak (*coffee, tea*).

Dunst *der* (PL die **Dünste**) haze.

Duo *das* (PL die **Duos**) duet.

durch *preposition* (+ ACC) **1** through; **er ist durch das Fernsehen bekannt geworden** he's become famous through television; **2** by; **durch Boten** by courier; **3 acht durch zwei ist vier** eight divided by two is four; **4** due to.

durch *adverb* **1** through; **die ganze Nacht durch** all through the night; **2 den Winter durch** throughout the winter; **3 durch und durch** completely; **4 es war acht Uhr**

durcharbeiten verb (PERF hat durchgearbeitet) **1** to work through; **die Nacht durcharbeiten** to work through the night; **2 sich durch etwas durcharbeiten** to work your way through something.

durchaus adverb absolutely.

durchblicken verb (PERF hat durchgeblickt) **1** (informal) to understand; **2 durchblicken lassen, dass …** to hint that ….

durchbrechen ◇verb (PRES **bricht durch**, IMPERF **brach durch**, PERF **hat durchgebrochen**) **1** to snap, to break in two; **2** (PERF **ist durchgebrochen**) **das Brett ist durchgebrochen** the board has snapped.

Durcheinander das **1** muddle; **2** mess; **in der Wohnung herrschte ein fürchterliches Durcheinander** the flat was a terrible mess; **3** confusion; **im allgemeinen Durcheinander** in the general confusion.

durcheinander adverb **1** in a mess; **mein Zimmer ist durcheinander** my room is (in) a mess; **2 die Akten durcheinander bringen** to muddle up the files; **Karl hat ihre Namen durcheinander gebracht** Karl got their names mixed up; **3** confused; **bring mich nicht durcheinander** don't confuse me; **4 sie haben alle durcheinander geredet** they all talked at once.

durcheinanderbringen SEE **durcheinander.**

durchfahren ◇verb (PRES **fährt durch**, IMPERF **fuhr durch**, PERF **ist durchgefahren**) **1** to drive through; **2** to go through; **3 der Zug fährt (in Stuttgart) durch** the train doesn't stop (in Stuttgart).

Durchfall der diarrhoea.

durchfallen ◇verb (PRES **fällt durch**, IMPERF **fiel durch**, PERF **ist durchgefallen**) **1** to fall through; **2** to fail (an exam).

durchführen verb (PERF hat durchgeführt) to carry out.

Durchgang der (PL die **Durchgänge**) **1** passage; **2 'Durchgang verboten'** 'no entry'; **3** round (in sport).

Durchgangsverkehr der through traffic.

durchgehen ◇verb (IMPERF **ging durch**, PERF **ist durchgegangen**) **1** to go through; **2** (informal) to escape; **3 jemandem etwas durchgehen lassen** to let somebody get away with something.

durchkommen ◇verb (IMPERF **kam durch**, PERF **ist durchgekommen**) **1** to come through; **2** to get through (on the phone, in an exam); **3** to pull through (after an illness).

durchlassen ◇verb (PRES **lässt durch**, IMPERF **ließ durch**, PERF **hat durchgelassen**) **1** to let through; **2** to let in.

durchmachen *verb* (PERF **hat durchgemacht**) **1** to go through; **2** to work through (*your lunch break, for example*); **3 wir haben die Nacht durchgemacht** we made a night of it.

Durchmesser *der* (PL *die* **Durchmesser**) diameter.

durchnehmen ◇*verb* (PRES **nimmt durch**, IMPERF **nahm durch**, PERF **hat durchgenommen**) to do (*a topic at school*).

durchs = durch das.

Durchsage *die* (PL *die* **Durchsagen**) announcement.

Durchschnitt *der* (PL *die* **Durchschnitte**) average; **im Durchschnitt** on average.

durchschnittlich *adjective* average.

durchschnittlich *adverb* on average.

durchsetzen *verb* (PERF **hat durchgesetzt**) **1** to carry through; **2 sich durchsetzen** to assert yourself; **3 sich durchsetzen** to catch on (*of a fashion, an idea*).

durchsichtig *adjective* transparent.

durchstreichen ◇*verb* (IMPERF **strich durch**, PERF **hat durchgestrichen**) to cross out.

Durchzug *der* draught.

dürfen ◇*verb* (PRES **darf**, IMPERF **durfte**, PERF **hat gedurft** or **hat dürfen**) **1** to be allowed; **sie darf das nicht** she's not allowed to do that; **er hat nicht gedurft** he wasn't allowed to; **2 Klaus hat sie im**

Krankenhaus besuchen dürfen Klaus was allowed to visit her in hospital; **3 darf ich?** may I?; **4 das dürfen Sie nicht vergessen** you mustn't forget that; **du darfst es nicht alles so ernst nehmen** you mustn't take it all so seriously; **5 du darfst froh sein, dass sonst nichts passiert ist** you should be glad that nothing else happened; **das darf einfach nicht passieren** that just shouldn't happen; **das dürfte nicht schwierig sein** that shouldn't be difficult; **6 das darf nicht wahr sein!** I don't believe it!; **7 was darf es sein?** can I help you?; **8 das dürfte der Grund sein** that's probably the reason.

durfte, durften, durftest, durftet SEE dürfen.

dürftig *adjective* poor, meagre.

Dürre *die* (PL *die* **Dürren**) drought.

Durst *der* thirst; **Durst haben** to be thirsty.

durstig *adjective* thirsty.

Dusche *die* (PL *die* **Duschen**) shower.

duschen *verb* (PERF **hat geduscht**) **1** to have a shower; **2 sich duschen** to have a shower.

Düsenflugzeug *das* (PL *die* **Düsenflugzeuge**) jet (plane).

düster *adjective* **1** gloomy (*future, thoughts*); **2** dark.

Dutzend *das* (PL *die* **Dutzende**) dozen.

duzen *verb* (PERF **hat geduzt**) to call somebody 'du'; **wollen wir uns duzen?** shall we say 'du' to each

a b c **d** e f g h i j k l m n o p q r s t u v w x y z

a

b other? (*du* is used when talking to family members, close friends, or people of your own age).

c **dynamisch** *adjective* dynamic.

D-Zug *der* (PL die **D-Züge**) fast train, express.

f

g # Ee

h

i **Ebbe** *die* (PL die **Ebben**) low tide; **es ist Ebbe** the tide is out.

eben *adjective* **1** flat; **2** level.

j **eben** *adverb* **1** just; **Gabi war eben hier** Gabi was just here; **eben noch** just now; **2 eben!** exactly!

k

l **Ebene** *die* (PL die **Ebenen**) **1** plain; **2** level; **3** plane (*in geometry*).

m **ebenso** *adverb* just as; **Ulla hat den Film ebenso oft gesehen wie du** Ulla's seen the film just as often as you; **ich habe ebenso viel Arbeit wie du** I've got just as much work as you.

n

o

p **Echo** *das* (PL die **Echos**) echo.

q **echt** *adjective* real, genuine; **die Kette ist aus echtem Gold** the necklace is real gold.

r **echt** *adverb* (*informal*) really; **das ist echt gut** that's really good.

s **Eckball** *der* (PL die **Eckbälle**) corner (kick).

t **Ecke** *die* (PL die **Ecken**) corner; **um die Ecke** round the corner.

u **eckig** *adjective* square.

v **Edelstein** *der* (PL die **Edelsteine**) precious stone.

w

x

y

z

EDV *die* (*elektronische Datenverarbeitung*) electronic data processing, EDP.

Efeu *der* (PL die **Efeus**) ivy.

Effekt *der* (PL die **Effekte**) effect.

effektiv *adjective* effective.

effektiv *adverb* really, actually.

EG *die* (*Europäische Gemeinschaft*) EC.

egal *adjective* **1 das ist mir egal** it's all the same to me; **2 egal, wie groß** no matter how big; **egal, ob er es will oder nicht** (it doesn't matter) whether he wants to or not.

egoistisch *adjective* selfish.

Ehe *die* (PL die **Ehen**) marriage.

ehe *conjunction* before; **ehe ich nicht weiß, was er will, mache ich nichts** I won't do anything before I know what he wants.

Ehefrau *die* (PL die **Ehefrauen**) wife.

ehemalig *adjective* former.

Ehemann *der* (PL die **Ehemänner**) husband.

Ehepaar *das* (PL die **Ehepaare**) married couple.

eher *adverb* **1** earlier, sooner; **je eher, desto besser** the sooner the better; **2** rather; **eher gehe ich zu Fuß, als Geld für ein Taxi auszugeben** I'd rather walk than pay for a taxi; **3** more; **das ist schon eher möglich** that's more likely.

Ehre *die* (PL die **Ehren**) honour.

ehrenamtlich *adjective* honorary.

Ehrgeiz *der* ambition.

ehrgeizig *adjective* ambitious.

ehrlich *adjective* honest.

Ehrlichkeit *die* honesty.

Ei *das* (PL die **Eier**) egg.

Eiche *die* (PL die **Eichen**) oak.

Eichhörnchen *das* (PL die **Eichhörnchen**) squirrel.

Eid *der* (PL die **Eide**) oath.

Eidechse *die* (PL die **Eidechsen**) lizard.

Eidotter *das* (PL die **Eidotter**) egg yolk.

Eierbecher *der* (PL die **Eierbecher**) egg-cup.

Eierschale *die* (PL die **Eierschalen**) eggshell.

Eifer *der* eagerness.

Eifersucht *die* jealousy.

eifersüchtig *adjective* jealous; **auf jemanden eifersüchtig sein** to be jealous of somebody.

eifrig *adjective* eager.

Eigelb *das* (PL die **Eigelb(e)**) egg yolk.

eigen *adjective* own; **sie ist erst siebzehn und hat schon ihr eigenes Auto** she's only seventeen and she's already got her own car.

Eigenart *die* (PL die **Eigenarten**) peculiarity.

eigenartig *adjective* peculiar.

Eigenschaft *die* (PL die **Eigenschaften**) 1 quality; 2 characteristic.

eigensinnig *adjective* obstinate.

eigentlich *adjective* actual.

eigentlich *adverb* actually; **eigentlich habe ich keine Lust, heute ins Kino zu gehen** actually I don't fancy going to the cinema today.

Eigentum *das* property.

Eigentümer *der* (PL die **Eigentümer**) owner.

eignen *verb* (PERF **hat sich geeignet**) **sich eignen** to be suitable.

Eile *die* hurry.

eilen *verb* 1 (PERF **ist geeilt**) to hurry; 2 (PERF **hat geeilt**) to be urgent; **das eilt nicht** it's not urgent.

eilig *adjective* 1 urgent; 2 hurried; 3 **es eilig haben** to be in a hurry.

Eilzug *der* (PL die **Eilzüge**) fast stopping train.

Eimer *der* (PL die **Eimer**) bucket.

ein, eine, ein *article* a, an, **ein Haus** a house; **eine Allergie** an allergy; **ein bisschen mehr** a bit more; **was für ein Kleid hast du gekauft?** what sort of dress did you buy?

ein *adjective* 1 one; **sie haben nur ein Kind** they've got just one child; **eines Abends** one evening; 2 **einer Meinung sein** to be of the same opinion; 3 **ein für alle Mal** once and for all.

einander *pronoun* each other, one another.

Einbahnstraße *die* (PL die **Einbahnstraßen**) one-way street.

Einband *der* (PL die **Einbände**) cover.

einbauen verb (PERF hat eingebaut) 1 to fit; 2 to install.

Einbauküche die (PL die Einbauküchen) fitted kitchen.

einbiegen ◇verb (IMPERF bog ein, PERF ist eingebogen) to turn; der Radfahrer bog langsam in die Seitenstraße ein the cyclist turned slowly down the side street.

einbilden verb (PERF hat sich eingebildet) 1 sich einbilden to imagine; das bildest du dir nur ein you're only imagining it; 2 Till bildet sich viel ein Till is very conceited.

Einbildung die imagination; das ist alles nur Einbildung it's all in the mind.

einbrechen ◇verb (PRES bricht ein, IMPERF brach ein, PERF ist eingebrochen) to break in; in unserem Haus sind Diebe eingebrochen thieves broke into our house; bei unseren Nachbarn ist eingebrochen worden our neighbours have been burgled.

Einbrecher der (PL die Einbrecher) burglar.

einbringen verb (IMPERF brachte ein, PERF hat eingebracht) to bring in; die Ernte einbringen to gather in the harvest.

Einbruch der (PL die Einbrüche) 1 burglary; 2 vor Einbruch der Dunkelheit before it gets dark; 3 bei Einbruch der Nacht at nightfall.

einchecken verb (PERF hat eingecheckt) am Flughafen einchecken to check in at the airport.

eindeutig adjective 1 clear; 2 definite (proof).

Eindruck der (PL die Eindrücke) impression; einen guten Eindruck auf jemanden machen to make a good impression on somebody.

eindrucksvoll adjective impressive.

eine SEE ein, einer.

eineinhalb number one and a half.

einer, eine, ein(e)s pronoun 1 one; einer von uns one of us; wie soll das einer wissen? how is one supposed to know?; 2 somebody; 3 kaum einer hardly anyone; 4 you; das macht einen müde it makes you tired.

einerseits adverb on the one hand; einerseits sagt sie, dass sie kein Geld hat, andererseits kauft sie sich dauernd neue Sachen on the one hand she claims to have no money, on the other hand she's constantly buying new things.

eines SEE einer.

einfach adjective 1 simple; 2 easy; 3 single (ticket, knot).

einfach adverb simply.

Einfachheit die simplicity.

Einfahrt die (PL die Einfahrten) 1 entrance; 2 arrival (of a train); 3 slip road (on a motorway).

Einfall der (PL die Einfälle) idea.

einfallen ◇verb (PRES fällt ein, IMPERF fiel ein, PERF ist eingefallen) 1 jemandem einfallen to occur to somebody; 2 ihr Name fällt mir nicht ein I can't think of her name; **3 was fällt dir eigentlich ein?** what do you think you're doing?; **4 sich etwas einfallen lassen** to think of something.

Einfamilienhaus *das* (PL die **Einfamilienhäuser**) detached family house.

Einfluss *der* (PL die **Einflüsse**) influence.

einfrieren ◇*verb* (IMPERF **fror ein**, PERF **ist eingefroren**) **1** to freeze; **2** (PERF **hat eingefroren**) to freeze (*food in the freezer*).

Einfuhr *die* (PL die **Einfuhren**) import.

einführen *verb* (PERF **hat eingeführt**) **1** to import; **2** to introduce.

Einführung *die* (PL die **Einführungen**) introduction.

Eingabe *die* input (*of data*).

Eingang *der* (PL die **Eingänge**) entrance.

Eingangshalle *die* (PL die **Eingangshallen**) hallway.

eingeben ◇*verb* (PRES **gibt ein**, IMPERF **gab ein**, PERF **hat eingegeben**) **1** to hand in; **2** to input, to key in.

eingebildet *adjective* **1** conceited; **2** imaginary (*illness*).

Eingeborene *der/die* (PL die **Eingeborenen**) native.

eingehen ◇*verb* (IMPERF **ging ein**, PERF **ist eingegangen**) **1** to shrink (*of clothes*); **2** to die (*of plants*); **3** to arrive (*of goods*); **4 auf etwas eingehen** to go into something; **sie**

ging näher darauf ein she went into it in more detail; **5 auf etwas nicht eingehen** to ignore something; **6 auf etwas eingehen** to agree to something; **Oliver ist auf unseren Plan eingegangen** Oliver agreed to our plan; **7 ein Risiko eingehen** to take a risk.

eingeschrieben *adjective* registered; **ein eingeschriebener Brief** a registered letter.

eingestellt *adjective* **1 auf etwas eingestellt sein** to be prepared for something; **2 fortschrittlich eingestellt sein** to be progressively minded.

eingewöhnen *verb* (PERF **hat sich eingewöhnt**) **sich eingewöhnen** to settle in.

eingießen ◇*verb* (IMPERF **goss ein**, PERF **hat eingegossen**) to pour.

Eingriff *der* (PL die **Eingriffe**) **1** intervention; **2** operation (*surgical*).

einheimisch *adjective* **1** native; **2** local.

Einheit *die* (PL die **Einheiten**) **1** unity; **2** unit (*of drink, soldiers*).

Einheitspreis *der* (PL die **Einheitspreise**) **1** standard price; **2** flat fare.

einholen *verb* (PERF **hat eingeholt**) **1** to catch up with; **2** to make up (*time, a delay*); **3** to buy; **einholen gehen** to go shopping.

einhundert *number* one hundred.

einige SEE **einiger**.

einigen *verb* (PERF **hat sich geeinigt**) **sich einigen** to come to

a *b* *c* *d* **e** *f* *g* *h* *i* *j* *k* *l* *m* *n* *o* *p* *q* *r* *s* *t* *u* *v* *w* *x* *y* *z* an agreement; **sich auf etwas einigen** to agree on something.

einiger, einige, einiges *adjective, pronoun* **1** some; **vor einiger Zeit** some time ago; **2** several; **3 nur einige waren noch da** there were only a few left; **4 einiges** quite a lot; **wir haben einiges gesehen** we saw quite a lot (of things); **5 einiges** some things; **einiges hat uns nicht gefallen** there were some things we didn't like.

einigermaßen *adverb* **1** fairly; **2** fairly well; **3 'wie geht es dir?'– 'einigermaßen'** 'how are you?'– 'so-so'.

einiges SEE einiger.

Einigung die agreement.

Einkauf der (PL die Einkäufe) **1** purchase; **2** shopping; **Einkäufe machen** to do some shopping.

einkaufen *verb* (PERF hat eingekauft) **1** to buy; **ich habe vergessen Milch einzukaufen** I forgot to buy milk; **2** to shop; **wir kaufen meist im Supermarkt ein** we usually shop at the supermarket; **einkaufen gehen** to go shopping.

Einkaufsbummel der (PL die Einkaufsbummel) shopping spree.

Einkaufswagen der (PL die Einkaufswagen) shopping trolley.

Einkaufszentrum das (PL die Einkaufszentren) shopping centre.

Einkommen das (PL die Einkommen) income.

einladen ⬦*verb* (PRES lädt ein, IMPERF lud ein, PERF hat eingeladen)

1 to invite; **jemanden zum Abendessen einladen** to invite somebody for dinner; **2 jemanden ins Kino einladen** to take sombody to the cinema; **3** to treat; **ich lade euch ein** I'll treat you; **4** to load (goods).

Einladung die (PL die Einladungen) invitation.

einleben *verb* (PERF hat sich eingelebt) **sich einleben** to settle down.

Einleitung die (PL die Einleitungen) introduction.

einlösen *verb* (PERF hat eingelöst) to cash.

einmal *adverb* **1** once (in the past); **es war einmal** ... once upon a time ...; **2** one day (in the future); **3 auf einmal** suddenly; **4 auf einmal** at the same time; **sie kamen alle auf einmal** they all came at the same time; **5 nicht einmal** not even; **6 noch einmal** again; **7 es geht nun einmal nicht** it's just not possible.

einmalig *adjective* **1** unique; **2** fantastic; **3** single, one-off (payment).

einmischen *verb* (PERF hat sich eingemischt) **sich einmischen** to interfere.

Einmündung die (PL die Einmündungen) **1** junction (of roads); **2** confluence (of rivers).

einordnen *verb* (PERF hat eingeordnet) **1** to put in order; **2 sich einordnen** to fit in (with *other people)*; **3 sich einordnen** to get in lane *(when driving)*.

einpacken *verb* (PERF **hat eingepackt**) **1** to pack; **2** to wrap.

einreichen *verb* (PERF **hat eingereicht**) to hand in.

Einreise *die* (PL *die* **Einreisen**) entry.

einreisen *verb* (PERF **ist eingereist**) to enter a country; **er reiste nach Italien ein** he entered Italy.

einrichten *verb* (PERF **hat eingerichtet**) **1** to furnish; **2** to set up *(an organisation)*; **3** to arrange; **kannst du es so einrichten, dass du vormittags da bist?** can you arrange to be here in the morning?; **4 sich einrichten** to furnish your home; **5 sich einrichten** to economize; **6 sich auf etwas einrichten** to prepare for something.

Einrichtung *die* (PL *die* **Einrichtungen**) **1** furnishing; **2** furnishings; **3** setting up; **4** institution; **staatliche Einrichtungen** state institutions.

Eins *die* (PL *die* **Einsen**) one.

eins *number* one; **eins zu eins** one all; **es ist eins** it's one o'clock.

oins *pronoun* SEE **einer**

eins *adjective* **mir ist alles eins** it's all the same to me.

einsam *adjective* lonely.

einsammeln *verb* (PERF **hat eingesammelt**) to collect.

Einsatz *der* **1** use; **2** stake *(when betting)*.

einschalten *verb* (PERF **hat eingeschaltet**) **1** to switch on *(a radio, TV)*; **2 sich einschalten** to intervene.

einschlafen ◇*verb* (PRES **schläft ein**, IMPERF **schlief ein**, PERF **ist eingeschlafen**) to go to sleep.

einschließen ◇*verb* (IMPERF **schloss ein**, PERF **hat eingeschlossen**) **1** to lock in; **2** to include; **3 sich einschließen** to lock yourself in.

einschließlich *preposition* (+ GEN) including; **einschließlich der Unkosten** including expenses.

einschließlich *adverb* inclusive.

einschränken *verb* (PERF **hat eingeschränkt**) **1** to restrict; **2** to cut back; **3 sich einschränken** to economize.

einschreiben ◇*verb* (IMPERF **schrieb sich ein**, PERF **hat sich eingeschrieben**) **1 sich einschreiben** to enrol *(at university)*; **2 sich einschreiben** to put your name down.

Einschreiben *das* (PL *die* **Einschreiben**) registered letter, registered parcel; **per Einschreiben** registered.

einsehen ◇*verb* (PRES **sieht ein**, IMPERF **sah ein**, PERF **hat eingesehen**) **1** to realize; **2** to see; **das sehe ich nicht ein** I don't see why.

einseitig *adjective* one-sided.

einsenden ◇*verb* (IMPERF **sendete ein/sandte ein**, PERF **hat**

a
b
c
d
e
f
g
h
i
j
k
l
m
n
o
p
q
r
s
t
u
v
w
x
y
z

eingesendet/hat eingesandt) to send in.

einsetzen *verb* (PERF **hat eingesetzt**) 1 to put in (*a missing part*) to insert; 2 to use; **während der Weltmeisterschaft wurden Sonderzüge eingesetzt** special trains were put on during the World Cup; 3 to stake (*money*); 4 to start (*of rain, snow*); 5 **sich für jemanden einsetzen** to support somebody.

Einsicht *die* 1 insight; 2 sense; 3 **zu der Einsicht kommen, dass ...** to come to realize that ....

einsperren *verb* (PERF **hat eingesperrt**) to lock up.

Einspruch *der* (PL die **Einsprüche**) objection.

einst *adverb* 1 once; 2 one day (*in the future*).

einstecken *verb* (PERF **hat eingesteckt**) 1 to put in (*a coin*); 2 **einen Brief einstecken** to post a letter; 3 to plug in; 4 **etwas einstecken** to put something in your pocket or bag, to take something; 5 (*informal*) to take (*insults*).

einsteigen ◇*verb* (IMPERF **stieg ein**, PERF **ist eingestiegen**) 1 to get in; 2 to get on (*a bus or train*).

einstellen *verb* (PERF **hat eingestellt**) 1 to employ (*in a job*); 2 to adjust (*a machine*); 3 to focus (*a camera*); 4 to tune into (*a radio station*); 5 to stop; 6 **sich auf etwas einstellen** to prepare yourself for something; 7 **sich schnell auf eine neue Situation einstellen** to adjust quickly to a new situation.

Einstellung *die* (PL die **Einstellungen**) 1 employment; 2 adjustment; 3 stopping; 4 take (*of a film*); 5 attitude; **seine politische Einstellung** his political views.

Einstieg *der* (PL die **Einstiege**) entrance.

einstürzen *verb* (PERF **ist eingestürzt**) to collapse.

einstweilen *adverb* 1 for the time being; 2 meanwhile.

eintausend *number* one thousand.

einteilen *verb* (PERF **hat eingeteilt**) 1 to divide up; 2 **sich seine Zeit gut einteilen** to organize your time well.

Eintopf *der* (PL die **Eintöpfe**) stew.

Eintrag *der* (PL die **Einträge**) entry.

eintragen ◇*verb* (PRES **trägt ein**, IMPERF **trug ein**, PERF **hat eingetragen**) 1 to enter, to write; 2 **sich eintragen** to put your name down.

einträglich *adjective* profitable.

eintreffen ◇*verb* (PRES **trifft ein**, IMPERF **traf ein**, PERF **ist eingetroffen**) 1 to arrive; 2 to come true.

eintreten ◇*verb* (PRES **tritt ein**, IMPERF **trat ein**, PERF **ist eingetreten**) 1 to enter; 2 **in einen Klub eintreten** to join a club; 3 **für jemanden eintreten** to stand up for somebody).

Eintritt der **1** entrance; **2** admission; **'Eintritt frei'** 'admission free'.

Eintrittskarte die (PL die **Eintrittskarten**) (admission) ticket.

Eintrittspreis der (PL die **Eintrittspreise**) admission charge.

einverstanden adjective **1 einverstanden sein** to agree; **einverstanden! okay!; 2 mit jemandem einverstanden sein** to approve of somebody.

Einwand der (PL die **Einwände**) objection.

Einwanderer der (PL die **Einwanderer**) immigrant.

Einwanderin die (PL die **Einwanderinnen**) immigrant.

einwandern verb (PERF **ist eingewandert**) to immigrate; **nach Europa einwandern** to immigrate into Europe.

Einwanderung die immigration.

einwärts adverb inwards.

einweichen verb (PERF **hat eingeweicht**) to soak (washing).

einwerfen ◇verb (PRES **wirft ein**, IMPERF **warf ein**, PERF **hat eingeworfen**) **1** to post; **2** to put in (a coin, money); **3** to throw in; **4** to smash.

Einwohner der (PL die **Einwohner**) inhabitant.

Einzahl die singular.

einzahlen verb (PERF **hat eingezahlt**) to pay in.

Einzel das (PL die **Einzel**) singles (in sport).

Einzelheit die (PL die **Einzelheiten**) detail.

Einzelkarte die (PL die **Einzelkarten**) single ticket.

Einzelkind das (PL die **Einzelkinder**) only child.

einzeln adjective **1** single; **2** individual; **3** odd (sock, for example).

einzeln adverb **1** individually; **2** separately, one at a time; **bitte einzeln eintreten** please enter one at a time.

Einzelne der/die/das (PL die **Einzelnen**) **1** der/die Einzelne the individual; **2 Einzelne** some; **3 ein Einzelner/eine Einzelne/ein Einzelnes** a single one; **jeder/jede/jedes Einzelne** every single one; **4 im Einzelnen** in detail; **ins Einzelne gehen** to go into detail.

Einzelzimmer das (PL die **Einzelzimmer**) single room.

einziehen ◇verb (IMPERF **zog ein**, PERF **hat eingezogen**) **1** to collect (payment); **2** to draw in (its feelers, claws); **3 den Kopf einziehen** to duck; **4** (PERF **ist eingezogen**) to move in; **wann zieht ihr in die neue Wohnung ein?** when are you moving into your new flat?; **5** (PERF **ist eingezogen**) to soak in.

einzig adjective only; **ein einziges Mal** only once.

Einzige der/die/das (PL die **Einzigen**) **1** der/die/das Einzige the only one; **2 ein Einziger/eine Einzige/ein**

Einziges a single one; **kein Einziger/keine Einzige/kein Einziges** not a single one; **3 das Einzige, was mich stört** the only thing that bothers me.

Eis das **1** ice; **2** ice cream.

Eisbahn die (PL die **Eisbahnen**) skating rink.

Eisbär der (PL die **Eisbären**) polar bear.

Eisbecher der (PL die **Eisbecher**) ice-cream sundae.

Eisdiele die (PL die **Eisdielen**) ice-cream parlour.

Eisen das iron.

Eisenbahn die (PL die **Eisenbahnen**) railway.

eisern adjective iron.

Eishockey das ice hockey.

eisig adjective icy.

eiskalt adjective **1** ice-cold (drink); **2** freezing cold.

Eislaufen das ice-skating.

Eisläufer der (PL die **Eisläufer**) skater (on ice).

Eisläuferin die (PL die **Eisläuferinnen**) skater (on ice).

Eisportionierer der (PL die **Eisportionierer**) scoop.

Eiswürfel der (PL die **Eiswürfel**) ice cube.

Eiszapfen der (PL die **Eiszapfen**) icicle.

eitel adjective vain.

Eitelkeit die of vanity.

Eiter der pus.

Eiweiß das **1** egg-white; **2** protein.

Ekel der disgust.

ekelhaft adjective disgusting.

ekeln verb (PERF **hat sich geekelt**) **sich vor etwas ekeln** to find something disgusting.

eklig adjective disgusting.

Ekzem das (PL die **Ekzeme**) eczema.

Elefant der (PL die **Elefanten**) elephant.

elegant adjective elegant, stylish.

Elektriker der (PL die **Elektriker**) electrician.

elektrisch adjective electrical.

Elektrizität die electricity.

Elektroherd der (PL die **Elektroherde**) electric cooker.

Elektronik die electronics.

elektronisch adjective electronic.

Elektrorasierer der (PL die **Elektrorasierer**) electric razor.

Elend das misery.

elend adjective **1** miserable; **2** terrible.

elf number eleven.

Elfe die (PL die **Elfen**) fairy.

Elfmeter der (PL die **Elfmeter**) penalty (in soccer).

Ellbogen der (PL die **Ellbogen**) elbow.

Eltern plural noun parents.

Email das (PL die **Emails**) enamel.

E-Mail die (PL die **E-Mails**) email.

empfahl SEE **empfehlen**.

Empfang der (PL die **Empfänge**) **1** reception; **2** receipt (of goods or a letter).

empfangen ✧verb (PRES **empfängt**, IMPERF **empfing**, PERF **hat empfangen**) to receive.

Empfängnisverhütung die contraception.

Empfangsdame die (PL die **Empfangsdamen**) receptionist.

empfehlen ✧verb (PRES **empfiehlt**, IMPERF **empfahl**, PERF **hat empfohlen**) to recommend.

empfindlich adjective **1** sensitive; **2** delicate; **3** touchy.

empfing SEE **empfangen**.

empfohlen SEE **empfehlen**.

empört adjective indignant.

Ende das (PL die **Enden**) **1** end; Ende April at the end of April; am Ende der Straße at the end of the road; **2** am Ende in the end; **3** ending (of a film, novel); **4** zu Ende sein to be finished, to be over; Ende gut, alles gut all's well that ends well.

enden verb (PERF **hat geendet**) to end.

endgültig adjective **1** final (consent, decision); **2** definite.

Endivie die (PL die **Endivien**) endive.

endlich adverb finally, at last; na endlich! at last!

endlos adjective endless.

Endspiel das (PL die **Endspiele**) final.

Endstation die (PL die **Endstationen**) terminus.

Endung die (PL die **Endungen**) ending.

Energie die energy.

energisch adjective energetic.

eng adjective **1** narrow; **2** tight; **3** close; eng befreundet sein to be close friends.

Engel der (PL die **Engel**) angel.

England das England; aus England from England.

Engländer der (PL die **Engländer**) Englishman.

Engländerin die (PL die **Engländerinnen**) Englishwoman.

englisch adjective English.

Englisch das English; auf Englisch in English.

Enkel der (PL die **Enkel**) grandson.

Enkelin die (PL die **Enkelinnen**) granddaughter.

Enkelkind das (PL die **Enkelkinder**) grandchild.

entdecken verb (PERF **hat entdeckt**) to discover.

Entdeckung die (PL die **Entdeckungen**) discovery.

Ente die (PL die **Enten**) duck.

entfernen verb (PERF **hat entfernt**) to remove.

entfernt adjective **1** distant; **2** zehn Kilometer entfernt ten kilometres away.

entfernt adverb entfernt verwandt sein to be distantly related.

Entfernung die (PL die **Entfernungen**) distance.

entführen verb (PERF hat entführt)
1 to kidnap; 2 to hijack.

Entführer der (PL die Entführer)
1 hijacker; 2 kidnapper.

Entführerin die (PL die
Entführerinnen) 1 hijacker;
2 kidnapper.

Entführung die (PL die
Entführungen) 1 hijacking;
2 kidnapping.

entgegen preposition (+ DAT)
contrary to.

entgegengesetzt adjective
1 opposite; 2 opposing (views).

entgegenkommen ◇verb
(IMPERF kam entgegen, PERF ist
entgegengekommen) 1 to come
towards; 2 jemandem
entgegenkommen to come to meet
somebody; 3 jemandem auf
halbem Wege entgegenkommen
to meet somebody halfway;
4 jemandem freundlich
entgegenkommen to be
accommodating towards
somebody.

entgegenkommend adjective
1 obliging; 2 der
entgegenkommende Verkehr the
oncoming traffic.

Entgelt das payment.

Enthaarungsmittel das (PL die
Enthaarungsmittel) hair remover,
depilatory.

enthalten ◇verb (PRES enthält,
IMPERF enthielt, PERF hat enthalten)
1 to contain; 2 sich einer Sache
enthalten to abstain from
something; sich der Stimme

enthalten to abstain; 3 (PERF ist
enthalten) in etwas enthalten
sein to be included in something;
im Preis enthalten included in the
price.

entkommen ◇verb (IMPERF
entkam, PERF ist entkommen) to
escape.

entlang preposition (+ ACC or + DAT)
along; die Straße entlang along
the road; am Fluss entlang along
the river.

entlanggehen ◇verb (IMPERF
ging entlang, PERF ist
entlanggegangen) to walk along.

entlanglaufen ◇verb (PRES läuft
entlang, IMPERF lief entlang, PERF ist
entlanggelaufen) to run along.

entlassen ◇verb (PRES entlässt,
IMPERF entließ, PERF hat entlassen)
1 to dismiss (from a job); 2 to
discharge (from hospital); 3 to
release (from prison).

Entlassung die (PL die
Entlassungen) 1 dismissal;
2 discharge; 3 release.

entmutigen verb (PERF hat
entmutigt) to discourage.

entschädigen verb (PERF hat
entschädigt) to compensate.

Entschädigung die
compensation.

entscheiden ◇verb (IMPERF
entschied, PERF hat entschieden)
1 to decide (on); 2 sich
entscheiden to decide.

entscheidend adjective decisive,
crucial.

Entscheidung die (PL die Entscheidungen) decision.

Entschiedenheit die decisiveness.

entschließen ⬦verb (IMPERF entschloss sich, PERF hat sich entschlossen) **1** sich entschließen to decide; **2** sich anders entschließen to change your mind; Karl hat sich anders entschlossen Karl has changed his mind.

entschlossen adjective determined.

Entschluss der (PL die Entschlüsse) decision.

entschuldigen verb (PERF hat entschuldigt) **1** to excuse; entschuldigen Sie bitte excuse me; **2** sich entschuldigen to apologize; ich habe mich bei Michi entschuldigt I apologized to Michi.

Entschuldigung die (PL die Entschuldigungen) **1** apology; **2** jemanden um Entschuldigung bitten to apologize to somebody; **3** Entschuldigung! sorry!; **4** Entschuldigung (with a question or request) excuse me; Entschuldigung, können Sie mir sagen, wie ich zum Bahnhof komme? excuse me, could you tell me the way to the station?; **5** excuse.

Entsetzen das horror.

entsetzlich adjective **1** horrible; **2** terrible.

entsetzt adjective horrified.

entspannen verb (PERF hat sich entspannt) **1** sich entspannen to relax; **2** sich entspannen to ease (of a situation).

entspannend adjective relaxing.

entsprechen ⬦verb (PRES entspricht, IMPERF entsprach, PERF hat entsprochen) **1** den Anforderungen entsprechen to meet the requirements; **2** einer Sache entsprechen to correspond to something; **3** to agree with (the truth, a description); **4** to comply with (certain standards).

entsprechend adjective **1** corresponding; **2** appropriate.

entsprechend preposition (+ DAT) in accordance with.

entstehen ⬦verb (IMPERF entstand, PERF ist entstanden) **1** to develop; **2** to result of (damage).

enttäuschen verb (PERF hat enttäuscht) to disappoint.

Enttäuschung die (PL die Enttäuschungen) disappointment.

entweder conjunction either; entweder heute oder morgen either today or tomorrow.

entwerten verb (PERF hat entwertet) **1** to devalue; **2** to punch (a ticket in a machine found on trains, trams, buses, and on the platform; you have to punch your ticket before each journey).

Entwerter der (PL die Entwerter) ticket-punching machine (these machines are found on trains, trams, buses, and on the platform;

you have to punch your ticket before each journey).

entwickeln verb (PERF hat entwickelt) 1 to develop; 2 to display (ability, a characteristic); 3 sich entwickeln to develop.

Entwicklung die (PL die Entwicklungen) 1 development; 2 developing.

Entwicklungsland das (PL die Entwicklungsländer) developing country.

Entwurf der (PL die Entwürfe) 1 design; 2 draft.

entzückend adjective delightful.

entzünden verb (PERF hat entzündet) 1 to light (a fire, match); 2 sich entzünden to become inflamed; 3 sich entzünden to ignite.

Entzündung die (PL die Entzündungen) inflammation.

Enzian der (PL die Enziane) gentian.

Epidemie die (PL die Epidemien) epidemic.

er pronoun 1 he; 2 it; 'wo ist mein Mantel?' – 'er liegt auf dem Stuhl' 'where's my coat?' – 'it's on the chair'; 3 him (stressed); **er war es** it was him.

erben verb (PERF hat geerbt) to inherit.

erblich adjective hereditary.

Erbschaft die (PL die Erbschaften) inheritance.

Erbse die (PL die Erbsen) pea.

Erdbeben das (PL die Erdbeben) earthquake.

Erdbeere die (PL die Erdbeeren) strawberry.

erbrechen verb (PRES erbricht, IMPERF erbrach, PERF hat erbrochen) 1 to brng up (food); 2 sich erbrechen to be sick.

Erde die 1 earth, soil; 2 ground; **auf der Erde** on the ground; 3 Earth; 4 earth (for electricity).

Erdgeschoss das (PL die Erdgeschosse) ground floor; **im Erdgeschoss** on the ground floor.

Erdkunde die geography.

Erdnuss die (PL die Erdnüsse) peanut.

ereignen verb (PERF hat sich ereignet) sich ereignen to happen.

Ereignis das (PL die Ereignisse) event.

erfahren ◇verb (PRES erfährt, IMPERF erfuhr, PERF hat erfahren) 1 to hear, to learn; 2 to experience.

erfahren adjective experienced.

Erfahrung die (PL die Erfahrungen) experience.

erfinden ◇verb (IMPERF erfand, PERF hat erfunden) to invent.

Erfindung die (PL die Erfindungen) invention.

Erfolg der (PL die Erfolge) 1 success; **Erfolg haben** to be successful; 2 Erfolg versprechend promising; 3 viel Erfolg! good luck!

erfolglos adjective unsuccessful.

erfolgreich adjective successful.

erfolgversprechend SEE Erfolg.

erforderlich adjective necessary.

erforschen verb (PERF **hat erforscht**) 1 to explore; 2 to investigate.

erfreulicherweise adverb happily.

erfreut adjective pleased.

Erfrischung die (PL die **Erfrischungen**) refreshment.

Erfrischungsgetränk das (PL die **Erfrischungsgetränke**) soft drink.

erfüllen verb (PERF **hat erfüllt**) to fulfil; **sich erfüllen** to come true.

Ergebnis das (PL die **Ergebnisse**) result.

ergreifen ◇verb (IMPERF **ergriff**, PERF **hat ergriffen**) 1 to seize, to grab; 2 to take (measures, an opportunity); 3 to take up (a job, career); 4 to move; **die Nachricht von ihrem Tod hat uns tief ergriffen** the news of her death moved us deeply; 5 **die Flucht ergreifen** to flee.

ergreifend adjective moving.

erhalten ◇verb (PRES **erhält**, IMPERF **erhielt**, PERF **hat erhalten**) 1 to receive; 2 to preserve.

erhältlich adjective obtainable.

Erhaltung die 1 preservation; 2 conservation; 3 maintenance.

erheben ◇verb (IMPERF **erhob**, PERF **hat erhoben**) 1 to raise; 2 to charge (a fee); 3 **Protest erheben** to protest; 4 **sich erheben** to rise up (in a rebellion).

erheblich adjective considerable.

erheitern verb (PERF **hat erheitert**) to amuse.

erhitzen verb (PERF **hat erhitzt**) to heat.

erhöhen verb (PERF **hat erhöht**) 1 to increase; 2 **sich erhöhen** to rise.

Erhöhung die (PL die **Erhöhungen**) increase.

erholen verb (PERF **hat sich erholt**) 1 **sich erholen** to have a rest; **ich habe mich in den Ferien gut erholt** I had a good rest on holiday; 2 **sich von einer Krankheit erholen** to recover from an illness.

erholsam adjective restful.

Erholung die rest; **Iris ist zur Erholung in die Berge gefahren** Iris went to the mountains for a rest.

erinnern verb (PERF **hat erinnert**) 1 to remind; 2 **sich erinnern** to remember.

Erinnerung die (PL die **Erinnerungen**) 1 memory; 2 souvenir.

erkälten verb (PERF **hat sich erkältet**) 1 **sich erkälten** to catch a cold; 2 **erkältet sein** to have a cold; **Ben ist erkältet** Ben has a cold.

Erkältung die (PL die **Erkältungen**) cold.

erkennbar adjective recognizable.

erkennen ◇verb (IMPERF **erkannte**, PERF **hat erkannt**) 1 to recognize; 2 to realize.

erklären verb (PERF **hat erklärt**) 1 to explain; 2 to declare; 3 **sich zu etwas bereit erklären** to agree to something.

a

b

c

d

e

f

g

h

i

j

k

l

m

n

o

p

q

r

s

t

u

v

w

x

y

z

Erklärung die (PL die **Erklärungen**)
1 explanation; 2 declaration;
3 eine öffentliche Erklärung a
public statement.

erkundigen verb (PERF **hat sich
erkundigt**) 1 **sich erkundigen** to
enquire; **ich werde mich nach den
Zügen erkundigen** I'm going to
enquire about the trains; 2 to ask
about; **Susi hat sich nach dir
erkundigt** Susi was asking about
you.

Erkundigung die (PL die
Erkundigungen) enquiry.

erlauben verb (PERF **hat erlaubt**)
1 to allow; **jemandem etwas
erlauben** to allow somebody to do
something; 2 **sich etwas erlauben**
to allow yourself something; 3 **sich
alles erlauben** to do as you please;
4 **erlauben Sie mal!** (informal) do
you mind!

Erlaubnis die permission.

erleben verb (PERF **hat erlebt**) 1 to
experience; 2 to have (a
disappointment, an experience);
eine Überraschung erleben to
have a surprise; 3 **er hat die
Geburt seines Enkels nicht mehr
erlebt** he didn't live to see the birth
of his grandson.

Erlebnis das (PL die **Erlebnisse**)
experience.

erledigen verb (PERF **hat erledigt**)
to deal with, to do.

erledigt adjective 1 settled;
2 (informal) worn out.

Erleichterung die relief.

erleiden ◇ verb (IMPERF **erlitt**, PERF
hat erlitten) to suffer.

Erlös der (PL die **Erlöse**) proceeds.

erloschen adjective 1 out,
extinguished; 2 extinct.

ermäßigen verb (PERF **hat
ermäßigt**) to reduce.

Ermäßigung die (PL die
Ermäßigungen) reduction.

ermorden verb (PERF **hat
ermordet**) to murder.

ermutigen verb (PERF **hat
ermutigt**) to encourage.

ernähren verb (PERF **hat ernährt**)
1 to feed; 2 **sich von Nudeln
ernähren** to live on pasta; 3 to
support (a family).

Ernährung die 1 diet; **eine
gesunde Ernährung** a healthy
diet; 2 nutrition.

erneuern verb (PERF **hat erneuer**
to renew.

erneut adjective renewed.

erneut adverb once again.

Ernst der 1 seriousness; 2 **im Ernst**
seriously; 3 **ist das dein Ernst?**
are you serious?

ernst adjective serious.

ernsthaft adjective serious.

ernstlich adjective serious.

Ernte die (PL die **Ernten**) harvest;
die Ernte einbringen to gather in
the harvest.

ernten verb (PERF **hat geerntet**) t
harvest.

erobern verb (PERF **hat erobert**) t
conquer.

Eroberung die (PL die Eroberungen) conquest.

eröffnen (PERF hat eröffnet) to open.

Eröffnung die (PL die Eröffnungen) opening.

erraten ◇verb (PRES errät, IMPERF erriet, PERF hat erraten) to guess.

erregen verb (PERF hat erregt) **1** to arouse; **2** to cause; **sie erregte viel Aufsehen** she caused a sensation.

Erreger der (PL die Erreger) germ.

Erregung die excitement.

erreichen verb (PERF hat erreicht) **1** to reach; **2 den Zug erreichen** to catch the train; **3** to achieve (a goal, aim); **4 Irene ist telefonisch zu erreichen** Irene can be contacted by phone.

erröten verb (PERF ist errötet) to blush.

Ersatz der replacement, substitute.

Ersatzmann der (PL die Ersatzmänner) substitute (in sport).

Ersatzmittel das (PL die Ersatzmittel) substitute (material, ingredient).

Ersatzreifen der (PL die Ersatzreifen) spare tyre.

Ersatzteil das (PL die Ersatzteile) spare part.

erschaffen verb (IMPERF erschuf, PERF erschaffen) to create.

erscheinen ◇verb (IMPERF erschien, PERF ist erschienen) to appear.

erschöpft adjective exhausted.

erschrecken verb **1** (PERF hat erschreckt) to scare; **2** (◇(PRES erschrickt, IMPERF erschrak, PERF ist erschrocken) to get a fright.

erschreckend adjective alarming.

erschrocken adjective **1** frightened; **2** startled.

ersetzen verb (PERF hat ersetzt) to replace; **jemandem einen Schaden ersetzen** to compensate somebody for damages.

Ersparnisse plural noun savings.

erst adverb **1** first; **erst einmal** first of all; **2** only; **eben erst** only just; **3** not until; **erst nächste Woche** not until next week; **Oma war erst zufrieden, als die ganze Familie da war** granny was not happy until all the family were there.

erstatten verb (PERF hat erstattet) to reimburse.

Erstattung die (PL die Erstattungen) reimbursement.

erstaunen verb (PERF hat erstaunt) to astonish.

erstaunlich adjective astonishing.

erstaunt adjective amazed; **über etwas erstaunt sein** to be amazed about something.

Erste der/die/das (PL die Ersten) **1 der/die Erste** the first (one); **das Erste** the first (thing); **2 Dirk kam als Erster** Dirk arrived first; **Marianne ging als Erste** Marianne left first; **3 als Erster/Erste etwas tun** to be the first to do something;

a
b
c
d
f
g
h
i
j
k
l
m
n
o
p
q
r
s
t
u
v
w
x
y
z

a
b
c
d
e
f
g
h
i
j
k
l
m
n
o
p
q
r
s
t
u
v
w
x
y
z

4 als Erstes first of all; **5 fürs Erste** for the time being.

erstens adverb firstly.

erster, erste, erstes adjective first; **mein erstes Rad war rot** my first bike was red; **der erste April** the first of April; **erste Hilfe** first aid.

erstklassig adjective first-class.

erstmals adverb for the first time.

erteilen verb (PERF **hat erteilt**) to give (advice, information).

ertragen ◇verb (PRES **erträgt**, IMPERF **ertrug**, PERF **hat ertragen**) to bear.

ertrinken ◇verb (IMPERF **ertrank**, PERF **ist ertrunken**) to drown; **sie ertrank im See** she drowned in the lake.

erwachsen adjective grown-up.

Erwachsene der/die (PL die **Erwachsenen**) adult, grown-up.

Erwachsenenbildung die adult education.

erwähnen verb (PERF **hat erwähnt**) to mention.

erwarten verb (PERF **hat erwartet**) to expect.

Erwartung die (PL die **Erwartungen**) expectation.

erwürgen verb (PERF **hat erwürgt**) to strangle.

erzählen verb (PERF **hat erzählt**) to tell.

Erzählung die (PL die **Erzählungen**) story.

Erzeugnis das (PL die **Erzeugnisse**) product.

erziehen ◇verb (IMPERF **erzog**, PERF **hat erzogen**) **1** to bring up; **2** to educate.

Erzieher der (PL die **Erzieher**) teacher.

Erzieherin die (PL die **Erzieherinnen**) teacher.

Erziehung die **1** upbringing; **2** education.

es pronoun **1** it; **es regnet** it is raining; **2 es gibt** there is, there are; **3 'wo ist das Baby?' – 'es schläft'** 'where's the baby?' – 'he's/ she's asleep'.

Esel der (PL die **Esel**) donkey.

essbar adjective edible.

essen ◇verb (PRES **isst**, IMPERF **aß**, PERF **hat gegessen**) to eat; **iss keine Bonbons** don't eat sweets.

Essen das **1** meal; **2** food.

Essig der vinegar.

Essiggurke die (PL die **Essiggurken**) gherkin.

Esskastanie die (PL die **Esskastanien**) sweet chestnut.

Esszimmer das (PL die **Esszimmer**) dining room.

Etage die (PL die **Etagen**) floor; **in der zweiten Etage** on the second floor.

Etagenbett das (PL die **Etagenbetten**) bunk beds.

ethnisch adjective ethnic.

Etikett das (PL die **Etikette(n)**) label.

Etui das (PL die **Etuis**) case.

etwa adverb **1** about; **er ist etwa so groß wie du** he's about as tall as you; **2** for example; **3 nicht etwa, dass** ... not that ...; **4 hat Klaus etwa Angst gehabt?** Klaus wasn't scared, was he?

etwas *pronoun, adverb* **1** something; **2** anything; **sonst noch etwas?** anything else?; **3** some; **etwas von dem Geld** some of the money; **noch etwas Kaffee?** (some) more coffee?; **4** a little; **nur etwas Zucker** only a little sugar; **etwas lauter singen** to sing a little louder.

EU *die* (*Europäische Union*) EU.

euch *pronoun* **1** you; **ich habe euch eingeladen** I've invited you; **2** to you; **Eva hat es euch geschenkt** Eva gave it to you; **3** (*reflexive*) yourselves.

euer *adjective* your.

Eule *die* (PL *die* Eulen) owl.

eurer, eure, eures *pronoun* yours.

Euro *der* (PL *die* Euros) euro; **ein Euro hat hundert Cent** the euro is divided into a hundred cents; **es kostet 3 Euro** it costs 3 euros.

Eurocent *der* (PL *die* Eurocents) cent; **50 Eurocent** 50 cents.

Euroland *das* eurozone.

Europa *das* Europe.

Europäer *der* (PL *die* Europäer) European.

Europäerin *die* (PL *die* Europäerinnen) European.

europäisch *adjective* European.

Eurostar *der* Eurostar; **mit dem Eurostar fahren** to go by Eurostar.

Eurostück *das* (PL *die* Eurostücke) one-euro coin.

evangelisch *adjective* Protestant.

eventuell *adjective* possible.

eventuell *adverb* possibly.

ewig *adjective* eternal.

ewig *adverb* forever.

Ewigkeit *die* eternity.

Examen *das* (PL *die* Examen) examination, exam.

Exemplar *das* (PL *die* Exemplare) **1** copy; **2** specimen.

existieren *verb* (PERF hat existiert) to exist.

Expedition *die* (PL *die* Expeditionen) expedition.

explodieren *verb* (PERF ist explodiert) to explode.

Explosion *die* (PL *die* Explosionen) explosion.

Export *der* (PL *die* Exporte) export.

exportieren *verb* (PERF hat exportiert) to export; **Russland exportiert viel Öl und Holz** Russia exports a lot of oil and timber.

extra *adverb* **1** separately; **2** extra; **3** specially; **4** (*informal*) on purpose.

extrem *adjective* extreme.

Ff

fabelhaft *adjective* fabulous, fantastic.

Fabrik *die* (PL *die* Fabriken) factory.

a
b
c
d
e
f
g
h
i
j
k
l
m
n
o
p
q
r
s
t
u
v
w
x
y
z

Fach das (PL die **Fächer**)
1 compartment; 2 drawer;
3 subject (*at school*).

Facharzt der (PL die **Fachärzte**)
specialist.

Fachärztin die (PL die
Fachärztinnen) specialist.

Fachfrau die (PL die **Fachfrauen**)
expert.

Fachmann der (PL die **Fachleute**)
expert.

fade *adjective* tasteless.

Faden der (PL die **Fäden**) thread.

fähig *adjective* 1 capable; 2 able.

Fähigkeit die (PL die **Fähigkeiten**)
ability.

Fahne die (PL die **Fahnen**) flag.

Fahrausweis der (PL die
Fahrausweise) ticket.

Fahrbahn die (PL die **Fahrbahnen**)
1 carriageway; 2 road.

Fähre die (PL die **Fähren**) ferry.

fahren ◇*verb* (PRES **fährt**, IMPERF
fuhr, PERF **ist gefahren**) 1 to go; mit
dem Zug nach Wien fahren to go
to Vienna by train; ich bin mit dem
Auto gefahren I went by car; ; 2 to
drive; Hanna ist sehr schnell
gefahren Hanna drove very fast;
3 to ride (*of a cyclist*); 4 to run (*of a
train, bus*); der Zug fährt nicht an
Sonn- und Feiertagen the train
doesn't run on Sundays and public
holidays; 5 to leave; wann fahrt
ihr? when are you leaving?; 6 was
ist in sie gefahren? (*informal*)
what's got into her?; 7 (PERF **hat
gefahren**) to drive; er hat Doris
nach Hause gefahren he drove

Doris home; ich habe das Auto in
die Garage gefahren I drove the
car into the garage.

Fahrer der (PL die **Fahrer**) driver.

Fahrerflucht die hit-and-run
driving; **Fahrerflucht begehen** to
be involved in a hit-and-run.

Fahrerin die (PL die **Fahrerinnen**)
driver.

Fahrgast der (PL die **Fahrgäste**)
passenger.

Fahrkarte die (PL die **Fahrkarten**)
ticket.

Fahrkartenausgabe die ticket
office.

Fahrkartenautomat der (PL die
Fahrkartenautomaten) ticket
machine.

Fahrkartenschalter der (PL die
Fahrkartenschalter) ticket office.

fahrlässig *adjective* negligent.

Fahrlehrer der (PL die **Fahrlehrer**)
driving instructor.

Fahrplan der (PL die **Fahrpläne**)
timetable.

Fahrpreis der (PL die **Fahrpreise**)
fare.

Fahrprüfung die (PL die
Fahrprüfungen) driving test; die
Fahrprüfung machen to take your
driving test.

Fahrrad das (PL die **Fahrräder**)
bicycle.

Fahrradfahrer der (PL die
Fahrradfahrer) cyclist.

Fahrradfahrerin die (PL die
Fahrradfahrerinnen) cyclist.

Fahrradweg der (PL die Fahrradwege) cycle lane.

Fahrschein der (PL die Fahrscheine) ticket.

Fahrschule die (PL die Fahrschulen) driving school.

Fahrstuhl der (PL die Fahrstühle) lift.

Fahrt die (PL die Fahrten) 1 journey; **gute Fahrt!** have a good journey!; 2 trip; 3 drive; 4 **in voller Fahrt** at full speed.

Fahrzeug das (PL die Fahrzeuge) vehicle.

fair adjective fair.

Faktor der (PL die Faktoren) factor.

Falke der (PL die Falken) falcon.

Fall der (PL die Fälle) 1 case; **in diesem Fall** in this case; **auf alle Fälle, auf jeden Fall** in any case; **für alle Fälle** just in case; 2 **auf jeden Fall** definitely; 3 **auf keinen Fall** on no account; 4 fall.

Falle die (PL die Fallen) trap.

fallen ◇verb (PRES fällt, IMPERF fiel, PERF ist gefallen) 1 to fall; 2 **etwas fallen lassen** to drop something; **wir haben den Plan fallen lassen** we've dropped the idea; 3 **eine Bemerkung fallen lassen** to make a comment.

fällen verb (PERF hat gefällt) to fell, to cut down (trees).

fallenlassen SEE fallen.

fällig adjective due.

falls conjunction 1 if; 2 in case.

Fallschirm der (PL die Fallschirme) parachute.

falsch adjective 1 wrong; **du hast ihn falsch verstanden** you got him wrong; 2 false (teeth, etc.); 3 forged.

fälschen verb (PERF hat gefälscht) to forge.

Fälschung die (PL die Fälschungen) 1 fake; 2 forgery.

Falte die (PL die Falten) 1 fold; 2 crease; 3 pleat; 4 wrinkle.

falten verb (PERF hat gefaltet) to fold.

faltig adjective 1 wrinkled; 2 creased.

familiär adjective familiar.

Familie die (PL die Familien) family.

Familienname der (PL die Familiennamen) surname.

Fan der (PL die Fans) fan.

fand SEE finden.

Fantasie die 1 imagination; 2 Fantasien (plural) fantasies.

fantasievoll adjective imaginative.

fangen ◇verb (PRES fängt, IMPERF fing, PERF hat gefangen) to catch.

Fantasie die 1 imagination; 2 Fantasien (plural) fantasies.

fantasievoll adjective imaginative.

fantastisch adjective fantastic.

Farbe die (PL die Farben) 1 colour; 2 paint; 3 dye; 4 suit (in playing cards).

farbecht adjective colour fast.

färben verb (PERF hat gefärbt) 1 to dye; 2 **sich die Haare färben** to dye

a
b
c
d
e
f
g
h
i
j
k
l
m
n
o
p
q
r
s
t
u
v
w
x
y
z

your hair; **3 das Sweatshirt färbt** this sweatshirt runs.

farbenblind *adjective* colour blind.

Farbfernsehen *das* colour television.

Farbfilm *der* (PL die **Farbfilme**) colour film.

farbig *adjective* coloured.

farblos *adjective* colourless.

Farbstift *der* (PL die **Farbstifte**) coloured pencil.

Farbstoff *der* (PL die **Farbstoffe**) **1** dye; **2** colouring (*for food*).

Farbton *der* (PL die **Farbtöne**) shade.

Fasan *der* (PL die **Fasane**) pheasant.

Fasching *der* (PL die **Faschinge**) carnival.

Faser *die* (PL die **Fasern**) fibre.

Fass *das* (PL die **Fässer**) barrel; **Bier vom Fass** draught beer.

fassen *verb* (PERF **hat gefasst**) **1** to grasp; **2 einen Dieb fassen** to catch a thief; **3** to hold (*of a container*); **4** to understand; **5 nicht zu fassen** unbelievable; **6 sich fassen** to compose yourself; **7 einen Entschluss fassen** to make a decision; **8 sich kurz fassen** to be brief.

Fassung *die* (PL die **Fassungen**) **1** version; **2** composure; **3 jemanden aus der Fassung bringen** to throw somebody, to upset somebody; **4** setting (*for gems*).

fassungslos *adjective* speechless.

Fastfood *das* fast food.

fast *adverb* **1** almost; **2 fast nie** hardly ever.

Fastenzeit *die* (PL die **Fastenzeiten**) Lent.

Fastnacht *die* carnival.

faul *adjective* **1** lazy; **2** rotten; **3 eine faule Ausrede** a lame excuse; **4 an der Sache ist etwas faul** (*informal*) there's something fishy about it.

faulen *verb* (PERF **ist gefault**) to rot.

faulenzen *verb* (PERF **hat gefaulenzt**) to laze about.

Faust *die* (PL die **Fäuste**) **1** fist; **2 auf eigene Faust** off your own bat.

Fax *das* (PL die **Fax(e)**) fax.

faxen *verb* (PERF **hat gefaxt**) to fax; **ich faxe Ihnen die Liste** I'll fax you the list.

Februar *der* February.

fechten ◇*verb* (PRES **ficht**, IMPERF **focht**, PERF **hat gefochten**) to fence.

Feder *die* (PL die **Federn**) **1** feather; **2** spring; **3** nib (*of a pen*).

Federball *der* (PL die **Federbälle**) **1** badminton; **2** shuttlecock.

Federhalter *der* (PL die **Federhalter**) fountain pen.

Federmäppchen *das* (PL die **Federmäppchen**) pencil case.

Fee *die* (PL die **Feen**) fairy.

fegen *verb* (PERF **hat gefegt**) to sweep.

fehl *adjective* **fehl am Platz** out of place.

fehlen verb (PERF **hat gefehlt**) 1 to be missing; 2 to be lacking; 3 to be absent (from school); 4 **mir fehlt die Zeit** I haven't got the time; **es fehlt ihnen einfach das Geld für ein neues Auto** they simply haven't got the money for a new car; 5 **was fehlt dir?** what's the matter?; 6 **Rudi fehlt mir** I miss Rudi.

Fehler der (PL die **Fehler**) 1 mistake; 2 fault.

Feier die (PL die **Feiern**) 1 party; 2 celebration.

Feierabend der (PL die **Feierabende**) 1 finishing time; 2 **nach Feierabend** after work.

Feierlichkeiten plural noun festivities.

feiern verb (PERF **hat gefeiert**) to celebrate.

Feiertag der (PL die **Feiertage**) 1 holiday; **ein gesetzlicher Feiertag** a public holiday; 2 **am ersten Feiertag** on Christmas Day; **der zweite Feiertag** Boxing Day.

Feige die (PL die **Feigen**) fig.

feige adjective cowardly; **du bist feige** you're a coward.

Feigenbaum der (PL die **Feigenbäume**) fig tree.

Feigling der (PL die **Feiglinge**) coward.

Feile die (PL die **Feilen**) file.

fein adjective 1 fine; 2 delicate; 3 refined; 4 **sich fein machen** to dress up.

Feind der (PL die **Feinde**) enemy.

feindlich adjective hostile.

Feld das (PL die **Felder**) 1 field; 2 pitch; 3 box (on a form); 4 square (on a board game).

Fell das (PL die **Felle**) fur, skin.

Fels der rock.

Felsen der (PL die **Felsen**) cliff.

feminin adjective feminine.

Feminist der (PL die **Feministen**) feminist.

Feministin die (PL die **Feministinnen**) feminist.

Fenster das (PL die **Fenster**) window.

Fensterladen der (PL die **Fensterläden**) shutter.

Ferien plural noun holidays; **Ferien haben** to be on holiday.

Ferienhaus das (PL die **Ferienhäuser**) holiday home.

fern adjective 1 distant; 2 **sich fern halten** to keep away; **jemanden von etwas fern halten** to keep somebody away from something.

fern adverb far away.

Fernbedienung die remote control.

Ferngespräch das (PL die **Ferngespräche**) long-distance call.

ferngesteuert adjective remote-controlled.

Fernglas das (PL die **Ferngläser**) binoculars.

fernhalten SEE **fern**.

Fernost das Far East.

Fernrohr das (PL die **Fernrohre**) telescope.

a
b
c
d
e
f
g
h
i
j
k
l
m
n
o
p
q
r
s
t
u
v
w
x
y
z

Fernsehapparat der (PL die Fernsehapparate) television set.

fernsehen ◇verb (PRES **sieht fern**, IMPERF **sah fern**, PERF **hat ferngesehen**) to watch television.

Fernsehen das television; **im Fernsehen** on television.

Fernseher der (PL die **Fernseher**) television (set).

Fernsehsendung die (PL die Fernsehsendungen) television programme.

Fernsehturm der (PL die Fernsehtürme) television tower.

Fernsprecher der (PL die Fernsprecher) telephone.

Ferse die (PL die **Fersen**) heel.

fertig adjective **1** finished; **mit den Hausaufgaben fertig werden** to finish your homework; **fertig sein** to be finished; **2 mit jemandem fertig sein** (informal) to be through with somebody; **3 völlig fertig sein** to be completely worn out; **4 mit etwas fertig werden** to cope with something (problems, for example); **5** ready; **das Essen ist fertig** food's ready; **6 etwas fertig machen** (prepare) to get something ready; (complete) to finish something; **sich fertig machen** to get ready; **7 jemanden fertig machen** to wear somebody out, to wear somebody down; **der ständige Stress macht mich fertig** this constant stress is wearing me down; **8 es fertig bringen, etwas zu tun** to bring yourself to do something; **ich**

bringe es einfach nicht fertig I just can't bring myself to do it.

fertig adverb **fertig essen** to finish eating.

fertigbringen SEE **fertig**.

Fertiggericht das (PL die Fertiggerichte) ready-to-serve meal.

fertigmachen SEE **fertig**.

Fest das (PL die **Feste**) **1** party; **2** celebration; **3** festival.

fest adjective **1** firm; **2** fixed (salary, address); **3** solid; **feste Nahrung** solids; **4 fest werden** to harden.

fest adverb **1 fest schlafen** to be fast asleep; **2 fest befreundet sein** to be close friends; **3 fest angestellt sein** to be in permanent employment.

festbinden ◇verb (IMPERF **band fest**, PERF **hat festgebunden**) to tie (up).

festhalten ◇verb (PRES **hält fest**, IMPERF **hielt fest**, PERF **hat festgehalten**) **1** to hold on to; **2 sich festhalten** to hold on; **halt dich an mir fest** hold on to me.

Festigkeit die strength.

festlegen verb (PERF **hat festgelegt**) **1** to fix; **2 sich auf etwas festlegen** to commit yourself to something.

Festlegung die (PL die Festlegungen) establishment.

festlich adjective festive.

festmachen verb (PERF **hat festgemacht**) **1** to fix; **ich mache**

gleich einen Termin fest I'll fix a date straight away; **2** to fasten.

Festnahme die (PL die Festnahmen) arrest.

festnehmen ◇verb (PRES nimmt fest, IMPERF nahm fest, PERF hat festgenommen) to arrest.

Festplatte die (PL die Festplatten) hard disk.

feststehen ◇verb (IMPERF stand fest, PERF hat festgestanden) to be certain; **eins steht fest, Daniel lade ich nicht mehr ein** one thing's certain, I'm not going to invite Daniel again.

feststellen verb (PERF hat festgestellt) **1** to establish; **2** to notice.

Fete die (PL die Feten) party.

Fett das (PL die Fette) **1** fat; **2** grease.

fett adjective **1** fat (person); **2** greasy, fatty (food); **3** bold (type).

fettarm adjective low-fat; **fettarme Milch** skimmed milk.

fettig adjective greasy.

Fetzen der (PL die Fetzen) **1** scrap; **2** rag.

feucht adjective **1** damp; **2** humid.

Feuchtigkeit die **1** moisture; **2** humidity.

Feuer das **1** fire; **2** hast du Feuer? have you got a light?

Feuerlöscher der (PL die Feuerlöscher) fire extinguisher.

Feuermelder der (PL die Feuermelder) fire alarm.

Feuertreppe die (PL die Feuertreppen) fire escape.

Feuerwehr die (PL die Feuerwehren) fire brigade.

Feuerwehrauto das (PL die Feuerwehrautos) fire engine.

Feuerwehrmann der (PL die Feuerwehrleute) fireman.

Feuerwerk das fireworks.

Feuerzeug das (PL die Feuerzeuge) lighter.

ficht SEE fechten.

Fieber das (high) temperature, fever; **(hohes) Fieber haben** to have a (high) temperature.

fiel SEE fallen.

fies adjective (informal) nasty.

Figur die (PL die Figuren) **1** figure; **2** character.

Filiale die (PL die Filialen) branch.

Film der (PL die Filme) film.

filmen verb (PERF hat gefilmt) to film.

Filter der (PL die Filter) filter.

Filzstift der (PL die Filzstifte) felt pen.

Finale das (PL die Finale) final.

finanziell adjective financial.

finanzieren verb (PERF hat finanziert) to finance.

finden ◇verb (IMPERF fand, PERF hat gefunden) **1** to find; **2** to think; **wie findest du das?** what do you think of it?; **findest du?** do you think so?; **3 ich finde nichts dabei** I don't mind.

fing SEE fangen.

Finger der (PL die Finger) finger.

a
b
c
d
e
f
g
h
i
j
k
l
m
n
o
p
q
r
s
t
u
v
w
x
y
z

a

Fingernagel der (PL die Fingernägel) fingernail.

b

Finne die (PL die Finnen) Finn.

c

Finnin die (PL die Finninnen) Finn.

d

Finnland das Finland.

finster adjective **1** dark; **im Finstern** in the dark; **2** sinister.

e

Finsternis die darkness.

f

Firma die (PL die Firmen) firm, company.

g

Fisch der (PL die Fische) **1** fish; **2 Fische** Pisces; **Helmut ist Fisch** Helmut is Pisces.

h

i

Fischer der (PL die Fischer) fisherman.

j

fit adjective fit; **er hält sich durch Jogging fit** he keeps fit by jogging.

k

Fitnesstraining das keep fit.

l

fix adjective **1** quick; **2 fix und fertig** all finished, all ready; **3 ich bin fix und fertig** (informal) I'm shattered.

m

n

flach adjective **1** flat; **2** low; **3** shallow; **die Erdbeeren kommen in die flache Schüssel** the strawberries go into the shallow bowl.

o

p

q

Fläche die (PL die Flächen) **1** surface; **2** area.

r

flackern verb (PERF hat geflackert) to flicker.

s

Flagge die (PL die Flaggen) flag.

t

Flamme die (PL die Flammen) flame.

u

v

Flasche die (PL die Flaschen) bottle.

w

x

Flaschenöffner der (PL die Flaschenöffner) bottle opener.

y

z

flauschig adjective **1** fluffy; **2** fleecy.

Fleck der (PL die Flecken) **1** stain; **2** spot; **3 ein blauer Fleck** a bruise.

fleckig adjective **1** stained; **2** blotchy (skin).

Fledermaus die (PL die Fledermäuse) bat.

Fleisch das **1** meat; **2** flesh.

Fleischer der (PL die Fleischer) butcher.

Fleischerei die (PL die Fleischereien) butcher's.

Fleiß der hard work.

fleißig adjective hard-working.

flicken verb (PERF hat geflickt) to mend.

Flicken der (PL die Flicken) patch (for mending).

Fliege die (PL die Fliegen) **1** fly; **2** bow tie.

fliegen ✧verb (IMPERF flog, PERF ist geflogen) **1** to fly; **2 ich bin geflogen** (informal) I fell; **3 Manfred ist geflogen** (informal) Manfred has been fired; **4** (PERF hat geflogen) to fly (a plane).

fliehen ✧verb (IMPERF floh, PERF ist geflohen) to flee.

Fliese die (PL die Fliesen) tile.

Fließband das (PL die Fließbänder) **1** conveyor belt; **2** assembly line.

fließen ✧verb (IMPERF floss, PERF ist geflossen) to flow.

fließend adjective **1** running; **2** fluent; **fließendes Deutsch** fluent German; **3** moving (traffic).

Flitterwochen *plural noun*
honeymoon; **sie fahren nach
Ägyten für ihre Flitterwochen**
they're going to Egypt for their
honeymoon.

flitzen *verb (informal)* (PERF **ist
geflitzt**) **1** to dash; **2** to whizz.

Flocke *die* (PL *die* **Flocken**) flake.

flog SEE **fliegen**.

Floh *der* (PL *die* **Flöhe**) flee.

floh SEE **fliehen**.

Flohmarkt *der* (PL *die* **Flohmärkte**)
flea market.

floss SEE **fließen**.

Flosse *die* (PL *die* **Flossen**) **1** fin;
2 flipper.

Flöte *die* (PL *die* **Flöten**) flute.

fluchen *verb* (PERF **hat geflucht**) to
curse.

Flüchtling *der* (PL *die* **Flüchtlinge**)
refugee.

Flug *der* (PL *die* **Flüge**) flight.

Flugbegleiter *der* (PL *die*
Flugbegleiter) flight attendant.

Flugbegleiterin *die* (PL *die*
Flugbegleiterinnen) flight
attendant.

Flugblatt *das* (PL *die* **Flugblätter**)
pamphlet.

Flugdienstleiter *der* (PL *die*
Flugdienstleiter) air-traffic
controller.

Flugdienstleiterin *die* (PL *die*
Flugdienstleiterinnen) air-traffic
controller.

Flügel *der* (PL *die* **Flügel**) **1** wing;
2 grand piano.

Fluggast *der* (PL *die* **Fluggäste**)
(air) passenger.

Fluggesellschaft *die* (PL *die*
Fluggesellschaften) airline.

Flughafen *der* (PL *die* **Flughäfen**)
airport.

Fluglotse *der* (PL *die* **Fluglotsen**)
air-traffic controller.

Fluglotsin *die* (PL *die*
Fluglotsinnen) air-traffic
controller.

Flugplatz *dor* (PL *die* **Flugplätze**)
1 airport; **2** airfield.

Flugzeug *das* (PL *die* **Flugzeuge**)
aeroplane; **mit dem Flugzeug
fliegen** to go by air.

Fluor *das* fluoride.

Flur *der* (PL *die* **Flure**) **1** hall;
2 corridor.

Fluss *der* (PL *die* **Flüsse**) river.

flüssig *adjective* liquid.

Flüssigkeit *die* (PL *die*
Flüssigkeiten) liquid.

flüstern *verb* (PERF **hat geflüstert**)
to whisper.

Flut *die* (PL *die* **Fluten**) **1** high tide;
bei Flut at high tide; **2** flood (*of
letters, complaints*).

Flutlicht *das* floodlight.

focht SEE **fechten**.

Föhn *der* (PL *die* **Föhne**) hair drier.

föhnen *verb* (PERF **hat geföhnt**) to
blow-dry.

Folge *die* (PL *die* **Folgen**)
1 consequence; **2** episode; **3** etwas
zur Folge haben to result in
something; **4 an den Folgen eines**

a
b
c
d
e
f
g
h
i
j
k
l
m
n
o
p
q
r
s
t
u
v
w
x
y
z

Unfalls sterben to die as the result of an accident.

folgen *verb* (PERF **ist gefolgt**) **1** to follow; **daraus folgt, dass** ... it follows that ...; **ich kann dir nicht folgen** I can't follow what you're saying; **2** (PERF **hat gefolgt**) to obey.

folgend *adjective* **1** following; **2 Folgendes** the following.

Folgerung die (PL die **Folgerungen**) conclusion.

folgsam *adjective* obedient.

Folie die (PL die **Folien**) foil.

Folienkartoffel die (PL die **Folienkartoffeln**) jacket potato.

Folterkammer die (PL die **Folterkammern**) torture chamber.

Fön™ SEE **Föhn**.

fönen SEE **föhnen**.

fördern *verb* (PERF **hat gefördert**) **1** to promote; **2** to sponsor.

fordern *verb* (PERF **hat gefordert**) to demand.

Forderung die (PL die **Forderungen**) **1** demand; **2** claim.

Forelle die (PL die **Forellen**) trout.

Form die (PL die **Formen**) **1** shape; **2** form; **in Form sein** to be on form; **3** tin (*for baking*).

Format das (PL die **Formate**) format.

formatieren *verb* (PERF **hat formatiert**) to format.

formen *verb* (PERF **hat geformt**) **1** to form; **2 sich formen** to take shape.

förmlich *adjective* formal.

förmlich *adverb* **1** formally; **2 jemanden förmlich zwingen, etwas zu tun** to positively force somebody to do something; **ich hätte förmlich schreien können** I really could have screamed.

Formular das (PL die **Formulare**) form.

Forscher der (PL die **Forscher**) **1** researcher, research scientist; **2** explorer.

Forschung die (PL die **Forschungen**) research.

Forst der (PL die **Forste(n)**) forest.

Förster der (PL die **Förster**) forester.

fort *adverb* **1** away; **2 fort sein** to have gone; **3 und so fort** and so on; **4 in einem fort** on and on.

fortbewegen *verb* (PERF **hat fortbewegt**) **1** to move; **2 sich fortbewegen** to move.

fortfahren ✧*verb* (PRES **fährt fort**, IMPERF **fuhr fort**, PERF **ist fortgefahren**) **1** to leave; **wann fahrt ihr fort?** when are you leaving?; **2** to continue.

fortgeschritten *adjective* advanced.

Fortpflanzung die (PL die **Fortpflanzungen**) **1** reproduction; **2** propagation.

Fortschritt der (PL die **Fortschritte**) progress; **Fortschritte machen** to make progress.

fortsetzen *verb* (PERF **hat fortgesetzt**) to continue.

Fortsetzung die (PL die Fortsetzungen) 1 continuation; 2 instalment.

Foto das (PL die Fotos) photo.

Fotoapparat der (PL die Fotoapparate) camera.

Fotograf der (PL die Fotografen) photographer.

Fotografie die (PL die Fotografien) 1 photography; 2 photograph.

fotografieren verb (PERF hat fotografiert) 1 to photograph, to take a photograph of; 2 to take photographs.

Fotografin die (PL die Fotografinnen) photographer.

Fotokopie die (PL die Fotokopien) photocopy.

fotokopieren verb (PERF hat fotokopiert) to photocopy.

Fracht die (PL die Frachten) freight, cargo.

Frage die (PL die Fragen) question; **eine Frage stellen** to ask a question; **etwas in Frage stellen** to question something; **das kommt nicht in Frage** that's out of the question.

Fragebogen der (PL die Fragebogen) questionnaire.

fragen verb (PERF hat gefragt) 1 to ask; 2 **sich fragen** to wonder.

Fragezeichen das (PL die Fragezeichen) question mark.

fraglich adjective doubtful.

Franken[1] der (PL die Franken) (Swiss) franc.

Franken[2] das Franconia.

Frankreich das France.

Franzose der (PL die Franzosen) Frenchman.

Französin die (PL die Französinnen) Frenchwoman.

Französisch das French.

französisch adjective French.

fraß SEE fressen.

Frau die (PL die Frauen) 1 woman; 2 wife; 3 Mrs, Ms ('Frau' is usually used to address both married and unmarried women).

Fräulein das (PL die Fräulein) 1 young lady; 2 Miss; **Fräulein Schmidt** Miss Schmidt.

frech adjective cheeky.

Frechheit die (PL die Frechheiten) 1 cheek; 2 cheeky remark.

Frechheit die (PL die Frechheiten) 1 cheeky remark; 2 cheekiness.

frei adjective 1 free; 2 freelance; 3 **ist dieser Platz frei?** is this seat taken?; 4 **ein freier Tag** a day off; **sich frei nehmen** to take a day off; 5 **'Zimmer frei'** 'vacancies'.

Freibad das (PL die Freibäder) open-air swimming pool.

Freie das **im Freien** in the open air.

freigebig adjective generous.

Freiheit die (PL die Freiheiten) 1 freedom; 2 liberty; **sich Freiheiten erlauben** to take liberties.

freimachen verb (PERF hat freigemacht) 1 to take time off; 2 **sich freimachen** to take time off.

Freistoß der (PL die Freistöße) free kick.

a **Freistunde** die (PL die Freistunden) free period.

b **Freitag** der (PL die Freitage) Friday.

c **freitags** adverb on Fridays.

d **freiwillig** adjective voluntary.

e **Freizeit** die 1 spare time; 2 leisure.

f **Freizeitkleidung** die leisure wear, casual clothes.

g **fremd** adjective 1 foreign; 2 strange; **fremde Leute** strangers; **ich bin hier fremd** I'm a stranger here.

h

i **Fremde** der/die (PL die Fremden) 1 foreigner; 2 stranger.

j

k **Fremdenverkehr** der tourism.

l **Fremdenverkehrsbüro** das (PL die Fremdenverkehrsbüros) tourist office.

m **Fremdenzimmer** das (PL die Fremdenzimmer) room (to let).

n **Fremdsprache** die (PL die Fremdsprachen) foreign language.

o

p **fressen** ◇verb (PRES frisst, IMPERF fraß, PERF hat gefressen) to eat.

q **Freude** die (PL die Freuden) 1 joy; 2 pleasure; **mit Freuden** with pleasure; **3 an etwas Freude haben** to be delighted with something; **4 jemandem eine Freude machen** to please somebody.

r

s

t

u

v

w **freuen** verb (PERF hat sich gefreut) 1 sich freuen to be pleased; **sich über etwas freuen** to be pleased about something; **2 sich auf etwas freuen** to look forward to something.

x

y

z

Freund der (PL die Freunde) 1 friend; 2 boyfriend.

Freundin die (PL die Freundinnen) 1 friend; 2 girlfriend.

freundlich adjective 1 friendly; 2 kind.

freundlicherweise adverb kindly.

Freundlichkeit die friendliness.

Freundschaft die (PL die Freundschaften) friendship; **mit jemandem Freundschaft schließen** to make friends with somebody.

Frieden der peace.

Friedhof der (PL die Friedhöfe) cemetery.

friedlich adjective peaceful.

frieren ◇verb (IMPERF fror, PERF hat gefroren) 1 to be cold; **frierst du?** are you cold?; **2 es friert** it's freezing, it's frosty; **3** (PERF **ist gefroren**) to freeze.

Frikadelle die (PL die Frikadellen) rissole.

frisch adjective fresh; **sich frisch machen** to freshen up.

frisch adverb freshly; **'frisch gestrichen'** 'wet paint'.

Friseur der (PL die Friseure) hairdresser.

Friseuse die (PL die Friseusen) hairdresser.

frisieren verb (PERF hat frisiert) 1 **jemanden frisieren** to do somebody's hair; **2 sich frisieren** to do your hair.

frisst SEE fressen.

Frisur die (PL die **Frisuren**) hairstyle, hairdo.

froh adjective 1 happy; **frohe Weihnachten!** happy Christmas!; 2 **über etwas froh sein** to be glad about something.

fröhlich adjective cheerful.

Fröhlichkeit die cheerfulness.

fromm adjective devout.

fror SEE **frieren**.

Frosch der (PL die **Frösche**) frog.

Frost der (PL die **Fröste**) frost.

frostig adjective frosty.

Frottee das (PL die **Frottees**) towelling.

Frottiertuch das (PL die **Frottiertücher**) towel.

Frucht die (PL die **Früchte**) fruit.

fruchtbar adjective fertile.

Fruchtsaft der (PL die **Fruchtsäfte**) fruit juice.

früh adjective, adverb 1 early; **von früh auf** from an early age; 2 **heute früh** this morning.

Frühe die **in aller Frühe** at the crack of dawn.

früher adjective 1 earlier, 2 former.

früher adverb 1 earlier; 2 formerly; 3 **früher war sie ganz anders** she used to be quite different; **das war früher ein Blumengeschäft** it used to be a florist's.

frühestens adverb at the earliest.

Frühjahr das (PL die **Frühjahre**) spring; **im Frühjahr** in spring.

Frühling der (PL die **Frühlinge**) spring; **im Frühling** in spring.

Frühstück das (PL die **Frühstücke**) breakfast.

frühstücken verb (PERF hat **gefrühstückt**) to have breakfast.

frühzeitig adjective early.

Fuchs der (PL die **Füchse**) fox.

fühlen verb (PERF hat **gefühlt**) 1 to feel; 2 **sich krank fühlen** to feel ill.

fuhr SEE **fahren**.

führen verb (PERF hat **geführt**) 1 to lead; **sie führt mit fünf Punkten** she is five points in the lead; **unsere Mannschaft führt** our team's winning; 2 to run (a shop or business); 3 to show round; 4 to keep (a diary, list); 5 **ein Telefongespräch führen** to make a phone call.

Führer der (PL die **Führer**) 1 leader; 2 guide.

Führerschein der (PL die **Führerscheine**) driving licence; **den Führerschein machen** to take your driving test.

Führung die (PL die **Führungen**) 1 leadership; 2 guided tour; 3 management (of a shop); 4 **in Führung** in the lead.

Führungsposition die (PL die **Führungspositionen**) 1 top position; 2 pole position.

füllen verb (PERF hat **gefüllt**) 1 to fill; 2 to stuff (a turkey, peppers); 3 **sich füllen** to fill (up).

Füller der (PL die **Füller**) fountain pen.

a
b
c
d
e
f
g
h
i
j
k
l
m
n
o
p
q
r
s
t
u
v
w
x
y
z

a **Füllfederhalter** der (PL die Füllfederhalter) fountain pen.

b **Füllung** die (PL die Füllungen) filling.

c **Fundament** das (PL die Fundamente) foundations.

d **Fundbüro** das (PL die Fundbüros) lost property office.

e **fünf** number five.

f **fünfhundert** number five hundred.

g **Fünftel** das (PL die Fünftel) fifth.

h **fünfter, fünfte, fünftes** adjective fifth.

i **fünfzehn** number fifteen.

j **fünfzig** number fifty.

k **Funkausstellung** die (PL die Funkausstellungen) radio and television exhibition.

l **Funke** der (PL die Funken) spark.

m **funkeln** verb (PERF hat gefunkelt) 1 to sparkle; 2 to twinkle (of a star).

n **funktionieren** verb (PERF hat funktioniert) to work.

o **für** preposition (+ ACC) 1 for; 2 was für ein ...? what sort of ... ?; 3 für sich by yourself; jetzt habe ich das Haus ganz für mich now I've got the house to myself; 4 das Für und Wider the pros and cons.

p **Furcht** die fear.

q **furchtbar** adjective terrible.

r **fürchten** verb (PERF hat gefürchtet) 1 to fear; 2 sich fürchten to be afraid; ich fürchte mich vor ihm I'm afraid of him; ich fürchte, das geht nicht I'm afraid that's not possible.

s

t

u

v

w

x

y

z

fürchterlich adjective dreadful.

füreinander adverb for each other.

fürs = für das.

Fürsorge die 1 care; 2 welfare; 3 (informal) social security.

Fuß der (PL die Füße) 1 foot; zu Fuß on foot; zu Fuß gehen to walk; 2 base.

Fußabdruck der (PL die Fußabdrücke) footprint.

Fußball der (PL die Fußbälle) football.

Fußballplatz der (PL die Fußballplätze) football pitch.

Fußballspiel das (PL die Fußballspiele) football match.

Fußballspieler der (PL die Fußballspieler) footballer.

Fußboden der (PL die Fußböden) floor.

Fußgänger der (PL die Fußgänger) pedestrian.

Fußgängerzone die (PL die Fußgängerzonen) pedestrian precinct.

Fußweg der (PL die Fußwege) footpath.

Futter das 1 feed; ich habe dem Hund schon Futter gegeben I've already given the dog his food; 2 lining (of clothes).

füttern verb (PERF hat gefüttert) 1 to feed; den Hund und die Katze füttern to feed the dog and the cat; 2 to line.

Futur das (PL die Future) future (tense).

Gg

gab SEE **geben**.

Gabel die (PL die **Gabeln**) fork.

gähnen verb (PERF **hat gegähnt**) to yawn.

Galerie die (PL die **Galerien**) gallery.

galoppieren verb (PERF **ist galoppiert**) to gallop.

Gammler der (PL die **Gammler**) drop-out.

Gammlerin die (PL die **Gammlerinnen**) drop-out.

Gang der (PL die **Gänge**) **1** walk; **2** errand; **3** corridor; **4 ein Platz am Gang** an aisle seat; **5** course (of a meal); **6** gear (of a car); **7 in Gang setzen** to get going; **8 im Gange** in progress.

gängig adjective **1** common; **2** popular (goods).

Gans die (PL die **Gänse**) goose.

Gänseblümchen das (PL die **Gänseblümchen**) daisy.

Gänsehaut die goose pimples.

ganz adjective whole **1 ganz Deutschland** the whole of Germany; **2 im Großen und Ganzon** on the whole; **3 eine ganze Menge** quite a lot; **4** all; **mein ganzes Geld** all my money; **die ganzen Leute** all the people; **5 etwas wieder ganz machen** to mend something.

ganz adverb **1** quite; **es war ganz gut** it was quite good; **2 ganz und**

gar completely; **3 ganz und gar nicht** not at all.

ganztägig adjective, adverb **1** full-time; **2** all-day; **ganztägig geöffnet** open all day.

ganztags adverb **1** full time; **2** all day.

Ganztagsschule die (PL die **Ganztagsschulen**) **1** all-day school; **2** all-day schooling.

gar adjective done, cooked.

gar adverb **1 gar nicht** not at all; **gar nichts** nothing; **2 oder gar** or even.

Garage die (PL die **Garagen**) garage.

Garantie die (PL die **Garantien**) guarantee.

garantieren verb (PERF **hat garantiert**) to guarantee.

Garderobe die (PL die **Garderoben**) cloakroom; **wir können die Mäntel an der Garderobe abgeben** we can leave the coats in the cloakroom.

Gardine die (PL die **Gardinen**) curtain.

Garn das (PL die **Garne**) thread.

Garnele die (PL die **Garnelen**) **1** shrimp; **2** prawn.

Garten der (PL die **Gärten**) garden.

Gärtner der (PL die **Gärtner**) gardener.

Gärtnerin die (PL die **Gärtnerinnen**) gardener.

Gas das (PL die **Gase**) **1** gas; **2 Gas geben** to accelerate.

Gasherd der (PL die **Gasherde**) gas cooker.

Gaspedal das (PL die **Gaspedale**) accelerator.

Gasse die (PL die **Gassen**) lane.

Gast der (PL die **Gäste**) 1 guest; **wir haben heute Abend Gäste** we've got guests tonight; **2 bei jemandem zu Gast sein** to be staying with somebody.

Gastarbeiter der (PL die **Gastarbeiter**) foreign worker, guest worker.

Gästezimmer das (PL die **Gästezimmer**) 1 (hotel) room; 2 spare room.

gastfreundlich adjective hospitable.

Gastfreundschaft die hospitality.

Gastgeber der (PL die **Gastgeber**) host.

Gastgeberin die (PL die **Gastgeberinnen**) host.

Gasthaus das (PL die **Gasthäuser**) inn.

Gasthof der (PL die **Gasthöfe**) inn.

Gaststätte die (PL die **Gaststätten**) restaurant.

Gauner der (PL die **Gauner**) crook.

Gebäck das 1 pastries; 2 biscuits.

gebären ✧verb (IMPERF gebar, PERF hat geboren) 1 to give birth to; 2 geboren werden to be born.

Gebäude das (PL die **Gebäude**) building.

geben ✧verb (PRES gibt, IMPERF gab, PERF hat gegeben) 1 to give; 2 to deal (cards); 3 to teach (at school); 4 geben Sie mir bitte Frau Scheck please put me through to Mrs Scheck; 5 es gibt there is, there are; es gibt viele gute Restaurants in München there are lots of good restaurants in Munich; was gibts or gibt's im Kino? what's on at the cinema?; was gibt es zum Mittagessen? what are we having for lunch?; 6 was gibts or gibt's Neues? what's the news?, what's new?; 7 sich geschlagen geben to admit defeat; 8 das gibt sich wieder it'll get better; 9 das gibts or gibt's doch nicht! I don't believe it!

Gebet das (PL die **Gebete**) prayer.

gebeten SEE bitten.

Gebiet das (PL die **Gebiete**) 1 area; 2 field.

gebildet adjective educated.

Gebirge das (PL die **Gebirge**) mountain range; **im Gebirge** in the mountains.

Gebiss das (PL die **Gebisse**) 1 teeth; 2 false teeth, dentures.

gebissen SEE beißen.

geblieben SEE bleiben.

geboren verb SEE gebären.

geboren adjective 1 born; 2 née; **Frau Hahn, geborene Müller** Mrs Hahn, née Müller.

geborgen adjective safe.

geboten SEE bieten.

gebracht SEE bringen.

gebraten adjective fried.

Gebrauch der (PL die Gebräuche)
1 use; **vor Gebrauch schütteln**
shake before use; 2 custom.

gebrauchen verb (PERF **hat
gebraucht**) to use.

Gebrauchsanweisung die (PL
die Gebrauchsanweisungen)
instructions (for use).

gebraucht adjective used, secondhand.

Gebrauchtwagen der (PL die
Gebrauchtwagen) second-hand
car.

gebrochen SEE brechen.

Gebühr die (PL die Gebühren) fee,
charge.

gebührenfrei adjective free (of
charge).

gebührenpflichtig adjective
1 subject to a charge; 2 eine
gebührenpflichtige Straße a toll
road.

gebunden SEE binden.

Geburt die (PL die Geburten) birth.

Geburtenregelung die birth
control.

Geburtsdatum das (PL die
Geburtsdaten) date of birth.

Geburtsort der (PL die
Geburtsorte) place of birth.

Geburtstag der (PL die
Geburtstage) birthday.

Geburtsurkunde die (PL die
Geburtsurkunden) birth
certificate.

gedacht SEE denken.

Gedächtnis das (PL die
Gedächtnisse) memory.

Gedanke der (PL die Gedanken)
1 thought; **in Gedanken
versunken sein** to be lost in
thought; 2 **sich Gedanken
machen** to worry; 3 **jemanden auf
andere Gedanken bringen** to take
somebody's mind off things.

gedankenlos adjective
thoughtless.

gedankenlos adverb without
thinking.

Gedeck das (PL die Gedecke)
1 place setting; 2 set meal.

Gedicht das (PL die Gedichte)
poem.

Geduld die patience.

geduldig adjective patient.

gedurft SEE dürfen.

geehrt adjective 1 honoured;
2 **Sehr geehrte Frau Ross** Dear
Mrs Ross.

geeignet adjective 1 suitable;
2 right.

Gefahr die (PL die Gefahren)
1 danger; **außer Gefahr** out of
danger; 2 **auf eigene Gefahr** at
your own risk; **Gefahr laufen,
etwas zu tun** to run the risk of
doing something.

gefährdet adjective at risk,
endangered; **eine gefährdete Art**
an endangered species.

gefährlich adjective dangerous.

gefallen¹ SEE fallen.

gefallen² ◇ verb (PRES **gefällt**,
IMPERF **gefiel**, PERF **hat gefallen**)
1 **es gefällt mir** I like it; **es hat mir
sehr gut gefallen** I liked it a lot;

2 sich etwas gefallen lassen to put up with something.

Gefallen[1] *der* (PL *die* **Gefallen**) favour.

Gefallen[2] *das* pleasure; **dir zu Gefallen** to please you.

Gefangene *der/die* (PL *die* **Gefangenen**) prisoner.

Gefängnis *das* (PL *die* **Gefängnisse**) prison.

Gefäß *das* (PL *die* **Gefäße**) container.

gefasst *adjective* **1** calm, composed; **2 auf etwas gefasst sein** to be prepared for something.

gefiel SEE **gefallen**.

geflogen SEE **fliegen**.

geflossen SEE **fließen**.

Geflügel *das* poultry.

gefochten SEE **fechten**.

gefräßig *adjective* (*informal*) greedy.

gefrieren ◇*verb* (IMPERF **gefror**, PERF **ist gefroren**) to freeze.

Gefrierfach *das* (PL *die* **Gefrierfächer**) freezer (compartment).

gefroren *adjective* frozen.

Gefühl *das* (PL *die* **Gefühle**) **1** feeling; **2 etwas im Gefühl haben** to have a feel for something.

gefüllt *adjective* stuffed (*peppers, for example*).

gefunden SEE **finden**.

gegangen SEE **gehen**.

gegeben SEE **geben**.

gegebenenfalls *adverb* if need be.

gegen *preposition* (+ACC) **1** against; **2 gegen die Mauer fahren** to drive into the wall; **3 ein Mittel gegen Grippe** a cure for flu; **4** towards; **gegen Abend** towards evening; **5 gegen vier Uhr** around four o'clock; **6** compared with; **7** versus (*in sport*).

Gegend *die* (PL *die* **Gegenden**) **1** area; **2** neighbourhood.

gegeneinander *adverb* against each other, against one another.

Gegenmittel *das* (PL *die* **Gegenmittel**) **1** remedy; **2** antidote.

Gegensatz *der* (PL *die* **Gegensätze**) **1** contrast; **2** opposite; **3 im Gegensatz zu mir** unlike me.

gegenseitig *adjective* mutual.

gegenseitig *adverb* **sich gegenseitig helfen** to help each other.

Gegenstand *der* (PL *die* **Gegenstände**) **1** object; **2** subject (*in grammar or of a discussion*).

Gegenteil *das* (PL *die* **Gegenteile**) **1** opposite; **2 im Gegenteil** on the contrary.

gegenüber *preposition* (+DAT) **1** opposite; **Susi saß mir gegenüber** Susi sat opposite me; **2** compared with; **3** towards; **jemandem gegenüber freundlich sein** to be friendly towards somebody.

gegenüber *adverb* opposite; **meine Freundin wohnt gegenüber** my friend lives opposite.

Gegenwart *die* 1 present; 2 presence.

gegessen SEE essen.

Gegner *der* (PL die Gegner) opponent.

Gegnerin *die* (PL die Gegnerinnen) opponent.

gegrillt *adjective* grilled.

Gehackte *das* mince.

Gehalt *das* (PL die Gehälter) salary.

gehässig *adjective* spiteful.

geheim *adjective* secret.

Geheimnis *das* (PL die Geheimnisse) secret.

geheimnisvoll *adjective* mysterious.

gehen ◇*verb* (IMPERF ging, PERF ist gegangen) 1 to go; **schlafen gehen** to go to bed; 2 to walk; 3 **über die Straße gehen** to cross the road; 4 **es geht ihr gut** she's well; **wie geht es ihnen?** how are you?; **es geht** it's not too bad; 5 **das geht nicht** that's impossible; 6 **um etwas gehen** to be about something; **worum geht or geht's hier?** what's it all about?; 7 **die Uhr geht falsch** the clock's wrong.

Gehirn *das* (PL die Gehirne) brain.

Gehirnerschütterung *die* (PL die Gehirnerschütterungen) concussion.

gehoben SEE heben.

geholfen SEE helfen.

Gehör *das* hearing.

gehorchen *verb* (PERF hat gehorcht) to obey.

gehören *verb* (PERF hat gehört) 1 to belong; **es gehört mir** it belongs to me; 2 **dazu gehört Mut** that takes courage; 3 **es gehört sich nicht** it isn't done.

gehorsam *adjective* obedient.

Gehsteig *der* (PL die Gehsteige) pavement.

Geier *der* (PL die Geier) vulture.

Geige *die* (PL die Geigen) violin.

Geisel *die* (PL die Geiseln) hostage.

Geist *der* (PL die Geister) 1 mind; 2 ghost; 3 wit.

geistesabwesend *adjective* absent-minded.

Geisteskrankheit *die* (PL die Geisteskrankheiten) mental illness.

Geisteswissenschaften (*plural noun*) arts, humanities.

geistig *adjective* mental.

geistreich *adjective* witty, clever.

gelzig *adjective* mean.

gekannt SEE kennen.

gekonnt SEE können.

Gel *das* (PL die Gele) gel.

Gelächter *das* (PL die Gelächter) laughter.

geladen SEE laden.

gelähmt *adjective* paralysed.

Gelände *das* (PL die Gelände) 1 ground; 2 area.

Geländer *das* (PL die Geländer) 1 banister(s); 2 railing(s).

a b c d e f g h i j k l m n o p q r s t u v w x y z

gelangweilt *adjective* bored.

gelassen *verb* SEE **lassen**

gelassen *adjective* calm.

geläufig *adjective* 1 common;
2 das ist mir nicht geläufig I'm
not familiar with it.

gelaunt *adjective* gut gelaunt sein
to be in a good mood.

gelb *adjective* yellow.

Geld *das* (PL die **Gelder**) money.

Geldautomat *der* (PL die
Geldautomaten) cash dispenser.

Geldbörse *die* (PL die **Geldbörsen**)
purse.

Geldschein *der* (PL die
Geldscheine) banknote.

Geldstrafe *die* (PL die **Geldstrafen**)
fine.

Geldwechsel *der* 1 bureau de
change; 2 currency exchange.

gelegen SEE **liegen**.

Gelegenheit *die* (PL die
Gelegenheiten) 1 opportunity;
2 occasion.

gelegentlich *adverb*
occasionally.

Gelenk *das* (PL die **Gelenke**) joint.

Geliebte *der/die* (PL die **Geliebten**)
lover.

geliehen SEE **leihen**.

gelingen ◇*verb* (IMPERF **gelang**,
PERF **ist gelungen**) to succeed; es
ist mir gelungen, sie zu
überreden I succeeded in
persuading her.

gelten ◇*verb* (PRES **gilt**, IMPERF **galt**,
PERF **hat gegolten**) 1 to be valid;
2 to apply (*of a rule*); 3 jemandem

gelten to be directed at somebody;
4 sein Wort gilt viel his word is
worth a lot; 5 das gilt nicht that
doesn't count; 6 als etwas gelten
to be regarded as something.

gelungen *verb* SEE **gelingen**

gelungen *adjective* successful.

Gemälde *das* (PL die **Gemälde**)
painting.

gemein *adjective* mean.

Gemeinde *die* (PL die **Gemeinden**)
1 community; 2 congregation.

gemeinsam *adjective* 1 common;
2 joint.

gemeinsam *adverb* together;
gemeinsam essen to eat together.

Gemeinschaft *die* (PL die
Gemeinschaften) community.

gemischt *adjective* mixed.

gemocht SEE **mögen**.

Gemüse *das* (PL die **Gemüse**)
vegetables.

Gemüsehändler *der* (PL die
Gemüsehändler) greengrocer.

Gemüseladen *der* (PL die
Gemüseläden) greengrocer's
shop.

gemusst SEE **müssen**.

gemustert *adjective* patterned.

gemütlich *adjective* 1 cosy;
2 mach es dir gemütlich make
yourself comfortable.

genannt SEE **nennen**.

genau *adjective* 1 exact;
2 accurate (*scales, description*);
3 meticulous; 4 ich weiß nichts
Genaues I don't know any details.

genau adverb 1 exactly; **sich etwas genau ansehen** to look at something carefully; 2 **genau genommen** strictly speaking.

Genauigkeit die accuracy.

genauso adverb 1 just the same; 2 **genauso gut** just as good; **genauso viel** just as much, just as many; **genauso lange** just as long.

Genehmigung die (PL die Genehmigungen) 1 permission; 2 permit; 3 licence.

Generation die (PL die Generationen) generation.

Generator der (PL die Generatoren) generator.

generell adjective general.

Genetik die genetics.

Genf das Geneva.

Genfer See der Lake Geneva.

genial adjective brilliant.

Genick das (PL die Genicke) (back of the) neck.

Genie das (PL die Genies) genius.

genießbar adjective edible.

genießen ◇verb (IMPERF genoss, PERF hat genossen) to enjoy.

genommen SEE nehmen.

genug adverb enough.

genügen verb (PERF hat genügt) to be enough.

genügend adjective 1 enough; 2 sufficient.

Genuss der (PL die Genüsse) 1 enjoyment; 2 consumption (of alcohol).

geöffnet adjective open.

Geometrie die geometry.

Gepäck das luggage.

Gepäckaufbewahrung die (PL die Gepäckaufbewahrungen) left-luggage office.

Gepäckausgabe die left-luggage office.

Gepäckträger der (PL die Gepäckträger) 1 porter; 2 roof rack; 3 carrier (on a bike).

gerade adjective 1 straight; 2 **etwas gerade biegen** to straighten something; 3 upright; 4 **eine gerade Zahl** an even number.

gerade adverb 1 just; **gerade erst** only just; 2 **es war nicht gerade billig** it wasn't exactly cheap.

geradeaus adverb straight ahead.

geradebiegen SEE gerade.

gerannt SEE rennen.

Gerät das (PL die Geräte) 1 appliance; 2 set (TV or radio); 3 tool; 4 gadget; 5 **die Geräte** apparatus (in gymnastics).

geraten ◇verb (PRES gerät, IMPERF geriet, PERF ist geraten) 1 to get (somewhere, the wrong side of the road etc.); **in etwas geraten** to get into something; **in Wut geraten** to get angry; 2 **an den Richtigen geraten** to come to the right person, 3 **gut/schlecht geraten** to turn out well/badly; 4 **nach jemandem geraten** to take after somebody.

Gerätetauchen das scuba diving.

geräuchert *adjective* smoked.

geräumig *adjective* spacious.

Geräusch *das* (PL die **Geräusche**) noise.

gerecht *adjective* 1 just; 2 fair.

Gerechtigkeit *die* justice.

Gerede *das* gossip.

Gericht *das* (PL die **Gerichte**) 1 court; 2 dish.

gerieben SEE **reiben**.

gering *adjective* 1 small (*amount*); 2 low (*value*); 3 short (*time, distance*).

Gerippe *das* (PL die **Gerippe**) skeleton.

gerissen *adjective* crafty.

geritten SEE **reiten**.

gern(e) *adverb* 1 gladly; 2 jemanden gern haben to like somebody; etwas gern tun to like doing something; ich tanze gern I like dancing; ich hätte gerne einen Kaffee I'd like a coffee; welchen Belag hättest du gerne? which topping would you like?; 3 ja, gern! yes, I'd love to!; 4 das glaube ich gern I can well believe that.

Gerste *die* barley.

Geruch *der* (PL die **Gerüche**) smell.

Gerücht *das* (PL die **Gerüchte**) rumour.

Gerümpel *das* junk.

gesalzen *verb* SEE **salzen**.

gesalzen *adjective* 1 salted; 2 gesalzene Preise (*informal*) steep prices.

gesamt *adjective* 1 whole; 2 die gesamten Kosten the total cost; 3 die gesamten Werke the complete works.

Gesamtschule *die* (PL die **Gesamtschulen**) comprehensive school.

gesandt SEE **senden**.

Geschäft *das* (PL die **Geschäfte**) 1 shop; 2 business; 3 deal.

Geschäftsführer *der* (PL die **Geschäftsführer**) manager.

Geschäftsführerin *die* (PL die **Geschäftsführerinnen**) manageress.

Geschäftszeiten *plural noun* business hours.

geschehen ◇*verb* (PRES geschieht, IMPERF geschah, PERF ist geschehen) to happen.

gescheit *adjective* clever.

Geschenk *das* (PL die **Geschenke**) present, gift.

Geschichte *die* (PL die **Geschichten**) 1 story; 2 history; 3 mach bloß keine große Geschichte daraus don't make such a thing of it.

Geschick *das* 1 skill; 2 fate.

geschickt *adjective* 1 skilful; 2 clever.

geschieden *verb* SEE **scheiden**.

geschieden *adjective* divorced; meine Eltern sind geschieden my parents are divorced.

geschienen SEE **scheinen**.

Geschirr *das* 1 crockery; 2 dishes.

Geschirrspülmaschine die (PL die **Geschirrspülmaschinen**) dishwasher.

Geschirrtuch das (PL die **Geschirrtücher**) tea towel.

Geschlecht das (PL die **Geschlechter**) 1 sex; 2 gender.

geschlossen verb SEE **schließen**.

geschlossen adjective closed.

Geschmack der (PL die **Geschmäcke**) taste.

geschmacklos adjective 1 tasteless; 2 geschmacklos sein to be in a bad taste.

geschnitten SEE **schneiden**.

geschossen SEE **schießen**.

geschrieben SEE **schreiben**.

geschrien SEE **schreien**.

Geschwätz das talk.

geschwätzig adjective talkative.

Geschwindigkeit die (PL die **Geschwindigkeiten**) speed.

Geschwindigkeitsbeschränkung die (PL die **Geschwindigkeitsbeschränkungen**) speed limit.

Geschwister plural noun brothers and sisters, siblings.

geschwommen SEE **schwimmen**.

Geschwür das (PL die **Geschwüre**) ulcer.

gesellig adjective sociable.

Gesellschaft die (PL die **Gesellschaften**) 1 society; 2 company; ich leiste dir Gesellschaft I'll keep you company; 3 party.

gesessen SEE **sitzen**.

Gesetz das (PL die **Gesetze**) law.

gesetzlich adjective legal; ein gesetzlicher Feiertag a public holiday.

gesetzlich adverb legally, by law.

Gesicht das (PL die **Gesichter**) face.

Gesichtsausdruck der (facial) expression.

gesollt SEE **sollen**.

gespannt adjective 1 eager; 2 auf etwas gespannt sein to look forward eagerly to something; auf jemanden gespannt sein to look forward to seeing somebody; 3 ich bin gespannt, ob ... I wonder whether ...; 4 tense; in Südafrika ist die Lage immer noch gespannt the situation in South Africa is still tense.

Gespenst das (PL die **Gespenster**) ghost.

Gespräch das (PL die **Gespräche**) 1 conversation; 2 call (on the phone).

gesprächig adjective talkative.

gesprochen SEE **sprechen**.

gesprungen SEE **springen**.

Gestalt die (PL die **Gestalten**) 1 figure; 2 form.

gestanden SEE **stehen**, **gestehen**.

Geständnis das (PL die **Geständnisse**) confession.

gestatten verb (PERF hat gestattet) 1 to permit; 2 nicht gestattet prohibited; 3 gestatten Sie? may I?

a

Geste die (PL die **Gesten**) gesture.

b

gestehen ✧verb (IMPERF **gestand**, PERF **hat gestanden**) to confess.

c

Gestell das (PL die **Gestelle**) **1** rack; **2** stand; **3** frame.

d

gestern adverb **1** yesterday; **2 gestern Nacht** last night.

e

f

gestohlen SEE **stehlen**.

g

gestorben SEE **sterben**.

gestreift adjective striped.

h

gesund adjective **1** healthy; **2 wieder gesund werden** to get well again; **3 Schwimmen ist gesund** swimming is good for you.

i

j

Gesundheit die **1** health; **2 Gesundheit!** bless you! (said after someone sneezes).

k

l

gesungen SEE **singen**.

m

getan SEE **tun**.

Getränk das (PL die **Getränke**) drink.

n

o

Getränkekarte die (PL die **Getränkekarten**) wine list.

p

getrauen verb (PERF **hat sich getraut**) **sich getrauen** to dare.

q

Getreide das grain.

r

Getriebe das (PL die **Getriebe**) gearbox.

s

getrieben SEE **treiben**.

getroffen SEE **treffen**.

t

u

getrunken SEE **trinken**.

Getue das fuss.

v

geübt adjective **1** accomplished; **2 mit geübtem Auge** with a practised eye.

w

x

Gewächshaus das (PL die **Gewächshäuser**) greenhouse.

y

z

Gewalt die **1** power; **2** force; **mit Gewalt** by force; **3** violence.

gewaltig adjective enormous.

gewalttätig adjective violent.

gewann SEE **gewinnen**.

Gewebe das (PL die **Gewebe**) **1** fabric; **2** tissue.

Gewehr das (PL die **Gewehre**) rifle, gun.

Gewerkschaft die (PL die **Gewerkschaften**) trade union.

gewesen SEE **sein**.

Gewicht das (PL die **Gewichte**) weight.

Gewinn der (PL die **Gewinne**) **1** profit; **2** winnings; **3** prize.

gewinnen ✧verb (IMPERF **gewann**, PERF **hat gewonnen**) **1** to win; **mit 3 zu 2 Toren gewinnen** to win by 3 goals to 2; **2** to gain (time or influence); **an Bedeutung gewinnen** to gain in importance.

Gewinner der (PL die **Gewinner**) winner.

Gewinnerin die (PL die **Gewinnerinnen**) winner.

gewiss adjective certain; **ein gewisser Herr Schmidt möchte Sie sprechen** a Mr Schmidt would like to speak to you.

gewiss adverb certainly; **'darf ich?' 'aber gewiss doch!'** 'may I?' 'but of course'.

Gewissen das (PL die **Gewissen**) conscience.

gewissenhaft adjective conscientious.

gewissermaßen *adverb* **1** more or less; **2** as it were.

Gewitter *das* (PL die **Gewitter**) thunderstorm.

gewittrig *adjective* thundery.

gewöhnen *verb* (PERF **hat gewöhnt**) **1** jemanden an etwas gewöhnen to get somebody used to something; **2** an etwas gewöhnt sein to be used to something; **3** sich an etwas gewöhnen to get used to something.

Gewohnheit *die* (PL die **Gewohnheiten**) habit.

gewöhnlich *adjective* **1** usual; **2** ordinary.

gewöhnlich *adverb* usually; **wie gewöhnlich** as usual.

gewohnt *adjective* **1** usual; **2** etwas gewohnt sein to be used to something; **Renate ist es nicht gewohnt, früh aufzustehen** Renate isn't used to getting up early.

gewollt SEE **wollen.**

gewonnen SEE **gewinnen.**

geworden SEE **werden.**

geworfen SEE **werfen.**

Gewürz *das* (PL die **Gewürze**) spice.

gewusst SEE **wissen.**

Gezeiten *plural noun* tides.

gezogen SEE **ziehen.**

gezwungen SEE **zwingen.**

gibt SEE **geben.**

gierig *adjective* greedy.

gießen ◇*verb* (IMPERF **goss**, PERF **hat gegossen**) **1** to pour; **es gießt** it's pouring; **2** to water; **vergiss**

nicht, die Blumen zu gießen don't forget to water the flowers.

Gießkanne *die* (PL die **Gießkannen**) watering can.

Gift *das* (PL die **Gifte**) poison.

giftig *adjective* **1** poisonous; **2** toxic.

Gigabyte *das* (PL die **Gigabytes**) gigabyte; **eine Festplatte mit 20 Gigabyte Speicherkapazität** a twenty gigabyte hard disk.

ging SEE **gehen.**

Gipfel *der* (PL die **Gipfel**) **1** peak, summit; **2** der Gipfel der Geschmacklosigkeit the height of bad taste.

Gips *der* plaster.

Giraffe *die* (PL die **Giraffen**) giraffe.

Girokonto *das* (PL die **Girokonten**) current account.

Gitarre *die* (PL die **Gitarren**) guitar.

Gitarrist *der* (PL die **Gitarristen**) guitarist, guitar player.

Gitter *das* (PL die **Gitter**) **1** grid; **2** bars.

glänzen *verb* (PERF **hat geglänzt**) to shine.

glänzend *adjective* **1** shining; **2** brilliant; **ein glänzender Erfolg** a brilliant success.

Glas *das* (PL die **Gläser**) **1** glass (*the material*); **2** glass (*for a drink*); **3** jar.

Glasscheibe *die* (PL die **Glasscheiben**) pane (of glass).

Glasur *die* **1** icing; **2** glaze.

a
b
c
d
e
f
g
h
i
j
k
l
m
n
o
p
q
r
s
t
u
v
w
x
y
z

a
b
c
d
e
f
g
h
i
j
k
l
m
n
o
p
q
r
s
t
u
v
w
x
y
z

glatt *adjective* **1** smooth;
2 slippery; **3 eine glatte Absage** a
flat refusal.

glatt *adverb* **1** smoothly; **2** flatly;
etwas glatt ablehnen to flatly
reject something; **3 das ist glatt
gelogen** that's a downright lie;
**4 ich habe ihren Geburtstag glatt
vergessen** I totally forgot about
her birthday.

Glatteis *das* (black) ice.

Glatze *die* (PL **die Glatzen**) **eine
Glatze haben** to be bald; **eine
Glatze bekommen** to go bald.

glauben *verb* (PERF **hat geglaubt**)
1 to believe; **an Gott glauben** to
believe in God; **2** to think; **3 nicht
zu glauben!** incredible!

gleich *adjective* **1** same;
2 identical; **3** equal bleibend
constant; **4 das ist mir gleich** it's
all the same to me; **ganz gleich,
wer anruft** no matter who calls.

gleich *adverb* **1** the same;
2 equally; **3** immediately; **gleich
danach** immediately afterwards;
gleich neben right next to; **ich
komme gleich** I'm coming (right
away); **er ist gleich fertig** he'll be
ready in a minute.

gleichartig *adjective* similar.

gleichberechtigt *adjective*
equal.

Gleichberechtigung *die*
equality.

gleichbleibend SEE **gleich**.

gleichen ◇*verb* (IMPERF **glich**, PERF
hat geglichen) **1** to be like; **2 sich
gleichen** to be alike.

gleichfalls *adverb* **1** also;
2 danke gleichfalls! the same to
you!

Gleichgewicht *das* balance.

gleichgültig *adjective* indifferent;
das ist doch gleichgültig it's not
important.

gleichwertig *adjective*
1 equivalent; **2** of the same value;
3 of the same standard.

gleichzeitig *adverb* at the same
time.

Gleis *das* (PL **die Gleise**) **1** track,
line; **2** platform; **Gleis vier**
platform four.

glich SEE **gleichen**.

Glied *das* (PL **die Glieder**) **1** limb;
2 link.

glitschig *adjective* slippery.

glitzern *verb* (PERF **hat geglitzert**)
to glitter.

global *adjective* global, general;
der globale Temperaturanstieg
global warming.

Glocke *die* (PL **die Glocken**) bell.

Glück *das* **1** luck; **viel Glück!** good
luck!; **Glück haben** to be lucky;
zum Glück luckily; **2** happiness.

glücklich *adjective* **1** lucky; **es
war ein glücklicher Zufall, dass
ich ihn heute in der Stadt
getroffen habe** it was a lucky
coincidence that I met him in town
today; **2** happy.

glücklicherweise *adverb*
luckily, fortunately.

Glückwunsch *der* (PL **die
Glückwünsche**) congratulations;

herzlichen Glückwunsch zum Geburtstag! happy birthday!

Glückwunschkarte die (PL die Glückwunschkarten) greetings card.

Glühbirne die (PL die Glühbirnen) light bulb.

glühen verb (PERF hat geglüht) to glow.

Gokart der (PL die Gokarts) go-kart; **Gokart gehen** to go karting.

Gold das gold.

golden adjective 1 gold; 2 golden.

Goldfisch der (PL die Goldfische) goldfish.

Golf[1] der (PL die Golfe) gulf.

Golf[2] das golf.

Golfplatz der (PL die Golfplätze) golf course.

Golfschläger der (PL die Golfschläger) golf club.

Golfspieler der (PL die Golfspieler) golfer.

Golfspielerin die (PL die Golfspielerinnen) golfer.

Gorilla der (PL die Gorillas) gorilla.

goss SEE gießen.

Gosse die (PL die Gossen) gutter (in street).

Gott der (PL die Götter) god.

Gottesdienst der (PL die Gottesdienste) service.

Göttin die (PL die Göttinnen) goddess.

Grab das (PL die Gräber) grave.

graben verb (PRES gräbt, IMPERF grub, PERF hat gegraben) to dig.

Grad der (PL die Grade) degree.

Grafik die (PL die Grafiken) graphics.

Gramm das (PL die Gramme) gram.

Grammatik die (PL die Grammatiken) grammar.

grammatikalisch adjective grammatical; **ein grammatikalischer Fehler** a grammatical error.

grantig adjective grumpy.

Gras das (PL die Gräser) grass.

grässlich adjective horrible.

Gräte die (PL die Gräten) (fish)bone.

gratis adverb free of charge.

gratulieren verb (PERF hat gratuliert) 1 to congratulate; 2 ich habe Gabi zum Geburtstag gratuliert I wished Gabi happy birthday; 3 wir gratulieren! congratulations!

grau adjective grey.

Gräuel der horror.

grauen verb (PERF hat gegraut) mir graut es davor I dread it.

grauenvoll adjective 1 grim; 2 horrific.

grauhaarig adjective grey-haired.

grausam adjective cruel.

Grausamkeit die cruelty.

graziös adjective graceful.

greifen ◇ verb (IMPERF griff, PERF hat gegriffen) 1 to take hold of; 2 to catch; 3 nach etwas greifen to reach for something; 4 um sich greifen to spread (of fire).

a b c d e f g h i j k l m n o p q r s t u v w x y z

grell *adjective* **1** glaring; **2** garish; **3** shrill.

Grenze *die* (PL **die Grenzen**) **1** border; **2** boundary; **3** limit.

grenzen *verb* (PERF **hat gegrenzt**) **an etwas grenzen** to border on something.

Greuel SEE **Gräuel**.

Grieche *der* (PL **die Griechen**) Greek.

Griechenland *das* Greece.

Griechin *die* (PL **die Griechinnen**) Greek.

griechisch *adjective* Greek.

Griff *der* (PL **die Griffe**) **1** grasp; **2** handle.

griff SEE **greifen**.

griffbereit *adjective* handy; **sie hat den Korkenzieher immer griffbereit** she always keeps the corkscrew handy.

Grill *der* (PL **die Grills**) **1** grill; **2** barbecue.

Grille *die* (PL **die Grillen**) cricket (*the insect*).

grillen *verb* (PERF **hat gegrillt**) **1** to grill; **2** to have a barbecue.

Grillfest *das* (PL **die Grillfeste**) barbecue.

grinsen *verb* (PERF **hat gegrinst**) to grin.

Grippe *die* (PL **die Grippen**) flu.

grob *adjective* **1** coarse; **2** rough; **3** rude; **4 ein grober Fehler** a bad mistake.

Groschen *der* (PL **die Groschen**) **1** groschen (*one hundredth of a Schilling in the former Austrian currency*) SEE **Schilling**; **2** (*informal*) **der Groschen ist gefallen** the penny's dropped.

groß *adjective* **1** big; **2** great; **Gisela hatte große Angst** Gisela was very frightened; **3** tall; **4 ein großer Buchstabe** a capital letter; **5 groß werden** to grow up; **6 die großen Ferien** the summer holidays; **7 im Großen und Ganzen** on the whole; **8 Groß und Klein** young and old.

groß *adverb* **was soll man da schon groß machen?** what are you supposed to do?

großartig *adjective* great.

Großbritannien *das* Great Britain.

Großbuchstabe *der* (PL **die Großbuchstaben**) capital (letter).

Größe *die* (PL **die Größen**) **1** size; **2** height; **3** greatness.

Großeltern *plural noun* grandparents.

großenteils *adverb* largely.

Großmarkt *der* (PL **die Großmärkte**) hypermarket.

Großmutter *die* (PL **die Großmütter**) grandmother.

großschreiben ✧*verb* (IMPERF **großschrieb**, PERF **hat großgeschrieben**) **ein Wort großschreiben** to write a word with a capital.

Großstadt *die* (PL **die Großstädte**) city.

Großvater *der* (PL **die Großväter**) grandfather.

großzügig *adjective* generous.

grub SEE **graben.**

grün *adjective* **1** green; **2 im Grünen** in the country; **3 die Grünen** the Greens.

Grund *der* (PL die **Gründe**) **1** ground; **2** bottom; **3** reason; **aus diesem Grund** for this reason; **4 im Grunde genommen** basically.

gründen *verb* (PERF **hat gegründet**) **1** to set up, to found; **2 sich auf etwas gründen** to be based on something.

Grundlage *die* (PL die **Grundlagen**) basis.

gründlich *adjective* thorough.

grundsätzlich *adjective* **1** fundamental; **2** basic.

grundsätzlich *adverb* **1** basically; **2** on principle.

Grundschule *die* (PL die **Grundschulen**) primary school.

Grundstück *das* (PL die **Grundstücke**) plot (of land).

Gruppe *die* (PL die **Gruppen**) group.

Gruß *der* (PL die **Grüße**) greeting; **einen schönen Gruß an Lars** give my regards to Lars; **mit herzlichen Grüßen** with best wishes.

grüßen *verb* (PERF **hat gegrüßt**) **1** to greet; **2** to say hello; **3 grüß Gott!** hello; **4 grüße Thomas von mir** give Thomas my regards; **Gisela lässt grüßen** Gisela sends her regards.

gucken *verb* (PERF **hat geguckt**) to look.

gültig *adjective* valid.

Gültigkeit *die* validity.

Gummi *der* (PL die **Gummis**) rubber.

Gummiband *das* (PL die **Gummibänder**) rubber band.

Gummistiefel *der* (PL die **Gummistiefel**) wellington (boot).

günstig *adjective* **1** favourable; **2** convenient.

Gurgel *die* (PL die **Gurgeln**) throat.

gurgeln *verb* (PERF **hat gegurgelt**) to gargle.

Gurke *die* (PL die **Gurken**) **1** cucumber; **2** gherkin.

Gürtel *der* (PL die **Gürtel**) belt.

Gürteltasche *die* (PL die **Gürteltaschen**) bum bag.

gut *adjective* **1** good; **2 guten Appetit!** enjoy your meal!; **3 schon gut** that's all right; **also gut** all right; **4 im Guten** amicably; **5 alles Gute!** all the best!.

gut *adverb* **1** well; **2 gut schmecken** to taste good; **3 gut zwei Stunden** a good two hours; **4 uns geht's gut** we're fine; **ihm geht es nicht gut** he's not well.

Gut *das* (PL die **Güter**) **1** property; **2** estate; **3** (*plural*) goods, freight.

Güte *die* **1** goodness; **du meine Güte!** my goodness!; **2** quality.

Güterzug *der* (PL die **Güterzüge**) goods train.

gutgehen SEE **gut.**

gutmütig *adjective* good-natured.

Gutschein *der* (PL die **Gutscheine**) **1** voucher; **2** coupon.

a
b
c
d
e
f
g
h
i
j
k
l
m
n
o
p
q
r
s
t
u
v
w
x
y
z

Gymnasium das (PL die Gymnasien) grammar school.

Gymnastik die 1 gymnastics; 2 keep-fit (exercises).

Hh

Haar das (PL die Haare) 1 hair; **sich die Haare waschen** to wash your hair; 2 **um ein Haar** (informal) very nearly.

Haarbürste die (PL die Haarbürsten) hairbrush.

haarig adjective hairy.

Haarschnitt der (PL die Haarschnitte) haircut.

Haarwaschmittel das (PL die Haarwaschmittel) shampoo.

haben ✧verb (PRES hat, IMPERF hatte, PERF hat gehabt) 1 to have (got); **ich habe ein neues Auto** I have (I've got) a new car; **etwas gegen jemanden haben** to have something against somebody; 2 (used with another verb, like 'have' in English, to form past tenses) **ich habe Werners Adresse verloren** I've lost Werner's address; **ich habe deine Mutter gestern angerufen** I rang your mother yesterday; 3 **Angst haben** to be frightened; **Hunger haben** to be hungry; **Husten haben** to have a cough; 4 **heute haben wir Mittwoch** it's Wednesday today; 5 **die Kinder haben Ferien** the children are on holiday; 6 **was ist sie?** what's the matter with her?;

7 **ich hätte gern ...** I'd like ...; **ich hätte ihr geholfen** I would have helped her; 8 **sich haben** (informal) to make a fuss.

Habicht der (PL die Habichte) hawk.

hacken verb (PERF hat gehackt) 1 to chop (up); 2 to peck (of a bird).

Hackfleisch das minced meat.

Hacksteak das (PL die Hacksteaks) beefburger (without bread).

Hafen der (PL die Häfen) harbour.

Haferflocken plural noun porridge oats.

haftbar adjective **für etwas haftbar sein** to be liable for something.

haften verb (PERF hat gehaftet) 1 to stick; 2 **für etwas haften** to be responsible for something.

Hagel der hail.

hageln verb (PERF hat gehagelt) to hail.

Hagelschauer der (PL die Hagelschauer) hailstorm.

Hahn der (PL die Hähne) 1 cock; 2 tap.

Hähnchen das (PL die Hähnchen) chicken.

Hai der (PL die Haie) shark.

Haken der (PL die Haken) 1 hook; 2 tick; 3 catch; **da muss ein Haken dran sein** there must be a catch.

halb adjective half; **zum halben Preis** at half price; **halb eins** half past twelve;

Halbbruder der (PL die Halbbrüder) half-brother.

Halbfinale das (PL die Halbfinale) semi-final.

halbieren verb (PERF hat halbiert) to halve.

Halbkreis der (PL die Halbkreise) semicircle.

Halbpension die half board.

Halbschwester die (PL die Halbschwestern) half-sister.

halbtags adverb part-time.

halbwegs adverb 1 half-way; 2 more or less.

Halbzeit die (PL die Halbzeiten) 1 half; 2 half-time; **während der Halbzeit** during half-time.

half SEE **helfen**.

Hälfte die (PL die Hälften) half; **zur Hälfte** half.

Halle die (PL die Hallen) 1 hall; 2 foyer.

Hallenbad das (PL die Hallenbäder) indoor swimming pool.

hallo exclamation hello!

Hals der (PL die Hälse) 1 neck; 2 throat; **mir tut der Hals weh** I've got a sore throat; 3 **aus vollem Hals schreien** to shout at the top of your voice; 4 **Hals über Kopf** in a rush.

Halsband das (PL die Halsbänder) collar.

Halsschmerzen plural noun sore throat; **Paul hat Halsschmerzen** Paul's got a sore throat.

Halstuch das (PL die Halstücher) scarf.

Halt der 1 hold; **jetzt hat es einen besseren Halt** it holds better now; 2 **Halt machen** to stop.

halt exclamation stop!

haltbar adjective 1 hard-wearing; 2 durable; 3 **mindestens haltbar bis** ... best before ....

halten ◇verb (PRES **hält**, IMPERF **hielt**, PERF **hat gehalten**) 1 to hold; 2 to keep; **sein Versprechen halten** to keep your promise; **warm halten** to keep warm; 3 to stop; **der Bus hält direkt vor seiner Haustür** the bus stops right outside his door; 4 to save (in sport); 5 to take (a paper, magazine); 6 **ich habe ihn für deinen Bruder gehalten** I took him for your brother; 7 **viel von jemandem halten** to think a lot of somebody; **jemanden für ehrlich halten** to think somebody is honest; 8 **zu jemandem halten** to stand by somebody; 9 **eine Rede halten** to make a speech; 10 **sich halten** to keep (of milk, fruit, etc.); 11 **sich links/rechts halten** to keep left/right; 12 **sich gut halten** to do well; 13 **sich an etwas halten** to keep to something.

Haltestelle die (PL die Haltestellen) stop.

haltmachen SEE **Halt**.

Haltung die (PL die Haltungen) 1 posture; 2 attitude; 3 composure.

Hammelfleisch das mutton.

Hammer der (PL die Hämmer) hammer.

a

hämmern verb (PERF hat gehämmert) to hammer.

b

Hamster der (PL die Hamster) hamster.

c

Hand die (PL die Hände) hand; **jemandem die Hand geben** to shake hands with somebody.

d

e

Handarbeit die (PL die Handarbeiten) 1 handicraft; 2 hand-made article.

f

g

Handball der handball.

h

Handbremse die (PL die Handbremsen) handbrake; **die Handbremse ziehen** to pull the handbrake.

i

j

Handbuch das (PL die Handbücher) manual.

k

l

Handel der 1 trade; 2 deal; 3 **in den Handel kommen** to come on the market.

m

handeln verb (PERF hat gehandelt) 1 to trade, to deal; 2 **mit jemandem handeln** to bargain with somebody; 3 **zu act**; 4 **von etwas handeln** to be about something; 5 **es handelt sich um** … it's about …; **worum handelt es sich?** what's it about?

n

o

p

q

r

s

Handelsschule die (PL die Handelsschulen) business school, vocational college.

t

u

Handfläche die (PL die Handflächen) palm.

Handgelenk das (PL die Handgelenke) wrist.

w

Handgepäck das hand luggage.

x

y

handhaben verb (PERF hat gehandhabt) to handle.

z

Händler der (PL die Händler) dealer.

handlich adjective handy.

Handlung die (PL die Handlungen) 1 act; 2 action; 3 plot.

Handschellen (plural noun) handcuffs.

Handschrift die (PL die Handschriften) handwriting.

Handschuh der (PL die Handschuhe) glove.

Handtasche die (PL die Handtaschen) bag.

Handtrommel die (PL die Handtrommeln) tambourine.

Handtuch das (PL die Handtücher) towel.

Handwerker der (PL die Handwerker) 1 craftsman; 2 workman.

Handwerkszeug das tools.

Handy das (PL die Handys) mobile (phone).

Hang der (PL die Hänge) slope.

Hängematte die (PL die Hängematten) hammock.

hängen¹ verb (PERF hat gehängt) 1 to hang; **Florian hat das Bild an die Wand gehängt** Florian hung the picture on the wall; **sie hängte ihren Mantel in den Schrank** she hung her coat up in the cupboard; 2 **sie haben den Wohnwagen an das Auto gehängt** they attached the caravan to the car; 3 **sich an jemanden hängen** to latch on to somebody.

hängen² ◇verb (IMPERF hing, PERF hat gehangen) 1 to hang; **mein**

Bild hat immer hier gehangen my picture used to hang here; **2 an seinen Eltern hängen** to be attached to your parents; **sie hängt sehr an ihrer Mutter** she's very attached to her mother; **3 an etwas hängen bleiben** to catch on something, to stick to something; **ich bin mit dem Ärmel am Zaun hängen geblieben** I got my sleeve caught on the fence.

hängenbleiben SEE **hängen**².

Hansaplast™ das plaster.

Happen der (PL die **Happen**) mouthful; **ich habe heute keinen Happen gegessen** I haven't had a bite to eat all day.

Harfe die (PL die **Harfen**) harp.

Harke die (PL die **Harken**) rake.

harmlos adjective harmless.

hart adjective **1** hard; **2** harsh.

hart gekocht adjective hard-boiled.

Häschen das (PL die **Häschen**) bunny rabbit.

Hase der (PL die **Hasen**) hare.

Haselnuss die (PL die **Haselnüsse**) hazelnut.

Hass der hatred.

hassen verb (PERF **hat gehasst**) to hate.

hässlich adjective **1** ugly; **sie hat ein hässliches Gesicht** she's got an ugly face; **2** nasty; **das war sehr hässlich von dir** that was very nasty of you.

hast SEE **haben**.

hastig adjective hasty.

hat, hatte, hatten, hattest, hattet SEE **haben**.

Haube die (PL die **Hauben**) **1** bonnet; **2** cap.

hauen ⬦verb (PRES **haut**, IMPERF **haute**, PERF **hat gehauen**) **1** to beat; **2** to thump, to bang; **3 sich hauen** to fight; **4 jemanden übers Ohr hauen** (informal) to cheat somebody.

Haufen der (PL die **Haufen**) **1** heap; **2** crowd (of people); **3 ein Haufen** (informal) heaps of; **ein Haufen Geld** heaps of money.

haufenweise adverb heaps of; **Gabi hat haufenweise CDs** Gabi has heaps of CDs.

häufig adjective frequent.

Häufigkeit die frequency.

Hauptbahnhof der (PL die **Hauptbahnhöfe**) main station.

Hauptgericht das (PL die **Hauptgerichte**) main course.

Hauptrolle die (PL die **Hauptrollen**) lead.

Hauptsache die (PL die **Hauptsachen**) main thing.

hauptsächlich adjective main.

hauptsächlich adverb mainly.

Hauptschule die secondary school.

Hauptstadt die (PL die **Hauptstädte**) capital.

Hauptstraße die (PL die **Hauptstraßen**) main road.

Hauptverkehrszeit die (PL die **Hauptverkehrszeiten**) rush hour.

a
b
c
d
e
f
g
h
i
j
k
l
m
n
o
p
q
r
s
t
u
v
w
x
y
z

a

Hauptwort das (PL die Hauptwörter) noun.

b

Haus das (PL die Häuser) **1** house; **2 nach Hause** home; **zu Hause** at home.

c

d

Hausarbeit die (PL die Hausarbeiten) **1** housework; **die Kinder müssen bei der Hausarbeit helfen** the children have to help with the housework; **2** homework.

e

f

g

h

Hausaufgaben plural noun homework; **hast du deine Hausaufgaben gemacht?** have you done your homework?

i

j

Hausfrau die (PL die Hausfrauen) housewife.

k

Haushalt der (PL die Haushalte) **1** household; **2 den Haushalt machen** to do the housework; **im Haushalt helfen** to help with the housework; **3** budget.

l

m

n

Haushaltswarengeschäft das (PL die Haushaltswarengeschäfte) hardware shop.

o

p

Hausmeister der (PL die Hausmeister) caretaker.

q

Hausnummer die house number.

r

s

Hausschlüssel der (PL die Hausschlüssel) front-door key.

t

Hausschuh der (PL die Hausschuhe) slipper.

u

v

Haustier das (PL die Haustiere) pet.

w

Haustür die (PL die Haustüren) front door.

x

y

Haut die (PL die Häute) skin; **aus der Haut fahren** (informal) to go up the wall.

z

Hebamme die (PL die Hebammen) midwife.

Hebel der (PL die Hebel) lever.

heben ✧verb (IMPERF hob, PERF hat gehoben) **1** to lift; **2 sich heben** to rise.

Hecke die (PL die Hecken) hedge.

Heer das (PL die Heere) army.

Hefe die (PL die Hefen) yeast.

Heft das (PL die Hefte) **1** exercise book; **2** issue (of a magazine).

heften verb (PERF hat geheftet) **1** to pin; **2** to tack (by sewing); **3** to clip; **4** to staple.

heftig adjective **1** violent; **2** heavy (snow, rain).

Heftklammer die (PL die Heftklammern) staple.

Heftpflaster das (PL die Heftpflaster) sticking plaster.

Heftzwecke die (PL die Heftzwecken) drawing pin.

Heide die heath.

Heidekraut das heather.

Heidelbeere die (PL die Heidelbeeren) bilberry.

heilen verb (PERF hat geheilt) **1** to cure; **2** to heal.

heilig adjective **1** holy; **2 heilig halten** to hold sacred; **3 der heilige Franz von Assisi** Saint Francis of Assisi.

Heiligabend der (PL die Heiligabende) Christmas Eve.

Heilige der/die (PL die Heiligen) saint.

Heilmittel das (PL die **Heilmittel**) remedy.

Heim das (PL die **Heime**) **1** home; **2** hostel.

heim adverb home.

Heimat die (PL die **Heimaten**) **1** home; **2** native land.

Heimatstadt die home town.

Heimfahrt die (PL die **Heimfahrten**) **1** journey home; **2** way home.

heimgehen ◇verb (IMPERF **ging heim**, PERF **ist heimgegangen**) to go home.

heimlich adjective secret.

heimlich adverb secretly.

Heimspiel das (PL die **Heimspiele**) home game.

Heimweg der (PL die **Heimwege**) way home.

Heimweh das homesickness; **Heimweh haben** to be homesick.

Heirat die (PL die **Heiraten**) marriage.

heiraten verb (PERF **hat geheiratet**) to marry.

heiser adjective hoarse.

heiß adjective hot.

heißen ◇verb (IMPERF **hieß**, PERF **hat geheißen**) **1** to be called; **wie heißt du?** what's your name?; **2** to mean; **3 das heißt** that is; **4 es heißt it is** said; **5 wie heißt 'dog' auf Deutsch?** what's the German for 'dog'?

heiter adjective **1** bright; **2** cheerful.

heizen verb (PERF **hat geheizt**) **1** to heat (a room); **2** to put the heating on; **3** to have the heating on.

Heizung die heating.

hektisch adjective hectic.

Held der (PL die **Helden**) hero.

Heldin die (PL die **Heldinnen**) heroine.

helfen ◇verb (PRES **hilft**, IMPERF **half**, PERF **hat geholfen**) **1** to help; **Lisa hilft mir** Lisa is helping me; **2 es hilft nichts** it's no good; **3 sich zu helfen wissen** to know what to do; **ich weiß mir nicht zu helfen** I don't know what to do.

Helfer der (PL die **Helfer**) **1** helper; **2** assistant.

Helferin die (PL die **Helferinnen**) **1** helper; **2** assistant.

hell adjective **1** light (colour); **2** bright; **3 eine helle Stimme** a clear voice; **4 helles Bier** lager; **5 da ist heller Wahnsinn** (informal) that's sheer madness.

hellwach adjective wide awake.

Helm der (PL die **Helme**) helmet.

Hemd das (PL die **Hemden**) **1** shirt; **2** vest.

Henkel der (PL die **Henkel**) handle.

Henne die (PL die **Hennen**) hen.

her adverb **1** here; **komm her** come here; **2 vor jemandem her** in front of somebody; **3 hinter etwas her sein** to be after something; **4 von der Farbe her** as far as the colour is concerned; **5 wo bist du her?** where do you come from?; **6 wo hat Klaus das her?** where did Klaus

a b c d e f g h i j k l m n o p q r s t u v w x y z

get it from?; **7 her damit!** (*informal*) give it to me!; **8** ago; **das ist schon lange her** it was a long time ago; **das ist drei Tage her** it was three days ago.

herab *adverb* down.

herablassend *adjective* condescending.

herabsetzen *verb* (PERF **hat herabgesetzt**) **1** to reduce; **2** to belittle.

heran *adverb* **1 an etwas heran** close to something, right up to something; **bis an die Wand heran** up to the wall; **2 immer heran!** come closer!

herankommen ⋄*verb* (IMPERF **kam heran**, PERF **ist herangekommen**) **1** to come near; **2 herankommen an** to come up to; **3 ich komme nicht heran** I can't get at it.

herauf *adverb* up.

heraufkommen ⋄*verb* (IMPERF **kam herauf**, PERF **ist heraufgekommen**) to come up.

heraus *adverb* out.

herausbekommen ⋄*verb* (IMPERF **bekam heraus**, PERF **hat herausbekommen**) **1** to get out; **2** to find out; **3** to solve; **4 Geld herausbekommen** to get change.

herausbringen *verb* (IMPERF **brachte heraus**, PERF **hat herausgebracht**) **1** to publish (*a book*); **2** to release (*an album*); **3** to launch.

herausfinden ⋄*verb* (IMPERF **fand heraus**, PERF **hat herausgefunden**) **1** to find out; **2** to find your way out.

herausgeben ⋄*verb* (PRES **gibt heraus**, IMPERF **gab heraus**, PERF **hat herausgegeben**) **1** to hand over; **2** to bring out.

herauskommen ⋄*verb* (IMPERF **kam heraus**, PERF **ist herausgekommen**) to come out.

herausnehmen ⋄*verb* (PRES **nimmt heraus**, IMPERF **nahm heraus**, PERF **hat herausgenommen**) **1** to take out; **sie hat ihren Lippenstift aus der Tasche herausgenommen** she took her lipstick out of the bag; **2 sich die Mandeln herausnehmen lassen** to have your tonsils out; **3 es sich herausnehmen, etwas zu tun** to have the nerve to do something; **du nimmst dir zu viel heraus** you're going too far.

herausstellen *verb* (PERF **hat herausgestellt**) **1** to put out; **2 sich herausstellen** to turn out; **es stellte sich heraus, dass ...** it turned out that ....

herausziehen ⋄*verb* (IMPERF **zog heraus**, PERF **hat herausgezogen**) to pull out.

herb *adjective* **1** sharp; **2** dry (*wine*).

herbei *adverb* over (here); **kommt herbei** come over here!

Herberge *die* (PL **die Herbergen**) hostel.

Herbergsmutter *die* (PL **die Herbergsmütter**) warden (*in a youth hostel*).

Herbergsvater der (PL die Herbergsväter) warden (*in a youth hostel*).

herbringen ✧*verb* (IMPERF **brachte her**, PERF **hat hergebracht**) to bring (here).

Herbst der (PL die Herbste) autumn; **im Herbst** in autumn.

Herd der (PL die Herde) cooker.

Herde die (PL die Herden) **1** herd; **2** flock.

herein *adverb* in; **herein!** come in!

hereinfallen ✧*verb* (PRES **fällt herein**, IMPERF **fiel herein**, PERF **ist hereingefallen**) to be taken in; **auf einen Betrüger hereinfallen** to be taken in by a swindler.

hereinkommen ✧*verb* (IMPERF **kam herein**, PERF **ist hereingekommen**) to come in.

hereinlassen ✧*verb* (PRES **lässt herein**, IMPERF **ließ herein**, PERF **hat hereingelassen**) to let in; **Max lässt mich nicht ins Zimmer herein** Max won't let me into the room.

Herfahrt die (PL die Herfahrten) **1** journey here; **2** way here.

hergeben ✧*verb* (PRES **gibt her**, IMPERF **gab her**, PERF **hat hergegeben**) **1** to hand over; **gib die Tasche her!** hand over the bag!; **2** to give away; **3** **sich für etwas hergeben** to get involved in something; **dazu gebe ich mich nicht her** I won't have anything to do with it.

Hering der (PL die Heringe) herring.

herkommen ✧*verb* (IMPERF **kam her**, PERF **ist hergekommen**) to come (here); **wo kommt das her?** where does it come from?

Herkunft die (PL die Herkünfte) **1** origin; **2** background.

Heroin das heroin.

Herr der (PL die Herren) **1** gentleman; **2** **Herr Huber** Mr Huber; **3** **Sehr geehrte Herren** Dear Sirs (*in a letter*); **4** **meine Herren!** gentlemen!; **5** master; **6** **der Herr** the Lord.

herrichten *verb* (PERF **hat hergerichtet**) to get ready, to prepare; **sie richtet die Betten für die Gäste her** she's getting the beds for the guests ready.

herrlich *adjective* marvellous.

herrschen *verb* (PERF **hat geherrscht**) **1** to rule; **2** to be; **es herrschte große Aufregung** there was great excitement.

herstellen *verb* (PERF **hat hergestellt**) to manufacture, to make; **in Deutschland hergestellt** made in Germany.

Herstellung die (PL die Herstellungen) manufacture, production.

herüber *adverb* over (here).

herum *adverb* **um ... herum** round; **falsch herum** the wrong way round; **im Kreis herum** in a circle.

herumdrehen *verb* (PERF **hat herumgedreht**) **1** to turn (over or round); **2** **sich herumdrehen** to turn round.

a
b
c
d
e
f
g
h
i
j
k
l
m
n
o
p
q
r
s
t
u
v
w
x
y
z

herumführen verb (PERF **hat herumgeführt**) to show around.

herumgehen ◇verb (IMPERF **ging herum**, PERF **ist herumgegangen**) **1** to go round; **2** to walk around; **im Park herumgehen** to walk around the park; **3** to pass (of time).

herunter adverb down; **die Treppe herunter** down the stairs.

herunterfallen ◇verb (PRES **fällt herunter**, IMPERF **fiel herunter**, PERF **ist heruntergefallen**) **1** to fall down; **2** to fall off.

herunterkommen ◇verb (IMPERF **kam herunter**, PERF **ist heruntergekommen**) **1** to come down; **2** (informal) to go to rack and ruin.

herunterlassen ◇verb (PRES **lässt herunter**, IMPERF **ließ herunter**, PERF **hat heruntergelassen**) to let down, to lower.

hervor adverb out.

hervorragend adjective outstanding.

hervorragend adverb outstandingly well.

hervorrufen ◇verb (IMPERF **rief hervor**, PERF **hat hervorgerufen**) to cause.

Herz das (PL die **Herzen**) **1** heart; **2** hearts (in cards).

Herzanfall der (PL die **Herzanfälle**) heart attack.

Herzinfarkt der (PL die **Herzinfarkte**) heart attack.

herzlich adjective **1** warm; **2** sincere; **3 herzlichen Dank** many thanks; **4 herzliche Grüße** best wishes; **5 herzlichen Glückwunsch!** congratulations!; **6 herzlich willkommen in Passau!** welcome to Passau!

herzlos adjective heartless.

Herzschlag der (PL die **Herzschläge**) **1** heartbeat; **2** heart failure; **er hat einen Herzschlag bekommen** he had a heart attack.

heterosexuell adjective heterosexual.

Heterosexuelle der/die (PL die **Heterosexuellen**) heterosexual.

Heu das the hay.

heulen verb (PERF **hat geheult**) **1** to howl; **2** (informal) to cry.

Heuschnupfen der hayfever; **ich habe Heuschnupfen** I suffer from hayfever.

heute adverb today; **heute Abend** this evening; **heute Morgen** this morning.

heutig adjective **1** today's; **2 in der heutigen Zeit** nowadays.

heutzutage nowadays; **heutzutage sind sie häufig** they're common nowadays.

Hexe die (PL die **Hexen**) witch.

Hexenschuss der lumbago.

hielt SEE **halten**.

hier adverb here.

hierher adverb here; **komm sofort hierher!** come here immediately!

hierhin adverb here.

hiesig adjective local.

hieß SEE **heißen**.

Hilfe die (PL die **Hilfen**) **1** help; **2** aid.

hilflos adjective helpless.

hilfsbereit adjective helpful.

hilft SEE **helfen**.

Himbeere die (PL die **Himbeeren**) raspberry.

Himmel der (PL die **Himmel**) **1** sky; **2** heaven.

himmlisch adjective heavenly.

hin adverb **1** there; **hin und zurück** there and back; **2 hin und wieder** now and again; **3 hin und her** back and forth, to and fro; **4 auf meinen Rat hin** on my advice; **auf Ihren Brief hin** in reply to your letter; **5 wo ist Dominik hin?** where's Dominik gone?; **6 es ist nicht mehr lange hin** it's not long to go; **7 ich bin hin** (informal) I'm worn out.

hinauf adverb up; **die Straße hinauf** up the road.

hinaufgehen ◇verb (IMPERF ging hinauf, PERF ist hinaufgegangen) to go up.

hinaus adverb **1** out; **2 auf Jahre hinaus** for years to come.

hinausbringen ◇verb (IMPERF brachte hinaus, PERF hat hinausgebracht) **1** to see out (a person); **2** to take out; **den Abfall hinausbringen** to take the rubbish out.

hinausgehen ◇verb (IMPERF ging hinaus, PERF ist hinausgegangen) **1** to go out; **2 über etwas hinausgehen** to exceed something; **3 das Zimmer geht nach Norden hinaus** the room faces north.

hindern verb (PERF hat gehindert) to stop; **jemanden daran hindern, etwas zu tun** to stop somebody from doing something.

Hindernis das (PL die **Hindernisse**) obstacle.

hinduistisch adjective Hindu.

hindurch adverb **1** through it/ them; **2 das ganze Jahr hindurch** throughout the year.

hinein adverb **1** in; **2 in etwas hinein** into something.

hineingehen ◇verb (IMPERF ging hinein, PERF ist hineingegangen) **1** to go in; **2 in etwas hineingehen** to go into something.

hinfahren ◇verb (PRES fährt hin, IMPERF fuhr hin, PERF ist hingefahren) **1** to go/drive there; **2** (PERF hat hingefahren) to take/ drive there.

Hinfahrt die (PL die **Hinfahrten**) **1** journey there, way there; **2** outward journey.

hinfallen ◇verb (PRES fällt hin, IMPERF fiel hin, PERF ist hingefallen) to fall over.

hing SEE **hängen**.

hingehen ◇verb (IMPERF ging hin, PERF ist hingegangen) **1** to go there; **wo geht ihr hin?** where are you going?; **2** to go by (of time).

hinken verb (PERF hat/ist gehinkt) to limp.

hinkommen ◇verb (IMPERF kam hin, PERF ist hingekommen) **1** to get there; **2** to go; **wo kommt das Buch hin?** where does the book go?; **3 mit etwas hinkommen**

a b c d e f g h i j k l m n o p q r s t u v w x y z

a   (*informal*) to manage (with something).

hinlegen *verb* (PERF **hat hingelegt**)
1 to put down; **leg die Zeitung unten hin** put the paper down there; **2 sich hinlegen** to lie down.

hinsetzen *verb* (PERF **hat sich hingesetzt**) **sich hinsetzen** to sit down; **Petra setzte sich neben ihm hin** Petra sat down next to him.

hinten *adverb* at the back; **von hinten** from behind.

hinter *preposition* (+ DAT *or* + ACC)
1 behind; **2 etwas hinter sich bringen** to get something over with.

hintere SEE **hinterer**.

hintereinander *adverb* **1** one behind the other; **2** one after the other; **dreimal hintereinander** three times in a row.

hinterer, **hintere**, **hinteres** *adjective* **1** back; **2 am hinteren Ende** at the far end.

Hintergrund *der* (PL die **Hintergründe**) background.

hinterher *adverb* afterwards.

Hintern *der* (PL die **Hintern**) bottom.

Hinterrad *das* (PL die **Hinterräder**) back wheel.

hinters = **hinter das**.

hinüber *adverb* **1** over (there), across (there); **2 das Radio ist hinüber** (*informal*) the radio has had it.

hinübergehen ❖*verb* (IMPERF **ging hinüber**, PERF **ist**

hinübergegangen) to go over, to go across.

hinunter *adverb* down.

Hinweg *der* (PL die **Hinwege**) way there; **auf dem Hinweg** on the way there.

Hinweis *der* (PL die **Hinweise**)
1 hint; **das war ein deutlicher Hinweis, dass er lieber allein fährt** it was an obvious hint that he prefers to go on his own;
2 reference; **3 Hinweise zur Bedienung** operating instructions.

hinweisen ❖*verb* (IMPERF **wies hin**, PERF **hat hingewiesen**) to point; **jemanden auf etwas hinweisen** to point something out to somebody.

Hirn *das* (PL die **Hirne**) brain.

Hirnhautentzündung *die* meningitis.

Hirsch *der* (PL die **Hirsche**) **1** deer; **2** stag; **3** venison.

Hirt *der* (PL die **Hirten**) shepherd.

Hirtin *die* (PL die **Hirtinnen**) shepherd.

Historiker *der* (PL die **Historiker**) historian.

historisch *adjective* historical.

Hitze *die* heat.

hitzefrei *adjective* **hitzefrei haben** to be sent home early from school because of hot weather.

Hitzewelle *die* (PL die **Hitzewellen**) heatwave.

Hitzschlag *der* (PL die **Hitzschläge**) heatstroke.

hob SEE **heben**.

Hobby das (PL die **Hobbys**) hobby.

Hoch das (PL die **Hochs**) 1 cheer; **ein dreifaches Hoch für das Geburtstagskind** three cheers for the birthday girl/boy; 2 high (*pressure*).

hoch adjective (*with endings 'hoch' becomes 'hoher/hohe/hohes'*) 1 high; **der Zaun ist zu hoch** the fence is too high; **ein hoher Zaun** a high fence; 2 deep (*snow*); 3 great (*age, weight*).

hoch adverb 1 highly; **hoch begabt** highly gifted; 2 **die Treppe hoch** up the stairs.

hochachtungsvoll adverb **Hochachtungsvoll** Yours faithfully.

hochhackig adjective high-heeled; **hochhackige Schuhe** high-heeled shoes.

Hochhaus das (PL die **Hochhäuser**) high-rise building.

hochheben ◇verb (IMPERF **hob hoch**, PERF **hat hochgehoben**) to lift up; **sie hob das Kind hoch** she lifted up the child.

hochnäsig adjective stuck-up.

Hochschule die (PL die **Hochschulen**) university, college.

Hochsprung der high jump.

höchst adverb extremely.

höchstens adverb 1 at most; 2 except perhaps.

höchster, höchste, höchstes adjective highest; **der Mount Everest ist der der höchste Berg der Welt** Mount Everest is the highest mountain in the world; **es ist höchste Zeit** it is high time.

Höchstgeschwindigkeit die maximum speed.

höchstmöglich adjective highest possible; **die höchstmögliche Geschwindigkeit** the highest possible speed.

Höchsttemperatur die (PL die **Höchsttemperaturen**) maximum temperature.

Hochzeit die (PL die **Hochzeiten**) wedding.

Hochzeitstag der (PL die **Hochzeitstage**) 1 wedding day; 2 wedding anniversary.

Hocker der (PL die **Hocker**) stool.

Hockey das hockey.

Hockeyschläger der (PL die **Hockeyschläger**) hockey stick.

Hof der (PL die **Höfe**) 1 yard; 2 farm.

hoffen verb (PERF **hat gehofft**) to hope; **auf etwas hoffen** to hope for something.

hoffentlich adverb hopefully; **hoffentlich nicht** I hope not.

Hoffnung die (PL die **Hoffnungen**) hope.

hoffnungslos adjective hopeless.

höflich adjective polite.

Höflichkeit die (PL die **Höflichkeiten**) politeness, courtesy.

Höhe die (PL die **Höhen**) 1 height; 2 **das ist die Höhe!** (*informal*) that's the limit!

hoher, hohe, hohes SEE **hoch**.

höher adjective 1 higher; 2 deeper.

a b c d e f g h i j k l m n o p q r s t u v w x y z

a

hohl *adjective* hollow.

b

Höhle die (PL die **Höhlen**) **1** cave; **2** den.

c

holen *verb* (PERF **hat geholt**) **1** to get, to fetch; **2 jemanden holen lassen** to send for somebody; **3 sich etwas holen** to get something.

d

e

f

Holland das Holland.

g

Holländer der (PL die **Holländer**) Dutchman.

h

Holländerin die (PL die **Holländerinnen**) Dutchwoman.

i

holländisch *adjective* Dutch.

j

Hölle die (PL die **Höllen**) hell.

k

Holz das (PL die **Hölzer**) wood.

l

Holzkohle die charcoal.

m

homöopathisch *adjective* homeopathic.

n

homosexuell *adjective* homosexual.

o

Homosexuelle der/die (PL die **Homosexuellen**) homosexual.

p

Honig der (PL die **Honige**) honey.

q

horchen *verb* (PERF **hat gehorcht**) **1** to listen; **2** to eavesdrop.

r

hören *verb* (PERF **hat gehört**) **1** to hear; **2** to listen (to); **Musik hören** to listen to music.

s

t

Hörer der (PL die **Hörer**) **1** listener; **2** receiver (*of a phone*).

u

Hörerin die (PL die **Hörerinnen**) listener.

v

w

Hörgerät das (PL die **Hörgeräte**) hearing aid.

x

Horizont der (PL die **Horizonte**) horizon.

y

z

horizontal *adjective* horizontal.

Horn das (PL die **Hörner**) horn.

Horoskop das (PL die **Horoskope**) horoscope.

Horrorfilm der (PL die **Horrorfilme**) horror film.

Hose die (PL die **Hosen**) trousers.

Hosenträger *plural noun* braces.

Hotdog das or der (PL die **Hotdogs**) hot dog.

Hotel das (PL die **Hotels**) hotel.

Hotelverzeichnis das (PL die **Hotelverzeichnisse**) list of hotels.

hübsch *adjective* **1** pretty; **2** nice.

Hubschrauber der (PL die **Hubschrauber**) helicopter.

Huf der (PL die **Hufe**) hoof.

Hufeisen das (PL die **Hufeisen**) horseshoe.

Hüfte die (PL die **Hüften**) hip.

Hügel der (PL die **Hügel**) hill.

Huhn das (PL die **Hühner**) **1** chicken; **2** hen.

Hummel die (PL die **Hummeln**) bumble-bee.

Hummer der (PL die **Hummer**) lobster.

Humor der humour; **Humor haben** to have a sense of humour.

Hund der (PL die **Hunde**) dog; **den Hund ausführen** to take the dog for a walk.

Hundehütte die (PL die **Hundehütten**) kennel.

hundemüde *adjective* (*informal*) dog-tired.

Hundepension die (PL die Hundepensionen) kennels (for boarding).

hundert number a hundred, one hundred.

Hunger der hunger; **Hunger haben** to be hungry.

hungrig adjective hungry.

Hupe die (PL die Hupen) horn.

hurra exclamation hooray!.

Husten der cough.

husten verb (PERF **hat gehustet**) to cough.

Hut der (PL die Hüte) hat.

hüten verb (PERF **hat gehütet**) **1** to look after (a child, children); **2 sich hüten** to be on your guard; **3 sich hüten, etwas zu tun** to take care not to do something.

Hütte die (PL die Hütten) hut.

Hygiene die **1** hygiene; **2** health care.

hygienisch adjective hygienic.

hypnotisieren verb (PERF **hat hypnotisiert**) to hypnotize.

Hypothek die (PL die Hypotheken) mortgage.

hysterisch adjective hysterical.

Ii

ich pronoun I.

Icon das (PL die Icons) icon; **das Icon anklicken** to click the icon.

IC-Zug der (PL die IC-Züge) (Intercityzug) intercity train.

ideal adjective ideal.

Idee die (PL die Ideen) idea.

identifizieren verb (PERF **hat identifiziert**) to identify.

identisch adjective identical.

Idiot der (PL die Idioten) idiot.

idiotisch adjective idiotic.

idyllisch adjective idyllic.

Igel der (PL die Igel) hedgehog.

ihm pronoun **1** him, to him; **2** it, to it.

ihn pronoun **1** him; **2** it.

ihnen pronoun them, to them.

Ihr adjective your; **Ihr Sohn hat mir geschrieben** your son wrote to me.

ihr pronoun **1** you (plural); **2** her, to her; **3** (standing for an object) it, to it.

ihr adjective **1** her; **2** its; **3** their; **sie haben ihr Auto verkauft** they sold their car.

ihrer, ihre, ihr(e)s pronoun **1** hers; **mein Rad ist rot, ihrs ist blau** my bike is red, hers is blue; **2** theirs; **das ist nicht ihre Katze, ihre ist schwarz** that's not their cat, theirs is black.

Ihrer, Ihre, Ihr(e)s pronoun yours; **mein Job ist nicht so interessant wie Ihrer** my job's not as interesting as yours.

ihretwegen adverb **1** for her sake; **2** for their sake; **3** because of her; **4** because of them.

Ihretwegen adverb **1** for your sake; **2** because of you.

Illusion die (PL die Illusionen) illusion.

a
b
c
d
e
f
g
h
i
j
k
l
m
n
o
p
q
r
s
t
u
v
w
x
y
z

Illustration 132 GERMAN-ENGLISH

a

Illustration die (PL die Illustrationen) illustration.

b

Illustrierte die (PL die Illustrierten) magazine.

c

d

im = in dem; was läuft im Kino? what's on at the cinema?; im August in August.

e

f

Imbiss der (PL die Imbisse) 1 snack; 2 snack bar.

g

Imbissstube die (PL die Imbissstuben) snack bar.

h

Imitator der (PL die Imitatoren) mimic, impressionist.

j

imitieren verb (PERF hat imitiert) to imitate.

k

l

immer adverb 1 always; 2 immer wieder again and again; 3 immer mehr more and more; immer dunkler darker and darker; 4 immer noch still; 5 immer, wenn er anruft every time he rings; 6 wo/wer/wann immer wherever/whoever/whenever; 7 für immer for ever.

m

n

o

p

immerhin adverb at least.

q

immerzu adverb all the time.

r

Imperfekt das imperfect; 'ich schlug' steht im Imperfekt 'ich schlug' is in the imperfect.

s

t

Impfausweis der (PL die Impfausweise) vaccination certificate.

u

v

impfen verb (PERF hat geimpft) to vaccinate.

w

x

Impfung die (PL die Impfungen) vaccination.

y

z

imponieren verb (PERF hat imponiert) to impress; jemandem imponieren to impress somebody.

Import der (PL die Importe) import.

Importeur der (PL die Importeure) importer.

importieren verb (PERF hat importiert) to import.

imprägniert adjective waterproof.

imstande adverb imstande sein, etwas zu tun to be able to do something; er ist nicht imstande, seine Hausaufgaben allein zu machen he's not able to do his homework on his own.

in preposition (+ DAT or + ACC) (the dative is used when talking about position; the accusative shows movement towards something) 1 in; es ist in der Küche it's in the kitchen; 2 into, in; ich habe es in meine Tasche gesteckt I've put it in my bag; 3 in die Schule gehen to go to school; 4 Susi ist in der Schule Susi is at school; 5 in diesem Jahr this year; 6 in sein to be in; Rap ist in rap is in.

inbegriffen adjective included; Essen ist inbegriffen food is included.

indem conjunction 1 while; 2 by.

Inder der (PL die Inder) Indian.

Inderin die (PL die Inderinnen) Indian.

Indianer der (PL die Indianer) (American) Indian, native American.

Indianerin die (PL die **Indianerinnen**)(American) Indian, native American.

indianisch adjective (American) Indian, native American.

Indien das India.

indisch adjective Indian.

indiskutabel adjective out of the question.

individuell adjective individual.

Individuum das (PL die **Individuen**) individual.

Industrie die (PL die **Industrien**) industry.

industriell adjective industrial.

Infektion die (PL die **Infektionen**) infection.

Infinitiv der (PL die **Infinitive**) infinitive.

infizieren verb (PERF **hat infiziert**) 1 to infect; 2 **sich bei jemandem infizieren** to be infected by somebody.

Inflation die (PL die **Inflationen**) inflation.

infolge preposition (+ GEN) as a result of.

infolgedessen adverb consequently.

Informatik die computer science.

Informatiker der (PL die **Informatiker**) computer scientist.

Informatikerin die (PL die **Informatikerinnen**) computer scientist.

Information die (PL die **Informationen**) (piece of) information.

Informationsbüro das (PL die **Informationsbüros**) (tourist) information office.

informieren verb (PERF **hat informiert**) 1 to inform; 2 **informiert sein** to be aware; **da bist du falsch informiert** you've been wrongly informed; 3 **sich über etwas informieren** to find out about something; **ich habe mich darüber genau informieren lassen** I found out all about it.

Ingenieur der (PL die **Ingenieure**) engineer.

Ingenieurin die (PL die **Ingenieurinnen**) engineer.

Ingwer der ginger.

Inhaber der (PL die **Inhaber**) 1 owner (of a shop); 2 holder (of an office).

Inhaberin die (PL die **Inhaberinnen**) 1 owner (of a shop); 2 holder (of a position).

Inhalt der (PL die **Inhalte**) 1 contents; **den Inhalt der Dose mit etwas Wasser verdünnen** dilute the contents of the tin with a little water; 2 content (of a story, film); **er hat den Inhalt der Geschichte kurz für uns zusammengefasst** he gave us a quick summary of the content of the story; 3 volume; 4 area (of a rectangle, circle, etc.).

Initiative die (PL die **Initiativen**) initiative; **die Initiative ergreifen** to take the initiative.

inklusive preposition (+ GEN) including.

a
b
c
d
e
f
g
h
i
j
k
l
m
n
o
p
q
r
s
t
u
v
w
x
y
z

inklusive *adverb* inclusive.

innen *adverb* inside; **nach innen** inwards.

Innenstadt *die* (PL *die* **Innenstädte**) town centre, city centre.

Innere *das* **1** interior; **2** inside.

innerer, innere, inneres *adjective* **1** inner; **2** inside; **3** internal (*injuries*).

innerhalb *preposition* (+ GEN) **1** within; **2** during.

innerhalb *adverb* **innerhalb von** within.

innerlich *adjective* **1** internal; **2** inner.

innerlich *adverb* **1** internally; **2** inwardly.

ins = **in das**; **ins Theater gehen** to go to the theatre.

Insekt *das* (PL *die* **Insekten**) insect.

Insel *die* (PL *die* **Inseln**) island.

Inserat *das* (PL *die* **Inserate**) advertisement.

inserieren *verb* (PERF **hat inseriert**) to advertise.

insgesamt *adverb* in all.

Instinkt *der* (PL *die* **Instinkte**) instinct.

instinktiv *adjective* instinctive.

Instrument *das* (PL *die* **Instrumente**) instrument; **ein Instrument spielen** to play an instrument.

intelligent *adjective* intelligent.

Intelligenz *die* intelligence.

Intensivpflege *die* intensive care.

Intensivstation *die* (PL *die* **Intensivstationen**) intensive care unit.

Intercityzug *der* (PL *die* **Intercityzüge**) intercity train.

interessant *adjective* interesting.

Interesse *das* (PL *die* **Interessen**) interest; **Interesse für jemanden/etwas haben** to be interested in somebody/something.

interessieren *verb* (PERF **hat interessiert**) **1** to interest; **2 sich für etwas interessieren** to be interested in something.

Internat *das* (PL *die* **Internate**) boarding school.

international *adjective* international.

Internet *das* Internet.

Internetcafé *das* (PL *die* **Internetcafés**) Internet cafe; **wo gibt es hier ein Internetcafé?** where is there an Internet cafe?

Interview *das* (PL *die* **Interviews**) interview.

inzwischen *adverb* in the meantime, meanwhile.

Ire *der* (PL *die* **Iren**) Irishman; **die Iren** the Irish.

irgend *adverb* **1** at all; **wenn irgend möglich** if at all possible; **wenn du irgend kannst** if you could possibly manage it; **2 irgend so ein Idiot** some such idiot.

irgendein *adjective* **1** some; **2** any; **3 irgendein anderer** someone else, anyone else.

irgendeiner, irgendeine, irgendein(e)s *pronoun* **1** any one; **'welche möchten Sie?' - 'irgendeine'** 'which one would you like?' - 'any one'; **2** somebody, someone; **3** anybody, anyone; **hat irgendeiner angerufen?** has anybody phoned?

irgendetwas *pronoun* **1** something; **2** anything.

irgendjemand *pronoun* **1** somebody; **2** anybody, anyone.

irgendwann *adverb* **1** some time, at some time; **2** any time, at any time.

irgendwas (*informal*) SEE **irgendetwas.**

irgendwie *adverb* somehow.

irgendwo *adverb* **1** somewhere; **2** anywhere.

Irin *die* (PL *die* **Irinnen**) Irishwoman.

irisch *adjective* Irish.

Irisch *das* Irish (*language*).

Irland *das* Ireland.

ironisch *adjective* ironic.

irre *adjective* **1** mad, **2** (*informal*) incredible, fantastic (*party, song*).

irre *adverb* **irre gut** incredibly good.

irren *verb* (PERF **ist geirrt**) **1** to wander (about) (*when lost*); **2** (PERF **hat sich geirrt**) **sich irren** to be mistaken, to be wrong.

irrsinnig *adjective* **1** mad; **2** (*informal*) incredible.

Irrtum *der* (PL *die* **Irrtümer**) mistake.

Islam *der* Islam.

isst SEE **essen.**

ist SEE **sein.**

Italien *das* Italy.

Italiener *der* (PL *die* **Italiener**) Italian.

Italienerin *die* (PL *die* **Italienerinnen**) Italian.

italienisch *adjective* Italian.

Jj

ja *adverb* **1** yes; **2 ich glaube ja** I think so; **3 du kommst doch, ja?** you'll come, won't you?; **es passt doch, ja?** it fits, doesn't it?; **4 sag's ihm ja nicht!** don't (you dare) tell him, whatever you do!; **seid ja vorsichtig!** do be careful!; **5 es ist ja noch früh** it's still early; **ich kann ihn ja mal fragen, ob er mitkommen will** I could always ask him if he wants to come.

Jacht *die* (PL *die* **Jachten**) yacht.

Jacke *die* (PL *die* **Jacken**) **1** jacket; **2** cardigan.

Jackett *das* (PL *die* **Jacketts**) jacket.

Jagd *die* (PL *die* **Jagden**) **1** hunt; **2** hunting.

jagen *verb* (PERF **hat gejagt**) **1** to hunt; **2** to chase; **drei Polizisten jagten den Einbrecher, aber er hängte sie schnell ab** three policemen chased the burglar, but he soon shook them off; **meine Mutter hat mich aus dem Bett gejagt** (*informal*) my mother chased me out of bed; **3 jemanden**

a
b
c
d
e
f
g
h
i
j
k
l
m
n
o
p
q
r
s
t
u
v
w
x
y
z

a aus dem Haus jagen to throw somebody out of the house; **4 damit**
b **kannst du mich jagen** (*informal*) I can't stand that.

Jäger der (PL die **Jäger**) **1** hunter;
c **2** fighter (*aircraft*).

d **jäh** *adjective* sudden.

e **Jahr** das (PL die **Jahre**) **1** year; **in**
f **den sechzigen Jahren** in the sixties; **Kinder bis zu zwölf**
g **Jahren** children up to the age of twelve; **2 ein freiwilliges soziales**
h **Jahr (FSJ)** gap year (*during which socially useful work is done for*
i *subsistence payment*).

jahrelang *adverb* for years.

j **Jahrestag** der (PL die **Jahrestage**)
k anniversary.

Jahrestag der (PL die **Jahrestage**)
l anniversary.

m **Jahreszeit** die (PL die
Jahreszeiten) season.

n **Jahrgang** der (PL die **Jahrgänge**)
o **1** year; **2** vintage.

p **Jahrhundert** das (PL die
Jahrhunderte) century.

q **-jährig** *adjective* **eine**
dreißigjährige Frau a woman aged
r thirty; **eine zweijährige**
Verspätung a two-year delay.

s **jährlich** *adjective, adverb* yearly;
t **zweimal jährlich** twice a year.

u **Jahrmarkt** der (PL die **Jahrmärkte**)
fair.

v **Jahrtausend** das (PL die
w **Jahrtausende**) millennium.

x **Jahrzehnt** das (PL die **Jahrzehnte**)
y decade.
z

jähzornig *adjective* hot-tempered.

jammern *verb* (PERF **hat**
gejammert) to moan.

Januar der January.

Japan das Japan.

Japaner der (PL die **Japaner**)
Japanese.

Japanerin die (PL die
Japanerinnen) Japanese.

japanisch *adjective* Japanese.

jawohl *adverb* **1** yes; **2** certainly.

je *adverb* **1** ever; **besser denn je**
better than ever; **2** each; **sie**
kosten je zwanzig Euro they are
twenty euros each; **3 seit eh und**
je always; **4 je nach** depending on.

je *preposition* (+ ACC) per.

je *conjunction* **1 je mehr, desto**
besser the more the better; **2 je**
nachdem it depends.

Jeans *plural noun* jeans.

jede SEE **jeder.**

jedenfalls *adverb* in any case.

jeder, jede, jedes *adjective*
1 every; **jedes Mal** every time;
2 each; **3** any; **ohne jeden Grund**
without any reason.

jedes *pronoun* **1** everybody,
everyone; **2** each one; **3** anybody,
anyone; **das kann jeder** anybody
can do that.

jedermann *pronoun* everybody,
everyone.

jederzeit *adverb* at any time.

jedes SEE **jeder.**

jedesmal SEE **jeder.**

jedoch *adverb* however.

jemals *adverb* ever.

jemand *pronoun* **1** somebody, someone; **jemand hat das für dich abgegeben** sombody left this for you; **2** anybody, anyone; **hat jemand angerufen?** did anybody call?

jener, jene, jenes *adjective (used in elevated language and in literature)* **1** that; **2** those *(plural)*.

jenes *pronoun* **1** that one; **2** those *(plural)*.

jenseits *preposition* (+ GEN) (on) the other side of.

Jetlag *der* jet lag.

jetzt *adverb* now.

Job *der* (PL die **Jobs**) job.

jobben *verb (informal)* (PERF **hat gejobbt**) to work.

joggen *verb* (PERF **ist gejoggt**) to jog.

Jogginganzug *der* (PL die **Jogginganzüge**) tracksuit.

Joghurt *der* (PL die **Joghurt(s)**) yoghurt.

Johannisbeere *die* (PL die **Johannisbeeren**) **1 rote Johannisbeeren** redcurrants; **2 schwarze Johannisbeeren** blackcurrants.

Journalist *der* (PL die **Journalisten**) journalist.

Journalistin *die* (PL die **Journalistinnen**) journalist.

Joystick *der* (PL die **Joysticks**) joystick *(for computer games)*.

jubeln *verb* (PERF **hat gejubelt**) **1** to cheer; **2 Beifall jubeln** to applaud.

Jubiläum *das* (PL die **Jubiläen**) **1** anniversary; **2** jubilee.

Jude *der* (PL die **Juden**) Jew.

Judentum *das* Judaism.

Jüdin *die* (PL die **Jüdinnen**) Jew.

jüdisch *adjective* Jewish.

Jugend *die* youth.

Jugendherberge *die* (PL die **Jugendherbergen**) youth hostel.

Jugendklub *der* (PL die **Jugendklubs**) youth club.

Jugendliche *der/die* (PL die **Jugendlichen**) **1** young man/woman; **2 die Jugendlichen** youth, young people.

Jugendzentrum *das* (PL die **Jugendzentren**) youth centre.

Jugoslawien *das* Yugoslavia.

jugoslawisch *adjective* Yugoslavian.

Juli *der* July.

jung *adjective* **1** young; **2 Jung und Alt** young and old.

Junge¹ *der* (PL die **Jungen**) boy.

Junge² *das* (PL die **Jungen**) young *(animal)*.

Jungfrau *die* (PL die **Jungfrauen**) **1** virgin; **2** Virgo.

jüngster, jüngste, jüngstes *adjective* **1** youngest; **2** latest *(news, developments)*; **3 in jüngster Zeit** recently.

Juni *der* June.

Jury *die* (PL die **Jurys**) **1** jury; **2** judges *(in sport)*.

a b c d e f g h i j k l m n o p q r s t u v w x y z

Juwelier der (PL die **Juweliere**) jeweller.

Jux der (*informal*) laugh; **aus Jux** for a laugh.

Kk

Kabel das (PL die **Kabel**) **1** cable; **2** wire.

Kabelfernsehen das cable television.

Kabeljau der (PL die **Kabeljaus**) cod.

Kabine die (PL die **Kabinen**) **1** cabin; **2** cubicle (*for changing*); **3** car (*of a cable car*).

Kachel die (PL die **Kacheln**) tile.

Käfer der (PL die **Käfer**) beetle.

Kaffee der (PL die **Kaffee(s)**) coffee; **zwei Kaffee mit Milch bitte** two white coffees please.

Kaffeekanne die (PL die **Kaffeekannen**) coffee-pot.

Käfig der (PL die **Käfige**) cage.

kahl *adjective* **1** bald (*head*); **2** bare (*tree, walls*).

Kahn der (PL die **Kähne**) **1** barge; **2** rowing boat.

Kaiser der (PL die **Kaiser**) emperor.

Kaiserin die (PL die **Kaiserinnen**) empress.

Kakao der (PL die **Kakao(s)**) cocoa; **zwei Kakao bitte** two cups of cocoa please.

Kakerlak der (PL die **Kakerlaken**) cockroach.

Kaktus der (PL die **Kakteen**) cactus.

Kalb das (PL die **Kälber**) **1** calf; **2** veal.

Kalbfleisch das veal.

Kalender der (PL die **Kalender**) **1** calendar; **2** diary.

Kalk der **1** lime; **2** limescale; **3** calcium.

Kalorie die (PL die **Kalorien**) calorie.

kalorienarm *adjective* low-calorie, low in calories.

kalorienreich *adjective* high-calorie, rich in calories.

kalt *adjective* cold; **ist dir kalt?** are you cold?; **stell die Heizung an, den Kindern ist kalt** put on the heating, the children are cold; **abends essen wir kalt** we have a cold meal in the evening; **den Wein kalt stellen** to chill the wine.

Kälte die **1** cold; **2** coldness; **3 fünf Grad Kälte** five degrees below zero.

kam SEE **kommen**.

Kamel das (PL die **Kamele**) camel.

Kamera die (PL die **Kameras**) camera.

Kamerad der (PL die **Kameraden**) friend.

Kameradin die (PL die **Kameradinnen**) friend.

Kameramann der (PL die **Kameramänner**) cameraman.

Kamin der (PL die **Kamine**) fireplace; **wir saßen am Kamin** we sat by the fire.

Kamm der (PL die **Kämme**) **1** comb; **2** ridge (*of a mountain*).

kämmen *verb* (PERF **hat gekämmt**)
1 to comb; 2 **sich kämmen** to comb your hair.

Kammer *die* (PL *die* **Kammern**)
1 store room; 2 chamber.

Kampagne *die* (PL *die* **Kampagnen**) campaign.

Kampf *der* (PL *die* **Kämpfe**) 1 fight; 2 contest; 3 struggle.

kämpfen *verb* (PERF **hat gekämpft**) to fight.

Kanada *das* Canada.

Kanadier *der* (PL *die* **Kanadier**) Canadian.

Kanadierin *die* (PL *die* **Kanadierinnen**) Canadian.

kanadisch *adjective* Canadian.

Kanal *der* (PL *die* **Kanäle**) 1 canal; 2 channel (*radio, TV*); 3 **der Kanal** the (English) Channel; 4 sewer, drain.

Kanalinseln *plural noun* Channel Islands.

Kanalisation *die* sewers, drains.

Kanarienvogel *der* (PL *die* **Kanarienvögel**) canary.

Kandidat *der* (PL *die* **Kandidaten**) candidate.

Kandidatin *die* (PL *die* **Kandidatinnen**) candidate.

Känguru *das* (PL *die* **Kängurus**) kangaroo.

Kaninchen *das* (PL *die* **Kaninchen**) rabbit.

kann SEE **können**.

Kännchen *das* (PL *die* **Kännchen**) 1 pot; **ein Kännchen Kaffee bitte** a pot of coffee please; 2 jug (*of milk*).

Kanne *die* (PL *die* **Kannen**) 1 pot (*for coffee, tea*); 2 jug (*for water*); 3 can (*for oil*); 4 churn (*for milk*); 5 watering can.

kannst SEE **können**.

kannte SEE **kennen**.

Kante *die* (PL *die* **Kanten**) edge.

Kantine *die* (PL *die* **Kantinen**) canteen; **wir essen immer in der Kantine zu Mittag** we always have lunch in the canteen.

Kanu *das* (PL *die* **Kanus**) canoe; **Kanu fahren** to go canoeing.

Kapelle *die* (PL *die* **Kapellen**) 1 chapel; 2 (brass) band.

kapieren *verb* (*informal*) (PERF **hat kapiert**) to understand; **er hat es mir schon dreimal erklärt, aber ich kapier es einfach nicht** he's already explained it to me three times, but I still don't get it.

Kapital *das* capital.

Kapitalismus *der* capitalism.

Kapitän *der* (PL *die* **Kapitäne**) captain.

Kapitel *das* (PL *die* **Kapitel**) chapter.

Kappe *die* (PL *die* **Kappen**) cap.

kaputt *adjective* 1 broken; 2 **an meinem Computer ist etwas kaputt** there's something wrong with my computer; 3 **ich bin kaputt** (*informal*) I'm shattered.

kaputtgehen ◇*verb* (*informal*) (IMPERF **ging kaputt**, PERF **ist kaputtgegangen**) 1 to break; 2 to pack up; **mein Fernseher ist mitten im Fußballspiel kaputtgegangen** the television

a b c d e f g h i j k l m n o p q r s t u v w x y z

packed up in the middle of the football match; **4** to wear out (*of clothing*); **4** to break up (*of a marriage or friendship*).

kaputtmachen *verb* (*informal*) (PERF **hat kaputtgemacht**) **1** to break; **er macht alle seine Spielsachen kaputt** he breaks all his toys; **2** to ruin (*clothes, furniture*); **3** to finish off (*a person*); **die viele Arbeit macht mich ganz kaputt** all this work is wearing me out; **4** sich kaputtmachen to wear yourself out.

Kapuze *die* (PL **die Kapuzen**) hood.

Karamell *der* (PL **die Karamells**) caramel.

Karfreitag *der* Good Friday.

Karibik *die* **die Karibik** the Caribbean.

karibisch *adjective* Caribbean.

kariert *adjective* **1** check; **ein karierter Rock** a check skirt; **2** squared (*paper*).

Karneval *der* (PL **die Karnevale**) carnival.

Karo *das* (PL **die Karos**) **1** square; **2** diamonds (*in cards*).

Karotte *die* (PL **die Karotten**) carrot.

Karpfen *der* (PL **die Karpfen**) carp.

Karriere *die* (PL **die Karrieren**) career; **Karriere machen** to get to the top.

Karte *die* (PL **die Karten**) **1** card; **ich schicke euch eine Karte aus Italien** I'll send you a card from Italy; **2** card (*for playing*); **wir haben den ganzen Abend Karten**

gespielt we played cards all evening; **gute/schlechte Karten haben** to have a good/bad hand; **3** ticket; **gibt es noch Karten für das Popfestival?** can you still get tickets for the pop festival?; **4** menu; **5** map; **ich kann Oberammergau nicht auf der Karte finden** I can't find Oberammergau on the map; **6** alles auf eine Karte setzen to put all your eggs in one basket.

Kartenspiel *das* (PL **die Kartenspiele**) **1** card game; **2** pack of cards.

Kartoffel *die* (PL **die Kartoffeln**) potato.

Kartoffelbrei *der* mashed potatoes.

Kartoffelchips *plural noun* potato crisps.

Karton *der* (PL **die Kartons**) **1** cardboard; **2** cardboard box.

Karussell *das* (PL **die Karussells**) merry-go-round; **Karussell fahren** to go on the merry-go-round.

Käse *der* cheese.

Käsekuchen *der* (PL **die Käsekuchen**) cheesecake.

Kaserne *die* (PL **die Kasernen**) barracks.

Kasse *die* (PL **die Kassen**) **1** till; **2** checkout; **an der Kasse zahlen** pay at the checkout; **3** cash desk (*in a bank*); **4** box-office; **Sie können die Karten an der Kasse abholen** you can collect the tickets from the box office; **5** ticket office (*at a sports stadium*); **Sie müssen sich**

an der Kasse anstellen you have to queue at the ticket office; **6** health insurance; **7 knapp bei Kasse sein** (*informal*) to be short of money; **gut bei Kasse sein** (*informal*) to be in the money.

Kassenzettel der (PL die **Kassenzettel**) receipt.

Kassette die (PL die **Kassetten**) **1** cassette, tape; **ich habe den neuen Song auf Kassette aufgenommen** I've taped the new song; **2** box (*for money, jewellery*).

Kassettenrekorder der (PL die **Kassettenrekorder**) cassette recorder.

kassieren verb (PERF **hat kassiert**) **1** to collect the money; **2** to collect the fares; **3 wie viel hat er kassiert?** how much did he charge you?; **4 darf ich bei Ihnen kassieren?** would you like to pay now? (*your bill in a restaurant*); **5** (*informal*) to take away (*a driving licence, for example*).

Kassierer der (PL die **Kassierer**) cashier.

Kassiererin die (PL die **Kassiererinnen**) cashier.

Kastanie die (PL die **Kastanien**) chestnut.

Kasten der (PL die **Kästen**) **1** box; **2** crate; **ein Kasten Bier** a crate of beer; **3** bin; **4** letter-box; **5 was auf dem Kasten haben** (*informal*) to be brainy.

Katalog der (PL die **Kataloge**) catalogue.

Katalysator der (PL die **Katalysatoren**) catalytic converter.

katastrophal adjective, adverb **1** catastrophic; **2 sie hat katastrophal schlecht abgeschnitten** she came out terribly badly.

Katastrophe die (PL die **Katastrophen**) catastrophe.

Kategorie die (PL die **Kategorien**) category.

Kater der (PL die **Kater**) **1** tom-cat; **2 einen Kater haben** (*informal*) to have a hangover.

Kathedrale die (PL die **Kathedralen**) cathedral.

Katholik der (PL die **Katholiken**) Catholic.

Katholikin die (PL die **Katholikinnen**) Catholic.

katholisch adjective Catholic.

Kätzchen das (PL die **Kätzchen**) kitten.

Katze die (PL die **Katzen**) cat.

kauen verb (PERF **hat gekaut**) to chew.

kauern verb (PERF **hat gekauert**) to crouch.

Kauf der (PL die **Käufe**) **1** purchase; **2 ein guter Kauf** a bargain; **3 etwas in Kauf nehmen** to put up with something.

kaufen verb (PERF **hat gekauft**) to buy.

Käufer der (PL die **Käufer**) buyer.

Käuferin die (PL die **Käuferinnen**) buyer.

a
b
c
d
e
f
g
h
i
j
k
l
m
n
o
p
q
r
s
t
u
v
w
x
y
z

Kauffrau die (PL die **Kauffrauen**) businesswoman.

Kaufhaus das (PL die **Kaufhäuser**) department store.

Kaufmann der (PL die **Kaufleute**) businessman.

Kaugummi der (PL die **Kaugummis**) chewing gum.

Kaulquappe die (PL die **Kaulquappen**) tadpole.

kaum adverb hardly, scarcely.

Kaution die (PL die **Kautionen**) 1 deposit; 2 bail.

Kegel der (PL die **Kegel**) 1 cone; 2 skittle.

Kegelbahn die skittle alley.

kegeln verb (PERF **hat gekegelt**) to play skittles.

Kehle die (PL die **Kehlen**) throat.

Keim der (PL die **Keime**) 1 shoot; 2 germ.

kein adjective 1 no; **auf keinen Fall** on no account; 2 **ich habe keine Zeit** I haven't got any time; **er hat kein Geld** he hasn't got any money; 3 **keine zehn Minuten** less than ten minutes.

keiner, keine, kein(e)s pronoun 1 nobody, no one; 2 none, not one; 3 **von diesen Kleidern gefällt mir keins** I don't like any of these dresses; 4 **keiner von beiden** neither (of them).

keinesfalls adverb on no account.

keineswegs adverb by no means.

keinmal adverb not once.

keins SEE **keiner**.

Keks der (PL die **Kekse**) biscuit.

Keller der (PL die **Keller**) cellar.

Kellergeschoss das (PL die **Kellergeschosse**) basement.

Kellner der (PL die **Kellner**) waiter.

Kellnerin die (PL die **Kellnerinnen**) waitress.

kennen ✧verb (IMPERF **kannte**, PERF **hat gekannt**) 1 to know; 2 **kennen lernen** to get to know; **sich kennen lernen** to get to know each other; 3 **kennen lernen** to meet; **ich habe Ulrike in London kennen gelernt** I met Ulrike in London; **wo habt ihr euch kennen gelernt?** where did you meet?

kennenlernen SEE **kennen**.

Kenntnis die (PL die **Kenntnisse**) 1 knowledge; 2 **etwas zur Kenntnis nehmen** to take note of something.

Kennzeichen das (PL die **Kennzeichen**) 1 mark; 2 characteristic; 3 registration (number) (of a vehicle).

Kerl der (PL die **Kerle**) 1 bloke; 2 **Eva ist ein netter Kerl** Eva's a nice girl.

Kern der (PL die **Kerne**) 1 pip; 2 stone (of an apricot, peach); 3 kernel (of a nut).

Kernenergie die nuclear power.

Kernkraftwerk das (PL die **Kernkraftwerke**) nuclear power station.

Kernwaffen plural noun nuclear weapons.

Kerze die (PL die **Kerzen**) candle.

Kerzenhalter der (PL die **Kerzenhalter**) candlestick.

Kessel der (PL die **Kessel**) 1 kettle;
2 boiler.

Kette die (PL die **Ketten**) chain.

Keule die (PL die **Keulen**) 1 club;
2 leg (of lamb); 3 drumstick (of
chicken).

kichern verb (PERF **hat gekichert**)
to giggle.

Kiefer[1] der (PL die **Kiefer**) jaw.

Kiefer[2] die (PL die **Kiefern**) pine
tree.

Kiefernzapfen der (PL die
Kiefernzapfen) cone.

Kieselstein der (PL die
Kieselsteine) pebble.

Kilo das (PL die **Kilo(s)**) kilo.

Kilogramm das (PL die
Kilogramme) kilogram.

Kilometer der (PL die **Kilometer**)
kilometre.

Kind das (PL die **Kinder**) child.

Kindergarten der (PL die
Kindergärten) nursery school.

Kindergeld das child benefit.

Kinderkrippe die (PL die
Kinderkrippen) crèche.

kinderleicht adjective very easy;
das ist kinderleicht it's child's play.

Kindertagesstätte die (PL die
Kindertagesstätten) day nursery.

Kinderwagen der (PL die
Kinderwagen) pram.

Kindheit die childhood.

kindisch adjective childish.

Kinn das (PL die **Kinne**) chin.

Kino das (PL die **Kinos**) cinema.

Kiosk das (PL die **Kioske**) kiosk (for
newspapers or snacks).

kippen verb (PERF **hat gekippt**) 1 to
tip; 2 (PERF **ist gekippt**) to topple.

Kirche die (PL die **Kirchen**) church.

Kirsche die (PL die **Kirschen**)
cherry.

Kissen das (PL die **Kissen**)
1 cushion; 2 pillow.

Kiste die (PL die **Kisten**) 1 crate;
2 box.

kitzeln verb (PERF **hat gekitzelt**) to
tickle.

kitzlig adjective ticklish.

Kiwi die (PL die **Kiwis**) kiwi fruit.

klagen verb (PERF **hat geklagt**) to
complain.

Klammer die (PL die **Klammern**)
1 peg (for washing); 2 grip (for
hair); 3 bracket.

Klammeraffe die (PL die
Klammeraffen) at, @ (in email
addresses); dieter-punkt-schmidt-
Klammeraffe-einfachkom-punkt-
com dieter-dot
schmidt@einfachkom-dot-com.

Klamotten plural noun gear
(clothes).

Klang der (PL die **Klänge**) sound.

klang SEE **klingen**.

Klappe die (PL die **Klappen**) 1 flap;
2 clapperboard; 3 (informal) trap
(mouth); halt die Klappe! shut up!

klappen verb (PERF **hat geklappt**)
1 nach vorne klappen to tilt
forward; 2 nach hinten klappen to
tip back; 3 nach oben klappen to
lift up; 4 nach unten klappen to

a
b
c
d
e
f
g
h
i
j
k
l
m
n
o
p
q
r
s
t
u
v
w
x
y
z

a
b
c
d
e
f
g
h
i
j
k
l
m
n
o
p
q
r
s
t
u
v
w
x
y
z

put down; **5** to work out;
hoffentlich klappt es I hope it'll
work out.

Klappstuhl der (PL die
Klappstühle) folding chair.

klar adjective **1** clear (water,
answer); **klar werden** to become
clear; **2 jetzt ist mir alles klar** now
I understand; **3 sich klar werden**
to make up your mind; **4 sich über
etwas im Klaren sein** to realize
something.

klar adverb clearly; **na klar!**
(informal) of course!

klären verb (PERF **hat geklärt**) **1** to
clarify; **2** to sort out; **3** to purify
(sewage); **4 sich klären** to clear (of
the weather or the sky); **5 sich
klären** to resolve itself, to be
settled.

Klarinette die (PL die **Klarinetten**)
clarinet.

klarwerden SEE **klar**.

Klasse die (PL die **Klassen**) **1** class;
erster Klasse reisen to travel first
class; **2** year; **in die sechste
Klasse gehen** to be in year six.

klasse adjective (informal) great,
smashing.

Klassenarbeit die (PL die
Klassenarbeiten) (written) test.

Klassenbuch das register (kept
by the teacher, it also contains notes
about students' achievements).

Klassenfahrt die (PL die
Klassenfahrten) school trip.

Klassenkamerad der (PL die
Klassenkameraden) class-mate.

Klassenkameradin die (PL die
Klassenkameradinnen) class-
mate.

Klassensprecher der (PL die
Klassensprecher) class
representative.

Klassensprecherin die (PL die
Klassensprecherinnen) class
representative.

Klassenzimmer das (PL die
Klassenzimmer) classroom.

klassisch adjective classical.

Klatsch der gossip.

klatschen verb (PERF **hat
geklatscht**) **1** to clap; **jemandem
Beifall klatschen** to applaud
somebody, to applaud somebody;
2 to slap; **3** to gossip.

klauen verb (informal) (PERF **hat
geklaut**) to pinch.

Klavier das (PL die **Klaviere**) piano.

kleben verb (PERF **hat geklebt**) **1** to
stick; **2** to glue; **3 jemandem eine
kleben** (informal) to belt somebody
one.

klebrig adjective sticky.

Klebstoff der (PL die **Klebstoffe**)
glue.

Klebstreifen der (PL die
Klebstreifen) sticky tape.

Klecks der (PL die **Kleckse**) stain.

Kleid das (PL die **Kleider**) **1** dress;
**Uschi hat sich zwei neue Kleider
gekauft** Uschi bought two new
dresses; **2 Kleider** clothes.

Kleiderbügel der (PL die
Kleiderbügel) coat hanger.

Kleiderschrank der (PL die Kleiderschränke) wardrobe.

Kleidung die clothes, clothing.

klein adjective **1** small, little; **etwas klein schneiden** to cut something up small; **2** short, **Peter ist kleiner als Klaus** Peter is shorter than Klaus.

Kleingarten der (PL die Kleingärten) allotment (used mainly as garden).

Kleingeld das change.

Klempner der (PL die Klempner) plumber.

klettern verb (PERF ist geklettert) to climb.

Klick der (PL die Klicks) click (with mouse).

Klicken das click (noise).

Klient der (PL die Klienten) client.

Klientin die (PL die Klientinnen) client.

Klima das (PL die Klimas) climate.

Klimaanlage die (PL die Klimaanlagen) air conditioning.

Klinge die (PL die Klingen) blade.

Klingel die (PL die Klingeln) bell.

klingeln verb (PERF hat geklingelt) to ring; **es klingelt** there's a ring at the door.

klingen ◇verb (IMPERF klang, PERF hat geklungen) to sound.

Klinik die (PL die Kliniken) clinic.

Klinke die (PL die Klinken) handle.

Klippe die (PL die Klippen) rock.

Klo das (informal) (PL die Klos) loo.

klopfen verb (PERF hat geklopft) **1** to knock; **2** to beat.

Klosett das (PL die Klosetts) lavatory.

Kloß der (PL die Klöße) dumpling.

Kloster das (PL die Kloster) **1** monastery; **2** convent.

Klotz der (PL die Klötze) block.

Klub der (PL die Klubs) club.

klug adjective **1** clever; **2 ich werde daraus nicht klug** I don't understand it.

Klugheit die cleverness.

Klumpen der (PL die Klumpen) lump.

knabbern verb (PERF hat geknabbert) to nibble.

Knäckebrot das (PL die Knäckebrote) crispbread.

knacken verb (PERF hat geknackt) to crack.

Knall der (PL die Knalle) bang.

knallen verb (PERF hat geknallt) **1** to go bang; **2** to pop (of a cork); **3** to slam (of a door); **4** to crack (of a whip).

knapp adjective **1** scarce, **2** tight (skirt, top); **3 knapp bei Kasse sein** to be short of money; **4 mit knapper Mehrheit** by a narrow majority; **5** just; **eine knappe Stunde** just under an hour; **sie haben knapp verloren** they only just lost; **6 das war knapp** (informal) that was a close shave.

knarren verb (PERF hat geknarrt) to creak.

Knauf der (PL die Knäufe) knob.

a
b
c
d
e
f
g
h
i
j
k
l
m
n
o
p
q
r
s
t
u
v
w
x
y
z

a

knautschen *verb* (PERF **hat geknautscht**) **1** to crumple; **2** to crease.

b

c

kneifen ⋄*verb* (IMPERF **kniff**, PERF **hat gekniffen**) **1** to pinch; **2** (*informal*) to chicken out; **sie hat mal wieder gekniffen und nichts gesagt** she's chickened out yet again and didn't say anything.

d

e

f

g

Kneipe *die* (PL *die* **Kneipen**) pub.

kneten *verb* (PERF **hat geknetet**) to knead.

h

i

knicken *verb* (PERF **hat geknickt**) **1** to bend; **2** to fold.

j

Knie *das* (PL *die* **Knie**) knee.

k

knien *verb* (PERF **hat gekniet**) **1** to kneel; **2 sich knien** to kneel down.

l

kniff SEE **kneifen.**

m

knipsen *verb* (PERF **hat geknipst**) (*to photograph*) to take a snap, to take snaps.

n

o

Knoblauch *der* garlic.

p

Knoblauchzehe *die* (PL *die* **Knoblauchzehen**) clove of garlic.

q

r

Knöchel *der* (PL *die* **Knöchel**) **1** ankle; **2** knuckle; **Mario hat sich beim Joggen den Knöchel verstaucht** Mario sprained his ankle when jogging.

s

t

u

Knochen *der* (PL *die* **Knochen**) bone.

v

Knopf *der* (PL *die* **Knöpfe**) button.

w

x

Knoten *der* (PL *die* **Knoten**) **1** knot; **2** bun (*as a hairstyle*); **3** lump.

y

z

Knüller *der* (PL *die* **Knüller**) scoop (*in journalism*).

knurren *verb* (PERF **hat geknurrt**) **1** to growl; **2** to rumble; **3** to grumble.

knusprig *adjective* crisp, crusty (*bread*).

Koalabär *der* (PL *die* **Koalabären**) koala bear.

Koch *der* (PL *die* **Köche**) **1** cook; **2** chef.

Kochbuch *das* (PL *die* **Kochbücher**) cookery book.

kochen *verb* (PERF **hat gekocht**) **1** to cook; **2** to boil; **das Wasser kocht** the water's boiling.

Köchin *die* (PL *die* **Köchinnen**) cook.

Kochtopf *der* (PL *die* **Kochtöpfe**) saucepan.

Koffer *der* (PL *die* **Koffer**) suitcase.

Kofferkuli *der* (PL *die* **Kofferkulis**) baggage trolley.

Kofferraum *der* (PL *die* **Kofferräume**) boot.

Kohl *der* **1** cabbage; **2** (*informal*) rubbish; **rede keinen Kohl** don't talk rubbish.

Kohle *die* (PL *die* **Kohlen**) coal.

Kohlrübe *die* (PL *die* **Kohlrüben**) swede.

Kokain *das* cocaine.

Kokosnuss *die* (PL *die* **Kokosnüsse**) coconut.

Kollege *der* (PL *die* **Kollegen**) colleague.

Kollegin *die* (PL *die* **Kolleginnen**) colleague.

Köln *das* Cologne.

Kölnischwasser das eau de cologne.

Kombination die (PL die **Kombinationen**) combination.

Komfort der comfort.

Komiker der (PL die **Komiker**) comedian.

komisch adjective funny.

Komma das (PL die **Kommas**) 1 comma; 2 decimal point; **zwei Komma fünf** two point five.

kommen ◇verb (IMPERF **kam**, PERF **ist gekommen**) 1 to come; 2 to get; **wie komme ich zur U-Bahn?** how do I get to the tube station?; **kommt gut nach Hause!** have a safe journey home!; 3 **etwas kommen lassen** to send for something; 4 **wie kommst du darauf?** what gave you that idea?; 5 **hinter etwas kommen** to find out about something; 6 **zur Schule kommen** to start school; 7 to go; **die Gabeln kommen in die Schublade** the forks go in the drawer; **ins Krankenhaus kommen** to go to hospital; 8 **wer kommt zuerst?** who's first?; **du kommst an die Reihe** it's your turn; 9 **wie kommt das?** why is that?; 10 **zu etwas kommen** to acquire something; 11 **wieder zu sich kommen** to come round (after fainting or anaesthetic); 12 **dazu kommen, etwas zu tun** to get round to doing something; **ich komme einfach nicht zum Einkaufen** I just can't get round to doing the shopping; 13 **das kommt davon!** see what happens!

Kommissar der (PL die **Kommissare**) superintendent.

Kommode die (PL die **Kommoden**) chest of drawers.

Kommunismus der communism.

Kommunist der (PL die **Kommunisten**) communist.

Kommunistin die (PL die **Kommunistinnen**) communist.

kommunizieren verb (PERF **hat kommuniziert**) to communicate.

Komödie die (PL die **Komödien**) comedy.

Kompass der (PL die **Kompasse**) compass.

komplett adjective complete.

Kompliment das (PL die **Komplimente**) compliment.

kompliziert adjective complicated.

Komponist der (PL die **Komponisten**) composer.

Komponistin die (PL die **Komponistinnen**) composer.

Kompott das (PL die **Kompotte**) stewed fruit.

Kompromiss der (PL die **Kompromisse**) compromise; **einen Kompromiss schließen** to compromise.

Konditional das (verb tense) conditional.

Konditorei die (PL die **Konditoreien**) patisserie, cake shop.

Kondom das (PL die **Kondome**) condom.

a b c d e f g h i j k l m n o p q r s t u v w x y z

a

Konfektion die ready-made clothes.

b

Konferenz die (PL die Konferenzen) conference.

c

Konflikt der (PL die Konflikte) conflict.

d

König der (PL die Könige) king.

e

Königin die (PL die Königinnen) queen.

f

königlich adjective royal.

g

Königreich das (PL die Königreiche) kingdom.

h

Konjunktion die (PL die Konjunktionen) conjunction.

i

Konkurrent der (PL die Konkurrenten) competitor.

j

Konkurrentin die (PL die Konkurrentinnen) competitor.

k

Konkurrenz die competition.

l

können ◇verb (PRES kann, IMPERF konnte, PERF hat gekonnt) **1** can; **kann ich Ihnen helfen?** can I help you?; **kannst du Auto fahren?** can you drive?; **kannst du Deutsch?** can you speak German?; **ich konnte nicht früher kommen** I couldn't come any earlier; **das kann ich nicht** I can't do that; **2 etwas können** to be able to do something; **er wird es vor Dienstag nicht machen können** he won't be able to do it before Tuesday; **3 das kann gut sein** that may well be so; **es kann sein, dass ... it may be that ...; **4 ich kann nichts dafür** it's not my fault.

m

n

o

p

q

r

s

t

u

v

w

x

y

Können das ability.

z

Könner der (PL die Könner) expert.

könnt SEE können.

konnte, konnten, konntest, konntet SEE können.

Konrektor der (PL die Konrektoren) deputy headteacher, deputy headmaster.

Konrektorin die (PL die Konrektorinnen) deputy headteacher.

Konserven plural noun tinned food.

Konsonant der (PL die Konsonanten) consonant.

Konstruktion die (PL die Konstruktionen) construction (in grammar).

Konsul der (PL die Konsuln) consul.

Konsulat das (PL die Konsulate) consulate.

konsultieren verb (PERF hat konsultiert) to consult.

Kontakt der (PL die Kontakte) contact.

Kontaktlinse die (PL die Kontaktlinsen) contact lens.

Kontinent der (PL die Kontinente) continent.

Konto das (PL die Konten) account.

Kontrolle die (PL die Kontrollen) **1** check; **2** control.

Kontrolleur der (PL die Kontrolleure) inspector.

kontrollieren verb (PERF hat kontrolliert) **1** to check; **2** to control.

konzentrieren verb (PERF hat konzentriert) **1** to concentrate;

2 sich konzentrieren to concentrate.

Konzert das (PL die **Konzerte**) **1** concert; **2** concerto.

Kopf der (PL die **Köpfe**) **1** head; **2 sich den Kopf zerbrechen** to rack your brains; **3 seinen Kopf durchsetzen** to get your own way; **4 sich den Kopf waschen** to wash your hair; **5 auf dem Kopf** upside down; **6 ein Kopf Salat** a lettuce.

köpfen verb (PERF hat **geköpft**) **1** to head (in football); **2** to behead.

Kopfhörer der (PL die **Kopfhörer**) headphones.

Kopfkissen das (PL die **Kopfkissen**) pillow.

Kopfsalat der (PL die **Kopfsalate**) lettuce.

Kopfschmerzen plural noun headache.

Kopie die (PL die **Kopien**) copy.

kopieren verb (PERF hat **kopiert**) **1** to copy; **2** to photocopy.

Kopiergerät das (PL die **Kopiergeräte**) photocopier.

Korb der (PL die **Körbe**) **1** basket; **2 jemandem einen Korb geben** to turn somebody down.

Kork der (PL die **Korke**) cork.

Korken der (PL die **Korken**) cork.

Korkenzieher der (PL die **Korkenzieher**) corkscrew.

Korn das (PL die **Körner**) **1** corn (in general); **2** grain (a seed).

Körper der (PL die **Körper**) body.

körperbehindert adjective disabled.

Körpergeruch der (PL die **Körpergerüche**) body odour.

körperlich adjective physical.

Korrektur die (PL die **Korrekturen**) correction.

korrigieren verb (PERF hat **korrigiert**) to correct.

Korsika das Corsica.

koscher adjective kosher.

Kosmetik die (PL die **Kosmetika**) **1** cosmetics; **2** beauty care.

Kost die food.

kostbar adjective precious.

Kosten plural noun **1** cost; **2** expenses.

kosten verb (PERF hat **gekostet**) **1** to cost; **2 wie viel kostet es?** how much is it?; **3** to taste.

kostenlos adjective free (of charge).

köstlich adjective **1** delicious; **2** funny.

Kostüm das (PL die **Kostüme**) **1** suit; **2** costume.

Kotelett das (PL die **Koteletts**) chop.

Krabbe die (PL die **Krabben**) **1** crab; **2** shrimp.

krabbeln verb (PERF ist **gekrabbelt**) to crawl.

Krach der **1** row; **2** noise; **3** crash.

krachen verb (PERF hat **gekracht**) **1** to crash; **2** (PERF ist **gekracht**) to crack; **er ist gegen die Mauer gekracht** he crashed into the wall.

krächzen verb (PERF hat **gekrächzt**) to croak.

Kraft die (PL die **Kräfte**) **1** strength; **er hat nicht viel Kraft** he's not very strong; **2** force; **in Kraft treten** to come into force; **3 geistige Kräfte** mental powers; **4** worker.

kräftig adjective **1** strong; **2** nourishing.

kräftig adverb **1** strongly; **2** hard; **kräftig schütteln** shake hard.

Kraftwerk das (PL die **Kraftwerke**) power station.

Kragen der (PL die **Kragen**) collar.

Krähe die (PL die **Krähen**) crow.

Kralle die (PL die **Krallen**) claw.

Kram der stuff; **mach deinen Kram allein!** (informal) do it yourself!

kramen verb (PERF **hat gekramt**) to rummage about.

Krampf der (PL die **Krämpfe**) cramp.

Kran der (PL die **Kräne**) crane (machine).

Kranich der (PL die **Kraniche**) crane (bird).

krank adjective ill, sick; **krank werden** to fall ill.

Kranke der/die (PL die **Kranken**) patient.

kränken verb (PERF **hat gekränkt**) to hurt.

Krankenhaus das (PL die **Krankenhäuser**) hospital; **sie haben ihn gestern ins Krankenhaus eingeliefert** he was taken to hospital yesterday.

Krankenkasse die health insurance; **bei welcher Krankenkasse sind Sie versichert?** what health insurance have you got?

Krankenpfleger der (PL die **Krankenpfleger**) (male) nurse.

Krankenpflegerin die (PL die **Krankenpflegerinnen**) nurse.

Krankenschwester die (PL die **Krankenschwestern**) nurse; **Ulrike ist Krankenschwester** Ulrike is a nurse.

Krankenversicherung die (PL die **Krankenversicherungen**) medical insurance.

Krankenwagen der (PL die **Krankenwagen**) ambulance.

Krankheit die (PL die **Krankheiten**) illness, disease.

kratzen verb (PERF **hat gekratzt**) to scratch.

Kratzer der (PL die **Kratzer**) scratch.

kraus adjective frizzy.

Kraut das (PL die **Kräuter**) **1** herb; **2** sauerkraut; **3** cabbage.

Kräutertee der (PL die **Kräutertees**) herbal tea.

Krawall der (PL die **Krawalle**) **1** riot; **2** row.

Krawatte die (PL die **Krawatten**) tie.

kreativ adjective creative.

Krebs der (PL die **Krebse**) **1** crab; **2** cancer; **3** Cancer.

Kredit der (PL die **Kredite**) **1** loan (by a bank); **auf Kredit** on credit; **2** credit (reputation).

Kreditkarte die (PL die **Kreditkarten**) credit card.

Kreide die (PL die **Kreiden**) chalk.

kreieren verb (PERF hat kreiert) to create.

Kreis der (PL die Kreise) 1 circle; 2 district.

Kreislauf der 1 cycle; 2 circulation.

Kreuz das (PL die Kreuze) 1 cross; 2 (small of the) back; 3 intersection (of a motorway); 4 clubs (in cards).

kreuzen verb (PERF hat gekreuzt) 1 to cross; 2 sich kreuzen to cross.

Kreuzfahrt die (PL die Kreuzfahrten) 1 cruise; eine Kreuzfahrt machen to go on a cruise; 2 crusade.

Kreuzung die (PL die Kreuzungen) 1 crossroads; 2 cross (of plants, animals).

Kreuzworträtsel das (PL die Kreuzworträtsel) crossword (puzzle).

kriechen ◇verb (IMPERF kroch, PERF ist gekrochen) to crawl.

Krieg der (PL die Kriege) war.

kriegen verb (Informal) (PERF hat gekriegt) 1 to get; 2 ein Kind kriegen to have a baby.

Krimi der (PL die Krimis) thriller.

Kriminalroman der (PL die Kriminalromane) crime novel.

kriminell adjective criminal.

Kriminelle der/die (PL die Kriminellen) criminal.

Krippe die (PL die Krippen) 1 manger; 2 crib; 3 crèche.

Krise die (PL die Krisen) crisis.

Kristall¹ der (PL die Kristalle) crystal.

Kristall² das (glass) crystal.

kritisch adjective critical.

kritisieren verb (PERF hat kritisiert) 1 to criticize; 2 to review.

kroch SEE kriechen.

Krokodil das (PL die Krokodile) crocodile.

Krone die (PL die Kronen) crown.

Kröte die (PL die Kröten) toad.

Krücke die (PL die Krücken) crutch.

Krug der (PL die Krüge) 1 jug; 2 mug.

Krümel der (PL die Krümel) crumb.

krümelig adjective crumbly.

krumm adjective 1 bent; 2 crooked.

Kruste die (PL die Krusten) crust.

Küche die (PL die Küchen) 1 kitchen; 2 cooking; die italienische Küche Italian cooking; 3 warme Küche hot food.

Kuchen der (PL die Kuchen) cake.

Kuckuck der (PL die Kuckucke) cuckoo.

Kugel die (PL die Kugeln) 1 ball; 2 bullet; 3 sphere; wieviele Kugeln Eis möchtest du? how many scoops of ice-cream would you like?

Kugelschreiber der (PL die Kugelschreiber) ballpoint pen, biro.

Kuh die (PL die Kühe) cow.

kühl adjective cool.

kühlen verb (PERF hat gekühlt) 1 to cool, to chill; 2 to refrigerate.

Kühler der (PL die Kühler) radiator.

a
b
c
d
e
f
g
h
i
j
l
m
n
o
p
q
r
s
t
u
v
w
x
y
z

a **Kühlerhaube** die (PL die Kühlerhauben) bonnet.

b **Kühlschrank** der (PL die Kühlschränke) fridge.

c **Kühltruhe** die (PL die Kühltruhen) freezer.

d **Küken** das (PL die Küken) chick.

e **Kuli** der (PL die Kulis) biro.

f **Kultur** die (PL die Kulturen) 1 culture; 2 civilization.

g **Kulturbeutel** der (PL die Kulturbeutel) toilet bag.

h **kulturell** adjective cultural.

Kummer der 1 sorrow; 2 worry; 3 trouble.

j

k **kümmern** verb (PERF hat gekümmert) 1 to concern; 2 sich um jemanden kümmern to look after somebody; sich um den Garten kümmern to look after the garden; 3 sich darum kümmern, dass … to see to it that …; 4 kümmere dich um deine eigenen Angelegenheiten mind your own business.

l

m

n

o

p **Kunde** der (PL die Kunden) 1 customer; 2 client.

q **Kundendienst** der 1 customer services (department); 2 after-sales service.

r

s

t **kündigen** verb (PERF hat gekündigt) 1 to cancel; 2 to give notice; die Firma hat ihm gekündigt the company gave him his notice; 3 seine Stellung kündigen to hand in your notice.

u

v

w

x

y **Kundin** die (PL die Kundinnen) 1 customer; 2 client.

z

Kundschaft die customers.

Kunst die (PL die Künste) 1 art; 2 skill.

Kunstausstellung die (PL die Kunstausstellungen) art exhibition.

Künstler der (PL die Künstler) artist.

Künstlerin die (PL die Künstlerinnen) artist.

künstlerisch adjective artistic.

künstlich adjective artificial.

Kunststoff der (PL die Kunststoffe) plastic.

Kunststück das (PL die Kunststücke) 1 trick; 2 feat.

Kunstwerk das (PL die Kunstwerke) work of art.

Kupfer das copper.

Kupplung die (PL die Kupplungen) 1 clutch (of a car); 2 coupling.

Kürbis der (PL die Kürbisse) pumpkin.

Kurier der (PL die Kuriere) courier (delivery person).

Kurierdienst der (PL die Kurierdienste) courier service.

Kurort der (PL die Kurorte) health resort.

Kurs der (PL die Kurse) 1 course; 2 exchange rate; 3 price (of shares).

Kurve die (PL die Kurven) 1 curve; 2 bend.

kurz *adjective* **1** short; **vor kurzem** a short time ago; **2 zu kurz kommen** to get less than your fair share, to come off badly.

kurz *adverb* **1** shortly; **2** briefly; **3 kurz gesagt** in a word.

Kurzarbeit *die* short-time working.

kurzärmelig *adjective* short-sleeved.

kürzen *verb* (PERF **hat gekürzt**) **1** to shorten; **2** to cut.

kurzfristig *adjective* short-term.

kurzfristig *adverb* at short notice.

kürzlich *adverb* recently.

kurzsichtig *adjective* short-sighted.

Kurzwaren *plural noun* haberdashery.

Kusine *die* (PL die **Kusinen**) cousin.

Kuss *der* (PL die **Küsse**) kiss.

küssen *verb* (PERF **hat geküsst**) **1** to kiss; **2 sich küssen** to kiss.

Küste *die* (PL die **Küsten**) coast.

Kuvert *das* (PL die **Kuverts**) envelope.

Ll

Labor *das* (PL die **Labors**) laboratory.

Lache *die* (PL die **Lachen**) pool.

lächeln *verb* (PERF **hat gelächelt**) to smile.

lachen *verb* (PERF **hat gelacht**) to laugh.

lächerlich *adjective* ridiculous.

Lachs *der* (PL die **Lachse**) salmon.

Lack *der* (PL die **Lacke**) **1** varnish; **2** paint.

lackieren *verb* (PERF **hat lackiert**) **1** to varnish; **2** to spray (*with paint*).

laden ◇*verb* (PRES **lädt**, IMPERF **lud**, PERF **hat geladen**) **1** to load; **wir haben die Möbel in den Möbelwagen geladen** we loaded the furniture into the removal van; **2 eine Batterie laden** to charge a battery; **3** to summon; **mein Bruder wurde als Zeuge geladen** my brother was summoned as a witness.

Laden *der* (PL die **Läden**) **1** shop; **wann macht der Laden zu?** when does the shop close?; **wenn es heiß ist, lassen wir die Läden den ganzen Tag zu** when it's hot we keep the shutters closed all day.

Ladendieb *der* (PL die **Ladendiebe**) shoplifter.

Ladung *die* (PL die **Ladungen**) **1** cargo; **2** charge (*of dynamite or shot*); **3** summons; **4** load.

lag SEE **liegen.**

Lage *die* (PL die **Lagen**) **1** situation; **nicht in der Lage sein, etwas zu tun** not be in a position to do something; **2** layer.

Lager *das* (PL die **Lager**) **1** camp; **2** warehouse; **3** stock; **etwas auf Lager haben** to have something in stock; **4** stock-room; **5** bearing (*in a machine*).

lagern verb (PERF **hat gelagert**)
1 to store; **2** to camp.

lahm adjective lame.

lähmen verb (PERF **hat gelähmt**) to
paralyse.

Lähmung die paralysis.

Laib der (PL die **Laibe**) loaf.

Laken das (PL die **Laken**) sheet.

Lakritze die liquorice.

Lamm das (PL die **Lämmer**) lamb.

Lampe die (PL die **Lampen**) lamp.

Lampenschirm der (PL die
Lampenschirme) lampshade.

Lancieren das launch (of
product).

Land das (PL die **Länder**) **1** country;
auf dem Land in the country;
2 land; **3** state (there are 16 Länder
in Germany).

Landebahn die (PL die
Landebahnen) runway.

landen verb (PERF **ist gelandet**)
1 to land; **2 im Krankenhaus
landen** (informal) to end up in
hospital.

Landkarte die (PL die **Landkarten**)
map.

Landkreis der (PL die **Landkreise**)
district.

ländlich adjective rural.

Landschaft die (PL die
Landschaften) **1** countryside;
2 landscape.

Landschaftsschutzgebiet
das (PL die
Landschaftsschutzgebiete)
conservation area.

Landstraße die (PL die
Landstraßen) country road.

landwirtschaftlich adjective
agricultural.

Landtag der state parliament.

Landwirtschaft die agriculture,
farming.

lang adjective **1** long; **seit langem**
for a long time; **2** tall.

lang adverb **eine Woche lang** for a
week.

langärmelig adjective long-
sleeved.

Länge die (PL die **Längen**) **1** length;
2 longitude.

lange adverb **1** a long time; **lange
nicht** not for a long time; **2 so
lange wie möglich** as long as
possible; **3 er ist lange nicht so
reich** he's nowhere near as rich.

langen verb (PERF **hat gelangt**) **1** to
be enough; **das Geld langt nicht**
(informal) it's not enough money;
mir langt's (informal) I've had
enough; **2** to reach; **nach etwas
langen** to reach for something;
3 jemandem eine langen
(informal) to slap somebody's face.

Langlauf der cross-country (in
skiing).

langsam adjective, adverb slow;
**die Musik geht mir langsam auf
die Nerven** the music is slowly
getting on my nerves.

längst adverb **1** a long time ago;
**das habe ich schon längst
gemacht** I did it a long time ago;
2 for a long time; **er weiß es schon
längst** he's known it for a long

time; **3 längst nicht** nowhere near, not nearly.

längster, **längste**, **längstes** *adjective* longest; **Marion hat den längsten Aufsatz geschrieben** Marion wrote the longest essay.

langweilen *verb* (PERF **hat gelangweilt**) **1** to bore; **sich langweilen** to be bored.

langweilig *adjective* boring.

Lappen der (PL die **Lappen**) cloth, rag.

Laptop der (PL die **Laptops**) laptop.

Lärm der noise; **sich über den Lärm beschweren** to complain about the noise.

las SEE **lesen**.

Laser der (PL die **Laser**) laser.

Lasordrucker der (PL die **Laserdrucker**) laser printer.

Laseroperation die laser surgery.

Laserstrahl der (PL die **Laserstrahlen**) laser beam.

lassen ◇*verb* (PRES **lässt**, IMPERF **ließ**, PERF **hat gelassen**) **1** to let; **jemanden schlafen lassen** to let somebody sleep; **lass uns jetzt gehen** let's go now; **2 jemandem etwas lassen** to let somebody have something; **3** to leave; **die Kinder zu Hause lassen** to leave the children at home; **lass mich!** leave me!; **4 jemanden warten lassen** to keep somebody waiting; **5 etwas reparieren lassen** to have something repaired; **6 lass das!** stop it!; **7 die Tür lässt sich leicht öffnen** the door opens easily; **das**

lässt sich alles machen that can all be arranged.

lässig *adjective* casual.

Last die (PL die **Lasten**) **1** load; **2 jemandem zur Last fallen** to be a burden on somebody.

lästig *adjective* troublesome.

Lastwagen der (PL die **Lastwagen**) lorry, truck.

Latein das Latin.

Laterne die (PL die **Laternen**) **1** lantern; **2** street lamp.

Laub das leaves.

Lauch der leek(s).

Lauf der (PL die **Läufe**) **1** run; **2** course; **im Laufe der Zeit** in the course of time; **im Laufe der Jahre** over the years; **3** race; **4** barrel (of a gun).

Laufbahn die (PL die **Laufbahnen**) career.

laufen ◇*verb* (PRES **läuft**, IMPERF **lief**, PERF **ist gelaufen**) **1** to run; **sie kann viel schneller laufen als ihr Bruder** she can run much faster than her brother; **2** to walk; **du kannst nach Hause laufen oder mit dem Bus fahren** you can walk home or go on the bus; **3** to be valid; **4 Ski laufen** to ski; **5** to be on (of a film, programme, or machine).

laufend *adjective* **1** running; **2** current (issue, month); **3 auf dem Laufenden sein** to be up to date; **Anita hält mich auf dem Laufenden** Anita keeps me up to date.

laufend *adverb* continually, constantly.

a b c d e f g h i j k l m n o p q r s t u v w x y z

Läufer der (PL die **Läufer**) **1** runner; **2** rug; **3** bishop (in chess).

Läuferin die (PL die **Läuferinnen**) runner.

Laufmasche die (PL die **Laufmaschen**) ladder (in your tights).

Laufwerk das (PL die **Laufwerke**) drive (on a computer).

Laune die (PL die **Launen**) mood.

launisch adjective moody.

Laus die (PL die **Läuse**) louse.

Laut der (PL die **Laute**) sound.

laut adjective **1** loud; **2** noisy.

laut adverb **1** loudly; **2** laut lesen to read aloud; **3** lauter stellen to turn up.

laut preposition (+ GEN or + DAT) according to.

lauten verb (PERF hat gelautet) **1** to be; **2** to go.

läuten verb (PERF hat geläutet) to ring.

lauter adjective nothing but.

Lautsprecher der (PL die **Lautsprecher**) (loud)speaker.

Lautstärke die volume.

lauwarm adjective lukewarm.

Lavendel der lavender.

Lawine die (PL die **Lawinen**) avalanche.

Leben das (PL die **Leben**) life; am Leben sein to be alive; ums Leben kommen to lose your life.

leben verb (PERF hat gelebt) **1** to live; **2** to be alive; **3** leb wohl! farewell!

lebend adjective living.

lebendig adjective **1** living; **2** lebendig sein to be alive; **3** lively.

Lebensgefahr die mortal danger; sein Vater ist in Lebensgefahr his father is critically ill.

lebensgefährlich adjective **1** extremely dangerous; **2** critical; lebensgefährlich verletzt critically injured.

Lebenshaltungskosten plural noun cost of living.

lebenslänglich adjective life.

lebenslänglich adverb for life.

Lebenslauf der (PL die **Lebensläufe**) CV.

Lebensmittel plural noun food, groceries.

Lebensmittelgeschäft das (PL die **Lebensmittelgeschäfte**) grocer's (shop).

Lebensmittelvergiftung die (PL die **Lebensmittelvergiftungen**) food poisoning.

Lebensunterhalt der livelihood; seinen Lebensunterhalt verdienen to earn one's living.

Leber die (PL die **Lebern**) liver.

Leberfleck der (PL die **Leberflecke**) mole.

Leberwurst die liver sausage.

Lebewesen das (PL die **Lebewesen**) living being, living thing.

lebhaft adjective **1** lively; **2** vivid (idea, colour).

Lebkuchen der (PL die Lebkuchen) gingerbread.

leblos adjective lifeless.

Leck das (PL die Lecks) leak.

lecken verb (PERF hat geleckt) 1 to lick; **die Katze leckte ihre Jungen** the cat licked the kittens; **an etwas lecken** to lick something; 2 to leak.

lecker adjective delicious.

Leder das (PL die Leder) leather.

ledig adjective single.

lediglich adverb merely.

leer adjective ompty; **leer machen** to empty.

leeren verb (PERF hat geleert) 1 to empty; 2 **ein leeres Blatt Papier** a blank sheet of paper; 3 **sich leeren** to empty.

Leerlauf der neutral (gear).

Leerung die (PL die Leerungen) collection.

legal adjective legal.

legen verb (PERF hat gelegt) 1 to put; 2 to lay; 3 **sich legen** to lie down; 4 **sich legen** to die down (of a storm, noise); **unsere Begeisterung hat sich gelegt** our enthusiasm has worn off.

loger adjective, adverb casual; **leger gekleidet sein** to be casually dressed.

Lehm der clay.

Lehne die (PL die Lehnen) 1 back (of a chair); 2 arm (of a sofa or chair).

lehnen verb (PERF hat gelehnt) 1 to lean; 2 **sich an etwas lehnen** to lean against something.

Lehrbuch das (PL die Lehrbücher) textbook.

lehren verb (PERF hat gelehrt) to teach.

Lehrer der (PL die Lehrer) 1 teacher; 2 instructor.

Lehrerin die (PL die Lehrerinnon) 1 teacher; 2 instructor.

Lehrerzimmer das (PL die Lehrerzimmer) staffroom.

Lehrling der (PL die Lehrlinge) 1 apprentice; 2 trainee.

Lehrplan der (PL die Lehrpläne) syllabus.

Lehrstelle die (PL die Lehrstellen) apprenticeship, trainee post.

Leibwächter der (PL die Leibwächter) bodyguard.

Leiche die (PL die Leichen) (dead) body, corpse.

leicht adjective 1 light; 2 easy; **jemandem leicht fallen** to be easy for somebody; **es ist ihm nicht leicht gefallen** it wasn't easy for him; **Markus macht es sich immer leicht** Markus always takes the easy way out; 3 **ein leichter Akzent** a slight accent.

Leichtathletik die athletics.

leichtfallen SEE leicht.

Leichtsinn der 1 carelessness; 2 recklessness.

leichtsinnig adjective 1 careless; 2 reckless.

Leid das 1 sorrow; 2 harm; 3 **es tut mir Leid** I'm sorry; **Andreas tut mir Leid** I feel sorry for Andreas.

a

b

c

d

e

f

g

h

i

j

k

l

m

n

o

p

q

r

s

t

u

v

w

x

y

z

leid *adjective* jemanden leid sein to be fed up with somebody; **etwas leid sein** to be fed up with something.

leiden ◇*verb* (IMPERF litt, PERF hat gelitten) 1 to suffer; 2 jemanden gut leiden können to like somebody; 3 ich kann Erika nicht leiden I can't stand Erika.

leider *adverb* 1 unfortunately; 2 leider ja I'm afraid so; leider nicht I'm afraid not.

leihen ◇*verb* (IMPERF lieh, PERF geliehen) 1 to lend; 2 sich etwas leihen to borrow something; ich habe mir das Buch von Alex geliehen I borrowed the book from Alex.

Leihgabe die (PL die Leihgaben) loan (*by a bank*).

Leihwagen der (PL die Leihwagen) hire car.

Leim der (PL die Leime) glue.

Leine die (PL die Leinen) 1 rope; 2 line (*for washing*); 3 lead (*for a dog*).

Leinen das (PL die Leinen) linen.

Leinwand die (PL die Leinwände) screen (*in a cinema*).

leise *adjective* quiet.

leise *adverb* 1 quietly; 2 die Musik leiser stellen to turn the music down.

leisten *verb* (PERF hat geleistet) 1 to achieve; 2 jemandem Hilfe leisten to help somebody; 3 jemandem Gesellschaft leisten to keep somebody company; 4 sich etwas leisten to treat yourself to

something; **5 sich etwas leisten können** to be able to afford something; **ich kann mir kein neues Auto leisten** I can't afford a new car.

Leistung die (PL die Leistungen) 1 achievement; 2 performance; 3 Leistungen payment.

Leistungskurs der (PL die Leistungskurse) main subject.

leiten *verb* (PERF hat geleitet) 1 to lead; 2 to direct; 3 to manage, run (*a business*); 4 to conduct.

Leiter[1] die (PL die Leitern) ladder.

Leiter[2] der (PL die Leiter) 1 leader; 2 head; 3 manager; 4 director; 5 conductor (*of an orchestra or electricity*).

Leiterin die (PL die Leiterinnen) 1 leader; 2 head; 3 manageress; 4 director.

Leitung die (PL die Leitungen) 1 direction; 2 management; 3 (*phone*) line; 4 (*electric*) lead; 5 cable; 6 pipe; 7 unter der Leitung von conducted by.

Leitungswasser das tap water.

Lektion die (PL die Lektionen) lesson.

lenken *verb* (PERF hat gelenkt) 1 to steer; 2 to guide; 3 den Verdacht auf jemanden lenken to throw suspicion on somebody.

Lenkrad das (PL die Lenkräder) steering wheel.

Lenkstange die (PL die Lenkstangen) handlebars.

lernen *verb* (PERF **hat gelernt**) **1** to learn; **schwimmen lernen** to learn to swim; **2** to study.

lesbisch *adjective* lesbian.

lesen ◊*verb* (PRES **liest**, IMPERF **las**, PERF **hat gelesen**) to read.

Leser *der* (PL die **Leser**) reader.

Leseratte *die* (PL die **Leseratten**) bookworm.

Leserin *die* (PL die **Leserinnen**) reader.

Letzte *der/die/das* (PL die **Letzten**) **1** der/die **Letzte** the last (one); **das Letzte** the last (thing); **2** Boris **kam als Letzter** Boris arrived last.

letzte SEE letzter.

letztens *adverb* **1** recently; **2** lastly.

letzter, letzte, letztes *adjective* **1** last; **zum letzten Mal** for the last time; **das letzte Mal** the last time; **2** latest (*news, information*); **3** in **letzter Zeit** recently.

leuchten *verb* (PERF **hat geleuchtet**) to shine.

Leuchter *der* (PL die **Leuchter**) candlestick.

Leuchtreklame *die* neon sign.

Leuchtturm *der* (PL die **Leuchttürme**) lighthouse.

leugnen *verb* (PERF **hat geleugnet**) to deny.

Leukämie *die* leukaemia.

Leute *plural noun* people.

Lexikon *das* (PL die **Lexika**) **1** encyclopaedia; **2** dictionary.

Licht *das* (PL die **Lichter**) light.

Lichtbild *das* (PL die **Lichtbilder**) photograph.

Lichtschalter *der* (PL die **Lichtschalter**) light switch.

Lid *das* (PL die **Lider**) (eye)lid.

Lidschatten *der* (PL die **Lidschatten**) eye shadow.

lieb *adjective* **1** dear; **liebe Gabi** dear Gabi; **2** nice; **das ist lieb von euch** that's nice of you; **3 jemanden lieb haben** to be fond of somebody; **4 es wäre mir lieber, wenn** ... I'd prefer it if ...; **5 ihr liebstes Spielzeug** her favourite toy.

Liebe *die* (PL die **Lieben**) love.

lieben *verb* (PERF **hat geliebt**) to love.

liebenswürdig *adjective* kind.

lieber *adverb* **1** rather; **2 lieber mögen** to like better; **3 lass das lieber** you'd better not do that; **4 ich trinke lieber Kaffee** I prefer coffee.

Liebesbrief *der* (PL die **Liebesbriefe**) love letter.

Liebesfilm *der* (PL die **Liebesfilme**) romantic film.

Liebeskummer *der* **Liebeskummer haben** to be lovesick.

liebevoll *adjective* loving.

liebhaben SEE lieb.

Liebling *der* (PL die **Lieblinge**) **1** darling; **2** favourite.

Lieblings- *prefix* favourite.

liebster, liebste, liebstes *adjective* **1** dearest; **2** favourite.

liebstes adverb am liebsten best (of all); **ich mag Max am liebsten** I like Max best.

Lied das (PL die **Lieder**) song.

lief SEE **laufen**.

liefern verb (PERF **hat geliefert**) 1 to deliver; 2 to supply.

Lieferung die (PL die **Lieferungen**) delivery.

Lieferwagen der (PL die **Lieferwagen**) (delivery) van.

liegen ◇verb (IMPERF **lag**, PERF **hat gelegen**) 1 to lie; **der Brief liegt auf dem Tisch** the letter is on the table; **es liegt viel Schnee** there's lots of snow; 2 to be, to be situated; 3 **liegen bleiben** to stay (in bed); **er ist liegen geblieben** he didn't get up; 4 **etwas bleibt liegen** something is left behind; **die Arbeit ist liegen geblieben** the job was left undone; 5 **der Schnee bleibt liegen** the snow is settling; 6 **liegen lassen** to leave; 7 **es liegt mir nicht** it doesn't suit me; 8 **an etwas liegen** to be due to something; 9 **das liegt an ihm** it's up to him.

liegenbleiben, **liegenlassen** SEE **liegen**.

Liegestuhl der (PL die **Liegestühle**) deckchair.

Liegewagen der (PL die **Liegewagen**) couchette (car).

ließ SEE **lassen**.

liest SEE **lesen**.

Lift der (PL die **Lifte**) lift.

Liga die (PL die **Ligen**) league.

lila adjective 1 purple; 2 mauve.

Limo die (PL die **Limo(s)**) SEE **Limonade**.

Limonade die (PL die **Limonaden**) 1 fizzy drink; 2 lemonade.

Limone die (PL die **Limonen**) lime.

Lineal das (PL die **Lineale**) ruler.

Linie die (PL die **Linien**) 1 line; 2 route (of a bus); **Linie 6** number 6.

Linienflug der (PL die **Linienflüge**) scheduled flight.

Linke die 1 left; **zu meiner Linken** on my left; 2 left hand; 3 left side; 4 **die Linke** the left (in politics).

linker, **linke**, **linkes** adjective 1 left; 2 left-wing.

links adverb 1 on the left; **links fahren** to drive on the left; **links abbiegen** to turn left; **nach links** left; **von links** from the left; 2 **links sein** to be left-wing; 3 **zwei links, zwei rechts stricken** to purl two, knit two; 4 (clothing) inside out.

Linkshänder der (PL die **Linkshänder**) left-hander.

Linkshänderin die (PL die **Linkshänderinnen**) left-hander.

Linse die (PL die **Linsen**) 1 lens; 2 lentil.

Lippe die (PL die **Lippen**) lip.

Lippenstift der (PL die **Lippenstifte**) lipstick.

Liste die (PL die **Listen**) list.

listig adjective cunning.

Liter der (PL die **Liter**) litre.

Literatur die literature.

litt SEE **leiden**.

Livesendung die (PL die
Livesendungen) live programme.

Lizenz die (PL die Lizenzen) licence.

Lkw der (PL die Lkws)
(*Lastkraftwagen*) lorry, truck.

Lob das praise.

loben verb (PERF hat gelobt) to
praise.

Loch das (PL die Löcher) hole.

Locke die (PL die Locken) curl.

locken verb (PERF hat gelockt) 1 to
tempt; 2 to curl.

locker adjective 1 loose; 2 slack
(*rope*); 3 relaxed (*atmosphere*,
person).

lockerlassen ◇verb (PRES lässt
locker, IMPERF ließ locker, PERF hat
lockergelassen) nicht
lockerlassen (*informal*) not to let
up.

lockig adjective curly.

Löffel der (PL die Löffel) 1 spoon;
2 ein Löffel Mehl a spoonful of
flour.

log SEE **lügen**.

Logik die logic.

logisch adjective 1 logical; 2 ja,
logisch! yes, of course!

Lohn der (PL die Löhne) 1 wages;
2 reward.

lohnen verb (PERF hat sich
gelohnt) sich lohnen to be worth
it.

Lokal das (PL die Lokale) 1 bar;
2 restaurant.

Lokomotive die (PL die
Lokomotiven) locomotive, engine.

Lorbeerblatt das (PL die
Lorbeerblätter) bay leaf.

Los das (PL die Lose) 1 (lottery)
ticket; 2 das große Los ziehen to
hit the jackpot; 3 lot.

los adjective 1 der Hund ist los the
dog is off the lead; 2 die Schraube
ist los the screw's loose; 3 es ist
viel los there's a lot going on;
4 etwas los sein to be rid of
something; 5 was ist los? what's
the matter?.

los adverb 1 los! go on!; 2 Achtung,
fertig, los! ready, steady, go!

losbinden ◇verb (IMPERF band los,
PERF hat losgebunden) to untie.

löschen verb (PERF hat gelöscht)
1 to put out; 2 seinen Durst
löschen to quench your thirst; 3 to
delete, to cancel; 4 to erase.

lose adjective loose.

lösen verb (PERF hat gelöst) 1 to
solve; 2 to undo; 3 to buy; eine
Fahrkarte lösen to buy a ticket;
4 to release; 5 to remove; 6 sich
lösen to come undone; 7 sich
lösen to be solved (*of a puzzle or
mystery*); sich von selbst lösen to
be resolved (*of a problem*); 8 sich in
Wasser lösen to dissolve in water.

losfahren ◇verb (PRES fährt los,
IMPERF fuhr los, PERF ist
losgefahren) 1 to set off; 2 to drive
off.

losgehen ◇verb (IMPERF ging los,
PERF ist losgegangen) 1 to set off;
2 to start; 3 to come off (*of a
button*); 4 to go off (*of a bomb*);
5 auf jemanden losgehen to go for
somebody.

a
b
c
d
e
f
g
h
i
j
k
l
m
n
o
p
q
r
s
t
u
v
w
x
y
z

a

b

c

d

e

f

g

h

i

j

k

l

m

n

o

p

q

r

s

t

u

v

w

x

z

loslassen ◇verb (PRES **lässt los**, IMPERF **ließ los**, PERF **hat losgelassen**) **1** to let go of; **2** to let go.

Lösung die (PL die **Lösungen**) solution.

Losung die (PL die **Losungen**) **1** slogan; **2** password; **die Losung nennen** to give the password.

loswerden ◇verb (PRES **wird los**, IMPERF **wurde los**, PERF **ist losgeworden**) to get rid of.

Lotterie die (PL die **Lotterien**) lottery.

Lotto das (PL die **Lottos**) (national) lottery.

Löwe der (PL die **Löwen**) **1** lion; **2** Leo; **Wilhelm ist Löwe** Wilhelm's a Leo.

Loyalität die loyalty.

Lücke die (PL die **Lücken**) gap.

Luft die (PL die **Lüfte**) **1** air; **2 die Luft anhalten** to hold your breath; **3 in die Luft gehen** (informal) to blow your top; **4 jemanden wie Luft behandeln** to ignore somebody.

Luftballon der (PL die **Luftballons**) balloon.

Luftdruck der air pressure.

Luftmatratze die (PL die **Luftmatratzen**) air-bed.

Luftpost die airmail; **per Luftpost** by airmail.

Luftverschmutzung die air pollution.

Luftwaffe die air force.

Lüge die (PL die **Lügen**) lie.

lügen ◇verb (IMPERF **log**, PERF **hat gelogen**) to lie.

Lügner der (PL die **Lügner**) liar.

Lügnerin die (PL die **Lügnerinnen**) liar.

Lunge die (PL die **Lungen**) lungs.

Lungenentzündung die pneumonia.

Lupe die (PL die **Lupen**) magnifying glass.

Lust die **1** pleasure; **2 Lust haben, etwas zu tun** to feel like doing something; **ich habe keine Lust** I don't feel like it; **Lust auf etwas haben** to feel like something.

lustig adjective **1** jolly; **2** funny; **3** Dieter hat sich über mich lustig gemacht Dieter made fun of me.

lutschen verb (PERF **hat gelutscht**) to suck.

Lutscher der (PL die **Lutscher**) lollipop.

Luxemburg das Luxembourg.

Luxus der luxury.

Mm

machen verb (PERF **hat gemacht**) **1** to make; **2** to do; **was machst du da?** what are you doing?; **3 was macht die Arbeit?** how's work?; **was macht Karin?** how's Karin?; **4 sich an die Arbeit machen** to get down to work; **5 schnell machen** to hurry; **6 das macht nichts** it doesn't matter; **7** to come to; **das macht fünf Euro** that comes to five euros; **8 sich nichts aus etwas machen** to not be very keen on something; **Gisela macht sich nichts aus Schokolade** Gisela isn't keen on chocolate.

Macht die (PL die **Mächte**) power; **an die Macht kommen** to come to power.

Mädchen das (PL die **Mädchen**) girl.

Mädchenname der (PL die **Mädchennamen**) maiden name.

Made die (PL die **Maden**) maggot.

mag SEE **mögen**.

Magazin das (PL die **Magazine**) magazine.

Magen der (PL die **Mägen**) stomach.

Magenschmerzen plural noun stomach-ache.

mager adjective **1** thin; **2** lean; **3** low-fat.

Magie die magic.

Magnet der (PL die **Magnete(n)**) magnet.

magnetisch adjective magnetic.

magst SEE **mögen**.

Mahagoni das mahogany.

mähen verb (PERF **hat gemäht**) to mow; **den Rasen mähen** to mow the lawn.

mahlen ✧verb (PERF **hat gemahlen**) to grind.

Mahlzeit die (PL die **Mahlzeiten**) meal; **Mahlzeit!** enjoy your meal!

Mai der May; **der Erste Mai** May Day.

Maiglöckchen das (PL die **Maiglöckchen**) lily of the valley.

Mais der maize.

Majonäse die mayonnaise.

Majoran der marjoram.

Makkaroni (plural noun) macaroni.

Makler der (PL die **Makler**) estate agent.

Makrele die (PL die **Makrelen**) mackerel.

Mal das (PL die **Male**) **1** time; **nächstes Mal** next time; **zum ersten Mal** for the first time; **2** mark; **3** mole.

mal adverb **1** times; **zwei mal drei** two times three; **2** by (with measurements); **3** sometime (in the future); **ich möchte mal nach Brasilien fahren** I'd like to go to Brazil sometime; **4** schon mal ever; **5** ich war schon mal da I've been once before; **6** nicht mal not even; **7** komm mal her! come here!

malen verb (PERF **hat gemalt**) to paint.

Maler der (PL die **Maler**) painter.

Malerei die painting.

Malerin die (PL die **Malerinnen**) painter.

Mallorca das Majorca.

Mama die (PL die **Mamas**) mum.

Mami die (PL die **Mamis**) mummy.

man pronoun **1** you, one; **wie macht man das?** how do you do it?; **man kann ja nie wissen** one can never tell; **2** they, people; **man**

sagt they say; **3 man hat mir gesagt** I was told.

mancher, manche, manches *adjective* **1** many a; **so manchen Tag** many a day; **2 manche** (*plural*) some; **an manchen Tagen** some days.

manches *pronoun* **1** many a person; **2 manche** (*plural*) some people; **3 manches** some things.

manchmal *adverb* sometimes.

Mandarine die (PL die **Mandarinen**) mandarin.

Mandel die (PL die **Mandeln**) **1** almond; **2** tonsil.

Mandelentzündung die tonsillitis.

Mangel der (PL die **Mängel**) **1** lack; **2** shortage; **3** defect, fault.

mangelhaft *adjective* **1** faulty; **2** unsatisfactory (*school mark*).

Manie die (PL die **Manien**) mania.

Manieren *plural noun* manners; **er hat keine Manieren** he's got no manners.

Mann der (PL die **Männer**) **1** man; **2** husband.

Männchen das (PL die **Männchen**) male (*animal*).

Mannequin das (PL die **Mannequins**) model.

männlich *adjective* **1** male; **2** manly; **3** masculine.

Mannschaft die (PL die **Mannschaften**) **1** team; **2** crew.

Manschette die (PL die **Manschetten**) cuff.

Mantel der (PL die **Mäntel**) coat.

Mappe die (PL die **Mappen**) **1** folder; **2** briefcase; **3** bag.

Märchen das (PL die **Märchen**) fairy tale.

Margarine die margarine.

Marienkäfer der (PL die **Marienkäfer**) ladybird.

Marine die (PL die **Marinen**) navy.

Mark die (PL die **Mark**) mark (*German currency until replaced by the euro; one hundred marks =* \51.13 *euros*).

Marke die (PL die **Marken**) **1** make, brand; **meine Mutter fährt seit Jahren die gleiche Marke** my mother has been driving the same make of car for years; **Adidas ist eine führende Marke** Adidas is a leading brand; **2** tag; **3** stamp (*for letters*); **4** coupon.

markieren *verb* (PERF **hat markiert**) **1** to mark; **2** to fake.

Markt der (PL die **Märkte**) market; **auf den Markt bringen** to launch (*a product*).

Marktplatz der (PL die **Marktplätze**) market-place.

Marmelade die (PL die **Marmeladen**) jam.

Marmor der marble.

Marokko das Morocco.

Marsch der (PL die **Märsche**) march.

März der March.

Masche die (PL die **Maschen**) **1** stitch; **2** mesh; **3** (*informal*) trick; **die Masche raushaben** to know how to do it; **das is die neueste Masche** that's the latest thing.

Maschine die (PL die Maschinen) 1 machine; 2 plane; 3 typewriter; **Maschine schreiben** to type.

Masern plural noun measles.

Maske die (PL die Masken) mask.

maskieren verb (PERF hat sich maskiert) 1 **sich maskieren** to dress up; 2 **sich maskieren** to disguise yourself.

Maß¹ das (PL die Maße) 1 measure; 2 measurement; 3 extent; **in hohem Maße** to a high degree; 4 **Maß halten** to show moderation.

Maß² die (PL die Maß) litre (of beer).

maß SEE messen.

Masse die (PL die Massen) 1 mass; **eine Masse Arbeit** masses of work; 2 crowd; 3 mixture (in cooking).

massenhaft adjective masses of.

Massenvernichtungswaffen plural noun weapons of mass destruction.

massieren verb (PERF hat massiert) to massage.

mäßig adjective moderate.

Maßnahme die (PL die Maßnahmen) measure.

Maßstab der (PL die Maßstäbe) 1 standard; 2 scale.

Mast der (PL die Masten) 1 mast; 2 pole; 3 pylon.

Material das (PL die Materialien) 1 material; 2 materials.

Mathe die (informal) maths.

Mathematik die mathematics.

Matratze die (PL die Matratzen) mattress.

Matrose der (PL die Matrosen) sailor.

Matsch der 1 mud; 2 slush.

matschig adjective 1 muddy; 2 slushy.

matt adjective 1 weak; 2 matt; 3 dull; 4 **matt!** checkmate!

Matte die (PL die Matten) mat.

Mauer die (PL die Mauern) wall.

Maul das (PL die Mäuler) mouth; **halt's Maul!** (informal) shut up!

Maulkorb der (PL die Maulkörbe) muzzle.

Maulwurf der (PL die Maulwürfe) mole.

Maulwurfshügel der (PL die Maulwurfshügel) molehill.

Maurer der (PL die Maurer) bricklayer.

Maus die (PL die Mäuse) mouse.

Maximum das (PL die Maxima) maximum.

Mayonnaise die mayonnaise.

Mechaniker der (PL die Mechaniker) mechanic.

Mechanikerin die (PL die Mechanikerinnen) mechanic.

mechanisch adjective mechanical.

meckern verb (PERF hat gemeckert) 1 to bleat; 2 to grumble.

Medaille die (PL die Medaillen) medal.

Medien plural noun media.

Medikament das (PL die Medikamente) medicine, drug.

Medizin die (PL die Medizinen) medicine.

Meer das (PL die Meere) sea.

Meeresfrüchte plural noun seafood.

Meerschweinchen das (PL die Meerschweinchen) guinea pig.

Megabyte das (PL die Megabytes) megabyte.

Mehl das flour.

mehr adverb, pronoun more; **nichts mehr** no more; **nie mehr** never again.

mehrere pronoun several.

mehreres pronoun several things.

mehrfach adjective **1** multiple, many; **2** repeated.

mehrfach adverb several times.

Mehrheit die (PL die Mehrheiten) majority.

mehrmalig adjective repeated.

mehrmals adverb several times.

Mehrwertsteuer die value added tax.

Mehrzahl die **1** majority; **2** plural.

meiden ✧verb (IMPERF **mied**, PERF **hat gemieden**) to avoid.

Meile die (PL die Meilen) mile.

mein adjective my.

meine SEE meiner.

meinen verb (PERF **hat gemeint**) **1** to think; **2** to mean; **es gut meinen** to mean well; **3** to say.

meiner, meine, mein(e)s pronoun mine.

meinetwegen adverb **1** for my sake; **2** because of me; **3** as far as I'm concerned; **'kann ich das Auto haben?' – 'meinetwegen'** 'can I take the car?' – 'I don't mind'.

meins SEE meiner.

Meinung die (PL die Meinungen) opinion.

meist adverb **1** mostly; **2** usually.

meiste adjective, pronoun der/die/das meiste most; **die meisten** most; **am meisten** most, the most.

meistens adverb **1** mostly; **2** usually.

Meister der (PL die Meister) **1** master; **2** champion.

Meisterin die (PL die Meisterinnen) champion.

Meisterschaft die (PL die Meisterschaften) championship.

Meisterstück das (PL die Meisterstücke) **1** masterpiece; **2** masterstroke.

Meisterwerk das (PL die Meisterwerke) masterpiece.

melden verb (PERF **hat gemeldet**) **1** to report; **2** to register; **3** sich melden to report, (on the phone) to answer; **Luise hat sich gemeldet** (in school) Luise put up her hand; **4** sich bei jemandem melden to get in touch with somebody.

Melodie die (PL die Melodien) melody, tune.

Melone die (PL die Melonen) **1** melon; **2** bowler (hat).

Menge die (PL die Mengen)
1 quantity; **eine Menge Geld** a lot
of money; 2 crowd; 3 set (in maths).

Mensch der (PL die Menschen)
1 human being; 2 person; **kein
Mensch** nobody; **jeder Mensch**
everybody; 3 **die Menschen**
people; **wie viele Menschen?** how
many people?; 4 (as an
exclamation) **Mensch!** (informal)
wow!, hey!; **Mensch, hab ich mich
geärgert!** (informal) I was damn
annoyed.

menschenleer adjective
deserted.

Menschenverstand der
gesunder Menschenverstand
common sense.

Menschheit die mankind.

menschlich adjective 1 human;
2 humane.

Mentalität die (PL die
Mentalitäten) mentality.

Menü das (PL die Menüs) 1 set menu
(in restaurant); 2 menu (of
computer program).

merken verb (PERF hat gemerkt)
1 to notice; 2 **sich etwas merken**
to remember something.

Merkmal das (PL die Merkmale)
feature.

merkwürdig adjective strange,
odd.

Messe die (PL die Messen) 1 mass;
2 trade fair.

messen ◇ verb (PRES misst, IMPERF
maß, PERF hat gemessen) 1 to
measure; **(bei jemandem) Fieber
messen** to take somebody's

temperature; 2 **sich mit
jemandem messen können** to be
as good as somebody.

Messer das (PL die Messer) knife.

Messing das brass.

Metall das (PL die Metalle) metal.

Meter der (PL die Meter) metre.

Metermaß das (PL die Metermaße)
tape measure.

Methode die (PL die Methoden)
method.

metrisch adjective metric.

Metzger der (PL die Metzger)
butcher.

Metzgerei die (PL die Metzgereien)
butcher's (shop).

Mexiko das Mexico.

miauen verb (PERF hat miaut) to
miaow.

mich pronoun 1 me; 2 myself.

mied SEE meiden.

Miete die (PL die Mieten) 1 rent; **zur
Miete wohnen** to live in rented
accommodation; 2 hire charge.

mieten verb (PERF hat gemietet)
1 to rent; 2 to hire.

Mieter der (PL die Mieter) tenant.

Mieterin die (PL die Mieterinnen)
tenant.

Mietshaus das (PL die
Mietshäuser) block of rented flats.

Mietvertrag der (PL die
Mietverträge) lease.

Mietwagen der (PL die Mietwagen)
hire car.

Migräne die (PL die Migränen)
migraine.

a
b
c
d
e
f
g
h
i
j
k
l
m
n
o
p
q
r
s
t
u
v
w
x
y
z

Mikrochip der (PL die **Mikrochips**) microchip.

Mikrofon das (PL die **Mikrofone**) microphone.

Mikroskop das (PL die **Mikroskope**) microscope.

Mikrowellenherd der (PL die **Mikrowellenherde**) microwave oven.

Milch die milk.

Milchshake der (PL die **Milchshakes**) milk shake.

mild adjective mild.

Militär das army.

militärisch adjective military.

Milliarde die (PL die **Milliarden**) thousand million, billion; **zwei Milliarden Euro** two billion euros.

Millimeter der (PL die **Millimeter**) millimetre.

Million die (PL die **Millionen**) million.

Millionär der (PL die **Millionäre**) millionaire.

Millionärin die (PL die **Millionärinnen**) millionairess.

Minderheit die (PL die **Minderheiten**) minority.

minderjährig adjective under age.

mindestens adverb at least.

mindester, mindeste, mindestes adjective least.

mindestes pronoun 1 der/die/das **Mindeste** the least; **zum Mindesten** at least; 2 **nicht im Mindesten** not in the least.

Mine die (PL die **Minen**) 1 mine; 2 lead (in a pencil); 3 refill (for a ball-point).

Mineralwasser das (PL die **Mineralwässer**) mineral water.

Minirock der (PL die **Miniröcke**) miniskirt.

Minister der (PL die **Minister**) minister.

Ministerin die (PL die **Ministerinnen**) minister.

Ministerium das (PL die **Ministerien**) ministry, department.

minus adverb minus.

Minute die (PL die **Minuten**) minute.

mir pronoun 1 me, to me; 2 myself.

mischen verb (PERF **hat gemischt**) 1 to mix; 2 **die Karten mischen** to shuffle the cards; 3 **sich mischen** to mix.

Mischung die (PL die **Mischungen**) 1 mixture; 2 blend.

miserabel adjective (informal) 1 hopeless; 2 dreadful.

missbilligen verb (PERF **hat missbilligt**) to disapprove.

Missbrauch der abuse.

missbrauchen verb (PERF **hat missbraucht**) to abuse.

Misserfolg der (PL die **Misserfolge**) failure.

Missgeschick das (PL die **Missgeschicke**) 1 misfortune; 2 mishap.

misshandeln verb (PRES **hat misshandelt**) to ill-treat.

misslingen ◊*verb* (IMPERF **misslang**, PERF **ist misslungen**) to fail; **es misslang ihr** she failed.

misst SEE **messen**.

Misstrauen *das* **1** mistrust; **2** distrust.

misstrauen *verb* (PERF **hat misstraut**) **jemandem misstrauen** to mistrust somebody.

misstrauisch *adjective* suspicious.

Missverständnis *das* (PL *die* **Missverständnisse**) misunderstanding.

missverstehen ◊*verb* (IMPERF **missverstand**, PERF **hat missverstanden**) to misunderstand.

Mist *der* **1** manure; **2** (*informal*) rubbish.

Mistel *die* (PL *die* **Misteln**) mistletoe.

mit *preposition* (+ DAT) **1** with; **2 mit der Bahn fahren** to go by train, **mit dem Boot fahren** to go by boat; **3 mit sechs Jahren** at the age of six; **4 mit jemandem sprechen** to speak to somebody; **5 mit Bleistift** in pencil; **6 mit lauter Stimme** in a loud voice.

mit *adverb* as well, too; **warst du mit dabei?** were you there too?

Mitarbeiter *der* (PL *die* **Mitarbeiter**) **1** colleague; **2** employee.

Mitarbeiterin *die* (PL *die* **Mitarbeiterinnen**) **1** colleague; **2** employee.

mitbringen ◊*verb* (IMPERF **brachte mit**, PERF **hat mitgebracht**) to

bring, to bring along; **ich bringe den Kindern Schokolade mit** I'm taking the children some chocolate.

miteinander *adverb* with each other, with one another.

Mitesser *der* (PL *die* **Mitesser**) blackhead.

mitfahren ◊*verb* (PRES **fährt mit**, IMPERF **fuhr mit**, PERF **ist mitgefahren**) **1 mit jemandem mitfahren** to go with somebody; **die Kinder fahren mit uns mit** the children are coming with us; **2 bei jemandem mitfahren** to get a lift with somebody; **jemanden mitfahren lassen** to give somebody a lift.

mitgeben ◊*verb* (PRES **gibt mit**, IMPERF **gab mit**, PERF **hat mitgegeben**) to give.

Mitglied *das* (PL *die* **Mitglieder**) member.

mithalten ◊*verb* (PRES **hält mit**, IMPERF **hielt mit**, PERF **hat mitgehalten**) to keep up.

mitkommen ◊*verb* (IMPERF **kam mit**, PERF **ist mitgekommen**) **1** to come too; **2** to keep up.

Mitleid *das* pity; **kein Mitleid mit jemandem haben** not to feel any sympathy for somebody.

mitmachen *verb* (PERF **hat mitgemacht**) **1** to join in, **hast du Lust, bei dem Spiel mitzumachen?** do you want to join in the game?; **2** to take part in; **3** to go through (*experiences, troubles*);

a b c d e f g h i j k l m n o p q r s t u v w x y z

sie hat viel mitgemacht she's gone through a lot.

mitnehmen ⬦*verb* (PRES **nimmt mit**, IMPERF **nahm mit**, PERF **hat mitgenommen**) **1** to take, to take along; **Anni hat die Kinder auf den Spielplatz mitgenommen** Anni has taken the children to the playground; **2** to give a lift to; **3** to affect (badly); **4 zum Mitnehmen** to take away.

Mitschüler *der* (PL *die* **Mitschüler**) schoolfriend.

Mitschülerin *die* (PL *die* **Mitschülerinnen**) schoolfriend.

mitsingen *verb* (IMPERF **sang mit**, PERF **hat mitgesungen**) to sing along.

mitspielen *verb* (PERF **hat mitgespielt**) **1** to play; **wer spielt bei dem Fußballspiel mit?** who's playing in the football match?; **willst du mitspielen?** do you want to join in?; **2 in einem Film mitspielen** to be in a film.

Mittag *der* (PL *die* **Mittage**) **1** midday; **2** lunch; **zu Mittag essen** to have lunch; **3** lunchbreak.

Mittagessen *das* (PL *die* **Mittagessen**) lunch; **beim Mittagessen** at lunch.

mittags *adverb* **1** at lunchtime, at midday; **2 um zwölf Uhr mittags** at noon.

Mittagspause *die* (PL *die* **Mittagspausen**) lunch-break.

Mitte *die* (PL *die* **Mitten**) **1** middle; **2** centre.

Mitteilung *die* (PL *die* **Mitteilungen**) **1** announcement; **2** communication.

Mittel *das* (PL *die* **Mittel**) **1** means; **2 ein Mittel gegen Husten** a cough remedy; **3 öffentliche Mittel** public funds.

Mittelalter *das* Middle Ages.

Mitteleuropa *das* Central Europe.

mittelgroß *adjective* medium-sized.

mittelmäßig *adjective* mediocre.

Mittelmeer *das* Mediterranean.

Mittelpunkt *der* (PL *die* **Mittelpunkte**) centre; **im Mittelpunkt stehen** to be the centre of attention.

Mittelstand *der* middle class.

Mittelstürmer *der* (PL *die* **Mittelstürmer**) centre-forward.

mitten *adverb* **mitten in/auf** in the middle of; **mitten in der Nacht** in the middle of the night.

Mitternacht *die* midnight.

mittlerer, mittlere, mittleres *adjective* **1** middle; **2** medium (*quality, size*); **3** average.

mittlerweile *adverb* **1** meanwhile; **2** by now.

Mittwoch *der* (PL *die* **Mittwoche**) Wednesday.

mittwochs *adverb* on Wednesdays.

Mixer *der* (PL *die* **Mixer**) liquidizer.

Möbel *plural noun* furniture.

Möbelwagen *der* (PL *die* **Möbelwagen**) removal van.

Mobiltelefon das (PL die Mobiltelefone) mobile phone.

möbliert adjective furnished.

mochte, möchte SEE **mögen**.

Mode die (PL die Moden) fashion.

Modell das (PL die Modelle) model.

Moderator der (PL die Moderatoren) presenter (on TV).

Moderatorin die (PL die Moderatorinnen) presenter (on TV).

modern adjective modern.

modernisieren verb (PERF hat modernisiert) to modernize.

modisch adjective fashionable.

Mofa die (PL die Mofas) moped.

mogeln verb (PERF hat gemogelt) to cheat.

mögen ✧verb (PRES mag, IMPERF mochte, PERF hat gemocht) 1 to like; **ich mag ihn nicht** I don't like him; **ich möchte** I'd like; **ich möchte gern wissen** I'd like to know; **möchtest du nach Hause?** would you like to go home?; 2 lieber mögen to prefer; **ich möchte lieber Tee** I would prefer tea; 3 etwas nicht tun mögen not to want to do something; **ich mag nicht fragen** I don't want to ask; **ich mag nicht mehr** I've had enough; 4 das mag sein maybe; 5 was mag das sein? whatever can it be?

möglich adjective possible; **alles Mögliche** all sorts of things.

möglicherweise adverb possibly.

Möglichkeit die (PL die Möglichkeiten) possibility.

möglichst adverb if possible; **möglichst früh** as early as possible.

Möhre die (PL die Möhren) carrot.

Mokka der (PL die Mokkas) mocca.

Molekül das (PL die Moleküle) molecule.

Moment der (PL die Momente) moment; **im Moment** at the moment; **Moment (mal)!** just a moment!

momentan adjective 1 temporary; 2 current.

momentan adverb 1 temporarily; 2 at the moment.

Monat der (PL die Monate) month.

monatelang adverb for months.

monatlich adjective, adverb monthly.

Mönch der (PL die Mönche) monk.

Mond der (PL die Monde) moon.

Mondschein der moonlight; **im Mondschein** by moonlight.

Montag der (PL die Montage) Monday.

montags adverb on Mondays.

Moped das (PL die Mopeds) moped.

Moral die 1 moral; 2 morale; 3 morals.

moralisch adjective moral.

Mord der (PL die Morde) murder.

Mörder der (PL die Mörder) murderer.

a
b
c
d
e
f
g
h
i
j
k
l
m
n
o
p
q
r
s
t
u
v
w
x
y
z

Mörderin die (PL die **Mörderinnen**) murderer.

Morgen der (PL die **Morgen**) morning; **am Morgen** in the morning; **heute Morgen** this morning; **guten Morgen!** good morning!

morgen adverb tomorrow; **morgen Abend** tomorrow evening.

morgens adverb in the morning.

Moschee die (PL die **Moscheen**) mosque.

Mosel die (River) Moselle.

Moskau das Moscow.

Moslem der (PL die **Moslems**) Muslim.

moslemisch adjective Muslim.

Moslenin die (PL die **Mosleninnen**) Muslim.

Motiv das (PL die **Motive**) 1 motive; 2 motif.

Motivation die motivation.

Motor der (PL die **Motoren**) engine, motor.

Motorrad das (PL die **Motorräder**) motorcycle, motorbike.

Mousse die (PL die **Mouses**) mousse.

Möwe die (PL die **Möwen**) seagull.

Mücke die (PL die **Mücken**) 1 midge; 2 mosquito.

müde adjective tired.

Müdigkeit die tiredness.

Mühe die (PL die **Mühen**) 1 effort; **sich Mühe geben** to make an effort; 2 trouble; **machen Sie sich keine Mühe** don't go to any

trouble; **3 mit Müh und Not** only just.

Mühle die (PL die **Mühlen**) 1 mill; 2 grinder (for coffee).

mühsam adjective laborious.

Müll der rubbish.

Müllabfuhr die refuse collection.

Mülleimer der (PL die **Mülleimer**) rubbish bin.

Mülltonne die (PL die **Mülltonnen**) dustbin.

Mumps der mumps.

München das Munich.

Mund der (PL die **Münder**) mouth; **halt den Mund!** (informal) shut up!

Mundharmonika die (PL die **Mundharmonikas**) mouth organ.

mündlich adjective oral.

Münster das (PL die **Münster**) cathedral.

Münze die (PL die **Münzen**) coin.

Münzfernsprecher der (PL die **Münzfernsprecher**) payphone.

murmeln verb (PERF **hat gemurmelt**) to mumble.

mürrisch adjective surly.

Muschel die (PL die **Muscheln**) 1 mussel; 2 (sea) shell; 3 mouthpiece (of a phone).

Museum das (PL die **Museen**) museum.

Musik die music.

Musikal das (PL die **Musikals**) musical.

musikalisch *adjective* musical.

Musiker der (PL die **Musiker**) musician.

Musikerin die (PL die **Musikerinnen**) musician.

Muskat der nutmeg.

Muskel der (PL die **Muskeln**) muscle.

Müsli das muesli.

muss SEE **müssen**.

müssen ✧*verb* (PRES **muss**, IMPERF **musste**, PERF **hat gemusst**) **1** etwas tun müssen to have to do something; **sie muss es tun** she's got to do it, she must do it; **muss ich?** do I have to?; **muss das sein?** is that necessary?; **2 Sie müssten es mal versuchen** you should try it; **3 sie müssen gleich hier sein** they'll be here at any moment; **4 ich muss mal** (*informal*) I need (to go to) the loo.

Muster das (PL die **Muster**) **1** pattern; **2** sample.

Mut der courage; **jemandem Mut machen** to encourage somebody.

mutig *adjective* courageous.

Mutter[1] die (PL die **Mütter**) mother.

Mutter[2] die (PL die **Muttern**) nut.

Muttersprache die (PL die **Muttersprachen**) mother tongue, native language.

Muttertag der (PL die **Muttertage**) Mother's Day.

Mutti die (PL die **Muttis**) mum.

Mütze die (PL die **Mützen**) cap.

MwSt. (*Mehrwertsteuer*) VAT.

Mythos der (PL die **Mythen**) myth.

Nn

na *exclamation* well; **na und?** so what?; **na gut** all right then.

Nabel der (PL die **Nabel**) navel.

nach *preposition* (+ DAT) **1** to; **nach Hause gehen** to go home; **nach oben** up; **nach hinten** back; **nach rechts abbiegen** to turn right; **2** after; **nach Ihnen** after you; **zehn nach eins** ten past one; **nach etwas greifen** to reach for something; **3** according to; **meiner Meinung nach** in my opinion.

nach *adverb* **nach und nach** bit by bit, gradually; **nach wie vor** still.

nachahmen *verb* (PERF **hat nachgeahmt**) to imitate.

Nachbar der (PL die **Nachbarn**) neighbour.

Nachbarin die (PL die **Nachbarinnen**) neighbour.

Nachbarschaft die neighbourhood.

nachdem *conjunction* **1** after; **2 je nachdem** it depends; **je nachdem, wie schnell du damit fertig wirst** it depends on how quicky you can finish it.

nachdenken ✧*verb* (IMPERF **dachte nach**, PERF **hat nachgedacht**) to think; **über etwas nachdenken** to think about something; **ich habe lange über ihr Angebot nachgedacht und mich schließlich dagegen entschieden** I've thought a long time about her offer and finally decided against it.

a
b
c
d
e
f
g
h
i
j
k
l
m
n
o
p
q
r
s
t
u
v
w
x
y
z

nachdenklich *adjective*
thoughtful.

nacheinander *adverb* one after
the other; **die Bewerber kamen
nacheinander herein** the
applicants came in one after the
other.

Nachfrage *die* (PL *die* **Nachfragen**)
demand; **es besteht keine
Nachfrage** there's no demand for
it.

nachgehen ◇*verb* (IMPERF **ging
nach**, PERF **ist nachgegangen**) **1** to
be slow; **meine Uhr geht nach** my
watch is slow; **2 jemandem
nachgehen** to follow somebody;
einer Sache nachgehen to look
into something.

nachher *adverb* afterwards; **erst
gehen wir ins Kino und nachher
könnten wir essen gehen** we go to
the cinema first and afterwards we
could go for a meal; **bis nachher!**
see you later!

nachholen *verb* (PERF **hat
nachgeholt**) **1** to catch up on; **ich
hatte Grippe und muss jetzt viel
Mathe nachholen** I've had flu and
now I've got a lot of maths to catch
up on; **2** to make up for (*something
missed*); **3 eine Prüfung
nachholen** to do an exam at a later
date.

nachkommen ◇*verb* (IMPERF **kam
nach**, PERF **ist nachgekommen**)
1 to come later, to follow; **2 ich
komme nicht nach** I can't keep up;
**3 einem Versprechen
nachkommen** to carry out a
promise; **seinen Verpflichtungen**

nachkommen to meet your
commitments.

nachlassen ◇*verb* (PRES **lässt
nach**, IMPERF **ließ nach**, PERF **hat
nachgelassen**) **1** to ease; **meine
Zahnschmerzen lassen langsam
nach** my toothache is getting
better; **2** to let go; **sobald die Kälte
nachlässt** as soon as it gets
warmer; **3** to deteriorate; **4 etwas
vom Preis nachlassen** to take
something off the price; **jemandem
zwanzig Euro nachlassen** to give
somebody twenty euros off.

nachlässig *adjective* careless.

nachlaufen ◇*verb* (PRES **läuft
nach**, IMPERF **lief nach**, PERF **ist
nachgelaufen**) **jemandem
nachlaufen** to run after somebody;
Philipp läuft allen Mädchen nach
(*informal*) Philipp chases all the
girls.

nachmachen *verb* (PERF **hat
nachgemacht**) to copy.

Nachmittag *der* (PL *die*
Nachmittage) afternoon.

nachmittags *adverb* in the
afternoon.

Nachnahme *die* per **Nachnahme**
cash on delivery.

Nachname *der* (PL *die*
Nachnamen) surname.

nachprüfen *verb* (PERF **hat
nachgeprüft**) to check; **er prüft
nach, ob es stimmt** he's going to
check if it is correct.

Nachricht *die* (PL *die* **Nachrichten**)
1 news; **ich warte noch immer auf
eine Nachricht von ihm** I'm still

waiting for news of him; **eine Nachricht hinterlassen** to leave a message; **2 die Nachrichten** the news; **das kam in den Nachrichten** it was on the news.

Nachrichtensprecher der (PL die Nachrichtensprecher) newsreader.

Nachrichtensprecherin die (PL die Nachrichtensprecherinnen) newsreader.

nachschlagen ◇verb (PRES schlägt nach, IMPERF schlug nach, PERF hat nachgeschlagen) to look up.

nachsehen ◇verb (PRES sieht nach, IMPERF sah nach, PERF hat nachgesehen) **1** to check; **sieh nach, wer da ist** go and see who's there; **2** to look up; **3 jemandem etwas nachsehen** to let somebody get away with something.

nachsitzen ◇verb (IMPERF saß nach, PERF hat nachgesessen) to be in detention; **Jan muss nachsitzen** Jan has detention.

Nachspeise die (PL die Nachspeisen) dessert, pudding.

nächste SEE nächstor.

nächstens adverb shortly.

nächster, nächste, nächstes adjective **1** next; **2** nearest; **am nächsten sein** to be nearest; **3 in nächster Nähe** close by.

nächstes pronoun der/die/das Nächste (the) next; **als Nächstes** next.

Nacht die (PL die Nächte) night.

Nachteil der (PL die Nachteile) disadvantage.

Nachtfalter der (PL die Nachtfalter) moth.

Nachthemd das (PL die Nachthemden) nightdress, nightshirt.

Nachtigall die (PL die Nachtigallen) nightingale.

Nachtisch der (PL die Nachtische) dessert, pudding.

Nachtklub der (PL die Nachtklubs) night club.

Nachtleben das nightlife.

nachträglich adjective **1** subsequent; **2** belated.

nachträglich adverb **1** later; **2** belatedly.

nachts adverb at night; **um zwei Uhr nachts** at two o'clock in the morning.

Nacken der (PL die Nacken) neck.

nackt adjective **1** naked; **2** bare.

Nacktschnecke die (PL die Nacktschnecken) slug.

Nadel die (PL die Nadeln) **1** needle; **2** pin.

Nagel der (PL die Nägel) nail.

Nagelbürste die (PL die Nagelbürsten) nailbrush.

Nagelfeile die (PL die Nagelfeilen) nailfile.

Nagellack der (PL die Nagellacke) nail varnish.

nagelneu adjective brand-new.

Nagelschere die (PL die Nagelscheren) nail scissors.

a b c d e f g h i j k l m n o p q r s t u v w x y z

a **Nähe** die 1 proximity; 2 in der Nähe der Kirche near the church; ganz in der Nähe nearby; 3 aus der Nähe close up.

b

c

nahe, nah adjective, adverb
1 near, nearby; der Nahe Osten the Middle East; nahe daran sein, etwas zu tun to nearly do something; 2 close; nahe bei close to; Nähe close up; nahe verwandt sein to be closely related; 3 jemandem nahe legen, etwas zu tun to urge somebody to do something; 4 nahe liegend obvious.

d

e

f

g

h

i

j **nah** preposition (+ DAT) near, close to.

k **nahelegen, naheliegend** SEE nahe.

l

m **nähen** verb (PERF hat genäht) 1 to sew; 2 to stitch (a wound).

näher adjective 1 closer; 2 nähere Einzelheiten further details; 3 shorter (way, road).

o **näher** adverb 1 closer; näher kommen to come closer; 2 more closely; 3 Näheres further details.

p

q **nähern** verb (PERF hat sich genähert) sich nähern to approach; wir näherten uns dem Dorf we were approaching the village.

r

s

t

u **Nähgarn** das cotton.

nahm SEE nehmen.

v **Nähmaschine** die (PL die Nähmaschinen) sewing machine.

w

Nahrung die food.

x **Naht** die (PL die Nähte) seam.

y **Nahverkehrszug** der (PL die Nahverkehrszüge) local train.

z

Name der (PL die Namen) name; im Namen von on behalf of; ich rufe im Namen von Herrn und Frau Schmidt an I'm calling on behalf of Mr and Mrs Schmidt.

nämlich adverb 1 because; 2 namely; 3 das war nämlich ganz anders it was quite different actually.

nannte SEE nennen.

nanu exclamation well, well!

Narbe die (PL die Narben) scar.

Narr der (PL die Narren) fool.

Närrin die (PL die Närrinnen) fool.

Nase die (PL die Nasen) nose; die Nase voll haben (informal) to have had enough.

Nasenbluten das nosebleed.

Nashorn das (PL die Nashörner) rhinoceros.

nass adjective wet.

Nation die (PL die Nationen) nation.

Nationalhymne die (PL die Nationalhymnen) national anthem.

Nationalität die (PL die Nationalitäten) nationality.

Natur die 1 nature; von Natur aus by nature; 2 die freie Natur the open countryside.

Naturlehrpfad der (PL die Naturlehrpfade) nature trail.

natürlich adjective natural.

natürlich adverb of course, naturally.

Natürlichkeit die naturalness.

Naturschützer der (PL die Naturschützer) conservationist.

Naturschützerin der (PL die Naturschützerinnen) conservationist.

Naturschutzgebiet das (PL die Naturschutzgebiete) nature reserve.

Naturwissenschaft die natural science.

Nebel der (PL die Nebel) 1 fog; 2 mist.

nebelig adjective SEE **neblig**.

neben preposition (+ DAT or + ACC with movement towards a place) 1 next to; **er hat neben mir gesessen** he sat next to me; **er hat sich neben mich gesetzt** he sat down next to me; 2 apart from.

nebenan adverb next door.

nebenbei adverb 1 as well, at the same time; **er liest die Zeitung und hört nebenbei Musik** he reads the newspaper and listens to music at the same time; 2 on the side; **nebenbei arbeite ich noch in einem Blumengeschäft** I work in a florist's on the side; **das mache ich so nebenbei** (informal) that's just a sideline; 3 in passing; **nebenbei bemerkt** by the way.

nebeneinander adverb next to each other.

nebenhergehen ◇verb (IMPERF ging nebenher, PERF ist nebenhergegangen) to walk alongside.

neblig adjective 1 foggy; 2 misty.

necken verb (PERF hat geneckt) to tease.

Neffe der (PL die Neffen) nephew.

Negativ das (PL die Negative) negative.

negativ adjective negative.

nehmen ◇verb (PRES nimmt, IMPERF nahm, PERF hat genommen) 1 to take; 2 **ich nehme eine Suppe** I'll have soup; 3 **was nehmen Sie dafür?** how much do you want for it? 4 **jemanden zu sich nehmen** to have somebody live with you; 5 **sich etwas nehmen** to take something; **nimm dir ein Stück Kuchen** help yourself to a piece of cake.

Neid der envy, jealousy.

neidisch adjective envious, jealous.

nein adverb no.

Nelke die (PL die Nelken) carnation.

nennen ◇verb (IMPERF nannte, PERF hat genannt) 1 to call; 2 to name; 3 **ihr Name wurde nicht genannt** her name wasn't mentioned; 4 **sich nennen** to call yourself.

Nerv der (PL die Nerven) nerve; **Gabi geht mir auf die Nerven** Gabi gets on my nerves.

nervig adjective nerve-wracking.

nervös adjective nervous.

Nervosität die nervousness.

Nessel die (PL die Nesseln) nettle.

Nest das (PL die Nester) 1 nest; 2 little place (a village).

nett adjective nice.

netto adverb net.

Netz das (PL die Netze) 1 net; 2 network; 3 string bag; 4 (spider's) web.

a
b
c
d
e
f
g
h
i
j
k
l
m
n
o
p
q
r
s
t
u
v
w
x
y
z

a **Netzkarte** die (PL die **Netzkarten**)
b unlimited travel ticket (*over a transport network*).

c **Netzwerk** das (PL die **Netzwerke**)
network.

d **neu** *adjective* 1 new; **wie neu** as
e good as new; **neue Sprachen**
modern languages; **2 seit**
f **neuestem** recently; **3 die neueste**
Mode the latest fashion; **das**
g **Neueste** the latest news; **das**
Neueste an Audioausrüstung the
h latest in audio equipment; **4 das**
ist mir neu that's news to me.

i **neu** *adverb* 1 newly; **2** only just; **es**
j **ist neu eingetroffen** it has only
just come in; **3 etwas neu**
k **schreiben** to rewrite something.

l **neuartig** *adjective* new; **ein**
neuartiger Flaschenöffner a new
m kind of bottle opener.

neuerdings *adverb* recently.

n **Neugier** die curiosity.

o **neugierig** *adjective* curious,
inquisitive.

p **Neuigkeit** die (PL die **Neuigkeiten**)
q piece of news; **gibt es**
irgendwelche Neuigkeiten? is
r there any news?

Neujahr das New Year, New Year's
s Day.

t **neulich** *adverb* the other day.

neun *number* nine.

u **neunter, neunte, neuntes**
v *adjective* ninth.

w **neunzehn** *number* nineteen.

neunzig *number* ninety.

x **Neuseeland** das New Zeal and.

nicht *adverb* 1 not; **ich kann nicht**
I can't; **Iris hat nicht angerufen**
Iris didn't ring; **bitte nicht** please
don't; **nicht! don't!; nicht**
berühren! don't touch!; **2 'ich mag**
das nicht' – 'ich auch nicht' 'I
don't like it' – 'neither do I'; **3 nicht**
(wahr)? isn't he/she/it?; **du**
kennst ihn doch, nicht? you know
him, don't you?; **4 gar nicht** not at
all; **5 nicht mehr** no more.

Nichte die (PL die **Nichten**) niece.

Nichtraucher der (PL die
Nichtraucher) non-smoker.

Nichtraucherabteil das (PL die
Nichtraucherabteile) no-smoking
compartment.

Nichtraucherin die (PL die
Nichtraucherinnen) non-smoker.

nichts *pronoun* 1 nothing; **2 ich**
habe nichts gewusst I didn't know
anything; **3 nichts mehr** no more;
4 das macht nichts it doesn't
matter; **5 nichts ahnend**
unsuspecting.

nichtsahnend SEE **nichts**.

Nichtschwimmerbecken das
(PL die **Nichtschwimmerbecken**)
shallow swimming pool (*for non-
swimmers and learners*).

nicken *verb* (PERF **hat genickt**) to
nod.

Nickerchen das (PL die
Nickerchen) nap; **ein Nickerchen**
machen to have a nap.

nie *adverb* never.

nieder *adjective* low.

nieder *adverb* down.

Niederlage die (PL die Niederlagen) defeat.

Niederlande plural noun die Niederlande the Netherlands.

Niederländer der (PL die Niederländer) Dutchman; **die Niederländer** the Dutch.

Niederländerin die (PL die Niederländerinnen) Dutchwoman.

niederländisch adjective Dutch.

niedlich adjective sweet.

niedrig adjective 1 low; 2 base.

niemals adverb never.

niemand pronoun nobody, **wir haben niemand** or **niemanden gesehen** we didn't see anybody.

Niere die (PL die Nieren) kidney.

nieseln verb (PERF **hat genieselt**) to drizzle; **es nieselt** it's drizzling.

niesen verb (PERF **hat geniest**) to sneeze.

Nil der der Nil the River Nile.

Nilpferd das (PL die Nilpferde) hippopotamus.

nimmt SEE nehmen.

nirgends, nirgendwo adverb nowhere.

Niveau das (PL die Niveaus) 1 level; 2 standard.

noch adverb 1 still; immer noch still; 2 even; **noch besser** even better; 3 **noch nicht** not yet; **noch nie** never; 4 gerade noch only just; 5 **wer war noch da?** who else was there?; **was noch?** what else?; 6 **noch einmal** again; 7 **noch ein Bier** another beer; **noch etwas Kaffee?** (would you like some) more coffee?; 8 **noch gestern** only yesterday; 9 **noch und noch Geld** loads of money.

noch conjunction nor; **weder ... noch** neither ... nor.

nochmals adverb again.

Nominativ der (PL die Nominative) nominative.

Nonne die (PL die Nonnen) nun.

Nordamerika das North America.

Nordamerikaner der (PL die Nordamerikaner) North American.

Nordamerikanerin die (PL die Nordamerikanerinnen) North American.

nordamerikanisch adjective North American.

Norden der north.

Nordirland das Northern Ireland.

nördlich adjective 1 northern; 2 northerly (direction).

nördlich adverb, preposition (+ GEN) **nördlich von Wien** to the north of Vienna; **nördlich der Stadt** north of the town.

Nordosten der north-east.

Nordpol der North Pole.

Nordsee die North Sea.

Nordwesten der north-west.

nörgeln verb (PERF **hat genörgelt**) to grumble.

Norm die (PL die Normen) 1 norm; 2 standard.

normal adjective normal.

normalerweise adverb normally.

Norwegen das Norway.

Norweger der (PL die **Norweger**) Norwegian.

Norwegerin die (PL die **Norwegerinnen**) Norwegian.

norwegisch adjective Norwegian.

Not die (PL die **Nöte**) **1** need; **zur Not** if necessary, at a pinch; **mit knapper Not** only just; **2** hardship.

Notaufnahme die (PL die **Notaufnahmen**) accident & emergency (hospital department).

Notausgang der (PL die **Notausgänge**) emergency exit.

Notdienst der **Notdienst haben** to be on call.

Note die (PL die **Noten**) **1** note; **Noten lesen** to read music; **2** mark.

Notfall der (PL die **Notfälle**) emergency.

notfalls adverb if need be.

notieren verb (PERF **hat notiert**) **1** to note down; **2 sich etwas notieren** to make a note of something.

nötig adjective necessary.

nötig adverb urgently.

Notiz die (PL die **Notizen**) **1** note; **2 keine Notiz von etwas nehmen** to take no notice of something; **3** item (in a newspaper).

Notizblock der (PL die **Notizblöcke**) notepad.

Notizbuch das (PL die **Notizbücher**) notebook.

Notlage die (PL die **Notlagen**) crisis.

Notruf der (PL die **Notrufe**) **1** emergency call; **2** emergency number.

notwendig adjective necessary.

November der November.

nüchtern adjective **1** sober; **wieder nüchtern werden** to sober up; **2 auf nüchternen Magen** on an empty stomach; **3** down-to-earth.

Nudeln plural noun **1** noodles; **2** pasta.

Null die (PL die **Nullen**) **1** zero, nought; **2** failure.

null number **1** nought; **unter null** below zero; **2** nil; **zwei zu null** two nil; **4 null Fehler haben** to have no mistakes; **ich habe null Ahnung** (informal) I haven't got a clue; **5 in null Komma nichts** (informal) in less than no time.

numerieren SEE nummerieren.

Nummer die (PL die **Nummern**) **1** number; **2** issue (of a magazine); **3** size (of clothing); **4** act; **5 auf Nummer sicher gehen** to play safe.

nummerieren verb (PERF **hat nummeriert**) to number.

Nummernschild das (PL die **Nummernschilder**) number plate.

nun adverb now.

nun exclamation well; **nun ja** ... well, yes ....

nur adverb **1** only; **2 was sollen wir nur tun?** what on earth are we going to do?; **sie soll es nur**

versuchen! just let her try!; **3 nur zu!** go ahead!

Nürnberg das Nuremberg.

Nuss die (PL die **Nüsse**) nut.

Nutzen der benefit; **von Nutzen sein** to be useful.

nutzen, nützen verb (PERF **hat genutzt/genützt**) **1** to use; **etwas nutzen** to take advantage of something; **2** to be useful; **3 nichts nutzen** to be no use; **das nutzt mir nichts** that won't help me; **4 das nutzt ja doch nichts** it's pointless.

nützlich adjective useful.

nutzlos adjective useless.

Oo

ob conjunction **1** whether; **wissen Sie, ob heute noch ein Zug nach Freising fährt?** do you know if there is another train to Freising today?; **2 ob Alex noch anruft?** I wonder if Alex will ring; **3 und ob!** you bet!

obdachlos adjective homeless.

Obdachlose der/die (PL die **Obdachlosen**) homeless person; **die Obdachlosen** the homeless.

oben adverb **1** on top; **oben auf** on top of; **die Vase steht oben auf dem Schrank** the vase is on top of the cupboard; **2** at the top; **von oben bis unten** from top to bottom; **er hat uns von oben bis unten gemustert** he looked us up and down; **3** upstairs; **4 nach oben** up, upstairs; **er ist nach oben ins Zimmer gegangen** he went up into his room; **geht der Fahrstuhl nach oben?** is the lift going up?; **hier oben** up here; **da oben** up there; **5 siehe oben** see above (on a page); **oben erwähnt** above mentioned; **6 oben ohne** (informal) topless.

obenerwähnt SEE oben.

Ober der (PL die **Ober**) waiter; **Herr Ober!** waiter!

oberer, obere, oberes adjective upper, top.

Oberfläche die (PL die **Oberflächen**) surface.

oberflächlich adjective superficial.

Oberhaupt das (PL die **Oberhäupter**) head.

Oberhemd das (PL die **Oberhemden**) shirt.

Oberschenkel der (PL die **Oberschenkel**) thigh.

Oberschule die (PL die **Oberschulen**) secondary school.

oberster, oberste, oberstes adjective top.

Oberstufe die (PL die **Oberstufen**) upper school.

Oberweite die (PL die **Oberweiten**) chest size, bust measurement.

Objekt das (PL die **Objekte**) object.

Objektiv das (PL die **Objektive**) lens.

objektiv adjective objective.

Oboe die (PL die **Oboen**) oboe; **Oboe spielen** to play the oboe.

Obst das fruit.

a
b
c
d
e
f
g
h
i
j
k
l
m
n
o
p
q
r
s
t
u
v
w
x
y
z

Obstbaum der (PL die **Obstbäume**) fruit tree.

Obstsalat der (PL die **Obstsalate**) fruit salad.

obszön adjective obscene.

obwohl conjunction although.

öde adjective 1 desolate; 2 dreary; **das ist so ein furchtbar öder Job** it's such terribly dull job.

oder conjunction 1 or; 2 **du kennst sie doch, oder?** you know her, don't you?

Ofen der (PL die **Öfen**) 1 oven; 2 stove; 3 heater.

offen adjective 1 open; **offen haben** to be open; **Tag der offenen Tür** open day; 2 frank; 3 vacant; **eine offene Stelle** a vacancy; 4 **offen bleiben** to stay open; 5 **offen bleiben** to remain open (of a question, possibility).

offen adverb 1 openly; 2 frankly; **offen gesagt** frankly.

offenbar adjective obvious.

offenbar adverb 1 apparently; 2 **da hast du dich offenbar geirrt** you seem to have made a mistake; **sie hat offenbar den Zug verpasst** she must have missed the train.

offenbleiben SEE **offen**.

offensichtlich adjective obvious.

öffentlich adjective public.

Öffentlichkeit die public; **in aller Öffentlichkeit** in public.

offiziell adjective official.

Offizier der (PL die **Offiziere**) officer.

öffnen verb (PERF **hat geöffnet**) to open; **jemandem die Tür öffnen** to open the door for somebody.

Öffner der (PL die **Öffner**) opener.

Öffnung die (PL die **Öffnungen**) opening.

Öffnungszeiten plural noun opening times.

oft adverb often.

öfter, öfters adverb quite often; **ich habe ihn öfters mal getroffen** I used to meet him quite often.

ohne preposition (+ ACC) 1 without; **ohne mich** count me out; 2 **ohne weiteres** easily; 3 **oben ohne** (informal) topless; 4 **das ist nicht ohne** (informal) it's not bad.

ohne conjunction without; **ohne zu überlegen** without thinking.

Ohnmacht die **in Ohnmacht fallen** to faint.

ohnmächtig adjective 1 unconscious; 2 **ohnmächtig werden** to faint; **Gisela ist ohnmächtig** Gisela's fainted.

Ohr das (PL die **Ohren**) ear.

Ohrenschmerzen plural noun earache.

Ohrring der (PL die **Ohrringe**) earring.

oje exclamation oh dear!

Ökoladen der (PL die **Ökoläden**) health-food shop.

Ökologie die ecology.

ökologisch adjective ecological.

Oktober der October.

Öl das (PL die Öle) oil.

Ölfarbe die (PL die Ölfarben) oil-paint.

Ölgemälde das (PL die Ölgemälde) oil painting.

ölig adjective oily.

Olive die (PL die Oliven) olive.

Olivenöl das (PL die Olivenöle) olive oil.

Ölteppich der (PL die Ölteppiche) oil slick.

Olympiade die (PL die Olympiaden) Olympic Games; **die Olympiade findet alle vier Jahre statt** the Olympic Games take place every four years.

olympisch adjective Olympic.

Oma die (PL die Omas) granny.

Omelett das (PL die Omeletts) omelette.

Omi die (PL die Omis) granny.

Onkel der (PL die Onkel) uncle.

Opa der (PL die Opas) grandpa.

Oper die (PL die Opern) opera.

Operation die (PL die Operationen) operation.

Operationssaal der (PL die Operationssäle) operating theatre.

operieren verb (PERF hat operiert) 1 to operate on; **sich operieren lassen** to have an operation; **sie wurde am Magen operiert** she had a stomach operation; 2 to operate.

Opfer das (PL die Opfer) 1 sacrifice; 2 victim; **das Erdbeben forderte viele Opfer** the earthquake claimed many victims.

Optiker der (PL die Optiker) optician.

Optikerin die (PL die Optikerinnen) optician.

Optimist der (PL die Optimisten) optimist.

optimistisch adjective optimistic.

Orange die (PL die Orangen) orange.

orange adjective orange.

Orangensaft der (PL die Orangensäfte) orange juice.

Orchester das (PL die Orchester) orchestra.

ordentlich adjective 1 tidy; 2 respectable; 3 proper (meal, job, salary); 4 **eine ordentliche Tracht Prügel** (informal) a good hiding.

ordentlich adverb 1 tidily; **ordentlich schreiben** to write neatly; 2 respectably; 3 properly; 4 **ordentlich feiern** (informal) to have a really good celebration; **wir sind ordentlich nass geworden** (informal) we got soaked.

ordinär adjective vulgar.

ordnen verb (PERF hat geordnet) 1 to arrange; 2 to put in order.

Ordner der (PL die Ordner) file.

Ordnung die 1 order; **Ordnung halten** to keep order; 2 **Ordnung machen** to tidy up; **die Wohnung in Ordnung bringen** to tidy up the flat; 3 **mit der Waschmaschine ist etwas nicht in Ordnung** there's something wrong with the washing

a
b
machine; **4 etwas in Ordnung bringen** to put something right; **die Waschmaschine in Ordnung bringen** to repair the washing
c
machine; **5 in Ordnung!** okay!; **6 er ist in Ordnung** he's all right.
d

e **Organ** das (PL die **Organe**) **1** organ;
2 (informal) voice.
f

Organisation die (PL die **Organisationen**) organization.
g

h **organisch** adjective organic.

i **organisieren** verb (PERF **hat organisiert**) **1** to organize;
2 (informal) to get (hold of).
j

k **Orgel** die (PL die **Orgeln**) organ.

l **orientieren** verb (PERF **hat sich orientiert**) **1 sich orientieren** to get your bearings; **2 sich über etwas orientieren** to inform yourself about something.
m
n

Orientierung die **1** orientation; **die Orientierung verlieren** to lose your bearings; **2 zu Ihrer Orientierung** for your information.
p
q

r **Orientierungsjahr** das (PL die **Orientierungsjahre**) gap year.

s **Orientierungspunkt** der (PL die **Orientierungspunkte**) landmark, reference point.
t

u **Orientierungsrennen** das orienteering.

v
w **Orientierungssinn** der sense of direction.

x **originell** adjective original.

y
z **Orkan** der (PL die **Orkane**) hurricane.

Ort der (PL die **Orte**) **1** place; **an Ort und Stelle** on the spot; **2** (small) town.

Orthografie, Orthographie die spelling.

örtlich adjective local.

Ortschaft die (PL die **Ortschaften**) village.

Ortsgespräch das (PL die **Ortsgespräche**) local call.

Ossi der (informal) (PL die **Ossis**) East German.

Osten der east.

Osterei das (PL die **Ostereier**) Easter egg.

Ostern das Easter.

Österreich das Austria.

Österreicher der (PL die **Österreicher**) Austrian.

Österreicherin die (PL die **Österreicherinnen**) Austrian.

österreichisch adjective Austrian.

östlich adjective **1** eastern; **2** easterly.

östlich adverb, preposition (+ GEN) **östlich von Wien** to the east of Vienna; **östlich der Stadt** east of the town.

Ostsee die Baltic (Sea).

oval adjective oval.

Ozean der (PL die **Ozeane**) ocean.

Ozon das ozone.

Ozonschicht die ozone layer.

Pp

Paar das (PL die **Paare**) **1** pair; **ein Paar Schuhe** a pair of shoes; **2** couple.

paar pronoun **ein paar** a few; **ein paar Mal** a few times; **alle paar Tage** every few days.

paarmal SEE **paar.**

paarweise adjective in pairs; **die Kinder stellten sich paarweise auf** the children lined up in pairs.

Päckchen das (PL die **Päckchen**) **1** package, packet; **2** small parcel.

packen verb (PERF **hat gepackt**) **1** to pack; **ich muss jetzt meinen Koffer packen** I must pack my case now; **2** to grab (hold of); **von Furcht gepackt** seized with fear.

Packung die (PL die **Packungen**) packet, pack.

Pädagoge der (PL die **Pädagogen**) **1** educationalist; **2** teacher.

pädagogisch adjective educational.

Paddel das (PL die **Paddel**) paddle.

paddeln verb **1** (PERF **hat gepaddelt**) to paddle (a canoe); **2** (PERF **ist gepaddelt**) to paddle (along a lake, river).

Paket das (PL die **Pakete**) **1** parcel; **Gabi hat mir ein Paket geschickt** Gabi sent me a parcel; **2** packet; **kaufe bitte ein Paket Waschpulver für mich** can you please buy a packet of washing powder for me.

Pakistan das Pakistan.

Pakistaner der (PL die **Pakistaner**) Pakistani.

Pakistanerin die (PL die **Pakistanerinnen**) Pakistani.

pakistanisch adjective Pakistani.

Palast der (PL die **Paläste**) palace.

Palme die (PL die **Palmen**) palm (tree).

Pampelmuse die (PL die **Pampelmusen**) grapefruit.

Panik die panic; **in Panik geraten** to panic.

Panne die (PL die **Pannen**) **1** breakdown; **wir haben auf dem Rückweg eine Panne gehabt** we had a breakdown on the way back; **2** mishap; **uns ist eine Panne passiert** we had a mishap.

Panzer der (PL die **Panzer**) tank (military).

Papa der (PL die **Papas**) daddy.

Papagei der (PL die **Papageien**) parrot.

Papier das (PL die **Papiere**) paper.

Papierkorb der (PL die **Papierkörbe**) waste-paper basket.

Papiertüte die (PL die **Papiertüten**) paper bag.

Pappe die (PL die **Pappen**) cardboard.

Paprika der (PL die **Paprikas**) **1** pepper; **2** paprika.

Papst der (PL die **Päpste**) pope.

Parabolantenne die (PL die **Parabolantennen**) satellite dish.

Paradies das paradise.

a b c d e f g h i j k l m n o p q r s t u v w x y z

a **Paragraph** der (PL die Paragraphen) **1** section; **2** clause.

b **parallel** adjective parallel.

c **Pärchen** das (PL die Pärchen) couple.

d **Parfüm** das (PL die Parfüms) perfume.

e **Park** der (PL die Parks) park.

f **Parkanlage** die (PL die Parkanlagen) park.

g **parken** verb (PERF hat geparkt) to park.

h **Parkett** das (PL die Parkette) **1** (in a theatre) stalls; **2** parquet floor.

i **Parkhaus** das (PL die Parkhäuser) multi-storey car park.

j **Parklücke** die (PL die Parklücken) parking space.

k **Parkplatz** der (PL die Parkplätze) **1** car park; **2** parking space.

l **Parkschein** der (PL die Parkscheine) car-park ticket.

m **Parkuhr** die (PL die Parkuhren) parking meter.

n **Parkverbot** das 'Parkverbot' 'no parking'; **in der Innenstadt ist Parkverbot** you can't park in the town centre.

o **Parlament** das (PL die Parlamente) parliament.

p **Parole** die (PL die Parolen) slogan.

q **Partei** die (PL die Parteien) **1** party; **2 für jemanden Partei ergreifen** to side with somebody.

r **Parterre** das (PL die Parterres) ground floor.

s **Partie** die (PL die Partien) **1** part; **2** game (of tennis, chess).

Partner der (PL die Partner) partner.

Partnerin die (PL die Partnerinnen) partner.

Partnerstadt die (PL die Partnerstädte) twin town.

Party die (PL die Partys) party.

Pass der (PL die Pässe) **1** passport; **2** pass.

Passage die (PL die Passagen) **1** shopping arcade; **2** passage (of text); **3** sequence (of music, film).

Passagier der (PL die Passagiere) passenger.

Passant der (PL die Passanten) passer-by.

Passantin die (PL die Passantinnen) passer-by.

passen (PERF hat gepasst) **1** to fit; **jemandem passen** to fit somebody; **2** to suit; **jemandem passen** to suit somebody; **Freitag passt mir nicht** Friday doesn't suit me; **seine Art passt mir nicht** I don't like his manner; **3 zu etwas passen** to go with something; **zu jemandem passen** to be right for somebody.

passend adjective **1** suitable; **2** matching.

passieren verb (PERF ist passiert) to happen.

Passiv das passive.

passiv adjective passive.

Passkontrolle die passport control.

Passwort das (PL die Passwörter) password (in computing); das

Passwort eingeben to give the password.

Paste die (PL die **Pasten**) paste.

Pastete die (PL die **Pasteten**) pie.

Pate der (PL die **Paten**) godfather.

Patenkind das (PL die **Patenkinder**) godchild.

patent adjective capable, clever.

Patentante die (PL die **Patentanten**) godmother.

Patient der (PL die **Patienten**) patient.

Patientin die (PL die **Patientinnen**) patient.

Patin die (PL die **Patinnen**) godmother.

patschnass adjective soaking wet.

pauken verb (informal) (PERF hat **gepaukt**) to swot.

pauschal adjective all-inclusive.

Pauschalreise die (PL die **Pauschalreisen**) package tour.

Pause die (PL die **Pausen**) 1 break; 2 pause; 3 interval.

Pazifik der der **Pazifik** the Pacific (Ocean).

PC der (PL die **PCs**) PC.

Pech das 1 bad luck; **Pech haben** to be unlucky; 2 pitch.

Pedal das (PL die **Pedale**) pedal.

peinlich adjective 1 embarrassing; **es war mir sehr peinlich** I felt very embarrassed about it; 2 awkward; 3 meticulous.

Peitsche die (PL die **Peitschen**) whip.

Pelle die skin.

Pelz der (PL die **Pelze**) fur.

pendeln verb 1 (PERF **ist gependelt**) to commute; 2 (PERF hat **gependelt**) to swing.

Pendelverkehr der 1 commuter traffic; 2 shuttle service.

Pendler der (PL die **Pendler**) commuter.

penetrant adjective 1 overpowering (odour, perfume); 2 pushy (person).

Penis der (PL die **Penisse**) penis.

pennen verb (informal) (PERF hat **gepennt**) to sleep, to kip.

Pension die (PL die **Pensionen**) 1 guesthouse; 2 **volle Pension** full board; 3 pension; **eine schöne Pension haben** to get a good pension; **in Pension gehen** to retire.

pensioniert adjective retired.

per preposition (+ ACC) 1 by; **per Luftpost** by airmail; 2 per.

Perfekt das (PL die **Perfekte**) perfect.

perfekt adjective perfect.

Perlode die (PL die **Perloden**) period.

Perle die (PL die **Perlen**) 1 pearl; 2 bead.

Person die (PL die **Personen**) person; **für vier Personen** for four people; **ich für meine Person** personally.

Personal das staff, personnel.

Personalausweis der (PL die **Personalausweise**) identity card.

a b c d e f g h i j k l m n o p q r s t u v w x y z

a Personenzug der (PL die Personenzüge) stopping train.

b persönlich adjective personal.

c persönlich adverb **1** personally; **2** in person.

d Persönlichkeit die (PL die Persönlichkeiten) personality.

e Perücke die (PL die Perücken) wig.

f Pessimist der (PL die Pessimisten) pessimist.

g pessimistisch adjective pessimistic.

h Petersilie die parsley.

i Petroleum das paraffin.

j Pfad der (PL die Pfade) path.

k Pfadfinder der (PL die Pfadfinder) (Boy) Scout.

l Pfadfinderin die (PL die Pfadfinderinnen) (Girl) Guide.

m Pfand das (PL die Pfänder) **1** forfeit; **2** deposit (on a bottle); **3** pledge.

n Pfandflasche die (PL die Pfandflaschen) returnable bottle.

o Pfanne die (PL die Pfannen) (frying) pan.

p Pfannkuchen der (PL die Pfannkuchen) pancake.

q Pfarrer der (PL die Pfarrer) **1** vicar; **2** priest.

r Pfau der (PL die Pfauen) peacock.

s Pfauhenne die (PL die Pfauhennen) peahen.

t Pfeffer der pepper.

u Pfefferkorn das (PL die Pfefferkörner) peppercorn.

v Pfefferkuchen der gingerbread.

Pfefferminzbonbon der (PL die Pfefferminzbonbons) mint.

Pfefferminze die peppermint.

Pfeffermühle die (PL die Pfeffermühlen) peppermill.

Pfeife die (PL die Pfeifen) **1** whistle; **2** pipe.

pfeifen ◊ verb (IMPERF pfiff, PERF hat gepfiffen) to whistle.

Pfeil der (PL die Pfeile) arrow.

Pfeiler der (PL die Pfeiler) **1** pillar; **2** pier.

Pfennig der (PL die Pfennige) pfennig (one hundredth of a mark in the former German currency) **ich habe keinen Pfennig mehr** I haven't got a penny left SEE **Mark.**

Pferd das (PL die Pferde) horse.

Pferderennen das (PL die Pferderennen) horse race.

Pferdeschwanz der (PL die Pferdeschwänze) ponytail.

pfiff SEE **pfeifen.**

Pfingsten das (PL die Pfingsten) Whitsun.

Pfirsich der (PL die Pfirsiche) peach.

Pflanze die (PL die Pflanzen) plant.

pflanzen verb (PERF hat gepflanzt) to plant; **pflanze mehr Bäume** plant more trees.

Pflaster das (PL die Pflaster) **1** pavement; **2** plaster.

Pflaume die (PL die Pflaumen) plum.

w x y z

Pflege *die* **1** care; **2** nursing; **3 ein Kind in Pflege nehmen** to foster a child.

Pflegeeltern *plural noun* foster parents.

Pflegeheim *das* (PL die **Pflegeheime**) nursing home.

Pflegekind *das* (PL die **Pflegekinder**) foster child.

pflegeleicht *adjective* easy-care (*fabric*).

pflegen *verb* (PERF **hat geflegt**) **1** to look after, to care for; **eine Freundschaft pflegen** to foster a friendship; **2** to nurse.

Pfleger *der* (PL die **Pfleger**) (male) nurse.

Pflicht *die* (PL die **Pflichten**) duty; **Pflicht sein** to be compulsory.

pflichtbewusst *adjective* conscientious.

Pflichtfach *das* (PL die **Pflichtfächer**) compulsory subject.

pflücken *verb* (PERF **hat gepflückt**) to pick.

Pflug *der* (PL die **Pflüge**) plough.

pflügen *verb* (PERF **hat gepflügt**) to plough.

Pforte *die* (PL die **Pforten**) gate.

Pförtner *der* (PL die **Pförtner**) porter.

Pfosten *der* (PL die **Pfosten**) post.

Pfote *die* (PL die **Pfoten**) paw.

pfui *exclamation* ugh!

Pfund *das* (PL die **Pfund(e)**) pound.

Pfütze *die* (PL die **Pfützen**) puddle.

Phantasie *die* SEE **Fantasie**.

phantasievoll *adjective* SEE **Fantasievoll**.

phantastisch *adjective* fantastic.

Philosoph *der* (PL die **Philosophen**) philosopher.

Philosophie *die* (PL die **Philosophien**) philosophy.

Photo *das* (PL die **Photos**) SEE **Foto**.

Phrase *die* (PL die **Phrasen**) **1** phrase; **2** cliché.

Physik *die* physics.

Physiker *der* (PL die **Physiker**) physicist.

Physikerin *die* (PL die **Physikerinnen**) physicist.

Pickel *der* (PL die **Pickel**) spot, pimple.

Picknick *das* (PL die **Picknicks**) picnic.

Pik *das* spades (*in cards*).

pikant *adjective* spicy.

Pille *die* (PL die **Pillen**) pill.

Pilot *der* (PL die **Piloten**) pilot

Pilotin *die* (PL die **Pilotinnen**) pilot.

Pilz *der* (PL die **Pilze**) **1** mushroom; **2** fungus.

Pinguin *der* (PL die **Pinguine**) penguin.

pinkeln *verb* (*informal*) (PERF **hat gepinkelt**) to pee.

Pinnwand *die* (PL die **Pinnwände**) noticeboard.

Pinsel *der* (PL die **Pinsel**) brush.

Pinzette *die* (PL die **Pinzetten**) tweezers.

Pirat *der* (PL die **Piraten**) pirate.

a
b
c
d
e
f
g
h
i
j
k
l
m
n
o
p
q
r
s
t
u
v
w
x
y
z

a
b
c
d
e
f
g
h
i
j
k
l
m
n
o
p
q
r
s
t
u
v
w
x
y
z

Piste die (PL die **Pisten**) 1 run, piste; 2 track; 3 runway.

Pizza die (PL die **Pizzas**) pizza.

Pkw der (PL die **Pkws**) (*Personenkraftwagen*) car.

plagen verb (PERF hat geplagt) 1 to bother, to torment; 2 to pester; 3 sich plagen to struggle; sich in der Schule plagen to struggle at school; er muss sich plagen he has to work hard.

Plakat das (PL die **Plakate**) poster.

Plan der (PL die **Pläne**) 1 plan; 2 map.

planen verb (PERF hat geplant) to plan.

Planierraupe die (PL die **Planierraupen**) bulldozer.

planmäßig adjective scheduled.

planmäßig adverb 1 according to plan; alles läuft planmäßig everything is going according to plan; 2 on schedule; der Zug ist planmäßig abgefahren the train left on schedule.

Plastik[1] das plastic.

Plastik[2] die (PL die **Plastiken**) sculpture.

Plastiktüte die (PL die **Plastiktüten**) plastic bag.

Platin das platinum.

platt adjective flat; platt sein (*informal*) to be flabbergasted.

plattdeutsch adjective low German.

Platte die (PL die **Platten**) 1 plate; 2 dish; kalte Platte cold meats and cheeses; 3 hotplate; 4 record;

5 board (*made of wood*); 6 slab (*made of stone*); 7 sheet (*made of metal or glass*); 8 top (*of a table*).

Plattenspieler der (PL die **Plattenspieler**) record player.

Platz der (PL die **Plätze**) 1 place; viel Platz haben to have a lot of room; Platz lassen to leave room; auf die Plätze, fertig, los! on your marks, get set, go!; 2 seat; Platz nehmen to take a seat; 3 square (*in a town*); 4 ground, pitch; einen Spieler vom Platz stellen to send a player off; 5 court (*for tennis*); 6 course (*for golf*).

Plätzchen das (PL die **Plätzchen**) 1 biscuit; 2 spot.

platzen verb (PERF ist geplatzt) 1 to burst; 2 der Plan ist geplatzt (*informal*) the plan fell through; 3 vor Neugier platzen to be bursting with curiosity.

plaudern verb (PERF hat geplaudert) to chat.

pleite adjective (*informal*) broke.

Plombe die (PL die **Plomben**) filling.

plombieren verb (PERF hat plombiert) to fill.

plötzlich adjective sudden.

plötzlich adverb suddenly.

plump adjective 1 plump; 2 clumsy.

Plural der (PL die **Plurale**) plural.

Plus das 1 plus; 2 profit; 3 advantage.

plus adverb plus.

PLZ SEE **Postleitzahl**.

Po der (*informal*) (PL die **Pos**) bottom.

Poesie die poetry.

Pokal der (PL die **Pokale**) **1** cup; **2** goblet.

Pokalspiel das (PL die **Pokalspiele**) cup-tie.

Pole der (PL die **Polen**) Pole.

Polen das Poland.

polieren verb (PERF **hat poliert**) to polish.

Polin die (PL die **Polinnen**) Pole.

Politik die **1** politics; **2** policy.

Politiker der (PL die **Politiker**) politician.

Politikerin die (PL die **Politikerinnen**) politician.

politisch adjective political.

Politur die (PL die **Polituren**) polish.

Polizei die police.

polizeilich adjective police.

polizeilich adverb by the police; **sich polizeilich anmelden** to register with the police.

Polizeiwache die (PL die **Polizeiwachen**) police station.

Polizist der (PL die **Polizisten**) policeman.

Polizistin die (PL die **Polizistinnen**) policewoman.

polnisch adjective Polish.

Pommes frites plural noun chips, French fries.

Pony[1] das (PL die **Ponys**) pony.

Pony[2] der (PL die **Ponys**) fringe.

Popmusik die pop music.

poppig adjective bright; **Natalie hat immer poppige Socken an** Natalie always wears bright socks.

Porree der (PL die **Porrees**) leek; **eine Stange Porree** a leek.

Portemonnaie das SEE **Portmonee**.

Portier der (PL die **Portiers**) porter.

Portion die (PL die **Portionen**) portion; **möchtest du eine zweite Portion?** would you like a second helping?

Portmonee das (PL die **Portmonees**) purse.

Porto das postage.

Porträt das (PL die **Porträts**) portrait.

Portugal das Portugal.

Portugiese der (PL die **Portugiesen**) Portuguese.

Portugiesin die (PL die **Portugiesinnen**) Portuguese.

portugiesisch adjective Portuguese.

Posaune die (PL die **Posaunen**) trombone.

Post die **1** post; **mit der Post** by post; **2** post office.

Postamt das (PL die **Postämter**) post office.

Postbote der (PL die **Postboten**) postman.

Poster das (PL die **Poster**) poster.

Postkarte die (PL die **Postkarten**) postcard.

Postleitzahl die (PL die **Postleitzahlen**) postcode.

Pracht die splendour.

prächtig adjective splendid.

a **prahlen** verb (PERF **hat geprahlt**) to boast.

b **praktisch** adjective **1** practical; **praktische Erfahrung** practical experience; **2** handy; **3 ein praktischer Arzt** a general practitioner.

c

d **praktisch** adverb **1** practically; **2** in practice.

e

f **Praline** die (PL die **Pralinen**) chocolate.

g **Präposition** die (PL die **Präpositionen**) preposition.

h **Präsens** das present (tense).

i **Präservativ** das (PL die **Präservative**) condom.

j **Präsident** der (PL die **Präsidenten**) president.

k

l **Präsidentin** die (PL die **Präsidentinnen**) president.

m **Pratikum** das (PL die **Praktika**) practical training.

n **Praxis** die (PL die **Praxen**) **1** practice; **2** practical experience; **3** surgery.

o **Preis** der (PL die **Preise**) **1** price; **um keinen Preis** not at any price; **2** prize.

p **Preisausschreiben** das (PL die **Preisausschreiben**) competition.

q **Preiselbeere** die (PL die **Preiselbeeren**) cranberry.

r **preiswert** adjective reasonable, cheap.

s **Prellung** die (PL die **Prellungen**) bruise.

t **Premierminister** der (PL die **Premierminister**) prime minister.

u

Presse die press.

v **Priester** der (PL die **Priester**) priest.

w **prima** adjective (informal) brilliant.

x **Prinz** der (PL die **Prinzen**) prince.

y **Prinzessin** die (PL die **Prinzessinnen**) princess.

z **Prise** die (PL die **Prisen**) pinch; **eine Prise Salz** a pinch of salt.

privat adjective private.

Privileg das (PL die **Privilegien**) privilege.

pro preposition (+ ACC) per.

Probe die (PL die **Proben**) **1** test; **jemanden auf die Probe stellen** to test somebody; **ein Auto Probe fahren** to test-drive a car; **2** sample; **3** rehearsal.

probefahren SEE **Probe**.

probieren verb (PERF **hat probiert**) **1** to try; **2** to taste.

Problem das (PL die **Probleme**) problem.

Produkt das (PL die **Produkte**) product.

Produzent der (PL die **Produzenten**) producer.

produzieren verb (PERF **hat produziert**) to produce.

Profi der (PL die **Profis**) pro.

Profil das (PL die **Profile**) **1** profile; **2** tread (of a tyre).

Programm das (PL die **Programme**) **1** programme; **2** program (in computing); **3** channel (on TV).

programmieren *verb* (PERF **hat programmiert**) to program.

Programmierer *der* (PL die **Programmierer**) programmer.

Programmiererin *die* (PL die **Programmiererinnen**) programmer.

Projekt *das* (PL die **Projekte**) project.

Promille *das* (PL die **Promille**) alcohol level; **zuviel Promille haben** to be over the limit.

Pronomen *das* (PL die **Pronomen**) pronoun.

Prospekt *der* (PL die **Prospekte**) brochure.

prost *exclamation* cheers!

Protein *das* (PL die **Proteine**) protein.

Protest *der* (PL die **Proteste**) protest.

protestantisch *adjective* Protestant.

protestieren *verb* (PERF **hat protestiert**) to protest.

Protokoll *das* (PL die **Protokolle**) 1 minutes, transcript; 2 record (*in court*); 3 protocol.

protzen *verb* (PERF **hat geprotzt**) to show off; **Klaus protzt mit seinem neuen Auto** Klaus is showing off with his new car.

Proviant *der* provisions.

Prozent *das* (PL die **Prozente**) 1 per cent; **zehn Prozent** ten per cent; **2 Prozente bekommen** (*informal*) to get a discount.

Prozentsatz *der* (PL die **Prozentsätze**) percentage.

Prozess *der* (PL die **Prozesse**) 1 court case; **einen Prozess gewinnen** to win a case; 2 trial; 3 process.

Prozession *die* (PL die **Prozessionen**) procession.

prüfen *verb* (PERF **hat geprüft**) 1 to test, to examine (*at school*); 2 to check; **hast du die Reifen geprüft?** have you checked the tyres?

Prüfung *die* (PL die **Prüfungen**) 1 examination, exam; **eine Prüfung bestehen** to pass an examination; **sie ist durch die Prüfung gefallen** she failed the exam; 2 check.

Prügel *der* (PL die **Prügel**) 1 stick; **2 Prügel bekommen** to get a beating.

Prügelei *die* (PL die **Prügeleien**) fight.

prügeln *verb* (PERF **hat geprügelt**) 1 to beat; **2 sich prügeln** to fight; **sich um etwas prügeln** to fight for something.

Psychiater *der* (PL die **Psychiater**) psychiatrist.

Psychiaterin *die* (PL die **Psychiaterinnen**) psychiatrist.

psychisch *adjective* psychological.

Psychologe *der* (PL die **Psychologen**) psychologist.

Psychologie *die* psychology.

Psychologin *die* (PL die **Psychologinnen**) psychologist.

a b c d e f g h i j k l m n o p q r s t u v w x y z

Publikum das **1** audience, crowd; **2** public.

Pudding der (PL die **Puddinge**) **1** blancmange; **2** pudding (steamed).

Pudel der (PL die **Pudel**) poodle.

Puder der (PL die **Puder**) powder.

Puffmais der popcorn.

Pulli der (PL die **Pullis**) pullover.

Pullover der (PL die **Pullover**) pullover.

Puls der (PL die **Pulse**) pulse; **der Arzt maß meinen Puls** the doctor took my pulse.

Pult das (PL die **Pulte**) desk.

Pulver das (PL die **Pulver**) powder.

Pulverkaffee der instant coffee.

Pumpe die (PL die **Pumpen**) pump.

pumpen verb (PERF hat gepumpt) **1** to pump; **2** (informal) to lend; **jemandem Geld pumpen** to lend somebody money; **3** (informal) to borrow; **sich etwas pumpen** to borrow something.

Punker der (PL die **Punker**) punk.

Punkerin die (PL die **Punkerinnen**) punk.

Punkt der (PL die **Punkte**) **1** dot, spot; **Punkt sechs Uhr** at six o'clock on the dot; **2** full stop; **3** point; **nach Punkten siegen** to win on points.

pünktlich adjective punctual.

Puppe die (PL die **Puppen**) **1** doll; **2** puppet.

pur adjective **1** pure; **2** Whisky pur neat whisky.

Purzelbaum der (PL die **Purzelbäume**) somersault.

pusten verb (PERF hat gepustet) to blow.

Pute die (PL die **Puten**) turkey.

putzen verb (PERF hat geputzt) **1** to clean; **putz dir die Zähne** clean your teeth; **putzen gehen** to work as a cleaner; **2** sich die Nase putzen to blow your nose.

Putzfrau die (PL die **Putzfrauen**) cleaning lady, cleaner.

putzig adjective cute.

Puzzle das (PL die **Puzzles**) jigsaw (puzzle).

Pyjama der (PL die **Pyjamas**) pyjamas.

Pyramide die (PL die **Pyramiden**) pyramid.

Pyrenäen (plural noun) die **Pyrenäen** the Pyrenees.

Qq

Quadrat das (PL die **Quadrate**) square.

quadratisch adjective square.

Quadratmeter der (PL die **Quadratmeter**) square metre.

quaken verb (PERF hat gequakt) **1** to quack; **2** to croak (of a frog).

Qual die (PL die **Qualen**) **1** torment; **2** agony; **es war eine Qual, das ansehen zu müssen** it was agony to watch.

quälen verb (PERF **hat gequält**) **1** to torment; **2** to torture; **3** to pester; **4 sich quälen** to suffer; **5 sich mit etwas quälen** to struggle with something; **sich durch ein Buch quälen** to struggle (your way) through a book.

Quälgeist der (informal) (PL die **Quälgeister**) pest.

Qualifikation die (PL die **Qualifikationen**) qualification.

qualifizieren verb (PERF **hat qualifiziert**) **sich qualifizieren** to qualify; **sie haben sich für die dritte Runde qualifiziert** they qualified for the third round.

Qualität die (PL die **Qualitäten**) quality.

Qualle die (PL die **Quallen**) jellyfish.

Qualm der thick smoke.

qualmen verb (PERF **hat gequalmt**) to give off clouds of smoke; **sie qualmt wie ein Schlot** (informal) she smokes like a chimney.

Quarantäne die quarantine.

Quark der (curd cheese) quark.

Quartett das (PL die **Quartette**) quartet.

Quartier das (PL die **Quartiere**) **1** accommodation; **2** quarters.

quasseln verb (informal) (PERF **hat gequasselt**) to natter.

Quatsch der (informal) rubbish.

quatschen verb (informal) (PERF **hat gequatscht**) to chat.

Quelle die (PL die **Quellen**) **1** source; **2** spring.

quer adverb **1** across; **2** crosswise; **3** diagonally; **quer gestreift** with diagonal stripes; **4 quer durch** straight through.

quergestreift SEE **quer**.

Querstraße die (PL die **Querstraßen**) side street; **die erste Querstraße rechts** the first turning on the right.

quetschen verb (PERF **hat gequetscht**) **1** to crush; **2** to squash; **3 ich habe mich in meine Jeans gequetscht** I squeezed into my jeans.

Quetschung die (PL die **Quetschungen**) bruise.

quietschen verb (PERF **hat gequietscht**) to squeak.

quitt adjective quits.

Quittung die (PL die **Quittungen**) receipt.

Quiz das (PL die **Quiz**) quiz.

Rr

Rabatt der (PL die **Rabatte**) discount.

Rache die revenge.

rächen verb (PERF **hat gerächt**) **1** to avenge; **2 sich an jemandem rächen** to take revenge on somebody; **3 das wird sich rächen** you'll have to pay for it.

Rad das (PL die **Räder**) **1** wheel; **2** bike; **Julia ist mit dem Rad gekommen** Julia came by bike; **3 Rad fahren** to cycle.

Radar der radar.

Radarschirm der (PL die Radarschirme) radar screen.

radeln verb (PERF **ist geradelt**) to cycle; **Max ist ins Dorf geradelt** Max cycled into the village.

radfahren SEE Rad.

Radfahrer der (PL die Radfahrer) cyclist.

Radfahrerin die (PL die Radfahrerinnen) cyclist.

Radfahrweg der (PL die Radfahrwege) cycle lane.

Radiergummi der (PL die Radiergummis) rubber.

Radieschen das (PL die Radieschen) radish.

Radio das (PL die Radios) radio.

radioaktiv adjective radioactive.

Radiosendung die (PL die Radiosendungen) radio broadcast.

Radler der (PL die Radler) cyclist.

Radlerin die (PL die Radlerinnen) cyclist.

Radrennen das **1** cycle race; **Maria hat das Radrennen gewonnen** Maria won the cycle race; **2** cycle racing.

Radweg der (PL die Radwege) cycle path.

raffiniert adjective crafty.

Rahm der cream.

Rahmen der (PL die Rahmen) **1** frame; **2** framework; **3** limits; **im Rahmen des Möglichen** within the bounds of possibility.

rahmen verb (PERF **hat gerahmt**) to frame (a picture).

Rakete die (PL die Raketen) rocket.

ran (informal) SEE heran.

Rand der (PL die Ränder) **1** edge; **2** rim; **der Rand der Tasse war angeschlagen** the rim of the cup was chipped; **3** ring, mark; **4** margin (of a page); **du musst einen Rand für die Korrekturen lassen** you must leave a margin for the corrections; **5** outskirts (of a town); **6 etwas am Rande erwähnen** to mention something in passing; **7 am Rande der Pleite sein** to be on the verge of bankruptcy; **8 außer Rand und Band geraten** (informal) to go wild.

Randstreifen der (PL die Randstreifen) hard shoulder.

Rang der (PL die Ränge) **1** rank; **2** (in a theatre) circle.

rannte SEE rennen.

rasch adjective quick.

Rasen der (PL die Rasen) lawn, grass.

rasen verb (PERF **ist gerast**) to tear along, to rush; **gegen eine Mauer rasen** to career into a wall.

Rasenmäher der (PL die Rasenmäher) lawnmower.

Rasierapparat der (PL die Rasierapparate) **1** shaver; **2** razor.

Rasiercreme die (PL die Rasiercremes) shaving cream.

rasieren verb (PERF **hat rasiert**) **1** to shave; **2 sich rasieren** to shave.

Rasierklinge die (PL die Rasierklingen) razor blade.

Rasierwasser das aftershave.

Rasse die (PL die Rassen) **1** race; **2** breed; **ich weiß nicht, was für eine Rasse unser Hund ist** I don't know what breed our dog is.

Rassenhass der racial hatred.

rassisch adjective racial.

Rassismus der racism.

Rassist der (PL die Rassisten) racist.

Rassistin die (PL die Rassistinnen) racist.

rassistisch adjective racist.

rasten verb (PERF hat gerastet) to rest.

Rastplatz der (PL die Rastplätze) picnic area (on a motorway).

Raststätte die (PL die Raststätten) services (on a motorway).

Rat der **1** advice; **ein Rat** a piece of advice; **jemanden zu Rate ziehen** to ask somebody's advice; **2 sich keinen Rat wissen** not to know what to do; **3** council.

Rate die (PL die Raten) instalment; **in monatlichen Raten abzahlen** to pay in monthly instalments.

raten ◇verb (PRES rät, IMPERF riet, PERF hat geraten) **1 jemandem raten** to advise somebody; **was rätst du mir?** what do you advise me to do?; **2** to guess; **richtig raten** to guess right.

Rathaus das (PL die Rathäuser) town hall.

rationell adjective efficient.

ratlos adjective helpless; **Emma hat mich ratlos angesehen** Emma gave me a helpless look; **ratlos sein** not to know what to do.

ratsam adjective advisable; **es wäre ratsam, früher zu fahren** it would be advisable to leave earlier.

Ratschlag der (PL die Ratschläge) piece of advice, advice; **deine klugen Ratschläge kannst du dir sparen** you can keep your advice to yourself.

Rätsel das (PL die Rätsel) **1** puzzle; **2** mystery.

rätselhaft adjective mysterious.

Ratte die (PL die Ratten) rat.

rau adjective **1** rough; **2** harsh; **3 eine raue Stimme** a husky voice; **4 einen rauen Hals haben** to have a sore throat.

Raub der robbery.

Raubdruck der (PL die Raubdrucke) pirated edition.

Räuber der (PL die Räuber) robber.

Rauch der smoke.

rauchen verb (PERF hat geraucht) to smoke; **'Rauchen verboten'** 'no smoking'.

Rauchen das smoking; **passives Rauchen** passive smoking.

Raucher der (PL die Raucher) smoker.

Raucherin die (PL die Raucherinnen) smoker.

Räucherlachs der smoked salmon.

räuchern verb (PERF hat geräuchert) to smoke (fish, meat).

a b c d e f g h i j k l m n o p q r s t u v w x y z

a

b

c

d

e

f

g

h

i

j

k

l

m

n

o

p

q

r

s

t

u

v

w

x

y

z

rauf (*informal*) SEE **herauf, hinauf.**

rauh *adjective* SEE **rau.**

Raum der (PL die **Räume**) **1** room; **das Haus hat sehr große Räume** the house has very big rooms; **2** space; **wir brauchen mehr Raum** we need more space; **3 die Rakete ist im Raum explodiert** the rocket exploded in space; **4** area; **im Raum Berlin** in the area of Berlin.

räumen *verb* (PERF **hat geräumt**) **1** to clear; **das Geschirr vom Tisch räumen** to clear away the dishes; **2 die Hemden in den Schrank räumen** to put the shirts in the cupboard; **seine Sachen beiseite räumen** to put your things to one side; **die Akten aus dem Schrank räumen** to take the files out of the cabinet; **3** to vacate.

Raumfahrt die space travel.

Raumschiff das (PL die **Raumschiffe**) space ship.

Räumungsverkauf der closing-down sale.

Raupe die (PL die **Raupen**) caterpillar.

raus (*informal*) SEE **heraus, hinaus.**

Rauschgift das (PL die **Rauschgifte**) drug; **Rauschgift nehmen** to take drugs.

Rauschgiftsüchtige der/die (PL die **Rauschgiftsüchtigen**) drug addict.

rauskriegen *verb* (*informal*) (PERF **hat rausgekriegt**) **1** to get out; **2 ein Geheimnis rauskriegen** to find out a secret; **3 ich kann die

Aufgabe nicht rauskriegen I can't do the exercise.

räuspern *verb* (PERF **hat sich geräuspert**) **sich räuspern** to clear your throat.

reagieren *verb* (PERF **hat reagiert**) to react.

Reaktion die (PL die **Reaktionen**) reaction.

realisieren *verb* (PERF **hat realisiert**) **1** to realize; **2** to implement.

Reality-Show die (PL die **Reality-Shows**) reality show.

Realschule die (PL die **Realschulen**) secondary school.

rebellieren *verb* (PERF **hat rebelliert**) to rebel.

Rechen der (PL die **Rechen**) rake.

Recherche die (PL die **Recherchen**) investigation.

rechnen *verb* (PERF **hat gerechnet**) **1** to do arithmetic; **Peter kann gut rechnen** Peter's good at arithmetic, Peter's good at figures; **2** to reckon; **mit etwas rechnen** to reckon with something; **3 er wird zu den besten Schauspielern gerechnet** he's reckoned to be one of the best actors; **4** to count; **jemanden zu seinen Freunden rechnen** to count somebody as a friend; **5 mit etwas rechnen** to expect something; **6 auf jemanden rechnen** to count on somebody.

Rechner der (PL die **Rechner**) **1** calculator; **2** computer.

Rechnung die (PL die Rechnungen) **1** bill; **2** invoice; **die Rechnung liegt bei** the invoice is enclosed; **3** calculation.

Recht das (PL die Rechte) **1** law; **nach deutschem Recht** under German law; **2** right; **Recht haben** to be right; **im Recht sein** to be in the right; **Recht bekommen** to be proved right; **Recht geben** to agree with somebody; **4 mit Recht** rightly; **du hast dich mit Recht beschwert** you were right to complain.

recht adjective **1** right; **jemandem recht sein** to be all right with somebody; **wenn es dir recht ist** if it's all right with you; **2 der/die Rechte** the right man/woman; **3 das Rechte** the right thing; **etwas Rechtes** something proper; **ich habe nichts Rechtes gegessen** I haven't had a proper meal; **etwas Rechtes lernen** to learn something useful; **4** real; **ich habe keine rechte Lust** I don't really feel like it.

recht adverb **1** correctly; **2** quite; **recht einfach** quite simple; **3** really; **4 recht vielen Dank** many thanks; **5 das geschieht dir recht!** (it) serves you right!; **6 man kann es nicht allen recht machen** you can't please everyone.

Rechte die **1** right (side); **zu meiner Rechten** on my right; **2** right hand; **3 die Rechte** the right (in politics).

rechte SEE rechter.

Rechteck das (PL die Rechtecke) rectangle.

rechteckig adjective rectangular.

rechter, rechte, rechtes adjective **1** right; **auf der rechten Seite** on the right; **2** right-wing.

rechtfertigen verb **1** (PERF **hat gerechtfertigt**) to justify; **2 sich rechtfertigen** to justify yourself.

rechtlich adjective legal.

rechts adverb on the right; **nimm die dritte Abzweigung rechts** take the third turning on the right; **von rechts** from the right; **rechts abbiegen** to turn right.

Rechtsanwalt der (PL die Rechtsanwälte) lawyer.

Rechtsanwältin die (PL die Rechtsanwältinnen) lawyer.

Rechtschreibprogramm das (PL die Rechtschreibprogramme) spell checker.

Rechtschreibung die spelling.

Rechtshänder der (PL die Rechtshänder) **Klaus ist Rechtshänder** Klaus is right-handed.

Rechtshänderin die (PL die Rechtshänderinnen) **Beate ist Rechtshänderin** Beate is right-handed.

rechtzeitig adjective timely.

rechtzeitig adverb in time; **wir sind gerade noch rechtzeitig angekommen** we got there just in time.

Redakteur der (PL die Redakteure) editor.

a b c d e f g h i j k l m n o p q **r** s t u v w x y z

Redakteurin die (PL die Redakteurinnen) editor.

Rede die (PL die Reden) 1 speech; **eine Rede halten** to make a speech; 2 **nicht der Rede wert** not worth mentioning; **davon kann keine Rede sein** it's out of the question; **jemanden zur Rede stellen** to take somebody to task.

reden verb (PERF hat geredet) 1 to talk; 2 to speak; **mit jemandem reden** to speak to somebody; 3 **sie hat kein Wort geredet** she didn't say a word; 4 **mir ist egal, was über mich geredet wird** I don't care what people say about me.

Redewendung die (PL die Redewendungen) idiom, expression.

redigieren verb (PERF hat redigiert) to edit.

redlich adjective honest.

Redlichkeit die honesty.

Redner der (PL die Redner) speaker.

Rednerin die (PL die Rednerinnen) speaker.

reduzieren verb (PERF hat reduziert) to reduce.

reflexiv adjective reflexive.

Reformhaus das (PL die Reformhäuser) health-food shop.

Regal das (PL die Regale) 1 shelf; 2 shelves, bookcase.

Regel die (PL die Regeln) 1 rule; **in der Regel** as a rule; 2 period (menstruation).

regelmäßig adjective regular.

regeln verb (PERF hat geregelt) 1 to regulate; 2 to direct (the traffic); 3 to settle (a matter); **wir haben die Sache so geregelt, dass ...** we've arranged things so that ...; 4 **sich von selbst regeln** to sort itself out.

Regelung die (PL die Regelungen) 1 regulation; 2 settlement.

Regen der rain.

Regenbogen der (PL die Regenbogen) rainbow.

Regenmantel der (PL die Regenmäntel) raincoat.

Regenschirm der (PL die Regenschirme) umbrella.

Regenwurm der (PL die Regenwürmer) earthworm.

regieren verb (PERF hat regiert) 1 to govern; 2 to rule, to reign.

Regierung die (PL die Regierungen) 1 government; 2 reign.

Regisseur der (PL die Regisseure) director.

Regisseurin die (PL die Regisseurinnen) director.

Register das (PL die Register) 1 index; 2 register.

regnen verb (PERF hat geregnet) to rain.

regnerisch adjective rainy.

Reh das (PL die Rehe) deer.

reiben ◊verb (IMPERF rieb, PERF hat gerieben) 1 to rub; 2 to grate.

reibungslos adjective smooth.

reich adjective rich.

Reich das (PL die **Reiche**) 1 empire;
das Römische Reich the Roman
Empire; 2 kingdom, realm.

reichen verb (PERF hat gereicht)
1 to hand, to pass; 2 to be enough;
mit dem Geld reichen to have
enough money; 3 bis zu etwas
reichen to reach up to something;
er reicht seinem Vater bis zur
Schulter he comes up to his
father's shoulder; die Felder
reichen bis zum Wald the fields
extend as far as go right up to the
forest; 4 mir reicht's! (informal)
I've had enough!

reichlich adjective 1 large;
2 ample (space).

reichlich adverb plenty of.

Reichtum der (PL die **Reichtümer**)
wealth.

Reichweite die 1 reach; außer
Reichweite out of reach; 2 range.

relf adjective 1 ripe; 2 mature.

Reife die maturity; mittlere Reife
exams taken after five years of
secondary schooling.

Reifen der (PL die **Reifen**) 1 tyre;
2 hoop.

Reifendruck der tyre pressure.

Reifenpanne die (PL die
Reifenpannen) puncture.

Reihe die (PL die **Reihen**) 1 row;
2 series; eine Reihe von
Erelgnissen a series of events;
3 der Reihe nach in turn; außer
der Reihe out of turn; du bist an
der Reihe it's your turn.

Reihenfolge die (PL die
Reihenfolgen) order; in der

richtigen Reihenfolge in the right
order.

Reihenhaus das (PL die
Reihenhäuser) terraced house.

Reim der (PL die **Reime**) rhyme.

reimen verb (PERF hat gereimt)
1 to rhyme; 2 sich reimen to
rhyme.

rein[1] adjective 1 pure; 2 clean;
3 sheer (madness); 4 etwas ins
Reine schreiben to make a fair
copy of something; etwas ins
Reine bringen to sort something
out.

rein adverb 1 purely; 2 absolutely;
rein gar nichts absolutely nothing.

rein[2] (informal) SEE herein, hinein.

reinigen verb (PERF hat gereinigt)
to clean.

Reinigung die (PL die
Reinigungen) 1 cleaning;
2 cleaner's.

Reis der of rice.

Reise die (PL die **Reisen**) 1 journey,
trip; gute Reise! have a good
journey!; auf meinen Reisen on
my travels; 2 voyage.

Reiseandenken das (PL die
Reiseandenken) souvenir.

Reisebüro das (PL die Reisebüros)
travel agency.

Reisebus der (PL die Reisebusse)
coach.

Reiseführer der (PL die
Reiseführer) 1 guidebook;
2 (travel) guide.

reisekrank *adjective* travel-sick; **reisekrank werden** to get travel-sick.

Reiseleiter der (PL die **Reiseleiter**) (travel) guide.

Reiseleiterin die (PL die **Reiseleiterinnen**) tourist guide.

reisen *verb* (PERF **ist gereist**) to travel.

Reisende der/die (PL die **Reisenden**) traveller.

Reisepass der (PL die **Reisepässe**) passport.

Reisescheck der (PL die **Reiseschecks**) traveller's cheque.

Reiseziel das (PL die **Reiseziele**) destination.

reißen ◇*verb* (IMPERF **riss**, PERF **hat gerissen**) 1 to tear; 2 to snatch; 3 to pull; **an etwas reißen** to pull at something; 4 **mit sich reißen** to sweep away; 5 **etwas an sich reißen** to snatch something; **die Macht an sich reißen** to seize power; 6 **Witze reißen** to crack jokes; 7 **sich um etwas reißen** to fight for something; 8 (PERF **ist gerissen**) to be torn; 9 (PERF **ist gerissen**) to tear, to break.

Reißverschluss der (PL die **Reißverschlüsse**) zip.

Reißzwecke die (PL die **Reißzwecken**) drawing pin.

reiten ◇*verb* (IMPERF **ritt**, PERF **hat/ ist geritten**) to ride.

Reiter der (PL die **Reiter**) rider.

Reiterin die (PL die **Reiterinnen**) rider.

Reitschule die (PL die **Reitschulen**) riding school.

Reiz der (PL die **Reize**) 1 attraction, appeal; 2 charm.

reizen *verb* (PERF **hat gereizt**) 1 to appeal to, to tempt; **das reizt mich sehr** it's very tempting; 2 to annoy; **jemanden zum Zorn reizen** to provoke somebody to anger; 3 to irritate (*the skin, eyes*); 4 to bid (*when playing cards*).

reizend *adjective* charming.

reizvoll *adjective* attractive.

Reklame die (PL die **Reklamen**) 1 advertisement, advert; **für etwas Reklame machen** to advertise something; 2 commercial (*on TV*).

Rekord der (PL die **Rekorde**) record.

Rektor der (PL die **Rektoren**) 1 head (*of a school*); 2 vice-chancellor (*of a university*).

Religion die (PL die **Religionen**) religion.

religiös *adjective* religious.

Rendezvous das (PL die **Rendezvous**) date.

Rennbahn die (PL die **Rennbahnen**) racetrack.

rennen ◇*verb* (IMPERF **rannte**, PERF **ist gerannt**) to run.

Rennen das (PL die **Rennen**) race.

Rennfahrer der (PL die **Rennfahrer**) racing driver.

Rennwagen der (PL die **Rennwagen**) racing car.

renovieren *verb* (PERF **hat renoviert**) to renovate, to redecorate.

rentabel *adjective* profitable.

Rente die (PL die **Renten**) pension; **in Rente gehen** to retire.

Rentner der (PL die **Rentner**) pensioner.

Rentnerin die (PL die **Rentnerinnen**) pensioner.

Reparatur die (PL die **Reparaturen**) repair.

reparieren *verb* (PERF **hat repariert**) to repair.

Reportage die (PL die **Reportagen**) 1 report; 2 live commentary.

Reporter der (PL die **Reporter**) reporter.

Reporterin die (PL die **Reporterinnen**) reporter.

Reptil das (PL die **Reptile**) reptile.

Republik die (PL die **Republiken**) republic.

Reservat das (PL die **Reservate**) reservation.

Reserverad das (PL die **Reserveräder**) spare wheel.

reservieren *verb* (PERF **hat reserviert**) to reserve.

Reservierung die (PL die **Reservierungen**) reservation.

Reservoir das (PL die **Reservoirs**) reservoir.

Respekt der respect.

respektieren *verb* (PERF **hat respektiert**) to respect.

Rest der (PL die **Reste**) 1 rest, remainder; 2 left-over; **zum Mittagessen gibts die Reste** we're having the leftovers for lunch; **3 die Reste** the remains.

Restaurant das (PL die **Restaurants**) restaurant.

restlich *adjective* remaining.

restlos *adjective* complete.

Resultat das (PL die **Resultate**) result.

retten *verb* (PERF **hat gerettet**) 1 to save, to rescue; **jemandem das Leben retten** to save somebody's life; 2 **sich retten** to escape.

Rettich der (PL die **Rettiche**) radish.

Rettung die rescue.

Rettungsboot das (PL die **Rettungsboote**) life boat.

Rettungsring der (PL die **Rettungsringe**) lifebelt.

Rettungsschwimmer der (PL die **Rettungsschwimmer**) lifeguard; **gibt es einen Rettungsschwimmer im Schwimmbad?** is there a lifeguard at the pool?

Rettungsschwimmerin die (PL die **Rettungsschwimmerinnen**) lifeguard.

Rettungswagen der (PL die **Rettungswagen**) ambulance.

Rezept das (PL die **Rezepte**) 1 prescription; 2 recipe.

Rezeption die (PL die **Rezeptionen**) reception; **bitte geben Sie Ihren Schlüssel an der Rezeption ab** please leave your key at reception.

R-Gespräch das (PL die **R-Gespräche**) reverse-charge call.

Rhabarber der rhubarb.

Rhein der Rhine.

Rheuma das rheumatism.

a
b
c
d
e
f
g
h
i
j
k
l
m
n
o
p
q
r
s
t
u
v
w
x
y
z

a

Rhythmus der (PL die **Rhythmen**) rhythm.

b

richten verb (PERF **hat gerichtet**)

c

1 to direct, to point (a torch, telescope, gun); **2 eine Frage an jemanden richten** to put a

d

question to somebody; **3** to address (a letter, remarks); **4** to prepare (a

e

meal, room); **5 sich auf etwas**

f

richten to be directed towards something; **6 sich nach**

g

jemandem richten to fit in with somebody's wishes; **sich nach den**

h

Vorschriften richten to follow the rules; **7 sich nach etwas richten**

i

to depend on something.

j

Richter der (PL die **Richter**) judge.

k

richtig adjective **1** right; **2 das**

l

Richtige the right thing; **der/die Richtige** the right man/woman;

m

3 real, proper.

n

richtig adverb **1** correctly; **hast du**

o

das Formular richtig ausgefüllt? have you filled in the form

p

correctly?; **2** really; **3 richtig stellen** to put right; **die Uhr geht**

q

richtig the clock is telling the right time.

r

Richtlinie die (PL die **Richtlinien**) guideline.

s

Richtung die (PL die **Richtungen**)

t

1 direction; **2** trend.

u

rieb SEE **reiben**.

v

riechen ⬦verb (IMPERF **roch**, PERF

w

hat gerochen) **1** to smell; **2 ich kann ihn nicht riechen** (informal)

x

I can't stand him.

y

rief SEE **rufen**.

z

Riegel der (PL die **Riegel**) **1** bolt; **2 ein Riegel Schokolade** a bar of chocolate.

Riemen der (PL die **Riemen**) strap.

Riese der (PL die **Riesen**) giant.

riesengroß adjective gigantic.

riesig adjective gigantic, huge; **ein riesiger Lastwagen** a gigantic lorry.

riet SEE **raten**.

Rind das (PL die **Rinder**) **1** ox; **2** cow; **Rinder** cattle; **3** beef.

Rinde die (PL die **Rinden**) **1** bark; **2** rind; **3** crust.

Rinderbraten der (PL die **Rinderbraten**) roast beef.

Rindfleisch das beef.

Ring der (PL die **Ringe**) ring.

Ringbuch das (PL die **Ringbücher**) ring binder.

Ringen das wrestling.

Rinne die (PL die **Rinnen**) **1** gutter; **2** drainpipe, channel.

Rippe die (PL die **Rippen**) rib.

Risiko das (PL die **Risiken**) risk.

riskant adjective risky.

riskieren verb (PERF **hat riskiert**) to risk, to put at risk.

Riss der (PL die **Risse**) **1** tear; **2** crack.

riss SEE **reißen**.

ritt SEE **reiten**.

Rivale der (PL die **Rivalen**) rival.

Rivalin die (PL die **Rivalinnen**) rival.

Robbe die (PL die **Robben**) seal.

Roboter der (PL die **Roboter**) robot.

roch SEE **riechen**.

Rock der (PL die **Röcke**) skirt.

Roggen der rye.

roh adjective **1** raw; **2** rough; **3** brutal.

Rohr das (PL die **Rohre**) **1** pipe; **2** reed; **3** cane.

Rohstoff der (PL die **Rohstoffe**) raw material.

Rollladen SEE **Rollladen**.

Rolle die (PL die **Rollen**) **1** roll; **2** reel; **3** role, part; **4 es spielt keine Rolle** it doesn't matter.

rollen verb (PERF **hat gerollt**) **1** to roll; **2** (PERF **ist gerollt**) to roll.

Roller der (PL die **Roller**) scooter.

Rollkragen der (PL die **Rollkragen**) polo neck.

Rollladen der (PL die **Rollläden**) shutter.

Rollschuh der (PL die **Rollschuhe**) roller-skate.

Rollschuhfahrer der (PL die **Rollschuhfahrer**) skater (on rollerskates).

Rollschuhfahrerin die (PL die **Rollschuhfahrerinnen**) skater (on rollerskates).

Rollschuhlaufen das roller-skating.

Rollstuhl der (PL die **Rollstühle**) wheelchair.

Rolltreppe die (PL die **Rolltreppen**) escalator.

Rom das Rome.

Roman der (PL die **Romane**) novel.

romantisch adjective romantic.

Römer der (PL die **Römer**) Roman.

Römerin die (PL die **Römerinnen**) Roman.

röntgen verb (PERF **hat geröntgt**) to X-ray.

rosa adjective pink.

Rose die (PL die **Rosen**) rose.

Rosenkohl der (Brussels) sprouts.

Rosine die (PL die **Rosinen**) raisin.

Rosmarin der rosemary.

Rosskastanie die (PL die **Rosskastanien**) horse-chestnut, conker.

Rost der (PL die **Roste**) **1** rust; **2** grate, grill.

rösten (PERF **hat geröstet**) **1** to roast; **2** to toast.

rosten verb (PERF **ist gerostet**) to rust.

rostig adjective rusty.

Röstkartoffeln plural noun roast potatoes.

rot adjective red.

Röteln plural noun German measles.

rothaarig adjective red-haired.

Rotkehlchen das (PL die **Rotkehlchen**) robin.

Rotkohl der red cabbage.

Rotwein der (PL die **Rotweine**) red wine.

Routine die routine.

rüber adverb (informal) over; **komm zu uns rüber** come over to us.

Rückblende die (PL die **Rückblenden**) flashback.

a
b
c
d
e
f
g
h
i
j
k
l
m
n
o
p
q
r
s
t
u
v
w
x
y
z

Rücken der (PL die **Rücken**) 1 back;
2 spine (of a book).

rücken verb (PERF **hat gerückt**) to
move; **kannst du ein wenig
rücken?** can you move over a bit?

Rückfahrkarte die (PL die
Rückfahrkarten) return ticket;
**eine Rückfahrkarte nach
München** a return ticket to
Munich.

Rückfahrt die return journey; **auf
der Rückfahrt** on the way back.

Rückgabe die (PL die **Rückgaben**)
return.

Rückgang der (PL die **Rückgänge**)
decrease; **ein Rückgang in der
Anzahl der Unfälle** a decrease in
the number of accidents.

rückgängig adjective etwas
rückgängig machen to cancel
something.

Rückhand die backhand (in
tennis).

Rückkehr die return.

Rückreise die return journey.

Rucksack der (PL die **Rucksäcke**)
rucksack.

Rückseite die (PL die **Rückseiten**)
back.

Rücksicht die consideration.

rücksichtslos adjective
1 inconsiderate; **ein
rücksichtsloser Fahrer** a reckless
driver; 2 ruthless.

rücksichtsvoll adjective
considerate.

Rücksitz der (PL die **Rücksitze**)
back seat.

rückwärts adverb backwards.

Rückwärtsgang der (PL die
Rückwärtsgänge) reverse (gear).

Rückweg der (PL die **Rückwege**)
1 way back; 2 return journey.

Rückzahlung die (PL die
Rückzahlungen) refund,
repayment.

Ruder das (PL die **Ruder**) 1 oar;
2 rudder.

Ruderboot das (PL die
Ruderboote) rowing boat.

rudern verb (PERF **ist gerudert**) 1 to
row; **ich bin über den See
gerudert** I rowed across the lake;
2 (PERF **hat gerudert**) to row; **ich
habe Monika über den See
gerudert** I rowed Monika across
the lake.

Rudern das rowing; **du bist mit
dem Rudern dran** it's your turn to
row.

Ruf der (PL die **Rufe**) 1 call, shout;
2 reputation; 3 phone number.

rufen ◇ verb (IMPERF **rief**, PERF **hat
gerufen**) to call; **den Arzt rufen** to
send for the doctor.

Rufnummer die (PL die
Rufnummern) phone number.

Ruhe die 1 silence; **Ruhe bitte!**
quiet please!; 2 rest; 3 peace;
jemanden in Ruhe lassen to leave
somebody in peace; **in aller Ruhe**
calmly; 4 **sich nicht aus der Ruhe
bringen lassen** to not get worked
up; 5 **sich zur Ruhe setzen** to
retire.

ruhen verb (PERF **hat geruht**) to
rest; **hier ruht ...** here lies ....

Ruhestand der **im Ruhestand** retired.

Ruhetag der (PL die **Ruhetage**) closing day; '**Dienstag Ruhetag**' 'closed on Tuesdays'.

ruhig adjective 1 quiet; 2 peaceful; 3 calm.

ruhig adverb 1 quietly; **sich ruhig verhalten** to keep quiet; 2 calmly; **ruhig bleiben** to remain calm; 3 **sehen Sie sich ruhig um** you're welcome to look around; **du kannst es ihm ruhig sagen** it's OK, you can tell him.

Ruhm der fame.

Rührei das scrambled eggs.

rühren verb (PERF **hat gerührt**) 1 to move; 2 to stir; 3 **sich rühren** to move; 4 **an etwas rühren** to touch, to touch on.

Ruine die (PL die **Ruinen**) ruin.

ruinieren verb (PERF **hat ruiniert**) to ruin.

rülpsen verb (PERF **hat gerülpst**) to belch.

Rum der rum.

Rumänien das Romania.

rumänisch adjective Romanian.

Rummel der 1 hustle and bustle; 2 fuss; 3 fair.

Rummelplatz der (PL die **Rummelplätze**) fairground.

rund adjective round.

rund adverb about; **rund um** around.

Runde die (PL die **Runden**) 1 round; 2 lap; 3 circle, group; 4 **über die Runden kommen** (informal) to get by.

Rundfahrt die (PL die **Rundfahrten**) tour.

Rundfrage die (PL die **Rundfragen**) poll.

Rundfunk der radio; **im Rundfunk** on the radio.

rundherum adverb all around.

Rundkurs der (PL die **Rundkurse**) (motor racing) circuit.

runter adverb (informal) SEE **herunter, hinunter; runter da!** get off!

runzlig adjective wrinkled.

Rüsche die (PL die **Rüschen**) frill.

Russe der (PL die **Russen**) Russian.

Rüssel der (PL die **Rüssel**) trunk.

Russin die (PL die **Russinnen**) Russian.

russisch adjective Russian.

Russland das Russia.

Rüstung die (PL die **Rüstungen**) 1 armament; 2 arms; 3 (suit of) armour.

Rutschbahn die (PL die **Rutschbahnen**) slide.

rutschen verb (PERF **ist gerutscht**) 1 to slide; 2 to slip; 3 **rutsch mal!** move over!

rutschig adjective slippery.

rütteln verb (PERF **hat gerüttelt**) to shake; **an der Tür rütteln** to rattle at the door.

Ss

Saal der (PL die **Säle**) hall.

Saatkrähe die (PL die **Saatkrähen**) rook.

Sabbat der (PL die **Sabbate**) Sabbath.

Sache die (PL die **Sachen**) 1 matter; **das ist eine andere Sache** that's a different matter; 2 business; **das ist seine Sache** that's his business; 3 thing; **meine Sachen** my things (clothing); **sie räumt nie ihre Sachen weg** she never puts away her things; 4 **zur Sache kommen** to get to the point; 5 **das ist so 'ne Sache** (informal) it's a bit tricky.

Sachgebiet das (PL die **Sachgebiete**) field, area.

sachlich adjective 1 objective; 2 factual.

sächlich adjective neuter.

Sachsen das Saxony.

Sack der (PL die **Säcke**) 1 sack; 2 bag.

Sackgasse die (PL die **Sackgassen**) dead end, cul-de-sac.

Saft der (PL die **Säfte**) 1 juice; 2 sap.

saftig adjective juicy.

Säge die (PL die **Sägen**) saw.

Sägemehl das sawdust.

sagen verb (PERF hat gesägt) 1 to say; **man sagt, dass … it's said that …**; 2 **was ich noch sagen wollte** by the way; **unter uns gesagt** between you and me; 3 to tell; **jemandem etwas sagen** to tell somebody something; **sag mal** tell me; **was sagen Sie dazu?** what do you think about it?; 4 to mean; **das hat nichts zu sagen** it doesn't mean anything; 5 **zu jemandem Tante sagen** to call somebody aunt; 6 **ihr Gesicht sagte alles** it was written all over her face.

sägen verb (PERF hat gesägt) to saw.

sagenhaft adjective 1 legendary; 2 (informal) brilliant.

sah SEE **sehen**.

Sahne die cream.

Saison die (PL die **Saisons**) season.

Saite die (PL die **Saiten**) string.

Sakko das (PL die **Sakkos**) jacket.

Salami die (PL die **Salamis**) salami.

Salat der (PL die **Salate**) 1 lettuce; **ein grüner Salat** a lettuce; 2 salad.

Salatsoße die (PL die **Salatsoßen**) salad dressing.

Salbe die (PL die **Salben**) ointment.

Salbei der sage.

salopp adjective casual, informal.

Salz das salt.

salzen verb (PERF hat gesalzen) to salt.

salzig adjective salty.

Salzkartoffeln plural noun boiled potatoes.

Salzwasser das 1 salt water; 2 salted water (for cooking).

Samen der (PL die **Samen**) 1 seed; 2 sperm, semen.

Sammelalbum das (PL die **Sammelalben**) scrapbook.

sammeln *verb* (PERF **hat gesammelt**) **1** to collect; **Martin sammelt Briefmarken** Martin collects stamps; **2** to gather; **3 sich sammeln** to gather; **seine Gedanken sammeln** to gather your thoughts.

Sammler *der* (PL die **Sammler**) collector.

Sammlerin *die* (PL die **Sammlerinnen**) collector.

Sammlung *die* (PL die **Sammlungen**) collection; **eine Sammlung für einen guten Zweck** a collection for a good cause.

Samstag *der* (PL die **Samstage**) Saturday.

samstags *adverb* on Saturdays.

Samt *der* (PL die **Samte**) velvet.

samt *preposition* (+ DAT) (together) with; **Mimi kam samt Puppen und Katze** Mimi arrived with her dolls and cat.

sämtlicher, sämtliche, sämtliches *adjective* all the; **meine sämtlichen Bücher** all my books.

Sand *der* sand.

Sandale *die* (PL die **Sandalen**) sandal.

sandig *adjective* sandy.

Sandpapier *das* (PL die **Sandpapiere**) sandpaper.

sandte SEE **senden**.

sanft *adjective* gentle; **eine sanfte Stimme** a soft voice.

sang SEE **singen**.

Sänger *der* (PL die **Sänger**) singer.

Sängerin *die* (PL die **Sängerinnen**) singer.

sank SEE **sinken**.

Sardelle *die* (PL die **Sardellen**) anchovy.

Sardine *die* (PL die **Sardinen**) sardine.

Sarg *der* (PL die **Särge**) coffin.

Sarkasmus *der* sarcasm.

sarkastisch *adjective* sarcastic.

SARS *das* SARS (*the disease*).

saß SEE **sitzen**.

Satellit *der* (PL die **Satelliten**) satellite.

Satellitenfernsehen *das* satellite television.

satt *adjective* **1** full (up); **bist du satt geworden?** have you had enough to eat?; **sich satt essen** to eat as much as one wants; **satt machen** to be filling; **2 etwas satt haben** (*informal*) to be fed up with something.

Sattel *der* (PL die **Sättel**) saddle.

Satteltasche *die* (PL die **Satteltaschen**) saddlebag.

Satz *der* (PL die **Sätze**) **1** sentence; **2** set (*of things or in tennis*); **ein Satz Reifen** a set of tyres; **3** movement (*in music*); **4** rate (*of tax, interest*); **5** leap.

sauber *adjective* **1** clean, **2** neat, **3** (*informal*) fine (*expressing irony*); **4 sauber machen** to clean.

Sauberkeit *die* cleanliness, cleanness.

saubermachen SEE **sauber**.

Sauce die (PL die **Saucen**) SEE **Soße**.

sauer adjective **1** sour; **2** pickled; **3** acid; **saurer Regen** acid rain; **4** **sauer sein** (informal) to be annoyed; **ich bin sauer auf Eva** I'm annoyed with Eva.

Sauerei die (informal) (PL die **Sauereien**) **1** mess; **2** disgrace, scandal; **3** obscenity.

Sauerstoff der oxygen.

saufen ✧verb (informal) (PRES **säuft**, IMPERF **soff**, PERF **hat gesoffen**) to drink, to booze.

saugen verb (PERF **hat gesaugt**) **1** to suck; **2** to vacuum, to hoover.

Säugetier das (PL die **Säugetiere**) mammal.

Säugling der (PL die **Säuglinge**) baby, infant.

Säule die (PL die **Säulen**) column, pillar.

Saum der (PL die **Säume**) hem.

Säure die (PL die **Säuren**) acid.

Saxofon das (PL die **Saxofone**) saxophone.

S-Bahn die (PL die **S-Bahnen**) city and suburban railway.

Scanner der (PL die **Scanner**) scanner.

schäbig adjective shabby.

Schach das chess; **Schach!** check!

Schachbrett das (PL die **Schachbretter**) chessboard.

Schachfigur die (PL die **Schachfiguren**) chess piece.

Schachtel die (PL die **Schachteln**) box.

schade adjective **1** **schade sein** to be a pity; **schade!** (what a) pity!; **2** **zu schade für jemanden sein** to be too good for somebody.

Schädel der (PL die **Schädel**) skull.

Schaden der (PL die **Schäden**) **1** damage; **2** disadvantage.

schaden verb (PERF **hat geschadet**) **1** to damage; **das hat seinem Ruf geschadet** it damaged his reputation; **2** **jemandem schaden** to harm somebody; **3** **das schadet nichts** it doesn't matter.

schädlich adjective harmful.

Schaf das (PL die **Schafe**) sheep.

Schäfer der (PL die **Schäfer**) shepherd.

Schäferhund der (PL die **Schäferhunde**) sheepdog.

schaffen[1] ✧verb (IMPERF **schuf**, PERF **hat geschaffen**) to create; **wie geschaffen für** made for.

schaffen[2] verb (PERF **hat geschafft**) **1** to manage; **es schaffen, etwas zu tun** to manage to do something; **2** **eine Prüfung schaffen** to pass an exam; **3** **jemandem zu schaffen machen** to cause somebody trouble; **4** **geschafft sein** (informal) to be worn out.

Schaffner der (PL die **Schaffner**) **1** conductor; **2** (ticket) inspector.

Schaffnerin die (PL die **Schaffnerinnen**) **1** conductress; **2** (ticket) inspector.

Schakal der (PL die **Schakale**) jackal.

Schal der (PL die **Schals**) scarf.

Schale die (PL die Schalen) 1 skin;
2 peel; 3 shell; 4 dish, bowl; **eine
Schale Obst** a bowl of fruit.

schälen verb (PERF hat geschält)
1 to peel; **er hat ihr eine Orange
geschält** he peeled an orange for
her; 2 **sich schälen** to peel; **mein
Rücken schält sich** my back's
peeling.

Schall der sound.

Schallplatte die (PL die
Schallplatten) record.

schalten verb (PERF hat
geschaltet) 1 to switch; **auf etwas
schalten** to turn to something; 2 to
change gear; 3 **schnell schalten**
(informal) to catch on quickly.

Schalter der (PL die Schalter)
1 switch; 2 counter.

Schaltjahr das (PL die Schaltjahre)
leap year.

schämen verb (PERF hat sich
geschämt) **sich schämen** to be
ashamed.

Schampon das (PL die
Schampons) SEE Shampoo.

Schande die 1 disgrace; 2 shame.

scharf adjective 1 sharp; 2 hot
(food); **ein scharfer Wind** a biting
wind; 3 fierce (dog, frost); 4 **scharf
nachdenken** to think hard; 5 (in
photography) **scharf sein** to be in
focus; **scharf einstellen** to focus;
6 **scharf schießen** to fire live
ammunition; 7 **scharf auf etwas
sein** (informal) to be really keen on
something; **sie ist scharf auf
Bernd** (informal) she fancies
Bernd.

Schaschlik der (PL die
Schaschliks) kebab.

Schatten der (PL die Schatten)
1 shadow; 2 shade.

schattig adjective shady.

Schatz der (PL die Schätze)
1 treasure; 2 darling.

Schätzchen das (PL die
Schätzchen) darling.

schätzen verb (PERF hat
geschätzt) 1 to estimate; 2 to
value; 3 to reckon, to guess; **schätz
mal!** guess!; 4 **etwas zu schätzen
wissen** to appreciate something.

Schau die (PL die Schauen) show.

schauen verb (PERF hat geschaut)
1 to look; 2 to watch; **Fernsehen
schauen** to watch television.

Schauer der (PL die Schauer)
shower.

Schauergeschichte die (PL die
Schauergeschichten) horror
story.

Schaufel die (PL die Schaufeln)
1 shovel; 2 dustpan.

Schaufenster das (PL die
Schaufenster) shop window.

Schaukel die (PL die Schaukeln)
swing.

schaukeln verb (PERF hat
geschaukelt) to swing.

Schaukelstuhl der (PL die
Schaukelstühle) rocking chair.

Schaum der 1 foam; 2 froth;
3 lather.

schäumen verb (PERF hat
geschäumt) 1 to foam; 2 to froth
(up).

a b c d e f g h i j k l m n o p q r s t u v w x y z

Schauplatz der (PL die Schauplätze) scene.

Schauspiel das (PL die Schauspiele) **1** play; **2** spectacle.

Schauspieler der (PL die Schauspieler) actor.

Schauspielerin die (PL die Schauspielerinnen) actress.

Schauspielkunst die dramatic art, acting.

Scheck der (PL die Schecks) cheque.

Scheckbuch das (PL die Scheckbücher) chequebook.

Scheckkarte die (PL die Scheckkarten) cheque card.

Scheibe die (PL die Scheiben) **1** pane (of a window, car); **2** slice; eine Scheibe Schinken a slice of ham; die Salami in Scheiben schneiden to slice the salami; du könntest dir eine Scheibe von ihr abschneiden (informal) you could take a leaf out of her book; **3** disc.

Scheibenwischer der (PL die Scheibenwischer) windscreen wiper.

scheiden ◇verb (IMPERF schied, PERF hat geschieden) **1** to separate; sich scheiden lassen to get divorced; sie haben sich im Juli scheiden lassen they got divorced in July; **2** geschieden sein to be divorced.

Scheidung die (PL die Scheidungen) divorce.

Schein der (PL die Scheine) **1** light; **2** appearance; etwas nur zum Schein machen to only pretend to do something; **3** certificate; **4** note (money).

scheinbar adverb apparently.

scheinen ◇verb (IMPERF schien, PERF hat geschienen) **1** to shine; **2** to seem; mir scheint it seems to me.

Scheinwerfer der (PL die Scheinwerfer) **1** headlamp, headlight; **2** floodlight, spotlight.

Scheitel der (PL die Scheitel) parting (in your hair).

scheitern verb (PERF ist gescheitert) to fail.

Schenkel der (PL die Schenkel) thigh.

schenken verb (PERF hat geschenkt) **1** to give; etwas geschenkt bekommen to be given something; **2** sich etwas schenken to give something a miss; **3** das ist ja geschenkt! (informal) it's a gift!

Schere die (PL die Scheren) **1** (pair of) scissors; **2** shears; **3** claw (of a crab).

scheren verb (informal) (PERF hat geschert) to bother; sich nicht um etwas scheren not to care about something; scher dich um deine eigenen Angelegenheiten! mind your own business!; scher dich zum Teufel! go to hell!

Scherz der (PL die Scherze) joke.

scheu adjective shy.

scheuern verb (PERF hat gescheuert) **1** to scrub; **2** to rub.

Scheune die (PL die Scheunen) barn.

scheußlich *adjective* horrible.

Schi *der* (PL die **Schi(er)**) SEE **Ski**.

Schicht *die* (PL die **Schichten**)
1 layer; 2 class; 3 shift.

Schicht *die* (PL die **Schichten**)
1 stratum; 2 section; 3 shift (*in factory etc*).

schick *adjective* 1 stylish, smart;
2 (*informal*) great.

schicken *verb* (PERF **hat geschickt**) to send.

Schicksal *das* (PL die **Schicksale**) fate.

Schiebedach *das* (PL die **Schiebedächer**) sunroof.

schieben ◇*verb* (IMPERF **schob**, PERF **hat geschoben**) 1 to push;
2 **etwas auf etwas schieben** to blame something for something;
die Schuld auf jemanden schieben to put the blame on somebody.

schied SEE **scheiden**.

Schiedsrichter *der* (PL die **Schiedsrichter**) referee, umpire.

schief *adjective* crooked, **ein schiefer Blick** a funny look.

schief *adverb* 1 **das Bild hängt schief** the picture is not straight;
2 **schief gehen** to go wrong.

Schiefer *der* slate.

schiefgehen SEE **schief**.

schielen *verb* (PERF **hat geschielt**) to squint.

schien SEE **scheinen**.

Schienbein *das* (PL die **Schienbeine**) shin.

Schiene *die* (PL die **Schienen**)
1 rail; 2 splint.

schießen ◇*verb* (IMPERF **schoss**, PERF **hat geschossen**) 1 to shoot;
auf jemanden schießen to shoot at somebody; **ein Tor schießen** to score a goal; 2 (PERF **ist geschossen**) to shoot (along);
Andrea ist in die Höhe geschossen Andrea's shot up (*has got a lot taller*).

Schiff *das* (PL die **Schiffe**) ship; **ein Schiff zu Wasser lassen** to launch a ship.

Schifffahrt *die* (PL die **Schifffahrten**) boat trip.

schikanieren *verb* (PERF **hat schikaniert**) to bully.

Schikoree *der* SEE **Chicorée**.

Schild[1] *das* (PL die **Schilder**) 1 sign;
2 badge; 3 label.

Schild[2] *der* (PL die **Schilde**) shield.

Schildkröte *die* (PL die **Schildkröten**) 1 tortoise; 2 turtle.

Schilling *der* (PL die **Schilling(e)**) Schilling (*the currency of Austria until replaced by the euro; 100 Schillings =* ℏ*7.26 euros*).

Schimmel *der* (PL die **Schimmel**)
1 mould; 2 white horse.

Schimpanse *der* (PL die **Schimpansen**) chimpanzee.

schimpfen *verb* (PERF **hat geschimpft**) 1 to tell off; 2 to grumble.

Schinken *der* (PL die **Schinken**) ham; **ein Schinkenbrötchen** a ham roll.

a b c d e f g h i j k l m n o p q r **s** t u v w x y z

Schirm der (PL die **Schirme**)
1 umbrella; **2** sunshade; **3** shade
(of a lamp); **4** peak (of a cap).

Schlaf der sleep.

Schlafanzug der (PL die
Schlafanzüge) pyjamas.

Schlafcouch die (PL die
Schlafcouchs) sofa bed.

schlafen ✧verb (PRES **schläft**,
IMPERF **schlief**, PERF **hat
geschlafen**) **1** to sleep; **2** to be
asleep; **das Baby schläft** the baby's
asleep; **3 schlafen gehen** to go to
bed.

schlaff adjective **1** slack (rope);
2 limp (handshake, body);
3 lethargic.

schläfrig adjective sleepy; **ich bin
schläfrig** I'm sleepy.

Schlafsaal der (PL die **Schlafsäle**)
dormitory.

Schlafsack der (PL die
Schlafsäcke) sleeping bag.

Schlafwagen der (PL die
Schlafwagen) sleeper.

Schlafzimmer das (PL die
Schlafzimmer) bedroom.

Schlag der (PL die **Schläge**) **1** blow,
punch; **Schläge kriegen** to get a
beating; **2** stroke; **3** (electric) shock;
4 Schlag auf Schlag in quick
succession; **auf einen Schlag** all at
once.

schlagen ✧verb (PRES **schlägt**,
IMPERF **schlug**, PERF **hat
geschlagen**) **1** to hit; **einen Nagel
in die Wand schlagen** to knock a
nail into the wall; **2** to beat; **3** to
bang; **mit dem Kopf gegen etwas
schlagen** to bang your head
against something; **4** to strike (of a
clock); **5** to whip (cream); **6 sich
schlagen** to fight; **7 sich
geschlagen geben** to admit defeat.

Schlager der (PL die **Schlager**) hit.

Schläger der (PL die **Schläger**)
1 racket (in tennis); **2** bat (in
baseball); **3** club (in golf); **4** stick
(in hockey); **5** thug.

Schlägerei die (PL die
Schlägereien) fight.

Schlagsahne die **1** whipping
cream; **2** whipped cream.

Schlagzeile die (PL die
Schlagzeilen) headline.

Schlagzeug das (PL die
Schlagzeuge) drums.

Schlagzeuger der (PL die
Schlagzeuger) drummer.

Schlamm der mud.

schlampen verb (PERF **hat
geschlampt**) to be sloppy.

Schlamperei die (PL die
Schlampereien) **1** sloppiness;
2 mess.

schlampig adjective sloppy.

Schlange die (PL die **Schlangen**)
1 snake; **2** queue; **Schlange
stehen** to queue.

schlank adjective slim.

Schlankheitskur die (PL die
Schlankheitskuren) diet; **eine
Schlankheitskur machen** to be on a
diet.

schlapp adjective worn out, tired
out.

schlau *adjective* **1** crafty; **2** clever; **ich werde nicht schlau daraus** I can't make head nor tail of it.

Schlauch *der* (PL *die* **Schläuche**) hose.

schlauchlos *adjective* tubeless.

schlecht *adjective* **1** bad; **schlecht werden** to go so bad; **2 mir ist schlecht** I feel sick; **3 jemanden schlecht machen** to run somebody down.

schlecht *adverb* **1** badly; **schlecht gelaunt** in a bad mood; **2 es geht ihm schlecht** he's not well.

schleichen ⬦*verb* (IMPERF **schlich**, PERF **ist geschlichen**) **1** to creep; **2** to crawl (*in traffic*); **3 sich schleichen** to creep.

Schleife *die* (PL *die* **Schleifen**) **1** bow; **2** loop.

Schlepper *der* (PL *die* **Schlepper**) **1** tug; **2** tractor.

Schleuder *die* (PL *die* **Schleudern**) **1** catapult; **2** spin-dryer.

schleudern *verb* (PERF **hat geschleudert**) **1** to hurl; **2** to spin (*washing*); **3** (PERF **ist geschleudert**) to skid.

schlich SEE **schleichen**.

schlicht *adjective* plain, simple.

schlief SEE **schlafen**.

schließen ⬦*verb* (IMPERF **schloss**, PERF **hat geschlossen**) **1** to close, to shut; **2** to close down; **3** to lock; **4** to conclude; **aus etwas schließen, dass** ... to conclude from something that ...; **5 einen Vertrag schließen** to enter into a contract;

6 Freundschaft mit jemandem schließen to make friends with somebody; **7 sich schließen** to close.

Schließfach *das* (PL *die* **Schließfächer**) locker.

schließlich *adverb* **1** finally; **2** after all; **er hat sie schließlich doch eingeladen** he's invited her after all.

schlimm *adjective* bad.

schlimmstenfalls *adverb* if the worst comes to the worst.

Schlips *der* (PL *die* **Schlipse**) tie.

Schlitten *der* (PL *die* **Schlitten**) sledge; **Schlitten fahren gehen** to go sledging.

Schlittschuh *der* (PL *die* **Schlittschuhe**) skate; **Schlittschuh laufen** to skate.

Schlittschuhlaufen *das* ice-skating.

Schlitz *der* (PL *die* **Schlitze**) **1** slit; **2** flies (*in trousers*); **3** slot.

Schloss *das* (PL *die* **Schlösser**) **1** lock; **2** castle.

schloss SEE **schließen**.

Schluck *der* (PL *die* **Schlucke**) **1** mouthful; **2** gulp.

Schluckauf *der* for hiccups.

schlucken *verb* (PERF **hat geschluckt**) to swallow.

schlug SEE **schlagen**.

Schlüpfer *der* (PL *die* **Schlüpfer**) knickers.

Schluss *der* (PL *die* **Schlüsse**) **1** end, ending; **zum Schluss** in the end; **Schluss machen** to stop; **mit**

a b c d e f g h i j k l m n o p q r s t u v w x y z

a
b
c
d
e
f
g
h
i
j
k
l
m
n
o
p
q
r
s
t
u
v
w
x
y
z

jemandem Schluss machen to finish with somebody; **2** conclusion.

Schlüssel der (PL die **Schlüssel**) **1** key; **2** spanner.

Schlussverkauf der sales.

schmal adjective **1** narrow; **2** thin (face, nose); **3** sie ist schmäler geworden she's lost weight.

schmecken verb (PERF hat geschmeckt) to taste; **die Suppe schmeckt gut** the soup tastes good; **das schmeckt mir nicht** I don't like it; **das Eis schmeckt nach Zitrone** the ice cream tastes of lemon.

schmeicheln verb (PERF hat geschmeichelt) to flatter; **jemandem schmeicheln** to flatter somebody.

schmeißen ◇verb (informal) (IMPERF schmiss, PERF hat geschmissen) to chuck; **mit etwas schmeißen** to chuck something.

schmelzen ◇verb (PRES schmilzt, IMPERF schmolz, PERF ist geschmolzen) **1** to melt; **der Schnee ist geschmolzen** the snow has melted; **2** (PERF hat geschmolzen) to melt (snow, ice); **3** (PERF hat geschmolzen) to smelt (ore).

Schmerz der (PL die **Schmerzen**) **1** pain; **2** grief.

schmerzen verb (PERF hat geschmerzt) to hurt; **mein Kopf schmerzt** my head is aching.

schmerzhaft adjective painful.

schmerzlos adjective painless.

Schmerzmittel das (PL die **Schmerzmittel**) painkiller.

Schmerzschwelle das (PL die **Schmerzschwellen**) painthreshold.

Schmetterling der (PL die **Schmetterlinge**) butterfly.

schmettern verb (PERF hat geschmettert) **1** to hurl; **2** to smash (in tennis); **3** to blare out (music, orders).

schmieren verb (PERF hat geschmiert) **1** to lubricate; **2** to spread (butter, jam); **Brote schmieren** to spread slices of bread; **jemandem eine schmieren** (informal) to clout somebody; **3** to scrawl; **4** to smudge.

schmilzt SEE **schmelzen**.

Schminke die make-up.

schminken verb (PERF hat geschminkt) **1** to make up; **2 sich schminken** to put on make-up.

schmiss SEE **schmeißen**.

schmolz SEE **schmelzen**.

Schmuck der **1** jewellery; **2** decoration.

schmücken verb (PERF hat geschmückt) to decorate.

schmuggeln verb (PERF hat geschmuggelt) to smuggle.

schmusen verb (PERF hat geschmust) to cuddle; **Gabi hat mit Max geschmust** Gabi cuddled Max.

Schmutz der dirt.

schmutzig adjective dirty.

Schmutzigkeit die dirtiness.

Schnabel der (PL die **Schnäbel**) beak.

Schnalle die (PL die **Schnallen**) buckle.

schnallen verb (PERF hat **geschnallt**) 1 to fasten; 2 to buckle.

schnarchen verb (PERF hat **geschnarcht**) to snore.

Schnauze die (PL die **Schnauzen**) 1 muzzle; **eine kalte Schnauze** a cold nose; 2 **die Schnauze halten** (informal) to keep your mouth shut.

schnäuzen (PERF hat sich **geschnäuzt**) **sich schnäuzen** to blow your nose.

Schnecke die (PL die **Schnecken**) snail.

Schnee der snow.

Schneeregen der sleet.

Schneesturm der (PL die **Schneestürme**) blizzard.

Schneewehe die (PL die **Schneewehen**) snow drift.

schneiden ◇verb (IMPERF schnitt, PERF hat geschnitten) 1 to cut; **Ich kann dir die Haare schneiden** I can cut your hair; **Evi hat sich die Haare kurz schneiden lassen** Evi had her hair cut short; **in Scheiben schneiden** to slice; 2 **sich schneiden** to cut yourself; **ich habe mich in den Finger geschnitten** I've cut my finger; 3 **sich schneiden** to intersect; 4 **Gesichter schneiden** to pull faces.

Schneider der (PL die **Schneider**) tailor.

Schneiderin die (PL die **Schneiderinnen**) dressmaker.

schneien verb (PERF hat **geschneit**) to snow; **es schneit** it's snowing.

schnell adjective quick, fast.

schnell adverb quickly; **mach schnell!** hurry up!

Schnelligkeit die speed.

Schnellimbiss der (PL die **Schnellimbisse**) snack bar.

schnellstens adverb as quickly as possible.

Schnellzug der (PL die **Schnellzüge**) express (train).

schneuzen SEE **schnäuzen**.

Schnitt der (PL die **Schnitte**) 1 cut; **er hat einen tiefen Schnitt im Finger** he's got a deep cut in his finger; **das Kostüm hat einen sehr guten Schnitt** the suit is well cut; 2 cutting (of a film); 3 **im Schnitt** on average, 4 pattern.

schnitt SEE **schneiden**.

Schnittlauch der chives.

Schnitzel das (PL die **Schnitzel**) 1 escalope; 2 scrap.

schnitzen verb (PERF hat **geschnitzt**) to carve.

Schnorchel der (PL die **Schnorchel**) snorkel.

schnüffeln verb (PERF hat **geschnüffelt**) 1 to sniff; 2 to snoop around.

Schnuller der (PL die **Schnuller**) dummy.

a b c d e f g h i j k l m n o p q r s t u v w x y z

Schnupfen der (PL die **Schnupfen**) cold.

Schnur die (PL die **Schnüre**) 1 (piece of) string; 2 flex; 3 cord.

Schnurrbart der (PL die **Schnurrbärte**) moustache.

schnurren verb (PERF hat **geschnurrt**) to purr.

Schnurrhaar das (PL die **Schnurrhaare**) whisker.

Schnürsenkel der (PL die **Schnürsenkel**) shoelace.

schob SEE schieben.

Schock der (PL die **Schocks**) shock.

schockieren verb (PERF hat **schockiert**) to shock.

Schokolade die (PL die **Schokoladen**) chocolate.

schön adjective 1 beautiful; 2 nice; **schönes Wochenende!** have a nice weekend!; 3 good; **na schön** all right then; 4 **schönen Dank** thank you very much; **schöne Grüße** best wishes.

schon adverb 1 already ('schon' is often not translated); **schon wieder** again; **schon oft** often; **du wirst schon sehen** you'll see; **ja schon, aber ... well yes, but ...; nun geh schon!** go on then!; 2 yet; **hast du sie schon gesehen?** have you seen her yet?; **du weißt schon** you know; 3 even; 4 **komm schon!** come on!; 5 **schon deshalb** for that reason alone; 6 **das ist schon möglich** that's quite possible; 7 **er war schon mal da** he's been there before.

schonen verb (PERF hat **geschont**) 1 to look after; 2 **sich schonen** to take things easy.

Schönheit die (PL die **Schönheiten**) beauty.

Schornstein der (PL die **Schornsteine**) chimney, funnel.

schoss SEE schießen.

Schoß der (PL die **Schöße**) lap.

Schotte der (PL die **Schotten**) Scot, Scotsman.

Schottin die (PL die **Schottinnen**) Scot, Scotswoman.

schottisch adjective Scottish.

Schottland das Scotland.

schräg adjective 1 diagonal; 2 sloping.

schräg adverb **etwas schräg halten** to tilt something; **etwas schräg stellen** to put something at an angle.

Schrank der (PL die **Schränke**) 1 cupboard; 2 wardrobe.

Schranke die (PL die **Schranken**) barrier.

Schraube die (PL die **Schrauben**) screw.

schrauben verb (PERF hat **geschraubt**) to screw.

Schraubenschlüssel der (PL die **Schraubenschlüssel**) spanner.

Schraubenzieher der (PL die **Schraubenzieher**) screwdriver.

Schreck der fright; **jemandem einen Schreck einjagen** to give somebody a fright; **ich habe einen Schreck bekommen** I got a fright.

schrecklich adjective terrible.

Schrei der (PL die Schreie) **1** cry, shout; **2** scream; **3 der letzte Schrei** (informal) the latest thing.

Schreibblock der (PL die Schreibblöcke) writing pad.

schreiben ◇verb (IMPERF **schrieb**, PERF **hat geschrieben**) **1** to write; **David hat mir einen Brief geschrieben** David wrote a letter to me; **einen Test schreiben** to do a test; **2** to spell; **wie schreibt man das?** how is it spelt?; **3** to type.

Schreibmaschine die (PL die Schreibmaschinen) typewriter.

Schreibpapier das writing paper.

Schreibtisch der (PL die Schreibtische) desk.

Schreibwaren plural noun stationery.

schreien ◇verb (IMPERF **schrie**, PERF **hat geschrien**) **1** to cry, to shout; **das Baby schreit** the baby's crying; **2** to scream; **vor Lachen schreien** to scream with laughter; **zum Schreien sein** (informal) to be a scream.

Schreiner der (PL die Schreiner) joiner.

schrie SEE schreien.

schrieb SEE schreiben.

Schrift die (PL die Schriften) **1** writing; **2** type; **3** script.

schriftlich adjective written.

schriftlich adverb in writing; **das lasse ich mir schriftlich geben** I'll get that in writing; **jemanden schriftlich einladen** to send somebody a written invitation.

Schriftsteller der (PL die Schriftsteller) writer.

Schriftstellerin die (PL die Schriftstellerinnen) writer.

Schritt der (PL die Schritte) **1** step; **2** footstep.

schrumpfen verb (PERF **ist geschrumpft**) **1** to shrink; **2** to shrivel.

Schublade die (PL die Schubladen) drawer.

schubsen verb (PERF **hat geschubst**) to shove.

schüchtern adjective shy.

schuf SEE schaffen.

Schuh der (PL die Schuhe) shoe.

Schuhgröße die (PL die Schuhgrößen) shoe size.

Schularbeiten plural noun homework.

Schulaufgaben plural noun homework.

Schulbuch das (PL die Schulbücher) schoolbook.

Schuld die (PL die Schulden) **1** blame; **Schuld haben** to be to blame; **Jemandem Schuld geben** to blame somebody; **2** fault; **es war seine Schuld** it was his fault; **3** guilt; **4** debt; **Schulden haben** to be in debt; **Schulden machen** to get into debt.

schuld adjective **schuld sein** to be to blame; **du bist schuld daran** it's your fault.

schulden verb (PERF **hat geschuldet**) to owe.

a
b
c
d
e
f
g
h
i
j
k
l
m
n
o
p
q
r
s
t
u
v
w
x
y
z

schuldig adjective **1** guilty; **2** jemandem etwas schuldig sein to owe somebody something.

Schule die (PL die Schulen) school; **in die Schule gehen** to go to school.

schulen verb (PERF hat geschult) to train.

Schüler der (PL die Schüler) pupil, student.

Schülerin die (PL die Schülerinnen) pupil, student.

Schulferien plural noun school holidays.

schulfrei adjective **ein schulfreier Tag** a day off school; **wir haben heute schulfrei** there's no school today.

Schulfreund der (PL die Schulfreunde) schoolfriend.

Schulfreundin die (PL die Schulfreundinnen) schoolfriend.

Schulheft das (PL die Schulhefte) exercise book.

Schulhof der (PL die Schulhöfe) playground.

Schuljahr das (PL die Schuljahre) school year.

Schulschwänzer der (PL die Schulschwänzer) truant.

Schulschwänzerin die (PL die Schulschwänzerinnen) truant.

Schulstunde die (PL die Schulstunden) period.

Schultasche die (PL die Schultaschen) schoolbag.

Schulter die (PL die Schultern) shoulder.

schummeln verb hat geschummelt) to cheat.

Schuppe die (PL die Schuppen) **1** scale; **2 Schuppen** dandruff.

Schuppen der (PL die Schuppen) shed.

Schürze die (PL die Schürzen) apron.

Schuss der (PL die Schüsse) **1** shot; **2** dash (of brandy, vinegar); **3** schuss (in skiing).

Schüssel die (PL die Schüsseln) bowl, dish.

Schuster der (PL die Schuster) shoemaker.

schütteln verb (PERF hat geschüttelt) **1** to shake; **2 sich schütteln** to shake yourself; **sich vor Ekel schütteln** to shudder.

schütten verb (PERF hat geschüttet) **1** to pour; **es schüttet** (informal) it's pouring (down); **2** to tip; **3** to spill.

Schutz der **1** protection; **2** shelter; **3** conservation.

Schutzbrille die (PL die Schutzbrillen) goggles.

Schütze der (PL die Schützen) **1** marksman; **2** Sagittarius; **Daniel ist Schütze** Daniel's Sagittarius.

schützen verb (PERF hat geschützt) **1** to protect; **die meisten Cremes schützen die Haut gegen Sonnenbrand** most creams protect the skin from sunburn; **2 gesetzlich geschützt** registered (as a trade-mark).

a
b
c
d
e
f
g
h
i
j
k
l
m
n
o
p
q
r
s
t
u
v
w
x
y
z

Schutzhütte die (PL die Schutzhütten) 1 mountain refuge; 2 shelter.

schwach adjective 1 weak; 2 dim (light); 3 poor (performance, memory).

Schwäche die (PL die Schwächen) weakness.

schwachsinnig adjective idiotic.

Schwager der (PL die Schwäger) brother-in-law.

Schwägerin die (PL die Schwägerinnen) sister-in-law.

Schwalbe die (PL die Schwalben) swallow.

Schwamm der (PL die Schwämme) sponge.

schwamm SEE schwimmen.

Schwan der (PL die Schwäne) swan.

schwanger adjective pregnant.

Schwangerschaft die (PL die Schwangerschaften) pregnancy.

schwanken verb (PERF hat geschwankt) 1 to sway; 2 to fluctuate; 3 to waver; 4 (PERF ist geschwankt) to stagger.

Schwanz der (PL die Schwänze) tail.

schwänzen verb (PERF hat geschwänzt) to skip, to skive off; die Schule schwänzen to play truant.

Schwarm der (PL die Schwärme) swarm.

schwarz adjective, adverb 1 black; schwarz gekleidet dressed in black; ein schwarz gestreiftes Kleid a dress with black stripes; das habe ich schwarz auf weiß I have it in black and white; 2 ins Schwarze treffen to hit the nail on the head, to score a bull's eye; 3 schwarz sehen to be pessimistic; 4 etwas schwarz machen to do something illegally.

Schwarze der/die (PL die Schwarzen) black.

schwarzsehen SEE schwarz.

Schwarzwald der Black Forest.

schwätzen verb (PERF hat geschwätzt) to chatter.

Schwede der (PL die Schweden) Swede.

Schweden das Sweden.

Schwedin die (PL die Schwedinnen) Swede.

schwedisch adjective Swedish.

schweigen ◇verb (IMPERF schwieg, PERF hat geschwiegen) to be silent; ganz zu schweigen von ... not to mention ....

Schwein das (PL die Schweine) 1 pig; 2 pork; 3 du Schwein! (informal) you swine!; Schwein haben (informal) to be lucky.

Schweinefleisch das pork.

Schweinekotelett das (PL die Schweinekoteletts) pork chop.

Schweiß der sweat.

Schweiz die die Schweiz Switzerland.

Schweizer der (PL die Schweizer) Swiss.

Schweizerin die (PL die Schweizerinnen) Swiss.

a
b
c
d
e
f
g
h
i
j
k
l
m
n
o
p
q
r
s
t
u
v
w
x
y
z

a

schweizerisch adjective Swiss.

b **Schwelle** der (PL die **Schwellen**) threshold.

c

Schwellung die (PL die **Schwellungen**) swelling.

d **schwer** adjective **1** heavy; **zwei Pfund schwer sein** to weigh two

e pounds; **2** difficult; **3** serious.

f **schwer** adverb **1** heavily; **2** seriously; **schwer krank**

g seriously ill; **3 schwer arbeiten** to work hard; **jemandem schwer**

h **fallen** to be hard for somebody; **4 sich mit etwas schwer tun** to

i have difficulty with something.

j **schwerfallen** SEE **schwer**.

k **schwerhörig** adjective hard of hearing.

l **Schwert** das (PL die **Schwerter**) sword.

m **schwertun** SEE **schwer**.

n **Schwester** die (PL die **Schwestern**) sister.

o **schwieg** SEE **schweigen**.

Schwiegereltern plural noun

p parents-in-law.

q **Schwiegermutter** die (PL die **Schwiegermütter**) mother-in-law.

r **Schwiegersohn** der (PL die **Schwiegersöhne**) son-in-law.

s **Schwiegertochter** die (PL die **Schwiegertöchter**) daughter-in-

t law.

u **Schwiegervater** der (PL die **Schwiegerväter**) father-in-law.

v **schwierig** adjective difficult.

w **Schwierigkeit** die (PL die **Schwierigkeiten**) difficulty.

x

y

z

Schwimmbad das (PL die **Schwimmbäder**) swimming baths.

schwimmen ◇verb (IMPERF **schwamm**, PERF **ist/hat geschwommen**) **1** to swim; **2** to float.

Schwimmer der (PL die **Schwimmer**) swimmer.

Schwimmbecken das (PL die **Schwimmbecken**) swimming pool (for experienced swimmers).

Schwimmerin die (PL die **Schwimmerinnen**) swimmer.

Schwimmweste die (PL die **Schwimmwesten**) life-jacket.

schwindlig adjective dizzy; **mir ist schwindlig** I feel dizzy.

Schwips der (PL die **Schwipse**) **einen Schwips haben** to be tipsy.

schwitzen verb (PERF **hat geschwitzt**) to sweat.

schwören ◇verb (IMPERF **schwor**, PERF **hat geschworen**) to swear.

schwul adjective close.

schwul adjective gay.

Schwule der (PL die **Schwulen**) gay.

Schwung der (PL die **Schwünge**) **1** swing; **2** drive; **die Party in Schwung bringen** to get the party going.

sechs number six.

sechster, **sechste**, **sechstes** adjective sixth.

sechzehn number sixteen.

sechzig number sixty.

See[1] der (PL die **Seen**) lake.

See[2] die sea.

Seehund der (PL die Seehunde) seal.

seekrank adjective seasick.

Seele die (PL die Seelen) soul.

Seemann der (PL die Seeleute) seaman, sailor.

Seetang der seaweed.

Segel das (PL die Segel) sail.

Segelboot das (PL die Segelboote) sailing boat.

Segelfliegen das gliding.

Segelflugzeug das (PL die Segelflugzeuge) glider.

Segellehrer der (PL die Segellehrer) sailing instructor.

Segellehrerin die (PL die Segellehrerinnen) sailing instructor.

segeln verb (PERF ist gesegelt) to sail.

sehen ⬦verb (PRES **sieht**, IMPERF **sah**, PERF **hat gesehen**) 1 to see; **jemanden wieder sehen** to see somebody again; **mal sehen, ob ...** let's see if ...; 2 to look; 3 **eine Fernsehsendung sehen** to watch a television programme; 4 **gut/ schlecht sehen** to have good/bad eyesight; 5 **nach jemandem sehen** to look after somebody.

sehenswert adjective worth seeing.

Sehenswürdigkeiten plural noun sights.

Sehnsucht die longing; **Sehnsucht nach jemandem haben** to long to see somebody.

sehr adverb 1 very; **sehr gut** very good; 2 **danke sehr** thank you very much; 3 **ich habe Karin sehr gern** I like Karin a lot; 4 **Sehr geehrte Frau Huber** Dear Mrs Huber.

seid SEE **sein**.

Seide die (PL die Seiden) silk.

Seife die (PL die Seifen) soap.

Seil das (PL die Seile) 1 rope; 2 cable.

Seilbahn die (PL die Seilbahnen) cable railway.

sein[1] ⬦verb (PRES **ist**, IMPERF **war**, PERF **ist gewesen**) 1 to be; **wir sind in der Küche** we're in the kitchen; **Rosi ist krank** Rosi is ill; **mir ist schlecht** I feel sick; **mir ist kalt/ heiß** I'm cold/hot; 2 **sie ist Lehrerin** she's a teacher; 3 **es ist drei Uhr** it's three o'clock; **Karl ist aus München** Karl's from Munich; **es war viel zu tun** there was a lot to be done; 4 **aus Seide sein** to be made of silk; 5 **etwas sein lassen** to stop something; **lass das sein!** stop it!; 6 **es sei denn, dass ... unless ...**; 7 (used with certain verbs to form past tenses) **ich bin nach Berlin gefahren** I went to Berlin; **wir sind kurz vor acht nach Hause gekommen** we got home shortly before eight o'clock; **er ist abgeholt worden** he's been collected.

sein[2] adjective 1 his; 2 (of a thing or animal) its; **der Hund ist in seiner Hütte** the dog is in its kennel; 3 (after the pronoun 'man') your, one's; **wenn man sich seine Eltern aussuchen könnte** if you could choose your parents.

a
b
c
d
e
f
g
h
i
j
k
l
m
n
o
p
q
r
s
t
u
v
w
x
y
z

seiner, seine, sein(e)s *pronoun* **1** his; **das ist nicht meine CD, das ist seine** it's not my CD, it's his; **du kannst seins nehmen** you can take his; **2** *(after the pronoun 'man')* your own, one's own; **das Seine tun** to do one's share.

seinetwegen *adverb* **1** for his sake; **2** because of him; **3** on his account.

seinlassen SEE **sein**.

seins SEE **seiner**.

seit *preposition* (+ DAT) *conjunction* **1** since; **seit etwa einer Woche** since about a week; **seit du hier wohnst** since you've been living here; **seit wann?** since when?; **2 ich bin seit zwei Wochen hier** I've been here for two weeks; **seit einiger Zeit** for some time.

seitdem *adverb* since then; **ich habe sie seitdem nicht mehr gesehen** I haven't seen her since.

seitdem *conjunction* since.

Seite die (PL die **Seiten**) **1** side; **auf der einen Seite** on the one hand; **2** page; **das steht auf Seite zwanzig** it's on page twenty.

Seitenstechen das stich; **ich habe Seitenstechen** I've got a stitch.

Seitenstraße die (PL die **Seitenstraßen**) side street.

seither *adverb* since then.

Sekretär der (PL die **Sekretäre**) secretary.

Sekretärin die (PL die **Sekretärinnen**) secretary.

Sekt der (PL die **Sekte**) sparkling wine.

Sekte die (PL die **Sekten**) sect.

Sekunde die (PL die **Sekunden**) second.

selbst *pronoun* **1 ich selbst** I myself; **er selbst** he himself; **wir selbst** we ourselves; **Sie selbst** you yourself, you yourselves; **2 von selbst** by itself; **3 sie schneidet sich die Haare selbst** she cuts her own hair; **4** on one's own; **ich kann es selbst machen** I can do it on my own; **5 selbst gemacht** home-made.

selbst *adverb* even; **selbst wenn** even if.

selbständig SEE **selbstständig**.

Selbstbedienung die self-service.

selbstbewusst *adjective* self-confident.

Selbstbewusstsein das **1** self-confidence; **2** self-awareness.

selbstgemacht SEE **selbst**.

Selbstmord der (PL die **Selbstmorde**) suicide; **Selbstmord begehen** to commit suicide.

selbstsicher *adjective* self-confident.

selbstständig *adjective* **1** independent; **2** self-employed; **sich selbstständig machen** to set up on your own.

selbstverständlich *adjective* natural; **etwas für selbstverständlich halten** to take something for granted; **das ist**

selbstverständlich it goes without saying.

selbstverständlich *adverb* naturally, of course; **wir haben ihn selbstverständlich auf die Party eingeladen** of course we invited him to the party.

selten *adjective* rare.

selten *adverb* rarely.

seltsam *adjective* strange, odd.

Semester das (PL die **Semester**) semester, term.

Semikolon das (PL die **Semikolons**) semicolon.

Semmel die (PL die **Semmeln**) roll.

senden *verb* (PERF **hat gesendet**) **1** to send; **etwas an jemanden senden** to send something to somebody; **2** to broadcast; **seine Rede wird im ersten Programm gesendet** his speech will be broadcast on channel one; **3** to transmit.

Sendung die (PL die **Sendungen**) **1** programme; **2** consignment.

Senf der (PL die **Senfe**) mustard.

Senior der (PL die **Senioren**) **1** senior; **2 Senioren** senior citizens.

senkrecht *adjective* vertical.

Sensation die (PL die **Sensationen**) sensation, stir.

sensationell *adjective* sensational.

sensibel *adjective* sensitive.

sentimental *adjective* sentimental.

September der September.

Sequenz die (PL die **Sequenzen**) sequence (*in a film*).

Serie die (PL die **Serien**) **1** series; **2** serial.

Service[1] das (PL die **Service**) set (*of china, for example*).

Service[2] der service; **das Essen im Hotel ist gut, aber der Service ist furchtbar** the food in the hotel is good but the service is appalling.

servieren *verb* (PERF **hat serviert**) to serve.

Serviette die (PL die **Servietten**) napkin.

Sessel der (PL die **Sessel**) armchair.

Sessellift der (PL die **Sessellifte**) chair-lift.

setzen *verb* (PERF **hat gesetzt**) **1** to put; **ein Komma setzen** to put a comma; **vergiss nicht, deinen Namen auf die Liste zu setzen** don't forget to put your name on the list; **2** to move (*a counter in games*); **3 auf etwas setzen** to bet on something; **auf ein Pferd setzen** to back a horse, **4 sich setzen** to sit down; **sich auf einen Stuhl setzen** to sit down on a chair.

seufzen *verb* (PERF **hat geseufzt**) to sigh.

Seufzer der (PL die **Seufzer**) sigh.

Sex der sex; **Sex mit jemandem haben** to have sex with somebody.

Sexismus der sexism.

sexistisch *adjective* sexist.

sexuell *adjective* sexual.

a b c d e f g h i j k l m n o p q r **s** t u v w x y z

a

Shampoo das (PL die **Shampoos**) shampoo.

b

Shuttledienst der (PL die **Shuttledienste**) shuttle service.

c

d

sich pronoun **1** (with 'er/sie/es') himself/herself/itself; **sie hat sich eingeschlossen** she locked herself in; **2** (with plural 'sie') themselves; **3** (with 'Sie') yourself, yourselves (plural); **4** each other, one another; **sich kennen** to know each other; **Petra und Werner lieben sich** Petra and Werner love each other; **5** (not translated with certain verbs) **sich freuen** to be pleased; **sich wundern** to be surprised; **6 Anita wäscht sich die Haare** Anita is washing her hair; **sich den Arm brechen** to break your arm; **7 sich gut verkaufen** to sell well; **8 von sich aus** of your own accord.

e

f

g

h

i

j

k

l

m

sicher adjective **1** safe; **2** certain; **bist du sicher?** are you sure?.

sicher adverb **1** safely; **2** certainly, surely; **sicher!** certainly!

n

o

Sicherheit die **1** safety; **zur Sicherheit** for safety's sake; **schnallen Sie sich zur Ihrer eigenen Sicherheit an** fasten your seat belt for your own safety; **etwas in Sicherheit bringen** to rescue something; **in Sicherheit sein** to be safe; **2** security; **die Sicherheit der Arbeitsplätze** job security; **3** certainty; **mit Sicherheit!** certainly! (as a reply).

p

q

r

s

t

u

v

Sicherheitsgurt der (PL die **Sicherheitsgurte**) seatbelt.

w

x

Sicherheitsnadel die (PL die **Sicherheitsnadeln**) safety pin.

y

z

sicherlich adverb certainly.

sichern verb (PERF **hat gesichert**) to secure; **jemandem etwas sichern** to secure something for somebody.

Sicherung die (PL die **Sicherungen**) **1** fuse; **die Sicherung ist durchgebrannt** the fuse has blown; **2** safeguard; **die Sicherung der Arbeitsplätze** safeguarding jobs; **3** safety catch.

Sicht die **1** view; **ich hatte eine gute Sicht auf den See** I had a good view of the lake; **auf lange Sicht** in the long term; **2 aus meiner Sicht** as I see it; **3** visibility; **gute/schlechte Sicht** good/poor visibility.

sichtbar adjective visible.

sie pronoun **1** she; **2** her; **ich kenne sie** I know her; **3** it; **so eine hübsche Bluse, war sie teuer?** what a pretty blouse, was it expensive?; **4** they; **sie sind in der Küche** they're in the kitchen; **5** them; **ich habe sie gestern abgeschickt** I posted them yesterday.

Sie pronoun you; **kommen Sie herein!** come in!

Sieb das (PL die **Siebe**) **1** sieve; **2** strainer.

sieben number seven.

siebter, siebte, siebtes adjective seventh.

siebzehn number seventeen.

siebzig number seventy.

Siedlung die (PL die **Siedlungen**) **1** (housing) estate; **2** settlement.

Sieg der (PL die **Siege**) victory, win.

Siegel das (PL die **Siegel**) seal.

siegen verb (PERF **hat gesiegt**) to win.

Sieger der (PL die **Sieger**) winner.

Siegerin die (PL die **Siegerinnen**) winner.

sieht SEE sehen.

Silbe die (PL die **Silben**) syllable.

Silber das silver.

silbern adjective silver.

Silvester das New Year's Eve.

sind SEE sein.

Sinfonie die (PL die **Sinfonien**) symphony.

singen ◇verb (IMPERF **sang**, PERF **hat gesungen**) to sing

sinken ◇verb (IMPERF **sank**, PERF **ist gesunken**) **1** to sink; **2** to go down.

Sinn der (PL die **Sinne**) **1** sense; **2** meaning; **3** point; **das hat keinen Sinn** there's no point.

sinnlos adjective pointless.

sinnvoll adjective **1** sensible; **2** meaningful.

Situation die (PL die **Situationen**) situation.

Sitz der (PL die **Sitze**) **1** seat; **2** fit (of clothes).

sitzen ◇verb (IMPERF **saß**, PERF **hat gesessen**) **1** to sit; **sitzen bleiben** to remain seated; **2** **sitzen bleiben** to have to repeat a year, to stay down (at school); **3** **er sitzt** (informal) he's in jail; **4** **jemanden sitzen lassen** (informal) to leave somebody in the lurch; **5** to fit (of

clothes); **der Mantel sitzt gut** the coat fits well.

Sitzplatz der (PL die **Sitzplätze**) seat.

Sitzung die (PL die **Sitzungen**) **1** meeting; **2** session.

Sizilien das Sicily.

Skandal der (PL die **Skandale**) scandal.

Skandinavien das Scandinavia.

skandinavisch adjective Scandinavian.

Skateboard der (PL die **Skateboards**) skateboard; **Skateboard fahren** to skateboard.

Skater der (PL die **Skater**) skater (on a skateboard).

Skelett das (PL die **Skelette**) skeleton.

skeptisch adjective sceptical.

Ski der (PL die **Ski(er)**) ski; **Ski fahren/laufen** to ski.

Skianzug der (PL die **Skianzüge**) ski suit.

Skibrille die (PL die **Skibrillen**) skiing goggles.

Skifahren das skiing.

Skifahrer der (PL die **Skifahrer**) skier.

Skifahrerin die (PL die **Skifahrerinnen**) skier.

Skilaufen das skiing.

Skiläufer der (PL die **Skiläufer**) skier.

Skiläuferin die (PL die **Skiläuferinnen**) skier.

a b c d e f g h i j k l m n o p q r s t u v w x y z

Skilehrer der (PL die **Skilehrer**) ski instructor.

Skizze die (PL die **Skizzen**) sketch.

Skooter der (PL die **Skooter**) bumper car, dodgem car.

Skorpion der (PL die **Skorpione**) 1 scorpion; 2 Scorpio.

Skulptur die (PL die **Skulpturen**) sculpture.

Slip der (PL die **Slips**) briefs, pants.

Slowake der (PL die **Slowaken**) Slovak.

Slowakei die Slovakia.

Slowakin die (PL die **Slowakinnen**) Slovak.

slowakisch adjective Slovak.

Slowenien das Slovenia.

Smoking der (PL die **Smokings**) dinner jacket.

SMS die (PL die **SMS**) text message.

so adverb 1 so; **nicht so viel** not so much; **und so weiter** and so on; 2 like this, like that; **so nicht** not like that; 3 as; **so bald wie** as soon as; 4 such; **so ein Zufall!** what a coincidence!; 5 **das kriegst du so** (informal) you get it for nothing; 6 **so um zwanzig Euro** (informal) about twenty euros.

so conjunction **so dass** so that.

so exclamation right!, well!; **so?** really?

sobald conjunction as soon as.

Socke die (PL die **Socken**) sock.

Sofa das (PL die **Sofas**) sofa.

sofort adverb immediately.

sogar adverb even.

sogleich adverb at once.

Sohle die (PL die **Sohlen**) sole.

Sohn der (PL die **Söhne**) son.

Soja die soy.

solange conjunction as long as.

solch pronoun such; **solch einer/eine/eins** one like that, somebody like that.

solcher, solche, solches adjective, pronoun such; **ich habe solche Angst** I'm so frightened; 2 **ein solcher Mann** a man like that; **eine solche Frage** a question like that; **ein solches Haus** a house like that; 3 **solche** (plural) those; **solche wie die** people like that.

Soldat der (PL die **Soldaten**) soldier.

solide adjective 1 solid; 2 respectable.

Solist der (PL die **Solisten**) soloist.

Solistin die (PL die **Solistinnen**) soloist.

sollen ◇verb (PRES soll, IMPERF sollte, PERF hat gesollt) 1 should; **sollte es regnen** if it should rain; 2 to be supposed to; **was soll das heißen?** what's that supposed to mean?; 3 **sagen Sie ihr, sie soll anrufen** tell her to ring; 4 **was soll ich machen?** what shall I do?; **soll ich?** shall I?; 5 **was soll's!** so what!

sollte, sollten, solltest, solltet SEE sollen.

Sommer der (PL die **Sommer**) summer.

sommerlich adjective summery, summer.

Sommersprossen *plural noun* freckles.

Sonderangebot *das* (PL *die* **Sonderangebote**) special offer; **im Sonderangebot** on special offer.

sonderbar *adjective* strange, odd.

sondern *conjunction* but; **nicht nur ..., sondern auch ...** not only ..., but also ...

Song *der* (PL *die* **Songs**) song.

Sonnabend *der* (PL *die* **Sonnabende**) Saturday.

sonnabends *adverb* on Saturdays.

Sonne *die* (PL *die* **Sonnen**) sun.

sonnen *verb* (PERF **hat sich gesonnt**) **sich sonnen** to sun yourself.

Sonnenaufgang *der* sunrise.

Sonnenbrand *der* sunburn.

Sonnenbrille *die* (PL *die* **Sonnenbrillen**) sunglasses.

Sonnencreme *die* (PL *die* **Sonnencremes**) suntan lotion.

Sonnenenergie *die* solar energy.

Sonnenmilch *die* suntan lotion.

Sonnenöl *das* suntan oil.

Sonnenschein *der* sunshine.

Sonnenstich *der* sunstroke.

sonnig *adjective* sunny.

Sonntag *der* (PL *die* **Sonntage**) Sunday.

sonntags *adverb* on Sundays.

sonst *adverb* **1** usually; **2** else; **wer sonst?** who else?; **was sonst?** what else?; **3** sonst noch etwas? anything else?; **sonst noch jemand?** anybody else?; **4 sonst wo** somewhere; **es kann sonst wo sein** it could be anywhere; **5** otherwise; **geh jetzt, sonst verpasst du den Bus** go now, otherwise you'll miss the bus.

sonstwo SEE **sonst**.

sooft *conjunction* whenever.

Sorge *die* (PL *die* **Sorgen**) worry; **sich Sorgen machen** to worry.

sorgen *verb* (PERF **hat gesorgt**) **1 für etwas sorgen** to take care of something; **für die Musik sorgen** to see to the music; **für jemanden sorgen** to look after somebody; **2 dafür sorgen, dass ...** to make sure that ...; **3 sich sorgen** to worry; **ich sorge mich um meine Eltern** I worry about my parents.

sorgfältig *adjective* careful.

Sorte *die* (PL *die* **Sorten**) **1** kind; **2** brand.

Soße *die* (PL *die* **Soßen**) **1** sauce; **2** gravy; **3** dressing.

Souvenir *das* (PL *die* **Souvenirs**) souvenir.

soviel *conjunction* as far as; **soviel ich weiß** as far as I know.

soviel *adverb* SEE **viel**.

soweit *conjunction* as far as; **soweit ich weiß, ist er in Ferien** as far as I know, he's on holiday.

soweit *adverb* SEE **weit**.

sowenig SEE **wenig**.

sowie *conjunction* **1** as well as; **2** as soon as.

sowieso *adverb* anyway.

a b c d e f g h i j k l m n o p q r s t u v w x y z

sowohl *adverb* **sowohl ... als auch ... both ... and ...; sowohl er wie auch sein Freund** both he and his friend.

sozial *adjective* social.

Sozialarbeiter *der* (PL die **Sozialarbeiter**) social worker.

Sozialarbeiterin *die* (PL die **Sozialarbeiterinnen**) social worker.

Sozialhilfe *die* social security.

Sozialismus *der* socialism.

sozialistisch *adjective* socialist.

Sozialkunde *die* social studies.

Sozialwohnung *die* (PL die **Sozialwohnungen**) council flat.

Soziologie *die* sociology.

sozusagen *adverb* so to speak.

Spalte *die* (PL die **Spalten**) **1** crack; **2** column (*in text*).

spalten *verb* (PERF **hat gespalten**) to split.

Spaniel *der* (PL die **Spaniels**) Spaniel.

Spanien *das* Spain.

Spanier *der* (PL die **Spanier**) Spaniard.

Spanierin *die* (PL die **Spanierinnen**) Spaniard.

spanisch *adjective* Spanish.

Spanisch *das* Spanish (*language*).

spann SEE **spinnen**.

spannend *adjective* exciting.

Spannung *die* (PL die **Spannungen**) **1** tension; **2** suspense (*in a film or novel, for example*); **ich erwarte**

seine Antwort mit Spannung I can't wait for his answer; **3** voltage.

Sparbüchse *die* (PL die **Sparbüchsen**) money box.

sparen *verb* (PERF **hat gespart**) **1** to save; **auf etwas sparen** to save up for something; **2 sich etwas sparen** not to bother with something; **sich die Mühe sparen** to save yourself the trouble; **3 an etwas sparen** to economize on something.

Spargel *der* asparagus.

Sparkasse *die* savings bank.

sparsam *adjective* **1** economical; **2** thrifty.

Sparschwein *das* (PL die **Sparschweine**) piggy bank.

Spaß *der* (PL die **Späße**) **1** fun; **zum/aus Spaß** for fun; **das macht Spaß** it's fun; **Segeln macht mir keinen Spaß** I don't like sailing; **2 viel Spaß!** have a good time!; **3** joke; **er macht nur Spaß** he's only joking.

spät *adjective, adverb* late; **zu spät kommen** to be late; **wie spät ist es?** what time is it?

Spaten *der* (PL die **Spaten**) spade.

später *adjective* later.

spätestens *adverb* at the latest.

Spatz *der* (PL die **Spatzen**) sparrow.

Spätzle *plural noun* noodles (*South German dish*).

spazieren *verb* (PERF **ist spaziert**) **1** to stroll; **2 spazieren gehen** to go for a walk; **hast du Lust, spazieren zu gehen?** would you like to go for a walk?

spazierengehen SEE **spazieren.**

Spaziergang der (PL die Spaziergänge) walk; **einen Spaziergang machen** to go for a walk.

Speck der bacon.

Speiche die (PL die Speichen) spoke.

Speicher der (PL die Speicher) **1** loft, attic; **2** memory (in computing).

Speicherkapazität die storage capacity (on hard disk).

speichern verb (PERF hat gespeichert) **1** to store; **2** to save (in computing).

Speise die (PL die Speisen) **1** food; **2** dish.

Speisekarte die (PL die Speisekarten) menu.

Speisesaal der (PL die Speisesäle) **1** dining hall; **2** dining room.

Speisewagen der (PL die Speisewagen) dining car.

Spende die (PL die Spenden) donation.

spenden verb (PERF hat gespendet) **1** to donate; **2** to give.

spendieren verb (PERF hat spendiert) **jemandem etwas spendieren** to treat somebody to something.

Sperling der (PL die Sperlinge) sparrow.

Sperre die (PL die Sperren) **1** barrier; **2** ban.

sperren verb (PERF hat gesperrt) **1** to close; **2** to block (an entrance,

access); **3 den Strom sperren** to cut off the electricity; **4 einen Scheck sperren** to stop a cheque; **5 ein Tier in einen Käfig sperren** to shut an animal (up) in a cage.

spezialisieren verb (PERF hat spezialisiert) **sich spezialisieren** to specialize.

Spezialität die (PL die Spezialitäten) speciality.

speziell adjective special.

Spezies die (PL die Spezies) species.

Spiegel der (PL die Spiegel) mirror.

Spiegelbild das (PL die Spiegelbilder) reflection.

Spiegelei das (PL die Spiegeleier) fried egg.

spiegeln verb (PERF hat gespiegelt) **1** to reflect; **2 sich spiegeln** to be reflected.

Spiel das (PL die Spiele) **1** game; **2 ein Spiel Karten** a pack of cards; **3 es steht viel auf dem Spiel** there's a lot at stake.

Spielautomat der (PL die Spielautomaten) gaming machine.

spielen verb (PERF hat gespielt) **1** to play; **wir spielen morgen Fußball** we're playing football tomorrow; **2** to gamble; **3** to act; **das Stück war gut gespielt** the play was well acted; **4 der Film spielt in Rom** the film is set in Rome.

spielend adverb easily.

Spieler der (PL die Spieler) **1** player; **2** gambler.

Spielerin die (PL die Spielerinnen)
1 player; 2 gambler.

Spielfeld das (PL die Spielfelder)
pitch, field.

Spielhalle die (PL die Spielhallen)
amusement arcade.

Spielplatz der (PL die Spielplätze)
playground.

Spielverderber der (PL die
Spielverderber) spoilsport.

Spielverderberin die (PL die
Spielverderberinnen) spoilsport.

Spielwaren plural noun toys.

Spielzeug das 1 toy; 2 toys.

Spinat der spinach.

Spinne die (PL die Spinnen) spider.

spinnen ◇verb (IMPERF spann, PERF
hat gesponnen) 1 to spin; 2 du
spinnst! (informal) you're mad!

Spinnennetz das (PL die
Spinnennetze) 1 spider's web;
2 cobweb.

Spion der (PL die Spione) spy.

Spionage die spying, espionage.

spionieren verb (PERF hat
spioniert) to spy.

Spirituosen plural noun spirits
(alcohol).

spitz adjective pointed.

Spitze die (PL die Spitzen) 1 point;
2 top; Schalke liegt jetzt an der
Spitze Schalke is top of the league
at the moment; 3 peak; von hier
kann man die schneebedeckten
Spitzen sehen you can see the
snow-covered peaks from here;
4 front; an der Spitze liegen to be

in the lead; 5 lace; 6 Spitze sein
(informal) to be great.

spitzen verb (PERF hat gespitzt)
1 to sharpen; 2 sich auf etwas
spitzen (informal) to look forward
to something.

Spitzname der (PL die
Spitznamen) nickname.

Splitter der (PL die Splitter)
splinter.

splittern verb (PERF hat/ist
gesplittert) 1 to splinter; 2 to
shatter.

sponsern verb (PERF hat
gesponsert) to sponsor.

Sport der sport.

Sportgeschäft das (PL die
Sportgeschäfte) sports shop.

Sporthalle die (PL die Sporthallen)
sports hall.

Sportler der (PL die Sportler)
sportsman.

Sportlerin die (PL die
Sportlerinnen) sportswoman.

sportlich adjective 1 sporting;
2 sporty.

Sportplatz der (PL die Sportplätze)
sports field, sports ground.

Sportschuh der (PL die
Sportschuhe) trainer.

Sportverein der (PL die
Sportvereine) sports club.

Sportwagen der (PL die
Sportwagen) 1 sports car;
2 pushchair.

Sportzentrum das (PL die
Sportzentren) sports centre.

spotten verb (PERF **hat gespottet**) to mock.

sprach SEE **sprechen**.

Sprache die (PL die **Sprachen**) 1 language; 2 speech; **etwas zur Sprache bringen** to bring something up.

Sprachführer der (PL die **Sprachführer**) phrase-book.

sprachlos adjective speechless.

sprang SEE **springen**.

Sprechblase die (PL die **Sprechblasen**) speech bubble.

sprechen ◇verb (PRES **spricht**, IMPERF **sprach**, PERF **hat gesprochen**) 1 to speak; **Deutsch sprechen** to speak German; **mit wem spreche ich?** who's speaking? (on the phone); **jemanden sprechen** to speak to somebody; 2 **Frau Hahn ist nicht zu sprechen** Mrs Hahn is not available; 3 to talk; **mit jemandem über etwas sprechen** to talk to somebody about something; 4 to say (a word, sentence).

Sprecher der (PL die **Sprecher**) 1 spokesman; 2 (on TV) announcer; 3 (in a film) narrator; 4 speaker.

Sprecherin die (PL die **Sprecherinnen**) 1 spokeswoman; 2 (on TV) announcer; 3 (in a film) narrator; 4 speaker.

Sprechstunde die (PL die **Sprechstunden**) surgery.

spricht SEE **sprechen**.

Sprichwort das (PL die **Sprichwörter**) proverb.

springen ◇verb (IMPERF **sprang**, PERF **ist gesprungen**) 1 to jump; 2 to bounce (of a ball); 3 to dive; 4 to crack.

Spritze die (PL die **Spritzen**) 1 syringe; 2 injection; 3 hose.

spritzen verb (PERF **hat gespritzt**) 1 to inject; 2 to splash; **du hast mich nass gespritzt** you've splashed me; 3 to spray; 4 to spit (of fat); 5 (PERF **ist gespritzt**) to splash up.

Sprudel der (PL die **Sprudel**) sparkling mineral water.

sprühen verb (PERF **hat gesprüht**) 1 to spray; 2 to sparkle (of eyes); 3 (PERF **ist gesprüht**) to fly (of sparks); **die Funken sind in alle Richtungen gesprüht** sparks flew in all directions.

Sprung der (PL die **Sprünge**) 1 jump; 2 dive; 3 crack (in china, glass).

Sprungbrett das (PL die **Sprungbretter**) diving board.

spucken verb (PERF **hat gespuckt**) to spit.

Spülbecken das (PL die **Spülbecken**) sink.

spülen verb (PERF **hat gespült**) 1 to rinse; 2 to wash up; 3 to flush.

Spülmaschine die (PL die **Spülmaschinen**) dishwasher.

Spülmittel das (PL die **Spülmittel**) washing-up liquid.

Spültuch das (PL die **Spültücher**) dishcloth.

Spur die (PL die **Spuren**) 1 track; **auf der falschen Spur sein** to be on the

a
b
c
d
e
f
g
h
i
j
k
l
m
n
o
p
q
r
s
t
u
v
w
x
y
z

wrong track; **jemandem auf die Spur kommen** to get on to somebody; **2** lane; **in der Spur bleiben** to keep in lane; **3** trail; **4** trace.

spüren verb (PERF **hat gespürt**)
1 to feel; **2** to sense.

Staat der (PL die **Staaten**) state.

staatlich adjective state; **eine staatliche Schule** a state school.

staatlich adverb by the state.

Staatsangehörigkeit die (PL die **Staatsangehörigkeiten**) nationality.

stabil adjective **1** stable; **2** sturdy.

stach SEE **stechen**.

Stachel der (PL die **Stacheln**)
1 spine; **2** spike; **3** sting.

Stachelbeere die (PL die **Stachelbeeren**) gooseberry.

Stacheldraht der barbed wire.

Stadion das (PL die **Stadien**) stadium.

Stadium das (PL die **Stadien**) stage.

Stadt die (PL die **Städte**) town, city.

städtisch adjective **1** urban; **2** municipal.

Stadtmitte die town centre.

Stadtplan der (PL die **Stadtpläne**) street map.

Stadtrand der outskirts (of town); **am Stadtrand von Lübeck** on the outskirts of Lübeck.

Stadtrat der (PL die **Stadträte**) town or city council.

Stadtrundfahrt die (PL die **Stadtrundfahrten**) sightseeing tour (of a town).

Stadtteil der (PL die **Stadtteile**) district.

Stahl der steel.

stahl SEE **stehlen**.

Stall der (PL die **Ställe**) **1** stable; **2** cowshed; **3** pigsty.

Stamm der (PL die **Stämme**)
1 trunk; **2** tribe; **3** stem (of a word).

Stammbaum der (PL die **Stammbäume**) family tree.

stammen verb (PERF **hat gestammt**) **aus Deutschland stammen** to come from Germany.

Stammgast der (PL die **Stammgäste**) regular customer (in a pub or restaurant).

stand SEE **stehen**.

Stand der (PL die **Stände**) **1** state; **etwas auf den neuesten Stand bringen** to bring something up to date; **2** score (in a game); **3** stall (for a horse); **4** stand (in a fair); **5** level (of water, of a river).

ständig adjective constant.

Standort der (PL die **Standorte**) position, location; **von ihrem Standort aus konnte sie nichts sehen** she couldn't see anything from where she was standing.

Stange die (PL die **Stangen**) **1** bar; **2** pole.

stank SEE **stinken**.

starb SEE **sterben**.

stark adjective **1** strong; **2** heavy (rain, traffic); **3** severe (frost, pain); **4** (informal) great; **das ist stark!** that's great!

Stärke die (PL die **Stärken**)
1 strength; 2 starch.

starrsinnig adjective obstinate.

Start der (PL die **Starts**) 1 start;
2 take-off.

Startbahn die (PL die **Startbahnen**)
runway.

starten verb (PERF **ist gestartet**)
1 (of a plane) to take off; 2 (PERF **hat gestartet**) to start, to launch (a campaign).

Station die (PL die **Stationen**)
1 station; 2 stop; **Station machen** to stop over; 3 ward (in hospital).

statt conjunction, preposition (+GEN)
instead of; **statt zu arbeiten** instead of working; **sie ging statt ihrer Schwester** she went instead of her sister.

stattdessen conjunction instead.

stattfinden verb (IMPERF **fand statt**, PERF **hat stattgefunden**) to take place.

Stau der (PL die **Staus**) 1 congestion; 2 traffic jam.

Staub der dust.

staubig adjective dusty.

staubsaugen verb (PERF **hat staubgesaugt**) to vacuum.

Staubsauger der (PL die **Staubsauger**) vacuum cleaner.

staunen verb (PERF **hat gestaunt**) to be amazed.

Steak das (PL die **Steaks**) steak.

stechen ◇verb (PRES **sticht**, IMPERF **stach**, PERF **hat gestochen**) 1 to prick; **sich in den Finger stechen** to prick your finger; 2 to sting, to

bite (of an insect); 3 **mit etwas in etwas stechen** to jab something into something.

Steckbrief der (PL die **Steckbriefe**) description (of a wanted person).

Steckdose die (PL die **Steckdosen**) socket.

stecken verb (PERF **hat gesteckt**)
1 to put; **du musst die Münze in den Schlitz stecken** put the coin into the slot; 2 to pin; 3 **wo steckt er?** where is he?; 4 **stecken bleiben** to get stuck; **den Schlüssel stecken lassen** to leave the key in the lock.

Stecker der (PL die **Stecker**) plug.

Stecknadel die (PL die **Stecknadeln**) pin.

Steckrübe die (PL die **Steckrüben**) turnip.

stehen ◇verb (IMPERF **stand**, PERF **hat gestanden**) 1 to stand; 2 to be; **es steht zwei zu zwei** the score is two all, **wie steht's?** what's the score?; 3 to have stopped (of a clock or a machine); 4 **es steht schlecht um ihn** he's in a bad way; **na, wie steht's?** how are you?; 5 **stehen bleiben** to stop; **die Uhr ist stehen geblieben** the clock has stopped; 6 **in der Zeitung steht, dass ...** it says in the paper that ...; 7 **jemandem (gut) stehen** to suit somebody; 8 **zu jemandem stehen** to stand by somebody; 9 **sich gut stehen** to be on good terms; 10 **zum Stehen kommen** to come to a standstill.

stehenbleiben SEE stehen.

stehlen ◇*verb* (PRES **stiehlt**, IMPERF **stahl**, PERF **hat gestohlen**) to steal.

steif *adjective* stiff.

steigen *verb* (IMPERF **stieg**, PERF **ist gestiegen**) 1 to climb; **auf eine Leiter steigen** to climb up a ladder; **auf ein Fahrrad steigen** to get on a bike; **in den Bus steigen** to get on the bus; 2 to rise.

steil *adjective* steep.

Stein *der* (PL **die Steine**) stone.

Steinbock *der* (PL **die Steinböcke**) 1 ibex; 2 Capricorn; **Petra ist Steinbock** Petra's Capricorn.

Steinbruch *der* (PL **die Steinbrüche**) quarry.

Stelle *die* (PL **die Stellen**) 1 place, spot; **an deiner Stelle** in your place; **an dritter Stelle liegen** to be in third place; 2 job; **eine freie Stelle** a vacancy; 3 authority; 4 **auf der Stelle** immediately.

stellen *verb* (PERF **hat gestellt**) 1 to put; 2 to set (*a watch, task*); 3 **zur Verfügung stellen** to provide; 4 **lauter stellen** to turn up; **leiser stellen** to turn down; **die Heizung höher stellen** to turn the heating up; 5 **sich krank stellen** to pretend to be ill; 6 **sich stellen** to give yourself up; 7 **die Kinder stellten sich an die Wand** the children stood against the wall.

Stellenanzeige *die* (PL **die Stellenanzeigen**) job advertisement.

Stellplatz *der* (PL **die Stellplätze**) pitch (*for a tent*).

Stellung *die* (PL **die Stellungen**) position.

stellvertretend *adjective* 1 acting; 2 deputy; **der stellvertretende Feuerwehrhauptmann** the deputy chief fire officer.

Stellvertreter *der* (PL **die Stellvertreter**) 1 deputy; 2 representative.

Stellvertreterin *die* (PL **die Stellvertreterinnen**) 1 deputy; 2 representative.

Stempel *der* (PL **die Stempel**) 1 stamp; 2 postmark.

stempeln *verb* (PERF **hat gestempelt**) to stamp.

Steppdecke *die* (PL **die Steppdecken**) quilt.

sterben ◇*verb* (PRES **stirbt**, IMPERF **starb**, PERF **ist gestorben**) to die.

Stereoanlage *die* (PL **die Stereoanlagen**) stereo (system).

Stern *der* (PL **die Sterne**) star.

Sternzeichen *das* (PL **die Sternzeichen**) star sign; **was ist dein Sternzeichen?** what star sign are you?

Steuer¹ *das* (PL **die Steuer**) 1 (steering) wheel; 2 helm.

Steuer² *die* (PL **die Steuern**) tax.

steuern *verb* (PERF **hat gesteuert**) 1 to steer; 2 to control; 3 (PERF **ist gesteuert**) to head.

Stewardess *die* (PL **die Stewardessen**) stewardess, air hostess.

Stich der (PL die **Stiche**) **1** prick; **2** stab; **3** sting, bite (of an insect); **4** stitch; **5** trick (when playing cards); **6** engraving; **7** jemanden im Stich lassen to leave somebody in the lurch.

sticht SEE **stechen**.

sticken verb (PERF hat gestickt) to embroider.

Stickstoff der nitrogen.

Stiefbruder der (PL die **Stiefbrüder**) stepbrother.

Stiefel der (PL die **Stiefel**) boot.

Stiefkind das (PL die **Stiefkinder**) stepchild.

Stiefmutter die (PL die **Stiefmütter**) stepmother.

Stiefschwester die (PL die **Stiefschwestern**) stepsister.

Stiefvater der (PL die **Stiefväter**) stepfather.

stieg SEE **steigen**.

stiehlt SEE **stehlen**.

Stiel der (PL die **Stiele**) **1** handle; **2** stem.

Stier der (PL die **Stiere**) **1** bull; **2** Taurus; Andrea ist Stier Andrea's Taurus.

stieß SEE **stoßen**.

Stift der (PL die **Stifte**) **1** pencil; **2** crayon; **3** tack (nail).

Stil der (PL die **Stile**) style.

still adjective **1** quiet; **2** still.

stillen verb (PERF hat gestillt) **1** to quench; **2** to breast-feed.

stillhalten ◇verb (PRES hält still, IMPERF hielt still, PERF hat stillgehalten) to keep still.

Stimme die (PL die **Stimmen**) **1** voice; **2** vote.

stimmen verb (PERF hat gestimmt) **1** to be right; stimmt das? is that right?; **2** to vote; **3** to tune.

Stimmung die (PL die **Stimmungen**) **1** mood; **2** atmosphere.

stinken ◇verb (IMPERF stank, PERF hat gestunken) to smell, to stink.

Stipendium das (PL die **Stipendien**) **1** scholarship; **2** grant.

stirbt SEE **sterben**.

Stirn die (PL die **Stirnen**) forehead.

Stock¹ der (PL die **Stöcke**) stick.

Stock² der (PL die **Stock**) floor; im ersten Stock on the first floor.

Stockwerk das (PL die **Stockwerke**) floor.

Stoff der (PL die **Stoffe**) **1** material, fabric; **2** substance.

stöhnen verb (PERF hat gestöhnt) to groan.

stolpern verb (PERF ist gestolpert) **1** to stumble; **2** to trip; ich bin über einen Stein gestolpert I tripped on a stone.

stolz adjective proud.

stoppen verb (PERF hat gestoppt) to stop.

Stöpsel der (PL die **Stöpsel**) **1** plug; **2** stopper.

stören verb (PERF hat gestört) **1** to disturb; Bitte nicht stören please do not disturb; **2** to bother; **das stört mich nicht** that doesn't bother me; **3 stört es Sie, wenn ich das Fenster aufmache?** do you mind if I open the window?; **der Empfang ist gestört** there's interference (on a TV).

Störung die (PL die **Störungen**) **1** disturbance, interruption; **entschuldigen Sie die Störung** I'm sorry to bother you; **2** interference; **eine technische Störung** a technical fault.

Stoß der (PL die **Stöße**) **1** push; **2** pile; **ein Stoß Handtücher** a pile of towels.

stoßen ◇verb (PRES **stößt**, IMPERF **stieß**, PERF **hat gestoßen**) **1** to push; **2** to kick; **3 sich den Kopf stoßen** to hit your head; **ich habe mir den Kopf an dem Balken gestoßen** I hit my head on the beam; **sich stoßen** to bump yourself; **4 sich an etwas stoßen** to object to something; **5** (PERF **ist gestoßen**) **gegen etwas stoßen** to bump into something; **6** (PERF **ist gestoßen**) **auf etwas stoßen** to come across something.

Stoßstange die (PL die **Stoßstangen**) bumper.

Stoßzeit die (PL die **Stoßzeiten**) rush hour.

stottern verb (PERF **hat gestottert**) to stutter.

Strafe die (PL die **Strafen**) **1** punishment; **2** fine; **3** penalty.

Straftat die (PL die **Straftaten**) crime.

Strahl der (PL die **Strahlen**) **1** ray, beam; **2** jet.

strahlen verb (PERF **hat gestrahlt**) **1** to shine; **2** to beam.

Strahlung die (PL die **Strahlungen**) radiation.

Strand der (PL die **Strände**) beach.

Straße die (PL die **Straßen**) street, road; **in welcher Straße ist der Supermarkt?** which street is the supermarket in?; **über die Straße gehen** to cross the road; **jemanden auf die Straße setzen** (informal) to give somebody the sack; **mein Wirt hat mich einfach auf die Straße gesetzt** (informal) my landlord just turned me out (of a flat or room).

Straßenbahn die (PL die **Straßenbahnen**) tram; **mit der Straßenbahn fahren** to go by tram.

Straßenraub der **1** mugging; **2** street robbery.

Straßenräuber der (PL die **Straßenräuber**) mugger.

Straßenüberführung die (PL die **Straßenüberführungen**) **1** footbrige; **2** roadbridge.

Straßenunterführung die (PL die **Straßenunterführungen**) **1** subway; **2** underpass.

Strauch der (PL die **Sträucher**) bush.

Strauß[1] der (PL die **Sträuße**) bunch of flowers, bouquet.

Strauß[2] der (PL die **Strauße**) ostrich.

Streber der (PL die **Streber**) swot.

Strecke die (PL die **Strecken**)
1 distance; 2 route; 3 line (rail).

strecken verb (PERF hat
gestreckt) 1 to stretch (your arms,
legs); 2 sich **strecken** to stretch.

Streich der (PL die **Streiche**) trick.

streicheln verb (PERF hat
gestreichelt) to stroke.

streichen ◇verb (IMPERF **strich**,
PERF hat **gestrichen**) 1 to paint;
'frisch gestrichen' 'wet paint'; 2 to
spread (with butter); 3 to delete;
4 to cancel (a flight); 5 jemandem
über den Kopf **streichen** to stroke
somebody's head.

Streichholz das (PL die
Streichhölzer) match.

Streifen der (PL die **Streifen**)
1 stripe; 2 strip.

Streik der (PL die **Streiks**) strike.

streiken verb (PERF hat **gestreikt**)
to strike.

Streit der (PL die **Streite**) quarrel,
argument.

streiten ◇verb (IMPERF **stritt**, PERF
hat **gestritten**) 1 to quarrel, to
argue; 2 sich **streiten** to quarrel, to
argue.

streng adjective strict.

Stress der stress.

stressig adjective stressful.

streuen verb (PERF hat **gestreut**)
1 to spread; die Straßen **streuen** to
grit the roads; 2 to sprinkle.

Strich der (PL die **Striche**) 1 line;
2 stroke.

strich SEE **streichen**.

Strichpunkt der (PL die
Strichpunkte) semicolon.

stricken verb (PERF hat **gestrickt**)
to knit.

Strickjacke die (PL die
Strickjacken) cardigan.

stritt SEE **streiten**.

Stroh das straw.

Strohhalm der (PL die **Strohhalme**)
straw (for drinking).

Strom der (PL die **Ströme**) 1 river;
2 stream (of people or blood); es
regnet in **Strömen** it's pouring
with rain; 3 current.

Stromausfall der (PL die
Stromausfälle) power failure.

strömen verb (PERF ist **geströmt**)
to stream.

Strömung die (PL die **Strömungen**)
current.

Strudel der (PL die **Strudel**) strudel
(kind of Austrian cake).

Strumpf der (PL die **Strümpfe**)
1 stocking; 2 sock.

Strumpfhose die (PL die
Strumpfhosen) tights.

Stube die (PL die **Stuben**) room

Stück das (PL die **Stücke**) 1 piece;
2 item; ein Euro das Stück one
euro each; 3 play.

Stückchen das (PL die **Stückchen**)
little piece.

Student der (PL die **Studenten**)
student.

Studentin die (PL die
Studentinnen) student.

studieren verb (PERF hat **studiert**)
to study; Horst studiert

Mathematik Horst is studying mathematics.

Studium das (PL die **Studien**) studies.

Stufe die (PL die **Stufen**) 1 step; 'Vorsicht Stufe' 'mind the step'; 2 stage (of development).

Stuhl der (PL die **Stühle**) chair.

stumm adjective 1 dumb; 2 silent.

stumpf adjective 1 blunt; 2 dull; 3 ein stumpfer Winkel an obtuse angle.

Stunde die (PL die **Stunden**) 1 hour; 2 lesson.

stundenlang adverb for hours.

Stundenplan der (PL die **Stundenpläne**) timetable.

stündlich adjective hourly.

stur adjective stubborn.

Sturm der (PL die **Stürme**) storm.

stürmisch adjective stormy.

Sturz der (PL die **Stürze**) 1 fall; 2 overthrow.

stürzen verb (PERF ist gestürzt) 1 to fall; 2 to rush (into a room); 3 (PERF hat gestürzt) to overthrow; 4 (PERF hat sich gestürzt) er hat sich aus dem Fenster gestürzt he threw himself out of the window; sich auf jemanden stürzen to pounce on somebody.

Sturzhelm der (PL die **Sturzhelme**) crash helmet.

stützen verb (PERF hat gestützt) to support; sich auf jemanden stützen to lean on somebody.

Subjekt das (PL die **Subjekte**) subject.

Substantiv das (PL die **Substantive**) noun.

subtil adjective subtle.

Subvention die (PL die **Subventionen**) subsidy.

subventionieren verb (PERF hat subventioniert) to subsidize.

Suche die (PL die **Suchen**) search.

suchen verb (PERF hat gesucht) 1 to look for; 'Zimmer gesucht' 'room wanted'; 2 to search.

süchtig adjective addicted.

Süchtige der/die (PL die **Süchtigen**) addict.

Südafrika das South Africa.

Südamerika das South America.

Süden der south.

südlich adjective 1 southern; 2 southerly.

südlich adverb, preposition (+ GEN) südlich von Wien south of Vienna; südlich der Stadt to the south of the town.

Südosten der south-east.

Südpol der South Pole.

Südwesten der south-west.

Summe die (PL die **Summen**) sum.

summen verb (PERF hat gesummt) 1 to hum; 2 to buzz.

Sünde die (PL die **Sünden**) sin.

super adjective (informal) great.

Supermarkt der (PL die **Supermärkte**) supermarket.

Suppe die (PL die **Suppen**) soup.

Surfen das surf.

surfen verb (PERF hat gesurft) to surf (in the sea, on the Internet); im

Internet surfen to surf the Internet.

Surfer der (PL die Surfer) surfer (*on the sea and Internet*).

Surferin die (PL die Surferinnen) surfer (*on the sea and Internet*).

süß *adjective* sweet.

Süßigkeit die (PL die Süßigkeiten) sweet.

Sweatshirt die (PL die Sweatshirts) sweatshirt.

symbolisch *adjective* symbolic.

sympathisch *adjective* likeable.

Symphonie die (PL die Symphonien) SEE Sinfonie.

Synagoge die (PL die Synagogen) synagogue.

synthetisch *adjective* synthetic.

System das (PL die Systeme) system.

Szene die (PL die Szenen) scene.

Tt

Tabak der (PL die Tabake) tobacco.

Tabelle die (PL die Tabellen) table.

Tablett das (PL die Tabletts) tray.

Tablette die (PL die Tabletten) tablet.

Tafel die (PL die Tafeln) **1** board, blackboard; **ein Wort an die Tafel schreiben** to write a word on the blackboard; **2 eine Tafel Schokolade** a bar of chocolate.

Tag der (PL die Tage) day; **guten Tag** hello; **am Tag** in the daytime.

Tagebuch das (PL die Tagebücher) diary.

tagelang *adverb* for days.

Tagesanbruch der dawn.

Tagesausflug der (PL die Tagesausflüge) day trip.

Tageskarte die (PL die Tageskarten) **1** today's menu; **2** day ticket.

Tageslicht das daylight.

Tageslichtprojektor der (PL die Tageslichtprojektoren) overhead projector.

Tagesmutter die (PL die Tagesmütter) childminder.

Tagesschau die (PL die Tagesschauen) news (*on television*).

Tageszeitung die (PL die Tageszeitungen) daily paper.

täglich *adjective* daily; **sein täglicher Besuch** his daily visit.

täglich *adverb* daily; **zweimal täglich** twice daily, twice a day.

tagsüber *adverb* during the day.

Taille die (PL die Taillen) waist.

Takt der (PL die Takte) **1** tact; **2** time; **im Takt** in time to the music; **3** rhythm.

taktlos *adjective* tactless.

taktvoll *adjective* tactful.

Tal das (PL die Täler) valley.

Talent das (PL die Talente) talent.

Tampon der (PL die Tampons) tampon.

Tang der seaweed.

Tank der (PL die Tanks) tank.

a
b
c
d
e
f
g
h
i
j
k
l
m
n
o
p
q
r
s
t
u
v
w
x
y
z

tanken verb (PERF hat getankt) to fill up (with petrol) to get petrol.

Tanker der (PL die Tanker) tanker (on sea).

Tankstelle die (PL die Tankstellen) petrol station.

Tankwagen der (PL die Tankwagen) tanker (on road).

Tankwart der (PL die Tankwarte) petrol-pump attendant.

Tanne die (PL die Tannen) fir.

Tannenbaum der (PL die Tannenbäume) 1 fir tree; 2 Christmas tree.

Tante die (PL die Tanten) aunt.

Tanz der (PL die Tänze) dance.

tanzen verb (PERF hat getanzt) to dance.

Tänzer der (PL die Tänzer) dancer.

Tänzerin die (PL die Tänzerinnen) dancer.

Tapete die (PL die Tapeten) wallpaper.

tapezieren verb (PERF hat tapeziert) to (wall)paper.

tapfer adjective brave.

Tapferkeit die bravery.

Tarif der (PL die Tarife) 1 tariff; 2 rate.

Tasche die (PL die Taschen) 1 bag; 2 pocket; **er hat es aus eigener Tasche bezahlt** he paid for it out of his own pocket; **Max hat mir fünf Euro aus der Tasche gezogen** (informal) Max wangled five euros out of me.

Taschenbuch das (PL die Taschenbücher) paperback.

Taschendieb der (PL die Taschendiebe) pickpocket.

Taschengeld das pocket money.

Taschenlampe die (PL die Taschenlampen) torch.

Taschenmesser das (PL die Taschenmesser) penknife.

Taschenrechner der (PL die Taschenrechner) pocket calculator.

Taschentuch das (PL die Taschentücher) handkerchief.

Tasse die (PL die Tassen) cup.

Tastatur die (PL die Tastaturen) keyboard.

Taste die (PL die Tasten) 1 key; 2 button (on a phone or a machine).

tasten verb (PERF hat getastet) 1 to feel; 2 **sich tasten** to feel your way.

Tat die (PL die Taten) 1 action; 2 eine gute Tat a good deed; 3 crime; 4 in der Tat indeed.

tat SEE tun.

Täter der (PL die Täter) 1 culprit; 2 offender.

Täterin die (PL die Täterinnen) 1 culprit; 2 offender.

tätig adjective active.

Tätigkeit die (PL die Tätigkeiten) 1 activity; 2 job.

Tätigkeit die (PL die Tätigkeiten) activity.

Tätowierung die (PL die Tätowierungen) tattoo.

Tatsache die (PL die Tatsachen) fact.

tatsächlich *adjective* actual.

tatsächlich *adverb* **1** actually; **2** really.

Tau[1] *der* the dew.

Tau[2] *das* (PL die **Taue**) rope.

taub *adjective* deaf.

Taube *die* (PL die **Tauben**) **1** pigeon; **2** dove.

tauchen *verb* (PERF **hat getaucht**) **1** to dip; **2** (PERF **hat/ist getaucht**) ('*ist getaucht*' is used when movement is described) to dive.

Taucher *der* (PL die **Taucher**) diver.

Taucherbrille *die* (PL die **Taucherbrillen**) diving goggles.

Taucherin *die* (PL die **Taucherinnen**) diver.

tauen *verb* (PERF **ist getaut**) **1** to melt; **2 es taut** it's thawing.

Taufe *die* (PL die **Taufen**) christening.

taufen *verb* (PERF **hat getauft**) **1** to christen; **2** to baptize.

taugen *verb* (PERF **hat getaugt**) **nichts taugen** to be no good.

tauschen *verb* (PERF **hat getauscht**) to exchange, to swap.

tausend *number* a thousand.

Taxi *das* (PL die **Taxis**) taxi.

Taxifahrer *der* (PL die **Taxifahrer**) taxi driver.

Taxifahrerin *die* (PL die **Taxifahrerinnen**) taxi driver.

Taxistand *der* (PL die **Taxistände**) taxi rank.

Technik *die* (PL die **Techniken**) **1** technology; **2** technique.

Techniker *der* (PL die **Techniker**) technician.

Technikerin *die* (PL die **Technikerinnen**) technician.

technisch *adjective* **1** technical; **2** technological.

Technologie *die* technology.

technologisch *adjective* technological.

Teddybär *der* (PL die **Teddybären**) teddy bear.

Tee *der* (PL die **Tee(s)**) tea; **ein Tee mit Zitrone** one lemon tea; **ein Tee mit Milch** one tea with milk.

Teebeutel *der* (PL die **Teebeutel**) tea bag.

Teekanne *die* (PL die **Teekannen**) teapot.

Teelöffel *der* (PL die **Teelöffel**) teaspoon.

Teenager *der* (PL die **Teenager**) teenager.

Teich *der* (PL die **Teiche**) pond.

Teig *der* (PL die **Teige**) **1** dough; **2** pastry; **3** mixture.

Teigwaren *plural noun* pasta.

Teil[1] *der* (PL die **Teile**) **1** part; **der zweite Teil** the second part; **zum größten Teil** for the most part; **2 zum Teil** partly; **3** share; **mein Teil am Gewinn** my share of the profit.

Teil[2] *das* (PL die **Teile**) **1** spare part; **2** part (*of a car, machine*); **3** unit (*of furniture*).

teilen *verb* (PERF **hat geteilt**) **1** to divide; **2 sich etwas mit**

a jemandem teilen to share something with somebody.

b **teilnehmen** ◇verb (PRES **nimmt teil**, IMPERF **nahm teil**, PERF **hat teilgenommen**) an etwas teilnehmen to take part in something.

Teilnehmer der (PL die **Teilnehmer**) 1 participant; 2 competitor.

Teilnehmerin die (PL die **Teilnehmerinnen**) 1 participant; 2 competitor.

teils adverb partly.

Teilung die (PL die **Teilungen**) division.

Teilzeitarbeit die part-time work.

Telefax das (PL die **Telefax(e)**) fax.

Telefon das (PL die **Telefone**) telephone.

Telefonanruf der (PL die **Telefonanrufe**) phone call.

Telefonbuch das (PL die **Telefonbücher**) telephone directory; phone book.

Telefongespräch das (PL die **Telefongespräche**) telephone call.

Telefonhörer der (PL die **Telefonhörer**) receiver.

telefonieren verb (PERF **hat telefoniert**) to telephone, to make a phone call.

telefonisch adjective telephone.

telefonisch adverb by telephone; er ist telefonisch nicht erreichbar he can't be contacted by phone.

Telefonkarte die (PL die **Telefonkarten**) phone card.

Telefonnummer die (PL die **Telefonnummern**) telephone number.

Telefonzelle die (PL die **Telefonzellen**) phone box, call box.

Teleskop das (PL die **Teleskope**) telescope.

Teller der (PL die **Teller**) plate.

Temperatur die (PL die **Temperaturen**) temperature.

Tempo das (PL die **Tempos**) speed; Tempo Tempo! (informal) hurry up!

Tendenz die (PL die **Tendenzen**) 1 trend; 2 tendency.

tendieren verb (PERF **hat tendiert**) zu etwas tendieren to tend towards something.

Tennis das tennis.

Tennisplatz der (PL die **Tennisplätze**) tennis court.

Tennisschläger der (PL die **Tennisschläger**) tennis racket.

Tennisspieler der (PL die **Tennisspieler**) tennis player.

Tennisspielerin die (PL die **Tennisspielerinnen**) tennis player.

Teppich der (PL die **Teppiche**) 1 carpet; 2 rug.

Termin der (PL die **Termine**) 1 date; einen Termin vereinbaren to fix a date; 2 appointment; 3 der letzte Termin the deadline.

Terminal¹ der (PL die **Terminals**) terminal.

Terminal² das (PL die **Terminals**) (computer) terminal.

Terrasse die (PL die **Terrassen**) terrace.

Terror der terror.

Terrorismus der terrorism.

Terrorist der (PL die **Terroristen**) terrorist.

Terroristin die (PL die **Terroristinnen**) terrorist.

Tesafilm™ der Sellotape™.

Test der (PL die **Tests**) test; **ein Test zum Hörverständnis** a listening comprehension test.

testen verb (PERF **hat getestet**) to test.

teuer adjective expensive; **wie teuer?** how much?

Teufel der (PL die **Teufel**) devil.

Text der (PL die **Texte**) **1** text; **2** lyrics; **3** caption.

Textverarbeitung die word processing.

Theater das (PL die **Theater**) **1** theatre; **2** (informal) fuss.

Theaterstück das (PL die **Theaterstücke**) play.

Theke die (PL die **Theken**) **1** bar; **2** counter.

Thema das (PL die **Themen**) subject, topic.

Themenpark der (PL die **Themenparks**) theme park.

Themse die Thames.

theoretisch adjective theoretical.

theoretisch adverb in theory.

Theorie die (PL die **Theorien**) theory.

Therapie die (PL die **Therapien**) therapy.

Thermometer das (PL die **Thermometer**) thermometer.

Thron der (PL die **Throne**) throne.

Thunfisch der (PL die **Thunfische**) tuna.

Thymian der thyme.

tief adjective **1** deep; **2** low.

Tiefe die (PL die **Tiefen**) depth.

Tiefgarage die (PL die **Tiefgaragen**) underground car park.

Tiefkühlfach das (PL die **Tiefkühlfächer**) freezer compartment.

Tiefkühlkost die frozen food.

Tiefkühltruhe die (PL die **Tiefkühltruhen**) freezer.

Tiefsttemperatur die (PL die **Tiefsttemperaturen**) minimum temperature.

Tier das (PL die **Tiere**) animal.

Tierarzt der (PL die **Tierärzte**) vet.

Tierärztin die (PL die **Tierärztinnen**) vet.

Tiergarten der (PL die **Tiergärten**) zoo.

Tierkreis der zodiac.

Tierpark der (PL die **Tierparks**) zoo.

Tiger der (PL die **Tiger**) tiger.

Tinte die (PL die **Tinten**) ink.

Tintenfisch der (PL die **Tintenfische**) **1** octopus; **2** squid.

Tipp der (PL die **Tipps**) tip.

a b c d e f g h i j k l m n o p q r s t u v w x y z

a **tippen** verb (PERF **hat getippt**) **1** to
type; **2** to tap; **3** **auf etwas tippen** to
bet on something; **ich tippe auf ihn**
I'm tipping him to win; **im Lotto
tippen** to do the lottery.

Tisch der (PL die **Tische**) **1** table;
2 **nach Tisch** after the meal.

Tischdecke die (PL die
Tischdecken) tablecloth.

Tischler der (PL die **Tischler**)
joiner, carpenter.

Tischtennis das table tennis.

Tischtuch das (PL die **Tischtücher**)
tablecloth.

Titel der (PL die **Titel**) title.

Toast der (PL die **Toasts**) toast.

toben verb (PERF **hat getobt**) **1** to
rage; **2** to go mad; **3** to charge
about.

Tochter die (PL die **Töchter**)
daughter.

Tod der (PL die **Tode**) death.

Todesstrafe die death penalty.

tödlich adjective **1** fatal; **2** deadly.

todmüde adjective (informal)
dead tired.

todschick adjective (informal)
trendy.

Toilette die (PL die **Toiletten**) toilet;
auf die Toilette gehen to go to the
toilet.

Toilettenpapier das toilet paper.

toll adjective (informal) brilliant.

Tollwut die rabies.

Tomate die (PL die **Tomaten**)
tomato.

Tomatenmark das tomato purée.

Ton¹ der (PL die **Töne**) **1** sound; **er
hat keinen Ton gesagt** he didn't
make a sound; **2** **große Töne
spucken** (informal) to talk big;
3 tone; **einen frechen Ton
anschlagen** to adopt a cheeky tone;
4 note; **5** shade (of colour); **6** stress
(in pronunciation).

Ton² der clay.

Tonband das (PL die **Tonbänder**)
tape.

Tonbandgerät das (PL die
Tonbandgeräte) tape recorder.

Tonne die (PL die **Tonnen**) **1** barrel;
2 bin (for rubbish); **3** tonne, ton.

Topf der (PL die **Töpfe**) **1** pot; **2** pan.

Töpferei die (PL die **Töpfereien**)
pottery.

Tor das (PL die **Tore**) **1** gate; **2** goal;
mit 3 zu 2 Toren gewinnen to win
by 3 goals to 2.

Torte die (PL die **Torten**) **1** gateau;
2 cake.

Torwart der (PL die **Torwarte**)
goalkeeper.

tot adjective dead.

total adjective complete.

total adverb completely; **du bist
total verrückt** you're totally mad.

Tote der/die (PL die **Toten**) **1** dead
man/woman; **die Toten** the dead;
2 fatality.

töten verb (PERF **hat getötet**) to kill.

totlachen verb (informal) (PERF
hat sich totgelacht) **sich
totlachen** to laugh your head off.

Tour die (PL die Touren) **1** tour;
2 trip; **3 auf diese Tour** (*informal*)
in this way.

Tourismus der tourism.

Tourist der (PL die Touristen)
tourist.

Touristeninformation die (PL
die Touristeninformationen)
1 tourist information office;
2 tourist information.

Touristin die (PL die Touristinnen)
tourist.

Tournee die (PL die Tournees) tour.

traben verb (PERF **ist getrabt**) to
trot.

Tradition die (PL die Traditionen)
tradition.

traditionell adjective traditional.

traf SEE **treffen**.

tragbar adjective **1** portable;
2 wearable.

tragen ◇verb (PRES **trägt**, IMPERF
trug, PERF **hat getragen**) **1** to carry;
2 to wear; **sie trug ein weißes
Kleid** she wore a white dress; **man
trägt wieder kurz short** skirts are
in fashion again; **3** to bear; **die
Verantwortung für etwas tragen**
to be responsible for something;
4 to support; **die Organisation
trägt sich selbst** the organization
is self-supporting.

Träger der (PL die Träger) **1** porter;
2 bearer (*of a name, title*); **3** strap
(*of a dress*); **4** girder.

Tragetasche die (PL die
Tragetaschen) carrier bag.

tragisch adjective tragic.

Tragödie die (PL die Tragödien)
tragedy.

Trainer der (PL die Trainer) coach,
trainer.

trainieren verb (PERF **hat
trainiert**) **1** to coach; **2** to train.

Training das training.

Trainingsanzug der (PL die
Trainingsanzüge) tracksuit.

Trainingsschuh der (PL die
Trainingsschuhe) trainer (*shoe*).

Traktor der (PL die Traktoren)
tractor.

trampen verb (PERF **ist getrampt**)
to hitchhike.

Trampen das hitchhiking.

Tramper der (PL die Tramper)
hitchhiker.

Tramperin die (PL die
Tramperinnen) hitchhiker.

Träne die (PL die Tränen) tear.

trank SEE **trinken**.

Transplantation die (PL die
Transplantationen) transplant.

Transport der (PL die Transporte)
1 transport; **2** consignment.

transportieren verb (PERF **hat
transportiert**) to transport.

trat SEE **treten**.

Traube die (PL die Trauben) grape.

trauen verb (PERF **hat getraut**) **1** to
trust; **jemandem trauen** to trust
somebody; **2 sich trauen** to dare;
Ich trau mich nicht I don't dare;
3 to marry.

Trauer die **1** grief; **2** mourning.

Traum der (PL die Träume) dream.

a
b
c
d
e
f
g
h
i
j
k
l
m
n
o
p
q
r
s
t
u
v
w
x
y
z

träumen verb (PERF **hat geträumt**) to dream.

traumhaft adjective fabulous.

traurig adjective sad.

Traurigkeit die sadness.

Trauung die (PL die **Trauungen**) wedding.

Trauzeuge der (PL die **Trauzeugen**) witness (at a wedding ceremony).

treffen ◇verb (PRES **trifft**, IMPERF **traf**, PERF **hat getroffen**) 1 to hit; 2 to meet; 3 to make (arrangements, a decision); 4 **sich mit jemandem treffen** to meet somebody; 5 **sich gut treffen** to be convenient; 6 (PERF **ist getroffen**) **auf etwas treffen** to meet with (resistance, difficulties).

Treffen das (PL die **Treffen**) meeting.

Treffer der (PL die **Treffer**) 1 hit; 2 winner; 3 goal.

Treffpunkt der (PL die **Treffpunkte**) meeting place.

treiben ◇verb (IMPERF **trieb**, PERF **hat getrieben**) 1 to drive; 2 to do; **viel Sport treiben** to do a lot of sport; **Handel treiben** to trade; 3 **jemanden zur Eile treiben** to hurry somebody up; 4 **Unsinn treiben** to mess about; 5 (PERF **ist getrieben**) to drift.

Treibhaus das (PL die **Treibhäuser**) hothouse.

Treibhauseffekt der greenhouse effect.

Treibstoff der fuel.

trennen verb (PERF **hat getrennt**) 1 to separate; 2 to divide (words, parts of a room); 3 **sich trennen** to separate; **wir haben uns getrennt** we've separated; **Jutta hat sich von ihm getrennt** Jutta has left him; 4 **sich von etwas trennen** to part with something.

Trennung die (PL die **Trennungen**) 1 separation; 2 division.

Treppe die (PL die **Treppen**) stairs; **eine Treppe** a flight of stairs.

Treppenhaus das stairwell; **im Treppenhaus** on the stairs.

treten ◇verb (PRES **tritt**, IMPERF **trat**, PERF **ist getreten**) 1 to step; 2 to tread; 3 to kick; 4 **mit jemandem in Verbindung treten** to get in touch with somebody.

treu adjective faithful.

Treuekarte die (PL die **Treuekarten**) loyalty card.

Tribüne die (PL die **Tribünen**) 1 stand (in a stadium); 2 platform.

Trick der (PL die **Tricks**) trick.

Trickfilm der (PL die **Trickfilme**) cartoon.

trieb SEE **treiben**.

trifft SEE **treffen**.

Trimm-dich-Pfad der (PL die **Trimm-dich-Pfade**) keep-fit trail.

trimmen verb (PERF **hat getrimmt**) 1 to trim; 2 **sich trimmen** to keep fit.

trinken ◇verb (IMPERF **trank**, PERF **hat getrunken**) to drink.

Trinkgeld das (PL die **Trinkgelder**) tip.

Trinkschokolade *die* drinking chocolate.

Trinkwasser *das* drinking water.

Tritt *der* (PL die **Tritte**) **1** step; **2** kick.

tritt SEE **treten**.

Triumph *der* (PL die **Triumphe**) triumph.

trocken *adjective* dry.

trockenlegen *verb* (PERF hat **trockengelegt**) to drain (*a marsh, a pond*).

trocknen *verb* (PERF hat **getrocknet**) to dry.

Trockner *der* (PL die **Trockner**) drier.

Trödel *der* (*informal*) junk.

Trödelmarkt *der* (PL die **Trödelmärkte**) flea market.

Trommel *die* (PL die **Trommeln**) drum.

trommeln *verb* (PERF hat **getrommelt**) to drum.

Trompete *die* (PL die **Trompeten**) trumpet.

Tropen (*plural noun*) die **Tropen** the tropics.

Tropfen *der* (PL die **Tropfen**) drop.

tropfen *verb* (PERF hat **getropft**) to drip.

Trophäe *die* (PL die **Trophäen**) trophy.

tropisch *adjective* tropical.

trösten *verb* (PERF hat **getröstet**) to console, to comfort.

trotz *preposition* (+ GEN) despite, in spite of.

trotzdem *adverb* nevertheless.

trüb *adjective* **1** dull, dismal; **2** cloudy (*liquid*).

trübsinnig *adjective* gloomy.

trug SEE **tragen**.

Truhe *die* (PL die **Truhen**) chest.

Trümmer *plural noun* ruins.

Trumpf *der* (PL die **Trümpfe**) **1** trump (*card*); **2** trumps.

Trunkenheit *die* drunkenness; **Trunkenheit am Steuer** drink-driving.

Truppen *plural noun* troops.

Truthahn *der* (PL die **Truthähne**) turkey.

Tscheche *der* (PL die **Tschechen**) Czech.

Tschechin *die* (PL die **Tschechinnen**) Czech.

tschechisch *adjective* Czech.

Tschechische Republik *die* Czech Republic.

tschüss *exclamation* bye!.

T-Shirt *das* (PL die **T-Shirts**) T-shirt.

Tube *die* (PL die **Tuben**) tube.

Tuberkulose *die* tuberculosis.

Tuch *das* (PL die **Tücher**) **1** cloth; **2** scarf.

tüchtig *adjective* **1** efficient; **2** competent.

Tüchtigkeit *die* **1** efficiency; **2** competence.

Tulpe *die* (PL die **Tulpen**) tulip.

Tumor *der* (PL die **Tumoren**) tumour.

tun ◇*verb* (PRES **tut**, IMPERF **tat**, PERF hat **getan**) **1** to do; **das tut man nicht** it isn't done; **das tut's**

a b c d e f g h i j k l m n o p q r s u v w x y z

(*informal*) that'll do; **2** to put; **die Butter in den Kühlschrank tun** to put the butter in the fridge; **3** to pretend; **er tut nur so** he's only pretending; **4** to act; **freundlich tun** to act friendly; **5 jemandem etwas tun** to hurt somebody; **6 mit jemandem etwas zu tun haben** to have dealings with somebody; **das hat nichts damit zu tun** it's got nothing to do with it; **7 das tut nichts** it doesn't matter; **es hat sich viel getan** lots has happened.

Tunesien *das* Tunisia.

Tunesier *der* (PL *die* **Tunesier**) Tunisian.

Tunesierin *die* (PL *die* **Tunesierinnen**) Tunisian.

tunesisch *adjective* Tunisian.

Tunfisch *der* (PL *die* **Tunfische**) tuna.

Tunnel *der* (PL *die* **Tunnel**) tunnel.

Tupfen *der* (PL *die* **Tupfen**) dot.

tupfen *verb* (PERF **hat getupft**) to dab.

Tür *die* (PL *die* **Türen**) door.

Türke *der* (PL *die* **Türken**) Turk.

Türkei *die* Turkey.

Türkin *die* (PL *die* **Türkinnen**) Turk.

türkis *adjective* turquoise.

türkisch *adjective* Turkish.

Turm *der* (PL *die* **Türme**) **1** tower; **2** steeple; **3** rook, castle (*in chess*).

Turnanzug *der* (PL *die* **Turnanzüge**) leotard.

Turnen *das* **1** gymnastics; **2** physical education, PE.

turnen *verb* (PERF **hat geturnt**) to do gymnastics.

Turnhalle *die* (PL *die* **Turnhallen**) gymnasium, gym.

Turnier *das* (PL *die* **Turniere**) tournament.

Turnschuh *der* (PL *die* **Turnschuhe**) **1** trainer; **2** gym shoe.

Turnverein *der* (PL *die* **Turnvereine**) gymnastics club.

tuscheln *verb* (PERF **hat getuschelt**) to whisper.

tut SEE **tun**.

Tüte *die* (PL *die* **Tüten**) bag.

Typ *der* (PL *die* **Typen**) **1** type; **2** (*informal*) bloke.

typisch *adjective* typical.

Uu

U-Bahn *die* (PL *die* **U-Bahnen**) underground.

übel *adjective* **1** bad; **2 mir ist übel** I feel sick; **3 etwas übel nehmen** to take offence at something; **jemandem etwas übel nehmen** to hold something against somebody.

Übelkeit *die* nausea.

übelnehmen SEE **übel.**

üben *verb* (PERF **hat geübt**) to practise.

über *preposition* (+ DAT, *or* + ACC *with movement towards a place*) **1** over; **über Weihnachten** over Christmas; **2** above; **er wohnt über uns** he lives above us; **fünf Grad**

über Null five degrees above zero;
3 about; **über etwas schreiben** to
write about something; **4** for; **ein
Scheck über hundert Euro** a
cheque for one hundred euros;
5 across (*a field, the street*); **6 über
Frankfurt fahren** to go via
Frankfurt; **7 über die Straße
gehen** to cross the road.

über *adverb* **1 über und über** over
and over; **2 jemandem über sein** to
be better than somebody; **3 über
sein** (*informal*) to be left over;
4 jemanden ist etwas über
(*informal*) somebody is fed up with
something; **5 etwas über haben**
(*informal*) to be fed up with
something; **Nudeln habe ich über**
I'm getting fed up with pasta.

überall *adverb* everywhere.

überarbeiten *verb* (PERF **hat
überarbeitet**)) to revise (*a text*).

Überblick *der* (PL *die* **Überblicke**)
**1 einen guten Überblick über
etwas haben** to have a good view of
something; **2** overall view; **den
Überblick verlieren** to lose track of
things; **3** summary.

überblicken *verb* (PERF **hat
überblickt**) **1** to overlook; **2** to
assess.

Überdosis *die* (PL *die* **Überdosen**)
overdose.

Überdruss *der* **bis zum Überdruss**
ad nauseam.

übereinander *adverb* **1** one on
top of the other; **2 übereinander
sprechen** to talk about each other.

übereinstimmen *verb* (PERF **hat
übereingestimmt**) to agree.

überempfindlich *adjective*
hypersensitive.

überfahren ◇*verb* (PRES
überfährt, IMPERF **überfuhr**, PERF
hat überfahren) to run over; **das
Kind ist von einem Auto
überfahren worden** the child was
run over by a car.

Überfahrt *die* (PL *die* **Überfahrten**)
crossing.

Überfall *der* (PL *die* **Überfälle**)
1 attack; **2** raid.

überfallen ◇*verb* (PRES **überfällt**,
IMPERF **überfiel**, PERF **hat
überfallen**) **1** to attack, to mug; **2** to
raid; **3 jemanden mit Fragen
überfallen** to bombard somebody
with questions.

überfällig *adjective* overdue.

überflüssig *adjective*
superfluous.

Überführung *die* (PL *die*
Überführungen) **1** transfer;
2 flyover; **3** footbridge.

überfüllt *adjective* **1** crowded;
2 oversubscribed.

Übergang *der* (PL *die* **Übergänge**)
1 crossing; **2** transition.

übergeben ◇*verb* (PRES **übergibt**,
IMPERF **übergab**, PERF **hat
übergeben**) **1** to hand over; **2 sich
übergeben** to be sick.

überhaben SEE **über**.

überhaupt *adverb* **1** in general;
2 anyway; **was will er anyway?**
what does he want anyway?;
3 überhaupt nicht not at all;
überhaupt nichts nothing at all;

überhaupt keine Zeit haben to have no time at all.

überholen verb (PERF hat überholt) **1** to overtake; **2** to overhaul.

überholt adjective out-of-date.

überlassen ◇verb (PRES überlässt, IMPERF überließ, PERF hat überlassen) **1** jemandem etwas überlassen to let somebody have something; **2** etwas jemandem überlassen to leave something up to somebody (a decision, for example); **das bleibt dir überlassen** it's up to you.

überlaufen ◇verb (PRES läuft über, IMPERF lief über, PERF ist übergelaufen) to overflow.

überleben verb (PERF hat überlebt) to survive.

überlegen[1] verb (PERF hat überlegt) **1** to think; **sich etwas überlegen** to think something over; **ohne zu überlegen** without thinking; **2 ich habe es mir anders überlegt** I've changed my mind.

überlegen[2] adjective **1** superior; **jemandem überlegen sein** to be superior to somebody; **2** convincing (victory).

überm = über dem.

übermäßig adjective excessive.

übermorgen adverb the day after tomorrow.

übernächster, **übernächste**, **übernächstes** adjective next but one; **übernächstes Jahr** the year after next.

übernachten verb (PERF hat übernachtet) to stay the night; **bei jemandem übernachten** to stay the night at somebody's house.

übernehmen ◇verb (PRES übernimmt, IMPERF übernahm, PERF hat übernommen) **1** to take over; **2** to take on; **3 sich übernehmen** to take on too much.

überqueren verb (PERF hat überquert) to cross.

überraschen verb (PERF hat überrascht) to surprise.

Überraschung die (PL die Überraschungen) surprise.

überreden verb (PERF hat überredet) to persuade.

übers = über das.

Überschrift die (PL die Überschriften) heading.

überschüssig adjective surplus.

überschütten verb (PERF hat überschüttet) jemanden mit etwas überschütten to shower somebody with something.

Überschwemmung die (PL die Überschwemmungen) flood.

übersehen[1] ◇verb (PRES übersieht, IMPERF übersah, PERF hat übersehen) **1** to overlook; (informal) einen Fehler übersehen to overlook a mistake; **2** to assess (consequences, damages).

übersehen[2] ◇verb (PRES sieht sich über, IMPERF sah sich über, PERF hat sich übergesehen) **sich etwas übersehen** (informal) to get fed up of seeing something.

übersetzen verb (PERF hat übersetzt) to translate.

Übersetzer der (PL die Übersetzer) translator.

Übersetzerin die (PL die Übersetzerinnen) translator.

Übersetzung die (PL die Übersetzungen) translation.

überspringen ✧verb (IMPERF übersprang, PERF hat übersprungen) **1** to jump (over); **2** to skip (a chapter).

überstehen ✧verb (IMPERF überstand, PERF hat überstanden) **1** to get over; **2** to survive.

Überstunden plural noun overtime; **Überstunden machen** to work overtime.

übertragen ✧verb (PRES überträgt, IMPERF übertrug, PERF hat übertragen) **1** to transfer; **2** to transmit; **3** to broadcast; **4** etwas ins Reine übertragen to make a fair copy of something; **5** sich auf jemanden übertragen to communicate itself to somebody (of enthusiasm or nervousness).

Übertragung die (PL die Übertragungen) **1** broadcast; **2** transmission.

übertreiben ✧verb (IMPERF übertrieb, PERF hat übertrieben) **1** to exaggerate, **2** to overdo.

Übertreibung die (PL die Übertreibungen) exaggeration.

überwältigend adjective overwhelming.

überweisen ✧verb (IMPERF überwies, PERF hat überwiesen) **1** to transfer; **2** to refer (a patient).

überzeugen verb (PERF hat überzeugt) **1** to convince; **2** sich selbst überzeugen to satisfy yourself.

überzeugend adjective convincing.

Überzeugung die (PL die Überzeugungen) conviction.

überziehen[1] ✧verb (IMPERF zog über, PERF hat übergezogen) to put on (a cardigan, jacket).

überziehen[2] ✧verb (IMPERF überzog, PERF hat überzogen) **1** to overdraw; **2** to cover (with icing, for example).

üblich adjective usual.

U-Boot das (PL die U-Boote) submarine.

übrig adjective **1** remaining; **2** übrig sein to be left over; **3** etwas übrig lassen to leave something (over); **4** uns blieb nichts anderes übrig we had no other choice; **5** alles Übrige the rest; die Übrigen the others; **6** im Übrigen besides.

übrigens adverb by the way.

übriglassen SEE übrig.

Übung die (PL die Übungen) **1** exercise; **2** practice; aus der Übung sein to be out of practice.

Ufer das (PL die Ufer) **1** bank (of a river); **2** shore.

Uhr die (PL die Uhren) **1** clock; **2** watch; **3** (in time phrases) es ist ein Uhr it's one o'clock; wie viel Uhr ist es? what's the time?; um

a
b
c
d
e
f
g
h
i
j
k
l
m
n
o
p
q
r
s
t
u
v
w
x
y
z

sechzehn Uhr at four o'clock (in the afternoon).

Uhrzeiger der (PL die **Uhrzeiger**) hand (of a clock or watch).

Uhrzeigersinn der im **Uhrzeigersinn** clockwise; **entgegen dem Uhrzeigersinn** anticlockwise.

Uhrzeit die time; **jemanden nach der Uhrzeit fragen** to ask somebody the time.

ulkig adjective funny.

um preposition (+ ACC) 1 round, around; **um das Haus herum** around the house; 2 at; **um fünf Uhr** at five o'clock; 3 around (about); 4 for; **um etwas bitten** to ask for something; **um seinetwillen** for his sake; 5 **sich um jemanden sorgen** to worry about somebody; 6 by (indicating difference); **um vieles besser** better by far; **um so besser** so much the better.

um adverb 1 about, around; **um die dreihundert Euro herum** about three hundred euros; **um Weihnachten** around Christmas; 2 **um sein** (informal) to be over.

um conjunction **um zu** (in order) to; **er ist noch zu klein, um in die Schule zu gehen** he's too young to go to school.

umarmen verb (PERF hat umarmt) to hug.

Umbau der (PL die **Umbauten**) 1 renovation; 2 conversion.

umbinden ◇verb (IMPERF band um, PERF hat umgebunden) to put on.

umblättern verb (PERF hat umgeblättert) to turn over.

umbringen ◇verb (IMPERF brachte um, PERF hat umgebracht) to kill.

umdrehen verb (PERF hat umgedreht) 1 to turn (round); 2 **sich umdrehen** to turn round, to turn over.

umfallen ◇verb (PRES fällt um, IMPERF fiel um, PERF ist umgefallen) to fall down.

Umfrage die (PL die **Umfragen**) survey.

umgänglich adjective sociable.

Umgangsformen plural noun manners.

Umgangssprache die slang, colloquial language.

umgeben ◇verb (PRES umgibt, IMPERF umgab, PERF hat umgeben) to surround.

Umgebung die (PL die **Umgebungen**) 1 surroundings; 2 neighbourhood.

umgehen[1] ◇verb (IMPERF ging um, PERF ist umgegangen) 1 to go round (of a rumour, an illness); 2 **mit jemandem streng umgehen** to treat somebody strictly; 3 **er kann mit Geld nicht umgehen** he can't handle money; **mit seinen Sachen sorgfältig umgehen** to handle one's things carefully.

umgehen[2] ◇verb (IMPERF umging, PERF hat umgangen) to avoid.

Umgehungsstraße die (PL die **Umgehungsstraßen**) bypass.

umgekehrt adjective 1 opposite; 2 reverse (order); 3 **es war**

umgekehrt it was the other way round.

umgekehrt *adverb* **1 und umgekehrt** and vice versa; **2** the other way round; **warum machst du es nicht umgekehrt?** why don't you do it the other way round?

umkehren *verb* (PERF **ist umgekehrt**) **1** to turn back; **nach zehn Minuten sind wir wieder umgekehrt** ten minutes later we turned back again; **2** to turn round (*a picture, book*); **3** to turn inside out (*a bag, for example*); **4 sie hat das ganze Zimmer umgekehrt** (*informal*) she turned the whole room upside down.

Umkleidekabine *die* (PL *die* **Umkleidekabinen**) changing cubicle.

Umkleideraum *der* (PL *die* **Umkleideräume**) changing room.

umkommen ◇*verb* (IMPERF **kam um**, PERF **ist umgekommen**) to be killed.

Umlaut *der* (PL *die* **Umlaute**) umlaut.

umlegen *verb* (PERF **hat umgelegt**) **1** to put on (*a scarf*); **2** to transfer (*a patient, call*); **3 jemanden umlegen** (*informal*) to bump somebody off.

Umleitung *die* (PL *die* **Umleitungen**) diversion.

umrechnen *verb* (PERF **hat umgerechnet**) to convert.

Umrechnung *die* conversion.

Umrechnungskurs *der* exchange rate.

Umriss *der* (PL *die* **Umrisse**) outline.

umrühren *verb* (PERF **hat umgerührt**) to stir.

ums = um das.

umschalten *verb* (PERF **hat umgeschaltet**) **1** to turn over; **vom ersten aufs zweite Programm umschalten** to turn from channel one to channel two; **2 auf Rot umschalten** to change to red.

Umschlag *der* (PL *die* **Umschläge**) **1** envelope; **2** cover.

umsehen ◇*verb* (PRES **sieht sich um**, IMPERF **sah sich um**, PERF **hat sich umgesehen**) **sich umsehen** to look round.

umso *adverb* **umso besser** all the better; **je mehr, umso besser** the more the better.

umsonst *adverb* **1** in vain; **2** free, for nothing.

Umstand *der* (PL *die* **Umstände**) **1** circumstance; **unter diesen Umständen** under these circumstances; **2 unter Umständen** possibly; **3 jemandem Umstände machen** to put somebody to trouble; **das macht gar keine Umstände** it's no trouble at all; **4 in anderen Umständen sein** to be pregnant.

umständlich *adjective* **1** laborious; **2** complicated.

umsteigen ◇*verb* (IMPERF **stieg um**, PERF **ist umgestiegen**) to change.

umstellen[1] *verb* (PERF **hat umgestellt**) **1** to rearrange; **2** to

a b c d e f g h i j k l m n o p q r s t u v w x y z

a reset; **3** to change over; **4 sich umstellen** to adjust.

umstellen[2] *verb* (PERF **hat umstellt**) to surround.

Umtausch *der* exchange.

umtauschen *verb* (PERF **hat umgetauscht**) to change, to exchange.

Umweg *der* (PL die **Umwege**) detour.

Umwelt *die* environment.

umweltfeindlich *adjective* environmentally unfriendly.

umweltfreundlich *adjective* environmentally friendly.

Umweltschützer *der* (PL die **Umweltschützer**) environmentalist.

Umweltschützerin *die* (PL die **Umweltschützerinnen**) environmentalist.

Umweltverschmutzung *die* pollution.

umwerfen ◇*verb* (PRES **wirft um**, IMPERF **warf um**, PERF **hat umgeworfen**) **1** to knock over; **2** to upset (*a plan*); **das hat mich umgeworfen** it's thrown me.

umwerfend *adjective* fantastic.

umziehen ◇*verb* (IMPERF **zog um**, PERF **ist umgezogen**) **1** to move; **sie ziehen nächste Woche um** they're moving next week; **2** (PERF **hat umgezogen**) to change; **3** (PERF **sich umgezogen**) **sich umziehen** to get changed.

Umzug *der* (PL die **Umzüge**) **1** move; **2** procession.

unabhängig *adjective* independent.

Unabhängigkeit *die* independence.

unangenehm *adjective* **1** unpleasant; **2** embarrassing (*question, situation*).

unartig *adjective* naughty.

unbedeutend *adjective* insignificant.

unbedeutend *adverb* slightly.

unbedingt *adjective* absolute.

unbedingt *adverb* really; **ich muss ihn unbedingt sprechen** I really must talk to him; **nicht unbedingt** not necessarily.

unbefriedigend *adjective* unsatisfactory.

unbefriedigt *adjective* unsatisfied.

unbegrenzt *adjective* unlimited.

unbehaglich *adjective* **1** uncomfortable; **2** uneasy.

unbekannt *adjective* unknown.

unbeliebt *adjective* unpopular.

unbequem *adjective* uncomfortable.

unbestimmt *adjective* **1** indefinite; **auf unbestimmte Zeit** for an indefinite period; **2** uncertain.

unbestimmt *adverb* vaguely; **etwas unbestimmt lassen** to leave something open.

unbewusst *adjective* unconscious.

und *conjunction* and; **und so weiter** and so on; **na und?** so what?

undankbar *adjective* ungrateful.

undeutlich *adjective* unclear.

undicht *adjective* leaking, leaky;
eine undichte Stelle a leak.

uneben *adjective* uneven.

unehrlich *adjective* dishonest.

unempfindlich *adjective* 1 hard-
wearing, easy-care; 2 immune;
gegen Kälte unempfindlich sein
not to feel the cold.

unentbehrlich *adjective*
indispensable.

unentschieden *adjective*
undecided; unentschieden spielen
to draw.

unerträglich *adjective*
unbearable.

unerwartet *adjective* unexpected.

unfähig *adjective* 1 incompetent;
2 unfähig sein, etwas zu tun to be
incapable of doing something.

unfair *adjective* unfair.

Unfall *der* (PL die **Unfälle**) accident.

unfreundlich *adjective*
unfriendly.

Unfug *der* 1 nonsense; 2 mischief;
Unfug machen to get up to
mischief.

Ungar *der* (PL die **Ungarn**)
Hungarian.

Ungarin *die* (PL die **Ungarinnen**)
Hungarian.

ungarisch *adjective* Hungarian.

Ungarn *das* Hungary.

Ungeduld *die* impatience.

ungeduldig *adjective* impatient.

ungeeignet *adjective* unsuitable.

ungefähr *adjective* approximate.

ungefähr *adverb* approximately,
about.

ungefährlich *adjective* safe,
harmless.

Ungeheuer *das* (PL die
Ungeheuer) monster.

ungeheuer *adjective* enormous.

ungehorsam *adjective*
disobedient.

ungelegen *adjective*
inconvenient.

ungemütlich *adjective*
uncomfortable.

ungenau *adjective* 1 inaccurate;
2 vague.

ungenießbar *adjective* 1 inedible;
2 undrinkable; 3 Bernd ist heute
aber ungenießbar (*Informal*)
Bernd is quite unbearable today.

ungenügend *adjective*
1 insufficient; 2 unsatisfactory
(*mark at school*).

ungerade *adjective* eine
ungerade Zahl an odd number.

ungerecht *adjective* unjust.

ungern *adverb* reluctantly.

ungeschickt *adjective* clumsy.

ungesund *adjective* unhealthy.

ungewöhnlich *adjective*
unusual.

Ungeziefer *das* vermin.

ungezwungen *adjective*
1 informal; 2 natural.

unglaublich *adjective* incredible.

Unglück *das* (PL die **Unglücke**)
1 accident; 2 misfortune; 3 bad

luck; **das bringt Unglück** that's unlucky.

unglücklich *adjective* **1** unhappy; **2** unfortunate.

unglücklicherweise *adverb* unfortunately.

unheilbar *adjective* incurable.

unheimlich *adjective* eerie.

unheimlich *adverb* **1** eerily; **2** (*informal*) incredibly; **unheimlich viel** an incredible amount.

unhöflich *adjective* impolite.

Uniform *die* (PL **die Uniformen**) uniform.

uninteressant *adjective* uninteresting.

Universität *die* (PL **die Universitäten**) university.

Unkenntnis *die* ignorance.

unklar *adjective* unclear.

Unkosten *plural noun* expenses.

Unkraut *das* weed.

unleserlich *adjective* illegible.

unlogisch *adjective* illogical.

unmittelbar *adjective* immediate, direct.

unmodern *adjective* old-fashioned.

unmöglich *adjective* impossible.

Unmöglichkeit *die* impossibility.

unnötig *adjective* unnecessary.

unordentlich *adjective* untidy.

Unordnung *die* **1** disorder; **2** mess.

unpraktisch *adjective* impractical.

unpünktlich *adjective* unpunctual; **unpünktlich sein** to be late.

Unrecht *das* **1** wrong; **zu Unrecht** wrongly; **Unrecht haben** to be wrong; **2** **jemandem Unrecht geben** to disagree with somebody.

unrecht *adjective* wrong; **jemandem unrecht tun** to do somebody an injustice.

unregelmäßig *adjective* irregular.

unreif *adjective* **1** unripe; **2** immature.

Unruhe *die* (PL **die Unruhen**) **1** restlessness; **2** agitation; **3** **Unruhen** unrest.

Unruhestifter *der* (PL **die Unruhestifter**) troublemaker.

unruhig *adjective* restless.

uns *pronoun* **1** us; **gib es uns** give it to us; **sie kommen mit uns** they're coming with us; **2** ourselves; **wir waschen uns die Hände** we are washing our hands; **3** each other; **wir kennen uns** we know each other.

unscharf *adjective* blurred, indistinct.

unschuldig *adjective* innocent.

unser *pronoun* our.

unserer, unsere, unser(e)s *pronoun* ours.

unsertwegen *adverb* **1** for our sake; **2** because of us; **3** as far as we're concerned.

unsicher *adjective* **1** uncertain; **2** insecure.

unsicher *adverb* unsteadily.

unsichtbar *adjective* invisible.

Unsinn *der* nonsense.

unsrer SEE **unserer**.

unsympathisch *adjective* unpleasant; **Tobias ist mir unsympathisch** I don't like Tobias.

unten *adverb* **1** at the bottom; **2** underneath; **3** downstairs; **hier unten** down here; **nach unten** down.

unter *preposition* (+ DAT *or* + ACC *with movement towards a place*) **1** under, below; **2** among; **unter anderem** among other things; **3** unter sich by themselves; **unter uns gesagt** between ourselves; **4** unter der Woche during the week.

Unterbewusstsein *das* subconscious.

unterbrechen ◇*verb* (PRES **unterbricht**, IMPERF **unterbrach**, PERF **hat unterbrochen**) to interrupt.

Unterbrechung *die* (PL *die* **Unterbrechungen**) interruption.

unterbringen ◇*verb* (IMPERF **brachte unter**, PERF **hat untergebracht**) **1** to put; **2** to put up (*a guest*).

untere SEE **unterer**.

untereinander *adverb* **1** among ourselves/yourselves/themselves; **2** one below the other.

unterer, untere, unteres *adjective* lower.

Unterführung *die* (PL *die* **Unterführungen**) subway.

untergehen ◇*verb* (IMPERF **ging unter**, PERF **ist untergegangen**) **1** to set (*of the sun*); **2** to sink, to drown; **3** to come to an end.

Untergrundbahn *die* (PL *die* **Untergrundbahnen**) underground.

unterhalb *preposition* (+ GEN) below.

unterhalten ◇*verb* (PRES **unterhält**, IMPERF **unterhielt**, PERF **hat unterhalten**) **1** to support; **2** to run (*a hotel, leisure centre*); **3** to entertain; **4** sich über etwas **unterhalten** to talk about something; **5** sich unterhalten to enjoy yourself.

unterhaltsam *adjective* entertaining.

Unterhaltung *die* (PL *die* **Unterhaltungen**) **1** conversation; **2** entertainment.

Unterhemd *das* (PL *die* **Unterhemden**) vest.

Unterhose *die* (PL *die* **Unterhosen**) underpants.

Unterkunft *die* (PL *die* **Unterkünfte**) accommodation.

Unterlagen *plural noun* documents, papers.

Untermieter *der* (PL *die* **Untermieter**) lodger.

Untermieterin *die* (PL *die* **Untermieterinnen**) lodger.

unternehmen ◇*verb* (PRES **unternimmt**, IMPERF **unternahm**, PERF **hat unternommen**) **1** to undertake; **2** nichts unternehmen

a
b
c
d
e
f
g
h
i
j
k
l
m
n
o
p
q
r
s
t
u
v
w
x
y
z

to do nothing; **was unternehmt ihr heute?** what are you doing today?

Unternehmen *das* (PL die **Unternehmen**) **1** enterprise; **2** concern.

Unterricht *der* **1** lessons; **heute haben wir keinen Unterricht** we've got no lessons today; **2** teaching.

unterrichten *verb* (PERF hat **unterrichtet**) **1** to teach; **2** to inform; **3 sich unterrichten** to inform yourself.

Unterrichtsfach *das* (PL die **Unterrichtsfächer**) subject.

Unterrock *der* (PL die **Unterröcke**) slip.

unterscheiden ◊*verb* (IMPERF **unterschied**, PERF hat **unterschieden**) **1** to distinguish, to tell apart; **2 sich unterscheiden** to differ.

Unterschied *der* (PL die **Unterschiede**) difference.

unterschiedlich *adjective* different; **das ist unterschiedlich** it varies.

unterschreiben ◊*verb* (IMPERF **unterschrieb**, PERF hat **unterschrieben**) to sign.

Unterschrift *die* (PL die **Unterschriften**) signature.

Unterseeboot (PL die **Unterseeboote**) submarine.

unterster, unterste, unterstes *adjective* bottom, lowest.

unterstreichen ◊*verb* (IMPERF **unterstrich**, PERF hat **unterstrichen**) to underline.

unterstützen *verb* (PERF hat **unterstützt**) to support.

Unterstützung *die* support.

untersuchen *verb* (PERF hat **untersucht**) **1** to examine; **2** to investigate.

Untersuchung *die* (PL die **Untersuchungen**) **1** examination, check-up; **2** investigation.

Untertasse *die* (PL die **Untertassen**) saucer.

Untertitel *der* (PL die **Untertitel**) subtitle.

Unterwäsche *die* underwear.

unterwegs *adverb* on the way; **den ganzen Tag unterwegs sein** to be out all day.

untreu *adjective* **1** unfaithful; **2** disloyal.

untüchtig *adjective* **1** inefficient; **2** incompetent.

ununterbrochen *adjective* uninterrupted.

unverbleit *adjective* unleaded.

unvergleichlich *adjective* incomparable.

unverheiratet *adjective* unmarried.

unverkäuflich *adjective* not for sale; **ein unverkäufliches Muster** a free sample.

unverschämt *adjective* impertinent.

unverständlich *adjective* incomprehensible.

unverzüglich *adjective* promptly; **bitte antworten Sie unverzüglich** please reply promptly.

unvorsichtig *adjective* careless.

unwahr *adjective* untrue.

unwahrscheinlich *adjective*
1 unlikely; 2 incredible.

unwahrscheinlich *adverb*
(*informal*) incredibly;
unwahrscheinlich schön
incredibly beautiful.

Unwetter *das* (PL die **Unwetter**)
storm.

unwichtig *adjective* unimportant.

unzählig *adjective* countless.

unzerbrechlich *adjective*
unbreakable.

unzertrennlich *adjective*
inseparable.

unzufrieden *adjective*
dissatisfied.

üppig *adjective* lavish.

uralt *adjective* ancient.

Urenkel *der* (PL die **Urenkel**) great-
grandson; **die Urenkel** the great-
grandchildren.

Urenkelin *die* (PL die
Urenkelinnen) great-
granddaughter.

Urkunde *die* (PL die **Urkunden**)
certificate.

Urlaub *der* (PL die **Urlaube**) holiday;
Urlaub haben to be on holiday; **auf/
im Urlaub** on holiday.

Urlauber *der* (PL die **Urlauber**)
holidaymaker.

Ursache *die* (PL die **Ursachen**)
cause; **keine Ursache!** don't
mention it!

Ursprung *der* (PL die **Ursprünge**)
origin.

ursprünglich *adjective* original.

ursprünglich *adverb* originally.

Urteil *das* (PL die **Urteile**)
1 judgement; 2 opinion; 3 verdict.

urteilen *verb* (PERF **hat geurteilt**)
to judge.

Urwald *der* (PL die **Urwälder**)
jungle.

USA *plural noun* USA.

usw. (*und so weiter*) etc.

Vv

vage *adjective* vague.

Vagina *die* (PL die **Vaginen**) vagina.

Valentinskarte *die* (PL die
Valentinskarten) valentine card.

Valentinstag *der* Valentine's Day.

Vanille *die* vanilla.

Variante *die* (PL die **Varianten**)
variety.

Vase *die* (PL die **Vasen**) vase.

Vater *der* (PL die **Väter**) father.

Vaterunser *das* Lord's Prayer.

Vati *der* (PL die **Vatis**) dad.

Veganer *der* (PL die **Veganer**)
vegan.

Vegetarier *der* (PL die **Vegetarier**)
vegetarian.

Vegetarierin *die* (PL die
Vegetarierinnen) vegetarian.

vegetarisch *adjective* vegetarian.

Veilchen *das* (PL die **Veilchen**)
violet.

Vene *die* (PL die **Venen**) vein.

a
b
c
d
e
f
g
h
i
j
k
l
m
n
o
p
q
r
s
u
v
w
x
y
z

a **Ventil** das (PL die **Ventile**) valve.

b **Ventilator** der (PL die **Ventilatoren**) fan.

c **verabreden** verb (PERF hat **verabredet**) 1 to arrange; **was habt ihr verabredet?** what did you arrange?; **mit jemandem verabredet sein** to have arranged to meet somebody; **Laura ist mit Frank verabredet** Laura has a date with Frank; 2 **sich mit jemandem verabreden** to arrange to meet somebody; **ich habe mich mit Oliver zum Tennis verabredet** I've arranged to play tennis with Oliver.

Verabredung die (PL die **Verabredungen**) 1 appointment; 2 date; 3 arrangement.

verabschieden verb (PERF hat **verabschiedet**) 1 to say goodbye to; 2 **sich verabschieden** to say goodbye.

Verachtung die contempt.

verallgemeinern verb (PERF hat **verallgemeinert**) to generalize.

veralten verb (PERF ist **veraltet**) to become obsolete.

veränderlich adjective changeable.

verändern verb (PERF hat **verändert**) 1 to change; 2 **sich verändern** to change.

Veränderung die (PL die **Veränderungen**) change.

veranstalten verb (PERF hat **veranstaltet**) to organize.

Veranstalter der (PL die **Veranstalter**) organizer.

Veranstaltung die (PL die **Veranstaltungen**) event.

verantwortlich adjective responsible.

Verantwortung die responsibility.

verantwortungsbewusst adjective responsible.

verantwortungslos adjective irresponsible.

verarbeiten verb (PERF hat **verarbeitet**) 1 to process; **etwas zu etwas verarbeiten** to make something into something; 2 to digest (food, information).

Verarbeitung die 1 use; 2 digestion; 3 processing of data.

verärgern verb (PERF hat **verärgert**) to annoy.

Verb das (PL die **Verben**) verb.

Verband der (PL die **Verbände**) 1 association; **sich zu einem Verband zusammenschließen** to form an association; 2 bandage, dressing; **einen Verband anlegen** to apply a dressing.

verband SEE **verbinden**.

verbergen ◊ verb (PRES **verbirgt**, IMPERF **verbarg**, PERF hat **verborgen**) 1 to hide; 2 **sich verbergen** to hide.

verbessern verb (PERF hat **verbessert**) 1 to improve; 2 to correct; 3 **sich verbessern** to improve.

Verbesserung die (PL die **Verbesserungen**) 1 improvement; 2 correction.

verbiegen ◇*verb* (IMPERF **verbog**, PERF **hat verbogen**) **1** to bend; **2 sich verbiegen** to bend.

verbieten ◇*verb* (IMPERF **verbot**, PERF **hat verboten**) **1** to forbid; **sie hat ihm verboten, das Haus zu betreten** she forbade him to enter the house; **meine Eltern verbieten mir, am Abend wegzugehen** my parents don't allow me to go out in the evening; **2** to ban.

verbilligt *adjective* reduced.

verbinden ◇*verb* (IMPERF **verband**, PERF **hat verbunden**) **1** to connect, to join; **2** to combine; **3** to bandage, to dress (*a wound*); **jemandem die Augen verbinden** to blindfold somebody; **4 jemanden verbinden** to put somebody through (*on the phone*); **ich verbinde** I'm putting you through.

verbindlich *adjective* **1** friendly; **2** binding (*agreement, decision*).

Verbindung *die* (PL *die* **Verbindungen**) **1** connection; **2 gute Verbindungen haben** to have good contacts; **sich mit jemandem in Verbindung setzen** to get in touch with somebody; **3** combination; **4 eine chemische Verbindung** a chemical compound.

verbirgt SEE **verbergen**.

verbleit *adjective* leaded.

verblüffen *verb* (PERF **hat verblüfft**) to amaze.

verbog SEE **verbiegen**.

verbogen *adjective* hidden.

Verbot *das* (PL *die* **Verbote**) ban.

verbot SEE **verbieten**.

verboten *adjective* forbidden; **'Rauchen verboten'** 'no smoking'.

verbracht, verbrachte SEE **verbringen**.

verbrannt, verbrannte SEE **verbrennen**.

Verbrauch *der* consumption.

verbrauchen *verb* (PERF **hat verbraucht**) to use, to use up; **die Waschmaschine verbraucht nicht viel Strom** the washing machine doesn't use up much electricity.

Verbraucher *der* (PL *die* **Verbraucher**) consumer.

Verbrechen *das* (PL *die* **Verbrechen**) crime.

Verbrecher *der* (PL *die* **Verbrecher**) criminal.

verbreiten *verb* (PERF **hat verbreitet**) **1** to spread; **eine Krankheit verbreiten** to spread an illness; **2 eine Meldung über den Rundfunk verbreiten** to broadcast a message; **3 sich verbreiten** to spread; **die Neuigkeit hat sich schnell verbreitet** the news spread quickly.

verbreitet *adjective* widespread.

verbrennen ◇*verb* (IMPERF **verbrannte**, PERF **ist verbrannt**) **1** to burn; **2** (PERF **hat verbrannt**) to burn (*rubbish, leaves*); **3** (PERF **hat verbrannt**) to cremate; **4** (PERF **hat verbrannt**) **sich die Hand verbrennen** to burn your hand.

verbringen ◇*verb* (IMPERF **verbrachte**, PERF **hat verbracht**) to spend; **wir haben schöne Ferien in**

a

Bayern verbracht we spent a nice holiday in Bavaria.

b

verbunden SEE **verbinden.**

c

Verdacht der suspicion.

d

verdächtig adjective suspicious.

e

verdächtigen verb (PERF **hat verdächtigt**) to suspect.

f

g

verdammt adjective, adverb (informal) damned; **verdammt!** damn!

h

verdarb SEE **verderben.**

i

Verdauung die digestion.

j

verderben ✧verb (PRES **verdirbt,** IMPERF **verdarb,** PERF **hat verdorben**) 1 to spoil, to ruin; **das hat mir den Abend verdorben** it ruined the evening for me; **ich habe mir den Magen verdorben** I have an upset stomach; 2 **es sich mit jemandem verderben** to get into somebody's bad books; 3 (PERF **ist verdorben**) to go off; **die Milch verdirbt, wenn du sie nicht in den Kühlschrank stellst** the milk will go off if you don't put it in the fridge.

k

l

m

n

o

p

q

r

verdienen verb (PERF **hat verdient**) 1 to earn; 2 to deserve.

s

Verdienst der (PL die **Verdienste**) 1 salary; 2 achievement.

t

u

verdirbt SEE **verderben.**

v

verdoppeln verb (PERF **hat verdoppelt**) 1 to double; 2 **sich verdoppeln** to double.

w

verdorben SEE **verderben.**

x

y

verdünnen verb (PERF **hat verdünnt**) to dilute.

z

verehren verb (PERF **hat verehrt**) to worship.

Verehrer der (PL die **Verehrer**) admirer.

Verehrerin die (PL die **Verehrerinnen**) admirer.

Verein der (PL die **Vereine**) 1 society; 2 organization; 3 club.

vereinbaren verb (PERF **hat vereinbart**) to arrange.

Vereinbarung die (PL die **Vereinbarungen**) 1 agreement; 2 arrangement.

vereinfachen verb (PERF **hat vereinfacht**) to simplify.

vereinigen verb (PERF **hat vereinigt**) to unite; **ein Land wieder vereinigen** to reunify a country.

Vereinigte Staaten plural noun United States.

Vereinigung die (PL die **Vereinigungen**) organization.

verfahren ✧verb (PRES **verfährt,** IMPERF **verfuhr,** PERF **ist verfahren**) 1 to proceed; 2 **ich habe mich verfahren** I've lost my way.

verfallen ✧verb (PRES **verfällt,** IMPERF **verfiel,** PERF **ist verfallen**) 1 to decay; 2 to expire (of a passport or ticket).

Verfallsdatum das (PL die **Verfallsdaten**) use-by date.

Verfassung die (PL die **Verfassungen**) 1 constitution; 2 state (of a person).

verfaulen verb (PERF **ist verfault**) to rot.

verfiel SEE **verfallen**.

verfolgen verb (PERF **hat verfolgt**)
1 to follow; 2 to persecute.

Verfolgung die (PL die
Verfolgungen) 1 pursuit, hunt;
2 persecution.

verfügbar adjective available.

Verfügung die **jemandem etwas
zur Verfügung stellen** to put
something at somebody's disposal;
jemandem zur Verfügung stehen
to be at somebody's disposal.

verfuhr SEE **verfahren**.

verführen verb (PERF **hat verführt**)
1 to tempt; 2 to seduce.

Verführung die (PL die
Verführungen) 1 temptation;
2 seduction.

vergab SEE **vergeben**.

vergangen verb SEE **vergehen**

vergangen adjective last.

Vergangenheit die 1 past; 2 past
tense.

vergaß SEE **vergessen**.

vergeben ◇verb (PRES **vergibt**,
IMPERF **vergab**, PERF **hat vergeben**)
1 to forgive; **jemandem etwas
vergeben** to forgive somebody for
something; 2 to give away, to
award, 3 **vergeben sein** to be
taken; **das Zimmer ist schon
vergeben** the room's already
taken.

vergeblich adverb in vain.

vergehen ◇verb (IMPERF **verging**,
PERF **ist vergangen**) to pass.

vergessen ◇verb (PRES **vergisst**,
IMPERF **vergaß**, PERF **hat vergessen**)
to forget.

vergesslich adjective forgetful.

vergewaltigen verb (PERF **hat
vergewaltigt**) to rape.

Vergewaltigung die (PL die
Vergewaltigungen) rape.

vergibt SEE **vergeben**.

vergiften verb (PERF **hat vergiftet**)
to poison.

verging SEE **vergehen**.

vergisst SEE **vergessen**.

Vergleich der (PL die **Vergleiche**)
comparison.

vergleichen ◇verb (IMPERF
verglich, PERF **hat verglichen**) to
compare.

Vergnügen das (PL die **Vergnügen**)
pleasure; **viel Vergnügen!** have
fun!

vergnügen verb (PERF **hat sich
vergnügt**) **sich vergnügen** to have
fun.

vergnügt adjective cheerful.

vergrößern verb (PERF **hat
vergrößert**) 1 to enlarge; 2 to
increase; 3 to magnify; 4 to extend
(a room, building); 5 **sich
vergrößern** to expand, to grow
bigger.

Vergrößerung die (PL die
Vergrößerungen) 1 expansion;
2 enlargement (of a photograph).

verhaften verb (PERF **hat
verhaftet**) to arrest; **er ist
verhaftet worden** he was arrested.

a
b
c
d
e
f
g
h
i
j
k
l
m
n
o
p
q
r
s
t
u
v
w
x
y
z

verhalten ✧*verb* (PRES **verhält sich**, IMPERF **verhielt sich**, PERF **hat sich verhalten**) **sich verhalten** to behave.

Verhalten *das* behaviour.

Verhältnis *das* (PL die **Verhältnisse**) **1** relationship; **sie hat ein gutes Verhältnis zu ihren Eltern** she has a good relationship with her parents; **2** affair; **Gabi hat ein Verhältnis mit einem verheirateten Mann** Gabi is having an affair with a married man; **3** ratio (*in maths*); **4 in keinem Verhältnis zu etwas stehen** to be out of all proportion to something; **5 Verhältnisse** conditions; **über seine Verhältnisse leben** to live beyond your means.

verhältnismäßig *adverb* relatively.

verhandeln *verb* (PERF **hat verhandelt**) to negotiate; **über etwas verhandeln** to negotiate something.

Verhandlung *die* (PL die **Verhandlungen**) **1** negotiation; **2** hearing; **3** trial.

verhauen *verb* (PERF **hat verhauen**) **1** to beat up; **2 die Prüfung verhauen** (*informal*) to make a mess of the exam.

verheimlichen *verb* (PERF **hat verheimlicht**) to keep secret.

verheiratet *adjective* married.

verhext *adjective* bewitched.

verhielt SEE **verhalten**.

verhindern *verb* (PERF **hat verhindert**) **1** to prevent;

2 verhindert sein to be unable to make it; **Petra ist verhindert** Petra won't be able to make it.

verhungern *verb* (PERF **ist verhungert**) to starve.

Verhütungsmittel *das* (PL die **Verhütungsmittel**) contraceptive.

verirren *verb* (PERF **hat sich verirrt**) **sich verirren** to get lost.

verkam SEE **verkommen**.

Verkauf *der* (PL die **Verkäufe**) sale; **zum Verkauf** for sale.

verkaufen *verb* (PERF **hat verkauft**) to sell; **zu verkaufen** for sale.

Verkäufer *der* (PL die **Verkäufer**) **1** seller; **2** sales assistant.

Verkäuferin *die* (PL die **Verkäuferinnen**) **1** seller; **2** sales assistant.

Verkaufsautomat *der* (PL die **Verkaufsautomaten**) vending machine.

Verkehr *der* traffic.

Verkehrsampel *die* (PL die **Verkehrsampeln**) traffic lights.

Verkehrsamt *das* (PL die **Verkehrsämter**) tourist office.

Verkehrsinsel *die* (PL die **Verkehrsinseln**) traffic island.

Verkehrsunfall *der* (PL die **Verkehrsunfälle**) road accident.

Verkehrszeichen *das* (PL die **Verkehrszeichen**) traffic sign, road sign.

verkehrt *adjective* **1** wrong; **2 verkehrt herum** inside out, the wrong way round.

verklagen verb (PERF hat verklagt) to sue.

verkleiden verb (PERF hat sich verkleidet) sich verkleiden to dress up.

Verkleidung die (PL die Verkleidungen) disguise, fancy dress.

verkommen ◇verb (IMPERF verkam, PERF ist verkommen) 1 to go off (of food); 2 to become dilapidated (of a house); 3 to go to the bad.

verkratzt adjective scratched.

Verlag der (PL die Verlage) publisher's.

verlangen verb (PERF hat verlangt) 1 to ask for, to require; am Telefon verlangt werden to be wanted on the phone; 2 to demand; 3 to charge.

verlängern verb (PERF hat verlängert) 1 to extend; 2 to lengthen; 3 to renew (a passport, driving licence).

Verlängerung die (PL die Verlängerungen) 1 extension; 2 renewal; 3 extra time (in sport).

verlassen[1] ◇verb (PRES verlässt, IMPERF verließ, PERF hat verlassen) 1 to leave; jemanden verlassen to leave somebody; 2 sich auf etwas verlassen to rely on something; du kannst dich auf ihn verlassen you can rely on him.

verlassen[2] adjective deserted.

verlaufen ◇verb (PRES verläuft, IMPERF verlief, PERF ist verlaufen) 1 to go; es ist gut verlaufen it went well; 2 sich verlaufen to lose your way; 3 die Menge verlief sich schnell the crowd quickly dispersed.

verlegen[1] adjective embarrassed.

verlegen[2] verb (PERF hat verlegt) 1 to mislay; 2 to postpone; 3 to publish; 4 to lay (a carpet, cable).

Verlegenheit die embarrassment.

Verleih der (PL die Verleihe) 1 renting out, hiring out; 2 rental firm, hire shop.

verleihen ◇verb (IMPERF verlieh, PERF hat verliehen) 1 to hire out; 2 to lend; 3 to award.

verlernen verb (PERF hat verlernt) to forget.

verletzen verb (PERF hat verletzt) 1 to injure; 2 to hurt; 3 to violate (a law); 4 sich verletzen to hurt yourself.

Verletzte der/die (PL die Verletzten) 1 injured person; 2 casualty.

Verletzung die (PL die Verletzungen) injury.

verlieben verb (PERF hat sich verliebt) sich verlieben to fall in love.

verlief SEE verlaufen.

verlieh SEE verleihen.

verlieren ◇verb (IMPERF verlor, PERF hat verloren) to lose.

verließ SEE verlassen.

verloben verb (PERF hat sich verlobt) sich verloben to get engaged.

a b c d e f g h i j k l m n o p q r s t u v w x y z

a

Verlobte der/die (PL die **Verlobten**) fiancé, fiancée.

b

Verlobung die (PL die **Verlobungen**) engagement.

c

verlocken verb (PERF hat **verlockt**) to tempt, to entice.

d

verlor, verloren SEE **verlieren**.

e

Verlosung die (PL die **Verlosungen**) prize draw.

f

Verlust der (PL die **Verluste**) loss.

g

vermeiden ✧verb (IMPERF **vermied**, PERF hat **vermieden**) to avoid.

h

vermieten verb (PERF hat **vermietet**) 1 to rent out, to hire out; 2 to let; **Zimmer zu vermieten** rooms to let.

i

Vermieter der (PL die **Vermieter**) landlord.

j

Vermieterin die (PL die **Vermieterinnen**) landlady.

k

vermissen verb (PERF hat **vermisst**) to miss.

l

Vermittlung die (PL die **Vermittlungen**) 1 arrangement; 2 agency; 3 switchboard; 4 telephone exchange; 5 mediation.

m

Vermögen das (PL die **Vermögen**) fortune; **ein Vermögen machen** to make a fortune.

n

vermuten verb (PERF hat **vermutet**) to suspect.

o

vermutlich adjective probable.

p

vermutlich adverb probably.

q

vernachlässigen verb (PERF hat **vernachlässigt**) to neglect.

r

s

t

u

v

w

x

y

z

vernichten verb (PERF hat **vernichtet**) 1 to destroy; 2 to exterminate.

Vernunft die reason.

vernünftig adjective sensible.

verpacken verb (PERF hat **verpackt**) 1 to pack; 2 to wrap up.

Verpackung die (PL die **Verpackungen**) packaging.

verpassen verb (PERF hat **verpasst**) to miss.

verpesten verb, (PERF hat **verpestet**) to pollute.

Verpflegung die food; **Unterkunft und Verpflegung** board and lodging.

verpflichten verb (PERF hat **verpflichtet**) 1 sich verpflichten to promise; 2 sich vertraglich verpflichten to sign a contract; 3 verpflichtet sein, etwas zu tun to be obliged to do something; jemandem zu Dank verpflichtet sein to be obliged to somebody; 4 verpflichtend binding.

Verpflichtung die (PL die **Verpflichtungen**) 1 obligation; 2 commitment.

verprügeln verb (PERF hat **verprügelt**) to beat up.

verraten ✧verb (PRES **verrät**, IMPERF **verriet**, PERF hat **verraten**) 1 to betray; 2 to give away; 3 to tell; 4 sich verraten to give yourself away.

verrechnen verb (PERF hat sich **verrechnet**) sich verrechnen to make a mistake.

verregnet adjective rainy.

verreisen verb (PERF **ist verreist**) to go away; **verreist sein** to be away.

verriet SEE **verraten.**

verrosten verb (PERF **ist verrostet**) to rust.

verrostet adjective rusty.

verrückt adjective mad, crazy.

Verrückte der/die (PL die **Verrückten**) maniac.

versagen verb (PERF **hat versagt**) to fail.

versammeln verb (PERF **hat versammelt**) 1 to assemble; 2 **sich versammeln** to assemble.

Versammlung die (PL die **Versammlungen**) meeting.

versäumen verb (PERF **hat versäumt**) to miss; **es versäumen, etwas zu tun** to fail to do something.

verschenken verb (PERF **hat verschenkt**) to give away.

verschieben ✧verb (IMPERF **verschob**, PERF **hat verschoben**) to postpone.

verschieden adjective 1 different; 2 various.

verschlafen ✧verb (PRES **verschläft**, IMPERF **verschlief**, PERF **hat verschlafen**) 1 to oversleep; 2 to sleep through (the day); 3 to miss (a date, the train).

verschlechtern verb (PERF **hat verschlechtert**) 1 to make worse; 2 **sich verschlechtern** to get worse.

verschlief SEE **verschlafen.**

verschließen ✧verb (IMPERF **verschloss**, PERF **hat verschlossen**) 1 to close (a tin, package); 2 to lock (a door, drawer).

verschlimmern verb (PERF **hat verschlimmert**) 1 to make worse; 2 **sich verschlimmern** to get worse.

verschloss SEE **verschließen.**

verschlucken verb (PERF **hat verschluckt**) 1 to swallow; 2 **sich verschlucken** to choke.

Verschluss der (PL die **Verschlüsse**) 1 fastener, clasp; 2 top (of a bottle).

verschmutzen verb (PERF **hat verschmutzt**) to soil; **die Umwelt verschmutzen** to pollute the environment.

Verschmutzung die pollution.

verschob SEE **verschieben.**

verschreiben ✧verb (IMPERF **verschrieb**, PERF **hat verschrieben**) 1 to prescribe; 2 **sich verschreiben** to make a mistake.

verschütten verb (PERF **hat verschüttet**) to spill.

verschwand SEE **verschwinden.**

verschwenden verb (PERF **hat verschwendet**) to waste.

Verschwendung die waste.

verschwinden ✧verb (IMPERF **verschwand**, PERF **ist verschwunden**) to disappear.

verschwommen adjective blurred.

a b c d e f g h i j k l m n o p q r s t u v w x y z

Versehen das (PL die **Versehen**) oversight; **aus Versehen** by mistake.

versehentlich adverb by mistake.

versetzen verb (PERF **hat versetzt**) **1** to move, to transfer (a person); **2** to move up (into the next class at school); **3 jemanden versetzen** to stand somebody up; **4 jemandem einen Schreck versetzen** to give somebody a fright; **jemandem einen Tritt versetzen** to kick somebody; **5 sich in jemandes Lage versetzen** to put yourself in somebody's position.

verseuchen verb (PERF **hat verseucht**) to contaminate.

Verseuchung die (PL die **Verseuchungen**) contamination.

versichern verb (PERF **hat versichert**) **1** to insure; **2** to assert; **jemandem versichern, dass …** to assure somebody that ….

Versicherung die (PL die **Versicherungen**) **1** insurance; **2** assurance.

Versicherungsgesellschaft die (PL die **Versicherungsgesellschaften**) insurance company.

Versicherungsschein der (PL die **Versicherungsscheine**) insurance policy document.

versöhnen verb (PERF **hat sich versöhnt**) **sich versöhnen** to make up; **sich mit jemandem versöhnen** to make it up with somebody.

versorgen verb (PERF **hat versorgt**) **1** to supply; **2** to provide for; **3** to look after.

verspäten verb (PERF **hat sich verspätet**) **sich verspäten** to be late.

Verspätung die lateness, delay; **Verspätung haben** to be late.

versprechen ✧verb (PRES **verspricht**, IMPERF **versprach**, PERF **hat versprochen**) **1** to promise; **2 sich viel von etwas versprechen** to have high hopes of something; **3 sich versprechen** to make a slip of the tongue.

Versprechen das (PL die **Versprechen**) promise.

Verstand der **1** mind; **den Verstand verlieren** to go out of your mind; **2** reason.

verstand SEE **verstehen**.

verstanden SEE **verstehen**.

verständigen verb (PERF **hat verständigt**) **1** to notify; **2 sich verständigen** to communicate, to make yourself understood; **3 sich über etwas verständigen** to agree on something.

Verständigung die **1** communication; **2** notification.

verständlich adjective **1** understandable; **jemandem etwas verständlich machen** to make something clear to somebody; **2** comprehensible.

Verständnis das (PL die **Verständnisse**) **1** comprehension; **2** understanding.

Verstärker *der* (PL *die* **Verstärker**) amplifier.

verstauchen *verb* (PERF **hat verstaucht**) to sprain; **sich den Fuß verstauchen** to sprain your ankle.

Versteck *das* (PL *die* **Verstecke**) hiding place.

verstecken *verb* (PERF **hat versteckt**) 1 to hide; 2 **sich verstecken** to hide.

verstehen ✧*verb* (IMPERF **verstand**, PERF **hat verstanden**) 1 to understand; **etwas falsch verstehen** to misunderstand something; 2 **sich gut verstehen** to get on well; 3 **das versteht sich von selbst** that goes without saying.

verstellbar *adjective* adjustable.

verstellen *verb* (PERF **hat verstellt**) 1 to adjust; 2 to block; 3 to disguise; 4 **sich verstellen** to pretend.

verstimmt *adjective* 1 out of tune; 2 peeved; 3 **ein verstimmter Magen** an upset stomach.

verstopft *adjective* constipated.

Versuch *der* (PL *die* **Versuche**) 1 attempt; 2 experiment.

versuchen *verb* (PERF **hat versucht**) to try.

verteidigen *verb* (PERF **hat verteidigt**) to defend.

Verteidiger *der* (PL *die* **Verteidiger**) 1 defender; 2 defence counsel.

Verteidigung *die* defence.

verteilen *verb* (PERF **hat verteilt**) to distribute.

Vertrag *der* (PL *die* **Verträge**) 1 contract; 2 treaty.

vertragen *verb* (PRES **verträgt**, IMPERF **vertrug**, PERF **hat vertragen**) 1 to stand, to take; 2 **ich vertrage keinen Kaffee** coffee disagrees with me; 3 **sich vertragen** to get on; **sich wieder vertragen** to make it up.

vertrat SEE **vertreten**.

Vertrauen *das* trust; **im Vertrauen** in confidence.

vertrauen *verb* (PERF **hat vertraut**) to trust.

vertraulich *adjective* 1 confidential; 2 familiar.

vertreten ✧*verb* (PRES **vertritt**, IMPERF **vertrat**, PERF **hat vertreten**) 1 to stand in for; 2 to represent; 3 **eine Meinung vertreten** to hold an opinion; 4 **sich die Beine vertreten** to stretch your legs.

Vertreter *der* (PL *die* **Vertreter**) 1 representative; 2 deputy.

Vertreterin *die* (PL *die* **Vertreterinnen**) 1 representative; 2 deputy.

vertritt SEE **vertreten**.

vertrug SEE **vertragen**.

verunglücken *verb* (PERF **ist verunglückt**) to have an accident.

verursachen *verb* (PERF **hat verursacht**) to cause.

verurteilen *verb* (PERF **hat verurteilt**) 1 to sentence; 2 to condemn.

a
b
c
d
e
f
g
h
i
j
k
l
m
n
o
p
q
r
s
t
u
v
w
x
y
z

Verwaltung die (PL die Verwaltungen) administration.

verwandt adjective related.

Verwandte der/die (PL die Verwandten) relative.

Verwandtschaft die relatives.

verwechseln verb (PERF hat verwechselt) to mix up, to confuse; **jemanden mit jemandem verwechseln** to mistake somebody for somebody; **ich verwechsele ihn mit seinem Bruder** I mistake him for his brother.

verwenden verb (PERF hat verwendet) to use.

Verwendung die use.

verwickelt adjective complicated.

verwirren verb (PERF hat verwirrt) **1** to confuse; **2** to tangle up.

verwirrt adjective confused.

verwöhnen verb (PERF hat verwöhnt) to spoil.

verwunden verb (PERF hat verwundet) to wound.

Verwundete der/die (PL die Verwundeten) casualty, injured person.

Verwundung die (PL die Verwundungen) injury, wound.

verzählen verb (PERF hat sich verzählt) **sich verzählen** to miscount.

Verzeichnis das (PL die Verzeichnisse) **1** list; **2** index.

verzeihen verb (IMPERF verzieh, PERF hat verziehen) to forgive; **verzeihen Sie, können Sie mir**

sagen ...? excuse me, could you tell me ...?

Verzeihung die forgiveness; **jemanden um Verzeihung bitten** to apologize to somebody; **Verzeihung!** sorry!

verzichten verb (PERF hat verzichtet) **1** to do without; **ich verzichte auf deine Hilfe** I can do without your help; **2 auf etwas verzichten** to give up something (*smoking or your share of something*); to relinquish something (*a right or privilege*).

verzieh, verziehen SEE verzeihen.

verzögern verb (PERF hat verzögert) **1** to delay; **2 sich verzögern** to be delayed.

Verzögerung die (PL die Verzögerungen) delay.

verzollen verb (PERF hat verzollt) to pay duty on; **haben Sie etwas zu verzollen?** have you anything to declare?

verzweifeln verb (PERF ist verzweifelt) to despair.

verzweifelt adjective desperate.

Verzweiflung die despair.

Vetter der (PL die Vettern) cousin.

Video das (PL die Videos) video.

Videokamera die (PL die Videokameras) video camera.

Videokassette die (PL die Videokassetten) video cassette.

Videorekorder der (PL die Videorekorder) video recorder.

Videospiel das (PL die Videospiele) video game.

Videothek die (PL die Videotheken) video shop.

Vieh das cattle.

viel adjective, pronoun **1** a lot of; **Erika hat viel Arbeit** Erika's got a lot of work; **2 viele** (plural) many, a lot of; **viele Leute** many people; **3** much, a lot; **wie viel?** how much?, how many?; **zu viel** too much; **vielen Dank** thank you very much; **viel Spaß!** have fun!; **viel Glück!** good luck!; **4 das viele Geld** all that money.

viel adverb **1** much, a lot; **viel weniger** much less; **so viel wie möglich** as much as possible; **sie redet viel** she talks a lot; **2 viel zu groß** far too big, much too big; **das dauert viel zu lange** it'll take far too long.

vielleicht adverb perhaps.

vielmals adverb **danke vielmals** thanks a lot.

vier number four.

Viereck das (PL die Vierecke) **1** rectangle; **2** square.

viereckig adjective **1** rectangular; **2** square.

vierte SEE **vierter.**

Viertel das (PL die Viertel) quarter; **es ist Viertel vor acht** it's quarter to eight.

viertel adjective quarter; **wir treffen uns um viertel acht** we'll meet at quarter past seven; **um drei viertel acht** at quarter to eight.

Viertelfinale das (PL die Viertelfinale) quarter finals.

Viertelstunde die (PL die Viertelstunden) quarter of an hour.

vierter, vierte, viertes adjective fourth.

vierzehn number fourteen.

vierzig number forty.

Villa die (PL die Villen) villa.

virtuell adjective virtual; **virtuelle Realität** virtual reality.

Virus das (PL die Viren) virus.

visuell adjective visual.

Visum das (PL die Visa) visa.

Vitamin das (PL die Vitamine) vitamin.

vitaminarm adjective low in vitamins.

vitaminreich adjective rich in vitamins.

Vogel der (PL die Vögel) bird.

Vogelbeobachter der (PL die Vogelbeobachter) birdwatcher.

Vogelbeobachterin die (PL die Vogelbeobachterinnen) birdwatcher.

Vogelscheuche die (PL die Vogelscheuchen) scarecrow.

Vokabel die (PL die Vokabeln) word; **Vokabeln** vocabulary.

Vokal der (PL die Vokale) vowel.

Volk das (PL die Völker) people.

Volkshochschule die adult education centre; **ein Kurs an der Volkshochschule** an adult education class.

a

b

c

d

e

f

g

h

i

j

k

l

m

n

o

p

q

r

s

t

u

v

w

x

y

z

Volkslied das (PL die **Volkslieder**) folk song.

Volkswirtschaft die economics.

voll adjective 1 full; ein Korb voll Äpfel a basket full of apples; die **volle Wahrheit** the whole truth; 2 etwas voll machen to fill something up; voll tanken to fill up with petrol.

voll adverb 1 fully, completely; voll und ganz completely; 2 jemanden nicht für voll nehmen (informal) not to take somebody seriously.

Volleyball der volleyball; Volleyball spielen to play volleyball.

völlig adjective complete.

völlig adverb completely.

vollkommen adjective 1 perfect; 2 complete.

vollkommen adverb completely.

Vollkornbrot das wholemeal bread.

vollmachen SEE voll.

Vollpension die full board.

vollständig adjective complete.

volltanken SEE voll.

vom = von dem.

von preposition (+ DAT) 1 from; von heute an from today; von hier bis ... from here to ...; 2 of; eine Freundin von mir a friend of mine; 3 about; Peter hat mir von dem neuen Haus erzählt Peter told me about the new house; 4 by; ein Theaterstück von Brecht a play by Brecht; 5 von mir aus I don't mind.

voneinander adverb from each other; sie sind voneinander abhängig they depend on each other.

vor preposition (+ DAT or + ACC with movement towards a place) 1 in front of; 2 before; Manfred war vor euch da Manfred arrived before you; kurz vor der Ampel shortly before the lights; 3 with; vor Angst zittern to tremble with fear; 4 (with clock time) zehn vor fünf ten to five; 5 ago; vor zwei Jahren two years ago; 6 sich vor jemandem fürchten to be frightened of somebody; 7 vor allen Dingen above all; 8 vor sich hin summen to hum to yourself.

vor adverb forward; vor und zurück backwards and forwards.

voraus adverb 1 ahead; 2 im Voraus in advance.

vorausgehen ◇verb (IMPERF ging voraus, PERF ist vorausgegangen) 1 to go on ahead; 2 to precede.

voraussetzen verb (PERF hat vorausgesetzt) 1 to take for granted; 2 to require; 3 vorausgesetzt, dass ... provided that ...

Voraussetzung die (PL die **Voraussetzungen**) 1 condition; 2 assumption.

vorbei adverb 1 past; 2 over; vorbei sein to be over.

vorbeifahren ◇verb (PRES fährt vorbei, IMPERF fuhr vorbei, PERF ist vorbeigefahren) to drive past, to pass.

vorbeigehen ⬦*verb* (IMPERF ging vorbei, PERF **ist vorbeigegangen**) **1** to go past, to pass; **2** to drop in; **ich gehe bei Anne vorbei** I'll drop in on Anne.

vorbeikommen ⬦*verb* (IMPERF kam vorbei, PERF **ist vorbeigekommen**) **1** to pass; **2** to get past; **3** to drop in.

vorbereiten *verb* (PERF **hat vorbereitet**) **1** to prepare; **2 sich vorbereiten** to prepare.

Vorbereitung *die* (PL die **Vorbereitungen**) preparation.

vorbeugen *verb* (PERF **hat vorgebeugt**) **1** to prevent; **2 sich vorbeugen** to lean forward.

Vorbild *das* (PL die **Vorbilder**) example.

vorderer, vordere, vorderes *adjective* front.

Vordergrund *der* foreground; **im Vordergrund** in the foreground.

Vorderseite *die* front.

vorderster, vorderste, vorderstes *adjective* front.

Vorfahr *der* (PL die **Vorfahren**) ancestor.

Vorfahrt *die* right of way; '**Vorfahrt beachten/gewähren**' 'give way'.

Vorfall *der* (PL die **Vorfälle**) incident.

Vorführung *die* (PL die **Vorführungen**) **1** performance; **2** demonstration.

Vorgänger *der* (PL die **Vorgänger**) predecessor.

Vorgängerin *die* (PL die **Vorgängerinnen**) predecessor.

vorgehen ⬦*verb* (IMPERF ging vor, PERF **ist vorgegangen**) **1** to go on ahead; **2** to go forward; **3** to proceed; **4 die Uhr geht vor** the clock is fast; **5 was geht hier vor?** what's going on here?

Vorgehensweise *die* (PL die **Vorgehensweisen**) policy.

vorgestern *adverb* the day before yesterday.

vorhaben ⬦*verb* (PRES **hat vor**, IMPERF **hatte vor**, PERF **hat vorgehabt**) **1** to intend; **2 etwas vorhaben** to have something planned.

Vorhang *der* (PL die **Vorhänge**) curtain.

Vorhängeschloss *das* (PL die **Vorhängeschlösser**) padlock.

vorhor *adverb* beforehand, before.

Vorhersage *die* (PL die **Vorhersagen**) **1** forecast; **2** prediction.

vorhin *adverb* just now.

voriger, vorige, voriges *adjective* last.

vorkommen ⬦*verb* (IMPERF kam vor, PERF **ist vorgekommen**) **1** to happen; **2** to occur; **3** to come forward; **4** to come out (*from behind somewhere*); **5** to seem; **jemandem bekannt vorkommen** to seem familiar to somebody; **6 sich alt vorkommen** to feel old.

Vorlauf *der* fast forward (*on video*).

vorläufig *adjective* temporary.

vorlesen ⬦*verb* (PRES **liest vor**, IMPERF **las vor**, PERF **hat vorgelesen**)

a b c d e f g h i j k l m n o p q r s t u v w x y z

a 1 to read (out); 2 jemandem vorlesen to read to somebody.

vorletzter, vorletzte, vorletztes *adjective* last but one; **vorletztes Jahr** the year before last.

Vormittag der (PL die **Vormittage**) morning.

vormittags *adverb* in the morning.

vorn *adverb* 1 at the front; **nach vorn** to the front; 2 **von vorn** from the beginning; **wieder von vorn anfangen** to start again at the beginning; **da vorn** over there.

Vorname der (PL die **Vornamen**) first name.

vorne SEE vorn.

vornehm *adjective* 1 elegant; 2 distinguished.

vornehmen ◇*verb* (PRES **nimmt vor**, IMPERF **nahm vor**, PERF **hat vorgenommen**) 1 to carry out; 2 **sich vornehmen, etwas zu tun** to plan to do something.

Vorort der (PL die **Vororte**) suburb.

Vorrat der (PL die **Vorräte**) supply, stock.

Vorsatz der (PL die **Vorsätze**) intention.

Vorschau die 1 preview; 2 trailer (of a film).

Vorschlag der (PL die **Vorschläge**) suggestion.

vorschlagen ◇*verb* (PRES **schlägt vor**, IMPERF **schlug vor**, PERF **hat vorgeschlagen**) to suggest.

Vorschrift die (PL die **Vorschriften**) 1 regulation; 2 instruction.

Vorschule die (PL die **Vorschulen**) infant school.

vorsehen ◇*verb* (PRES **sieht sich vor**, IMPERF **sah sich vor**, PERF **hat sich vorgesehen**) **sich vorsehen** to be careful.

Vorsicht die care; **Vorsicht!** careful!, (on a sign) caution!

vorsichtig *adjective* careful.

vorsichtshalber *adverb* to be on the safe side.

Vorsichtsmaßnahme die (PL die **Vorsichtsmaßnahmen**) precaution; **Vorsichtsmaßnahmen gegen etwas ergreifen** to take precautions against something.

Vorspeise die (PL die **Vorspeisen**) starter.

Vorsprung der (PL die **Vorsprünge**) 1 ledge (of a rock); 2 lead (over somebody).

vorstellen *verb* (PERF **hat vorgestellt**) 1 to introduce; **darf ich Ihnen Herrn Schulz vorstellen?** may I introduce Mr Schulz?; 2 **die Uhr vorstellen** to put the clock forward; 3 **sich vorstellen** to introduce yourself; 4 **sich beim Personalchef vorstellen** to go for an interview with the personnel manager; 5 **sich etwas vorstellen** to imagine something; **stell dir vor!** can you imagine?

Vorstellung die (PL die **Vorstellungen**) 1 performance;

2 introduction; **3** interview (*for a job*); **4** idea; **5** imagination.

Vorstellungsgespräch *das* (PL die **Vorstellungsgespräche**) interview.

Vorteil *der* (PL die **Vorteile**) advantage.

Vortrag *der* (PL die **Vorträge**) talk.

vorüber *adverb* **vorüber sein** to be over.

vorübergehend *adjective* temporary.

vorübergehend *adverb* temporarily.

Vorurteil *das* (PL die **Vorurteile**) prejudice.

Vorwahl *die* (PL die **Vorwahlen**) dialling code; **wählen Sie die Vorwahl 00 44 für Großbritannien** dial 00 44 for Britain.

vorwärts *adverb* forward(s).

vorwiegend *adverb* predominantly.

Vorwurf *der* (PL die **Vorwürfe**) reproach; **jemandem Vorwürfe machen** to reproach somebody.

vorzeigen *verb* (PERF hat **vorgezeigt**) to show.

vorziehen ✧*verb* (PRES **zieht vor**, IMPERF **zog vor**, PERF hat **vorgezogen**) **1** to prefer; **2** to pull up (*a chair*); **3** den **Vorhang vorziehen** to draw the curtain.

vorzüglich *adjective* excellent.

vulgär *adjective* vulgar.

Vulkan *der* (PL die **Vulkane**) volcano.

Ww

Waage *die* (PL die **Waagen**) **1** scales; **2** Libra; **Gabi ist Waage** Gabi's Libra.

waagerecht *adjective* horizontal.

wach *adjective* awake; **wach sein** to be awake; **wach werden** to wake up.

Wache *die* (PL die **Wachen**) **1** guard; **2** (police) station.

Wachhund *der* (PL die **Wachhunde**) guard dog.

Wachs *das* wax.

wachsen ✧*verb* (PRES **wächst**, IMPERF **wuchs**, PERF **ist gewachsen**) to grow.

Wachstum *das* growth.

wackelig *adjective* wobbly.

wackeln *verb* (PERF hat **gewackelt**) to wobble.

Wade *die* (PL die **Waden**) calf.

Waffe *die* (PL die **Waffen**) weapon.

Waffel *die* (PL die **Waffeln**) waffle.

Waffenhandel *der* arms trade.

Wagen *der* (PL die **Wagen**) **1** car; **nimmst du den Wagen?** are you going by car? **2** carriage (*of a train*); **3** cart.

wagen *verb* (PERF hat **gewagt**) **1** to risk; **2** es **wagen, etwas zu tun** to dare to do something; **sich nicht irgendwohin wagen** not dare to go somewhere.

Wagenheber *der* (PL die **Wagenheber**) jack.

a b c d e f g h i j k l m n o p q r s t u v w x y z

Wahl die (PL die Wahlen) **1** choice; **er hat die Wahl** it's his choice; **2** election; **die nächsten Wahlen sind im Herbst** the next election is in autumn.

wählen verb (PERF **hat gewählt**) **1** to choose; **zwischen zwei Möglichkeiten wählen** to choose between two possibilities; **2 haben Sie schon gewählt?** are you ready to order? (in a restaurant); **3** to elect; **4** to vote, to vote for; **sie wählt immer grün** she always votes green; **wählt Schröder!** vote for Schröder; **5** to dial; **ich muss die falsche Nummer gewählt haben** I must have dialled the wrong number.

Wahlfach das (PL die **Wahlfächer**) optional subject, option.

Wahnsinn der madness.

wahnsinnig adjective **1** mad; **wahnsinnig werden** to go mad; **2 wahnsinnigen Durst haben** to be terribly thirsty; **der Film war wahnsinnig gut** the film was incredibly good.

wahr adjective **1** true; **2 du kommst doch, nicht wahr?** you're coming, aren't you?

während preposition (+ GEN) during.

während conjunction **1** while; **2** whereas.

Wahrheit die (PL die **Wahrheiten**) truth.

Wahrsager der (PL die **Wahrsager**) fortune-teller.

Wahrsagerin die (PL die **Wahrsagerinnen**) fortune-teller.

wahrscheinlich adjective probable, likely.

wahrscheinlich adverb probably.

Währung die (PL die **Währungen**) currency.

Waise die (PL die **Waisen**) orphan; **er ist Waise** he's an orphan.

Wal der (PL die **Wale**) whale.

Wald der (PL die **Wälder**) wood, forest.

Waliser der (PL die **Waliser**) Welshman.

Waliserin die (PL die **Waliserinnen**) Welshwoman.

walisisch adjective Welsh.

Walkman™ der (PL die **Walkmans**) walkman™.

Walnuss die (PL die **Walnüsse**) walnut.

Wand die (PL die **Wände**) wall.

Wanderer der (PL die **Wanderer**) **1** hiker; **2** rambler.

Wanderin die (PL die **Wanderinnen**) **1** hiker; **2** rambler.

wandern verb (PERF **ist gewandert**) **1** to hike; **2** to go walking.

Wandern das hiking.

Wanderung die (PL die **Wanderungen**) **1** hike; **2** walking tour.

Wandteppich der (PL die **Wandteppiche**) tapestry.

wann *adverb* when.

Wanne *die* (PL die **Wannen**) **1** tub; **2** bath.

war SEE **sein.**

warb SEE **werben.**

Ware *die* (PL die **Waren**) **1** article; **2 Waren** goods.

waren SEE **sein.**

Warenhaus *das* (PL die **Warenhäuser**) department store.

warf SEE **werfen.**

warm *adjective* warm; **eine warme Mahlzeit** a hot meal, **das Essen warm machen** to heat up the food.

Wärme *die* warmth.

wärmen *verb* (PERF **hat gewärmt**) to warm, to heat.

Warndreieck *das* (PL die **Warndreiecke**) warning triangle.

warnen *verb* (PERF **hat gewarnt**) to warn; **jemanden vor etwas warnen** to warn somebody of something.

Warnung *die* (PL die **Warnungen**) warning.

warst, wart SEE **sein.**

Warteliste *die* (PL die **Wartelisten**) waiting list.

warten *verb* (PERF **hat gewartet**) **1** to wait; **auf jemanden warten** to wait for somebody; **2 auf sich warten lassen** to take your time.

Wärter *der* (PL die **Wärter**) **1** keeper; **2** attendant; **3** warder.

Warteraum *der* (PL die **Warteräume**) waiting room.

Wärterin *die* (PL die **Wärterinnen**) **1** keeper; **2** attendant; **3** warder.

Wartezeit *die* wait; **eine Stunde Wartezeit** an hour's wait.

Wartezimmer *das* (PL die **Wartezimmer**) waiting room.

warum *adverb* why.

Warze *die* (PL die **Warzen**) wart.

was *pronoun* **1** what; **was für ein/ eine …?** what kind of …?; **was für ein Fahrrad hast du?** what kind of bike do you have?; **was für ein Glück!** what luck!; **was kostet das?** how much is it?; **2** that; **alles, was wir brauchen** all (that) we need; **alles, was du willst** all (that) you want; **3** (*short for 'etwas'*) something, **heute gibts was Gutes im Fernsehen** there's something good on television today; **4** (*short for 'etwas' in questions and negatives*) anything; **hast du was für mich?** have you got anything for me?

Waschbecken *das* (PL die **Waschbecken**) washbasin.

Wäsche *die* **1** washing; **2** underwear.

waschen ◇*verb* (PRES **wäscht**, IMPERF **wusch**, PERF **hat gewaschen**) **1** to wash; **2 sich waschen** to have a wash; **sich die Hände waschen** to wash your hands.

Wäscheraum *der* (PL die **Wäscheräume**) laundry room.

Wäscherei *die* (PL die **Wäschereien**) laundry.

a b c d e f g h i j k l m n o p q r s t u v x y z

a

Waschlappen der (PL die Waschlappen) flannel.

b

Waschmaschine die (PL die Waschmaschinen) washing machine.

c

d

Waschpulver das (PL die Waschpulver) washing powder.

e

Waschsalon der (PL die Waschsalons) launderette.

f

g

Wasser das water.

h

wasserdicht adjective waterproof.

i

Wasserfall der (PL die Wasserfälle) waterfall.

j

Wasserfarbe die (PL die Wasserfarben) watercolour.

k

Wasserhahn der (PL die Wasserhähne) tap.

l

m

Wassermann der Aquarius; **Lisa ist Wassermann** Lisa's Aquarius.

n

Wassermelone die (PL die Wassermelonen) water melon.

o

Wasserskifahren das water-skiing.

p

Wassersport der water sport.

q

Wassertiefe die depth (of water); **Wassertiefe: 2 Meter** depth: 2 metres.

r

s

Watte die cotton wool.

t

wattiert adjective padded.

u

WC das (PL die WCs) WC, toilet.

v

weben verb (PERF hat gewebt) to weave.

x

Webseite die (PL die Webseiten) web page.

y

z

Website die (PL die Websites) web site.

Wechselkurs der (PL die Wechselkurse) exchange rate.

wechseln verb (PERF hat gewechselt) **1** to change; **kannst du mir zehn Euro wechseln?** have you got change for ten euros?; **2** to exchange (glances, letters).

Wechselstube die (PL die Wechselstuben) bureau de change.

wecken verb (PERF hat geweckt) to wake (up).

Wecker der (PL die Wecker) alarm clock; **Max geht mir auf den Wecker** (informal) Max gets on my nerves.

weder conjunction **weder ... noch** neither ... nor.

Weg der (PL die Wege) **1** way; **auf dem Weg nach Hause** on the way home; **2** path; **3 sich auf den Weg machen** to set off; **4 im Weg sein** to be in the way.

weg adverb **1** away; **geh weg!** go away!; **Hände weg!** hands off!; **2** gone; **der Ring ist weg** the ring's gone; **Heidi ist schon weg** Heidi's already gone.

wegen preposition (+ GEN) because of.

wegfahren ◇verb (PRES **fährt weg**, IMPERF **fuhr weg**, PERF **ist weggefahren**) **1** to leave; **sie fahren gerade weg** they are leaving just now; **2** (PERF **hat weggefahren**) to drive away (a car or things).

weggehen ◇verb (IMPERF **ging weg**, PERF **ist weggegangen**) **1** to

go away; **2** to leave; **3** to go out; **wir gehen heute Abend weg** we're going out tonight; **4** to come out (*of a stain*).

weglassen ◇*verb* (PRES **lässt weg**, IMPERF **ließ weg**, PERF **hat weggelassen**) **1** to let go; **2** to leave out.

weglaufen ◇*verb* (PRES **läuft weg**, IMPERF **lief weg**, PERF **ist weggelaufen**) to run away.

weglegen *verb* (PERF **hat weggelegt**) **1** to put down; **2** to put away.

wegmachen *verb* (PERF **hat weggemacht**) to get rid of (*a stain or wart, for example*).

wegmüssen ◇*verb* (*informal*) (PRES **muss weg**, IMPERF **musste weg**, PERF **hat weggemusst**) to have to go.

wegnehmen ◇*verb* (PRES **nimmt weg**, IMPERF **nahm weg**, PERF **hat weggenommen**) to take away.

wegräumen *verb* (PERF **hat weggeräumt**) to clear away.

wegschicken *verb* (PERF **hat weggeschickt**) **1** to send away; **2** to send off.

wegtun ◇*verb* (IMPERF **tat weg**, PERF **hat weggetan**) to put away.

Wegweiser *der* (PL die **Wegweiser**) signpost.

wegwerfen ◇*verb* (PRES **wirft weg**, IMPERF **warf weg**, PERF **hat weggeworfen**) to throw away.

weh *adjective* **1** sore; **2** oh weh! oh dear!; **3** es tut weh it hurts.

wehen *verb* (PERF **hat geweht**) to blow.

Wehrdienst *der* military service.

wehren *verb* (PERF **hat sich gewehrt**) **sich wehren** to defend yourself.

wehrlos *adjective* defenceless.

wehtun ◇*verb* (PRES **tut weh**, IMPERF **tat weh**, PERF **hat wehgetan**) **1** to hurt; **mein Arm tut weh** my arm hurts; **jemandem wehtun** to hurt somebody; **2 sich wehtun** to hurt yourself.

Weibchen *das* (PL die **Weibchen**) female.

weiblich *adjective* **1** female; **2** feminine (*noun*).

weich *adjective* soft.

Weide *die* (PL die **Weiden**) **1** willow; **2** pasture.

weigern *verb* (PERF **hat sich geweigert**) **sich weigern** to refuse.

Weihnachten *das* (PL die **Weihnachten**) Christmas; **Frohe Weihnachten!** Merry Christmas!

Weihnachtskrippe *die* (PL die **Weihnachtskrippen**) Christmas crib scene.

Weihnachtslied *das* (PL die **Weihnachtslieder**) Christmas carol.

Weihnachtsmann *der* (PL die **Weihnachtsmänner**) Father Christmas.

Weihnachtstag *der* (PL die **Weihnachtstage**) Christmas Day; **zweiter Weihnachtstag** Boxing Day.

a
b
c
d
e
f
g
h
i
j
k
l
m
n
o
p
q
r
s
t
u
v
x
y
z

weil *conjunction* because.

Weile *die* while.

Wein *der* (PL die **Weine**) wine.

Weinberg *der* (PL die **Weinberge**) vineyard.

Weinbergschnecke *die* (PL die **Weinbergschnecken**) snail.

Weinbrand *der* (PL die **Weinbrände**) brandy.

weinen *verb* (PERF **hat geweint**) to cry.

Weinkarte *die* (PL die **Weinkarten**) wine list.

Weinkeller *der* (PL die **Weinkeller**) wine cellar.

Weinstube *die* (PL die **Weinstuben**) wine bar.

Weintraube *die* (PL die **Weintrauben**) grape.

Weise *die* (PL die **Weisen**) way; **auf diese Weise** in this way.

weise *adjective* wise.

Weisheit *die* (PL die **Weisheiten**) wisdom.

weiß[1] SEE **wissen**.

weiß[2] *adjective* white.

Weißwein *der* (PL die **Weißweine**) white wine.

weit *adjective, adverb* **1** wide, loose (*clothes*); **2** long; **eine weite Reise** a long journey; **3** far; **wie weit ist es?** how far is it?; **ist es noch weit?** is it much further?; **so weit wie möglich** as far as possible; **bei weitem** by far; **4 von weitem** from a distance; **5 ich bin so weit** I'm ready; **6 weit verbreitet**

widespread; **7 zu weit gehen** to go too far.

weiten *verb* (PERF **hat sich geweitet**) **sich weiten** to stretch.

weiter *adjective, adverb* **1** further; **2** in addition; **3 etwas weiter tun** to go on doing something; **weiter nichts** nothing else; **weiter niemand** nobody else; **4 und so weiter** and so on.

weiterer, weitere, weiteres *adjective* **1** further; **2 ohne weiteres** just like that, easily; **3 bis auf weiteres** for the time being.

weiterfahren ⋄*verb* (PRES **fährt weiter**, IMPERF **fuhr weiter**, PERF **ist weitergefahren**) to go on.

weitergehen ⋄*verb* (IMPERF **ging weiter**, PERF **ist weitergegangen**) to go on.

weiterhin *adverb* **1** still; **2** in future; **3 etwas weiterhin tun** to go on doing something.

weitermachen *verb* (PERF **hat weitergemacht**) to carry on.

Weitsprung *der* long jump.

Weizen *der* wheat.

welcher, welche, welches *adjective* which; **welches Kleid?** which dress?; **um welche Zeit?** at what time?.

welches *pronoun* **1** which (one); **2** some; **brauchst du Briefmarken? ich habe welche** do you need stamps?; **I've got some; 3** any; **hast du welche?** have you got any?

Welle *die* (PL die **Wellen**) wave.

Wellensittich *der* (PL die **Wellensittiche**) budgerigar.

wellig *adjective* wavy.

Welt *die* (PL die **Welten**) world; **auf der ganzen Welt** in the whole world.

Weltall *das* universe.

Weltkrieg *der* (PL die **Weltkriege**) world war.

Weltmeister *der* (PL die **Weltmeister**) world champion.

Weltmeisterin *die* (PL die **Weltmeisterinnen**) world champion.

Weltmeisterschaft *die* (PL die **Weltmeisterschaften**) 1 world championship; 2 die **Weltmeisterschaft** (*football*) the World Cup.

Weltraum *der* space.

Weltreise *die* (PL die **Weltreisen**) world tour.

wem *pronoun* to whom; **wem hat er das Geld gegeben?** who did he give the money to?

wen *pronoun* whom, who; **wen hast du eingeladen?** who did you invite?

Wende *die* 1 change; 2 reunification (*of Germany*).

wenig *pronoun, adjective* 1 little; **zu wenig** too little, not enough; 2 wenige few; **in wenigen Wochen** in a few weeks.

wenig *adverb* little; **so wenig wie möglich** as little as possible.

weniger *pronoun, adjective* less, fewer; **sie hat weniger Geschenke bekommen** she got fewer presents; **immer weniger Geld** less and less

money; **immer weniger Häuser** fewer and fewer houses.

weniger *adverb, conjunction* less; **zehn weniger fünf** ten minus five.

wenigste SEE **wenigster**.

wenigstens *adverb* at least.

wenigster, wenigste, wenigstes *adjective, pronoun* least; **am wenigsten** least; **sein Geschenk hat mir am wenigsten gefallen** I liked his present least.

wenn *conjunction* 1 when; **wenn ich in München bin, schreibe ich dir** I'll write to you when I'm in Munich; **immer, wenn** whenever; 2 if; **wenn es regnet** if it rains; 3 außer **wenn** unless.

wer *pronoun* who.

werben ◊*verb* (PRES **wirbt**, IMPERF **warb**, PERF **hat geworben**) 1 to advertise; 2 to recruit (*members*).

Werbespot *der* (PL die **Werbespots**) commercial, advert.

Werbung *die* 1 advertising; **in der Werbung arbeiten** to work in advertising; 2 advertisement; **im Fernsehen kommt viel Werbung** there are many advertisements on television; **Werbung für etwas machen** to advertise something.

werden ◊*verb* (PRES **wird**, IMPERF **wurde**, PERF **ist geworden**) 1 to become; **Arzt werden** to become a doctor; 2 müde **werden** to get tired; **alt werden** to get old; **mir wird kalt** I'm getting cold; 3 mir **wurde schlecht** I felt sick; **blass werden** to turn pale; 4 wach **werden** to wake up; 5 (*used to form the future*) *tense*) will, shall; **sie wird anrufen** she'll ring; **sie wird gleich da sein** she'll be here in a minute; **6** (*used to form the passive*) to be; **gerufen werden** to be called; **er wurde gefragt** he was asked; **7** (*used to form the conditional*) **sie würde kommen** she would come; **ich würde gern kommen, aber** ... I'd like to come but ....

werfen ⋄*verb* (PRES **wirft**, IMPERF **warf**, PERF **hat geworfen**) to throw.

Werk *das* (PL *die* **Werke**) **1** work; **2** works (*a factory*).

Werken *das* handicraft.

Werkstatt *die* (PL *die* **Werkstätten**) workshop.

Werktag *der* (PL *die* **Werktage**) weekday.

werktags *adverb* on weekdays.

Werkzeug *das* (PL *die* **Werkzeuge**) tool.

Werkzeugkasten *der* (PL *die* **Werkzeugkästen**) tool box.

wert *adjective* **viel wert sein** to be worth a lot; **nichts wert sein** to be worthless.

Wert *der* (PL *die* **Werte**) **1** value; **im Wert von hundert Euro** worth one hundred euros; **2 auf etwas Wert legen** to attach importance to something; **3 es hat doch keinen Wert** there's no point.

wertlos *adjective* worthless.

wertvoll *adjective* valuable.

Wesen *das* (PL *die* **Wesen**) **1** nature, manner; **2** creature.

wesentlich *adjective* essential; **im Wesentlichen** essentially.

wesentlich *adverb* considerably.

weshalb *adverb* why.

Wespe *die* (PL *die* **Wespen**) wasp.

wessen *pronoun* whose.

Wessi *der* (*informal*) (PL *die* **Wessis**) West German.

Weste *die* (PL *die* **Westen**) waistcoat.

Westen *der* west.

Western *der* (PL *die* **Western**) western (*film*).

Westinder *der* (PL *die* **Westinder**) West Indian.

Westinderin *die* (PL *die* **Westinderinnen**) West Indian.

westlich *adjective* **1** western; **2** westerly.

westlich *adverb, preposition* (+ GEN) **westlich von Wien** west of Vienna; **westlich der Stadt** to the west of the town.

weswegen *adverb* why.

Wettbewerb *der* (PL *die* **Wettbewerbe**) competition, contest.

Wette *die* (PL *die* **Wetten**) bet; **mit jemandem um die Wette laufen** to race somebody.

wetten *verb* (PERF **hat gewettet**) to bet; **mit jemandem um etwas wetten** to bet somebody something.

Wetter *das* weather.

Wetterbericht *der* (PL *die* **Wetterberichte**) weather report.

Wettervorhersage *die* weather forecast.

Wettkampf *der* (PL *die* **Wettkämpfe**) contest.

Wettlauf der race.

wichtig adjective important; **das wichtigste Exportgut ist Wolle** the most important export is wool.

wickeln verb (PERF **hat gewickelt**) **1** to wind; **2 ein Kind wickeln** to change a baby.

Widder der (PL **die Widder**) **1** ram; **2** Aries; **Jan ist Widder** Jan's Aries.

widerlich adjective disgusting.

widersprechen ◇verb (PRES **widerspricht**, IMPERF **widersprach**, PERF **hat widersprochen**) to contradict.

Widerspruch der (PL **die Widersprüche**) contradiction.

Widerstand der resistance.

widerstehen ◇verb (IMPERF **widerstand**, PERF **hat widerstanden**) to resist.

widmen verb (PERF **hat gewidmet**) **1** to dedicate; **2** to devote; **3 sich einer Sache widmen** to devote yourself to something.

wie adverb **1** how; **wie geht's?** how are you?; **wie viel?** how much?, how many?; **wie viele Leute waren da?** how many people were there?; **um wie viel Uhr kommst du?** (at) what time are you coming?; **2 wie ist Ihr Name?** what is your name?; **wie ist das Wetter?** what's the weather like?; **3 wie bitte?** sorry?.

wie conjunction **1** as; **so schnell wie möglich** as quickly as possible; **2** like; **wie du** like you; **3 wie zum Beispiel** such as.

wieder adverb **1** again; **sie ist wieder da** she's back again; **2 jemanden wieder erkennen** to recognize somebody; **etwas wieder finden** to find something (again); **etwas wieder verwerten** to recycle something; **jemanden wieder beleben** to revive somebody.

wiederbekommen ◇verb (IMPERF **bekam wieder**, PERF **hat wiederbekommen**) to get back.

wiederbeleben verb (PERF **hat wiederbelebt**) SEE **wieder**.

wiedererkennen SEE **wieder**.

wiederfinden SEE **wieder**.

wiederholen verb (PERF **hat wiederholt**) **1** to repeat; **2** to bring back; **3** to revise (schoolwork); **4 sich wiederholen** to recur; **er hat sich wiederholt** he's repeated himself.

Wiederholung die (PL **die Wiederholungen**) **1** repetition; **2** repeat performance; **3** replay; **4** revision (at school).

Wiederhören das auf **Wiederhören!** (said on the phone) goodbye!

wiederkommen ◇verb (IMPERF **kam wieder**, PERF **ist wiedergekommen**) **1** to come back; **2** to come again.

Wiedersehen das (PL **die Wiedersehen**) **1** reunion; **2 auf Wiedersehen!** goodbye!

wiedersehen SEE **sehen**.

wiedervereinigen SEE **vereinigen**.

a
b
c
d
e
f
g
h
i
j
k
l
m
n
o
p
q
r
s
t
u
v
x
y
z

Wiedervereinigung die reunification.

wiederverwerten SEE wieder.

Wiege die (PL die Wiegen) cradle.

wiegen ✧verb (IMPERF wog, PERF hat gewogen) to weigh.

Wiegenlied das (PL die Wiegenlieder) lullaby.

Wien das Vienna.

Wiese die (PL die Wiesen) meadow.

wieso adverb why.

wieviel SEE wie.

wievielmal adverb how often.

wievielter, wievielte, wievieltes adjective **1** which; **2 die wievielte Querstraße ist das von hier aus?** how many roads is that from here?; **der Wievielte ist heute?** what's the date today?

wild adjective wild.

Wildleder das suede.

Wildpark der (PL die Wildparks) wildlife park.

Wildschwein das (PL die Wildschweine) wild boar.

will SEE wollen.

Wille der will; **seinen Willen durchsetzen** to get your own way.

willkommen adjective welcome.

willst SEE wollen.

Wimper die (PL die Wimpern) eyelash.

Wimperntusche die (PL die Wimperntuschen) mascara.

Wind der (PL die Winde) wind.

Windel die (PL die Windeln) nappy.

Windhund der (PL die Windhunde) greyhound.

windig adjective windy.

Windmühle die (PL die Windmühlen) windmill.

Windpark der (PL die Windparks) wind farm.

Windpocken plural noun chickenpox.

Windschutzscheibe die (PL die Windschutzscheiben) windscreen.

Windsurfen das windsurfing; **Windsurfen gehen** to go windsurfing.

Winkel der (PL die Winkel) **1** angle; **2** corner.

winken verb (PERF hat gewinkt) to wave.

Winter der (PL die Winter) winter.

winzig adjective tiny.

Wippe die (PL die Wippen) seesaw.

wir pronoun we; **wir sind es** it's us; **wir alle** all of us.

Wirbel der (PL die Wirbel) **1** whirl; **2** whirlwind; **3** whirlpool; **4** commotion.

Wirbelsäule die (PL die Wirbelsäulen) spine.

wirbt SEE werben.

wird SEE werden.

wirft SEE werfen.

wirken verb (PERF hat gewirkt) **1** to have an effect; **2 gegen etwas wirken** to be effective against something; **3** to seem (sad, happy).

wirklich adjective real.

wirklich *adverb* really.

Wirklichkeit *die* reality.

wirksam *adjective* effective.

Wirkung *die* (PL *die* **Wirkungen**) effect.

wirst SEE **werden**.

Wirt *der* (PL *die* **Wirte**) landlord.

Wirtin *die* (PL *die* **Wirtinnen**) landlady.

Wirtschaft *die* (PL *die* **Wirtschaften**) 1 economy; 2 pub.

wirtschaftlich *adjective* economic.

Wirtschaftswissenschaften *plural noun* business studies.

Wirtshaus *das* (PL *die* **Wirtshäuser**) pub.

wischen *verb* (PERF **hat gewischt**) to wipe.

wissen ◇*verb* (PRES **weiß**, IMPERF **wusste**, PERF **hat gewusst**) to know; **ich weiß, dass er in London wohnt** I know he lives in London; **ich wüsste gern** ... I'd like to know ...; **von etwas wissen** to know about something; **weißt du was?** you know what?

Wissen *das* knowledge.

Wissenschaft *die* (PL *die* **Wissenschaften**) science.

Wissenschaftler *der* (PL *die* **Wissenschaftler**) scientist.

Wissenschaftlerin *die* (PL *die* **Wissenschaftlerinnen**) scientist.

wissenschaftlich *adjective* scientific.

Witwe *die* (PL *die* **Witwen**) widow.

Witwer *der* (PL *die* **Witwer**) widower.

Witz *der* (PL *die* **Witze**) joke.

witzig *adjective* funny.

wo *adverb* whore; **wo seid ihr gewesen?** where havo you been?; **in München, wo Markus seit einem Jahr lebt** in Munich, where Markus has been living for a year; **wo immer** wherever.

wo *conjunction* 1 seeing that; 2 although; **jetzt ist sie mir böse, wo ich doch so nett zu ihr war** now she's angry with me, although I've been so nice to her.

woanders *adverb* elsewhere.

Woche *die* (PL *die* **Wochen**) week.

Wochenende *das* (PL *die* **Wochenenden**) weekend.

wochenlang *adverb* for weeks.

Wochentag *der* (PL *die* **Wochentage**) weekday.

wochentags *adverb* on weekdays.

wöchentlich *adjective* weekly.

wofür *adverb* what ... for; **wofür brauchst du das Geld?** what do you need the money for?

wog SEE **wiegen**.

woher *adverb* where ... from; **woher ist er?** where does he come from?; **woher weißt du das?** how do you know?

wohin *adverb* where .. (to); **wohin geht ihr?** where are you going?

Wohl *das* 1 welfare, well-being; 2 **zu seinem Wohl** for his benefit; 3 **zum Wohl!** cheers!

wohl *adverb* **1** well; **sich wohl fühlen** to feel well; **ich fühle mich heute nicht wohl** I don't feel well today; **2 sich wohl fühlen** to be happy; **Anni fühlt sich in London wohl** Anni is happy in London; **3 jemandem wohl tun** to do somebody good; **4** probably; **er hat den Zug wohl verpasst** he probably missed the train; **du bist wohl verrückt!** you must be mad!; **5 wohl kaum** hardly.

wohlhabend *adjective* well-off.

wohltun SEE **wohl**.

wohnen *verb* (PERF **hat gewohnt**) **1** to live; **2** to stay (*for a short time*).

Wohngemeinschaft die (PL die **Wohngemeinschaften**) people sharing a flat/house; **wir wohnen in einer Wohngemeinschaft** we share a flat.

wohnhaft *adjective* resident.

Wohnheim das (PL die **Wohnheime**) **1** hostel; **2** home (*for old people*).

Wohnmobil das (PL die **Wohnmobile**) motor home.

Wohnort der (PL die **Wohnorte**) place of residence.

Wohnsitz der (PL die **Wohnsitze**) place of residence.

Wohnung die (PL die **Wohnungen**) flat, apartment.

Wohnwagen der (PL die **Wohnwagen**) caravan.

Wohnzimmer das (PL die **Wohnzimmer**) living room.

Wolf der (PL die **Wölfe**) wolf.

Wolke die (PL die **Wolken**) cloud.

Wolkenkratzer der (PL die **Wolkenkratzer**) skyscraper.

wolkig *adjective* cloudy.

Wolldecke die (PL die **Wolldecken**) blanket.

Wolle die wool.

wollen ◇*verb* (PRES **will**, IMPERF **wollte**, PERF **hat gewollt**) **1** to want; **Anne will einen Hund** Anne wants a dog; **ich will nach Hause** I want to go home; **2 sie wollte gerade gehen** she was just about to go; **3 ganz wie du willst** as you like.

womit *adverb* **1** what ... with; **womit hast du das gewaschen?** what did you wash it with?; **2** with which.

womöglich *adverb* possibly.

wonach *adverb* **1** what ... for; **wonach suchst du?** what are you looking for?; **wonach riecht es?** what does it smell of?; **2** after which, according to which; **eine Regelung, wonach wir eine Stunde mehr arbeiten müssen** a rule according to which we have to work an extra hour.

woran *adverb* what ... of **1 woran denkst du?** what are you thinking of?; **woran hast du ihn erkannt?** how did you recognize him?; **2** on which, of which; **nichts, woran man sich verletzen könnte** nothing you could hurt yourself on.

worauf *adverb* **1** what ... on, what ... for; **worauf hast du die Vase gestellt?** what did you put the vase on?; **worauf wartet ihr?** what are you waiting for?; **2** on which, for which; **das Regal, worauf das Radio steht** the shelf the radio is on; **das Einzige, worauf ich mich freue** the only thing I'm looking forward to.

woraus *adverb* **1** what ... from, what ... of; **woraus ist das?** what's it made of?; **2** from which; **es gibt nichts, woraus wir trinken können** there isn't anything we can drink out of.

worin *adverb* **1** what ... in, in what; **2** in which; **die Punkte, worin ich mit dir übereinstimme** the points I agree with you on.

Wort *das* (PL **die Worte/Wörter**) word; **mir fehlen die Worte** I'm lost for words; **ich habe heute zwanzig neue Wörter gelernt** I've learnt twenty new words today.

Wörterbuch *das* (PL **die Wörterbücher**) dictionary.

wörtlich *adjective* word for word.

Wortschatz *der* vocabulary.

Wortspiel *das* (PL **die Wortspiele**) pun.

Wortstellung *die* word order.

worüber *adverb* **1** over, what ... about; **worüber lacht ihr?** what are you laughing about?; **2** over which, about which.

worum *adverb* **1** about what; **worum geht es?** what's it about?; **worum hat sie dich gebeten?** what did she ask you for?; **2** for which; **3** round which.

wovon *adverb* **1** what ... from, what ... about; **wovon redet ihr?**

what are you talking about?; **2** from which, about which; **der Geruch, wovon mir schlecht geworden ist** the smell which made me feel sick.

wovor *adverb* **1** what ... of; **wovor hast du Angst?** what are you frightened of?; **2** in front of what; **3** of which; **4** in front of which; **der Turm, wovor wir stehen** the tower we are standing in front of.

wozu *adverb* **1** what ... for, why; **wozu brauchst du das?** what do you need it for?; **wozu?** what for?; **2** to which, for which; **wozu ich dir raten würde** which I would advise.

Wrack *das* (PL **die Wracks**) wreck.

Wuchs *der* growth.

wuchs SEE **wachsen**.

wund *adjective* sore.

Wunde *die* (PL **die Wunden**) wound.

Wunder *das* (PL **die Wunder**) miracle; **kein Wunder!** no wonder!

wunderbar *adjective* wonderful.

wundern *verb* (PERF **hat sich gewundert**) **sich wundern** to be surprised.

wunderschön *adjective* beautiful.

wundervoll *adjective* wonderful.

Wundschorf *der* (PL **die Wundschorfe**) scab.

Wunsch *der* (PL **die Wünsche**) wish; **auf Wunsch** on request; **haben Sie sonst noch einen Wunsch?** will there be anything else?

wünschen *verb* (PERF **hat gewünscht**) **1** to wish; **ich**

wünsche dir alles Gute zum Geburtstag I wish you a happy birthday; **ich wünschte, ich könnte ... I wish I could ...; was wünschen Sie?** can I help you?; **2 sich etwas wünschen** to want something.

wünschenswert *adjective* desirable.

wurde, würde, wurden, würden, wurdest, würdest, wurdet, würdet SEE **werden**.

Wurf *der* (PL *die* **Würfe**) throw.

Würfel *der* (PL *die* **Würfel**) **1** dice (*in games*); **2** cube.

würfeln *verb* (PERF **hat gewürfelt**) to throw the dice.

Würfelspiel *das* (PL *die* **Würfelspiele**) game of dice.

Wurm *der* (PL *die* **Würmer**) worm.

Wurst *die* (PL *die* **Würste**) **1** sausage; **2 das ist mir Wurst** (*informal*) I couldn't care less.

Würstchen *das* (PL *die* **Würstchen**) (little) sausage.

Wurzel *die* (PL *die* **Wurzeln**) root.

würzen *verb* (PERF **hat gewürzt**) to season.

würzig *adjective* spicy.

wusch SEE **waschen**.

wusste SEE **wissen**.

Wüste *die* (PL *die* **Wüsten**) desert.

Wut *die* rage; **eine Wut auf jemanden haben** to be furious with somebody.

wütend *adjective* furious.

Xx

x-beliebig *adjective* (*informal*) any; **eine x-beliebige Zahl** any number (you like).

x-mal *adverb* (*informal*) umpteen times; **zum x-ten Mal** for the umpteenth time.

Xylophon *das* (PL *die* **Xylophone**) xylophone.

Yy

Yoga *das* yoga.

Ypsilon *das* (PL *die* **Ypsilons**) Y.

Zz

zaghaft *adjective* **1** timid; **2** tentative.

zäh *adjective* tough.

Zahl *die* (PL *die* **Zahlen**) **1** number; **2** figure.

zahlen *verb* (PERF **hat gezahlt**) **1** to pay; **hast du schon gezahlt?** have you paid?; **2** to pay for; **bitte zahlen!** the bill please!

zählen *verb* (PERF **hat gezählt**) **1** to count; **auf jemanden zählen** to count on somebody; **jemanden zu seinen Freunden zählen** to count somebody among your friends; **2 zählen zu** to be one of.

Zähler *der* (PL *die* **Zähler**) meter.

zahlreich *adjective* numerous.

Zahlung die (PL die **Zahlungen**) payment.

Zählung die (PL die **Zählungen**) 1 count; 2 census.

zahm *adjective* tame.

Zahn der (PL die **Zähne**) tooth.

Zahnarzt der (PL die **Zahnärzte**) dentist.

Zahnärztin die (PL die **Zahnärztinnen**) dentist.

Zahnbürste die (PL die **Zahnbürsten**) toothbrush.

Zahnfleisch das gums.

Zahnpasta die (PL die **Zahnpasten**) toothpaste.

Zahnschmerzen *plural noun* toothache.

Zange die (PL die **Zangen**) pliers.

zanken *verb* (PERF **hat sich gezankt**) **sich zanken** to squabble.

Zapfen der (PL die **Zapfen**) 1 cone; 2 icicle.

zappeln *verb* (PERF **hat gezappelt**) 1 to wriggle; 2 to fidget.

zart *adjective* 1 delicate, soft; 2 gentle; 3 tender.

zärtlich *adjective* affectionate.

Zauber der 1 magic; 2 spell.

Zauberer der (PL die **Zauberer**) magician, conjurer.

Zauberin die (PL die **Zauberinnen**) magician, conjurer.

zauberhaft *adjective* enchanting.

zaubern *verb* (PERF **hat gezaubert**) to do magic.

Zaumzeug das (PL die **Zaumzeuge**) bridle.

Zaun der (PL die **Zäune**) fence.

z. B. (*zum Beispiel*) e.g.

Zebra das (PL die **Zebras**) zebra.

Zebrastreifen der (PL die **Zebrastreifen**) zebra crossing.

Zeh der (PL die **Zehen**) toe.

Zehe die (PL die **Zehen**) 1 toe; 2 clove (*of garlic*).

Zehenspitze die (PL die **Zehenspitzen**); **auf Zehenspitzen** on tiptoes.

zehn *number* ten.

Zehntel das (PL die **Zehntel**) tenth.

zehnter, zehnte, zehntes *adjective* tenth.

Zeichen das (PL die **Zeichen**) 1 sign; 2 signal.

Zeichentrickfilm der (PL die **Zeichentrickfilme**) cartoon film.

zeichnen *verb* (PERF **hat gezeichnet**) to draw.

Zeichnung die (PL die **Zeichnungen**) drawing.

Zeigefinger der (PL die **Zeigefinger**) index finger.

zeigen *verb* (PERF **hat gezeigt**) 1 to show; **Peter hat uns sein neues Auto gezeigt** Peter showed us his new car; 2 to point; **auf jemanden zeigen** to point to somebody; 3 **sich zeigen** to appear; 4 **es hat sich gezeigt, dass ...** it has become clear that ...; **es wird sich zeigen** time will tell.

Zeiger der (PL die **Zeiger**) hand.

Zeile die (PL die **Zeilen**) line.

Zeit die (PL die **Zeiten**) **1** time; **sich Zeit lassen** to take your time; **ich habe keine Zeit mehr** I haven't got any more time; **eine Zeit lang** for a time; **2 es hat Zeit** there's no hurry; **die erste Zeit** at first; **in nächster Zeit** in the near future.

Zeitalter das (PL die **Zeitalter**) age.

Zeitlang die SEE **Zeit**.

Zeitlupe die slow motion; **in Zeitlupe** in slow motion.

Zeitraum der (PL die **Zeiträume**) period.

Zeitschrift die (PL die **Zeitschriften**) magazine.

Zeitung die (PL die **Zeitungen**) newspaper.

Zeitungshändler der (PL die **Zeitungshändler**) newsagent.

Zeitverschwendung die waste of time.

zeitweise adverb at times.

Zelle die (PL die **Zellen**) **1** cell; **2** booth.

Zelt das (PL die **Zelte**) tent.

zelten verb (PERF **hat gezeltet**) to camp.

Zeltplatz der (PL die **Zeltplätze**) campsite.

Zement der cement.

Zentimeter der (PL die **Zentimeter**) centimetre.

Zentimetermaß das (PL die **Zentimetermaße**) tape measure.

zentral adjective central.

Zentrale die (PL die **Zentralen**) **1** central office, head office; **2** headquarters; **3** (telephone) exchange, switchboard.

Zentralheizung die central heating.

Zentrum das (PL die **Zentren**) centre.

zerbrechen ✧verb (PRES **zerbricht**, IMPERF **zerbrach**, PERF **hat zerbrochen**) **1** to break; **sie hat meine Vase zerbrochen** Irene broke my vase; **2** (PERF **ist zerbrochen**) to break; **die Untertasse ist zerbrochen** the saucer broke.

zerbrechlich adjective fragile.

Zerbrechlichkeit die fragility.

Zeremonie die (PL die **Zeremonien**) ceremony.

zerfallen verb (PRES **zerfällt**, IMPERF **zerfiel**, PERF **ist zerfallen**) to disintegrate, to decay.

zerreißen ✧verb (IMPERF **zerriss**, PERF **hat zerrissen**) **1** to tear; **sie hat sich das Kleid zerrissen** she tore her dress; **2** to tear up; **Anna hat seinen Brief zerrissen** Anna tore up his letter; **3** (PERF **ist zerrissen**) to tear; **das Hemd ist in der Wäsche zerrissen** the shirt got torn in the washing.

zerschlagen ✧verb (PRES **zerschlägt**, IMPERF **zerschlug**, PERF **hat zerschlagen**) **1** to smash, to smash up; **2 sich zerschlagen** to fall through (of plans); **meine Hoffnungen haben sich zerschlagen** my hopes were dashed.

zerschneiden *verb* (IMPERF **zerschnitt**, PERF **zerschnitten**) to cut up, to cut to pieces.

zerstören *verb* (PERF **hat zerstört**) to destroy.

Zerstörung *die* destruction.

zerstreuen *verb* (PERF **hat zerstreut**) 1 to scatter; 2 **jemanden zerstreuen** to entertain somebody; 3 **sich zerstreuen** to take your mind off things; 4 **die Menge hat sich zerstreut** the crowd's dispersed.

zerstreut *adjective* absent-minded.

Zettel *der* (PL die **Zettel**) 1 piece of paper; 2 note; 3 leaflet.

Zeug *das* (*informal*) 1 stuff; 2 things, gear; 3 **dummes Zeug** nonsense.

Zeuge *der* (PL die **Zeugen**) witness.

Zeugin *die* (PL die **Zeuginnen**) witness.

Zeugnis *das* (PL die **Zeugnisse**) 1 certificate; 2 report (*at school*).

Zickzack *der* (PL die **Zickzacke**) zigzag; **im Zickzack laufen** to zigzag.

Ziege *die* (PL die **Ziegen**) goat.

Ziegel *der* (PL die **Ziegel**) 1 brick; 2 tile.

ziehen ✧*verb* (IMPERF **zog**, PERF **hat gezogen**) 1 to pull; **an etwas ziehen** to pull on something; **einen Zahn ziehen** to pull out a tooth; 2 to draw; **einen Strich ziehen** to draw a line; **eine Niete ziehen** to draw a blank; 3 **die Bremse ziehen** to put on the brakes; 4 to grow

(*vegetables, flowers*); 5 **sich ziehen** to run (*of a path, road*); 6 (PERF **ist gezogen**) to move; **sie sind nach Berlin gezogen** they've moved to Berlin.

Ziel *das* (PL die **Ziele**) 1 destination; 2 goal, aim; 3 finish (*in sport*).

zielen *verb* (PERF **hat gezielt**) to aim; **auf etwas zielen** to aim at something.

Zielscheibe *die* (PL die **Zielscheiben**) target.

zielstrebig *adjective* determined.

ziemlich *adjective* fair.

ziemlich *adverb* 1 quite; **ziemlich viel** quite a lot; 2 fairly; **ihre Eltern haben ein ziemlich großes Haus** her parents have a fairly large house.

zierlich *adjective* dainty.

Ziffer *die* (PL die **Ziffern**) figure.

Zifferblatt *das* (PL die **Zifferblätter**) face, dial.

zig *adjective* (*informal*) umpteen.

Zigarette *die* (PL die **Zigaretten**) cigarette.

Zigarre *die* (PL die **Zigarren**) cigar.

Zigeuner *der* (PL die **Zigeuner**) gypsy.

Zigeunerin *die* (PL die **Zigeunerinnen**) gypsy.

Zimmer *das* (PL die **Zimmer**) room; **Zimmer mit Frühstück** bed and breakfast; '**Zimmer frei**' 'vacancies'.

Zimmermädchen *das* (PL die **Zimmermädchen**) chambermaid.

Zimt *der* cinnamon.

a b c d e f g h i j k l m n o p q r s t u v w x y z

Zink das zinc.

zirka adverb about.

Zirkel der (PL die **Zirkel**) pair of compasses.

Zirkus der (PL die **Zirkusse**) circus.

zischen verb (PERF **hat gezischt**) to hiss.

Zitat das (PL die **Zitate**) quotation.

zitieren verb (PERF **hat zitiert**) to quote.

Zitrone die (PL die **Zitronen**) lemon.

Zitronensaft der (PL die **Zitronensäfte**) lemon juice.

zittern verb (PERF **hat gezittert**) to tremble; **vor Kälte zittern** to shiver.

Zivildienst der community service.

Zivilisation die (PL die **Zivilisationen**) civilization.

zog SEE **ziehen**.

zögern verb (PERF **hat gezögert**) to hesitate.

Zoll der (PL die **Zölle**) 1 customs; **am Zoll** at customs; 2 duty; **Zoll auf etwas bezahlen** to pay duty on something.

Zollbeamte der (PL die **Zollbeamten**) customs officer.

Zollbeamtin die (PL die **Zollbeamtinnen**) customs officer.

zollfrei adjective duty-free.

Zollkontrolle die (PL die **Zollkontrollen**) customs check.

Zone die (PL die **Zonen**) zone.

Zoo der (PL die **Zoos**) Zoo.

Zoomobjektiv das (PL die **Zoomobjektive**) zoom lens.

Zopf der (PL die **Zöpfe**) plait.

Zorn der anger.

zornig adjective angry.

zu preposition (+ DAT) 1 to; **ich gehe zum Arzt** I'm going to the doctor's; **zu einer Party eingeladen sein** to be invited to a party; 2 **zu ... hin** towards; **zum Fenster hin** towards the window; **er kam zu dieser Tür herein** he came in through this door; 3 **das passt nicht zu meinem Mantel** it doesn't go with my coat; **es gab Wein zum Käse** there was wine with the cheese; 4 at; **zu Weihnachten** at Christmas; **zu Hause** at home; 5 **zu etwas werden** to turn into something; 6 **zu diesem Zweck** for this purpose; **was schenkst du Karin zum Geburtstag?** what are you giving Karin for her birthday?; **zum Spaß** for fun; **zum ersten Mal** for the first time; 7 **sich zu etwas äußern** to comment on something; **Papier zum Schreiben** paper to write on; 8 **nett zu jemandem sein** to be nice to somebody; 9 **sie waren zu zweit** there were two of them; **eine Marke zu achtzig Cent** an 80-Cent stamp; **es steht drei zu zwei** the score is 3-2; 10 **zu Fuß** on foot.

zu adverb 1 too; **zu groß** too big; 2 closed; **zu haben** to be closed; **Tür zu!** (informal) shut the door!; 3 **zu sein** to be closed; **alle Läden sind zu gewesen** the shops were all closed; 4 towards (indicating direction); 5 **mach zu!** (informal) hurry up!

zu *conjunction* to; **nichts zu essen** nothing to eat; **zu verkaufen** for sale.

zuallererst *adverb* first of all.

zuallerletzt *adverb* last of all.

Zubehör *das* accessories.

zubereiten *verb* (PERF **hat zubereitet**) to prepare; **sie bereitet das Essen zu** she's preparing the meal.

zubinden ✧*verb* (IMPERF **band zu**, PERF **hat zugebunden**) to tie, to tie up.

zubringen ✧*verb* (IMPERF **brachte zu**, PERF **hat zugebracht**) to spend; **sie bringt viel Zeit bei ihrem Freund zu** she spends a lot of time with her boyfriend.

Zucchini *plural noun* courgettes.

Zucht *die* (PL **die Zuchten**) 1 breed, species; 2 breeding (*of animals*); 3 breeding establishment.

züchten *verb* (PERF **hat gezüchtet**) to breed.

zucken *verb* (PERF **hat gezuckt**) to twitch.

Zucker *der* sugar.

Zuckerguss *der* icing.

zuckerkrank *adjective* diabetic.

zudecken *verb* (PERF **hat zugedeckt**) 1 to cover up, to cover; 2 to tuck up (*in bed*).

zueinander *adverb* 1 to one another; **lieb zueinander sein** to be nice to one another; 2 together; **zueinander passen** to go together; **zueinander halten** to stick together.

zuerst *adverb* 1 first; 2 at first.

Zufahrt *die* (PL **die Zufahrten**) 1 access; 2 drive(way).

Zufall *der* (PL **die Zufälle**) 1 chance; **durch Zufall** by chance; 2 coincidence; **so ein komischer Zufall** such a strange coincidence; **per Zufall traf ich ihn in der U-Bahn** by coincidence I met him in the tube.

zufällig *adjective* chance; **das war rein zufällig** it was purely by chance.

zufällig *adverb* by chance; **kannst du mir zufällig zehn Euro leihen?** could you lend me ten euros by any chance?

Zuflucht *die* refuge.

zufrieden *adjective* 1 content; 2 satisfied; **mit etwas zufrieden sein** to be satisfied with something.

zufrieden *adverb* **jemanden zufrieden lassen** to leave somebody in peace; **jemanden zufrieden stellen** to satisfy somebody.

zufriedenlassen, **zufriedenstellen** SEE **zufrieden**.

Zug *der* (PL **die Züge**) 1 train; 2 procession; 3 characteristic, trait; 4 move (*in games*); 5 swig (*when drinking*); 6 drag (*when smoking*); 7 **in einem Zug** in one go.

Zugabe *die* (PL **die Zugaben**) 1 free gift; 2 encore.

a b c d e f g h i j k l m n o p q r s t u v w x y z

a

Zugang der (PL die **Zugänge**) access.

b

c

zugeben ◇verb (PRES **gibt zu**, IMPERF **gab zu**, PERF **hat zugegeben**) 1 to add; 2 to admit.

d

e

zugehen ◇verb (IMPERF **ging zu**, PERF **ist zugegangen**) 1 to close, to shut; **die Tür geht nicht zu** the door won't shut; 2 **auf etwas zugehen** to go towards something; **auf jemanden zugehen** to walk up to somebody; 3 **jemandem zugehen** to be sent to somebody; 4 **auf der Party ging es lustig zu** the party was good fun; 5 **dem Ende zugehen** to be nearing the end.

f

g

h

i

j

zügig adjective quick.

k

zugreifen ◇verb (IMPERF **griff zu**, PERF **hat zugegriffen**) 1 to grab it/ them; 2 to help yourself; 3 to lend a hand.

l

m

zugunsten preposition (+ GEN) in favour of.

n

o

zuhaben SEE zu.

Zuhause das home.

p

zuhören verb (PERF **hat zugehört**) to listen.

q

r

Zuhörer der (PL die **Zuhörer**) listener.

s

Zuhörerin die (PL die **Zuhörerinnen**) listener.

t

u

zukleben verb (PERF **hat zugeklebt**) to seal (an envelope).

v

zukommen ◇verb (IMPERF **kam zu**, PERF **ist zugekommen**) 1 **auf jemanden zukommen** to come up to somebody; **nächstes Jahr kommt eine Menge Arbeit auf mich zu** I'm in for a lot of work next

w

x

y

z

year; 2 **jemandem etwas zukommen lassen** to give somebody something; 3 **etwas auf sich zukommen lassen** to take things as they come.

Zukunft die future.

zukünftig adjective future.

zulassen ◇verb (PRES **lässt zu**, IMPERF **ließ zu**, PERF **hat zugelassen**) 1 to allow; 2 to register (a car); 3 to leave closed.

Zulassung die (PL die **Zulassungen**) 1 registration; 2 admission.

zuletzt adverb 1 last; 2 in the end.

zum = zu dem; 1 **etwas zum Lesen** something to read; 2 **spätestens zum fünften März** by 5 March at the latest; 3 **er hat es zum Fenster hinausgeworfen** he threw it out of the window.

zumachen verb (PERF **hat zugemacht**) 1 to close, to shut; 2 to fasten.

zumindest adverb at least.

zunächst adverb 1 first (of all); 2 at first.

Zunahme die (PL die **Zunahmen**) increase.

Zuname der (PL die **Zunamen**) surname.

zunehmen ◇verb (PRES **nimmt zu**, IMPERF **nahm zu**, PERF **hat zugenommen**) 1 to increase; 2 to put on weight.

Zunge die (PL die **Zungen**) tongue.

zur = zu der.

zurechtkommen ◇*verb* (IMPERF **kam zurecht**, PERF **ist zurechtgekommen**) to cope, to manage.

zurechtlegen *verb* (PERF **hat zurechtgelegt**) 1 to put out ready; 2 **sich eine Ausrede zurechtlegen** to think up an excuse.

zurück *adverb* 1 back; 2 **Hamburg, hin und zurück** a return to Hamburg.

zurückbekommen ◇*verb* (IMPERF **bekam zurück**, PERF **hat zurückbekommen**) to get back; **zehn Pfennig zurückbekommen** to get 10 pfennig change.

zurückbringen ◇*verb* (IMPERF **brachte zurück**, PERF **hat zurückgebracht**) 1 to bring back; 2 to take back.

zurückfahren ◇*verb* (PRES **fährt zurück**, IMPERF **fuhr zurück**, PERF **ist zurückgefahren**) 1 to go back; 2 to drive back; 3 (PERF **hat zurückgefahren**) to drive back; **jemanden zurückfahren** to drive somebody back.

zurückgeben ◇*verb* (PRES **gibt zurück**, IMPERF **gab zurück**, PERF **hat zurückgegeben**) to give back.

zurückgehen ◇*verb* (IMPERF **ging zurück**, PERF **ist zurückgegangen**) 1 to go back; **zurückgehen auf** to go back to; 2 to go down; 3 to decrease.

zurückhalten ◇*verb* (PRES **hält zurück**, IMPERF **hielt zurück**, PERF **hat zurückgehalten**) 1 to hold back; 2 **sich zurückhalten** to restrain yourself.

zurückkommen ◇*verb* (IMPERF **kam zurück**, PERF **ist zurückgekommen**) 1 to come back; **nach Hause zurückkommen** to return home; 2 to get back.

zurücklassen ◇*verb* (PRES **lässt zurück**, IMPERF **ließ zurück**, PERF **hat zurückgelassen**) to leave behind.

zurücklegen *verb* (PERF **hat zurückgelegt**) 1 to put back; 2 to keep, to put aside; 3 **Geld für etwas zurücklegen** to put money by for something; 4 to cover (*a distance*); 5 **sich zurücklegen** to lie back.

zurücknehmen ◇*verb* (PRES **nimmt zurück**, IMPERF **nahm zurück**, PERF **hat zurückgenommen**) to take back.

zurückrufen ◇*verb* (IMPERF **rief zurück**, PERF **hat zurückgerufen**) to call back.

zurücktreten ◇*verb* (PRES **tritt zurück**, IMPERF **trat zurück**, PERF **ist zurückgetreten**) 1 to step back; 2 to resign.

zurückzahlen *verb* (PERF **hat zurückgezahlt**) to pay back.

zurückziehen ◇*verb* (IMPERF **zog zurück**, PERF **hat zurückgezogen**) 1 to draw back; 2 to withdraw (*an offer*); 3 **sich zurückziehen** to withdraw, to retire.

zurzeit *adverb* at the moment.

Zusage *die* (PL **die Zusagen**) acceptance.

zusammen *adverb* 1 together; **zusammen sein** to be together; 2 altogether.

Zusammenarbeit die co-operation.

zusammenarbeiten verb (PERF hat zusammengearbeitet) to co-operate.

zusammenbleiben ◇verb (IMPERF blieb zusammen, PERF ist zusammengeblieben) to stay together.

zusammenbrechen ◇verb (PRES bricht zusammen, IMPERF brach zusammen, PERF ist zusammengebrochen) to collapse.

zusammenfassen verb (PERF hat zusammengefasst) to summarize.

Zusammenfassung die (PL die Zusammenfassungen) summary.

zusammenhalten ◇verb (PRES hält zusammen, IMPERF hielt zusammen, PERF hat zusammengehalten) 1 to hold together; 2 to keep together; 3 die Kinder haben zusammengehalten the children stuck together.

Zusammenhang der (PL die Zusammenhänge) 1 context; 2 connection.

zusammenkommen ◇verb (IMPERF kam zusammen, PERF ist zusammengekommen) 1 to meet; 2 to accumulate.

Zusammenkunft die (PL die Zusammenkünfte) meeting.

zusammenlegen verb (PERF hat zusammengelegt) 1 to put together; 2 to fold up; 3 to club together.

zusammennehmen ◇verb (PRES nimmt zusammen, IMPERF nahm zusammen, PERF hat zusammengenommen) 1 to gather up; 2 to summon up; to collect; 3 sich zusammennehmen to pull yourself together.

zusammenpassen verb (PERF hat zusammengepasst) 1 to match; 2 to be well matched (of people); 3 to fit together.

Zusammensein das get-together.

Zusammenstoß der (PL die Zusammenstöße) collision, crash.

zusammenstoßen ◇verb (PRES stößt zusammen, IMPERF stieß zusammen, PERF ist zusammengestoßen) to collide, to crash.

zusammenzählen verb (PERF hat zusammengezählt) to add up.

zusätzlich adjective additional, extra.

zusätzlich adverb in addition, extra.

zuschauen verb (PERF hat zugeschaut) to watch.

Zuschauer der (PL die Zuschauer) 1 spectator; 2 viewer; 3 die Zuschauer the audience.

Zuschauerin die (PL die Zuschauerinnen) 1 spectator; 2 viewer.

Zuschlag der (PL die Zuschläge) 1 surcharge; 2 supplement.

Zuschuss der (PL die Zuschüsse) 1 contribution; 2 grant.

zusehen ◇*verb* (PRES **sieht zu**, IMPERF **sah zu**, PERF **hat zugesehen**) **1** to watch; **2 zusehen, dass** ... to see (to it) that ...

zusein SEE **zu**.

zusenden *verb* (PERF **hat zugesendet**) to send; **jemandem etwas zusenden** to send something to somebody.

Zustand *der* (PL **die Zustände**) **1** condition; **2** state.

zustande *adverb* **zustande bringen** to bring about; **zustande kommen** to come about.

zuständig *adjective* responsible.

Zustellung *die* (PL **die Zustellungen**) delivery.

zustimmen *verb* (PERF **hat zugestimmt**) to agree.

Zustimmung *die* (PL **die Zustimmungen**) **1** agreement; **2** approval.

zustoßen ◇*verb* (PRES **stößt zu**, IMPERF **stieß zu**, PERF **ist zugestoßen**) to happen.

Zutat *die* (PL **die Zutaten**) ingredient.

zutreffen ◇*verb* (PRES **trifft zu**, IMPERF **traf zu**, PERF **hat zugetroffen**) **auf etwas zutreffen** to apply to something.

Zutritt *der* entry; **Zutritt haben** to have access.

zuverlässig *adjective* reliable.

zuversichtlich *adjective* confident, optimistic.

Zuversichtlichkeit *die* confidence.

zuviel SEE **viel**.

zuvor *adverb* **1** before; **der Tag zuvor** the day before; **2** first.

zuwenig SEE **wenig**.

zuzahlen *verb* (PERF **hat zugezahlt**) to pay extra.

zuziehen ◇*verb* (IMPERF **zog zu**, PERF **hat zugezogen**) **1** to pull tight; **2** to draw (*curtains*); **3** to call in (*an expert etc.*); **4** (PERF **ist zugezogen**) to move into an area; **5 sich eine Verletzung zuziehen** to sustain an injury; **sich eine Erkältung zuziehen** to catch a cold.

zuzüglich *preposition* (+ GEN) plus.

Zwang *der* (PL **die Zwänge**) **1** compulsion; **2** urge; **3** obligation.

zwang SEE **zwingen**.

zwängen *verb* (PERF **hat gezwängt**) to squeeze.

zwanglos *adjective* casual, informal.

zwar *adverb* **1** admittedly; **2 ich war zwar dabei, habe aber nichts gesehen** I was there, but I didn't see anything; **3 und zwar** to be exact.

Zweck *der* (PL **die Zwecke**) **1** purpose; **2** point; **es hat keinen Zweck** there's no point.

zwecklos *adjective* pointless.

zwei *number* two.

zweideutig *adjective* ambiguous.

zweifach *adjective* twice.

Zweifel *der* (PL **die Zweifel**) doubt.

zweifelhaft *adjective* **1** doubtful; **2** dubious.

zweifellos *adverb* undoubtedly

a
b
c
d
e
f
g
h
i
j
k
l
m
n
o
p
q
r
s
t
u
v
w
x
y

a

zweifeln verb (PERF **hat gezweifelt**) to doubt; **an etwas zweifeln** to doubt something.

b

Zweig der (PL die **Zweige**) 1 branch; 2 twig.

c

d

zweihundert number two hundred.

e

zweimal adverb twice.

f

zweisprachig adjective bilingual.

g

h

zweispurig adjective two-track (railway, recording, road); **eine zweispurige Straße** a dual carriageway.

i

j

zweit adverb **zu zweit** in twos; **wir sind zu zweit** there are two of us.

k

l

zweite SEE **zweiter.**

zweitens adverb secondly.

m

n

zweiter, zweite, zweites adjective second; **Mario kam als Zweiter** Mario was the second to arrive.

o

p

Zwerg der (PL die **Zwerge**) dwarf.

q

Zwiebel die (PL die **Zwiebeln**) 1 onion; 2 bulb.

r

s

Zwilling der (PL die **Zwillinge**) 1 twin; 2 **Zwillinge** Gemini; **Markus ist Zwilling** Markus is Gemini.

t

u

zwingen ◇verb (IMPERF **zwang**, PERF **hat gezwungen**) 1 to force; 2 **sich zwingen** to force yourself.

v

w

zwinkern verb (PERF **hat gezwinkert**) to wink.

x

y

zwischen preposition (+ DAT , or + ACC with movement towards a place) 1 between; 2 among (a crowd).

z

zwischendurch adverb 1 in between; 2 now and again.

Zwischenfall der (PL die **Zwischenfälle**) incident.

Zwischenlandung die (PL die **Zwischenlandungen**) stop-over.

Zwischenraum der (PL die **Zwischenräume**) gap, space.

Zwischenzeit die **in der Zwischenzeit** in the meantime.

zwo number two.

zwölf number twelve.

zwoter, zwote, zwotes adjective second.

VERB TABLES AND FORMS

On the following pages you will find forms for a regular German verb **machen** followed by the forms for a reflexive verb **sich waschen** and then the forms for twelve important irregular verbs in alphabetical order: **dürfen, essen, fahren, gehen, haben, kommen, können, müssen, sein, sollen, werden, wissen.**

After these are given the main forms for other irregular verbs. Note that the forms for separable verbs such as **aufstehen** are not given as they can be looked up under the base form, for example **stehen.**

Guide to the Verb tables

Personal pronouns

ich	=	I
du	=	you (singular)
er/sie/es	=	he/she/it
wir	=	we
ihr	=	you (plural)
Sie	=	you (polite form/singular and plural)
sie	=	they

Perfect and Imperfect tense

In German, both these tenses are past tenses. The Perfect tense is usually used in spoken German or informal letters. The Imperfect tense is usually used when writing formal letters or stories. When you are translating sentences with 'already' or 'yet' in them (German **schon**), the English Perfect tense should be translated with the German Perfect tense, not the Imperfect. For example:

I saw the film yesterday.
Ich habe den Film gestern gesehen or **Ich sah den Film gestern.**

I have seen the film already.
Ich habe den Film schon gesehen.

Translation of Perfect and Imperfect tense

Both German past tenses can sometimes be translated into English with the 'I was doing' form of the verb. For example:

Wir spielten Tischtennis, als er ankam. / Wir haben Tischtennis gespielt, als er ankam. We were playing table tennis when he arrived.

Imperative

The imperative form does not make sense with all verbs. Therefore it has only been given where it makes sense. For example:

Frag!	Ask!	(speaking to one friend)
Fragt!	Ask!	(speaking to two or more friends)
Fragen Sie!	Ask!	(polite form)
Fragen wir!	Let's ask!	(speaking to yourself and others)

1
machen
to make *or* to do

Imperative
Mach!
Make! *or* Do!
Macht!
Make! *or* Do!
Machen Sie!
Make! *or* Do!
Machen wir! Let's
make! *or* Let's do!

Past participle
gemacht
made *or* done

Present

ich	mache	I make *or* I do
du	machst	
er*	macht	
wir	machen	
ihr	macht	
sie*	machen	

Perfect

ich	habe gemacht	I made *or* I did
du	hast gemacht	
er	hat gemacht	
wir	haben gemacht	
ihr	habt gemacht	
sie	haben gemacht	

Future

ich	werde machen	I will make *or* I will do
du	wirst machen	
er	wird machen	
wir	werden machen	
ihr	werdet machen	
sie	werden machen	

Present subjunctive

ich	mache	I make *or* I do
du	machest	
er	mache	
wir	machen	
ihr	machet	
sie	machen	

Imperfect

ich	machte	I made *or* I did
du	machtest	
er	machte	
wir	machten	
ihr	machtet	
sie	machten	

Conditional

ich	würde machen	I would make *or* I would do
du	würdest machen	
er	würde machen	
wir	würden machen	
ihr	würdet machen	
sie	würden machen	

---

* In these tables *er* should be read as *er/sie/es* and *sie* should be read as *sie/Sie*

Imperative
Wasch dich!
Wash!
Wascht euch!
Wash!
Waschen Sie sich!
Wash!
Waschen wir uns!
Let's wash!

Past participle
gewaschen
washed

2
sich waschen
to wash (yourself)

Present

ich	wasche mich	I wash
du	wäschst dich	
er*	wäscht sich	
wir	waschen uns	
ihr	wascht euch	
sie*	waschen sich	

Present subjunctive

ich	wasche mich	I wash
du	waschest dich	
er	wasche sich	
wir	waschen uns	
ihr	waschet euch	
sie	waschen sich	

Perfect

ich	habe mich gewaschen	
	I washed	
du	hast dich gewaschen	
er	hat sich gewaschen	
wir	haben uns gewaschen	
ihr	habt euch gewaschen	
sie	haben sich gewaschen	

Imperfect

ich	wusch mich	I washed
du	wuschst dich	
er	wusch sich	
wir	wuschen uns	
ihr	wuscht euch	
sie	wuschen sich	

Future

ich	werde mich waschen	
	I will wash	
du	wirst dich waschen	
er	wird sich waschen	
wir	werden uns waschen	
ihr	werdet euch waschen	
sie	werden sich waschen	

Conditional

ich	würde mich waschen	
	I would wash	
du	würdest dich waschen	
er	würde sich waschen	
wir	würden uns waschen	
ihr	würdet euch waschen	
sie	würden sich waschen	

---

* In these tables *er* should be read as *er/sie/es* and *sie* should be read as *sie/Sie*

3

dürfen
to be allowed

Imperative
The imperative of
dürfen is not used.

Past participle
gedurft
allowed
dürfen
allowed

Present

ich	darf	I am allowed
du	darfst	
er*	darf	
wir	dürfen	
ihr	dürft	
sie*	dürfen	

Present subjunctive

ich	dürfe	I am allowed
du	dürfest	
er	dürfe	
wir	dürfen	
ihr	dürfet	
sie	dürfen	

Perfect

ich	habe gedurft	I was allowed
du	hast gedurft	
er	hat gedurft	
wir	haben gedurft	
ihr	habt gedurft	
sie	haben gedurft	

Imperfect

ich	durfte	I was allowed
du	durftest	
er	durfte	
wir	durften	
ihr	durftet	
sie	durften	

Future

ich	werde dürfen	I will be allowed
du	wirst dürfen	
er	wird dürfen	
wir	werden dürfen	
ihr	werdet dürfen	
sie	werden dürfen	

Conditional

ich	würde dürfen	I would be allowed
du	würdest dürfen	
er	würde dürfen	
wir	würden dürfen	
ihr	würdet dürfen	
sie	würden dürfen	

---

* In these tables *er* should be read as *er/sie/es* and *sie* should be read as *sie/Sie*

305

Imperative		Past participle
Iss!	Eat!	gegessen
Esst!	Eat!	eaten
Essen Sie!	Eat!	
Essen wir!	Let's eat!	

4

essen
to eat

Present

ich	esse	I eat
du	isst	
er*	isst	
wir	essen	
ihr	esst	
sie*	essen	

Present subjunctive

ich	esse	I eat
du	essest	
er	esse	
wir	essen	
ihr	esset	
sie	essen	

Perfect

ich	habe gegessen	I ate
du	hast gegessen	
er	hat gegessen	
wir	haben gegessen	
ihr	habt gegessen	
sie	haben gegessen	

Imperfect

ich	aß	I ate
du	aßest	
er	aß	
wir	aßen	
ihr	aßt	
sie	aßen	

Future

ich	werde essen	I will eat
du	wirst essen	
er	wird essen	
wir	werden essen	
ihr	werdet essen	
sie	werden essen	

Conditional

ich	würde essen	I would eat
du	würdest essen	
er	würde essen	
wir	würden essen	
ihr	würdet essen	
sie	würden essen	

* In these tables *er* should be read as *er/sie/es* and *sie* should be read as *sie/Sie*

5
fahren
to drive or to go

Imperative	Past participle
Fahr!	gefahren
Drive! or Go!	driven or gone
Fahrt!	
Drive! or Go!	
Fahren Sie!	
Drive! or Go!	
Fahren wir! Let's drive! or Let's go!	

Present

ich	fahre	I drive or I go
du	fährst	
er*	fährt	
wir	fahren	
ihr	fahrt	
sie*	fahren	

Present subjunctive

ich	fahre	I drive or I go
du	fahrest	
er	fahre	
wir	fahren	
ihr	fahret	
sie	fahren	

Perfect

ich	bin gefahren	I drove or I went
du	bist gefahren	
er	ist gefahren	
wir	sind gefahren	
ihr	seid gefahren	
sie	sind gefahren	

Imperfect

ich	fuhr	I drove or I went
du	fuhrst	
er	fuhr	
wir	fuhren	
ihr	fuhrt	
sie	fuhren	

Future

ich	werde fahren	I will drive or I will go
du	wirst fahren	
er	wird fahren	
wir	werden fahren	
ihr	werdet fahren	
sie	werden fahren	

Conditional

ich	würde fahren	I would drive or I would go
du	würdest fahren	
er	würde fahren	
wir	würden fahren	
ihr	würdet fahren	
sie	würden fahren	

* In these tables *er* should be read as *er/sie/es* and *sie* should be read as *sie/Sie*

Imperative		Past participle
Geh!	Go!	gegangen
Geht!	Go!	gone
Gehen Sie!	Go!	
Gehen wir!	Let's go!	

6

gehen
to go

Present

ich	gehe	I go
du	gehst	
er*	geht	
wir	gehen	
ihr	geht	
sie*	gehen	

Present subjunctive

ich	gehe	I go
du	gehest	
er	gehe	
wir	gehen	
ihr	gehet	
sie	gehen	

Perfect

ich	bin gegangen	I went
du	bist gegangen	
er	ist gegangen	
wir	sind gegangen	
ihr	seid gegangen	
sie	sind gegangen	

Imperfect

ich	ging	I went
du	gingst	
er	ging	
wir	gingen	
ihr	gingt	
sie	gingen	

Future

ich	werde gehen	I will go
du	wirst gehen	
er	wird gehen	
wir	werden gehen	
ihr	werdet gehen	
sie	werden gehen	

Conditional

ich	würde gehen	I would go
du	würdest gehen	
er	würde gehen	
wir	würden gehen	
ihr	würdet gehen	
sie	würden gehen	

* In these tables *er* should be read as *er/sie/es* and *sie* should be read as *sie/Sie*

7

haben
to have

Imperative		Past participle
Hab!	Have!	gehabt
Habt!	Have!	had
Haben Sie!	Have!	
Haben wir!	Let's have!	

Present

ich habe	I have
du hast	
er* hat	
wir haben	
ihr habt	
sie* haben	

Perfect

ich habe gehabt	I had
du hast gehabt	
er hat gehabt	
wir haben gehabt	
ihr habt gehabt	
sie haben gehabt	

Future

ich werde haben	I will have
du wirst haben	
er wird haben	
wir werden haben	
ihr werdet haben	
sie werden haben	

Present subjunctive

ich habe	I have
du habest	
er habe	
wir haben	
ihr habet	
sie haben	

Imperfect

ich hatte	I had
du hattest	
er hatte	
wir hatten	
ihr hattet	
sie hatten	

Imperfect subjunctive

ich hätte	I would have*
du hättest	
er hätte	
wir hätten	
ihr hättet	
sie hätten	

Conditional

ich würde haben	I would have
du würdest haben	
er würde haben	
wir würden haben	
ihr würdet haben	
sie würden haben	

* In these tables *er* should be read as *er/sie/es* and *sie* should be read as *sie/Sie*

* 'Ich hätte' can also be translated as 'I had', e.g. **Wenn ich viel Geld hätte**... If I had lots of money...

Imperative		**Past participle**
Komm!	Come!	gekommen
Kommt!	Come!	come
Kommen Sie!	Come!	
Kommen wir!	Let's come!	

Present		**Present subjunctive**	
ich komme	I come	ich komme	I come
du kommst		du kommest	
er* kommt		er komme	
wir kommen		wir kommen	
ihr kommt		ihr kommet	
sie* kommen		sie kommen	

Perfect		**Imperfect**	
ich bin gekommen	I came	ich kam	I came
du bist gekommen		du kamst	
er ist gekommen		er kam	
wir sind gekommen		wir kamen	
ihr seid gekommen		ihr kamt	
sie sind gekommen		sie kamen	

Future		**Conditional**	
ich werde kommen	I will come	ich würde kommen	I will come
du wirst kommen		du würdest kommen	
er wird kommen		er würde kommen	
wir werden kommen		wir würden kommen	
ihr werdet kommen		ihr würdet kommen	
sie werden kommen		sie würden kommen	

* In these tables *er* should be read as *er/sie/es* and *sie* should be read as *sie/Sie*

9
können
can *or* to be able to

Imperative
The imperative
of können is not
used.

Past participle
gekonnt
been able to
hätte können
been able to

Present

ich kann	I can *or* I am able to
du kannst	
er* kann	
wir können	
ihr könnt	
sie* können	

Perfect

ich habe gekonnt	I could *or* I was able to
du hast gekonnt	
er hat gekonnt	
wir haben gekonnt	
ihr habt gekonnt	
sie haben gekonnt	

Future

ich werde können	I will be able to
du wirst können	
er wird können	
wir werden können	
ihr werdet können	
sie werden können	

Present subjunctive

ich könne	I can *or* I am able to
du könnest	
er könne	
wir können	
ihr könnet	
sie können	

Imperfect

ich konnte	I could *or* I was able to
du konntest	
er konnte	
wir konnten	
ihr konntet	
sie konnten	

Imperfect subjunctive

ich könnte	I could *or* I would be able to
du könntest	
er könnte	
wir könnten	
ihr könntet	
sie könnten	

Conditional

ich würde können	I could *or* I would be able to
du würdest können	
er würde können	
wir würden können	
ihr würdet können	
sie würden können	

* In these tables *er* should be read as
er/sie/es and *sie* should be read as *sie/Sie*

Imperative	Past participle	
The imperative of müssen is not used.	gemusst had to müssen had to	**10** **müssen** must *or* to have to

Present

ich	muss	I must *or* I have to
du	musst	
er*	muss	
wir	müssen	
ihr	müsst	
sie*	müssen	

Present subjunctive

ich	müsse	I must *or* I have to
du	müssest	
er	müsse	
wir	müssen	
ihr	müsset	
sie	müssen	

Perfect

ich	habe gemusst	I had to
du	hast gemusst	
er	hat gemusst	
wir	haben gemusst	
ihr	habt gemusst	
sie	haben gemusst	

Imperfect

ich	musste	I had to
du	musstest	
er	musste	
wir	mussten	
ihr	musstet	
sie	mussten	

Future

ich	werde müssen	I will have to
du	wirst müssen	
er	wird müssen	
wir	werden müssen	
ihr	werdet müssen	
sie	werden müssen	

Imperfect subjunctive

ich	müsste	I would have to
du	müsstest	
er	müsste	
wir	müssten	
ihr	müsstet	
sie	müssten	

Conditional

ich	würde müssen	I would have to
du	würdest müssen	
er	würde müssen	
wir	würden müssen	
ihr	würdet müssen	
sie	würden müssen	

* In these tables *er* should be read as *er/sie/es* and *sie* should be read as *sie/Sie*

11
sein
to be

Imperative		Past participle	
Sei!	Be!	gewesen	been
Seid!	Be!		
Seien Sie!	Be!		
Seien wir!	Let's be!		

Present

ich	bin	I am
du	bist	
er*	ist	
wir	sind	
ihr	seid	
sie*	sind	

Perfect

ich	bin gewesen	I was
du	bist gewesen	
er	ist gewesen	
wir	sind gewesen	
ihr	seid gewesen	
sie	sind gewesen	

Future

ich	werde sein	I will be
du	wirst sein	
er	wird sein	
wir	werden sein	
ihr	werdet sein	
sie	werden sein	

Present subjunctive

ich	sei	I am
du	seist/seiest	
er	sei	
wir	seien	
ihr	seiet	
sie	seien	

Imperfect

ich	war	I was
du	warst	
er	war	
wir	waren	
ihr	wart	
sie	waren	

Imperfect subjunctive

ich	wäre	I would be*
du	wärst/wärest	
er	wäre	
wir	wären	
ihr	wärt/wäret	
sie	wären	

Conditional

ich	würde sein	I would be
du	würdest sein	
er	würde sein	
wir	würden sein	
ihr	würdet sein	
sie	würden sein	

* In these tables er should be read as er/sie/es
and sie should be read as sie/Sie

* 'Ich wäre' can also be translated as 'I were',
e.g. Wenn ich du wäre... If I were you...

Imperative	Past participle
The imperative of sollen is not used.	gesollt had to sollen had to

Present

ich	soll	I should
du	sollst	
er*	soll	
wir	sollen	
ihr	sollt	
sie*	sollen	

Perfect

ich	habe gesollt	I had to
du	hast gesollt	
er	hat gesollt	
wir	haben gesollt	
ihr	habt gesollt	
sie	haben gesollt	

Future

ich	werde sollen	I will have to
du	wirst sollen	
er	wird sollen	
wir	werden sollen	
ihr	werdet sollen	
sie	werden sollen	

Present subjunctive

ich	solle	I should
du	sollest	
er	solle	
wir	sollen	
ihr	sollet	
sie	sollen	

Imperfect

ich	sollte	I had to
du	solltest	
er	sollte	
wir	sollten	
ihr	solltet	
sie	sollten	

Imperfect subjunctive

ich	sollte	I should
du	solltest	
er	sollte	
wir	sollten	
ihr	solltet	
sie	sollten	

Conditional

ich	würde sollen	I would have to
du	würdest sollen	
er	würde sollen	
wir	würden sollen	
ihr	würdet sollen	
sie	würden sollen	

* In these tables *er* should be read as *er/sie/es* and *sie* should be read as *sie/Sie*

13

werden
to become or to get

Imperative	Past participle
Werde!	geworden
Become! or Get!	become or got
Werdet!	
Become! or Get!	
Werden Sie!	
Become! or Get!	
Werden wir! Let's	
become! or Let's get!	

Present

ich	werde	I become or I get
du	wirst	
er*	wird	
wir	werden	
ihr	werdet	
sie*	werden	

Present subjunctive

ich	werde	I become or I get
du	werdest	
er	werde	
wir	werden	
ihr	werdet	
sie	werden	

Perfect

ich	bin geworden	I became or I got
du	bist geworden	
er	ist geworden	
wir	sind geworden	
ihr	seid geworden	
sie	sind geworden	

Imperfect

ich	wurde	I became or I got
du	wurdest	
er	wurde	
wir	wurden	
ihr	wurdet	
sie	wurden	

Future

ich	werde werden	I will become or I will get
du	wirst werden	
er	wird werden	
wir	werden werden	
ihr	werdet werden	
sie	werden werden	

Conditional

ich	würde werden	I would become or I would get
du	würdest werden	
er	würde werden	
wir	würden werden	
ihr	würdet werden	
sie	würden werden	

* In these tables *er* should be read as *er/sie/es* and *sie* should be read as *sie/Sie*

Imperative	Past participle	
The imperative of wissen is not used.	gewusst known	**14** **wissen** to know

Present

ich	weiß	I know
du	weißt	
er*	weiß	
wir	wissen	
ihr	wisst	
sie*	wissen	

Present subjunctive

ich	wisse	I know
du	wissest	
er	wisse	
wir	wissen	
ihr	wisset	
sie	wissen	

Perfect

ich	habe gewusst	I knew
du	hast gewusst	
er	hat gewusst	
wir	haben gewusst	
ihr	habt gewusst	
sie	haben gewusst	

Imperfect

ich	wusste	I knew
du	wusstest	
er	wusste	
wir	wussten	
ihr	wusstet	
sie	wussten	

Future

ich	werde wissen	I will know
du	wirst wissen	
er	wird wissen	
wir	werden wissen	
ihr	werdet wissen	
sie	werden wissen	

Conditional

ich	würde wissen	I would know
du	würdest wissen	
er	würde wissen	
wir	würden wissen	
ihr	würdet wissen	
sie	würden wissen	

* In these tables *er* should be read as *er/sie/es* and *sie* should be read as *sie/Sie*

German irregular verb forms

This list shows the main forms of other irregular verbs.

Infinitive	Present ich, du, er/sie/es	Imperfect er/sie/es	Perfect er/sie/es
bekommen	bekomme, bekommst, bekommt	bekam	hat bekommen
bergen	berge, birgst, birgt	barg	hat geborgen
besitzen	besitze, besitzst, besitzt	besaß	hat besessen
betrügen	betrüge, betrügst, betrügt	betrog	hat betrogen
biegen	biege, biegst, biegt	bog	hat or ist gebogen
bieten	biete, bietest, bietet	bot	hat geboten
binden	binde, bindest, bindet	band	hat gebunden
bitten	bitte, bittest, bittet	bat	hat gebeten
blasen	blase, bläst, bläst	blies	hat geblasen
bleiben	bleibe, bleibst, bleibt	blieb	ist geblieben
braten	brate, brätst, brät	briet	hat gebraten
brechen	breche, brichst, bricht	brach	hat or ist gebrochen
brennen	brenne, brennst, brennt	brannte	hat gebrannt
bringen	bringe, bringst, bringt	brachte	hat gebracht
denken	denke, denkst, denkt	dachte	hat gedacht
dürfen	darf, darfst, darf	durfte	hat gedurft
einladen	lade ein, lädst ein, lädt ein	lud ein	hat eingeladen
empfangen	empfange, empfängst, empfängt	empfing	hat empfangen
empfehlen	empfehle, empfiehlst, empfiehlt	empfahl	hat empfohlen
entscheiden	entscheide, entscheidest, entscheidet	entschied	hat entschieden
erfahren	erfahre, erfährst, erfährt	erfuhr	hat erfahren

Infinitive	Present ich, du, er/sie/es	Imperfect er/sie/es	Perfect er/sie/es
erfinden	erfinde, erfindest, erfindet	erfand	hat erfunden
erschrecken	erschrecke, erschrickst, erschrickt	erschrak	ist erschrocken
ertrinken	ertrinke, ertrinkst, ertrinkt	ertrank	ist ertrunken
essen	esse, isst, isst	aß	hat gegessen
fahren	fahre, fährst, fährt	fuhr	ist or hat gefahren
fallen	falle, fällst, fällt	fiel	ist gefallen
fangen	fange, fängst, fängt	fing	hat gefangen
fechten	fechte, fichtst, ficht	focht	hat gefochten
finden	finde, findest, findet	fand	hat gefunden
fliegen	fliege, fliegst, fliegt	flog	ist or hat geflogen
fliehen	fliehe, fliehst, flieht	floh	ist geflohen
fließen	fließe, fließt, fließt	floss	ist geflossen
fressen	fresse, frisst, frisst	fraß	hat gefressen
frieren	friere, frierst, friert	fror	hat or ist gefroren
geben	gebe, gibst, gibt	gab	hat gegeben
gefallen	gefalle, gefällst, gefällt	gefiel	hat gefallen
gehen	gehe, gehst, geht	ging	ist gegangen
gelingen	es gelingt mir/dir/ihm, ihr, ihm	gelang	ist gelungen
gelten	gelte, giltst, gilt	galt	hat gegolten
genießen	genieße, genießt, genießt	genoss	hat genossen
geraten	gerate, gerätst, gerät	geriet	ist geraten
geschehen	es geschieht	geschah	ist geschehen
gewinnen	gewinne, gewinnst, gewinnt	gewann	hat gewonnen
gießen	gieße, gießt, gießt	goss	hat gegossen
gleichen	gleiche, gleichst, gleicht	glich	hat geglichen
graben	grabe, gräbst, gräbt	grub	hat gegraben
greifen	greife, greifst, greift	griff	hat gegriffen

Infinitive	Present ich, du, er/sie/es	Imperfect er/sie/es	Perfect er/sie/es
helfen	helfe, hilfst, hilft	half	hat geholfen
hinweisen	weise hin, weist hin, weist hin	wies hin	hat hingewiesen
kennen	kenne, kennst, kennt	kannte	hat gekannt
klingen	klinge, klingst, klingt	klang	hat geklungen
kneifen	kneife, kneifst, kneift	kniff	hat gekniffen
kommen	komme, kommst, kommt	kam	ist gekommen
können	kann, kannst, kann	konnte	hat gekonnt
kriechen	krieche, kriechst, kriecht	kroch	ist gekrochen
lassen	lasse, lässt, lässt	ließ	hat gelassen
laufen	laufe, läufst, läuft	lief	ist gelaufen
leiden	leide, leidest, leidet	litt	hat gelitten
leihen	leihe, leihst, leiht	lieh	hat geliehen
lesen	lese, liest, liest	las	hat gelesen
liegen	liege, liegst, liegt	lag	hat gelegen
lügen	lüge, lügst, lügt	log	hat gelogen
mahlen	mahle, mahlst, mahlt	mahlte	hat gemahlen
meiden	meide, meidest, meidet	mied	hat gemieden
messen	messe, mißt, mißt	maß	hat gemessen
misslingen	misslinge, misslingst, misslingt	misslang	ist misslungen
mögen	mag, magst, mag	mochte	hat gemocht
müssen	muss, musst, muss	musste	hat gemusst
nehmen	nehme, nimmst, nimmt	nahm	hat genommen
nennen	nenne, nennst, nennt	nannte	hat genannt
pfeifen	pfeife, pfeifst, pfeift	pfiff	hat gepfiffen

Infinitive	Present ich, du, er/sie/es	Imperfect er/sie/es	Perfect er/sie/es
raten	rate, rätst, rät	riet	hat geraten
reiben	reibe, reibst, reibt	rieb	hat gerieben
reißen	reiße, reißt, reißt	riss	hat or ist gerissen
reiten	reite, reitest, reitet	ritt	hat or ist geritten
rennen	renne, rennst, rennt	rannte	ist gerannt
riechen	rieche, riechst, riecht	roch	hat gerochen
rufen	rufe, rufst, ruft	rief	hat gerufen
saufen	saufe, säufst, säuft	soff	hat gesoffen
schaffen	schaffe, schaffst, schafft	schuf	hat geschaffen
scheiden	scheide, scheidest, scheidet	schied	hat or ist geschieden
scheinen	scheine, scheinst, scheint	schien	hat geschienen
schieben	schiebe, schiebst, schiebt	schob	hat geschoben
schießen	schieße, schießt, schießt	schoss	hat or ist geschossen
schlafen	schlafe, schläfst, schläft	schlief	hat geschlafen
schlagen	schlage, schlägst, schlägt	schlug	hat geschlagen
schleichen	schleiche, schleichst, schleicht	schlich	ist geschlichen
schließen	schließe, schließt, schließt	schloss	hat geschlossen
schmeißen	schmeiße, schmeißt, schmeißt	schmiss	hat geschmissen
schmelzen	schmelze, schmilzt, schmilzt	schmolz	ist geschmolzen
schneiden	schneide, schneidest, schneidet	schnitt	hat geschnitten
schreiben	schreibe, schreibst, schreibt	schrieb	hat geschrieben
schreien	schreie, schreist, schreit	schrie	hat geschrien
schweigen	schweige, schweigst, schweigt	schwieg	hat geschwiegen
schwimmen	schwimme, schwimmst, schwimmt	schwamm	ist or hat geschwommen
schwören	schwöre, schwörst, schwört	schwor	hat geschworen
sehen	sehe, siehst, sieht	sah	hat gesehen
sein	bin, bist, ist	war	ist gewesen

Infinitive	Present ich, du, er/sie/es	Imperfect er/sie/es	Perfect er/sie/es
singen	singe, singst, singt	sang	hat gesungen
sinken	sinke, sinkst, sinkt	sank	ist gesunken
sitzen	sitze, sitzt, sitzt	saß	hat gesessen
sollen	soll, sollst, soll	sollte	hat gesollt
spinnen	spinne, spinnst, spinnt	spann	hat gesponnen
springen	springe, springst, springt	sprang	ist gesprungen
stechen	steche, stichst, sticht	stach	hat gestochen
stehen	stehe, stehst, steht	stand	hat gestanden
sprechen	spreche, sprichst, spricht	sprach	hat gesprochen
stehlen	stehle, stiehlst, stiehlt	stahl	hat gestohlen
steigen	steige, steigst, steigt	stieg	ist gestiegen
sterben	sterbe, stirbst, stirbt	starb	ist gestorben
stinken	stinke, stinkst, stinkt	stank	hat gestunken
stoßen	stoße, stößt, stößt	stieß	hat *or* ist gestoßen
streichen	streiche, streichst, streicht	strich	hat gestrichen
streiten	streite, streitest, streitet	stritt	hat gestritten
tragen	trage, trägst, trägt	trug	hat getragen
treffen	treffe, triffst, trifft	traf	hat getroffen
treiben	treibe, treibst, treibt	trieb	hat getrieben
treten	trete, trittst, tritt	trat	hat *or* ist getreten
trinken	trinke, trinkst, trinkt	trank	hat getrunken
tun	tue, tust, tut	tat	hat getan
überweisen	überweise, überweist, überweist	überwies	hat überwiesen
umziehen	ziehe um, ziehst um, zieht um	zog um	ist *or* hat umgezogen
verbieten	verbiete, verbietest, verbietet	verbot	hat verboten

Infinitive	Present ich, du, er/sie/es	Imperfect er/sie/es	Perfect er/sie/es
verderben	verderbe, verdirbst, verdirbt	verdarb	hat *or* ist verdorben
vergessen	vergesse, vergißt, vergißt	vergaß	hat vergessen
verlieren	verliere, verlierst, verliert	verlor	hat verloren
verschwinden	verschwinde, verschwindest, verschwindet	verschwand	ist verschwunden
verzeihen	verzeihe, verzeihst, verzeiht	verzieh	hat verziehen
verstehen	verstehe, verstehst, versteht	verstand	hat verstanden
wachsen	wachse, wächst, wächst	wuchs	ist gewachsen
waschen	wasche, wäscht, wäscht	wusch	hat gewaschen
werben	werbe, wirbst, wirbt	warb	hat geworben
werden	werde, wirst, wird	wurde	ist geworden
werfen	werfe, wirfst, wirft	warf	hat geworfen
wiegen	wiege, wiegst, wiegt	wog	hat gewogen
wissen	weiß, weißt, weiß	wusste	hatgewusst
wollen	will, willst, will	wollte	hat gewollt
ziehen	ziehe, ziehst, zieht	zog	hat *or* ist gezogen
zwingen	zwinge, zwingst, zwingt	zwang	hat gezwungen

Aa

a *indefinite article* **1** (*before a noun which is masculine in German*) ein; **a tree** ein Baum; **2** (*before a noun which is feminine in German*) eine; **a story** eine Geschichte; **3** (*before a noun which is neuter in German*) ein; **a dress** ein Kleid; **4 not a** kein; **the party was not a success** die Party war kein Erfolg; **he didn't say a word** er hat kein Wort gesagt; **5 ten euros a metre** zehn Euro den Meter; **6 fifty kilometres an hour** fünfzig Stundenkilometer; **7 three times a day** dreimal täglich.

abandon *verb* **1** aufgeben ❖ SEP; **they abandoned the plan** sie gaben den Plan auf; **2** verlassen ❖; **they abandoned the city** sie verließen die Stadt.

abbey *noun* Abtei *die* (PL die Abteien)

abbreviation *noun* Abkürzung *die* (PL die Abkürzungen).

ability *noun* Fähigkeit *die* (PL die Fähigkeiten); **to have the ability to do something** etwas tun können.

able *adjective* fähig; **to be able to do something** etwas tun können; **she wasn't able to come** sie konnte nicht kommen.

abortion *noun* Abtreibung *die* (PL die Abtreibungen).

about *preposition* **1** über (+ ACC); **a film about space** ein Film über den Weltraum; **to be about something/somebody** über etwas/jemanden reden; **what is she talking about?** worüber redet sie?; **2** um (+ ACC); **to be about**

something um etwas gehen; **what's it about?** worum geht es?; **3 to know about something** von etwas (DAT) wissen; **she didn't know about the party** sie wusste nichts von der Party; **he knows nothing about it** er weiß nichts davon; **4 to think about something/somebody** an etwas/jemanden (+ ACC) denken; **I'm thinking about you** ich denke an dich.

about *adverb* **1** (*approximately*) ungefähr; **about sixty people** ungefähr sechzig Leute; **in about a week** in ungefähr einer Woche; **2** (*when talking about time*) gegen; **about three o'clock** gegen drei Uhr; **3 to be about to do something** gerade etwas tun wollen; **I was (just) about to leave** ich wollte gerade gehen.

above *preposition* **1** über (+ DAT); **the lamp above the table** die Lampe über dem Tisch; **2 above all** vor allem.

abroad *adverb* im Ausland; **to live abroad** im Ausland leben, **to go abroad** ins Ausland fahren.

abscess *noun* Abszess *der* (PL die Abszesse).

abseiling *noun* Abseilen *das*.

absent *adjective* abwesend; **to be absent from school** in der Schule fehlen.

absent-minded *adjective* zerstreut.

absolute *adjective* absolut; **an absolute disaster** eine absolute Katastrophe.

absolutely *adverb* **1** wirklich; **it's absolutely dreadful** das ist

a b c d e f g h i j k l m n o p q r s t u v w x y z

a

wirklich furchtbar; **2** völlig; **you're absolutely right** du hast völlig Recht.

b

abuse noun **1** Missbrauch der; **drug abuse** Der Drogenmissbrauch; **2** (insults) Beschimpfungen (plural).

c

d

abuse verb **1** **to abuse somebody** jemanden missbrauchen; **2** (to insult) beschimpfen.

e

f

accelerate verb beschleunigen.

accelerator noun Gaspedal das (PL die Gaspedale).

g

h

accent noun Akzent der (PL die Akzente); **to speak with a German accent** mit deutschem Akzent sprechen.

i

j

accept verb annehmen⋄ SEP; **he accepted the invitation** er nahm die Einladung an.

k

l

acceptable adjective annehmbar.

m

access noun Zugang der.

access verb **to access data** auf Daten zugreifen.

n

o

accessory noun **1** Zubehörteil das; **accessories** Zubehör das; **2 accessories** (fashion items) Accessoires (plural).

p

q

r

accident noun **1** Unfall der (PL die Unfälle); **to have an accident** einen Unfall haben; **road accident** der Verkehrsunfall; **car accident** der Autounfall; **2** Zufall der (PL die Zufälle); **by accident** zufällig; **I found it by accident** ich habe es zufällig gefunden.

s

t

u

v

w

accidental adjective zufällig; **an accidental discovery** eine zufällige Entdeckung.

x

y

z

accidentally adverb **1** (without meaning to) versehentlich; **I accidentally threw it away** ich habe es versehentlich weggeworfen; **2** (by chance) zufällig; **I accidentally discovered that ...** ich habe zufällig herausgefunden, dass ....

accident & emergency noun Notaufnahme die.

accommodation noun Unterkunft die; **accommodation is free** Unterkunft ist kostenlos; **I'm looking for accommodation** (when looking for a room) ich suche ein Zimmer.

accompany verb begleiten; **to accompany somebody** jemanden begleiten.

according in phrase **according to** laut (+ DAT); **according to Sophie** laut Sophie.

accordion noun Akkordeon das (PL die Akkordeons).

account noun **1** (in a bank, shop, or post office) Konto das (PL die Konten); **bank account** das Bankkonto; **to open an account** ein Konto eröffnen; **I have fifty pounds in my account** ich habe fünfzig Pfund auf meinem Konto; **2** (an explanation) Darstellung die (PL die Darstellungen); **I want to hear his account of what happened** ich möchte seine Darstellung der Ereignisse hören; **3 on account of** wegen (+ GEN); **4** **to take something into account** etwas berücksichtigen.

accountant noun Buchhalter der (PL die Buchhalter), Buchhalte die (PL die Buchhalterinnen); **she's an accountant** sie ist Buchhalterin.

accurate *adjective* genau.

accurately *adverb* genau.

accuse *verb* beschuldigen; **she accused me of stealing her pen** sie beschuldigte mich, ihren Kugelschreiber gestohlen zu haben.

ace *noun* Ass *das* (PL die Asse); **the ace of hearts** das Herzass.

ace *adjective* klasse (*informal*); **he's an ace drummer** er spielt klasse Schlagzeug.

ache *verb* schmerzen; **my head aches** mein Kopf schmerzt.

achieve *verb* 1 leisten; **she's achieved a great deal** sie hat eine Menge geleistet; 2 erreichen (*an aim*); **he achieved what he wanted** er hat erreicht, was er wollte.

achievement *noun* Leistung *die* (PL die Leistungen); **it's a great achievement** das ist eine große Leistung.

acid *noun* Säure *die* (PL die Säuren).

acne *noun* Akne *die*.

across *preposition* 1 (*over to the other side of*) über (+ ACC); **to run across the road** über die Straße laufen; **we walked across the park** wir sind durch den Park gegangen; 2 (*on the other side of*) auf der anderen Seite (+ GEN); **he lives across the river** er wohnt auf der anderen Seite des Flusses; 3 **they live across the street** sie wohnen gegenüber.

act *noun* (*deed*) Tat *die* (PL die Taten).

act *verb* (*in a play or film*) spielen; **to act the part of the hero** die Rolle des Helden spielen.

action *noun* 1 Handlung *die* (PL die Handlungen); 2 **to take action** etwas unternehmen.

action replay *noun* Wiederholung *die* (PL die Wiederholungen).

active *adjective* aktiv.

activity *noun* Aktivität *die* (PL die Aktivitäten).

actor *noun* Schauspieler *der* (PL die Schauspieler).

actress *noun* Schauspielerin *die* (PL die Schauspielerinnen).

actual *adjective* **what were his actual words?** was genau hat er gesagt?; **in actual fact** eigentlich.

actually *adverb* 1 (*in fact, as it happens*) eigentlich; **actually, I've changed my mind** ich habe mich eigentlich anders entschlossen; 2 (*really and truly*) wirklich; **did she actually say that?** hat sie das wirklich gesagt?

AD (*Anno Domini*) n. Chr. (*nach Christus*); **in 400 AD** 400 n.Chr.

ad *noun* 1 (*on TV*) Werbespot *der* (PL die Werbespots); 2 (*in a newspaper*) Anzeige *die* (PL die Anzeigen); **to put an ad in the paper** eine Anzeige in die Zeitung setzen; **the small ads** die Kleinanzeigen.

adapt *verb* 1 **to adapt something** (*a book or film*) etwas bearbeiten; 2 **to adapt to** sich anpassen SEP (+ DAT); **she's adapted to her new surroundings** sie hat sich der neuen Umgebung angepasst.

adaptor *noun* 1 Adapter *der* (PL die Adapter); 2 (*for two plugs*)

a
b
c
d
e
f
g
h
i
j
k
l
m
n
o
p
q
r
s
t
u
v
w
x
y
z

Doppelstecker der (PL die Doppelstecker).

add verb 1 hinzufügen SEP; **to add an introduction to something** etwas (DAT) eine Einleitung hinzufügen; 2 dazugeben✧ SEP; **add three eggs** geben Sie drei Eier dazu.

● **to add up** zusammenzählen SEP.

addict noun 1 (drug addict) Süchtige der/die (PL die Süchtigen); 2 **she's a telly addict** sie ist fernsehsüchtig; **he's a football addict** er ist ein Fußballnarr.

addicted adjective 1 **to become addicted to drugs** drogensüchtig werden; 2 **he's addicted to football** Fußball ist bei ihm zur Sucht geworden; 3 **I'm addicted to sweets** ich bin nach Süßigkeiten süchtig.

addition noun 1 (adding up) Addition die; 2 **in addition** außerdem; 3 **in addition to** zusätzlich zu (+ DAT).

additional adjective zusätzlich.

additive noun Zusatz der (PL die Zusätze).

address noun Adresse die (PL die Adressen); **do you know his address?** weißt du seine Adresse?; **to change address** die Adresse wechseln.

address book noun Adressbuch das (PL die Adressbücher).

adequate adjective angemessen.

adhesive noun Klebstoff der.

adhesive adjective **adhesive tape** der Klebstreifen.

adjective noun Adjektiv das (PL die Adjektive).

adjust verb 1 **to adjust something** etwas einstellen SEP; **he adjusted the set** er stellte das Gerät ein; **to adjust the distance** auf die (richtige) Entfernung einstellen; 2 **to adjust to something** sich an etwas (ACC) gewöhnen.

adjustable adjective verstellbar.

administration noun Verwaltung die.

admiration noun Bewunderung die.

admire verb bewundern.

admission noun Eintritt der, **'admission free'** 'Eintritt frei'.

admit verb 1 (confess, concede) zugeben✧ SEP; **she admits she lied** sie gibt zu, dass sie gelogen hat; 2 (allow to enter) hereinlassen✧ SEP; **to admit somebody to a restaurant** jemanden in ein Restaurant lassen; 3 **to be admitted to hospital** ins Krankenhaus eingeliefert werden.

adolescence noun Jugend die.

adolescent noun Jugendliche der/die (PL die Jugendlichen).

adopt verb adoptieren.

adopted adjective adoptiert.

adoption noun Adoption die (PL die Adoptionen).

adore verb lieben.

adult noun Erwachsene der/die (PL die Erwachsenen).

adult adjective **the adult population** Erwachsene (plural).

Adult Education noun Erwachsenenbildung die.

advance noun Fortschritt der (PL die Fortschritte); **advances in technology** technologische Fortschritte.

advance verb **1** (make progress) Fortschritte machen; **2** (move forward) (of a group or an army) vorrücken SEP (PERF sein).

advanced adjective fortgeschritten (student, age).

advantage noun **1** Vorteil der (PL die Vorteile); **there are several advantages** es gibt verschiedene Vorteile; **2 to take advantage of something** etwas ausnutzen SEP; **I always take advantage of the sales to buy myself some shoes** ich warte immer bis zum Schlussverkauf, um mir Schuhe zu kaufen; **3 to take advantage of somebody** (unfairly) jemanden ausnutzen SEP.

Advent noun Advent der.

adventure noun Abenteuer das (PL die Abenteuer).

adverb noun Adverb das (PL die Adverbien).

advert, advertisement noun **1** (at the cinema or on television) Werbespot der (PL die Werbespots); **2** (in a newspaper for a job, article for sale, etc.) Anzeige die (PL die Anzeigen); **she answered a job advertisement** sie meldete sich auf eine Stellenanzeige.

advertise verb **to advertise something in the newspaper** (in the small ads) etwas in der Zeitung inserieren; **I saw a bike advertised in the paper** ich habe ein Rad in der Zeitung inseriert gesehen.

advertising noun Werbung die.

advice noun Rat der; **to ask somebody's advice** jemanden um Rat fragen; **a piece of advice** ein Ratschlag.

advise verb raten ✧ (+ DAT); **to advise somebody to do something** jemandem raten, etwas zu tun; **I advised him to stop** ich riet ihm anzuhalten; **I advised her not to buy the car** ich habe ihr geraten, das Auto nicht zu kaufen.

aerial noun Antenne die (PL die Antennen).

aerobics noun Aerobic das; **to do aerobics** Aerobic machen.

aeroplane noun Flugzeug das (PL die Flugzeuge).

aerosol noun **an aerosol can** eine Spraydose.

affair noun **1** Angelegenheit die (PL die Angelegenheiten); **international affairs** internationale Angelegenheiten; **current affairs** die Tagespolitik; **2 love affair** das Liebesverhältnis.

affect verb beeinflussen.

affectionate adjective liebevoll.

afford verb **to be able to afford something** sich (DAT) etwas leisten können; **we can't afford to go out much** wir können es uns nicht leisten, oft auszugehen; **I can't afford a new bike** ich kann mir kein neues Rad leisten.

afraid adjective **1 to be afraid of something** Angst vor etwas (DAT) haben; **she's afraid of dogs** sie hat Angst vor Hunden; **2 I'm afraid I can't help you** ich kann dir leider nicht helfen; **I'm afraid so** leider ja; **I'm afraid not** leider nicht.

Africa noun Afrika das; **to Africa** nach Afrika.

African noun Afrikaner der (PL die Afrikaner), Afrikanerin die (PL die Afrikanerinnen).

a

African *adjective* afrikanisch; **she is African** sie ist Afrikanerin.

after *preposition, adverb* **1** nach (+ DAT); **after 10 o'clock** nach zehn Uhr; **after lunch** nach dem Mittagessen; **after school** nach der Schule; **2 the day after tomorrow** übermorgen; **soon after** kurz danach; **3 to run after somebody** jemandem hinterherlaufen ✧ SEP.

after *conjunction* nachdem; **after I'd finished my homework** nachdem ich meine Hausaufgaben gemacht hatte.

after all *adverb* schließlich; **after all, she's only six** sie ist schließlich erst sechs.

afternoon *noun* **1** Nachmittag *der* (PL *die* Nachmittage); **in the afternoon** am Nachmittag; **every afternoon** jeden Nachmittag; **2 this afternoon** heute Nachmittag; **on Sunday afternoon** am Sonntagnachmittag; **3 on Saturday afternoons** samstagsnachmittags; **at four o' clock in the afternoon** um vier Uhr nachmittags.

after-shave *noun* Rasierwasser *das* (PL *die* Rasierwasser).

afterwards *adverb* danach; **shortly afterwards** kurz danach.

again *adverb* **1** wieder; **she's ill again** sie ist wieder krank; **2 I saw her again yesterday** ich habe sie gestern wieder gesehen; **3 never again!** nie wieder!; **again and again** immer wieder; **4** (*one more time*) noch einmal; **try again** versuche es noch einmal; **you**

should ask her again du solltest sie noch einmal fragen.

against *preposition* gegen (+ ACC); **against the wall** gegen die Wand; **to lean against the wall** sich gegen die Wand lehnen; **I'm against the idea** ich bin gegen die Idee.

age *noun* **1** Alter *das*; **at the age of fifty** im Alter von fünfzig; **she's the same age as me** sie ist genauso alt wie ich; **to be under age** minderjährig sein; **2 I haven't seen Johnny for ages** ich habe Johnny schon ewig nicht mehr gesehen; **I haven't been to London for ages** ich bin schon ewig nicht mehr in London gewesen.

aged *adjective* alt; **a woman aged thirty** eine dreißigjährige Frau.

agent *noun* Vertreter *der* (PL *die* Vertreter), Vertreterin *die* (PL *die* Vertreterinnen); **an estate agent** ein Immobilienmakler; **a travel agent's** ein Reisebüro.

aggressive *adjective* aggressiv.

ago *adverb* vor (+ DAT); **an hour ago** vor einer Stunde; **three days ago** vor drei Tagen; **a long time ago** vor langer Zeit; **not long ago** vor kurzem; **how long ago was it?** wie lange ist das her?

agree *verb* **1 to agree with somebody** mit jemandem gleicher Meinung sein; **I agree with Laura** ich stimme Laura zu; **2 I agree** ich bin der gleichen Meinung; **I don't agree** ich bin anderer Meinung; **3 to agree that ...** zugeben ✧ SEP, dass ...; **I agree that it's too late now** ich gebe zu, dass es jetzt zu spät ist; **4 to agree to something** mit etwas einverstanden sein;

Steve's agreed to help me Steve hat sich einverstanden erklärt, mir zu helfen; **5 coffee doesn't agree with me** Kaffee bekommt mir nicht.

agreement *noun* **1** (*when sharing an opinion*) Übereinstimmung *die*; **2** (*contract*) Abkommen *das* (PL *die* Abkommen).

agriculture *noun* Landwirtschaft *die*.

ahead *adverb* **1 go ahead!** bitte!; **2 straight ahead** geradeaus; **keep going straight ahead until you get to the crossroads** gehen Sie immer geradeaus bis zur Kreuzung; **3 our team was ten points ahead** unsere Mannschaft hatte zehn Punkte Vorsprung; **4 ahead of time** früher als geplant; **5 the people ahead of me** die Leute vor mir.

aid *noun* **1** Hilfe *die*; **aid to developing countries** die Entwicklungshilfe; **2 in aid of** zugunsten (+ GEN); **in aid of the homeless** zugunsten der Obdachlosen.

Aids *noun* Aids *das*; **to have Aids** Aids haben.

aim *noun* Ziel *das* (PL die Ziele); **their aim is to control pollution** ihr Ziel ist es, die Umweltverschmutzung unter Kontrolle zu bringen.

aim *verb* **1 to aim to do something** beabsichtigen, etwas zu tun; **we're aiming to finish it today** wir beabsichtigen, es heute fertig zu machen; **2 the campaign is aimed at young people** die Kampagne zielt auf junge Leute ab.

air *noun* **1** Luft *die*; **in the open air** im Freien; **to go out for a breath of air** frische Luft schöpfen gehen; **2 to travel by air** fliegen✧ (PERF sein).

air-conditioned *adjective* klimatisiert.

air conditioning *noun* Klimaanlage *die*.

Air Force *noun* Luftwaffe *die*.

air hostess *noun* Stewardess *die* (PL die Stewardessen); **she's an air hostess** sie ist Stewardess.

airline *noun* Fluggesellschaft *die* (PL die Fluggesellschaften).

airmail *noun* **by airmail** per Luftpost.

air pollution *noun* Luftverschmutzung *die*.

airport *noun* Flughafen *der* (PL die Flughäfen).

alarm *noun* Alarm *der* (PL die Alarme); **fire alarm** der Feuermelder; **burglar alarm** die Alarmanlage.

alarm clock *noun* Wecker *der* (PL die Wecker).

album *noun* Album *das* (PL die Alben).

alcohol *noun* Alkohol *der*.

alcoholic *noun* Alkoholiker *der* (PL die Alkoholiker), Alkoholikerin *die* (PL die Alkoholikerinnen).

alcoholic *adjective* alkoholisch.

A levels *noun* Abitur *das* (*Students take 'Abitur' at about 19 years of age. You can explain A levels briefly as follows: Diese Prüfungen werden in zwei Schritten abgelegt: AS und A2. AS Prüfungen finden nach einjähriger Vorbereitungszeit statt, und umfassen normalerweise vier*

a
b
c
d
e
f
g
h
i
j
k
l
m
n
o
p
q
r
s
t
u
v
w
x
y
z

bis fünf Fächer. A2 Prüfungen macht man in weniger Fächern als man für die AS Prüfungen belegt hatte. AS und A2 Prüfungen werden benotet von A (beste Note) bis N (nicht bestanden). A levels stellen eine Zugangsberechtigung für die Universität dar) SEE **Abitur**.

alien *noun* **1** *(foreigner)* Ausländer *der* (PL die Ausländer), Ausländerin *die* (PL die Ausländerinnen); **2** *(from outer space)* Außerirdische *der/die* (PL die Außerirdischen).

alike *adjective* **1** gleich; **2 they're all alike** sie sind alle gleich; **3 to look alike** (DAT) ähnlich sehen; **the two brothers look alike** die beiden Brüder sehen sich ähnlich.

alive *adjective* **1 to be alive** leben; **to stay alive** am Leben bleiben; **2** *(lively)* lebendig.

all *adjective* **1** *(with a singular noun)* ganz; **all the time** die ganze Zeit; **all day** den ganzen Tag; **2** *(with a plural noun)* alle; **all the knives** alle Messer; **all our friends** alle unsere Freunde.

all *pronoun* **1** *(everything)* alles; **they've eaten it all** sie haben alles aufgegessen; **2** *(everybody)* **all of us** wir alle; **they're all there** sie sind alle da; **3 not at all** gar nicht.

all *adverb* **1** ganz; **all alone** ganz allein; **2 three all** drei beide.

all along *adverb* die ganze Zeit; **I knew it all along** ich habe es die ganze Zeit gewusst.

allergic *adjective* allergisch; **to be allergic to something** gegen etwas (ACC) allergisch sein.

allow *verb* **1 to allow somebody to do something** jemandem erlauben, etwas zu tun; **the teacher allowed them to go home** der Lehrer erlaubte ihnen, nach Hause zu gehen; **2 to be allowed to** dürfen◇; **I'm not allowed to go to the cinema during the week** ich darf während der Woche nicht ins Kino gehen.

all right *adverb* **1** *(yes)* ist gut, okay *(informal)*; **'come round to my house around six' - 'all right'** 'komm um sechs bei mir vorbei' - 'okay'; **2** *(fine)* in Ordnung, okay *(informal)*; **is everything all right?** ist alles okay?; **she's all right again** es geht ihr wieder gut; **it's all right by me** das geht in Ordnung; **is it all right if I come later?** ist es in Ordnung, wenn ich später komme?; **3** *(not bad)* okay, okay *(informal)*; **the meal was all right** das Essen war okay; **4 'how are you?' - 'all right'** 'wie geht's dir?' - 'mir geht's gut'.

almost *adverb* fast; **almost every day** fast jeden Tag; **almost everybody** fast alle.

alone *adjective* **1** allein; **he lives alone** er lebt allein; **2 leave me alone!** lass mich in Ruhe!

along *preposition* entlang (+ ACC, or + DAT); **there are trees all along the river** am Fluss entlang stehen Bäume; **to go for a walk along the beach** am Strand entlang spazieren gehen; **2** *(there is often no direct translation for 'along', so the sentence has to be expressed differently)* **she lives along the road from me** sie wohnt in der gleichen Straße wie ich; **I'll bring it along** ich bringe es mit.

aloud *adverb* laut; **to read something aloud** etwas vorlesen✧ SEP.

alphabet *noun* Alphabet *das* (PL *die* Alphabete).

Alps *plural noun* **the Alps** die Alpen.

already *adverb* schon; **they've already left** sie sind schon weggegangen; **it's six o'clock already** es ist schon sechs Uhr.

Alsatian *noun* Schäferhund *der* (PL *die* Schäferhunde).

also *adverb* auch; **I've also invited Karen** ich habe Karen auch eingeladen.

alter *verb* **1** ändern (*a report, a dress*); **2** (*to change*) sich verändern.

alternative *noun* **1** Alternative *die* (PL *die* Alternativen); **there are several alternatives** es gibt mehrere Alternativen; **2 we have no alternative** wir haben keine andere Wahl.

alternative *adjective* anderer/ andere/anderes (*masculine/ feminine/neuter*); **to find an alternative solution** eine andere Lösung finden.

alternative medicine *noun* Alternativmedizin *die*.

although *conjunction* obwohl; **although she's ill, she wants to help us** obwohl sie krank ist, will sie uns helfen.

altogether *adverb* **1** insgesamt; **I've spent thirty pounds altogether** insgesamt habe ich dreißig Pfund ausgegeben; **2** (*completely*) ganz; **I'm not altogether convinced** ich bin nicht ganz überzeugt.

always *adverb* immer; **I always leave at five** ich gehe immer um fünf (weg).

am *verb* SEE be.

a.m. *abbreviation* vormittags; **at 8 a.m.** um acht Uhr morgens.

amateur *noun* **1** Amateur *der* (PL *die* Amateure), Amateurin *die* (PL *die* Amateurinnen); **2 amateur dramatics** *das* Laientheater.

amaze *verb* erstaunen; **what amazes me is ...** was mich erstaunt, ist ....

amazed *adjective* erstaunt; **I was amazed to see her** ich war erstaunt, sie zu sehen.

amazing *adjective* **1** (*terrific*) fantastisch; **they've got an amazing house** sie haben ein fantastisches Haus; **2** (*extraordinary*) erstaunlich; **she has an amazing number of friends** sie hat erstaunlich viele Freunde.

ambition *noun* Ehrgeiz *der*.

ambitious *adjective* ehrgeizig.

ambulance *noun* Krankenwagen *der* (PL *die* Krankenwagen).

America *noun* Amerika *das*; **in America** in Amerika; **to America** nach Amerika.

American *noun* Amerikaner *der* (PL *die* Amerikaner), Amerikanerin *die* (PL *die* Amerikanerinnen).

American *adjective* amerikanisch; **she's American** sie ist Amerikanerin.

among, amongst *preposition* **1** unter (+ DAT); **I found it amongst my books** ich habe das unter

meinen Büchern gefunden;
amongst other things unter
anderem; **2** (*between*) among
yourselves untereinander.

amount *noun* **1** Menge die (PL die
Mengen); **a huge amount of work**
eine Menge Arbeit; **2** (*of money*)
Betrag der (PL die Beträge); **a large
amount of money** ein sehr hoher
Betrag.

amount *verb* **1 to amount to** sich
belaufen◇; **the bill amounts to five
hundred euros** die Rechnung
beläuft sich auf fünfhundert Euro.

amp *noun* (*amplifier*) Verstärker
der (PL die Verstärker).

amplifier *noun* Verstärker der (PL
die Verstärker).

amuse *verb* amüsieren.

amusement arcade *noun*
Spielhalle die (PL die Spielhallen).

amusing *adjective* amüsant.

an *article* SEE **a**.

anaesthetic *noun* Narkose die (PL
die Narkosen).

analyse *verb* analysieren.

ancestor *noun* Vorfahr der (PL die
Vorfahren).

anchovy *noun* Sardelle die (PL die
Sardellen).

ancient *adjective* **1** alt; **ancient
Greece** das alte Griechenland; **
2** (*very old*) uralt; **an ancient pair
of jeans** uralte Jeans.

and *conjunction* **1** und; **Rosie and I**
Rosie und ich; **girls and boys**
Mädchen und Jungen; **2 louder
and louder** immer lauter; **3 try and
come** versuche zu kommen.

angel *noun* Engel der (PL die Engel).

anger *noun* Zorn der.

angle *noun* Winkel der (PL die
Winkel).

angrily *adverb* wütend.

angry *adjective* **to be angry** böse
sein; **she was angry with me** sie
war böse auf mich; **to get angry**
böse werden.

animal *noun* Tier das (PL die Tiere).

ankle *noun* Knöchel der (PL die
Knöchel).

anniversary *noun* **1** Jahrestag
der (PL die Jahrestage); **2 our
wedding anniversary** unser
Hochzeitstag.

announce *verb* bekanntgeben
◇ SEP; **she announced her
engagement** sie gab ihre
Verlobung bekannt.

annoy *verb* **to be annoyed**
verärgert sein; **to get annoyed
with somebody** sich über
jemanden ärgern; **she got
annoyed about it** sie hat sich
darüber geärgert.

annoying *adjective* ärgerlich.

annual *adjective* jährlich.

anorak *noun* Anorak der (PL die
Anoraks).

anorexia *noun* Magersucht die.

another *adjective* **1** (*additional*)
noch ein/noch eine/noch ein; **
would you like another cup
of tea?** möchtest du noch eine
Tasse Tee?; **we need another
three chairs** wir brauchen noch
drei Stühle; **2** (*different*) ein
anderer/eine andere/ein anderes;
we saw another film wir haben
einen anderen Film gesehen; **3 in
another two years** in zwei
weiteren Jahren.

answer noun 1 Antwort die (PL die Antworten); **the right answer** die richtige Antwort; **the wrong answer** die falsche Antwort; **2 the answer to a problem** die Lösung eines Problems.

answer verb 1 antworten (+ DAT); **why don't you answer him?** warum antwortest du ihm nicht?; **2** beantworten (a letter, a question); **he hasn't answered our letter** er hat unseren Brief nicht beantwortet.

answering machine noun Anrufbeantworter der (PL die Anrufbeantworter).

ant noun Ameise die (PL die Ameisen).

anthem noun **the national anthem** die Nationalhymne.

antibiotic noun Antibiotikum das (PL die Antibiotika).

antique noun antiques Antiquitäten (plural).

antique adjective antik; **an antique table** ein antiker Tisch.

antique shop noun Antiquitätengeschäft das (PL die Antiquitätengeschäfte).

antiseptic noun Antiseptikum das (PL die Antiseptika).

anxious adjective 1 (worried) besorgt; **2** (keen) **she was anxious to see him** sie wollte ihn unbedingt sehen.

anxiously adverb ängstlich.

any adjective 1 irgendein; **if they had any plan** wenn sie irgendeinen Plan hätten; **2** (with plural nouns) irgendwelche; **if they had any plans** wenn sie irgendwelche Pläne

hätten; **3** (in questions 'any' is often not translated) **have you got any stamps?** haben Sie Briefmarken?; **have we got any milk?** haben wir Milch?; **4** not any kein; **they haven't made any plans** sie haben nichts geplant; **we haven't got any milk** wir haben keine Milch; **5** (no matter which) jeder beliebige/jede beliebige/jedes beliebige; **you can have any colour** du kannst jede beliebige Farbe haben.

any pronoun 1 (in questions, replacing the noun) welcher/ welche/welches, (replacing a plural noun) welche; **I need some flour, have you got any?** ich brauche Mehl, hast du welches?; **2** not any keiner/keine/keins, (replacing a plural noun) keine; **I don't want any** ich will keins haben; **there aren't any** es gibt keine; **3** (no matter which one) irgendein; **'which chair can I take?' – 'take any of them'** 'welchen Stuhl kann ich nehmen?' – 'nimm irgendeinen'.

any adverb 1 (in questions) noch; **would you like any more?** möchtest du noch etwas?; **2** (with negatives) **I can't see him any more** ich kann ihn nicht mehr sehen.

anybody, anyone pronoun 1 (in questions) jemand; **does anybody want some tea?** möchte jemand Tee?; **Is anybody in?** ist irgendjemand da?; **2** not anybody niemand; **there isn't anybody in the office** niemand ist im Büro; **3** (absolutely anybody) jeder; **anybody can do it** das kann jeder.

a b c d e f g h i j k l m n o p q r s t u v w x y z

a

anyhow *adverb* SEE **anyway**.

anyone *pronoun* SEE **anybody**.

b

c

anything *pronoun* **1** (*in questions*) irgendetwas; **is there anything I can do to help?** kann ich irgendwie helfen?; **2 not anything** nichts; **there isn't anything on the table** auf dem Tisch liegt nichts; **3** (*anything at all*) alles; **I'll do anything to help him** ich werde alles tun, um ihm zu helfen.

d

e

f

g

anyway, anyhow *adverb* **1** jedenfalls; **anyway, I'll ring you before I leave** jedenfalls ruf ich dich an, bevor ich fahre; **2** sowieso.

h

i

j

k

anywhere *adverb* **1** (*in questions*) irgendwo; **have you seen my keys anywhere?** hast du meine Schlüssel irgendwo gesehen?; **2 not anywhere** nirgends; **I can't find my keys anywhere** ich kann meine Schlüssel nirgends finden; **3** (*to any place*) irgendwohin; **are you going anywhere tomorrow?** fahrt ihr morgen irgendwohin?; **put your cases down anywhere** stell deine Koffer irgendwohin; **4** (*in any place*) überall; **you can get that anywhere** das kann man überall kriegen.

l

m

n

o

p

q

r

s

apart *adjective, adverb* **1** (*separate*) auseinander; **they've been apart for some time** sie sind schon lange auseinander; **2 to be two metres apart** zwei Meter auseinander liegen; **3 apart from** außer (+ DAT); **apart from my brother everybody was there** außer meinem Bruder waren alle da.

t

u

v

w

x

apologize *verb* sich entschuldigen; **he apologized for**

y

z

his mistake er entschuldigte sich für seinen Fehler; **he apologized to Sam** er hat sich bei Sam entschuldigt.

apology *noun* Entschuldigung die (PL die Entschuldigungen).

apostrophe *noun* Apostroph der (PL die Apostrophe).

apparent *adjective* offensichtlich.

apparently *adverb* offensichtlich.

appeal *noun* Appell der (PL die Appelle).

appeal *verb* **1 to appeal for something** um etwas (ACC) bitten✧; **2 to appeal to somebody** sich an jemanden wenden✧; **horror films don't appeal to me** Horrorfilme sind nicht mein Geschmack.

appear *verb* **1** erscheinen✧ (PERF sein); **Mick appeared at breakfast** Mick erschien zum Frühstück; **2 to appear on television** im Fernsehen auftreten✧ SEP (PERF sein); **3** (*seem*) scheinen✧; **it appears that somebody has stolen the key** es scheint, dass jemand den Schlüssel gestohlen hat.

appendicitis *noun* Blinddarmentzündung die.

appetite *noun* Appetit der; **it'll spoil your appetite** das verdirbt dir den Appetit.

applaud *verb* Beifall klatschen.

applause *noun* Beifall der.

apple *noun* Apfel der (PL die Äpfel).

apple tree *noun* Apfelbaum der (PL die Apfelbäume).

applicant *noun* Bewerber der (PL die Bewerber), Bewerberin die (PL die Bewerberinnen).

application noun (for a job) Bewerbungsformular das (PL die Bewerbungsformulare).

application noun Bewerbung die (PL die Bewerbungen).

apply verb 1 to apply for a job sich um eine Stelle bewerben✧; 2 to apply for university sich um einen Studienplatz bewerben✧; 3 to apply for a passport einen Pass beantragen; 4 to apply to zutreffen✧ SEP auf (+ACC); that doesn't apply to students das trifft nicht auf Studenten zu.

appointment noun Termin der (PL die Termine); to make a dental appointment einen Zahnarzttermin vereinbaren; I've got a hair appointment at four ich habe um vier einen Friseurtermin.

appreciate verb I appreciate your advice ich bin dir für deinen Rat dankbar; I'd appreciate it if you could tidy up afterwards es wäre nett von dir, wenn du danach aufräumen würdest.

apprentice noun Lehrling der (PL die Lehrlinge).

apprenticeship noun Lehre die (PL die Lehren).

approach verb sich nähern (+DAT) (PERF sein); we were approaching the village wir näherten uns dem Dorf.

approve verb to approve of something mit etwas (DAT) einverstanden sein; they don't approve of her friends sie lehnen ihre Freunde ab.

approximate adjective ungefähr.

approximately adverb ungefähr; approximately fifty people ungefähr fünfzig Personen.

apricot noun Aprikose die (PL die Aprikosen).

April noun April der; in April im April.

April Fool noun (trick) Aprilscherz der (PL die Aprilscherze); April fool! April, April!

April Fool's Day noun der erste April.

apron noun Schürze die (PL die Schürzen).

aquarium noun Aquarium das (PL die Aquarien).

Aquarius noun Wassermann der; Sharon's Aquarius Sharon ist Wassermann.

Arab noun Araber der (PL die Araber), Araberin die (PL die Araberinnen).

Arab adjective arabisch; the Arab countries die arabischen Länder.

arch noun Bogen der (PL die Bogen).

archaeologist noun Archäologe der (PL die Archäologen), Archäologin die (PL die Archäologinnen); she's an archaeologist sie ist Archäologin.

archaeology noun Archäologie die.

architect noun Architekt der (PL die Architekten), Architektin die (PL die Architektinnen); he's an architect er ist Architekt.

architecture noun Architektur die.

are verb SEE be.

area noun 1 (part of a town, a region) Gegend die (PL die

a
b
c
d
e
f
g
h
i
j
k
l
m
n
o
p
q
r
s
t
u
v
w
x
y
z

Gegenden); **a nice area** eine nette Gegend; **in the Leeds area** in der Gegend von Leeds; **2 picnic area** der Picknickplatz.

argue verb sich streiten◇; **to argue about something** sich über etwas (ACC) streiten; **they're arguing about the result** sie streiten sich über das Ergebnis.

argument noun Streit der (PL die Streite); **to get into an argument with somebody** mit jemandem in Streit geraten◇; **to have an argument** sich streiten◇.

Aries noun Widder der; **Pauline's Aries** Pauline ist Widder.

arm noun Arm der (PL die Arme); **arm in arm** Arm in Arm; **to break your arm** sich (DAT) den Arm brechen.

armchair noun Sessel der (PL die Sessel).

armed adjective bewaffnet.

army noun **1** Heer das (PL die Heere); **2** (profession) Militär das; **to join the army** zum Militär gehen.

around preposition, adverb **1** (with time of day) gegen (+ ACC); **we'll be there around ten** wir werden gegen zehn da sein; **2** (with ages or amounts) etwa; **she's around fifteen** sie ist etwa fünfzehn; **we need around six kilos** wir brauchen etwa sechs Kilo; **3** (with dates) um (+ ACC); **around 10 August** um den 10. August herum; **4** (surrounding) um ... herum; **the countryside around Edinburgh** die Landschaft um Edinburgh herum; **5** (near) **is there a post office around here?** gibt es hier in der

Gegend eine Post?; **is Phil around?** ist Phil da?

arrange verb **to arrange something** etwas vereinbaren; **we've arranged to go to the cinema on Saturday** wir haben vereinbart, am Samstag ins Kino zu gehen.

arrest noun **to be under arrest** verhaftet sein.

arrest verb verhaften.

arrival noun Ankunft die (PL die Ankünfte).

arrive verb ankommen◇ SEP (PERF sein); **they arrived at 3 p.m.** sie kamen um fünfzehn Uhr an.

arrow noun Pfeil der (PL die Pfeile).

art noun **1** Kunst die (PL die Künste); **modern art** moderne Kunst; **2** (school subject) Kunsterziehung die.

artery noun Arterie die (PL die Arterien).

art gallery noun Kunstgalerie die (PL die Kunstgalerien).

article noun **1** (in a newspaper or magazine) Artikel der (PL die Artikel); **2** (object) Stück das (PL die Stücke).

artificial adjective künstlich.

artist noun Künstler der (PL die Künstler), Künstlerin die (PL die Künstlerinnen); **he's an artist** er ist Künstler.

artistic adjective künstlerisch.

art school noun Kunsthochschule die (PL die Kunsthochschulen).

as conjunction, adverb **1** wie; **as you know** wie du weißt; **as usual** wie üblich; **as I told you** wie ich dir gesagt habe; **2** (because) da; **as there was no bus, we took a taxi**

da es keinen Bus gab, nahmen wir ein Taxi; **3 as ... as** so ...wie; **he's as tall as his brother** er ist so groß wie sein Bruder; **come as quickly as possible** komm so schnell wie möglich; **4 as much ... as** so viel ...wie; **you have as much time as I do** du hast so viel Zeit wie ich; **5 as many ... as** so viele ... wie; **we have as many problems as he does** wir haben genauso viele Probleme wie er; **6 as long as** vorausgesetzt; **we'll go tomorrow, as long as it's a nice day** wir gehen morgen, vorausgesetzt es ist schönes Wetter; **7 for as long as** solange; **you can stay for as long as you like** du kannst bleiben, solange du willst; **8 as soon as possible** so bald wie möglich; **9 to work as** arbeiten als; **he works as a waiter in the evenings** abends arbeitet er als Kellner; **as well** auch.

ash *noun* **1** Asche *die* (PL die Aschen); **2** (*tree*) Esche *die* (PL die Eschen).

ashamed *adjective* **to be ashamed of something** sich wegen etwas (DAT) schämen; **you should be ashamed of yourself!** du solltest dich schämen!

ashtray *noun* Aschenbecher *der* (PL die Aschenbecher).

Asia *noun* Asien *das*; **in Asia** in Asien.

Asian *noun* Asiate *der* (PL die Asiaten), Asiatin *die* (PL die Asiatinnen).

Asian *adjective* asiatisch.

ask *verb* **1** fragen; **to ask somebody something** jemanden nach etwas (DAT) fragen; **I asked**

him the way ich fragte ihn nach dem Weg; **2 to ask something** um etwas (ACC) bitten; **to ask somebody a favour** jemanden um einen Gefallen bitten; **to ask somebody to do something** jemanden bitten, etwas zu tun; **ask Danny to give you a hand** bitte Danny, dir zu helfen; **3 to ask somebody a question** jemandem eine Frage stellen; **I asked him a few questions** ich habe ihm ein paar Fragen gestellt; **4** einladen◊ SEP; **they've asked us to a party** sie haben uns auf eine Party eingeladen; **Paul's asked Janie out on Friday** Paul hat Janie Freitag eingeladen; **5 to ask for** verlangen; **how much are they asking for the car?** wieviel verlangen sie für das Auto?

asleep *adjective* **to be asleep** schlafen ◊; **the baby's asleep** das Baby schläft; **to fall asleep** einschlafen ◊ SEP (PERF *sein*).

asparagus *noun* Spargel *der* (PL die Spargel).

aspirin *noun* Aspirin *das*.

assembly *noun* (*at school*) Morgenandacht *die* (PL die Morgenandachten).

assess *verb* beurteilen.

assignment *noun* (*at school*) Aufgabe *die* (PL die Aufgaben).

assist *verb* helfen (+ DAT) .

assistance *noun* Hilfe *die*.

assistant *noun* **1** Helfer *der* (PL die Helfer), Helferin *die* (PL die Helferinnen); **2** (*in school*) Assistent *der* (PL die Assistenten), Assistentin *die* (PL die

Assistentinnen); **3 shop assistant**
der Verkäufer, die Verkäuferin.

association noun Verband der (PL
die Verbände).

assorted adjective gemischt.

assortment noun Auswahl die.

assume verb annehmen◇ SEP; **I**
assume ich nehme an.

asthma noun Asthma das.

astrology noun Astrologie die.

astronaut noun Astronaut der (PL
die Astronauten), Astronautin die
(PL die Astronautinnen).

astronomy noun Astronomie die.

at preposition **1** in (+ DAT); **at school**
in der Schule; **at my office** in
meinem Büro; **at the supermarket**
im Supermarkt; **2 an** (+ DAT); **at the**
station am Bahnhof; **at the bus**
stop an der Bushaltestelle; **3** bei
(+ DAT); **at the dentist** beim
Zahnarzt; **at Emma's** bei Emma's;
she's at her brother's this evening
sie ist heute Abend bei ihrem
Bruder; **at the hairdresser's** beim
Friseur; **4 at a party** auf einer
Party; **5 at home** zu Hause;
6 (talking about the time) um; **at**
eight o'clock um acht Uhr; **7 at**
night nachts; **at Christmas** zu
Weihnachten; **at the weekend** am
Wochenende; **8** (@ in e-mail
addresses) Klammeraffe der; **john-**
dot-smith@easycom-dot-com
john-punkt-smith-Klammeraffe-
easycom-punkt-com; **9 at last**
endlich; **she's found a job at last**
sie hat endlich einen Job gefunden.

athlete noun Athlet der (PL die
Athleten), Athletin die (PL die
Athletinnen).

athletic adjective sportlich.

athletics noun Leichtathletik die.

Atlantic noun **the Atlantic**
(Ocean) der Atlantik.

atlas noun Atlas der (PL die
Atlanten).

atmosphere noun Atmosphäre
die (PL die Atmosphären).

atom noun Atom das (PL die Atome).

atomic adjective Atom-; **an atomic**
bomb eine Atombombe.

attach verb befestigen.

attached adjective (emotionally)
to be attached to somebody/
something an jemandem/etwas
(DAT) hängen◇.

attachment noun **1** (in a letter)
Anlage die (PL die Anlagen); **2** (in an
email) Attachment das (PL die
Attachments).

attack noun Angriff der (PL die
Angriffe).

attack verb **1** angreifen◇ SEP;
2 (mug or raid) überfallen◇.

attempt noun Versuch der (PL die
Versuche); **at the first attempt**
beim ersten Versuch.

attempt verb **to attempt to do**
something versuchen, etwas zu
tun.

attend verb teilnehmen◇ SEP an
(+ DAT); **to attend a meeting** an
einer Besprechung teilnehmen; **to**
attend an evening class einen
Abendkurs besuchen.

attention noun
1 Aufmerksamkeit die; **to pay**
attention aufpassen SEP; **I wasn't**
paying attention ich habe nicht
aufgepasst; **2 he wasn't paying**
attention to the teacher er hörte
dem Lehrer nicht zu.

attic noun Dachboden der (PL die Dachböden); **in the attic** auf dem Dachboden.

attitude noun 1 (way of thinking) Einstellung die; 2 (way of acting) Haltung die.

attract verb anziehen ⋄ SEP.

attraction noun 1 Anziehung die; 2 (a thing that attracts) Attraktion die (PL die Attraktionen); **the whale was a big attraction** der Wal war eine große Attraktion.

attractive adjective attraktiv.

aubergine noun Aubergine die (PL die Auberginen).

audience noun Publikum das; **the television audience** die Fernsehzuschauer (plural).

August noun August der; **in August** im August.

aunt, auntie noun Tante die (PL die Tanten).

au pair noun Aupairmädchen das (PL die Aupairmädchen); **I'm looking for a job as an au pair** ich suche eine Aupair-Stelle.

Australia noun Australien das; **to Australia** nach Australien.

Australian noun Australier der (PL die Australier), Australierin die (PL die Australierinnen).

Australian adjective australisch; **she's Australian** sie ist Australierin.

Austria noun Österreich das; **in Austria** in Österreich.

Austrian noun Österreicher der (PL die Österreicher), Österreicherin die (PL die Österreicherinnen).

Austrian adjective österreichisch; **he's Austrian** er ist Österreicher.

author noun Autor der (PL die Autoren), Autorin die (PL die Autorinnen).

autograph noun Autogramm das (PL die Autogramme).

automatic adjective automatisch.

automatically adverb automatisch.

autumn noun Herbst der (PL die Herbste); **in autumn** im Herbst.

available adjective (on sale) erhältlich.

average noun Durchschnitt der (PL die Durchschnitte); **on average** im Durchschnitt; **above average** über dem Durchschnitt.

average adjective durchschnittlich; **the average height** die durchschnittliche Größe.

avocado noun Avocado die (PL die Avocados).

avoid verb 1 vermeiden ⋄; **to avoid doing something** es vermeiden, etwas zu tun; **I avoid speaking to him** ich vermeide es, mit ihm zu reden; 2 (keep away from somebody or a place) meiden ⋄; **she avoids me** sie meidet mich.

awake adjective **to be awake** wach sein; **are you still awake?** bist du noch wach?

award noun Preis der (PL die Preise); **to win an award** einen Preis gewinnen.

aware adjective **to be aware of a problem** sich (DAT) eines Problems bewusst sein; **I'm aware of the danger** ich bin mir der Gefahr

a
b
c
d
e
f
g
h
i
j
k
l
m
n
o
p
q
r
s
t
u
v
w
x
y
z

bewusst; **as far as I'm aware** soweit ich weiß.

away *adverb* **1 to be away** nicht da sein; **I'll be away next week** ich bin nächste Woche nicht da; **2 to go away** verreisen (PERF *sein*); **Laura's gone away for a week** Laura ist auf eine Woche verreist; **go away!** geh weg!; **3 to run away** weglaufen◇ SEP (PERF *sein*); **the thieves ran away** die Diebe liefen weg; **4 the school is two kilometres away** die Schule ist zwei Kilometer entfernt; **how far away is it?** wie weit entfernt ist es?; **not far away** nicht weit entfernt; **5 to put something away** etwas wegräumen SEP; **I'm just putting my books away** ich räume gerade meine Bücher weg; **6 to give something away** etwas weggeben◇ SEP, (*as a present*) etwas verschenken; **she's given away all her cassettes** sie hat alle ihre Kassetten verschenkt.

away match *noun* Auswärtsspiel das (PL die Auswärtsspiele).

awful *adjective* furchtbar; **the film was awful** der Film war furchtbar; **I feel awful** (*ill*) ich fühle mich furchtbar; **I feel awful about it** es ist mir furchtbar unangenehm; **an awful lot of mistakes** furchtbar viele Fehler.

awkward *adjective* **1** schwierig; **it's an awkward situation** das ist eine schwierige Situation; **it's a bit awkward** das ist ein bisschen schwierig; **an awkward child** ein schwieriges Kind; **2 an awkward question** eine peinliche Frage.

axe *noun* Axt die (PL die Äxte).

Bb

baby *noun* Baby das (PL die Babys).

babysit *verb* babysitten.

babysitter *noun* Babysitter der (PL die Babysitter), Babysitterin die (PL die Babysitterinnen).

babysitting *noun* Babysitten das.

back *noun* **1** (*of a person or animal*) Rücken der (PL die Rücken); **he did it behind my back** er hat es hinter meinem Rücken getan; **2** (*of a piece of paper, cheque, or building*) Rückseite die (PL die Rückseiten); **on the back** auf der Rückseite; **3 the back of your hand** der Handrücken; **4 at the back** hinten; **at the back of the room** hinten im Zimmer; **we sat at the back** wir saßen hinten; **a garden at the back of the house** ein Garten hinter dem Haus; **5** (*of a chair or sofa*) Rückenlehne die (PL die Rückenlehnen); **6** (*in football or hockey*) Verteidiger der (PL die Verteidiger), Verteidigerin die (PL die Verteidigerinnen); **left back** der Linksverteidiger.

back *adjective* **1 the back seat** (*of a car*) der Rücksitz; **2 the back door** die Hintertür; **the back garden** der Garten hinter dem Haus.

back *adverb* **1** zurück; **there and back** hin und zurück; **to go back** (*on foot*) zurückgehen◇ SEP (PERF *sein*) (*in a vehicle*) zurückfahren◇ SEP (PERF *sein*); **2 to come back** zurückkommen◇ SEP (PERF *sein*); **they've come back from Italy** sie sind aus Italien zurückgekommen;

I'll be back at 8 o'clock ich bin um acht Uhr zurück; **Sue's not back yet** Sue ist noch nicht zurück; **3 to phone back** zurückrufen ✧ SEP; **I'll ring back later** ich rufe dich später zurück; **4 to give something back to somebody** jemandem etwas zurückgeben ✧ SEP; **give it back!** gib es zurück!

back verb (bet on) setzen auf (+ ACC).

● **to back up** (computing) sichern; **to back up a file** eine Sicherungskopie machen.

● **to back somebody up** jemanden unterstützen.

backache noun
Rückenschmerzen (plural).

background noun **1** (of a person) Verhältnisse (plural); **she comes from a poor background** sie kommt aus ärmlichen Verhältnissen; **2** (in a picture, view, or situation) Hintergrund der (PL die Hintergründe); **background noise** Hintergrundgeräusche (plural); **3** (to events or problems) Hintergründe (plural).

backhand noun Rückhand die.

backing noun **1** (on sticky-back plastic, for example) Verstärkung die (PL die Verstärkungen); **2** (moral support) Unterstützung die; **3** (in music) Begleitung die; **a backing group** eine Begleitband.

backpack noun Rucksack der (PL die Rucksäcke).

backpack verb **to go backpacking** trampen (PERF sein).

back seat noun Rücksitz der (PL die Rücksitze).

backstroke noun
Rückenschwimmen das.

back to front adverb verkehrt herum; **your jumper's back to front** du hast deinen Pullover verkehrt herum an.

backup noun **1** (support) Unterstützung die; **2** (in computing) Sicherungskopie die (PL die Sicherungskopien); **a backup disk** eine Sicherungsdiskette.

backwards adverb **1** rückwärts; **2 to lean backwards** sich nach hinten lehnen; **to fall backwards** nach hinten fallen.

bacon noun Speck der; **bacon and eggs** Eier mit Speck.

bad adjective **1** (not good) schlecht; **a bad idea** eine schlechte Idee; **a bad meal** ein schlechtes Essen; **his new film's not bad** sein neuer Film ist nicht schlecht; **it's bad for your health** das ist ungesund; **I'm bad at physics** ich bin schlecht in Physik; **2** (serious) schlimm; **a bad mistake** ein schlimmer Fehler; **a bad cold** eine schlimme Erkältung; **3 a bad accident** ein schwerer Unfall; **4** (rotten) schlecht; **to go bad** schlecht werden; **5 a bad apple** ein fauler Apfel; **6 bad language** Kraftausdrücke (plural); ★ **too bad!** schade!, so ein Pech!

badge noun Abzeichen das (PL die Abzeichen).

badly adverb **1** (poorly) schlecht; **he writes badly** er schreibt schlecht; **I slept badly** ich habe schlecht geschlafen; **2** (seriously) schwer; **they were badly injured** sie waren schwer verletzt; **3** (very much) dringend; **to need something badly** etwas dringend brauchen.

a b c d e f g h i j k l m n o p q r s t u v w x y z

a

bad-mannered *adjective* to be bad-mannered schlechte Manieren haben.

b

badminton *noun* Badminton das.

c

bad-tempered *adjective* schlecht gelaunt; **a bad-tempered old man** ein schlecht gelaunter alter Mann.

d

e

bag *noun* **1** Tasche die (PL die Taschen); **2** (*made of paper or plastic*) Tüte die (PL die Tüten).

f

baggage *noun* Gepäck das.

g

bagpipes *noun* Dudelsack der (PL die Dudelsäke).

h

bags *plural noun* Gepäck das; **to pack your bags** (sein Gepäck) packen; ★ **to have bags under your eyes** Ringe unter den Augen haben (*informal*).

i

j

k

bake *verb* **1** backen; **to bake a cake** einen Kuchen backen; **2 I'm baking** mir ist furchtbar heiß.

l

m

baked *adjective* **1** (*fish or fruit*) überbacken; **baked apples** Bratäpfel; **2 baked potatoes** die Ofenkartoffeln.

n

o

baked beans *plural noun* Bohnen in Tomatensoße.

p

baker *noun* Bäcker der (PL die Bäcker); **to go to the baker's** zum Bäcker gehen.

q

r

bakery *noun* Bäckerei die (PL die Bäckereien).

s

balance *noun* **1** Gleichgewicht das; **to lose your balance** das Gleichgewicht verlieren; **2** (*in a bank account*) Kontostand der.

t

u

v

balanced *adjective* ausgeglichen.

balcony *noun* Balkon der (PL die Balkons).

w

bald *adjective* **1** kahl; **2** (*of a person*) kahlköpfig; **to go bald** eine Glatze bekommen.

x

y

z

ball *noun* **1** (*for tennis, football, or golf*) Ball der (PL die Bälle); **2** (*for billiards, croquet*) Kugel die (PL die Kugeln); **3** (*of string or wool*) Knäuel das (PL die Knäuel).

ballet *noun* Ballett das (PL die Ballette).

ballet dancer *noun* Balletttänzer der (PL die Balletttänzer), Balletttänzerin die (PL die Balletttänzerinnen).

balloon *noun* **1** Luftballon der (PL die Luftballons); **2** (*hot-air*) Ballon der (PL die Ballons).

ballpoint (pen) *noun* Kugelschreiber der (PL die Kugelschreiber).

ban *noun* Verbot das (PL die Verbote); **a ban on smoking** ein Rauchverbot.

ban *verb* verbieten✧; **to ban someone from smoking** jemandem verbieten zu rauchen.

banana *noun* **1** Banane die (PL die Bananen); **2 a banana yoghurt** ein Bananenjoghurt.

band *noun* **1** (*playing music*) Band die (PL die Bands); **rock band** die Rockband; **brass band** die Blaskapelle; **2 rubber band** das Gummiband.

bandage *noun* Verband der (PL die Verbände).

bandage *verb* verbinden✧.

bang *noun* (*noise*) Knall der (PL die Knalle).

bang *verb* **1** (*hit, knock*) schlagen✧; **he banged his fist on the table** er schlug mit der Faust auf den Tisch; **to bang on the door** gegen die Tür schlagen; **2 I**

banged my head on the door ich habe mir den Kopf an der Tür gestoßen; **3 to bang into something** gegen etwas (ACC) knallen; **4** (shut loudly) zuknallen SEP; **he banged the door** er knallte die Tür zu.

bang exclamation peng!.

bank noun **1** (for money) Bank die (PL die Banken); **I'm going to the bank** ich gehe auf die Bank; **2** (of a river or lake) Ufer das (PL die Ufer).

bank account noun Bankkonto das (PL die Bankkonten).

bank balance noun Kontostand der (PL die Kontostände).

bank card noun Scheckkarte die (PL die Scheckkarten).

bank holiday noun gesetzliche Feiertag der (PL die gesetzlichen Feiertage).

banknote noun Geldschein der (PL die Geldscheine).

bank statement noun Kontoauszug der (PL die Kontoauszüge).

bar noun **1** (selling drinks) Bar die (PL die Bars); **Janet works in a bar** Janet arbeitet in einer Bar; **2** (counter) Theke die (PL die Theken); **on the bar** auf der Theke; **3 a bar of chocolate** eine Tafel Schokolade; **4 a bar of soap** ein Stück Seife; **5** (made of wood or metal) Stange die (PL die Stangen); **an iron bar** eine Eisenstange; **6** (in music) Takt der (PL die Takte).

barbecue noun **1** (apparatus) Grill der (PL die Grills); **2** (party) Grillfest das (PL die Grillfeste).

barbecue verb to barbecue a **chicken** ein Hühnchen grillen; **barbecued chicken** gegrilltes Hühnchen.

bare adjective nackt.

barefoot adjective **to be barefoot** barfuß sein; **to walk barefoot** barfuß gehen.

bargain noun (a good buy) gute Kauf der (PL die Käufe); **I got a bargain** ich habe einen guten Kauf gemacht; **it's a bargain!** das ist ein Schnäppchen!

barge noun Kahn der (PL die Kähne).

bark noun **1** (of a tree) Rinde die (PL die Rinden); **2** (of a dog) Bellen das.

bark verb bellen.

barmaid noun Bardame die (PL die Bardamen).

barman noun Barkeeper der (PL die Barkeeper).

barn noun Scheune die (PL die Scheunen).

barrel noun Fass das (PL die Fässer).

barrier noun Absperrung die (PL die Absperrungen).

base noun (bottom part) Fuß der (PL die Füße).

baseball noun Baseball der.

based adjective **1 to be based on** basieren auf (+ DAT); **the film is based on a true story** der Film basiert auf einer wahren Geschichte; **2 to be based in** wohnen in (+ DAT); **he's based in Bristol** er wohnt in Bristol.

basement noun Kellergeschoss das (PL die Kellergeschosse).

bash noun 1 Schlag der (PL die Schläge); 2 I'll have a bash ich probier's mal.

bash verb I bashed my head ich habe mir den Kopf angestoßen.

basic adjective 1 grundlegend, Grund-; basic knowledge Grundkenntnisse (plural); her basic salary ihr Grundgehalt; 2 the basic problem das Hauptproblem; 3 (not luxurious) einfach.

basically adverb 1 grundsätzlich; it's basically all right grundsätzlich ist es okay; 2 basically, I don't want to come eigentlich will ich nicht kommen.

basics plural noun the basics das Wesentliche.

basin noun Becken das (PL die Becken).

basis noun 1 Basis die; 2 on a regular basis regelmäßig.

basket noun Korb der (PL die Körbe); a basket of apples ein Korb Äpfel; waste-paper basket der Papierkorb.

basketball noun Basketball der.

bass noun 1 Bass der (PL die Bässe); 2 double bass der Kontrabass.

bass guitar noun Bassgitarre die (PL die Bassgitarren).

bassoon noun Fagott das (PL die Fagotte).

bat noun 1 (for games) Schläger der (PL die Schläger); 2 (animal) Fledermaus die (PL die Fledermäuse).

bath noun 1 Bad das (PL die Bäder); to have a bath baden; 2 (tub) Badewanne die (PL die Badewannen).

bathroom noun Badezimmer das (PL die Badezimmer).

baths plural noun Badeanstalt die (PL die Badeanstalten).

bath towel noun Badetuch das (PL die Badetücher).

batter noun Teig der (PL die Teige); fish in batter ausgebackener Fisch.

battery noun Batterie die (PL die Batterien).

battle noun 1 (in war) Schlacht die (PL die Schlachten); 2 (contest) Kampf der (PL die Kämpfe).

Bavaria noun Bayern das.

bay noun 1 (on coast) Bucht die (PL die Buchten); 2 (in bus station) Haltebucht die (PL die Haltebuchten).

BC (before Christ) v.Chr. (vor Christus).

be verb 1 sein◇ (PERF sein); Melanie is in the kitchen Melanie ist in der Küche; where is the butter? wo ist die Butter?; I'm tired ich bin müde; when we were in Germany als wir in Deutschland waren; 2 (with jobs and professions) sein◇ (PERF sein); she's a teacher sie ist Lehrerin; he's a taxi driver er ist Taxifahrer; 3 (in clock times, days of the week, dates, and age) sein◇ (PERF sein); it's three o'clock es ist drei Uhr; it's half past five es ist halb sechs; what day is it today? welcher Tag ist heute?; it's Tuesday today heute ist Dienstag; it's the twentieth of May heute ist der zwanzigste Mai; what's the date today? der Wievielte ist heute?; how old are you? wie alt bist du?; I'm fifteen ich bin fünfzehn; 4 (cold, hot, ill) sein◇ (PERF sein);

I'm **hot** mir ist heiß; **I'm cold** mir
ist kalt; **to be ill** krank sein;
5 (weather) sein ✧ (PERF sein); **it's
cold today** heute ist es kalt; **it's a
nice day** es ist schönes Wetter; **it's
raining** es regnet; **6 I have** Hunger; **she's thirsty** sie hat
Durst; **7** (saying how much
something costs) kosten; **how much
are the bananas?** wie viel kosten
die Bananen?; **8** (go, come, or visit)
sein ✧ (PERF sein); **I've never been
to Berlin** ich war noch nie in Berlin
gewesen; **have you been to
England before?** warst du schon
einmal in England?; **has the
postman been?** ist der
Briefträger schon da?; **9** (forming
the passive) werden ✧ (PERF sein); **to
be loved** geliebt werden; **he has
been promoted** er ist befördert
worden; **10 there is/are** es gibt; **is
there a bank near here?** gibt es
hier in der Nähe eine Bank?

beach noun Strand der (PL die
Strände); **to go to the beach** zum
Strand gehen; **on the beach** am
Strand.

bead noun Perle die (PL die Perlen).

beak noun Schnabel der (PL die
Schnäbel).

beam noun **1** (of light) Strahl der (PL
die Strahlen); **2** (for a roof) Balken
der (PL die Balken).

bean noun Bohne die (PL die
Bohnen); **green beans** grüne
Bohnen.

bear noun Bär der (PL die Bären).

bear verb **1** ertragen ✧; **I can't bear
the idea** ich kann den Gedanken
nicht ertragen; **2 to bear
something in mind** an etwas (ACC)

denken; **I'll bear it in mind** ich
denke daran.

beard noun Bart der (PL die Bärte).

bearded adjective bärtig.

bearings plural noun **to get one's
bearings** sich orientieren.

beast noun **1** (animal) Tier das (PL
die Tiere); **2 you beast!** du Biest!

beat noun (in music) Takt der.

beat verb **1** (defeat) schlagen ✧; **we
beat them!** wir haben sie
geschlagen; **2 you can't beat a
good meal** es geht doch nichts
über ein gutes Essen.

● **to beat somebody up**
jemanden verprügeln.

beautiful adjective schön.

beauty noun **1** Schönheit die (PL die
Schönheiten); **2 the beauty of it is
that ...** das Schöne daran ist, dass
....

because conjunction **1** weil;
because it's cold weil es kalt ist;
2 because of wegen (+ GEN);
because of the accident wegen
des Unfalls; **because of you**
deinetwegen.

become verb werden ✧ (PERF sein);
she's become a painter sie ist
Malerin geworden.

bed noun **1** Bett das (PL die Betten);
double bed das Doppelbett; **in bed**
im Bett; **to go to bed** ins Bett
gehen; **2** (flower bed) Beet das (PL die
Beete).

bedclothes plural noun
Bettwäsche die.

bedding noun Bettzeug das.

bedroom noun Schlafzimmer das
(PL die Schlafzimmer); **bedroom
furniture** Schlafzimmermöbel

a
b
c
d
e
f
g
h
i
j
k
l
m
n
o
p
q
r
s
t
u
v
w
x
y
z

a

(plural); **my bedroom window** mein Schlafzimmerfenster.

bedside table noun Nachttisch der (PL die Nachttische).

c

bedsit, bedsitter noun möbliertes Zimmer das (PL die möblierten Zimmer).

d

bedspread noun Tagesdecke die (PL die Tagesdecken).

f

bedtime noun Schlafenszeit die; **at bedtime** vor dem Schlafengehen.

g

bee noun Biene die (PL die Bienen).

h

beech noun Buche die (PL die Buchen).

i

beef noun Rindfleisch das; **we had roast beef** wir haben Rinderbraten gegessen.

j

beefburger noun Hamburger der (PL die Hamburger).

k

beer noun Bier das (PL die Biere); **two beers please** zwei Bier bitte; **beer can** die Bierdose.

l

beetle noun Käfer der (PL die Käfer).

m

beetroot noun Rote Bete die.

o

before preposition vor (+ DAT); **before Monday** vor Montag; **he left before me** er ist vor mir gegangen; **the day before the wedding** am Tag vor der Hochzeit; **2 the day before** am Tag zuvor; **the day before yesterday** vorgestern; **3** (already) schon einmal; **I've seen him before somewhere** ich habe ihn schon einmal irgendwo gesehen; **I had seen the film before** ich hatte den Film schon einmal gesehen.

before conjunction bevor; **I closed the windows before leaving** (or **before I left**) ich habe die Fenster zugemacht, bevor ich wegging;

before the train leaves bevor der Zug abfährt; **oh, before I forget ...** oh, bevor ich es vergesse ....

beforehand adverb (ahead of time) vorher; **phone beforehand** rufe vorher an.

beg verb **1** betteln; **to beg for money** um Geld betteln; **2** (ask) bitten◇; **he begged her not to say anything** er bat sie, nichts zu sagen; **3 I beg your pardon** entschuldigen Sie bitte.

begin verb anfangen◇ SEP, beginnen◇; **the meeting begins at ten** die Besprechung fängt um zehn an; **the words beginning with P** die Wörter, die mit P anfangen; **to begin to do something** anfangen, etwas zu tun; beginnen, etwas zu tun; **I'm beginning to understand why ...** ich beginne zu verstehen, warum ....

beginner noun Anfänger der (PL die Anfänger), Anfängerin die (PL die Anfängerinnen).

beginning noun Anfang der (PL die Anfänge); **at the beginning** am Anfang; **at the beginning of the holidays** am Anfang der Ferien.

behalf noun **on behalf of** im Namen von (+ DAT); **on behalf of Mr and Mrs Smith** im Namen von Herrn und Frau Smith.

behave verb **1** sich benehmen◇; **he behaved badly** er hat sich schlecht benommen; **2 to behave oneself** sich benehmen◇; **behave yourself!** benimm dich!

behaviour noun Benehmen das.

behind noun Hintern der (informal) (PL die Hintern).

behind *preposition, adverb*
1 hinter (+ DAT, *or* + ACC *when there is movement towards a place*); **behind the sofa** hinter dem Sofa; **behind them** hinter ihnen; **the car behind** das Auto hinter ihnen/uns; **2 to leave something behind** (*belongings*) etwas vergessen.
beige *adjective* beige.
Belgian *noun* Belgier *der* (PL die Belgier), Belgierin *die* (PL die Belgierinnen).
Belgian *adjective* belgisch; **he's Belgian** er ist Belgier.
Belgium *noun* Belgien *das*; **to Belgium** nach Belgien.
belief *noun* Glaube *der* (PL die Glauben); **his political beliefs** seine politische Überzeugung.
believe *verb* **1** glauben; **I believe so** ich glaube schon; **they believed what I said** sie glaubten, was ich sagte; **I don't believe you** das glaube ich dir nicht; **2 to believe in something** an etwas (ACC) glauben; **to believe in God** an Gott glauben.
bell *noun* **1** (*in a church*) Glocke *die* (PL die Glocken); **2** (*on a door*) Klingel *die* (PL die Klingeln); **to ring the bell** klingeln; **3** (*for a cat or toy*) Glöckchen *das* (PL die Glöckchen); ★ **that name rings a bell** der Name sagt mir etwas (*literally: says something to me*).
belong *verb* **1 to belong to** gehören (+ DAT); **that belongs to my mother** das gehört meiner Mutter; **2 to belong to a club** einem Klub angehören; **3** (*go*) gehören; **where does this vase belong?** wo gehört diese Vase hin?

belongings *plural noun* Sachen (*plural*); **all my belongings** alle meine Sachen.
below *preposition* unter (+ DAT, *or* + ACC *when there is movement towards a place*); **below the window** unter dem Fenster; **the flat below yours** die Wohnung unter dir.
below *adverb* **1** (*further down*) unten; **he called from below** er rief von unten herauf; **2 the flat below** die Wohnung darunter.
belt *noun* Gürtel *der* (PL die Gürtel).
bench *noun* Bank *die* (PL die Bänke).
bend *noun* **1** (*in a road*) Kurve *die* (PL die Kurven); **2** (*in a river*) Biegung *die* (PL die Biegungen).
bend *verb* **1** (*make a bend in*) biegen✧ (*a pipe or wire*) beugen (*your knee, arm, or head*); **2** (*curve*) eine Biegung machen; **3 to bend down** sich bücken.
beneath *preposition* unter (+ DAT).
benefit *noun* **1** Vorteil *der* (PL die Vorteile); **2 unemployment benefit** die Arbeitslosenunterstützung.
bent *adjective* verbogen.
beret *noun* Baskenmütze *die* (PL die Baskenmützen).
beside *preposition* (*next to*) neben (+ DAT, *or* + ACC *when there is movement towards a place*); **she was sitting beside me** sie saß neben mir; **she sat down beside me** sie hat sich neben mich gesetzt; ★ **that's beside the point** das hat nichts damit zu tun.
besides *adverb* (*anyway*) außerdem; **besides, it's too late** außerdem ist es zu spät; (*as well*)

a
b
c
d
e
f
g
h
i
j
k
l
m
n
o
p
q
r
s
t
u
v
w
x
y
z

four dogs, and six cats besides vier Hunde und außerdem sechs Katzen.

best *adjective* **1** bester/beste/ bestes; **she's my best friend** sie ist meine beste Freundin; **2 she's the best at tennis** im Tennis ist sie die Beste; **it's best to wait** das Beste ist zu warten.

best *adverb* am besten; **he plays best** er spielt am besten; **I like Munich best** München gefällt mir am besten; **best of all** am allerbesten; **I like grapes best** ich mag Weintrauben am liebsten; ★ **all the best!** alles Gute!; ★ **to make the best of it** das Beste daraus machen; ★ **to do your best** sein Bestes tun;; **I did my best to help her** ich habe mein Bestes getan, um ihr zu helfen.

best man *noun* Trauzeuge der (PL die Trauzeugen).

bet *noun* Wette die (PL die Wetten).

bet *verb* wetten; **to bet on a horse** auf ein Pferd wetten; **I bet you he'll forget** ich wette mit dir, dass er es vergisst.

better *adjective, adverb* **1** besser; **she's found a better flat** sie hat eine bessere Wohnung gefunden; **2 it works better than the other one** dieser geht besser als der andere; **even better** noch besser; **it's even better than before** das ist noch besser als vorher; **3** (*less ill*) I'm better es geht mir besser; **he's a bit better today** es geht ihm heute ein bisschen besser; **I feel better** ich fühle mich besser; **4 to get better** besser werden; **my**

German is getting better mein Deutsch wird besser; **5 so much the better** umso besser; **the sooner the better** je eher, desto besser.

better *adverb* **it's better to phone at once** es wäre besser, sofort anzurufen; **he'd better not go** er sollte besser nicht gehen; **I'd better go now** ich gehe jetzt besser.

better off *adjective* **1** (*richer*) besser gestellt; **they're better off than us** sie sind besser gestellt als wir; **2** (*more comfortable*) to be better off besser dran sein; **you'd be better off in bed** im Bett wärst du besser aufgehoben.

between *preposition* **1** zwischen (+ DAT, *or* + ACC *when there is movement towards a place*); **between London and Dover** zwischen London und Dover; **between Monday and Friday** zwischen Montag und Freitag; **2** (*sharing*) unter (+ DAT); **between ourselves** unter uns; **between the two of them** unter sich.

beyond *preposition* **1** (*in space*) jenseits (+ GEN); **beyond the border** jenseits der Grenze; **2** (*in time*) nach (+ DAT); **beyond midnight** nach Mitternacht; **3 it's beyond me!** das ist mir unverständlich.

Bible *noun* the Bible die Bibel.

bicycle *noun* Fahrrad das (PL Fahrräder); **she rides a bicycle** sie fährt Rad.

bicycle lane *noun* Fahrradweg der (PL die Fahrradwege).

big *adjective* groß; **a big house** ein großes Haus; **my big sister** meine große Schwester; **a big mistake** ein

großer Fehler; **it's too big for me** das ist mir zu groß.

big toe noun große Zehe die (PL die großen Zehen).

bike noun **1** (with pedals) Rad das (PL die Räder); **by bike** mit dem Rad; **2** (with motor) Motorrad das (PL die Motorräder).

bikini noun Bikini der (PL die Bikinis).

bilingual adjective zweisprachig.

bill noun Rechnung die (PL die Rechnungen); **can we have the bill, please?** die Rechnung bitte.

billiards noun Billard das; **to play billiards** Billard spielen.

billion noun Milliarde die (PL die Milliarden), Billion die (PL die Billionen); **two billion euros** zwei Milliarden Euro.

bin noun Mülleimer der (PL die Mülleimer).

binoculars plural noun Fernglas das (PL die Ferngläser).

biochemistry noun Biochemie die.

biology noun Biologie die.

bird noun Vogel der (PL die Vögel).

bird sanctuary noun Vogelschutzgebiet das (PL die Vogelschutzgebiete).

birdwatching noun Beobachten von Vögeln; **to go birdwatching** Vögel beobachten.

Biro noun Kugelschreiber der (PL die Kugelschreiber).

birth noun Geburt die (PL die Geburten).

birth certificate noun Geburtsurkunde die (PL die Geburtsurkunden).

birthday noun Geburtstag der (PL die Geburtstage); **happy birthday!** herzlichen Glückwunsch zum Geburtstag!

birthday party noun Geburtstagsfeier die (PL die Geburtstagsfeiern).

biscuit noun Keks der (PL die Kekse).

bishop noun **1** (churchman) Bischof der (PL die Bischöfe); **2** (in chess) Läufer der (PL die Läufer).

bit noun **1** (piece) Stückchen das (PL die Stückchen); **a bit of chocolate** ein Stückchen Schokolade; **2** (a small amount) **a bit of** ein bisschen; **a bit of sugar** ein bisschen Zucker; **3** (in a book, film, etc.) Teil der (PL die Teile); **this bit is brilliant** dieser Teil ist hervorragend; **4 a bit** ein bisschen; **a bit too early** ein bisschen zu früh; **wait a bit!** warte ein bisschen!; **5 he's a bit of a show-off** er ist ein ziemlicher Angeber; **6 bit by bit** nach und nach.

bite noun **1** (snack) Happen der (PL die Happen); **we'll just have a bite before we go** wir essen noch einen kleinen Happen, bevor wir gehen; **2** (from an insect) Stich der (PL die Stiche); **mosquito bite** der Mückenstich; **3** (from a dog) Biss der (PL die Bisse).

bite verb **1** (person or dog) beißen◇; **2** (insect) stechen◇.

bitter adjective (taste) bitter.

black adjective **1** schwarz; **my black jacket** meine schwarze Jacke; **2 a black man** ein Schwarzer; **a black woman** eine Schwarze.

a b c d e f g h i j k l m n o p q r s t u v w x y z

a
b
c
d
e
f
g
h
i
j
k
l
m
n
o
p
q
r
s
t
u
v
w
x
y
z

blackberry noun Brombeere die (PL die Brombeeren).

blackbird noun Amsel die (PL die Amseln).

blackboard noun Tafel die (PL die Tafeln).

blackcurrant noun Schwarze Johannisbeere die (PL die Schwarzen Johannisbeeren).

black pudding noun Blutwurst die (PL die Blutwürste).

blade noun Klinge die (PL die Klingen).

blame noun Schuld die; **to take the blame for something** die Schuld für etwas (ACC) auf sich (ACC) nehmen; **to put the blame on somebody** die Schuld auf jemanden schieben.

blame verb **to blame somebody for something** jemandem die Schuld an etwas (DAT) geben; **they blamed him for the accident** sie haben ihm die Schuld an dem Unfall gegeben; **she is to blame for it** sie ist daran schuld; **I blame the parents** ich gebe den Eltern Schuld; **I don't blame you** ich kann es dir nicht verdenken.

blank noun Lücke die (PL die Lücken).

blank adjective **1** (page) leer (tape or disk) unbespielt; **2 blank cheque** der Blankoscheck.

blanket noun Decke die (PL die Decken).

blaze noun Feuer das (PL die Feuer).

blaze verb brennen✧.

bleach noun Bleichmittel das (PL die Bleichmittel).

bleed verb bluten; **my nose is bleeding** meine Nase blutet.

blend verb mischen.

blender noun Mixer der (PL die Mixer).

bless verb segnen; **bless you!** (after a sneeze) Gesundheit!

blind noun (in a window) Rollo das (PL die Rollos).

blind adjective blind.

blink verb (mit den Augen) blinzeln.

blister noun Blase die (PL die Blasen).

blizzard noun Schneesturm der (PL die Schneestürme).

block noun (a building or buildings) Block der (PL die Blocks); **block of flats** der Wohnblock; **office block** das Bürohaus; **to drive round the block** um den Block fahren.

block verb **1** sperren (an exit or a road); **2 the sink's blocked** das Spülbecken ist verstopft.

blonde adjective blond.

blood noun Blut das.

blood test noun Blutprobe die (PL die Blutproben).

blouse noun Bluse die (PL die Blusen).

blow noun Schlag der (PL die Schläge).

blow verb **1** (a person) blasen✧; **2** (the wind) wehen; **3 the bomb blew the bridge to pieces** die Bombe hat die Brücke in die Luft gesprengt; **4 to blow your nose** sich (DAT) die Nase putzen.

● **to blow something out** etwas ausblasen✧ SEP.

• **to blow up** (*explode*) explodieren (PERF *sein*).
• **to blow something up** (*a tyre or balloon*) etwas aufblasen✧ SEP, (*with explosives*) etwas sprengen.

blow-dry *noun* Föhnen *das*; **a cut and blow-dry** Schneiden und Föhnen *das*.

blue *adjective* blau; **blue eyes** blaue Augen.

blunder *noun* Fehler *der* (PL die Fehler).

blunt *adjective* **1** (*a knife, pencil, or scissors*) stumpf; **2** (*a person or question*) direkt.

blurred *adjective* **1** (*not distinct*) verschwommen; **2** (*photo*) unscharf.

blush *verb* erröten (PERF *sein*).

board *noun* **1** (*plank, notice board, game*) Brett *das* (PL die Bretter); **chess board** das Schachbrett; **2** (*blackboard*) Tafel *die* (PL die Tafeln); **3** (*accommodation in a hotel*) **full board** die Vollpension; **half board** die Halbpension; **board and lodging** Unterkunft und Verpflegung.

boarder *noun* (*in a school*) Internatsschüler *der* (PL die Internatsschüler), Internatsschülerin *die* (PL die Internatsschülerinnen).

board game *noun* Brettspiel *das* (PL die Brettspiele).

boarding *noun* (*on a plane, train*) Einsteigen *das*.

boarding card *noun* Bordkarte *die* (PL die Bordkarten).

boarding school *noun* Internat *das* (PL die Internate).

boast *verb* prahlen; **he was boasting about his new bike** er prahlte mit seinem neuen Rad.

boat *noun* **1** Boot *das* (PL die Boote); **rowing boat** das Ruderboot; **2** (*larger boat*) Schiff *das* (PL die Schiffe); **to go by boat** mit dem Schiff fahren.

body *noun* **1** Körper *der* (PL die Körper); **2** (*corpse*) Leiche *die* (PL die Leichen).

bodybuilding *noun* Bodybuilding *das*.

bodyguard *noun* Leibwächter *der* (PL die Leibwächter).

body odour *noun* Körpergeruch *der*.

boil *noun* **1 to bring the water to the boil** das Wasser zum Kochen bringen; **2** (*swelling*) Furunkel *der* (PL die Furunkel).

boil *verb* **1** kochen; **the water's boiling** das Wasser kocht; **to boil vegetables** Gemüse kochen; **2** (*put the kettle on*) **to boil some water** Wasser aufsetzen SEP.
• **to boil over** überkochen SEP (PERF *sein*).

boiled egg *noun* gekochte Ei *das* (PL die gekochten Eier).

boiled potato *noun* Salzkartoffel *die* (PL die Salzkartoffeln).

boiler *noun* (*for central heating*) Heizkessel *der* (PL die Heizkessel).

boiling *adjective* **1** (*water*) kochend; **2 it's boiling hot today** heute ist es wahnsinnig heiß.

bolt *noun* (*on a door*) Riegel *der* (PL die Riegel).

bolt verb **1** (lock) verriegeln;
2 (gobble down) runterschlingen◇
SEP (informal).

bomb noun Bombe die (PL die
Bomben).

bomb verb bombardieren.

bombing noun **1** (in war)
Bombardierung die (PL die
Bombardierungen); **2** (a terrorist
attack) Bombenattentat das (PL die
Bombenattentate).

bone noun **1** Knochen der (PL die
Knochen); **2** (of a fish) Gräte die (PL
die Gräten).

bonfire noun Feuer das (PL die
Feuer).

bonnet noun **1** (of a car)
Kühlerhaube die (PL die
Kühlerhauben); **2** (clothing) Haube
die (PL die Hauben).

boo verb ausbuhen SEP; **the crowd
booed the referee** die Menge
buhte den Schiedsrichter aus.

book noun **1** Buch das (PL die
Bücher); **a book about dinosaurs**
ein Buch über Dinosaurier; **my
biology book** mein Biologiebuch;
2 (of stamps, tickets) Heft das (PL die
Hefte); **3 exercise book** das Heft;
cheque book das Scheckbuch.

book verb **1** buchen (holiday,
flight); **2** bestellen (a table, theatre,
or cinema tickets); **I booked a table
for 8 p.m.** ich habe einen Tisch für
zwanzig Uhr bestellt.

bookcase noun Bücherregal das
(PL die Bücherregale).

booking noun (for a flight or a
holiday, for example) Buchung die
(PL die Buchungen).

booking office noun **1** (at a train
station) Fahrkartenschalter der (PL
die Fahrkartenschalter); **2** (in a
theatre or cinema) Kasse die (PL die
Kassen).

booklet noun Broschüre die (PL die
Broschüren).

bookshelf noun Bücherregal das
(PL die Bücherregale).

bookshop noun Buchhandlung
die (PL die Buchhandlungen).

boot noun **1** Stiefel der (PL die
Stiefel); **2** (for football, walking,
climbing, or skiing) Schuh der (PL die
Schuhe); **football boots**
Fußballschuhe; **3** (of a car)
Kofferraum der (PL die
Kofferräume).

border noun (between countries)
Grenze die (PL die Grenzen); **at the
border** an der Grenze.

bore noun **1** (a boring person)
langweiliger Mensch der (PL die
langweiligen Menschen); **2** (a
nuisance) **what a bore!** wie
ärgerlich!

bored adjective **to be bored** sich
langweilen; **I'm bored** ich
langweile mich.

boring adjective langweilig.

born adjective geboren; **to be born**
geboren werden; **she was born in
Germany** sie ist in Deutschland
geboren.

borrow verb sich (DAT) borgen; **can
I borrow your bike?** kann ich mir
dein Rad borgen?; **to borrow
something from somebody** sich
etwas von jemandem borgen; **I
borrowed some money from Dad**
ich habe mir Geld von Vati geborgt.

boss noun Chef der (PL die Chefs), Chefin die (PL die Chefinnen).

bossy adjective herrisch.

both pronoun beide; **they both came** sie kamen beide; **both my sisters were there** meine beiden Schwestern waren da; **both of us** wir beide; **they are both sold** beide sind verkauft.

both adverb **both at home and at school** sowohl zu Hause als auch in der Schule; **both in summer and in winter** sowohl im Sommer als auch im Winter.

bother noun 1 (minor trouble) Ärger der; **I've had a lot of bother with the car** ich hatte viel Ärger mit dem Auto; 2 **if it isn't too much bother** wenn es nicht zu viel Mühe macht; **it's no bother** das ist kein Problem; **the children were no bother** die Kinder waren kein Problem; **without any bother** ohne irgendwelche Schwierigkeiten.

bother verb 1 (disturb) stören; **I'm sorry to bother you** es tut mir Leid, dich zu stören; 2 (worry) stören; **what's bothering you?** was stört dich?; **it doesn't bother me at all** das stört mich überhaupt nicht; 3 (take trouble) **don't bother to write** du brauchst nicht zu schreiben; **she didn't even bother to wait** sie hat nicht einmal gewartet; **don't bother!** lass es! (informal) **I can't be bothered** ich habe keine Lust.

bottle noun Flasche die (PL die Flaschen).

bottle bank noun Altglascontainer der (PL die Altglascontainer).

bottle opener noun Flaschenöffner der (PL die Flaschenöffner).

bottom noun 1 (of a bag, bottle, hole, or stretch of water) Boden der (PL die Böden); **at the bottom of the lake** am Boden des Sees; **at the bottom of the well** auf dem Grund des Brunnens; 2 (of a hill or building) Fuß der (PL die Füße); **at the bottom of the tower** am Fuß des Turms; 3 (of a garden, street, list) Ende das (PL die Enden); **at the bottom of the street** am Ende der Straße; 4 **at the bottom of the page** unten auf der Seite; 5 (buttocks) Hintern der (informal) (PL die Hintern).

bottom adjective 1 unterster/unterste/unterstes; **the bottom shelf** das unterste Regalbrett; 2 **the bottom flat** die Wohnung im Erdgeschoss.

bounce verb (jump) springen ◇ (PERF sein).

bouncer noun Rausschmeißer der (PL die Rausschmeißer).

bound adjective (certain) **he's bound to be late** er kommt ganz bestimmt zu spät; **that was bound to happen** das musste ja kommen.

boundary noun Grenze die (PL die Grenzen).

bow noun 1 (in a shoelace or ribbon) Schleife die (PL die Schleifen); 2 (for a violin or with arrows) Bogen der (PL die Bogen); **with bow and arrow** mit Pfeil und Bogen.

bowl noun **1** (large, for salad, mixing, or washing up) Schüssel die (PL die Schüsseln); **2** (smaller) Schale die (PL die Schalen).

bowler noun (in cricket) Werfer der (PL die Werfer), Werferin die (PL die Werferinnen).

bowling noun (tenpin) Bowling das; **to go bowling** kegeln gehen.

bow tie noun Fliege die (PL die Fliegen).

box noun **1** Schachtel die (PL die Schachteln); **a box of chocolates** eine Schachtel Pralinen; **2 cardboard box** der Karton; **3** (on a form) Kästchen das (PL die Kästchen).

boxer noun Boxer der (PL die Boxer).

boxing noun **1** Boxen das; **2 boxing match** der Boxkampf.

Boxing Day noun zweite Weihnachtsfeiertag der.

box office noun Kasse die (PL die Kassen).

boy noun Junge der (PL die Jungen); **a little boy** ein kleiner Junge.

boyfriend noun Freund der (PL die Freunde).

bra noun BH der (PL die BHs).

brace noun (for teeth) Spange die (PL die Spangen).

bracelet noun Armband das (PL die Armbänder).

bracket noun Klammer die (PL die Klammern); **in brackets** in Klammern.

brain noun Gehirn das (PL die Gehirne).

brainwave noun Geistesblitz der (PL die Geistesblitze).

brake noun Bremse die (PL die Bremsen).

brake verb bremsen.

branch noun **1** (of a tree) Ast der (PL die Äste); **2** (of a shop) Filiale die (PL die Filialen); **3** (of a bank) Zweigstelle die (PL die Zweigstellen).

brand noun Marke die (PL die Marken).

brand new adjective nagelneu.

brandy noun Weinbrand der (PL die Weinbrände).

brass noun **1** (metal) Messing das; **2** (in an orchestra) **the brass** die Blechbläser.

brass band noun Blaskapelle die (PL die Blaskapellen).

brave adjective tapfer.

bravery noun Tapferkeit die.

Brazilian adjective brasilianisch.

Brazilian noun Brasilianer der (PL die Brasilianer), Brasilianerin die (PL die Brasilianerinnen).

bread noun Brot das (PL die Brote); **a slice of bread** eine Scheibe Brot; **a piece of bread and butter** ein Butterbrot.

break noun **1** (a short rest or at school) Pause die (PL die Pausen); **ten minutes' break** eine Pause von zehn Minuten; **to take a break** Pause machen; **at break** in der Pause; **2 the Christmas break** die Weihnachtsferien (plural).

break verb **1** zerbrechen✧, kaputtmachen SEP (informal); **he broke a glass** er hat ein Glas zerbrochen; **don't break the doll** mach die Puppe nicht kaputt; **2** (get damaged) zerbrechen✧ (PERF sein), kaputtgehen✧ SEP (informal) PERF sein); **the glass broke** das Glas zerbrach; **the eggs broke** die Eier sind kaputtgegangen; **3 to break your arm** sich (DAT) den Arm brechen; **4** brechen ✧ (*rules, promise*); **to break one's promise** sein Versprechen brechen; **5 to break the record** den Rekord brechen ✧; **6 to break the news that** ... melden, dass ....

● **to break down 1** (*car*) eine Panne haben; **the car broke down** das Auto hatte eine Panne; **2** (*talks, negotiations*) scheitern (PERF *sein*).

● **to break in** einbrechen ✧ (PERF *sein*).

● **to break up 1** (*couple*) sich trennen; **2** (*crowd*) sich auflösen SEP; **3 we break up on Thursday** die Ferien fangen Donnerstag an.

breakdown *noun* **1** (*of a vehicle*) Panne die (PL die Pannen); **we had a breakdown on the motorway** wir hatten eine Panne auf der Autobahn; **2** (*in talks or negotiations*) Scheitern das; **3** (*a nervous collapse*) Zusammenbruch der (PL die Zusammenbrüche); **to have a nervous breakdown** einen Nervenzusammenbruch haben.

breakdown truck *noun* Abschleppwagen der (PL die Abschleppwagen).

breakfast *noun* Frühstück das (PL die Frühstücke); **we have breakfast at eight** wir frühstücken um acht Uhr.

break-in *noun* Einbruch der (PL die Einbrüche).

breast *noun* Brust die (PL die Brüste).

breaststroke *noun* Brustschwimmen das.

breath *noun* Atem der; **out of breath** außer Atem; **to hold your breath** den Atem anhalten; **to get your breath back** wieder zu Atem kommen; **to take a deep breath** tief einatmen.

breathe *verb* atmen.

breathing *noun* Atmen das

breed *noun* (*of animal*) Rasse die (PL die Rassen).

breeze *noun* Brise die (PL die Brisen).

brew *verb* **1** brauen (*beer*); **2** aufbrühen SEP (*tea*); **the tea's brewing** der Tee zieht noch.

brewery *noun* Brauerei die (PL die Brauereien).

brick *noun* Ziegel der (PL die Ziegel); **a brick wall** eine Ziegelmauer.

bride *noun* Braut die (PL die Bräute); **the bride and groom** das Brautpaar.

bridegroom *noun* Bräutigam der (PL die Bräutigame).

bridesmaid *noun* Brautjungfer die (PL die Brautjungfern).

bridge *noun* **1** (*over a river*) Brücke die (PL die Brücken); **2** (*card game*) Bridge das.

bridle *noun* Zaumzeug das (PL die Zaumzeuge).

brief *adjective* kurz.

briefcase *noun* Aktentasche die (PL die Aktentaschen).

briefly *adverb* kurz.

briefs *plural noun* Slip der (PL die Slips).

bright *adjective* **1** (*colour*) leuchtend; **bright green socks** leuchtend grüne Socken; **2** (*eyes, sunshine*) strahlend; **3** (*light*) hell; **4** (*clever*) intelligent; **she's not**

a
b
c
d
e
f
g
h
i
j
k
l
m
n
o
p
q
r
s
t
u
v
w
x
y
z

very bright sie ist nicht sehr intelligent; ★ **to look on the bright side** die Sache positiv sehen (*literally: to see things positively*).

brilliant *adjective* **1** (*very clever*) glänzend; **he's a brilliant surgeon** er ist ein glänzender Chirurg; **2** (*wonderful*) toll; **the party was brilliant!** die Party war toll!

bring *verb* **1** mitbringen✧ SEP; **he brought a present** er brachte ein Geschenk mit; **bring your camera** bring deinen Fotoapparat mit; **2** (*to a place*) bringen✧; **she's bringing the children home** sie bringt die Kinder nach Hause.

● **to bring somebody up** jemanden großziehen✧ SEP; **he was brought up by his aunt** er wurde von seiner Tante großgezogen.

Britain *noun* Großbritannien *das*; **to Britain** nach Großbritannien.

British *plural noun* **the British** die Briten.

British *adjective* **1** britisch; **the British Isles** die Britischen Inseln; **2 he's British** er ist Brite; **she's British** sie ist Britin.

broad *adjective* **1** (*wide*) breit; **2** (*extensive*) weit.

broad bean *noun* dicke Bohne *die* (PL die dicken Bohnen).

broadcast *noun* Sendung *die* (PL die Sendungen).

broadcast *verb* senden.

broccoli *noun* Brokkoli *der* (PL die Brokkolis).

brochure *noun* Broschüre *die* (PL die Broschüren).

broke *adjective* **to be broke** pleite sein (*informal*).

broken *adjective* zerbrochen, kaputt (*informal*); **the window's broken** das Fenster ist kaputt; **to have a broken leg** ein gebrochenes Bein haben.

bronchitis *noun* Bronchitis die.

brooch *noun* Brosche die (PL die Broschen).

broom *noun* Besen der (PL die Besen).

brother *noun* Bruder der (PL die Brüder); **my mother's brother** der Bruder meiner Mutter.

brother-in-law *noun* Schwager der (PL die Schwäger).

brown *adjective* braun; **my brown shoes** meine braunen Schuhe; **light brown** hellbraun; **dark brown** dunkelbraun; **to go brown** (*suntanned*) braun werden.

brown bread *noun* Mischbrot das (PL die Mischbrote).

bruise *noun* **1** (*on a person*) blaue Fleck der (PL die blauen Flecken); **2** (*on fruit*) Druckstelle die (PL die Druckstellen).

brush *noun* **1** (*for your hair, clothes, nails, or shoes*) Bürste die (PL die Bürsten); **my hair brush** meine Haarbürste; **2** (*for sweeping*) Besen der (PL die Besen); **3** (*for paint*) Pinsel der (PL die Pinsel).

brush *verb* **1** bürsten; **to brush your hair** sich (DAT) die Haare bürsten; **I brushed my hair** ich habe mir die Haare gebürstet; **2 to brush your teeth** sich (DAT) die Zähne putzen.

Brussels *noun* Brüssel das.

Brussels sprout *noun* Rosenkohl der; **he likes Brussels sprouts** er mag Rosenkohl.

bubble noun Blase die (PL die Blasen).

bubble bath noun Badeschaum der.

bucket noun Eimer der (PL die Eimer).

buckle noun Schnalle die (PL die Schnallen).

Buddhism noun Buddhismus der.

Buddhist noun Buddhist der (PL die Buddhisten), Buddhistin die (PL die Buddhistinnen).

budget noun Budget das (PL die Budgets).

budgie noun Wellensittich der (PL die Wellensittiche).

buffet noun Büffet das (PL die Büffets).

buffet car noun Speisewagen der (PL die Speisewagen).

bug noun 1 (insect) Wanze die (PL die Wanzen); 2 (germ) Bazillus der (PL die Bazillen); a stomach bug eine Magengrippe; 3 a computer bug ein Programmierfehler.

build verb bauen.

builder noun Bauarbeiter der (PL die Bauarbeiter).

building noun Gebäude das (PL die Gebäude).

building site noun Baustelle die (PL die Baustellen).

building society noun Bausparkasse die (PL die Bausparkassen).

built-up adjective 1 bebaut; 2 built-up area das Wohngebiet.

bulb noun 1 (lightbulb) Glühbirne die (PL die Glühbirnen); 2 (flower bulb) Blumenzwiebel die (PL die Zwiebeln).

bull noun Bulle der (PL die Bullen).

bulldozer noun Planierraupe die (PL die Planierraupen).

bullet noun Kugel die (PL die Kugeln).

bulletin noun 1 (written) Bulletin das (PL die Bulletins); 2 (on TV, radio) news bulletin die Kurzmeldung.

bully noun 1 (in school) Rabauke der (PL die Rabauken); 2 (adult) Tyrann der (PL die Tyrannen).

bully verb schikanieren.

bum noun Hintern der (informal) (PL die Hintern).

bump noun 1 (on a surface) Unebenheit die (PL die Unebenheiten); there are lots of bumps in the road die Straße ist sehr uneben; 2 (swelling) Beule die (PL die Beulen); a bump on the head eine Beule am Kopf; 3 (jolt) Stoß der (PL die Stöße); 4 (noise) Bums der (PL die Bumse).

bump verb 1 (bang) stoßen✧; I bumped my head ich habe mir den Kopf gestoßen; to bump into something gegen etwas (ACC) stoßen; 2 to bump into somebody (meet by chance) jemanden zufällig treffen.

bumper noun Stoßstange die (PL die Stoßstangen).

bumpy adjective holperig.

bun noun 1 (for a burger) Brötchen das (PL die Brötchen), Semmel die (PL die Semmeln); 2 (sweet) süße Brötchen das (PL die süßen Brötchen).

bunch noun 1 (of flowers) Strauß der (PL die Sträuße); 2 (of carrots, radishes) Bund das (PL die Bunde); a

bunch of keys ein Schlüsselbund; **3 a bunch of grapes** eine ganze Weintraube.

bundle noun Bündel das (PL die Bündel).

bungalow noun Bungalow der (PL die Bungalows).

bunk noun 1 (on a boat) Koje die (PL die Kojen); 2 (on a train) Bett das (PL die Betten).

bunk bed noun Etagenbett das (PL die Etagenbetten).

burger noun Hamburger der (PL die Hamburger).

burglar noun Einbrecher der (PL die Einbrecher), Einbrecherin die (PL die Einbrecherinnen).

burglar alarm noun Alarmanlage die (PL die Alarmanlagen).

burglary noun Einbruch der (PL die Einbrüche).

burn noun 1 (on the skin) Verbrennung die (PL die Verbrennungen); 2 (on fabric, object) Brandstelle die (PL die Brandstellen).

burn verb 1 verbrennen✧; **she burnt his letters** sie hat seine Briefe verbrannt; 2 (fire, candle) brennen✧; 3 (injure) verbrennen✧; **to burn yourself** sich verbrennen; **you'll burn your fingers!** du verbrennst dir die Finger!; 4 (cake, meat, etc.) anbrennen✧ SEP; **Mum's burnt the cake** Mutti hat den Kuchen anbrennen lassen.

burnt adjective 1 (papers, rubbish) verbrannt; 2 (cake, meat, etc.) angebrannt.

burst verb 1 platzen lassen (a balloon); **the tyre has burst** der Reifen ist geplatzt; 2 **to burst out laughing** in Lachen ausbrechen✧ SEP (PERF sein); **to burst into tears** in Tränen ausbrechen✧ SEP (PERF sein); 3 **to burst into flames** in Flammen aufgehen✧ SEP (PERF sein).

bury verb 1 begraben✧ (a dead person); 2 vergraben✧ (treasure or a bone).

bus noun Bus der (PL die Busse); **on the bus** im Bus; **by bus** mit dem Bus.

bus driver noun Busfahrer der (PL die Busfahrer), Busfahrerin die (PL die Busfahrerinnen).

bush noun Busch der (PL die Büsche).

business noun 1 (commercial dealings) Geschäfte (plural); **business is bad** die Geschäfte gehen schlecht; **he's in Leeds on business** er ist geschäftlich in Leeds; 2 (a line of business or profession) Branche die (PL die Branchen); **he's in the insurance business** er ist in der Versicherungsbranche; 3 (firm or company) Betrieb der (PL die Betriebe); **small businesses** kleine Betriebe; 4 (personal concern) Angelegenheit die (PL die Angelegenheiten); **mind your own business!** kümmere dich um deine eigenen Angelegenheiten!

businessman noun Geschäftsmann der (PL die Geschäftsleute).

business trip noun Geschäftsreise die (PL die Geschäftsreisen).

businesswoman noun Geschäftsfrau die (PL die Geschäftsfrauen).

bus pass noun Zeitkarte die (PL die Zeitkarten).

bus route noun Buslinie die (PL die Buslinien).

bus shelter noun Wartehäuschen das (PL die Wartehäuschen).

bus station noun Busbahnhof der (PL die Busbahnhöfe).

bus stop noun Bushaltestelle die (PL die Bushaltestellen).

bus ticket noun Busfahrkarte die (PL die Busfahrkarten).

busy adjective 1 beschäftigt; **he's busy** er ist beschäftigt; **she was busy packing** sie war mit Packen beschäftigt; 2 **to have a busy day** viel zu tun haben; 3 **the shops were busy** in den Läden war sehr viel los; 4 (phone) besetzt.

but conjunction 1 aber; **small but strong** klein aber stark, 2 (after a negative statement) sondern; **not Thursday but Friday** nicht Donnerstag, sondern Freitag; **not only ... but also** nicht nur ... sondern auch.

but preposition 1 außer (+ DAT); **everyone but Winston** alle außer Winston; **anything but that!** nur das nicht!; 2 **the last but one** der/die/das Vorletzte.

butcher noun 1 Fleischer der (PL die Fleischer), Fleischerin die (PL die Fleischerinnen), Metzger der (PL die Metzger), Metzgerin die (PL die Metzgerinnen); **he's a butcher** er

ist Fleischer, er ist Metzger; 2 **the butcher's** die Fleischerei, die Metzgerei.

butter noun Butter die.

butter verb buttern.

butterfly noun Schmetterling der (PL die Schmetterlinge).

button noun Knopf der (PL die Knöpfe); **the record button** die Aufnahmetaste.

buttonhole noun Knopfloch das (PL die Knopflöcher).

buy noun Kauf der (PL die Käufe); **a bad buy** ein schlechter Kauf.

buy verb kaufen; **I bought the tickets** ich habe die Karten gekauft; **to buy something for somebody** jemandem etwas kaufen; **Sarah bought him a sweater** Sarah hat ihm einen Pullover gekauft.

buzz verb (a fly or bee) summen.

buzzer noun Summer der (PL die Summer).

by preposition 1 von (+ DAT); **I was bitten by a dog** ich bin von einem Hund gebissen worden; **by Mozart** von Mozart; 2 **by mistake** versehentlich; 3 (travel) mit (+ DAT); **to come by bus** mit dem Bus kommen; **to go by train** mit dem Zug fahren; **by bike** mit dem Rad; 4 (near) an (+ DAT); **by the sea** am Meer; **the stop by the school** die Haltestelle an der Schule; 5 (before) bis; **it'll be ready by Monday** es wird bis Montag fertig sein; **I'll be back by four** ich bin bis vier Uhr zurück; 6 **by now** inzwischen; 7 **by yourself** ganz allein; **I was by myself in the house** ich war ganz

a
b
c
d
e
f
g
h
i
j
k
l
m
n
o
p
q
r
s
t
u
v
w
x
y
z

a
b
c

allein im Haus; **she did it by herself** sie hat es ganz allein gemacht; **8 by the way** übrigens; **9 to go by** vorbeigehen ◇ SEP (PERF sein).

d
bye *exclamation* tschüs! (*informal*).

e
bypass *noun* Umgehungsstraße die (PL die Umgehungsstraßen).

f

g
h

Cc

i
j
k
l

cab *noun* 1 Taxi das (PL die Taxis); **to call a cab** ein Taxi rufen; 2 (*on a lorry*) Führerhaus das (PL die Führerhäuser).

cabbage *noun* Kohl der.

cable *noun* Kabel das (PL die Kabel).

café *noun* Café das (PL die Cafés).

m
cage *noun* Käfig der (PL die Käfige).

n
cagoule *noun* Anorak der (PL die Anoraks).

o
p

cake *noun* Kuchen der (PL die Kuchen); **would you like a piece of cake?** möchtest du ein Stück Kuchen?

q
calculate *verb* berechnen.

r
calculation *noun* Rechnung die (PL die Rechnungen).

s
calculator *noun* Taschenrechner der (PL die Taschenrechner).

t
calendar *noun* Kalender der (PL die Kalender).

u
calf *noun* 1 (*animal*) Kalb das (PL die Kälber); 2 (*of your leg*) Wade die (PL die Waden).

v
w
x

call *noun* (*telephone*) Anruf der (PL die Anrufe); **I had several calls this morning** ich erhielt heute Morgen mehrere Anrufe; **thank**

y
z

you for your call danke für deinen Anruf; **a phone call** ein Telefonanruf.

call *verb* 1 rufen ◇; **to call a taxi** ein Taxi rufen; **to call the doctor** einen Arzt rufen; **they called the police** sie riefen die Polizei; 2 (*phone*) anrufen ◇ SEP; **call me later** ruf mich später an; **thank you for calling** danke für deinen Anruf; **I'll call you back later** ich rufe dich später zurück; 3 nennen ◇; **they've called the baby Julie** sie haben das Baby Julie genannt; 4 **to be called** heißen ◇; **her brother is called Dan** ihr Bruder heißt Dan; **what's he called?** wie heißt er?

call box *noun* Telefonzelle die (PL die Telefonzellen).

calm *adjective* ruhig.

calm *verb* beruhigen.

● **to calm down** sich beruhigen; **he's calmed down a bit** er hat sich etwas beruhigt.

● **to calm somebody down** jemanden beruhigen; **I tried to calm her down** ich habe versucht, sie zu beruhigen.

calmly *adverb* ruhig.

calorie *noun* Kalorie die (PL die Kalorien).

camcorder *noun* Camcorder der (PL die Camcorder).

camel *noun* Kamel das (PL die Kamele).

camera *noun* 1 Fotoapparat der (PL die Fotoapparate); 2 (*film or video camera*) Kamera die (PL die Kameras).

camp *noun* Lager das (PL die Lager).

camp *verb* campen, zelten.

campaign *noun* Kampagne *die* (PL die Kampagnen).

camper *noun* **1** (*person*) Camper *der* (PL die Camper), Camperin *die* (PL die Camperinnen); **2** (*vehicle*) Campingbus *der* (PL die Campingbusse).

camper van *noun* Wohnmobil *das* (PL die Wohnmobile).

camping *noun* Camping *das*; **to go camping** zelten; **we're going camping in Bavaria this summer** diesen Sommer zelten wir in Bayern.

campsite *noun* Campingplatz *der* (PL die Campingplätze).

can[1] *noun* **1** Dose *die* (PL die Dosen); **a can of tomatoes** eine Dose Tomaten; **2** (*for petrol or oil*) Kanister *der* (PL die Kanister).

can[2] *verb* **1** können◇; **I can't be there before ten** ich kann vor zehn Uhr nicht da sein; **can you open the door, please?** kannst du die Tür bitte aufmachen?; **can I help you?** kann ich Ihnen helfen?; **they couldn't come** sie konnten nicht kommen; **you could have told me** das hättest du mir wirklich sagen können; **I can't see him** ich kann ihn nicht sehen; **I can't remember it** ich kann mich nicht daran erinnern; **she can't drive** sich kann nicht Auto fahren; **2** (*be allowed*) dürfen◇; **you can't smoke here** Sie dürfen hier nicht rauchen.

Canada *noun* Kanada *das*; **to Canada** nach Kanada.

Canadian *noun* Kanadier *der* (PL die Kanadier), Kanadierin *die* (PL die Kanadierinnen).

Canadian *adjective* kanadisch; **he is Canadian** er ist Kanadier.

canal *noun* Kanal *der* (PL die Kanäle).

cancel *verb* absagen SEP; **the concert's been cancelled** das Konzert ist abgesagt worden.

cancer *noun* Krebs *der*; **to have lung cancer** Lungenkrebs haben.

Cancer *noun* Krebs *der* (PL die Krebse); **I'm Cancer** ich bin Krebs.

candidate *noun* Kandidat *der* (PL die Kandidaten), Kandidatin *die* (PL die Kandidatinnen).

candle *noun* Kerze *die* (PL die Kerzen).

candlestick *noun* Kerzenständer *der* (PL die Kerzenständer).

canned *adjective* in Dosen; **canned tomatoes** Tomaten in Dosen.

canoe *noun* Kanu *das* (PL die Kanus).

canoeing *noun* **to go canoeing** Kanu fahren◇ (PERF *sein*); **I like canoeing** ich fahre gerne Kanu.

can-opener *noun* Dosenöffner *der* (PL die Dosenöffner).

canteen *noun* Kantine *die* (PL die Kantinen).

canvas *noun* **1** (*of a tent or bag*) Segeltuch *das*; **2** (*for painting on*) Leinwand *die*.

cap *noun* **1** (*hat*) Kappe *die* (PL die Kappen); **baseball cap** die Baseballkappe; **2** (*on a bottle or tube*) Verschluss *der* (PL die Verschlüsse).

capable *adjective* fähig.

capital noun 1 (city) Hauptstadt die (PL die Hauptstädte); **Berlin is the capital of Germany** Berlin ist die Hauptstadt von Deutschland; 2 (letter) Großbuchstabe der (PL die Großbuchstaben); **in capitals** mit Großbuchstaben.

capitalism noun Kapitalismus der.

Capricorn noun Steinbock der (PL die Steinböcke); **Linda's Capricorn** Linda ist Steinbock.

captain noun Kapitän der (PL die Kapitäne).

capture verb festnehmen ✧ SEP.

car noun Auto das (PL die Autos); **to park the car** das Auto einparken; **we're going by car** wir fahren mit dem Auto; **car crash** der Autounfall.

caramel noun Karamell der (PL die Karamells).

caravan noun Wohnwagen der (PL die Wohnwagen).

card noun Karte die (PL die Karten); **card game** das Kartenspiel; **to have a game of cards** Karten spielen.

cardboard noun Pappe die.

cardigan noun Strickjacke die (PL die Strickjacken).

cardphone noun Kartentelefon das (PL die Kartentelefone).

care noun 1 Vorsicht die; **to take care crossing the road** beim Überqueren der Straße vorsichtig sein; **take care!** (be careful) sei vorsichtig!, (when saying goodbye) mach's gut!; 2 **to take care to do something** darauf achten, dass man etwas tut; **to take care of**

somebody auf jemanden aufpassen.

care verb 1 **to care about something** sich für etwas (ACC) interessieren; **she cares about the environment** sie kümmert sich um die Umwelt; **liegt ihr am Herzen**; 2 **she doesn't care** es ist ihr egal; **I couldn't care less!** das ist mir völlig egal!

career noun Karriere die (PL die Karrieren).

careful adjective vorsichtig; **a careful driver** ein vorsichtiger Fahrer, eine vorsichtige Fahrerin; **be careful!** sei vorsichtig!

carefully adverb 1 sorgfältig; **to read the instructions carefully** die Anweisungen sorgfältig lesen; 2 vorsichtig; **she put the vase down carefully** sie stellte die Vase vorsichtig hin; **drive carefully!** fahr vorsichtig!; 3 **listen carefully!** hören Sie gut zu!

careless adjective 1 he's very careless er ist sehr nachlässig; **this is careless work** das ist eine schlampige Arbeit; 2 **a careless mistake** ein Flüchtigkeitsfehler; 3 **a careless driver** ein leichtsinniger Fahrer.

car ferry noun Autofähre die (PL die Autofähren).

car hire noun Autovermietung die.

Caribbean noun **the Caribbean (islands)** die Karibik (singular).

carnation noun Nelke die (PL die Nelken).

carnival noun Karneval der (PL die Karnevale).

car park noun Parkplatz der (PL die Parkplätze), (multi-storey) Parkhaus das (PL die Parkhäuser).

carpenter noun Tischler der (PL die Tischler), Tischlerin die (PL die Tischlerinnen).

carpentry noun Tischlerhandwerk das.

carpet noun Teppich der (PL die Teppiche).

car phone noun Autotelefon das (PL die Autotelefone).

car radio noun Autoradio das (PL die Autoradios).

carriage noun (of a train) Abteil das (PL die Abteile).

carrier bag noun Tragetasche die (PL die Tragetaschen).

carrot noun Karotte die (PL die Karotten), Möhre die (PL die Möhren).

carry verb tragen; she was carrying a case sie trug einen Koffer.

● **to carry on** weitermachen SEP; they carried on working sie arbeiteten weiter.

carrycot noun Babytragetasche die (PL die Babytragetaschen).

carsick adjective he gets carsick ihm wird beim Autofahren schlecht.

carton noun 1 (of cream or yoghurt) Becher der (PL die Becher); 2 (of milk or orange) Tüte die (PL die Tüten).

cartoon noun 1 (a film) Zeichentrickfilm der (PL die Zeichentrickfilme); 2 (a comic strip) Cartoon der (PL die Cartoons); 3 (a drawing) Karikatur die (PL die Karikaturen).

cartridge noun (for a pen) Patrone die (PL die Patronen).

case¹ noun 1 (suitcase) Koffer der (PL die Koffer); to pack a case einen Koffer packen; 2 (a large wooden box) Kiste die (PL die Kisten); 3 (for spectacles or small things) Etui das (PL die Etuis).

case² noun 1 Fall der (PL die Fälle); in that case in dem Fall; that's not the case das ist nicht der Fall; in case of fire bei Feuer; 2 in case falls; in case he comes falls er kommt; 3 just in case für alle Fälle; 4 in any case sowieso; in any case, it's too late es ist sowieso zu spät.

cash noun 1 (money in general) Geld das; I haven't any cash on me ich habe kein Geld dabei; 2 (money rather than a cheque) Bargeld das; to pay in cash bar zahlen; £50 in cash fünfzig Pfund in bar.

cash card noun Bankkarte die (PL die Bankkarten).

cash desk noun Kasse die (PL die Kassen); to pay at the cash desk an der Kasse zahlen.

cash dispenser noun Geldautomat der (PL die Geldautomaten).

cashier noun Kassierer der (PL die Kassierer), Kassiererin die (PL die Kassiererinnen).

cash point noun Geldautomat der (PL die Geldautomaten).

cassette noun Kassette die (PL die Kassetten).

cassette recorder noun Kassettenrekorder der (PL die Kassettenrekorder).

cast noun (of a play) Besetzung die.

castle noun 1 (*in an accident*) Burg die (PL die Burgen); 2 (*in chess*) Turm der (PL die Türme).

casual adjective zwanglos.

casualty noun 1 (*in an accident*) Verletzte der/die (PL die Verletzten); 2 (*hospital department*) Unfallstation die (PL die Unfallstationen); **he's in casualty** er ist auf der Unfallstation.

cat noun Katze die (PL die Katzen), (*tomcat*) Kater der (PL die Kater); ★ **it's raining cats and dogs** es regnet in Strömen (*literally: it's raining in streams*).

catalogue noun Katalog der (PL die Kataloge).

catastrophe noun Katastrophe die (PL die Katastrophen).

catch noun 1 (*on a door*) Schnappriegel der (PL die Schnappriegel); 2 (*a drawback*) Haken der (PL die Haken); **where's the catch?** wo ist der Haken?

catch verb 1 fangen◇; **Tom caught the ball** Tom hat den Ball gefangen; **she caught a fish** sie hat einen Fisch gefangen; **catch me!** fang mich!; 2 **to catch somebody doing something** jemanden bei etwas (DAT) erwischen; **he was caught stealing money** er wurde beim Geldstehlen erwischt; 3 (*be in time for*) noch erreichen; **did Tim catch his plane?** hat Tim sein Flugzeug noch erreicht?; 4 (*become ill with*) bekommen◇; **she's caught chickenpox** sie hat die Windpocken bekommen; 5 verstehen◇ (*what somebody says*); **I didn't catch your name** ich

habe Ihren Namen nicht verstanden.

● **to catch up with somebody** jemanden einholen SEP.

category noun Kategorie die (PL die Kategorien).

catering noun 1 (*trade*) Gastronomie die; 2 **who's doing the catering?** wer liefert das Essen und die Getränke?

caterpillar noun Raupe die (PL die Raupen).

cathedral noun Kathedrale die (PL die Kathedralen); **Cologne cathedral** der Kölner Dom.

Catholic noun Katholik der (PL die Katholiken), Katholikin die (PL die Katholikinnen).

Catholic adjective katholisch.

cattle plural noun Vieh das.

cauliflower noun Blumenkohl der; **cauliflower cheese** mit Käse überbackener Blumenkohl.

cause noun 1 Ursache die (PL die Ursachen); **the cause of the accident** die Unfallursache; 2 **for a good cause** für eine gute Sache.

cause verb verursachen; **to cause difficulties** Schwierigkeiten verursachen.

cave noun Höhle die (PL die Höhlen).

caving noun Höhlenforschung die; **to go caving** auf Höhlenforschung gehen.

CD noun CD die (PL die CDs).

CD player noun CD-Player der (PL die CD-Player).

CD-ROM noun CD-ROM die (PL die CD-ROMs).

ceiling noun Decke die (PL die Decken); **on the ceiling** an der Decke.

celebrate verb feiern; **he's celebrating his birthday** er feiert seinen Geburtstag.

celebrity noun Berühmtheit die (PL die Berühmtheiten).

celery noun Sellerie der (PL die Sellerie).

cell noun Zelle die (PL die Zellen).

cellar noun Keller der (PL die Keller).

cello noun Cello das (PL die Cellos); **to play the cello** Cello spielen.

cement noun Zement der.

cemetery noun Friedhof der (PL die Friedhöfe).

cent noun 1 (in euro system) Eurocent der (PL die Eurocents), Cent der (PL die Cents); **50 cents** 50 (Euro)cent; 2 (in dollar system) Cent der (PL die Cents); **25 cents** 25 Cent.

centigrade adjective Celsius; **ten degrees centigrade** zehn Grad Celsius.

centimetre noun Zentimeter der (PL die Zentimeter).

central adjective 1 zentral; **the office is very central** das Büro ist sehr zentral gelegen; 2 **in central London** im Zentrum von London.

Central Europe noun Mitteleuropa das.

central heating noun Zentralheizung die.

centre noun Zentrum das (PL die Zentren); **in the centre of** im Zentrum von (+ DAT); **in the town centre** im Stadtzentrum; a **shopping centre** ein Einkaufszentrum.

century noun Jahrhundert das (PL die Jahrhunderte); **in the twentieth century** im zwanzigsten Jahrhundert.

cereal noun breakfast cereal Frühstücksflocken (plural).

ceremony noun Zeremonie die (PL die Zeremonien).

certain adjective 1 (definite) bestimmt; **a certain number of** eine bestimmte Zahl von (+ DAT); 2 (confident) sicher; **to be certain** sich (DAT) sicher sein; **are you certain of the address?** bist du sicher, dass das die richtige Adresse ist?; **I'm absolutely certain** ich bin mir ganz sicher; **to be certain that ...** sicher sein, dass ...; 3 **nobody knows for certain** niemand weiß es genau.

certainly adverb bestimmt; **certainly not** bestimmt nicht.

certificate noun 1 Bescheinigung die (PL die Bescheinigungen); 2 **birth certificate** die Geburtsurkunde; 3 (at school) Zeugnis das (PL die Zeugnisse).

chain noun Kette die (PL die Ketten).

chair noun 1 (upright) Stuhl der (PL die Stühle); **a kitchen chair** ein Küchenstuhl; 2 (with arms) Sessel der (PL die Sessel).

chair lift noun Sessellift der (PL die Sessellifte).

chalet noun 1 (in the mountains) Chalet das (PL die Chalets); 2 (in a holiday camp) Ferienhaus das (PL die Ferienhäuser).

a b c d e f g h i j k l m n o p q r s t u v w x y z

challenge noun Herausforderung die (PL die Herausforderungen).

champion noun Meister der (PL die Meister), Meisterin die (PL die Meisterinnen); **the world slalom champion** der Weltmeister im Slalom, die Weltmeisterin im Slalom.

chance noun 1 (opportunity) Gelegenheit die (PL die Gelegenheiten); **to have the chance to do something** die Gelegenheit haben, etwas zu tun; **if you have the chance to go to New York** wenn du die Gelegenheit hast, nach New York zu fahren; **I had no chance to speak to him** ich hatte keine Gelegenheit, mit ihm zu reden; 2 (likelihood) Aussicht die (PL die Aussichten); **he's got no chance of winning** er hat keine Aussicht zu gewinnen; 3 (luck) Zufall der; **by chance** zufällig; **do you have her address, by any chance?** hast du zufällig ihre Adresse?

change noun 1 (from one thing to another) Änderung die (PL die Änderungen); **a change of address** eine Adressänderung; **there's been a change of plan** der Plan ist geändert worden; 2 (alteration) Veränderung die (PL die Veränderungen); **they've made some changes to the house** sie haben im Haus ein paar Veränderungen vorgenommen; **a change in the weather** eine Wetterumschwung; 3 (for the sake of variety) **for a change, we could go to a restaurant** zur Abwechslung könnten wir in ein

Restaurant gehen; **it makes a change from hamburgers** das ist mal etwas anderes als Hamburger; **a change of clothes** etwas anderes zum Anziehen; 4 (cash) Wechselgeld das; **I haven't any change** ich habe kein Wechselgeld.

change verb 1 (make different) ändern; **you can't change her** du kannst sie nicht ändern; **to change your address** seine Adresse ändern; 2 (become different) sich verändern; **Liz has changed a lot** Liz hat sich sehr verändert; 3 (transform completely) verwandeln; **the prince changed into a frog** der Prinz verwandelte sich in einen Frosch; 4 (exchange in a shop) umtauschen; **just change it for a larger size** tauschen Sie es einfach gegen eine Nummer größer um; 5 (change clothes) sich umziehen ◇ SEP; **Mike's just changing** Mike zieht sich gerade um; 6 (switch from one train or bus to another) umsteigen ◇ SEP (PERF sein); **we changed trains at Crewe** wir stiegen in Crewe um; 7 (switch one thing for another) wechseln; **I want to change my job** ich möchte meinen Arbeitsplatz wechseln; **they changed places** sie haben die Plätze gewechselt; 8 **to change your mind** sich anders entschließen ◇.

changing room noun (for sport or swimming) Umkleideraum der (PL die Umkleideräume).

channel noun 1 (on TV) Kanal der (PL die Kanäle); **to change channels** auf einen anderen Kanal umschalten; **2 the Channel** der Ärmelkanal.

Channel Tunnel noun Eurotunnel der.

chaos noun Chaos das; **it was chaos!** das war ein Chaos!

chapel noun Kapelle die (PL die Kapellen).

chapter noun Kapitel das (PL die Kapitel); **in chapter two** im zweiten Kapitel.

character noun **1** (personality) Charakter der; **2** (somebody in a book) Charakter der (PL die Charaktere); **3** (part in a play or film) Rolle die (PL die Rollen); **the main character** die Hauptrolle.

charcoal noun **1** (for burning) Holzkohle die; **2** (for drawing) Kohle die.

charge noun **1** (what you pay) Gebühr die (PL die Gebühren); **a booking charge** eine Buchungsgebühr; **an extra or additional charge** eine zusätzliche Gebühr; **there's no charge** das ist kostenlos; **2 to be in charge** für etwas (ACC) verantwortlich sein; **who's in charge of the children?** wer ist für die Kinder verantwortlich?; **3 to be on a charge of theft** wegen Diebstahls angeklagt sein.

charge verb **1** (ask to pay) berechnen; **they charge us fifteen pounds an hour** sie berechnen uns fünfzehn Pfund pro Stunde; **they didn't charge for delivery** sie haben die Lieferung nicht berechnet; **we won't charge you for it** wir berechnen Ihnen nichts dafür; **2 to charge somebody with**

something jemanden wegen etwas (+ GEN) anklagen SEP.

charity noun Wohltätigkeitsverein der (PL die Wohltätigkeitsvereine).

charming adjective reizend.

chart noun **1** (table) Tabelle die (PL die Tabellen); **2 the weather chart** die Wetterkarte; **3 the charts** die Hitparade.

charter flight noun Charterflug der (PL die Charterflüge).

chase noun Verfolgungsjagd die (PL die Verfolgungsjagden); **a car chase** eine Verfolgungsjagd mit dem Auto.

chase verb jagen.

chat noun Plauderei die (PL die Plaudereien); **to have a chat with somebody** mit jemandem plaudern.

chatroom noun Chatroom der (PL die Chatrooms).

chat show noun Talkshow die (PL die Talkshows).

chatter verb **1** (talk) schwatzen; **2 my teeth were chattering** ich klapperte mit den Zähnen.

cheap adjective billig; **cheap shoes** billige Schuhe; **that's very cheap** das ist sehr billig.

cheaply adverb billig; **to eat cheaply** billig essen.

cheap-rate adjective verbilligt; **a cheap-rate phone call** ein Gespräch zum Billigtarif

cheat noun **1** Betrüger der (PL die Betrüger), Betrügerin die (PL die Betrügerinnen); **2** (in games) Mogler der (PL die Mogler), Moglerin die (PL die Moglerinnen).

a b c d e f g h i j k l m n o p q r s t u v w x y z

cheat verb **1** betrügen✧; **2** (in games) mogeln.

check noun **1** (in a factory or at a border control) Kontrolle die (PL die Kontrollen); **passport check** die Passkontrolle; **2** (in chess) **check!** Schach!

check verb **1** (make sure) prüfen; **he checked their statements** er prüfte ihre Aussagen; **2** (make sure by looking) nachsehen✧ SEP; **to check the time** auf die Uhr sehen; **check they're all back** sieh nach, ob alle wieder da sind; **3** (inspect) kontrollieren; **to check the tickets** die Fahrkarten kontrollieren.

● **to check in** sich anmelden SEP; **to check in at the airport** am Flughafen einchecken.

● **to check out** abreisen✧ SEP (PERF sein); **to check out of the hotel** das Hotel verlassen.

check-in noun Abfertigungsschalter der (PL die Abfertigungsschalter).

checkout noun Kasse die (PL die Kassen); **at the checkout** an der Kasse.

check-up noun Untersuchung die (PL die Untersuchungen).

cheek noun **1** (part of face) Backe die (PL die Backen); **2** (nerve) Frechheit die; **what a cheek!** so eine Frechheit!

cheeky adjective frech.

cheer noun **1** three cheers for Tom! ein dreifaches Hoch auf Tom!; **2** (when drinking) cheers! prost!

cheer verb (shout hurray) Hurra schreien✧.

● **to cheer somebody up** jemanden aufmuntern SEP; **your visits always cheer me up** deine Besuche muntern mich immer auf; **cheer up!** Kopf hoch!.

cheerful adjective fröhlich.

cheese noun Käse der; **a cheese sandwich** ein Käsebrot.

chef noun Koch der (PL die Köche), Köchin die (PL die Köchinnen).

chemical noun Chemikalie die (PL die Chemikalien).

chemist noun **1** (in a pharmacy) Apotheker der (PL die Apotheker), Apothekerin die (PL die Apothekerinnen); **2** chemist's (dispensing) Apotheke die (PL die Apotheken); **at the chemist's** in der Apotheke; **3** (scientist) Chemiker der (PL die Chemiker), Chemikerin die (PL die Chemikerinnen).

chemistry noun Chemie die.

cheque noun Scheck der (PL die Schecks); **to pay by cheque** mit Scheck bezahlen; **to write a cheque** einen Scheck ausstellen.

cheque book noun Scheckbuch das (PL die Scheckbücher).

cherry noun Kirsche die (PL die Kirschen).

chess noun Schach das; **to play chess** Schach spielen.

chessboard noun Schachbrett das (PL die Schachbretter).

chest noun **1** (part of the body) Brust die (PL die Brüste); **2** (box) Truhe die (PL die Truhen); **3** a chest of drawers eine Kommode.

chestnut noun Esskastanie die (PL die Esskastanien).

chestnut tree noun 1 (horse-chestnut) Rosskastanie die (PL die Rosskastanien); 2 (sweet chestnut) Edelkastanie die (PL die Edelkastanien).

chew verb kauen.

chewing gum noun Kaugummi der (PL die Kaugummis).

chicken noun Huhn das (PL die Hühner); **roast chicken** das Brathähnchen; **chicken breast** die Hühnerbrust.

chickenpox noun Windpocken (plural).

child noun Kind das (PL die Kinder); **when I was a child** ... als Kind ....

childish adjective kindisch.

childminder noun Tagesmutter die (PL die Tagesmütter).

chill noun 1 Kälte die; 2 **to have a chill** eine Erkältung haben.

chilled adjective gekühlt.

chilli noun Chili der.

chimney noun Schornstein der (PL die Schornsteine).

chimpanzee noun Schimpanse der (PL die Schimpansen).

chin noun Kinn das (PL die Kinne).

China noun China das.

china noun Porzellan das; **the china bowl** die Porzellanschüssel.

Chinese noun 1 **the Chinese** (people) die Chinesen; 2 (language) Chinesisch das.

Chinese adjective 1 chinesisch; **a Chinese man** ein Chinese; **a Chinese woman** eine Chinesin; 2 **to have a Chinese meal** chinesisch essen.

chip noun 1 (fried potato) **chips** Pommes frites (plural); **fish and chips** ausgebackener Fisch mit Pommes frites; 2 (microchip) Chip der (PL die Chips); 3 (in glass or china) angeschlagene Stelle die (PL die angeschlagenen Stellen).

chipped adjective angeschlagen.

chocolate noun 1 Schokolade die; **a box of chocolates** eine Schachtel Pralinen; 2 **chocolate ice cream** das Schokoladeneis; 3 **a cup of hot chocolate** eine Tasse Kakao.

choice noun 1 Wahl die (PL die Wahlen); **to make a good choice** eine gute Wahl treffen; 2 (variety) Auswahl die; **you have a choice of two flights** du hast zwei Flüge zur Auswahl.

choir noun Chor der (PL die Chöre).

choke noun (on a car) Choke der (PL die Chokes).

choke verb (by yourself) sich verschlucken; **she choked on a bone** sie hat sich an einer Gräte verschluckt.

choose verb 1 wählen; **you chose well** du hast gut gewählt; **it's hard to choose from all these colours** es ist schwer, unter allen diesen Farben zu wählen; 2 (select from a group of things) sich (DAT) aussuchen SEP; **Cathy chose the red skirt** Cathy suchte sich den roten Rock aus.

chop noun Kotelett das (PL die Koteletts); **a pork chop** ein Schweinekotelett.

chop verb hacken.

chord noun Akkord der (PL die Akkorde).

a
b
c
d
e
f
g
h
i
j
k
l
m
n
o
p
q
r
s
t
u
v
w
x
y
z

chorus noun **1** (when you all join in the song) Refrain der (PL die Refrains); **2** (a group of singers) Chor der (PL die Chöre).

Christ noun Christus der.

christening noun Taufe die (PL die Taufen).

Christian noun Christ der (PL die Christen), Christin die (PL die Christinnen).

Christian adjective christlich.

Christianity noun Christentum das.

Christian name noun Vorname der (PL die Vornamen).

Christmas noun Weihnachten das (PL die Weihnachten); **at Christmas** zu Weihnachten; **what did you get for Christmas?** was hast du zu Weihnachten bekommen?; **Happy Christmas!** Frohe Weihnachten!

Christmas card noun Weihnachtskarte die (PL die Weihnachtskarten).

Christmas carol noun Weihnachtslied das (PL die Weihnachtslieder).

Christmas cracker noun Knallbonbon der (PL die Knallbonbons).

Christmas Day noun erste Weihnachtstag der.

Christmas Eve noun Heiligabend der; **on Christmas Eve** Heiligabend.

Christmas present noun Weihnachtsgeschenk das (PL die Weihnachtsgeschenke).

Christmas tree noun Weihnachtsbaum der (PL die Weihnachtsbäume).

church noun Kirche die (PL die Kirchen); **to go to church** in die Kirche gehen.

chute noun (in a swimming pool or playground) Rutsche die (PL die Rutschen).

cider noun Apfelwein der (PL die Apfelweine).

cigar noun Zigarre die (PL die Zigarren).

cigarette noun Zigarette die (PL die Zigaretten).

cinema noun Kino das (PL die Kinos); **to go to the cinema** ins Kino gehen.

circle noun Kreis der (PL die Kreise); **to sit in a circle** im Kreis sitzen; **to go round in circles** sich im Kreis drehen.

circuit noun **1** (for athletes) Bahn die (PL die Bahnen); **2** (for cars) Rennbahn die (PL die Rennbahnen).

circumstance noun Umstand der (PL die Umstände); **under these circumstances** unter diesen Umständen.

circus noun Zirkus der (PL die Zirkusse).

citizen noun Bürger der (PL die Bürger), Bürgerin die (PL die Bürgerinnen).

city noun Stadt die (PL die Städte); **the city of Berlin** die Stadt Berlin.

city centre noun Stadtzentrum das (PL die Stadtzentren); **in the city centre** im Stadtzentrum, in der Innenstadt.

civil servant noun Beamte der (PL die Beamten), Beamtin die (PL die Beamtinnen); **she's a civil servant** sie ist Beamtin.

civilization *noun* Zivilisation *die* (PL *die* Zivilisationen).

claim *verb* behaupten; **he claims to know who ...** er behauptet zu wissen, wer ....

claim *noun* **1** (*statement*) Behauptung *die* (PL *die* Behauptungen); **2** (*for compensation*) Anspruch *der* (PL *die* Ansprüche); **to make a claim on insurance** seine Versicherungsansprüche geltend machen.

clap *verb* **1** klatschen; **everyone clapped** alle klatschten; **2 to clap your hands** in die Hände klatschen.

clarinet *noun* Klarinette *die* (PL *die* Klarinetten); **to play the clarinet** Klarinette spielen.

clash *noun* (*between two groups*) Zusammenstoß *der* (PL *die* Zusammenstöße).

clash *verb* **1** (*rival groups*) zusammenstoßen✧ SFP; **2** (*colours*) sich beißen✧; **the curtains clash with the wallpaper** die Vorhänge passen farblich nicht zur Tapete.

class *noun* **1** (*a group of students or pupils*) Klasse *die* (PL *die* Klassen); **she's in my class** sie geht in meine Klasse; **2** (*a lesson*) Stunde *die* (PL *die* Stunden); **history class** die Geschichtsstunde; **in class** im Unterricht; **3** (*category*) Klasse *die* (PL *die* Klassen); **social class** die Gesellschaftsschicht.

classic *adjective* klassisch.

classical *adjective* klassisch; **classical music** die klassische Musik.

classroom *noun* Klassenzimmer *das* (PL *die* Klassenzimmer).

clay *noun* Ton *der*.

clean *adjective* sauber; **a clean shirt** ein sauberes Hemd; **my hands are clean** ich habe saubere Hände.

clean *verb* **1** putzen; **I cleaned the windows** ich habe die Fenster geputzt; **2 to clean your teeth** sich (DAT) die Zähne putzen; **I'm going to clean my teeth** ich putze mir jetzt die Zähne.

cleaner *noun* **1** (*cleaning lady*) Putzfrau *die* (PL *die* Putzfrauen); **2** (*in a public place*) Reinigungskraft *die* (PL *die* Reinigungskräfte); **3 dry cleaner's** die (chemische) Reinigung.

cleaning *noun* **to do the cleaning** putzen.

cleanser *noun* **1** (*for the house*) Reinigungsmittel *das* (PL *die* Reinigungsmittel); **2** (*for your face*) Reinigungsmilch *die*.

clear *adjective* **1** (*that you can see through*) klar; **clear water** klares Wasser; **2** (*cloudless*) klar; **3** (*easy to understand*) klar; **clear instructions** klare Anweisungen; **is that clear?** ist das klar? (*informal*); **to make something clear** etwas klar machen.

clear *verb* **1** räumen; **have you cleared your stuff out of your room?** hast du deine Sachen aus deinem Zimmer geräumt?; **2 can I clear the table?** kann ich den Tisch abräumen SEP?; **3 to clear your throat** sich räuspern.

● **to clear up 1** (*tidy up*) aufräumen SEP; **2** (*the weather*) sich aufklären SEP; **the weather's**

clearing up a bit das Wetter klärt sich ein bisschen auf.

clearly adverb **1** (to think, speak, or hear) deutlich; **2** (obviously) eindeutig; **she was clearly better** sie war eindeutig besser.

clementine noun Klementine die (PL die Klementinen).

clever adjective **1** klug; **their children are all very clever** ihre Kinder sind alle sehr klug; **2** (ingenious) clever; **a clever idea** eine clevere Idee.

click noun **1** (noise) Klicken das; **2** (with mouse) Klick der (PL die Klicks); **a double click** ein Doppelklick.

click verb **to click on something** etwas anklicken SEP; **click on the icon twice!** doppelklicken Sie das Icon!

client noun Klient der (PL die Klienten), Klientin die (PL die Klientinnen).

cliff noun Klippe die (PL die Klippen).

climate noun Klima das (PL die Klimata).

climb verb **1** (the stairs, a hill) hinaufgehen◇ SEP (PERF sein); **to climb a mountain** einen Berg besteigen◇ (PERF sein); **2** (a wall, tree, or rock) klettern (PERF sein), auf (+ ACC); **to climb a tree** auf einen Baum klettern.

climber noun Bergsteiger der (PL die Bergsteiger), Bergsteigerin die (PL die Bergsteigerinnen).

climbing noun Bergsteigen das; **they go climbing in Italy** sie gehen in Italien bergsteigen.

clinic noun Klinik die (PL die Kliniken).

clip noun **1** (from a film) Ausschnitt der (PL die Ausschnitte); **2** (for your hair) Klammer die (PL die Klammern).

cloakroom noun (for coats) Garderobe die (PL die Garderoben).

clock noun **1** Uhr die (PL die Uhren); **to put the clocks forward an hour** die Uhr eine Stunde vorstellen; **to put the clocks back** die Uhr zurückstellen; **2 an alarm clock** ein Wecker.

close¹ adjective, adverb **1** (result) knapp; **2** (friend, connection) eng; **3** (relation or acquaintance) nahe; **4** (near) in der Nähe; **the station's very close** der Bahnhof ist ganz in der Nähe; **she lives close by** sie wohnt in der Nähe; **5 close to** nahe, nah (informal) (+ DAT); **close to the cinema** nahe am Kino; **not very close** nicht sehr nah.

close² noun Ende das; **at the close** am Ende.

close verb zumachen SEP, schließen◇; **close your eyes!** mach die Augen zu!; **she closed the door** sie machte die Tür zu; **the post office closes at six** die Post macht um sechs zu, die Post schließt um sechs.

closed adjective geschlossen; **'closed on Mondays'** 'Montags geschlossen'.

closely adverb **1** (in distance) eng; **2** (carefully) genau; **to look at something closely** sich etwas genau ansehen.

closing date noun **the closing date for entries** (for a competition) der Einsendeschluss, (for a sporting event) der Meldeschluss.

closing time noun
1 Ladenschluss der; 2 (of a pub)
Polizeistunde die.

cloth noun 1 (for drying up and
polishing) Tuch das (PL die Tücher);
2 (for the floor) Lappen der (PL die
Lappen); 3 (fabric) Stoff der (PL die
Stoffe).

clothes plural noun 1 Kleider
(plural); 2 to put your clothes on
sich anziehen ◇ SEP; to take your
clothes off sich ausziehen ◇ SEP; to
change your clothes sich
umziehen ◇ SEP.

clothes peg noun
Wäscheklammer die (PL die
Wäscheklammern).

clothing noun Kleidung die.

cloud noun Wolke die (PL die
Wolken).

cloudy adjective bewölkt.

clown noun Clown der (PL die
Clowns).

club noun 1 (association, for tennis-
players, golfers) Klub der (PL die
Klubs), (for footballers) Verein der
(PL die Vereine); a football club ein
Fußballverein; 2 (in cards) Kreuz
das (PL die Kreuze); the four of
clubs die Kreuz-Vier; 3 (golfing
iron) Schläger der (PL die Schläger).

clue noun Anhaltspunkt der (PL
die Anhaltspunkte); they have a
few clues sie haben ein paar
Anhaltspunkte; 2 (in a crossword)
Frage die (PL die Fragen); ★ I
haven't a clue ich habe keine
Ahnung.

clumsy adjective ungeschickt.

clutch noun (in a car) Kupplung
die (PL die Kupplungen).

clutch verb to clutch something
etwas festhalten ◇ SEP.

coach noun 1 (bus) Bus der (PL die
Busse); on the coach im Bus; to
travel by coach mit dem Bus
fahren; 2 (sports trainer) Trainer
der (PL die Trainer), Trainerin die (PL
die Trainerinnen); 3 (railway
carriage) Wagen der (PL die Wagen).

coach station noun Busbahnhof
der (PL die Busbahnhöfe).

coach trip noun Busausflug der
(PL die Busausflüge); to go on a
coach trip einen Busausflug
machen.

coal noun Kohle die (PL die Kohlen).

coarse adjective grob.

coast noun Küste die (PL die
Küsten); on the east coast an der
Ostküste.

coat noun 1 Mantel der (PL die
Mäntel); 2 coat of paint der
Anstrich.

coat hanger noun Kleiderbügel
der (PL die Kleiderbügel).

cobweb noun Spinnennetz das (PL
die Spinnennetze).

cocaine noun Kokain das.

cock noun Hahn der (PL die Hähne).

cocoa noun Kakao das.

coconut noun Kokosnuss die (PL die
Kokosnüsse).

cod noun Kabeljau der (PL die
Kabeljaue).

code noun 1 (in law) Gesetzbuch
das; the highway code die
Straßenverkehrsordnung; 2 the
dialling code for Hull die Vorwahl
für Hull.

coffee noun Kaffee der (PL die
Kaffees); a cup of coffee eine
Tasse Kaffee; a black coffee,

a
b
c
d
e
f
g
h
i
j
k
l
m
n
o
p
q
r
s
t
u
v
w
x
y
z

please einen Kaffee ohne Milch bitte; **a white coffee, please** einen Kaffee mit Milch bitte.

coffee break noun Kaffeepause die (PL die Kaffeepausen).

coffee cup noun Kaffeetasse die (PL die Kaffeetassen).

coffee machine noun Kaffeemaschine die (PL die Kaffeemaschinen).

coffin noun Sarg der (PL die Särge).

coin noun 1 Münze die (PL die Münzen); **she collects old coins** sie sammelt alte Münzen; **2 a pound coin** ein Einpfundstück.

coincidence noun Zufall der (PL die Zufälle).

Coke noun Cola die; **two Cokes please** zwei Cola bitte.

cold noun 1 (cold weather) Kälte die; **to be out in the cold** draußen in der Kälte sein; **2** (illness) Schnupfen der (PL die Schnupfen), Erkältung die (PL die Erkältungen); **to have a cold** Schnupfen haben; **Carol's got a cold** Carol hat Schnupfen; **a bad cold** eine schlimme Erkältung.

cold adjective 1 kalt; **your hands are cold** du hast kalte Hände; **cold milk** kalte Milch; **2** (weather, temperature) **it's cold today** heute ist es kalt; **3** (feeling) **I'm cold** mir ist kalt.

collapse verb 1 (a roof or wall) einstürzen SEP (PERF sein); **2** (a person) zusammenbrechen◇ SEP (PERF sein); **he collapsed in his office** er brach in seinem Büro zusammen.

collar noun 1 (on a garment) Kragen der (PL die Kragen); **2** (for an animal) Halsband das (PL die Halsbänder).

colleague noun Kollege der (PL die Kollegen), Kollegin die (PL die Kolleginnen).

collect verb 1 (as a hobby) sammeln; **do you collect stamps?** sammelst du Briefmarken?; **2** (fetch) abholen SEP; **she collects the children from school** sie holt die Kinder von der Schule ab; **3 to collect up the exercise books** Hefte einsammeln SEP.

collection noun (of stamps, CDs, money, etc.) Sammlung die (PL die Sammlungen).

collector noun Sammler der (PL die Sammler), Sammlerin die (PL die Sammlerinnen).

college noun 1 (for higher education) Hochschule die (PL die Hochschulen); **to go to college** studieren; **2** (a school) College das (PL die Colleges).

Cologne noun Köln das.

colour noun Farbe die (PL die Farben); **what colour is it?** welche Farbe hat es?; **do you have it in a different colour?** haben Sie es in einer anderen Farbe?

colour verb 1 (with paints or crayons) anmalen SEP; **to colour something red** etwas rot anmalen; **2** (with dye) färben.

colour blind adjective farbenblind.

colour film noun Farbfilm der (PL die Farbfilme).

colourful adjective bunt.

column noun 1 (of a building) Säule die (PL die Säulen); **2** (on a page) Spalte die (PL die Spalten).

comb noun Kamm der (PL die Kämme).

comb verb kämmen; **to comb your hair** sich (DAT) die Haare kämmen; **I'll just comb my hair** ich kämme mir nur die Haare.

come verb 1 kommen ✧ (PERF sein); **come quick!** komm schnell!; **come here!** komm mal her!; **Nick came by car** Nick kam mit dem Auto; **can you come over for a coffee?** kannst du auf eine Tasse Kaffee kommen?; **did Jess come to school yesterday?** war Jess gestern in der Schule?; **2** (arrive) **coming!** ich komme schon!; **the bus is coming** der Bus kommt gerade; **come along!** komm schon!

● **to come back** zurückkommen ✧ SEP (PERF sein); **he's coming back to collect us** er kommt zurück, um uns abzuholen.

● **to come down** herunterkommen ✧ SEP (PERF sein).

● **to come for** (collect) abholen SEP; **my father's coming for me** mein Vater holt mich ab.

● **to come in** hereinkommen ✧ SEP (PERF sein); **come in!** herein!; **she came into the kitchen** sie kam in die Küche.

● **to come off** (a button) abgehen ✧ SEP (PERF sein).

● **to come out** herauskommen ✧ SEP (PERF sein); **they came out when I called** als ich rief, kamen sie heraus; **the new CD's coming out soon** die neue CD kommt bald heraus.

● **to come up** heraufkommen ✧ SEP (PERF sein); **can you come up a moment?** kannst du eine Sekunde heraufkommen?

● **to come up to somebody** auf jemanden zukommen ✧ SEP (PERF sein).

comedian noun Komiker der (PL die Komiker), Komikerin die (PL die Komikerinnen).

comedy noun Komödie die.

comfortable adjective **1** bequem; **this chair's really comfortable** dieser Sessel ist wirklich bequem; **2 to feel comfortable** (a person) sich wohl fühlen.

comfortably adverb bequem.

comic noun (magazine) Comicheft das (PL die Comichefte).

comic strip noun Comic der (PL die Comics).

comma noun Komma das (PL die Kommas).

command noun Befehl der (PL die Befehle).

comment noun (remark) Bemerkung die (PL die Bemerkungen); **he made some rude comments about my friends** er hat ein paar unhöfliche Bemerkungen über meine Freunde gemacht.

commentary noun Reportage die (PL die Reportagen); **the commentary on the soccer match** die Reportage über das Fußballspiel.

commentator noun Reporter der (PL die Reporter), Reporterin die (PL die Reporterinnen); **sports commentator** der Sportreporter.

commercial noun Werbespot der (PL die Werbespots).

commercial adjective kommerziell.

commit verb **1** begehen ✧ (a crime); **2 to commit yourself to** sich festlegen SEP: auf (+ ACC) .

committee noun Ausschuss der (PL die Ausschüsse).

common adjective **1** häufig; **it's a common problem** das Problem kommt häufig vor; **2 in common** gemeinsam; **they have nothing in common** sie haben nichts gemeinsam.

common sense noun gesunde Menschenverstand der.

communicate verb kommunizieren.

communication noun Verständigung die.

communion noun (in a Catholic church) Kommunion die, (in a Protestant church) Abendmahl das.

communism noun Kommunismus der.

community noun Gemeinschaft die (PL die Gemeinschaften); **the European Community** die Europäische Gemeinschaft.

commute verb **to commute between Oxford and London** zwischen Oxford und London pendeln (PERF sein).

commuter noun Pendler der (PL die Pendler), Pendlerin die (PL die Pendlerinnen).

compact disc noun Compactdisc die (PL die Compactdiscs).

compact disc player noun Compactdisc-Player der (PL die Compactdisc-Player).

company noun **1** (business) Gesellschaft die (PL die Gesellschaften); **an airline company** eine Fluggesellschaft;

she's set up a company sie hat eine Firma gegründet; **2** (group) Truppe die (PL die Truppen); **a theatre company** eine Theatertruppe; **3 to keep somebody company** jemandem Gesellschaft leisten; **the dog keeps me company** der Hund leistet mir Gesellschaft.

compare verb vergleichen✧; **if you compare the German phrase with the English** wenn man den deutschen mit dem englischen Ausdruck vergleicht; **our house is small compared with yours** verglichen mit eurem ist unser Haus klein.

compartment noun Abteil das (PL die Abteile).

compass noun Kompass der (PL die Kompasse).

compatible adjective **1** zueinander passend; **2** (in computing) kompatibel.

compete verb **1 to compete in something** (race, event) an etwas (DAT) teilnehmen✧ SEP; **2 to compete with each other** miteinander konkurrieren; **3 to compete for something** um etwas (ACC) kämpfen; **thirty people are competing for one job** dreißig Leute kämpfen um eine Stelle.

competent adjective fähig.

competition noun **1** (a contest) Wettbewerb der (PL die Wettbewerbe); **2** (in a magazine) Preisausschreiben das (PL die Preisausschreiben).

competitor noun Konkurrent der (PL die Konkurrenten),

Konkurrentin die (PL die Konkurrentinnen).

complain verb sich beschweren; **we complained about the meals** wir haben uns über das Essen beschwert.

complaint noun Beschwerde die (PL die Beschwerden); **to make a complaint** sich beschweren; **she made a complaint to the manager about the poor service** sie beschwerte sich bei dem Geschäftsführer über den schlechten Service.

complete adjective **1** (whole) vollständig; **the complete collection** die vollständige Sammlung; **2** (absolute) völlig; **a complete idiot** ein völliger Idiot (informal).

complete verb (to finish) beenden.

completely adverb völlig.

complexion noun Teint der (PL die Teints).

complicated adjective kompliziert.

compliment noun Kompliment das (PL die Komplimente); **to pay somebody a compliment** jemandem ein Kompliment machen.

composer noun Komponist der (PL die Komponisten), Komponistin die (PL die Komponistinnen).

comprehension noun Vorständnis das, **a comprehension test** ein Test zum Textverständnis.

comprehensive school noun Gesamtschule die (PL die Gesamtschulen).

compulsory adjective **1** obligatorisch; **2** (at school)

compulsory subject das Pflichtfach.

computer noun Computer der (PL die Computer); **to work on a computer** am Computer arbeiten; **to have something on computer** etwas im Computer gespeichert haben.

computer engineer noun Computertechniker der (PL die Computertechniker), Computertechnikerin die (PL die Computertechnikerinnen).

computer game noun Computerspiel das (PL die Computerspiele).

computer program noun Computerprogramm das (PL die Computerprogramme).

computer programmer noun Programmierer der (PL die Programmierer), Programmiererin die (PL die Programmiererinnen).

computer science noun Informatik die.

computing noun Informatik die.

concentrate verb sich konzentrieren; **I can't concentrate** ich kann mich nicht konzentrieren; **I was concentrating on the film** ich konzentrierte mich auf den Film.

concentration noun Konzentration die.

concern verb (to affect) betreffen◇; **this doesn't concern you** das betrifft Sie nicht; **as far as I'm concerned** was mich betrifft.

concert noun **1** Konzert das (PL die Konzerte); **to go to a concert** ins

Konzert gehen; **2** concert ticket die Konzertkarte.

conclusion noun Schluss der (PL die Schlüsse).

concrete noun Beton der; **the concrete floor** der Betonboden.

condemn verb verurteilen; **to condemn somebody to death** jemanden zum Tode verurteilen.

condition noun **1** Zustand der (PL die Zustände); **in good condition** in gutem Zustand; **weather conditions** die Wetterlage; **2** (something you insist on) Bedingung die (PL die Bedingungen); **on condition that you let me pay** unter der Bedingung, dass du mich zahlen lässt.

conditional noun Konditional das.

conditioner noun (for your hair) Spülung die (PL die Spülungen).

condom noun Kondom das (PL die Kondome).

conduct noun Benehmen das.

conduct verb dirigieren (an orchestra or a piece of music).

conductor noun (of an orchestra) Dirigent der (PL die Dirigenten), Dirigentin die (PL die Dirigentinnen).

cone noun **1** (for ice cream) Eistüte die (PL die Eistüten); **2** (for traffic) Verkehrshütchen das (PL die Verkehrshütchen).

conference noun Konferenz die (PL die Konferenzen).

confess verb gestehen✧.

confession noun Geständnis das (PL die Geständnisse).

confidence noun **1** (self-confidence) Selbstvertrauen das; **to be lacking in confidence** kein Selbstvertrauen haben; **2** (faith in somebody else) Vertrauen das; **to have confidence in somebody** jemandem vertrauen.

confident adjective **1** (sure of yourself) selbstbewusst; **2** (sure that something will happen) zuversichtlich.

confirm verb bestätigen; **he confirmed the date** er bestätigte das Datum.

confuse verb **1** verwirren (a person); **2** to confuse someone with somebody else jemanden (mit jemandem anderem) verwechseln; **I confuse him with his brother** ich verwechsle ihn immer mit seinem Bruder.

confused adjective **1** wirr; **a confused story** eine wirre Geschichte; **2** durcheinander; **I'm confused about the holiday plans** ich bin mit den Ferienplänen durcheinander; **now I'm completely confused** jetzt bin ich völlig durcheinander.

confusing adjective verwirrend; **the instructions are confusing** die Anweisungen sind verwirrend.

confusion noun Verwirrung die.

congratulate verb gratulieren; **I congratulated Tim on passing his exam** ich gratulierte Tim zur bestandenen Prüfung.

congratulations plural noun Glückwünsche (plural); **congratulations on the baby!** herzlichen Glückwunsch zum Baby!

connect *verb* (*to plug in to the mains*) anschließen❖ SEP (*a dishwasher or TV, for example*).

connection *noun* **1** (*between two ideas or events*) Zusammenhang der (PL die Zusammenhänge); **there's no connection** between his letter and my decision es besteht kein Zusammenhang zwischen seinem Brief und meiner Entscheidung; **2** (*between trains, planes, on phone, and electrical*) Anschluss der (PL die Anschlüsse); **Sally missed her connection** Sally hat ihren Anschluss verpasst.

conscience *noun* Gewissen das; **to have a guilty conscience** ein schlechtes Gewissen haben.

conscious *adjective* bei Bewusstsein sein❖; **she is not fully conscious yet** sie ist noch nicht wieder bei vollem Bewusstsein; **I was conscious that he was a policeman** es war mir bewusst, dass er Polizist war.

conservation *noun* (*of nature*) Schutz der, **environmental conservation** der Umweltschutz.

conservative *noun* Konservative der/die (PL die Konservativen).

conservative *adjective* konservativ.

conservatory *noun* Wintergarten der (PL die Wintergärten).

consider *verb* **1** sich (DAT) überlegen (*a suggestion or idea*) **all things considered** alles in allem; **2** (*think about (doing)*) erwägen❖; **we are considering buying a flat** wir erwägen, eine Wohnung zu kaufen.

considerate *adjective* rücksichtsvoll.

considering *preposition* wenn man bedenkt; **considering her age** wenn man ihr Alter bedenkt; **considering he did it all himself** wenn man bedenkt, dass er es ganz allein gemacht hat.

consist *verb* **to consist of** bestehen❖ aus (+ DAT).

consonant *noun* Konsonant der (PL die Konsonanten).

constant *adjective* ständig.

constipated *adjective* verstopft.

construct *verb* bauen.

construction *noun* **1** (*building*) Gebäude das (PL die Gebäude); **a construction site** eine Baustelle; **2** (*in grammar*) Konstruktion die (PL die Konstruktionen).

consul *noun* Konsul der (PL die Konsuln).

consulate *noun* Konsulat das (PL die Konsulate).

consult *verb* konsultieren.

consumer *noun* Verbraucher der (PL die Verbraucher), Verbraucherin die (PL die Verbraucherinnen).

contact *noun* Kontakt der (PL die Kontakte); **to be in contact with somebody** mit jemandem in Kontakt sein; **we've lost contact** wir haben den Kontakt verloren; **Rob has contacts in the music business** Rob hat Kontakte zur Musikindustrie.

contact *verb* sich in Verbindung setzen mit (+ DAT); **I'll contact you tomorrow** ich setze mich morgen mit dir in Verbindung.

a b c d e f g h i j k l m n o p q r s t u v w x y z

contact lens noun Kontaktlinse die (PL die Kontaktlinsen).

contain verb enthalten✧.

container noun Behälter der (PL die Behälter).

contaminate verb verseuchen.

contemporary adjective
1 (around today) zeitgenössisch;
2 (modern) modern.

contents plural noun Inhalt der; **the contents of my suitcase** der Inhalt meines Koffers.

contest noun Wettbewerb der (PL die Wettbewerbe).

contestant noun Teilnehmer der (PL die Teilnehmer), Teilnehmerin die (PL die Teilnehmerinnen).

continent noun Kontinent der (PL die Kontinente).

continue verb 1 fortsetzen SEP; **we continued (with) our journey** wir setzten unsere Reise fort; 2 **to continue to do something** etwas weiter tun; **Jill continued talking** Jill redete weiter; 3 **'to be continued'** 'Fortsetzung folgt'.

continuous adjective ununterbrochen.

contraception noun Verhütung die.

contraceptive noun Verhütungsmittel das (PL die Verhütungsmittel).

contract noun Vertrag der (PL die Verträge).

contradict verb widersprechen✧ (+ DAT).

contradiction noun Widerspruch der (PL die Widersprüche).

contrary noun Gegenteil das; **on the contrary** im Gegenteil.

contrast noun Kontrast der (PL die Kontraste).

contribute verb beisteuern SEP (money).

contribution noun (to charity or an appeal) Spende die (PL die Spenden).

control noun (of a crowd or animals) Kontrolle die; **the police are in control of the situation** die Polizei hat die Situation unter Kontrolle; **keep your dogs under control** halten Sie Ihre Hunde unter Kontrolle; **everything's under control** alles ist unter Kontrolle; **to get out of control** außer Kontrolle geraten.

control verb **to control yourself** sich beherrschen.

convenient adjective 1 praktisch; **frozen food is very convenient** Tiefkühlkost ist sehr praktisch; 2 **to be convenient for somebody** jemandem passen; **whenever's convenient for you** wann immer es dir passt.

conventional adjective konventionell.

conversation noun Gespräch das (PL die Gespräche).

convert verb 1 umwandeln SEP; 2 (adapt a building) umbauen SEP; **we're going to convert the garage into a workshop** wir wollen die Garage zu einer Werkstatt umbauen.

convince verb überzeugen; **I'm convinced he's wrong** ich bin davon überzeugt, dass er sich irrt.

convincing adjective überzeugend.

cook noun Koch der (PL die Köche), Köchin die (PL die Köchinnen).

cook verb **1** kochen; **who's cooking tonight?** wer kocht heute Abend?; **I like cooking** ich koche gern; **to cook vegetables and pasta** Gemüse und Nudeln kochen; **cook the cabbage for five minutes** lass den Kohl fünf Minuten kochen; **2** (prepare food or a meal) machen; **Fran's busy cooking supper** Fran macht gerade Abendessen; **how do you cook duck?** wie macht man Ente?; **3** (boil) kochen, (fry or roast) braten❖; **the potatoes are cooking** die Kartoffeln kochen; **the sausages are cooking** die Würstchen braten.

cooker noun Herd der (PL die Herde); **electric cooker** der Elektroherd; **gas cooker** der Gasherd.

cookery noun Kochen das.

cookery book noun Kochbuch das (PL die Kochbücher).

cooking noun **1** (preparing food) Kochen das; **cooking is fun** Kochen macht Spaß; **who's doing the cooking?** wer kocht?; **2** (food) Küche die; **Italian cooking** die italienische Küche.

cool noun **1** (coldness) Kühle die; **2** (calm) **to lose one's cool** durchdrehen SEP (PERF sein) (informal); **don't lose your cool!** dreh nicht durch!; **he kept his cool** er blieb gelassen.

cool adjective **1** (cold) kühl; **it's cool inside** drinnen ist es kühl; **2** (laid back) gelassen; **to stay cool** gelassen bleiben (PERF sein).

cool verb abkühlen SEP (PERF sein).

cop noun Polizist der (PL die Polizisten).

cope verb zurechtkommen❖ SEP (PERF sein); **she copes well** sie kommt gut zurecht; **to cope with the children** mit den Kindern zurechtkommen; **she's had a lot to cope with** sie musste mit viel fertig werden.

copy noun **1** (photocopy) Kopie die (PL die Kopien); **2** (of a book) Exemplar das (PL die Exemplare).

copy verb **1** (imitate) kopieren; **2** (make a copy of) abschreiben❖ SEP; **I copied (down) the address** ich habe die Adresse abgeschrieben; (in an exam) **to copy from somebody** bei jemandem abschreiben.

cord noun (for a blind, for example) Schnur die (PL die Schnüre).

cordless telephone noun schnurlose Telefon das (PL die schnurlosen Telefone).

core noun (of an apple or a pear) Kerngehäuse das (PL die Kerngehäuse).

cork noun **1** (in a bottle) Korken der (PL die Korken); **2** (material) Kork der.

corkscrew noun Korkenzieher der (PL die Korkenzieher).

corn noun **1** (wheat) Korn das; **2** (sweetcorn) Mais der.

corner noun **1** Ecke die (PL die Ecken); **at the corner of the street** an der Straßenecke; **it's just round the corner** es ist gleich um die Ecke; **2** (of mouth) Mundwinkel; **3** (of eye) Augenwinkel der (PL die

a
b
c
d
e
f
g
h
i
j
k
l
m
n
o
p
q
r
s
t
u
v
w
x
y
z

Augenwinkel); **out of the corner of your eye** aus den Augenwinkeln heraus; **4** (*bend in the road*) Kurve die (PL die Kurven); **5** (*in football*) Eckball der (PL die Eckbälle).

cornflakes *plural noun* die Cornflakes (*plural*).

corpse *noun* Leiche die (PL die Leichen).

correct *adjective* **1** richtig; **the correct answer** die richtige Antwort; **2 yes, that's correct** ja, das stimmt.

correct *verb* **1** verbessern; **2** (*teacher*) korrigieren; **the teacher has already corrected our homework** der Lehrer hat unsere Hausaufgaben schon korrigiert.

correction *noun* Verbesserung die (PL die Verbesserungen).

correctly *adverb* richtig; **have you filled in the form correctly?** hast du das Formular richtig ausgefüllt?

corridor *noun* Korridor der (PL die Korridore).

cosmetics *plural noun* Kosmetik die.

cost *noun* **1** Kosten (*plural*); **the cost of living** die Lebenshaltungskosten (*plural*); **2 the cost of a new computer** der Preis für einen neuen Computer.

cost *verb* kosten; **how much does it cost?** was kostet es?; **the tickets cost £10** die Karten kosten zehn Pfund; **it costs too much** das ist zu teuer.

costume *noun* Kostüm das (PL die Kostüme).

cosy *adjective* (*a room*) gemütlich.

cot *noun* Kinderbett das (PL die Kinderbetten).

cottage *noun* Häuschen das (PL die Häuschen).

cotton *noun* **1** (*fabric*) Baumwolle die; **cotton shirt** das Baumwollhemd; **2** (*thread*) Nähgarn das (PL die Nähgarne).

cotton wool *noun* Watte die.

couch *noun* Couch die (PL die Couchs).

cough *noun* Husten der; **a nasty cough** ein schlimmer Husten; **to have a cough** Husten haben.

cough *verb* husten.

could *verb* **1** (*the past tense of können is used to translate 'was able to'*) **I couldn't open it** ich konnte es nicht aufmachen; **they couldn't come** sie konnten nicht kommen; **she did all she could** sie hat getan, was sie konnte; **he couldn't drive** er konnte nicht Auto fahren; **she couldn't see anything** sie konnte überhaupt nichts sehen; **2** (*the past tense of dürfen is used to translate 'was allowed to'*) **they couldn't smoke there** sie durften dort nicht rauchen; **3** (*might*) (*the subjunctive of können is used to translate a wish or suggestion*) **could I speak to David?** könnte ich mit David sprechen?; **you could try phoning** du könntest versuchen anzurufen; **if he could pay** wenn er zahlen könnte; **he could be right** er könnte recht haben.

council *noun* Stadtrat der (PL die Stadträte).

count *verb* **1** (*reckon up*) zählen; **I counted my money** ich habe mein Geld gezählt; **2** (*include*) mitzählen

SEP; **thirty-five not counting the children** fünfunddreißig, die Kinder nicht mitgezählt.

counter noun 1 (in a shop) Ladentisch der (PL die Ladentische); 2 (in a post office or bank) Schalter der (PL die Schalter); 3 (in a bar or café) Theke die (PL die Theken); 4 (for board games) Spielmarke die (PL die Spielmarken).

country noun 1 (Germany, etc.) Land das (PL die Länder); **a foreign country** ein fremdes Land; **from another country** aus einem anderen Land; 2 (not town) Land das; **in the country** auf dem Land; **country road** die Landstraße.

country dancing noun Volkstanz der.

countryside noun 1 (not town) Land das; 2 (scenery) Landschaft die.

county noun Grafschaft die (PL die Grafschaften).

couple noun 1 (a pair) Paar das (PL die Paare); **a couple of** ein paar; **a couple of times** ein paar Mal; **I've got a couple of things to do** ich habe ein paar Sachen zu tun.

courage noun Mut der.

courgette noun Zucchini die (PL die Zucchini).

courier noun 1 (for tourist group) Reiseleiter der (PL die Reiseleiter), Reiseleiterin die (PL die Reiseleiterinnen); 2 (delivery person) Kurier der (PL die Kuriere); **it will be delivered by courier** es wird mit Kurierdienst gebracht.

course noun 1 (lessons) Kurs der (PL die Kurse); **computer course** der Computerkurs; **to go on a course**

einen Kurs machen; 2 (part of a meal) Gang der (PL die Gänge); **the main course** der Hauptgang; 3 **golf course** der Golfplatz; 4 **of course** natürlich; **yes, of course!** ja, natürlich!; **he's forgotten, of course** er hat es natürlich vergessen.

court noun 1 (for playing sports) Platz der (PL die Plätze); 2 (law court) Gericht das; **to go to court** vor Gericht gehen.

cousin noun Cousin der (PL die Cousins), Kusine die (PL die Kusinen); **my cousin Sonia** meine Kusine Sonia.

cover noun 1 (of a book) Einband der (PL die Einbände); 2 (for a duvet or cushion) Bezug der (PL die Bezüge).

cover verb 1 (to cover up) zudecken SEP; **he covered her with a blanket** er hat sie mit einer Decke zugedeckt; 2 **he was covered in spots** er war mit Pickeln übersät; **the room was covered in dust** das Zimmer war völlig verstaubt; 3 (with leaves, snow, or for protection) bedecken; **the ground was covered with snow** der Boden war mit Schnee bedeckt; 4 (with fabric) beziehen✦.

cow noun Kuh die (PL die Kühe); **mad cow disease** der Rinderwahn.

coward noun Feigling der (PL die Feiglinge).

cowboy noun Cowboy der (PL die Cowboys).

crab noun Krabbe die (PL die Krabben).

crack noun 1 (in a glass or cup) Sprung der (PL die Sprünge); 2 (in

a
b
c
d
e
f
g
h
i
j
k
l
m
n
o
p
q
r
s
t
u
v
w
x
y
z

wood or a wall) Riss der (PL die Risse); **3** *(a cracking noise)* Knacks der (PL die Knackse).

crack verb **1** *(to make a crack in)* anschlagen ✧ SEP; **2** *(to break)* zerbrechen ✧; **3** *(to make a noise)* *(a twig)* knacken.

cracker noun **1** *(biscuit)* Cracker der (PL die Cracker); **2** *(Christmas cracker)* Knallbonbon der (PL die Knallbonbons).

craft noun *(at school)* Werken das.

cramp noun Krampf der (PL die Krämpfe); **to have cramp in your leg** einen Krampf im Bein haben.

crane noun Kran der (PL die Kräne).

crash noun **1** *(an accident)* Unfall der (PL die Unfälle); **car crash** der Autounfall; **2** *(a noise)* Krachen das.

crash verb **1** *(a plane)* abstürzen SEP (PERF sein); **the plane crashed** das Flugzeug ist abgestürzt; **2** *(have a collision in a car)* einen Unfall haben; **3 to crash into something** gegen etwas (ACC) krachen (PERF sein); **the car crashed into a tree** das Auto krachte gegen einen Baum.

crash course noun Schnellkurs der (PL die Schnellkurse).

crash helmet noun Sturzhelm der (PL die Sturzhelme).

crate noun Kiste der (PL die Kisten).

crawl noun *(in swimming)* Kraulen das.

crawl verb **1** *(a person)* kriechen ✧ (PERF sein), *(a baby)* krabbeln (PERF sein); **2** *(cars in a jam)* im Schneckentempo fahren ✧ (PERF

sein); **we were crawling along** wir fuhren im Schneckentempo.

crayon noun **1** *(wax)* Wachsmalstift der (PL die Wachsmalstifte); **2** *(coloured pencil)* Buntstift der (PL die Buntstifte).

craze noun Mode die; **the craze for rollerblades** die Inlinerwelle.

crazy adjective verrückt; **to be crazy for something** verrückt auf etwas (ACC) sein.

cream noun Sahne die; **strawberries and cream** Erdbeeren mit Sahne.

cream cheese noun Frischkäse der.

creased adjective zerknittert.

create verb (er)schaffen ✧.

creative adjective kreativ.

creature noun Geschöpf das (PL die Geschöpfe).

crèche noun Kinderkrippe die (PL die Kinderkrippen).

credit noun Kredit der; **to buy something on credit** etwas auf Kredit kaufen.

credit card noun Kreditkarte die (PL die Kreditkarten).

cress noun Kresse die.

crew noun *(on a ship or plane)* Besatzung die; **2 camera crew** das Kamerateam; **3** *(in water sports)* Mannschaft die (PL die Mannschaften).

crew cut noun Bürstenschnitt der (PL die Bürstenschnitte).

cricket noun **1** *(game)* Kricket das; **to play cricket** Kricket spielen; **2** *(insect)* Grille die (PL die Grillen).

cricket bat noun Kricketschläger der (PL die Kricketschläger).

crime noun 1 Verbrechen das (PL die Verbrechen); **theft is a crime** Diebstahl ist ein Verbrechen; 2 (criminality) Kriminalität die; **to fight crime** die Kriminalität bekämpfen.

criminal noun Kriminelle der/die (PL die Kriminellen).

criminal adjective kriminell.

crisis noun Krise die (PL die Krisen).

crisp noun Chip der (PL die Chips); **a packet of potato crisps** eine Tüte Kartoffelchips.

crisp adjective 1 (biscuit) knusprig; 2 (apple) knackig.

critical adjective 1 kritisch (remark, medical condition); 2 entscheidend (moment).

criticism noun Kritik die.

criticize verb kritisieren.

crocodile noun Krokodil das (PL die Krokodile).

crook noun (criminal) Gauner der (PL die Gauner), Gaunerin die (PL die Gaunerinnen).

crop noun Ernte die.

cross noun Kreuz das (PL die Kreuze).

cross adjective ärgerlich; **she was very cross** sie war sehr ärgerlich; **I'm cross with you** ich bin sehr ärgerlich auf dich.

cross verb 1 (to cross over) überqueren; **to cross the road** die Straße überqueren; **to cross your legs** die Beine übereinander schlagen✧; 3 (to cross each other) sich kreuzen; **the two roads cross here** die beiden Straßen kreuzen sich hier.

● **to cross out** durchstreichen✧ SEP.

cross-Channel adjective a cross-Channel ferry eine Fähre über den Ärmelkanal.

cross-country noun 1 Crosslauf der; 2 cross-country skiing der Langlauf.

crossing noun 1 (from one place to another) Überquerung die (PL die Überquerungen); 2 (a sea journey) Überfahrt die (PL die Überfahrten); **Channel crossing** die Überfahrt über den Ärmelkanal; 3 pedestrian crossing der Fußgängerübergang; **level crossing** der Bahnübergang.

crossroads noun Kreuzung die (PL die Kreuzungen); **at the crossroads** an der Kreuzung.

crossword noun Kreuzworträtsel das (PL die Kreuzworträtsel); **to do the crossword** ein Kreuzworträtsel machen.

crow noun Krähe die (PL die Krähen).

crow verb (a cock) krähen.

crowd noun 1 Menschenmenge die (PL die Menschenmengen); **in the crowd** in der Menschenmenge; 2 (spectators) **a crowd of five thousand** fünftausend Zuschauer (plural).

crowd verb to crowd into or onto something sich in etwas (ACC) drängen; **we all crowded into the train** wir drängten uns alle in den Zug.

crowded adjective überfüllt.

crown noun Krone die (PL die Kronen).

crude adjective **1** (rough and ready) primitiv; **2** (vulgar) ordinär.

cruel adjective grausam.

cruise noun Kreuzfahrt die (PL die Kreuzfahrten); **to go on a cruise** eine Kreuzfahrt machen.

crumb noun Krümel der (PL die Krümel).

crumpled adjective zerknittert.

crunchy adjective knusprig.

crush verb zerquetschen.

crust noun Kruste die (PL die Krusten).

crusty adjective knusprig.

crutch noun Krücke die (PL die Krücken); **to be on crutches** an Krücken gehen.

cry noun Schrei der (PL die Schreie).

cry verb **1** (weep) weinen; **2** (call out) schreien✧.

cub noun **1** (animal) Junge das (PL die Jungen); **2** (boy scout) Wölfling der (PL die Wölflinge).

cube noun Würfel der (PL die Würfel); **ice cube** der Eiswürfel.

cubic adjective (in measurements) Kubik-; **three cubic metres** drei Kubikmeter.

cubicle noun **1** (in a changing room) Kabine die; **2** (in a public lavatory) Toilette die (PL die Toiletten).

cuckoo noun Kuckuck der (PL die Kuckucke).

cucumber noun Gurke die (PL die Gurken).

cuddle noun **to give somebody a cuddle** jemanden in den Arm nehmen.

cuddle verb schmusen.

cue noun (billiards, pool, snooker) Queue das (PL die Queues).

cuff noun (on a shirt) Manschette die (PL die Manschetten).

cul-de-sac noun Sackgasse die (PL die Sackgassen).

culture noun Kultur die (PL die Kulturen).

cunning adjective listig.

cup noun **1** (for drinking) Tasse die (PL die Tassen); **a cup of tea** eine Tasse Tee; **2** (a trophy) Pokal der (PL die Pokale).

cupboard noun Schrank der (PL die Schränke); **in the kitchen cupboard** im Küchenschrank.

cup tie noun Pokalspiel das (PL die Pokalspiele).

cure noun Heilmittel das (PL die Heilmittel).

cure verb heilen.

curiosity noun Neugier die.

curious adjective neugierig.

curl noun Locke die (PL die Locken).

curl verb **1** locken (hair); **2** (of hair) sich locken.

currant noun Korinthe die (PL die Korinthen).

currency noun Währung die (PL die Währungen); **the Japanese currency** die japanische Währung; **foreign currencies** Devisen (plural).

current noun **1** (electricity) Strom der, **2** (in water or air) Strömung die (PL die Strömungen).

current adjective aktuell.

current affairs noun Tagespolitik die.

curriculum noun Lehrplan der (PL die Lehrpläne).

curry noun Curry das; **vegetable curry** das Gemüse in Currysoße.

cursor noun Cursor der (PL die Cursors).

curtain noun Vorhang der (PL die Vorhänge).

cushion noun Kissen das (PL die Kissen).

custard noun Vanillesoße die (PL die Vanillesoßen).

custom noun Brauch der (PL die Bräuche).

customer noun Kunde der (PL die Kunden), Kundin die (PL die Kundinnen); **customer services** Kundendienst der.

customs hall noun Zollabfertigung die.

customs officer noun Zollbeamte der (PL die Zollbeamten), Zollbeamtin die (PL die Zollbeamtinnen).

customs plural noun Zoll der; **to go through customs** durch den Zoll gehen.

cut noun 1 (injury) Schnittwunde die (PL die Schnittwunden); 2 (haircut) Schnitt der (PL die Schnitte).

cut verb 1 schneiden◇; **can you cut the bread please?** kannst du bitte das Brot schneiden?; **you'll cut yourself!** du schneidest dich!; **Kevin's cut his finger** Kevin hat sich in den Finger geschnitten; 2 **to cut the grass** den Rasen mähen; 3 **to get your hair cut** sich (DAT) die Haare schneiden lassen; **I had my hair cut** ich habe mir die Haare schneiden lassen; 4 **to cut prices** die Preise senken.

● **to cut down** 1 fällen (a tree); 2 **to cut down on cigarettes** seinen Zigarettenkonsum einschränken SEP.

● **to cut out something** 1 etwas ausschneiden◇ SEP (a shape, a newspaper article); 2 etwas streichen◇ (sugar, fatty food, holidays, for example).

● **to cut something up** etwas klein schneiden◇ (food).

cutlery noun Besteck das (PL die Bestecke).

CV noun Lebenslauf der (PL die Lebensläufe).

cycle noun (bike) Rad das (PL die Räder).

cycle verb Rad fahren◇ (PERF sein); **do you like cycling?** fährst du gerne Rad?; **we cycle to school** wir fahren mit dem Rad zur Schule.

cycle lane noun Fahrradweg die (PL die Fahrradwege).

cycle race noun Radrennen das (PL die Radrennen).

cycling noun Radfahren das.

cycling shorts noun Radlerhose die (PL die Radlerhosen).

cyclist noun Radfahrer der (PL die Radfahrer), Radfahrerin die (PL die Radfahrerinnen).

Dd

dad noun Vati der (PL die Vatis).

daffodil noun Osterglocke die (PL die Osterglocken).

a
b
c
d
e
f
g
h
i
j
k
l
m
n
o
p
q
r
s
t
u
v
w
x
y
z

daily *adjective* täglich; **his daily visit** sein täglicher Besuch.

daily *adverb* täglich; **she visits him daily** sie besucht ihn täglich.

dairy products *plural noun* Milchprodukte (*plural*).

daisy *noun* Gänseblümchen *das* (PL die Gänseblümchen).

dam *noun* Damm *der* (PL die Dämme).

damage *noun* Schaden *der* (PL die Schäden); **to do a lot of damage** großen Schaden anrichten.

damage *verb* beschädigen.

damn *noun* **I don't give a damn** das ist mir piepegal (*informal*).

damn *exclamation* **damn!** verdammt!

damp *adjective* feucht.

damp *noun* Feuchtigkeit *die*.

dance *noun* Tanz *der* (PL die Tänze); **a folk dance** ein Volkstanz.

dance *verb* tanzen; **I like dancing** ich tanze gerne.

dancer *noun* Tänzer *der* (PL die Tänzer), Tänzerin *die* (PL die Tänzerinnen).

dancing class *noun* Tanzstunde *die* (PL die Tanzstunden); **to go to dancing classes** in die Tanzstunde gehen.

dancing *noun* Tanzen *das*.

dandruff *noun* Schuppen (*plural*).

danger *noun* Gefahr *die* (PL die Gefahren); **to be in danger** in Gefahr sein.

dangerous *adjective* gefährlich; **it's dangerous to drive too fast** es ist gefährlich, zu schnell zu fahren.

Danish *noun* Dänisch *das*.

Danish *adjective* dänisch; **he's Danish** er ist Däne; **she's Danish** sie ist Dänin.

dare *verb* **1** wagen; **to dare to do something** es wagen, etwas zu tun; **I didn't dare suggest it** ich habe es nicht gewagt, das vorzuschlagen; **2 don't you dare tell her I'm here!** untersteh dich, ihr zu sagen, dass ich hier bin!; **3 I dare you!** trau dich doch nicht!; **I dare you to tell him!** sag's ihm doch wenn du dich traust!

daring *adjective* gewagt; **that was a bit daring** das war etwas gewagt.

dark *noun* **in the dark** im Dunkeln; **after dark** nach Einbruch der Dunkelheit; **to be afraid of the dark** Angst im Dunkeln haben.

dark *adjective* **1** (*colour*) dunkel (*adjectives ending in -el drop the e when followed by a vowel, which means that* dunkel *becomes* dunkler/dunkle/dunkles); **a dark colour** eine dunkle Farbe; **it gets dark around five** es wird gegen fünf dunkel; **2 a dark blue skirt** ein dunkelblauer Rock; **she has dark brown hair** sie hat dunkelbraune Haare.

darkness *noun* Dunkelheit *die*; **in darkness** in der Dunkelheit.

darling *noun* Liebling *der* (PL die Lieblinge); **see you later, darling!** bis später, Liebling!

dart *noun* **1** Wurfpfeil der (PL die Wurfpfeile); **2** (*game*) darts Darts das; **to play darts** Darts spielen.

data *plural noun* Daten (*plural*).

database *noun* Datenbank die (PL die Datenbanken).

date *noun* **1** Datum das (PL die Daten); **what's the date today?** welches Datum haben wir heute?; **the date of the meeting** das Datum für das Treffen; **what date is he coming?** wann kommt er?; **2** Termin der (PL die Termine); **the last date for payment** der letzte Zahlungstermin; **3 out of date** ungültig; **my passport's out of date** mein Pass ist ungültig; **4** (*appointment*) Verabredung die (PL die Verabredungen); **Laura's got a date with Frank** Laura ist mit Frank verabredet; **5** (*fruit*) Dattel die (PL die Datteln).

date of birth *noun* Geburtsdatum das (PL die Geburtsdaten).

daughter *noun* Tochter die (PL die Töchter); **Tina's daughter** Tinas Tochter.

daughter-in-law *noun* Schwiegertochter die (PL die Schwiegertöchter).

dawn *noun* Morgendämmerung die (PL die Morgendämmerungen).

day *noun* **1** Tag der (PL die Tage); **three days later** drei Tage später; **a few days ago** vor ein paar Tagen; **the day I went to London** an dem Tag, an dem ich nach London gefahren bin; **we spent the day in London** wir haben den Tag in London verbracht; **it rained all day** es hat den ganzen Tag geregnet; **the day after** am Tag danach; **the day**

after the wedding am Tag nach der Hochzeit; **the day before** am Tag davor; **the day before the wedding** am Tag vor der Hochzeit; **2 the day after tomorrow** übermorgen; **my sister's arriving the day after tomorrow** meine Schwester kommt übermorgen an; **3 the day before yesterday** vorgestern; **my brother arrived the day before yesterday** mein Bruder kam vorgestern an; **4 during the day** tagsüber.

dead *adjective* tot; **her father's dead** ihr Vater ist tot.

dead *adverb* (*really*) irre (*informal*); **he's dead nice** er ist irre nett; **it was dead good** es war irre gut; **it was dead easy** es war kinderleicht; **you're dead right** du hast völlig Recht; **she arrived dead on time** sie kam auf die Minute pünktlich an.

dead end *noun* Sackgasse die (PL die Sackgassen).

deadline *noun* letzte Termin der (PL die letzten Termine).

deaf *adjective* taub.

deafening *adjective* ohrenbetäubend.

deal *noun* **1** (*involving money*) Geschäft das (PL die Geschäfte); **it's a good deal** das ist ein gutes Geschäft; **2** (*agreement*) Vereinbarung die (PL die Voreinbarungen); **to make a deal with somebody** mit jemandem eine Vereinbarung treffen; **it's a deal!** abgemacht!; **3 a great deal of** viel; **I don't have a great deal of time** ich habe nicht viel Zeit.

a
b
c
d
e
f
g
h
i
j
k
l
m
n
o
p
q
r
s
t
u
v
w
x
y
z

deal verb (in cards) geben; **it's you to deal** du gibst.

● **to deal with something** sich um etwas (ACC) kümmern; **Linda deals with the accounts** Linda kümmert sich um die Buchführung; **I'll deal with it as soon as possible** ich kümmere mich so schnell wie möglich darum.

dear adjective **1** lieb; **Dear Franz** Lieber Franz; **Dear Mr Smith** Sehr geehrter Herr Smith; **2** (expensive) teuer.

death noun Tod der; **after his father's death** nach dem Tod seines Vaters; **three deaths** drei Todesfälle; ★ **I was bored to death** ich habe mich zu Tode gelangweilt; ★ **I'm sick to death of it** ich habe es gründlich satt.

death penalty noun Todesstrafe die.

debate noun Debatte die (PL die Debatten).

debate verb debattieren.

debt noun (money owed) Schulden (plural); **to get into debt** in Schulden geraten.

decade noun Jahrzehnt das (PL die Jahrzehnte).

decaffeinated adjective koffeinfrei.

deceive verb betrügen✧.

December noun Dezember der (PL die Dezember); **in December** im Dezember.

decent adjective anständig; **a decent salary** ein anständiges Gehalt; **a decent meal** ein anständiges Essen.

decide verb **1** entscheiden✧; **to decide on something** sich für etwas (ACC) entscheiden; **he's decided against buying a new car** er hat sich entschieden, kein neues Auto zu kaufen; **2 to decide to do something** sich entschließen✧, etwas zu tun; **they've decided to buy a house** sie haben sich entschlossen, ein Haus zu kaufen.

decimal adjective Dezimal-; **decimal number** die Dezimalzahl.

decimal point noun Komma das (PL die Kommas).

decision noun Entscheidung die (PL die Entscheidungen); **to make a decision** eine Entscheidung treffen.

deckchair noun Liegestuhl der (PL die Liegestühle).

declare verb **1** erklären; **2** (at customs) **nothing to declare** nichts zu verzollen.

decorate verb **1** schmücken; **to decorate the Christmas tree** den Weihnachtsbaum schmücken; **2** (with paint) streichen✧, (with wallpaper) tapezieren; **we're decorating the kitchen this weekend** wir streichen dieses Wochenende die Küche.

decoration noun Verzierung die (PL die Verzierungen); **Christmas decorations** der Weihnachtsschmuck.

decrease noun Rückgang der (PL die Rückgänge); **a decrease in the number of accidents** ein Rückgang in der Anzahl der Unfälle.

decrease *verb* zurückgehen ✧ SEP (PERF *sein*), abnehmen ✧ SEP.

deep *adjective* tief; **a deep feeling of gratitude** ein tiefes Dankbarkeitsgefühl; **how deep is the swimming pool?** wie tief ist das Schwimmbecken?; **a hole two metres deep** ein zwei Meter tiefes Loch.

deep end *noun* Schwimmbecken *das* (PL *die* Schwimmbecken); **deep end: 2 metres** Wassertiefe: 2 Meter.

deep freeze *noun* Tiefkühltruhe *die* (PL *die* Tiefkühltruhen), (*upright*) Tiefkühlschrank *der* (PL *die* Tiefkühlschränke).

deeply *adverb* tief.

deer *noun* **1** Hirsch *der* (PL *die* Hirsche); **2** (*roe deer*) Reh *das* (PL *die* Rehe).

defeat *noun* Niederlage *die* (PL *die* Niederlagen).

defeat *verb* schlagen✧.

defence *noun* Verteidigung *die*.

defend *verb* vorteidigen.

defender *noun* Verteidiger *der* (PL *die* Verteidiger), Verteidigerin *die* (PL *die* Verteidigerinnen).

definite *adjective* **1** eindeutig; **a definite improvement** eine eindeutige Besserung; **2** (*certain*) sicher; **it's not definite yet** es ist noch nicht sicher; **3** (*exact*) klar; **a definite answer** eine klare Antwort.

definite article *noun* bestimmter Artikel *der* (PL *die* bestimmten Artikel).

definitely *adverb* **1** (*when giving your opinion about something*) eindeutig; **your German is definitely better than mine** dein Deutsch ist eindeutig besser als meins; **2** (*without doubt*) bestimmt; **she's definitely going to be there** sie wird bestimmt dort sein; **I'm definitely not coming** ich komme ganz bestimmt nicht; **3** '**are you sure you like this one better?**' – '**definitely!**' 'gefällt dir diese wirklich besser?' · 'auf jeden Fall!'

definition *noun* Definition *die* (PL *die* Definitionen).

degree *noun* **1** Grad *der* (PL *die* Grade); **thirty degrees** dreißig Grad; **2 a university degree** ein akademischer Grad.

delay *noun* Verspätung *die* (PL *die* Verspätungen); **a two-hour delay** eine zweistündige Verspätung.

delay *verb* **1** (*hold up*) aufhalten✧ SEP; **she was delayed in the office** sie ist im Büro aufgehalten worden; **2** (*train, plane*) **to be delayed** Verspätung haben; **the flight was delayed by bad weather** der Flug hatte wegen des schlechten Wetters Verspätung; **3** (*postpone*) aufschieben✧ SEP; **the decision has been delayed until Thursday** die Entscheidung wurde bis Donnerstag aufgeschoben.

delete *verb* **1** streichen✧; **2** (*in computing*) löschen.

deliberate *adjective* absichtlich.

deliberately *adverb* absichtlich; **she did it deliberately** sie hat das absichtlich getan.

delicate *adjective* **1** (*fabric, health*) zart; **2** (*situation, question*) heikel; **3** (*taste, smell*) fein.

delicatessen noun
Feinkostgeschäft das (PL die
Feinkostgeschäfte).

delicious adjective köstlich.

delighted adjective hocherfreut;
to be delighted begeistert sein;
**they're delighted with their new
flat** sie sind von ihrer neuen
Wohnung begeistert; **I'm delighted
that you can come** ich freue mich
sehr, dass ihr kommen könnt.

deliver verb 1 liefern; **they're
delivering the washing machine
tomorrow** die Waschmaschine
wird morgen geliefert; 2 (mail,
newspapers) zustellen SEP.

delivery noun 1 Lieferung die (PL
die Lieferungen); 2 (of mail,
newspapers) Zustellung die (PL die
Zustellungen).

demand noun Nachfrage die (PL die
Nachfragen); **much in demand**
sehr gefragt.

demand verb verlangen.

demo noun (protest) Demo die
(informal) (PL die Demos).

democracy noun Demokratie die
(PL die Demokratien).

democratic adjective
demokratisch.

demolish verb abreißen ◇ SEP.

demonstrate verb 1 (a machine,
product, or technique) vorführen
SEP; 2 (protest) demonstrieren; **to
demonstrate against something**
gegen etwas (ACC) demonstrieren.

demonstration noun 1 (of a
machine, product, or technique)
Vorführung die (PL die
Vorführungen); 2 (protest)
Demonstration die (PL die
Demonstrationen).

demonstrator noun
Demonstrant der (PL die
Demonstranten), Demonstrantin
die (PL die Demonstrantinnen).

denim noun Jeansstoff der (PL die
Jeansstoffe); **a denim jacket** eine
Jeansjacke.

Denmark noun Dänemark das.

dental adjective 1 Zahn-; **dental
floss** die Zahnseide; **dental hygiene**
die Zahnpflege; 2 **to have a dental
appointment** einen Zahnarzt
Termin haben.

dental surgeon noun Zahnarzt
der (PL die Zahnärzte), Zahnärztin die
(PL die Zahnärztinnen).

dentist noun Zahnarzt der (PL die
Zahnärzte), Zahnärztin die (PL die
Zahnärztinnen); **my mum's a
dentist** meine Mutter ist
Zahnärztin.

deny verb bestreiten ◇.

deodorant noun Deodorant das
(PL die Deodorants).

depart verb 1 (set out on a journey)
abreisen SEP; 2 (train,
coach) abfahren ◇ SEP (PERF sein);
3 (plane) abfliegen ◇ SEP (PERF sein).

department noun 1 (in a shop,
firm, or hospital) Abteilung die (PL
die Abteilungen); **the men's
department** die Herrenabteilung;
2 (of a university) Seminar das (PL
die Seminare); **the history
department** das Seminar für
Geschichte; 3 (in school)
Fachbereich der (PL die
Fachbereiche).

department store noun
Kaufhaus das (PL die Kaufhäuser).

departure noun 1 (of a person)
Abreise die; 2 (of a car, train)

Abfahrt die; 3 (of a plane) Abflug der.

departure lounge noun Abflughalle die (PL die Abflughallen).

depend verb 1 to depend on abhängen ❖ SEP von (+ DAT); it depends on the price das hängt vom Preis ab; it depends on what you want das hängt davon ab, was du willst; 2 it depends es kommt darauf an.

deposit noun 1 (when renting or hiring) Kaution die (PL die Kautionen); 2 (when booking a holiday or hotel room) Anzahlung die (PL die Anzahlungen); to pay a deposit eine Anzahlung leisten; 3 (on a bottle) Pfand das.

depressed adjective deprimiert.

depressing adjective deprimierend.

depth noun Tiefe die.

deputy noun Stellvertreter der (PL die Stellvertreter), Stellvertreterin die (PL die Stellvertreterinnen); the deputy headteacher Konrektor der (PL die Konrektoren), Konrektorin die (PL die Konrektorinnen).

describe verb beschreiben ❖.

description noun Beschreibung die (PL die Beschreibungen).

desert noun Wüste die (PL die Wüsten).

desert island noun verlassene Insel die (PL die verlassenen Inseln).

deserve verb verdienen.

design noun 1 Konstruktion die (PL die Konstruktionen); the design of the plane die Flugzeugkonstruktion; 2 (artistic

design) Design das (PL die Designs); **modern design** modernes Design; 3 (pattern) Muster das (PL die Muster); **a floral design** ein Blumenmuster; 4 (sketch) Entwurf der (PL die Entwürfe).

design verb 1 konstruieren (a machine, plane, system); 2 entwerfen ❖ (costumes, fabric, scenery).

designer noun Designer der (PL die Designer), Designerin die (PL die Designerinnen).

desk noun 1 (in an office or at home) Schreibtisch der (PL die Schreibtische); 2 (pupil's) Pult das (PL die Pulte); 3 the reception desk die Rezeption; the information desk die Auskunft.

despair noun Verzweiflung die.

despair verb to despair of doing something alle Hoffnung aufgeben ❖ SEP, etwas zu tun.

desperate adjective 1 verzweifelt; **a desperate attempt** ein verzweifelter Versuch; 2 to be desperate to do something etwas dringend tun müssen; **I'm desperate to speak to you** ich muss dich dringend sprechen; to be desperate for something etwas dringend brauchen.

dessert noun Nachtisch der (PL die Nachtische); **what's for dessert?** was gibts zum Nachtisch?

destination noun Ziel das (PL die Ziele).

destroy verb zerstören.

destruction noun Zerstörung die.

a b c d e f g h i j k l m n o p q r s t u v w x y z

detached house noun
Einfamilienhaus das (PL die
Einfamilienhäuser).

detail noun Einzelheit die (PL die
Einzelheiten).

detailed adjective ausführlich.

detective noun 1 (in the police)
Kriminalbeamte der (PL die
Kriminalbeamten),
Kriminalbeamtin die (PL die
Kriminalbeamtinnen); 2 private
detective der Detektiv, die
Detektivin.

detective story noun
Detektivgeschichte die (PL die
Detektivgeschichten).

detention noun 1 (at school)
Nachsitzen das; 2 (in prison) Haft
die.

detergent noun Waschmittel das
(PL die Waschmittel).

determined adjective
entschlossen; he's determined to
leave er ist fest entschlossen zu
gehen.

detour noun Umweg der (PL die
Umwege).

develop verb 1 entwickeln; to get
a film developed einen Film
entwickeln lassen; 2 sich
entwickeln; how children develop
wie Kinder sich entwickeln.

developing country noun
Entwicklungsland das (PL die
Entwicklungsländer).

development noun Entwicklung
die (PL die Entwicklungen).

devil noun Teufel der (PL die Teufel).

devoted adjective treu.

diabetes noun Zuckerkrankheit
die.

diabetic noun Diabetiker der (PL
die Diabetiker), Diabetikerin die (PL
die Diabetikerinnen).

diabetic adjective zuckerkrank; to
be diabetic zuckerkrank sein.

diagnosis noun Diagnose die (PL
die Diagnosen).

diagonal adjective diagonal.

diagram noun Diagramm das (PL
die Diagramme).

dial verb wählen; I dialled the
wrong number ich habe die falsche
Nummer gewählt; dial 00 49 for
Germany wählen Sie die Vorwahl
00 49 für Deutschland.

dialling tone noun Freizeichen
das.

dialogue noun Dialog der (PL die
Dialoge).

diamond noun 1 Diamant der (PL
die Diamanten), (gemstone) Brillant
der (PL die Brillanten); 2 (in cards)
Karo das; the jack of diamonds der
Karobube; 3 (shape) Raute die (PL
die Rauten).

diarrhoea noun Durchfall der.

diary noun 1 (for appointments)
Terminkalender der (PL die
Terminkalender); 2 Tagebuch das
(PL die Tagebücher); to keep a diary
ein Tagebuch führen.

dice noun Würfel der (PL die Würfel);
to throw the dice würfeln.

dictation noun Diktat das (PL die
Diktate).

dictionary noun Wörterbuch das
(PL die Wörterbücher).

did verb SEE DO.

die verb 1 sterben ✧ (PERF sein); my
grannie died in January meine
Oma starb im Januar; 2 to be
dying to do something darauf

brennen, etwas zu tun; **I'm dying to meet her** ich brenne darauf, sie kennen zu lernen.

diesel *noun* **1** Dieselöl *das*; **2 diesel engine** der Dieselmotor; **diesel car** der Diesel.

diet *noun* **1** Ernährung *die*; **a healthy diet** eine gesunde Ernährung; **2** (*slimming or special*) Diät *die* (PL die Diäten); **to be on a diet** Diät machen.

difference *noun* **1** Unterschied der (PL die Unterschiede); **I can't see any difference between the two** ich erkenne keinen Unterschied zwischen den beiden; **what's the difference between ...?** was ist der Unterschied zwischen ...?; **2 it makes a difference** es ist ein Unterschied; **it makes no difference** es ist egal; **it makes no difference what I say** es ist egal, was ich sage.

different *adjective* **1** verschieden; **the two sisters are very different** die beiden Schwestern sind sehr verschieden; **2 to be different from** anders sein als; **she's very different from her sister** sie ist ganz anders als ihre Schwester; **3** (*separate*) anderer/andere/anderes; **she reads a different book every day** sie liest jeden Tag ein anderes Buch.

difficult *adjective* schwer; **it's really difficult** es ist sehr schwer; **he finds it difficult** es fällt ihm schwer.

difficulty *noun* Schwierigkeit *die* (PL die Schwierigkeiten); **to have difficulty doing something** Schwierigkeiten haben, etwas zu

tun; **I had difficulty finding your house** ich hatte Schwierigkeiten, dein Haus zu finden.

dig *verb* graben✧; **to dig a hole** ein Loch graben.

digestion *noun* Verdauung *die*.

digital *adjective* digital; **digital watch** die Digitaluhr; **digital recording** die Digitalaufnahme.

dim *adjective* **1** schwach; **a dim light** ein schwaches Licht; **2** beschränkt; **she's a bit dim** sie ist ein bisschen beschränkt.

din *noun* Lärm der; **stop making such a din!** hör auf, so einen Lärm zu machen!

dinghy *noun* **1 sailing dinghy** das Dingi; **2 rubber dinghy** das Schlauchboot.

dining room *noun* Esszimmer das (PL die Esszimmer); **in the dining room** im Esszimmer.

dinner *noun* **1** (*evening*) Abendessen das (PL die Abendessen); **to invite somebody to dinner** jemanden zum Abendessen einladen; **2** (*midday*) Mittagessen das (PL die Mittagessen); **to have school dinner** in der Schulkantine zu Mittag essen.

dinner party *noun* Abendessen das (PL die Abendessen).

dinner time *noun* Essenszeit die.

dinosaur *noun* Dinosaurier der (PL die Dinosaurier).

diploma *noun* Diplom das (PL die Diplome).

direct *adjective* direkt; **a direct flight** ein Direktflug.

direct adverb direkt; **the bus goes direct to the airport** der Bus fährt direkt zum Flughafen.

direct verb **1** to direct a film or a play bei einem Film oder einem Theaterstück Regie führen; **2** regeln (traffic).

direction noun **1** Richtung die (PL die Richtungen); **to go in the other direction** in die andere Richtung gehen; **2** to ask somebody for directions jemanden nach dem Weg fragen; **3** directions for use die Gebrauchsanweisung (singular).

directly adverb direkt; **directly afterwards** gleich danach.

director noun **1** (of a company) Direktor der (PL die Direktoren), Direktorin die (PL die Direktorinnen); **2** (of a play, film) Regisseur der (PL die Regisseure), Regisseurin die (PL die Regisseurinnen); **3** (of a programme) Leiter der (PL die Leiter), Leiterin die (PL die Leiterinnen).

directory noun Telefonbuch das (PL die Telefonbücher); **he's ex-directory** seine Nummer steht nicht im Telefonbuch.

dirt noun Schmutz der.

dirty adjective schmutzig; **my hands are dirty** ich habe schmutzige Hände; **to get something dirty** etwas schmutzig machen; **you'll get your dress dirty** du machst dir das Kleid schmutzig; **to get dirty** schmutzig werden; **the curtains get dirty quickly** die Vorhänge werden sehr schnell schmutzig.

disability noun Behinderung die (PL die Behinderungen); **does he have a disability?** ist er behindert?

disabled adjective behindert; **disabled people** Behinderte (plural).

disadvantage noun **1** Nachteil der (PL die Nachteile); **2** to be at a disadvantage im Nachteil sein.

disagree verb **1** I disagree ich bin anderer Meinung; **2** to disagree with somebody mit jemandem nicht übereinstimmen SEP; **I disagree with James** ich stimme mit James nicht überein.

disappear verb verschwinden✧ (PERF sein).

disappearance noun Verschwinden das.

disappointed adjective enttäuscht; **I'm disappointed with my marks** ich bin über meine Noten enttäuscht.

disappointment noun Enttäuschung die (PL die Enttäuschungen).

disaster noun Katastrophe die (PL die Katastrophen); **it was a complete disaster** es war eine komplette Katastrophe.

disastrous adjective katastrophal.

disc noun **1** compact disc die Compactdisc; **2** tax disc (for a vehicle) die Steuerplakette; **3** slipped disc der Bandscheibenvorfall.

discipline noun Disziplin die.

disc-jockey noun Diskjockey der (PL die Diskjockeys).

disco *noun* **1** Disko *die* (PL die Diskos); **they're having a disco** sie veranstalten eine Disko; **2** (*club*) Disko *die* (PL die Diskos); **to go to a disco** in eine Disko gehen.

discount *noun* Rabatt *der* (PL die Rabatte).

discover *verb* entdecken.

discovery *noun* Entdeckung *die* (PL die Entdeckungen).

discreet *adjective* diskret.

discrimination *noun* Diskriminierung *die*; **discrimination against women** die Diskriminierung von Frauen; **racial discrimination** die Rassendiskriminierung.

discuss *verb* **to discuss something** etwas besprechen✧; **we'll discuss the problem tomorrow** wir besprechen das Problem morgen; **I'm going to discuss it with Phil** ich werde es mit Phil besprechen.

discussion *noun* Gespräch *das* (PL die Gespräche).

disease *noun* Krankheit *die* (PL die Krankheiten).

disguise *noun* Verkleidung *die* (PL die Verkleidungen); **to be in disguise** verkleidet sein.

disguise *verb* verkleiden; **disguised as a woman** als Frau verkleidet.

disgust *noun* Ekel *der*.

disgusted *adjective* **1** (*filled with indignation*) empört, **2** (*nauseated*) angeekelt.

disgusting *adjective* eklig.

dish *noun* **1** Schüssel *die* (PL die Schüsseln); **a large white dish** eine große weiße Schüssel; **satellite**

dish die Satellitenschüssel; **2** (*type of food*) Gericht *das* (PL die Gerichte); **risotto is my favourite dish** Risotto ist mein Lieblingsgericht; **3** (*crockery*) **the dishes** das Geschirr; **to do the dishes** Geschirr spülen.

dishcloth *noun* Spültuch *das* (PL die Spültücher).

dishonest *adjective* unehrlich.

dishonesty *noun* Unehrlichkeit *die*.

dishwasher *noun* Geschirrspülmaschine *die* (PL die Geschirrspülmaschinen).

disinfect *verb* desinfizieren.

disinfectant *noun* Desinfektionsmittel *das*.

disk *noun* Diskette *die* (PL die Disketten); **floppy disk** die Diskette; **hard disk** die Festplatte.

diskdrive *noun* Diskettenlaufwerk *das* (PL die Diskettenlaufwerke).

diskette *noun* Diskette *die* (PL die Disketten).

dismiss *verb* entlassen✧ (*an employee*).

disobedient *adjective* ungehorsam.

display *noun* **1** Ausstellung *die* (PL die Ausstellungen); **handicrafts display** die Handarbeitsausstellung; **to be on display** ausgestellt sein; **2** window display die Auslage; **3** firework display *das* Feuerwerk.

display *verb* ausstellen SEP.

disposable *adjective* Wegwerf-; **disposable towel** *das* Wegwerfhandtuch.

disqualify *verb* disqualifizieren.

disrupt *verb* stören.

dissolve *verb* auflösen SEP.

distance *noun* Entfernung die (PL die Entfernungen); **from this distance** aus dieser Entfernung; **from a distance** von weitem; **in the distance** in der Ferne; **it's within walking distance** es ist zu Fuß erreichbar.

distant *adjective* fern.

distinct *adjective* deutlich.

distinctly *adverb* **1** deutlich; **2 it's distinctly odd** es ist äußerst komisch.

distract *verb* ablenken SEP.

distribute *verb* verteilen.

district *noun* **1** (*of a town*) Stadtteil der (PL die Stadtteile); **a poor district of Berlin** ein ärmlicher Stadtteil von Berlin; **2** (*in the country*) Gebiet das (PL die Gebiete).

disturb *verb* stören; **sorry to disturb you** Entschuldigung, dass ich störe.

dive *noun* Kopfsprung der (PL die Kopfsprünge).

dive *verb* **1** einen Kopfsprung machen; **2** (*swim underwater*) tauchen (PERF sein).

diver *noun* **1** (*underwater*) Taucher der (PL die Taucher), Taucherin die (PL die Taucherinnen); **2** (*from a diving board*) Kunstspringer der (PL die Kunstspringer), Kunstspringerin die (PL die Kunstspringerinnen).

diversion *noun* (*of traffic*) Umleitung die (PL die Umleitungen).

divide *verb* teilen.

diving *noun* **1** (*underwater*) Tauchen das; **2** (*from a diving board*) Kunstspringen das.

diving board *noun* Sprungbrett das (PL die Sprungbretter).

division *noun* **1** Teilung die (PL die Teilungen); **2** (*in maths*) Division die (PL die Divisionen); **3** (*sports league*) Liga die (PL die Ligen).

divorce *noun* Scheidung die (PL die Scheidungen).

divorce *verb* sich scheiden lassen◇; **they divorced in May** sie haben sich im Mai scheiden lassen.

divorced *adjective* geschieden.

DIY *noun* **1** Heimwerken das; **2 to do DIY** heimwerken; **3 DIY shop** der Baumarkt (PL die Baumärkte).

dizzy *adjective* **I feel dizzy** mir ist schwindlig.

DJ *noun* DJ der (PL die DJs).

do *verb* **1** tun◇, machen; **what are you doing?** was machst du?; **I'm doing my homework** ich mache meine Hausaufgaben; **what have you done with the hammer?** was hast du mit dem Hammer gemacht?; **can you do me a favour?** kannst du mir einen Gefallen tun?; **do as I say** tu was ich sage; **2 she's doing the cleaning** sie putzt; **I'll do the washing up** ich wasche ab; **I must do the shopping** ich muss einkaufen gehen; **3** (*in questions*) **do you like it?** gefällt es dir?; **when does the film start?** wann fängt der Film an?; **how do you open the door?** wie macht man die Tür auf?; **do you know him?** kennst du ihn?; **4** (*in negative sentences*) **I don't like mushrooms** ich mag keine Pilze; **Rosie doesn't like spinach** Rosie mag keinen Spinat; **you didn't shut the door** du hast die Tür nicht zugemacht; **it doesn't matter** das macht nichts; **5** (*when it refers back to another verb, 'do' is not translated*) **'do you live here?' – 'yes, I do'** 'wohnst du hier?' – 'ja'; **she has more money than I do** sie hat mehr Geld als ich; **'I live in Oxford' – 'so do I'** 'ich wohne in Oxford' – 'ich auch'; **'I didn't phone Gemma' – 'neither did I'** 'ich habe Gemma nicht angerufen' – 'ich auch nicht'; **6 don't you?, doesn't he?** nicht wahr?; **you know Helen, don't you?** du kennst Helen, nicht wahr?; **she left on Thursday, didn't she?** sie ist Donnerstag abgefahren, nicht wahr?; **7 that'll do** das reicht; **it'll do like that** das geht so.

● **to do something up 1** etwas zubinden✧ SEP (*shoes*); **2** etwas zumachen SEP (*a cardigan, jacket*); **3** etwas renovieren SEP (*a house*).

● **to do without something** ohne etwas (ACC) auskommen✧ SEP (PERF *sein*); **we can do without knives** wir können ohne Messer auskommen.

doctor *noun* Arzt *der* (PL die Ärzte), Ärztin *die* (PL die Ärztinnen); **her mother's a doctor** ihre Mutter ist Ärztin.

document *noun* Dokument *das* (PL die Dokumente).

documentary *noun* Dokumentarfilm *der* (PL die Dokumentarfilme).

dodgems *plural noun* **the dodgems** Autoskooter *der* (PL die Autoskooter).

dog *noun* Hund *der* (PL die Hunde).

do-it-yourself *noun* Heimwerken *das*.

dole *noun* Arbeitslosgeld *das*; **to be on the dole** arbeitslos sein.

doll *noun* Puppe *die* (PL die Puppen).

dollar *noun* Dollar *der* (PL die Dollars).

dolphin *noun* Delfin *der* (PL die Delfine).

domino *noun* **1** Dominostein *der* (PL die Dominosteine); **2** (*game*) **dominoes** Domino *das*; **to play dominoes** Domino spielen.

donkey *noun* Esel *der* (PL die Esel).

don't SEE do.

door *noun* Tür *die* (PL die Türen); **to open the door** die Tür aufmachen; **to shut the door** die Tür zumachen.

doorbell *noun* Türklingel *die* (PL die Türklingeln); **to ring the doorbell** klingeln.

dot *noun* **1** Punkt *der* (PL die Punkte); **at ten on the dot** Punkt zehn Uhr; **2** (*small dot on fabric*) Pünktchen *das* (PL die Pünktchen).

double *adjective, adverb* **1** doppelt; **a double helping** eine doppelte Portion; **double the size** doppelt so groß; **double the time** doppelt so viel Zeit; **at double the price** zum doppelten Preis; **2 double room** das Doppelzimmer; **3 double bed** das Doppelbett.

double bass *noun* Kontrabass *der* (PL die Kontrabässe).

double-decker bus *noun* Doppeldeckerbus *der* (PL die Doppeldeckerbusse).

doubles *noun* (*in tennis*) Doppel *das* (PL die Doppel).

doubt noun Zweifel der (PL die Zweifel); **there's no doubt about it** es besteht kein Zweifel daran; **I have my doubts** ich habe gewisse Zweifel.

doubt verb to doubt something etwas bezweifeln; **I doubt it** das bezweifle ich; **I doubt that ...** ich bezweifle, dass ...; **I doubt they'll buy it** ich bezweifle, dass sie es kaufen.

doubtful adjective **1** fraglich; **it's doubtful** es ist fraglich; **2 to be doubtful about doing something** Bedenken haben, ob man etwas tun soll; **I'm doubtful about inviting them together** ich habe Bedenken, ob ich sie zusammen einladen soll.

dough noun Teig der.

doughnut noun Krapfen der (PL die Krapfen).

down adverb, preposition **1** unten; **he's down in the cellar** er ist unten im Keller; **it's down there** es ist da unten; **2 down the road** (nearby) in der Nähe; **there's a chemist's just down the road** eine Apotheke ist ganz in der Nähe; **3 to go down** nach unten gehen; **I went down to open the door** ich ging nach unten, um die Tür aufzumachen; **to walk down the street** die Straße entlanggehen ◇ SEP (PERF sein); **to run down the stairs** die Treppe runterrennen SEP (PERF sein) (informal); **4 to come down** herunterkommen ◇ SEP (PERF sein); **she came down into the kitchen** sie kam in die Küche herunter; **5 to sit down** sich setzen; **she sat down on the chair** sie setzte sich auf den Stuhl; **6 to write something down** etwas aufschreiben ◇ SEP.

downstairs adverb **1** unten; **she's downstairs** sie ist unten; **2** (with movement) nach unten; **to go downstairs** nach unten gehen; **3 im Erdgeschoss; the flat downstairs** die Wohnung im Erdgeschoss.

doze verb dösen.

dozen noun Dutzend das (PL die Dutzende).

drag noun **1 what a drag!** so'n Mist! (informal); **2 what a drag she is!** Mann, ist die langweilig! (informal).

drag verb schleppen.

dragon noun Drache der (PL die Drachen).

drain noun **1** (outlet pipe) Abflussrohr das (PL die Abflussrohre); **2 the drains:** Kanalisation die (PL die Kanalisationen).

drain verb abgießen ◇ SEP (vegetables); trockenlegen SEP (fields, land).

drama noun **1** (play) Drama das (PL die Dramen); **he made a big drama out of it** er hat ein großes Drama daraus gemacht (informal); **2** (dramatic nature) Dramatik die.

dramatic adjective dramatisch.

draught noun Luftzug der; **there's a draught in here** hier zieht es.

draughts noun Damespiel das; **to play draughts** Dame spielen.

draw noun **1** (in a match) Unentschieden das; **to end in a draw** mit einem Unentschieden enden; **2** (*lottery*) Ziehung die (PL die Ziehungen).

draw *verb* **1** zeichnen; **she can draw really well** sie kann wirklich sehr gut zeichnen; **2 to draw the curtains** (*open*) die Vorhänge aufziehen✧ SEP, (*close*) die Vorhänge zuziehen✧ SEP; **3** (*in a match*) unentschieden spielen; **we drew three all** wir haben drei zu drei unentschieden gespielt.

drawer *noun* Schublade die (PL die Schubladen).

drawing *noun* Zeichnung die (PL die Zeichnungen).

drawing pin *noun* Reißzwecke die (PL die Reißzwecken).

dreadful *adjective* furchtbar.

dreadfully *adverb* furchtbar; **I'm dreadfully late** ich habe mich furchtbar verspätet; **I'm dreadfully sorry** es tut mir furchtbar Leid.

dream *noun* Traum der (PL die Träume); **to have a dream** einen Traum haben.

dream *verb* träumen; **to dream about something** von etwas (DAT) träumen.

dress *noun* Kleid das (PL die Kleider).

dress *verb* **to dress a child** ein Kind anziehen✧ SEP.

• **to dress up** sich verkleiden; **to dress up as a vampire** sich als Vampir verkleiden.

dressed *adjective* **1** angezogen; **Is Tom dressed yet?** ist Tom schon angezogen?; **2 she was dressed in black trousers and a yellow shirt** sie trug eine schwarze Hose und ein gelbes Hemd; **3 to get dressed**

sich anziehen✧ SEP; **I got dressed quickly** ich zog mich schnell an.

dressing gown *noun* Morgenrock der (PL die Morgenröcke).

dressing table *noun* Frisierkommode die (PL die Frisierkommoden).

drier *noun* **hair drier** der Föhn; **tumble drier** der Wäschetrockner.

drill *noun* Bohrer der (PL die Bohrer).

drink *noun* Getränk das (PL die Getränke) **1 to have a drink** etwas trinken; **would you like a drink of water?** möchtest du etwas Wasser trinken?; **2** (*an alcoholic drink*) Drink der (PL die Drinks); **they've invited us round for drinks** sie haben uns auf einen Drink eingeladen; **let's have a drink!** trinken wir einen! (*informal*).

drink *verb* trinken✧; **he drank a glass of water** er trank ein Glas Wasser.

drive *noun* **1 to go for a drive** eine Autofahrt machen; **2** (*in front of a house*) Einfahrt die (PL die Einfahrten).

drive *verb* **1** fahren✧ (PERF *sein*); **she drives very fast** sie fährt sehr schnell; **to drive a car** Auto fahren; **I'd like to learn to drive** ich möchte Autofahren lernen; **can you drive?** kannst du Auto fahren?; **2 we drove to Berlin** wir sind mit dem Auto nach Berlin gefahren; **3 to drive somebody (to a place)** jemanden (irgendwohin) fahren (PERF *haben*); **Mum drove me to the station** Mutti hat mich zum Bahnhof gefahren; **to drive**

a b c d e f g h i j k l m n o p q r s t u v w x y z

driver

somebody home jemanden nach Hause fahren; ★ **she drives me mad!** sie macht mich verrückt!.

driver noun **1** Fahrer der (PL die Fahrer), Fahrerin die (PL die Fahrerinnen); **2** (of a locomotive) Lokomotivführer der (PL die Lokomotivführer), Lokomotivführerin die (PL die Lokomotivführerinnen).

driving instructor noun Fahrlehrer der (PL die Fahrlehrer), Fahrlehrerin die (PL die Fahrlehrerinnen).

driving lesson noun Fahrstunde die (PL die Fahrstunden).

driving licence noun Führerschein der (PL die Führerscheine).

driving test noun Fahrprüfung die; **to take your driving test** die Fahrprüfung machen; **Jenny's passed her driving test** Jenny hat die Fahrprüfung bestanden.

drop noun Tropfen der (PL die Tropfen).

drop verb **1 to drop something** etwas fallen lassen; **I dropped my glasses** ich habe meine Brille fallen lassen; **2 drop it!** lass das!; **3 I'm going to drop history next year** nächstes Jahr lege ich Geschichte ab; **4** absetzen SEP (a person); **could you drop me at the station?** könntest du mich am Bahnhof absetzen?

drought noun Dürre die (PL die Dürren).

drown verb ertrinken ⋄ (PERF sein); **she drowned in the lake** sie ertrank im See.

drug noun **1** (medicine) Medikament das (PL die Medikamente); **2** (illegal) **drugs** Drogen (plural).

drug abuse noun Drogenmissbrauch der.

drug addict noun Drogenabhängige der/die (PL die Drogenabhängigen).

drug addiction noun Drogenabhängigkeit die.

drum noun **1** Trommel die (PL die Trommeln); **2 drums** das Schlagzeug; **to play drums** Schlagzeug spielen.

drummer noun Schlagzeuger der (PL die Schlagzeuger), Schlagzeugerin die (PL die Schlagzeugerinnen).

drunk noun Betrunkene der/die (PL die Betrunkenen).

drunk adjective betrunken; **to get drunk** sich betrinken ⋄.

dry adjective trocken.

dry verb **1** trocknen; **to let something dry** etwas trocknen lassen; **to dry your hair** sich (DAT) die Haare trocknen; **to dry the washing** die Wäsche trocknen; **2 to dry your hands** sich (DAT) die Hände abtrocknen SEP; **I dried my feet** ich trocknete mir die Füße ab; **to dry the dishes** das Geschirr abtrocknen.

dry cleaner's noun chemische Reinigung die.

dryer noun SEE **drier**.

dual carriageway noun zweispurige Straße die (PL die zweispurigen Straßen).

dubbed *adjective* **a dubbed film** ein synchronisierter Film.

duck *noun* Ente die (PL die Enten).

due *adjective, adverb* **1 to be due to do something** etwas tun müssen; **Paul's due back soon** Paul muss bald zurück sein; **we're due to leave on Thursday** wir müssen Donnerstag abfahren; **2 due to** wegen (+ GEN); **due to bad weather** wegen schlechten Wetters.

dull *adjective* **1 dull weather** trübes Wetter; **it's a dull day today** heute ist ein trüber Tag; **2** (*boring*) langweilig.

dumb *adjective* **1** stumm; **2** (*stupid*) dumm; **he asked some dumb questions** er hat ein paar dumme Fragen gestellt.

dump *verb* **1** abladen ✧ SEP (*rubbish*); **2** (*put down*) hinwerfen ✧ SEP; **he dumped it in the rubbish** er hat es in den Müll geworfen; **3** abschieben ✧ SEP (*a person*) (*informal*); **she's dumped her boyfriend** she hat ihren Freund abgeschoben.

dungarees *plural noun* Latzhose die (PL die Latzhosen).

during *preposition* während (+ GEN); **during the night** während der Nacht; **I saw her during the holidays** ich habe sie während der Ferien gesehen.

dusk *noun* Dämmerung die (PL die Dämmerungen); **at dusk** bei Einbruch der Dunkelheit.

dust *noun* Staub der.

dust *verb* **1** abstauben SEP (*furniture, objects*); **2** (*in a room*) Staub wischen; **she's dusting** sie wischt Staub.

dustbin *noun* Mülltonne die (PL die Mülltonnen).

dustman *noun* Müllmann der (PL die Müllmänner).

dusty *adjective* staubig.

Dutch *noun* **1** (*language*) Holländisch das; **2 the Dutch** (*people*) die Holländer.

Dutch *adjective* holländisch; **he's Dutch** er ist Holländer; **she's Dutch** sie ist Holländerin.

duty *noun* **1** Pflicht die (PL die Pflichten); **to have a duty to do something** die Pflicht haben, etwas zu tun; **you have a duty to inform us** du hast die Pflicht, uns zu benachrichtigen; **2 to be on duty** Dienst haben; **to be on night duty** Nachtdienst haben; **I'm off duty tonight** ich habe heute Abend keinen Dienst.

duty-free *adjective* zollfrei; **duty-free shop** der Dutyfreeshop; **duty-free goods** zollfreie Waren (*plural*).

duvet *noun* Bettdecke die (PL die Bettdecken).

duvet cover *noun* Bettbezug der (PL die Bettbezüge).

dye *noun* Färbemittel das (PL die Färbemittel).

dye *verb* färben; **to dye your hair** sich die Haare färben; **I'm going to dye my hair black** ich werde mir die Haare schwarz färben; **I'm going to have my hair dyed pink** ich lasse mir die Haare rosa färben.

dynamic *adjective* dynamisch.

a b c d e f g h i j k l m n o p q r s t u v w x y z

a
b
c
d
e
f
g
h
i
j
k
l
m
n
o
p
q
r
s
t
u
v
w
x
y
z

dyslexia noun Legasthenie die.

dyslexic adjective legasthenisch;
to be dyslexic Legastheniker sein,
Legasthenikerin sein.

Ee

each adjective, pronoun **1** jeder/
jede/jedes; **each Sunday** jeden
Sonntag; **each time** jedes Mal;
at the beginning of each year am
Anfang jedes Jahres; **we each have
an invitation** jeder von uns hat eine
Einladung; **my sisters each have a
computer** jede meiner Schwestern
hat einen Computer; **she gave us
an apple each** sie hat jedem von
uns einen Apfel gegeben; **each of
you** jeder von euch/jede von euch;
we each got a present jeder
Einzelne hat ein Geschenk
bekommen; **2 the tickets cost ten
pounds each** die Karten kosten je
zehn Pfund; **£5 each** (per person)
fünf Pfund pro Person, (per item)
fünf Pfund pro Stück.

each other pronoun ('each other'
is usually translated using a
reflexive pronoun) **they love each
other** sie lieben sich; **we know
each other** wir kennen uns; **do you
see each other often?** seht ihr
euch oft?

eagle noun Adler der (PL die Adler).

ear noun Ohr das (PL die Ohren).

earache noun **to have earache**
Ohrenschmerzen haben.

earlier adverb **1** (a while ago) vor
kurzem; **your brother phoned
earlier** dein Bruder hat vor kurzem
angerufen; **2** (not as late) früher;
we should have started earlier wir
hätten früher anfangen sollen.

early adverb **1** (in the morning)
früh; **to get up early** früh
aufstehen; **it's too early** es ist zu
früh; **2** (for an appointment) **to be
early** (zu) früh dran sein; **we're
early, the train doesn't leave until
ten** wir sind früh dran, der Zug
fährt erst um zehn Uhr ab.

early adjective **1** (one of the first) **in
the early months** während der
ersten Monate; **I'm getting the
early train** ich nehme den früheren
Zug; **2 to have an early lunch** früh
zu Mittag essen; **Jan's having an
early night** Jan geht früh zu Bett;
3 in the early afternoon am frühen
Nachmittag; **in the early hours** in
den frühen Morgenstunden.

earn verb verdienen; **Richard
earns five pounds an hour** Richard
verdient fünf Pfund die Stunde.

earring noun Ohrring der (PL die
Ohrringe).

earth noun Erde die; **life on earth**
das Leben auf der Erde; **★ what on
earth are you doing?** was in aller
Welt machst du da?

earthquake noun Erdbeben das
(PL die Erdbeben).

easily adverb leicht; **he's easily
the best** er ist mit Abstand der
Beste.

east noun Osten der; **in the east** im Osten.

east adjective, adverb östlich, Ost-; **the east side** die Ostseite; **an east wind** ein Ostwind; **east of Munich** östlich von München.

Easter noun Ostern das (PL die Ostern); **they're coming at Easter** sie kommen zu Ostern; **Happy Easter** Frohe Ostern.

Easter Day noun Ostersonntag der (PL die Ostersonntage).

Easter egg noun Osterei das (PL die Ostereier).

Eastern Europe noun Osteuropa das.

easy adjective leicht; **it's easy!** das ist leicht!; **it was easy to decide** die Entscheidung fiel uns leicht.

eat verb 1 essen✧; **he was eating a banana** er aß eine Banane; **we're going to have something to eat** wir essen jetzt etwas; **2 to eat your breakfast** frühstücken.

EC noun EG die (Europäische Gemeinschaft).

echo noun Echo das (PL die Echos).

echo verb wiederholen.

ecological adjective ökologisch.

ecology noun Ökologie die.

economical adjective sparsam.

economics noun Wirtschaftswissenschaften (plural).

economy noun Wirtschaft die.

edge noun 1 Kante die (PL die Kanten); **the edge of the table** die Tischkante; **2** (of a road, sheet of paper, or cliff) Rand der (PL die Ränder); **at the edge of the forest** am Waldrand.

edible adjective essbar.

edit verb redigieren.

editor noun 1 (of a newspaper or magazine) Chefredakteur der (PL die Chefredakteure), Chefredakteurin die (PL die Chefredakteurinnen); **2** (of a book) Redakteur der (PL die Redakteure), Redakteurin die (PL die Redakteurinnen).

educate verb erziehen✧.

education noun Ausbildung die.

effect noun 1 Wirkung die (PL die Wirkungen); **the effect of the explosion was horrific** die Wirkung der Explosion war entsetzlich; **2 to have an effect on something** eine Auswirkung auf etwas (ACC) haben; **it had a good effect on the whole family** es hatte eine gute Auswirkung auf die ganze Familie; **3** (in a film) Effekt der (PL die Effekte); **special effects** die Specialeffekte.

effective adjective effektiv.

efficient adjective 1 (person) tüchtig; **2** (machine or organization) leistungsfähig.

effort noun 1 Mühe die (PL die Mühen); **2 to make an effort** sich bemühen; **Toya made an effort to help us** Toya hat sich bemüht, uns zu helfen; **he didn't even make the effort to apologize** er hat sich nicht einmal die Mühe gemacht, sich zu entschuldigen.

e.g. abbreviation z.B. (zum Beispiel).

egg noun Ei das (PL die Eier); **a fried egg** ein Spiegelei; **a hard-boiled egg** ein hart gekochtes Ei.

egg-cup noun Eierbecher der (PL die Eierbecher).

a
b
c
d
e
f
g
h
i
j
k
l
m
n
o
p
q
r
s
t
u
v
w
x
y
z

a

eggshell *noun* Eierschale die (PL die Eierschalen).

b

egg-white *noun* Eiweiß das (PL die Eiweiße).

c

egg-yolk *noun* Eigelb das (PL die Eigelbe).

d

e

eight *number* acht; **Maya's eight** Maya ist acht; **at eight o'clock** um acht Uhr.

f

eighteen *number* achtzehn; **Jason's eighteen** Jason ist achtzehn.

g

h

eighth *number* achter/achte/ achtes; **on the eighth of July** am achten Juli.

i

j

eighty *number* achtzig; **eighty-five** fünfundachtzig.

k

l

either *pronoun* **1** (*one or the other*) einer von beiden/eine von beiden/ eins von beiden; **take either (of them)** nimm einen von beiden/ eine von beiden/eins von beiden; **I don't like either (of them)** ich mag keinen von beiden/keine von beiden/keins von beiden; **2** (*both*) beide (*plural*); **either is possible** beide sind möglich; **on either side** auf beiden Seiten.

m

n

o

p

q

either *conjunction* **1** **either ... or** entweder ... oder; **either Susie or Judy** entweder Susie oder Judy; **2** (*with a negative*) **either ... or** weder ... noch; **he didn't ring either Sam or Emma** er hat weder Sam noch Emma angerufen; **3 I don't know them either** ich kenne sie auch nicht.

r

s

t

u

v

w

x

elastic *noun* Gummiband das (PL die Gummibänder).

y

elastic band *noun* Gummiband das (PL die Gummibänder).

z

elbow *noun* Ellbogen der (PL die Ellbogen).

elder *adjective* älterer/ältere/ älteres; **her elder brother** ihr älterer Bruder.

elderly *adjective* alt; **the elderly** ältere Menschen (*plural*).

eldest *adjective* ältester/älteste/ ältestes; **her eldest brother** ihr ältester Bruder.

elect *verb* wählen; **she has been elected** sie ist gewählt worden.

election *noun* Wahl die (PL die Wahlen); **in the election** bei den Wahlen; **to call an election** allgemeine Wahlen ausrufen SEP.

electric *adjective* elektrisch.

electrical *adjective* elektrisch, Elektro-; **electrical equipment** Elektrogeräte (*plural*).

electrician *noun* Elektriker der (PL die Elektriker), Elektrikerin die (PL die Elektrikerinnen).

electricity *noun* Strom der.

electronic *adjective* elektronisch.

electronics *noun* Elektronik die.

elegant *adjective* elegant.

elephant *noun* Elefant der (PL die Elefanten).

eleven *number* elf; **Josh is eleven** Josh ist elf; **at eleven o'clock** um elf Uhr; **a football eleven** eine Fußballelf.

eleventh *number* elfter/elfte/ elftes; **the eleventh of September** der elfte September; **on the eleventh floor** im elften Stock.

else *adverb* **1** (*in addition*) sonst; **who else?** wer sonst?; **did you see anyone else?** hast du sonst noch jemanden gesehen?; **nothing else** sonst nichts; **I don't want anything**

else ich will sonst nichts; **2 would you like something else?** möchten Sie sonst noch etwas?; **3** (*instead or different*) anderer/andere/anderes; **somewhere else** irgendwo anders; **everyone else** alle anderen; **somebody else** jemand anders; **something else** etwas anderes; **4 or else** sonst; **hurry up, or else we'll be late** beeil dich, sonst kommen wir zu spät.

email *noun* E-Mail *die* (PL die E-Mails).

embarrassed *adjective* verlegen; **he was very embarrassed** er war ganz verlegen.

embarrassing *adjective* peinlich.

embassy *noun* Botschaft *die* (PL die Botschaften); **the German Embassy** die Deutsche Botschaft.

emergency exit *noun* Notausgang *der* (PL die Notausgänge).

emergency *noun* Notfall *der* (PL die Notfälle).

emotion *noun* Gefühl *das* (PL die Gefühle).

emotional *adjective* **1** (*person*) emotional; **2** (*speech or occasion*) emotionsgeladen.

emperor *noun* Kaiser *der* (PL die Kaiser).

emphasize *verb* betonen; **he emphasized that it was voluntary** er betonte, dass es freiwillig war.

empire *noun* Reich *das* (PL die Reiche); **the Roman Empire** das Römische Reich.

employ *verb* **1** (*have working for you*) beschäftigen; **2** (*take on a worker*) einstellen SEP.

employee *noun* Angestellte *der/ die* (PL die Angestellten).

employer *noun* Arbeitgeber *der* (PL die Arbeitgeber), Arbeitgeberin *die* (PL die Arbeitgeberinnen).

employment *noun* Arbeit *die*.

empty *adjective* leer; **an empty bottle** eine leere Flasche.

empty *verb* **1** (*empty out*) ausleeren SEP; **2** (*pour*) schütten.

enclose *verb* (*in a letter*) beilegen SEP; **please find enclosed a cheque** ein Scheck liegt bei.

encourage *verb* ermutigen; **to encourage somebody to do something** jemanden (dazu) ermutigen, etwas zu tun; **Mum encouraged me to try again** Mutti hat mich dazu ermutigt, es noch einmal zu versuchen.

encouragement *noun* Ermutigung *die* (PL die Ermutigungen).

encouraging *adjective* ermutigend.

encyclopedia *noun* Lexikon *das* (PL die Lexika).

end *noun* **1** Ende *das* (PL die Enden); **'The End' 'Ende'; at the end of the film** am Ende des Films; **by the end of the lesson** als die Stunde zu Ende war; **in the end I went home** schließlich bin ich nach Hause gegangen; **Sally's coming at the end of June** Sally kommt Ende Juni; **I read to the end of the page** ich habe die Seite zu Ende gelesen; **hold the other end** halte das andere Ende fest; **at the end of the street** am Ende der Straße; **2** (*in sports*) Spielfeldhälfte *die* (PL

a b c d e f g h i j k l m n o p q r s t u v w x y z

die Spielfeldhälften); **to change ends** die Seiten wechseln.

end *verb* **1** (*to put an end to*) beenden; **they've ended the strike** sie haben den Streik beendet; **2** (*to come to an end*) enden; **the day ended with a meal** der Tag endete mit einem Essen.

● **to end up 1 to end up doing something** am Ende etwas tun; **we ended up taking a taxi** am Ende haben wir ein Taxi genommen; **2 to end up somewhere** irgendwo landen (PERF *sein*) (*informal*); **Rob ended up in Berlin** Rob landete schließlich in Berlin.

endangered *adjective* gefährdet; **an endangered species** eine von Aussterben bedrohte Art.

ending *noun* **1** Ende *das* (PL die Enden); **2** (*in grammar*) Endung *die* (PL die Endungen).

endless *adjective* endlos (*day or journey, for example*).

enemy *noun* Feind *der* (PL die Feinde); **to make enemies** sich (DAT) Feinde machen.

energetic *adjective* energiegeladen.

energy *noun* Energie *die*.

engaged *adjective* **1** (*to be married*) verlobt; **they're engaged** sie sind verlobt; **to get engaged** sich verloben; **2** (*a phone or toilet*) besetzt; **it's engaged, I'll ring later** es ist besetzt, ich rufe später an.

engagement *noun* (*to marry*) Verlobung *die* (PL die Verlobungen).

engagement ring *noun* Verlobungsring *der* (PL die Verlobungsringe).

engine *noun* **1** (*in a car*) Motor *der* (PL die Motoren); **2** (*pulling a train*) Lokomotive *die* (PL die Lokomotiven).

engineer *noun* **1** (*who comes for repairs*) Techniker *der* (PL die Techniker), Technikerin *die* (PL die Technikerinnen); **2** (*who builds roads and bridges*) Ingenieur *der* (PL die Ingenieure), Ingenieurin *die* (PL die Ingenieurinnen).

England *noun* England *das*; **I'm from England** ich bin Engländer, ich bin Engländerin.

English *noun* **1** (*the language*) Englisch *das*; **do you speak English?** sprechen Sie Englisch?; **he answered in English** er hat auf Englisch geantwortet; **2** (*the people*) **the English** die Engländer.

English *adjective* **1** (*of or from England*) englisch; **the English team** die englische Mannschaft; **he's English** er ist Engländer; **she's English** sie ist Engländerin; **2 an English lesson** eine Englischstunde; **our English teacher** unser Englischlehrer, unsere Englischlehrerin.

English Channel *noun* **the English Channel** der Ärmelkanal.

Englishman *noun* Engländer *der* (PL die Engländer).

Englishwoman *noun* Engländerin *die* (PL die Engländerinnen).

enjoy *verb* **1** **did you enjoy the party?** hat dir die Party gefallen?; **we really enjoyed the concert** das Konzert hat uns wirklich gut gefallen; **2 to enjoy doing something** etwas gerne tun✧; **I**

enjoy reading ich lese gerne; **do you enjoy living in York?** wohnst du gerne in York?; **3 to enjoy oneself** sich gut amüsieren; **we really enjoyed ourselves** wir haben uns richtig gut amüsiert; **enjoy yourselves!** viel Vergnügen!; **did you enjoy yourself?** hast du dich gut amüsiert?

enjoyable adjective nett.

enormous adjective riesig.

enough adverb, adjective, pronoun **1** genug; **there's enough for everyone** es gibt genug für alle; **big enough** groß genug; **have we got enough bread?** haben wir genug Brot?; **2 that's enough** das reicht.

enquire verb to enquire about sich erkundigen nach (+ DAT); **I'm going to enquire about the trains** ich werde mich nach den Zügen erkundigen.

enrol verb sich anmelden SEP; **I want to enrol on the course** ich möchte mich zu dem Kurs anmelden.

enter verb **1** (to go inside) gehen ✧ PERF sein) in (+ ACC) (a room or a building); **we all entered the church** wir gingen alle in die Kirche hinein; **2** (in computing) eingeben ✧ SEP; **3 to enter for** sich anmelden SEP zu (+ DAT) (an exam or a race); **to enter for a competition** an einem Preisausschreiben teilnehmen ✧ SEP.

entertain verb **1** (to keep amused) unterhalten ✧; **2** (to have people round) Gäste haben ✧; **they don't entertain much** sie haben selten Gäste.

entertainment noun (fun) Unterhaltung die; **there wasn't much entertainment in the evenings** abends war wenig Unterhaltung geboten.

enthusiasm noun Begeisterung die.

enthusiast noun **1** Enthusiast der (PL die Enthusiasten), Enthusiastin die (PL die Enthusiastinnen); **2** (for sports) Fan der (PL die Fans); **he's a rugby enthusiast** er ist ein Rugbyfan.

enthusiastic adjective begeistert.

entire adjective ganz; **the entire class** die ganze Klasse.

entirely adverb ganz.

entrance noun **1** (fee) Eintritt der; **2** (way in) Eingang der (PL die Eingänge).

entry noun **1** (way in) Eingang der (PL die Eingänge), (for cars) Einfahrt die (PL die Einfahrten); **2 'no entry'** 'Zutritt verboten', (to cars) 'Einfahrt verboten'.

entry phone noun Sprechanlage die (PL die Sprechanlagen).

envelope noun Briefumschlag der (PL die Briefumschläge).

environment noun Umwelt die.

environmental adjective Umwelt-; **environmental pollution** die Umweltverschmutzung.

environment-friendly adjective umweltfreundlich.

epidemic noun Epidemie die (PL die Epidemien).

epileptic adjective epileptisch.

episode noun **1** (an event) Episode die (PL die Episoden); **2** (on TV or radio) Folge die (PL die Folgen).

a b c d e f g h i j k l m n o p q r s t u v w x y z

equal *adjective* gleich; **milk and water in equal quantities** gleich viel Milch und Wasser.

equal *verb* gleichen ✧ (+ DAT).

equality *noun* Gleichberechtigung die.

equalize *verb* ausgleichen ✧ SEP; **they equalized in the last minute** sie haben in der letzten Minute ausgeglichen.

equally *adverb* (to share) gleichmäßig; **we divided it equally** wir haben es gleichmäßig verteilt.

equator *noun* Äquator der.

equip *verb* ausrüsten SEP; **well equipped for the hike** für die Wanderung gut ausgerüstet; **equipped with rucksacks** mit Rucksäcken ausgerüstet.

equipment *noun* **1** (for sport) Ausrüstung die (PL die Ausrüstungen); **2** Ausstattung die (PL die Ausstattungen); **laboratory equipment** die Laborausstattung; **3** (something needed for an activity) Geräte (plural); **recording equipment** Aufnahmegeräte.

equivalent *adjective* gleichwertig; **to be equivalent to** etwas (DAT) entsprechen; **1 litre is equivalent to about 1.75 pints** ein Liter entspricht ungefähr 1,75 Pints.

error *noun* **1** (in spelling, typing, on a computer, or in maths) Fehler der (PL die Fehler); **spelling error** der Rechtschreibfehler; **2** (wrong opinion) Irrtum der (PL die Irrtümer).

error message *noun* Fehlermeldung die (PL die Fehlermeldungen).

escalator *noun* Rolltreppe die (PL die Rolltreppen).

escape *noun* (from prison) Ausbruch der (PL die Ausbrüche).

escape *verb* **1** (from prison) ausbrechen ✧ SEP (PERF sein); **2** entkommen ✧ (PERF sein); **to escape from somebody** jemandem entkommen.

especially *adverb* besonders.

essay *noun* Aufsatz der (PL die Aufsätze); **an essay on German reunification** ein Aufsatz über die deutsche Wiedervereinigung.

essential *adjective* unbedingt erforderlich; **it's essential to reply quickly** es ist unbedingt erforderlich, sofort zu antworten.

estate *noun* **1** (a housing estate) Wohnsiedlung die (PL die Wohnsiedlungen); **2** (a big house and grounds) Landsitz der (PL die Landsitze).

estate agent *noun* Immobilienmakler der (PL die Immobilienmakler), Immobilienmaklerin die (PL die Immobilienmaklerinnen).

estate car *noun* Kombiwagen der (PL die Kombiwagen).

estimate *noun* **1** (a quote for work) Kostenvoranschlag der (PL die Kostenvoranschläge); **2** (a rough guess) Schätzung die (PL die Schätzungen).

estimate *verb* schätzen.

etc. *abbreviation* usw. (und so weiter).

ethnic *adjective* ethnisch; **an ethnic minority** eine ethnische Minderheit.

EU noun EU die (*Europäische Union*).

euro noun Euro der (PL die Euros); **the euro is divided into 100 cents** ein Euro hat 100 Cent.

Europe noun Europa das.

European noun Europäer der (PL die Europäer), Europäerin die (PL die Europäerinnen).

European adjective europäisch.

European Union noun Europäische Union die.

eurozone noun Euroland das

even[1] adverb **1** sogar; **even Lisa is coming** sogar Lisa kommt; **2 not even** nicht einmal; **I don't like animals, not even dogs** ich mag keine Tiere, nicht einmal Hunde; **3 without even asking** ohne wenigstens zu fragen; **4 even if** selbst wenn; **even if they arrive late** selbst wenn sie spät ankommen; **5** (*with a comparison*) (sogar) noch; **even bigger** sogar noch größer; **even faster** noch schneller; **even better than** sogar noch besser als; **the song is even better than their last one** das Lied ist sogar noch besser als ihr letztes; **6 even so** trotzdem; **even so, we had a good time** trotzdem haben wir uns gut amüsiert.

even[2] adjective **1** (*surface or layer*) eben; **2** (*number*) gerade; **six is an even number** sechs ist eine gerade Zahl; **3** (*equal*) gleich (*distance, value*); **the score is even** die Punktzahl ist gleich; **4 to get even with somebody** es jemandem heimzahlen.

evening noun **1** Abend der (PL die Abende); **in the evening** am Abend;

this evening heute Abend; **tomorrow evening** morgen Abend; **on Monday evening** am Montagabend; **every Thursday evening** jeden Donnerstagabend; **the evening before** am Abend zuvor; **the evening meal** das Abendessen; **2 at six o'clock in the evening** um sechs Uhr abends; **the other evening** neulich abends; **I work in the evening(s)** ich arbeite abends.

evening class noun Abendkurs der (PL die Abendkurse).

event noun **1** (*a happening*) Ereignis das (PL die Ereignisse); **2** (*in athletics*) Disziplin die (PL die Disziplinen).

eventually adverb schließlich.

ever adverb **1** (*at any time*) je; **have you ever noticed that?** hast du das je bemerkt?; **more than ever** mehr denn je; **colder than ever** kälter denn je; **he drove more slowly than ever** er fuhr langsamer als je zuvor; **2 not ever** nie; **nobody ever came** es kam nie jemand; **hardly ever** fast nie; **3** (*always*) immer; **as cheerful as ever** so vergnügt wie immer; **the same as ever** so wie immer; **4 ever since** seitdem; **and it's been raining ever since** und seitdem regnet es.

every adjective **1** jeder/jede/jedes; **every house has a garden** jedes Haus hat einen Garten; **every day** jeden Tag; **every Monday** jeden Montag; **every time** jedes Mal; **2 every few days** alle paar Tage; **every ten kilometres** alle zehn Kilometer; **3 every one** jeder Einzelne/jede Einzelne/jedes

a b c d e f g h i j k l m n o p q r s t u v w x y z

Einzelne; **I've seen every one of his films** ich habe jeden Einzelnen seiner Filme gesehen; **4 every now and then** ab und zu.

everybody, everyone *pronoun* **1** alle (*plural*); **everybody knows that ...** alle wissen, dass ...; **everyone else** alle anderen; **2** (*each one*) jeder; **not everybody can afford it** das kann sich nicht jeder leisten.

everything *pronoun* alles; **everything is ready** es ist alles fertig; **everything's fine** es ist alles okay (*informal*); **everything else** alles andere; **he gets everything he wants** er bekommt alles, was er will.

everywhere *adverb* **1** überall; **there was dirt everywhere** überall war Dreck; **she went everywhere** sie ist überall hingegangen; **everywhere else** sonst überall; **2 everywhere she went** wohin sie auch ging.

evidently *adverb* offensichtlich.

evil *noun* Böse *das*.

evil *adjective* böse.

exact *adjective* genau; **the exact fare** das genaue Fahrgeld; **it's the exact opposite** das ist das genaue Gegenteil.

exactly *adverb* genau; **they're exactly the right age** sie sind genau im richtigen Alter; **yes, exactly!** ja, genau!

exaggerate *verb* übertreiben❖.

exaggeration *noun* Übertreibung *die* (PL die Übertreibungen).

exam *noun* Prüfung *die* (PL die Prüfungen); **history exam** die

Geschichtsprüfung; **to sit an exam** eine Prüfung machen; **to pass an exam** eine Prüfung bestehen; **to fail an exam** durch eine Prüfung fallen.

examination *noun* Prüfung *die* (PL die Prüfungen).

examine *verb* **1** (*at school or university*) prüfen; **2** (*at the doctor's*) untersuchen.

examiner *noun* Prüfer *der* (PL die Prüfer), Prüferin *die* (PL die Prüferinnen).

example *noun* Beispiel *das* (PL die Beispiele); **for example** zum Beispiel; **to set a good example** ein gutes Beispiel geben.

excellent *adjective* ausgezeichnet.

except *preposition* **1** außer (+ DAT); **every day except Tuesday** täglich außer Dienstag; **we play except when it rains** wir spielen, außer wenn es regnet; **except in March** außer März; **2 except for** außer (+ DAT); **except for the children** außer den Kindern.

exception *noun* Ausnahme *die* (PL die Ausnahmen); **without exception** ohne Ausnahme; **with the exception of** mit Ausnahme von (+ DAT).

exchange *noun* **1** Austausch *der*; **the students are coming to London on an exchange** die Schüler kommen auf einen Schüleraustausch nach London; **exchange student** der Austauschstudent, die Austauschstudentin; **an exchange of pupils** ein Schüleraustausch;

2 in exchange for his help für seine Hilfe.

exchange *verb* umtauschen SEP; **can I exchange this shirt for a smaller one?** kann ich dieses Hemd gegen ein kleineres umtauschen?

exchange rate *noun* Wechselkurs der (PL die Wechselkurse).

excite *verb* **1** (*thrill*) begeistern; **2** (*agitate*) aufregen SEP.

excited *adjective* **1** aufgeregt; **the children are excited** die Kinder sind aufgeregt; **the dogs get excited when they hear the car** die Hunde geraten in Aufregung, wenn sie das Auto hören; **2** (*annoyed or angry*) **to get excited** sich aufregen SEP.

exciting *adjective* aufregend; **a very exciting film** ein sehr aufregender Film.

exclamation mark *noun* Ausrufezeichen das (PL die Ausrufezeichen).

excursion *noun* Ausflug der (PL die Ausflüge).

excuse *noun* Entschuldigung die (PL die Entschuldigungen).

excuse *verb* (*apologizing*) **excuse me!** Entschuldigung!

exercise *noun* **1** Übung die (PL die Übungen); **a maths exercise** eine Matheübung; **2 physical exercise** körperliche Bewegung; **to get exercise** sich Bewegung verschaffen.

exercise bike *noun* Heimtrainer der (PL die Heimtrainer).

exercise book *noun* Heft das (PL die Hefte); **my German exercise book** mein Deutschheft.

exhaust (pipe) *noun* Auspuff der (PL die Auspuffe).

exhaust fumes *noun* Abgase die (*plural*).

exhausted *adjective* erschöpft.

exhibition *noun* Ausstellung die (PL die Ausstellungen); **the Dürer exhibition** die Dürer-Ausstellung.

exist *verb* existieren.

exit *noun* **1** Ausgang der (PL die Ausgänge); **2** (*from a motorway*) Ausfahrt die (PL die Ausfahrten).

expect *verb* **1** erwarten (*guests or a baby*); **we're expecting thirty visitors** wir erwarten dreißig Besucher; **2** (*require something*) **to expect somebody to do something** von jemandem erwarten, dass er etwas tut; **3** rechnen mit (+ DAT) (*something to happen*); **I didn't expect that** damit habe ich nicht gerechnet; **I didn't expect it at all** damit habe ich überhaupt nicht gerechnet; **4** (*suppose*) glauben; **I must she'll bring her boyfriend** ich glaube, sie bringt ihren Freund mit; **yes, I expect so** ich glaube ja.

expedition *noun* Expedition die (PL die Expeditionen).

expel *verb* **to be expelled** (*from school*) von der Schule verwiesen werden.

expensive *adjective* teuer; **those shoes are too expensive for me** diese Schuhe sind mir zu teuer; **the most expensive CDs** die teuersten CDs.

experience noun 1 Erfahrung die (PL die Erfahrungen); 2 (an event) Erlebnis das (PL die Erlebnisse).

experienced adjective erfahren.

experiment noun Experiment das (PL die Experimente); **to do an experiment** ein Experiment machen.

expert noun Experte der (PL die Experten), Expertin die (PL die Expertinnen); **he's a computer expert** er ist ein Computerexperte.

expire verb ablaufen◇ SEP (PERF sein).

expiry date noun Verfallsdatum das (PL die Verfallsdaten).

explain verb erklären.

explanation noun Erklärung die (PL die Erklärungen).

explode verb explodieren (PERF sein).

explore verb erforschen.

explosion noun Explosion die (PL die Explosionen).

export noun Export der (PL die Exporte); **the chief export is wool** das wichtigste Exportgut ist Wolle.

export verb exportieren; **Russia exports a lot of oil and timber** Russland exportiert viel Öl und Holz.

exposure noun (of a film) Belichtung die; **a 24-exposure film** ein Film mit 24 Aufnahmen.

express noun (train) Schnellzug der (PL die Schnellzüge).

express verb 1 ausdrücken SEP; 2 **to express yourself** sich ausdrücken.

expression noun Ausdruck der (PL die Ausdrücke).

extend verb 1 verlängern; 2 ausbauen SEP (a house).

extension noun 1 (to a house) Anbau der (PL die Anbauten); 2 (telephone) Apparat der (PL die Apparate); **can I have extension 2347 please?** bitte verbinden Sie mich mit Apparat 2347? (note that in spoken German telephone numbers are usually broken down into groups of two figures); 3 (electrical) Verlängerung die (PL die Verlängerungen).

extension number noun Apparatnummer die (PL die Apparatnummern).

exterior adjective äußerer/ äußere/äußeres.

extinct adjective 1 (animal) ausgestorben; 2 (volcano) erloschen.

extinguish verb 1 löschen (a fire); 2 **to extinguish a cigarette** eine Zigarette ausmachen SEP.

extinguisher noun Feuerlöscher der (PL die Feuerlöscher).

extra adjective 1 zusätzlich, extra (informal) (extra never has an ending); **extra homework** zusätzliche Hausaufgaben; **wine is extra** Wein kostet extra; **you have to pay extra** das wird extra berechnet; 2 **at no extra charge** ohne Aufschlag.

extra adverb 1 besonders; **he was extra careful** er war besonders vorsichtig; 2 **extra large** extragroß.

extraordinary adjective außerordentlich.

extra time noun (in football) Verlängerung die (PL die

Verlängerungen); **to go into extra time** in die Verlängerung gehen.

extravagant *adjective* verschwenderisch (*person*).

extreme *noun* Extrem *das* (PL die Extreme); **to go from one extreme to another** von einem Extrem ins andere fallen.

extreme *adjective* extrem.

extremely *adverb* äußerst; **extremely fast** äußerst schnell.

eye *noun* Auge *das* (PL die Augen); **a girl with blue eyes** ein Mädchen mit blauen Augen; **shut your eyes!** mach die Augen zu!; ★ **to keep an eye on something** auf etwas (ACC) aufpassen SEP.

eyebrow *noun* Augenbraue *die* (PL die Augenbrauen).

eyelash *noun* Augenwimper *die* (PL die Augenwimpern).

eyelid *noun* Augenlid *das* (PL die Augenlider).

eyeliner *noun* Eyeliner *der* (PL die Eyeliner).

eye shadow *noun* Lidschatten *der* (PL die Lidschatten).

eyesight *noun* **to have good eyesight** gute Augen haben; **to have bad eyesight** schlechte Augen haben.

Ff

fabric *noun* (*cloth*) Stoff *der* (PL die Stoffe).

fabulous *adjective* phantastisch.

face *noun* **1** (*of a person*) Gesicht *das* (PL die Gesichter); **to pull a face** eine Grimasse schneiden; **2** (*of a clock or watch*) Zifferblatt *das* (PL die Zifferblätter).

face *verb* **1** gegenüberstehen✧ SEP (PERF *sein*) (+ DAT); **she was facing him** sie stand ihm gegenüber; **2** the **house faces the park** das Haus befindet sich gegenüber dem Park; **3** (*to stand the idea of*) verkraften; **I can't face going back** ich bringe es nicht über mich zurückzugehen; **4** **to face up to something** sich etwas (DAT) stellen.

facilities *plural noun* **1** the **school has good sports facilities** die Schule hat gute Sportanlagen; **2** the **flat has no cooking facilities** die Wohnung hat keine Kochgelegenheit.

fact *noun* Tatsache *die* (PL die Tatsachen); **the fact is that ...** Tatsache ist, dass ...; **in fact** tatsächlich; **is that a fact?** Tatsache?

factory *noun* Fabrik *die* (PL die Fabriken).

fade *verb* **1** (*fabric*) ausbleichen✧ SEP (PERF *sein*); **faded jeans** ausgeblichene Jeans; **2** (*a colour or memory*) verblassen (PERF *sein*); **the colours have faded** die Farben sind verblasst.

fail *verb* **1** nicht bestehen✧ (*a test or an exam*); **I failed my driving test** ich habe meine Fahrprüfung nicht bestanden; **2** (*in a test or an exam*) durchfallen✧ SEP (PERF *sein*); **three students failed** drei Studenten sind durchgefallen; **3** **to fail to do something** etwas nicht tun; **he failed to inform us** er hat uns nicht benachrichtigt; ★ **without fail** auf

a
b
c
d
e
f
g
h
i
j
k
l
m
n
o
p
q
r
s
t
u
v
w
x
y
z

a

jeden Fall;; **ring me without fail** ruf mich auf jeden Fall an.

b

failure noun **1** Misserfolg der (PL die Misserfolge); **it was a terrible failure** es war ein schrecklicher Misserfolg; **2** (of equipment) Ausfall der (PL die Ausfälle); **a power failure** ein Stromausfall.

c

d

e

f

faint adjective **1** (slight) leicht; **a faint smell of gas** ein leichter Gasgeruch; **I haven't the faintest idea** ich habe nicht die blasseste Ahnung (informal); **2** (voice or sound) leise.

g

h

i

faint verb ohnmächtig werden; **Lisa fainted** Lisa wurde ohnmächtig.

j

k

fair noun Jahrmarkt der (PL die Jahrmärkte).

l

fair adjective **1** (not unfair) gerecht; **2** (hair) blond; **he's fair-haired** er ist blond; **3** (skin) hell; **fair-skinned** hellhäutig; **4** (fairly good) ganz gut (chance, condition, or performance); **5** (weather) schön; **if it's fair tomorrow** wenn es morgen schön ist.

m

n

o

p

q

fairground noun Jahrmarkt der (PL die Jahrmärkte).

r

fairly adverb (quite) ziemlich.

s

fairy noun Fee die (PL die Feen).

fairy tale noun Märchen das (PL die Märchen).

t

u

faith noun **1** (trust) Vertrauen das; **to have faith in somebody** Vertrauen zu jemandem haben; **2** (religious belief) Glaube der (PL die Glauben).

v

w

x

faithful adjective treu; **to be faithful to somebody** jemandem treu sein.

y

z

faithfully adverb Yours faithfully Hochachtungsvoll.

fake noun **1** Imitation die (PL die Imitationen); **the diamonds were fakes** die Brillanten waren eine Imitation; **2** (a painting or money) Fälschung die (PL die Fälschungen).

fake adjective gefälscht; **a fake passport** ein gefälschter Pass.

fall noun Fall der (PL die Fälle); **to have a fall** stürzen (PERF sein).

fall verb **1** fallen◇ (PERF sein); mind, **you'll fall** pass auf, dass du nicht hinfällst; **Tony fell off his bike** Tony ist vom Rad gefallen; **she fell down the stairs** sie ist die Treppe hinuntergefallen; **2** (of temperature, prices) sinken◇ (PERF sein).

false adjective falsch; **a false alarm** ein falscher Alarm.

fame noun Ruhm der.

familiar adjective bekannt; **his face is familiar** sein Gesicht kommt mir bekannt vor.

family noun Familie die (PL die Familien); **a family of six** eine sechsköpfige Familie; **Ben's one of the family** Ben gehört zur Familie; **the Morris family** Familie Morris.

famous adjective berühmt.

fan noun **1** (a supporter) Fan der (PL die Fans); **Will's a Chelsea fan** Will ist ein Fan von Chelsea; **2** (electric, for cooling) Ventilator der (PL die Ventilatoren); **3** (hand-held) Fächer der (PL die Fächer).

fanatic noun Fanatiker der (PL die Fanatiker), Fanatikerin die (PL die Fanatikerinnen).

fancy noun to take somebody's fancy jemandem gefallen✧; the picture took his fancy das Bild hat es ihm angetan.

fancy adjective (equipment) ausgefallen.

fancy verb 1 (to want) (do you) fancy a coffee? hast du Lust auf einen Kaffee?; do you fancy going to the cinema? hast du Lust, ins Kino zu gehen?; 2 I really fancy him ich stehe total auf ihn; 3 (just) fancy that! stell dir vor!; fancy you being here! na so was, dich hier zu treffen!

fancy dress noun in fancy dress verkleidet; **fancy-dress party** das Kostümfest.

fantastic adjective fantastisch; really? that's fantastic! wirklich? das ist ja fantastisch!; a fantastic holiday fantastische Ferien.

far adverb, adjective 1 weit; it's not far es ist nicht weit; is it far to Carlisle? ist es weit nach Carlisle?; how far is it to Bristol? wie weit ist es bis nach Bristol?; 2 he took us as far as Newport er hat uns bis Newport mitgenommen; 3 by far bei weitem; the prettiest by far bei weitem das hübscheste; 4 (much) viel; far better viel besser; far faster viel schneller; far too many people viel zu viele Leute; 5 so far bis jetzt; so far everything's going well bis jetzt läuft alles gut; 6 as far as I know soweit ich weiß.

fare noun 1 (on a bus, train, or the underground) Fahrpreis der (PL die Fahrpreise); 2 (on a plane) Flugpreis der (PL die Flugpreise);

half fare der halbe Fahrpreis; **full fare** der volle Fahrpreis.

Far East noun der Ferne Osten, Fernost das

farm noun Bauernhof der (PL die Bauernhöfe).

farmer noun Bauer der (PL die Bauern), Bäuerin die (PL die Bäuerinnen).

farming noun Landwirtschaft die.

fascinating adjective faszinierend.

fashion noun Mode die (PL die Moden); in fashion in Mode; to go out of fashion aus der Mode kommen.

fashionable adjective modisch.

fashion model noun Mannequin das (PL die Mannequins).

fashion show noun Modenschau die (PL die Modenschauen).

fast adjective 1 schnell; a fast car ein schnelles Auto; 2 (of a clock or watch) to be fast vorgehen✧ SEP (PERF sein), my watch is fast meine Uhr geht vor; you're ten minutes fast deine Uhr geht zehn Minuten vor.

fast adverb 1 schnell; he swims fast er schwimmt schnell; 2 to be fast asleep fest schlafen.

fast food noun Fastfood das.

fast forward noun Vorlauf der.

fat noun Fett das (PL die Fette).

fat adjective 1 (meat) fett; 2 (person) dick, fett (informal); a fat man ein dicker Mann; to get fat fett werden (informal).

fatal adjective tödlich.

a b c d e f g h i j k l m n o p q r s t u v w x y z

father noun Vater der (PL die Väter);
my father's office das Büro von
meinem Vater.

Father Christmas noun der
Weihnachtsmann.

father-in-law noun
Schwiegervater der (PL die
Schwiegerväter).

fault noun 1 (when you are
responsible) Schuld die; it's
Stephen's fault Stephen ist schuld;
it's not my fault es ist meine
Schuld; 2 (in tennis) double fault
der Doppelfehler.

favour noun 1 (a kindness)
Gefallen der (PL die Gefallen); to do
somebody a favour jemandem
einen Gefallen tun; can you do me
a favour? kannst du mir einen
Gefallen tun?; to ask a favour of
somebody jemanden um einen
Gefallen bitten; 2 to be in favour of
something für etwas (ACC) sein.

favourite adjective Lieblings-; my
favourite band meine
Lieblingsband.

fax noun Fax das (PL die Faxe).

fax verb faxen.

fear noun Angst die (PL die Ängste).

fear verb fürchten.

feather noun Feder die (PL die
Federn).

feature noun 1 (of your face)
Gesichtszug der (PL die
Gesichtszüge); to have delicate
features feine Gesichtszüge haben;
2 (of a car or a machine) Merkmal
das (PL die Merkmale).

February noun Februar der; in
February im Februar.

fed up adjective 1 I'm fed up ich
habe die Nase voll (informal); he's
fed up with her er hat die Nase voll
von ihr; 2 to be fed up with
something etwas (ACC) satt haben
(informal); I'm fed up with
working every day ich habe es satt,
jeden Tag zu arbeiten.

feed verb füttern; have you fed the
dog? hast du den Hund gefüttert?

feel verb 1 sich fühlen; I don't feel
well ich fühle mich nicht gut;
2 spüren; I didn't feel a thing ich
habe nichts gespürt; 3 I feel tired
ich bin müde; I feel cold mir ist
kalt; 4 to feel afraid Angst haben;
to feel thirsty Durst haben; 5 to
feel like doing something Lust
haben, etwas zu tun; I feel like
going to the cinema ich habe Lust,
ins Kino zu gehen; 6 (touch) fühlen;
7 (to the touch) sich anfühlen SEP; to
feel soft sich weich anfühlen.

feeling noun 1 Gefühl das (PL die
Gefühle); to show your feelings
seine Gefühle zeigen; a dizzy
feeling ein Schwindelgefühl; I
have the feeling James doesn't
like me ich habe das Gefühl, dass
James mich nicht mag; 2 to hurt
somebody's feelings jemanden
verletzen.

felt-tip (pen) noun Filzstift der (PL
die Filzstifte).

female noun (animal) Weibchen
das (PL die Weibchen).

female adjective weiblich.

feminine adjective weiblich.

feminist noun Feministin die (PL
die Feministinnen), Feminist der
(PL die Feministen).

feminist *adjective* feministisch.

fence *noun* Zaun der (PL die Zäune).

ferry *noun* Fähre die (PL die Fähren).

fertilizer *noun* Dünger der.

festival *noun* (*of films, art, or music*) Festspiele (*plural*).

fetch *verb* **1** (*collect*) abholen SEP; **Tom's fetching the children** Tom holt die Kinder ab; **2** holen; **fetch me the other knife** hol mir das andere Messer.

fever *noun* Fieber das.

few *adjective, pronoun* **1** wenige; **few people know that ...** wenige Leute wissen, dass ...; **2** a few (*several*) ein paar (*ein paar never changes*); **a few weeks** ein paar Wochen; **in a few minutes** in ein paar Minuten; **have you got any tomatoes? we want a few for the salad** haben Sie Tomaten? wir brauchen ein paar für den Salat; **3 quite a few** eine ganze Menge; **there were quite a few questions** es gab eine ganze Menge Fragen.

fewer *adjective* weniger; **there are fewer mosquitoes this year** dieses Jahr gibt es weniger Mücken.

fiancé *noun* Verlobte der (PL die Verlobten).

fiancée *noun* Verlobte die (PL die Verlobten).

field *noun* **1** (*with grass or crops*) Feld das (PL die Felder); **a field of wheat** ein Kornfeld; **2** (*for sport*) Spielfeld das (PL die Spielfelder).

fierce *adjective* **1** wild (*animal or person*); **2** heftig (*storm or battle*).

fifteen *number* fünfzehn.

fifth *number* fünfter/fünfte/ fünftes; **the fifth of January** der

fünfte Januar; **on the fifth floor** im fünften Stock.

fifty *number* fünfzig.

fig *noun* Feige die (PL die Feigen).

fight *noun* **1** (*a scuffle*) Schlägerei die (PL die Schlägereien); **2** (*in boxing or against illness*) Kampf der (PL die Kämpfe).

fight *verb* **1** (*to have a fight*) sich prügeln; **they were fighting** sie haben sich geprügelt; **2** (*to quarrel*) sich streiten❖; **they're always fighting** sie streiten sich immer; **3** (*struggle against*) kämpfen gegen (+ ACC) (*poverty or a disease*).

figure *noun* **1** (*number*) Zahl die (PL die Zahlen); **a four-figure number** eine vierstellige Zahl; **2** (*body shape*) Figur die; **good for your figure** gut für die Figur; **3** (*a person*) Gestalt die (PL die Gestalten).

figure *verb* **to figure something out** etwas herausfinden❖ SEP (*the answer or reason*).

file *noun* **1** (*for records of a person or case*) Akte die (PL die Akten); **2** (*ring binder or folder*) Ordner der (PL die Ordner); **3** (*on a computer*) Datei die (PL die Dateien); **4 a nail file** eine Nagelfeile.

file *verb* **1** ablegen SEP (*documents*); **2 to file your nails** sich (DAT) die Nägel feilen.

fill *verb* **1** füllen (*a container*); **she filled my glass** sie füllte mein Glas; **2 to be filled with people** voller Menschen sein; **filled with smoke** voller Rauch.

● **to fill in** ausfüllen SEP (*a form*).

a
b
c
d
e
f
g
h
i
j
k
l
m
n
o
p
q
r
s
t
u
v
w
x
y
z

filling noun 1 (of a pie) Füllung die (PL die Füllungen); 2 (in a tooth) Füllung die (PL die Füllungen).

film noun (in a cinema and for a camera) Film der (PL die Filme); **shall we go and see the new film about Freud?** wollen wir uns den neuen Film über Freud ansehen?; **to make a film** einen Film drehen; **a 24-exposure colour film** ein Farbfilm mit 24 Aufnahmen.

film star noun Filmstar der (PL die Filmstars).

filter noun Filter der (PL die Filter).

filthy adjective dreckig.

final noun (in sport) Endspiel das (PL die Endspiele).

final adjective letzter/letzte/letztes; **the final instalment** die letzte Folge; **the final result** das Endergebnis.

finally adverb schließlich.

find verb finden◇; **did you find your passport?** hast du deinen Pass gefunden?; **I can't find my keys** ich kann meine Schlüssel nicht finden.

● **to find out** 1 (to enquire) sich informieren; **I don't know, I'll find out** das weiß ich nicht, ich werde mich informieren; 2 **to find something out** etwas (ACC) herausfinden◇ SEP (the facts or an answer); **when she found out the truth** als sie die Wahrheit herausfand.

fine noun Bußgeld das (PL die Bußgelder) (for parking or speeding).

fine adjective 1 (in good health) gut; **'how are you?' – 'fine, thanks'** 'wie

gehts?' – 'danke, gut'; **I'm fine** mir geht es gut; 2 (convenient) in Ordnung; **ten o'clock? yes, that's fine!** zehn Uhr? ja, in Ordnung!; **Friday will be fine** Freitag geht in Ordnung; 3 (sunny) schön; (weather or day) **if it's fine** wenn es schön ist; **in fine weather** bei schönem Wetter; 4 (not coarse or thick) fein.

finely adverb fein (chopped or grated).

finger noun Finger der (PL die Finger); ★ **I'll keep my fingers crossed for you** ich drücke dir den Daumen.

fingernail noun Fingernagel der (PL die Fingernägel).

finish noun 1 (end) Schluss der (PL die Schlüsse); 2 (in a race) Ziel das (PL die Ziele).

finish verb 1 beenden (a conversation or quarrel); **to finish a discussion** ein Gespräch beenden; **to be finished with something** mit etwas (DAT) fertig sein (work or a project); **have you finished your homework?** bist du mit den Hausaufgaben fertig?; **wait, I haven't finished!** warte, ich bin noch nicht fertig!; 2 (to finish off) **to finish doing something** etwas zu beenden; **have you finished (reading) the letter?** hast du den Brief zu Ende gelesen?; **he hasn't yet finished (writing) the report** er hat den Bericht noch nicht zu Ende geschrieben; 3 (come to an end) zu Ende sein, aus sein (informal) (a meeting or performance); **the film finishes at ten o'clock** der Film ist um zehn

Uhr zu Ende; **when does school finish?** wann ist die Schule aus?

● **to finish with** (*complete your use of*) nicht mehr brauchen; **when you've finished with these clothes, give them back to me** wenn du die Sachen nicht mehr brauchst, gib sie mir zurück; **have you finished with the computer?** brauchen Sie den Computer noch?

Finland *noun* Finnland *das*.

Finnish *noun* (*the language*) Finnisch *das*.

Finnish *adjective* finnisch; **he's Finnish** er ist Finne; **she's Finnish** sie ist Finnin.

fire *noun* **1** (*in a grate*) Kaminfeuer *das* (PL die Kaminfeuer); **to light the fire** das Feuer im Kamin anmachen; **2** (*accidental*) Feuer *das* (PL die Feuer); **to catch fire** (*fabric, furnishings*) Feuer fangen; **3** (*in a building or forest*) Brand der (PL die Brände); **to set fire to a factory** eine Fabrik in Brand stecken; **4** **to be on fire** brennen✧.

fire *verb* **1** (*with a gun*) schießen✧; **to fire at somebody** auf jemanden schießen; **2** abfeuern SEP (▸ gun).

fire alarm *noun* Feuermelder der (PL die Feuermelder).

fire brigade *noun* Feuerwehr die.

fire engine *noun* Feuerwehrauto *das* (PL die Feuerwehrautos).

fire escape *noun* Feuertreppe die (PL die Feuertreppen).

fire extinguisher *noun* Feuerlöscher der (PL die Feuerlöscher).

firefighter *noun* Feuerwehrmann der (PL die Feuerwehrleute).

fireplace *noun* Kamin der (PL die Kamine).

fire station *noun* Feuerwache die (PL die Feuerwachen).

firework *noun* Feuerwerkskörper der (PL die Feuerwerkskörper); **firework display** das Feuerwerk.

firm *noun* (*business*) Firma die (PL die Firmen).

firm *adjective* **1** fest; **2** (*strict*) streng.

first *adjective* erster/erste/erstes; **the first of May** der erste Mai; **for the first time** zum ersten Mal; **I was the first to arrive** ich kam als Erster/Erste an; **Susan was first** Susan war die Erste; **to come first in the 100 metres** beim Hundertmeterlauf Erster/Erste werden.

first *adverb* **1** (*to begin with*) zuerst; **first, I'm going to make some tea** zuerst mache ich Tee; **2** **at first** zuerst; **at first he was shy** er war zuerst schüchtern.

first aid *noun* erste Hilfe die.

first class *adjective* (*ticket, carriage, or hotel*) erster Klasse (*goes after the noun*); **a first-class hotel** ein Hotel erster Klasse; **he always travels first class** er reist immer erster Klasse; **a first-class compartment** ein Erste-Klasse-Abteil.

first floor *noun* erste Stock der; **on the first floor** im ersten Stock.

firstly *adverb* zunächst.

first name *noun* Vorname der (PL die Vornamen).

fir tree *noun* Tanne die (PL die Tannen).

a
b
c
d
e
f
g
h
i
j
k
l
m
n
o
p
q
r
s
t
u
v
w
x
y
z

a
b
c
d
e
f
g
h
i
j
k
l
m
n
o
p
q
r
s
t
u
v
w
x
y
z

fish noun Fisch der (PL die Fische).

fish verb fischen, (with a rod) angeln.

fish and chips noun ausgebackener Fisch mit Pommes frites.

fisherman noun Fischer der (PL die Fischer).

fishing noun Fischen das, (with a rod) Angeln das; **to go fishing** fischen/angeln gehen.

fishing rod noun Angel die (PL die Angeln).

fishing tackle noun Angelausrüstung die.

fist noun Faust die (PL die Fäuste).

fit noun 1 (of rage) Anfall der (PL die Anfälle); **your dad'll have a fit when he sees your hair** dein Vater kriegt bestimmt einen Anfall, wenn er deine Haare sieht; **2 an epileptic fit** ein epileptischer Anfall.

fit adjective (healthy) fit; **I feel really fit** ich fühle mich richtig fit; **to keep fit** fit bleiben.

fit verb 1 (be the right size for) (of shoes or a garment) passen (+ DAT); **this skirt doesn't fit me** der Rock passt mir nicht; **2** (be able to be put into) passen in (+ ACC); **will my cases all fit in the car?** passen meine Koffer alle in das Auto?; **the key doesn't fit in the lock** der Schlüssel passt nicht ins Schloss; **3** (install) einbauen SEP.

fitted carpet noun Teppichboden der (PL die Teppichböden).

fitted kitchen noun Einbauküche die (PL die Einbauküchen).

fitting room noun Umkleidekabine die (PL die Umkleidekabinen).

five number fünf; **it's five o'clock** es ist fünf Uhr.

fix verb 1 (repair) reparieren; **Mum's fixed the computer** Mutti hat den Computer repariert; **2** (decide on) festlegen ✧ SEP; **to fix a date** einen Termin festlegen; **3** machen (a meal); **I'll fix supper** ich mache Abendessen.

fizzy adjective sprudelnd; **fizzy water** das Sprudelwasser.

flag noun Fahne die (PL die Fahnen).

flame noun Flamme die (PL die Flammen).

flan noun Torte die (PL die Torten); **fruit flan** die Obsttorte.

flap verb (of a bird) **to flap its wings** mit den Flügeln schlagen ✧.

flash noun (on a camera) Blitz der (PL die Blitze); **flash of lightning** der Blitz.

flash verb 1 (a light) aufleuchten SEP, (repeatedly) blinken; **2 to flash by** or **past** vorbeiflitzen SEP (informal).

flashback noun Rückblende die (PL die Rückblenden).

flat noun Wohnung die (PL die Wohnungen); **a third-floor flat** eine Wohnung im dritten Stock.

flat adjective 1 flach; **flat shoes** flache Schuhe; **a flat landscape** eine flache Landschaft; **2 a flat tyre** ein platter Reifen.

flatmate noun Mitbewohner der (PL die Mitbewohner), Mitbewohnerin die (PL die Mitbewohnerinnen).

flatter noun schmeicheln (+ DAT).

flavour noun 1 Geschmack der (PL die Geschmäcke); **the sauce has a bitter flavour** die Soße hat einen bitteren Geschmack; **strawberry flavour** Erdbeergeschmack; 2 (of drinks, coffee, or tea) Aroma das (PL die Aromen).

flavour verb würzen; **vanilla-flavoured** mit Vanillegeschmack.

flea noun Floh der (PL die Flöhe).

flesh noun Fleisch das.

flex noun Kabel das (PL die Kabel).

flight noun 1 Flug der (PL die Flüge); **the flight was delayed** der Flug hatte Verspätung; **charter flight** der Charterflug; **the flight from Munich to London takes an hour and a half** die Flugzeit von München nach London beträgt eineinhalb Stunden; 2 **flight of stairs** die Treppe.

flight attendant noun Flugbegleiter der (PL die Flugbegleiter), Flugbegleiterin die (PL die Flugbegleiterinnen).

flipper noun Flosse die (PL die Flossen).

flirt verb flirten.

float verb 1 (on water) treiben◇; 2 (in the air) schweben.

flood noun 1 (of water) Überschwemmung die (PL die Überschwemmungen); 2 **to be in floods of tears** in Tränen aufgelöst sein; 3 (of letters or complaints) Flut die.

flood verb überschwemmen.

floodlight noun Flutlicht das.

floor noun 1 Boden der (PL die Böden); **your glasses are on the floor** deine Brille liegt auf dem Boden; 2 **to sweep the floor** fegen; **to sweep the kitchen floor** die Küche fegen; 3 (a storey) Stock der (PL die Stock); **on the second floor** im zweiten Stock.

floppy disk noun Diskette die (PL die Disketten).

florist noun Blumenhändler der (PL die Blumenhändler), Blumenhändlerin die (PL die Blumenhändlerinnen).

flour noun Mehl das.

flow verb fließen◇ (PERF sein).

flower noun Blume die (PL die Blumen); **bunch of flowers** der Blumenstrauß.

flower verb blühen.

flu noun Grippe die (PL die Grippen); **to have flu** die Grippe haben.

fluent adjective **she speaks fluent Italian** sie spricht fließend Italienisch.

fluently adverb fließend.

flute noun Flöte die (PL die Flöten); **to play the flute** Flöte spielen.

fly noun Fliege die (PL die Fliegen).

fly verb 1 fliegen◇ (PERF sein), **we flew to Berlin** wir sind nach Berlin geflogen; 2 **steigen lassen** (a kite); 3 fliegen◇ (PERF haben) (a plane or helicopter); 4 (to pass quickly) schnell vergehen◇ (PERF sein).

foam noun 1 (foam rubber) Schaumgummi der; **foam mattress** die Schaumgummimatratze; 2 (on a drink) Schaum der.

focus noun Brennpunkt der (PL die Brennpunkte) **to be in focus** scharf sein; **to be out of focus** unscharf sein.

focus verb scharf stellen (a camera).

fog noun Nebel der.

foggy adjective neblig.

foil noun (kitchen foil) Alufolie die.

fold noun 1 (in fabric or skin) Falte die (PL die Falten); 2 (in paper) Falz der (PL die Falze).

fold verb falten; **to fold something up** etwas zusammenfalten SEP.

folder noun Mappe die (PL die Mappen).

follow verb 1 folgen (PERF sein) (+ DAT); **follow me!** folgen Sie mir!; **2 do you follow me?** verstehst du, was ich meine?

following adjective folgend; **the following evening** am folgenden Abend.

fond adjective **to be fond of somebody** jemanden gern haben; **I'm very fond of him** ich habe ihn sehr gern.

food noun 1 Essen das; **I have to buy some food** ich muss noch etwas zu essen einkaufen; **2 I like German food** ich mag die deutsche Küche; **3** (stocks) Lebensmittel (plural); **we bought food for the holiday** wir haben Lebensmittel für die Ferien eingekauft.

food poisoning noun Lebensmittelvergiftung.

fool noun Dummkopf der (PL die Dummköpfe).

foot noun Fuß der (PL die Füße); **Lucy came on foot** Lucy ist zu Fuß gekommen.

football noun 1 Fußball der (PL die Fußbälle); **to play football** Fußball spielen.

footballer noun Fußballspieler der (PL die Fußballspieler), Fußballspielerin die (PL die Fußballspielerinnen).

footpath noun Fußweg der (PL die Fußwege).

footprint noun Fußabdruck der (PL die Fußabdrücke).

footstep noun Schritt der (PL die Schritte).

for preposition **1** für (+ ACC); **a present for my mother** ein Geschenk für meine Mutter; **what's it for?** wofür ist das?; **2** (for a particular occasion or event) zu (+ DAT); **sausages for lunch** Würstchen zum Mittagessen; **Sam got a bike for Christmas** Sam hat zu Weihnachten ein Rad bekommen; **what for?** wozu?; **3** (time expressions in the past but continuing in the present) seit (+ DAT); **I've been waiting here for an hour** (and I'm still waiting) ich warte hier seit einer Stunde; **my brother's been living in Berlin for three years** (and he still lives there) mein Bruder wohnt seit drei Jahren in Berlin; **4** (time expressions in the past or the future) **I studied French for six years** (but I no longer do) ich habe sechs Jahre lang Französisch gelernt; **I'll be away for four days** ich werde vier Tage nicht da sein; **5** (with a price) für (+ ACC); **I sold my bike for fifty pounds** ich habe mein Rad für fünfzig Pfund verkauft; **6 what's the German for 'bee'?** wie heißt 'bee' auf Deutsch?

forbid verb verbieten✧; **to forbid somebody to do something** jemandem verbieten, etwas zu tun.

forbidden adjective verboten.

force noun Kraft die (PL die Kräfte).

force verb zwingen✧; **to force somebody to do something** jemanden zwingen, etwas zu tun.

forecast noun Vorhersage die (PL die Vorhersagen).

foreground noun Vordergrund der; **in the foreground** im Vordergrund.

forehead noun Stirn die (PL die Stirnen).

foreign adjective **1** ausländisch; **in a foreign country** im Ausland; **from a foreign country** aus dem Ausland; **2 foreign language** die Fremdsprache.

foreigner noun Ausländer der (PL die Ausländer), Ausländerin die (PL die Ausländerinnen).

forest noun Wald der (PL die Wälder).

forever adverb **1** immer; **I'd like to stay here forever** ich möchte für immer hier bleiben; **2** (non-stop) ständig; **he's forever asking questions** er fragt ständig.

forget verb vergessen✧; **to forget about something** etwas vergessen; **we've forgotten the bread** wir haben das Brot vergessen; **to forget to do something** vergessen, etwas zu tun; **I forgot to phone** ich habe vergessen anzurufen.

forgive verb verzeihen✧ (+ DAT); **to forgive somebody** jemandem verzeihen; **I forgave him** ich habe ihm verziehen; **to forgive somebody for doing something** jemandem verzeihen, dass er/sie etwas getan hat; **I forgave her for losing my ring** ich habe ihr verziehen, dass sie meinen Ring verloren hat.

fork noun Gabel die (PL die Gabeln).

form noun **1** Formular das (PL die Formulare); **to fill in a form** ein Formular ausfüllen; **2** (shape or kind) Form die (PL die Formen); **in the form of** in Form von; **to be on form** gut in Form sein; **3** (in school) Klasse die (PL die Klassen).

form verb bilden.

formal adjective formell (invitation, event).

format noun Format das (PL die Formate).

former adjective ehemalig; **a former pupil** ein ehemaliger Schüler, eine ehemalige Schülerin.

fortnight noun vierzehn Tage (plural); **we're going to Spain for a fortnight** wir fahren vierzehn Tage nach Spanien.

fortunately adverb glücklicherweise.

fortune noun Vermögen das (PL die Vermögen); **to make a fortune** ein Vermögen machen.

forty number vierzig.

forward noun (in sport) Stürmer der (PL die Stürmer).

forward adverb ✧ (to the front) nach vorn; **to move forward** vorrücken SEP (PERF sein); **a seat further forward** ein Platz weiter vorn.

foster child noun Pflegekind das (PL die Pflegekinder).

foul noun (in sport) Foul das (PL die Fouls).

a
b
c
d
e
f
g
h
i
j
k
l
m
n
o
p
q
r
s
t
u
v
w
x
y
z

foul *adjective* scheußlich; **the weather's foul** das Wetter ist scheußlich.

fountain *noun* Brunnen der (PL die Brunnen).

fountain pen *noun* Füllfederhalter der (PL die Füllfederhalter).

four *number* vier; **it's four o'clock** es ist vier Uhr; ★ **on all fours** auf allen vieren.

fourteen *number* vierzehn.

fourth *number* vierter/vierte/viertes; **the fourth of July** der vierte Juli; **on the fourth floor** im vierten Stock.

fox *noun* Fuchs der (PL die Füchse).

fragile *adjective* zerbrechlich.

frame *noun* 1 Rahmen der (PL die Rahmen); 2 (of spectacles) Gestell das (PL die Gestelle).

franc *noun* 1 (Swiss) Franken der (PL die Franken); **a fifty-franc note** ein Fünfzig-Franken-Schein; 2 (former French and Belgian currencies) Franc der (PL die Francs).

France *noun* Frankreich das; **to France** nach Frankreich.

frantic *adjective* 1 (very upset) **to be frantic** außer sich (DAT) sein; **I was frantic with worry** ich war außer mir vor Sorge; 2 (desperate) fieberhaft (effort or search).

freckle *noun* Sommersprosse die (PL die Sommersprossen).

free *adjective* 1 (when you don't pay) kostenlos; **a free ride** eine kostenlose Fahrt; **a free ticket** eine Freikarte; 2 (without charge) umsonst; **to do something for free** etwas umsonst machen; 3 (not

occupied) frei; **are you free on Thursday?** haben Sie am Donnerstag Zeit?; 4 **sugar-free** ohne Zucker; **lead-free** bleifrei.

free *verb* befreien.

freedom *noun* Freiheit die.

free gift *noun* Werbegeschenk das (PL die Werbegeschenke).

free kick *noun* Freistoß der (PL die Freistöße).

freeze *verb* 1 (in a freezer) einfrieren◇ SEP; **to freeze raspberries** Himbeeren einfrieren; 2 (in cold weather) frieren◇; **it's freezing** es friert; 3 (become covered with ice) zufrieren◇ SEP (PERF sein); **the pond is frozen** der Teich ist zugefroren.

freezer *noun* Gefrierschrank der (PL die Gefrierschränke).

freezing *noun* below freezing unter Null; **three degrees above freezing** drei Grad über Null.

freezing *adjective* 1 **I'm freezing** ich friere sehr; 2 **it's freezing outside** es ist eiskalt draußen.

French *noun* 1 (the language) Französisch das; 2 (the people) **the French** die Franzosen.

French *adjective* 1 französisch; **Jean-Marc is French** Jean-Marc ist Franzose; 2 (teacher or lesson) Französisch-; **the French class** der Französischunterricht.

French bean *noun* grüne Bohne die (PL die grünen Bohnen).

French dressing *noun* Vinaigrette die.

French fries *plural noun* Pommes frites (plural).

Frenchman *noun* Franzose *der* (PL die Franzosen).

French window *noun* Terrassentür *die* (PL die Terrassentüren).

Frenchwoman *noun* Französin *die* (PL die Französinnen).

frequent *adjective* häufig.

fresh *adjective* frisch; **fresh eggs** frische Eier; **I'm going out for some fresh air** ich gehe ein bisschen frische Luft schnappen.

Friday *noun* 1 Freitag *der* (PL die Freitage); **next Friday** nächsten Freitag; **last Friday** letzten Freitag; **on Friday** (am) Freitag; **I'll phone you on Friday evening** ich rufe dich Freitagabend an; **every Friday** jeden Freitag; **Good Friday** Karfreitag; 2 **on Fridays** freitags; **closed on Fridays** freitags geschlossen.

fridge *noun* Kühlschrank *der* (PL die Kühlschränke); **put it in the fridge** stell es in den Kühlschrank.

friend *noun* 1 Freund *der* (PL die Freunde), Freundin *die* (PL die Freundinnen); **a friend of mine** ein Freund von mir; 2 **to make friends** sich anfreunden; **he made friends with Danny** er hat sich mit Danny angefreundet; **he is friends with Danny** er ist mit Danny befreundet.

friendly *adjective* freundlich.

friendship *noun* Freundschaft *die* (PL die Freundschaften).

fries *plural noun* Pommes frites (*plural*).

fright *noun* 1 Schreck *der* (PL die Schrecke); **to have** or **get a fright** einen Schreck bekommen; 2 **you**

gave me a fright! du hast mich erschreckt!

frighten *verb* 1 (*of an explosion or shot*) erschrecken; 2 (*scare or threaten*) **to frighten somebody** jemandem Angst machen.

frightened *adjective* **to be frightened** Angst haben; **Martin's frightened of snakes** Martin hat Angst vor Schlangen.

frightening *adjective* beängstigend.

fringe *noun* 1 (*hairstyle*) Pony *der* (PL die Ponys); 2 (*on clothes or a curtain*) Fransen (*plural*).

frog *noun* Frosch *der* (PL die Frösche).

from *preposition* 1 von (+ DAT); **ten metres from the cinema** zehn Meter vom Kino; **a letter from Tom** ein Brief von Tom; **from Monday to Friday** von Montag bis Freitag; **from now on** von jetzt an; 2 aus (+ DAT); **he comes from Dublin** er kommt aus Dublin; **the train from London** der Zug aus London; 3 **from seven o'clock onwards** ab sieben Uhr; **from then on** von da ab.

front *noun* 1 (*of a cupboard, card, or envelope*) Vorderseite *die* (PL die Vorderseiten); (*of a building*) Vorderfront *die* (PL die Vorderfronten); 2 (*of a garment or in an interior*) Vorderteil *das* (PL die Vorderteile); 3 (*at the seaside*) Strandpromenade *die* (PL die Strandpromenaden); 4 (*of a car*) **to sit in (the) front** vorne sitzen; 5 (*of a train or queue*) vordere Ende *das*; 6 (*of a procession or in a race*) Spitze *die*; 7 **in/at the front** vorne;

a b c d e f g h i j k l m n o p q r s t u v w x y z

in/at the front of vorne in (+ DAT, or + ACC *with movement towards a place*); **there are still seats at the front of the train** es gibt noch Plätze vorne im Zug; **we got on at the front of the train** wir sind vorne in den Zug eingestiegen; **8 in front of** vor (+ DAT, or + ACC *with movement towards a place*); **in front of the TV** vor dem Fernseher; **in front of me** vor mir.

front *adjective* **1** vorderer/vordere/vorderes; **in the front rows** in den vorderen Reihen; **2** Vorder-; **front seat** (*of a car*) der Vordersitz; **front wheel** das Vorderrad.

front door *noun* Haustür die (PL die Haustüren).

frontier *noun* Grenze die (PL die Grenzen).

frost *noun* Frost der.

frosty *adjective* frostig.

frown *verb* die Stirn runzeln; **he frowned at us** er blickte uns mit gerunzelter Stirn an.

frozen *adjective* (*in a freezer*) tiefgekühlt; **a frozen pizza** eine Tiefkühlpizza.

fruit *noun* **1** (*a single fruit or type of fruit*) Frucht die (PL die Früchte); **2** (*various fruits*) Obst das; **we bought cheese and fruit** wir haben Käse und Obst gekauft.

fruit juice *noun* Fruchtsaft der (PL die Fruchtsäfte).

fruit machine *noun* Spielautomat der (PL die Spielautomaten).

fruit salad *noun* Obstsalat der (PL die Obstsalate).

frustrated *adjective* frustriert.

fry *verb* braten❖; **we fried fish** wir haben Fisch gebraten; **fried potatoes** Bratkartoffeln; **fried egg** das Spiegelei.

frying pan *noun* Bratpfanne die (PL die Bratpfannen).

fuel *noun* (*for a car*) Kraftstoff der.

full *adjective* **1** voll; **the glass is full** das Glas ist voll; **I'm full** ich bin voll (*informal*); **2 full of** voller (+ GEN); **the train was full of tourists** der Zug war voller Touristen; **3 at full speed** in voller Fahrt; **4 to write something out in full** etwas voll ausschreiben.

full stop *noun* Punkt der (PL die Punkte).

full-time *adjective* **a full-time job** eine Ganztagsstelle.

fully *adverb* voll.

fun *noun* **1** Spaß der; **have fun!** viel Spaß!; **we had fun catching the ponies** die Ponys einzufangen machte uns Spaß; **skiing is fun** Skifahren macht Spaß; **I do it for fun** ich mache es aus Spaß; **2 to have fun** sich amüsieren; ★ **to make fun of somebody** sich über jemanden lustig machen.

funds *plural noun* Geldmittel (*plural*).

funeral *noun* Beerdigung die (PL die Beerdigungen).

funfair *noun* Jahrmarkt der (PL die Jahrmärkte).

funny *adjective* **1** (*amusing*) lustig; **a funny story** eine lustige Geschichte; **he's so funny** er ist so witzig; **2** (*strange*) komisch; **a funny noise** ein komisches Geräusch; **that's funny, I'm sure I**

paid das ist komisch, ich bin mir sicher, dass ich gezahlt habe.

fur noun **1** (on an animal) Fell das (PL die Felle); **2** (for a coat) Pelz der (PL die Pelze); **fur coat** der Pelzmantel.

furious adjective wütend; **she was furious with Steve** sie war wütend auf Steve.

furniture noun Möbel (plural); **to buy some furniture** Möbel kaufen; **piece of furniture** das Möbelstück.

further adverb weiter; **further than the station** weiter als der Bahnhof; **ten kilometres further on** zehn Kilometer weiter; **further off** weiter entfernt; **further forward** weiter vorn; **further back** weiter hinten.

fuse noun Sicherung die (PL die Sicherungen).

fuss noun Theater das; **to make a fuss** ein Theater machen; **to make a big fuss about the bill** ein großes Theater um die Rechnung machen.

fussy adjective **to be fussy about something** wählerisch in etwas (DAT) sein (food, for example).

future noun Zukunft die; **in future** in Zukunft.

Gg

gadget noun Gerät das (PL die Geräte).

gain verb **1** gewinnen◇; **in order to gain time** um Zeit zu gewinnen; **2** profitieren; **to gain by something** von etwas profitieren.

gale noun Sturm der (PL die Stürme).

gallery noun Galerie die (PL die Galerien).

gamble verb spielen (for money).

game noun **1** Spiel das (PL die Spiele); **game of chance** das Glücksspiel; **board game** das Brettspiel; **2 to have a game of cards** eine Partie Karten spielen; **3 to have a game of football** Fußball spielen; **4 games** (at school) Sport der.

gang noun Bande die (PL die Banden); **all the gang were there** die ganze Bande war da.

gap noun **1** (hole) Lücke die (PL die Lücken); **2** (in time) Pause die (PL die Pausen); **a two-hour gap** eine zweistündige Pause; **3 age gap** der Altersunterschied.

gap year noun Orientierungsjahr das (PL die Orientierungsjahre).

garage noun **1** (for keeping your car) Garage die (PL die Garagen); **2** (for repairing cars) Autowerkstatt die (PL die Autowerkstätten); **3** (for petrol) Tankstelle die (PL die Tankstellen).

garden noun Garten der (PL die Gärten).

gardener noun Gärtner der (PL die Gärtner), Gärtnerin die (PL die Gärtnerinnen).

gardening noun Gartenarbeit die.

garlic noun Knoblauch der.

garment noun Kleidungsstück das (PL die Kleidungsstücke).

gas noun Gas das.

gas cooker noun Gasherd der (PL die Gasherde).

a b c d e f g h i j k l m n o p q r s t u v w x y z

gas fire noun Gasofen der (PL die Gasöfen).

gas meter noun Gaszähler der (PL die Gaszähler).

gate noun 1 (in garden) Pforte die (PL die Pforten); 2 (in field) Gatter das (PL die Gatter); 3 (at an airport) Flugsteig der (PL die Flugsteige).

gather verb 1 (of people) sich versammeln, sammeln (fruit, vegetables, flowers); 3 as far as I can gather soweit ich weiß.

gay adjective (homosexual) schwul (informal).

gaze verb to gaze at something etwas anstarren SEP.

GCSEs noun plural (You can explain GCSEs briefly as follows: Dies sind Prüfungen, die im Alter von ca 16 Jahren in bis zu 12 Fächern abgelegt werden. Sie werden von A* (beste Note) bis N (nicht bestanden) benotet. Viele Schüler und Schülerinnen machen nach den GCSEs weiter und legen die A-level Prüfungen ab) SEE **A levels**.

gear lever noun Schalthebel der (PL die Schalthebel).

gear noun 1 (in a car) Gang der (PL die Gänge); to change gear schalten; 2 (equipment) Ausrüstung die; camping gear die Campingausrüstung; 3 (things) Sachen (plural); I've left all my gear at Gary's ich habe alle meine Sachen bei Gary gelassen.

gel noun Gel das (PL die Gele).

Gemini noun Zwillinge (plural); Steph's Gemini Steph ist Zwilling.

gender noun (of a word) Geschlecht das (PL die Geschlechter); what is the gender of 'Haus'? welches Geschlecht hat 'Haus'?

general noun General der (PL die Generäle).

general adjective allgemein; in general im Allgemeinen; the general election die allgemeinen Wahlen.

general knowledge noun Allgemeinwissen das.

generally adverb im Allgemeinen.

generation noun Generation die (PL die Generationen).

generator noun Generator der (PL die Generatoren).

generous adjective großzügig.

genetics noun Genetik die.

Geneva noun Genf das; Lake Geneva der Genfer See.

genius noun Genie das (PL die Genies); Lisa, you're a genius! Lisa, du bist ein Genie!

gentle adjective sanft.

gentleman noun Herr der (PL die Herren); ladies and gentlemen! meine Damen und Herren!

gently adverb sanft.

gents noun (lavatory) Herrentoilette die (PL die Herrentoiletten); (on a sign) 'Gents' 'Herren'; where's the gents? wo ist die Herrentoilette?

genuine adjective 1 (real, authentic) echt; a genuine diamond ein echter Brillant; 2 aufrichtig (person); she's very genuine sie ist sehr aufrichtig.

geography noun Geographie die, (at school) Erdkunde die.

get

germ noun **1** Keim der (PL die Keime); **2** (causing a cold) **germs** Bazillen (plural).

German noun **1** (person) Deutsche der/die (PL die Deutschen); **2** (language) Deutsch das; **in German** auf Deutsch.

German adjective deutsch; **he is German** er ist Deutscher; **she is German** sie ist Deutsche; **our German teacher** unser Deutschlehrer, unsere Deutschlehrerin.

Germany noun Deutschland das; **to Germany** nach Deutschland; **from Germany** aus Deutschland.

get verb **1** (obtain, receive) bekommen, kriegen (informal); **I got a bike for my birthday** ich habe ein Rad zum Geburtstag bekommen; **Fred got the job** Fred hat die Stelle bekommen; **she got a shock** sie hat einen Schreck gekriegt; **I got a good mark for my German homework** ich habe auf meine Deutschhausaufgaben eine gute Note bekommen; **2 he's got lots of money** er hat viel Geld; **she's got long hair** sie hat lange Haare; **I've got a headache** ich habe Kopfschmerzen; **3** (fetch) holen; **I'll get some bread** ich hole Brot; **I'll get your bag for you** ich hole dir deine Tasche; **4 to have got to do something** etwas tun müssen◇; **I've got to phone before midday** ich muss vor Mittag anrufen; **5 to get (to) somewhere** irgendwo ankommen◇ SEP (PERF sein); **when I got to London** als ich in London ankam; **we got here this morning** wir sind heute Morgen angekommen; **what time did they get there?** wann sind sie angekommen?; **6** (become) werden◇ (PERF sein); **it's getting late** es wird spät; **it's getting dark** es wird dunkel; **7 to get something done** etwas machen lassen◇; **I'm getting my hair cut today** ich lasse mir heute die Haare schneiden.

● **to get back** zurückkommen◇ SEP (PERF sein); **Mum gets back at six** Mutti kommt um sechs zurück.

● **to get something back** etwas zurückbekommen◇ SEP, etwas zurückkriegen SEP (informal); **did you get your books back?** hast du deine Bücher zurückbekommen?

● **to get into something** (a vehicle) in etwas (ACC) einsteigen◇ SEP (PERF sein); **he got into the car** er ist ins Auto eingestiegen.

● **to get off something** (a vehicle) aus etwas (DAT) aussteigen◇ SEP (PERF sein); **I got off the train at Banbury** ich bin in Banbury aus dem Zug ausgestiegen.

● **to get on: how's Amanda getting on?** wie gehts Amanda?

● **to get on something** (a vehicle) in etwas (ACC) einsteigen◇ SEP (PERF sein); **she got on the train at Reading** sie ist in Reading in den Zug eingestiegen.

● **to get on with somebody** sich mit jemandem verstehen◇; **she doesn't get on with her brother** sie versteht sich nicht mit ihrem Bruder.

a
b
c
d
e
f
g
h
i
j
k
l
m
n
o
p
q
r
s
t
u
v
w
x
y
z

a
b
c
d
e
f
g
h
i
j
k
l
m
n
o
p
q
r
s
t
u
v
w
x
y
z

• **to get out of something** (*a vehicle*) aus etwas (DAT) austeigen✧ SEP (PERF *sein*); **Laura got out of the car** Laura ist aus dem Auto ausgestiegen.

• **to get together** sich wieder sehen✧ SEP; **we must get together soon** wir müssen uns bald mal wieder sehen.

• **to get up** aufstehen✧ SEP (PERF *sein*); **I get up at seven** ich stehe um sieben auf.

ghost noun Geist der (PL die Geister).

giant noun Riese der (PL die Riesen).

giant adjective riesig; **a giant lorry** ein riesiger Lastwagen.

gift noun **1** Geschenk das (PL die Geschenke); **a Christmas gift** ein Weihnachtsgeschenk; **2** Begabung die; **to have a gift for something** für etwas (ACC) begabt sein; **Jo has a real gift for languages** Jo ist wirklich sprachbegabt.

gigabyte noun Gigabyte das (PL die Gigabytes); **a fifty gigabyte hard disk** eine Festplatte mit fünfzig Gigabyte Speicherkapazität.

gigantic adjective riesig.

gin noun Gin der (PL die Gins).

ginger noun Ingwer der (PL die Ingwer).

gipsy noun Zigeuner der (PL die Zigeuner), Zigeunerin die (PL die Zigeunerinnen).

giraffe noun Giraffe die (PL die Giraffen).

girl noun Mädchen das (PL die Mädchen); **three boys and four girls** drei Jungen und vier Mädchen; **when I was a little girl** ich ... als kleines Mädchen hatte ich ....

girlfriend noun Freundin die (PL die Freundinnen).

give verb **1** geben✧; **to give something to somebody** jemandem etwas geben; **I'll give you my address** ich gebe dir meine Adresse; **give me the key** gib mir den Schlüssel; **Yasmin's dad gave her the money** Yasmins Vater hat ihr das Geld gegeben; **2** (*give as a gift*) schenken; **to give somebody a present** jemandem etwas schenken.

• **to give something away** etwas weggeben✧ SEP; **she's given away all her books** sie hat alle ihre Bücher weggegeben.

• **to give something back to somebody** jemandem etwas zurückgeben✧ SEP; **I gave her back the keys** ich habe ihr die Schlüssel zurückgegeben.

• **to give in** nachgeben✧ SEP; **my mum said no but she gave in in the end** meine Mutti hat nein gesagt, aber schließlich hat sie nachgegeben.

• **to give up** aufgeben✧ SEP; **I give up!** ich gebe auf!

• **to give up doing something** etwas aufgeben✧ SEP; **she's given up smoking** sie hat das Rauchen aufgegeben.

glad adjective froh; **I'm glad to hear he's better** ich bin froh, dass es ihm besser geht; **I'm glad to be back** ich bin froh, dass ich wieder zurück bin.

go

glass noun Glas das (PL die Gläser); **a glass of water** ein Glas Wasser; **a glass table** ein Glastisch.

glasses plural noun Brille die (PL die Brillen); **to wear glasses** eine Brille tragen.

glider noun Segelflugzeug das (PL die Segelflugzeuge).

global warming noun globale Temperaturanstieg der.

glove noun Handschuh der (PL die Handschuhe); **a pair of gloves** ein Paar Handschuhe.

glove compartment noun Handschuhfach das (PL die Handschuhfächer).

glue noun Klebstoff der (PL die Klebstoffe).

go noun **1** (in a game) whose go is it? wer ist dran?; **it's my go** ich bin dran; **2 to have a go at doing something** versuchen, etwas zu tun; **I'll have a go at mending it** ich versuche, es zu reparieren.

go verb **1** (on foot) gehen ✧ (PERF sein); **to go to school** in die Schule gehen; **Mark's gone to the dentist's** Mark ist zum Zahnarzt gegangen; **to go shopping** einkaufen gehen ✧ (in a vehicle) fahren ✧ (PERF sein); **we're going to London** wir fahren nach London; **we're planning to go early** wir wollen früh losfahren; **to go on holiday** in die Ferien fahren; **3** (by plane) fliegen ✧ (PERF sein); **4 to go for a walk** spazieren gehen ✧ (PERF sein); **5** (with another verb) **I'm going to do it** ich werde es tun; **I'm going to make some tea** ich mache Tee; **he was going to phone you** er wollte dich anrufen;

6 (leave) gehen ✧ (PERF sein); **Pauline's already gone** Pauline ist schon gegangen; **7** (on a journey) abfahren ✧ SEP (PERF sein); **when does the train go?** wann fährt der Zug ab?; **8** (turn out) verlaufen ✧ (PERF sein) (event); **how did your evening go?** wie ist dein Abend verlaufen?; **the party went well** die Party war gut.

● **to go away 1** weggehen ✧ SEP (PERF sein); **go away!** geh weg!; **2** (on holiday) verreisen (PERF sein).

● **to go back 1** zurückgehen ✧ SEP (PERF sein); **I'm going back to Germany in March** ich werde im März nach Deutschland zurückkehren; **I'm not going back there again!** ich gehe da nicht wieder zurück!; **2 I went back home** ich bin nach Hause gegangen.

● **to go down 1** hinuntergehen ✧ SEP (PERF sein); **she's gone down to the kitchen** sie ist in die Küche hinuntergegangen; **to go down the stairs** die Treppe hinuntergehen; **2** (price, temperature) fallen ✧ (PERF sein); **3** (tyre, balloon, airbed) Luft verlieren ✧.

● **to go in** hineingehen ✧ SEP (PERF sein); **he went in and shut the door** er ist hineingegangen und hat die Tür zugemacht.

● **to go into 1** (person) gehen in (+ ACC) PERF sein); **Fran went into the kitchen** Fran ging in die Küche; **2** (object) passen in (+ ACC); **this book won't go into my bag** dieses Buch passt nicht in meine Tasche.

● **to go off 1** (bomb) explodieren

a
b
c
d
e
f
g
h
i
j
k
l
m
n
o
p
q
r
s
t
u
v
w
x
y
z

(PERF *sein*); **2** (*alarm clock*) klingeln; **my alarm clock went off at six** mein Wecker hat um sechs geklingelt; **3** (*fire or burglar alarm*) losgehen ✧ SEP (PERF *sein*); **the fire alarm went off** der Feuermelder ging los.

● **to go on 1 what's going on?** was ist los?; **2 to go on doing something** weiter etwas tun; **she went on talking** sie hat weitergeredet; **3 to go on about something** stundenlang von etwas (DAT) reden; **he's always going on about his dog** er redet stundenlang von seinem Hund.

● **to go out 1** (*for an evening*) ausgehen ✧ SEP, weggehen ✧ SEP (PERF *sein*) (*informal*); **we're going out tonight** wir gehen heute Abend aus; **2** (*leave*) **she went out of the kitchen** sie ist aus der Küche gegangen; **3 to be going out with somebody** mit jemandem gehen ✧ (PERF *sein*) (*informal*); **she's going out with my brother** sie geht mit meinem Bruder; **4** (*light, fire*) ausgehen ✧ SEP (PERF *sein*); **the light went out** das Licht ist ausgegangen.

● **to go past something** an etwas (DAT) vorbeigehen ✧ SEP; **we went past your house** wir sind an eurem Haus vorbeigegangen.

● **to go round: to go round to somebody's house** jemanden besuchen; **we went round to Fred's last night** wir haben gestern Abend Fred besucht.

● **to go round something 1** um etwas (ACC) herumgehen ✧ SEP (PERF *sein*) (*building, park, garden*); **2** besichtigen (*museum, monument*).

● **to go through 1 the train goes through Cologne** der Zug fährt durch Köln; **2 to go through a room** durch ein Zimmer gehen; **3** (*search*) durchsuchen.

● **to go up 1** (*person*) hinaufgehen ✧ SEP (PERF *sein*); **she's gone up to her room** sie ist in ihr Zimmer hinaufgegangen; **to go up the stairs** die Treppe hinaufgehen; **2** (*prices*) steigen ✧ (PERF *sein*); **the price of petrol has gone up** die Benzinpreise sind gestiegen.

goal *noun* Tor *das* (PL die Tore); **to score a goal** ein Tor schießen; **to win by 3 goals to 2** mit 3 zu 2 Toren gewinnen.

goalkeeper *noun* Torwart *der* (PL die Torwarte), Torfrau *die* (PL die Torfrauen).

goat *noun* Ziege *die* (PL die Ziegen).

God *noun* Gott *der*; **to believe in God** an Gott glauben.

god *noun* Gott *der* (PL die Götter).

godchild *noun* Patenkind *das* (PL die Patenkinder).

goddaughter *noun* Patentochter *die* (PL die Patentöchter).

goddess *noun* Göttin *die* (PL die Göttinnen).

godfather *noun* Pate *der* (PL die Paten).

godmother *noun* Patin *die* (PL die Patinnen).

godson *noun* Patensohn *der* (PL die Patensöhne).

goggles *plural noun* Schutzbrille *die* (PL die Schutzbrillen); **swimming**

goggles Schwimmbrille die (PL die Schwimmbrillen); **skiing goggles** Skibrille die (PL die Skibrillen).

gold noun Gold das; **a gold bracelet** ein Goldarmband.

goldfish noun Goldfisch der (PL die Goldfische).

golf noun Golf das; **to play golf** Golf spielen.

golf club noun 1 (place) Golfklub der (PL die Golfklubs); 2 (iron) Golfschläger der (PL die Golfschläger).

golf course noun Golfplatz der (PL die Golfplätze).

golfer noun Golfspieler der (PL die Golfspieler), Golfspielerin die (PL die Golfspielerinnen).

good adjective 1 gut; **she's a good teacher** sie ist eine gute Lehrerin; **the cherries are very good** die Kirschen sind sehr gut; **2 to be good for you** gesund sein; **tomatoes are good for you** Tomaten sind gesund; **3 good at** gut in (+ DAT); **she's good at maths** sie ist gut in Mathe; **he's good at drawing** er kann gut zeichnen; **4** (well-behaved) brav; **be good!** sei brav!; **5** (kind) nett; **she's been very good to me** sie ist sehr nett zu mir gewesen; **6 for good** endgültig; **I've stopped smoking for good** ich habe das Rauchen endgültig aufgegeben.

good afternoon exclamation guten Tag!

goodbye exclamation auf Wiedersehen!

good evening exclamation guten Abend!.

Good Friday noun Karfreitag der (PL die Karfreitage).

good-looking adjective gut aussehend.

good morning exclamation guten Morgen!

goodness exclamation meine Güte!; **for goodness sake!** um Himmels willen!

good night exclamation gute Nacht!

goods plural noun Waren (plural).

goods train noun Güterzug der (PL die Güterzüge).

goose noun Gans die (PL die Gänse).

gorgeous adjective herrlich; **it's a gorgeous day** es ist ein herrlicher Tag.

gorilla noun Gorilla der (PL die Gorillas).

gosh exclamation Mensch!

gossip noun 1 (person) Klatschbase die (PL die Klatschbasen); 2 (scandal) Klatsch der.

gossip verb klatschen.

government noun Regierung die (PL die Regierungen).

grab verb 1 packen; **she grabbed my arm** sie packte mich am Arm; **2 to grab something from somebody** jemandem etwas (ACC) entreißen◇; **he grabbed the book from me** er hat mir das Buch entrissen.

grade noun (mark) Note die (PL die Noten), **to get good grades** gute Noten bekommen.

gradual adjective allmählich.

gradually adverb allmählich; **the weather got gradually better** das Wetter wurde allmählich besser.

graffiti plural noun Graffiti (plural).

grain noun Korn das (PL die Körner).

gram noun Gramm das; **100 grams of salami** hundert Gramm Salami.

grammar noun Grammatik die.

grammar school noun Gymnasium das (PL die Gymnasien).

grammatical adjective grammatikalisch; **a grammatical error** eine Grammatikfehler.

gran noun Oma die (PL die Omas).

grandchildren plural noun Enkelkinder (plural).

granddad noun Opa der (PL die Opas).

granddaughter noun Enkelin die (PL die Enkelinnen).

grandfather noun Großvater der (PL die Großväter).

grandma noun Oma die (PL die Omas).

grandmother noun Großmutter die (PL die Großmütter).

grandpa noun Opa der (PL die Opas).

grandparents plural noun Großeltern (plural).

grandson noun Enkel der (PL die Enkel).

granny noun Omi die (PL die Omis).

grape noun Weintraube die (PL die Weintrauben); **a grape** eine Weintraube; **to buy some grapes** Weintrauben kaufen; **do you like grapes?** magst du Weintrauben?; **a bunch of grapes** eine ganze Weintraube.

grapefruit noun Grapefruit die (PL die Grapefruits).

graph noun Grafik die (PL die Grafiken).

grasp verb festhalten ✧ SEP.

grass noun 1 Gras das; **to lie on the grass** im Gras liegen; 2 (lawn) Rasen der (PL die Rasen); **to cut the grass** den Rasen mähen.

grasshopper noun Heuschrecke die (PL die Heuschrecken).

grate verb reiben ✧; **grated cheese** geriebener Käse.

grateful adjective dankbar; **to be grateful to somebody** jemandem dankbar sein.

grater noun Reibe die (PL die Reiben).

grave noun Grab das (PL die Gräber).

graveyard noun Friedhof der (PL die Friedhöfe).

gravy noun Soße die (PL die Soßen).

grease noun Fett das.

greasy adjective 1 fettig; **to have greasy skin** fettige Haut haben; 2 (food) fett.

great adjective 1 groß; **a great poet** ein großer Dichter; 2 (terrific) großartig; **it was a great party** das war eine großartige Party; **great!** großartig!, prima! (informal) 3 **a great deal of** sehr viel; **a great many** sehr viele.

Great Britain noun Großbritannien das.

Greece noun Griechenland das.

greedy adjective gierig, (with food) gefräßig.

Greek noun 1 (person) Grieche der (PL die Griechen), Griechin die (PL die Griechinnen); 2 (language) Griechisch das.

Greek *adjective* griechisch; **she's Greek** sie ist Griechin.

green *noun* **1** (*colour*) Grün *das*; **a pale green** ein Hellgrün; **2 the Greens** (*ecologists*) die Grünen.

green *adjective* **1** grün; **a green door** eine grüne Tür; **2 the Green Party** die Grünen (*plural*).

greengrocer *noun* Obst- und Gemüsehändler *der* (PL die Obst- und Gemüsehändler).

greenhouse *noun* Gewächshaus *das* (PL die Gewächshäuser).

greenhouse effect *noun* Treibhauseffekt *der*.

greetings *plural noun* Grüße (*plural*); **Season's Greetings** fröhliche Weihnachten und ein glückliches neues Jahr.

greetings card *noun* Glückwunschkarte die (PL die Glückwunschkarten).

grey *adjective* grau.

greyhound *noun* Windhund *der* (PL die Windhunde).

grid *noun* **1** (*grating*) Gitter *das* (PL die Gitter); **2** (*network*) Netz *das* (PL die Netze).

grief *noun* Trauer die.

grill *noun* Grill der (PL die Grills).

grill *verb* grillen; **I'm going to grill the sausages** ich grille die Würstchen.

grim *adjective* grauenvoll.

grin *verb* grinsen.

grind *verb* mahlen.

grip *verb* (*hold on to*) festhalten✧ SEP.

groan *noun* Stöhnen das.

groan *verb* stöhnen.

grocer *noun* Lebensmittelhändler *der* (PL die Lebensmittelhändler).

groceries *plural noun* Lebensmittel (*plural*).

grocer's *noun* Lebensmittelgeschäft *das* (PL die Lebensmittelgeschäfte).

groom *noun* Bräutigam *der* (PL die Bräutigame); **the bride and groom** das Brautpaar.

gross *adjective* **1 a gross injustice** eine schreiende Ungerechtigkeit; **2** grob; **a gross error** ein grober Fehler; **3** (*disgusting*) ekelhaft; **the food was gross!** das Essen war ekelhaft!

ground *noun* **1** Boden *der*; **to sit on the ground** auf dem Boden sitzen; **2** (*for sport*) Sportplatz *der* (PL die Sportplätze); **football ground** *der* Fußballplatz.

ground *adjective* gemahlen; **ground coffee** gemahlener Kaffee.

ground floor *noun* Erdgeschoss *das*; **they live on the ground floor** sie wohnen im Erdgeschoss.

group *noun* Gruppe die (PL die Gruppen).

grow *verb* **b** (*get bigger*) **1** wachsen✧ (PERF sein); **your hair grows very quickly** deine Haare wachsen sehr schnell; **my little sister's grown quite a bit this year** meine kleine Schwester ist dieses Jahr ein ganzes Stück gewachsen; **the number of students is still growing** die Zahl der Studenten wächst noch; **2** anbauen SEP (*fruit, vegetables*); **3 to grow a beard** sich (DAT) einen Bart wachsen lassen; **4** (*become*) werden✧ (PERF sein); **to grow old** alt werden.

a
b
c
d
e
f
g
h
i
j
k
l
m
n
o
p
q
r
s
t
u
v
w
x
y
z

● **to grow up 1** erwachsen werden; **the children are growing up** die Kinder werden erwachsen; **2** aufwachsen✧ SEP (PERF *sein*); **she grew up in Scotland** sie ist in Schottland aufgewachsen.

growl *verb* knurren.

grown-up *noun* Erwachsene der/die (PL die Erwachsenen).

growth *noun* Wachstum das.

grudge *noun* **to bear a grudge against somebody** etwas gegen jemanden haben; **she bears me a grudge** sie hat etwas gegen mich.

grumble *verb* **1** murren; **he's always grumbling** er murrt immer; **2** to grumble about something sich über etwas (ACC) beklagen; **what's she grumbling about?** worüber beklagt sie sich?

guarantee *noun* Garantie die (PL die Garantien); **a year's guarantee** ein Jahr Garantie.

guarantee *verb* garantieren.

guard *noun* **1 prison guard** der Gefängniswärter, die Gefängniswärterin; **2** (*on a train*) Zugführer der (PL die Zugführer), Zugführerin die (PL die Zugführerinnen); **3 security guard** der Wächter, die Wächterin.

guard *verb* bewachen.

guard dog *noun* Wachhund der (PL die Wachhunde).

guess *noun* **have a guess!** rate mal!; **it's a good guess** gut geraten.

guess *verb* **1** raten✧; **guess who I saw last night** rate mal, wen ich gestern Abend gesehen habe; **2** (*guess something correctly*) es

erraten✧; **you'll never guess!** du errätst es nie!

guest *noun* Gast der (PL die Gäste); **we've got guests coming tonight** wir haben heute Abend Gäste; **a paying guest** ein zahlender Gast.

guide *noun* **1** (*person*) Führer der (PL die Führer), Führerin die (PL die Führerinnen); **2** (*book*) Reiseführer der (PL die Reiseführer); **3** (*girl guide*) Pfadfinderin die (PL die Pfadfinderinnen).

guidebook *noun* **1** Reiseführer der (PL die Reiseführer); **2** (*to a museum or monument*) Handbuch das (PL die Handbücher).

guide dog *noun* Blindenhund der (PL die Blindenhunde).

guideline *noun* Richtlinie die (PL die Richtlinien).

guilty *adjective* **1** schuldig; **2 to feel guilty** ein schlechtes Gewissen haben; **I felt guilty about the noise** ich hatte ein schlechtes Gewissen wegen des Lärms.

guinea pig *noun* **1** (*pet*) Meerschweinchen das (PL die Meerschweinchen); **2** (*in an experiment*) Versuchskaninchen das (PL die Versuchskaninchen).

guitar *noun* Gitarre die (PL die Gitarren); **to play the guitar** Gitarre spielen.

gum *noun* **1** (*in your mouth*) Zahnfleisch das; **2** (*chewing gum*) Kaugummi der (PL die Kaugummi).

gun *noun* **1** Pistole die (PL die Pistolen); **2** (*rifle*) Gewehr das (PL die Gewehre).

gutter *noun* **1** (*in the street*) Rinnstein der (PL die Rinnsteine);

2 (*on roof edge*) Dachrinne die (PL die Dachrinnen).

guy noun Typ der (PL die Typen) (*informal*); **he's a nice guy** er ist ein netter Typ; **that guy from Newcastle** der Typ aus Newcastle.

gym noun **1** (*school lesson*) Turnen das; **2** (*building*) Turnhalle die (PL die Turnhallen); **3** (*health club*) Fitnesscenter das (PL die Fitnesscenter); **to go to the gym** ins Fitnesscenter gehen.

gym shoe noun Turnschuh der (PL die Turnschuhe).

gymnasium noun Turnhalle die (PL die Turnhallen).

gymnast noun Turner der (PL die Turner), Turnerin die (PL die Turnerinnen).

gymnastics noun Turnen das.

Hh

habit noun Gewohnheit die (PL die Gewohnheiten); **it's a bad habit** es ist eine schlechte Gewohnheit.

haddock noun Schellfisch der; **smoked haddock** geräucherter Schellfisch.

hail noun Hagel der.

hailstone noun Hagelkorn das (PL die Hagelkörner).

hailstorm noun Hagelschauer der (PL die Hagelschauer).

hair noun **1** Haare (*plural*); **to comb your hair** sich (DAT) die Haare kämmen; **to wash your hair** sich (DAT) die Haare waschen; **to have your hair cut** sich (DAT) die Haare

schneiden lassen; **she's had her hair cut** sie hat sich die Haare schneiden lassen; **2 a hair** ein Haar.

hairbrush noun Haarbürste die (PL die Haarbürsten).

haircut noun **1** Haarschnitt der (PL die Haarschnitte); **2 to have a haircut** sich (DAT) die Haare schneiden lassen.

hairdresser noun Friseur der (PL die Friseure), Friseurin die (PL die Friseurinnen); **at the hairdresser's** beim Friseur.

hair drier noun Föhn der (PL die Föhne).

hair gel noun Haargel das (PL die Haargele).

hairgrip noun Haarklemme die (PL die Haarklemmen).

hairslide noun Haarspange die (PL die Haarspangen).

hairspray noun Haarspray das (PL die Haarsprays).

hairstyle noun Frisur die (PL die Frisuren).

hairy adjective behaart.

half noun **1** Hälfte die (PL die Hälften); **half of** die Hälfte von (+ DAT); **I gave him half of the money** ich habe ihm die Hälfte von dem Geld gegeben; **half of it** die Hälfte davon; **2 half an apple** ein halber Apfel; **3 to cut something in half** etwas halbieren; **4** (*as a fraction*) halb; **three and a half** dreieinhalb; **5** (*in time*) halb; **half an hour** eine halbe Stunde; **an hour and a half** anderthalb Stunden; **it's half past three** es ist halb vier (*literally: half on the way to four*);

a b c d e f i j k l m n o p q r s t u v w x y z

a

6 (in weights and measures) halb;
half a litre ein halber Liter.

b

half hour noun halbe Stunde die;
every half hour jede halbe Stunde.

c

half price adjective, adverb zum
halben Preis; **half-price CDs** CDs
zum halben Preis.

d

e

half-time noun Halbzeit die; **at
half-time the score is 0-0** zur
Halbzeit steht es null zu null.

f

g

halfway adverb 1 auf halbem Weg;
halfway to Frankfurt auf halbem
Weg nach Frankfurt; **2 to be
halfway through doing something**
mit etwas halb fertig sein; **I'm
halfway through my homework**
ich bin mit meinen Hausaufgaben
halb fertig.

h

i

j

k

hall noun 1 (in a house) Diele die (PL
die Dielen); 2 (public) Saal der (PL die
Säle); **village hall** der
Gemeindesaal; **concert hall** der
Konzertsaal.

l

m

n

Hallowe'en noun der Tag vor
Allerheiligen (in Germany there
are no particular customs for this
date).

o

p

ham noun Schinken der; **a ham
sandwich** ein Schinkenbrot.

q

r

hamburger noun Hamburger der
(PL die Hamburger).

s

hammer noun Hammer der (PL die
Hammer).

t

hamster noun Hamster der (PL die
Hamster).

u

v

hand noun 1 Hand die (PL die
Hände); **to have something in
your hand** etwas in der Hand
haben; **to hold somebody's hand**
jemandes Hand halten; **2 to give
somebody a hand** jemandem
helfen◇; **can you give me a hand**

w

x

y

z

**to move the table into the
corner?** kannst du mir helfen, den
Tisch in die Ecke zu rücken?; **do
you need a hand?** kann ich dir
helfen?; **3 on the other hand** ...
andererseits ...; **4** (of a watch or
clock) Zeiger der (PL die Zeiger); **the
hour hand** der Stundenzeiger.

hand verb **to hand something to
somebody** jemandem etwas
geben◇; **I handed him the keys**
ich gab ihm die Schlüssel.

● **to hand something in** etwas
abgeben◇ SEP; **hand in your
homework** gebt eure
Hausaufgaben ab.

● **to hand something out** etwas
austeilen SEP.

handbag noun Handtasche die (PL
die Handtaschen).

handcuffs plural noun
Handschellen (plural).

handful noun **a handful of** eine
Hand voll.

handicapped adjective
behindert.

handkerchief noun Taschentuch
das (PL die Taschentücher).

handle noun 1 (of a door, drawer,
bag, or knife) Griff der (PL die
Griffe); 2 (on a cup, jug, or basket)
Henkel der (PL die Henkel); 3 (of a
frying pan or broom) Stiel der (PL
die Stiele).

handle verb 1 erledigen; **Gina
handles the correspondence** Gina
erledigt die Korrespondenz;
2 umgehen◇ SEP (PERF sein) mit;
she's good at handling people sie
kann gut mit Menschen umgehen;
3 fertig werden◇ (PERF sein) mit; **he**

can't handle problems er kann mit Problemen nicht fertig werden.

handlebars *plural noun* Lenkstange *die* (PL *die* Lenkstangen).

hand luggage *noun* Handgepäck *das.*

handmade *adjective* handgemacht.

handsome *adjective* gut aussehend; **he's a handsome guy** er ist ein gut aussehender Typ.

handwriting *noun* Handschrift *die* (PL *die* Handschriften).

handy *adjective* 1 praktisch; **this little knife's very handy** dieses kleine Messer ist sehr praktisch; 2 griffbereit; **I always keep a notebook handy** ich habe immer ein kleines Notizbuch griffbereit.

hang *verb* 1 hängen✧; **there was a mirror hanging on the wall** an der Wand hing ein Spiegel; 2 aufhängen SEP; **to hang a mirror on the wall** einen Spiegel an der Wand aufhängen.

● **to hang around** 1 umhängen✧ SEP (PERF *sein*) (*informal*); **we were hanging around outside the cinema** wir haben vor dem Kino rumgehangen.

● **to hang on** warten; **hang on a second!** warten Sie einen Moment!

● **to hang up** (*on the phone*) auflegen SEP; **she hung up on me** sie hat einfach aufgelegt.

● **to hang something up** etwas aufhängen SEP.

hang-gliding *noun* Drachenfliegen *das*; **to go hang-gliding** Drachenfliegen gehen.

hangover *noun* Kater *der* (PL *die* Kater).

happen *verb* 1 passieren (PERF *sein*); **what happened?** was ist passiert?; **it happened in June** es ist im Juni passiert; 2 **what's happening?** was ist los?; **what's happened to Jill?** was ist mit Jill los?; 3 **what's happened to the can-opener?** wo ist der Dosenöffner?; 4 **if you happen to see him** wenn du ihn zufällig triffst; **Leila happened to be there** Leila war zufällig da.

happily *adverb* 1 glücklich; 2 (*willingly*) gerne; **I'll happily do it for you** ich tu es gerne für dich.

happiness *noun* Glück *das.*

happy *adjective* glücklich; **a happy child** ein glückliches Kind; **Happy Birthday** herzlichen Glückwunsch zum Geburtstag.

harbour *noun* Hafen *der* (PL *die* Häfen).

hard *adjective* 1 hart; 2 (*difficult*) schwer; **a hard question** eine schwere Frage; **it's hard to say** es ist schwer zu sagen.

hard *adverb* 1 **to work hard** hart arbeiten; 2 **to try hard** sich sehr bemühen.

hard disk *noun* Festplatte *die* (PL *die* Festplatten).

hardly *adverb* 1 kaum; **I can hardly hear him** ich kann ihn kaum hören; **there was hardly anybody there** es war kaum jemand da; **we've got hardly any milk** wir haben kaum Milch; **hardly anything** kaum etwas; **he ate hardly anything** er hat kaum etwas gegessen; 2 **hardly ever** fast nie; **I**

a b c d e f g h i j k l m n o p q r s t u v w x y z

a

hardly ever see him ich sehe ihn fast nie.

b

hard up *adjective* **to be hard up** knapp bei Kasse sein.

c

hare *noun* Hase der (PL die Hasen).

harm *noun* **it won't do any harm** es kann nichts schaden.

d

e

harm *verb* **1 to harm somebody** jemandem etwas tun; **they didn't harm him** sie haben ihm nichts getan; **2** schaden (+ DAT) (*health, environment, reputation*); **a cup of coffee won't harm you** eine Tasse Kaffee schadet nicht.

f

g

h

i

harmful *adjective* schädlich.

harmless *adjective* unschädlich.

j

harvest *noun* Ernte die (PL die Ernten); **to get the harvest in** die Ernte einbringen.

k

l

hat *noun* Hut der (PL die Hüte).

hate *verb* hassen; **I hate geography** ich hasse Erdkunde.

m

hatred *noun* Hass der.

n

o

have *verb* **1** haben✧; **Anna has three brothers** Anna hat drei Brüder; **how many sisters do you have?** wie viele Schwestern hast du?; **2 what have you got in your hand?** was hast du in der Hand?; **he has (got) flu** er hat die Grippe; **3** (*to form past tenses, some verbs in German take 'haben' and others 'sein'*) **I've finished** ich bin fertig; **have you seen the film?** hast du den Film gesehen?; **Rosie hasn't arrived yet** Rosie ist noch nicht angekommen; **4 to have to do something** etwas tun müssen✧; **I have to phone my mum** ich muss meine Mutter anrufen; **5** (*'have' is often translated by a more specific German verb*) **we had a coffee** wir

p

q

r

s

t

u

v

w

x

y

z

haben einen Kaffee getrunken; **what will you have?** was nehmen Sie?; **I'll have an omelette** ich nehme ein Omelett; **I'm going to have a shower** ich dusche jetzt; **to have lunch** zu Mittag essen; **to have dinner** (*in the evening*) zu Abend essen; **6** (*get*) bekommen✧; **Emma had a letter from Sam yesterday** gestern bekam Emma einen Brief von Sam; **she had a baby** sie hat ein Baby bekommen; **7 to have something done** etwas machen lassen✧; **I'm going to have my hair cut** ich lasse mir die Haare schneiden; **8 to have on** (*be wearing*) anhaben✧ SEP; **to have nothing on** nichts anhaben.

hawk *noun* Habicht der (PL die Habichte).

hay *noun* Heu das.

hay fever *noun* Heuschnupfen der.

hazelnut *noun* Haselnuss die (PL die Haselnüsse).

he *pronoun* er; **he lives in Manchester** er wohnt in Manchester.

head *noun* **1** Kopf der (PL die Köpfe); **he shook his head** er schüttelte den Kopf; **2** (*of a school*) Direktor der (PL die Direktoren), Direktorin die (PL die Direktorinnen); **3** (*of a firm*) Chef der (PL die Chefs), Chefin die (PL die Chefinnen); **4** (*when tossing a coin*) **'heads or tails?'** 'Kopf oder Zahl?'

● **to head for something** auf etwas (ACC) zusteuern SEP (PERF sein); **Liz headed for the door** Liz steuerte auf die Tür zu.

headache noun Kopfschmerzen (plural); **I've got a headache** ich habe Kopfschmerzen.

headlight noun Scheinwerfer der (PL die Scheinwerfer).

headline noun Schlagzeile die (PL die Schlagzeilen).

headmaster noun Direktor der (PL die Direktoren).

headmistress noun Direktorin die (PL die Direktorinnen).

headphones noun Kopfhörer der (PL die Kopfhörer).

headteacher noun Direktor der (PL die Direktoren), Direktorin die (PL die Direktorinnen).

health noun Gesundheit die.

health centre noun Ärztezentrum das (PL die Ärztezentren).

healthy adjective gesund.

heap noun Haufen der (PL die Haufen); **I've got heaps of work** ich habe einen Haufen Arbeit (informal).

hear verb hören; **I can't hear anything** ich kann überhaupt nichts hören; **I hear you've bought a dog** ich habe gehört, dass ihr einen Hund gekauft habt.

● **to hear about something** von etwas (DAT) hören; **have you heard about the concert?** hast du von dem Konzert gehört?.

● **to hear from somebody** von jemandem hören.

hearing aid noun Hörgerät das (PL die Hörgeräte).

heart noun 1 Herz das (PL die Herzen); **2 to learn something by heart** etwas auswendig lernen; **3** (in cards) Herz das; **the jack of hearts** der Herzbube.

heart attack noun Herzinfarkt der (PL die Herzinfarkte).

heat noun Hitze die.

heat verb 1 **to heat something** etwas heiß machen; **I'll go and heat the soup** ich mache die Suppe heiß; **2 the soup's heating** die Suppe wird warm; **3** heizen (a room).

● **to heat something up** etwas aufwärmen SEP; **I'm heating the sauce up** ich wärme die Soße auf.

heater noun Heizgerät das (PL die Heizgeräte).

heather noun Heidekraut das.

heating noun Heizung die.

heatwave noun Hitzewelle die (PL die Hitzewellen).

heaven noun Himmel der.

heavy adjective 1 schwer; **my rucksack's really heavy** mein Rucksack ist sehr schwer; **2** (busy) **I've got a heavy day tomorrow** ich habe morgen viel zu tun; **3** (in quantity) stark; **heavy rain** starker Regen.

hectic adjective hektisch; **a hectic day** ein hektischer Tag.

hedge noun Hecke die (PL die Hecken).

hedgehog noun Igel der (PL die Igel).

heel noun 1 (of foot or sock) Ferse die (PL die Fersen); **2** (of a shoe) Absatz der (PL die Absätze).

height noun 1 (of a person) Größe die; **what height are you?** wie groß bist du?; **2** (of a building, mountain) Höhe die; **what height is it?** wie hoch ist es?

helicopter *noun* Hubschrauber der (PL die Hubschrauber).

hell *noun* Hölle die; **hell!** verdammt! (*informal*).

hello *exclamation* **1** (*polite*) guten Tag!; **2** (*informal, and on the phone*) hallo!

helmet *noun* Helm der (PL die Helme).

help *noun* Hilfe die; **do you need any help?** kann ich dir helfen?, (*in a shop*) kann ich Ihnen behilflich sein?

help *verb* **1** helfen✧ (+ DAT); **to help somebody (to) do something** jemandem helfen, etwas zu tun; **can you help me lay the table?** kannst du mir helfen, den Tisch zu decken?; **2 to help yourself to something** sich (DAT) etwas nehmen✧; **help yourself to vegetables** nimm dir Gemüse; **help yourself!** greif zu!; **3 help!** Hilfe!; **4 he can't help it** er kann nichts dafür.

helper *noun* Helfer der (PL die Helfer), Helferin die (PL die Helferinnen).

helpful *adjective* (*person*) hilfsbereit.

helping *noun* Portion die (PL die Portionen); **would you like a second helping?** möchtest du eine zweite Portion?

hem *noun* Saum der (PL die Säume).

hen *noun* Henne die (PL die Hennen).

her *pronoun* (in German this pronoun changes according to the function it has in the sentence or the preposition it follows) **1** (*as a direct object in the accusative*) sie; **I know her** ich kenne sie; **I saw her last week** ich habe sie letzte Woche gesehen; **2** (*after prepositions* + ACC) sie; **without her** ohne sie; **we've heard a lot about her** wir haben viel über sie gehört; **3** (*as an indirect object or after verbs that take the dative*) ihr; **I gave her my address** ich habe ihr meine Adresse gegeben; **we helped her** wir haben ihr geholfen; **4** (*after prepositions* + DAT) ihr; **with her** mit ihr; **5** (*in comparisons*) sie; **he's older than her** er ist älter als sie; **6** (*in the nominative*) sie; **it was her** sie war es.

her *adjective* **1** (*before a masculine noun*) ihr; **her brother** ihr Bruder; **2** (*before a feminine noun*) ihre; **her sister** ihre Schwester; **3** (*before a neuter noun*) ihr; **her house** ihr Haus; **4** (*before a plural noun*) ihre; **her children** ihre Kinder; **5** (*with parts of the body*) der/die/das, die (*plural*); **she had a glass in her hand** sie hatte ein Glas in der Hand; **she's washing her hands** sie wäscht sich die Hände.

herb *noun* Kraut das (PL die Kräuter).

herd *noun* (*of cattle, goats*) Herde die (PL die Herden).

here *adverb* **1** (*in or at this place*) hier; **not far from here** nicht weit von hier; **here's my address** hier ist meine Adresse; **I want to stay here** ich möchte hier bleiben; **2** (*to this place*) hierher; **when Peter came here** als Peter hierher kam; **3 here they are!** da sind sie!; **Tom isn't here at the moment** Tom ist im Moment nicht da.

hero *noun* Held der (PL die Helden).

heroin noun Heroin das.

heroine noun Heldin die (PL die Heldinnen).

herring noun Hering der (PL die Heringe).

hers pronoun **1** (for a masculine noun) ihrer; **my coat is blue and hers is red** mein Mantel ist blau und ihrer ist rot; **I took my hat and she took hers** ich nahm meinen Hut und sie nahm ihren; **2** (for a feminine noun) ihre; **I gave Ann my address and she gave me hers** ich habe Ann meine Adresse gegeben und sie hat mir ihre gegeben; **3** (for a neuter noun) ihr(e)s; **my bike is new but hers is old** mein Rad ist neu, aber ihrs ist alt; **4** (for masculine/ feminine/neuter plural nouns) ihre; **I showed Emma my photos and she showed me hers** ich habe Emma meine Fotos gezeigt und sie hat mir ihre gezeigt; **5 the CDs are hers** die CDs gehören ihr; **it's hers** das gehört ihr.

herself pronoun **1** (reflexive) sich; **she's hurt herself** sie hat sich wehgetan; **2** (stressing something) selbst; **she said it herself** sie hat es selbst gesagt; **3 she did it by herself** sie hat es ganz allein gemacht.

hesitate verb zögern.

heterosexual adjective heterosexuell.

heterosexual noun Heterosexuelle der/die (PL die Heterosexuellen).

hi exclamation hallo!.

hiccups plural noun **to have the hiccups** einen Schluckauf haben.

hidden adjective verborgen.

hide verb **1** sich verstecken; **she hid behind the door** sie hat sich hinter der Tür versteckt; **2 to hide something** etwas verstecken.

hi-fi noun Hi-Fi-Anlage die (PL die Hi-Fi-Anlagen).

high adjective **1** hoch; **how high is the wall?** wie hoch ist die Mauer?; **the wall is two metres high** die Mauer ist zwei Meter hoch; **the shelf is too high** das Regal ist zu hoch; (the adjective 'hoch' loses its c when it has an ending, becoming hoher/hohe/hohes) **a high tower** ein hoher Turm; **a high wall** eine hohe Mauer; **at high speed** mit hoher Geschwindigkeit; **a high voice** eine hohe Stimme; **2 high winds** starker Wind.

high adverb hoch.

Highers, Advanced Highers noun plural Abitur das ((Students take 'Abitur' at about 19 years of age. You can explain Highers briefly as follows: Highers werden im vorletzten Jahr der Sekundarstufe in bis zu fünf Fächern abgelegt. Manche Schüler legen zusätzlich Advanced Highers in ihrem letzten Schuljahr ab. Advanced Highers werden in bis zu drei Fächern, die bereits für Highers belegt wurden, abgelegt. Beide Qualifikationen werden von A bis C benotet und sind Hochschulzugangsberechtigung)) SEE Abitur.

high-heeled adjective hochhackig.

high jump noun Hochsprung der.

hijack verb **to hijack a plane** ein Flugzeug entführen.

a
b
c
d
e
f
g
h
i
j
k
l
m
n
o
p
q
r
s
t
u
v
w
x
y
z

hijacker noun Entführer der (PL die Entführer).

hijacking noun Entführung die (PL die Entführungen).

hike noun Wanderung die (PL die Wanderungen).

hiker noun Wanderer der (PL die Wanderer), Wanderin die (PL die Wanderinnen).

hiking noun Wandern das

hilarious adjective lustig.

hill noun 1 (large hill) Berg der (PL die Berge); **you can see the hills** man kann die Berge sehen; 2 (smaller) Hügel der (PL die Hügel); **to walk up the hill** den Hügel hinaufgehen; 3 (hillside) Hang der (PL die Hänge); **the house on the hill** das Haus am Hang.

him pronoun (in German this pronoun changes according to the function it has in the sentence or the preposition it follows) 1 (as a direct object in the accusative) ihn; **I know him** ich kenne ihn; **I saw him last week** ich habe ihn letzte Woche gesehen; 2 (after prepositions + ACC) ihn; **he fought against him** er hat gegen ihn gekämpft; **without him** ohne ihn; 3 (as an indirect object or after verbs that take the dative) ihm; **I gave him my address** ich habe ihm meine Adresse gegeben; **you must help him** du musst ihm helfen; 4 (after prepositions + DAT) ihm; **with him** mit ihm; 5 (in comparisons) er; **she's older than him** sie ist älter als er; 6 (in the nominative) er; **it was him** er war es.

himself pronoun 1 (reflexive) sich; **he's hurt himself** er hat sich

wehgetan; 2 (stressing something) selbst; **he said it himself** er hat es selbst gesagt; 3 **he did it by himself** er hat es ganz allein gemacht.

Hindu adjective hinduistisch.

hip noun Hüfte die (PL die Hüften).

hippie noun Hippie der (PL die Hippies).

hippopotamus noun Nilpferd das (PL die Nilpferde).

hire noun 1 Vermietung die; **car hire** die Autovermietung; 2 **for hire** zu vermieten.

hire verb mieten.

his adjective 1 (before a masculine noun) sein; **his brother** sein Bruder; 2 (before a feminine noun) seine; **his sister** seine Schwester; 3 (before a neuter noun) sein; **his house** sein Haus; 4 (before a plural noun) seine; **his children** seine Kinder; 5 (with parts of the body) der/die/das, die (plural); **he had a glass in his hand** er hatte ein Glas in der Hand; **he's washing his hands** er wäscht sich (DAT) die Hände.

his pronoun 1 (for a masculine noun) seiner; **my hat is red and his is blue** mein Hut ist rot und seiner ist blau; 2 (for a feminine noun) seine; **I gave him my address and he gave me his** ich habe ihm meine Adresse gegeben und er hat mir seine gegeben; 3 (for a neuter noun) sein(e)s; **my book is new but his is old** mein Buch ist neu, aber seins ist alt; 4 (for masculine/feminine/ neuter plural nouns) seine; **I've invited my parents and Steve's invited his** ich habe meine Eltern eingeladen und Steve hat seine eingeladen; **5 the green car's his** das grüne Auto gehört ihm; **it's his** das gehört ihm.

historic *adjective* historisch.

history *noun* Geschichte *die*.

hit *noun* **1** (*song*) Hit *der* (PL *die* Hits); **their latest hit** ihr neuester Hit; **2** (*success*) Erfolg *der* (PL *die* Erfolge); **the film is a huge hit** der Film ist ein großer Erfolg.

hit *verb* **1** treffen✧; **to hit the ball** den Ball treffen; **2 to hit your head on something** sich (DAT) den Kopf an etwas (DAT) stoßen; **I hit my head on the door** ich habe mir den Kopf an der Tür gestoßen; **3** prallen gegen (+ ACC) (PERF *sein*); **the car hit a wall** das Auto ist gegen eine Wand geprallt; **4 to be hit by a car** von einem Auto angefahren werden.

hitch *noun* Problem *das* (PL *die* Probleme); **there's been a slight hitch** ein kleines Problem ist aufgetaucht.

hitch *verb* **to hitch a lift** per Anhalter fahren✧ (PERF *sein*).

hitchhike *verb* per Anhalter fahren✧ (PERF *sein*); **we hitchhiked to Heidelberg** wir sind per Anhalter nach Heidelberg gefahren.

hitchhiker *noun* Anhalter *der* (PL *die* Anhalter), Anhalterin *die* (PL *die* Anhalterinnen).

hitchhiking *noun* Trampen *das*.

HIV-negative *adjective* HIV-negativ.

HIV-positive *adjective* HIV-positiv.

hobby *noun* Hobby *das* (PL *die* Hobbys).

hockey *noun* Hockey *das*.

hockey stick *noun* Hockeyschläger *der* (PL *die* Hockeyschläger).

hold *verb* **1** halten✧; **to hold something in your hand** etwas in der Hand halten; **can you hold the torch?** kannst du die Taschenlampe halten?; **2** (*be able to contain*) fassen; **the jug holds a litre** der Krug fasst einen Liter; **3 to hold a meeting** eine Versammlung abhalten✧ SEP; **4 can you hold the line, please?** bleiben Sie bitte am Apparat; **5 hold on!** (*wait*) warten Sie! (*on the phone*) bleiben Sie am Apparat.

● **to hold on to something** (*to stop yourself from falling*) sich an etwas (DAT) festhalten✧ SEP.

● **to hold somebody up** (*delay*) jemanden aufhalten✧ SEP; **I was held up at the dentist's** ich bin beim Zahnarzt aufgehalten worden.

● **to hold something up** (*raise*) etwas hochhalten✧ SEP.

hold-up *noun* **1** Verzögerung *die* (PL *die* Verzögerungen); **2** (*traffic jam*) Stau *der* (PL *die* Staus); **3** (*robbery*) Überfall *der* (PL *die* Überfälle).

hole *noun* Loch *das* (PL *die* Löcher).

holiday *noun* **1** Ferien (*plural*) Urlaub *der* (PL *die* Urlaube); (*students, schoolchildren, and families usually have 'Ferien'; people in paid employment usually have 'Urlaub'*); **where are you going for your holiday?** wo fahrt

a
b
c
d
e
f
g
h
i
j
k
l
m
n
o
p
q
r
s
t
u
v
w
x
y
z

ihr in den Ferien hin?; **have a good holiday!** schöne Ferien!, schönen Urlaub!; **to be away on holiday** auf Urlaub sein, in den Ferien sein; **to go on holiday** in Urlaub fahren, in die Ferien fahren; **the school holidays** die Schulferien; **2** (day off work) freie Tag der (PL die freien Tage); **I'm taking two days' holiday next week** ich nehme mir nächste Woche zwei Tage frei; **3 public holiday** der Feiertag; **Monday's a holiday** Montag ist ein Feiertag.

holiday home noun Ferienhaus das (PL die Ferienhäuser).

Holland noun Holland das.

hollow adjective hohl.

holy adjective heilig.

home noun **1** I **was at home** ich war zu Hause; **to stay at home** zu Hause bleiben; **2 make yourself at home** mach es dir bequem.

home adverb **1** (to home) nach Hause; **Susie's gone home** Susie ist nach Hause gegangen; **on my way home** auf dem Weg nach Hause; **to get home** nach Hause kommen; **we got home at midnight** wir sind um Mitternacht nach Hause gekommen; **2** (at home) zu Hause; **I'll be home in the afternoon** ich bin am Nachmittag zu Hause.

homeless adjective obdachlos; **the homeless** die Obdachlosen.

homemade adjective selbst gemacht; **homemade biscuits** selbst gebackene Kekse.

homeopathic adjective homöopathisch.

homesick adjective **to be homesick** Heimweh haben.

homework noun Hausaufgaben (plural); **I did my homework** ich habe meine Hausaufgaben gemacht; **my German homework** meine Deutschhausaufgaben.

homosexual adjective homosexuell.

homosexual noun Homosexuelle der/die (PL die Homosexuellen).

honest adjective ehrlich.

honestly adverb ehrlich.

honesty noun Ehrlichkeit die.

honey noun Honig der (PL die Honige).

honeymoon noun Flitterwochen die (plural); **they're going to Italy on their honeymoon** sie fahren nach Italien in die Flitterwochen.

honour noun Ehre die.

hood noun **1** Kapuze die (PL die Kapuzen); **2** (on a car) Verdeck das (PL die Verdecke).

hook noun **1** Haken der (PL die Haken); **2 to take the phone off the hook** das Telefon aushängen SEP.

hooligan noun Hooligan der (PL die Hooligans).

hooray exclamation hurra!.

Hoover noun Staubsauger der (PL die Staubsauger).

hoover verb saugen; **I hoovered my bedroom** ich habe mein Schlafzimmer gesaugt.

hope noun Hoffnung die (PL die Hoffnungen); **to give up hope** die Hoffnung aufgeben.

hope verb **1** hoffen; **we hope you'll be able to come** wir hoffen, ihr könnt kommen; **I'm hoping to see you on Friday** ich hoffe, dich am Freitag zu sehen; **2 I hope so** hoffentlich; **I hope not** hoffentlich nicht.

hopefully *adverb* hoffentlich; **hopefully, the film won't have started** hoffentlich hat der Film noch nicht angefangen.

hopeless *adjective* miserabel (*informal*); **I'm hopeless at geography** ich bin miserabel in Erdkunde.

horizontal *adjective* horizontal, waagrecht; **the flag has three horizontal bars** die Flagge hat drei waagrechte Streifen.

horn *noun* **1** (*of an animal, instrument*) Horn *das* (PL die Hörner); **2** (*of a car*) Hupe *die* (PL die Hupen).

horoscope *noun* Horoskop *das* (PL die Horoskope).

horrible *adjective* **1** furchtbar; **the weather was horrible** das Wetter war furchtbar; **2** (*person*) gemein; **she's really horrible** sie ist richtig gemein; **he was really horrible to me** er war richtig gemein zu mir.

horror *noun* Entsetzen *das*.

horror film *noun* Horrorfilm *der* (PL die Horrorfilme).

horse *noun* Pferd *das* (PL die Pferde).

horse chestnut *noun* (*tree and nut*) Rosskastanie *die* (PL die Rosskastanien).

horseshoe *noun* Hufeisen *das* (PL die Hufeisen).

hose *noun* Schlauch *der* (PL die Schläuche).

hosepipe *noun* Schlauch *der* (PL die Schläuche).

hospital *noun* Krankenhaus *das* (PL die Krankenhäuser); **in hospital** im Krankenhaus; **to be taken into hospital** ins Krankenhaus kommen.

hospitality *noun* Gastfreundschaft *die*.

host *noun* **1** Gastgeber *der* (PL die Gastgeber); **2** (*on a TV programme*) Moderator *der* (PL die Moderatoren).

hostage *noun* Geisel *die* (PL die Geiseln).

hostel *noun* youth hostel *die* Jugendherberge.

hostess *noun* **1** Gastgeberin *die* (PL die Gastgeberinnen); **2** (*on a TV programme*) Moderatorin *die* (PL die Moderatorinnen); **3** air hostess *die* Stewardess.

hot *adjective* **1** heiß; **be careful, the plates are hot** sei vorsichtig, die Teller sind heiß; **it's hot today** heute ist es heiß; **2** (*person*) **I'm very hot** mir ist sehr heiß; **3** (*spicy*) scharf; **the curry's too hot for me** das Curry ist mir zu scharf; **4 a hot meal** ein warmes Essen.

hot dog *noun* Hotdog *das* (*or*) *der* (PL die Hotdogs).

hotel *noun* Hotel *das* (PL die Hotels).

hour *noun* Stunde *die* (PL die Stunden); **two hours later** zwei Stunden später; **we waited for two hours** wir haben zwei Stunden lang gewartet; **I've been waiting for hours** ich warte schon seit Stunden; **two hours ago** vor zwei Stunden; **to be paid by the hour** pro Stunde bezahlt werden; **every hour** jede Stunde; **half an hour** eine

a
b
c
d
e
f
g
h
i
j
k
l
m
n
o
p
q
r
s
t
u
v
w
x
y
z

halbe Stunde; **a quarter of an hour** eine Viertelstunde; **an hour and a half** anderthalb Stunden.

house *noun* **1** Haus *das* (PL die Häuser); **2 at somebody's house** bei jemandem; **I'm at Judy's house** ich bin bei Judy; **I'm going to Sid's house tonight** ich gehe heute Abend zu Sid; **I phoned from Jill's house** ich habe von Jill aus angerufen.

housewife *noun* Hausfrau *die* (PL die Hausfrauen).

housework *noun* Hausarbeit *die*; **he does the housework** er macht den Haushalt (*informal*).

hovercraft *noun* Luftkissenfahrzeug *das* (PL die Luftkissenfahrzeuge).

how *adverb* **1** wie; **how did you do it?** wie hast du das gemacht?; **how are you?** wie geht es dir?; **how many?** wie viele?; **how many brothers do you have?** wie viele Brüder hast du?; **how old are you?** wie alt bist du?; **how far is it?** wie weit ist es?; **how far is it to York?** wie weit ist es bis York?; **how long will it take?** wie lange dauert es?; **how long have you known her?** wie lange kennst du sie?; **2 how much?** wie viel?; **how much money do you have?** wie viel Geld hast du?; **how much is it?** wie viel kostet das?

however *adverb* **1** jedoch; **2** (*in questions*) however did she do it? wie hat sie das nur gemacht?; **3 however famous he is** wie berühmt er auch sein mag.

hug *noun* **to give somebody a hug** jemanden umarmen; **she gave me a hug** sie hat mich umarmt.

huge *adjective* riesig.

hum *verb* summen.

human *adjective* menschlich.

human being *noun* Mensch *der* (PL die Menschen).

humour *noun* Humor *der*; **to have a sense of humour** Humor haben.

hundred *number* hundert; **two hundred** zweihundert; **two hundred and ten** zweihundertzehn; **a hundred people** hundert Menschen; **about a hundred** um die hundert; **hundreds of people** hunderte von Menschen.

Hungary *noun* Ungarn *das*.

hunger *noun* Hunger *der*.

hungry *adjective* **to be hungry** Hunger haben; **I'm hungry** ich habe Hunger.

hunt *verb* **1** jagen (*an animal*); **2** suchen (*a person*).

hunting *noun* Jagd *die*; **fox-hunting** die Fuchsjagd.

hurry *noun* **to be in a hurry** es eilig haben; **I'm in a hurry** ich habe es eilig; **there's no hurry** es eilt nicht.

hurry *verb* **1** sich beeilen; **I must hurry** ich muss mich beeilen; **hurry up!** beeil dich!; **2** he hurried home er ging schnell nach Hause.

hurt *verb* **1** **to hurt somebody** jemandem wehtun⋄ SEP; **you're hurting me!** du tust mir weh!; **that hurts!** das tut weh!; **2 my arm hurts** der Arm tut mir weh; **3 to hurt yourself** sich (DAT) wehtun⋄ SEP; **did you hurt yourself?** hast du dir wehgetan?

hurt *adjective* **1** (*in an accident*) verletzt; **three people were hurt** drei Menschen wurden verletzt; **2** (*in feelings*) gekränkt; **she felt hurt** sie fühlte sich gekränkt.

husband *noun* Ehemann der (PL die Ehemänner).

hygienic *adjective* hygienisch.

hymn *noun* Kirchenlied das (PL die Kirchenlieder).

hypermarket *noun* Großmarkt der (PL die Großmärkte).

hyphen *noun* Bindestrich der (PL die Bindestriche).

Ii

I *pronoun* ich; **I have two sisters** ich habe zwei Schwestern.

ice *noun* Eis das.

ice cream *noun* Eis das; **two chocolate ice creams** zwei Schokoladeneis.

ice hockey *noun* Eishockey das.

ice rink *noun* Eisbahn die (PL die Eisbahnen).

ice-skating *noun* **to go ice-skating** Schlittschuh laufen ◆ (PERF sein).

icy *adjective* **1** vereist (*road*); **2** (*very cold*) eiskalt.

idea *noun* **1** Idee die (PL die Ideen); **what a good idea!** was für eine gute Idee!; **2 I've no idea** ich habe keine Ahnung.

ideal *adjective* ideal.

identical *adjective* identisch.

identification *noun* **1** Identifizierung die; **2** (*proof of identity*) Ausweispapiere (*plural*).

identity card *noun* Personalausweis der (PL die Personalausweise).

idiot *noun* Idiot der (PL die Idioten).

idiotic *adjective* idiotisch.

i.e. *abbreviation* d. h. (*das heißt*).

if *conjunction* **1** wenn; **if it rains** wenn es regnet; **if I won the lottery** wenn ich in der Lotterie gewinnen sollte; **if not** wenn nicht; **if only** wenn nur; **if only you'd told me** wenn du mir das nur gesagt hättest; **2 even if** selbst wenn; **even if it snows** selbst wenn es schneit; **3 if I were you** an deiner Stelle; **4** (*whether*) ob; **I wonder if he'll come** ich bin gespannt, ob er kommt; **as if** als ob.

ignore *verb* **1** ignorieren; **2** überhören (*what somebody says*).

ill *adjective* krank; **to fall ill,to be taken ill** krank werden; **I feel ill** ich fühle mich krank.

illegal *adjective* illegal.

illness *noun* Krankheit die (PL die Krankheiten).

illusion *noun* Illusion die (PL die Illusionen).

illustration *noun* Illustration die (PL die Illustrationen).

image *noun* Bild das (PL die Bilder); ★ **he's the spitting image of his father** er ist das Ebenbild seines Vaters.

imagination *noun* Phantasie die.

imaginative *adjective* phantasievoll.

imagine *verb* sich (DAT) vorstellen; **imagine that you're very rich** stell

a
b
c
d
e
f
g
h
i
j
k
l
m
n
o
p
q
r
s
t
u
v
w
x
y
z

dir vor, du bist sehr reich; **you can't imagine how hard it was** du kannst dir nicht vorstellen, wie schwer es war.

imitate verb nachahmen SEP.

immediate adjective 1 (without delay) unmittelbar; **2 the immediate family** die engste Familie.

immediately adverb 1 sofort; **I rang them immediately** ich habe sie sofort angerufen; **2 immediately before** unmittelbar davor; **immediately after** unmittelbar danach.

immigrant noun Einwanderer der (PL die Einwanderer), Einwanderin die (PL die Einwanderinnen).

immigration noun Einwanderung die.

impatience noun Ungeduld die.

impatient adjective 1 ungeduldig; **2 to be impatient with somebody** ungeduldig mit jemandem sein.

impatiently adverb ungeduldig.

imperfect noun (verb tense) Imperfekt das; **"ich schlug" is in the imperfect** "ich schlug" steht im Imperfekt.

import noun Import der (PL die Importe).

import verb importieren.

importance noun Wichtigkeit die.

important adjective wichtig.

impossible adjective unmöglich; **it's impossible to find a telephone** es ist unmöglich, ein Telefon zu finden.

impressed adjective beeindruckt; **to be impressed by something** von etwas (DAT) beeindruckt sein.

impression noun Eindruck der (PL die Eindrücke); **to make a good impression on somebody** einen guten Eindruck auf jemanden machen; **I got the impression he was hiding something** ich hatte den Eindruck, dass er etwas verheimlichte.

impressive adjective eindrucksvoll.

improve verb 1 **to improve something** etwas verbessern; **2** (get better) besser werden; **the weather is improving** das Wetter wird besser.

improvement noun Verbesserung die (PL die Verbesserungen).

in preposition 1 in (+ DAT or, with movement into, + ACC); **it is in my pocket** es ist in meiner Tasche; (with movement) **he put it in his pocket** er hat es in die Tasche gesteckt; **she sat in the sun** sie saß in der Sonne; **I read it in the newspaper** ich habe es in der Zeitung gelesen; **in Oxford** in Oxford; **in Germany** in Deutschland; **2 the biggest city in the world** die größte Stadt der Welt; **a house in the country** ein Haus auf dem Land; **in the street** auf der Straße; **3** (wearing and with colours) in (+ DAT); **the girl in the pink shirt** das Mädchen im rosa Hemd; **4 in German** auf Deutsch; **5** (time expressions) in (+ DAT); **in May** im Mai; **in 1994** (im Jahre) 1994; **in winter** im Winter; **in summer** im Sommer; **in the night** in der Nacht; **I'll phone you in ten minutes** ich rufe dich in zehn

a
b
c
d
e
f
g
h
i
j
k
l
m
n
o
p
q
r
s
t
u
v
w
x
y
z

Minuten an; **she was ready in five minutes** sie war in fünf Minuten fertig; **6 in the morning** am Morgen; **at eight in the morning** um acht Uhr morgens; **7** (*among people or in literature*) bei (+ DAT); **it's rare in children** das ist selten bei Kindern; **in Shakespeare** bei Shakespeare; **in the army** beim Militär; **8 in time** rechtzeitig.

in *adverb* **1** (*inside*) hinein-, herein-, rein- (*informal*) (*Herein-, hinein-, and rein- form prefixes to separable verbs. 'Herein-' is used with verbs like* kommen, *which have the sense of moving towards the speaker. 'Hinein-' is used with verbs like* gehen, *which have the sense of going away from the speaker. The informal 'rein-' can be used with either movement*); **to come in** hereinkommen⟡ SEP (PERF *sein*); **to go in** hineingehen⟡ SEP (PERF *sein*); **he was not allowed to go into the room** er durfte nicht ins Zimmer reingehen; **to run in** reinlaufen⟡ SEP (PERF *sein*) (*informal*); **2 to be in** da sein; **Mick's not in at the moment** Mick ist im Moment nicht da; **3** (*at home*) zu Hause; **4** (*indoors*) drinnen; **in here** hier drinnen; **in there** da drinnen.

include *verb* einschließen⟡ SEP; **service is included in the price** die Bedienung ist im Preis inbegriffen.

including *preposition* **1** einschließlich (+ GEN); **everyone, including the children** alle, einschließlich der Kinder; **£50 including postage** fünfzig Pfund einschließlich Porto; **including Sundays** einschließlich sonntags;

2 not including Sundays außer sonntags.

income *noun* Einkommen *das* (PL die Einkommen).

income tax *noun* Einkommenssteuer *die* (PL die Einkommenssteuern).

increase *noun* Erhöhung *die* (PL die Erhöhungen) (*in price, for example*).

increase *verb* **1** steigen⟡ (PERF *sein*); **the price has increased by £10** der Preis ist um zehn Pfund gestiegen; **2** erhöhen (*salary*).

incredible *adjective* unglaublich.

incredibly *adverb* (*very*) unglaublich; **the film's incredibly boring** der Film ist unglaublich langweilig.

indeed *adverb* **1** (*to emphasize*) wirklich; **she's very pleased indeed** sie hat sich wirklich sehr gefreut; **2** (*certainly*) natürlich; **'can you hear the radio?' – 'indeed I can!'** 'kannst du das Radio hören?' · 'ja, natürlich!'; **3 thank you very much indeed** vielen herzlichen Dank.

indefinite article *noun* unbestimmte Artikel *der* (PL die umbestimmten Artikel).

independence *noun* Unabhängigkeit *die*.

independent *adjective* unabhängig; **independent school** die Privatschule.

index *noun* Register *das* (PL die Register).

India *noun* Indien *das*.

Indian *noun* **1** Inder *der* (PL die Inder), Inderin *die* (PL die Inderinnen); **2** (*a Native American*)

Indian Indianer der (PL die Indianer), Indianerin die (PL die Indianerinnen).

Indian adjective **1** indisch; he's Indian er ist Inder; **2** (*Native American*) indianisch; she's Indian sie ist Indianerin.

indicate verb **1** zeigen auf (+ ACC) (*a person or a thing*); **2** (*of a car or driver*) blinken.

indigestion noun Magenverstimmung die (PL die Magenverstimmungen).

individual noun Einzelne der/die (PL die Einzelnen).

individual adjective **1** einzeln (*serving, contribution*); **2** individual tuition der Einzelunterricht.

indoor adjective an indoor swimming pool ein Hallenbad; indoor games Spiele im Haus, (*in sports*) Hallenspiele.

indoors adverb drinnen; it's cooler indoors drinnen ist es kühler; to go indoors ins Haus gehen.

industrial adjective industriell.

industrial estate noun Industriegebiet das (PL die Industriegebiete).

industry noun Industrie die (PL die Industrien); the car industry die Autoindustrie.

inefficient adjective uneffektiv.

inevitable adjective unvermeidlich.

inevitably adverb zwangsläufig.

inexperienced adjective unerfahren.

infant school noun Vorschule die (PL die Vorschulen).

infection noun Infektion die (PL die Infektionen); eye infection die Augeninfektion; throat infection die Halsentzündung.

infectious adjective ansteckend.

infinitive noun Infinitiv der (PL die Infinitive).

inflammable adjective leicht entflammbar.

inflatable adjective inflatable mattress die Luftmatratze; inflatable boat das Schlauchboot.

inflate verb aufblasen ✧ SEP (*a mattress or boat*).

inflation noun Inflation die (PL die Inflationen).

influence noun Einfluss der (PL die Einflüsse); to be a good influence on somebody einen guten Einfluss auf jemanden haben.

influence verb beeinflussen.

inform verb informieren; to inform somebody of something jemanden über etwas (ACC) informieren.

informal adjective **1** zwanglos (*meal or event*); **2** ungezwungen (*language, tone*).

information noun Auskunft die; where can I get information about flights to Berlin? wo kann ich Auskunft über Flüge nach Berlin bekommen?

information desk, **information office** noun Auskunftsbüro das (PL die Auskunftsbüros).

information technology noun Informatik die.

ingredient noun Zutat die (PL die Zutaten).

inhabitant noun Einwohner der (PL die Einwohner), Einwohnerin die (PL die Einwohnerinnen).

initials plural noun Initialen (plural).

initiative noun Initiative die (PL die Initiativen); **you must use your initiative** du musst die Initiative ergreifen.

injection noun Spritze die (PL die Spritzen).

injure verb verletzen.

injury noun Verletzung die (PL die Verletzungen).

ink noun Tinte die (PL die Tinten).

in-laws noun Schwiegereltern (plural).

inner adjective inner.

innocent adjective unschuldig.

insane adjective 1 geisteskrank; 2 (foolish) wahnsinnig.

insect noun Insekt das (PL die Insekten); **insect bite** der Insektenstich.

insect repellent noun Insektenvertilgungsmittel das.

inside noun on the inside innen; **the inside of the oven is black** innen ist der Herd schwarz.

inside preposition in (+ DAT, or, with movement towards a place, + ACC); **inside the cinema** im Kino; **to go inside (the house)** ins Haus gehen.

inside adverb drinnen; **she's inside, I think** ich glaube, sie ist drinnen.

inside out adjective, adverb (clothing) links.

insist verb darauf bestehen◇; **if you insist** wenn du darauf bestehst; **to insist on doing**

something darauf bestehen, etwas zu tun; **he insists on paying** er besteht darauf zu zahlen; **to insist that ...** darauf bestehen, dass ...; **Ruth insisted I was wrong** Ruth hat darauf bestanden, dass ich Unrecht hatte.

inspector noun 1 (on a bus or train) Kontrolleur der (PL die Kontrolleure), Kontrolleurin die (PL die Kontrolleurinnen); 2 (in the police) Kommissar der (PL die Kommissare), Kommissarin die (PL die Kommissarinnen).

install verb installieren.

instalment noun (of a story or serial) Folge die (PL die Folgen).

instance noun **for instance** zum Beispiel.

instant noun Augenblick der (PL die Augenblicke); **come here this instant!** komm sofort her!

instant adjective 1 Instant- (coffee, tea); 2 (immediate) sofortig.

instantly adverb sofort.

instead adverb 1 Ted couldn't come, so I came instead (of him) Ted konnte nicht kommen, also bin ich an seiner Stelle gekommen; 2 instead of statt (+ GEN or + DAT); he bought a bike instead of a car statt eines Autos hat er ein Fahrrad gekauft; instead of cake I had cheese statt Kuchen habe ich Käse genommen; instead of playing tennis we went swimming statt Tennis zu spielen, sind wir schwimmen gegangen.

instinct noun Instinkt der (PL die Instinkte).

institute noun Institut das (PL die Institute).

instructions *plural noun*
Anweisung *die* (PL die
Anweisungen); **follow the
instructions on the packet**
befolgen Sie die Anweisung auf der
Packung; **'instructions for use'**
'Gebrauchsanweisung'.

instructor *noun* Lehrer *der* (PL die
Lehrer), Lehrerin *die* (PL die
Lehrerinnen); **my skiing
instructor** mein Skilehrer.

instrument *noun* Instrument *das*
(PL die Instrumente); **to play an
instrument** ein Instrument spielen.

insulin *noun* Insulin *das*.

insult *noun* Beleidigung *die* (PL die
Beleidigungen).

insult *verb* beleidigen.

insurance *noun* Versicherung *die*
(PL die Versicherungen); **travel
insurance** *die* Reiseversicherung;
**do you have holiday medical
insurance?** bist du
urlaubskrankenversichert?

intelligence *noun* Intelligenz *die*.

intelligent *adjective* intelligent.

intend *verb* beabsichtigen; **as I
intended** wie beabsichtigt; **to
intend to do something**
beabsichtigen, etwas zu tun; **we
intend to spend the night in Rome**
wir beabsichtigen, in Rom zu
übernachten.

intensive care *noun*
Intensivpflege *die*; **he's now in
intensive care** er ist jetzt auf der
Intensivstation.

intention *noun* Absicht *die* (PL die
Absichten); **I have no intention of
paying** ich habe nicht die Absicht
zu zahlen.

interest *noun* 1 Interesse *das* (PL
die Interessen); **to have lots of
interests** viele Interessen haben;
he has an interest in jazz er hat
Interesse an Jazz; 2 (*financial*)
Zinsen (*plural*).

interest *verb* interessieren; **that
doesn't interest me** das
interessiert mich nicht.

interested *adjective* **to be
interested in something** sich für
etwas (ACC) interessieren; **Sean's
interested in cooking** Sean
interessiert sich für Kochen.

interesting *adjective* interessant.

interfere *verb* 1 **to interfere with
something** (*to fiddle with it*) sich
(DAT) an etwas (DAT) zu schaffen
machen; **don't interfere with my
computer!** mach dir nicht an
meinem Computer zu schaffen!;
2 **to interfere in something** sich in
etwas (ACC) einmischen SEP
(*somebody else's affairs*).

interior designer *noun*
Innenarchitekt *der* (PL die
Innenarchitekten),
Innenarchitektin *die* (PL die
Innenarchitektinnen).

international *adjective*
international.

Internet *noun* Internet *das*; **on the
Internet** im Internet.

Internet cafe *noun* Internetcafé
das (PL die Internetcafés); **where is
there an Internet cafe?** wo gibt es
hier ein Internetcafé?

interpret *verb* (*act as an
interpreter*) dolmetschen.

interpreter *noun* Dometscher *der*
(PL die Dolmetscher),

Dolmetscherin die (PL die Dometscherinnen).

interrupt verb unterbrechen✷.

interruption noun
Unterbrechung die (PL die Unterbrechungen).

interval noun (in a play or concert)
Pause die (PL die Pausen).

interview noun 1 (for a job)
Vorstellungsgespräch das (PL die Vorstellungsgespräche); **to go for an interview** sich vorstellen SEP;
2 (in a newspaper, on TV, or radio)
Interview das (PL die Interviews).

interview verb interviewen (on TV, radio).

interviewer noun Interviewer der (PL die Interviewer), Interviewerin die (PL die Interviewerinnen).

into preposition 1 in (+ ACC); **he's gone into the garden** er ist in den Garten gegangen; **I put the ball into the bag** ich habe den Ball in die Tasche gelegt; **we all got into the car** wir sind alle ins Auto gestiegen; **to go into town** in die Stadt gehen; **to get into bed** ins Bett gehen; **to translate into German** ins Deutsche übersetzen; **to change pounds into euros** Pfund in Euro wechseln;
2 (against) gegen (+ ACC); **he drove into the wall** er ist gegen die Wand gefahren; 3 **to be into jazz** auf Jazz abfahren✷ SEP (PERF sein) (informal).

introduce verb vorstellen SEP; **she introduced me to her brother** sie hat mich ihrem Bruder vorgestellt; **she introduced her brother to me** sie hat mir ihren Bruder vorgestellt; **can I introduce you to**

my mother? darf ich Sie meiner Mutter vorstellen?

introduction noun (in a book)
Einleitung die (PL die Einleitungen).

invade verb einfallen✷ SEP in (PERF sein) (+ ACC).

invalid noun Kranke der/die (PL die Kranken).

invent verb erfinden✷.

invention noun Erfindung die (PL die Erfindungen).

inverted commas plural noun
Anführungszeichen (plural); **in inverted commas** in Anführungszeichen.

investigation noun
Untersuchung die (PL die Untersuchungen); **an investigation into the incident** eine Untersuchung des Vorfalls.

invisible adjective unsichtbar.

invitation noun Einladung die (PL die Einladungen); **an invitation to dinner** eine Einladung zum Abendessen.

invite verb einladen✷ SEP; **Kirsty invited me to lunch** Kirsty hat mich zum Mittagessen eingeladen; **he's invited me out on Tuesday** er hat mich eingeladen, Dienstag mit ihm auszugehen; **they invited us round** sie haben uns zu sich eingeladen.

inviting adjective verlockend.

involve verb 1 erfordern; **it involves a lot of time** es erfordert viel Zeit; 2 (include) beteiligen; **the game will involve everybody** alle können sich an dem Spiel beteiligen; **to be involved in something** an etwas (DAT) beteiligt sein; **I am involved in the new**

a

project ich bin an dem neuen Projekt beteiligt; **3** (*implicate*) verwickeln; **to get involved in something** in etwas (ACC) verwickelt werden; **two cars were involved in the accident** zwei Autos waren in den Unfall verwickelt; **4 to get involved with somebody** sich mit jemandem einlassen✧ SEP.

Iran *noun* Iran *der*.

Iraq *noun* Irak *der*.

Ireland *noun* Irland *das*; **the Republic of Ireland** die Republik Irland.

Irish *noun* **1** (*the language*) Irisch *das*; **2** (*the people*) **the Irish** die Iren.

Irish *adjective* irisch; **he's Irish** er ist Ire; **she's Irish** sie ist Irin.

Irishman *noun* Ire *der* (PL die Iren).

Irish Sea *noun* Irische See *die*.

Irishwoman *noun* Irin *die* (PL die Irinnen).

iron *noun* **1** (*for clothes*) Bügeleisen *das* (PL die Bügeleisen); **2** (*the metal*) Eisen *das*.

iron *verb* bügeln.

ironing *noun* Bügeln *das*; **to do the ironing** bügeln.

ironing board *noun* Bügelbrett *das* (PL die Bügelbretter).

ironmonger's *noun* Haushaltswarengeschäft *das* (PL die Haushaltswarengeschäfte).

irregular *adjective* unregelmäßig.

irritable *adjective* reizbar.

irritate *verb* ärgern.

irritating *adjective* ärgerlich.

Islam *noun* Islam *der*.

Islamic *adjective* islamisch.

island *noun* Insel *die* (PL die Inseln).

isolated *adjective* **1** (*remote*) abgelegen; **2** (*single*) einzeln; **isolated cases** Einzelfälle.

Israel *noun* Israel *das*.

Israeli *noun* Israeli *der/die* (PL die Iraelis).

Israeli *adjective* israelisch.

issue *noun* **1** (*something you discuss*) Frage *die* (PL die Fragen); **a political issue** eine politische Frage; **2** (*of a magazine*) Ausgabe *die* (PL die Ausgaben).

issue *verb* (*hand out*) ausgeben✧ SEP.

it *pronoun* **1** (*as the subject*) er (*standing for a masculine noun*), sie (*standing for a feminine noun*), es (*standing for a neuter noun*); **'where's my key?' – 'it's in the kitchen'** 'wo ist mein Schlüssel?' – 'er ist in der Küche'; **'where's my bag?' – 'it's in the living-room'** 'wo ist meine Tasche?' – 'sie ist im Wohnzimmer?'; **'how old is your car?' – 'it's five years old'** 'wie alt ist dein Auto?' – 'es ist fünf Jahre alt'; **2** (*as the direct object, in the accusative*) ihn (*standing for a masculine noun*), sie (*standing for a feminine noun*), es (*standing for a neuter noun*); **'where's your umbrella?' –'I've lost it'** 'wo ist dein Regenschirm?'- 'ich habe ihn verloren'; **'have you seen my bag?' -'I saw it in the kitchen'** 'hast du meine Tasche gesehen?' - 'ich habe sie in der Küche gesehen'; **'have you read his new book?' - 'I've just bought it'** 'hast du sein neues Buch gelesen?' - 'ich habe es gerade gekauft'; **3 to it** ihm (*masculine*), ihr (*feminine*), ihm (*neuter*); **4 yes, it's true** ja, das stimmt; **it doesn't matter** das macht nichts; **5 who is it?** wer ist da?; **it's me** ich bins; **what is it?** was ist los?; **6 it's raining** es regnet; **it's Monday** es ist Montag; **it's two o'clock** es ist zwei Uhr; **7 of it** davon; **8 out of it** daraus.

Italian noun **1** (*the language*) Italienisch *das*; **2** (*person*) Italiener *der* (PL die Italiener), Italienerin *die* (PL die Italienerinnen).

Italian food die italienische Küche; **2 my Italian class** mein Italienischunterricht.

italics noun Kursivschrift *die*; **in italics** kursiv.

Italy noun Italien *das*.

itch verb **1 my back's itching** mein Rücken juckt; **2 this jumper itches** dieser Pullover kratzt.

item noun **1** Gegenstand *der* (PL die Gegenstände); **2** (*for sale in a shop*) Artikel *der* (PL die Artikel).

its adjective **1** sein (*for a masculine noun*), ihr (*for a feminine noun*), sein (*for a neuter noun*); **the dog has lost its collar** der Hund hat sein Halsband verloren; **the cat's in its basket** die Katze ist in ihrem Korb; **the horse is brown and its mane is black** das Pferd ist braun und seine Mähne ist schwarz; **2** (*for a plural noun*) seine (*standing for a feminine noun*), seine (*standing for a masculine noun*), ihre, seine (*standing for a neuter noun*); **its toys** seine Spielsachen, ihre Spielsachen.

itself pronoun **1** (*reflexive*) sich; **the cat's washing itself** die Katze putzt sich; **2 he left the dog by itself** er hat den Hund allein gelassen.

ivy noun Efeu *der*.

Jj

jack noun **1** (*in cards*) Bube *der* (PL die Buben); **the jack of clubs** der Kreuzbube; **2** (*for a car*) Wagenheber *der* (PL die Wagenheber).

jacket noun Jacke *die* (PL die Jacken).

jacket potatoes noun in der Schale gebackenen Kartoffeln.

jackpot noun Jackpot *der* (PL die Jackpots); **to win the jackpot** den Hauptgewinn bekommen; **to hit the jackpot** das große Los ziehen.

jam noun **1** Marmelade *die* (PL die Marmeladen), **raspberry jam** die Himbeermarmelade; **2 traffic jam** der Stau.

January noun Januar *der*; **in January** im Januar.

Japan noun Japan *das*.

Japanese noun **1** (*the language*) Japanisch *das*; **2** (*person*) Japaner *der* (PL die Japaner), Japanerin *die* (PL die Japanerinnen); **the Japanese** die Japaner.

Japanese adjective japanisch.

jar noun **1** (*small*) Glas *das* (PL die Gläser); **a jar of jam** ein Glas Marmelade; **2** (*large*) Topf *der* (PL die Töpfe).

a b c d e f g h i j k l m n o p q r s t u v w x y z

javelin noun Speer der (PL die Speere).

jaw noun Kiefer der (PL die Kiefer).

jazz noun Jazz der.

jealous adjective eifersüchtig; **to be jealous of somebody** eifersüchtig auf jemanden sein.

jeans plural noun Jeans (plural); **my jeans** meine Jeans; **a pair of jeans** ein Paar Jeans.

jelly noun 1 Gelee das (PL die Gelees); 2 (dessert) Götterspeise die (PL die Götterspeisen).

jellyfish noun Qualle die (PL die Quallen).

jersey noun 1 (jumper) Pullover der (PL die Pullover); 2 (for football) Trikot das (PL die Trikots).

Jesus noun Jesus der; **Jesus Christ** Jesus Christus.

jet noun (a plane) Jet der (PL die Jets).

jet lag noun Jetlag der.

Jew noun Jude der (PL die Juden), Jüdin die (PL die Jüdinnen).

jewel noun Edelstein der (PL die Edelsteine).

jeweller noun Juwelier der (PL die Juweliere).

jeweller's noun Juweliergeschäft das.

jewellery noun Schmuck der.

Jewish adjective jüdisch.

jigsaw noun Puzzlespiel das (PL die Puzzlespiele).

job noun 1 (paid work) Stelle die (PL die Stellen), Job der (PL die Jobs) (informal); **a job as a secretary** eine Stelle als Sekretärin; 2 (a task) Arbeit die (PL die Arbeiten); **it's not an easy job** das ist keine leichte Arbeit; 3 **she made a good job of it** sie hat es gut gemacht.

jobless adjective arbeitslos.

jog verb joggen ⋄ (PERF sein).

join verb 1 (become a member of) beitreten ⋄ SEP (+DAT) (PERF sein); **I've joined the tennis club** ich bin dem Tennisklub beigetreten; 2 (to meet up with) treffen ⋄; **I'll join you later** ich treffe euch später.

● **to join in** mitmachen SEP; **Kylie never joins in** Kylie macht nie mit; 2 **to join in something** bei etwas (DAT) mitmachen SEP; **won't you join in the game?** willst du bei dem Spiel nicht mitmachen?

joint noun 1 (of meat) Braten der (PL die Braten); **a joint of beef** ein Rinderbraten; 2 (in your body) Gelenk das (PL die Gelenke).

joke noun Witz der (PL die Witze); **to tell a joke** einen Witz erzählen.

joke verb Witze machen; **you must be joking!** du machst wohl Witze!

joker noun (in cards) Joker der (PL die Joker).

journalism noun Journalismus der.

journalist noun Journalist der (PL die Journalisten), Journalistin die (PL die Journalistinnen); **Sean's a journalist** Sean ist Journalist.

journey noun 1 (a long one) Reise die (PL die Reisen); **on our journey to Italy** auf unserer Reise nach Italien; 2 (shorter; to work or school) Fahrt die (PL die Fahrten); **bus journey** die Busfahrt.

joy noun Freude die (PL die Freuden).

joystick noun (for computer games) Joystick der (PL die Joysticks).

Judaism noun Judentum das.

judge *noun* **1** (*in court*) Richter der (PL die Richter); **2** (*in sporting events*) Schiedsrichter der (PL die Schiedsrichter); **3** (*in a competition*) Preisrichter der (PL die Preisrichter).

judge *verb* schätzen (*time or distance*).

judo *noun* Judo das; **he does judo** er macht Judo.

jug *noun* Krug der (PL die Krüge).

juice *noun* Saft der; **two orange juices please** zwei Orangensaft bitte.

juicy *adjective* saftig.

jukebox *noun* Jukebox die (PL die Jukeboxes).

July *noun* Juli der; **in July** im Juli.

jumble sale *noun* Basar der (PL die Basare).

jump *noun* Sprung der (PL die Sprünge); **parachute jump** der Fallschirmsprung.

jump *verb* springen◇ (PERF sein).

jumper *noun* Pullover der (PL die Pullover).

junction *noun* **1** (*of roads*) Kreuzung die (PL die Kreuzungen); **2** (*on railway*) Gleisanschluss der (PL die Gleisanschlüsse).

June *noun* Juni der; **in June** im Juni.

jungle *noun* Dschungel der.

junior *adjective* jünger; **junior school** die Grundschule; **the juniors** (*at primary school*) die Grundschüler, die Grundschülerinnen.

junk *noun* Trödel der.

junk food *noun* ungesunde Essen das.

just *adverb* **1** (*very recently*) gerade; **to have just done something** gerade etwas getan haben; **Tom has just arrived** Tom ist gerade angekommen; **2** **to be just doing something** gerade dabei sein, etwas zu tun; **I'm just doing the food** ich bin gerade dabei, Essen zu machen; **3** **just before midday** kurz vor Mittag; **just after 4 o'clock** kurz nach vier Uhr; **4** (*only*) nur; **just for fun** nur zum Vergnügen; **he's just a child** er ist doch nur ein Kind; **just me and Justine are coming** nur ich und Justine kommen; **5** **just a minute!** einen Moment!; **6** **just coming!** ich komme schon!; **7** (*exactly*) **just as** genauso wie.**he's got just as many friends** er hat genauso viele Freunde.

justice *noun* Gerechtigkeit die.

Kk

kangaroo *noun* Känguru das (PL die Kängurus).

karate *noun* Karate das.

karting *noun* Gokarten das; **to go go-karting** Gokarten gehen.

kebab *noun* Kebab der (PL die Kebabs).

keen *adjective* **1** (*enthusiastic or committed*) begeistert; **he's a keen photographer** er ist ein begeisterter Fotograf; **you don't seem too keen** du scheinst nicht gerade begeistert zu sein; **2** **to be keen on** mögen◇; **I'm not keen on**

a
b
c
d
e
f
g
h
i
j
k
l
m
n
o
p
q
r
s
t
u
v
w
x
y
z

fish ich mag Fisch nicht; **3 to be keen on doing** (or **to do**) **something** etwas gerne tun.

keep verb **1** behalten◇; **you can keep the book** du kannst das Buch behalten; **to keep a secret** ein Geheimnis für sich behalten; **2 will you keep my seat?** können Sie meinen Platz freihalten?; **3 to keep somebody waiting** jemanden warten lassen; **4** (store) aufbewahren SEP; **can I keep my watch in your desk?** kann ich meine Uhr in deinem Schreibtisch aufbewahren?; **where do you keep saucepans?** wo sind die Töpfe?; **5** (not throw away) aufheben◇ SEP; **I kept all his letters** ich habe alle seine Briefe aufgehoben; **6 to keep on doing something** etwas weiter tun; **she kept on talking** sie hat weitergeredet; **keep straight on** weiter geradeaus gehen; **7 to keep on doing something** (time after time) dauernd etwas tun; **he keeps on ringing me up** er ruft mich dauernd an; **8** (maintain) halten◇; **to keep the food warm** das Essen warm halten; **to keep a promise** ein Versprechen halten; **9** (stay) bleiben◇ (PERF sein); **to keep calm** ruhig bleiben; **to keep out of the sun** im Schatten bleiben.

kennel noun **1** (for one dog) Hundehütte die (PL die Hundehütten); **2** (for boarding) **kennels** Hundepension die (PL die Hundepensionen).

kerb noun Randstein der.

kettle noun Kessel der (PL die Kessel); **to put the kettle on** Wasser aufsetzen.

key noun **1** (for a lock) Schlüssel der (PL die Schlüssel); **bunch of keys** ein Schlüsselbund; **2** (on a piano or keyboard) Taste die.

keyboard noun (for a computer) Tastatur die (PL die Tastaturen).

keyring noun Schlüsselring der (PL die Schlüsselringe).

kick noun **1** (from a person or a horse) Tritt der (PL die Tritte); **to give somebody a kick** jemandem einen Tritt geben; **2** (in football) Schuss der (PL die Schüsse); ★ **to get a kick out of doing something** etwas leidenschaftlich gerne tun.

kick verb **1 to kick somebody** jemandem einen Tritt geben; **2 to kick the ball** den Ball kicken.

● **to kick off** anstoßen◇ SEP.

kick-off noun Anstoß der.

kid noun (child) Kind das (PL die Kinder); **Dad's looking after the kids** Vati passt auf die Kinder auf.

kidnap verb entführen.

kidnapper noun Entführer der (PL die Entführer), Entführerin die (PL die Entführerinnen).

kidney noun Niere die (PL die Nieren).

kill verb **1** töten (an animal); **2** (murder) umbringen◇ SEP; **he killed the girl** er brachte das Mädchen um; **3 she was killed in a car accident** sie kam bei einem Autounfall ums Leben.

killer noun Mörder der (PL die Mörder), Mörderin die (PL die Mörderinnen).

kilo noun Kilo das (PL die Kilo); **a kilo of sugar** ein Kilo Zucker; **two euros a kilo** zwei Euro das Kilo.

kilogram noun Kilogramm das (PL die Kilogram).

kilometre noun Kilometer der (PL die Kilometer).

kilt noun Kilt der (PL die Kilts).

kind noun 1 (for newspapers or snacks) Kiosk das (PL die Kioske; 2 (for a phone) Telefonzelle die (PL die Telefonzellen).

kind noun 1 Art die (PL die Arten); this kind of book diese Art Buch; all kinds of people alle möglichen Leute; 2 (brand) Sorte die (PL die Sorten).

kind adjective nett; she was very kind to me sie war sehr nett zu mir.

kindness noun Freundlichkeit die.

king noun König der (PL die Könige); the king of hearts der Herzkönig.

kingdom noun Königreich das (PL die Königreiche); the United Kingdom das Vereinigte Königreich.

kiosk noun 1 (for newspapers or snacks) Kiosk das (PL die Kioske; 2 (for a phone) Telefonzelle die (PL die Telefonzellen).

kipper noun Räucherhering der (PL die Räucherheringe).

kiss noun Kuss der (PL die Küsse); to give somebody a kiss jemandem einen Kuss geben.

kiss verb küssen; kiss me! küss mich!; we kissed each other wir haben uns geküsst.

kit noun 1 (of tools) Werkzeug das; 2 (in a box) a tool kit ein Werkzeugkasten; 3 (clothes) Sachen (plural); where's my football kit? wo sind meine Fußballsachen?; 4 (for making a model, a piece of furniture, etc.) Bausatz der (PL die Bausätze).

kitchen noun Küche die (PL die Küchen); the kitchen table der Küchentisch.

kitchen foil noun Alufolie die.

kitchen roll noun Küchenrolle die (PL die Küchenrollen).

kite noun Drachen der; to fly a kite einen Drachen steigen lassen.

kitten noun Kätzchen das (PL die Kätzchen).

kiwi fruit noun Kiwi die (PL die Kiwis).

knee noun Knie das (PL die Knie); on (your) hands and knees auf allen vieren.

kneel verb knien◇; to kneel (down) sich hinknien SEP.

knickers plural noun Schlüpfer der (PL die Schlüpfer); two pairs of knickers zwei Schlüpfer.

knife noun Messer das (PL die Messer).

knife verb einstechen◇ SEP auf (+ ACC), (kill) erstechen◇.

knight noun (in chess) Springer der (PL die Springer).

knit verb stricken.

knitting noun Strickerei die.

knob noun 1 (on a door or walking stick) Knauf der (PL die Knäufe); 2 (control on a radio or machine) Knopf der (PL die Knöpfe); 3 knob of butter das kleine Stückchen Butter.

knock noun Schlag der (PL die Schläge); a knock on the head ein Schlag auf den Kopf; a knock at the door ein Klopfen an der Tür.

knock verb 1 (to bang) stoßen◇; I knocked my arm on the table ich habe mir den Arm am Tisch gestoßen; **2 to knock on something** an etwas (ACC) klopfen.

● **to knock down 1** (*in a traffic accident*) anfahren✧ SEP (*a person*); **2** (*to demolish*) abreißen✧ SEP (*an old building*).

● **to knock out 1** (*to make unconscious*) bewusstlos schlagen✧; **2** (*in sport, to eliminate*) k.o. schlagen✧.

knot *noun* Knoten der (PL die Knoten); **to tie a knot** einen Knoten machen.

know *verb* **1** (*know a fact*) wissen✧; **do you know where Tim is?** weißt du, wo Tim ist?; **I know they've moved house** ich weiß, dass sie umgezogen sind; **yes, I know** ja, weiß ich; **you never know!** man kann nie wissen!; **I know how to get to town** ich weiß, wie man in die Stadt kommt; **2** (*be personally acquainted with*) kennen✧; **do you know the Jacksons?** kennst du die Jacksons?; **all the people I know** alle Leute, die ich kenne; **I don't know his mother** ich kenne seine Mutter nicht; **3 to know how to do something** wissen, wie man etwas macht; **Steve knows how to make potato salad** Steve kann Kartoffelsalat machen; **Liz knows how to mend it** Liz kann es reparieren; **4 to know about** Bescheid wissen über (+ ACC) (*items in the news*); **5 to know about** sich auskennen✧ SEP mit (*machines, cars, etc.*); **Lindy knows about computers** Lindy kennt sich mit Computern aus; **6 to get to know**

somebody jemanden kennen lernen.

knowledge *noun* Wissen das.

Koran *noun* Koran der.

kosher *adjective* koscher.

LI

lab *noun* Labor das (PL die Labors).

label *noun* Etikett das (PL die Etikette).

laboratory *noun* Labor das (PL die Labors).

lace *noun* **1** (*for a shoe*) Schnürsenkel der (PL die Schnürsenkel); **to tie your laces** sich (DAT) die Schnürsenkel binden; **2** (*fabric or trimming*) Spitze die.

ladder *noun* **1** (*for climbing*) Leiter die (PL die Leitern); **2** (*in your tights*) Laufmasche die (PL die Laufmaschen).

ladies *noun* (*lavatory*) Damentoilette die (PL die Damentoiletten); (*on a sign*) '**Ladies**' Damen'.

lady *noun* Dame die (PL die Damen); **ladies and gentlemen** meine Damen und Herren.

ladybird *noun* Marienkäfer der (PL die Marienkäfer).

lager *noun* helle Bier das (PL die hellen Biere), Helle das (PL die Hellen) (*informal*); **a lager, please** ein Helles bitte.

laid-back *adjective* gelassen.

lake *noun* See der (PL die Seen); **Lake Geneva** der Genfer See.

landlady noun 1 (of a house or room) Vermieterin die (PL die Vermieterinnen); 2 (of a pub) Gastwirtin die (PL die Gastwirtinnen).

landlord noun 1 (of a house or room) Vermieter der (PL die Vermieter); 2 (of a pub) Gastwirt der (PL die Gastwirte).

lane noun 1 (small road) Weg der (PL die Wege); 2 (of a motorway) Spur die (PL die Spuren).

language noun 1 (German, Italian, etc.) Sprache die (PL die Sprachen); **foreign language** die Fremdsprache; 2 (way of speaking) Ausdrucksweise die; **bad language** Kraftausdrücke (plural).

lap noun 1 Schoß der (PL die Schöße); 2 (in races) Runde die (PL die Runden).

laptop noun Laptop der (PL die Laptops).

larder noun Speisekammer die (PL die Speisekammern).

large adjective groß.

laser noun Laser der (PL die Laser).

laser beam noun Laserstrahl der (PL die Laserstrahlen).

laser printer noun Laserdrucker der (PL die Laserdrucker).

laser surgery noun Laseroperation die (PL die Laseroperationen).

last adjective letzter/letzte/letztes; **last week** letzte Woche; **for the last time** zum letzten Mal; **last night** gestern Nacht.

last adverb 1 (in final position) als Letzter/als Letzte/als Letztes; **Rob arrived last** Rob kam als Letzter an; 2 **at last!** endlich!; 3 (most

recently) zuletzt; **I last saw him in May** ich habe ihn zuletzt im Mai gesehen.

last verb dauern; **the film lasted two hours** der Film dauerte zwei Stunden.

late adjective, adverb 1 spät; **I'm late** ich bin spät dran; **we were five minutes late** wir haben uns fünf Minuten verspätet; **they arrived late** sie sind zu spät angekommen; **to be late for something** zu spät zu etwas (DAT) kommen; **we were late for the party** wir kamen zu spät zur Party; 2 **to be late** (of a bus or train) Verspätung haben; **the train was an hour late** der Zug hatte eine Stunde Verspätung; 3 (late in the day) spät; **we got up late** wir sind spät aufgestanden; **the chemist is open late** die Apotheke hat bis spät auf; **late last night** gestern spät in der Nacht; **too late!** zu spät!

lately adverb in letzter Zeit.

later adverb später; **I'll explain later** ich erkläre es später; **see you later!** bis später!

latest adjective 1 neuester/neueste/neuestes; **the latest news** die neuesten Nachrichten; **the latest in audio equipment** das Neueste an Audioausrüstung; 2 **at the latest** spätestens.

Latin noun Latein das.

laugh noun Lachen das; **to do something for a laugh** etwas aus Spaß machen.

laugh verb 1 lachen; **everybody laughed** alle haben gelacht; **to laugh about something** über etwas (ACC) lachen; 2 **to laugh at**

a
b
c
d
e
f
g
h
i
j
k
l
m
n
o
p
q
r
s
t
u
v
w
x
y
z

a

somebody jemanden auslachen SEP; **they'll only laugh at me** sie lachen mich bestimmt aus.

b

launch noun **1** (*of a ship*) Stapellauf der ; **2** (*of a product*) Einführung die; **3** (*of a spacecraft*) Abschuss der.

c

d

launch verb **1** auf den Markt bringen✧ (*a product*); **2** ins All schiessen✧ (*a spacecraft*); **3** zu Wasser lassen ✧ (*a ship*).

e

f

g

launderette noun Waschsalon der (PL die Waschsalons).

h

lavatory noun Toilette die (PL die Toiletten); **to go to the lavatory** auf die Toilette gehen.

i

j

lavender noun Lavendel der.

k

law noun **1** Gesetz das (PL die Gesetze); **to break the law** gegen das Gesetz verstoßen; **2 it's against the law** das ist verboten; **3** (*subject of study*) Jura die (*no plural*).

l

m

lawn noun Rasen der (PL die Rasen).

lawnmower noun Rasenmäher der (PL die Rasenmäher).

n

o

lawyer noun Rechtsanwalt der (PL die Rechtsanwälte), Rechtsanwältin die (PL die Rechtsanwältinnen).

p

q

lay verb **1** (*put*) legen; **she laid the cards on the table** sie legte die Karten auf den Tisch; **2 to lay the table** den Tisch decken.

r

s

lay-by noun Parkplatz der (PL die Parkplätze).

t

layer noun Schicht die (PL die Schichten).

u

lazy adjective faul.

v

lead[1] noun **1** (*when you are ahead*) Führung die; **to be in the lead** in Führung liegen; **Baxter's in the lead** Baxter liegt in Führung; **to**

w

x

y

z

take the lead in Führung gehen; **2** (*electric*) Kabel das (PL die Kabel); **3** (*for a dog*) Leine die (PL die Leinen); **on a lead** an der Leine; **4** (*role*) Hauptrolle die (PL die Hauptrollen); **5** (*an actor*) Hauptdarsteller der (PL die Hauptdarsteller), Hauptdarstellerin die (PL die Hauptdarstellerinnen).

lead verb **1** führen; **the path leads to the sea** der Weg führt zum Meer; **to lead by three points** mit drei Punkten führen; **2 to lead the way** vorangehen✧ SEP (PERF *sein*); **3 to lead to something** zu etwas (DAT) führen (*an accident or problems, for example*).

lead[2] noun (*metal*) Blei das.

lead singer noun Leadsänger der (PL die Leadsänger), Leadsängerin die (PL die Leadsängerinnen).

leader noun **1** (*of a political party*) Vorsitzende der/die (PL die Vorsitzenden); **2** (*of an expedition or group*) Leiter der (PL die Leiter), Leiterin die (PL die Leiterinnen); **3** (*in a competition*) Erste der/die (PL die Ersten); **4** (*of a gang*) Anführer der (PL die Anführer), Anführerin die (PL die Anführerinnen).

leaf noun Blatt das (PL die Blätter).

leaflet noun **1** (*with instructions*) Merkblatt das (PL die Merkblätter); **2** (*for advertising*) Reklameblatt das (PL die Reklameblätter).

leak noun **1** (*in a roof, tent*) undichte Stelle die (PL die undichten Stellen); **2 gas leak** die undichte Gasleitung; **3** (*in a boat*) Leck das (PL die Lecks).

leave

a
b
c
d
e
f
g
h
i
j
k
l
m
n
o
p
q
r
s
t
u
v
w
x
y
z

leak verb (bottle or roof) undicht sein.

lean adjective (meat) mager.

lean verb 1 to lean on something sich an etwas (ACC) lehnen; he leaned against the door er hat sich gegen die Tür gelehnt; 2 sich lehnen; she was leaning out of the window sie lehnte sich aus dem Fenster; 3 to lean forward sich vorbeugen SEP.

leap year noun Schaltjahr das (PL die Schaltjahre).

learn verb lernen; to learn German Deutsch lernen; to learn (how) to drive Autofahren lernen.

learner noun 1 Lerner der (PL die Lerner); to be a fast learner schnell lernen; 2 (beginner) Anfänger der (PL die Anfänger), Anfängerin die (PL die Anfängerinnen).

least adjective, pronoun 1 wenigster/wenigste/wenigstes; to have least time am wenigsten Zeit haben; Tony has the least money Tony hat das wenigste Geld; 2 (the slightest) geringster/geringste/geringstes; I haven't the least idea ich habe nicht die geringste Ahnung.

least adverb 1 am wenigsten; I like the blue shirt least ich mag das blaue Hemd am wenigsten; 2 the least expensive hotel das billigste Hotel; 3 at least (at a minimum) mindestens; at least twenty people mindestens zwanzig Leute; 4 at least (at any rate) wenigstens; she's a teacher, at least I think

she is sie ist Lehrerin, glaube ich wenigstens.

leather noun Leder das; **leather jacket** noun Lederjacke.

leave noun Urlaub der; three days' leave drei Tage Urlaub.

leave verb 1 (go away) gehen◇ (PERF sein), (by car) fahren◇ SEP (PERF sein), (a train or bus) abfahren◇ SEP (PERF sein); they're leaving tomorrow evening sie fahren morgen Abend; we left at six wir sind um sechs Uhr gegangen; the train leaves Munich at ten der Zug fährt um zehn Uhr von München ab; 2 (go away from or go out of) verlassen◇; I left the office at five ich habe das Büro um fünf verlassen; he left his wife er hat seine Frau verlassen; 3 (deposit or allow to remain in the same state) lassen◇; you can leave your coats in the hall Sie können Ihre Mäntel in der Diele lassen; to leave the door open die Tür offen lassen; leave it until tomorrow lass es bis morgen; 4 to leave somebody something jemandem etwas hinterlassen◇ (a message or money); he didn't leave a message er hat keine Nachricht hinterlassen; 5 (not do) stehen lassen◇; leave the washing up lass den Abwasch stehen; 6 (forget) vergessen◇; he left his umbrella on the train er hat seinen Regenschirm im Zug vergessen; 7 be left übrig sein (PERF sein); there are two pancakes left zwei Pfannkuchen sind noch übrig; I don't have any money left ich habe kein Geld mehr übrig; we have ten

a

minutes left wir haben noch zehn Minuten Zeit.

b

lecture noun **1** (*at university*) Vorlesung die (PL die Vorlesungen); **2** (*public*) Vortrag der (PL die Vorträge).

c

d

leek noun Lauch der.

e

left noun **on the left** links; **to drive on the left** links fahren; **on my left** links von mir.

f

g

left adverb links; **turn left at the church** an der Kirche links abbiegen.

h

left adjective linker/linke/linkes; **his left foot** sein linker Fuß.

i

j

left-click noun Klick der (mit der linken Maustaste).

k

left-click verb **left-click the icon** das Icon mit der linken Maustaste anklicken.

l

m

left-hand adjective **the left-hand side** die linke Seite.

n

left-handed adjective linkshändig.

o

left-luggage office noun Gepäckaufbewahrung die (PL die Gepäckaufbewahrungen).

p

q

leg noun **1** Bein das (PL die Beine); **my left leg** mein linkes Bein; **to break your leg** sich (DAT) das Bein brechen; **2** (*in cooking*) Keule die (PL die Keulen); **leg of lamb** die Lammkeule; ★ **to pull somebody's leg** jemanden auf den Arm nehmen.

r

s

t

u

legal adjective gesetzlich.

v

leggings plural noun Leggings (*plural*).

w

x

leisure noun Freizeit die; **in my leisure time** in meiner Freizeit.

y

z

lemon noun Zitrone die (PL die Zitronen).

lemonade noun Limonade die (PL die Limonaden).

lemon juice noun Zitronensaft der.

lend verb leihen✧; **to lend something to somebody** jemandem etwas leihen; **I lent Judy my bike** ich habe Judy mein Rad geliehen; **will you lend it to me?** kannst du es mir leihen?

length noun Länge die (PL die Längen).

lens noun **1** (*in a camera*) Objektiv das (PL die Objektive); **2** (*in spectacles*) Brillenglas das (PL die Brillengläser); **3 contact lenses** Kontaktlinsen (*plural*).

Lent noun Fastenzeit die.

lentil noun Linse die (PL die Linsen).

Leo noun Löwe der (PL die Löwen); **I'm a Leo** ich bin Löwe.

leotard noun Turnanzug der (PL die Turnanzüge).

lesbian adjective lesbisch.

less pronoun, adjective, adverb weniger ('*weniger' never changes*); **Ben eats less** Ben isst weniger; **less time** weniger Zeit; **less than** weniger als; **less than three hours** weniger als drei Stunden; **you spent less than me** du hast weniger als ich ausgegeben; **less and less** immer weniger.

lesson noun (*class*) Stunde die (PL die Stunden); **German lesson** die Deutschstunde; **driving lesson** die Fahrstunde.

let[1] verb **1** (*allow*) lassen✧; **to let somebody do something** jemanden etwas tun lassen; **she**

lets me drive her car sie lässt mich mit ihrem Auto fahren; **the police let us through** die Polizei hat uns durchgelassen; **let me in** lass mich hinein; **2** (*as a suggestion or a command*) **let's go!** gehen wir!; **let's not talk about it** reden wir nicht mehr darüber; **let's eat out** essen wir im Restaurant.

● **to let off 1** abfeuern◇ (*fireworks*); **2** (*to excuse from*) befreien von (+ DAT) (*homework*).

let² *verb* (*to rent out*) vermieten; **'flat to let'** 'Wohnung zu vermieten'.

letter *noun* **1** Brief *der* (PL die Briefe); **a letter for you from Delia** ein Brief für dich von Delia; **2** (*of the alphabet*) Buchstabe *der* (PL die Buchstaben).

letter box *noun* Briefkasten *der* (PL die Briefkästen).

lettuce *noun* Salat *der*; **two lettuces** zwei Salatköpfe.

leukaemia *noun* Leukämie die.

level *noun* Höhe *die*; **at eye level** in Augenhöhe.

level *adjective* **1** eben (*ground or floor*); **2** (*horizontal*) waagerecht (*shelf*); **3** (*at the same height*) auf gleicher Höhe; **to be level with the ground** auf gleicher Höhe mit dem Boden sein.

level crossing *noun* Bahnübergang *der* (PL die Bahnübergänge).

lever *noun* Hebel *der* (PL die Hebel).

liar *noun* Lügner *der* (PL die Lügner), Lügnerin die (PL die Lügnerinnen).

liberal *adjective* **1** tolerant; **2** (*in politics*) liberal; **the Liberal**

Democrats die Liberaldemokraten.

Libra *noun* Waage die; **Sean's Libra** Sean ist Waage.

librarian *noun* Bibliothekar *der* (PL die Bibliothekare), Bibliothekarin die (PL die Bibliothekarinnen).

library *noun* Bibliothek die (PL die Bibliotheken); **public library** die öffentliche Bücherei.

licence *noun* **1** (*for a TV*) Genehmigung die (PL die Genehmigungen); **2** (*driving licence*) Führerschein *der* (PL die Führerscheine).

lick *verb* lecken.

lid *noun* Deckel *der* (PL die Deckel).

lie *noun* Lüge die (PL die Lügen); **to tell a lie** (or **lies**) lügen◇.

lie *verb* **1** (*to be stretched out*) liegen◇; **he's lying on the sofa** er liegt auf dem Sofa; **my coat lay on the bed** mein Mantel lag auf dem Bett; **2** to lie down (*for a rest*) sich hinlegen SEP; **I'm going to lie down for a little** ich lege mich ein bisschen hin; **3** (*tell lies*) lügen◇.

lie-in *noun* **to have a lie-in** ausschlafen◇ SEP.

life *noun* Leben das (PL die Leben); **all her life** ihr ganzes Leben lang; **full of life** voller Leben; **that's life!** so ist das Leben!

lifeboat *noun* Rettungsboot das (PL die Rettungsboote).

lifeguard *noun* Rettungsschwimmer *der* (PL die Rettungsschwimmer), Rettungsschwimmerin die (PL die Rettungsschwimmerinnen); **is there a lifeguard at the pool?** gibt es einen Bademeister im Schwimmbad?

life jacket *noun* Schwimmweste die (PL die Schwimmwesten).

life-style *noun* Lebensstil der (PL die Lebensstile).

lift *noun* **1** Aufzug der (PL die Aufzüge); **let's take the lift** fahren wir mit dem Aufzug; **2** (*a ride*) **to give somebody a lift to the station** jemanden zum Bahnhof mitnehmen⧫ SEP; **Khaled's giving me a lift** Khaled nimmt mich mit; **would you like a lift?** möchtest du mitfahren?

lift *verb* hochheben⧫ SEP; **he lifted the box** er hob die Kiste hoch.

light *noun* **1** Licht das; **will you turn the light on?** kannst du das Licht anmachen?; **to turn off the light** das Licht ausmachen; **are your lights on?** hast du das Licht an?; **2** (*in the street*) Straßenlampe die (PL die Straßenlampen); **3** (*a lamp*) Lampe die (PL die Lampen); **4** **traffic lights** die Ampel (*singular*); **the lights are green** die Ampel ist grün; **5** (*for a cigarette*) **have you got a light?** hast du Feuer?

light *adjective* **1** (*not dark*) hell; **a light blue dress** ein hellblaues Kleid; **it gets light at six** es wird um sechs hell; **2** (*not heavy*) leicht; **a light coat** ein leichter Mantel; **a light breeze** eine leichte Brise.

light *verb* **1** anzünden SEP (*the fire, a match, the gas*); **we lit a fire** wir zündeten ein Feuer an; **2 to light a cigarette** sich (DAT) eine Zigarette anzünden.

light bulb *noun* Glühbirne die (PL die Glühbirnen).

lighter *noun* Feuerzeug das (PL die Feuerzeuge).

lighthouse *noun* Leuchtturm der (PL die Leuchttürme).

lightning *noun* Blitz der; **flash of lightning** der Blitz; **to be struck by lightning** vom Blitz getroffen werden.

like[1] *preposition, conjunction* **1** wie; **like me** wie ich; **like a duck** wie eine Ente; **like I said** wie gesagt; **what's it like?** wie ist es?; **what was the weather like?** wie war das Wetter?; **2 like this/that** so; **3** ähnlich (+ DAT); **to look like somebody** jemandem ähnlich sehen; **Cindy looks like her father** Cindy sieht ihrem Vater ähnlich.

like[2] *verb* **1** mögen⧫; **I like vegetables** ich mag Gemüse; **I don't like meat** ich mag kein Fleisch; **I like Dürer best** ich mag Dürer am liebsten; **2 to like doing something** etwas gerne tun; **Mum likes reading** Mutti liest gerne; **3 I would like ...** ich möchte gerne ...; **would you like a coffee?** möchten Sie einen Kaffee?; **what would you like to eat?** was möchten Sie essen?; **yes, if you like** ja, wenn du willst; **4 I like the dress** das Kleid gefällt mir; **how do you like it?** wie gefällt es dir?

likely *adjective* wahrscheinlich; **she's likely to phone** wahrscheinlich ruft sie an.

lime *noun* Kalk der.

limit *noun* Grenze die (PL die Grenzen); **speed limit** die Geschwindigkeitsbeschränkung.

limp noun to have a limp hinken.

line noun **1** Linie die (PL die Linien); **a straight line** eine gerade Linie; **to draw a line** eine Linie ziehen; **2** (in writing) Zeile die (PL die Zeilen); **six lines of text** sechs Zeilen Text; **3** (railway) Bahnlinie die (PL die Bahnlinien) (from one place to another); **on the line** (the track) auf der Strecke; **4** (a queue of people or cars) Schlange die (PL die Schlangen); **to stand in line** in der Schlange stehen; **5** (telephone) Leitung die (PL die Leitungen); **the line's bad** die Verbindung ist schlecht; **hold the line, please** bitte bleiben Sie am Apparat.

line verb füttern (a coat).

linen noun Leinen das; **a linen jacket** eine Leinenjacke.

lining noun Futter das (PL die Futter).

link noun Verbindung die (PL die Verbindungen); **what's the link between the two?** was für eine Verbindung besteht zwischen den beiden?

link verb verbinden✧ (two places); **the two towns are linked by a railway line** die beiden Städte sind durch eine Bahnlinie miteinander verbunden.

lion noun Löwe der (PL die Löwen).

lip noun Lippe die (PL die Lippen).

lip-read verb von den Lippen lesen✧.

lipstick noun Lippenstift der (PL die Lippenstifte).

liquid noun Flüssigkeit die (PL die Flüssigkeiten).

liquid adjective flüssig.

liquidizer noun Mixer der (PL die Mixer).

list noun Liste die (PL die Listen).

listen verb **1** zuhören SEP; **I wasn't listening** ich habe nicht zugehört; **to listen to somebody** jemandem zuhören; **you're not listening to me** du hörst mir nicht zu; **2** to listen to something etwas (ACC) hören; **to listen to the radio** Radio hören.

listener noun (to the radio) Hörer der (PL die Hörer), Hörerin die (PL die Hörerinnen).

literature noun Literatur die (PL die Literaturen).

litre noun Liter der (PL die Liter); **a litre of milk** ein Liter Milch.

litter noun (rubbish) Abfall der.

litter bin noun Abfalleimer der (PL die Abfalleimer).

little adjective, pronoun **1** (small) klein; **a little boy** ein kleiner Junge; **a little break** eine kleine Pause; **2** (not much) wenig; **we have very little time** wir haben sehr wenig Zeit; **3** a little ein wenig; **we have a little left** wir haben ein wenig übrig; **4** just a little, please nur ein bisschen, bitte; **it's a little late** es ist ein bisschen spät; **a little more** ein bisschen mehr; **a little less** ein bisschen weniger; ★ **little by little** nach und nach.

little finger noun kleine Finger der (PL die kleinen Finger).

live¹ verb **1** (in a house or town) wohnen; **she lives in York** sie wohnt in York; **we live in a flat** wir wohnen in einer Wohnung; **2** (be or stay alive, spend one's life) leben;

we're living in the country now wir leben jetzt auf dem Land; they live on fruit sie leben von Obst; they live apart sie leben getrennt.

live² *adjective, adverb* **1** live (*broadcast*); **a live programme** eine Livesendung; **live music** die Livemusik; **a broadcast live from Wembley** eine Liveübertragung aus Wembley; **to broadcast a concert live** ein Konzert live senden; **2** (*alive*) lebend.

lively *adjective* lebhaft.

liver *noun* Leber die (PL die Lebern).

living *noun* Lebensunterhalt der; **to earn a living** sich (DAT) seinen Lebensunterhalt verdienen.

living room *noun* Wohnzimmer das (PL die Wohnzimmer).

lizard *noun* Eidechse die (PL die Eidechsen).

load *noun* **1** (*on a lorry*) Ladung die (PL die Ladungen); **a (lorry-)load of bricks** eine Ladung Ziegelsteine; **2 a bus-load of tourists** ein Bus voll Touristen; **3 loads of** massenhaft (*informal*); **loads of tourists** massenhaft Touristen; **they've got loads of money** sie haben einen Haufen Geld (*informal*).

load *verb* **1** beladen ❖ (*a vehicle*); **2 to load a camera** einen Film einlegen SEP.

loaf *noun* Brot das (PL die Brote); **a loaf of white bread** ein Weißbrot.

loan *noun* **1** (*from a person*) Leihgabe die (PL die Leihgaben); **2** (*by a bank*) Kredit der (PL die Kredite).

loan *verb* leihen ❖.

loathe *verb* hassen; **I loathe getting up early** ich hasse es, früh aufzustehen.

local *noun* **1** (*a pub*) Stammkneipe die (PL die Stammkneipen); **2 the locals** (*people*) die Einheimischen.

local *adjective* **1** hiesig; **the local library** die hiesige Bücherei; **2 local newspaper** die Lokalzeitung.

lock *noun* Schloss das (PL die Schlösser).

lock *verb* abschließen ❖ SEP (*a door, room, or bicycle*); **have you locked the door?** hast du abgeschlossen?

lodger *noun* Untermieter der (PL die Untermieter), Untermieterin die (PL die Untermieterinnen).

loft *noun* Dachboden der (PL die Dachböden).

log *noun* **1** Baumstamm der (PL die Baumstämme); **2** (*as firewood*) Holzscheit das (PL die Holzscheite); **a log fire** ein offenes Feuer.

lollipop *noun* Lutscher der (PL die Lutscher).

London *noun* London das.

Londoner *noun* Londoner der (PL die Londoner), Londonerin die (PL die Londonerinnen).

lonely *adjective* einsam; **to feel lonely** sich einsam fühlen.

long *adjective, adverb* **1** lang; **a long film** ein langer Film; **a long day** ein langer Tag; **it's five metres long** es ist fünf Meter lang; **the film is an hour long** der Film dauert eine Stunde; **2 a long time** lange; **he stayed for a long time** er ist lange geblieben; **I've been here for a long time** ich bin schon lange hier; **a long time ago** vor langer Zeit; **this won't take long** das dauert nicht lange; **3 how long?** wie lange?; **how long have you been here?** wie lange sind Sie schon hier?; **long ago** vor langer Zeit; **4 a long way** weit; **it's a long way to the cinema** bis zum Kino ist es weit; **5 all night long** die ganze Nacht; **6 no longer** nicht mehr; **he doesn't work here any longer** er arbeitet nicht mehr hier.

long verb **to long to do something** sich danach sehnen, etwas zu tun; **I'm longing to see you** ich sehne mich danach, dich zu sehen.

long-distance call noun (*within the country*) Ferngespräch das (PL die Ferngespräche).

long jump noun Weitsprung der.

longlife milk noun H-Milch die.

loo noun Klo das (PL die Klos) (*informal*).

look noun 1 (*a glance*) Blick der (PL die Blicke); **to take a look at somebody** einen Blick auf jemanden werfen; 2 (*a tour*) **to have a look at the school** sich (DAT) die Schule ansehen; **to have a look round the town** sich (DAT) die Stadt ansehen; 3 **to have a look for** suchen.

look verb 1 sehen◇; **to look out of the window** aus dem Fenster sehen; **I wasn't looking** ich habe nicht hingesehen; 2 **to look at** ansehen◇ SEP; **he looked at the girl** er hat das Mädchen angesehen; **to look at something** sich (DAT) etwas ansehen; **I'm looking at the photos** ich sehe mir

die Fotos an; 3 (*to seem*) aussehen◇ SEP; **she looks sad** sie sieht traurig aus; **the salad looks delicious** der Salat sieht köstlich aus; **to look like** aussehen wie; **what does the house look like?** wie sieht das Haus aus?; 4 (*resemble*) **to look like somebody** jemandem ähnlich sehen; **she looks like her aunt** sie sieht ihrer Tante ähnlich; **they look like each other** sie sehen sich ähnlich.

● **to look after** 1 sich kümmern um (+ ACC); **Dad's looking after the children** Vati kümmert sich um die Kinder; 2 aufpassen SEP auf (+ ACC) (*luggage*).

● **to look for** suchen; **I'm looking for my keys** ich suche meine Schlüssel.

● **to look forward to** sich freuen auf (+ ACC) (*a party or a trip, for example*).

● **to look out** (*to be careful*) aufpassen SEP; **look out, it's hot!** pass auf, das ist heiß!

● **to look up** nachschlagen◇ SEP (*in a dictionary or directory*); **he's looking it up in the dictionary** er schlägt es im Wörterbuch nach.

loose adjective 1 (*screw or knot*) locker; 2 (*garment*) weit; 3 **loose change** das Kleingeld; ★ **I'm at a loose end** ich habe nichts zu tun.

lorry noun Lastwagen der (PL die Lastwagen).

lorry driver noun Lastwagenfahrer der (PL die Lastwagenfahrer),

a b c d e f g h i j k l m n o p q r s t u v w x y z

Lastwagenfahrerin die (PL die Lastwagenfahrerinnen).

lose verb **1** verlieren◇; we lost wir haben verloren; we lost the match wir haben das Spiel verloren; Sam's lost his watch Sam hat seine Uhr verloren; **2** to get lost sich verlaufen◇; we got lost in the woods wir haben uns im Wald verlaufen; **3** to lose weight abnehmen◇ SEP.

loss noun Verlust der (PL die Verluste).

lost property noun Fundsachen (plural).

lot noun **1** a lot viel; Wilbur eats a lot Wilbur isst viel; I spent a lot ich habe viel ausgegeben; he's a lot better es geht ihm viel besser; a lot of viel; a lot of coffee viel Kaffee; **2** (many) a lot of viele; a lot of books viele Bücher; **3** lots of eine Menge (informal); lots of people eine Menge Leute.

lottery noun Lotterie die (PL die Lotterien); to win the lottery in der Lotterie gewinnen.

loud adjective **1** laut; in a loud voice mit lauter Stimme; **2** to say something out loud etwas laut sagen.

loudly adverb laut.

loudspeaker noun Lautsprecher der (PL die Lautsprecher).

lounge noun **1** (in a house) Wohnzimmer das (PL die Wohnzimmer); **2** (in a hotel or an airport) Halle die (PL die Hallen); departure lounge die Abflughalle.

love noun **1** Liebe die; for love aus Liebe; **2** to be in love with somebody in jemanden verliebt

sein; she's in love with Jake sie ist in Jake verliebt; **3** Gina sends her love Gina lässt grüßen; with love from Charlie herzliche Grüße von Charlie; **4** (in tennis) null.

love verb **1** lieben (a person); I love you ich liebe dich; (a place or food) mögen◇ (a place or food); she loves London sie mag London sehr gerne; Wayne loves chocolate Wayne mag Schokolade sehr gerne; **3** to love doing something etwas sehr gerne tun; I love dancing ich tanze sehr gerne; **4** I'd love to come ich würde sehr gerne kommen.

lovely adjective schön; a lovely dress ein schönes Kleid; we had lovely weather wir hatten schönes Wetter; we had a lovely day der Tag war sehr schön.

low adjective **1** niedrig; a low table ein niedriger Tisch; at a low price zu einem niedrigen Preis; **2** (not loud) leise; in a low voice mit leiser Stimme.

lower adjective (not as high) tiefer.

lower verb senken.

loyalty noun Loyalität die (PL die Loyalitäten).

loyalty card noun Treuekarte die (PL die Treuekarten).

luck noun **1** Glück das; good luck! viel Glück!; with a bit of luck wenn wir Glück haben; **2** bad luck! so ein Pech!

luckily adverb zum Glück; luckily for them zu ihrem Glück.

lucky adjective **1** to be lucky Glück haben; we were lucky wir haben Glück gehabt; **2** to be lucky (*bringing luck*) Glück bringen; **it's supposed to be lucky** es soll Glück bringen; **my lucky number** meine Glückszahl.

luggage *noun* Gepäck *das*; **my luggage is in the boot** mein Gepäck ist im Kofferraum.

lump *noun* **1** Klumpen *der* (PL die Klumpen); **2** (*of sugar or butter*) Stück *das* (PL die Stücke).

lunch *noun* Mittagessen *das* (PL die Mittagessen); **to have lunch** zu Mittag essen; **we had lunch in Oxford** wir haben in Oxford zu Mittag gegessen.

lunch break *noun* Mittagspause *die* (PL die Mittagspausen).

lunch hour, lunch time *noun* Mittagszeit *die*.

lung *noun* Lungenflügel *der*; **lungs** die Lunge (*singular*).

luxurious *adjective* luxuriös.

lyrics *plural noun* Text *der*.

Mm

mac *noun* Regenmantel *der* (PL die Regenmäntel).

macaroni *noun* Makkaroni (*plural*).

machine *noun* **1** Maschine *die* (PL die Maschinen); **2** (*a slot machine*) Automat *der* (PL die Automaten).

machinery *noun* die Maschinen (*plural*).

mackerel *noun* Makrele *die* (PL die Makrelen).

mad *adjective* **1** verrückt; **she's completely mad!** sie ist total

verrückt!; **2** (*angry*) wütend; **to be mad at somebody** wütend auf jemanden sein; **3 to be mad about something** ganz verrückt auf etwas (ACC) sein; **she's mad about horses** sie ist ganz verrückt auf Pferde.

madman *noun* Verrückte *der* (PL die Verrückten).

madness *noun* Wahnsinn *der*.

magazine *noun* Zeitschrift *die* (PL die Zeitschriften), (*with mostly photos*) Magazin *das* (PL die Magazine).

magic *noun* Zauber *der*, (*conjuring tricks*) Zauberei *die*.

magic *adjective* **1** Zauber-; **magic wand** der Zauberstab; **2** (*great*) super (*informal*).

magician *noun* **1** (*wizard*) Zauberer *der* (PL die Zauberer); **2** (*conjurer*) Zauberkünstler *der* (PL die Zauberkünstler).

magnificent *adjective* wundervoll.

magnifying glass *noun* Lupe *die* (PL die Lupen).

maiden name *noun* Mädchenname *der* (PL die Mädchennamen).

mail *noun* Post *die*.

mail order *noun* Bestellung per Post *die*; **to buy something by mail order** etwas bei einem Versandhaus bestellen; **mail order catalogue** der Versandhauskatalog.

main *adjective* Haupt-; **main entrance** der Haupteingang.

main course *noun* Hauptgericht *das* (PL die Hauptgerichte).

mainly *adverb* hauptsächlich.

a b c d e f g h i j k l m n o p q r s t u v w x y z

a

main road noun Hauptstraße die (PL die Hauptstraßen).

b

maize noun Mais der

c

major adjective **1** (important) groß; **2** (serious) schwer; **a major accident** ein schwerer Unfall.

d

Majorca noun Mallorca das.

majority noun Mehrheit die.

e

make noun Marke die (PL die Marken); **the make of a car** die Automarke.

f

g

make verb **1** machen; **to make a meal** Essen machen; **I made breakfast** ich habe Frühstück gemacht; **she made her bed** sie hat ihr Bett gemacht; **to make somebody happy** jemanden glücklich machen; **it makes you tired** das macht einen müde; **2** herstellen SEP; **they make computers** sie stellen Computer her; **'made in Germany'** 'in Deutschland hergestellt'; **3** he made me wait er ließ mich warten; **she makes me laugh** sie bringt mich zum Lachen; **4** verdienen; **he makes forty pounds a day** er verdient vierzig Pfund pro Tag; **to make a living** seinen Lebensunterhalt verdienen; **5** (force) zwingen✧; **to make somebody do something** jemanden zwingen, etwas zu tun; **she made him do the money back** sie hat ihn gezwungen, das Geld zurückzugeben; **6** (the verb 'make' is often translated by a more specific verb) **to make a cake** einen Kuchen backen; **to make a phone call** telefonieren; **to make a dress** ein Kleid nähen; **7** to make friends with somebody sich mit

h

i

j

k

l

n

o

p

q

r

s

t

u

v

w

x

y

z

jemandem anfreunden SEP; **8 I can't make it tonight** ich kann heute Abend nicht kommen; **9 two and three make five** zwei und drei ist fünf.

● **to make something up 1** etwas erfinden✧; **she made up an excuse** sie hat eine Ausrede erfunden; **2 to make it up** (after a quarrel) sich versöhnen; **they've made it up again** sie haben sich wieder versöhnt.

make-up noun **1** Make-up das; **I don't wear make-up** ich trage kein Make-up; **2 to put on your make-up** sich schminken; **Jo's putting on her make-up** Jo schminkt sich.

male adjective **1** männlich; **male voice** die Männerstimme; **2 male animal** das Männchen; **male rat** das Rattenmännchen; **3 male student** der Student.

male chauvinist noun Chauvinist der (PL die Chauvinisten).

man noun **1** Mann der (PL die Männer); **an old man** ein alter Mann; **2** (the human race) der Mensch.

manage verb **1** leiten (a business, team); **she manages a travel agency** sie leitet ein Reisebüro; **2** (cope) zurechtkommen✧ SEP (PERF sein); **I can manage** ich komme schon zurecht; **3 to manage to do something** es schaffen, etwas zu tun; **he managed to push the door open** er hat es geschafft, die Tür aufzustoßen; **I didn't manage to get in touch with her** ich habe es nicht geschafft, sie zu erreichen;

management noun
1 Management das (PL die Managements); **management course** der Managementkurs;
2 Leitung die.

manager noun 1 (of a company or bank) Direktor der (PL die Direktoren), Direktorin die (PL die Direktorinnen); 2 (of a shop or restaurant) Geschäftsführer der (PL die Geschäftsführer), Geschäftsfürerin die (PL die Geschäftsführerinnen); 3 (in football) Trainer der (PL die Trainer), Managerin die (PL die Managerinnen), Trainerin die (PL die Trainerinnen); 4 (in entertainment) Manager der (PL die Manager), Managerin die (PL die Managerinnen).

manageress noun (of a shop or restaurant) Geschäftsführerin die (PL die Geschäftsführerinnen).

mania noun Manie die (PL die Manien).

maniac noun Wahnsinnige der/die (PL die Wahnsinnigen); **she drives like a maniac** sie fährt wie eine Wahnsinnige.

man-made adjective **man-made fibre** die Kunstfaser.

manner noun 1 **in a manner of speaking** mehr oder weniger; 2 **manners** Manieren (plural); **to have good manners** gute Manieren haben; **it's bad manners to talk like that** es gehört sich nicht, so zu reden.

mantelpiece noun Kaminsims der (PL die Kaminsimse).

manual noun Handbuch das (PL die Handbücher).

manufacture verb herstellen SEP.

manufacturer noun Hersteller der (PL die Hersteller).

many adjective, pronoun 1 viele; **does she have many friends?** hat sie viele Freunde?; **we didn't see many people** wir haben nicht viele Leute gesehen; **not many** nicht viele; **many of them forgot** viele haben es vergessen; **there were too many people** es waren zu viele (Leute) da; **how many?** wie viele?; **how many were there?** wie viele waren da?; **how many sisters have you got?** wie viele Schwestern hast du?; **how many are there left?** wie viele sind übrig geblieben?; **I've never had so many presents** ich habe noch nie so viele Geschenke bekommen; **2 (a lot) so many** so viel; **I have so many things to do** ich habe so viel zu tun; **3 (as much as) as many as** so viel wie; **take as many as you like** nimm so viel wie du willst; **4 (too much) that's far too many** das ist viel zu viel.

map noun 1 Karte die (PL die Karten); **2 (of a town)** Stadtplan (PL die Stadtpläne).

marathon noun Marathonlauf der (PL die Marathonläufe).

marble noun 1 Marmor der; **2 (for playing)** Murmel die (PL die Murmeln); **to play marbles** Murmeln spielen.

march noun Marsch der (PL die Marsche).

march verb marschieren (PERF sein).

March noun März der; **in March** im März.

mare noun Stute die (PL die Stuten).

margarine noun Margarine die.

margin noun Rand der (PL die Ränder).

marijuana noun Marihuana das.

mark noun 1 (at school) Note die (PL die Noten); **I got a good mark in German** ich habe eine gute Note in Deutsch bekommen; 2 (stain) Fleck der (PL die Flecke); 3 (German currency until replaced by the euro; one hundred marks = 51.13 euros) Mark die (PL die Mark).

mark verb 1 korrigieren; **the teacher marks our homework** die Lehrerin korrigiert unsere Hausaufgaben; 2 (in sports) decken.

market noun Markt der (PL die Märkte).

marketing noun Marketing das.

marmalade noun Orangenmarmelade die.

maroon adjective kastanienbraun.

marriage noun 1 Ehe die; 2 (wedding) Hochzeit die (PL die Hochzeiten).

married adjective 1 verheiratet; **they've been married for twenty years** sie sind seit zwanzig Jahren verheiratet; 2 **married couple** das Ehepaar.

marry verb 1 **to marry somebody** jemanden heiraten; **she married a Frenchman** sie hat einen Franzosen geheiratet; 2 **to get married** heiraten; **they got married in July** sie haben im Juli geheiratet.

marvellous adjective wunderbar.

marzipan noun Marzipan das.

mascara noun Wimperntusche die.

masculine noun (in German and other grammars) männlich.

mash verb stampfen.

mashed potatoes plural noun Kartoffelbrei der (singular).

mask noun Maske die (PL die Masken).

mass noun 1 **a mass of** eine Menge; 2 **masses of** massenhaft (informal); **they've got masses of money** sie haben massenhaft Geld; **there's masses left over** es ist massenhaft übrig geblieben; 3 (religious) Messe die (PL die Messen); **to go to mass** zur Messe gehen.

massage noun Massage die (PL die Massagen).

massive adjective riesig.

master verb 1 meistern; 2 **to master a language** eine Sprache beherrschen.

masterpiece noun Meisterwerk das (PL die Meisterwerke).

mat noun 1 (doormat) Matte die (PL die Matten); 2 (to put under a hot dish) Untersetzer der (PL die Untersetzer); 3 **table mat** das Platzdeckchen.

match noun 1 (for lighting) Streichholz das (PL die Streichhölzer); **box of matches** die Streichholzschachtel; 2 (in sports) Spiel das (PL die Spiele); **football match** das Fußballspiel; **to watch the match** das Spiel sehen; **to win the match** das Spiel gewinnen; **to lose the match** das Spiel verlieren.

match verb passen zu (+ DAT); **the jacket matches the skirt** die Jacke passt zu dem Rock.

mate *noun* Freund der (PL die Freunde); **I'm going to the pub with my mates** ich gehe mit meinen Freunden in die Kneipe.

material *noun* 1 (*fabric, also information*) Stoff der (PL die Stoffe); 2 (*substance*) Material das (PL die Materialien).

mathematics *noun* Mathematik die.

maths *noun* Mathe die (*informal*); **I like maths** ich mag Mathe gerne; **Anna's good at maths** Anna ist gut in Mathe.

matter *noun* **what's the matter?** was ist los?.

matter *verb* 1 **that's what matters most** das ist am wichtigsten; **it matters a lot to me** es ist mir sehr wichtig; **does it really matter?** ist das wirklich so wichtig?; 2 **it doesn't matter** es macht nichts; **it doesn't matter if it rains** es macht nichts, wenn es regnet; 3 **you can write it in German or English, it doesn't matter** du kannst es auf Deutsch oder Englisch schreiben, das ist egal; 4 **to matter to somebody** jemandem etwas ausmachen SEP; **does it matter to you if I leave earlier?** macht es dir etwas aus, wenn ich früher gehe?.

mattress *noun* Matratze die (PL die Matratzen).

maximum *noun* Maximum das (PL die Maxima); **the maximum number/speed possible is 200** die Höchstzahl/ Höchstgeschwindigkeit ist 200.

maximum *adjective* maximal; **the maximum temperature** die Höchsttemperatur; **she got the maximum points** sie erreichte die Höchstpunktzahl.

may *verb* 1 **she may be ill** vielleicht ist sie krank; **we may go to Spain** wir fahren vielleicht nach Spanien; 2 (*expressing permission*) dürfen◇; **may I close the door?** darf ich die Tür zumachen?.

May *noun* Mai der; **in May** im Mai.

maybe *adverb* vielleicht; **maybe they've got lost** vielleicht haben sie sich verlaufen.

May Day *noun* der Erste Mai.

mayonnaise *noun* Majonäse die.

mayor *noun* Bürgermeister der (PL die Bürgermeister); Bürgermeisterin die (PL die Bürgermeisterinnen).

me *pronoun* (in German this pronoun changes according to the function it has in the sentence or the preposition it follows) 1 (*as a direct object in the accusative*) mich; **she knows me** sie kennt mich; 2 (*after a preposition that takes the accusative*) mich; **they left without me** sie sind ohne mich losgefahren; **wait for me!** warte auf mich!; 3 (*as an indirect object or following a verb that takes the dative*) mir; **can you give me your address?** kannst du mir deine Adresse geben?; **he helped me** er hat mir geholfen; 4 (*after a preposition that takes the dative*) mir; **she never talks to me** sie redet nie mit mir; 5 (*in comparisons*) than me als ich; **she's older than me** sie ist älter als ich; 6 (*in the nominative*) ich; **it's me** ich bin's; **not me** ich nicht.

a
b
c
d
e
f
g
h
i
j
k
l
m
n
o
p
q
r
s
t
u
v
w
x
y
z

meadow noun Wiese die (PL die Wiesen).

meal noun 1 Essen das (PL die Essen); **to cook a meal** Essen kochen; 2 **to go for a meal** essen gehen.

mean verb 1 (signify) bedeuten; **what does that mean?** was bedeutet das?; 2 (intend to say) meinen; 3 **what do you mean?** was meinst du?; **that's not what I meant** das habe ich nicht gemeint; 4 **to mean to do something** etwas tun wollen; **I meant to phone my mother** ich wollte meine Mutter anrufen; 5 **to be meant to do something** etwas tun sollen; **she was meant to be here at six** sie sollte um sechs hier sein.

mean adjective 1 (with money) geizig; 2 (unkind) gemein; **she's really mean to her brother** sie ist richtig gemein zu ihrem Bruder; **what a mean thing to do!** das ist gemein!

meaning noun Bedeutung die (PL die Bedeutungen).

means noun 1 Mittel das (PL die Mittel); **a means of transport** das Verkehrsmittel; 2 **a means of** eine Möglichkeit; **a means of earning money** eine Möglichkeit, Geld zu verdienen; 3 **by means of** mit Hilfe (+ GEN); 4 **by all means!** selbstverständlich!

meantime adverb **for the meantime** einstweilen; **in the meantime** in der Zwischenzeit.

meanwhile adverb in der Zwischenzeit; **meanwhile she was waiting at the station** in der Zwischenzeit wartete sie am Bahnhof.

measles noun Masern (plural).

measure verb messen✧.

measurements plural noun Maße (plural); **the measurements of the room** die Maße des Zimmers; **my measurements** meine Maße.

meat noun Fleisch das; **I don't like meat** ich mag kein Fleisch.

mechanic noun Mechaniker der (PL die Mechaniker), Mechanikerin die (PL die Mechanikerinnen).

mechanical adjective mechanisch.

medal noun Medaille die (PL die Medaillen); **the gold medal** die Goldmedaille.

media noun **the media** die Medien (plural).

medical noun 1 ärztliche Untersuchung die (PL die ärztlichen Untersuchungen); 2 **to have a medical** sich untersuchen lassen.

medical adjective 1 medizinisch; 2 ärztlich (examination, treatment).

medicine noun 1 (drug) Medikament das (PL die Medikamente); 2 (subject of study) Medizin die; **she's studying medicine** sie studiert Medizin; 3 **alternative medicine** die Alternativmedizin.

Mediterranean noun **the Mediterranean (Sea)** das Mittelmeer.

medium adjective mittlerer/mittlere/mittleres.

medium-sized adjective mittelgroß.

meet verb 1 (by chance) treffen◇; I met Rosie at the baker's ich habe Rosie beim Bäcker getroffen; 2 (by appointment) sich treffen mit (+ DAT); **I'll meet you outside the cinema** ich treffe mich mit dir vor dem Kino; 3 sich treffen; **we're meeting at six** wir treffen uns um sechs; 4 (get to know) kennen lernen; **I met a German girl last week** ich habe letzte Woche eine Deutsche kennen gelernt; 5 **I've never met Oskar** ich kenne Oskar nicht; 6 (off a train or bus, for example) abholen SEP; **my dad's meeting me at the station** mein Vater holt mich vom Bahnhof ab.

meeting noun 1 (by arrangement) Treffen das (PL die Treffen); 2 (in business) Besprechung die (PL die Besprechungen); **she's in a meeting** sie ist in einer Besprechung; 3 (by chance, in sports) Begegnung die (PL die Begegnungen).

megabyte noun Megabyte das (PL die Megabytes).

melon noun Melone die (PL die Melonen).

melt verb 1 schmelzen◇ (PERF sein); **the snow has melted** der Schnee ist geschmolzen; 2 (in cookery) zerlassen◇ (butter, fat); **melt the butter in a saucepan** Butter im Topf zerlassen.

member noun Mitglied das (PL die Mitglieder).

Member of Parliament noun Abgeordnete der/die (PL die Abgeordneten).

membership noun Mitgliedschaft die.

membership card noun Mitgliedskarte die (PL die Mitgliedskarten).

membership fee noun Mitgliedsbeitrag der (PL die Mitgliedsbeiträge).

memorial noun Denkmal das (PL die Denkmäler); **a war memorial** ein Kriegsdenkmal.

memorize verb to memorize something etwas auswendig lernen.

memory noun 1 (of a person) Gedächtnis das; **you have a good memory** du hast ein gutes Gedächtnis; 2 (of the past) Erinnerung die (PL die Erinnerungen); **I have good memories of our stay in Italy** ich habe schöne Erinnerungen an unseren Urlaub in Italien; 3 (of a computer) Speicher der.

mend verb 1 reparieren; 2 (by sewing) ausbessern SEP.

meningitis noun Hirnhautentzündung die.

mental adjective 1 geistig; 2 **mental illness** die Geisteskrankheit; **mental hospital** die psychiatrische Klinik.

mention verb erwähnen.

menu noun 1 (in a restaurant) Speisekarte die (PL die Speisekarten); **is there a set menu?** gibt es ein Menü?; 2 (in computing) Menü das (PL die Menüs).

meringue noun Baiser das (PL die Baisers).

merit noun 1 Verdienst das (PL die Verdienste); 2 (good feature or

a b c d e f g h i j k l **m** n o p q r s t u v w x y z

advantage) Vorzug der (PL die Vorzüge).

merry *adjective* **1** fröhlich; **Merry Christmas** fröhliche Weihnachten; **2** *(from drinking)* angeheitert.

merry-go-round *noun* Karussell das (PL die Karussells).

mess *noun* **1** Durcheinander das; **my papers are in a complete mess** meine Unterlagen sind ein einziges Durcheinander; **what a mess!** was für ein Durcheinander!; **2 to make a mess** Unordnung machen; **3 to clear up the mess** aufräumen SEP.

● **to mess about** herumalbern SEP; **stop messing about!** hör auf herumzualbern!

● **to mess about with something** mit etwas (DAT) herumspielen SEP; **it's dangerous to mess about or with matches** es ist gefährlich, mit Streichhölzern herumzuspielen.

● **to mess something up 1** etwas durcheinander bringen✧; **you've messed up all my papers** sie haben meine Unterlagen völlig durcheinander gebracht; **2** *(make dirty)* etwas schmutzig machen; **3** *(botch)* etwas verpfuschen.

message *noun* **1** Nachricht die (PL die Nachrichten); **a telephone message** eine telefonische Nachricht; **2 to give somebody a message** jemandem etwas ausrichten SEP.

messy *adjective* **1** *(dirty)* **it's a messy job** das ist eine schmutzige Arbeit; **2 he's a messy eater** er bekleckert sich beim Essen; **3 her**

writing's really messy sie hat eine furchtbare Schrift; **4** *(untidy)* **she's very messy** sie ist sehr unordentlich.

metal *noun* Metall das (PL die Metalle).

meter *noun* **1** *(electricity, gas, taxi)* Zähler der (PL die Zähler); **to read the meter** den Zähler ablesen ✧ SEP; **2 parking meter** die Parkuhr.

method *noun* Methode die (PL die Methoden).

Methodist *noun* Methodist der (PL die Methodisten), Methodistin die (PL die Methodistinnen).

metre *noun* Meter der (PL die Meter).

metric *adjective* metrisch.

microchip *noun* Mikrochip der (PL die Mikrochips).

microphone *noun* Mikrofon das (PL die Mikrofone).

microscope *noun* Mikroskop das (PL die Mikroskope).

microwave (oven) *noun* Mikrowellenherd der (PL die Mikrowellenherde).

midday *noun* Mittag der; **at midday** mittags.

middle *noun* **1** Mitte die; **in the middle of the room** in der Mitte des Zimmers; **in the middle of June** Mitte Juni; **in the middle of the night** mitten in der Nacht; **2 to be in the middle of doing something** gerade dabei sein, etwas zu tun; **when she phoned I was in the middle of washing my hair** als sie anrief, war ich gerade dabei, mir die Haare zu waschen.

middle-aged *adjective* mittleren Alters; **a middle-aged lady** eine Dame mittleren Alters.

middle-class *adjective* der Mittelschicht; **a middle-class family** eine Familie der Mittelschicht.

Middle-East *noun* **the Middle East** der Nahe Osten.

midge *noun* Mücke *die* (PL die Mücken).

midnight *noun* Mitternacht *die*; **at midnight** um Mitternacht.

Midsummer's Day *noun* Sommersonnenwende *die*.

might *verb* 1 **'are you going to phone him?' — 'I might'** 'rufst du ihn an?' — 'vielleicht'; **I might invite Jo** vielleicht lade ich Jo ein; **he might have forgotten** vielleicht hat er es vergessen; 2 **she might be right** sie könnte Recht haben.

migraine *noun* Migräne *die*.

mike *noun* (microphone) Mikro *das* (PL die Mikros) (informal).

mild *adjective* mild

mile *noun* 1 Meile *die* (PL die Meilen) (Germans use kilometres for distances; to convert miles to kilometres, multiply by 8 and divide by 5); **it's ten miles to Oxford** es sind sechzehn Kilometer bis Oxford; 2 **it's miles better** das ist viel besser.

military *adjective* militärisch.

milk *noun* Milch *die*; **full-cream milk** die Vollmilch; **skimmed milk** die Magermilch; **semi-skimmed milk** die fettarme Milch.

milk *verb* melken.

milk chocolate *noun* Milchschokolade *die*.

milkman *noun* Milchmann *der* (PL die Milchmänner).

milk shake *noun* Milchshake *der* (PL die Milchshakes).

millennium *noun* Jahrtausend *das* (PL die Jahrtausende).

millimetre *noun* Millimeter *der* (PL die Millimeter).

million *noun* Million *die* (PL die Millionen); **a million people** eine Million Menschen; **two million people** zwei Millionen Menschen.

millionaire *noun* Millionär *der* (PL die Millionäre), Millionärin *die* (PL die Millionärinnen).

mimic *verb* nachmachen SEP.

mince *noun* Hackfleisch *das*.

mind *noun* 1 Sinn *der*; **it never crossed my mind to ask them for help** es kam mir überhaupt nicht in den Sinn, sie um Hilfe zu bitten; 2 Meinung *die*; **to change your mind** seine Meinung ändern; **I've changed my mind** ich habe meine Meinung geändert; 3 **to make up your mind to do something** sich entschließen◇, etwas zu tun; **I can't make up my mind which dress to wear** ich kann mich nicht entschließen, welches Kleid ich anziehe; 4 **I've made up my mind** ich habe mich entschieden.

mind *verb* 1 aufpassen SEP auf (+ ACC); **can you mind my bag for me?** können Sie auf meine Handtasche aufpassen?; **could you mind the baby for ten minutes?** könntest du zehn Minuten auf das Baby aufpassen?; 2 **do you mind closing the door?** würden Sie bitte die Tür zumachen?; 3 **do you mind if ...?** würde es Ihnen etwas

a
b
c
d
e
f
g
h
i
j
k
l
m
n
o
p
q
r
s
t
u
v
w
x
y
z

ausmachen SEP, **wenn ...?**; **do you mind if I open the window?** würde es Ihnen etwas ausmachen, wenn ich das Fenster aufmache?; **I don't mind** es macht mir nichts aus; **I don't mind the heat** die Hitze macht mir nichts aus; **4 never mind** macht nichts.

mine[1] noun Bergwerk das (PL die Bergwerke); **coal mine** das Kohlenbergwerk.

mine[2] pronoun **1** (for a masculine noun) mein; **she took her coat and I took mine** sie hat ihren Mantel genommen und ich habe meinen genommen; **2** (for a feminine noun) meine; **she gave me her address and I gave her mine** sie hat mir ihre Adresse gegeben und ich habe ihr meine gegeben; **3** (for a neuter noun) meins; **her dress is red and mine is blue** ihr Kleid ist rot und meins ist blau; **4** (for masculine/feminine/neuter plural nouns) meine; **she showed me her photos and I showed her mine** sie hat mir ihre Fotos gezeigt und ich habe ihr meine gezeigt; **5 a friend of mine** ein Freund von mir; **it's mine** das gehört mir.

miner noun Bergarbeiter der (PL die Bergarbeiter).

mineral water noun Mineralwasser das.

miniature noun Miniatur die (PL die Miniaturen).

miniature adjective Miniatur-; **miniature model** Miniaturmodell das.

minibus noun Kleinbus der (PL die Kleinbusse).

minimum noun Minimum das (PL die Minima); **a minimum of** ein Minimum von.

minimum adjective Mindest-; **the minimum age** das Mindestalter; **minimum wage** der Mindestlohn.

miniskirt noun Minirock der (PL die Miniröcke).

minister noun **1** (in government) Minister der (PL die Minister), Ministerin die (PL die Ministerinnen); **2** (of a church) Geistliche der/die (PL die Geistlichen).

ministry noun Ministerium das (PL die Ministerien).

minor adjective kleiner.

minority noun Minderheit die (PL die Minderheiten).

mint noun **1** (a herb) Minze die (PL die Minzen); **2** (sweet) Pfefferminzbonbon der (PL die Pfefferminzbonbons).

minus preposition minus (+ GEN); **seven minus three is four** sieben minus drei ist vier; **it was minus ten this morning** es war minus zehn heute Morgen.

minute[1] noun **1** Minute die (PL die Minuten); **I'll be ready in two minutes** ich bin in zwei Minuten fertig; **it's five minutes' walk from here** es ist fünf Minuten zu Fuß von hier; **2** Moment der; **just a minute!** einen Moment bitte!; **3 in a minute** gleich.

minute[2] adjective winzig; **the bedrooms are minute** die Schlafzimmer sind winzig.

miracle noun Wunder das (PL die Wunder).

mirror noun Spiegel der (PL die Spiegel); **he looked at himself in the mirror** er hat sich im Spiegel betrachtet.

misbehave verb sich schlecht benehmen✧.

miserable adjective **1** elend; **he was miserable without her** ohne sie fühlte er sich elend; **2 I feel really miserable today** ich fühle mich heute richtig elend; **3** mies; **it's miserable weather** das Wetter ist mies; **she gets paid a miserable salary** sie bekommt ein mieses Gehalt.

Miss noun Fräulein das; **Miss Jones** Fräulein Jones, Frau Jones (adult women are usually addressed as 'Frau', whether or not they are married).

miss verb **1** verpassen; **she missed her train** sie hat ihren Zug verpasst; **I missed the film** ich habe den Film verpasst; **to miss an opportunity** eine Gelegenheit verpassen; **2** nicht treffen✧; **the stone missed me** der Stein hat mich nicht getroffen; **the ball missed the goal** der Schuss ging am Tor vorbei; **missed!** nicht getroffen!; **3** versäumen; **he's missed his classes** er hat den Unterricht versäumt; **4** vermissen (a person or thing); **I miss you** ich vermisse dich; **she's missing her sister** sie vermisst ihre Schwester; **I miss England** ich vermisse England.

missing adjective **1** fehlend; **she's found the missing pieces** sie hat die fehlenden Teile gefunden; **the missing link** das fehlende Glied; **2 to be missing** fehlen; **there's a plate missing** ein Teller fehlt; **there are three forks missing** drei Gabeln fehlen; **3 to go missing** verschwinden✧ (PERF sein); **several things have gone missing lately** mehrere Sachen sind kürzlich verschwunden; **4 three children are missing** drei Kinder werden vermisst.

missionary noun Missionar der (PL die Missionare), Missionarin die (PL die Missionarinnen).

mist noun Nebel der.

mistake noun **1** Fehler der (PL die Fehler); **spelling mistake** der Rechtschreibfehler; **you've made lots of mistakes** du hast viele Fehler gemacht; **2 to make a mistake** (be mistaken) sich irren; **sorry, I made a mistake** Entschuldigung, ich habe mich geirrt; **3 by mistake** aus Versehen.

mistake verb **I mistook you for your brother** ich habe dich mit deinem Bruder verwechselt.

mistaken adjective **to be mistaken** sich täuschen; **you're mistaken** du täuschst dich.

mistletoe noun Mistel die (PL die Misteln).

misty adjective dunstig; **a misty morning** ein dunstiger Morgen.

misunderstand verb missverstehen✧; **I misunderstood** ich habe es missverstanden.

misunderstanding noun Missverständnis das (PL die Missverständnisse); **there's been a misunderstanding** da liegt ein Missverständnis vor.

a b c d e f g h i j k l m n o p q r s t u v w x y z

a

mix noun Mischung die (PL die Mischungen); **a good mix** eine gute Mischung; **cake mix** die Backmischung.

b

c

mix verb **1** vermischen; **mix the ingredients together** die Zutaten vermischen; **mix the cream into the sauce** die Sahne in die Soße rühren; **2 to mix with** verkehren mit (+ DAT); **she mixes with lots of interesting people** sie verkehrt mit vielen interessanten Leuten.

d

e

f

g

h

● **to mix up 1** durcheinander bringen✧; **you've mixed up all the papers** du hast alle Unterlagen durcheinander gebracht; **you've got it all mixed up** du hast alles durcheinander gebracht; **2** (confuse) verwechseln; **I get him mixed up with his brother** ich verwechsele ihn mit seinem Bruder.

i

j

k

l

m

mixed adjective **1** bunt; **a mixed programme** ein buntes Programm; **2** gemischt; **a mixed salad** ein gemischter Salat.

n

o

mixture noun Mischung die (PL die Mischungen); **it's a mixture of jazz and rock** es ist eine Mischung aus Jazz und Rock.

p

q

r

moan verb (complain) jammern; **stop moaning!** hör auf zu jammern!

s

t

mobile home noun Wohnwagen der (PL die Wohnwagen).

u

mobile phone noun Handy das (PL die Handys).

v

w

x

mock noun (mock exam) Übungsprüfung die (PL die Übungsprüfungen).

y

z

mock verb sich lustig machen über (+ ACC); **stop mocking me** hör auf, dich über mich lustig zu machen.

model noun **1** Modell das (PL die Modelle); **his car is the latest model** sein Auto ist das neueste Modell; **a model of Westminster Abbey** ein Modell von der Westminsterabtei; **2** (fashion model) Mannequin das (PL die Mannequins); **she's a model** sie ist Fotomodell.

model aeroplane noun Modellflugzeug das (PL die Modellflugzeuge).

model railway noun Modelleisenbahn die (PL die Modelleisenbahnen).

modem noun Modem der (PL die Modems).

modern adjective modern.

modernize verb modernisieren.

modern languages noun neuere Sprachen (plural).

modest adjective bescheiden.

modify verb abändern SEP.

moisture noun Feuchtigkeit die.

moisturizer noun Feuchtigkeitscreme die.

mole noun **1** (animal) Maulwurf der (PL die Maulwürfe); **2** (on the skin) Leberfleck der (PL die Leberflecke).

molecule noun Molekül das (PL die Moleküle).

molehill noun Maulwurfshügel der (PL die Maulwurfshügel).

moment noun **1** Moment der (PL die Momente); **at any moment** jeden Moment; **at the moment** im Moment, im Augenblick; **at the right moment** im richtigen

Moment; **2** Augenblick der (PL die Augenblicke); **wait a moment!** einen Augenblick!; **3 he'll be ready in a moment** er ist gleich fertig.

monarchy noun Monarchie die.

monastery noun Kloster das (PL die Klöster).

Monday noun **1** Montag der; **on Monday** am Montag; **I'm going to see him on Monday** ich sehe ihn am Montag; **see you on Monday!** bis Montag!; **every Monday** jeden Montag; **last Monday** letzten Montag; **next Monday** nächsten Montag; **2 on Mondays** montags; **the museum is closed on Mondays** das Museum ist montags geschlossen.

money noun Geld das; **I don't have enough money** ich habe nicht genug Geld; **to make money** Geld verdienen.

money box noun Sparbüchse die (PL die Sparbüchsen).

monitor noun (of a computer) Monitor der (PL die Monitoren).

monk noun Mönch der (PL die Mönche).

monkey noun Affe der (PL die Affen).

monotonous adjective eintönig.

monster noun Ungeheuer das (PL die Ungeheuer).

month noun Monat der; **in the month of May** im Mai; **this month** diesen Monat; **next month** nächsten Monat; **last month** letzten Monat; **for three months** drei Monate lang; **every month** jeden Monat; **every three months** alle drei Monate; **in two months'**

time in zwei Monaten; **at the end of the month** am Monatsende.

monthly adjective monatlich; **monthly payment** die monatliche Zahlung; **monthly ticket** die Monatskarte.

monument noun Denkmal das (PL die Denkmäler).

mood noun Laune die (PL die Launen); **to be in a good mood** gute Laune haben; **to be in a bad mood** schlechte Laune haben; **2 I'm not in the mood** ich habe keine Lust dazu; **I'm not in the mood for working** ich habe keine Lust zum Arbeiten.

moon noun Mond der (PL die Monde); **by the light of the moon** im Mondschein; **★ to be over the moon** im siebten Himmel sein (literally: to be in seventh heaven)

moonlight noun Mondschein der; **by moonlight** im Mondschein.

moped noun Moped das (PL die Mopeds).

moral noun Moral die; **the moral of the story** die Moral der Geschichte.

moral adjective moralisch.

morals noun Moral die.

more adverb **1** (followed by an adjective) (in German the ending '-er' is added to the adjective to show the comparative) **more interesting** interessanter; **the book's more interesting than the film** das Buch ist interessanter als der Film; **more difficult** schwieriger; **more slowly** langsamer; **more easily** einfacher; **books are getting more and more expensive** Bücher werden immer teurer; **2 not any**

a b c d e f g h i j k l **m** n o p q r s t u v w x y z

more (*no longer*) nicht mehr; **she doesn't live here any more** sie wohnt nicht mehr hier.

more *adjective* **1** mehr (*'mehr' never changes*); **more friends** mehr Freunde; **more ... than** mehr ... als; **they have more money than we do** sie haben mehr Geld als wir; **2 no more** kein; **there's no more milk** es ist keine Milch mehr da; **3** (*of something you have already*) noch; **would you like some more cake?** möchtest du noch etwas Kuchen?; **a few more glasses** noch ein paar Gläser.

more *pronoun* **1** mehr; **he eats more than me** er isst mehr als ich; **no more, thank you** ich will nichts mehr, danke; **2** (*of something you have already*) noch; **we need three more** wir brauchen noch drei; **any more?** noch etwas?; **3 more and more** immer mehr; **it takes more and more time** es beansprucht immer mehr Zeit; **4 more or less** mehr oder weniger; **it's more or less finished** es ist mehr oder weniger fertig.

morning *noun* **1** Morgen *der* (PL die Morgen); **in the morning** am Morgen; **this morning** heute Morgen; **tomorrow morning** morgen früh; **yesterday morning** gestern Morgen; **on Friday morning** am Freitagmorgen; **2 in the morning** (*regularly*) morgens; **she doesn't work in the morning** sie arbeitet morgens nicht; **on Friday mornings** freitagmorgens; **at six o'clock in the morning** um sechs Uhr morgens; **3** (*as opposed to afternoon*) Vormittag *der* (PL die Vormittage); **I spent the whole morning waiting for him** ich habe den ganzen Vormittag auf ihn gewartet.

Moscow *noun* Moskau *das*.

Moslem *noun* Moslem *der* (PL die Moslems), Moslemin *die* (PL die Moslems), Moslemin *die* (PL die Mosleminnen).

mosque *noun* Moschee *die* (PL die Moscheen).

mosquito *noun* Mücke *die* (PL die Mücken); **mosquito bite** *der* Mückenstich.

most *adjective, pronoun* **1** (*followed by a plural noun*) die meisten; **most children like chocolate** die meisten Kinder mögen Schokolade; **most of my friends** die meisten meiner Freunde; **2** (*followed by a singular noun*) der meiste/die meiste/das meiste; **they've eaten most of the ice-cream** sie haben das meiste Eis gegessen; **3 the most** (*followed by a noun or a verb*) am meisten; **I've got the most time** ich habe am meisten Zeit; **4 most of the time** die meiste Zeit; **most of them** die meisten.

most *adverb* **1** (*followed by an adjective*) (*in German the ending '-(e)st' is added to the adjective to show the superlative*) the most **interesting film** der interessanteste Film; **the most exciting story** die spannendste Geschichte; **the most boring book** das langweiligste Buch; **2** am meisten; **the noise bothers me most** der Lärm stört mich am meisten; **3** (*very*) höchst; **it's most**

unlikely es ist höchst unwahrscheinlich.

moth noun **1** Nachtfalter der (PL die Nachtfalter); **2** (clothes moth) Motte die (PL die Motten).

mother noun Mutter die (PL die Mütter); **Kate's mother** Kates Mutter.

mother-in-law noun Schwiegermutter die (PL die Schwiegermütter).

Mother's Day noun Muttertag der (PL die Muttertage).

motivation noun Motivation die.

motor noun Motor der (PL die Motoren).

motorbike noun Motorrad das (PL die Motorräder).

motorcyclist noun Motorradfahrer der (PL die Motorradfahrer), Motorradfahrerin die (PL die Motorradfahrerinnen).

motorist noun Autofahrer der (PL die Autofahrer), Autofahrerin die (PL die Autofahrerinnen).

motor racing noun Autorennsport der.

motorway noun Autobahn die (PL die Autobahnen).

mouldy adjective schimmelig.

mountain noun Berg der (PL die Berge); **in the mountains** in den Bergen.

mountain bike noun Mountainbike das (PL die Mountainbikes).

mountaineer noun Bergsteiger der (PL die Bergsteiger), Bergsteigerin die (PL die Bergsteigerinnen).

mountaineering noun Bergsteigen das; **to go mountaineering** Bergsteigen gehen.

mountainous adjective gebirgig.

mouse noun Maus die (PL die Mäuse) (also for a computer).

mousse noun Mousse die (PL die Mousses).

moustache noun Schnurrbart der (PL die Schnurrbärte).

mouth noun **1** (of a person) Mund der (PL die Münder); **2** (of an animal) Maul das (PL die Mäuler); **3** (of a river) Mündung der (PL die Mündungen).

mouthful noun (food) Bissen der (PL die Bissen) (informal).

mouth organ noun Mundharmonika die (PL die Mundharmonikas); **to play the mouth organ** Mundharmonika spielen.

move noun **1** (to a different house) Umzug der (PL die Umzüge); **2** (in a game) Zug der (PL die Züge); **your move!** du bist am Zug!

move verb **1** sich bewegen; **she didn't move** sie hat sich nicht bewegt; **2 to move up** vorrücken SEP (PERF sein); **move up a bit** rücken Sie etwas vor; **3** wegnehmen✧ SEP; **can you move your bag, please?** können Sie Ihre Handtasche bitte wegnehmen?; **4 to move something somewhere else** etwas woanders hin stellen; **I've moved the chest into the cellar** ich habe die Truhe in den Keller gestellt; **5** (car) fahren✧ (PERF sein); **6** (traffic) vorwärtskommen✧ SEP (PERF sein);

a
b
c
d
e
f
g
h
i
j
k
l
m
n
o
p
q
r
s
t
u
v
w
x
y
z

7 (*driver*) wegfahren ◇ SEP; **could you move your car, please?** würden Sie bitte Ihr Auto wegfahren?; **8 to move forward** (*person*) vorrücken SEP (PERF *sein*) (*vehicle*) vorwärts fahren ◇ SEP (PERF *sein*); **9** (*move house*) umziehen ◇ SEP (PERF *sein*); **we're moving on Tuesday** wir ziehen am Dienstag um; **they've moved to London** sie sind nach London umgezogen.

● **to move away** wegziehen SEP (PERF *sein*).

● **to move in** einziehen SEP (PERF *sein*); **she's moving in with friends** sie zieht bei Freunden ein.

● **to move out** ausziehen SEP (PERF *sein*); **we're moving out next week** wir ziehen nächste Woche aus.

movement *noun* Bewegung die (PL die Bewegungen).

movie *noun* Film der (PL die Filme); **to go to the movies** ins Kino gehen.

moving *adjective* **1** fahrend; **a moving car** ein fahrendes Auto; **2** (*emotionally*) ergreifend.

mow *verb* mähen.

mower *noun* Rasenmäher der (PL die Rasenmäher).

MP *noun* Abgeordnete der/die (PL die Abgeordneten).

Mr *noun* Herr der; (*in an address*) **Mr Angus Brown** Herrn Angus Brown; (*in a letter*) **Dear Mr Brown** Sehr geehrter Herr Brown.

Mrs *noun* Frau die; **Mrs Mary Hendry** Frau Mary Hendry; (*in a letter*) **Dear Mrs Hendry** Sehr geehrte Frau Hendry.

Ms *noun* Frau die (there is no direct equivalent to 'Ms' in German, but 'Frau' may be used whether the woman is married or not).

much *adjective, adverb, pronoun* **1** viel; **she doesn't eat much for breakfast** sie isst nicht viel zum Frühstück; **much more** viel mehr; **much quicker** viel schneller; **we don't have much time** wir haben nicht viel Zeit; **2 not much** nicht viel; **'do you have a lot of work?'** – **'no, not much'** 'hast du viel Arbeit?' – ' 'nein, nicht viel'; **3 so much** so viel; **I have so much to do** ich habe so viel zu tun; **you shouldn't have given me so much** du hättest mir nicht so viel geben sollen; **4 as much as** so viel; **take as much as you like** nimm so viel du willst; **5 too much** zu viel; **she gets too much money from her parents** sie bekommt zu viel Geld von ihren Eltern; **that's far too much** das ist viel zu viel; **6 how much?** wie viel?; **how much is it?** wie viel kostet es?; **how much do you want?** wie viel möchten Sie?; **how much money do you need?** wie viel Geld brauchst du?; **7** (*greatly*) sehr; **he loved her very much** er hat sie sehr geliebt; **so much** zu sehr; **so much** (so) sehr; **we liked it so much** es hat uns sehr gefallen; **8** (*often*) **I don't watch television much** ich sehe nicht oft fern; **we don't go out much** wir gehen nicht oft aus; **9 thank you very much** vielen Dank.

mud *noun* Schlamm der.

muddle noun **1** Durcheinander das; **2 to be in a muddle** durcheinander sein.

mug noun Becher der (PL die Becher); **a mug of milk** ein Becher Milch.

mug verb **to mug somebody** jemanden überfallen✧; **to be mugged** überfallen werden.

mugging noun Straßenraub der.

multiplication noun Multiplikation die.

multiply verb multiplizieren; **six multiplied by four** sechs multipliziert mit vier.

mum, mummy noun Mutti die (PL die Muttis); **Tom's mum** Toms Mutti; **I'll ask my mum** ich frage Mutti.

mumps noun Mumps der.

Munich noun München das.

murder noun Mord der (PL die Morde).

murder verb ermorden.

murderer noun Mörder der (PL die Mörder), Mörderin die (PL die Mörderinnen).

muscle noun Muskel der (PL die Muskeln).

muscular adjective muskulös.

museum noun Museum das (PL die Museen); **to go to the museum** ins Museum gehen.

mushroom noun Pilz der (PL die Pilze), Champignon der (PL die Champignons); **mushroom salad** der Champignonsalat.

music noun Musik die; **pop music** die Popmusik; **classical music** die klassische Musik.

musical noun Musical das (PL die Musicals).

musical adjective **1** musical instrument das Musikinstrument; **2 they're a very musical family** sie sind eine sehr musikalische Familie.

musician noun Musiker der (PL die Musiker), Musikerin die (PL die Musikerinnen).

Muslim noun Muslem der (PL die Muslim), Muslimin die (PL die Musliminnen).

mussel noun Muschel die (PL die Muscheln).

must verb **1** müssen✧; **we must leave now** wir müssen jetzt gehen; **you must learn the vocabulary** du musst die Vokabeln lernen; **2** (with a negative) **you mustn't do that** das darfst du nicht tun; **3** (expressing probability) müssen✧; **you must be tired** ihr müsst müde sein; **it must be five o'clock** es muss fünf Uhr sein; **he must have forgotten** er muss es vergessen haben.

mustard noun Senf der (PL die Senfe).

mutter verb murmeln.

my adjective **1** (before a masculine noun) mein; **my brother** mein Bruder; **they don't like my dog** sie mögen meinen Hund nicht; **2** (before a feminine noun) meine; **my sister** meine Schwester; **3** (before a neuter noun) mein; **that's my new car** das ist mein neues Auto; **we can go in my car** wir können mit meinem Auto fahren; **4** (before masculine/feminine/neuter plural nouns)

meine; **my children** meine Kinder;
5 (*with parts of the body*) der/die/
das; **I had a glass in my hand** ich
hatte ein Glas in der Hand; **I'm
washing my hands** ich wasche mir
die Hände.

myself *pronoun* **1** (*reflexive and
after a preposition taking the
accusative*) mich; **I've cut myself**
ich habe mich geschnitten; **I've
addressed the letter to myself** ich
habe den Brief an mich adressiert;
2 (*reflexive and after a preposition
taking the dative*) mir; **I've hurt
myself** ich habe mir wehgetan; **I
said to myself** ich habe mir gesagt;
3 (*stressing something*) selbst; **I
said it myself** ich habe es selbst
gesagt; **4 by myself** allein.

mysterious *adjective* rätselhaft.

mystery *noun* **1** Rätsel das (PL die
Rätsel); **2** (*book*) Krimi der (PL die
Krimis) (*informal*).

myth *noun* Mythos der (PL die
Mythen).

mythology *noun* Mythologie die
(PL die Mythologien).

Nn

nail *noun* (*on your finger or toe, also
metal*) Nagel der (PL die Nägel).

nail *verb* nageln.

nailbrush *noun* Nagelbürste die
(PL die Nagelbürsten).

nailfile *noun* Nagelfeile die (PL die
Nagelfeilen).

nail polish *noun* Nagellack der.

nail polish remover *noun*
Nagellackentferner der.

naked *adjective* nackt.

name *noun* **1** Name der (PL die
Namen); **I've forgotten her name**
ich habe ihren Namen vergessen;
what's your name? wie heißt du?;
my name's Joy ich heiße Joy; **2** (*of
a book or film*) Titel der (PL die Titel).

napkin *noun* Serviette die (PL die
Servietten).

nappy *noun* Windel die (PL die
Windeln).

narrow *adjective* schmal; **a narrow
street** eine schmale Straße.

nasty *adjective* **1** (*mean*) gemein;
that was a nasty thing to do das
war gemein; **2** (*unpleasant, bad*)
scheußlich; **that's a nasty job** das
ist eine scheußliche Arbeit; **a nasty
smell** ein scheußlicher Geruch.

nation *noun* Nation die (PL die
Nationen).

national *adjective* national.

national anthem *noun*
Nationalhymne die (PL die
Nationalhymnen).

nationality *noun* Nationalität die
(PL die Nationalitäten).

national park *noun*
Nationalpark der (PL die
Nationalparks).

natural *adjective* natürlich.

naturally *adverb* natürlich.

nature *noun* Natur die.

nature reserve *noun*
Naturschutzgebiet das (PL die
Naturschutzgebiete).

naughty *adjective* unartig.

navy *noun* Marine die; **my uncle's
in the navy** mein Onkel ist bei der
Marine.

navy-blue *adjective* marineblau.

near *adjective* **1** nah(e); **2** (*the superlative of nah(e) is der/die/das nächste*) **the nearest park** der nächste Park; **the nearest bank** die nächste Bank; **the nearest shop** das nächste Geschäft.

near *preposition* nahe an (+ DAT); **near (to) the station** nahe am Bahnhof.

near *adverb* **1** nah(e) (*in spoken German 'nah' is more common*); **they live quite near** sie wohnen ganz nah; **2 to come nearer** näher kommen.

nearby *adverb* nahe gelegen; **there's a park nearby** hier in der Nähe ist ein Park.

nearly *adverb* fast; **nearly empty** fast leer.

neat *adjective* **1** (*well organized, tidy*) ordentlich; **a neat room** ein ordentliches Zimmer; **2** adrett (*clothes or the way you look*).

necessarily *adverb* not necessarily nicht unbedingt.

necessary *adjective* nötig; **if necessary** falls nötig.

neck *noun* **1** (*of a person*) Hals *der* (PL die Hälse); **2** (*of a garment*) Kragen *der* (PL die Kragen).

necklace *noun* Halskette die (PL die Halsketten).

need *noun* **there's no need, I've already done it** das ist nicht nötig, ich habe es schon gemacht; **there's no need to wait** du brauchst nicht zu warten.

need *verb* **1** brauchen; **we need bread** wir brauchen Brot; **everything you need** alles, was

man braucht; **2** (*to have to*) müssen ◊; **I need to go to the bank** ich muss zur Bank gehen; **3** (*with a negative*) **you needn't wait** du brauchst nicht zu warten.

needle *noun* Nadel die (PL die Nadeln).

negative *noun* (*of a photo*) Negativ das (PL die Negative).

neglected *adjective* vernachlässigt.

neighbour *noun* Nachbar der (PL die Nachbarn), Nachbarin die (PL die Nachbarinnen); **we're going round to the neighbours'** wir besuchen die Nachbarn.

neighbourhood *noun* Nachbarschaft die; **in our neighbourhood** in unserer Nachbarschaft.

neither *conjunction* **1 neither ... nor** weder ... noch; **I have neither the time nor the money** ich habe weder die Zeit noch das Geld; **2 neither do I** ich auch nicht; **'I don't like fish'** – **'neither do I'** 'ich mag keinen Fisch' – 'ich auch nicht'; **'I didn't like the film'** – **'neither did Kirsty'** 'mir hat der Film nicht gefallen' – 'Kirsty hat er auch nicht gefallen'.

neither *pronoun* keiner von beiden/keine von beiden/keins von beiden; **'which do you like?'** – **'neither'** 'welches gefällt dir?' – 'keins von beiden'.

nephew *noun* Neffe der (PL die Neffen).

nerve *noun* **1** Nerv der (PL die Nerven); **2 to lose your nerve** die Nerven verlieren; **you've got a nerve!** du hast Nerven! (*informal*);

a
b
c
d
e
f
g
h
i
j
k
l
m
n
o
p
q
r
s
t
u
v
w
x
y
z

a

b
3 **what a nerve!** so eine Frechheit!
★ **he gets on my nerves** er geht
mir auf die Nerven (*informal*).

c **nervous** *adjective* 1 (*afraid*)
ängstlich; **to feel nervous about**
something Angst vor etwas (DAT)

d haben; 2 (*highly strung*) nervös
(*person*).

e **nest** *noun* Nest das (PL die Nester).

f **net** *noun* Netz das (PL die Netze).

g **Netherlands** *noun* Niederlande
(*plural*); **in the Netherlands** in den
Niederlanden.

h **nettle** *noun* Nessel die (PL die
Nesseln).

i

j **network** *noun* Netzwerk das (PL die
Netzwerke).

k **neutral** *noun* (*neutral gear*)
Leerlauf der; **to be in neutral** im
Leerlauf sein.

l
neutral *adjective* neutral.

m **never** *adverb* 1 nie; **Ben never**
smokes Ben raucht nie; **I've never**

n **told him** ich habe es ihm nie gesagt;
never again nie wieder; 2 noch nie;

o **'have you ever been to Spain?'** –
'no, never' 'warst du schon mal in
Spanien?' – 'nein, noch nie';

p 3 **never mind** macht nichts.

q **new** *adjective* neu; **have you seen**
their new house? hast du ihr
neues Haus gesehen?

r

s **news** *noun* 1 (*new information*)
Nachricht die (PL die Nachrichten);
I've got good news ich habe gute

t Nachrichten; 2 **a piece of news**
eine Neuigkeit; **any news?** was

u gibt es Neues?; 3 (*on TV or the*
radio) Nachrichten (*plural*); **we**

v **saw it on the news** wir haben es in

w den Nachrichten gesehen.

x

y

z

newsagent *noun*
Zeitungshändler der (PL die
Zeitungshändler).

newspaper *noun* Zeitung die (PL
die Zeitungen).

newsreader *noun*
Nachrichtensprecher der (PL die
Nachrichtensprecher),
Nachrichtensprecherin die (PL die
Nachrichtensprecherinnen).

New Year *noun* Neujahr das;
Happy New Year! ein gutes neues
Jahr!

New Year's Day *noun* Neujahr
das.

New Year's Eve *noun* Silvester
der.

New Zealand *noun* Neuseeland
das.

next *adjective* 1 nächster/nächste/
nächstes; **the next train leaves at**
ten der nächste Zug fährt um zehn
ab; **next week** nächste Woche;
next Thursday nächsten Donnerstag;
next year nächstes Jahr; **next time**
I see you nächstes Mal, wenn ich
dich sehe; 2 (*following*) **next**
please! der Nächste bitte/die
Nächste bitte; **the next thing** das
Nächste; **the next day** am
nächsten Tag; **the letter arrived**
the next day der Brief kam am
nächsten Tag an; 3 **the week after**
next übernächste Woche; 4 (*next-*
door) nebenan; **I'm in the next**
room ich bin nebenan.

next *adverb* 1 (*afterwards*) danach;
what did he say next? was hat er
danach gesagt?; 2 (*now*) als
Nächstes; **what shall we do next?**
was machen wir als Nächstes?;
3 **next to** neben (+ DAT, *or* + ACC *with*

movement towards a place); **the house next to the baker's** das Haus neben dem Bäcker; **I sat down next to her** ich habe mich neben sie gesetzt.

next door *adverb* neben*an*; **they live next door** sie wohnen nebenan; **the girl next door** das Mädchen von nebenan.

nice *adjective* **1** *(pleasant)* schön; **we had a nice evening** wir haben einen schönen Abend verbracht; **Brighton's a nice town** Brighton ist eine schöne Stadt; **we had nice weather** wir hatten schönes Wetter; **2 to have a nice time** sich amüsieren; **have a nice day!** viel Spaß!; **3** *(attractive to look at)* hübsch; **that's a nice dress** das ist ein hübsches Kleid; **4** *(kind, friendly)* nett *(person)*; **she's really nice** sie ist wirklich nett; **5 to be nice to somebody** nett zu jemandem sein; **she's been very nice to me** sie war sehr nett zu mir; **6** *(tasting good)* gut, **it tastes nice** es schmeckt gut.

nickname *noun* Spitzname *der* (PL die Spitznamen).

niece *noun* Nichte *die* (PL die Nichten).

night *noun* **1** *(after bedtime)* Nacht *die* (PL die Nächte); **during the night** während der Nacht; **Sunday night** Sonntag Nacht; **it's cold at night** nachts ist es kalt; **to stay the night** über Nacht bleiben, **I stayed the night at Emma's** ich habe bei Emma übernachtet; **2** *(before you go to bed)* Abend *der* (PL die Abende); **what are you doing tonight?** was macht ihr heute Abend?; **one night**

eines Abends; **tomorrow night** morgen Abend; **I met Greg last night** ich habe Greg gestern Abend getroffen; **on Friday night** am Freitagabend; **see you tonight!** bis heute Abend!

night club *noun* Nachtklub *der* (PL die Nachtklubs).

nightie *noun* Nachthemd *das* (PL die Nachthemden).

nightmare *noun* Albtraum *der* (PL die Albträume).

nil *noun* *(in sport)* null; **they won four-nil** sie haben vier zu null gewonnen.

nine *number* neun.

nineteen *number* neunzehn.

ninety *number* neunzig.

ninth *number* neunte/neunte/neuntes; **on the ninth floor** im neunten Stock; **on the ninth of June** am neunten Juni.

no *adverb* nein; **I said no** ich habe nein gesagt; **no thank you** nein danke.

no *adjective* **1** kein; **we've got no bread** wir haben kein Brot; **no problem!** kein Problem!; **2** *(on a notice)* **'no smoking'** 'Rauchen verboten'; **'no parking'** 'Parken verboten'.

nobody *pronoun* niemand; **'who's there?' - 'nobody'** 'wer ist da?' - 'niemand'; **there's nobody in the kitchen** es ist niemand in der Küche; **nobody was at home** niemand war zu Hause.

nod *verb* nicken; **he nodded in agreement** er hat zustimmend genickt.

noise *noun* Lärm *der*; **to make a noise** Lärm machen.

noise pollution noun
Lärmbelästigung die

noisy adjective laut.

none pronoun 1 (not one) keiner/
keine/keins; **none of us** keiner von
uns/ keine von uns; **'how many
students failed the exam?' –
'none'** 'wie viele Schüler sind
durch die Prüfung gefallen?' –
'keine'; **none of the boys knows
him** keiner der Jungen kennt ihn;
2 there's none left es ist nichts
mehr übrig.

nonsense noun Unsinn der; **to
talk nonsense** Unsinn reden;
nonsense! Unsinn!

non-smoker noun Nichtraucher
der (PL die Nichtraucher
Nichtraucherin die (PL die
Nichtraucherinnen).

non-stop adjective durchgehend
(train), Nonstop- (flight).

non-stop adverb ununterbrochen;
she talks non-stop sie redet
ununterbrochen.

noodles plural noun Nudeln die
(plural).

noon noun Mittag der; **at (twelve)
noon** um zwölf (Uhr mittags).

no-one pronoun niemand; **'who's
there?' – 'no-one'** 'wer ist da?' –
'niemand'; **there's no-one in the
kitchen** es ist niemand in der
Küche; **no-one was at home**
niemand war zu Hause.

nor conjunction 1 **neither ...nor**
weder ...noch; **I have neither the
time nor the money** ich habe
weder die Zeit noch das Geld; **2 nor
do I** ich auch nicht; **'I don't like
fish' – 'nor do I'** 'ich mag keinen

Fisch' - 'ich auch nicht'; **nor do we**
wir auch nicht.

normal adjective normal.

normally adverb 1 (usually)
normalerweise; **2** (in a normal
way) normal.

north noun Norden der; **in the
north** im Norden.

north adjective nördlich, Nord-; **the
north side** die Nordseite; **north
wind** der Nordwind.

north adverb 1 (towards the north)
nach Norden; **to travel north** nach
Norden fahren; **2 north of London**
nördlich von London.

North America noun
Nordamerika das.

North American noun
Nordamerikaner der (PL die
Nordamerikaner),
Nordamerikanerin die (PL die
Nordamerikanerinnen).

North American adjective
nordamerikanisch.

northeast noun Nordosten der.

northeast adjective in northeast
England in Nordostengland.

Northern Ireland noun
Nordirland das.

North Pole noun Nordpol der.

North Sea noun **the North Sea**
die Nordsee.

northwest noun Nordwesten der.

northwest adjective in northwest
England in Nordwestengland.

Norway noun Norwegen das.

Norwegian noun 1 (person)
Norweger der (PL die Norweger),
Norwegerin die (PL die
Norwegerinnen); **2** (language)
Norwegisch das.

Norwegian *adjective* norwegisch.

nose *noun* Nase die (PL die Nasen);
to blow your nose sich (DAT) die
Nase putzen.

not *adverb* **1** nicht; **not on Sundays**
sonntags nicht; **not all alone!** nicht
ganz allein!; **not bad** nicht
schlecht; **not at all** überhaupt
nicht; **not yet** noch nicht; **Sam
didn't phone** Sam hat nicht
angerufen; **I hope not** hoffentlich
nicht; **2 not a** kein/keine; **he's not
a specialist** er ist kein Fachmann;
not a bit kein bisschen.

note *noun* **1** (*a short letter*) Zettel
der (PL die Zettel), (*informal*) Brief
der (PL die Briefe); **2** (*in a class*)
Notiz die (PL die Notizen); **to take
notes** sich (DAT) Notizen machen;
3 (*a banknote*) Schein der (PL die
Scheine); **a ten-pound note** ein
Zehnpfundschein; **4** (*in music*)
Note die (PL die Noten).

notebook *noun* Notizbuch das (PL
die Notizbücher).

notepad *noun* Notizblock der (PL
die Notizblöcke).

nothing *pronoun* nichts; **'what did
you say?' – 'nothing'** 'was hast du
gesagt?' – 'nichts'; **nothing special**
nichts Besonderes; **nothing new**
nichts Neues; **I saw nothing** ich
habe nichts gesehen; **there's
nothing left** es ist nichts mehr
übrig.

notice *noun* **1** (*a sign*) Schild das
(PL die Schilder); **2** (*an
advertisement*) Anzeige die (PL die
Anzeigen); **3** (*advance warning*)
Ankündigung die; **don't take any
notice of her** nimm keine Notiz

von ihr; **5 at short notice**
kurzfristig.

notice *verb* bemerken; **I didn't
notice anything** ich habe nichts
bemerkt.

notice board *noun*
Anschlagbrett das (PL die
Anschlagbretter).

nought *noun* Null die (PL die
Nullen).

noun *noun* Substantiv das (PL die
Substantive).

novel *noun* Roman der (PL die
Romane).

novelist *noun* Romanautor der (PL
die Romanautoren), Romanautorin
die (PL die Romanautorinnen).

November *noun* November der; **in
November** im November.

now *adverb* **1** jetzt; **where is he
now?** wo ist er jetzt?; **from now on**
von jetzt an; **2 he left just now** er
ist gerade eben gegangen; **I saw
her just now in the corridor** ich
habe sie gerade eben im Gang
gesehen; **3 do it right now!** mach es
sofort!; **4 now and then** hin und
wieder.

nowadays *adverb* heutzutage;
nowadays they are quite common
heutzutage sind sie ziemlich
häufig.

nowhere *adjective* nirgends;
there's nowhere to park man kann
nirgends parken.

nuclear *adjective* Kern-; **nuclear
power** die Kernenergie; **nuclear
power station** das Kernkraftwerk.

nude *noun* **in the nude** nackt.

nude *adjective* nackt.

a
b
c
d
e
f
g
h
i
j
k
l
m
n
o
p
q
r
s
t
u
v
w
x
y
z

nuisance *noun* it's a nuisance das ist ärgerlich; **what a nuisance!** wie ärgerlich!

numb *adjective* **1** (*with cold*) gefühllos; **2** (*emotionally*) benommen.

number plate *noun* Nummernschild das (PL die Nummernschilder).

number *noun* **1** (*of a house, telephone, or account*) Nummer die (PL die Nummern); **I live at number five** ich wohne in der Nummer fünf; **my new phone number** meine neue Telefonnummer; **2** (*a written figure*) Zahl die (PL die Zahlen); **3** (*amount*) Anzahl die; **the number of visitors** die Anzahl der Besucher.

nun *noun* Nonne die (PL die Nonnen).

nurse *noun* **1** (*female*) Krankenschwester die (PL die Krankenschwestern); **Janet's a nurse** Janet ist Krankenschwester; **2** (*male*) Krankenpfleger der (PL die Krankenpfleger).

nursery *noun* **1** (*for children*) Kindertagesstätte die (PL die Kindertagesstätten); **2** (*for plants*) Gärtnerei die (PL die Gärtnereien).

nursery school *noun* Kindergarten der (PL die Kindergärten).

nut *noun* **1** Nuss die (PL die Nüsse); **2** (*for a bolt*) Mutter die (PL die Muttern).

nylon *noun* Nylon das.

Oo

oak *noun* Eiche die (PL die Eichen).

oar *noun* Ruder das (PL die Ruder).

oats *noun* Hafer der; **porridge oats** Haferflocken (*plural*).

obedient *adjective* gehorsam.

obey *verb* **1** gehorchen (+ DAT); **to obey somebody** jemandem gehorchen; **2** to obey the rules sich an die Vorschriften halten❖.

object *noun* **1** (*thing*) Gegenstand der (PL die Gegenstände); **2** (*aim*) Zweck der; **3** (*in grammar*) Objekt das (PL die Objekte).

object *verb* etwas dagegen haben❖; **if you don't object** wenn Sie nichts dagegen haben.

objection *noun* Einwand der (PL die Einwände).

oboe *noun* Oboe die (PL die Oboen); **to play the oboe** Oboe spielen.

obscene *adjective* obszön.

observe *verb* beobachten.

obsessed *adjective* besessen; **she's really obsessed with her diet** sie ist von ihrer Schlankheitskur ganz besessen.

obstacle *noun* Hindernis das (PL die Hindernisse).

obstinate *adjective* starrsinnig.

obtain *verb* erhalten❖.

obvious *adjective* eindeutig.

obviously *adverb* **1** (*of course*) natürlich; **2** (*looking at something*) offensichtlich; **the house is obviously empty** das Haus steht offensichtlich leer.

occasion *noun* Gelegenheit die (PL die Gelegenheiten); **on special**

a

occasions zu besonderen Gelegenheiten.

occasionally *adverb* gelegentlich.

occupation *noun* Beruf der (PL die Berufe).

occupied *adjective* **1** (*taken*) besetzt; **the seat is occupied** der Platz ist besetzt; **2** (*lived in*) bewohnt.

occur *verb* **1 to occur to somebody** jemandem einfallen✧ SEP (PERF *sein*); **it occurs to me that** ... mir fällt ein, dass ...; **2 it never occurred to me** darauf wäre ich nie gekommen; **3** (*happen*) sich ereignen.

ocean *noun* Ozean der (PL die Ozeane).

o'clock *adverb* **at ten o'clock** um zehn Uhr; **it's three o'clock** es ist drei Uhr.

October *noun* Oktober der; **in October** im Oktober.

octopus *noun* Tintenfisch der (PL die Tintenfische).

odd *adjective* **1** (*strange*) komisch; **that's odd, I'm sure I heard the bell** das ist komisch, ich habe es bestimmt klingeln gehört; **2** (*number*) ungerade; **three is an odd number** drei ist eine ungerade Zahl; **3 the odd one out** die Ausnahme.

odds and ends *plural noun* Kleinkram der.

of *preposition* **1** von (+ DAT); (*instead of translating 'of' with 'von', the genitive case can be used*) **the parents of the children** die Eltern von den Kindern, die Eltern der Kinder; **the name of the flower** der

Name der Blume; **it's very kind of you** das ist sehr nett von Ihnen; **2** (*with quantities 'of' is not translated*) **a kilo of tomatoes** ein Kilo Tomaten; **a bottle of milk** eine Flasche Milch; **the three of us** wir drei; **3 of it/them** davon (*things*); **of them** von ihnen (*people*); **how many of them didn't pay?** wie viele von ihnen haben nicht gezahlt?; **Ray has four cars but he's selling three of them** Ray hat vier Autos, aber er verkauft drei davon; **half of it** die Hälfte davon; **we ate a lot of it** wir haben viel davon gegessen; **4 the sixth of June** der sechste Juni; **5 made of** aus; **a bracelet made of silver** ein Armband aus Silber.

off *adverb, adjective, preposition* **1** (*switched off*) aus; **is the telly off?** ist der Fernseher aus?; **to turn off the lights** das Licht ausmachen SEP; **2** (*electricity, water, gas*) abgestellt; **the gas and electricity were off** Gas und Strom waren abgestellt; **to turn off the tap** den Wasserhahn zudrehen SEP; **3 to be off** (*to leave*) gehen✧ (PERF *sein*), (*in a vehicle*) fahren✧ (PERF *sein*); **I must be off** ich muss gehen; **4 on my day off** an meinem freien Tag; **to take three days off work** sich (DAT) drei Tage frei nehmen; **we were given two days of school** wir hatten zwei Tage schulfrei; **to be off sick** wegen Krankheit fehlen; **Maya's off school today** Maya fehlt heute in der Schule; **5** (*cancelled*) abgesagt; **the match is off** das Spiel ist abgesagt worden; **6 '20% off shoes'** 'Schuhe 20% reduziert'.

b
c
d
e
f
g
h
i
j
k
l
m
n
o
p
q
r
s
t
u
v
w
x
y
z

offence noun 1 (crime) Straftat die (PL die Straftaten); **2 to take offence** beleidigt sein; **he takes offence easily** er ist schnell beleidigt.

offer noun 1 Angebot das (PL die Angebote); **job offer** das Stellenangebot; **2 on special offer** im Sonderangebot.

offer verb anbieten ◇ SEP (a present, a reward, or a job); **he offered her a chair** er bot ihr einen Stuhl an; **to offer to do something** anbieten, etwas zu tun; **he offered to drive me to the station** er hat angeboten, mich zum Bahnhof zu fahren.

office noun Büro das (PL die Büros); **he's still at the office** er ist noch im Büro.

office block noun Bürohaus das (PL die Bürohäuser).

officer noun Offizier der (PL die Offiziere).

official adjective offiziell.

off-licence noun Wein- und Spirituosenhandlung die (PL die Wein- und Spirituosenhandlungen).

often adverb 1 oft; **he's often late** er kommt oft zu spät; **how often?** wie oft?; **2 more often** öfter; **couldn't you come more often?** könntest du nicht öfter kommen?

oil noun 1 (crude oil) Öl das; **2 olive oil** das Olivenöl; **suntan oil** das Sonnenöl.

oil slick noun Ölteppich der (PL die Ölteppiche).

ointment noun Salbe die (PL die Salben).

okay adjective 1 okay (informal); **tomorrow at ten, okay?** morgen

um zehn, okay?; **is it okay if I don't come till Friday?** ist es okay, wenn ich erst Freitag komme?; **2** (person) in Ordnung; **Daisy's okay** Daisy ist in Ordnung; **3** (nothing special, not ill) ganz gut; **the film was okay** der Film war ganz gut; **I've been ill but I'm okay now** ich war krank, aber jetzt geht es mir ganz gut; **'how are you?' – 'okay'** 'wie geht's?' – 'ganz gut'; **4 it's okay by me** mir ist es recht.

old adjective 1 (not young, not new, previous) alt; **an old man** ein alter Mann; **an old lady** eine alte Dame; **an old tree** ein alter Baum; **old people** alte Leute; **bring some old clothes** bring ein paar alte Sachen mit; **I've only got their old address** ich habe nur ihre alte Adresse; **2** (talking about age) **how old are you?** wie alt bist du?; **James is ten years old** James ist zehn Jahre alt; **3 a two-year-old child** ein zweijähriges Kind; **4 my older sister** meine ältere Schwester; **she's older than me** sie ist älter als ich; **he's a year older than me** er ist ein Jahr älter als ich.

old age noun Alter das.

old age pensioner noun Rentner der (PL die Rentner), Rentnerin die (PL die Rentnerinnen).

old-fashioned noun altmodisch.

olive noun Olive die (PL die Oliven).

olive oil noun Olivenöl das (PL die Olivenöle).

Olympic Games, Olympics plural noun Olympische Spiele (plural).

omelette noun Omelett das (PL die Omelette); **a cheese omelette** ein Käseomelett.

on preposition **1** auf (+ DAT, or + ACC with movement towards a place); **it's on the desk** es ist auf dem Schreibtisch; **2** (attached to) an (+ DAT, or + ACC with movement towards a place); **on the wall** an der Wand; **3 on the beach** am Strand; **on the right/left** rechts/links; **4** (in expressions of time) **on March 21st** am 21. März; **he's arriving on Tuesday** er kommt am Dienstag an; **it's shut on Sundays** es ist sonntags geschlossen; **on rainy days** an Regentagen; **5** (for buses, trains, etc.) **to go on the bus** mit dem Bus fahren; **I met Jackie on the train** ich habe Jackie im Zug getroffen; **let's go on our bikes** fahren wir mit dem Rad; **6 on TV** im Fernsehen; **on the radio** im Radio; **on video** auf Video; **7 on holiday** in den Ferien.

on adjective **1** (switched on) **to be on** an sein; **the lights are on** das Licht ist an; **is the radio on?** ist das Radio an?; **2** (happening) **what's on TV?** was gibts im Fernsehen?; **what's on this week at the cinema?** was läuft diese Woche im Kino?

once adverb **1** einmal; **I've tried once already** ich habe es schon einmal versucht; **try once more** versuch es noch einmal; **once a day** einmal täglich; **once upon a time** ... es war einmal ...; **2 more than once** mehrmals; **3 at once** (immediately) sofort; **the doctor came at once** der Arzt kam sofort;

4 at once (at the same time) gleichzeitig; **I can't do two things at once** ich kann nicht zwei Sachen gleichzeitig machen.

one number (when counting) eins, (with a noun) ein; **one son** ein Sohn; **one apple** ein Apfel; **if you want a biro I've got one** falls du einen Kugelschreiber brauchst, habe ich einen; **at one o'clock** um ein Uhr.

one pronoun **1** einer/eine/eins; **I saw the photos, can I have one of them?** ich habe die Fotos gesehen, kann ich eins davon haben?; **2 this one** dieser/diese/dieses; **I'd prefer that bike, but this one's cheaper** ich würde lieber das Rad haben, aber dieses ist billiger; **3 that one** der da/die da/das da; **'which video?' – 'that one'** welches Video?' – 'das da'; **4 which one?** welcher/welche/welches?; **'my foot's hurting' – 'which one?'** 'mir tut der Fuß weh' – 'welcher?'; **'she borrowed a skirt from me' – 'which one?'** 'sie hat sich einen Rock von mir geliehen' – 'welchen?'; **5** (you) man; **one never knows** man kann nie wissen.

one's adjective sein/seine/sein; **one pays for one's car** man zahlt für sein Auto.

oneself pronoun **1** (reflexive) sich; **to wash oneself** sich waschen; **2** (stressing something) selbst; **one has to do everything oneself** man muss alles selbst machen.

one-way street noun Einbahnstraße die (PL die Einbahnstraßen).

onion noun Zwiebel die (PL die Zwiebeln).

only adjective **1** einziger/einzige/einziges; **the only free seat** der einzige freie Platz; **the only thing you could do** das Einzige, was du machen könntest; **2 an only child** ein Einzelkind.

only adverb, conjunction **1** nur; **they've only got two bedrooms** sie haben nur zwei Schlafzimmer; **Anne's only free on Fridays** Anne hat nur freitags Zeit; **there are only three left** es sind nur noch drei übrig; **I'd walk, only it's raining** ich würde zu Fuß gehen, nur regnet es; **2** (very recently) gerade erst; **he's only just got the message** er hat die Nachricht gerade erst bekommen; **3** (barely) gerade noch; **we've only just made it on time** wir sind gerade noch rechtzeitig angekommen.

onto preposition auf (+ ACC).

open noun **in the open** im Freien.

open adjective **1** offen; **the door's open** die Tür ist offen; **the baker's is not open** die Bäckerei ist nicht geöffnet; **2 in the open air** im Freien.

open verb **1** aufmachen SEP; **can you open the door for me?** kannst du mir die Tür aufmachen?; **the bank opens at nine** die Bank macht um neun auf; **2** (open up) sich öffnen; **the door opened slowly** die Tür öffnete sich langsam.

opera noun Oper die (PL die Opern).

operate verb **1** (medically) operieren; **will they have to operate (on him/her)?** werden sie ihn/sie operieren müssen?; **2** bedienen (a machine).

operation noun **1** Operation die (PL die Operationen); **2 to have an operation** operiert werden.

opinion noun Meinung die (PL die Meinungen); **in my opinion** meiner Meinung nach.

opinion poll noun Meinungsumfrage die (PL die Meinungsumfragen).

opponent noun Gegner der (PL die Gegner), Gegnerin die (PL die Gegnerinnen).

opportunity noun Gelegenheit die (PL die Gelegenheiten); **to have the opportunity of doing something** die Gelegenheit haben, etwas zu tun.

opposite noun Gegenteil das (PL die Gegenteile); **no, quite the opposite** nein, ganz im Gegenteil.

opposite adjective **1** entgegengesetzt (direction); **she went off in the opposite direction** sie ging in die entgegengesetzte Richtung; **2** (facing) gegenüberliegend; **in the house opposite** im gegenüberliegenden Haus.

opposite adverb gegenüber; **they live opposite** sie wohnen gegenüber.

opposite preposition gegenüber (+ DAT); **opposite the station** gegenüber dem Bahnhof.

optician noun Optiker der (PL die Optiker), Optikerin die (PL die Optikerinnen).

optimistic *adjective*
zuversichtlich, optimistisch.

option *noun* Wahl *die*; **we have no
option** wir haben keine andere
Wahl.

optional *adjective* auf Wunsch
erhältlich; **optional subject** *das*
Wahlfach.

or *conjunction* **1** oder; **English or
German?** Englisch oder Deutsch?;
today or Tuesday? heute oder
Dienstag?; **2** (*in negatives*) noch; **I
don't have a cat or a dog** ich habe
weder eine Katze noch einen Hund;
not in June or July weder im Juni
noch im Juli; **3** (*or else*) sonst;
phone Mum, or she'll worry ruf
Mutti an, sonst macht sie sich
Sorgen.

oral *noun* (*an exam*) Mündliche *das*
(*informal*); **my German oral** meine
mündliche Deutschprüfung.

orange *noun* (*the fruit*) Orange *die*
(PL *die* Orangen); **orange juice** *der*
Orangensaft.

orange *adjective* orange ('*orange*'
never changes); **my orange socks**
meine orange Socken.

orchestra *noun* Orchester *das* (PL
die Orchester).

order *noun* **1** (*sequence*)
Reihenfolge *die* (PL *die*
Reihenfolgen); **in the right order** in
der richtigen Reihenfolge; **in the
wrong order** in der falschen
Reihenfolge; **in alphabetical order**
in alphabetischer Reihenfolge;
2 (*in a restaurant or a shop*)
Bestellung *die* (PL *die* Bestellungen);
3 'out of order' 'außer Betrieb';
4 in order to do something um
etwas zu tun.

order *verb* **1** (*in a restaurant or a
shop*) bestellen; **we ordered soup**
wir haben Suppe bestellt; **have you
ordered?** haben Sie schon
bestellt?; **2** bestellen (*a taxi*).

ordinary *adjective* normal.

organ *noun* **1** (*the instrument*)
Orgel *die* (PL *die* Orgeln); **2** (*of the
body*) Organ *das* (PL *die* Organe).

organic *adjective* Bio- (*food*);
organic food *die* Biokost.

organization *noun* Organisation
die (PL *die* Organisationen).

organize *verb* **1** organisieren;
2 veranstalten (*a conference or a
festival*).

orienteering *noun*
Orientierungslauf *der*

original *adjective* **1** ursprünglich;
the original plan was better der
ursprüngliche Plan war besser;
2 originell; **it's a really original
novel** das ist ein wirklich
origineller Roman.

originally *adverb* ursprünglich;
originally we wanted to go by car
ursprünglich wollten wir mit dem
Auto fahren.

orphan *noun* Waise *die* (PL *die*
Waisen); **he is an orphan** er ist
Waise.

ostrich *noun* Strauß *der* (PL *die*
Strauße).

other *adjective* **1** anderer/andere/
anderes; **we took the other road**
wir haben die andere Straße
genommen; **where are the others?**
wo sind die anderen?; **the other
two cars** die anderen beiden Autos;
2 give me the other one gib mir
den anderen/die andere/das
andere (*the translation of 'the other*

one' depends on the gender of the noun it refers to); **3 the other day** neulich; **4 every other week** jede zweite Woche; **5 somebody or other** irgendjemand; **something or other** irgendetwas; **somewhere or other** irgendwo; **6 any other questions?** sonst noch Fragen?

otherwise adverb, conjunction sonst.

ought verb ('ought' is usually translated by the subjunctive of 'sollen') **I ought to go** ich sollte eigentlich gehen; **they ought to have known the address** sie hätten die Adresse kennen sollen; **you oughtn't to have any problems** du solltest keine Probleme haben.

our adjective **1** (before a masculine noun) unser; **our father** unser Vater; **2** (before a feminine noun) unsere; **our mother** unsere Mutter; **3** (before a neuter noun) unser; **our house** unser Haus; **4** (before masculine/feminine/neuter plural nouns) unsere; **our parents** unsere Eltern; **5** (with parts of the body) der/die/das (plural: die) ; **we'll go and wash our hands** wir waschen uns die Hände.

ours pronoun **1** (for a masculine noun) unserer; **their garden's bigger than ours** ihr Garten ist größer als unserer; **2** (for a feminine noun) unsere; **their kitchen is smaller than ours** ihre Küche ist kleiner als unsere; **3** (for a neuter noun) unseres; **their child is younger than ours** ihr Kind ist jünger als unseres; **4** (for plural nouns) unsere; **they've invited**

their friends and we've invited **ours** sie haben ihre Freunde eingeladen und wir haben unsere eingeladen; **5 the green car is ours** das grüne Auto gehört uns; **it's ours** es gehört uns; **a friend of ours** ein Freund von uns.

ourselves pronoun **1** (reflexive) uns; **we introduced ourselves** wir haben uns vorgestellt; **2** (for emphasis) selbst; **in the end we did it ourselves** schließlich haben wir es selbst gemacht.

out adverb **1** (outside) draußen; **it's cold out there** es ist kalt da draußen; **they're out in the garden** sie sind draußen im Garten; **2 to go out** hinausgehen ⋄ SEP (PERF sein), rausgehen ⋄ SEP (PERF sein) (informal); **to go out shopping** einkaufen gehen; **3 get out!** raus! (informal); **4 the ball is out** der Ball ist aus; **5** (absent) **to be out** nicht da sein; **Mr Barnes is out** Herr Barnes ist nicht da; **6 to go out** (for an evening or to the theatre or cinema) ausgehen ⋄ SEP (PERF sein), weggehen ⋄ SEP (PERF sein) (informal); **are you going out this evening?** gehst du heute Abend weg?; **to be going out with somebody** mit jemandem gehen; **Alison's going out with Danny now** Alison geht jetzt mit Danny; **7 to ask somebody out** jemanden einladen ⋄ SEP; **he's asked me out** er hat mich eingeladen; **8** (light, fire) aus; **are all the lights out?** ist das Licht aus?

out preposition **out of** aus (+ DAT); **to go out of the room** aus dem Zimmer gehen; **he threw it out of**

the window er hat es aus dem Fenster geworfen; **to drink out of a glass** aus einem Glas trinken; **she took the photo out of her bag** sie hat das Foto aus der Tasche genommen.

outdoor adjective (activity or sport) im Freien; **outdoor games** Spiele im Freien.

outdoors adverb draußen; **to go outdoors** nach draußen gehen.

outing noun Ausflug der (PL die Ausflüge); **to go on an outing** einen Ausflug machen.

outline noun (of an object) Umriss der (PL die Umrisse).

out-of-date adjective **1** (no longer valid) ungültig; **my passport's out of date** mein Pass ist ungültig; **2** (old-fashioned) altmodisch (clothes, music).

outside noun Außenseite die; **it's blue on the outside** außen ist es blau.

outside adjective Außen-.

outside adverb draußen; **it's cold outside** es ist kalt draußen.

outside preposition vor (+ DAT); **I'll meet you outside the cinema** ich treffe mich vor dem Kino mit dir.

outskirts plural noun Stadtrand der; **on the outskirts of Lübeck** am Stadtrand von Lübeck.

oven noun Ofen der (PL die Öfen); **to put something in the oven** etwas in den Ofen tun.

over preposition **1** (above) über (+ DAT); **there's a mirror over the sink** über dem Waschbecken hängt ein Spiegel; **2** (involving movement) über (+ ACC); **he threw**

the ball over the wall er hat den Ball über die Mauer geworfen; **3 over here** hier drüben; **the food is over here** das Essen ist hier drüben; **4 over there** da drüben; **she's over there** sie ist da drüben; **5** (more than) über; **it will cost over a hundred pounds** es wird über hundert Pfund kosten; **he's over sixty** er ist über sechzig; **6** (during) über (+ ACC); **over Christmas** über Weihnachten; **over the weekend** übers Wochenende; **7** (finished) zu Ende; **when the meeting's over** wenn die Besprechung zu Ende ist; **it's all over** es ist vorbei; **8 over the phone** am Telefon; **to ask someone over** jemanden einladen ◇ SEP; **to come over** herüberkommen ◇ SEP; **come over on Saturday** komm am Samstag zu uns herüber; **9 all over the place** überall; **I've been looking for it all over** ich habe überall danach gesucht.

overdose noun Überdosis die (PL die Überdosen).

overtake verb überholen.

overtime noun **to work overtime** Überstunden machen.

overweight adjective **to be overweight** Übergewicht haben.

owe verb schulden; **I owe him ten pounds** ich schulde ihm zehn Pfund.

owing adjective **1** (outstanding) ausstehend; **there's five pounds owing** fünf Pfund stehen aus; **2 owing to** wegen (+ GEN); **owing to the snow** wegen des Schnees.

owl noun Eule die (PL die Eulen).

own *adjective* **1** eigen; **my own computer** mein eigener Computer; **I've got my own room** ich habe mein eigenes Zimmer; **2 on your own** allein; **Annie did it on her own** Annie hat es allein gemacht.

own *verb* besitzen✧.

owner *noun* Besitzer *der* (PL die Besitzer), Besitzerin *die* (PL die Besitzerinnen).

oxygen *noun* Sauerstoff *der*.

oyster *noun* Auster *die* (PL die Austern).

ozone layer *noun* Ozonschicht *die*.

Pp

pace *noun* **1** (a step) Schritt *der* (PL die Schritte); **2** (the speed you walk at) Tempo *das* (PL die Tempos).

Pacific *noun* **the Pacific (Ocean)** der Pazifik.

pack *noun* **1** Packung *die* (PL die Packungen); **2 pack of cards** das Kartenspiel.

pack *verb* **1** packen (your case); **I haven't packed yet** ich habe noch nicht gepackt; **I'll pack my case tonight** ich packe meinen Koffer heute Abend; **2** einpacken SEP (clothes, shoes, etc.); **have you packed my red shirt?** hast du mein rotes Hemd eingepackt?

package *noun* Paket *das* (PL die Pakete).

package holiday *noun* Pauschalurlaub *der* (PL die Pauschalurlaube).

packed lunch *noun* Lunchpaket *das* (PL die Lunchpakete).

packet *noun* **1** Päckchen *das* (PL die Päckchen); **a packet of tea** ein Päckchen Tee; **2** (box) Schachtel *die* (PL die Schachteln); **3** (bag) Tüte *die* (PL die Tüten); **a packet of crisps** eine Tüte Chips.

pad *noun* (of paper) Block *der* (PL die Blöcke).

paddle *noun* (for a canoe) Paddel *das* (PL die Paddel).

paddle *verb* **1** (at the seaside) plauschen (PERF sein); **to go paddling** plauschen gehen; **2** (a canoe) paddeln.

padlock *noun* Vorhängeschloss *das* (PL die Vorhängeschlösser).

page *noun* Seite *die* (PL die Seiten); **on page seven** auf Seite sieben.

pain *noun* Schmerz *der* (PL die Schmerzen); **to be in pain** Schmerzen haben; **I've got a pain in my leg** ich habe Schmerzen im Bein; ★ **Eric's a real pain in the neck** Eric geht einem richtig auf den Wecker (informal).

painful *adjective* schmerzhaft.

painkiller *noun* Schmerzmittel *das* (PL die Schmerzmittel).

paint *noun* Farbe *die* (PL die Farben); **'wet paint'** 'frisch gestrichen'.

paint *verb* malen (a picture), streichen✧ (a room); **to paint a room pink** ein Zimmer rosa streichen.

paintbrush *noun* Pinsel *der* (PL die Pinsel).

painter noun Maler der (PL die Maler), Malerin die (PL die Malerinnen).

painting noun (picture) Gemälde das (PL die Gemälde); **a painting by Picasso** ein Gemälde von Picasso.

pair noun **1** Paar das (PL die Paare); **a pair of socks** ein Paar Socken; **2 a pair of scissors** eine Schere; **3 a pair of trousers** eine Hose; **a pair of knickers** eine Unterhose; **4 to work in pairs** paarweise arbeiten.

Pakistan noun Pakistan das.

palace noun Palast der (PL die Paläste).

pale adjective blass; **to turn pale** blass werden; **pale green** zartgrün.

palm noun **1** (of your hand) Handfläche die (PL die Handflächen); **2** (a palm tree) Palme die (PL die Palmen).

pan noun **1** (saucepan) Topf der (PL die Töpfe); **a pan of water** ein Topf Wasser; **2** (frying-pan) Pfanne die (PL die Pfannen).

pancake noun Pfannkuchen der (PL die Pfannkuchen).

panel noun **1** (for a discussion) Diskussionsrunde die, (for a quiz) Rateteam das; **2** (a piece of wood) Tafel die (PL die Tafeln).

panic noun Panik die.

panic verb in Panik geraten◊; **don't panic!** keine Panik!

pantomime noun Märchenvorstellung die (PL die Märchenvorstellungen).

pants plural noun Unterhose die (PL die Unterhosen).

paper noun **1** Papier das; **a sheet of paper** ein Blatt Papier; **2 paper hanky** das Papiertaschentuch;

3 paper cup der Pappbecher; **4** (newspaper) Zeitung die (PL die Zeitungen); **it was in the paper** es stand in der Zeitung; **5 papers** (documents) Unterlagen (plural).

paperback noun Taschenbuch das (PL die Taschenbücher).

paperclip noun Büroklammer die (PL die Büroklammern).

paper towel noun Papierhandtuch das (PL die Papierhandtücher).

parachute noun Fallschirm der (PL die Fallschirme).

parade noun Umzug der (PL die Umzüge).

paraffin noun Petroleum das .

paragraph noun Absatz der (PL die Absätze); **'new paragraph'** 'Absatz'.

parallel adjective parallel.

paralysed adjective gelähmt.

parcel noun Paket das (PL die Pakete).

pardon noun **I beg your pardon** (as an apology) Entschuldigung!; **pardon?** wie bitte?

parent noun Elternteil der; **parents** Eltern (plural); **my parents live in Germany** meine Eltern wohnen in Deutschland; **parents' evening** der Elternabend.

park noun **1** Park der (PL die Parks); **theme park** der (thematische) Freizeitpark; **2 car park** der Parkplatz.

park verb **1** parken; **you can park outside the house** du kannst vor dem Haus parken; **2 to find somewhere to park** einen Parkplatz finden.

parking noun Parken das; **'no parking'** 'Parken verboten'.

a b c d e f g h i j k l m n o p q r s t u v w x y z

a **parking meter** noun Parkuhr die
(PL die Parkuhren).

b **parking space** noun Parklücke
die (PL die Parklücken).

c **parking ticket** noun Strafzettel
der (PL die Strafzettel).

d **parliament** noun Parlament das
(PL die Parlamente).

e **parrot** noun Papagei der (PL die
Papageien).

f **parsley** noun Petersilie die.

g **part** noun 1 Teil der (PL die Teile);
part of the garden Teil des
Gartens; **the last part of the book**
der letzte Teil des Buches; 2 **that's
part of your job** das gehört dazu;
3 **to take part in something** an
etwas (DAT) teilnehmen ✧ SEP;
4 (spare part) Teil das (PL die Teile)
(for a machine or an engine); 5 (a
role in a play) Rolle die (PL die
Rollen).

particular adjective besonderer/
besondere/besonderes; **nothing in
particular** nichts Besonderes.

p **particularly** adverb besonders;
not particularly interesting nicht
besonders interessant.

parting noun 1 (in your hair)
Scheitel der (PL die Scheitel);
2 (departure) Abschied. der (PL die
Abschiede).

partly adverb teilweise.

partner noun Partner der (PL die
Partner), Partnerin die (PL die
Partnerinnen).

part-time adjective Teilzeit-; **part-
time work** die Teilzeitarbeit.

part-time adverb **to work part-
time** Teilzeit arbeiten.

party noun 1 (small, private) Party
die (PL die Partys), Feier die (PL die
Feiern); **a Christmas party** eine
Weihnachtsfeier; **to have a
birthday party** eine
Geburtstagsparty machen; 2 (more
formal, in the evening) Gesellschaft
die (PL die Gesellschaften); **we've
been invited to a party at the
Smiths' house** wir sind zu einer
Gesellschaft bei Smiths eingeladen
worden; 3 (group) Gruppe die (PL die
Gruppen); **a party of
schoolchildren** eine Gruppe
Schulkinder; 4 (in politics) Partei
die (PL die Parteien).

party game noun
Gesellschaftsspiel das (PL die
Gesellschaftsspiele).

pass noun 1 (to let you in) Ausweis
der (PL die Ausweise); 2 **bus pass** die
Buskarte; 3 (over the mountains)
Pass der (PL die Pässe); 4 (in an
exam) **to get a pass in maths** die
Mathematikprüfung bestehen.

pass verb 1 (walk past)
vorbeigehen ✧ SEP (PERF sein) an
(+ DAT) (a place or building); **we
passed your house** wir sind an
deinem Haus vorbeigegangen;
2 (drive past) vorbeifahren ✧ SEP
(PERF sein) an (+ DAT) (a place or
building); 3 (overtake) überholen
(a car); 4 (give) reichen; **could you
pass me the sugar please?**
könnten Sie mir bitte den Zucker
reichen?; 5 (time) vergehen ✧ (PERF
sein); **the time passed slowly** die
Zeit verging langsam; 6 bestehen ✧
(an exam); **to pass an exam** eine
Prüfung bestehen; **did you pass in
German?** hast du die
Deutschprüfung bestanden?

passage noun **1** (*corridor*) Gang der (PL die Gänge); **2** (*a piece of text*) Passage. die (PL die Passagen).

passenger noun **1** (*in a plane or ship*) Passagier der (PL die Passagiere); **2** (*in a train or bus*) Fahrgast der (PL die Fahrgäste); **3** (*in a car*) Mitfahrer der (PL die Mitfahrer).

passive noun Passiv das.

passive adjective passiv.

Passover noun Passah das.

passport noun Reisepass der (PL die Reisepässe), Pass der (PL die Pässe).

password noun **1** (*to gain entry*) Kennwort das (PL die Kennwörter); **2** (*for access to data*) Passwort das (PL die Passwörter); **to give the password** das Passwort eingeben.

past noun Vergangenheit die; **in the past** in der Vergangenheit.

past adjective (*recent*) letzter/letzte/letztes; **in the past few weeks** in den letzten paar Wochen; **2** (*over*) vorbei; **winter is past** der Winter ist vorbei.

past preposition, adverb **1** **to walk past something** an etwas (DAT) vorbeigehen✧ SEP (PERF *sein*); **we went past the school** wir sind an der Schule vorbeigegangen; **to go past** vorbeifahren✧ (PERF *sein*); **2** (*after*) nach (+ DAT); **it's just past the post office** es ist kurz nach der Post; **3** (*talking about time*) **ten past six** zehn nach sechs; **half past four** halb fünf; **a quarter past two** Viertel nach zwei.

pasta noun Nudeln (*plural*); **I don't like pasta** ich mag keine Nudeln.

pastry noun **1** (*for baking*) Teig der; **2** (*cake*) Gebäck das.

patch noun **1** (*for mending*) Flicken der (PL die Flicken); **2** (*of snow or ice*) Stelle die (PL die Stellen); **3** (*of blue sky*) Stückchen das (PL die Stückchen).

path noun Weg der (PL die Wege), (*very narrow*) Pfad der (PL die Pfade).

pathetic adjective (*useless, hopeless*) jämmerlich.

patience noun **1** Geduld die; **2** (*card game*) Patience die.

patient noun Patient der (PL die Patienten), Patientin die (PL die Patientinnen).

patient adjective geduldig.

patiently adverb geduldig.

patio noun Terrasse die (PL die Terrassen).

pattern noun **1** (*on wallpaper or fabric*) Muster das (PL die Muster); **2** (*dressmaking, knitting*) Schnitt der (PL die Schnitte).

pause noun Pause die (PL die Pausen).

pavement noun Bürgersteig der (PL die Bürgersteige); **on the pavement** auf dem Bürgersteig.

paw noun Pfote die (PL die Pfoten).

pawn noun (*in chess*) Bauer der (PL die Bauern).

pay noun (*wage*) Lohn der (PL die Löhne), (*salary*) Gehalt das (PL die Gehälter)

pay verb **1** zahlen; **I'm paying** ich zahle; **to pay cash** bar zahlen; **to pay by credit card** mit Kreditkarte zahlen; **they pay £8 an hour** sie zahlen acht Pfund die Stunde; **to**

pay by cheque mit Scheck zahlen; **2** bezahlen ('*bezahlen*' is used when you pay a person, a bill or for something); **to pay for something** etwas bezahlen; Tony paid for the drinks Tony hat die Getränke bezahlt; **it's all paid for** es ist alles bezahlt; **3 to pay somebody back** (money) jemandem Geld zurückzahlen SEP; **4 to pay attention** aufpassen SEP; **5 to pay a visit to somebody** jemanden besuchen.

pay phone noun Münzfernsprecher der (PL die Münzfernsprecher).

payment noun **1** Bezahlung die (of sum, bill, debt, or fine); **2** Zahlung die (PL die Zahlungen) (of interest, tax, or fee).

PC noun (computer) PC der (PL die PC).

pea noun Erbse die (PL die Erbsen).

peace noun Frieden der.

peaceful adjective friedlich.

peach noun Pfirsich der (PL die Pfirsiche).

peacock noun Pfau der (PL die Pfauen).

peak period (for holidays) Hauptferienzeit die (PL die Hauptferienzeiten).

peak rate noun (for phoning) Höchsttarif der (PL die Höchsttarife).

peak time noun (for traffic) Stoßzeit die (PL die Stoßzeiten).

peanut noun Erdnuss die (PL die Erdnüsse).

peanut butter noun Erdnussbutter die.

pear noun Birne die (PL die Birnen).

pearl noun Perle die (PL die Perlen).

pebble noun Kieselstein der (PL die Kieselsteine).

peculiar adjective komisch.

pedal noun Pedal das (PL die Pedale).

pedal verb (on a bike) **to pedal off** (mit dem Rad) wegfahren ✧ (PERF sein).

pedestrian noun Fußgänger der (PL die Fußgänger), Fußgängerin die (PL die Fußgängerinnen).

pedestrian crossing noun Fußgängerüberweg der (PL die Fußgängerüberwege).

pedestrian precinct noun Fußgängerzone die (PL die Fußgängerzonen).

pee noun **to have a pee** pinkeln (informal).

peel noun Schale die (PL die Schalen).

peel verb schälen (fruit, vegetables).

peg noun **1** (hook) Haken der (PL die Haken); **2 clothes peg** die Wäscheklammer (PL die Wäscheklammern); **3** (for a tent) Hering der (PL die Heringe).

pen noun (ball-point) Kugelschreiber der (PL die Kugelschreiber); **felt pen** der Filzstift.

penalty noun **1** (a fine) Geldstrafe die (PL die Geldstrafen); **2** (in football) Elfmeter der (PL die Elfmeter).

pence plural noun Pence (plural).

pencil noun Bleistift der (PL die Bleistifte); **to write in pencil** mit Bleistift schreiben.

pencil case noun Federmäppchen das (PL die Federmäppchen).

pencil sharpener noun Bleistiftanspitzer der (PL die Bleistiftanspitzer).

penfriend noun Brieffreund der (PL die Brieffreunde), Brieffreundin die (PL die Brieffreundinnen); **my German pen-friend is called Heidi** meine deutsche Brieffreundin heißt Heidi.

penguin noun Pinguin der (PL die Pinguine).

penis noun Penis der (PL die Penisse).

penknife noun Taschenmesser das (PL die Taschenmesser).

penny noun Penny der (PL die Pence).

pension noun Rente die (PL die Renten).

pensioner noun Rentner der (PL die Rentner), Rentnerin die (PL die Rentnerinnen).

people plural noun 1 Leute (plural), Menschen (plural) ('Menschen' is used in a more formal context); **most people round here** die meisten Leute hier; **several people** verschiedene Leute; **nice people** nette Leute; **all the people in the world** alle Menschen auf der Welt; **a crowd of people** eine Menschenmenge; 2 (when you're counting them) Personen (plural); **for ten people** für zehn Personen; **how many people have you invited?** wie viele Personen hast du eingeladen?; 3 **people say that** ... man sagt, dass ....

pepper noun 1 (spice) Pfeffer der; 2 (vegetable) Paprikaschote die (PL die Paprikaschoten).

peppermill noun Pfeffermühle die (PL die Pfeffermühlen).

peppermint noun (plant) Pfefferminze die; **peppermint tea** der Pfefferminztee.

per preposition pro (+ ACC); **ten pounds per person** zehn Pfund pro Person.

per cent adverb Prozent das; **sixty per cent of students** sechzig Prozent der Studenten.

percentage noun Prozentsatz der (PL die Prozentsätze).

percussion noun Schlagzeug das; **to play percussion** Schlagzeug spielen.

perfect adjective 1 perfekt; **she speaks perfect English** sie spricht perfekt Englisch; 2 (ideal) herrlich (day or weather).

perfectly adverb 1 (absolutely) vollkommen; 2 (faultlessly) perfekt.

perform verb 1 spielen (a piece of music or a part); 2 singen ✧ (a song); 3 **to perform a play** ein Theaterstück aufführen SEP.

performance noun 1 (playing or acting) Darstellung die (PL die Darstellungen); **his performance as Hamlet** seine Darstellung des Hamlet; 2 (show or film) Vorstellung die (PL die Vorstellungen); **the performance starts at eight** die Vorstellung fängt um acht Uhr an; 3 (of a play or opera) Aufführung die (PL die Aufführungen).

a b c d e f g h i j k l m n o p q r s t u v w x y z

a **performer** noun Künstler der (PL die Künstler), Künstlerin die (PL die Künstlerinnen).

b **perfume** noun Parfüm das (PL die Parfüme).

c

d **perhaps** adverb vielleicht; **perhaps he's missed the train** vielleicht hat er den Zug verpasst.

e

f **period** noun 1 (length of time) Zeit die (PL die Zeiten); **trial period** die Probezeit; 2 (a portion of time) Zeitraum der; **a two-year period** ein Zeitraum von zwei Jahren; 3 (in school) Stunde die (PL die Stunden); 4 (menstruation) Periode die (PL die Perioden).

g

h

i

j **perm** noun Dauerwelle die (PL die Dauerwellen).

k **permanent** adjective 1 ständig; 2 fest (job or address, for example).

l

m **permanently** adverb 1 dauernd; 2 **to be permanently employed** fest angestellt sein.

n **permission** noun Erlaubnis die; **to get permission to do something** Erlaubnis zu etwas (DAT) erhalten.

o

p **permit** noun Genehmigung die (PL die Genehmigungen).

q **permit** verb 1 erlauben; **to permit somebody to do something** jemandem erlauben, etwas zu tun; **smoking is not permitted** Rauchen ist nicht gestattet; 2 **weather permitting** bei entsprechendem Wetter.

r

s

t **person** noun 1 Person die (PL die Personen); **there's still room for one more person** wir haben noch Platz für eine Person; 2 **in person** persönlich.

u

v

w

x **personal** adjective persönlich.

y

z

personality noun Persönlichkeit die (PL die Persönlichkeiten).

personally adverb persönlich; **personally, I'm against it** ich persönlich bin dagegen.

perspiration noun Schweiß der.

persuade verb überreden; **to persuade somebody to come** jemanden überreden zu kommen.

pessimistic adjective pessimistisch.

pest noun 1 (greenfly, for example) Schädling der (PL die Schädlinge); 2 (annoying person) Nervensäge die (PL die Nervensägen) (informal).

pet noun 1 Haustier das (PL die Haustiere); **do you have a pet?** habt ihr Haustiere?; **a pet dog** ein Hund; 2 **Julie is teacher's pet** Julie ist der Liebling des Lehrers.

petrol noun Benzin das (PL die Benzine); **to fill up with petrol** tanken; **to run out of petrol** kein Benzin mehr haben.

petrol station noun Tankstelle die (PL die Tankstellen).

pharmacy noun Apotheke die (PL die Apotheken).

pheasant noun Fasan der (PL die Fasane).

philosophy noun Philosophie die (PL die Philosophien).

phone noun Telefon das (PL die Telefone); **she's on the phone** sie telefoniert; **I was on the phone to Sophie** ich habe mit Sophie telefoniert; **you can book by phone** du kannst telefonisch buchen.

phone verb 1 telefonieren; **while I was phoning** während ich telefonierte; 2 **to phone somebody**

jemanden anrufen◇ SEP; **I'll phone you tonight** ich rufe dich heute Abend an.

phone book noun Telefonbuch das (PL die Telefonbücher).

phone box noun Telefonzelle die (PL die Telefonzellen).

phone call noun 1 Anruf der (PL die Anrufe); **to get a phone call** einen Anruf erhalten; 2 **to make a phone call** ein Telefongespräch führen; **phone calls are free** Telefongespräche sind gebührenfrei.

phone card noun Telefonkarte die (PL die Telefonkarten).

phone number noun Telefonnummer die (PL die Telefonnummern).

photo noun Foto das (PL die Fotos); **to take a photo** ein Foto machen; **to take a photo of somebody** ein Foto von jemandem machen.

photocopier noun Fotokopiergerät das (PL die Fotokopiergeräte).

photocopy noun Fotokopie die (PL die Fotokopien).

photocopy verb fotokopieren.

photograph noun Fotografie die (PL die Fotografien); **to take a photograph** ein Foto machen.

photograph verb fotografieren.

photographer noun Fotograf der (PL die Fotografen), Fotografin die (PL die Fotografinnen).

photography noun Fotografie die.

phrase noun Phrase die (PL die Phrasen); **an idiomatic phrase** eine Redewendung.

phrase-book noun Sprachführer der (PL die Sprachführer).

physical adjective körperlich.

physics noun Physik die.

physiotherapist noun Physiotherapeut der (PL die Physiotherapeuten), Physiotherapeutin die (PL die Physiotherapeutinnen).

physiotherapy noun Physiotherapie die.

piano noun Klavier das (PL die Klaviere); **to play the piano** Klavier spielen; **piano lesson** die Klavierstunde.

pick noun **to take your pick** sich (DAT) etwas aussuchen SEP.

pick verb 1 (to select) wählen; **he picked his words carefully** er wählte seine Worte mit Bedacht; 2 (choose for oneself) sich (DAT) aussuchen SEP; **pick any book** such dir irgendein Buch aus; 3 **to pick a team** eine Mannschaft aufstellen; 4 pflücken (fruit); **to pick strawberries** Erdbeeren pflücken.

• **to pick up 1** (lift) (in die Hand) nehmen◇; **he picked up the papers** er nahm die Unterlagen; 2 (collect) abholen SEP; **I'll pick you up at six** ich hole dich um sechs Uhr ab; **I'll pick up the keys tomorrow** ich hole die Schlüssel morgen ab.

pickpocket noun Taschendieb der (PL die Taschendiebe).

picnic noun Picknick das (PL die Picknicke); **to have a picnic** ein Picknick machen.

picture noun 1 Bild das (PL die Bilder); 2 **to go to the pictures** (the cinema) ins Kino gehen.

a b c d e f g h i j k l m n o p q r s t u v w x y z

pie noun 1 (*sweet*) Kuchen der (PL die Kuchen); **apple pie** der Apfelkuchen; 2 (*savoury*) Pastete die (PL die Pasteten).

piece noun 1 (*a bit*) Stück das (PL die Stücke); **a big piece of cheese** ein großes Stück Käse; 2 (*that you fit together*) Teil das (PL die Teile); **the pieces of a jigsaw** die Teile von einem Puzzle; **to take something to pieces** etwas in Einzelteile zerlegen; 3 **piece of furniture** das Möbelstück; **a piece of information** eine Information; **a piece of luck** ein Glücksfall; 4 (*coin*) Stück das (PL die Stücke); **a five-pence piece** ein Fünf-Pence-Stück.

pierce verb 1 durchstechen◇ SEP; 2 **to have pierced ears** Löcher in den Ohrläppchen haben.

pig noun Schwein das (PL die Schweine).

pigeon noun Taube die (PL die Tauben).

piggy bank noun Sparschwein das (PL die Sparschweine).

pigtail noun Zopf der (PL die Zöpfe).

pile noun 1 (*a neat stack*) Stapel der (PL die Stapel); **a pile of plates** ein Stapel Teller; 2 (*a heap*) Haufen der (PL die Haufen).

● **to pile something up** (*neatly*) etwas aufstapeln SEP, (*in a heap*) etwas auftürmen SEP.

pill noun Pille die (PL die Pillen).

pillar noun Säule die (PL die Säulen).

pillow noun Kopfkissen das (PL die Kopfkissen).

pilot noun Pilot der (PL die Piloten), Pilotin die (PL die Pilotinnen).

pimple noun Pickel der (PL die Pickel).

pin noun 1 (*for sewing*) Stecknadel die (PL die Stecknadeln); 2 **a three-pin plug** ein dreipoliger Stecker.

● **to pin up** 1 hochstecken SEP (*a hem*); 2 anschlagen◇ SEP (*a notice*).

PIN noun (*personal identification number*) Geheimnummer die.

pinball noun Flippern das; **to play pinball** flippern; **pinball machine** der Flipper.

pinch noun (*of salt, for example*) Prise die (PL die Prisen).

pinch verb 1 kneifen◇; **she pinched my arm** sie hat mich in den Arm gekniffen; 2 (*to steal*) klauen; **somebody's pinched my bike** jemand hat mein Rad geklaut.

pine noun Kiefer die (PL die Kiefern); **pine furniture** Kiefernmöbel (*plural*).

pineapple noun Ananas die (PL die Ananas).

pine cone noun Kiefernzapfen der (PL die Kiefernzapfen).

ping-pong noun Tischtennis das; **to play ping-pong** Tischtennis spielen.

pink adjective rosa ('*rosa*' *never changes*); **pink hats** rosa Hüte.

pip noun (*in a fruit*) Kern der (PL die Kerne).

pipe noun 1 (*for gas or water*) Rohr das (PL die Rohre); 2 (*for smoking*) Pfeife die (PL die Pfeifen); **he smokes a pipe** er raucht Pfeife.

pirate noun Pirat der (PL die Piraten).

Pisces noun Fische (*plural*); **Amanda is Pisces** Amanda ist Fisch.

pitch noun Platz der (PL die Plätze); **football pitch** der Fußballplatz.

pitch verb **to pitch a tent** ein Zelt aufstellen SEP.

pity noun 1 (feeling sorry for somebody) Mitleid das; 2 **what a pity!** wie schade!; **it would be a pity to miss the beginning** es wäre schade, den Anfang zu verpassen.

pity verb **to pity somebody** jemanden bemitleiden.

pizza noun Pizza die (PL die Pizzas).

place noun 1 Ort der (PL die Orte); **Salzburg is a wonderful place** Salzburg ist ein sehr schöner Ort; **in place** an Ort und Stelle; 2 **all over the place** überall; 3 (a space) Platz der (PL die Plätze); **a place for the car** ein Platz für das Auto; **is there a place for me?** ist Platz für mich?; **will you keep my place?** kannst du mir den Platz freihalten?; **to change places** die Plätze tauschen; 4 (spot) Stelle die (PL die Stellen); **this is a good place to stop** das ist eine gute Stelle zum Halten; 5 (in a race) Platz der (PL die Plätze); **to gain first place** den ersten Platz belegen; 6 **at your place** bei dir; **we'll go round to Zafir's place** wir gehen zu Zafir; 7 **to take place** stattfinden◇ SEP; **the competition will take place at four** der Wettbewerb findet um vier Uhr statt

place verb (upright) stellen, (lying flat) legen.

plain noun Ebene die (PL die Ebenen).

plain adjective 1 einfach; **plain food** einfaches Essen; 2 (unflavoured)

Natur-; **plain yoghurt** der Naturjoghurt; 3 (not patterned) einfarbig; **plain curtains** einfarbige Vorhänge.

plait noun Zopf der (PL die Zöpfe).

plan noun Plan der (PL die Pläne); **we've made plans for the summer** wir haben Pläne für den Sommer gemacht; **to go according to plan** nach Plan gehen; **everything went according to plan** alles ging nach Plan.

plan verb 1 **to plan to do something** etwas vorhaben◇ SEP; **we're planning to leave at eight** wir haben vor, um acht abzufahren; 2 (make plans for, organize, design) planen; **she's planning a trip to Italy** sie plant eine Reise nach Italien.

plane noun Flugzeug das (PL die Flugzeuge); **we went by plane** wir sind geflogen.

planet noun Planet der (PL die Planeten).

plant noun Pflanze die (PL die Pflanzen); **a house plant** eine Topfpflanze.

plant verb pflanzen.

plaster noun 1 (sticking plaster) Pflaster das (PL die Pflaster); 2 (for walls) Verputz der; 3 Gips der; **to have your leg in plaster** das Bein in Gips haben.

plastic noun Plastik das; **plastic bag** die Plastiktüte.

plate noun Teller der (PL die Teller).

platform noun 1 (in a station) Bahnsteig der (PL die Bahnsteige); 2 **the train is arriving at platform six** der Zug fährt auf Gleis sechs ein; **3** (*for lecturing or performing*) Podium das (PL die Podien).

play noun (*in the theatre*) Stück das (PL die Stücke); **television play** das Fernsehspiel; **we are putting on a play by Brecht at school** wir führen ein Stück von Brecht in der Schule auf.

play verb **1** spielen; **the children are playing with a ball** die Kinder spielen Ball; **they play the piano and the guitar** sie spielen Klavier und Gitarre; **who's playing Hamlet?**; **to play tennis** Tennis spielen; **they were playing cards** sie haben Karten gespielt; **2** (*in sport*) **to play somebody** gegen jemanden spielen; **Italy are playing Germany** Italien spielt gegen Deutschland; **3** spielen (*a tape, CD, or record*); **play your new CD** spiel mal deine neue CD.

player noun **1** Spieler der (PL die Spieler), Spielerin die (PL die Spielerinnen); **football player** der Fußballspieler; **2** (*in the theatre*) Schauspieler der (PL die Schauspieler), Schauspielerin die (PL die Schauspielerinnen).

playground noun **1** Spielplatz der (PL die Spielplätze); **school playground** der Schulhof.

playgroup noun Spielgruppe die (PL die Spielgruppen).

playing field noun Sportplatz der (PL die Sportplätze).

pleasant adjective angenehm.

please adverb bitte; **two coffees, please** zwei Kaffee bitte; **could you turn the TV off, please?** könntest

du bitte den Fernseher ausmachen?

pleased adjective **1** erfreut; **I'm really pleased!** das freut mich wirklich!; **2 she was pleased with her present** sie hat sich über ihr Geschenk gefreut; **3 pleased to meet you!** freut mich!

pleasure noun **1** (*amusement*) Vergnügen das; **2** (*joy*) Freude die; **to get a lot of pleasure out of something** viel Freude an etwas (DAT) haben.

plenty pronoun **1** (*lots*) viel; **he's got plenty of money** er hat viel Geld; **2** (*enough*) genug; **that's plenty!** das ist genug!; **we've got plenty of time left** wir haben noch genug Zeit.

plot noun (*of a film or novel*) Handlung die.

plough noun Pflug der (PL die Pflüge).

plough verb pflügen.

plug noun **1** (*electrical*) Stecker der (PL die Stecker); **2** (*in a bath or sink*) Stöpsel der (PL die Stöpsel); **to pull out the plug** den Stöpsel herausziehen.

plum noun Pflaume die (PL die Pflaumen); **plum tart** der Pflaumenkuchen.

plumber noun Installateur der (PL die Installateure).

plural noun Mehrzahl die Plural der; **in the plural** in der Mehrzahl, im Plural.

plus preposition plus (+ DAT); **three children plus a baby** drei Kinder und ein Baby.

p.m. abbreviation nachmittags (*for times up to 6 p.m.*), abends (*for times* *after 6 p.m.*; **at two p.m.** um zwei Uhr nachmittags, um vierzehn Uhr; **at nine p.m.** um neun Uhr abends, um einundzwanzig Uhr (*in German you usually express times after midday in terms of the 24-hour clock*).

pocket *noun* Tasche die (PL die Taschen).

pocket money *noun* Taschengeld das.

poem *noun* Gedicht das (PL die Gedichte).

poet *noun* Dichter der (PL die Dichter), Dichterin die (PL die Dichterinnen).

poetry *noun* Dichtung die.

point *noun* 1 (*tip*) Spitze die (PL die Spitzen); **the point of a nail** die Spitze eines Nagels; 2 (*a tiny mark or dot*) Punkt der (PL die Punkte); 3 (*in time*) Zeitpunkt der (PL die Zeitpunkte); **at that point** zu diesem Zeitpunkt; **to be on the point of doing something** gerade etwas tun wollen; 4 **that's not the point** darum geht es nicht; **there's no point phoning, he's out** es hat keinen Sinn anzurufen, er ist nicht da; **what's the point?** wozu?; 5 **that's a good point!** das stimmt!; **the point is ...** es geht darum ...; 6 **point of view** der Standpunkt; **from my point of view** von meinem Standpunkt aus; 7 **her strong point** ihre Stärke; 8 (*in scoring*) Punkt der (PL die Punkte); **to win by fifteen points** mit fünfzehn Punkten Vorsprung gewinnen; 9 (*in decimals*) **6 point 4** sechs Komma vier (*in German, a comma is used for the decimal point*).

point *verb* 1 hinweisen ✧ SEP auf (+ ACC); **a notice pointing to the station** ein Schild, das in Richtung Bahnhof zeigt; 2 (*with your finger*) zeigen auf (+ ACC); **he pointed at Tom** er zeigte auf Tom.

pointless *adjective* sinnlos; **it's pointless to keep on ringing** es ist sinnlos, dauernd zu klingeln.

poison *noun* Gift das (PL die Gifte).

poison *verb* vergiften.

poisonous *adjective* giftig.

Poland *noun* Polen das.

polar bear *noun* Eisbär der (PL die Eisbären).

pole *noun* 1 (*for a tent*) Stange die (PL die Stangen); 2 (*for skiing*) Stock der (PL die Stöcke); 3 **the North Pole** der Nordpol.

Pole *noun* (*a Polish person*) Pole der (PL die Polen), Polin die (PL die Polinnen).

police *noun* **the police** die Polizei; **the police are coming** die Polizei kommt.

police car *noun* Streifenwagen der (PL die Streifenwagen).

policeman *noun* Polizist der (PL die Polizisten).

police station *noun* Polizeiwache die (PL die Polizeiwachen).

policewoman *noun* Polizistin die (PL die Polizistinnen).

policy *noun* 1 (*plan of action*) Vorgehensweise die (PL die Vorgehensweisen); **the policy on immigration** die Einwanderungspolitik;

2 (*document*) Versicherungsschein der (PL die Versicherungsscheine).

polish noun 1 (*for furniture*) Politur die; 2 (*for shoes*) Schuhcreme die; 3 (*for the floor*) Bohnerwachs das.

polish verb 1 polieren (*furniture, silver*); 2 to polish your shoes seine Schuhe putzen.

Polish noun (*language*) Polnisch das.

Polish adjective polnisch.

polite adjective höflich; to be polite to somebody höflich zu jemandem sein.

political adjective politisch.

politician noun Politiker der (PL die Politiker), Politikerin die (PL die Politikerinnen).

politics noun Politik die.

pollen noun Pollen der; the pollen count for today is ... die Pollenzahl heute ist ....

polluted adjective verschmutzt.

pollution noun Umweltverschmutzung die.

polo-necked adjective Rollkragen-; a polo-necked jumper ein Rollkragenpullover.

pond noun Teich der (PL die Teiche).

pony noun Pony das (PL die Ponys).

ponytail noun Pferdeschwanz der (PL die Pferdeschwänze).

poodle noun Pudel der (PL die Pudel).

pool noun 1 (*swimming pool*) Schwimmbecken das (PL die Schwimmbecken); 2 (*pond*) Tümpel der (PL die Tümpel); 3 (*puddle*) Lache die (PL die Lachen); 4 (*game*) Poolbillard das; 5 the

football pools das Toto; to do the pools Toto spielen.

poor adjective 1 arm; a poor country ein armes Land; a poor family eine arme Familie; 2 poor Tanya's failed her exam die arme Tanya ist durch die Prüfung gefallen; 3 (*bad*) schlecht; that's a poor result das ist ein schlechtes Ergebnis; the weather was pretty poor das Wetter war ziemlich schlecht.

pop noun Popmusik die; pop concert das Popkonzert; pop star der Popstar; pop song der Popsong.

● to pop into: I'll just pop into the bank ich gehe kurz auf die Bank.

popcorn noun Popcorn das.

pope noun Papst der (PL die Päpste).

poppy noun Mohn der.

popular adjective beliebt.

population noun Bevölkerung die.

porch noun Vorbau der (PL die Vorbauten).

pork noun Schweinefleisch das; pork chop das Schweinekotelett.

porridge noun Haferbrei der.

port noun 1 Hafen der (PL die Häfen); 2 (*wine*) Portwein der (PL die Portweine).

porter noun 1 (*at a station or an airport*) Gepäckträger der (PL die Gepäckträger); 2 (*in a hotel*) Portier der (PL die Portiers).

portion noun (*of food*) Portion die (PL die Portionen).

portrait noun Porträt das (PL die Porträts).

Portugal noun Portugal das.

Portuguese noun 1 (*language*) Portugiesisch das; 2 (*a person*) Portugiese der (PL die Portugiesen),

Portugiesin die (PL die Portugiesinnen).

Portuguese adjective portugiesisch.

posh adjective vornehm; **a posh area** eine vornehme Gegend.

position noun 1 Platz der (PL die Plätze); 2 (situation) Lage die (PL die Lagen); 3 (status, job) Stellung die (PL die Stellungen).

positive adjective 1 (sure) sicher; **I'm positive he's left** ich bin mir sicher, dass er gegangen ist; 2 (enthusiastic) positiv; **her reaction was very positive** ihre Reaktion war sehr positiv.

possess verb besitzen✧.

possessions plural noun Sachen (plural); **all my possessions are in the flat** alle meine Sachen sind in der Wohnung.

possibility noun Möglichkeit die (PL die Möglichkeiten).

possible adjective möglich; **it's possible** es ist gut möglich; **if possible** wenn möglich; **as quickly as possible** so schnell wie möglich.

possibly adverb 1 (maybe) möglicherweise; **'will you be at home at midday?' - 'possibly'** 'bist du mittags zu Hause?' - 'möglicherweise'; 2 **how can you possibly believe that?** wie kannst du das nur glauben?; **I can't possibly arrive before Thursday** ich kann unmöglich vor Donnerstag ankommen.

post noun 1 Post die; **to send something by post** etwas per Post schicken; (letters) **is there any post for me?** ist Post für mich gekommen?; 2 (a pole) Pfosten der (PL die Pfosten); 3 (a job) Stelle die (PL die Stellen).

post verb **to post a letter** einen Brief abschicken SEP.

postbox noun Briefkasten der (PL die Briefkästen).

postcard noun Postkarte die (PL die Postkarten).

postcode noun Postleitzahl die (PL die Postleitzahlen).

poster noun 1 (for decoration) Poster das (PL die Poster); **I've bought an Oasis poster** ich habe ein Poster von Oasis gekauft; 2 (advertising) Plakat das (PL die Plakate); **I saw a poster for the concert** ich habe ein Plakat für das Konzert gesehen.

postman noun Briefträger der (PL die Briefträger).

post office noun Post die; **the post office is on the right** die Post ist auf der rechten Seite.

postpone verb verschieben✧; **we've postponed the meeting until next week** wir haben die Besprechung auf nächste Woche verschoben.

postwoman noun Briefträgerin die (PL die Briefträgerinnen).

pot noun 1 (jar) Topf der (PL die Töpfe); **a pot of honey** ein Topf Honig; 2 (teapot) Kanne die (PL die Kannen); 3 **the pots and pans** die Töpfe und Pfannen.

potato noun Kartoffel die (PL die Kartoffeln); **fried potatoes** Bratkartoffeln (plural); **mashed potatoes** der Kartoffelbrei.

potato crisps plural noun Kartoffelchips (plural).

a
b
c
d
e
f
g
h
i
j
k
l
m
n
o
p
q
r
s
t
u
v
w
x
y
z

pottery noun **1** (craft) Töpferei die; **2** (objects) Töpferwaren (plural).

pound noun **1** (money) Pfund das (PL die Pfunde); **fourteen pounds** vierzehn Pfund; **1.6 euros to the pound** 1,6 Euro für ein Pfund; **a five pound note** ein Fünfpfundschein; **2** (in weight) Pfund das; **two pounds of apples** zwei Pfund Äpfel.

pour verb **1** gießen◇ (liquid); **he poured milk into the pan** er hat Milch in den Topf gegossen; **2** eingießen◇ SEP (a drink); **to pour the tea** den Tee eingießen; **I poured him a drink** ich habe ihm etwas zu trinken eingeschenkt; **3** (with rain) **it's pouring** es gießt.

poverty noun Armut die.

powder noun **1** Pulver das (PL die Pulver); **2** (for face or body) Puder der (PL die Puder).

power noun **1** (electricity) Strom der; **a power cut** eine Stromsperre; **2** (energy) Energie die; **nuclear power** die Kernenergie; **3** (strength) Kraft die; **4** (over other people) Macht die; **to be in power** an der Macht sein.

power point noun Steckdose die (PL die Steckdosen).

power station noun Kraftwerk das (PL die Kraftwerke).

powerful adjective (strong) stark, (influential) mächtig.

practical adjective praktisch.

practically adverb fast.

practice noun **1** (for sport) Training das; **hockey practice** das Hockeytraining; **2** Übung die; **to do your piano practice** Klavier üben;

to be out of practice aus der Übung sein.

practise verb **1** üben (an instrument, exercise, or skill); **to practise the piano** Klavier üben; **2** anwenden SEP (a language); **a week in Berlin to practise my German** eine Woche in Berlin, um mein Deutsch anzuwenden; **3** (in sport) trainieren; **the team practises on Wednesday** die Mannschaft trainiert mittwochs.

praise verb loben; **to praise somebody for something** jemanden für etwas (ACC) loben.

pram noun Kinderwagen der (PL die Kinderwagen).

prawn noun Garnele die (PL die Garnelen).

pray verb beten.

prayer noun Gebet das (PL die Gebete).

precaution noun Vorsichtsmaßnahme die (PL die Vorsichtsmaßnahmen); **to take precautions against something** Vorsichtsmaßnahmen gegen (+ ACC) etwas ergreifen.

precinct noun **shopping precinct** das Einkaufszentrum; **pedestrian precinct** die Fußgängerzone.

precisely adverb genau; **at eleven o'clock precisely** um genau elf Uhr.

prefer verb **1** vorziehen◇ SEP; **I prefer Anna to her sister** ich mag Anna lieber als ihre Schwester; **2** to prefer to do something etwas lieber tun; **I prefer to stay at home** ich bleibe lieber zu Hause.

pregnant adjective schwanger.

prejudice noun Vorurteil das (PL die Vorurteile); **to fight against racial prejudice** gegen Rassenvorurteile ankämpfen.

prejudiced adjective **to be prejudiced** voreingenommen sein.

prep noun Hausaufgaben (plural); **my English prep** meine Englischhausaufgaben.

prep school noun private Grundschule die.

preparation noun Vorbereitung die (PL die Vorbereitungen); **in preparation for something** in Vorbereitung auf etwas (ACC); **our preparations for Christmas** unsere Weihnachtsvorbereitungen.

prepare verb 1 vorbereiten SEP; **to prepare somebody for something** jemanden auf etwas (ACC) vorbereiten; **2 to be prepared for the worst** sich auf das Schlimmste gefasst machen.

prepared adjective bereit; **I'm prepared to pay half** ich bin bereit, die Hälfte zu zahlen.

preposition noun Präposition die (PL die Präpositionen).

prescription noun Rezept das (PL die Rezepte); **on prescription** auf Rezept.

presence noun Anwesenheit die; **he admitted it in my presence** er gab es in meiner Anwesenheit zu.

present noun **1** (a gift) Geschenk das (PL die Geschenke); **to give somebody a present** jemandem ein Geschenk machen; **2** (the time now) Gegenwart die; **in the present** (tense) im Präsens; **3 that's all for the present** das ist vorläufig alles.

present adjective **1** (attending) anwesend; **Mr Blair is not present** Herr Blair ist nicht anwesend; **to be present at something** bei etwas (DAT) anwesend sein; **fifty people were present at the funeral** fünfzig Personen waren bei der Beerdigung anwesend; **2** (existing now) gegenwärtig; **the present situation** die gegenwärtige Lage; **3 at the present time** zur Zeit.

present verb **1** überreichen (a prize); **2** (introduce) vorstellen SEP; **3** (on TV, radio) moderieren (a programme).

presenter noun (on TV) Moderator der (PL die Moderatoren), Moderatorin die (PL die Moderatorinnen).

presently adverb **1** (now) momentan; **2** (soon) bald.

president noun Präsident der (PL die Präsidenten), Präsidentin die (PL die Präsidentinnen).

press noun **the press** die Presse.

press verb **1** (to push) drücken; **press here!** hier drücken!; **2** drücken auf (+ ACC) (a button or switch); **she pressed the button** sie hat auf den Knopf gedrückt.

press conference noun Pressekonferenz die (PL die Pressekonferenzen).

pressure noun Druck der; **to put pressure on somebody** jemanden unter Druck setzen.

pressure gauge noun Druckluftmesser der (PL die Druckluftmesser).

pressure group noun
Interessengruppe die (PL die
Interessengruppen).

pretend verb **to pretend that** ... so
tun, als ob ...; **he's pretending not
to hear** er tut so, als ob er nicht
hört.

pretty adjective hübsch; **a pretty
dress** ein hübsches Kleid.

pretty adverb ziemlich; **it was
pretty silly** das war ziemlich blöd.

prevent verb **to prevent
somebody from doing something**
jemanden daran hindern, etwas zu
tun; **there's nothing to prevent you
from leaving** niemand kann dich
daran hindern zu gehen.

previous adjective **1** (earlier)
früher (years, opportunity, or job);
2 (immediately preceding) vorig; **on
the previous Tuesday** am vorigen
Dienstag.

price noun Preis der (PL die Preise);
the price per kilo der Preis pro
Kilo; **CDs have gone up in price**
CDs sind im Preis gestiegen; **what
is the price of this?** was kostet das?

price list noun Preisliste die (PL die
Preislisten).

price ticket noun Preisschild das
(PL die Preisschilder).

prick verb stechen✧; **to prick your
finger** sich in den Finger stechen.

pride noun Stolz der.

priest noun Priester der (PL die
Priester).

primary school noun
Grundschule die (PL die
Grundschulen).

primary (school) teacher
noun Grundschullehrer der (PL die
Grundschullehrer),

Grundschullehrerin die (PL die
Grundschullehrerinnen).

prime minister noun
Premierminister der (PL die
Premierminister),
Premierministerin die (PL die
Premierministerinnen).

prince noun Prinz der (PL die
Prinzen).

princess noun Prinzessin die (PL
die Prinzessinnen).

principal noun (of a college)
Direktor der (PL die Direktoren),
Direktorin die (PL die
Direktorinnen).

principal adjective (main) Haupt-.

principle noun Prinzip das (PL die
Prinzipien); **on principle** im
Prinzip; **that's true in principle** im
Prinzip stimmt das.

print noun **1** (letters) Druck der; **in
small print** klein gedruckt; **2** (a
photo) Abzug der (PL die Abzüge);
colour print der Farbabzug.

printer noun (for a computer)
Drucker der (PL die Drucker).

print-out noun Ausdruck der (PL die
Ausdrucke).

prison noun Gefängnis das (PL die
Gefängnisse); **in prison** im
Gefängnis.

prisoner noun Gefangene der/die
(PL die Gefangenen).

private adjective **1** Privat-, privat;
private school die Privatschule;
private property das
Privateigentum; **to have private
lessons** Privatstunden nehmen;
2 in private privat.

prize noun Preis der (PL die Preise);
to win a prize einen Preis
gewinnen.

prize-giving noun
Preisverleihung die (PL die
Preisverleihungen).

prizewinner noun Gewinner der
(PL die Gewinner), Gewinnerin die
(PL die Gewinnerinnen).

probable adjective
wahrscheinlich.

probably adverb wahrscheinlich.

problem noun Problem das (PL die
Probleme); **it's a serious problem**
das ist ein ernstes Problem; **no
problem!** kein Problem!

process noun 1 Prozess der (PL die
Prozesse); 2 **to be in the process of
doing something** dabei sein, etwas
zu tun.

procession noun 1 (in parade)
Umzug der (PL die Umzüge); 2 (at
religious festival) Prozession die (PL
die Prozessionen).

produce noun (food) Erzeugnisse
(plural).

produce verb 1 herstellen SEP
(goods, food); 2 vorzeigen SEP (a
ticket, document); **I produced my
passport** ich habe meinen Pass
vorgezeigt; 3 erzeugen (interest,
tension); **it produces heat** es
erzeugt Wärme; 4 **to produce a
film** einen Film produzieren; 5 **to
produce a play** ein Theaterstück
inszenieren.

producer noun (of a film or
programme) Produzent der (PL die
Produzenten).

product noun Produkt das (PL die
Produkte).

production noun 1 (of a film or an
opera) Produktion die (PL die
Produktionen); 2 (of a play)
Inszenierung die (PL die

Inszenierungen); **a new
production of Hamlet** eine neue
Inszenierung von Hamlet; 3 (by a
factory) Produktion die.

profession noun Beruf der (PL die
Berufe).

professional noun 1 (a trained
person) Fachmann der (PL die
Fachleute); 2 (in sport) Profi der (PL
die Profis).

professional adjective
1 professionell (work, sportsman);
a professional footballer ein
professioneller Fußballer;
2 beruflich (career, success); **she's a
professional singer** sie ist
Sängerin von Beruf.

professor noun Professor der (PL
die Professoren), Professorin die (PL
die Professorinnen).

profile noun Profil das (PL die
Profile).

profit noun Gewinn der (PL die
Gewinne).

profitable adjective rentabel.

program noun **computer program**
das Programm.

programme noun 1 (for a play or
an event) Programm das (PL die
Programme); 2 (on TV or radio)
Sendung die (PL die Sendungen).

programmer noun
Programmierer der (PL die
Programmierer),
Programmiererin die (PL die
Programmiererinnen).

progress noun 1 Fortschritt der
(PL die Fortschritte); **to make
progress** Fortschritte machen; 2 **to
be in progress** im Gange sein.

project noun 1 (at school) Arbeit
die (PL die Arbeiten); 2 (a plan)

Projekt das (PL die Projekte); **a project to build a bridge** ein Brückenbauprojekt.

promise noun Versprechen das (PL die Versprechen); **to make somebody a promise** jemandem ein Versprechen geben; **to keep a promise** ein Versprechen halten; **it's a promise!** versprochen!

promise verb **to promise something** etwas versprechen✧; **I've promised to ring my mother** ich habe versprochen, meine Mutter anzurufen.

promote verb **to be promoted** (in football) aufsteigen✧ SEP (PERF sein), (at work) befördert werden.

promotion noun **1** Beförderung die; **2** (in football) Aufstieg der; **3** (in advertising) Werbung die.

promptly adverb **1** (at once) sofort; **he promptly fell off again** er fiel sofort wieder herunter; **2** (quickly) schnell; **please reply promptly** bitte antworten Sie unverzüglich; **3** (punctually) pünktlich; **they left promptly at five o'clock** sie fuhren pünktlich um 5 Uhr ab.

pronoun noun Pronomen das (PL die Pronomen).

pronounce verb aussprechen✧ SEP; **you don't pronounce the 'c'** das 'c' spricht man nicht aus.

pronunciation noun Aussprache die.

proof noun Beweis der (PL die Beweise); **there's no proof that ...** es gibt keine Beweise dafür, dass ....

propaganda noun Propaganda die.

propeller noun Propeller der (PL die Propeller).

proper adjective **1** (correct, real, genuine) richtig; **the proper answer** die richtige Antwort; **he's not a proper doctor** er ist kein richtiger Arzt; **2** (decent) anständig; **I need a proper meal** ich brauche ein anständiges Essen; **3 in its proper place** an den richtigen Ort.

properly adverb **1** richtig; **2** (decent) anständig.

property noun **1** (your belongings) Eigentum das; **2** (land, premises) Besitz der; **'private property'** 'Privatbesitz'; **3** (house) Haus das (PL die Häuser).

propose verb **1** (suggest) vorschlagen✧ SEP; **2** (marriage) **he proposed to her** er hat ihr einen Heiratsantrag gemacht.

protect verb schützen; **to protect somebody from something** jemanden vor etwas (DAT) schützen.

protection noun Schutz der.

protein noun Protein das (PL die Proteine).

protest noun **1** Beschwerde die (PL die Beschwerden); **to make a protest** eine Beschwerde einlegen SEP; **2** (disapproval) Protest der (PL die Proteste); **in protest against something** aus Protest gegen etwas (ACC).

protest verb protestieren; **to protest about something** gegen etwas (ACC) protestieren.

protest march noun Protestmarsch der (PL die Protestmärsche).

Protestant *noun* Protestant der (PL die Protestanten), Protestantin die (PL die Protestantinnen).

Protestant *adjective* protestantisch.

proud *adjective* stolz; **to be proud about something** stolz auf etwas (ACC) sein.

prove *verb* beweisen✧.

proverb *noun* Sprichwort das (PL die Sprichwörter).

provide *verb* zur Verfügung stellen.

provided, providing *conjunction* vorausgesetzt; **provided it doesn't rain** vorausgesetzt, es regnet nicht.

prune *noun* Backpflaume die (PL die Backpflaumen).

psychiatrist *noun* Psychiater der (PL die Psychiater), Psychiaterin die (PL die Psychiaterinnen).

psychological *adjective* psychologisch.

psychologist *noun* Psychologe der (PL die Psychologen), Psychologin die (PL die Psychologinnen).

psychology *noun* Psychologie die.

PTO *abbreviation* b.w. (*bitte wenden*).

pub *noun* Kneipe die (PL die Kneipen) (*informal*).

public *noun* **the public** die Öffentlichkeit; **in public** in aller Öffentlichkeit.

public *adjective* öffentlich.

public holiday *noun* gesetzliche Feiertag der (PL die gesetzlichen Feiertage); **January 1st is a public holiday** der erste Januar ist ein gesetzlicher Feiertag.

publicity *noun* **1** Publicity die; **2** (*advertising*) Werbung die.

public school *noun* Privatschule die (PL die Privatschulen).

public transport *noun* öffentliche Verkehrsmittel (*plural*).

publish *verb* veröffentlichen.

publisher *noun* **1** Verleger der (PL die Verleger), Verlegerin die (PL die Verlegerinnen); **2** (*company*) Verlag der (PL die Verlage).

pudding *noun* (*dessert*) Nachtisch der (PL die Nachtische); **for pudding we've got strawberries** zum Nachtisch gibt es Erdbeeren.

puddle *noun* Pfütze die (PL die Pfützen).

puff *noun* (*of smoke*) Wölkchen das (PL die Wölkchen).

puff pastry *noun* Blätterteig der.

pull *verb* **1** ziehen✧; **to pull a cart** einen Wagen ziehen; **2** ziehen an (+ DAT); **to pull a rope** an einem Seil ziehen; **he pulled a letter out of his pocket** er hat einen Brief aus der Tasche gezogen; ★ **he's pulling your leg!** er nimmt dich auf den Arm (*literally: he's picking you up in his arms*).

● **to pull down 1** herunterziehen✧ SEP; **2** (*demolish*) abreißen✧ SEP (*a building*).

● **to pull in** (*at the roadside*) an den Straßenrand fahren✧ (PERF *sein*).

pullover *noun* Pullover der (PL die Pullover).

pulse *noun* Puls der; **the doctor took my pulse** der Arzt maß meinen Puls.

a
b
c
d
e
f
g
h
i
j
k
l
m
n
o
p
q
r
s
t
u
v
w
x
y
z

pump noun Pumpe die (PL die Pumpen); **bicycle pump** die Fahrradpumpe.

pump verb pumpen.
- **to pump up** aufpumpen SEP.

pumpkin noun Kürbis der (PL die Kürbisse).

punch noun 1 (in boxing) Faustschlag der (PL die Faustschläge); 2 (drink) Bowle die (PL die Bowlen).

punch verb 1 he punched me in the stomach er hat mich in den Magen geboxt; 2 lochen (a ticket).

punctual adjective pünktlich.

punctuation noun Zeichensetzung die.

punctuation mark noun Satzzeichen das (PL die Satzzeichen).

puncture noun (flat tyre) Reifenpanne die (PL die Reifenpannen).

punish verb bestrafen.

punishment noun Strafe die (PL die Strafen).

pupil noun Schüler der (PL die Schüler), Schülerin die (PL die Schülerinnen).

puppet noun Puppe die (PL die Puppen).

puppy noun junge Hund der (PL die jungen Hunde); **a boxer puppy** ein junger Boxer.

pure adjective rein.

purple adjective lila ('lila' never changes).

purpose noun 1 Zweck der (PL die Zwecke); **what's the purpose of it?** was hat das für einen Zweck?; 2 on purpose absichtlich; **she did it on**

purpose das hat sie absichtlich getan; **he closed the door on purpose** er hat die Tür absichtlich zugemacht.

purr verb schnurren.

purse noun Portemonnaie das (PL die Portemonnaies).

push noun **to give something a push** etwas schieben◇.

push verb 1 he schubsen; **he pushed me** er hat mich geschubst; 2 (to press) drücken auf (+ ACC) (a bell or button); 3 **to push somebody to do something** jemanden zu etwas drängen; **his teacher is pushing him to sit the exam** sein Lehrer drängt ihn, die Prüfung zu machen; 4 **to push your way through the crowd** sich durch die Menge drängeln.
- **to push something away** etwas wegschieben◇ SEP; she pushed her plate away sie schob ihren Teller weg.

pushchair noun Sportwagen der (PL die Sportwagen).

put verb 1 (place generally) tun◇; **put some milk in your tea** tu etwas Milch in den Tee; **you can put the butter in the fridge** du kannst die Butter in den Kühlschrank tun; 2 (lay flat) legen; **she put the pencil on the desk** sie hat den Bleistift auf den Schreibtisch gelegt; 3 (place upright) stellen; **where did you put my bag?** wo hast du meine Handtasche hingestellt?; 4 (write) schreiben◇; **put your address here** schreiben Sie Ihre Adresse hierhin.
- **to put away** wegräumen SEP; **put**

away your things räume deine Sachen weg.

● **to put back 1** zurücktun SEP, zurücklegen SEP, zurückstellen SEP (*the translation of 'put back' depends on the way it is done. if it's placed lying down, use 'zurücklegen', if placed upright use 'zurückstellen' and if it could be either, use 'zurücktun'*); **I put it back in the drawer** ich habe es in die Schublade zurückgetan; **2** (*postpone*) verschieben ⬧; **the meeting has been put back until Thursday** die Besprechung ist auf Donnerstag verschoben worden.

● **to put down** (*lying down*) hinlegen SEP, (*upright*) hinstellen SEP; **where can I put the vase down?** wo kann ich die Vase hinstellen?

● **to put off 1** (*postpone*) verschieben ⬧; **he's put off my lesson till Thursday** er hat meine Stunde auf Donnerstag verschoben; **2** (*turn off*) ausmachen SEP; **don't forget to put off the lights** vergiss nicht, das Licht auszumachen; **3 to put somebody off something** jemandem die Lust an etwas (DAT) verderben ⬧; **it really put me off my food** das hat mir wirklich den Appetit verdorben; **4 to put somebody off doing something** jemanden davon abbringen ⬧ SEP, etwas zu tun; **don't put off let** dich nicht davon abbringen.

● **to put on 1** anziehen ⬧ SEP (*clothes*); **I'll just put my shoes on** ich ziehe nur schnell meine Schuhe

an; **2** auflegen SEP (*a CD or record*); **I'm putting on Oasis** ich lege Oasis auf; **3** (*switch on*) anmachen SEP (*a light or the heating*); **could you put the lamp on?** kannst du die Lampe anmachen?

● **to put out 1** (*put outside*) nach draußen tun ⬧, raustun ⬧ SEP (*informal*); **have you put the rubbish out?** hast du den Müll rausgebracht?; **2** ausmachen SEP (*a light or cigarette*); **I've put the lights out** ich habe das Licht ausgemacht; **3 to put out your hand** die Hand ausstrecken SEP.

● **to put up 1** heben ⬧ (*your hand*); **2** aufhängen SEP (*a picture or poster*); **we've put up some posters in my room** ich habe ein paar Poster in meinem Zimmer aufgehängt; **3** anschlagen ⬧ SEP (*a notice*); **4** erhöhen (*the price*); **they've put up the fare** sie haben den Fahrpreis erhöht; **5** (*for the night*) **friends put me up** ich habe bei Freunden übernachtet; **can you put me up on Friday?** kannst du Freitag bei euch übernachten?

● **to put up with something** etwas aushalten ⬧ SEP; **I don't know how she puts up with it** ich weiß nicht, wie sie das aushält.

puzzle *noun* (*jigsaw*) Puzzle *das* (PL *die* Puzzles).

puzzled *adjective* verdutzt.

pyjamas *plural noun* Schlafanzug *der* (PL *die* Schlafanzüge); **a pair of pyjamas** ein Schlafanzug; **where are my pyjamas?** wo ist mein Schlafanzug?

a b c d e f g h i j k l m n o p q r s t u v w x y z

Qq

qualification noun **1** (*ability, experience*) Qualifikation die (PL die Qualifikationen); **2** (*on paper*) Zeugnis das (PL die Zeugnisse).

qualified adjective **1** ausgebildet; **she's a qualified ski instructor** sie ist eine ausgebildete Skilehrerin; **2** (*having a degree or a diploma*) Diplom-; **a qualified engineer** ein Diplomingenieur.

qualify verb **1** (*to be eligible*) berechtigt sein; **we don't qualify for a reduction** wir bekommen keine Ermäßigung; **2** (*in sport*) sich qualifizieren; **they qualified for the third round** sie haben sich für die dritte Runde qualifiziert.

quality noun Qualität die; **good quality products** Waren von guter Qualität.

quantity noun Menge die (PL die Mengen).

quarrel noun Streit der (PL die Streite); **to have a quarrel** Streit haben.

quarrel verb sich streiten✧; **they're always quarrelling** sie streiten sich dauernd.

quarry noun Steinbruch der (PL die Steinbrüche).

quarter noun **1** Viertel das (PL die Viertel); **a quarter of the price** ein Viertel des Preises; **three quarters of the class** drei Viertel der Klasse; **it's a quarter past ten** es ist Viertel nach zehn; **it's a quarter to ten** es ist Viertel vor zehn; **2 we meet at quarter to eight** wir treffen uns um Viertel vor acht; **3 a quarter of an**

hour eine Viertelstunde; **4 three quarters of an hour** eine Dreiviertelstunde; **5 an hour and a quarter** eineinviertel Stunden.

quarter finals noun Viertelfinale das (PL die Viertelfinale).

queen noun **1** Königin die (PL die Königinnen); **2** (*in chess, cards*) Dame die (PL die Damen).

query noun Frage die (PL die Fragen); **are there any queries?** gibt es irgendwelche Fragen?

question noun Frage die (PL die Fragen); **to ask somebody a question** jemandem eine Frage stellen; **I asked her a question** ich habe ihr eine Frage gestellt; **it's out of the question** das kommt nicht in Frage.

question verb befragen (*a person*).

question mark noun Fragezeichen das (PL die Fragezeichen).

questionnaire noun Fragebogen der (PL die Fragebögen).

queue noun (*of people, cars*) Schlange die (PL die Schlangen); **to stand in a queue** Schlange stehen; **a queue of cars** eine Autoschlange.

quick adjective schnell; **to have a quick lunch** schnell etwas zu Mittag essen; **it's quicker on the motorway** auf der Autobahn geht es schneller; **to have a quick look at something** sich (DAT) etwas schnell ansehen; **be quick!** mach schnell!

quickly adverb schnell; **I'll just quickly phone my mother** ich rufe nur schnell meine Mutter an.

quiet *adjective* **1** (*silent*) still; **to keep quiet** still sein; **please keep quiet** sei bitte still; **2** (*not loud*) leise; **the children are very quiet** die Kinder sind ganz leise; **in a quiet voice** mit leiser Stimme; **3** (*peaceful*) ruhig; **a quiet street** eine ruhige Straße.

quietly *adverb* **1** (*speak, move*) leise; **he got up quietly** er ist leise aufgestanden; **2** (*read or play*) ruhig; **to sit quietly** ruhig sitzen.

quilt *noun* Steppdecke die (PL die Steppdecken).

quite *adverb* **1** (*fairly*) ziemlich; **it's quite cold outside** es ist ziemlich kalt draußen; **quite often** ziemlich oft; **quite a few** ziemlich viele; **quite a few of our friends came** ziemlich viele unserer Freunde sind gekommen; **quite a few people** ziemlich viele Leute; **that's quite a good idea** das ist eine ganz gute Idee; **2** (*completely*) völlig; it was quite amazing es war einfach fantastisch; **not quite** nicht ganz; **she's not quite ready** sie ist noch nicht ganz fertig; **3** genau; **I don't quite know what he wants** ich weiß nicht genau, was er will; **quite!** genau!

quiz *noun* Quiz das (PL die Quiz).

quotation *noun* (*from a book*) Zitat das (PL die Zitate).

quotation marks *plural noun* Anführungszeichen (*plural*); **in quotation marks** in Anführungszeichen.

quote *noun* **1** (*from a book*) Zitat das (PL die Zitate); **2** (*estimate*)

Kostenvoranschlag der (PL die Kostenvoranschläge).

quote *verb* zitieren.

Rr

rabbi *noun* Rabbi der (PL die Rabbis).

rabbit *noun* Kaninchen das (PL die Kaninchen).

rabies *noun* Tollwut die.

race *noun* **1** (*a sports event*) Rennen das (PL die Rennen); **cycle race** das Radrennen; **2** (*running*) um die Wette laufen✧ (PERF sein), (*swimming*) um die Wette schwimmen✧ (PERF sein); **3** (*an ethnic group*) Rasse die (PL die Rassen).

racetrack *noun* Rennbahn die (PL die Rennbahnen).

racial *adjective* rassisch, Rassen-; **racial discrimination** die Rassendiskriminierung.

racing car *noun* Rennwagen der (PL die Rennwagen), Rennfahrerin die (PL die Rennfahrerinnen).

racing driver *noun* Rennfahrer der (PL die Rennfahrer).

racism *noun* Rassismus der.

racist *noun* Rassist der (PL die Rassisten), Rassistin die (PL die Rassistinnen).

racist *adjective* rassistisch.

racket *noun* **1** (*for tennis*) Schläger der (PL die Schläger); **my tennis racket** mein Tennisschläger; **2** (*noise*) Krach der.

radiation *noun* Strahlung die (PL die Strahlungen).

a b c d e f g h i j k l m n o p q r s t u v w x y z

radiator noun Heizkörper der (PL die Heizkörper).

radio noun Radio das (PL die Radios); **to listen to the radio** Radio hören; **to hear something on the radio** etwas im Radio hören.

radioactive adjective radioaktiv.

radio-controlled adjective ferngesteuert.

radio station noun Rundfunkstation die (PL die Rundfunkstationen).

radish noun Radieschen das (PL die Radieschen).

rag noun Lumpen der (PL die Lumpen).

rage noun Wut die; **to fly into a rage** in Wut geraten◇ (PERF sein); **she's in a rage** sie ist wütend; ★ **it's all the rage** das ist der letzte Schrei (literally: it's the last scream).

rail noun 1 (for a train) Schiene die (PL die Schienen); 2 (the railway) **to go by rail** mit der Bahn fahren; 3 (on a balcony, bridge, or stairs) Geländer das (PL die Geländer).

rail card noun Bahnpass der (PL die Bahnpässe).

railing(s) noun Geländer das (PL die Geländer).

railway noun 1 (the system) Bahn die; **the railways** die Bahn; 2 **railway line** (from one place to another) die Bahnstrecke; 3 **on the railway line** (the track) auf dem Gleis.

railway carriage noun Eisenbahnwagen der (PL die Eisenbahnwagen).

railway station noun Bahnhof der (PL die Bahnhöfe).

rain noun Regen der; **in the rain** im Regen.

rain verb regnen; **it's raining** es regnet; **it's going to rain** es wird regnen.

rainbow noun Regenbogen der (PL die Regenbogen).

raincoat noun Regenmantel der (PL die Regenmäntel).

rainy adjective regnerisch.

raise verb 1 (lift up) hochheben◇ SEP; 2 (increase) erhöhen (prices); 3 **to raise money for something** Geld für etwas aufbringen◇ SEP.

raisin noun Rosine die (PL die Rosinen).

rake noun Rechen der (PL die Rechen).

rally noun 1 (a meeting) Versammlung die (PL die Versammlungen); 2 (for cars) Rallye die (PL die Rallyes); 3 (in tennis) Ballwechsel der (PL die Ballwechsel).

rambler noun Wanderer der (PL die Wanderer), Wanderin die (PL die Wanderinnen).

rambling noun Wandern das.

range noun 1 (a choice) Auswahl die; **a wide range of travel brochures** eine große Auswahl an Reiseprospekten; 2 **a range of subjects** verschiedene Fächer; **in a range of colours** in verschiedenen Farben; 3 **a computer in this price range** ein Computer in dieser Preislage; **that's out of my price range** das kann ich mir nicht leisten.

rap noun Rap der (music).

rape noun Vergewaltigung die (PL die Vergewaltigungen).

rape *verb* vergewaltigen.

rare *adjective* 1 selten; **a rare bird** ein seltener Vogel; 2 englisch gebraten (*steak*).

rarely *adverb* selten.

rash *noun* Ausschlag der (PL die Ausschläge).

rash *adjective* voreilig.

raspberry *noun* Himbeere die (PL die Himbeeren); **raspberry jam** die Himbeermarmelade.

rat *noun* Ratte die (PL die Ratten).

rate *noun* 1 (*a charge*) Gebühren (*plural*); **postage rates** Postgebühren; 2 **are there special rates for children?** gibt es Sonderpreise für Kinder?; **at reduced rates** zu ermäßigten Preisen; 3 **rate of exchange** der Wechselkurs; 4 **rate of pay** der Lohnsatz; 5 (*a level*) Rate die (PL die Raten); **a high cancellation rate** eine hohe Absagerate; 6 **at any rate** auf jeden Fall.

rather *adverb* 1 lieber; **I'd rather wait** ich warte lieber; **I'd rather you didn't go** es wäre mir lieber, wenn du nicht gingest; 2 ziemlich; **I'm rather busy** ich habe ziemlich viel zu tun; **I've got rather a lot of shopping to do** ich muss noch ziemlich viel einkaufen; 3 **rather than** eher als; **in summer rather than winter** eher im Sommer als im Winter.

rave *noun* (*party*) Fete die (PL die Feten) (*informal*).

raw *adjective* roh.

razor *noun* Rasierapparat der (PL die Rasierapparate).

razor blade *noun* Rasierklinge die (PL die Rasierklingen).

RE *noun* Religionsunterricht der.

reach *noun* Reichweite die; **out of reach** außer Reichweite; **within reach** leicht erreichbar; **to be within easy reach of Munich** von München aus leicht erreichbar sein.

reach *verb* 1 ankommen✧ SEP (PERF sein) an (+ DAT) a place or point, ankommen✧ SEP (PERF sein) in (+ DAT) (*a town or country*); **when you reach the station** wenn du am Bahnhof ankommst; 2 kommen✧ (PERF sein) zu (+ DAT) (*an agreement, a conclusion*); **to reach a decision** zu einer Entscheidung kommen; 3 **to reach for something** nach etwas (DAT) greifen✧.

react *verb* reagieren.

reaction *noun* Reaktion die (PL die Reaktionen).

read *verb* 1 lesen✧; **what are you reading at the moment?** was liest du zur Zeit?; **I'm reading a detective novel** ich lese einen Krimi; 2 **to read out** vorlesen✧ SEP; **he read out the list to the students** er hat die Liste den Studenten vorgelesen.

reading *noun* 1 (*action*) Lesen das; 2 (*reading matter*) Lektüre die; **some easy reading for the holidays** eine leichte Lektüre für die Ferien.

ready *adjective* 1 fertig; **supper's not ready yet** das Essen ist noch nicht fertig; **we are not quite ready** wir sind noch nicht ganz fertig; **are you ready to leave?** seid ihr fertig?, (*on a journey*) seid ihr reisefertig?; **to get ready** sich fertig machen; **I'm getting ready to play tennis** ich mache mich zum Tennisspielen fertig; **I was getting ready for bed** ich war gerade dabei, ins Bett zu gehen; **2 to get something ready** (*complete*) etwas fertig machen, etwas vorbereiten SEP (*a room or food*); **I'll get your room ready** ich bereite dein Zimmer vor.

real *adjective* **1** (*genuine*) echt; **it's a real diamond** das ist ein echter Brillant; **he's a real coward** er ist ein echter Feigling; **I was getting** (*true*) etwas richtig; **is that her real name?** ist das ihr richtiger Name?; **3** (*not imagined*) wirklich; **it's a real pity you can't come** es ist wirklich schade, dass du nicht kommen kannst.

realistic *adjective* realistisch.

reality *noun* Wirklichkeit *die*; **a reality show** eine Reality-Show.

realize *verb* wissen◇; **I hadn't realized** das wusste ich nicht; **I didn't realize he was French** ich wusste nicht, dass er Franzose ist; **do you realize what time it is?** weißt du, wie viel Uhr es ist?

really *adverb* **1** wirklich; **the film was really good** der Film war wirklich gut; **really?** wirklich?; **2 not really** eigentlich nicht.

reason *noun* Grund *der* (PL *die* Gründe); **for that reason** aus diesem Grund; **the reason why I phoned** der Grund meines Anrufs.

reasonable *adjective* vernünftig.

receipt *noun* Quittung *die* (PL *die* Quittungen).

receive *verb* erhalten◇.

receiver *noun* Hörer *der* (PL *die* Hörer); **to pick up the receiver** den Hörer abnehmen◇ SEP.

recent *adjective* **1** kürzlich erfolgter/kürzlich erfolgte/kürzlich erfolgtes; **the recent closure** die kürzlich erfolgte Schließung; **2 in recent years** in den letzten Jahren.

recently *adverb* **1** (*at a time not long ago*) kürzlich; **2** (*over the recent period*) in letzter Zeit.

reception *noun* **1** Rezeption *die* (PL *die* Rezeptionen); **he's waiting at reception** er wartet an der Rezeption; **2** Empfang *der* (PL *die* Empfänge); **a big wedding reception** ein großer Hochzeitsempfang; **3 to get a good reception** gut aufgenommen werden.

receptionist *noun* **1** Empfangsdame *die* (PL *die* Empfangsdamen); **2** (*in a doctor's surgery*) Sprechstundenhilfe *die* (PL *die* Sprechstundenhilfen).

recipe *noun* Rezept *das* (PL *die* Rezepte).

reckon *verb* glauben; **I reckon it's a good idea** ich glaube, das ist eine gute Idee.

recognize *verb* erkennen◇.

recommend *verb* empfehlen◇; **can you recommend a dentist?** kannst du mir einen Zahnarzt empfehlen?; **I recommend the fish soup** ich empfehle die Fischsuppe.

record *noun* **1** Rekord *der* (PL *die* Rekorde); **it's a world record** das ist ein Weltrekord; **record sales** Verkaufsrekorde; **2** (*of events*) Aufzeichnung *die* (PL *die*

Aufzeichnungen); **on record** aufgezeichnet; **to keep a record of something** über etwas Buch führen; **3** (music) Platte die (PL die Platten); **a Miles Davis record** eine Platte von Miles Davis; **4 records** (office files) Unterlagen (plural); **I'll just check your records** ich prüfe nur Ihre Unterlagen.

record verb (on tape) aufnehmen✧ SEP; **I'm recording it on cassette** ich nehme es auf Kassette auf.

recorder noun **1** Blockflöte die (PL die Blockflöten); **to play the recorder** Blockflöte spielen; **2 cassette recorder** der Kassettenrekorder; **video recorder** der Videorekorder.

recording noun (on tape or CD) Aufnahme die (PL die Aufnahmen), (on video) Aufzeichnung die (PL die Aufzeichnungen).

record player noun Plattenspieler der (PL die Plattenspieler).

recover verb sich erholen; **she's recovered now** sie hat sich wieder erholt.

recovery noun (from an illness) Erholung die; **to make a good recovery** sich gut erholen.

rectangle noun Rechteck das (PL die Rechtecke).

rectangular adjective rechteckig.

recycle verb recyceln.

red adjective rot; **a red car** ein rotes Auto; **to go red** rot werden, **to have red hair** rote Haare haben.

Red Cross noun **the Red Cross** das Rote Kreuz.

redcurrant noun Johannisbeere die (PL die Johannisbeeren);

redcurrant jelly das Johannisbeergelee.

redecorate verb (with paint) neu streichen✧, (with wallpaper) neu tapezieren; **they've redecorated the kitchen** sie haben die Küche neu gestrichen.

redo verb noch einmal machen.

reduce verb **1 to reduce prices** die Preise herabsetzen SEP; **2 to reduce speed** die Geschwindigkeit verringern.

reduction noun **1** (in price) Ermäßigung die (PL die Ermäßigungen); **2** (in speed or number) Reduzierung die.

redundant adjective **to be made redundant** entlassen werden.

referee noun (in sport) Schiedsrichter der (PL die Schiedsrichter), Schiedsrichterin die (PL die Schiedsrichterinnen).

reference noun Referenz die (PL die Referenzen); (for a job) **she gave me a good reference** sie hat mir eine gute Referenz gegeben.

reference book noun Nachschlagewerk das (PL die Nachschlagewerke).

refill verb nachfüllen SEP.

reflect verb spiegeln; **to be reflected** sich spiegeln.

reflection noun **1** (in a mirror or on water) Spiegelung die (PL die Spiegelungen); **to see your reflection in the mirror** sich im Spiegel sehen; **2** (thought) Überlegung die; **on reflection** nach nochmaliger Überlegung.

reflexive adjective **a reflexive verb** ein reflexives Verb.

refreshing adjective erfrischend.

a b c d e f g h i j k l m n o p q r s t u v w x y z

refreshment noun Erfrischung die (PL die Erfrischungen).

refrigerator noun Kühlschrank der (PL die Kühlschränke).

refuge noun Zuflucht die; **a mountain refuge** eine Schutzhütte; **to take refuge in** sich flüchten in (+ DAT).

refugee noun Flüchtling der (PL die Flüchtlinge).

refund noun Rückzahlung die (PL die Rückzahlungen).

refund verb zurückerstatten SEP.

refusal noun **1** Weigerung die (PL die Weigerungen); **2** (for a job) Absage die (PL die Absagen); **to get a refusal** eine Absage bekommen.

refuse noun (rubbish) Abfall der.

refuse verb sich weigern; **I refused** ich habe mich geweigert; **he refuses to help** er weigert sich zu helfen.

regards plural noun Grüße (plural); **regards to your parents** viele Grüße an deine Eltern; **Nat sends his regards** Nat lässt grüßen.

reggae noun Reggae der.

region noun Gebiet das (PL die Gebiete).

regional adjective regional.

register noun (in school) Anwesenheitsliste die (PL die Anwesenheitslisten).

register verb **1** eintragen◇ SEP (a name); **2** (report) anmelden SEP.

registered letter noun Einschreiben das (PL die Einschreiben).

registration number noun Autonummer die (PL die Autonummern).

regret verb bedauern.

regular adjective regelmäßig; **regular visits** regelmäßige Besuche.

regularly adverb regelmäßig.

regulation noun Vorschrift die (PL die Vorschriften).

rehearsal noun Probe die (PL die Proben).

rehearse verb proben.

reheat verb aufwärmen SEP.

reject verb ablehnen SEP.

related adjective verwandt; **we're not related** wir sind nicht verwandt.

relation noun Verwandte der/die (PL die Verwandten).

relationship noun Beziehung die (PL die Beziehungen); **I have a good relationship with my parents** ich habe eine gute Beziehung zu meinen Eltern.

relative noun Verwandte der/die (PL die Verwandten).

relatively adverb relativ.

relax verb entspannen; **I'm going to relax and watch telly tonight** heute Abend entspanne ich mich und sehe fern.

relaxed adjective entspannt.

relaxing adjective entspannend.

relay race noun Staffel die (PL die Staffeln).

release noun (a film, CD, or book) **1** Neuerscheinung die (PL die Neuerscheinungen); **this week's new releases** die neuen Filme der Woche; **2** (of a prisoner or hostage)

Freilassung die (PL die Freilassungen).

release verb **1** herausbringen✧ SEP (a record, film, or video); **2** freilassen✧ SEP (a person).

reliable adjective zuverlässig.

relief noun Erleichterung die; **what a relief!** da bin ich aber erleichtert!

relieve verb stillen (pain).

relieved adjective erleichtert; **I was relieved to hear you'd arrived** ich war erleichtert zu hören, dass du angekommen bist.

religion noun Religion die (PL die Religionen).

religious adjective religiös.

rely verb **1** (trust) **to rely on somebody** sich auf jemanden verlassen✧; **I'm relying on your help for Saturday** ich verlasse mich darauf, dass du mir am Samstag hilfst; **2** (be dependent on) **to rely on** angewiesen sein auf (+ ACC).

remain verb (be left over) übrig bleiben✧ (PERF sein), (stay) bleiben✧ (PERF sein).

remark noun Bemerkung die (PL die Bemerkungen); **to make remarks about something** Bemerkungen über etwas (ACC) machen.

remarkable adjective bemerkenswert.

remarkably adverb bemerkenswert.

remember verb **1** sich erinnern an (+ ACC) (a person or an occasion); **I don't remember** daran kann ich mich nicht erinnern; **do you remember the holiday in Italy?** erinnerst du dich noch an die Ferien in Italien? **2 I can't**

remember his number seine Nummer fällt mir nicht ein; **3** to remember to do something daran denken✧, etwas zu tun; **remember to lock the door** denk daran abzuschließen; **I remembered to bring the CDs** ich habe daran gedacht, die CDs mitzubringen.

remind verb erinnern; **to remind somebody to do something** jemanden daran erinnern, etwas zu tun; **remind your mother to pick me up** erinnere deine Mutter daran, mich abzuholen; **he reminds me of my brother** er erinnert mich an meinen Bruder; **2 oh, that reminds me ...** dabei fällt mir ein ....

remote adjective abgelegen.

remote control noun **1** (for a car or plane) Fernsteuerung die (PL die Fernsteuerungen); **2** (for TV or video) Fernbedienung die (PL die Fernbedienungen).

remove verb **1** entfernen (a stain, mark, or obstacle); **2** ausziehen✧ SEP (clothes).

renew verb verlängern (a passport or licence).

rent noun Miete die (PL die Mieten).

rent verb mieten; **Simon's rented a flat** Simon hat eine Wohnung gemietet.

reorganize verb umorganisieren.

repair noun Reparatur die (PL die Reparaturen).

repair verb reparieren; **to get something repaired** etwas reparieren lassen; **we've had the television repaired** wir haben

a b c d e f g h i j k l m n o p q r s t u v w x y z

a unseren Fernseher reparieren lassen.

b **repay** verb zurückzahlen SEP.

repeat noun Wiederholung die (PL die Wiederholungen).

c **repeat** verb wiederholen.

d **repeatedly** adverb wiederholt.

e **repetitive** adjective eintönig.

f **replace** verb ersetzen.

reply noun Antwort die (PL die Antworten); **I didn't get a reply to my letter** ich habe keine Antwort auf meinen Brief bekommen; **there's no reply** niemand antwortet.

g
h
i

reply verb antworten; **I still haven't replied to the letter** ich habe immer noch nicht auf den Brief geantwortet.

j
k
l

report noun 1 (of an event) Bericht der (PL die Berichte); 2 (school report) Zeugnis das (PL die Zeugnisse).

m
n

report verb 1 melden (a problem or an accident); **we've reported the theft** wir haben den Diebstahl gemeldet; 2 sich melden; **I had to report to reception** ich musste mich an der Rezeption melden; 3 (in the news) berichten; **to report on the strike** über den Streik berichten.

o
p
q

r

s

reporter noun Reporter der (PL die Reporter), Reporterin die (PL die Reporterinnen).

t
u

represent verb 1 darstellen SEP (a word, a thing, an idea); 2 vertreten⬦ (a group or company).

v
w
x

representative noun Vertreter der (PL die Vertreter), Vertreterin die (PL die Vertreterinnen).

y
z

reproduction noun 1 (process) Fortpflanzung die (PL die Fortpflanzungen); 2 (of sound etc) Wiedergabe die; 3 (copy) Reproduktion. die (PL die Reproduktionen).

republic noun Republik die (PL die Republiken).

reputation noun 1 Ruf der; **to have a good reputation** einen guten Ruf haben; 2 **she has a reputation for honesty** sie gilt als ehrlich.

request noun Bitte die (PL die Bitten); **at my mother's request** auf Bitte meiner Mutter.

request verb bitten⬦; **to request something** um etwas (ACC) bitten.

rescue noun Rettung die; **rescue operation** die Rettungsaktion; **to come to somebody's rescue** jemandem zu Hilfe kommen.

rescue verb retten; **they rescued the dog** sie haben den Hund gerettet.

rescue party noun Rettungsmannschaft die (PL die Rettungsmannschaften).

research noun 1 Forschung die; **for research into Aids** für die Aidsforschung; 2 **to do research** forschen.

research verb **to research into something** etwas erforschen.

resemblance noun Ähnlichkeit die (PL die Ähnlichkeiten).

reservation noun (a booking) Reservierung die (PL die Reservierungen); **to make a reservation (for a room)** (ein Zimmer) reservieren lassen.

reserve noun 1 Reserve die (PL die Reserven); **we have a few in reserve** wir haben ein paar in Reserve; 2 **nature reserve** das Naturschutzgebiet; 3 (for a match) Reservespieler der (PL die Reservespieler), Reservespielerin die (PL die Reservespielerinnen).

reserve verb reservieren; **this table is reserved** dieser Tisch ist reserviert.

reservoir noun Reservoir das (PL die Reservoirs).

resident noun Bewohner der (PL die Bewohner), Bewohnerin die (PL die Bewohnerinnen).

residential adjective Wohn-; **a residential area** eine Wohngegend.

resign verb 1 (from your job) kündigen; 2 (from an official post) zurücktreten ◇ SEP.

resignation noun 1 Kündigung die (PL die Kündigungen); 2 (from an official post) Rücktritt der.

resist verb widerstehen ◇ (+ DAT) (an offer or temptation).

resit verb wiederholen (an exam).

resort noun 1 (for holidays) holiday resort der Urlaubsort; **ski resort** der Wintersportort; **seaside resort** das Seebad; 2 **as a last resort** als letzter Ausweg.

respect noun Respekt der.

respect verb respektieren.

respectable adjective anständig.

responsibility noun Verantwortung die (PL die Verantwortungen).

responsible adjective 1 verantwortlich; **he was responsible for the accident** er war für den Unfall verantwortlich; **I'm responsible for booking the rooms** ich bin für die Zimmerreservierung verantwortlich; 2 (reliable) verantwortungsbewusst; **he's not very responsible** er ist nicht sehr verantwortungsbewusst.

rest noun 1 **the rest** der Rest; **the rest of the day** der Rest des Tages; **the rest of the bread** der Brotrest, der Rest von dem Brot; 2 (the others) **the rest** die Übrigen; **the rest have gone home** die Übrigen sind nach Hause gegangen; 3 Erholung die; **he's going to the mountains for a rest** er fährt zur Erholung ins Gebirge; **ten days' rest** zehn Tage Erholung; **to have a rest** sich ausruhen SEP; 4 (a short break) Pause die (PL die Pausen); **to stop for a rest** eine Pause machen.

rest verb (have a rest) sich ausruhen SEP.

restaurant noun Restaurant das (PL die Restaurants).

restful adjective erholsam.

restless adjective unruhig.

restrain verb zurückhalten ◇ SEP.

result noun 1 Ergebnis das (PL die Ergebnisse); **the exam results** die Prüfungsergebnisse; 2 **as a result** infolgedessen; **as a result we missed the train** infolgedessen haben wir den Zug verpasst.

retire verb 1 (from work) in den Ruhestand gehen ◇, (civil servant, teacher, soldier) in Pension gehen ◇; **she retires in June** sie geht im Juni in Pension; 2 **to be retired** im Ruhestand sein ◇.

a b c d e f g h i j k l m n o p q r s t u v w x y z

a

retirement noun Ruhestand der, since his retirement seitdem er in den Ruhestand gegangen ist.

b

c

return noun 1 (coming back) Rückkehr die; the return journey die Rückreise; 2 by return of post postwendend; 3 in return für für; in return for his help für seine Hilfe; 4 in return dafür; ★ many happy returns! herzlichen Glückwunsch zum Geburtstag!

d

e

f

g

return verb 1 (come back) zurückkommen◇ SEP (PERF sein); he returned ten minutes later er kam zehn Minuten später zurück; to return from holiday aus den Ferien zurückkommen; 2 (go back) zurückgehen◇ SEP (PERF sein), (drive) zurückfahren◇ SEP (PERF sein); we are planning to return in the evening wir wollen am Abend zurückfahren; 3 (to give back) zurückgeben◇ SEP; Gemma's never returned the video Gemma hat das Video nie zurückgegeben.

h

i

j

k

l

m

n

o

return fare noun Preis für eine Rückfahrkarte der, (for a flight) Preis für einen Rückflugschein der.

p

q

r

return ticket noun Rückfahrkarte die (PL die Rückfahrkarten); (for a flight) Rückflugticket das (PL die Rückflugtickets).

s

t

reveal verb enthüllen.

u

v

reverse verb 1 (in a car) rückwärts fahren◇ (PERF sein); 2 to reverse the charges ein R-Gespräch führen.

w

x

y

review noun (of a book, play, or film) Kritik die (PL die Kritiken).

z

review verb rezensieren (a book, play, or film).

revise verb 1 lernen (for an exam); Tessa's busy revising for her exams Tessa lernt jetzt für ihre Prüfung; 2 wiederholen; to revise maths Mathe wiederholen.

revision noun Wiederholung die.

revive verb 1 (a person) wiederbeleben SEP; 2 (to recover) sich erholen.

revolting adjective eklig.

revolution noun Revolution die (PL die Revolutionen).

reward noun Belohnung die (PL die Belohnungen).

reward verb belohnen.

rewind verb zurückspulen SEP (a cassette or video).

rhinoceros noun Nashorn das (PL die Nashörner).

rhubarb noun Rhabarber der.

rhyme noun Reim der (PL die Reime).

rhythm noun Rhythmus der (PL die Rhythmen).

rib noun Rippe die (PL die Rippen).

ribbon noun Band das (PL die Bänder).

rice noun Reis der, rice pudding der Milchreis.

rich adjective 1 reich; they are very rich sie sind sehr reich; 2 the rich die Reichen.

rid adjective to get rid of something etwas loswerden◇ SEP (PERF sein) (informal); we got rid of the car wir sind das Auto losgeworden.

riddle noun Rätsel das (PL die Rätsel).

ride noun Fahrt die (PL die Fahrten); **to go for a ride (on a bike)** eine Fahrt machen; **to go for a ride (on a horse)** reiten gehen✧ (PERF *sein*).

ride verb 1 **to ride a bike** Rad fahren✧ (PERF *sein*); **can you ride a bike?** kannst du Rad fahren?; **I've never ridden a bike** ich bin noch nie Rad gefahren; 2 **to ride (a horse)** reiten✧ (PERF *sein*); **I've never ridden a horse** ich bin noch nie auf einem Pferd geritten.

rider noun 1 (*on a horse*) Reiter der (PL die Reiter), Reiterin die (PL die Reiterinnen); 2 (*on a bike*) Radler der (PL die Radler), Radlerin die (PL die Radlerinnen); 3 (*on a motorbike*) Fahrer der (PL die Fahrer), Fahrerin die (PL die Fahrerinnen).

ridiculous adjective lächerlich.

riding noun Reiten das; **to go riding** reiten gehen✧.

riding school noun Reitschule die (PL die Reitschulen).

rifle noun Gewehr das (PL die Gewehre).

right noun 1 (*not left*) rechte Seite die; **on the right** auf der rechten Seite; **on my right** rechts von mir; 2 (*to do something*) Recht das (PL die Rechte); **to have the right to something** ein Recht auf etwas (ACC) haben; **the right to work** das Recht auf Arbeit; **you have no right to say that** du hast kein Recht, das zu sagen.

right adjective 1 (*not left*) rechter/rechte/rechtes; **my right hand** meine rechte Hand; 2 (*correct*) richtig; **the right answer** die richtige Antwort; **is this the right address?** ist das die richtige Adresse?; 3 **to be right** (*of a person*) Recht haben; **you see, I was right** siehst du, ich hatte Recht; 4 **you were right not to say anything** du hattest Recht, nichts zu sagen; 5 **the clock is right** die Uhr geht richtig; 6 **yes, that's right** ja, das stimmt; **is that right?** stimmt das?

right adverb 1 (*direction*) rechts; **turn right at the lights** biege an der Ampel rechts ab; 2 (*correctly*) richtig; **you're not doing it right** du machst das nicht richtig; 3 (*completely*) ganz; **right at the bottom** ganz unten; **right at the beginning** ganz am Anfang; 4 (*exactly*) genau; **right in the middle** genau in der Mitte; 5 **right now** sofort; 6 (*okay*) gut; **right, let's go** gut, gehen wir.

right-click noun Klick der mit der rechten Maustaste (PL die Klicks mit der rechten Maustaste).

right-hand adjective **on the right-hand side** rechts.

right-handed adjective rechtshändig.

ring noun 1 (*on the phone*) **to give somebody a ring** jemanden anrufen✧ SEP; 2 (*for your finger*) Ring der (PL die Ringe); 3 (*circle*) Kreis der (PL die Kreise); 4 **there was a ring at the door** es hat geklingelt.

ring verb 1 (*a bell or phone*) klingeln; **the phone rang** das Telefon klingelte; 2 (*phone*) anrufen✧ SEP; **I'll ring you**

a b c d e f g h i j k l m n o p q r s t u v w x y z

tomorrow ich rufe dich morgen an; **3 to ring for a taxi** ein Taxi rufen.

● **to ring back** zurückrufen✧ SEP; **I'll ring you back later** ich rufe dich später zurück.

● **to ring off** auflegen SEP.

ring road noun Ringstraße die (PL die Ringstraßen).

rinse verb spülen.

riot noun Aufstand der (PL die Aufstände).

rioting noun Unruhen (plural).

rip verb zerreißen✧.

ripe adjective reif; **are the tomatoes ripe?** sind die Tomaten reif?

rip-off noun **it's a rip-off** das ist Nepp (informal).

rise noun **1** Anstieg der; **a rise in temperature** ein Temperaturanstieg; **2 pay rise** die Gehaltserhöhung.

rise verb **1** (the sun) aufgehen✧ SEP (PERF sein); **2** (prices) steigen✧ (PERF sein).

risk noun Risiko das (PL die Risiken); **to take a risk** ein Risiko eingehen.

risk verb riskieren; **he risks losing his job** er riskiert es, seine Stelle zu verlieren.

river noun Fluss der (PL die Flüsse).

road noun **1** Straße die (PL die Straßen); **the road to London** die Straße nach London; **2 the baker's is on the other side of the road** die Bäckerei ist auf der anderen Straßenseite; **3 across the road** gegenüber; **they live across the**

road from us sie wohnen uns gegenüber.

road accident noun Verkehrsunfall der (PL die Verkehrsunfälle).

road map noun Straßenkarte die (PL die Straßenkarten).

roadside noun **by the roadside** am Straßenrand.

road sign noun Straßenschild das (PL die Straßenschilder).

roadworks plural noun Straßenarbeiten (plural).

roast noun Braten der (PL die Braten).

roast adjective gebraten; **roast potatoes** Bratkartoffeln; **roast beef** der Rinderbraten.

rob verb **1** berauben (a person); **2** ausrauben SEP (a bank).

robber noun Räuber der (PL die Räuber).

robbery noun Raub der (PL die Raube); **bank robbery** der Bankraub.

robot noun Roboter der (PL die Roboter).

rock climbing noun Klettern das; **to go rock climbing** (zum) Klettern gehen.

rock noun **1** (a big stone) Felsen der (PL die Felsen); **2** (the material) Fels der; **3** (music) Rock der; **rock band** die Rockband; **to dance rock and roll** Rock 'n' Roll tanzen.

rocket noun Rakete die (PL die Raketen).

rock music noun Rockmusik die.

rock star noun Rockstar der (PL die Rockstars).

rocky adjective felsig.

rod noun **a fishing rod** eine Angel.

role *noun* Rolle die (PL die Rollen); **to play the role of Hamlet** die Rolle des Hamlet spielen.

roll *noun* **1** Rolle die (PL die Rollen); **a roll of film** eine Rolle Film; **a toilet roll** eine Rolle Toilettenpapier; **2 bread roll** das Brötchen, die Semmel (*South German*).

roll *verb* rollen (PERF *sein*).

roller *noun* **1** (*for hair*) Lockenwickler der (PL die Lockenwickler); **2** (*for paint*) Rolle die (PL die Rollen).

rollerblades *plural noun* Inlineskates (*plural*), Inliners (*plural*).

rollercoaster *noun* Achterbahn die (PL die Achterbahnen).

roller skates *plural noun* Rollschuhe (*plural*).

Roman Catholic *adjective* römisch-katholisch.

romantic *adjective* romantisch.

roof *noun* Dach das (PL die Dächer).

roof rack *noun* Gepäckträger der (PL die Gepäckträger).

rook *noun* **1** (*in chess*) Turm der (PL die Türme); **2** (*bird*) Saatkrähe die (PL die Saatkrähen).

room *noun* **1** Zimmer das (PL die Zimmer); **she's in the other room** sie ist im anderen Zimmer; **a three-room flat** eine Dreizimmerwohnung; **2** (*space*) Platz der; **enough room for two** genug Platz für zwei; **very little room** wenig Platz; **to make room** Platz machen.

root *noun* Wurzel die (PL die Wurzeln).

rope *noun* Seil das (PL die Seile).

rose *noun* Rose die (PL die Rosen).

rot *verb* verfaulen (PERF *sein*).

rotten *adjective* verfault.

rough *adjective* **1** (*scratchy*) rau; **2** (*vague*) grob (*plan or estimate*); **3 a rough idea** eine vage Vorstellung; **4** (*stormy*) stürmisch; **a rough sea** eine stürmische See; **5** (*difficult*) **to have a rough time** es schwer haben; **6 to sleep rough** im Freien schlafen.

roughly *adverb* (*approximately*) ungefähr; **roughly ten per cent** ungefähr zehn Prozent; **it takes roughly three hours** es dauert ungefähr drei Stunden.

round *noun* Runde die (PL die Runden); **a round of talks** eine Gesprächsrunde; **a round of drinks** eine Runde.

round *adjective* rund; **a round table** ein runder Tisch.

round *preposition* **1** um (+ ACC); **round the city** um die Stadt; **round my arm** um meinen Arm; **they were sitting round the table** sie haben um den Tisch gesessen; **it's just round the corner** es ist gleich um die Ecke; **2 to go round a museum** ein Museum besuchen.

round *adverb* **1 to go round to somebody's house** jemanden besuchen (+ DAT); **2 to invite somebody round** jemanden zu sich (DAT) einladen❖ SEP; **we invited Sally round for lunch** wir haben Sally zum Mittagessen eingeladen; **3 to look round the shops** sich in den Geschäften umsehen❖ SEP; **4 all the year round** das ganze Jahr hindurch.

roundabout noun 1 (for traffic) Kreisverkehr der; 2 (in a fairground) Karussell das (PL die Karussells).

route noun 1 (that you plan) Route die (PL die Routen); **the best route is via Calais** die beste Route führt über Calais; 2 **bus route** die Buslinie.

routine noun Routine die (PL die Routinen).

row¹ noun 1 Reihe die (PL die Reihen); **in the front row** in der ersten Reihe; **in the back row** in der letzten Reihe; 2 **in a row** hintereinander; **four times in a row** viermal hintereinander.

row verb (in a boat) rudern (PERF sein), (a boat, a person) rudern (PERF haben); **we rowed across the lake** wir sind über den See gerudert; **he rowed us across the lake** er hat uns über den See gerudert.

row² noun 1 (a quarrel) Krach der (informal) (PL die Kräche); **to have a row** Krach haben; **they've had a row** sie haben Krach gehabt; **I had a row with my parents** ich habe Krach mit meinen Eltern gehabt; 2 (noise) Krach der; **they were making a terrible row** sie haben einen furchtbaren Krach gemacht.

rowing noun Rudern das; **to go rowing** rudern gehen.

rowing boat noun Ruderboot das (PL die Ruderboote).

royal adjective königlich; **the royal family** die königliche Familie.

rub verb reiben✧; **to rub your eyes** sich (DAT) die Augen reiben.

● **to rub something out** etwas ausradieren SEP.

rubber noun 1 (an eraser) Radiergummi der (PL die Radiergummis); 2 (material) Gummi der; **rubber soles** Gummisohlen.

rubbish noun 1 (for the bin) Müll der; 2 (nonsense) Quatsch der (informal); **you're talking rubbish!** du redest Quatsch.

rubbish adjective schlecht; **the film was rubbish** der Film war schlecht; **they're a rubbish band** sie sind eine lausige Band.

rubbish bin noun Mülleimer der (PL die Mülleimer).

rucksack noun Rucksack der (PL die Rucksäcke).

rude adjective 1 unhöflich; **that's rude** das ist unhöflich; 2 unanständig; **a rude joke** ein unanständiger Witz.

rug noun 1 Teppich der (PL die Teppiche); 2 (a blanket) Decke die (PL die Decken).

rugby noun Rugby das.

ruin noun (remains) Ruine die (PL die Ruinen); **in ruins** in Trümmern.

ruin verb 1 ruinieren; **you'll ruin your jacket** du ruinierst dir die Jacke; 2 verderben✧ (day, holiday); **it ruined my evening** das hat mir den Abend verdorben.

rule noun 1 Regel die (PL die Regeln); **the rules of the game** die Spielregeln; **as a rule** in der Regel; 2 (administrative) Vorschrift die (PL die Vorschriften); **according to the school rules** nach den Schulvorschriften.

ruler noun Lineal das (PL die Lineale); **I've lost my ruler** ich habe mein Lineal verloren.

rum noun Rum der.

rumour noun Gerücht das (PL die Gerüchte).

run noun 1 (in games, sport, and for fitness) Lauf der (PL die Läufe); **to go for a run** laufen gehen (PERF sein), joggen gehen (PERF sein); **2** (of a play) Laufzeit die; **3** (in skiing) Abfahrt die (PL die Abfahrten); **4 in the long run** auf lange Sicht.

run verb 1 laufen◇ (PERF sein); **I ran ten kilometres** ich bin zehn Kilometer gelaufen; **he ran across the pitch** er ist über das Spielfeld gelaufen, **2** (run fast) rennen◇ (PERF sein); **Kitty ran for the bus** Kitty rannte, um den Bus zu kriegen; **3** (drive) fahren◇; **I'll run you home later** ich fahre dich später nach Hause; **4** (organize) veranstalten (a course or competition); **who's running this competition?** wer veranstaltet diesen Wettbewerb?; **5** (manage) leiten (a business); **she's been running the firm for years** sie leitet die Firma schon seit Jahren; **to run a shop** ein Geschäft leiten; **6** (a train or a bus) fahren◇ (PERF sein); **the buses don't run on Sundays** sonntags fahren keine Busse; **7 to run a bath** ein Bad einlaufen lassen.

● **to run away** weglaufen◇ SEP (PERF sein).

● **to run into something** gegen etwas (ACC) fahren◇ (PERF sein); **the car ran into a tree** das Auto ist gegen einen Baum gefahren.

● **to run out of something: we've run out of bread** wir haben kein Brot mehr; **I'm running out of money** ich habe kaum noch Geld.

● **to run somebody over** jemanden überfahren◇; **he nearly got run over** er ist beinahe überfahren worden.

runner noun Läufer der (PL die Läufer), Läuferin die (PL die Läuferinnen).

runner-up noun Zweite der/die (PL die Zweiten).

running noun (for exercise) Laufen das, Jogging das.

running adjective 1 running water fließendes Wasser; **2 three days running** drei Tage hintereinander; **to win three times running** dreimal hintereinander gewinnen.

runway noun 1 (for take-off) Startbahn die (PL die Startbahnen); **2** (for landing) Landebahn die (PL die Landebahnen).

rush noun (a hurry) **to be in a rush** in Eile sein; **sorry, I'm in a rush** Entschuldigung, ich bin in Eile.

rush verb 1 (hurry) sich beeilen, **I must rush!** ich muss mich beeilen; **2** (run) hetzen (PERF sein); **she rushed out** sie stürmte raus (informal); **3 Louise was rushed to hospital** Louise ist schnellstens ins Krankenhaus gebracht worden.

a b c d e f g h i j k l m n o p q r s t u v w x y z

rush hour noun Stoßzeit die (PL die Stoßzeiten); **in the rush hour** während der Stoßzeit.

Russia noun Russland das.

Russian noun 1 (a person) Russe der (PL die Russen), Russin die (PL die Russinnen); 2 (the language) Russisch das.

Russian adjective russisch; **he's Russian** er ist Russe.

rust noun Rost der.

rusty adjective rostig.

rye noun Roggen der.

Ss

Sabbath noun 1 (Jewish) Sabbat der (PL die Sabbate); 2 (Christian) Sonntag der (PL die Sonntage).

sack noun 1 Sack der (PL die Säcke); 2 **to get the sack** rausgeschmissen werden (informal).

sack verb **to sack somebody** jemanden rausschmeißen✧ SEP (informal).

sad adjective traurig.

saddle noun Sattel der (PL die Sättel).

saddlebag noun Satteltasche die (PL die Satteltaschen).

sadly adverb 1 traurig; **she looked at me sadly** sie hat mich traurig angesehen; 2 (unfortunately) leider.

safe adjective 1 (out of danger) sicher; **to feel safe from something** sich vor etwas (DAT) sicher fühlen; 2 **she's safe** sie ist in

Sicherheit; 3 (not dangerous) ungefährlich; **the path is safe** der Weg ist ungefährlich; **it's not safe** das ist gefährlich.

safety noun Sicherheit die.

safety belt noun Sicherheitsgurt der (PL die Sicherheitsgurte).

safety pin noun Sicherheitsnadel die (PL die Sicherheitsnadeln).

Sagittarius noun Schütze der; **Kylie's Sagittarius** Kylie ist Schütze.

sail noun Segel das (PL die Segel).

sailing noun Segeln das; **to go sailing** segeln.

sailing boat noun Segelboot das (PL die Segelboote).

sailor noun Seemann der (PL die Seeleute).

saint noun Heilige der/die (PL die Heiligen).

sake noun 1 **for your mother's sake** deiner Mutter zuliebe; 2 **for heaven's sake** um Gottes willen.

salad noun Salat der (PL die Salate); **tomato salad** der Tomatensalat.

salad dressing noun Salatsoße die (PL die Salatsoßen).

salami noun Salami die (PL die Salamis).

salary noun Gehalt das (PL die Gehälter).

sale noun 1 (selling) Verkauf der (PL die Verkäufe); **the sale of the house** der Verkauf des Hauses; **'for sale'** 'zu verkaufen'; 2 **the sales** der Ausverkauf; **I bought it in the sales** ich habe es im Ausverkauf gekauft.

sales assistant noun Verkäufer der (PL die Verkäufer), Verkäuferin die (PL die Verkäuferinnen).

salesman noun Verkäufer der (PL die Verkäufer).

saleswoman noun Verkäuferin die (PL die Verkäuferinnen).

salmon noun Lachs der (PL die Lachse).

salt noun Salz das.

salty adjective salzig.

same adjective **the same** der gleiche/die gleiche/das gleiche; **she said the same thing** sie hat das gleiche gesagt; **her birthday's the same day as mine** sie hat am gleichen Tag Geburtstag wie ich; **at the same time** zur gleichen Zeit; **their car's the same as ours** sie haben das gleiche Auto wie wir.

same adverb **1 the same** gleich; **the two bikes look the same** die beiden Fahrräder sehen gleich aus; **2 all the same** trotzdem.

sample noun Muster das (PL die Muster); **a free sample** ein unverkäufliches Muster, eine Warenprobe.

sand noun Sand der.

sandal noun Sandale die (PL die Sandalen); **a pair of sandals** ein Paar Sandalen.

sandpaper noun Sandpapier das (PL die Sandpapiere).

sandwich noun Sandwich das (PL die Sandwichs), belegte Brot das (PL die belegten Brote); **ham sandwich** das Schinkenbrot.

sanitary towel noun Damenbinde die (PL die Damenbinden).

Santa Claus noun der Weihnachtsmann.

sarcastic adjective sarkastisch.

sardine noun Sardine die (PL die Sardinen).

SARS noun SARS das.

satchel noun Ranzen der (PL die Ranzen).

satellite noun Satellit der (PL die Satelliten).

satellite dish noun Satellitenschüssel die (PL die Satellitenschüsseln).

satellite television noun Satellitenfernsehen das.

satisfactory adjective befriedigend.

satisfied adjective zufrieden.

satisfy verb befriedigen.

satisfying adjective **1** befriedigend; **2 a satisfying meal** ein sättigendes Essen.

Saturday noun **1** Samstag der (PL die Samstage), Sonnabend der (North German) der Sonnabende); **on Saturday** am Sonnabend/am Samstag; **I'm going out on Saturday** ich gehe Sonnabend aus; **see you on Saturday!** bis Samstag!; **every Saturday** jeden Samstag; **last Saturday** vorigen Sonnabend; **next Saturday** nächsten Sonnabend; **2 on Saturdays** samstags, sonnabends (North German); **the museum is closed on Saturdays** das Museum ist sonnabends/samstags geschlossen; **to have a Saturday job** sonnabends/samstags arbeiten.

sauce noun Soße die (PL die Soßen).

saucepan noun Kochtopf der (PL die Kochtöpfe).

saucer noun Untertasse die (PL die Untertassen).

a
b
c
d
e
f
g
h
i
j
k
l
m
n
o
p
q
r
s
t
u
v
w
x
y
z

sausage 546 ENGLISH - GERMAN

a

b

c

d

e

f

g

h

i

j

k

l

m

n

o

p

q

r

s

t

u

v

w

x

y

z

sausage noun Wurst die (PL die Würste).

save verb 1 retten (life); **to save somebody's life** jemandem das Leben retten; **the doctors saved his life** die Ärzte haben ihm das Leben gerettet; 2 sparen (money); **I've saved £60** ich habe sechzig Pfund gespart; **I cycle to school to save money** ich fahre mit dem Rad zur Schule, um Geld zu sparen; **we'll take a taxi to save time** um Zeit zu sparen, nehmen wir ein Taxi; 3 (stop) abwehren SEP (a shot); **to save a penalty** einen Elfmeter abwehren.

● **to save up** sparen; **I'm saving up for a car** ich spare auf ein Auto.

savings plural noun Ersparnisse (plural).

savoury adjective (not sweet) pikant.

saw noun Säge die (PL die Sägen).

sax noun Saxophon das (PL die Saxophone).

saxophone noun Saxophon das (PL die Saxophone); **to play the saxophone** Saxophon spielen.

say verb 1 sagen; **what did you say?** was hast du gesagt?; **she says she's tired** sie sagt, dass sie müde ist; **he said to wait here** er hat gesagt, wir sollen hier warten; **they say** man sagt; 2 **to say something again** etwas wiederholen; 3 **that's to say** das heißt.

saying noun Redensart die (PL die Redensarten); **it's just a saying** das ist so eine Redensart; **as the saying goes** wie man so sagt.

scab noun Wundschorf der (PL die Wundschorfe).

scale noun 1 (of a map or model) Maßstab der (PL die Maßstäbe); 2 (extent) Ausmaß das (PL die Ausmaße); **the scale of the disaster** das Ausmaß der Katastrophe; 3 (in music) Tonleiter die (PL die Tonleitern).

scales noun Waage die (PL die Waagen); **bathroom scales** die Personenwaage.

scandal noun 1 Skandal der (PL die Skandale); 2 (gossip) Klatsch der (informal).

Scandinavia noun Skandinavien das.

Scandinavian adjective skandinavisch.

scanner noun Scanner der (PL die Scanner).

scar noun Narbe die (PL die Narben).

scarce adjective knapp.

scare noun 1 Schrecken der (PL die Schrecken); **to give somebody a scare** jemandem einen Schrecken einjagen SEP; 2 (general alarm) Panik die (PL die Paniken); **to cause a scare** eine Panik auslösen; **3 bomb scare** die Bombendrohung.

scare verb **to scare somebody** jemanden erschrecken; **you scared me!** du hast mich erschreckt!

scarecrow noun Vogelscheuche die (PL die Vogelscheuchen).

scared adjective 1 **to be scared** Angst haben; **I'm scared** ich habe Angst; **to be scared of something** vor etwas (DAT) Angst haben; **he's scared of dogs** er hat vor Hunden Angst; 2 **to be scared of doing**

something sich nicht trauen, etwas zu tun; **I'm scared of telling him the truth** ich traue mich nicht, ihm die Wahrheit zu sagen.

scarf noun **1** (silky) Tuch das (PL die Tücher); **2** (long, warm) Schal der (PL die Schals).

scary adjective unheimlich.

scene noun **1** (of an incident or event) Schauplatz der (PL die Schauplätze); **to be on the scene** am Schauplatz sein; **the scene of the crime** der Tatort; **2** (world) the **music scene** die Musikszene; **on the fashion scene** in der Modewelt; **3** (argument) Szene die (PL die Szenen); **to make a scene** eine Szene machen.

scenery noun **1** (landscape) Landschaft die; **2** (in the theatre) Bühnenbild das.

schedule noun Programm das (PL die Programme).

scheduled flight noun Linienflug der (PL die Linienflüge).

scheme noun Projekt das (PL die Projekte).

scholarship noun Stipendium das (PL die Stipendien).

school noun Schule die (PL die Schulen); **at school** in der Schule; **to go to school** zur Schule gehen.

schoolbook noun Schulbuch das (PL die Schulbücher).

schoolboy noun Schüler der (PL die Schüler).

schoolchildren plural noun Schulkinder (plural).

schoolfriend noun Schulfreund der (PL die Schulfreunde), Schulfreundin die (PL die Schulfreundinnen).

schoolgirl noun Schülerin die (PL die Schülerinnen).

science noun Wissenschaft die (PL die Wissenschaften).

science fiction noun Sciencefiction die.

scientific adjective wissenschaftlich.

scientist noun Wissenschaftler der (PL die Wissenschaftler), Wissenschaftlerin die (PL die Wissenschaftlerinnen).

scissors plural noun Schere die (PL die Scheren); **a pair of scissors** eine Schere.

scoop noun **1** (implement) Eisportionierer der (PL die Eisportionierer); **2** (quantity) Eiskugel die (PL die Eiskugeln); **how many scoops would you like?** wieviele Kugeln Eis möchtest du?; **3** (in journalism) Knüller der (PL die Knüller).

scooter noun **1** (motor scooter) Motorroller der (PL die Motorroller); **2** (for a child) Roller der (PL die Roller).

score noun Spielstand der (PL die Spielstände); **the score was three two** es stand drei zu zwei.

score verb **1 to score a goal** ein Tor schießen✧; **2 to score three points** drei Punkte erzielen; **3** (keep score) zählen.

Scorpio noun Skorpion der; **Neil is Scorpio** Neil ist Skorpion.

Scot noun Schotte der (PL die Schotten), Schottin die (PL die Schottinnen); **the Scots** die Schotten.

Scotland noun Schottland das; **from Scotland** aus Schottland;

a b c d e f g h i j k l m n o p q r s t u v w x y z

Pauline's from Scotland Pauline kommt aus Schottland; **to Scotland** nach Schottland.

Scots *adjective* schottisch.

Scotsman *noun* Schotte der (PL die Schotten).

Scotswoman *noun* Schottin die (PL die Schottinnen).

Scottish *adjective* schottisch; **he's Scottish** er ist Schotte.

scout *noun* Pfadfinder der (PL die Pfadfinder).

scrambled eggs *noun* Rührei das.

scrap *noun* Stück das (PL die Stücke); **a scrap of paper** ein Stück Papier.

scrapbook *noun* Sammelalbum das (PL die Sammelalben).

scrape *verb* 1 schaben (*potatoes or carrots*); 2 (*remove dirt or paint*) abkratzen SEP; 3 (*damage*) schrammen.

scratch *noun* (*on your skin or a surface*) Kratzer der (PL die Kratzer); ★ **to start from scratch** von vorn anfangen✧ SEP.

scratch *verb* (*scratch yourself*) sich kratzen; **to scratch your head** sich am Kopf kratzen.

scream *noun* Schrei der (PL die Schreie).

scream *verb* schreien✧.

screen *noun* Bildschirm der (PL die Bildschirme) (*of a TV or computer*); **on the screen** auf dem Bildschirm; 2 (*in the cinema*) Leinwand die (PL die Leinwände).

screw *noun* Schraube die (PL die Schrauben).

screw *verb* schrauben.

screwdriver *noun* Schraubenzieher der (PL die Schraubenzieher).

scribble *verb* kritzeln.

scrub *verb* scheuern (*a saucepan or the floor*); **to scrub your nails** sich (DAT) die Nägel bürsten.

scuba diving *noun* Gerätetauchen das.

sculptor *noun* Bildhauer der (PL die Bildhauer), Bildhauerin die (PL die Bildhauerinnen); **Rebecca's a sculptor** Rebecca ist Bildhauerin.

sculpture *noun* Skulptur die (PL die Skulpturen).

sea *noun* Meer das (PL die Meere), See die; **by the sea** am Meer, an der See.

seafood *noun* Meeresfrüchte (*plural*); **I love seafood** ich esse Meeresfrüchte sehr gern.

seagull *noun* Möwe die (PL die Möwen).

seal *noun* (*animal*) Robbe die (PL die Robben), Seehund der (PL die Seehunde).

seal *verb* zukleben SEP (*an envelope*).

search *verb* 1 absuchen SEP; **I've searched my desk but I can't find the letter** ich habe meinen Schreibtisch abgesucht, aber ich kann den Brief nicht finden; 2 durchsuchen; **they searched the building for him** sie haben das Gebäude nach ihm durchsucht; 3 suchen; **to search for something** nach etwas (DAT) suchen; **I've been searching everywhere for my scissors** ich habe überall nach meiner Schere gesucht.

seashell noun Muschel die (PL die Muscheln).

seasick adjective to be seasick seekrank sein.

seaside noun at the seaside am Meer.

season noun 1 Jahreszeit die (PL die Jahreszeiten); the four seasons die vier Jahreszeiten; 2 (period of social or sporting activity) Saison die (PL die Saisons); the tennis season die Tennissaison; off-season prices Preise außerhalb der Saison; 3 strawberries are not in season at the moment jetzt ist nicht die richtige Zeit für Erdbeeren.

season ticket noun Dauerkarte die (PL die Dauerkarten).

seat noun 1 Sitz der (PL die Sitze); the front seat (in a car) der Vordersitz; the back seat der Rücksitz; take a seat nehmen Sie Platz (formal), setz dich (informal); 2 (on a bus, in the theatre, etc.) Platz der (PL die Plätze); to book a seat einen Platz reservieren; can you keep my seat? kannst du mir meinen Platz freihalten?

seatbelt noun Sicherheitsgurt der (PL die Sicherheitsgurte).

seaweed noun Tang der.

second noun Sekunde die (PL die Sekunden); can you wait a second? kannst du eine Sekunde warten?

second adjective 1 zweiter/zweite/zweites; for the second time zum zweiten Mal; 2 the second of July der zweite Juli.

secondary school noun 1 weiterführende Schule die (PL die weiterführenden Schulen) (Germans define the type of secondary school); 2 Gymnasium das (PL die Gymnasien) (grammar school, from age 10 to 19 when Abitur is taken); 3 Realschule die (PL die Realschulen) (from age 10 to 16, less academic than a Gymnasium).

secondhand adjective, adverb gebraucht; a secondhand bike ein gebrauchtes Fahrrad; secondhand car der Gebrauchtwagen; I bought it secondhand ich habe es gebraucht gekauft.

secondly adverb zweitens.

secret noun Geheimnis das (PL die Geheimnisse); to tell somebody a secret jemandem ein Geheimnis verraten; in secret heimlich.

secret adjective geheim; a secret plan ein geheimer Plan; to keep something secret etwas geheim halten.

secretary noun Sekretär der (PL die Sekretäre), Sekretärin die (PL die Sekretärinnen); the secretary's office das Sekretariat.

secretly adverb heimlich.

sect noun Sekte die (PL die Sekten).

section noun Teil der (PL die Teile).

security noun Sicherheit die.

security guard noun Wächter der (PL die Wächter), Wächterin die (PL die Wächterinnen).

see verb 1 sehen✧; I saw Lindy yesterday ich habe Lindy gestern gesehen; have you seen the film? hast du den Film gesehen?; I can't see anything ich kann überhaupt nichts sehen; to go and see nachsehen✧ SEP; I'll go and see ich sehe nach; **3** (*visit*) besuchen; **why don't you come and see us in the summer?** warum besucht ihr uns nicht im Sommer?; **4** to see **somebody home** jemanden nach Hause begleiten; **5 see you!** tschüs! (*informal*); **see you on Saturday!** bis Samstag!; **see you soon!** bis bald!

● **to see to something** sich um etwas (ACC) kümmern; **Jo's seeing to the drinks** Jo kümmert sich um die Getränke.

seed *noun* Samen der (PL die Samen).

seem *verb* **1** scheinen◇; **his story seems odd to me** seine Geschichte kommt mir komisch vor; **he seems shy** er scheint schüchtern zu sein; **the museum seems to be closed** das Museum scheint geschlossen zu sein; **2 it seems (that)** ... anscheinend ...; **it seems he's left** anscheinend ist er weggegangen; **it seems that there are problems** anscheinend gibt es Probleme.

seesaw *noun* Wippe die (PL die Wippen).

select *verb* auswählen SEP.

self-confidence *noun* Selbstbewusstsein das; **she doesn't have much self-confidence** sie hat sehr wenig Selbstbewusstsein.

self-employed *adjective* **to be self-employed** selbstständig sein; **my parents are self-employed** meine Eltern sind selbstständig.

selfish *adjective* egoistisch.

self-service *adjective* a self-service restaurant ein Selbstbedienungsrestaurant.

sell *verb* **1** verkaufen; **to sell something to somebody** jemandem etwas verkaufen; **I sold him my bike** ich habe ihm mein Rad verkauft; **the house sold for a million** das Haus wurde für eine Million verkauft; **2** the concert's **sold out** das Konzert ist ausverkauft; **the tickets sold out very quickly** die Karten waren schnell ausverkauft.

sell-by date *noun* Verfallsdatum das (PL die Verfallsdaten).

Sellotape™ *noun* Tesafilm der.

sellotape *verb* **to sellotape something** etwas mit Tesafilm kleben.

semi *noun* Doppelhaushälfte die (PL die Doppelhaushälften).

semicircle *noun* Halbkreis der (PL die Halbkreise).

semicolon *noun* Strichpunkt der (PL die Strichpunkte).

semi-detached house *noun* Doppelhaushälfte die (PL die Doppelhaushälften).

semi-final *noun* Halbfinale das (PL die Halbfinale).

send *verb* schicken; **to send something to somebody** jemandem etwas schicken; **I sent her a present for her birthday** ich habe ihr zum Geburtstag ein Geschenk geschickt.

● **to send somebody back** jemanden zurückschicken SEP.

● **to send something back** etwas zurückschicken SEP.

sender *noun* Absender der (PL die Absender).

senior citizen noun Senior der (PL die Senioren), Seniorin die (PL die Seniorinnen).

sensation noun 1 (feeling) Gefühl das; 2 (impact) Sensation die (PL die Sensationen); **she caused a sensation** sie erregte viel Aufsehen.

sensational adjective sensationell.

sense noun 1 (common sense) Verstand der; 2 (faculty) Sinn der (PL die Sinne); **sense of smell** der Geruchssinn; **sense of touch** der Tastsinn; **to have a sense of humour** Humor haben; **she has no sense of humour** sie hat keinen Sinn für Humor; 3 (meaning) Sinn der; **this sentence makes no sense** dieser Satz ergibt keinen Sinn; **it doesn't make sense to do that** es ist Unsinn, das zu machen; **it makes sense to collect her first** es ist sinnvoll, sie erst abzuholen.

sensible adjective vernünftig; **be sensible** sei vernünftig; **that's a sensible suggestion** das ist ein vernünftiger Vorschlag.

sensitive adjective empfindlich; **for sensitive skin** für empfindliche Haut.

sentence noun 1 (words) Satz der (PL die Sätze); 2 (prison) Strafe die (PL die Strafen); **the death sentence** die Todesstrafe.

sentence verb verurteilen; **to be sentenced to death** zum Tode verurteilt werden; **to sentence somebody to a year in prison** jemanden zu einem Jahr Gefängnis verurteilen.

sentimental adjective sentimental.

separate adjective 1 extra ('extra' never has an ending); **a separate pile** ein extra Stapel; **she wrote it on a separate sheet of paper** sie hat es auf ein anderes Blatt Papier geschrieben; **the drinks are separate** die Getränke gehen extra; 2 (different) verschieden; **two separate problems** zwei verschiedene Probleme; 3 **they have separate rooms** sie haben getrennte Zimmer.

separate verb 1 trennen; 2 (a couple) sich trennen.

separately adverb 1 extra; 2 getrennt; **they live separately** sie leben getrennt.

separation noun Trennung die (PL die Trennungen).

September noun September der; **in September** im September.

sequel noun Folge die (PL die Folgen).

sequence noun 1 (series) Reihe die (PL die Reihen); **a sequence of events** eine Reihe von Ereignissen; **in sequence** in der richtigen Reihenfolge; 2 (in a film) Sequenz die (PL die Sequenzen).

sergeant noun 1 (in the police) Polizeimeister der (PL die Polizeimeister), Polizeimeisterin die (PL die Polizeimeisterinnen); 2 (in the army) Feldwebel der (PL die Feldwebel).

serial noun 1 Fortsetzungsgeschichte die (PL die Fortsetzungsgeschichten); 2 (on TV or radio) Serie die (PL die Serien).

a b c d e f g h i j k l m n o p q r s t u v w x y z

series noun Serie die (PL die Serien); **television series** die Fernsehserie.

serious adjective 1 ernst; **a serious discussion** eine ernste Unterhaltung; **to be serious about something** etwas ernst nehmen; **are you serious?** ist das dein Ernst?; 2 schwer (accident or mistake).

seriously adverb 1 im Ernst; **seriously, I have to go now** im Ernst, ich muss jetzt gehen; **seriously?** im Ernst?; 2 **to take somebody seriously** jemanden ernst nehmen; 3 (gravely) schwer; **she is seriously ill** sie ist schwer krank.

servant noun Bedienstete der / die (PL die Bediensteten).

serve noun (in tennis) Aufschlag der (PL die Aufschläge); **it's my serve** ich habe Aufschlag.

serve verb 1 (in tennis) aufschlagen◇ SEP; **Becker is serving** Becker schlägt auf; 2 servieren; **can you serve the vegetables, please?** können Sie bitte das Gemüse servieren? ★ **it serves him right** das geschieht ihm recht.

service noun 1 (in a restaurant, shop, etc.) Bedienung die; **service is included** inklusive Bedienung; 2 (from a company or firm to a customer) Service der; 3 **the emergency services** der Notdienst; 4 (church service) Gottesdienst der (PL die Gottesdienste); 5 (of a car or machine) Wartung die (PL die Wartungen).

service area noun Raststätte die (PL die Raststätten).

service charge noun Bedienung die; **there is no service charge** die Bedienung wird nicht extra berechnet.

service station noun Tankstelle die (PL die Tankstellen).

serviette noun Serviette die (PL die Servietten).

session noun Sitzung die (PL die Sitzungen).

set noun 1 (for playing a game) Spiel das (PL die Spiele); **chess set** das Schachspiel; **train set** die Spielzeugeisenbahn; 3 (in tennis) Satz der (PL die Sätze).

set adjective 1 fest (hours, habits); **a set date** ein festes Datum; **at a set time** zu einer festgesetzten Zeit; 2 **set menu** das Menü.

set verb 1 festlegen SEP (a date, time); 2 aufstellen SEP (a record); 3 **to set the table** den Tisch decken; **to set an alarm clock** einen Wecker stellen; **I've set my alarm for seven** ich habe meinen Wecker auf sieben gestellt; 4 **to set your watch** seine Uhr richtig stellen; 5 (sun) untergehen◇ SEP.

● **to set off** aufbrechen◇ SEP (PERF sein); **we're setting off at ten** wir brechen um zehn auf; **they set off for Vienna yesterday** sie sind gestern nach Wien aufgebrochen.

● **to set off something** 1 etwas auslösen SEP (an alarm, reaction); 2 etwas abbrennen SEP (a firework); 3 etwas explodieren lassen (a bomb).

● **to set out** aufbrechen✧ SEP (PERF sein); **they set out for Hamburg at ten** sie sind um zehn nach Hamburg aufgebrochen.

settee noun Sofa das (PL die Sofas).

settle verb **1** bezahlen (a bill); **2** lösen (a problem); **3** beilegen SEP (an argument).

seven number sieben; **Rosie's seven** Rosie ist sieben.

seventeen number siebzehn; **I'm seventeen** ich bin siebzehn.

seventh adjective siebter/siebte/ siebtes; **on the seventh floor** im siebten Stock; **the seventh of July** der siebte Juli.

seventies plural noun **the seventies** die Siebzigerjahre; **in the seventies** in den Siebzigerjahren.

seventieth adjective siebzigster/ siebzigste/siebzigstes; **it's her seventieth birthday** es ist ihr siebzigster Geburtstag.

seventy number siebzig; **my granny's seventy** meine Oma ist siebzig.

several adjective, pronoun **1** mehrere; **I've read several of her novels** ich habe mehrere ihrer Romane gelesen; **2 I've seen her several times** ich habe sie mehrmals gesehen.

sew verb nähen.

sewing noun Nähen das; **I like sewing** ich nähe gern.

sewing machine noun Nähmaschine die (PL die Nähmaschinen).

sex noun **1** (gender) Geschlecht das (PL die Geschlechter); **2** (intercourse) Sex der; **to have sex with someone** mit jemandem Sex haben.

sex education noun Aufklärungsunterricht der.

sexism noun Sexismus der.

sexist adjective sexistisch; **sexist remarks** sexistische Bemerkungen.

sexual adjective sexuell.

sexual harassment noun sexuelle Belästigung die.

sexuality noun Sexualität die.

sexy adjective sexy.

shabby adjective schäbig.

shade noun **1** Ton der (PL die Töne); **a shade of green** ein Grünton; **2** Schatten der; **in the shade** im Schatten.

shadow noun Schatten der (PL die Schatten).

shake verb **1** (tremble) zittern; **I was shaking with fear** ich zitterte vor Angst; **2 to shake something** etwas schütteln; **to shake your head** (meaning no) den Kopf schütteln; **3 to shake hands with somebody** jemandem die Hand geben✧; **she shook hands with me** sie hat mir die Hand gegeben; **we shook hands** wir gaben uns die Hand.

shaken adjective erschüttert; **I was shaken by the news** die Nachricht hat mich erschüttert.

shall verb **shall I come with you?** soll ich mitkommen?; **shall we stop now?** sollen wir jetzt aufhören?

shallow adjective flach; **stay in the shallow end of the pool** bleib am flachen Ende des Beckens.

a b c d e f g h i j k l m n o p q r s t u v w x y z

shambles noun Chaos das; **it was a total shambles!** es war ein völliges Chaos!

shame noun 1 Schande die; **the shame of it!** was für eine Schande!; 2 **what a shame!** wie schade!; **it's a shame she can't come** schade, dass sie nicht kommen kann.

shampoo noun Shampoo das (PL die Shampoos); **I bought some shampoo** ich habe Shampoo gekauft.

shamrock noun Klee der.

shandy noun Radler der (PL die Radler) (South German), Alsterwasser das (PL die Alsterwasser) (North German).

shape noun Form die (PL die Formen).

share noun 1 Anteil der (PL die Anteile); **your share of the money** dein Anteil am Geld; **he paid his share** er hat seinen Anteil gezahlt; 2 (in a company) Aktie die (PL die Aktien).

share verb teilen; **I'm sharing a room with Lucy** ich teile ein Zimmer mit Lucy.

shark noun Hai der (PL die Haie), Haifisch der (PL die Haifische).

sharp adjective 1 (knife) scharf; **this knife isn't very sharp** dieses Messer ist nicht sehr scharf; 2 (pointed) spitz; **a sharp pencil** ein spitzer Bleistift; 3 **a sharp bend** eine scharfe Kurve; 4 (clever) clever.

shave verb 1 (have a shave) sich rasieren; 2 **to shave your legs** sich (DAT) die Beine rasieren; 3 **to shave off your beard** den Bart abrasieren SEP.

shaver noun Rasierapparat der (PL die Rasierapparate); **electric shaver** der Elektrorasierer.

shaving cream noun Rasiercreme die (PL die Rasiercremes).

shaving foam noun Rasierschaum der.

she pronoun sie; **she's a student** sie ist Studentin; **she's a very good teacher** sie ist eine sehr gute Lehrerin.

shed noun Schuppen der (PL die Schuppen).

sheep noun Schaf das (PL die Schafe).

sheepdog noun Schäferhund der (PL die Schäferhunde).

sheer adjective rein; **it's sheer stupidity** das ist reine Dummheit.

sheet noun 1 (for a bed) Laken das (PL die Laken); 2 **a sheet of paper** ein Blatt Papier; **a blank sheet** ein leeres Blatt; 3 (of glass or metal) Platte die (PL die Platten); ★ **to be as white as a sheet** leichenblass sein.

shelf noun 1 (in the home or a shop) Regal das (PL die Regale); **a set of shelves** ein Regal; 2 (in an oven) Schiene die (PL die Schienen).

shell noun 1 (of an egg or a nut) Schale die (PL die Schalen); 2 (seashell) Muschel die (PL die Muscheln).

shellfish noun 1 Schalentier das (PL die Schalentiere); 2 (in cookery) Meeresfrüchte (plural).

shelter noun Schutz der; **in the shelter of** im Schutz (+ GEN); **to take shelter from the rain** sich unterstellen SEP.

shepherd noun Schäfer der (PL die Schäfer).

sherry noun Sherry der (PL die Sherrys).

Shetland Islands noun Shetlandinseln (plural).

shield noun Schild der (PL die Schilde).

shift noun Schicht die (PL die Schichten); **the night shift** die Nachtschicht; **to be on night shift** Nachtschicht haben.

shift verb **to shift something** etwas verrücken.

shifty adjective verschlagen; **he looks shifty** er sieht verschlagen aus; **a shifty-looking guy** ein verschlagener Typ.

shin noun Schienbein das (PL die Schienbeine).

shine verb scheinen✧; **the sun is shining** die Sonne scheint.

shiny adjective glänzend.

ship noun Schiff das (PL die Schiffe).

shipyard noun Werft die (PL die Werften).

shirt noun **1** (man's) Hemd das (PL die Hemden); **2** (woman's) Bluse die (PL die Blusen).

shiver verb zittern.

shock noun **1** Schock der (PL die Schocks); **to get a shock** einen Schock bekommen; **it gave me a shock** das hat mir einen Schock versetzt; **2 electric shock** der elektrische Schlag.

shock verb (upset) erschüttern; (cause scandal) schockieren.

shocked adjective schockiert.

shocking adjective schockierend.

shoe noun Schuh der (PL die Schuhe); **a pair of shoes** ein Paar Schuhe.

shoelace noun Schnürsenkel der (PL die Schnürsenkel).

shoe polish noun Schuhcreme die (PL die Schuhcremes).

shoe shop noun Schuhgeschäft das (PL die Schuhgeschäfte).

shoot verb **1** (fire) schießen✧; **to shoot at somebody** auf jemanden schießen; **she shot him in the leg** sie hat ihm ins Bein geschossen; **he was shot in the arm** er wurde am Arm getroffen; **2** (kill, execute) erschießen✧; **he was shot by terrorists** er wurde von Terroristen erschossen; **3** (in football, hockey) schießen✧; **4 to shoot a film** einen Film drehen.

shop noun Geschäft das (PL die Geschäfte), Laden der (PL die Läden); **shoe shop** das Schuhgeschäft; **to go round the shops** einen Einkaufsbummel machen.

shop assistant noun Verkäufer der (PL die Verkäufer), Verkäuferin die (PL die Verkäuferinnen).

shopkeeper noun Ladenbesitzer der (PL die Ladenbesitzer), Ladenbesitzerin die (PL die Ladenbesitzerinnen).

shoplifter noun Ladendieb der (PL die Ladendiebe), Ladendiebin die (PL die Ladendiebinnen).

shoplifting noun Ladendiebstahl der.

shopping noun **1** Einkäufe (plural); **can you put the shopping away?** kannst du die Einkäufe wegräumen?; **2** (activity)

a b c d e f g h i j k l m n o p q r s t u v w x y z

shopping trolley 556

ENGLISH - GERMAN

shopping trolley noun
Einkaufen *das*; **shopping is fun**
Einkaufen macht Spaß; **to go
shopping** einkaufen gehen✧.

shopping trolley noun
Einkaufswagen der (PL die
Einkaufswagen).

shop window noun Schaufenster
das (PL die Schaufenster).

short *adjective* **1** kurz; **a short
dress** ein kurzes Kleid; **she has
short hair** sie hat kurze Haare; **2 a
short break** eine kurze Pause; **to
go for a short walk** einen kurzen
Spaziergang machen; **it's a short
walk from the bus stop** es ist nicht
weit zu Fuß von der Bushaltestelle;
3 to be short of something knapp
mit etwas (DAT) sein; **we're a bit
short of money at the moment** wir
sind im Moment etwas knapp bei
Kasse; **we're getting short of time**
die Zeit wird uns knapp.

shortage noun Mangel der.

shortbread noun Buttergebäck
das.

shortcrust pastry noun
Mürbeteig der.

short cut noun Abkürzung die (PL
die Abkürzungen).

shortly *adverb* gleich; **shortly
before I left** kurz bevor ich ging;
shortly after kurz danach.

shorts *plural noun* Shorts (*plural*);
a pair of shorts ein Paar Shorts;
my red shorts meine roten Shorts.

short-sighted *adjective*
kurzsichtig; **I'm short-sighted** ich
bin kurzsichtig.

shot noun **1** (*from a gun*) Schuss
der (PL die Schüsse); **2** (*a photo*)
Aufnahme die (PL die Aufnahmen).

should *verb* **1** sollen✧ ('*should*' *is
usually translated by the imperfect
subjunctive of* '*sollen*'); **you should
ask Simon** du solltest Simon
fragen; **the potatoes should be
ready now** die Kartoffeln sollten
jetzt fertig sein; **2** ('*should have*' *is
translated by* '*hätte sollen*') **you
should have told me** du hättest es
mir sagen sollen; **I shouldn't have
stayed** ich hätte nicht bleiben
sollen; **you shouldn't have said
that** das hättest du nicht sagen
sollen; **3** ('*should meaning would*'
is translated by '*würde*') **I should
forget it if I were you** an deiner
Stelle würde ich es vergessen; **4 I
should think** ich würde sagen; **I
should think he's forgotten** ich
würde sagen, er hat's vergessen;
5 this should be enough das
müsste eigentlich reichen.

shoulder noun Schulter die (PL die
Schultern).

shoulder bag noun
Umhängetasche die (PL die
Umhängetaschen).

shout noun Schrei der (PL die
Schreie).

shout *verb* **1** schreien✧; **stop
shouting!** hör auf zu schreien!;
2 (*call*) rufen✧; **he shouted at us
to come back** er rief uns zu, wir
sollten zurückkommen.

shovel noun Schaufel die (PL die
Schaufeln).

show noun **1** (*on stage*) Show die
(PL die Shows); **we went to see a
show** wir haben eine Show
gesehen; **2** (*on TV, radio*) Sendung
die (PL die Sendungen);
3 (*exhibition*) Ausstellung die (PL

die Ausstellung); **fashion show** die Modenschau.

show *verb* **1** zeigen; **to show something to somebody** jemandem etwas zeigen; **I'll show you my photos** ich zeige dir meine Fotos; **to show somebody how something works** jemandem zeigen, wie etwas funktioniert; **he showed me how to make pancakes** er hat mir gezeigt, wie man Pfannkuchen macht; **2 it shows!** das sieht man!

● **to show off** angeben ✧ SEP.

shower *noun* **1** (*in a bathroom*) Dusche die (PL die Duschen); **to have a shower** duschen; **2** (*of rain*) Schauer der (PL die Schauer).

show-jumping *noun* Springreiten das.

show-off *noun* Angeber der (PL die Angeber), Angeberin die (PL die Angeberinnen).

shriek *verb* kreischen.

shrimp *noun* Krabbe die (PL die Krabben).

shrink *verb* **1** schrumpfen (PERF *sein*); **2** (*clothes*) einlaufen ✧ SEP (PERF *sein*); **my sweater has shrunk** mein Pullover ist eingelaufen.

Shrove Tuesday *noun* Fastnachtsdienstag der.

shrug *verb* **to shrug your shoulders** mit den Achseln zucken.

shuffle *verb* **to shuffle the cards** die Karten mischen.

shut *adjective* zu; **the shops are shut** die Geschäfte haben zu.

shut *verb* zumachen SEP; **can you shut the door please?** kannst du die Tür bitte zumachen?; **the**

shops shut at six die Geschäfte machen um sechs zu.

● **to shut up** den Mund halten ✧ (*informal*); **shut up!** halt den Mund!.

shuttlecock *noun* Federball der (PL die Federbälle).

shuttle service *noun* Pendelverkehr der; **there's a shuttle service from the airport** es gibt einen Shuttledienst vom Flughafen.

shy *adjective* schüchtern.

shyness *noun* Schüchternheit die.

Sicily *noun* Sizilien das.

sick *adjective* **1** (*ill*) krank; **2 to be sick** (*vomit*) sich übergeben ✧; **I was sick several times** ich habe mich mehrmals übergeben; **3 I feel sick** mir ist schlecht; **4** übel; **a sick joke** ein übler Witz; **5 to be sick of something** etwas satt haben; **I'm sick of staying at home every day** ich habe es satt, jeden Tag zu Hause zu sitzen.

sickness *noun* Krankheit die (PL die Krankheiten).

side *noun* **1** Seite die (PL die Seiten); **on the other side of the street** auf der anderen Straßenseite; **on the wrong side** auf der falschen Seite; **I'm on your side** (*I agree with you*) ich bin auf deiner Seite; **2** (*edge*) Rand der (PL die Ränder) (*of a pool, river*); **at the side of the road** am Straßenrand; **3** (*team*) Mannschaft die (PL die Mannschaften); **the winning side** die siegreiche Mannschaft; **she plays on our side** sie spielt bei uns mit; **4 to take sides** Partei ergreifen ✧; **he always takes sides against her** er ergreift

a
b
c
d
e
f
g
h
i
j
k
l
m
n
o
p
q
r
s
t
u
v
w
x
y
z

immer gegen sie Partei; **5 side by side** nebeneinander.

sideboard noun Anrichte die (PL die Anrichten).

sideburns noun Koteletten (plural).

side-effect noun Nebenwirkung die (PL die Nebenwirkungen).

side street noun Seitenstraße die (PL die Seitenstraßen).

sieve noun Sieb das (PL die Siebe).

sigh noun Seufzer der (PL die Seufzer).

sigh verb seufzen.

sight noun **1** Anblick der; **it was a marvellous sight** es war ein herrlicher Anblick; **2 at first sight** auf den ersten Blick; **3** (eyesight) **to have poor sight** schlechte Augen haben; **to know somebody by sight** jemanden vom Sehen kennen; **out of sight** außer Sicht; **to lose sight of somebody** jemanden aus den Augen verlieren; **4 the sights** die Sehenswürdigkeiten; **to see the sights** die Sehenswürdigkeiten besichtigen.

sightseeing noun Sightseeing das; **to do some sightseeing** einige Sehenswürdigkeiten besichtigen.

sign noun **1** (notice) Schild das (PL die Schilder); **there's a sign on the door** da ist ein Schild an der Tür; **2** (trace, indication) Zeichen das (PL die Zeichen); **3** (of the zodiac) Sternzeichen das (PL die Sternzeichen); **what sign are you?** was für ein Sternzeichen bist du?

sign verb **1** unterschreiben✧; **to sign a cheque** einen Scheck unterschreiben; **2** (using sign language) sich durch Zeichensprache verständigen.

● **to sign on** sich arbeitslos melden.

signal noun Signal das (PL die Signale).

signature noun Unterschrift die (PL die Unterschriften).

significant adjective bedeutend.

sign language noun Zeichensprache die (PL die Zeichensprachen).

signpost noun Wegweiser der (PL die Wegweiser).

silence noun Stille die.

silent adjective still.

silk noun Seide die.

silk adjective Seiden-; **a silk blouse** eine Seidenbluse.

silky adjective seidig.

silly adjective dumm; **it was a really silly thing to do** das war wirklich dumm.

silver noun Silber das.

silver adjective Silber-; **a silver medal** eine Silbermedaille.

similar adjective ähnlich; **it looks similar to my old bike** es sieht so ähnlich wie mein altes Rad aus.

similarity noun Ähnlichkeit die (PL die Ähnlichkeiten).

simple adjective einfach.

simply adverb einfach.

sin noun Sünde die (PL die Sünden).

since preposition **1** seit (+ DAT) (notice that German uses the present tense for an action starting in the past and still going on in the present); **I have been in Berlin since Saturday** ich bin seit Samstag in Berlin; **since when?**

seit wann?; **2** (*with a negative the perfect tense is used*) **I haven't seen her since Monday** ich habe sie seit Montag nicht gesehen.

since *conjunction* **1** seit; **since I have known him** seit ich ihn kenne; **since I've been learning German** seitdem ich Deutsch lerne; **2** (*because*) da; **since it was raining, the match was cancelled** da es regnete, wurde das Spiel abgesagt.

since *adverb* seitdem; **I haven't seen him since** ich habe ihn seitdem nicht mehr gesehen.

sincere *adjective* aufrichtig.

sincerely *adverb* **Yours sincerely** Mit freundlichen Grüßen.

sing *verb* singen✧

singer *noun* Sänger der (PL die Sänger), Sängerin die (PL die Sängerinnen).

singing *noun* **1** Singen das; **a singing lesson** eine Singstunde; **2 I like singing** ich singe gern.

single *noun* **1** (*ticket*) einfache Fahrkarte die (PL die einfachen Fahrkarten); **a single to Munich, please** eine einfache Fahrkarte nach München bitte; **2** (*record, CD*) Single die (PL die Singles).

single *adjective* **1** (*not married*) allein stehend; **a single woman** eine allein stehende Frau, (*on forms*) ledig; **2** (*just one*) einzig; **I haven't had a single reply** ich habe keine einzige Antwort bekommen; **3 not a single one** kein Einziger/ keine Einzige/kein Einziges; **4 single room** *das* Einzelzimmer; **single bed** *das* Einzelbett.

single parent *noun* allein Erziehende der/die (PL die allein Erziehenden); **she's a single parent** sie ist allein erziehende Mutter; **a single-parent family** eine Einelternfamilie.

singles *plural noun* (*in tennis*) Einzel das (PL die Einzel); **the women's singles** das Dameneinzel; **the men's singles** das Herreneinzel.

singular *noun* Einzahl die; **in the singular** in der Einzahl.

sink *noun* Spülbecken das (PL die Spülbecken).

sink *verb* sinken✧ (PERF sein).

sir *noun* Herr der (PL die Herren); (*in German,* '*Sir' is usually not translated*) **would you like another one, sir?** möchten Sie noch eins?; **yes, sir** ja, mein Herr.

sister *noun* Schwester die (PL die Schwestern); **my sister's ten** meine Schwester ist zehn.

sister-in-law *noun* Schwägerin die (PL die Schwägerinnen).

sit *verb* **1** (*to sit down*) sich setzen; **you can sit on the sofa** ihr könnt euch aufs Sofa setzen; **sit on the floor** setz dich auf den Boden; **2** (*to be sitting*) sitzen✧; **Leila was sitting on the sofa** Leila saß auf dem Sofa; **to sit on the floor** auf dem Boden sitzen; **3 to sit an exam** eine Prüfung machen.

● **to sit down** sich setzen; **he sat down on the chair** er setzte sich auf den Stuhl; **do sit down** setzen Sie sich.

sitcom *noun* Situationskomödie die (PL die Situationskomödien).

a
b
c
d
e
f
g
h
i
j
k
l
m
n
o
p
q
r
s
t
u
v
w
x
y
z

a

site noun 1 **building site** die Baustelle; 2 **camping site** der Campingplatz; 3 **archaeological site** die archäologische Stätte.

b

c

sitting room noun Wohnzimmer das (PL die Wohnzimmer).

d

situated adjective **to be situated** sich befinden⋄; **the house is situated in a small village** das Haus befindet sich in einem kleinen Dorf.

e

f

g

situation noun 1 (location) Lage die (PL die Lagen); 2 (circumstances) Situation die (PL die Situationen).

h

i

six number sechs; **Harry's six** Harry ist sechs.

j

sixteen number sechzehn; **Alice is sixteen** Alice ist sechzehn.

k

l

sixth adjective sechster/sechste/ sechstes; **on the sixth floor** im sechsten Stock; **on the sixth of July** am sechsten Juli.

m

n

sixty number sechzig; **she's sixty** sie ist sechzig.

o

size noun 1 Größe die (PL die Größen); **it depends on the size of the house** es kommt auf die Größe des Hauses an; 2 **what size is the window?** wie groß ist das Fenster?; 3 (in clothes) Größe die (PL die Größen); **what size do you take?** welche Größe haben Sie?; 4 (of shoes) Schuhgröße die (PL die Schuhgrößen); **I take a size thirty-eight** ich habe Schuhgröße achtunddreißig.

p

q

r

s

t

u

skate noun 1 (an ice skate) Schlittschuh der (PL die Schlittschuhe); 2 (a roller skate) Rollschuh der (PL die Rollschuhe).

v

w

x

y

skate verb 1 (ice-skate) Schlittschuh laufen⋄; (PERF sein);

z

2 (roller-skate) Rollschuh laufen⋄ (PERF sein).

skateboard noun Skateboard das (PL die Skateboards).

skateboarding noun Skateboardfahren das; **to go skateboarding** Skateboard fahren⋄ (PERF sein).

skater noun 1 (on rollerskates) Rollschuhfahrer der (PL die Rollschuhfahrer), Rollschuhfahrerin die (PL die Rollschuhfahrerinnen); 2 (on ice) Eisläufer der (PL die Eisläufer), Eisläuferin die (PL die Eisläuferinnen); 3 (on a skateboard) Skater der (PL die Skater).

skating noun 1 (on ice) Schlittschuhlaufen das; **to go skating** Schlittschuh laufen⋄ (PERF sein); 2 (roller-skating) Rollschuhlaufen das; **to go roller-skating** Rollschuh laufen⋄ (PERF sein).

skating rink noun 1 (ice rink) Eisbahn die (PL die Eisbahnen); 2 (for roller-skating) Rollschuhbahn die (PL die Rollschuhbahnen).

skeleton noun Skelett das (PL die Skelette).

sketch noun 1 Skizze die (PL die Skizzen); 2 (comedy routine) Sketch der (PL die Sketche).

ski noun Ski der (PL die Skier).

ski verb Ski fahren⋄ (PERF sein); **he can ski** er kann Ski fahren.

ski boot noun Skistiefel der (PL die Skistiefel).

skid *verb* schleudern (PERF *sein*); **the car skidded** das Auto kam ins Schleudern.

skier *noun* Skifahrer der (PL die Skifahrer), Skifahrerin die (PL die Skifahrerinnen).

skiing *noun* Skifahren das; **to go skiing** Ski fahren◇ (PERF *sein*).

ski lift *noun* Skilift der (PL die Skilifte).

ski suit *noun* Skianzug der (PL die Skianzüge).

skimmed milk *noun* fettarme Milch die.

skin *noun* Haut die (PL die Häute).

skinhead *noun* Skinhead der (PL die Skinheads).

skinny *adjective* dünn.

skip *noun* (*for rubbish*) Container der (PL die Container).

skip *verb* 1 auslassen◇ SEP (*a meal, part of a book*); **I skipped a few chapters** ich ließ ein paar Kapitel aus; **2 to skip a lesson** eine Stunde schwänzen (*informal*).

skirt *noun* Rock der (PL die Röcke); **a long skirt** ein langer Rock; **a tight skirt** ein enger Rock; **a mini-skirt** ein Minirock.

skittles *plural noun* Kegeln das.

skull *noun* Schädel der (PL die Schädel).

sky *noun* Himmel der (PL die Himmel).

skyscraper *noun* Wolkenkratzer der (PL die Wolkenkratzer).

slam *verb* zuknallen SEP; **she slammed the door** sie hat die Tür zugeknallt; **the door slammed** die Tür ist zugeknallt.

slang *noun* Slang der (PL die Slangs).

slap *noun* Klaps der (PL die Klapse), (*in the face*) Ohrfeige die (PL die Ohrfeigen).

slap *verb* **to slap somebody** (*across the face*) jemanden ohrfeigen, (*on the bottom*) jemandem einen Klaps geben.

sledge *noun* Schlitten der (PL die Schlitten).

sledging *noun* **to go sledging** Schlitten fahren◇ (PERF *sein*).

sleep *noun* Schlaf der; **you need more sleep** du brauchst mehr Schlaf; **I had a good sleep** ich habe gut geschlafen; **to go to sleep** einschlafen◇ SEP (PERF *sein*); **he's gone back to sleep** er ist wieder eingeschlafen.

sleep *verb* schlafen◇; **she's sleeping** sie schläft.

sleeping bag *noun* Schlafsack der (PL die Schlafsäcke).

sleeping pill *noun* Schlaftablette die (PL die Schlaftabletten).

sleepy *adjective* **to be sleepy** schläfrig sein; **he was getting sleepy** er wurde schläfrig.

sleet *noun* Schneeregen der.

sleeve *noun* Ärmel der (PL die Ärmel); **a long-sleeved jumper** ein Pullover mit langen Ärmeln; **a short-sleeved shirt** ein Hemd mit kurzen Ärmeln; **to roll up your sleeves** die Ärmel hochkrempeln.

slice *noun* Scheibe die (PL die Scheiben); **a slice of bread** eine Scheibe Brot.

slice *verb* **to slice something** etwas in Scheiben schneiden◇.

slide *noun* 1 (*photo*) Dia das (PL die Dias); 2 (*hairslide*) Haarspange die

a b c d e f g h i j k l m n o p q r s t u v w x y z

(PL die Haarspangen); **3** (for sliding down) Rutschbahn die (PL die Rutschbahnen).

slight adjective klein; **there is a slight problem** es gibt ein kleines Problem.

slightly adverb etwas.

slim adjective schlank.

slim verb abnehmen◆ SEP; **I'm slimming** ich mache eine Schlankheitskur.

sling noun Schlinge die (PL die Schlingen); **to have your arm in a sling** den Arm in der Schlinge haben.

slip noun **1** (mistake) Fehler der (PL die Fehler); **2** (petticoat) Unterrock der (PL die Unterröcke).

slip verb **1** (slide) ausrutschen SEP (PERF sein); **2 it slipped my mind** es ist mir entfallen.

● **to slip up** einen Fehler machen.

slipper noun Hausschuh der (PL die Hausschuhe).

slippery adjective glatt.

slope noun Hang der (PL die Hänge).

slot noun Schlitz der (PL die Schlitze).

slot machine noun **1** (vending machine) Automat der (PL die Automaten); **2** (games machine) Spielautomat der (PL die Spielautomaten).

slow adjective **1** langsam; **the service is a bit slow** die Bedienung ist etwas langsam; **2** (of a clock or watch) **to be slow** nachgehen◆ SEP (PERF sein); **my watch is slow** meine Uhr geht nach.

● **to slow down** langsamer werden.

slowly adverb langsam; **he got up slowly** er ist langsam aufgestanden; **can you speak more slowly, please?** können Sie bitte etwas langsamer sprechen?

slug noun Nacktschnecke die (PL die Nacktschnecken).

sly adjective gerissen (a person); ★ **on the sly** heimlich.

smack noun Klaps der (PL die Klapse).

smack verb **to smack somebody** jemandem einen Klaps geben◆.

small adjective klein; **a small dog** ein kleiner Hund.

smart adjective **1** (well-dressed, posh) elegant; **a smart restaurant** ein elegantes Restaurant; **2** (clever) clever.

smash noun (collision) Zusammenstoß der (PL die Zusammenstöße).

smash verb **1** (break) zerschlagen◆; **they smashed a window pane** sie haben eine Fensterscheibe zerschlagen; **2** (get broken) zerbrechen◆ (PERF sein); **the plate smashed** der Teller ist zerbrochen.

smashing adjective klasse (informal).

smell noun Geruch der (PL die Gerüche); **a nasty smell** ein scheußlicher Geruch; **a smell of gas** ein Gasgeruch.

smell verb **1** riechen◆; **I can't smell anything** ich kann nichts riechen; **to smell of perfume** nach Parfüm riechen; **2** (smell bad) stinken✧; **the drains smell** der Abfluss stinkt.

smelly *adjective* **1** stinkend; **her smelly dog** ihr stinkender Hund; **2 to be smelly** stinken✧.

smile *noun* Lächeln *das*.

smile *verb* lächeln; **to smile at somebody** jemanden anlächeln SEP.

smoke *noun* Rauch *der*.

smoke *verb* rauchen; **she doesn't smoke** sie raucht nicht.

smoked *adjective* geräuchert; **smoked salmon** Räucherlachs *der*.

smoker *noun* Raucher *der* (PL die Raucher), Raucherin *die* (PL die Raucherinnen).

smoking *noun* 'no smoking' 'Rauchen verboten'; **to give up smoking** mit dem Rauchen aufhören.

smooth *adjective* **1** glatt; **a smooth surface** eine glatte Oberfläche; **2** (*person*) aalglatt.

smug *adjective* selbstgefällig.

smuggle *verb* **to smuggle something** etwas schmuggeln.

smuggler *noun* **1** Schmuggler *der* (PL die Schmuggler), Schmugglerin *die* (PL die Schmugglerinnen); **2 drugs smuggler** der Drogenschmuggler.

snack *noun* Snack *der* (PL die Snacks).

snail *noun* Schnecke *die* (PL die Schnecken).

snake *noun* Schlange *die* (PL die Schlangen).

snap *noun* (*card game*) Schnippschnapp *das* (PL die Schnippschnapp).

snap *verb* **1** (*break*) brechen✧ (PERF sein); **2 to snap something** etwas zerbrechen✧; **3 to snap your fingers** mit den Fingern schnalzen.

snapshot *noun* Schnappschuss *der* (PL die Schnappschüsse).

snarl *verb* knurren.

snatch *verb* **1** entreißen✧; **to snatch something from somebody** jemandem etwas entreißen; **she had her bag snatched** man hat ihr die Handtasche entrissen; **2 he snatched it out of my hand** er hat es mir aus der Hand gerissen.

sneak *verb* **1 to sneak in** sich hineinschleichen✧ SEP; **to sneak out** sich hinausschleichen✧ SEP; **2 to sneak on somebody** jemanden verpetzen (*informal*).

sneeze *verb* niesen.

sniff *verb* schnüffeln.

snob *noun* Snob *der* (PL die Snobs).

snobbery *noun* Snobismus *der*.

snooker *noun* Snooker *das*.

snooze *verb* Nickerchen *das* (PL die Nickerchen); **to have a snooze** ein Nickerchen machen.

snore *verb* schnarchen.

snow *noun* Schnee *der*.

snow *verb* schneien; **it's snowing** es schneit.

snowball *noun* Schneeball *der* (PL die Schneebälle).

snow drift *noun* Schneewehe *die* (PL die Schneewehen).

snowman *noun* Schneemann *der* (PL die Schneemänner).

so *conjunction, adverb* **1** so; **he's so lazy** er ist so faul; **not so** nicht so; **our house is a bit like yours, but**

not so big unser Haus ist so ähnlich wie eures, aber nicht so groß; **2 so much** so sehr; **I hate it so much** ich hasse es so sehr; **3 so much** so viel; **I have so much work** ich habe so viel Arbeit; **4 so many** so viele; **we've got so many problems** wir haben so viele Probleme; **5** (*therefore*) also; **he got up late, so he missed his train** er ist zu spät aufgestanden und hat deshalb den Zug verpasst; **so what shall we do?** also, was machen wir?; **6 so what?** na und?; **7** (*also*) so do I, so did I ich auch; **'I live in Leeds'- 'so do I'** 'ich wohne in Leeds' - 'ich auch'; **I liked the film and so did he** ich fand den Film gut und er auch; **so am I** ich auch; **so do we** wir auch; **8 I think so** ich glaube schon; **9 I hope so** hoffentlich.

soak *verb* einweichen SEP.

soaked *adjective* patschnass; ★ **to be soaked to the skin** patschnass sein.

soap *noun* **1** Seife, die (PL die Seifen); **2** (*soap opera*) Seifenoper die (PL die Seifenopern).

soap powder *noun* Seifenpulver das.

sober *adjective* nüchtern.

● **to sober up** nüchtern werden⋄ (PERF *sein*).

soccer *noun* Fußball der.

social *adjective* **1** sozial; **social problems** soziale Probleme; **2** gesellschaftlich (*engagement, ambition*); **social engagements** gesellschaftliche Verpflichtungen; **social class** die gesellschaftliche

Schicht; **3** (*sociable*) gesellig (*evening, person*).

socialism *noun* Sozialismus der.

socialist *noun* Sozialist der (PL die Sozialisten), Sozialistin die (PL die Sozialistinnen).

social security *noun* **1** Sozialhilfe die; **to be on social security** Sozialhilfe bekommen; **2** (*the system*) Sozialversicherung die.

social worker *noun* Sozialarbeiter der (PL die Sozialarbeiter), Sozialarbeiterin die (PL die Sozialarbeiterinnen).

society *noun* Gesellschaft die (PL die Gesellschaften).

sociology *noun* Soziologie die.

sock *noun* Socke die (PL die Socken); **a pair of socks** ein Paar Socken.

socket *noun* (*power point*) Steckdose die (PL die Steckdosen).

sofa *noun* Sofa das (PL die Sofas).

sofa bed *noun* Schlafcouch die (PL die Schlafcouchs).

soft *adjective* **1** weich; **2 a soft option** eine bequeme Lösung; ★ **to have a soft spot for somebody** eine Schwäche für jemanden haben.

soft drink *noun* alkoholfreie Getränk das (PL die alkoholfreien Getränke).

soft toy *noun* Stofftier das (PL die Stofftiere).

software *noun* Software die.

soil *noun* Erde die.

solar energy *noun* Sonnenenergie die.

soldier *noun* Soldat der (PL die Soldaten).

solicitor noun **1** (*dealing with lawsuits*) Rechtsanwalt der (PL die Rechtsanwälte), Rechtsanwältin die (PL die Rechtsanwältinnen); **2** (*dealing with property or documents*) Notar der (PL die Notare), Notarin die (PL die Notarinnen).

solid adjective **1** (*not flimsy*) stabil; **a solid structure** ein stabiler Bau; **2** massiv; **a table made of solid oak** ein Tisch aus massiver Eiche; **solid silver** massives Silber.

solo noun Solo das (PL die Solos); **guitar solo** das Gitarrensolo.

solo adjective Solo-; **a solo act** eine Solonummer.

solo adverb solo.

soloist noun Solist der (PL die Solisten), Solistin die (PL die Solistinnen).

solution noun Lösung die (PL die Lösungen).

solve verb lösen.

some adjective, adverb **1** (*followed by a singular noun*) etwas; **would you like some salad?** möchtest du etwas Salat?; **can you lend me some money?** kannst du mir etwas Geld leihen?; **have you got some bread?** hast du Brot?; (*some is often not translated*) hast du Brot?; **2** (*followed by a plural noun*) (*a few*) ein paar; **I've bought some apples** ich habe ein paar Äpfel gekauft; **3** (*followed by a plural noun*) (*a certain number but not all*) einige; **some of his films are too violent** einige von seinen Filmen sind zu brutal; **4** (*referring to something that has been mentioned*) 'would

you like tea?' — 'thanks, I've got some' 'möchten Sie Tee?' — 'nein danke, ich habe schon welchen'; **he's eaten some of it** er hat etwas davon gegessen; **I'd like some** ich möchte etwas; (*with a plural noun*) ich möchte welche; **5** (*certain people or things*) manche; **some people think he's right** manche Leute glauben, dass er Recht hat; **6** **some day** eines Tages.

somebody, someone pronoun jemand; **there's somebody in the garden** da ist jemand im Garten.

somehow adverb irgendwie; **I've got to finish this essay somehow** ich muss diesen Aufsatz irgendwie fertig schreiben.

something pronoun **1** etwas; **there's something I've got to tell you** ich muss dir etwas erzählen; **something new** etwas Neues; **something interesting** etwas Interessantes; **there's something wrong** irgendetwas stimmt nicht; **2 their house is really something!** ihr Haus ist einfach Klasse!

sometime adverb irgendwann; **give me a ring sometime next week** ruf mich irgendwann nächste Woche an.

sometimes adverb manchmal; **I sometimes take the train** manchmal fahre ich mit der Bahn.

somewhere adverb **1** (*in a place*) irgendwo; **I've left my bag somewhere here** ich habe meine Handtasche hier irgendwo liegen lassen; **2** (*to a place*) irgendwohin; **I'd like to go somewhere warm** ich möchte irgendwohin fahren, wo es warm ist.

a b c d e f g h i j k l m n o p q r s t u v w x y z

son noun Sohn der (PL die Söhne).

song noun Lied das (PL die Lieder).

son-in-law noun Schwiegersohn der (PL die Schwiegersöhne).

soon adverb **1** bald; **we'll soon be on holiday** wir haben bald Ferien; **see you soon!** bis bald!; **2 as soon as she arrives** sobald sie ankommt; **as soon as possible** so bald wie möglich; **3 it's too soon** es ist zu früh.

sooner adverb **1** früher; **we should have started sooner** wir hätten früher anfangen sollen; **sooner or later** früher oder später; **2 I'd sooner wait** ich würde lieber warten.

soprano noun Sopran der (PL die Soprane).

sore noun wunde Stelle die (PL die wunden Stellen).

sore adjective **1** (inflamed) wund; **to have a sore throat** Halsschmerzen haben; **2 he has a sore leg** ihm tut das Bein weh; **my arm's sore** mir tut der Arm weh; ★ **it's a sore point** das ist ein wunder Punkt.

sorry adjective **1 I'm really sorry** es tut mir wirklich Leid; **sorry to disturb you** es tut mir Leid, dass ich dich störe; **I'm sorry I forgot your birthday** es tut mir Leid, dass ich deinen Geburtstag vergessen habe; **I'm sorry, were closing** es tut mir Leid, aber wir machen jetzt zu; **2 sorry!** Entschuldigung!; **3 sorry?** wie bitte?; **4 I feel sorry for him** er tut mir Leid.

sort noun Art die (PL die Arten); **a sort of dance music** eine Art Tanzmusik; **what sort of car have you got?** was für ein Auto hast

du?; **all sorts of people** alle möglichen Leute; **for all sorts of reasons** aus allen möglichen Gründen.

● **to sort something out 1** Ordnung schaffen✧ in (+ DAT) (papers, desk, room, possessions); **I must sort out my room tonight** ich muss heute Abend in meinem Zimmer Ordnung schaffen; **2** klären (a problem, arrangement); **Liz is sorting it out** Liz klärt es.

so-so adjective so lala (informal); **'how was the film?'— 'so-so'** 'wie war der Film?'— 'mittelmäßig'.

soul noun **1** Seele die (PL die Seelen); **2** (music) Soul der.

sound noun **1** (noise) Geräusch das (PL die Geräusche); **2** (of voices, laughter, bell) Klang der; **the sound of her voice** der Klang ihrer Stimme; **I can hear the sound of voices** ich kann Stimmen hören; **3 without a sound** lautlos; **4** (volume) Lautstärke die; **to turn the sound down** leiser stellen.

sound verb **1** it sounds easy es hört sich einfach an; **2 it sounds as if she's happy** sie scheint glücklich zu sein.

sound asleep adverb **to be sound asleep** fest schlafen✧.

sound effect noun Geräuscheffekt der (PL die Geräuscheffekte).

soundtrack noun Soundtrack der (PL die Soundtracks).

soup noun Suppe die (PL die Suppen); **mushroom soup** die Pilzsuppe.

soup plate noun Suppenteller der (PL die Suppenteller).

soup spoon noun Suppenlöffel der (PL die Suppenlöffel).

sour adjective sauer.

south noun Süden der; **in the south** im Süden.

south adjective Süd-, südlich; **the south side** die Südseite; **south wind** der Südwind.

south adverb **south of Berlin** südlich von Berlin; **they went south** sie sind nach Süden gefahren.

South Africa noun Südafrika das.

South America noun Südamerika das.

southeast noun Südosten der.

southeast adjective **in southeast England** in Südostengland.

South Pole noun Südpol der.

southwest noun Südwesten der.

southwest adjective **in southwest England** in Südwestengland.

souvenir noun Souvenir das (PL die Souvenirs).

soya noun Soja die.

space noun 1 (room) Platz der, **there's enough space** es ist genug Platz; **we've got enough space for two** wir haben genug Platz für zwei; 2 (gap) Zwischenraum der (PL die Zwischenräume); **to leave a large space between lines** viel Platz zwischen den Zeilen lassen; 3 (parking) space die Parklücke; 4 (outer space) Weltraum der; **in space** im Weltraum.

spacecraft noun Raumschiff das (PL die Raumschiffe).

spade noun 1 Spaten der (PL die Spaten); 2 (in cards) Pik das; **the queen of spades** die Pikdame.

Spain noun Spanien das; **from Spain** aus Spanien; **to Spain** nach Spanien.

Spaniard noun Spanier der (PL die Spanier), Spanierin die (PL die Spanierinnen).

spaniel noun Spaniel der (PL die Spaniels).

Spanish noun 1 (language) Spanisch das; **I'm learning Spanish** ich lerne Spanisch; 2 **the Spanish** (people) die Spanier.

Spanish adjective spanisch; **Pedro is Spanish** Pedro ist Spanier.

spanner noun Schraubenschlüssel der (PL die Schraubenschlüssel).

spare adjective Extra-; **we have a spare ticket** wir haben eine Karte übrig.

spare verb **to have time to spare** Zeit haben; **can you spare a moment?** hast du einen Moment Zeit?

spare part noun Ersatzteil das (PL die Ersatzteile).

spare room noun Gästezimmer das (PL die Gästezimmer).

spare time noun Freizeit die; **in my spare time** in meiner Freizeit.

spare wheel noun Reserverad das (PL die Reserveräder).

sparkling adjective **sparkling mineral water** Mineralwasser mit Kohlensäure; **sparkling wine** der Schaumwein.

sparrow noun Spatz der (PL die Spatzen).

speak verb 1 sprechen✧; **do you speak German?** sprechen Sie Deutsch?; **spoken German**

a b c d e f g h i j k l m n o p q r s t u v w x y z

gesprochenes Deutsch; **to speak to somebody about something** mit jemandem über etwas (ACC) sprechen; **she's speaking to Mike about it** sie spricht mit Mike darüber; **2 who's speaking?** (on the phone) wer ist am Apparat?

speaker noun **1** (on a music system) Lautsprecher der (PL die Lautsprecher); **2** (at a public lecture) Redner der (PL die Redner), Rednerin die (PL die Rednerinnen).

special adjective **1** besonderer/ besondere/besonderes; **on special occasions** bei besonderen Anlässen; **2 special offer** das Sonderangebot.

specialist noun Fachmann der (PL die Fachleute), Fachfrau die (PL die Fachfrauen).

specialize verb sich spezialisieren auf (+ ACC); **to specialize in I'm specializing in business studies** ich spezialisiere mich auf Wirtschaftswissenschaften.

specially adverb **1** besonders; **not specially** nicht besonders; **it's specially good for babies** es ist besonders gut für Babys; **2** (specifically) speziell; **I made this cake specially for you** ich habe diesen Kuchen speziell für dich gebacken.

species noun Art die (PL die Arten).

spectacles noun Brille die (PL die Brillen).

spectacular adjective spektakulär.

spectator noun Zuschauer der (PL die Zuschauer), Zuschauerin die (PL die Zuschauerinnen).

speech noun Rede die (PL die Reden); **to make a speech** eine Rede halten.

speechless adjective sprachlos; **to be speechless: she was speechless with rage** sie war sprachlos vor Wut.

speed noun **1** Geschwindigkeit die (PL die Geschwindigkeiten); **at top speed** mit Höchstgeschwindigkeit; **what speed was he doing?** wie schnell ist er gefahren?; **2** (gear) Gang der (PL die Gänge); **a twelve-speed bike** ein Rad mit zwölf Gängen.

● **to speed up 1** beschleunigen (a car); **2** (of a person, car) schneller werden.

speeding noun zu schnelle Fahren das; **he was fined for speeding** er hat wegen zu schnellen Fahrens ein Bußgeld bekommen.

speed limit noun Geschwindigkeitsbeschränkung die.

spell noun **1** (of time) Weile die; **for a spell** eine Weile; **2 cold spell** die Kälteperiode; **sunny spells** sonnige Abschnitte.

spell verb **1** (in writing) schreiben◇; **how do you spell it?** wie schreibt man das?; **how do you spell your surname?** wie schreibt man Ihren Nachnamen?; **2** (out loud) buchstabieren.

spell checker noun Rechtschreibprogramm das (PL die Rechtschreibprogramme).

spelling noun Rechtschreibung die; **spelling mistake** der Rechtschreibfehler.

spend verb 1 ausgeben✧ SEP (money); **I've spent all my money** ich habe mein ganzes Geld ausgegeben; 2 verbringen✧ (time); **we spent three days in Munich** wir haben drei Tage in München verbracht; **she spends her time reading** sie verbringt ihre Zeit mit Lesen.

spice noun Gewürz das (PL die Gewürze).

spicy adjective scharf; **he doesn't like spicy food** er mag kein scharfes Essen.

spider noun Spinne die (PL die Spinnen).

spill verb verschütten; **I've spilled my wine on the carpet** ich habe meinen Wein auf dem Teppich verschüttet.

spinach noun Spinat der.

spine noun Wirbelsäule die (PL die Wirbelsäulen).

spire noun Kirchturm der (PL die Kirchtürme).

spirit noun 1 (energy) Energie die; 2 **in the right spirit** mit der richtigen Einstellung.

spirits noun 1 (alcohol) Spirituosen (plural); 2 **to be in good spirits** guter Laune sein.

spit verb 1 spucken; 2 **to spit something out** etwas ausspucken SEP; **spit it out!** spuck es aus!

spite noun 1 **in spite of** trotz (+ GEN); **we decided to go in spite of the rain** wir beschlossen trotz des Regens zu gehen; 2 (nastiness) Boshaftigkeit die; **to do something out of spite** etwas aus Boshaftigkeit tun.

spiteful adjective gehässig.

splash noun 1 (noise) Platsch der; 2 **splash of colour** der Farbfleck.

splash verb bespritzen.

splendid adjective herrlich.

splinter noun Splitter der (PL die Splitter).

split verb 1 (with an axe or a knife) spalten; **to split wood** Holz spalten; 2 (come apart) zerreißen✧ (PERF sein); **the lining has split** das Futter ist zerrissen; 3 (divide up) teilen; **they split the money between them** sie haben das Geld untereinander geteilt.

● **to split up** 1 (a group or crowd) sich auflösen SEP; 2 (a couple) sich trennen; **she's split up with her husband** sie hat sich von ihrem Mann getrennt; **she's split up with Sam** sie hat mit Sam Schluss gemacht (informal).

spoil verb verderben✧; **it completely spoiled our evening** das hat uns den Abend völlig verdorben; **to spoil somebody's fun** jemandem den Spaß verderben.

spoiled adjective verwöhnt; **a spoiled child** ein verwöhntes Kind.

spoilsport noun Spielverderber der (PL die Spielverderber), Spielverderberin die (PL die Spielverderberinnen).

spoke noun (of a wheel) Speiche die (PL die Speichen).

spokesman noun Sprecher der (PL die Sprecher).

spokeswoman noun Sprecherin die (PL die Sprecherinnen).

sponge noun Schwamm der (PL die Schwämme).

sponge cake noun Rührkuchen der (PL die Rührkuchen).

a b c d e f g h i j k l m n o p q r s t u v w x y z

sponsor noun Sponsor der (PL die Sponsoren).

sponsor verb sponsern.

spooky adjective gruselig; **a spooky story** eine gruselige Geschichte.

spoon noun Löffel der (PL die Löffel); **a spoon of sugar** ein Löffel Zucker; **soup spoon** der Suppenlöffel; **teaspoon** der Teelöffel.

spoonful noun Löffel der (PL die Löffel).

sport noun 1 Sport der; **to be good at sport** gut im Sport sein; **my favourite sport** mein Lieblingssport; 2 (in games) **to be a good sport** ein guter Verlierer sein.

sports bag noun Sporttasche die (PL die Sporttaschen).

sports car noun Sportwagen der (PL die Sportwagen).

sports centre noun Sportzentrum das (PL die Sportzentren).

sports club noun Sportverein der (PL die Sportvereine).

sportsman noun Sportler der (PL die Sportler).

sportswear noun Sportbekleidung die.

sportswoman noun Sportlerin die (PL die Sportlerinnen).

sporty adjective sportlich; **she's very sporty** sie ist sehr sportlich.

spot noun 1 (pattern in fabric) Punkt der (PL die Punkte); **a red shirt with black spots** ein rotes Hemd mit schwarzen Punkten; 2 (on your skin) Pickel der (PL die Pickel); **I've got spots** ich habe Pickel; **to be covered in spots**

völlig verpickelt sein; 3 (stain) Fleck der (PL die Flecke); **you've got a spot on your shirt** du hast einen Fleck auf dem Hemd; 4 (spotlight) Scheinwerfer der (PL die Scheinwerfer); (in the home) Spot der (PL die Spots); 5 **on the spot** (immediately) auf der Stelle; **we'll do it for you on the spot** wir machen es Ihnen auf der Stelle; 6 (at hand) **on the spot** zur Stelle; 7 (at the same place) **on the spot** an Ort und Stelle.

spot verb entdecken; **he spotted his friend in the crowd** er entdeckte seinen Freund in der Menge.

spotlight noun 1 Scheinwerfer der (PL die Scheinwerfer); 2 (in the home) Spot der (PL die Spots).

spotty adjective (pimply) pickelig.

spouse noun 1 (male) Ehemann der (PL die Ehemänner); 2 (female) Ehefrau die (PL die Ehefrauen).

sprain noun Verstauchung die (PL die Verstauchungen).

sprain verb **to sprain your ankle** sich (DAT) den Fuß verstauchen.

spray noun (spray can) Spray das (PL die Sprays).

spray verb sprühen.

spread noun Brotaufstrich der; **cheese spread** der Streichkäse.

spread verb 1 (of news or a disease) sich verbreiten; 2 streichen◇ (butter, jam, glue).

spreadsheet noun (on a computer) Tabellenkalkulation die.

spring noun 1 (the season) Frühling der (PL die Frühlinge); **in the spring** im Frühling; **spring**

flowers Frühlingsblumen; **2** (*made of metal*) Feder die (PL die Federn); **3** (*providing water*) Quelle die (PL die Quellen).

springtime noun Frühjahr das; **in springtime** im Frühjahr.

spring water noun Quellwasser das.

sprint noun Sprint der (PL die Sprints).

sprint verb rennen✧ (PERF sein).

sprinter noun Sprinter der (PL die Sprinter), Sprinterin die (PL die Sprinterinnen).

sprout (Brussels sprout) Rosenkohl der; **he likes sprouts** er mag Rosenkohl.

spy noun Spion der (PL die Spione), Spionin die (PL die Spioninnen).

spy verb **to spy on somebody** jemandem nachspionieren SEP; **he's spying on me** er spioniert mir nach.

squabble verb sich zanken.

square noun **1** (*shape*) Quadrat das (PL die Quadrate); **2** (*in a town or village*) Platz der (PL die Plätze); **the village square** der Dorfplatz.

square adjective quadratisch; **a square box** eine viereckige Schachtel; **three square metres** drei Quadratmeter; **the room is four metres square** das Zimmer ist vier mal vier Meter; ★ **to go back to square one** noch einmal von vorn anfangen.

squash noun **1** (*drink*) Saft der; **orange squash** der Orangensaft; **2** (*sport*) Squash das.

squash verb zerquetschen.

squeak verb **1** (*door, hinge*) quietschen; **2** (*person, animal*) quieken.

squeeze verb **1** drücken; **to squeeze somebody's hand** jemandem die Hand drücken; **2** drücken (*toothpaste*).

squirrel noun Eichhörnchen das (PL die Eichhörnchen).

stab verb stechen✧; **to stab somebody** (*kill*) jemanden erstechen✧.

stable noun Stall der (PL die Ställe).

stable adjective stabil.

stack noun **1** Stapel der (PL die Stapel); **2 stacks of** ein Haufen; **she's got stacks of CDs** sie hat einen Haufen CDs.

stadium noun Stadion das (PL die Stadien).

staff noun **1** (*of a company*) Personal das; **2** (*in a school*) Lehrkräfte (*plural*).

stage noun **1** (*for a performance*) Bühne die (PL die Bühnen); **on stage** auf der Bühne; **2** (*phase*) Phase die (PL die Phasen); **at this stage of the project** in dieser Phase des Projekts; **at this stage it's hard to say** im Augenblick ist es schwer zu sagen.

staggered adjective (*amazed*) verblüfft.

stain noun Fleck der (PL die Flecke).

stain verb beflecken.

stainless steel noun Edelstahl der; **a stainless steel sink** ein Spülbecken aus Edelstahl.

stair noun **1** (*step*) Stufe die (PL die Stufen); **2 the stairs** die Treppe (*singular*); **I met her on the stairs**

a b c d e f g h i j k l m n o p q r s t u v w x y z

ich habe sie auf der Treppe getroffen.

staircase noun Treppe die (PL die Treppen).

stale adjective alt.

stalemate noun (in chess) Patt das (PL die Patts).

stall noun 1 (at a market or fair) Stand der (PL die Stände); 2 (in a theatre) the stalls das Parkett.

stammer noun to have a stammer stottern.

stamp noun Briefmarke die (PL die Briefmarken).

stamp verb 1 frankieren (a letter); 2 to stamp your foot mit dem Fuß aufstampfen.

stamp album noun Briefmarkenalbum das (PL die Briefmarkenalben).

stamp collection noun Briefmarkensammlung die (PL die Briefmarkensammlungen).

stand¹ verb 1 stehen✧; **several people were standing** viele Leute standen; **we stood outside the cinema** wir haben vor dem Kino gestanden; 2 (bear) ausstehen✧ SEP; **I can't stand her** ich kann sie nicht ausstehen; **I can't stand waiting** ich kann es nicht ausstehen, wenn man warten muss; 3 (keep going) aushalten✧ SEP; **I can't stand it any longer** ich halte es nicht mehr aus.

stand noun (in a stadium) Tribüne die (PL die Tribünen).

● **to stand for something** (be short for) bedeuten; **UN stands for United Nations** UN bedeutet United Nations.

● **stand up** aufstehen✧ SEP (PERF sein); **everybody stood up** alle standen auf.

stand² noun 1 (in a stadium) Tribüne die (PL die Tribünen); 2 (in fair) Stand der (PL die Stände).

standard noun 1 (level) Niveau das; **of high standard** von hohem Niveau; 2 **standard of living** der Lebensstandard; 3 **she sets herself high standards** sie stellt hohe Ansprüche an sich selbst.

standard adjective normal; **the standard size** die Normalgröße.

Standard grades noun plural (You can explain Standard grades as follows: Diese Prüfungen werden im Alter von ca 16 Jahren in sechs oder sieben Fächern abgelegt. Sie werden von 1 (beste Note) bis 7 (Kurs abgeschlossen) benotet. Viele Schüler machen nach Standard Grades weiter, und legen Highers und Advanced Highers ab) SEE **Highers.**

staple noun Heftklammer die (PL die Heftklammern).

staple verb heften; **to staple the pages together** die Seiten zusammenheften.

stapler noun Hefter der (PL die Hefter).

star noun 1 (in the sky) Stern der (PL die Sterne); 2 (person) Star der (PL die Stars); **he's a film star** er ist ein Filmstar.

star verb **to star in a film** in einem Film die Hauptrolle spielen; **starring ... in der Hauptrolle ....**

stare verb 1 starren; **what are you staring at?** was starrst du so?; 2 **to**

stare at somebody jemanden anstarren SEP; **he's staring at the wall** er starrt die Wand an.

start noun **1** Anfang der; **at the start** am Anfang; **at the start of the film** am Anfang des Films; **from the start** von Anfang an; **we knew from the start that it was dangerous** wir wussten von Anfang an, dass es gefährlich war; **2 to make a start on something** mit etwas (DAT) anfangen✧ SEP; **I've made a start on my homework** ich habe mit meinen Hausaufgaben angefangen; **3** (of a race) Start der (PL die Starts).

start verb **1** anfangen✧ SEP; **the film starts at eight** der Film fängt um acht an; **I've started the book** ich habe das Buch angefangen; **to start doing something** anfangen, etwas zu tun; **I've started learning Spanish** ich habe angefangen, Spanisch zu lernen; **to start crying** anfangen zu weinen; **2 to start a business** ein Geschäft gründen; **3 to start a car** ein Auto starten; **she started the car** sie hat das Auto gestartet; **4 the car won't start** das Auto springt nicht an.

starter noun (first course) Vorspeise die (PL die Vorspeisen).

starve verb verhungern; **I'm starving!** ich bin schon am Verhungern!

state noun **1** Zustand der (PL die Zustände); **the house is in a very bad state** das Haus ist in einem sehr schlechten Zustand; **2** (country) Staat der (PL die Staaten); **the state** der Staat; **3 the States** (USA) die Staaten; **they live**

in the States sie leben in den Staaten.

state verb **1** erklären (intention, reason); **2** angeben✧ SEP (an address, income, a reason).

stately home noun herrschaftliche Anwesen das (PL die herrschaftlichen Anwesen).

statement noun Erklärung die (PL die Erklärungen).

station noun **1** Bahnhof der (PL die Bahnhöfe); **at the railway station** am Bahnhof; **bus station** der Busbahnhof; **2 police station** die Polizeiwache; **3 radio station** der Rundfunksender.

stationer's noun Schreibwarengeschäft das (PL die Schreibwarengeschäfte).

statistics noun (subject) Statistik die; **the statistics** (figures) die Statistik.

statue noun Statue die (PL die Statuen).

stay noun Aufenthalt der (PL die Aufenthalte); **our stay in Cologne** unser Aufenthalt in Köln; **enjoy your stay!** einen schönen Aufenthalt!

stay verb **1** bleiben✧ (PERF sein); **I'll stay here** ich bleibe hier; **how long are you staying?** wie lange bleibst du?; **2** (spend the night) **you can stay with us** du kannst bei uns übernachten; **to stay the night with friends** bei Freunden übernachten; **3** (be temporarily lodged) wohnen; **where are you staying?** wo wohnst du?; **I'm staying in a hotel** ich wohne im Hotel; **4** (be on a visit) sein✧ (PERF

a
b
c
d
e
f
g
h
i
j
k
l
m
n
o
p
q
r
s
t
u
v
w
x
y
z

sein); **I'm going to stay with my sister this weekend** ich bin am Wochenende bei meiner Schwester; **I stayed in Munich for a couple of days** ich war in ein paar Tage in München.

● **to stay in** zu Hause bleiben✧ (PERF *sein*); **I'm staying in tonight** heute Abend bleibe ich zu Hause.

steady *adjective* **1** fest; **a steady job** eine feste Stelle; **2** gleichmäßig; **at a steady pace** mit gleichmäßiger Geschwindigkeit; **3** (*hand, voice*) ruhig; **to hold something steady** etwas ruhig halten; **4** (*dependable*) zuverlässig.

steak *noun* Steak *das* (PL die Steaks); **steak and chips** Steak mit Pommes frites.

steal *verb* stehlen✧.

steam *noun* Dampf *der*.

steel *noun* Stahl *der*.

steep *adjective* steil; **a steep slope** ein steiler Hang.

steeple *noun* (*spire*) Kirchturm *der* (PL die Kirchtürme).

steering wheel *noun* Lenkrad *das* (PL die Lenkräder).

step *noun* **1** Schritt *der* (PL die Schritte); **to take a step forwards** einen Schritt nach vorn machen; **to take a step backwards** einen Schritt zurück machen; **2** (*stair*) Stufe die (PL die Stufen).

● **to step back** zurücktreten✧ SEP (PERF *sein*).

● **to step forward** vortreten✧ SEP (PERF *sein*).

stepbrother *noun* Stiefbruder *der* (PL die Stiefbrüder).

stepdaughter *noun* Stieftochter *die* (PL die Stieftöchter).

stepfather *noun* Stiefvater *der* (PL die Stiefväter).

stepladder *noun* Trittleiter *die* (PL die Trittleitern).

stepmother *noun* Stiefmutter *die* (PL die Stiefmütter).

stepsister *noun* Stiefschwester *die* (PL die Stiefschwestern).

stepson *noun* Stiefsohn *der* (PL die Stiefsöhne).

stereo *noun* Stereoanlage *die* (PL die Stereoanlagen).

sterling *noun* Sterling *der*; **in sterling** in Pfund (Sterling).

stew *noun* Eintopf *der* (PL die Eintöpfe).

steward *noun* Steward *der* (PL die Stewards).

stewardess *noun* Stewardess *die* (PL die Stewardessen).

stick *noun* **1** Stock *der* (PL die Stöcke); **2** hockey stick Hockeyschläger *der*.

stick *verb* **1** (*with glue*) kleben; **2** (*put*) tun✧; **stick them on my desk** tu sie auf meinen Schreibtisch.

sticker *noun* Aufkleber *der* (PL die Aufkleber).

sticky tape *noun* Klebestreifen *der*.

sticky *adjective* **1** klebrig; **I've got sticky hands** ich habe klebrige Hände; **2** a sticky label ein Aufkleber.

stiff *adjective* **1** steif; **to feel stiff** steif sein, (*after exercise*)

Muskelkater haben; to have a stiff neck einen steifen Hals haben; **2 to be bored stiff** sich zu Tode langweilen; **3 to be scared stiff** furchtbare Angst haben.

still adjective **1 sit still!** sitz still!; **keep still!** halt still!!; **2 still mineral water** Mineralwasser ohne Kohlensäure.

still adverb **1** noch; **do you still live in London?** wohnst du noch in London?; **I've still not finished** ich bin immer noch nicht fertig; **he's still working** er arbeitet noch; **2** (nevertheless) trotzdem; **I told her not to, but she still did it** ich habe es ihr verboten, aber sie hat es trotzdem gemacht; **3 better still** noch besser.

sting noun Stich der (PL die Stiche).

sting verb stechen◇.

stink noun Gestank der.

stink verb stinken◇; **it stinks of fish in here** es stinkt hier nach Fisch.

stir verb rühren.

stitch noun **1** (in sewing, surgical) Stich der (PL die Stiche); **2** (in knitting) Masche die (PL die Maschen); **3** (pain) Seitenstechen das.

stock noun **1** (in a shop) Warenbestand der; **to have something in stock** etwas auf Lager haben; **to be out of stock** ausverkauft sein; **2** (supply) Vorrat der (PL die Vorräte); **I always have a stock of pencils** ich habe immer einen Bleistiftvorrat; **3** (for cooking) Brühe die; **chicken stock** die Hühnerbrühe.

stock verb (in a shop) führen; **they don't stock books** sie führen keine Bücher.

stock cube noun Brühwürfel der (PL die Brühwürfel).

stock exchange noun Börse die (PL die Börsen).

stocking noun Strumpf der (PL die Strümpfe).

stomach noun Magen der (PL die Mägen).

stomach-ache noun Magenschmerzen (plural); **to have stomach-ache** Magenschmerzen haben.

stone noun Stein der (PL die Steine); **stone wall** die Steinmauer.

stool noun Hocker der (PL die Hocker).

stop noun Haltestelle die (PL die Haltestellen); **bus stop** die Bushaltestelle.

stop verb **1** halten◇; **does the train stop in Stuttgart?** hält der Zug in Stuttgart?; **2 to stop somebody/ something** jemanden/etwas anhalten◇ SEP; **the police stopped the car** die Polizei hielt den Wagen an; **3** (cease) aufhören SEP; **the noise has stopped** der Lärm hat aufgehört; **to stop doing something** aufhören, etwas zu tun; **he's stopped smoking** er hat aufgehört zu rauchen; **she never stops asking questions** sie hört nie auf, Fragen zu stellen; **stop it!** hör auf!; **4 to stop somebody doing something** jemanden daran hindern, etwas zu tun; **I can't stop her ringing him** ich kann sie nicht daran hindern, ihn anzurufen;

5 (*prevent*) verhindern (*an accident, a crime*).

stopwatch noun Stoppuhr die (PL die Stoppuhren).

store noun (*shop*) Geschäft das (PL die Geschäfte); **department store** das Kaufhaus.

store verb **1** aufbewahren SEP, (*in a warehouse*) lagern; **2** (*on a computer*) speichern.

storey noun Stockwerk das (PL die Stockwerke); **a four-storey house** ein vierstöckiges Haus.

storm noun **1** Sturm der (PL die Stürme); **2** (*thunderstorm*) Gewitter das (PL die Gewitter).

stormy adjective stürmisch.

story noun Geschichte die (PL die Geschichten); **to tell a story** eine Geschichte erzählen.

stove noun (*cooker*) Herd der (PL die Herde).

straight adjective **1** gerade; **a straight line** eine gerade Linie; **2 to have straight hair** glatte Haare haben.

straight adverb **1** (*in direction*) **straight ahead** geradeaus; **to go straight ahead** geradeaus gehen; **2** (*immediately, directly*) sofort; **straight away** sofort; **he went straight to the doctor's** er ging sofort zum Arzt.

straightforward adjective einfach.

strain noun Stress der; **the strain of the last few weeks** der Stress in den letzten Wochen; **to be a strain** anstrengend sein.

strain verb **1** zerren (*a muscle*); **2** verrenken (*your arm, back*); **he's**

strained his back er hat sich (DAT) den Rücken verrenkt.

strange adjective seltsam; **his strange behaviour** sein seltsames Verhalten.

stranger noun Fremde der/die (PL die Fremden).

strangle verb erwürgen.

strap noun **1** (*on a case, bag, camera*) Riemen der (PL die Riemen); **2** (*on a garment*) Träger der (PL die Träger); **3** (*of a watch*) Armband das (PL die Armbänder).

strapless adjective trägerlos.

straw noun **1** (*for drinking*) Strohhalm der (PL die Strohhalme); **2** (*the material*) Stroh das; **straw hat** der Strohhut.

strawberry noun Erdbeere die (PL die Erdbeeren); **strawberry jam** die Erdbeermarmelade.

stray adjective **a stray dog** ein streunender Hund.

stream noun Bach der (PL die Bäche).

street noun Straße die (PL die Straßen); **I met Simon in the street** ich habe Simon auf der Straße getroffen.

streetlamp noun Straßenlaterne die (PL die Straßenlaternen).

street map noun Stadtplan der (PL die Stadtpläne).

streetwise adjective gewieft.

strength noun Kraft die (PL die Kräfte).

stress noun Stress der.

stress verb betonen; **to stress the importance of something** die Wichtigkeit von etwas betonen.

stretch verb **1** (*garment, shoes*) sich dehnen; **this jumper has**

stretched der Pullover hat sich gedehnt; **2 to stretch your legs** sich (DAT) die Beine vertreten✧.

stretcher *noun* Trage *die* (PL die Tragen).

stretchy *adjective* elastisch.

strict *adjective* streng.

strike *noun* Streik *der* (PL die Streiks); **to go on strike** in den Streik treten✧ (PERF sein); **to be/go on strike** streiken.

strike *verb* **1** (*hit*) schlagen✧; **the clock struck six** die Uhr schlug sechs; **2** (*be/go on strike*) streiken.

striker *noun* **1** (*in football*) Stürmer *der* (PL die Stürmer), Stürmerin *die* (PL die Stürmerinnen); **2** (*person on strike*) Streikende *der/die* (PL die Streikenden).

string *noun* **1** (*for tying*) Schnur *die* (PL die Schnüre); **2** (*on a musical instrument*) Saite *die* (PL die Saiten).

strip *noun* Streifen *der* (PL die Streifen).

strip *verb* **1** (*undress*) sich ausziehen✧ SEP; **2** (*remove paint from*) abbeizen SEP.

strip cartoon *noun* Comicstrip *der* (PL die Comicstrips).

stripe *noun* Streifen *der* (PL die Streifen).

striped *adjective* gestreift.

stroke *noun* **1** (*style of swimming*) Stil *der* (PL die Stile); **2** (*medical*) Schlaganfall *der* (PL die Schlaganfälle); **to have a stroke** einen Schlaganfall bekommen; **★ a stroke of luck** ein Glücksfall; **to have a stroke of luck** Glück haben.

stroke *verb* streicheln.

strong *adjective* **1** (*person, drink, feeling*) stark; **2** (*sturdy*) stabil (*furniture*); **strong shoes** feste Schuhe.

strongly *adverb* **1** (*believe, oppose*) fest; **2** (*support*) nachdrücklich; **3** (*advise, recommend*) dringend; **4 she smelt strongly of garlic** sie hat stark nach Knoblauch gerochen.

struggle *noun* Kampf *der* (PL die Kämpfe); **the struggle for freedom** der Kampf für die Freiheit; **it's been a struggle** es war ein Kampf.

struggle *verb* **1** (*to obtain something*) kämpfen; **to struggle to do something** kämpfen, um etwas zu tun; **she struggled for a place** sie kämpfte um einen Platz; **2** (*physically, in order to escape or reach something*) sich wehren; **3** (*have difficulty in doing something*) sich abmühen SEP; **they are struggling to pay the rent** sie mühen sich ab, ihre Miete zu zahlen; **he's struggling with his homework** er müht sich mit seinen Hausaufgaben ab.

stub *noun* **cigarette stub** *die* Kippe.

● **to stub out** ausdrücken SEP.

stubborn *adjective* stur.

stuck *adjective* **1** (*jammed*) **it's stuck** es klemmt; **the drawer's stuck** die Schublade klemmt; **2 to get stuck** (*person*) stecken bleiben✧ (*in a lift, traffic jam, or place*).

stud *noun* **1** (*on clothes*) Niete *die* (PL die Nieten); **2** (*on a boot*) Stollen *der*

a b c d e f g h i j k l m n o p q r s t u v w x y z

(PL die Stollen); 3 (earring) Ohrstecker der (PL die Ohrstecker).

student noun 1 (at college or university) Student der (PL die Studenten), Studentin die (PL die Studentinnen); 2 (at school) Schüler der (PL die Schüler), Schülerin die (PL die Schülerinnen).

studio noun 1 (film, TV) Studio das (PL die Studios); 2 (artist's) Atelier das (PL die Ateliers).

study verb 1 lernen; he's busy studying for his exams er lernt fleißig für seine Prüfung; 2 studieren; she's studying medicine sie studiert Medizin.

stuff noun (things, personal belongings) Zeug das (informal); we can put all that stuff in the attic wir können das ganze Zeug auf den Dachboden bringen; you can leave your stuff at my house du kannst dein Zeug bei mir lassen.

stuff verb 1 (shove) stopfen; she stuffed some things into a suitcase sie hat ein paar Sachen in einen Koffer gestopft; 2 füllen (vegetables, turkey); stuffed peppers gefüllte Paprikaschoten.

stuffing noun (in cooking) Füllung die (PL die Füllungen).

stuffy adjective (airless) stickig.

stumble verb stolpern (PERF sein).

stunned adjective sprachlos.

stunning adjective toll (informal).

stunt noun (in a film) Stunt der (PL die Stunts).

stuntman noun Stuntman der (PL die Stuntmen).

stupid adjective dumm; that was really stupid das war wirklich dumm; I did something stupid ich habe etwas Blödes gemacht.

stutter noun to have a stutter stottern.

stutter verb stottern.

style noun 1 Stil der (PL die Stile); style of living der Lebensstil; he has his own style er hat seinen eigenen Stil; 2 (fashion) Mode die; it's the latest style das ist die neueste Mode.

subject noun 1 Thema das (PL die Themen); the subject of my talk das Thema meiner Rede; 2 (at school) Fach das (PL die Fächer); my favourite subject is biology mein Lieblingsfach ist Biologie.

submarine noun Unterseeboot das (PL die Unterseeboote), U-Boot das (PL die U-Boote).

subscription noun Abonnement das (PL die Abonnements); to take out a subscription to a magazine eine Zeitschrift abonnieren.

subsidize verb subventionieren.

subsidy noun Subvention die (PL die Subventionen).

substance noun Substanz die (PL die Substanzen).

substitute noun (in sport) Ersatzspieler der (PL die Ersatzspieler), Ersatzspielerin die (PL die Ersatzspielerinnen).

substitute verb ersetzen.

subtitled adjective mit Untertiteln.

subtitles plural noun Untertitel (plural).

subtle adjective subtil.

subtract verb abziehen ✧ SEP.

suburb noun Vorort der (PL die Vororte); **a suburb of Edinburgh** ein Vorort von Edinburgh; **in the suburbs of London** in den Londoner Vororten.

suburban adjective Vorort-; **a suburban train** ein Vorortzug.

subway noun (underpass) Unterführung die (PL die Unterführungen).

succeed verb gelingen ✧ (PERF sein); **we've succeeded in contacting her** es ist uns gelungen, sie zu erreichen.

success noun Erfolg der (PL die Erfolge); **a great success** ein großer Erfolg.

successful adjective
1 erfolgreich; **he's a successful writer** er ist ein erfolgreicher Schriftsteller; **2 to be successful in doing something** etwas mit Erfolg tun.

successfully adverb mit Erfolg.

such adjective, adverb **1** so; **they're such nice people** das sind so nette Leute; **I've had such a busy day** ich habe so einen hektischen Tag gehabt; **it's such a long way** es ist so weit; **it's such a pity** es ist so schade; **2 such a lot of** (followed by a singular noun) so viel; **they've got such a lot of money** sie haben so viel Geld; **3 such a lot of** (followed by a plural noun) so viele; **she's got such a lot of problems** sie hat so viele Probleme; **4 such as** wie; **in big cities such as Glasgow** in großen Städten wie Glasgow; **5 there's no such thing** so etwas gibt es nicht.

suck verb lutschen; **to suck your thumb** am Daumen lutschen.

sudden adjective plötzlich; ★ **all of a sudden** plötzlich.

suddenly adverb plötzlich; **he suddenly started to laugh** plötzlich hat er angefangen zu lachen; **suddenly the light went out** plötzlich ging das Licht aus.

suede noun Wildleder das; **suede jacket** die Wildlederjacke.

suffer verb leiden ✧; **to suffer from asthma** an Asthma leiden.

sufficiently adverb genug.

sugar noun Zucker der; **do you take sugar?** nimmst du Zucker?

suggest verb vorschlagen ✧ SEP; **he suggested I should speak to you about it** er hat vorgeschlagen, dass ich mit dir darüber sprechen soll.

suggestion noun Vorschlag der (PL die Vorschläge); **to make a suggestion** einen Vorschlag machen.

suicide noun Selbstmord der (PL die Selbstmorde); **to commit suicide** Selbstmord begehen.

suit noun **1** (man's) Anzug der (PL die Anzüge); **2** (woman's) Kostüm das (PL die Kostüme).

suit verb **1** (be convenient) passen (+ DAT); **does Monday suit you?** passt Ihnen Montag?; **2** (look good on) stehen ✧ (+ DAT); **hats suit her** ihr stehen Hüte.

suitable adjective **1** geeignet; **to be suitable for something** für etwas geeignet sein; **it's suitable for children** es ist für Kinder geeignet; **2** (convenient) passend; **at a suitable time** zur passenden Zeit;

Saturday is the most suitable day for me Samstag passt mir am besten; **3** (*for a social occasion*) angemessen (*clothes*).

suitcase *noun* Koffer der (PL die Koffer).

sulk *verb* schmollen.

sum *noun* **1** Summe die (PL die Summen); **a sum of money** eine Geldsumme; **2** (*calculation*) Rechenaufgabe die (PL die Rechenaufgaben).

● **to sum up** zusammenfassen SEP.

summarize *verb* zusammenfassen SEP.

summary *noun* Zusammenfassung die (PL die Zusammenfassungen).

summer *noun* Sommer der (PL die Sommer); **in summer** im Sommer; **summer clothes** die Sommerkleidung; **the summer holidays** die Sommerferien.

summertime *noun* Sommer der; **in summertime** im Sommer.

summit *noun* Gipfel der (PL die Gipfel).

sun *noun* Sonne die (PL die Sonnen); **in the sun** in der Sonne.

sunbathe *verb* sich sonnen.

sunblock *noun* Sunblocker der (PL die Sunblocker).

sunburn *noun* Sonnenbrand der (PL die Sonnenbrände).

sunburned *adjective* **to get sunburned** einen Sonnenbrand bekommen.

Sunday *noun* **1** Sonntag der (PL die Sonntage); **on Sunday** am Sonntag; **I'm going to the cinema on Sunday** ich gehe (am) Sonntag ins Kino; **see you on Sunday!** bis Sonntag!; **every Sunday** jeden Sonntag; **last Sunday** vorigen Sonntag; **next Sunday** nächsten Sonntag; **2 on Sundays** sonntags; **the museum is closed on Sundays** das Museum ist sonntags geschlossen.

sunflower *noun* Sonnenblume die (PL die Sonnenblumen); **sunflower oil** das Sonnenblumenöl.

sunglasses *plural noun* Sonnenbrille die (PL die Sonnenbrillen).

sunlight *noun* Sonnenlicht das.

sunny *adjective* sonnig; **a sunny day** ein sonniger Tag; **sunny intervals** sonnige Abschnitte.

sunrise *noun* Sonnenaufgang der (PL die Sonnenaufgänge).

sunroof *noun* Schiebedach das (PL die Schiebedächer).

sunscreen *noun* Sonnenschutzcreme die (PL die Sonnenschutzcremes).

sunset *noun* Sonnenuntergang der (PL die Sonnenuntergänge).

sunshine *noun* Sonnenschein der.

sunstroke *noun* Sonnenstich der (PL die Sonnenstiche); **to get sunstroke** einen Sonnenstich bekommen.

suntan *noun* Bräune die; **to have a suntan** braun sein; **to get a suntan** braun werden.

suntan lotion *noun* Sonnenmilch die.

suntan oil *noun* Sonnenöl das.

super *adjective* klasse (*informal*) (*'klasse' never changes*); **we had a super time** es war wirklich klasse.

supermarket noun Supermarkt der (PL die Supermärkte).

supernatural adjective übernatürlich.

superstitious adjective abergläubisch.

supervise verb beaufsichtigen.

supervisor noun Aufseher der (PL die Aufseher), Aufseherin die (PL die Aufseherinnen).

supper noun Abendessen das (PL die Abendessen); **I had supper at Sandy's** ich war bei Sandy zum Abendessen.

supplement noun 1 (to newspaper) Beilage die (PL die Beilagen); 2 (to fare) Zuschlag der (PL die Zuschläge).

supplies plural noun Vorrat der (PL die Vorräte).

supply noun 1 (stock) Vorrat der (PL die Vorräte); 2 **to be in short supply** knapp sein.

supply verb 1 stellen; **the school supplies the books** die Schule stellt die Bücher; 2 (deliver) liefern; **to supply somebody with something** jemandem etwas liefern.

supply teacher noun Aushilfslehrer der (PL die Aushilfslehrer), Aushilfslehrerin die (PL die Aushilfslehrerinnen).

support noun Unterstützung die; **in support** zur Unterstützung.

support verb 1 (back up) unterstützen; **her teachers have really supported her** die Lehrer haben sie sehr unterstützt; **to support somebody financially** jemanden finanziell unterstützen; **2 Will supports Chelsea** Will ist ein Chelsea-Fan; **what team do you support?** für welche Mannschaft bist du?; 3 (keep, provide for) ernähren; **to support a family** eine Familie ernähren.

supporter noun 1 Fan der (PL die Fans); **she's a Manchester United supporter** sie ist ein Manchester-United-Fan; 2 (of a party or cause) Anhänger der (PL die Anhänger), Anhängerin die (PL die Anhängerinnen).

suppose verb annehmen◊ SEP; **I suppose she's forgotten** ich nehme an, sie hat es vergessen.

supposed adjective **to be supposed to do something** etwas tun sollen; **you were supposed to be here at six** du solltest um sechs hier sein.

sure adjective 1 sicher; **are you sure?** bist du sicher?; **are you sure you saw her?** bist du sicher, dass du sie gesehen hast?; **2 sure!** klar!

surely adverb doch sicherlich; **surely she hasn't forgotten** sie hat es doch sicherlich nicht vergessen.

surf noun Surfen das.

surf verb **to surf the Net/Web** im Internet surfen.

surface noun Oberfläche die (PL die Oberflächen).

surfboard noun Surfbrett das (PL die Surfbretter).

surfer noun (on the sea and Internet) Surfer der (PL die Surfer), Surferin die (PL die Surferinnen).

surfing noun Surfen das.

surgeon noun Chirurg der (PL die Chirurgen), Chirurgin die (PL die Chirurginnen).

a b c d e f g h i j k l m n o p q r s t u v w x y z

surgery noun **1** to have surgery operiert werden; **2** (doctor's) Praxis die (PL die Praxen); **the dentist's surgery** die Zahnarztpraxis; **3** (surgery hours) Sprechstunde die.

surname noun Nachname der (PL die Nachnamen).

surprise noun Überraschung die (PL die Überraschungen); **what a surprise!** was für eine Überraschung!

surprised adjective überrascht; **I was surprised to see her** ich war überrascht, sie zu sehen.

surprising adjective überraschend.

surround verb umgeben; **surrounded by** umgeben von (+ DAT); **she was surrounded by friends** sie war von Freunden umgeben.

survey noun Umfrage die (PL die Umfragen).

survive verb überleben.

survivor noun Überlebende der/die (PL die Überlebenden).

suspect noun Verdächtige der/die (PL die Verdächtigen).

suspect adjective verdächtig.

suspect verb verdächtigen.

suspend verb **1** to be suspended (from school) vom Unterricht ausgeschlossen werden; **2** (from a team) sperren; **to suspend a player for four weeks** einen Spieler für vier Wochen sperren.

suspense noun Spannung die.

suspicious adjective **1** misstrauisch; **to be suspicious of somebody** jemandem

misstrauen; **2** (suspicious looking) verdächtig.

swallow noun (bird) Schwalbe die (PL die Schwalben).

swallow verb schlucken.

swan noun Schwan der (PL die Schwäne).

swap verb tauschen; **do you want to swap?** willst du tauschen?; **he swapped his bike for a computer** er hat sein Rad gegen einen Computer getauscht; **we swapped seats** wir tauschten die Plätze.

swear verb (use bad language) fluchen.

swearword noun Kraftausdruck der (PL die Kraftausdrücke).

sweat noun Schweiß der.

sweat verb schwitzen.

sweater noun Pullover der (PL die Pullover).

Swede noun Schwede der (PL die Schweden), Schwedin die (PL die Schwedinnen).

swede noun Kohlrübe die (PL die Kohlrüben).

Sweden noun Schweden das; **from Sweden** aus Schweden; **to Sweden** nach Schweden.

Swedish noun (the language) Schwedisch das.

Swedish adjective schwedisch; **he's Swedish** er ist Schwede; **she's Swedish** sie ist Schwedin.

sweep verb fegen.

sweet noun **1** Bonbon der (PL die Bonbons); **2** (dessert) Nachtisch der (PL die Nachtische).

sweet adjective **1** süß; **I try not to eat sweet things** ich versuche nichts Süßes zu essen; **she looks**

really sweet in that hat mit dem Hut sieht sie richtig süß aus; **2** (*kind*) lieb; **she's a really sweet person** sie ist wirklich ein sehr lieber Mensch; **how sweet of him** wie lieb von ihm.

sweetcorn *noun* Mais der.

swell *verb* (*part of the body*) anschwellen◇ SEP (PERF sein).

swelling *noun* Schwellung die (PL die Schwellungen).

swim *noun* **to go for a swim** schwimmen gehen◇ (PERF sein).

swim *verb* schwimmen◇ (PERF sein); **can he swim?** kann er schwimmen?; **to swim across a lake** an die gegenüberliegende Seite des Sees schwimmen.

swimmer *noun* Schwimmer der (PL die Schwimmer), Schwimmerin die (PL die Schwimmerinnen); **she's a strong swimmer** sie ist eine gute Schwimmerin.

swimming *noun* Schwimmen das; **to go swimming** schwimmen gehen◇.

swimming cap *noun* Badekappe die (PL die Badekappen).

swimming costume *noun* Badeanzug der (PL die Badeanzüge).

swimming pool *noun* Schwimmbecken das (PL die Schwimmbecken).

swimming trunks *noun* Badehose die (PL die Badehosen).

swimsuit *noun* Badeanzug der (PL die Badeanzüge).

swindle *noun* Betrug der (PL die Betrüge); **what a swindle!** was für ein Betrug!

swindle *verb* betrügen.

swing *noun* Schaukel die (PL die Schaukeln).

Swiss *noun* (*person*) Schweizer der (PL die Schweizer), Schweizerin die (PL die Schweizerinnen); **the Swiss** die Schweizer.

Swiss *adjective* schweizerisch; **she is Swiss** sie ist Schweizerin.

switch *noun* (*for a light, radio, etc.*) Schalter der (PL die Schalter).

switch *verb* (*change*) wechseln; **to switch places** die Plätze wechseln.

● **to switch something off** etwas ausschalten SEP.

● **to switch something on** etwas anschalten SEP.

Switzerland *noun* die Schweiz; **from Switzerland** aus der Schweiz, **in Switzerland** in der Schweiz; **to Switzerland** in die Schweiz.

swollen *adjective* geschwollen.

swop *verb* SEE swap.

sword *noun* Schwert das (PL die Schwerter).

syllabus *noun* Lehrplan der (PL die Lehrpläne); **to be on the syllabus** auf dem Lehrplan stehen.

symbol *noun* Symbol das (PL die Symbole).

symbolic *adjective* symbolisch.

sympathetic *adjective* verständnisvoll.

sympathize *verb* **to sympathize with somebody** mit jemandem mitfühlen SEP; **I sympathize with you** ich kann mit Ihnen mitfühlen.

sympathy *noun* Mitleid das.

symphony *noun* Sinfonie die (PL die Sinfonien).

a b c d e f g h i j k l m n o p q r **s** t u v w x y z

a

symptom noun Symptom das (PL die Symptome).

b

synagogue noun Synagoge die (PL die Synagogen).

c

synthesizer noun Synthesizer der (PL die Synthesizer).

d

synthetic adjective synthetisch.

e

syringe noun Spritze die (PL die Spritzen).

f

system noun System das (PL die Systeme).

g

h

i

Tt

j

k

table noun Tisch der (PL die Tische); **to lay the table** den Tisch decken; **to clear the table** den Tisch abräumen SEP.

l

tablecloth noun Tischdecke die (PL die Tischdecken).

m

n

tablespoon noun Esslöffel der (PL die Esslöffel); **a tablespoon of flour** ein Esslöffel Mehl.

o

table tennis noun Tischtennis das.

p

q

tablet noun Tablette die (PL die Tabletten).

r

tackle verb 1 (in football or hockey) angreifen♦ SEP; 2 angehen♦ SEP (PERF sein) (a job or a problem).

s

t

tact noun Takt der.

u

tactful adjective taktvoll; **that wasn't very tactful** das war nicht sehr taktvoll.

v

w

tadpole noun Kaulquappe die (PL die Kaulquappen).

x

tail noun 1 Schwanz der (PL die Schwänze); 2 'heads or tails?' — 'tails' 'Kopf oder Zahl?' — 'Zahl'.

y

z

take verb 1 nehmen♦; he took a sweet er nahm einen Bonbon; **take my hand** nimm meine Hand; **I took the bus** ich habe den Bus genommen; **do you take sugar?** nimmst du Zucker?; 2 (with time) dauern; **it takes two hours** es dauert zwei Stunden; 3 (react to) aufnehmen♦ SEP; **he took the news calmly** er hat die Nachricht gelassen aufgenommen; 4 (take to a place) bringen♦; **I'm taking Jake to my parents** ich bringe Jake zu meinen Eltern; **I must take the car to the garage** ich muss das Auto in die Werkstatt bringen; **to take somebody home** jemanden nach Hause bringen; 5 **to take something up(stairs)** etwas hinaufbringen♦ SEP; **could you take the towels up?** könntest du die Handtücher heraufbringen?; 6 **to take something down(stairs)** etwas hinunterbringen♦ SEP; **Cheryl's taken the cups down** Cheryl hat die Tassen heruntergebracht; 7 (carry with you) mitnehmen♦ SEP; **she's taken some of the files home** sie hat einige der Akten mit nach Hause genommen; **I'm taking my Walkman** ich nehme meinen Walkman mit; **I'll take him next time** nächstes Mal nehme ich ihn mit; 8 nehmen♦ SEP (a credit card or a cheque); **do you take cheques?** nehmen Sie Schecks?; 9 machen♦ (an exam, a holiday, or a photo); **she's taking her driving test tomorrow** sie macht morgen ihre Fahrprüfung; **to take a holiday** Ferien machen; 10 (need) brauchen; **it takes a lot of courage** dazu braucht man viel Mut; **it takes me at least two hours to read it** ich brauche mindestens zwei Stunden, um es zu lesen; **11 haben**✧ (*clothes size*); **what size do you take?** welche Größe haben Sie?

● **to take something apart** etwas auseinander nehmen✧.

● **to take something back** etwas zurückbringen✧ SEP.

● **to take off 1** (*plane*) abfliegen✧ SEP (PERF *sein*); **2** ausziehen✧ SEP (*clothes, shoes*); **take your jacket off** zieh die Jacke aus; **to take your clothes off** sich ausziehen; **3** abziehen✧ SEP (*money*); **he took five pounds off the price** er hat fünf Pfund vom Preis abgezogen.

● **to take out something** (*from a bag or pocket*) etwas herausnehmen✧ SEP; **Eric took out his wallet** Eric nahm seine Brieftasche heraus.

● **to take somebody out** jemanden ausführen✧ SEP; **to take somebody out for a meal** jemanden zum Essen in ein Restaurant einladen✧ SEP.

takeaway *noun* **1** (*meal*) Essen zum Mitnehmen *das* (PL die Essen zum Mitnehmen); **an Indian takeaway** ein indisches Essen zum Mitnehmen; **2** (*where you buy it*) Restaurant mit Straßenverkauf *das* (PL die Restaurants mit Straßenverkauf).

take-off *noun* (*of a plane*) Abflug *der* (PL die Abflüge).

talent *noun* Talent *das* (PL die Talente); **to have a talent for painting** ein Talent zum Malen haben.

talented *adjective* talentiert; **he's really talented** er ist wirklich talentiert.

talk *noun* **1** (*a chat*) Gespräch *das* (PL die Gespräche); **we had a serious talk about it** wir hatten ein ernstes Gespräch darüber; **2** Vortrag *der* (PL die Vorträge); **she's giving a talk on Hungary** sie hält einen Vortrag über Ungarn.

talk *verb* **1** reden; **to talk to somebody** mit jemandem reden; **we talked about football** wir haben über Fußball geredet; **what's he talking about?** wovon redet er?; **we'll talk about it later** darüber reden wir später; **they're always talking** sie reden immer; **2 to talk to somebody on the phone** mit jemandem telefonieren.

tall *adjective* **1** groß; **she's very tall** sie ist sehr groß; **I'm 1.7 metres tall** ich bin ein Meter siebzig groß; **2** hoch (*building or tree*).

tame *adjective* zahm.

tampon *noun* Tampon *der* (PL die Tampons).

tan *noun* **1** Bräune *die*; **to have a tan** braun sein; **to get a tan** braun werden.

tank *noun* **1** (*for petrol or water*) Tank *der* (PL die Tanks); **2** (*for fish*) Aquarium *das* (PL die Aquarien); **3** (*military*) Panzer *der* (PL die Panzer).

tanker *noun* **1** (*on sea*) Tanker *der* (PL die Tanker); **2** (*on the road*) Tankwagen *der* (PL die Tankwagen).

a
b
c
d
e
f
g
h
i
j
k
l
m
n
o
p
q
r
s
t
u
v
w
x
y
z

tanned *adjective* braun.

tap *noun* Wasserhahn *der* (PL *die* Wasserhähne); **to turn on the tap** den Wasserhahn aufdrehen SEP; **to turn off the tap** den Wasserhahn zudrehen SEP; **the hot tap** der Warmwasserhahn.

tap *verb* klopfen; **to tap on the door** an die Tür klopfen.

tap-dancing *noun* Stepptanzen *das*.

tape *noun* **1** Kassette *die* (PL *die* Kassetten); **my tape of the Stones** meine Kassette von den Stones; **I've got it on tape** ich habe es auf Kassette; **2 sticky tape** der Klebestreifen.

tape *verb* aufnehmen✧ SEP; **I want to tape the film** ich will den Film aufnehmen.

tape measure *noun* Metermaß *das* (PL *die* Metermaße).

tape recorder *noun* Tonbandgerät *das* (PL *die* Tonbandgeräte).

tapestry *noun* Wandteppich *der* (PL *die* Wandteppiche).

target *noun* Ziel *das* (PL *die* Ziele).

tart *noun* Kuchen *der* (PL *die* Kuchen); **apple tart** der Apfelkuchen.

tartan *adjective* Schotten-; **a tartan skirt** ein Schottenrock.

task *noun* Aufgabe *die* (PL *die* Aufgaben).

taste *noun* **1** Geschmack *der* (PL *die* Geschmäcke); **a taste of onions** ein Zwiebelgeschmack; **she's got no taste** sie hat keinen Geschmack; **2 in bad taste** geschmacklos.

taste *verb* **1** schmecken; **the soup tastes horrible** die Suppe schmeckt furchtbar; **2 to taste of something** nach etwas (DAT) schmecken; **it tastes of garlic** es schmeckt nach Knoblauch; **3** (*try a little*) probieren; **do you want to taste?** möchtest du mal probieren?

tasty *adjective* schmackhaft.

tattoo *noun* Tätowierung *die* (PL *die* Tätowierungen); **he's got a tattoo on his arm** er hat eine Tätowierung am Arm.

Taurus *noun* Stier *der*; **Josephine's Taurus** Josephine ist (ein) Stier.

tax *noun* Steuer *die* (PL *die* Steuern); (*on goods, income*).

taxi *noun* Taxi *das* (PL *die* Taxis); **to go by taxi** mit dem Taxi fahren; **to take a taxi** ein Taxi nehmen.

taxi driver *noun* Taxifahrer *der* (PL *die* Taxifahrer), Taxifahrerin *die* (PL *die* Taxifahrerinnen).

taxi rank *noun* Taxistand *der* (PL *die* Taxistände).

tea *noun* **1** Tee *der* (PL *die* Tees); **a cup of tea** eine Tasse Tee; **to have tea** Tee trinken; **2** (*evening meal*) Abendessen *das* (PL *die* Abendessen).

teabag *noun* Teebeutel *der* (PL *die* Teebeutel).

teach *verb* **1** beibringen✧ SEP; **she's teaching me to drive** sie bringt mir das Autofahren bei; **2 to teach yourself something** (DAT) etwas beibringen✧ SEP; **I taught myself Italian** ich habe mir Italienisch beigebracht; **3 that'll teach you!** das wird dir eine Lehre sein!; **4** unterrichten; **her mum**

teaches maths ihre Mutter unterrichtet Mathematik.

teacher noun Lehrer der (PL die Lehrer), Lehrerin die (PL die Lehrerinnen).

teaching noun Unterrichten das.

team noun Mannschaft die (PL die Mannschaften); **football team** die Fußballmannschaft.

teapot noun Teekanne die (PL die Teekannen).

tear[1] noun (a rip) Riss der (PL die Risse).

tear verb 1 zerreißen✧; **she tore up my letter** sie hat meinen Brief zerrissen; 2 reißen✧ (PERF sein); **the net has torn** das Netz ist gerissen; **be careful, it tears easily** sei vorsichtig, es reißt leicht.

tear[2] noun (when you cry) Träne die (PL die Tränen); **to be in tears** in Tränen aufgelöst sein; **to burst into tears** in Tränen ausbrechen.

tease verb 1 necken (a person); 2 quälen (an animal).

teaspoon noun Teelöffel der (PL die Teelöffel); **a teaspoon of vinegar** ein Teelöffel Essig.

teatime noun (evening meal) Abendessenszeit die; **it's teatime!** es gibt Abendessen!

tea towel noun Geschirrtuch das (PL die Geschirrtücher).

technical adjective technisch.

technical college noun Fachhochschule die (PL die Fachhochschulen).

technician noun Techniker der (PL die Techniker), Technikerin die (PL die Technikerinnen).

technique noun Technik die (PL die Techniken).

techno noun (music) Techno der.

technological adjective technologisch.

technology noun 1 Technologie die; 2 **information technology** die Informatik.

teddy bear noun Teddybär der (PL die Teddybären).

teenage adjective 1 Teenage-; 2 **they have a teenage son** sie haben einen Sohn im Teenageralter; 3 (films, magazines, etc.) für Teenager; **a teenage magazine** eine Jugendzeitschrift.

teenager noun Teenager der (PL die Teenager); **a group of teenagers** eine Gruppe von Teenagern.

teens plural noun **the teens** die Teenagerjahre; **he's in his teens** er ist ein Teenager.

tee-shirt noun T-Shirt das (PL die T-Shirts).

telephone noun Telefon das (PL die Telefone); **on the telephone** am Telefon.

telephone verb anrufen✧ SEP; **I'll telephone the bank** ich rufe die Bank an.

telephone box noun Telefonzelle die (PL die Telefonzellen).

telephone call noun Telefongespräch das (PL die Telefongespräche).

telephone directory noun Telefonbuch das (PL die Telefonbücher).

telephone number noun Telefonnummer die (PL die Telefonnummern).

telescope noun Fernrohr das (PL die Fernrohre), Teleskop das (PL die Teleskope).

a
b
c
d
e
f
g
h
i
j
k
l
m
n
o
p
q
r
s
t
u
v
w
x
y
z

televise verb im Fernsehen übertragen◇; **they're televising the match** sie übertragen das Spiel im Fernsehen.

television noun 1 Fernsehen das; **I saw it on television** ich habe es im Fernsehen gesehen; **to watch television** fernsehen◇ SEP; **I'm watching television** ich sehe fern.

television programme noun Fernsehsendung die (PL die Fernsehsendungen).

tell verb 1 sagen; **to tell somebody something** jemandem etwas sagen; **if she asks, tell her** sag's ihr, wenn sie fragt; 2 **to tell somebody to do something** jemandem sagen, er/ sie soll etwas tun; **he told me to do it myself** er hat mir gesagt, ich soll es selbst machen; **she told me not to wait** sie sagte ich solle nicht warten; 3 (explain) **can you tell me how to do it?** kannst du mir sagen, wie man das macht?; 4 erzählen (a story); **tell me about your holiday** erzähl mir von deinen Ferien; 5 (to see) sehen◇; **you can tell it's old** man sieht, dass es alt ist; **I can't tell them apart** ich kann sie nicht unterscheiden.

telly noun 1 (set) Fernseher der (PL die Fernseher); 2 **to watch telly** fernsehen◇ SEP; **I saw her on telly** ich habe sie im Fernsehen gesehen.

temp noun Aushilfskraft die (PL die Aushilfskräfte).

temper noun **to lose your temper** wütend werden.

temperature noun 1 Temperatur die (PL die Temperaturen); **what is the temperature?** wie viel Grad sind es?; 2 **to have a temperature** Fieber haben.

temporary adjective vorübergehend.

temptation noun Versuchung die (PL die Versuchungen).

tempted adjective versucht; **I'm really tempted to come** ich würde am liebsten kommen.

tempting adjective verlockend.

ten number zehn; **Harry's ten** Harry ist zehn.

tend verb **to tend to do something** dazu neigen, etwas zu tun.

tender adjective 1 (loving) zärtlich; 2 (painful) empfindlich.

tennis noun Tennis das; **to play tennis** Tennis spielen.

tennis ball noun Tennisball der (PL die Tennisbälle).

tennis court noun Tennisplatz der (PL die Tennisplätze).

tennis player noun Tennisspieler der (PL die Tennisspieler), Tennisspielerin die (PL die Tennisspielerinnen).

tennis racket noun Tennisschläger der (PL die Tennisschläger).

tenor noun Tenor der (PL die Tenöre).

tenpin bowling noun Bowling das.

tense noun Zeit die; **the present tense** das Präsens; **in the future tense** im Futur.

tense adjective gespannt.

tent noun Zelt das (PL die Zelte).

tenth *number* zehnter/zehnte/zehntes; **on the tenth floor** im zehnten Stock; **the tenth of April** der zehnte April.

term *noun* (*in school*) Halbjahr *das* (PL die Halbjahre), (*at university*) Semester *das* (PL die Semester).

terminal *noun* **1** (*at an airport*) Terminal *der* (PL die Terminals); **2 bus terminal** die Endstation; **3** (*computer terminal*) Terminal *das* (PL die Terminals).

terrace *noun* **1** (*outside a house*) Terrasse *die* (PL die Terrassen); **2** (*row of houses*) Häuserreihe die (PL die Häuserreihen); **3 the terraces** (*at a stadium*) die Ränge (*plural*).

terrible *adjective* furchtbar.

terribly *adverb* **1** (*very*) sehr; **not terribly clean** nicht sehr sauber; **2** (*badly*) furchtbar; **I played terribly** ich habe furchtbar gespielt.

terrific *adjective* **1** irre (*informal*); **a terrific amount** eine irre Menge; **2 terrific!** super! (*informal*).

terrified *adjective* verängstigt; **to be terrified** furchtbare Angst haben.

terrorism *noun* Terrorismus der.

terrorist *noun* Terrorist der (PL die Terroristen), Terroristin die (PL die Terroristinnen).

test *noun* **1** (*in school*) Klassenarbeit die (PL die Klassenarbeiten); **we've got a maths test tomorrow** wir schreiben morgen eine Mathearbeit; **2** (*medical check*, *trial*) Test der (PL die Tests); **eye test** der Sehtest; **blood test** die Blutprobe; **3 driving test** die Fahrprüfung; **she's taking her driving test on Friday** sie macht am Freitag ihre Fahrprüfung; **he passed his driving test** er hat seine Fahrprüfung bestanden.

test *verb* (*in school*) prüfen; **can you test me?** kannst du mich abfragen?

test tube *noun* Reagenzglas *das* (PL die Reagenzgläser).

text *noun* Text der (PL die Texte).

textbook *noun* Lehrbuch *das* (PL die Lehrbücher).

text message *noun* SMS die (PL die SMS).

Thames *noun* **the Thames** die Themse.

than *conjunction* als; **they have more money than we do** sie haben mehr Geld als wir; **more than forty** mehr als vierzig; **more than thirty years** mehr als dreißig Jahre.

thank *verb* **1 to thank somebody for something** sich bei jemandem für etwas (ACC) bedanken; **2 thank you** danke; **thank you for looking after the children** danke, dass du auf die Kinder aufgepasst hast.

thanks *plural noun* **1 thanks;** **thanks a lot!** vielen Dank!; **many thanks** vielen Dank; **2 no thanks** nein danke; **thanks for your letter** danke für deinen Brief; **3 thanks to** dank (+ DAT); **it was thanks to him that we made it** dank ihm haben wir es geschafft.

a b c d e f g h i j k l m n o p q r s **t** u v w x y z

a
b
c
d
e
f
g
h
i
j
k
l
m
n
o
p
q
r
s
t
u
v
w
x
y
z

thank you adverb danke; **thank you very much for the cheque** herzlichen Dank für den Scheck; **no thank you** nein danke; **a thank-you letter** ein Dankbrief.

that adjective **1** dieser/diese/dieses; **that boy** dieser Junge; **that woman** diese Frau; **that house** dieses Haus; **2 that one** der da/die da/das da; **'which cake would you like?' – 'that one, please'** 'welchen Kuchen möchten Sie?' - 'den da, bitte'; **I like all the dresses but I'm going to buy that one** mir gefallen alle Kleider, aber ich kaufe das da.

that adverb so; **it's not that easy** es ist nicht so einfach.

that pronoun **1** das; **what's that?** was ist das?; **who's that?** wer ist das?; **where's that?** wo ist das?; **is that Mandy?** ist das Mandy?; **2** das; **did you see that?** hast du das gesehen?; **that's my bedroom** das ist mein Schlafzimmer; **3** (in relative clauses) der/die/das (depending on the gender of the noun 'that' refers to); **the train that's leaving now** der Zug, der jetzt abfährt; **the flower that I picked** die Blume, die ich gepflückt habe; **the car that's red** das Auto, das rot ist.

that conjunction dass; **I knew that he was lying** ich wußte, dass er log.

the definite article **1** der/die/das (the article changes according to the gender of the noun); (before a masculine noun) **the dog** der Hund; (before a feminine noun) **the cat** die Katze; (before a neuter noun) **the car** das Auto; **2** (before all plural

nouns) die; **the windows** die Fenster.

theatre noun Theater das (PL die Theater); **to go to the theatre** ins Theater gehen.

theft noun Diebstahl der (PL die Diebstähle).

their adjective ihr, (plural) ihre; **their son** ihr Sohn; **their daughter** ihre Tochter; **their car** ihr Auto; **their presents** ihre Geschenke.

theirs pronoun **1** ihrer (when standing for a masculine noun); **our garden's smaller than theirs** unser Garten ist kleiner als ihrer; **2** ihre (when standing for a feminine noun); **your flat is bigger than theirs** deine Wohnung ist größer als ihre; **3** ihrs (when standing for a neuter noun); **our car was cheaper than theirs** unser Auto war billiger als ihrs; **4** (when standing for a plural noun); **our children are older than theirs** unsere Kinder sind älter als ihre; **5 the yellow car's theirs** das gelbe Auto gehört ihnen; **it's theirs** das gehört ihnen.

them pronoun **1** (as a direct object in the accusative) sie; **I know them** ich kenne sie; **I don't know them** ich kenne sie nicht; **2** (after prepositions + ACC) sie; **it's for them** das ist für sie; **3** (as an indirect object or following a verb that takes the dative) ihnen; **I told them a story** ich habe ihnen eine Geschichte erzählt; **4** (to them) ihnen; **I gave them my address** ich habe ihnen meine Adresse gegeben; **5** (after prepositions + DAT) ihnen; **I'll go with them** ich gehe mit ihnen mit; 6 (*in comparisons*) he's older than them er ist älter als sie.

theme *noun* Thema *das* (PL *die* Themen).

theme park *noun* Themenpark *der* (PL *die* Themenparks).

themselves *pronoun* 1 sich; they enjoyed themselves sie haben sich amüsiert; 2 (*for emphasis*) selbst; the boys can do it themselves die Jungen können es selbst machen.

then *adverb* 1 (*next*) dann; I get up and then I make the bed ich stehe auf und dann mache ich das Bett; I went to the post office and then the bank ich bin zur Post und dann auf die Bank gegangen; 2 (*at that time*) damals; we were living in York then wir haben damals in York gewohnt; 3 (*in that case*) dann; then why worry? warum machst du dir dann Sorgen?; 4 since then seitdem; 5 from then on von da an.

theory *noun* 1 Theorie *die* (PL *die* Theorien); 2 in theory theoretisch.

there *adverb* 1 (*in a fixed location*) da; up there da oben; down there da unten; in there da drin; stay there bleib da; over there da drüben; she's over there with Mark sie ist da drüben mit Mark; 3 (*with movement to a place*) dahin; put it there leg es dahin; we're going there on Tuesday wir fahren am Dienstag dahin; 4 (*further away*) dort; I've seen photos of Oxford but I've never been there ich habe Fotos von Oxford gesehen, aber ich war noch nie dort; 5 there is (*there exists*) da ist, es ist; there's a cat in the garden da ist eine Katze im Garten; there's enough bread es ist genug Brot da; no, there's not enough nein, es ist nicht genug da; 6 there is es gibt; there's only one hospital in this town in dieser Stadt gibt es nur ein Krankenhaus; 7 there are da sind, es sind; there were lots of people in town es waren viele Leute in der Stadt; there are (*there exist*) es gibt; there are lots of museums here es gibt hier viele Museen; 9 (*when drawing attention*) da; there they are! da sind sie!; there's the bus coming! da kommt der Bus!

therefore *adverb* deshalb.

thermometer *noun* Thermometer *das* (PL *die* Thermometer).

these *adjective* diese; these glasses diese Gläser.

these *pronoun* die; these are cheaper die sind billiger.

they *pronoun* 1 sie; 'where are the knives?' – 'they're in the drawer' 'wo sind die Messer?' - 'sie sind in der Schublade'; 2 man; they say man sagt.

thick *adjective* dick; a thick layer of butter eine dicke Schicht Butter.

thief *noun* Dieb *der* (PL *die* Diebe), Diebin *die* (PL *die* Diebinnen).

thigh *noun* Oberschenkel *der* (PL *die* Oberschenkel).

thin *adjective* dünn.

thing *noun* 1 (*an object*) Ding *das* (PL *die* Dinge); they have lots of

nice things sie haben viele schöne Dinge; **she told me some strange things** sie hat mir ein paar seltsame Dinge erzählt; **that thing next to the hammer** das Ding da neben dem Hammer; **2** (*belongings*) Sachen (*plural*); **you can leave your things in my room** du kannst deine Sachen in meinem Zimmer lassen; **3 the best thing to do is** ... am besten wäre es ...; **4** (*subject, affair*) Sache die (PL die Sachen); **the thing is, I've lost her address** die Sache ist, ich habe ihre Adresse verloren; **5 how are things?** wie geht's?

think *verb* **1** (*believe*) glauben; **do you think they'll come?** glaubst du, sie kommen?; **no, I don't think so** nein, ich glaube nicht; **I think so** ich glaube schon; **I think he's already paid** ich glaube, er hat schon gezahlt; **2** denken ✧; **I'm thinking about you** ich denke an dich; **what are you thinking about?** woran denkst du?; **3 what do you think of that?** was halten Sie davon?; **I don't think much of her proposal** ich halte nicht viel von ihrem Vorschlag; **4 what do you think of my new jacket?** wie findest du meine neue Jacke?; **5** (*remember*) **to think to do something** daran denken, etwas zu tun; **he didn't think of locking the door** er hat nicht daran gedacht, die Tür abzuschließen; **6** (*to think carefully*) nachdenken ✧ SEP; **he thought for a moment** er hat einen Moment lang nachgedacht; **think about it!** denk darüber nach!; **7 I've**

thought it over carefully ich habe es mir genau überlegt; **8** (*imagine*) sich (DAT) vorstellen SEP; **just think, we'll soon be in Spain!** stell dir nur vor, bald sind wir in Spanien!; **I never thought it would be like this** so habe ich es nie vorgestellt, dass es so sein würde.

third *noun* Drittel das (PL die Drittel); **a third of the population** ein Drittel der Bevölkerung.

third *adjective* dritter/dritte/ drittes; **on the third floor** im dritten Stock; **on the third of March** am dritten März.

thirdly *adverb* drittens.

Third World *noun* Dritte Welt die.

thirst *noun* Durst der.

thirsty *adjective* durstig; **to be thirsty** Durst haben; **I'm thirsty** ich habe Durst; **we were all thirsty** wir hatten alle Durst.

thirteen *number* dreizehn; **Ahmed's thirteen** Ahmed ist dreizehn.

thirty *number* dreißig.

this *adjective* **1** dieser/diese/ dieses; **this boy** dieser Junge; **this flower** diese Blume; **this car** dieses Auto; **at the end of this week** Ende dieser Woche; **2 this morning** heute Morgen; **this evening** heute Abend; **this afternoon** heute Nachmittag; **3 this one** der/die/ das, (*with more emphasis*) dieser/ diese/dieses; **if you need a pen you can have this one** wenn du einen Kugelschreiber brauchst, kannst du den haben; **I'll take this one** ich nehme diesen.

this *pronoun* **1** das; **can you hold this?** kannst du das festhalten?; **what's this?** was ist das?; **2 this is my sister Carla** (*in introductions*) das ist meine Schwester Carla; **3 this is Tracy speaking** (*on the phone*) hier spricht Tracy.

thistle *noun* Distel *die* (PL die Disteln).

thorn *noun* Dorn *der* (PL die Dornen).

those *adjective* diese; **those books** diese Bücher.

those *pronoun* die da; **if you need more knives you can take those** wenn du mehr Messer brauchst, kannst du die da nehmen.

though *conjunction* obwohl; **though it's cold** obwohl es kalt ist.

though *adverb* dennoch; **it was a good idea, though** es war dennoch eine gute Idee.

thought *noun* Gedanke *der* (PL die Gedanken).

thousand *number* **1** tausend; **a thousand** eintausend; **three thousand** dreitausend; **2 thousands of** Tausende von; **there were thousands of tourists in Venice** Tausende von Touristen waren in Venedig.

thread *noun* Faden *der* (PL die Fäden).

thread *verb* einfädeln (*u needle*).

threat *noun* Drohung *die* (PL die Drohungen); **is that a threat?** soll das eine Drohung sein?

threaten *verb* drohen (+ DAT); **he threatened her** er hat ihr gedroht;

to threaten to do something damit drohen, etwas zu tun.

three *number* drei; **Oskar's three** Oskar ist drei.

three-quarters *noun* drei Viertel *die*.

three-quarters *adverb* **three-quarters full** drei viertel voll.

thrilled *adjective* **to be thrilled** sich wahnsinnig freuen.

thriller *noun* Thriller *der* (PL die Thriller).

thrilling *adjective* spannend.

throat *noun* Hals *der* (PL die Hälse); **to have a sore throat** Halsschmerzen haben.

through *preposition* **1** (*across, via*) durch (+ ACC); **through the forest** durch den Wald; **the train goes through Leeds** der Zug fährt durch Leeds; **through the window** durch das Fenster; **2 to let somebody through** jemanden durchlassen◇ SEP; **the police let us through** die Polizei ließ uns durch, **3 I know them through my cousin** ich kenne sie über meinen Vetter.

throw *verb* **1** werfen◇; **I threw the letter in the bin** ich habe den Brief in den Mülleimer geworfen; **2 to throw something to somebody** jemandem etwas zuwerfen◇ SEP; **throw me the ball** wirf mir den Ball zu; **to throw something at somebody** etwas nach jemandem werfen.

● **to throw something away** etwas wegwerfen◇ SEP; **I'm throwing away the old newspapers** ich werfe die alten

Zeitungen weg.

● **to throw somebody out**
jemanden rauswerfen✧ SEP.

● **to throw something out** etwas
wegwerfen✧ SEP (*rubbish*).

thumb *noun* Daumen der (PL die
Daumen).

thump *verb* schlagen ✧, auf (+ ACC);
**he thumped the radio to see if it
would work** er schlug auf das
Radio, um zu sehen ob es dann
funktionierte.

thunder *noun* Donner der; **peal of
thunder** der Donnerschlag.

thunderstorm *noun* Gewitter
das (PL die Gewitter).

thundery *adjective* gewittrig.

Thursday *noun* **1** Donnerstag der
(PL die Donnerstage); **on Thursday**
(am) Donnerstag; **I'm leaving on
Thursday** ich fahre am Donnerstag
ab; **see you on Thursday** bis
Donnerstag; **every Thursday** jeden
Donnerstag; **last Thursday** vorigen
Donnerstag; **next Thursday**
nächsten Donnerstag; **2 on
Thursdays** donnerstags; **the
museum is closed on Thursdays**
das Museum ist donnerstags
geschlossen.

thyme *noun* Thymian der.

tick *verb* **1** (*clock, watch*) ticken;
2 (*on paper*) abhaken SEP.

ticket *noun* **1** (*for an exhibition,
theatre, or cinema*) Karte die (PL die
Karten); **two tickets for the
concert** zwei Karten für das
Konzert; **2** (*for the underground, a
bus, or a train*) Fahrkarte die (PL die
Fahrkarten); **a plane ticket** ein

Flugschein, ein Ticket; **3** (*for left
luggage, parking*) Zettel der (PL die
Zettel); **4** (*for a lottery or raffle*) Los
das (PL die Lose); **5 parking ticket**
der Strafzettel.

ticket inspector *noun* Schaffner
der (PL die Schaffner), Schaffnerin
die (PL die Schaffnerinnen).

ticket office *noun* (*at a station*)
Fahrkartenschalter der (PL die
Fahrkartenschalter).

tickle *verb* kitzeln.

tide *noun* **1** (*high*) Flut die
(Fluten); **at high tide** bei Flut;
2 (*low*) Ebbe die (PL die Ebben); **the
tide is out** es ist Ebbe.

tidy *adjective* ordentlich.

tidy *verb* aufräumen SEP; **I'll tidy
(up) the kitchen** ich räume die
Küche auf.

tie *noun* **1** (*necktie*) Krawatte die (PL
die Krawatten); **2** (*in a match*)
Unentschieden das.

tie *verb* **1** binden✧; **to tie your
shoelaces** sich (DAT) die
Schnürsenkel binden; **2 to tie a
knot in something** einen Knoten in
etwas (ACC) machen; **3** (*in a match*)
we tied two all wir haben zwei zu
zwei gespielt.

tiger *noun* Tiger der (PL die Tiger).

tight *adjective* (*close-fitting*) eng;
the skirt's a bit tight der Rock ist
etwas eng; **these shoes are too
tight** diese Schuhe sind zu eng; **she
was wearing tight jeans** sie hatte
enge Jeans an.

tighten *verb* anziehen✧ SEP (*a
screw, knot*); **he tightened his belt**
er schnallte seinen Gürtel enger;

he tightened his grip er griff fester zu.

tightly adverb fest.

tights plural noun Strumpfhose die (PL die Strumpfhosen); **a pair of purple tights** eine lila Strumpfhose.

tile noun 1 (on a floor) Fliese die (PL die Fliesen); 2 (on a wall) Kachel die (PL die Kacheln); 3 (on a roof) Ziegel der (PL die Ziegel).

till[1] preposition, conjunction 1 bis; **they're staying till Sunday** sie bleiben bis Sonntag; **till then** bis dann; **till now** bis jetzt; 2 (when 'till' is followed by a noun it is usually translated as 'bis zu' + DAT) **till the evening** bis zum Abend; **not till** erst; **she won't be back till ten** sie kommt erst um zehn zurück; **we won't know till Monday** wir werden erst am Montag Bescheid wissen.

till[2] noun Kasse die (PL die Kassen); **please pay at the till** bitte zahlen Sie an der Kasse.

time noun 1 (on the clock) Zeit die; **it's time for breakfast** es ist Zeit zum Frühstücken; **what time is it?** wie viel Uhr ist es?; **at what time does it start?** um wie viel Uhr fängt es an?; **ten o'clock German time** zehn Uhr, deutsche Zeit; 3 **on time** pünktlich; 4 (an amount of time) Zeit die; **we've got lots of time** wir haben viel Zeit; **I haven't got time now** ich habe jetzt keine Zeit; **there's no time left to do it** dafür bleibt keine Zeit mehr; **from time to time** von Zeit zu Zeit; **for a long time** lange; 5 (moment) Moment der

(PL die Momente); **this isn't a good time to discuss it** das ist kein guter Moment, um darüber zu sprechen; **at the right time** im richtigen Moment; **for the time being** im Moment; **any time now** jeden Moment; 6 **at times** manchmal; 7 (in a series) Mal das (PL die Male); **eight times** achtmal; **for the first time** zum ersten Mal; **the first time I saw you** das erste Mal, als ich dich sah; **three times a year** dreimal jährlich; 8 **three times two is six** drei mal zwei ist sechs; 9 **to have a good time** sich amüsieren; **we had a really good time** wir haben uns richtig gut amüsiert; **have a good time!** viel Vergnügen!

timetable noun 1 (in school) Stundenplan der (PL die Stundenpläne); 2 (for trains or buses) Fahrplan der (PL die Fahrpläne); **bus timetable** der Busfahrplan.

tin noun Dose die (PL die Dosen); **a tin of tomatoes** eine Dose Tomaten.

tinned adjective in Dosen; **tinned peas** Erbsen in Dosen.

tin opener noun Dosenöffner der (PL die Dosenöffner).

tiny adjective winzig.

tip noun 1 (end) Spitze die (PL die Spitzen); 2 (money) Trinkgeld das; 3 (useful hint) Tipp der (PL die Tipps) (informal).

tip verb (give money) ein Trinkgeld geben ✧ (+ DAT); **we tipped the waiter** wir haben dem Kellner ein Trinkgeld gegeben.

a

tiptoe *noun* **on tiptoe** auf Zehenspitzen.

b

tired *adjective* **1** müde; **I'm tired** ich bin müde; **you look tired** du siehst müde aus; **2 to be tired of something** etwas satt haben; **I'm tired of London** ich habe London satt; **I'm tired of watching TV every evening** ich habe es satt, jeden Abend fernzusehen.

c

d

e

f

g

tiring *adjective* ermüdend.

h

tissue *noun* (*a paper hanky*) Papiertaschentuch *das* (PL *die* Papiertaschentücher).

i

j

tissue paper *noun* Seidenpapier *das.*

k

title *noun* Titel *der* (PL *die* Titel).

l

to *preposition* **1** (*to a country or town*) nach; **to go to London** nach London fahren; **the motorway to Italy** die Autobahn nach Italien; **they're going to Switzerland** sie fahren in die Schweiz; **2** (*to the cinema, theatre, school, office*) in (+ ACC); **I'm going to school** ich gehe in die Schule; **she's gone to the office** sie ist ins Büro gegangen; **we want to go to town** wir wollen in die Stadt gehen; **3** (*to a wedding, party, university, the toilet*) auf (+ ACC); **she's gone to the toilet** sie ist auf die Toilette gegangen; **4** (*addressed or attached to*) an (+ ACC); **a letter to my parents** ein Brief an meine Eltern; **5 give the book to her** gib ihr das Buch; **he said to me that ...** er hat mir gesagt, dass ...; **6** (*to somebody's house, a particular place, or person*) zu (+ DAT); **I went round to Paul's house** ich bin zu Paul nach Hause

m

n

o

p

q

r

s

t

u

v

w

x

y

z

gegangen; **we're going to the Browns' for supper** wir gehen zu Browns zum Abendessen; **I'm going to the dentist tomorrow** morgen gehe ich zum Zahnarzt; **7** (*talking about the time*) **it's ten to nine** es ist zehn vor neun; **from eight to ten** von acht bis zehn; **from Monday to Friday** von Montag bis Freitag; **8** (*in order to*) um ... zu (+ *infinitive*); **he gave me some money to buy a sandwich** er hat mir Geld gegeben, um ein Sandwich zu kaufen; **9** (*in verbal phrases with the infinitive*) zu; **I have nothing to do** ich habe nichts zu tun; **have you got something to eat?** hast du etwas zu essen?

toast *noun* **1** Toast *der* (PL *die* Toasts); **two slices of toast** zwei Scheiben Toast; **2** (*to your health*) Toast *der* (PL *die* Toasts); **to drink a toast to somebody** auf jemanden trinken.

toaster *noun* Toaster *der* (PL *die* Toaster).

tobacco *noun* Tabak *der.*

tobacconist's *noun* Tabakladen *der* (PL *die* Tabakläden).

today *adverb* heute; **today's her birthday** sie hat heute Geburtstag.

toe *noun* Zeh *der* (PL *die* Zehen).

toffee *noun* Karamell *der.*

together *adverb* **1** zusammen; **we did it together** wir haben es zusammen gemacht; **2** (*at the same time*) gleichzeitig; **they all left together** sie sind alle gleichzeitig weggegangen.

toilet noun Toilette die (PL die Toiletten); **she's gone to the toilet** sie ist auf die Toilette gegangen.

toilet paper noun Toilettenpapier das.

toilet roll noun Rolle Toilettenpapier die (PL die Rollen Toilettenpapier).

token noun 1 (for a machine or game) Marke die (PL die Marken); 2 (voucher) Gutschein der (PL die Gutscheine); **gift token** der Geschenkgutschein.

tolerant adjective tolerant.

toll noun 1 (payment) Gebühr die (PL die Gebühren); 2 (number) Zahl die; **the death toll has risen to 25** die Zahl der Todesopfer ist jetzt bei 25.

tomato noun Tomate die (PL die Tomaten); **tomato salad** der Tomatensalat; **tomato sauce** die Tomatensoße.

tomorrow adverb 1 morgen; **I'll do it tomorrow** ich mache es morgen; **tomorrow afternoon** morgen Nachmittag; **tomorrow morning** morgen früh; **tomorrow night** morgen Abend; 2 **the day after tomorrow** übermorgen.

tone noun (on an answerphone, of a voice, or letter) Ton der (PL die Töne).

tongue noun Zunge die (PL die Zungen), **to stick your tongue out at somebody** jemandem die Zunge herausstrecken; ★ **it's on the tip of my tongue** es liegt mir auf der Zunge.

tonic noun Tonic das (PL die Tonics); **a gin and tonic** ein Gin Tonic.

tonight adverb 1 (this evening) heute Abend; **I'm going out with my friends tonight** ich gehe heute Abend mit meinen Freunden weg; 2 (after bedtime) heute Nacht.

tonsillitis noun Mandelentzündung die; **Ahlem's got tonsillitis** Ahlem hat eine Mandelentzündung.

too adverb 1 zu; **it's too expensive** es ist zu teuer; **too often** zu oft; **2 too much** zu viel; **I've spent too much** ich habe zu viel ausgegeben; **too many** zu viele; 3 (as well) auch; **Karen's coming too** Karen kommt auch; **me too!** ich auch!

tool noun Werkzeug das (PL die Werkzeuge).

tool box noun Werkzeugkasten der (PL die Werkzeugkästen).

tool kit noun Werkzeug das.

tooth noun Zahn der (PL die Zähne); **to brush your teeth** sich (DAT) die Zähne putzen.

toothache noun Zahnschmerzen (plural).

toothbrush noun Zahnbürste die (PL die Zahnbürsten).

toothpaste noun Zahnpasta die (PL die Zahnpasten).

top noun 1 (highest part) Spitze die (PL die Spitzen) (of a tree); 2 **at the top of** oben auf (+ DAT); **at the top of the ladder** oben auf der Leiter; **it's on top of the chest of drawers** es liegt oben auf der Kommode; 3 **at the top** oben; **there are four rooms at the top** oben sind vier Zimmer; **from top to bottom** von oben bis unten; 4 (of a container, jar, or box)

Deckel der (PL die Deckel); **5** (of a mountain) Gipfel der (PL die Gipfel); **6** (a lid) Kappe die (PL die Kappen) (of a pen), Verschluss der (PL die Verschlüsse) (of a bottle); **7** (of a garment) Oberteil das (PL die Oberteile); **8** (in sport) **the top of the table** die Tabellenspitze; ★ **and on top of all that** obendrein; ★ **it was a bit over the top** es war leicht übertrieben.

top adjective oberster/oberste/oberstes (step or floor); **on the top floor** im obersten Stockwerk.

topic noun Thema das (PL die Themen).

topping noun Belag der (PL die Beläge); **which topping would you like?** welchen Belag hättest du gerne?

torch noun Taschenlampe die (PL die Taschenlampen).

torn adjective zerrissen.

tortoise noun Schildkröte die (PL die Schildkröten).

torture noun **1** Folter die (PL die Foltern); **2 the exam was torture** die Prüfung war die Hölle (informal).

torture verb quälen.

Tory noun Konservative der/die (PL die Konservativen).

total noun **1** (number) Gesamtzahl die (PL die Gesamtzahlen); **2** (result of addition) Summe die (PL die Summen).

total adjective gesamt.

totally adverb völlig.

touch noun **1** (contact) **to get in touch with somebody** sich mit

jemandem in Verbindung setzen; **to stay in touch with somebody** mit jemandem Kontakt halten; **2 we've lost touch** wir haben keinen Kontakt mehr; **I've lost touch with Peter** ich habe keinen Kontakt mehr zu Peter; **3** (a little bit) **a touch of salt** eine Spur Salz; **it was a touch embarrassing** es war ein bisschen peinlich.

touch verb **1** berühren; **2** (get hold of) anfassen SEP; **don't touch that** fass das nicht an.

touched adjective gerührt.

touching adjective rührend.

tough adjective **1** hart; **she's had a tough time** sie hat eine harte Zeit hinter sich; **a tough guy** ein harter Kerl; **2** zäh; **the meat's tough** das Fleisch ist zäh; **3** fest (material, shoes, etc.); **4 tough luck!** Pech!; **tough, you're too late** so'n Pech, du bist zu spät dran.

tour noun **1** Besichtigung die (PL die Besichtigungen); **a tour of the city** eine Stadtbesichtigung; **we did a tour of the castle** wir haben das Schloss besichtigt; **2 guided tour** die Führung; **3 package tour** die Pauschalreise; **4** (by a band or theatre group) Tournee die (PL die Tournees); **to go on tour** auf Tournee gehen.

tour verb (performer) auf Tournee sein◇ (PERF sein); **they're touring America** sie sind auf Tournee in Amerika.

tour guide noun Reiseleiter der (PL die Reiseleiter), Reiseleiterin die (PL die Reiseleiterinnen).

tourism noun Tourismus der.

tourist *noun* Tourist der (PL die Touristen), Touristin die (PL die Touristinnen).

tourist information office *noun* Fremdenverkehrsbüro das (PL die Fremdenverkehrsbüros).

tournament *noun* Turnier das (PL die Turniere); **tennis tournament** das Tennisturnier.

tow *verb* **to be towed away** abgeschleppt werden✧ (PERF *sein*).

towards *preposition* zu (+ DAT); **she went off towards the lake** sie ist zum See gegangen; **to come towards somebody** auf jemanden zukommen✧ SEP (PERF *sein*).

towel *noun* Handtuch das (PL die Handtücher).

tower *noun* Turm der (PL die Türme).

tower block *noun* Hochhaus das (PL die Hochhäuser).

town *noun* Stadt die (PL die Städte); **to go into town** in die Stadt gehen.

town centre *noun* Stadtmitte die (PL die Stadtmitten).

town hall *noun* Rathaus das (PL die Rathäuser).

toy *noun* Spielzeug das.

toyshop *noun* Spielzeuggeschäft das (PL die Spielzeuggeschäfte).

trace *noun* Spur die (PL die Spuren); **there was no trace of the thieves** es fehlte jede Spur von den Dieben.

trace *verb* **1** (*find*) finden✧; **2** (*follow*) verfolgen; **3** (*copy*) durchpausen SEP.

tracing paper *noun* Pauspapier das.

track *noun* **1** (*for sport*) Bahn die (PL die Bahnen); **cycling track** die Radrennbahn; **racing track** (*for cars*) die Rennstrecke; **2** (*a path*) Weg der (PL die Wege); **3** (*song*) Stück das (PL die Stücke); **this is my favourite track** das ist mein Lieblingsstück.

track suit *noun* Trainingsanzug der (PL die Trainingsanzüge).

tractor *noun* Traktor der (PL die Traktoren).

trade *noun* **1** (*a profession*) Gewerbe das; **2** (*skill, craft*) Handwerk das; **to learn a trade** ein Handwerk erlernen.

trade union *noun* Gewerkschaft die (PL die Gewerkschaften).

tradition *noun* Tradition die (PL die Traditionen).

traditional *adjective* traditionell.

traffic *noun* Verkehr der.

traffic island *noun* Verkehrsinsel die (PL die Verkehrsinseln).

traffic jam *noun* Stau der (PL die Staus).

traffic lights *plural noun* Ampel die (PL die Ampeln).

traffic warden *noun* Verkehrsüberwacher der (PL die Verkehrsüberwacher), Politesse die (PL die Politessen).

tragedy *noun* Tragödie die (PL die Tragödien).

tragic *adjective* tragisch.

trail *noun* (*a path*) Pfad der (PL die Pfade); **a nature trail** ein Naturlehrpfad.

a b c d e f g h i j k l m n o p q r s t u v w x y z

trailer noun Anhänger der (PL die Anhänger).

train noun Zug der (PL die Züge); **he's coming by train** er kommt mit dem Zug; **I met her on the train** ich habe sie im Zug getroffen; **the train for York** der Zug nach York.

train verb **1** (for a career) ausbilden SEP; **she's training to be a nurse** sie macht eine Ausbildung zur Krankenschwester; **3** (in sport) trainieren; **the team trains on Wednesdays** die Mannschaft trainiert mittwochs.

trainee noun Auszubildende der/die (PL die Auszubildenden).

trainer noun **1** (of an athlete or horse) Trainer der (PL die Trainer), Trainerin die (PL die Trainerinnen); **2 trainers** Turnschuhe (plural).

training noun **1** (for a career) Ausbildung die; **2** (for sport) Training das.

train ticket noun Zugfahrkarte die (PL die Zugfahrkarten).

train timetable noun Bahnfahrplan der (PL die Bahnfahrpläne).

tram noun Straßenbahn die (PL die Straßenbahnen).

tramp noun Landstreicher der (PL die Landstreicher), Landstreicherin die (PL die Landstreicherinnen).

transfer noun Abziehbild das (PL die Abziehbilder).

transform verb verwandeln.

transistor noun Transistor der (PL die Transistoren).

translate verb übersetzen; **to translate something into German** etwas ins Deutsche übersetzen.

translation noun Übersetzung die (PL die Übersetzungen).

translator noun Übersetzer der (PL die Übersetzer), Übersetzerin die (PL die Übersetzerinnen).

transparent adjective durchsichtig.

transplant noun Transplantation die (PL die Transplantationen).

transport noun Transport der (PL die Transporte); **the transport of goods** der Warentransport; **public transport** öffentliche Verkehrsmittel (plural).

trap noun Falle die (PL die Fallen).

travel noun Reisen das; **foreign travel** Auslandsreisen (plural).

travel verb reisen (PERF sein).

travel agency noun Reisebüro das (PL die Reisebüros).

travel agent's noun Reisebüro das (PL die Reisebüros).

traveller noun **1** Reisende der/die (PL die Reisenden); **2** (gypsy) Zigeuner der (PL die Zigeuner), Zigeunerin die (PL die Zigeunerinnen).

traveller's cheque noun Reisescheck der (PL die Reiseschecks).

travel-sick adjective reisekrank; **I get travel-sick** ich werde reisekrank.

tray noun Tablett das (PL die Tabletts).

tread *verb* **to tread on something** auf etwas (ACC) treten✧ (PERF *sein*); **she trod on my foot** sie ist mir auf den Fuß getreten.

treasure *noun* Schatz der (PL die Schätze).

treat *noun* **1 I took them to the circus as a treat** ich habe ihnen eine besondere Freude gemacht und sie in den Zirkus eingeladen; **2** (*food*) Leckerbissen der (PL die Leckerbissen).

treat *verb* **1** behandeln; **he treats his dog well** er behandelt seinen Hund gut; **the doctor who treated you** der Arzt, der dich behandelt hat; **2 to treat somebody to something** jemandem etwas spendieren; **I'll treat you to an ice cream** ich spendiere euch ein Eis.

treatment *noun* Behandlung die (PL die Behandlungen).

tree *noun* Baum der (PL die Bäume).

tremble *verb* zittern.

trend *noun* **1** (*a fashion*) Trend der (PL die Trends); **2** (*a tendency*) Tendenz die (PL die Tendenzen).

trendy *adjective* modern.

trial *noun* (*in court*) Prozess der (PL die Prozesse).

triangle *noun* Dreieck das (PL die Dreiecke).

trick *noun* **1** (*a joke*) Streich der (PL die Streiche); **to play a trick on somebody** jemandem einen Streich spielen; **2** (*a knack or by a conjuror*) Trick der (PL die Tricks); **there must be a trick to it** da muss ein Trick dabei sein.

trick *verb* hereinlegen SEP; **he tricked me!** er hat mich hereingelegt!

tricky *adjective* verzwickt; **it's a tricky situation** das ist eine verzwickte Situation.

tricycle *noun* Dreirad das (PL die Dreiräder).

trim *verb* schneiden✧ (*hair*).

trip *noun* **1** Reise die (PL die Reisen); **a trip to Florida** eine Reise nach Florida; **he's going on a business trip** er macht eine Geschäftsreise; **2** (*a day out*) Ausflug der (PL die Ausflüge); **a day trip to France** ein Tagesausflug nach Frankreich.

trip *verb* (*to stumble*) stolpern (PERF *sein*); **Nicky tripped over a stone** Nicky ist über einen Stein gestolpert.

triumph *noun* Triumph der (PL die Triumphe).

trolley *noun* **1** (*for shopping*) Einkaufswagen der (PL die Einkaufswagen), **2** (*for luggage*) Kofferkuli der (PL die Kofferkulis).

trombone *noun* Posaune die (PL die Posaunen).

troops *plural noun* Truppen (*plural*).

trophy *noun* Trophäe die (PL die Trophäen), (*in competitions*) Pokal der (PL die Pokale).

trot *verb* traben (PERF *sein*).

trouble *noun* **1** (*general difficulties*) Ärger der; **to make trouble** Ärger machen; **to get into trouble** Ärger bekommen; **we had trouble with the travel agency** wir hatten Ärger mit dem Reisebüro;

a
b
c
d
e
f
g
h
i
j
k
l
m
n
o
p
q
r
s
t
u
v
w
x
y
z

2 (*problem*) Problem das (PL die Probleme); **the trouble is, I've lost his phone number** das Problem ist, dass ich seine Telefonnummer verloren habe; **Steph's in trouble** Steph hat Probleme; **what's the trouble?** was ist los?; **it's no trouble!** das ist kein Problem!; **3** (*difficulty, effort*) Mühe die; **to have trouble doing something** Mühe haben, etwas zu tun; **I had trouble finding a seat** ich hatte Mühe, einen Platz zu finden; **it's not worth the trouble** das ist nicht der Mühe wert.

trousers *plural noun* Hose die (PL die Hosen); **my old trousers** meine alte Hose; **a new pair of trousers** eine neue Hose.

trout *noun* Forelle die (PL die Forellen).

truant *noun* Schulschwänzer der (PL die Schulschwänzer), Schulschwänzerin die (PL die Schulschwänzerinnen); **she's playing truant** sie schwänzt die Schule.

truck *noun* Lastwagen der (PL die Lastwagen).

true *adjective* **1** wahr; **a true story** eine wahre Geschichte; **2 is that true?** stimmt das?; **it's true she's absent-minded** das stimmt, sie ist sehr vergesslich.

trump *noun* Trumpf der (PL die Trümpfe); **hearts are trumps** Herz ist Trumpf.

trumpet *noun* Trompete die (PL die Trompeten).

trunk *noun* **1** (*of a tree*) Stamm der (PL die Stämme); **2** (*of an elephant*) Rüssel der (PL die Rüssel).

trunks *plural noun* swimming trunks Badehose die (PL die Badehosen).

trust *noun* Vertrauen das.

trust *verb* **1** (*believe*) **to trust somebody** jemandem vertrauen; **2** (*rely on*) **you can trust him** man kann sich auf ihn verlassen.

truth *noun* Wahrheit die.

try *noun* Versuch der (PL die Versuche); **it's my first try** es ist mein erster Versuch; **to have a try** es versuchen; **give it a try!** versuch's doch mal!.

try *verb* **1** versuchen; **to try to do something** versuchen, etwas zu tun; **I'm trying to open the door** ich versuche, die Tür aufzumachen; **2** (*taste*) probieren.

● **to try something on** etwas anprobieren SEP (*a garment*).

T-shirt *noun* T-Shirt das (PL die T-Shirts).

tube *noun* **1** Tube die (PL die Tuben); **2** (*the Underground*) **the Tube** die U-Bahn.

tuberculosis *noun* Tuberkulose die.

Tuesday *noun* **1** Dienstag der (PL die Dienstage); **on Tuesday** (am) Dienstag; **I'm going to the cinema on Tuesday** ich gehe Dienstag ins Kino; **see you on Tuesday!** bis Dienstag!; **every Tuesday** jeden Dienstag; **last Tuesday** vorigen Dienstag; **next Tuesday** nächsten Dienstag; **2 on Tuesdays**

dienstags; **the museum is closed on Tuesdays** das Museum ist dienstags geschlossen.

tuition noun 1 Unterricht der; **piano tuition** der Klavierunterricht; 2 **extra tuition** Nachhilfestunden (plural).

tulip noun Tulpe die (PL die Tulpen).

tumble-drier noun Wäschetrockner der (PL die Wäschetrockner).

tumbler noun Becherglas das (PL die Bechergläser).

tuna noun Thunfisch der.

tune noun Melodie die (PL die Melodien).

tunnel noun Tunnel der (PL die Tunnel); **the Channel Tunnel** der Eurotunnel.

turkey noun Pute die (PL die Puten).

Turkey noun die Türkei; **from Turkey** aus der Türkei; **in Turkey** in der Türkei; **to Turkey** in die Türkei.

Turkish noun (language) Türkisch das.

Turkish adjective türkisch; **he is Turkish** er ist Türke; **she is Turkish** sie ist Türkin.

turn noun 1 (in a game) **it's your turn** du bist an der Reihe; **whose turn is it?** wer ist an der Reihe?; **it's Jane's turn** Jane ist an der Reihe. 2 **to take turns** sich abwechseln; **to take it in turns to do something** abwechselnd etwas tun; 3 (in a road) Kurve die (PL die Kurven); **to take a right/left turn** nach rechts/links abbiegen.

turn verb 1 drehen; **turn the key to the right** dreh den Schlüssel nach rechts; **turn your chair round** dreh deinen Stuhl herum; 2 (person, car) abbiegen✧ SEP (PERF sein); **turn left at the next set of lights** biegen Sie an der nächsten Ampel links ab; 3 (become) werden✧ (PERF sein); **she turned red** sie wurde rot.

● **to turn back** umkehren SEP (PERF sein).

● **to turn off** 1 (from a road) abbiegen✧ SEP (PERF sein); 2 (switch off) ausmachen SEP (a light, an oven, a TV, or radio), zudrehen SEP (a tap), abstellen SEP (gas, electricity, or water), ausschalten SEP (an engine).

● **to turn on** anmachen SEP (a TV, radio, or light), aufdrehen SEP (a tap), anschalten SEP (an oven), anlassen✧ SEP (an engine).

● **to turn out** 1 **to turn out well** gut ausgehen✧ SEP (PERF sein); **the discussions turned out badly** die Gespräche sind schlecht ausgegangen; **it all turned out all right in the end** am Ende ging alles gut aus; 2 **it turned out that I was right** es stellte sich heraus, dass ich Recht hatte.

● **to turn up** 1 (to arrive) aufkreuzen SEP (PERF sein); **they turned up an hour later** sie sind eine Stunde später aufgekreuzt; 2 (to make louder) lauter machen.

turning noun Abzweigung die (PL die Abzweigungen); **take the third turning on the right** nimm die dritte Abzweigung rechts.

a b c d e f g h i j k l m n o p q r s t u v w x y z

turnip noun Steckrübe die (PL die Steckrüben).

turquoise adjective türkis.

turtle noun Schildkröte die (PL die Schildkröten).

TV noun Fernsehen das; **I saw her on TV** ich habe sie im Fernsehen gesehen.

tweezers noun Pinzette die (PL die Pinzetten).

twelfth number zwölfter/zwölfte/zwölftes; **on the twelfth floor** im zwölften Stock; **the twelfth of May** der zwölfte Mai.

twelve number 1 zwölf; **Tara's twelve** Tara ist zwölf; **2 at twelve o'clock** um zwölf Uhr.

twenty number ist zwanzig; **Marie's twenty** Marie ist zwanzig; **twenty-one** einundzwanzig.

twice adverb 1 zweimal; **I've asked him twice** ich habe ihn zweimal gefragt; **twice a day** zweimal täglich; **2 twice as much** doppelt so viel.

twig noun Zweig der (PL die Zweige).

twin noun Zwilling der (PL die Zwillinge); **Helen and Tim are twins** Helen und Tim sind Zwillinge; **her twin sister** ihre Zwillingsschwester.

twin verb **Richmond is twinned with Konstanz** Richmond und Konstanz sind Partnerstädte.

twist verb 1 (bend out of shape) verbiegen✧; **2** verdrehen (words, meaning); **3 to twist your ankle** sich den Knöchel verrenken.

two number zwei; **Ben's two** Ben ist zwei; **two by two** zu zweit.

type noun Art die; **what type of computer is it?** welche Art Computer ist es?.

type verb (on a typewriter) Schreibmaschine schreiben✧, tippen (informal); **I'm learning to type** ich lerne Schreibmaschine schreiben; **I'm just typing some letters** ich tippe gerade ein paar Briefe.

typewriter noun Schreibmaschine die (PL die Schreibmaschinen).

typical adjective typisch.

tyre noun Reifen der (PL die Reifen).

Uu

ugly adjective hässlich.

UK noun (United Kingdom) Vereinigte Königreich das.

ulcer noun Geschwür das (PL die Geschwüre).

Ulster noun Ulster; **from Ulster** aus Ulster, aus Nordirland.

umbrella noun Regenschirm der (PL die Regenschirme).

umpire noun Schiedsrichter der (PL die Schiedsrichter), Schiedsrichterin die (PL die Schiedsrichterinnen).

UN noun (United Nations) UN (plural).

unable adjective **to be unable to do something** etwas nicht tun können; **he's unable to come** er kann nicht kommen.

unavoidable *adjective*
unvermeidlich.

unbearable *adjective*
unerträglich.

unbelievable *adjective*
unglaublich.

uncertain *adjective* **1** (*not sure*) **to
be uncertain whether** ... sich (DAT)
nicht sicher sein, ob ...; **
2** (*unpredictable*) ungewiss (*future
or result*).

uncle *noun* Onkel *der* (PL *die* Onkel).

uncomfortable *adjective*
1 unbequem (*shoes, chair, or
journey*); **2** unangenehm (*situation,
heat*).

unconscious *adjective* (*out cold*)
bewusstlos.

under *preposition* **1** (*underneath*)
unter (+ DAT, *or* + ACC *when there is
movement towards a place*); **the
dog's under the bed** der Hund ist
unter dem Bett; **the ball rolled
under the bed** der Ball ist unter
das Bett gerollt; **2 under there** da
drunter; **perhaps it's under there**
vielleicht ist es da drunter; **3** (*less
than*) unter (+ DAT); **under £20** unter
zwanzig Pfund; **children under five**
Kinder unter fünf.

under-age *adjective* **to be under-
age** minderjährig sein.

underclothes *plural noun*
Unterwäsche *die*.

undercooked *adjective* nicht gar.

underestimate *verb*
unterschätzen.

underground *noun* (*railway*) U-
Bahn *die* (PL *die* U-Bahnen); **I saw
her on the underground** ich habe

sie in der U-Bahn gesehen; **shall
we go by underground?** fahren
wir mit der U-Bahn?

underground *adjective*
unterirdisch (*cave*); **underground
car park** *die* Tiefgarage.

underline *verb* unterstreichen❖.

underneath *preposition* unter
(+ DAT, *or* + ACC *when there is
movement towards a place*); **it's
underneath the newspaper** es ist
unter der Zeitung; **I put it
underneath the newspaper** ich
habe es unter die Zeitung gelegt.

underneath *adverb* darunter;
check underneath sieh darunter
nach.

underpants *plural noun*
Unterhose *die* (PL *die* Unterhosen);
my underpants meine Unterhose.

underpass *noun* Unterführung
die (PL *die* Unterführungen).

understand *verb* verstehen❖; **do
you understand?** verstehst du?; **I
couldn't understand what he was
saying** ich konnte ihn nicht
verstehen; **I can't understand why
she doesn't want to see him** ich
kann nicht verstehen, warum sie
ihn nicht sehen will.

understandable *adjective* **that's
understandable** das ist
verständlich.

understanding *noun*
Verständnis *das*.

understanding *adjective*
verständnisvoll.

underwear *noun* Unterwäsche
die.

undo *verb* aufmachen SEP.

a b c d e f g h i j k l m n o p q r s t v w x y z

undone *adjective* **to come undone** aufgehen◇ SEP (PERF *sein*).

undress *verb* **to get undressed** sich ausziehen◇ SEP.

unemployed *noun* **the unemployed** die Arbeitslosen (*plural*).

unemployed *adjective* arbeitslos.

unemployment *noun* Arbeitslosigkeit *die*.

uneven *adjective* uneben (*surface*); **her pulse is uneven** ihr Puls ist unregelmäßig; **your writing is very uneven** deine Schrift ist sehr ungleichmäßig; **the icing is uneven** diese Kuchenglasur ist nicht glatt.

unexpected *adjective* unerwartet.

unexpectedly *adverb* (*to happen, arrive*) überraschend.

unfair *adjective* unfair; **it's unfair on young people** es ist jungen Leuten gegenüber unfair.

unfashionable *adjective* unmodern.

unfasten *verb* aufmachen SEP.

unfit *adjective* nicht fit; **I'm terribly unfit** ich bin nicht sehr fit.

unfold *verb* **1** (*a map*) ausbreiten SEP; **2** (*to develop*) spielen; **the story unfolds in Africa** die Geschichte spielt in Afrika.

unfortunate *adjective* unglücklich.

unfortunately *adverb* leider.

unfriendly *adjective* unfreundlich.

ungrateful *adjective* undankbar.

unhappy *adjective* **1** unglücklich; **2** (*not satisfied*) unzufrieden; **to be unhappy about something** mit etwas unzufrieden sein.

unhealthy *adjective* ungesund.

uniform *noun* Uniform *die* (PL die Uniformen).

union *noun* (*trade union*) Gewerkschaft *die* (PL die Gewerkschaften).

Union Jack *noun* **the Union Jack** die britische Nationalflagge.

unique *adjective* einzigartig.

unit *noun* **1** (*for measuring, for example*) Einheit *die* (PL die Einheiten); **2** (*in a kitchen*) Einbauschrank *der* (PL die Einbauschränke); **3** (*a department*) Abteilung *die* (PL die Abteilungen); **the research unit** die Forschungsabteilung.

United Kingdom *noun* Vereinigte Königreich *das*.

United Nations *noun* Vereinte Nationen (*plural*).

United States (of America) *plural noun* Vereinigte Staaten (von Amerika) (*plural*).

universe *noun* Universum *das*, Weltall *das*.

university *noun* Universität *die* (PL die Universitäten); **to go to university** auf die Universität gehen.

unkind *adjective* unfreundlich.

unknown *adjective* unbekannt.

unleaded petrol *noun* bleifreie Benzin *das*.

unless *conjunction* es sei denn; **unless he does it** es sei denn, er macht es; **unless you write** es sei denn, du schreibst.

unlike *adjective* **1** im Gegensatz zu (+ DAT); **unlike me, she hates dogs** im Gegensatz zu mir hasst sie Hunde; **2 it's unlike her to be late** es sieht ihr gar nicht ähnlich, zu spät zu kommen.

unlikely *adjective* unwahrscheinlich.

unlimited *adjective* unbegrenzt.

unload *verb* **1** ausladen ✧ SEP (*luggage, car*); **2** entladen ✧ SEP (*lorry*).

unlock *verb* aufschließen ✧ SEP.

unlucky *adjective* **1 to be unlucky** (*person*) Pech haben; **I was unlucky, the shop was shut** ich hatte Pech, das Geschäft war zu; **2** (*bringing bad luck*) Unglücks-; **thirteen is an unlucky number** dreizehn ist eine Unglückszahl; **it's unlucky** es bringt Unglück.

unmarried *adjective* ledig.

unnecessary *adjective* unnötig.

unpack *verb* auspacken SEP; **I'm just unpacking my rucksack** ich packe gerade meinen Rucksack aus; **I'll just unpack and then come down** ich packe nur noch aus und dann komme ich runter.

unpaid *adjective* unbezahlt.

unpleasant *adjective* unangenehm.

unplug *verb* **to unplug the lamp** den Stecker der Lampe herausziehen ✧ SEP.

unpopular *adjective* unbeliebt.

unreasonable *adjective* uneinsichtig; **he's being really unreasonable** er ist so uneinsichtig.

unrecognizable *adjective* nicht wieder zu erkennen.

unreliable *adjective* unzuverlässig; **he's unreliable** er ist unzuverlässig.

unsafe *adjective* gefährlich (*wiring, for example*).

unsatisfactory *adjective* unbefriedigend.

unscrew *verb* aufschrauben SEP.

unshaven *adjective* unrasiert.

unsuccessful *adjective* **1** erfolglos; **an unsuccessful attempt** ein erfolgloser Versuch; **2 to be unsuccessful** keinen Erfolg haben; **I tried, but I was unsuccessful** ich habe es versucht, aber ich hatte keinen Erfolg.

unsuitable *adjective* unpassend.

untidy *adjective* unordentlich; **the house is always untidy** das Haus ist immer unordentlich.

until *preposition, conjunction* **1** bis; **until Monday** bis Montag; **until now** bis jetzt; **until then** bis dahin; **2** (*when 'until' is followed by a noun it is usually translated as 'bis zu'* + DAT) **until the tenth** bis zum Zehnten; **until the morning** bis zum Morgen; **3 not until** erst; **not until September** erst im September; **it won't be finished until Friday** es wird erst Freitag fertig sein.

unusual *adjective* ungewöhnlich; **an unusual face** ein ungewöhnliches Gesicht.

a b c d e f g h i j k l m n o p q r s t **u** v w x y z

unwilling *adjective* **to be unwilling to do something** etwas nicht tun wollen.

unwrap *verb* auspacken SEP.

up *preposition, adverb* **1** *(out of bed)* **to be up** auf sein ✧ *(PERF sein)*; **Liz isn't up yet** Liz ist noch nicht auf; **I was up late last night** ich war gestern bis spät auf; **2 to get up** aufstehen ✧ SEP *(PERF sein)*; **we got up at six** wir sind um sechs aufgestanden; **3** *(higher up)* auf (+ DAT, *or* + ACC *when there is movement towards a place*); **up on the roof** oben auf dem Dach; **4 up here** hier oben; **up there** da oben; **to go up** *(upstairs)* nach oben gehen; **I went up** ich bin nach oben gegangen; **5 to go up the road** die Straße entlanggehen ✧ SEP *(PERF sein)*; **it's further up the road** es ist weiter die Straße entlang; **6 to go up the hill** *(on foot)* hinaufgehen ✧ SEP *(PERF sein)*, *(in a vehicle)* hinauffahren ✧ SEP *(PERF sein)*; *(in spoken German the prefix 'rauf-' is most common)* **does the bus go up the hill?** fährt der Bus den Berg rauf?; **7 to come up** heraufkommen ✧ SEP *(PERF sein)*, raufkommen ✧ SEP *(PERF sein)* *(informal)*; **8** *(wrong)* **what's up?** was ist los?; *(informal)* **what's up with him?** was ist mit ihm los?; **9 up to** bis; **up to here** bis hier; **up to last week** bis zur letzten Woche; **10 she came up to me** sie kam auf mich zu; **11 what's she up to?** was hat sie vor?; **12 it's up to you** *(it's for you to decide)* das hängt von dir ab; *(it concerns only you)* das ist

deine Sache; ★ **time's up!** die Zeit ist um.

up-date *noun* Aktualisierung *die* *(PL die Aktualisierungen)*; **here's an up-date on our plans** dies ist der neueste Stand unserer Pläne.

up-date *verb* **1** *(to revise)* überarbeiten *(timetables, information)*; **2** *(to modernize)* auf den neuesten Stand bringen ✧ *(styles, furnishings)*.

upheaval *noun* Unruhe *die* *(PL die Unruhen)*.

upper-class *adjective* der Oberschicht; **an upper-class family** eine Familie der Oberschicht.

upright *adjective* aufrecht; **put it upright** stell es aufrecht; **to stand upright** aufrecht stehen.

upset *noun* **stomach upset** die Magenstimmung.

upset *adjective* **1** *(annoyed)* ärgerlich; **he's upset** er ist ärgerlich; **2** *(distressed)* bestürzt, *(sad)* betrübt.

upset *verb* **to upset somebody** *(hurt)* jemanden kränken, *(annoy)* jemanden ärgern.

upside down *adjective* verkehrt herum.

upstairs *adverb* **1** oben; **Mum's upstairs** Mutti ist oben; **2** *(with movement)* nach oben; **to go upstairs** nach oben gehen.

up-to-date *adjective* **1** *(in fashion)* modern; **2** *(information)* aktuell.

upwards *adjective* nach oben.

urgent *adjective* dringend.

us *pronoun* uns; **she knows us** sie kennt uns; **they saw us** sie haben uns gesehen; **with us** mit uns.

US *noun* USA (*plural*).

USA *noun* USA (*plural*).

use *noun* 1 Gebrauch der; **instructions for use** die Gebrauchsanweisung (*singular*); **2 it's no use** es hat keinen Zweck; **it's no use phoning** es hat keinen Zweck anzurufen.

use *verb* benutzen; **we used the dictionary** wir haben das Wörterbuch benutzt; **to use something to do something** etwas zu etwas (DAT) benutzen; **I used a towel to dry myself** ich habe ein Handtuch zum Abtrocknen benutzt.

● **to use up 1** aufbrauchen SEP (*food*); **2** verbrauchen (*money*).

used *adjective* 1 **to be used to something** an etwas (ACC) gewöhnt sein; **I'm used to cats** ich bin an Katzen gewöhnt; **I'm not used to it!** das bin ich nicht gewohnt!; **I'm not used to eating in restaurants** ich bin nicht daran gewöhnt, in Restaurants zu essen; **2 to get used to something** sich an etwas (ACC) gewöhnen; **you'll soon get used to the new car** du wirst dich schnell an das neue Auto gewöhnen, **I've got used to living here** ich habe mich daran gewöhnt, hier zu wohnen; **you'll get used to it** du wirst dich schon daran gewöhnen.

used *verb* **they used to live in the country** sie haben früher auf dem Land gewohnt; **she used to smoke** sie hat früher geraucht.

useful *adjective* nützlich.

useless *adjective* 1 unbrauchbar; **this knife's useless** dieses Messer ist unbrauchbar; **you're completely useless!** du bist wirklich zu nichts zu gebrauchen!; **2** nutzlos (*advice, information, or facts, for example*); **useless knowledge** nutzloses Wissen; **3** (*pointless*) zwecklos.

user *noun* Benutzer der (PL die Benutzer), Benutzerin die (PL die Benutzerinnen).

user-friendly *adjective* benutzerfreundlich.

usual *adjective* 1 üblich; **it's the usual problem** es ist das übliche Problem; **as usual** wie üblich; **2 it's colder than usual** es ist kälter als gewöhnlich.

usually *adjective* normalerweise; **I usually leave at eight** normalerweise gehe ich um acht weg.

Vv

vacancy *noun* 1 (*in a hotel*) **'vacancies'** 'Zimmer frei'; **'no vacancies'** 'belegt'; **2** job vacancy die freie Stelle.

vacant *adjective* frei.

vaccinate *noun* impfen.

vaccination *noun* Impfung die (PL die Impfungen).

a

vacuum *verb* saugen; **I'm going to vacuum my room** ich sauge mein Zimmer.

b

vacuum cleaner *noun* Staubsauger der (PL die Staubsauger).

c

d

vagina *noun* Vagina die (PL die Vaginen).

e

vague *adjective* vage.

f

vain *adjective* eitel; **in vain** vergeblich.

g

h

valentine card *noun* Valentinskarte die (PL die Valentinskarten).

i

Valentine's Day *noun* Valentinstag der (PL die Valentinstage).

j

k

valid *adjective* gültig.

l

valley *noun* Tal das (PL die Täler).

valuable *adjective* wertvoll.

m

value *noun* Wert der (PL die Werte).

n

value *verb* schätzen.

o

van *noun* Lieferwagen der (PL die Lieferwagen).

p

vandal *noun* Rowdy der (PL die Rowdys).

q

r

vandalism *noun* Vandalismus der.

s

vandalize *verb* mutwillig zerstören.

t

vanilla *noun* Vanille die; **vanilla ice cream** das Vanilleeis.

u

v

vanish *verb* verschwinden◇ (PERF sein).

w

variety *noun* 1 Abwechslung die (*in a routine, diet, or style*); **for the sake of variety** zur Abwechslung; 2 (*kind*) Sorte die (PL die Sorten); **a new variety of apple** eine neue

x

y

z

Apfelsorte; 3 (*assortment*) Auswahl die.

various *adjective* verschieden; **there are various ways of doing it** man kann es auf verschiedene Art und Weise machen.

vary *verb* 1 (*become different*) sich ändern; 2 **it varies a lot** es ist sehr unterschiedlich; 3 (*make different*) ändern (*a programme or method*).

vase *noun* Vase die (PL die Vasen).

VAT *noun* Mehrwertsteuer die.

VCR *noun* Videorekorder der (PL die Videorekorder).

VDU *noun* Bildschirm der (PL die Bildschirme).

veal *noun* Kalbfleisch das.

vegan *noun* Veganer der, Veganerin die (PL die Veganerinnen).

vegetable *noun* Gemüse das; **fresh vegetables** frisches Gemüse.

vegetarian *noun* Vegetarier der (PL die Vegetarier), Vegetarierin die (PL die Vegetarierinnen).

vegetarian *adjective* vegetarisch.

vehicle *noun* Fahrzeug das (PL die Fahrzeuge).

vein *noun* Vene die (PL die Venen).

velvet *noun* Samt der.

vending machine *noun* Automat der (PL die Automaten).

verb *noun* Verb das (PL die Verben).

verdict *noun* Urteil das (PL die Urteile).

verge *noun* 1 (*roadside*) Bankett das (PL die Banketten); 2 **to be on the verge of doing something** im Begriff sein, etwas zu tun; **I was on**

rge of leaving ich war im
...f zu gehen.

...on noun Version die (PL die
...onen).

...s preposition gegen (+ ACC);
...al versus Chelsea Arsenal
...n Chelsea.

...ical adjective senkrecht.

... adverb sehr; **it's very difficult**
...st sehr schwer; **very much** sehr
...; **very little** sehr wenig.

...ry adjective **1 the very person** I
...eed! genau der Mann, den ich
...rauche, genau die Frau, die ich
...brauche; **the very thing he's
looking for** genau das, was er
sucht; **in the very middle** genau in
der Mitte; **2 at the very end** ganz
am Ende; **at the very front** ganz
vorne.

vest noun Unterhemd das (PL die
Unterhemden).

vet noun Tierarzt der (PL die
Tierärzte), Tierärztin die (PL die
Tierärztinnen); **she's a vet** sie ist
Tierärztin.

via preposition über (+ ACC); **we're
going to Frankfurt via Brussels**
wir fahren über Brüssel nach
Frankfurt.

vicar noun Pfarrer der (PL die
Pfarrer).

vicious adjective **1** bösartig (dog);
2 brutal (attack).

victim noun Opfer das (PL die
Opfer).

victory noun Sieg der (PL die Siege).

video noun **1** (film, cassette) Video
das (PL die Videos); **to watch a
video** ein Video ansehen; **I've got it**

on video ich habe es auf Video; **it's
out on video** das gibts als Video;
2 (video recorder) Videorekorder
der (PL die Videorekorder).

video verb aufzeichnen SEP; **I'll
video it for you** ich zeichne es für
dich auf.

video camera noun
Videokamera die (PL die
Videokameras).

video cassette noun
Videokassette die (PL die
Videokassetten).

video game noun Videospiel das
(PL die Videospiele).

video recorder noun
Videorekorder der (PL die
Videorekorder).

video shop noun Videothek die (PL
die Videotheken).

Vienna noun Wien das; **to Vienna**
nach Wien.

view noun **1** Aussicht die; **a room
with a view of the lake** ein Zimmer
mit Aussicht auf den See; **2** (opinion) Meinung die (PL die
Meinungen); **in my view** meiner
Meinung nach; **point of view** der
Standpunkt.

viewer noun Zuschauer der (PL die
Zuschauer), Zuschauerin die (PL die
Zuschauerinnen).

vile adjective ekelhaft.

villa noun Villa die (PL die Villen).

village noun Dorf das (PL die
Dörfer).

vine noun Weinrebe die (PL die
Weinreben).

vinegar noun Essig der.

a b c d e f g h i j k l m n o p q r s t u v w x y z

a

vineyard noun Weinberg der (PL die Weinberge).

b

violence noun Gewalt die.

c

violent adjective **1** gewalttätig (person, film, behaviour); **2** heftig (jolt, punch).

d

violin noun Geige die (PL die Geigen); **to play the violin** Geige spielen.

e

f

violinist noun Geiger der (PL die Geiger), Geigerin die (PL die Geigerinnen).

g

h

virgin noun Jungfrau die (PL die Jungfrauen).

i

Virgo noun Jungfrau die; **Robert's Virgo** Robert ist Jungfrau.

j

k

virtual reality noun virtuelle Realität die.

l

virus noun (in medicine and IT) Virus der (PL die Viren); **anti-virus software** Antivirenprogramm das (PL die Antivirenprogramme).

m

n

visa noun Visum das (PL die Visa).

o

visible adjective sichtbar.

p

visit noun Besuch der (PL die Besuche); **I was in Berlin on a visit to friends** ich war in Berlin bei Freunden zu Besuch; **my last visit to Germany** mein letzter Deutschlandbesuch.

q

r

s

visit verb **1** besuchen (a person); **2** besichtigen (a building, town).

t

u

visitor noun **1** Besucher der (PL die Besucher), Besucherin die (PL die Besucherinnen); **2 we've got visitors tonight** wir haben heute Abend Besuch; **3** (in a hotel) Gast der (PL die Gäste).

v

w

x

y

z

visual adjective visuell.

vital adjective unbedingt erforderlich; **it's vital to boo** muss unbedingt buchen.

vitamin noun Vitamin das (Vitamine).

vivid adjective lebhaft (colou memory); **to have a vivid imagination** eine lebhafte Phantasie haben.

vocabulary noun Wortscha

vocational adjective beruflich.

vodka noun Wodka der (PL die Wodkas).

voice noun Stimme die (PL die Stimmen).

volcano noun Vulkan der (PL die Vulkane).

volleyball noun Volleyball der; **to play volleyball** Volleyball spielen.

volume noun **1** Lautstärke die; **could you turn down the volume?** könntest du etwas leiser stellen?; **2** (book) Band der (PL die Bände).

voluntary adjective **1** freiwillig; **a voluntary worker** ein freiwilliger Helfer, eine freiwillige Helferin; **2 to do voluntary work** für einen wohltätigen Zweck arbeiten.

volunteer noun Freiwillige der/die (PL die Freiwilligen).

volunteer verb **to volunteer to do something** sich bereit erklären, etwas zu tun.

vomit verb sich übergeben ✧.

vote verb wählen; **to vote for somebody** jemanden wählen; **she always votes Green** sie wählt immer die Grünen.

voucher noun Gutschein der (PL die Gutscheine).

vowel noun Vokal der (PL die Vokale).

vulgar adjective vulgär.

Ww

waffle noun Waffel die (PL die Waffeln).

wage(s) noun Lohn der (PL die Löhne).

waist noun Taille die (PL die Taillen).

waistcoat noun Weste die (PL die Westen).

waist measurement noun Taillenweite die.

wait noun Wartezeit die; **an hour's wait** eine Stunde Wartezeit.

wait verb 1 warten; **they're waiting in the car** sie warten im Auto; **she kept me waiting** sie hat mich warten lassen; 2 **to wait for somebody** auf jemanden warten; **wait for me** warte auf mich, **to wait for something** auf etwas (ACC) warten; **we waited for a taxi** wir haben auf ein Taxi gewartet; 3 **to wait for somebody to do something** darauf warten, dass jemand etwas tut; **I'm waiting for him to ring** ich warte darauf, dass er anruft; 4 **I can't wait to open it** ich kann's kaum erwarten, es aufzumachen.

waiter noun Kellner der (PL die Kellner); **waiter!** Herr Ober!

waiting list noun Warteliste die (PL die Wartelisten).

waiting room noun Wartezimmer das (PL die Wartezimmer), (at a station) Warteraum der (PL die Warteräume).

waitress noun Kellnerin die (PL die Kellnerinnen); **waitress!** Fräulein!

wake verb 1 wecken (somebody); **Jess woke me at six** Jess hat mich um sechs geweckt; 2 aufwachen SEP (PERF sein); **I woke (up) at six** ich bin um sechs aufgewacht; **wake up!** wach auf!

Wales noun Wales das; **from Wales** aus Wales; **to Wales** nach Wales.

walk noun 1 Spaziergang der (PL die Spaziergänge); **to go for walk** einen Spaziergang machen; **we'll go for a little walk round the village** wir machen einen kleinen Spaziergang durchs Dorf; 2 **to take the dog for a walk** mit dem Hund spazieren gehen✧ (PERF sein); 3 **it's about five minutes' walk from here** es ist ungefähr fünf Minuten zu Fuß von hier.

walk verb 1 (go, not run) gehen✧ (PERF sein); **he walks very slowly** er geht sehr langsam; **I'll walk to the bus stop with you** ich gehe mit dir zur Bushaltestelle; 2 (on foot rather than by car or bus) zu Fuß gehen✧ (PERF sein); **it's not far, we can walk** es ist nicht weit, wir können zu Fuß gehen; 3 (walk around) spazieren gehen✧ (PERF sein); **we walked around the old town** wir sind in der Altstadt spazieren gegangen; 4 (move on foot) laufen✧ (PERF sein);

a
b
c
d
e
f
g
h
i
j
k
l
m
n
o
p
q
r
s
t
u
v
w
x
y
z

to learn to walk laufen lernen; **the child can't walk yet** das Kind kann noch nicht laufen.

walking distance noun **to be within walking distance** zu Fuß zu erreichen sein; **it's within walking distance of the sea** man kann das Meer zu Fuß erreichen.

walking noun (*hiking*) Wandern das; **to go walking** wandern (PERF sein).

walkman noun Walkman der (PL die Walkmen).

wall noun **1** (*inside a building*) Wand die (PL die Wände); **there's a picture on every wall** an jeder Wand hängt ein Bild; **2** (*outside*) Mauer die (PL die Mauern).

wallet noun Brieftasche die (PL die Brieftaschen).

wallpaper noun Tapete die (PL die Tapeten).

walnut noun Walnuss die (PL die Walnüsse).

wander verb **to wander around town** durch die Stadt bummeln (PERF sein); **to wander off** weggehen✧ SEP (PERF sein).

want verb **1** wollen✧; **do you want to come?** willst du mitkommen?; **what do you want to do?** was willst du machen?; **I don't want to bother him** ich will ihn nicht stören; **2** (*more polite*) mögen✧ ('ich möchte' is much politer than 'ich will'); **do you want some more coffee?** möchtest du noch Kaffee?; **I want two pounds of apples please** ich möchte gern zwei Pfund Äpfel ('*möchte gern*' *is particularly used when shopping*).

war noun Krieg der (PL die Kriege).

ward noun Station die (PL die Stationen).

wardrobe noun Kleiderschrank der (PL die Kleiderschränke).

warm adjective **1** warm; **a warm coat** ein warmer Mantel; **it's warm today** heute ist es warm; **I'll keep your dinner warm** ich halte dir das Essen warm; **it's warm inside** drinnen ist es warm; **I am warm** mir ist warm; **2** (*friendly*) herzlich; **a warm welcome** ein herzlicher Empfang.

warm verb wärmen; **to warm the plates** die Teller wärmen.

● **to warm up 1** (*weather*) warm werden; **2** (*an athlete*) sich aufwärmen SEP; **3** (*to heat up*) aufwärmen SEP; **I'll warm the soup up for you** ich wärme dir die Suppe auf.

warmth noun Wärme die.

warn verb **1** warnen; **I warn you, it's expensive** ich warne dich, es ist teuer; **to warn somebody not to do something** jemanden davor warnen, etwas zu tun; **she warned me not to let him drive** sie hat mich davor gewarnt, ihn fahren zu lassen; **2 he warned me to lock the car** er hat mich ermahnt, das Auto abzuschließen.

warning noun Warnung die (PL die Warnungen).

wart noun Warze die (PL die Warzen).

wash noun to give something a wash etwas waschen◇; to have a wash sich waschen.

wash verb 1 waschen◇; I've washed your jeans ich habe deine Jeans gewaschen; 2 (have a wash) sich waschen◇; to get washed sich waschen◇; 3 to wash your hands sich (DAT) die Hände waschen; I washed my hands ich habe mir die Hände gewaschen; to wash your hair sich (DAT) die Haare waschen; 4 to wash the dishes abwaschen◇ SEP.

● to wash up abwaschen◇ SEP.

washbasin noun Waschbecken das (PL die Waschbecken).

washing noun Wäsche die; to do the washing Wäsche waschen.

washing machine noun Waschmaschine die (PL die Waschmaschinen).

washing powder noun Waschpulver das.

washing-up liquid noun Spülmittel das (PL die Spülmittel).

washing-up noun Abwasch der; to do the washing-up den Abwasch machen.

wasp noun Wespe die (PL die Wespen).

waste noun Verschwendung die; it's a waste of time das ist eine Zeitverschwendung.

waste verb verschwenden.

waste-bin noun Mülltonne die (PL die Mülltonnen).

waste-paper basket noun Papierkorb der (PL die Papierkörbe).

watch noun Uhr die (PL die Uhren); my watch is fast meine Uhr geht vor; my watch is slow meine Uhr geht nach.

watch verb 1 (to look at) sich (DAT) ansehen◇ SEP; I was watching a film ich habe mir einen Film angesehen; 2 to watch TV fernsehen◇ SEP; 3 (keep a check on, look after) achten auf (+ ACC) ; watch the children achte auf die Kinder; 4 (to be careful) aufpassen◇ SEP; watch you don't spill it pass auf, dass du es nicht verschüttest; watch out! pass auf!; 5 (observe) beobachten; they were being watched sie wurden beobachtet.

water noun Wasser das.

water verb gießen◇ (plants).

waterfall noun Wasserfall der (PL die Wasserfälle).

watering can noun Gießkanne die (PL die Gießkannen).

water melon noun Wassermelone die (PL die Wassermelonen).

waterproof adjective wasserdicht.

water-skiing noun Wasserskifahren das; to go water-skiing Wasserski fahren◇.

water sports plural noun Wassersport der.

wave noun 1 (in the sea) Welle die (PL die Wellen); 2 (with your hand) to give somebody a wave jemandem zuwinken SEP; she gave him a wave from the bus sie winkte ihm vom Bus zu.

wave verb **1** (*with your hand*) winken; **2** (*flap*) schwenken (*a flag, for example*).

wax noun Wachs das.

way noun **1** (*a route or road*) Weg der (PL die Wege); **the way to town** der Weg in die Stadt; **we asked the way to the station** wir haben gefragt, wie man zum Bahnhof kommt; **on the way back** auf dem Rückweg; **on the way** unterwegs; **to be in the way** im Weg sein; **to be in somebody's way** jemandem im Weg sein; **to get out of the way** aus dem Weg gehen; **2 to lose your way** sich verlaufen✧, (*in a car*) sich verfahren✧; **3 'way in'** 'Eingang'; **'way out'** 'Ausgang'; **4** (*direction*) Richtung die (PL die Richtungen); **which way did he go?** in welche Richtung ist er gegangen?; **this way** in diese Richtung; **5** (*side*) **the right way up** richtig herum; **the wrong way round** falsch herum; **the other way round** andersherum; **6** (*distance*) **it's a long way** es ist weit weg; **we still had a little way to go** wir mussten noch ein kleines Stück gehen; **7** (*manner*) Art und Weise die; **my way of learning German** meine Art und Weise, Deutsch zu lernen; **he does it his way** er macht es auf seine Art und Weise; **I've done it the wrong way** ich habe es falsch gemacht; **in a way** in gewisser Weise; **8 no way!** auf keinen Fall!; **9 by the way** übrigens.

we pronoun wir; **we're going to the cinema tonight** wir gehen heute Abend ins Kino.

weak adjective **1** (*feeble*) schwach; **in a weak voice** mit schwacher Stimme; **2** (*coffee or tea*) dünn.

wealthy adjective reich.

weapon noun Waffe die (PL die Waffen); **weapons of mass destruction** Massenvernichtungswaffen die (*plural*).

wear noun **children's wear** die Kinderkleidung; **sports wear** die Sportkleidung.

wear verb tragen✧, anhaben✧ SEP (*informal*); **she often wears red** sie trägt oft Rot; **Tamsin's wearing her jeans** Tamsin hat ihre Jeans an.

weather noun **1** Wetter das; **what's the weather like?** wie ist das Wetter?; **in fine weather** bei schönem Wetter; **the weather is terrible** das Wetter ist furchtbar; **2 in wet weather** wenn es regnet; **the weather was cold** es war kalt.

weather forecast noun Wettervorhersage die; **the weather forecast says it will rain** der Wettervorhersage zufolge soll es regnen.

web noun **1** (*spider's*) Spinnennetz das (PL die Spinnennetze); **2 the Web** Netz das.

web page noun Webseite die (PL die Webseiten).

web site noun Website die (PL die Websites).

wedding noun Hochzeit die (PL die Hochzeiten).

Wednesday noun **1** Mittwoch der (PL die Mittwoche); **on Wednesday** (am) Mittwoch; **I'm going to the**

cinema on Wednesday ich gehe Mittwoch ins Kino; **see you on Wednesday!** bis Mittwoch!; **every Wednesday** jeden Mittwoch; **last Wednesday** vorigen Mittwoch; **next Wednesday** nächsten Mittwoch; **2 on Wednesdays** mittwochs; **the museum is closed on Wednesdays** das Museum ist mittwochs geschlossen.

weed *noun* Unkraut das.

week *noun* Woche die (PL die Wochen); **last week** vorige Woche; **next week** nächste Woche; **this week** diese Woche; **for weeks** wochenlang; **a week today** heute in einer Woche; **in three weeks' time** in drei Wochen.

weekday *noun* **on weekdays** wochentags.

weekend *noun* Wochenende das (PL die Wochenenden); **last weekend** voriges Wochenende; **next weekend** nächstes Wochenende; **they're coming for the weekend** sie kommen übers Wochenende; **I'll do it at the weekend** ich mache es am Wochenende; **have a nice weekend!** (ein) schönes Wochenende!

weigh *verb* **1** wiegen◇; **to weigh something** etwas wiegen; **to weigh yourself** sich wiegen; **2 how much do you weigh?** wie viel wiegst du?; **I weigh 50 kilos** ich wiege fünfzig Kilo.

weight *noun* **1** Gewicht das (PL die Gewichte); **2 to put on weight** zunehmen◇ SEP; **3 to lose weight** abnehmen◇ SEP.

weird *adjective* seltsam.

welcome *noun* **1 they gave us a warm welcome** sie haben uns herzlich empfangen; **2 welcome to Oxford!** herzlich willkommen in Oxford!

welcome *adjective* willkommen; **you're welcome any time** du bist immer willkommen; **'thank you!' – 'you're welcome!'** 'danke!' – 'bitte!'.

welcome *verb* begrüßen; **to welcome somebody** jemanden begrüßen.

well[1] *adverb* **1 to be well** gesund sein; **I'm very well, thank you** danke, es geht mir gut; **get well soon!** gute Besserung!; **2 well; Terry played well** Terry hat gut gespielt; **it's well paid** es wird gut bezahlt; **well done!** gut gemacht!; **3 as well** auch; **Kevin's coming as well** Kevin kommt auch; **4 na ja; well, never mind** na ja, macht nichts; **5 gut; it may well be that ...** es ist gut möglich, dass ...; **very well then, you can go** also gut, du kannst gehen.

well[2] *noun* Brunnen der (PL die Brunnen).

well-behaved *adjective* artig.

well-done *adjective* durchgebraten (steak).

wellington (boot) *noun* Gummistiefel der (PL die Gummistiefel).

well-known *adjective* bekannt.

well-off *adjective* wohlhabend.

Welsh *noun* **1 the Welsh** (people) die Waliser (plural); **2** (language) Walisisch das.

a

Welsh adjective walisisch; **he's Welsh** er ist Waliser; **she's Welsh** sie ist Waliserin.

b

Welshman noun Waliser der (PL die Waliser).

c

Welshwoman noun Waliserin die (PL die Waliserinnen).

d

west noun Westen der; **in the west** im Westen.

e

f

west adjective West-; **the west side** die Westseite; **west wind** der Westwind; **west of** westlich von; **it's west of Munich** es liegt westlich von München.

g

h

west adverb nach Westen.

i

western noun (film) Western der (PL die Western).

j

k

West Indian noun Westinder der (PL die Westinder), Westinderin die (PL die Westinderinnen).

l

West Indian adjective westindisch.

m

n

West Indies plural noun die Westindischen Inseln (plural); **in the West Indies** auf den Westindischen Inseln.

o

wet adjective 1 nass; **we got wet** wir sind nass geworden; 2 **a wet day** ein regnerischer Tag.

p

q

whale noun Wal der (PL die Wale).

r

s

what pronoun, adjective 1 (in questions) was; **what did you say?** was hast du gesagt?; **what's she doing?** was macht sie?; **what did you buy?** was hast du gekauft?; **what is it?** was ist das?; **what's the matter?** was ist los?; **what's happened?** was ist passiert?; **what?** was?; 2 **what's your address?** wie ist Ihre Adresse?;

t

u

v

w

x

y

z

what's her name? wie heißt sie?; **what was it like?** wie war's?; 3 (asking for an amount) wie viel; **at what time?** um wie viel Uhr?; 4 (that which) was (relative pronoun); **she told me what had happened** sie hat mir gesagt, was passiert ist; **do what I tell you** tu, was ich dir sage; 5 (which) welcher/welche/welches; **what country is it in?** in welchem Land ist es?; **what colour is it?** welche Farbe hat es?; **what make is it?** welche Marke ist es?; 6 **what for?** wozu?

wheat noun Weizen der.

wheel noun Rad das (PL die Räder); **the spare wheel** das Reserverad; **the steering wheel** das Lenkrad.

wheelbarrow noun Schubkarre die (PL die Schubkarren).

wheelchair noun Rollstuhl der (PL die Rollstühle).

when adverb wann; **when is she arriving?** wann kommt sie an?; **when's your birthday?** wann hast du Geburtstag?

when conjunction 1 (with the past) als; **I was out shopping when you rang** ich war beim Einkaufen, als du anriefst; 2 (with the present or future) wenn; **when she comes I'll ring** wenn sie kommt, rufe ich an.

where adverb, conjunction wo; **where do you live?** wo wohnst du?; **where are you going?** wo gehst du hin?; **I don't know where they live** ich weiß nicht, wo sie wohnen.

whether *conjunction* ob; **I don't know whether he's back** ich weiß nicht, ob er schon zurück ist.

which *adjective, pronoun*
1 welcher/welche/welches; **which CD did you buy?** welche CD hast du gekauft?; **2 which (one)** welcher/welche/welches (*depending on the gender of the noun the question refers back to*); **'I met your brother' - 'which one?'** 'ich habe deinen Bruder getroffen' - 'welchen?'; **'I met your sister' - 'which one?'** 'ich habe deine Schwester getroffen' - 'welche?'; **'have you seen my book?' -'which one?'** 'hast du mein Buch gesehen?' - 'welches?'; **3** (*relative pronoun*) der/die/das (*depending on the gender of the noun 'which' refers to*), (*plural*) die; **the film which is showing now** der Film, der gerade läuft; **the lamp which is on the table** die Lampe, die auf dem Tisch steht; **the book which I lent you** das Buch, das ich dir geliehen habe; **the books which I've read** die Bücher, die ich gelesen habe.

while *noun* **for a while** eine Weile; **she worked here for a while** sie hat eine Weile hier gearbeitet; **after a while** nach einer Weile.

while *conjunction* während; **you can make some coffee while I'm finishing my homework** du kannst Kaffee kochen, während ich meine Hausaufgaben fertig mache.

whip *noun* Peitsche *die* (PL *die* Peitschen).

whip *verb* schlagen✧ (*cream*); **whipped cream** *die* Schlagsahne.

whisker *noun* Schnurrhaar *das* (PL *die* Schnurrhaare).

whisky *noun* Whisky *der* (PL *die* Whiskys).

whisper *noun* Flüstern *das*; **in a whisper** im Flüsterton.

whisper *verb* flüstern.

whistle *noun* Pfeife *die* (PL *die* Pfeifen).

whistle *verb* pfeifen✧.

white *noun* Weiß *das*; **egg white** das Eiweiß.

white *adjective* weiß; **a white shirt** ein weißes Hemd.

white coffee *noun* Kaffee mit Milch *der* (PL *die* Kaffees mit Milch).

Whitsun *noun* Pfingsten *das* (PL *die* Pfingsten).

who *pronoun* **1** (*in questions*) wer; **who wants some chocolate?** wer möchte Schokolade?; **2** (*in the accusative*) wen; **who did you ring?** wen hast du angerufen?; **3** (*in the dative*) wem; **who did you give it to?** wem hast du es gegeben?; **4** (*relative pronoun*) der/die/das (*depending on the gender of the noun 'who' refers to*), (*plural*) die; **my boy friend who lives in Liverpool** mein Freund, der in Liverpool wohnt; **my girl friend who lives in Berlin** meine Freundin, die in Berlin wohnt; **the child who's staying with us** das Kind, das bei uns wohnt; **the friends who are coming to see us tonight** die Freunde, die heute Abend zu Besuch kommen.

whole *noun* **the whole of the class** die ganze Klasse; **the whole**

a b c d e f g h i j k l m n o p q r s t u v w x y z

of Germany ganz Deutschland; **on the whole** im Großen und Ganzen.

whole *adjective* ganz; **the whole family** die ganze Familie; **the whole morning** den ganzen Morgen; **the whole time** die ganze Zeit; **the whole world** die ganze Welt.

wholemeal *adjective* Vollkorn-; **wholemeal bread** *das* Vollkornbrot.

whom *pronoun* **1** den/die/das, *(plural)* die; **the man whom I saw** der Mann, den ich sah; **the woman whom I saw** die Frau, die ich sah; **the child whom I saw** das Kind, das ich sah; **2** *(in the dative)* dem/ der/dem, *(plural)* denen; **the girl to whom I wrote** das Mädchen, dem ich geschrieben habe; **3** *(in questions)* wen; **whom did you see?** wen haben Sie gesehen?; **4 to whom did you give it?** wem haben Sie es gegeben?

whose *pronoun, adjective* **1** *(in questions)* wessen; **whose is this jacket?** wessen Jacke ist das?; **whose shoes are these?** wessen Schuhe sind das?; **2 whose is it?** wem gehört das?; **I know whose it is** ich weiß, wem es gehört; **3** *(as a relative pronoun)* dessen/deren/ dessen *(depending on the gender of the noun 'whose' refers to)*, *(plural)* deren; **the man whose car I'm buying** der Mann, dessen Auto ich kaufe; **the woman whose bag I found** die Frau, deren Tasche ich gefunden habe; **the girl whose sister I know** das Mädchen, dessen Schwester ich kenne; **the people**

whose children he teaches die Leute, deren Kinder er unterrichtet.

why *adverb* **1** warum; **why did she phone?** warum hat sie angerufen?; **why not?** warum nicht?; **2 that's why I don't want to come** deswegen will ich nicht kommen.

wicked *adjective* **1** *(bad)* böse; **2** *(brilliant)* geil *(informal)*.

wide *adjective* **1** breit; **it's a very wide road** es ist eine sehr breite Straße; **the shelf is 30 cm wide** das Regal ist dreißig Zentimeter breit; **wide screen** *das* Breitbild; **2** groß; **a wide range** eine große Auswahl.

wide *adverb* **the door was wide open** die Tür stand weit offen.

wide awake *adjective* hellwach.

widow *noun* Witwe *die* (PL *die* Witwen).

widower *noun* Witwer *der* (PL *die* Witwer).

width *noun* Breite *die*.

wife *noun* Ehefrau *die* (PL *die* Ehefrauen).

wig *noun* Perücke *die* (PL *die* Perücken).

wild *adjective* **1** wild; **wild animals** wilde Tiere; **2** *(crazy)* verrückt *(idea, party, person)*; **3 to be wild about something** scharf auf etwas (ACC) sein.

wildlife *noun* Tierwelt *die*; **a programme on wildlife in Africa** eine Sendung über die afrikanische Tierwelt.

wildlife park *noun* Wildpark *der* (PL *die* Wildparks).

will verb **1** (in German the present tense is often used to express future actions and intentions) **I'll wait for you at the bus stop** ich warte an der Bushaltestelle auf dich; **he'll be pleased to help you** er hilft dir gern; **that won't be a problem** das ist kein Problem; **I'll phone them at once** ich rufe sie sofort an; **2** (the German future tense is used when firm intention is stressed, when referring to the more distant future and when some doubt about the future is expressed) werden✧; **he will definitely come** er wird ganz bestimmt kommen; **she'll probably ring before leaving** sie wird wahrscheinlich anrufen, bevor sie geht; **3** (in questions and requests) **will you have some more tea?** möchten Sie noch Tee?; **will you help me?** hilfst du mir?; **'will you write to me?' — 'of course I will!'** 'schreibst du mir?' — 'ja, natürlich!'; **'he won't like it' — 'yes he will'** 'es wird ihm nicht gefallen' — 'doch'; **4** wollen✧; **he won't help us** er will uns nicht helfen; **the car won't start** das Auto will nicht anspringen.

willing adjective **to be willing to do something** bereit sein, etwas zu tun; **I'm willing to pay half** ich bin bereit, die Hälfte zu zahlen.

willingly adverb gern.

willow noun Weide die (PL die Weiden).

win noun Sieg der (PL die Siege); **our win over Everton** unser Sieg über Everton.

win verb **1** gewinnen✧; **we won!** wir haben gewonnen!; **2 to win a prize** einen Preis bekommen.

wind[1] noun Wind der (PL die Winde).

wind[2] verb **1** wickeln (a wire or rope, for example); **2** aufziehen✧ SEP (a clock).

wind farm noun Windpark der (PL die Windparks).

wind instrument noun Blasinstrument das (PL die Blasinstrumente).

window noun **1** Fenster das (PL die Fenster); **to look out of the window** aus dem Fenster sehen; **2** (in a shop) Schaufenster das (PL die Schaufenster).

windscreen noun Windschutzscheibe die (PL die Windschutzscheiben).

windscreen wiper noun Scheibenwischer der (PL die Scheibenwischer).

windsurfing noun Windsurfen das; **to go windsurfing** windsurfen gehen.

windy adjective windig; **it's windy today** heute ist es windig.

wine noun Wein der (PL die Weine); **a glass of white wine** ein Glas Weißwein.

wing noun Flügel der (PL die Flügel).

wink verb **to wink at somebody** jemandem zuzwinkern SEP.

winner noun Sieger der (PL die Sieger), Siegerin die (PL die Siegerinnen).

winning adjective siegreich.

winnings plural noun Gewinn der.

a b c d e f g h i j k l m n o p q r s t u v w x y z

winter noun Winter der (PL die Winter); **in winter** im Winter.

wipe verb 1 abwischen SEP; **I'll just wipe the table** ich wische schnell den Tisch ab; **to wipe your nose** sich (DAT) die Nase abwischen; 2 **to wipe the floor** den Boden wischen; 3 **to wipe your feet** sich (DAT) die Schuhe abtreten SEP.

• **to wipe up** abtrocknen SEP (dishes).

wire noun Draht der (PL die Drähte); **electric wire** die Leitung.

wise adjective weise.

wish noun 1 Wunsch der (PL die Wünsche); **to make a wish** sich (DAT) etwas wünschen; **make a wish!** wünsch dir was!; 2 **best wishes on your birthday** alles Gute zum Geburtstag; 3 (in a letter) **with best wishes** mit freundlichen Grüßen.

wish verb 1 **I wish she were here** ich wünschte, sie wäre hier; 2 **to wish for something** sich (DAT) etwas wünschen; 3 **to wish somebody a happy Christmas** jemandem frohe Weihnachten wünschen; **I wished him happy birthday** ich habe ihm alles Gute zum Geburtstag gewünscht.

wit noun Geist der.

with preposition 1 mit (+ DAT); **with me** mit mir; **with pleasure** mit Vergnügen; **he went on holiday with his friends** er ist mit seinen Freunden in die Ferien gefahren; **a girl with red hair** ein Mädchen mit roten Haaren; 2 (at the house of) bei (+ ACC); **we're staying the night with friends** wir übernachten bei

Freunden; 3 vor (+ DAT); **to shiver with cold** vor Kälte zittern; **to tremble with fear** vor Angst zittern; 4 **I haven't got any money with me** ich habe kein Geld dabei.

without preposition ohne (+ ACC); **without you** ohne dich; **without a sweater** ohne einen Pullover; **without knowing** ohne zu wissen.

witness noun Zeuge der (PL die Zeugen), Zeugin die (PL die Zeuginnen).

witty adjective geistreich.

wolf noun Wolf der (PL die Wölfe).

woman noun Frau die (PL die Frauen); **a woman friend** eine Freundin; **a woman doctor** eine Ärztin.

wonder noun Wunder das (PL die Wunder); **it's no wonder you're tired** es ist kein Wunder, dass du müde bist.

wonder verb 1 sich fragen; **I wonder why she did that** ich frage mich, warum sie das getan hat; 2 **I wonder who?** wer wohl?; **I wonder where Jake is** wo Jake wohl ist?; 3 (in polite requests) **I wonder if you could tell me ...?** könnten Sie mir vielleicht sagen ...?

wonderful adjective wunderbar.

wood noun Holz das; **the lamp is made of wood** die Lampe ist aus Holz.

wooden adjective Holz-, hölzern; **wooden toys** das Holzspielzeug.

woodwork noun (craft) Tischlerei die.

wool noun Wolle die.

word noun **1** Wort das (PL die Wörter) (*the plural 'Wörter' is used when the words are unrelated*); **a long word** ein langes Wort; **what's the German word for 'window'?** wie heißt 'window' auf Deutsch?; **I've learned ten German words today** ich habe heute zehn deutsche Wörter gelernt; **words in the dictionary** Wörter im Wörterbuch; **2** Wort das (PL die Worte) (*the plural 'Worte' is used when the words are connected in a text or conversation*); **he wanted to say a few words** er wollte ein paar Worte sagen; **in other words** mit anderen Worten; **to have a word with somebody** mit jemandem sprechen; **3** (*promise*) Wort das; **to keep your word** sein Wort halten; **he broke his word** er hat sein Wort gebrochen; **4** the words of a song der Text von einem Lied.

word processing noun Textverarbeitung die.

word processor noun Textverarbeitungssystem das (PL die Textverarbeitungssysteme).

work noun Arbeit die; **I enjoy my work** meine Arbeit macht mir Spaß; **she's looking for work** sie sucht Arbeit; **I've got some work to do** ich habe noch etwas Arbeit; **he's out of work** er hat keine Arbeit; **to be off work** nicht arbeiten; **Ben's off work** (*sick*) Ben ist krank; **to go to work on the tube** mit der U-Bahn zur Arbeit fahren.

work verb **1** arbeiten; **she works in an office** sie arbeitet in einem Büro; **Mum works as a dentist** Mutti ist Zahnärztin; **he works part-time** er arbeitet halbtags; **2** (*to operate*) sich auskennen ◆ SEP mit; **can you work the video?** kennst du dich mit dem Videorekorder aus?; **3** (*function*) funktionieren; **the washing machine's not working** die Waschmaschine funktioniert nicht; **4** (*a plan or idea*) klappen; **that worked really well** das hat prima geklappt.

● **to work out 1** (*understand*) verstehen◆; **I can't work out why** ich kann nicht verstehen, warum; **2** (*exercise*) trainieren; **3** (*to go well*) klappen; **4** (*calculate*) ausrechnen SEP (*a sum*), **I'll work out how much it would cost** ich rechne aus, wie viel es kosten würde; **5** (*solve*) lösen (*a problem*).

worker noun Arbeiter der (PL die Arbeiter), Arbeiterin die (PL die Arbeiterinnen).

work experience noun Praktikum das (PL die Praktika); **to do work experience** ein Praktikum machen.

working-class adjective der Arbeiterschicht; **a working-class family** eine Familie der Arbeiterschicht.

work of art noun Kunstwerk das (PL die Kunstwerke).

workshop noun Werkstatt die (PL die Werkstätten).

world noun Welt die; **the biggest tree in the world** der größte Baum der Welt; **all over the world** auf der

a b c d e f g h i j k l m n o p q r s t u v w x y z

ganzen Welt; **the Western world** die westliche Welt.

World Cup noun **the World Cup** die Weltmeisterschaft.

world war noun Weltkrieg der (PL die Weltkriege); **the Second World War** der Zweite Weltkrieg.

worm noun Wurm der (PL die Würmer).

worn out adjective **1** (person) erschöpft; **2** (clothes or shoes) abgetragen.

worried adjective **1** besorgt; **his worried parents** seine besorgten Eltern; **2 to be worried about somebody** sich (DAT) um jemanden Sorgen machen; **we're worried about Susan** wir machen uns um Susan Sorgen.

worry noun Sorge die (PL die Sorgen).

worry verb sich (DAT) Sorgen machen; **don't worry!** keine Sorge!; **don't worry about it** mach dir darum keine Sorgen.

worrying adjective beunruhigend.

worse adjective **1** (more unpleasant) schlimmer (problem, pain, illness); **things couldn't be worse** es kann nicht schlimmer kommen; **2** (less good) schlechter; **it was even worse than the last time** es war noch schlechter als letztes Mal; **to get worse** schlechter werden; **the weather's getting worse** das Wetter wird schlechter; **she's getting worse** (in health) es geht ihr schlechter.

worst adjective **1** (most unpleasant) schlimmster/schlimmste/

schlimmstes; **the worst** der/die/ das schlimmste; **it was the worst day of my life** es war der schlimmste Tag meines Lebens; **if the worst comes to the worst** wenn es zum Schlimmsten kommt; **2** (least good) schlechtester/ schlechteste/schlechtestes; **it's his worst film** das ist sein schlechtester Film; **French is my worst subject** in Französisch bin ich am schlechtesten.

worth adjective **to be worth** wert sein; **how much is it worth?** wie viel ist es wert?; **it's worth buying** das lohnt sich zu kaufen; **it's worth it** das lohnt sich; **it's not worth it** es lohnt sich nicht.

would verb **1 would you like something to eat?** möchtest du etwas essen?; **what would you like?** was möchten Sie?; **2 I wouldn't do it** ich würde das nicht machen; **I would buy it, but I haven't got any money at the moment** ich würde es kaufen, aber ich habe zur Zeit kein Geld; **I'd like to go to the cinema** ich würde gern ins Kino gehen; **she said she'd help us** sie hat gesagt, sie würde uns helfen; **3 that would be a good idea** das wäre ein gute Idee; **if we had asked her she would have helped us** wenn wir sie gefragt hätten, hätte sie uns geholfen; **4 he wouldn't answer** er wollte nicht antworten; **the car wouldn't start** das Auto wollte nicht anspringen.

wound *noun* Wunde *die* (PL *die* Wunden).

wound *verb* verwunden.

wrap *verb* einwickeln SEP; **I'm going to wrap (up) my presents** ich wickele meine Geschenke ein; **could you wrap it for me please?** können Sie es bitte in Geschenkpapier einwickeln?

wrapping paper *noun* Geschenkpapier *das*.

wreck *noun* 1 Wrack *das* (PL *die* Wracks); **2 I feel a wreck** ich bin völlig kaputt.

wreck *verb* 1 zerstören (*a building or machinery*); 2 kaputtfahren✧ SEP (*a car*); 3 verderben✧ (*a party, holidays*); **it completely wrecked my evening** das hat mir den Abend völlig verdorben; 4 zunichte machen (*plans*).

wrestler *noun* Ringer *der* (PL *die* Ringer), Ringerin *die* (PL *die* Ringerinnen).

wrestling *noun* Ringen *das*.

wrist *noun* Handgelenk *das* (PL *die* Handgelenke).

write *verb* schreiben✧; **to write to somebody** jemandem schreiben; **I'll write her a letter** ich schreibe ihr einen Brief; **to write to a firm** an eine Firma schreiben.

● **to write down** aufschreiben✧ SEP; **I wrote down her name** ich schrieb ihren Namen auf; **she wrote it down for me** sie hat es mir aufgeschrieben.

writer *noun* Schriftsteller *der* (PL *die* Schriftsteller), Schriftstellerin *die* (PL *die* Schriftstellerinnen).

writing *noun* Schrift *die*.

wrong *adjective* 1 (*not correct*) falsch; **the wrong answer** die falsche Antwort; **it's the wrong address** das ist die falsche Adresse; **2 you've got the wrong number** Sie haben sich verwählt; **3 to be wrong** (*be mistaken*) sich irren; **I must have been wrong** ich muss mich geirrt haben; **4** (*out of order*) **to be wrong** nicht stimmen; **there's something wrong** etwas stimmt nicht; **5** (*dishonest*) nicht richtig; **it's wrong to make him pay for it** es ist nicht richtig, dass er dafür zahlen muss; **he's wrong** er hat Unrecht; **you're quite wrong there, cars pollute the environment** da haben Sie aber Unrecht, Autos verschmutzen die Umwelt; **6 what's wrong?** was ist los?

wrong *adverb* 1 (*false*) falsch; **he's got it wrong** er hat es falsch gemacht; **2 to go wrong** (*break*) kaputtgehen✧ SEP (PERF *sein*) (*informal*); **3 to go wrong** schief gehen✧ (*plan*).

Xx

xerox *noun* Fotokopie *die* (PL *die* Fotokopien).

xerox *verb* fotokopieren.

X-ray *noun* Röntgenaufnahme *die* (PL *die* Röntgenaufnahmen); **to have an X-ray** geröntgt werden✧ (PERF *sein*).

a b c d e f g h i j k l m n o p q r s t u v **w** **x** y z

a
b
c
d
e
f
g
h
i
j
k
l
m
n
o
p
q
r
s
t
u
v
w
x
y
z

X-ray verb röntgen; **they X-rayed her ankle** sie haben ihren Knöchel geröntgt.

Yy

yacht noun 1 (sailing boat) Segelboot das (PL die Segelboote); 2 (large luxury boat) Jacht die (PL die Jachten).

yawn verb gähnen.

year noun 1 Jahr das (PL die Jahre); **six years ago** vor sechs Jahren; **the whole year** das ganze Jahr; 2 **they lived in Moscow for years** sie haben jahrelang in Moskau gewohnt; 3 **to be seventeen years old** siebzehn Jahre alt sein; **a two-year-old child** ein zweijähriges Kind; 4 (in school) Klasse die (PL die Klassen) (in German secondary schools the years go from the 'fünfte Klasse' to the 'dreizehnte Klasse'); **I'm in Year 10** (in Britain) ich gehe in die zehnte Klasse; **he'll be in Year 11** (in Britain) er kommt in die elfte Klasse.

yell verb schreien✧.

yellow adjective gelb.

yes adverb 1 ja; **yes please** ja bitte; **'is Tom in his room?' – 'yes, he is'** 'ist Tom im Zimmer?' – 'ja'; 2 (answering a negative) doch; **'you don't want to come with us, do you?' – ' yes, I do!'** 'du willst nicht mitkommen?' - 'doch!'; **'you haven't finished, have you?' – 'yes, I have'** 'Sie sind noch nicht fertig, oder?' - 'doch!'.

yesterday adverb 1 gestern; **I saw her yesterday** ich habe sie gestern gesehen; **yesterday afternoon** gestern Nachmittag; **yesterday morning** gestern früh; 2 **the day before yesterday** vorgestern.

yet adverb 1 **not yet** noch nicht; **it's not ready yet** es ist noch nicht fertig; 2 (in questions) schon; **has she mentioned it yet?** hat sie es schon erwähnt?

yoghurt noun Joghurt der (PL die Joghurt).

yolk noun Eigelb das (PL die Eigelbe).

you pronoun 1 (as the subject of the sentence and in comparisons) du (familiar form, singular); Sie (polite form, singular and plural); ('du' is the familiar way of talking to family members, close friends, and people of your own age; 'Sie' is more polite) **do you want to go to the cinema tonight?** möchtest du heute Abend ins Kino gehen?; **can you tell me where the station is, please?** können Sie mir bitte sagen, wo der Bahnhof ist?; **he's older than you** er ist älter als du, er ist älter als Sie; 2 (the object form of 'du' and 'Sie', in the dative) dir (familiar form, singular), Ihnen (polite form, singular and plural); **I'll lend you my bike** ich leihe dir mein Rad; **I'll write to you** ich schreibe Ihnen; **I'll come with you** ich komme mit Ihnen mit; 3 (the object form of 'du' and 'Sie', in the accusative) dich (familiar form, singular), Sie (polite form, singular and plural); **I saw you** ich habe dich gesehen, ich habe Sie gesehen; **4** (*as the subject of the sentence*) ihr (*familiar form, plural*); **do you all want to come?** wollt ihr alle kommen?; **5** (*the object form, in the accusative and the dative*) euch; **I'll invite you all!** ich lade euch alle ein!; **I'll give it to you later** ich gebe es euch später.

young *adjective* jung; **young people** junge Leute; **he's younger than me** er ist jünger als ich; **Tessa's two years younger than me** Tessa ist zwei Jahre jünger als ich.

your *adjective* **1** (*familiar form, singular*) dein (*this is the familiar way of talking to family members, close friends, and people of your own age; 'Ihr' is more polite*); **I met your brother** ich habe deinen Bruder getroffen; **I met your sister** ich habe deine Schwester getroffen; **I drove your car** ich bin mit deinem Auto gefahren; **I know your brothers** ich kenne deine Brüder; **2** (*familiar form, plural*) euer; **your brother** euer Bruder; **your sister** eure Schwester; **your car** euer Auto; **your friends are waiting downstairs** eure Freunde warten unten; **3** (*polite form, singular and plural*) Ihr; **your brother** Ihr Bruder; **your sister** Ihre Schwester; **your car is in the garage** Ihr Auto ist in der Garage; **you can all bring your friends** Sie können alle Ihre Freunde mitbringen.

yours *pronoun* **1** (*familiar form, singular*) deiner/deine/deins (*this*

is the familiar way of talking to family members, close friends, and people of your own age, 'Ihrer/Ihre/Ihrs' is more polite); **my brother's younger than yours** mein Bruder ist jünger als deiner; **my sister is older than yours** meine Schwester ist älter als deine; **I enjoyed that book - is it yours?** das Buch hat mir gefallen - ist es deins?; **my shoes are more expensive than yours** meine Schuhe sind teurer als deine; **2** (*familiar form, plural*) euer/eure/eures; **my children are younger than yours** meine Kinder sind jünger als eure; **3** (*polite form, singular and plural*) Ihrer/Ihre/Ihrs; **his father must be older than yours** sein Vater muss älter als Ihrer sein; **4 she's a friend of yours** sie ist eine Freundin von Ihnen; **these books are yours** diese Bücher gehören Ihnen; **5** (*in letters*) **Yours sincerely** Mit freundlichen Grüßen.

yourself *pronoun* **1** (*when translated by a reflexive verb in German*) dich, (*formal*) sich; **ask yourself** frage dich, fragen Sie sich; **2** (*as a reflexive dative pronoun*) dir, (*formal*) sich; **did you hurt yourself?** hast du dir wehgetan?, haben Sie sich wehgetan?; **3** (*for emphasis*) selbst; **did you do it yourself?** hast du es selbst gemacht?; **4 all by yourself** ganz allein.

yourselves *pronoun* **1** euch, (*formal*) sich; **make yourselves comfortable** macht es euch gemütlich, machen Sie sich

a
b
c
d
e
f
g
h
i
j
k
l
m
n
o
p
q
r
s
t
u
v
w
x
y
z

a gemütlich; **2** (*for emphasis*) selbst;
did you do it yourselves? habt ihr
b es selbst gemacht?; **3 by _____**
yourselves allein.

c **youth** *noun* **1** (*stage in life*) Jugend
d die; **2** (*young people*) die
Jugendlichen; **today's youth** die
e Jugend von heute; **3** (*young male*)
f Jugendliche *der* (PL *die*
Jugendlichen).

g **youth hostel** *noun*
Jugendherberge *die* (PL *die*
h Jugendherbergen).

i **Yugoslavia** *noun* Jugoslawien
das; **in the former Yugoslavia** im
j ehemaligen Jugoslawien.

k

l

Zz

m

n **zany** *adjective* verrückt.

o **zebra** *noun* Zebra *das* (PL *die*
Zebras).

p **zebra crossing** *noun*
q Zebrastreifen *der* (PL *die*
Zebrastreifen).

r **zero** *noun* Null *die* (PL *die* Nullen).

s **zigzag** *verb* **1** im Zickzack laufen✧
(PERF *sein*); **2** (*in a car*) im Zickzack
t fahren✧ (PERF *sein*).

u **zip** *noun* Reißverschluss *der* (PL *die*
Reißverschlüsse).

v **zodiac** *noun* Tierkreis *der*; **the**
w **signs of the zodiac** die
Sternzeichen (*plural*).

x **zone** *noun* Zone *die* (PL *die* Zonen).

y **zoo** *noun* Zoo *der* (PL *die* Zoos).

z **zoom lens** *noun* Zoomobjektiv *das*
(PL *die* Zoomobjektive).

GERMAN LIFE AND CULTURE

At school

das Abitur This is the exam taken by students who have stayed at school to the age of 18 or 19. The equivalent exam in Austria and Switzerland is called *die Matura*.

hitzefrei This means literally 'heat free'. In many schools, students are sent home early if the thermometer reaches 27° C.

die Klassen As most German students begin school when they are six, they are usually in Klasse 6 at the age of 11:

  6. Klasse = Year 7
  7. Klasse = Year 8
  8. Klasse = Year 9
  9. Klasse = Year 10

die Noten These are school marks. In Germany, Note 1 is the best and Note 6 is the worst.
In Austria, Note 1 is the best and Note 5 is the worst.
In Switzerland, Note 1 is the worst and Note 6 is the best; *Halbnoten* such as 3,5 (3.5) may also be given.

die Schule At the age of 10, students in Germany move from primary school (*Grundschule* or *Volksschule*) to one of three types of secondary school: *Gymnasium* (the most academic), *Hauptschule* (the most vocational), or *Realschule* (between the other two). In some areas, there are comprehensive schools (*Gesamtschulen*).
In Switzerland, some cantons have only one type of secondary school, whilst other cantons have three types. In Austria, students move to a *Hauptschule*, a *Gymnasium*, or a *neue Mittelschule*.

die Schulferien These are the school holidays. Different parts of Germany have their summer holidays at different times. There may be:

  – one or two weeks in October / November
  – two weeks at Christmas
  – one or two weeks in February
  – two weeks at Easter
  – a week at Whitsun
  – six or seven weeks in summer

der Schultag This is the school day. The German school day is usually from 8.00 a.m. to 1 p.m. for younger students, with older students often having afternoon classes on one or more afternoons a week.

Ich gehe zu Fuß zur Schule.	I walk to school.
Ich bin in der sechsten (6.) Klasse.	I'm in Year 7.
In meiner Klasse sind 25 Schüler.	There are 25 students in my class.
Der Unterricht beginnt um neun Uhr.	Lessons start at 9 o'clock.
Mittags esse ich in der Schulkantine.	At lunchtime, I have lunch in the canteen.
Ich bin in ... gut.	I'm good at ...
Ich bin in ... nicht sehr gut.	I'm not very good at ...
Ich lerne für eine Prüfung, die ... genannt wird.	I'm working towards an exam called...
Wir haben viele Hausaufgaben.	We have a lot of homework.
Herein!	Come in!
Packt eure Hefte aus.	Take out your exercise books.
Schlagt eure Bücher auf Seite 23 auf.	Open your books at page 23.
Arbeitet mit einem Partner.	Work in pairs.
Hört zu und wiederholt.	Listen and repeat.

Ich brauche...
I need...

mein Schulbuch.	my textbook.	*meinen Bleistiftspitzer.*	my pencil sharpener.
meinen Bleistift.	my pencil.		
meinen Kuli.	my Biro®.	*meine Schere.*	my scissors.
meine Filzstifte.	my felt-tips.	*meinen Taschenrechner.*	my calculator.
mein Lineal.	my ruler.		
mein Radiergummi.	my rubber.	*mein Federmäppchen.*	my pencil case.
		mein Heft.	my exercise book.

Mein Lieblingsfach ist...
My favourite subject is...

Biologie.	Biology.	*Kunst.*	Art.
Chemie.	Chemistry.	*Mathe.*	Maths.
Deutsch.	German.	*Musik.*	Music.
Englisch.	English.	*Naturwissenschaften.*	Science.
Französisch.	French.	*Physik.*	Physics.
Geschichte.	History.	*Religion.*	RE.
Geografie /	Geography.	*Spanisch.*	Spanish.
Geographie.		*Sport.*	PE.
Informatik.	IT.		

Später möchte ich...
Later, I want to...

auf die Universität gehen.	go to university.	*Arzt / Ärztin werden...*	become a doctor...
...studieren	study...	*...denn...*	...because...
ins Ausland gehen...	go abroad...	*es ist interessant.*	it's interesting.
		es ist gut bezahlt.	it's well paid.

At home

Wir sind zu fünft in unserer Familie.	There are five of us in our family.
Ich habe...	I've got...
einen Bruder / eine Schwester.	a brother / a sister.
einen Halbbruder / eine Halbschwester.	a half-brother / a half-sister.
einen Zwillingsbruder / eine Zwillingsschwester.	a twin brother / a twin sister.
Ich bin (ein) Einzelkind.	I'm an only child.

632

Ich wohne...
I live...

in einem Haus.	in a house.	*in einer Wohnung.*	in a flat.

Es gibt...
There is...

eine Küche.	a kitchen.	*drei Schlafzimmer.*	three bedrooms.
ein Wohnzimmer.	a living room.	*ein Bad / Badezimmer.*	a bathroom.
eine Toilette.	a toilet.	*einen Garten.*	a garden.

Meine Lieblingsbeschäftigung ist..
My favourite pastime is...

mit Freunden ausgehen.	going out with friends.	*Mountainbike fahren.*	mountain biking.
lesen.	reading.		
Musik hören.	listening to music.	*Fußball / Volleyball spielen.*	playing football / volleyball.
fernsehen.	watching TV.		
an einer Spielkonsole spielen.	playing on a games console.	*Skateboard fahren.*	skateboarding.
Radfahren gehen.	going cycling.	*inlineskaten.*	roller-blading.

Ich werde mir ... ansehen.
I'm going to watch...

einen Film	a film.	*eine Spielshow*	a game show.
einen sportsendung	a sports programme.	*meine Lieblingsserie*	my favourite series.

Ich habe...
I've got...

eine Spielkonsole.	a games console.	*ein iPod®*	an Ipod®
ein Handy.	a (mobile) phone.	*einen Flachbildfernseher.*	a flat-screen TV.
einen Laptop.	a laptop.	*eine Satellitenschüssel.*	a satellite dish.
eine Digitalkamera.	a digital camera.	*eine Webcam.*	a webcam.
		einen Computer.	a computer.

On the computer

Mit meinem Computer...	On my computer...
mache ich Hausaufgaben.	I do my homework.
lade ich Musik herunter.	I download music.
schaue ich etwas im Internet nach.	I look something up on the Internet.
chatte ich mit meinen Freunden.	I chat with my friends.
besuche ich Chatrooms.	I visit chatrooms.
gehe ich auf soziale Netzwerk-Sites.	I go on social networking sites.
twittere ich.	I tweet.

Email

eine E-Mail	an email
eine E-Mail-Adresse	an email address
eine E-Mail schicken	to send an email
eine E-Mail bekommen	to get an email

On the phone

Hallo!	Hello!
Kann ich... sprechen?	Can I speak to...?
Wer ist am Apparat?	Who's calling?
Einen Moment, bitte.	Hold on, please.
Kann ich eine Nachricht hinterlassen?	Can I leave a message?
Ich rufe später zurück.	I'll call back later.
eine SMS	a text
eine SMS schicken	to send a text

634

Shopping

Ich gehe ... einkaufen.
I go shopping (for food)...

in der Konditorei	at the cake shop.
beim Lebensmittelhändler	at the grocer's.
beim Bäcker	at the baker's.
beim Metzger	at the butcher's.
im Feinkostgeschäft	at the delicatessen.
auf dem Markt	at the market.
im Supermarkt	at the supermarket.
im Internet	on the Internet.

Ich möchte ...
I'd like ...

ein Brot.	a loaf of bread.	*ein Kilo Zucker.*	a kilo of sugar.
vier Brötchen.	four rolls.		

Was kostet es?   How much is it?

eine Bäckerei	This is a baker's shop which usually sells many different types of bread, e.g. some with whole cereal seeds. They also sell rolls, called *Brötchen* in the north of Germany, and *Semmeln* in the south.
eine Konditorei	This is a cake shop which will sell a wide range of cakes (*Kuchen*) and gateaux (*Torten*).

Food and eating out

Was darf es sein?   What would you like?

Ich möchte...
I'd like...

einen	*an*	*eine Tasse Tee.*	a cup of tea.
Orangensaft.	orange juice.	*einen Kaffee.*	a coffee.

Haben Sie Vanilleeis?   Have you got any vanilla ice cream?

Als Vorspeise nehme ich...
For a starter I'll have...

Zwiebelsuppe.	onion soup.	*Tomatensalat.* tomato salad.

Als Hauptgericht möchte ich...
For my main course I'll have...

Hähnchen in Sahnesoße.	chicken in cream sauce.	*einen Hamburger.* a burger.
mit... with...		
Pommes.	chips.	*Salat.* salad.

Zum Nachtisch möchte ich...
For dessert I'd like...

Apfelstrudel.	apple strudel.	*Milchreis.* rice pudding.

Zu trinken nehme ich...
To drink I'll have...

Mineralwasser.	mineral water.	*eine* apple juice with
ein Cola.	a Coke®.	*Apfelschorle.* mineral water

Ich habe Hunger.	I'm hungry.
Ich habe Durst.	I'm thirsty.
Das ist lecker!	It's delicious!
Ich habe eine Allergie.	I have an allergy.
Zahlen, bitte.	The bill, please.

Meals

Frühstück	breakfast	Abendessen /	
Mittagessen	lunch	Abendbrot	dinner

Food

Apfelschorle This is a drink consisting of apple juice and fizzy mineral water. In Austria it is known as *Apfelsaft gespritzt*.

Apfelstrudel This is a traditional Austrian dessert made of thin pastry rolled around a filling of apples and raisins. It is often served with whipped cream.

Brötchen These are bread rolls. They are also called *Semmeln*, especially in southern Germany and Austria. People often go out early to buy them for breakfast.

Brezeln twisted pieces of firm, salted bread

Chips These are crisps. Chips are called *Pommes frites*, or just *Pommes*.

Eis ice cream

Emmentaler a Swiss cheese with a strong flavour and holes

Käsefondue This is a cheese fondue. It is made from cheese melted in white wine, and is eaten by dipping bread into a communal pot.

Lebkuchen Lebkuchen is gingerbread and it is traditionally made at Christmas, and may be covered with icing or chocolate.

Sauerkraut Sauerkraut is boiled pickled cabbage and it has a strong, vinegary flavour and is usually eaten with sausages. Many people consider it to be Germany's most typical dish.

Sachertorte rich chocolate cake, originally from Vienna

Schlagsahne This is whipped cream. In Austria it is also called *Schlagobers* or *Schlag*.

Schnitzel /
Wiener Schnitzel a slice of veal or pork, fried in breadcrumbs

Stollen A rich bread-like cake, often containing dried fruit and marzipan. It is traditionally eaten at Christmas.

Wurst	Germany has a huge range of *Wurst* or sausages which, can be boiled (*Bockwurst*), fried or grilled (*Bratwurst*), or served cold like salami.

Did you know...?

- that a *Berliner* is a doughnut, a *Wiener* a sausage, and a *Hamburger*, of course, a hamburger?
- that, in Austria, potatoes are often called *Erdäpfel* (apples of the earth) and tomatoes *Paradeiser* (fruits of paradise)?
- that chocolates are *Pralinen*, and chocolate is *Schokolade*?

On holiday

Letzten Sommer bin ich nach Deutschland gefahren.	Last summer, I went to Germany.
Nächsten Sommer werde ich nach Berlin fahren.	Next summer, I'll be going to Berlin.

Ich war...
I stayed...

in einem Hotel.	in a hotel.
in einem Ferienhaus auf dem Land.	in a holiday home in the country.
auf einem Campingplatz.	on a campsite.

Wir sind mit... gefahren.
We travelled by...

dem Schiff	ship.	*dem (Reise) bus*	coach.
dem Zug	train.		
dem Auto	car.	*dem Fahrrad*	bike.
		Wir sind geflogen.	We flew.

Biergärten	These are beer gardens. In a *Biergarten* coffee, cake, soft drinks, and small meals can be ordered, as well as beer.
der Föhn	This is a wind which brings warm air from the Mediterranean to Austria, Southern Germany, and parts of Switzerland. Some people believe that it causes headaches and other health problems.
ins Freibad gehen	This means going to the outdoor swimming pool. *Freibäder* are very popular because the weather gets very hot in summer.
Hochdeutsch	This means High German (standard German). Each area of Germany, Austria, and German-speaking Switzerland has its own dialect.
Kaffee und Kuchen	This means coffee and cake. Germany, Switzerland, and Austria are all famous for their mouth-watering cakes.
Kantone	Each of the 26 individual states in Switzerland is called a *Kanton* (canton).
Länder	Each of the individual states in Germany and Austria is called a *Land*. Germany has 16 *Länder*; Austria has nine.
der Marktplatz	This is the market square.
Personalausweise	These are identity cards. German, Austrian, and Swiss citizens can use their *Personalausweis* instead of a passport for travel within Europe.
das Rathaus	This is the town hall. It is often a grand building in the main square.

Did you know...
- that you can be fined if you cross the road when the traffic light (*Ampel*) is red for pedestrians?
- that German letter boxes (*Briefkästen*) are yellow?
- that the usual way of greeting people is:
  - *Guten Tag* in northern Germany,
  - *Grüß Gott* in southern Germany,
  - *Grüezi* in Switzerland,
  - *Servus* in Austria,

  but that you can also say *Hallo* everywhere?
- that a minority of Swiss people speak *Romantsch*, a language derived from Latin?
- that, in towns which have several railway stations, the main railway station is usually called the *Hauptbahnhof*?
- that Germany's fastest trains are called *InterCity Express*? You pay a supplement to travel in them, and have to book a seat.
- that many towns have a tram system (*die Straßenbahn*)?
- that underground trains are called the *U-Bahn*?
- that services on the motorway (*Autobahn*) are called *Raststätte* or *Autohof*?
- that to travel on Swiss or Austrian motorways, you have to buy a sticker called a *Vignette*, and display the sticker on the car windscreen?
- that the biggest city in Switzerland is Zürich, but the capital city (*Hauptstadt*) is Bern?
- that the capital of Austria is Vienna?
- that West and East Germany were reunified in 1990, having been divided into two states after World War II?
- that before reunification, the West German government had its seat in Bonn, and that after reunification Berlin was re-established as the capital?

Places of interest

die Alpen	The Alps cover much of Austria and Switzerland, and stretch along the southern border of Germany.

They are a popular holiday area in both summer and winter. The highest points in the three countries are:

Germany:	**Zugspitze** 2964m
Austria:	**Großglockner** 3798m
Switzerland:	**Monte Rosa** 4634m

Bayern — Bavaria, Germany's biggest *Land*, is in the south, with the Alps along its southern border. Its capital is Munich. Bavaria is famous for its big wooden farmhouses and its many local beers.

Brandenburger Tor — This gateway, built in 1791, is Berlin's most famous landmark.

Berliner Mauer — The Berlin Wall. East Germany was separated from West Germany, and governed by a Communist government, from 1948 to 1990. In Berlin, the Communists built a wall around West Berlin, to prevent people from East Germany fleeing to the West. The wall was taken down in 1989; some parts of it remain, as a reminder of the past.

Liechtenstein — A tiny country of 160 km² bordering Switzerland and Austria. It has its own government and issues its own stamps, but uses Swiss francs.

Neuschwanstein — A fairy-tale castle in the Bavarian Alps. Many people in Britain recognize Neuschwanstein as the castle from the film 'Chitty Chitty Bang Bang'.

Ostsee — The Baltic Sea. With large sandy beaches, this is a popular holiday area, especially as it is within easy reach of Berlin.

Reichstag — Built in 1894, the Reichstag was the seat of the German parliament. Destroyed by fire in 1933, it was rebuilt following the reunification of Germany, and the German parliament now sits there again.

Olympiastadion	This is the Olympic Stadium in Munich, which for many years was home to the football team Bayern München.
Rhein	The River Rhine. It cuts through the hills in a deep valley, with vines on the hillsides and castles on the tops. Barges carry goods along the Rhine.
Südtirol	South Tyrol: part of Italy, in the Alps, where people speak both German and Italian.
Wien	Vienna, the capital of Austria. It is known for its music, its museums and cafes, the white horses in the Spanish Riding School and the Riesenrad, an enormous Ferris wheel built in 1897.

Festivals and celebrations

Neujahr	New Year's Day
Heilige Drei Könige	Epiphany, or Twelfth Night, 6th January. In Austria and parts of Germany, teenagers dress up as kings and collect money to help children in developing countries.
Valentinstag	St Valentine's Day
Fasching / Fastnacht / Karneval	This is the celebration before Lent, with fancy dress parties and elaborate processions. Shrove Tuesday is known as *Fastnachtsdienstag* or *Faschingsdienstag*, and the Monday before as *Rosenmontag*.
Ostern	This is Easter. Children hunt for chocolate eggs brought by the *Osterhase* (the Easter Hare), and many families decorate their dining room with intricately painted eggs. Good Friday is known as *Karfreitag* and Easter Monday as *Ostermontag*.
der 1. Mai: Maifeiertag	May Day. The public holiday is always on May 1st, whereas in Britain it is on the first Monday in May.
Christi Himmelfahrt	Ascension Day. This is a public holiday on the Thursday that is forty days after Easter.

Pfingsten	Whitsun (Pentecost). This is fifty days after Easter. *Pfingstmontag* (Whit Monday) is a public holiday.
Schweizer Nationalfeiertag	1st August: Swiss National Day
Oktoberfest	This is a famous festival in Munich, with funfairs and beer tents. It actually begins in September.
Tag der Deutschen Einheit	3rd October. A public holiday that commemorates the reunification of East and West Germany in 1989.
Österreichischer Nationalfeiertag	26th October: Austrian National Day
Reformationstag	31st October: Reformation Day. This is a public holiday in the Protestant parts of Germany.
Allerheiligen	1st November: All Saints' Day. On this day many people put flowers on the graves of loved ones. It is a public holiday in most Roman Catholic parts of Germany and Switzerland, and in Austria.
Nikolaus	6th December: The Feast of Saint Nicholas. On the evening before, children put a shoe outside their door. In the morning, they find that *der Nikolaus* (Saint Nicholas) has filled the shoe with chocolates, nuts, and other goodies. (Traditionally, this happens only if they have been good.)
der Heiligabend / der Heilige Abend	Christmas Eve. Most families have a real Christmas tree. The main celebration is in the evening. Many people go to midnight mass.
Weihnachtsmärkte	Christmas markets. These are stalls decorated with greenery and smelling of mulled wine and roast chestnuts. A *Weihnachtsmarkt* is a beautiful setting for buying Christmas gifts.
Weihnachten	Christmas. *Der erste Weihnachtstag* (Christmas Day) often begins with a lie-in after the celebrations of the night before. There is a big midday meal. *Der zweite Weihnachtstag* (Boxing Day) is also a public holiday.
Silvester	New Year's Eve

Dates

am ersten Januar	on January 1st	*elfte*	11th
der erste Januar	the 1st of January	*zwölfte*	12th
		dreizehnte	13th
zweite (2.)	2nd	*vierzehnte*	14th
dritte (3.)	3rd	*fünfzehnte*	15th
vierte (4.)	4th	*sechzehnte*	16th
fünfte	5th	*siebzehnte*	17th
sechste	6th	*achtzehnte*	18th
siebte	7th	*neunzehnte*	19th
achte	8th	*zwanzigste*	20th
neunte	9th	*einundzwanzigste*	21st
zehnte	10th	*dreißigste*	30th

Days

Montag	Monday	*Freitag*	Friday
Dienstag	Tuesday	*Samstag/ Sonnabend*	Saturday
Mittwoch	Wednesday		
Donnerstag	Thursday	*Sonntag*	Sunday

Months

Januar	January	*Juli*	July
Februar	February	*August*	August
März	March	*September*	September
April	April	*Oktober*	October
Mai	May	*November*	November
Juni	June	*Dezember*	December

Seasons

der Winter	winter	*der Sommer*	summer
der Frühling	spring	*der Herbst*	autumn

Time

Wie spät ist es?
What time is it?

Es ist ein Uhr.	It's one o'clock.
Es ist halb fünf.	It's half past four.
Es ist Viertel nach sechs.	It's quarter past six.
Es ist Viertel vor sechs.	It's quarter to six.
Es ist zehn nach neun.	It's ten past nine.
Es ist zehn vor neun.	It's ten to nine.
Es ist Mittag.	It's midday.
Es ist Mitternacht.	It's midnight.
Es ist 7 Uhr abends (19 Uhr).	It's 7 p.m. (19.00).
Es ist 1 Uhr 15 nachmittags (13.15 Uhr).	It's 1.15 p.m. (13.15).

jeden Tag	every day
einmal die Woche	once a week
gelegentlich	from time to time
nie	never
immer	always

Numbers

null	0	vierzig	40
eins	1	fünfzig	50
zwei	2	sechzig	60
drei	3	siebzig	70
vier	4	einundsiebzig	71
fünf	5	achtzig	80
sechs	6	einundachtzig	81
sieben	7	zweiundachtzig	82
acht	8	neunzig	90
neun	9	einundneunzig	91
zehn	10	zweiundneunzig	92
elf	11	neunundneunzig	99
zwölf	12	hundert	100
dreizehn	13	hunderteins	101
vierzehn	14	hundertzwei	102
fünfzehn	15	zweihundert	200
sechzehn	16	zweihunderteins	201
siebzehn	17	zweihundertzwei	202
achtzehn	18		
neunzehn	19		
zwanzig	20	tausend	1000
einundzwanzig	21	tausendeins	1001
zweiundzwanzig	22	tausendzwei	1002
dreiundzwanzig	23	zweitausend	2000
vierundzwanzig	24	eine Million	1 000 000
fünfundzwanzig	25		
sechsundzwanzig	26		
siebenundzwanzig	27		
achtundzwanzig	28		
neunundzwanzig	29		
dreißig	30		

States

Germany and Austria are divided into *Bundesländer* (states).
Germany has sixteen *Bundesländer*, and Austria has nine.

Bundesland	German State
Baden-Württemberg	Baden-Württemberg
Bayern	Bavaria
Berlin	Berlin
Brandenburg	Brandenburg
Bremen	Bremen
Hamburg	Hamburg
Hessen	Hesse
Mecklenburg-Vorpommern	Mecklenburg-Western Pomerania
Niedersachsen	Lower Saxony
Nordrhein-Westfalen	North-Rhine Westphalia
Rheinland-Pfalz	Rhineland-Palatinate
Saarland	Saarland
Sachsen	Saxony
Sachsen-Anhalt	Saxony-Anhalt
Schleswig-Holstein	Schleswig-Holstein
Thüringen	Thuringia

Bundesland	Austrian State
Burgenland	Burgenland
Kärnten	Carinthia
Niederösterreich	Lower Austria
Oberösterreich	Upper Austria
Salzburg	Salzburg
Steiermark	Styria
Tirol	Tyrol
Vorarlberg	Vorarlberg
Wien	Vienna

European countries

Europa	Europe
Land	Country
Albanien	Albania
Andorra	Andorra
Belgien	Belgium
Bosnien-Herzogowina	Bosnia-Herzegovina
Bulgarien	Bulgaria
Danemark	Denmark
Deutschland	Germany
Estland	Estonia
Finnland	Finland
Frankreich	France
Griechenland	Greece
GroKbritannien	United Kingdom; Great Britain
England	England
Nordirland	Northern Ireland
Schottland	Scotland
Wales	Wales
Kroatien	Croatia
Island	Iceland
Italien	Italy
Jugoslawien	Yugoslavia
Lettland	Latvia
Liechtenstein	Liechtenstein
Litauen	Lithuania
Luxemburg	Luxembourg
Mazedonien (Ehmalige Jugoslawische Republik Mazedonien)	FYROM (Former Yugoslav Republic of Macedonia)
Monaco	Monaco
Moldawien	Moldavia
Niederlande	Netherlands
Norwegen	Norway
Osterreich	Austria
Polen	Poland

Portugal	Portugal
Republik Irland	Republic of Ireland
Rumänien	Romania
Russland	Russia
San Marino	San Marino
Schweden	Sweden
Schweiz	Switzerland
Slowakei	Slovakia
Slowenien	Slovenia
Spanien	Spain
Tschechische Republik	Czech Republic
Tiirkei	Turkey
Ukraine	Ukraine
Ungarn	Hungary
Weissrussland	Belarus

NOTES

NOTES

NOTES

NOTES

NOTES

NOTES